Also by Harvey Rachlin

The Songwriter's Handbook
The Encyclopedia of the Music Business

The Money Encyclopedia

The
·Money Encyclopedia·

Edited by
Harvey Rachlin

1817

HARPER & ROW, PUBLISHERS, New York

Cambridge, Philadelphia, San Francisco,
London, Mexico City, São Paulo, Sydney

Copyright acknowledgments appear on page 671.

THE MONEY ENCYCLOPEDIA. Copyright © 1984 by Harvey
Rachlin. All rights reserved. Printed in the United States
of America. No part of this book may be used or
reproduced in any manner whatsoever without written
permission except in the case of brief quotations embodied
in critical articles and reviews. For information address
Harper & Row, Publishers, Inc., 10 East 53rd Street, New
York, N.Y. 10022. Published simultaneously in Canada by
Fitzhenry & Whiteside Limited, Toronto.

Designer: Abigail Sturges

Library of Congress Cataloging in Publication Data
Main entry under title:

The Money encyclopedia.

　1. Finance—United States—Dictionaries.　2. Financial
institutions—United States—Dictionaries.　3. Money—
United States—Dictionaries.　I. Rachlin, Harvey.
HG181.M574　1984　　332.4′03′21　　83-48801
ISBN 0-06-181711-2

85 86 87 88 10 9 8 7 6 5 4 3

To
Mazie, Phil, Steven,
Craig and Gary

Preface

The changing world in which we live is no more remarkably embraced than in the dynamic field of money. We can look back with nostalgia to the banking days of the 1960s—only two decades ago—when the passbook savings account was the focal point of activity for most people. The economic currents that began in the 1970s, precipitated by the technological revolution, permanently altered our money practices and ushered in a financial services industry that continues to evolve almost on a daily basis.

The financial services industry—the network of companies that provides a plethora of investment options and services for customers—is an exciting and emerging area shepherded by politics, culture, and technology. Industry pressure results in financial laws being changed at both federal and state levels; public demand creates an ever-increasing array of investment vehicles; the electronic and computer systems supplied by the high-tech industries provide the means for effecting cashless and checkless transactions geared toward the convenience of the public.

Today, banking is no longer a matter of depositing savings in a regular passbook account for safekeeping and a small yield and keeping a no-interest checking account to pay bills. In the 1980s, it is the investment in instruments giving the highest possible return while meeting the needs and wants of the consumer that more closely defines banking.

The financial services industry (now a more appropriate name than "banking industry") is complex and will continue to grow ever more so. There are many investment options from which to choose (and no doubt these will continue to grow and evolve into even newer products that better cater to the individual needs and wants of our changing society). The financial instruments themselves take on catchy and oftimes confusing names, such as "money market deposit accounts," "asset-based management accounts," "no-load mutual funds," and "Felines." Surely, one cannot afford not to stay on top of the latest developments and investment offerings and their implications for individual financial growth. What with inflation, cost-of-living spirals, and other factors, money

that doesn't earn money loses money.

Not only has the range of investment instruments expanded, the way we effect our daily monetary transactions has changed. Rather than checks or cash, electronic fund transfer (EFT) systems, such as automated teller machines (ATM's) and point-of-sale (POS) terminals, are becoming more and more commonplace. These high-tech innovations provide for payment or transfer of funds between parties by the entering of codes electronically through computers, electronic terminals, telephones, and other data-transmittal devices. Thus, consumers can do banking without the assistance of a teller, or they can transfer funds directly from their own accounts to the merchant's to pay for goods and services.

What does the future hold? We'll probably have universally accepted debit cards; be able to purchase stocks, bonds, annuities, and other financial products in shared branches and outlets, such as supermarkets and department stores; and be able to bank at home via computer terminals and television hookups. This last development will enable us not only to make banking transactions in the comfort of our living rooms but also to make retail purchases; order and buy airplane tickets, hotel accommodations, concert tickets, baseball tickets; and perform myriad other functions all by pushing buttons from our easy chairs. Cashless and checkless financial transactions will eventually be possible from practically anywhere!

Government deregulation has changed the roles of institutions engaged in the financial marketplace, blurring the traditional distinctions between banks, thrifts, brokerage houses, insurance companies, and others. Like a rebuilt house, the industry's form and structure have changed. Many diversified companies, from retail chain operators to piano manufacturers, have jumped on the financial bandwagon. To paraphrase a rye-bread-manufacturer's well-known advertising slogan, "You don't have to be a bank to be a banker."

To be knowledgeable about—and independent in—today's and tomorrow's complex financial world requires understanding economic concepts and the language, practices, and products of business and investment. It mandates comprehending such kindred areas as taxes, real estate, health insurance, life insurance, retirement programs, and estate planning.

Keeping current with new developments should be an essential part of daily life. Newspapers, magazines, and other media, as well as local financial institutions, are the vehicles for this, but first one must have a basic, concrete understanding of money and its many applications. Hence, the raison d'être of *The Money Encyclopedia*.

It is hoped one will be able to put together all the facts and concepts presented herein and see them in a larger light—a unified perspective where they weave and intertwine with one another to form the tapestry that is our economic system. For ultimately the story of today's financial systems is nothing less than the story of the progress, growth, and evolution of our American culture.

About this book

The goal of *The Money Encyclopedia* is to present a comprehensive, information-packed work that is, at the same time, of practical value to a wide range of readers. To the degree this has been accomplished, many share in the credit. Contributors were selected with great care, and each is an expert or authority in the subject he or she has written about.

Unless otherwise stated, entries are current through the end of 1983 (for example, the products traded on the commodity-futures exchanges). Information deemed datable, particularly interest rates, fees, and other financial figures, has been purposely omitted to avoid dating the text.

In many entries, words or terms are cited which require further explanation. Such words or terms are capitalized, and for further explanation the reader should refer to the entry of such a cross-reference.

Reproduced in the text is the Federal Reserve Bank of New York's excellent "Fedpoints" series by Arthur Samansky. This particular set was prepared in the late 1970s and early 1980s and in some instances information may have changed because of revisions in banking operations and laws. The latest information about subjects discussed in "Fedpoints" is available from the Federal Reserve. The same holds true for other articles reproduced from Federal Reserve bank publications.

As an encyclopedia, this book serves to present information factually and objectively; it does not purport to give investment advice. In some instances, where decisions are based on individual circumstances, both the pros and cons of a situation are given.

The Money Encyclopedia contains many diverse entries—from actuary to zero-coupon bonds. Learning to be financially knowledgeable requires a study of several areas and keeping up with the latest developments. A person's objective, of course, is to apply information in a practical way to maximize savings and investment yields and gain peace of mind concerning his financial security. This book, it is hoped, will provide the basic background—and more—to help in approaching the financial world—as both a consumer and investor—with greater awareness, understanding, and perspicacity.

Harvey Rachlin

Acknowledgments

I would like to express my very special gratitude to the contributors of this book, as well as to the institutions where they are employed—Federal Reserve banks; federal government agencies, departments and bureaus; stock and commodity exchanges; trade and professional associations; academic institutions; publications; and companies and corporations.

I am indebted most of all to Harriet Rubin at Harper & Row. The quintessential business-book editor, Harriet was magnanimous in her advice, counsel, guidance, and support, and no words could express my utmost appreciation to her. She is the silent hero behind the fruition of this work.

Ineffable praise is also to be lavished upon Diana Perez, copyeditor; Toni Rachiele and Jim Armstrong, production editors; and Margie Bowen, editorial assistant. The seeds of this book were planted with Bernard Skydell, the copesetic editor who signed it up. I am also deeply appreciative to my agent, Lynn Seligman.

Deserving special mention are Darla Mendales (Fidelity Group), Marvin Kaplan (the Kaplan Company), Sidney Robbins (Health Care Financing Administration), Richard Torrenzano (New York Stock Exchange), and Bob Shabazian (American Stock Exchange).

Grateful acknowledgment is given to:

Richard Hoenig (Federal Reserve Bank of New York), Arthur Meyers (Federal Reserve Bank of Richmond), Gail Yost (Federal Reserve Bank of Minneapolis), Alan Friedman (U.S. League of Savings Institutions), Carol M. Stansfield (Food and Nutrition Service, U.S. Department of Agriculture), Harvey Seymour (Insurance Information Institute), Henry Tishman (Moore & Schley Cameron & Co.), Mary Lee Fox (New York Mercantile Exchange), Beth Van Houten (formerly of Federal National Mortgage Association), Mickey Fardella (Moody's Investors Service, Inc.), Ron Erickson (Farm Credit Administration), Dan E. Day (U.S. Department of Housing and Urban Development), Vance Clark (Federal Home Loan Mortgage Corporation).

Gary Garrity (American Land Title Association),

Jay Kobler (formerly of the Home Insurance Company), Ceil Frank (U.S. Department of Health and Human Services), John Trollinger (Social Security Administration), Ed Harvey (Insurance Institute of America), Joan Pinkerton (National Credit Union Administration), Dan Buser (American Bankers Association), Bruce Stoner (Commodity Futures Trading Commission), James Nagle (Chicago Board Options Exchange), Robert L. Jordan (Overseas Private Investors Corporation), Jack Queeney (Midwest Stock Exchange), Rab Bertlesen (Fidelity Group), William J. Henderson (International Consumer Credit Association), Amy J. Biderman and Jennifer Stockdale (Health Insurance Association of America), Neil Swan (formerly of Health Insurance Association of America), and Lou Dombrowski (National Association of Realtors).

William Kats (Pacific Stock Exchange), Steve Reed (Philadelphia Stock Exchange), Gene Podrazik and Debra Lopez (Chicago Board of Trade), Timothy Cook (Federal Reserve Bank of Richmond), Charlotte Gilbert (formerly of Rowland Company), Joseph Raftery (Boston Stock Exchange), Thomas Humphrey (Federal Reserve Bank of Richmond), Jim Brown (Social Security Administration), Jack Lipsky (Equitable Life Assurance Society of the United States), Catherine H. Jensen (Food and Nutrition Service, U.S. Department of Agriculture).

Wayne Burt (Federal Home Loan Mortgage Corporation), Louis Kirschbaum (Value Line Investment Survey), Ross Kleiman (Student Loan Mortgage Association), Eleanor Hayden (Bureau of the Mint, U.S. Department of the Treasury), and Sara W. Woodard (Council of Better Business Bureaus).

Warren Matthews (Mortgage Bankers Association of America), Brad Smith (American Institute of Certified Public Accountants), Pat Henderson (Minneapolis Grain Exchange), Donna Andrews (Student Loan Marketing Association), Tim Whitacre (Minneapolis Grain Exchange), Robert Solberg (Mortage Guarantee Insurance Corporation), Ken Swoyer (Allstate Insurance Company), Gwen King (Securities Industry Association), Jane Fleming (formerly of New York

Mercantile Exchange), Enno Hobbing (National Association of Securities Dealers), David Cheney (International Monetary Fund), Belle V. Brannner (of the now-defunct New Orleans Commodity Exchange), and Marlo Mitchell (Social Security Administration).

I owe much to my friends and family whose patience was pushed to the limit yet who were inexorable sources of understanding and encouragement—Alice French, Agnes Dubin, Sally Shiller, Steven Schulman, Elliott Miller, Lou Stevens, Pearl Bernstein, Jeanne Rachlin, Sharon Rachlin, Max Dubin, Sidney Bernstein, Roy Shiller, Jeff Luckman, Jay Cohen, Bonnie Schachter, Lonnie Grosswald, Stephanie Rachlin, Alan Goodman, David Copper, Khris Kellow, Phyllis Levine, Walter R. Andrews, Henry J. Hausch, A. Mitchell Liftig, and Eric Traub.

Finally, heartfelt thanks are understated and overdue my typist, Margaret Dyke.

Contributors

James A. Ambrose is editor of *Consumer Trends,* a twice-monthly newsletter of the International Consumer Credit Association (ICCA) in St. Louis and a veteran of more than 30 years in association management, publishing, and public relations. A former director of legislation and research for ICCA, he is a recognized expert on consumer economics and consumer credit legislation and regulation. He has previously served as the public-relations director of the St. Louis Council and the Boy Scouts of America.

Walter E. Auch is chairman and chief executive officer of the Chicago Board Options Exchange (CBOE). Prior to joining the CBOE, Mr. Auch was executive vice-president of Paine Webber, Jackson & Curtis and was the principal architect of that firm's large branch office network. He was also a director and member of the Executive Committee of Paine Webber, Inc., the parent company.

David B. Axelrod is a free-lance writer who has devoted the past ten years to a study of corporate and tax law. His journalistic efforts, including tax advice for teachers, have won him two national press awards. He is a frequent lecturer throughout the United States. Dr. Axelrod is on the faculty at Suffolk Community College on Long Island. He holds an M.A. from The Johns Hopkins University, an M.F.A. from the University of Iowa, and a Ph.D. from Union Graduate School.

Victoria J. Baker is editor/publications coordinator at the National Association of Real Estate Investment Trusts, Inc., in Washington, D.C.

Phil Battey is editorial manager for the American Bankers Association. He was previously a Washington correspondent for *American Banker,* the daily newspaper for the banking industry. He holds a master's degree in journalism from the University of Missouri.

Phillip J. Bayer is president of the National Creditors Association, Inc., a Long Island collection agency. He has served as president of the New York State Unit of the American Collectors Association, Inc., the trade association for collection agencies, and was an auditor for the National Bank of North America.

William J. Beahan, vice-president of Samuel A. Ramirez Company, Inc., has been in the municipal-bond business for 35 years. He has been active in all phases of the industry, including selling, trading, and underwriting. Mr. Beahan is a member of the Municipal Bond Club of New York and the Municipal Forum.

H. Phillip Becker is president of Hedged Portfolio Advisors, a registered investment adviser; chairman of Chronometrics, Inc., a registered commodity-trading adviser; and president of Becker, Williams & Company, a commodity-options brokerage firm. A veteran of more than 20 years' experience in equity- and futures-markets analysis, Mr. Becker is an options member of the Chicago Board of Trade and the Chicago Mercantile Exchange and was a member for seven years of the Chicago Board Options Exchange. He is frequently quoted in trade publications and is the editor of the *Becker Letter,* a guide to commodity-options markets. Mr. Becker received his J.D. from the University of Illinois Law School.

Karen M. Benedetti is senior research analyst, options and index products, at the New York Stock Exchange. She was formerly a research analyst at the New York Futures Exchange in the areas of economic analysis and new-product development.

Robert J. Birnbaum is president and chief operating officer of the American Stock Exchange, Inc. (ASE). He joined the ASE in 1967 and served in various executive positions. Previously, Mr. Birnbaum was with the U.S. Securities and Exchange Commission, where he served as branch chief of regulation and inspection, and with the U.S. General Accounting Office, where he was a law clerk on the staff of the general counsel. Mr. Birnbaum holds an LL.B. from Georgetown University Law School.

Samuel W. Bodman is president and chief operating officer of the Fidelity Group. In this role, he manages Fidelity Brokerage Services, Fidelity Management & Research Company, Fidelity Service Company, Fidelity Venture Associates, and BOSCOM. He also serves as a director of Fidelity Management & Research company, and as president and director of the Fidelity Group of Funds.

Dr. Bodman is a director of Dymo Business Systems, Inc.; Haemonetics Corporation; WellTech, Inc.; Guardian Oil Corporation; Mardrill, Inc.; and Brinadd Company. Prior to joining Fidelity, he was an associate professor of chemical engineering at the Massachusetts Institute of Technology, and continues to lecture there. He is a former director of the School of Engineering Practice, American Cyanamid Company, and a former member of the MIT Commission on Education. Dr. Bodman also served as technical director of the American Research & Development Corporation. He received his doctorate from MIT.

Jim Bowman is manager of public relations of Financial Shares Corporation in Chicago and writes a weekly column for the *Chicago Tribune* Sunday magazine. He has written for *Advertising Age, Crain's Chicago Business, Speechwriter's Newsletter,* and other publications. He was a reporter for nine years with the now-defunct *Chicago Daily News.*

Norman N. Bowsher is research officer of the Federal Reserve Bank of St. Louis. He began with the Reserve Bank in 1950 as an economist, and has taught at Indiana University and Washington University. Dr. Bowsher received an LL.B. from Ohio Northern University and a master's degree in law and a doctorate in business administration from Indiana University.

Hugh A. Brodkey is vice-president and associate general counsel of the Chicago Title Insurance Company. He is a member of many orgaizations dealing with real-property law and practice, including the American College of Real Property Lawyers, and has written and lectured extensively in the United States and Europe on real-estate matters. He received his J.D. from the University of Chicago.

John M. Buckley, Jr., is director of the secretariat Planning and Management Coordination Office of the Federal Home Loan Bank Board, where his responsibilities include assisting the chairman in developing the agency's goals and overall strategies for dealing with problems of the savings and loan industry and for processing all official Bank Board decisions. He has taught at several universities, was a member of the board of trustees of Augustinian College, and holds a J.C.D. from Catholic University.

Edgar F. Callahan is chairman of the National Credit Union Administration Board. Under his leadership federal credit unions became the first of the federal depository institutions to be deregulated with respect to savings accounts. As chairman of NCUA, he is a voting member of the Depository Institutions Deregulation Committee. President Reagan nominated Mr. Callahan to a six-year term on the National Credit Union Administration Board in September 1981. Mr. Callahan was confirmed by the Senate, sworn into office, and designated chairman the following month.

From 1977 until his presidential appointment, Mr. Callahan served as director of the Illinois Department of Financial Institutions. As director, he was responsible for the supervision of Illinois-chartered credit unions, consumer finance companies, and currency exchanges. Mr. Callahan has also served as Illinois deputy secretary of state and was superintendent of Catholic Schools for the Rockford, Illinois, area, the second-largest private school system in the state.

Randy Cepuch is assistant director of public information for the Investment Company Institute, the Washington, D.C.–based national association of mutual funds. Prior to his affiliation with ICI, he was a newspaper reporter, a radio announcer, a television producer, and an assistant director of press relations with the American Iron and Steel Institute.

Gary G. Chandler is founder and principal of Management Decision Systems, Inc., where he is a specialist in the development of credit-scoring systems and in the impact of the Equal Credit Opportunity Act on credit-scoring systems. He is also an associate professor of finance at Georgia State University. He has published several articles in the area of credit and is a member of the Editorial Review Board of the *Journal of Retail Banking.* Dr. Chandler served as consultant to the Federal Reserve Board during the drafting of the revisions of Regulation B and has been a member of the Federal Credit Legislative Subcommittee of the American Bar Association. He received his M.S. and Ph.D. (in finance) from Purdue University.

David M. Cheney is in the External Relations Department of the International Monetary Fund. He is assistant editor of *IMF Survey* and editor of the *IMF Memorandum,* a monthly review of statistical developments for the press. He was formerly editor of

Chase Manhattan Bank's biweekly *International Finance* and financial analyst in the Policy Analysis Division of the U.S. Export-Import Bank. He holds a master's degree in international economics from Temple University.

Joseph Chorun is an associate professor of economics and finance at Adelphi University's School of Business and School of Banking and Money Management. Previously he was a material project manager in the Elastimold Division of Amerace Corporation. Dr. Chorun received his Ph.D. in economics from Columbia University.

A. W. (Tom) Clausen is president of the World Bank. The World Bank consists of three affiliated institutions—the International Bank for Reconstruction and Development (IBRD), the International Development Association (IDA), and the International Finance Corporation (IFC). Mr. Clausen came to the World Bank after serving 32 years with Bank of America and BankAmerica Corporation, the last 11 years as president and chief executive officer of both institutions. He received his LL.B. from the University of Minnesota and is a graduate of the Fiftieth Advanced Management Program of the Harvard Business School. He has received honorary Doctor of Laws degrees from Carthage College, Lewis and Clark College, Gonzaga University, and the University of Notre Dame, and a Doctor of Public Services degree from the University of Santa Clara.

James B. Cloonan is president of the nonprofit American Association of Individual Investors. He has been chairman of Heinold Securities, president of Investment Information Services, and a university professor. Dr. Cloonan has an M.B.A. from the University of Chicago and a Ph.D. from Northwestern University.

D. Barry Connelly is senior vice-president of Associated Credit Bureaus, Inc., the trade association for the credit-bureau and debt-collection industry; and vice-president of the Merchants Research Council. Mr. Connelly is a recognized expert on federal regulations and legislation relating to consumer credit reporting and debt collection.

Virgil L. Conrad is the deputy administrator for family nutrition programs of the Food and Nutrition Service, where he is responsible for administering the food-stamp program. Previously he was commissioner of the South Carolina Department of Social Services and held various managerial and executive positions in the West Virginia Department of Welfare. During his career, Mr.

Conrad has been responsible for developing and implementing policies and procedures for public-assistance programs including social-service block grants, food stamps, aid to families with dependent children, Medicaid, child welfare, work-incentive, and state general assistance programs. He holds a master's degree in public administration from West Virginia University.

Bennett J. Corn is president of the Coffee, Sugar & Cocoa Exchange, Inc. His Wall Street career began in 1967 when he joined Hayden Stone, Inc. Prior to joining the exchange staff, he also held positions at Bear Stearns & Company, Dean Witter & Company, and Hornblower & Weeks–Hemphill, Noyes, Inc. Mr. Corn is a member of the Futures Industry Association, the Swiss Commodity Industry Association, the AEI Advisory Committee for the Study of Regulation of Commodity Futures Markets, and the Sugar Club of New York. He also serves on the board of trustees of Baruch College.

Howard Cosgrove is manager of press relations for the Credit Union National Association. Previously he was a speechwriter for Wisconsin Acting Governor Martin J. Schreiber and was also a newspaper reporter.

Steven P. Doehler is executive vice-president of Mortgage Insurance Companies of America (MICA), the Washington, D.C.–based trade association. His finance background in the nation's capital includes experience with the Senate Banking, Housing, and Urban Affairs Committee; the Federal Home Loan Bank Board as congressional liaison; the National Association of Home Builders; and the National Association of Realtors.

Thomas R. Donovan is president and chief executive officer of the Chicago Board of Trade (CBOT). A widely regarded and highly respected administrator, he has played a significant role in the expansion of the world's largest and oldest commodity-futures exchange. Before his affiliation with CBOT, Mr. Donovan served as administrative assistant for two Chicago mayors—Richard J. Daley and Michael A. Bilandic. Mr. Donovan holds a master's degree in public administration from the Illinois Institute of Technology, Chicago.

Virginia T. Douglas is a former writer/editor at the Health Care Financing Administration of the Department of Health and Human Services, Washington, D.C. She has many years experience in writing about health care and social services, and was the editor of *HFCA Forum,* a government magazine in the health-care field. She received a master's degree in journalism from the University of California, Los Angeles.

Franklin R. Edwards is professor and director of the Center for the Study of Futures Markets at Columbia University. He is a consultant to several government agencies and was previously employed by the Federal Reserve Board and the comptroller of the currency. His major area of expertise is in the regulation of futures markets and other financial markets and he has written extensively in these areas. Dr. Edwards is associate editor of the *Journal of Futures Markets* and editor of *Issues in Financial Regulations.* He holds a Ph.D. from Harvard University and a J.D. from New York University.

Charles B. Epstein is vice-president institutional sales for Lind-Waldock, a commodities discount firm. He was formerly the financial editor in the public-affairs department of the Chicago Mercantile Exchange. Mr. Epstein has written for numerous publications and has reported on commodity developments through television, radio, and print. He is a former reporter and a Jacob Scher Investigative Reporting Award nominee. He received a masters in communications arts from the University of Illinois, Urbana.

Dana F. Ferrell is director of marketing for the New York Cotton Exchange. Previously she was with the New York Mercantile Exchange. She is a member of the Association of Energy Professionals in New York City.

Roxanne P. Fischetti is a writer/editor with the Office of Public Affairs of the U.S. Securities and Exchange Commission. She is responsible for the SEC Annual Report to Congress and various other consumer and information publications. Previously, she worked for Foreign Affairs Studies, a research branch of American University.

Edward A. Fox is president and chief executive officer of the Student Loan Marketing Association (Sallie Mae). Prior to his election, Mr. Fox served as director of finance and chief financial officer of the Federal Home Loan Banks from 1970 to 1973. Mr. Fox holds an M.B.A. from New York University.

George D. Friedlander is vice-president of the Research Division of Smith Barney, Harris Upham & Company, Inc. He has had articles published in a number of periodicals, including *Municipal Finance Journal* and *Bond Buyer.* Mr. Friedlander is a member of the Public Securities Association Research Committee, the Municipal Analysts Group of New York, and the Southern Municipal Finance Group. He received his M.B.A. from Pace University.

David H. Friedman is special planning coordinator for the Federal Reserve Bank of New York. In that post he assists bank management in multiyear planning efforts and provides staff support for planning initiatives of key committees within the Federal Reserve system. Mr. Friedman has been a member of the Department of Economics at Brooklyn College, serving as an adjunct lecturer in money and banking, and is also on the faculty of the American Institute of Banking, in New York.

James S. Gallagher is president and chief operating officer of the Pacific Stock Exchange, Inc. (PSE). He is also a member of the board of directors of the Options Clearing Corporation in Chicago. Mr. Gallagher was previously vice-president for market operations of the New York Futures Exchange, a subsidiary of the New York Stock Exchange, with responsibilites for all floor operation, and held a variety of positions at the New York Stock Exchange, including vice-president, systems support. He had also been a floor broker on the New York and American stock exchanges. He received an M.B.A. from St. John's University.

Griffith L. Garwood is director of the Division of Consumer and Community Affairs of the Federal Reserve Board in Washington, D.C. He was previously in the private practice of law and served in various capacities at the Federal Reserve Board, including deputy secretary. He has authored articles published in *Business Lawyer, Banking Law Journal, Uniform Commercial Code Law Journal,* and other banking and legal publications. Mr. Griffith is a graduate of the University of Michigan Law School and the Stonier Graduate School of Banking.

Louis C. Gasper is executive assistant to the president of the Government National Mortgage Association ("Ginnie Mae"). Previously he was the economist for the United States Committee on Finance and for the Republican minority on the House of Representatives banking Committee. Dr. Gasper has worked as a private financial consultant and taught undergraduate and graduate economics for several years at the University of Arizona. He received his Ph.D. from Duke University.

David M. Geliebter is president of ZERO Capital Corp., a consulting firm to the securities community, specializing in the tax-shelter area, and president of Harvard Capital Group Inc., an NASD broker/dealer firm. Mr. Geliebter was previously associated with Merrill Lynch as the senior manager of its national tax-shelter operation. He has written two books on the subject, authored over 200 articles, and has been quoted in such leading publications as *Fortune, Business Week,* and *Money* magazines.

Nicholas A. Giordano is president of the Philadelphia Stock Exchange, chairman of the board of the exchange's three subsidiaries (Stock Clearing Corporation of Philadelphia, Philadelphia Depository Trust Company, and Financial Automation Corporation of Philadelphia), and a member of the board of the Options Clearing Corporation. Prior to joining the Philadelphia Stock Exchange in 1971, Mr. Giordano, a certified public accountant, was with various brokerage firms. He is a member of the board of trustees of La-Salle College, from which he holds a B.S.

Marvin Goodfriend is research officer and economist at the Federal Reserve Bank of Richmond. He is responsible for current policy analysis and monetary-policy research and has written numerous articles on these subjects for professional journals. In 1982-83, Dr. Goodfriend was visiting economist in the Econometric and Computer Applications section at the board of governors of the Federal Reserve system in Washington, D.C. He received his Ph.D. in economics from Brown University.

Reginald F. D. Green is vice-president of public information for the Investment Company Institute, the national association of mutual funds. Before coming to the United States from England in 1970, Mr. Green was a business editor with the *Manchester Guardian,* the *The Times* (London), and the *London Daily Telegraph.*

Charles Hamilton, owner of Charles Hamilton Galleries, Inc., a major firm among autograph dealers, is an internationally recognized authority in his field. He has written numerous books on autographs and has himself been the subject of many magazine articles. He has tracked down and helped send to prison over a dozen forgers and thieves, has been involved in skirmishes with the FBI and Secret Service, and has often made front-page headlines. He is a member of many philographic societies throughout the United States.

Doris E. Harless is associate economist and Money Museum curator at the Federal Reserve Bank of Richmond. She is the author of two books—*Nonbank Financial Institutions* and *South Carolina: An Economic Profile*—and of a number of articles published in the Richmond Reserve Bank's *Economic Review.* Her civic activities include membership on the board of directors of the Mary Washington College Foundation and the Mary Washington College Board of Visitors Selection Committee. Prior to joining the Federal Reserve Bank of Richmond in 1954, she was assistant dean at Sweet Briar College in Virginia. Ms. Harless received an M.S. degree from the Graduate School of Business of Columbia University, where she was a Samuel Bronfman Fellow in Democratic Business Enterprise.

Benjamin Harrison is secretary of the Spokane Stock Exchange. He began his career in the silver-mining industry in 1929.

Thomas R. Harter is the chief economist and senior staff vice-president of the Mortgage Bankers Association of America (MBA) in Washington, D.C. He is responsible for the association's economic and policy research. He is also a frequent speaker and lecturer at real-estate-industry meetings, conventions, and educational programs, and has published extensively in such areas as capital formation, financial institutions, and economic forecasting.

Prior to joining MBA, Dr. Harter was the senior economist and manager of program development at the Federal Home Loan Bank of San Francisco. From 1968 to 1974, he served as an associate professor of finance at the University of Colorado, School of Business, and worked as a private consultant to numerous financial institutions.

Dr. Harter received his Ph.D. in finance from Northwestern University and his B.A. and M.B.A. from Washington University in St. Louis, Missouri.

Mildred M. Hermann is secretary and treasurer of the Financial Analysts Federation (FAF). She is editor of both the FAF newsletter and FAF's annual *Corporate Information Committee Report* of evaluations of corporate financial reporting. She holds master's degrees from Union Theological Seminary.

C. Whitman Hobbs is an attorney/writer. A member of the New York Bar for the past 30 years, he has been an active general practitioner. In addition, he has been a daily newspaper reporter and a writer/editor with the television and radio news departments of a major network. He has also been a magazine editor.

A graduate of St. John's Law School, Mr. Hobbs has taught commercial law and has served as general counsel of a publicly held corporation. He has also served as a municipal attorney and has done graduate studies in international, copyright, and the communications law fields.

Douglas R. Hoffmann is an attorney at law and the secretary-treasurer at Glacken-Hoffmann Ltd., and vice-president of Hei Real Estate Funding, Inc. He is also a licensed insurance and real-estate broker and state-approved instructor in real estate and insurance. Mr. Hoffmann received his J.D. from St. John's University School of Law.

Marvin A. Holland is a partner in the law firm of Holland & Zinker, practicing exclusively in bankruptcy and debt-related matters. He is a member of the Suffolk County Bar Association, Nassau County Bar Association, New York State Bar Association, and Bankruptcy Lawyers Bar association, and has lectured for the Practicing Law Institute, American Academy of Matrimonial Lawyers, Nassau County Academy of Law, and Suffolk County Academy of Law. He is a member of the National Law Committee of the Anti-Defamation League, and has written extensively on bankruptcy.

Howard D. Hosbach is president and chief executive officer of Standard & Poor's Corporation. Mr. Hosbach joined McGraw-Hill, Inc., S&P's parent company, in 1955 as advertising manager of its medical-book division. After serving as general manager of dealer and library sales for McGraw-Hill, he joined Standard & Poor's in 1970 as group vice-president. Mr. Hosback received an M.B.A. from Fairleigh Dickinson University.

Samuel C. Hoyt is a senior staff writer in the public-relations division of the American Institute of Certified Public Accountants, where he prepares material for use by practitioners in small C.P.A. firms. He has also done public-relations work for the insurance and recreational marine industries.

Mary Ann Irvine is manager of public information in the public-relations department of the United States League of Savings Institutions, where she serves as liaison with textbook and encyclopedia publishers to provide current information on the savings and loan business.

Robert L. Isaacson is president of Future Funding Consultants and principal stockholder in Commodity Investment Consultants Ltd., a registered commodity adviser. He is the director of the board of directors of both the Futures Industry Association (FIA) and the National Association of Futures Trading Advisors (NAFTA) and a member of the board of directors and the Executive Committee of the National Futures Association (NFA). He is also a consultant to and member of the Executive Advisory committee to Transcorp. Ltd., a diversified conglomerate, and on the board of directors of Toolmac Mfg. Company, Inc.

Edwin M. Jones is executive director of the Pension Benefit Guaranty Corporation (PBGC). Mr. Jones's experience covers a wide range of legal, insurance, and investment matters directly related to his responsibilities for PBGC and its purposes and functions. For ten years prior to joining PBGC, Mr. Jones was a partner in the New York law firms of Lane & Mittendorf and Shea & Gould, specializing in ERISA, employee-benefit, tax, and insurance matters. Before that, for 20 years, he was a lawyer and officer of New York Life Insurance Company, and had been the president of a private investment company. Mr. Jones has been active on American Bar Association and New York State Bar Association committees concerned with employee benefits and retirement plans. He is also a lifetime member of the Association of Life Insurance Counsel. He has a law degree and Master of Laws in taxation from New York University School of Law.

Frank J. Jones is senior vice-president, options and index products, at the New York Stock Exchange and chairman of the board of the New York Futures Clearing Corporation. Previously he was executive vice-president and chief operating officer of the New York Futures Exchange, vice-president of research and chief economist of the Chicago Mercantile Exchange, and associate professor at the School of Business at San Jose University. Dr. Jones has authored several books, including *Macro Finance—The Financial System and the Economy,* and several articles and chapters in books on financial futures markets, the financial system, and other related topics. Dr. Jones holds a master's degree in business administration from the University of Pittsburgh, a master's degree in nuclear engineering from Cornell University, and a doctorate in economics from Stanford University.

Richard C. Kane is a senior vice-president at Citibank and general manager of its New York Banking Division. Previously he was president of Citicorp Credit Services, Inc., which handles Citibank MasterCard, Citibank Visa, and related payment transaction services, and vice-president in the Check Processing Division. Mr. Kane holds an M.B.A. from Harvard University.

Phil Kaufman has been a professional numismatist for over ten years, three of which he spent as a buyer for one of the largest rare-coin investment firms in the U.S. He has written numerous articles and research papers for trade and professional journals and is a frequent instructor at seminars. He holds a master's degree from Adelphi University.

Frederick W. Kilbourne, an actuary, is a member of the American Academy of Actuaries and is chairman of its Committee on Government Relations. He is also a Fellow of the Casualty Actuarial Society, the Society of Actuaries, the Conference of Actuaries in Public Practice, and the Canadian Institute of Actuaries.

Joseph F. Kissel is vice-president and an officer of the Vanguard Group of Investment Companies. Prior to joining Vanguard, Mr. Kissel held key marketing, advertising, research, and business-planning positions at three major marketing and research organizations. He is currently executive vice-president and a member of the Executive Committee and board of governors of the No-Load Mutual Fund Association and vice-president and a director of the Philadelphia Direct Marketing Association. He holds an M.B.A. from Temple University.

Duane Kline is public information representative of the Federal Reserve Bank of Atlanta. He is author and coauthor of a number of pamphlets on the Federal Reserve system and it operations. Mr. Kline is one of the original developers of the Federal Reserve Bank of Atlanta's Monetary Museum. He is a member of the Advisory Council for the Center for Business and Economic Education at Georgia State University and the Special Task Force of the Georgia Council on Economic Education.

Scott M. Krantz is options-marketing strategist and commodity trading adviser at ContiCommodity Services, Inc. He is also a consultant and lecturer for the Chicago Board of Trade, an instructor in finance, economics, and investments at Loyola University (Chicago) and an instructor in options on futures for the Futures Industry Association. Mr. Krantz holds an M.B.A. in finance from the University of Chicago.

Sheila Lambert is senior vice-president and publisher of Moody's Investors Service. Ms. Lambert served as publisher of Moody's for two years, although her association with Moody's and with Dun & Bradstreet Corporation, of which Moody's is a part, spans 12 years. She is a member of the Information Industry Association.

Harold C. Luckstone, Jr., is an assistant professor at the College of Insurance. A chartered life underwriter, Mr. Luckstone has been in the life-insurance business as an agent, assistant general agent, director of agencies, consultant, writer, and educator for over 25 years. He holds a master's degree from New York University.

Leonard Machlis is executive director of the National Commercial Finance Conference, Inc., in New York City, where he has been employed for 28 years. He is a member of various other organizations, such as both the New York and American Societies of Association Executives, the Commercial Law League, and the New York Credit & Financial Mangement Association.

Gordon S. Macklin is president of the National Association of Securities Dealers, Inc. Previously he was chairman of the National Clearing Corporation and a partner in McDonald & Company, investment bankers. He has also been a member of the board of directors of the Midwest Stock Exchange, the State of Ohio Chamber of Commerce, and 11 companies, the majority of which held publicly traded securities, as well as a member of the Banking and Securities Industry Committee and the National Advisory Council of the Small Business Administration.

Seth P. Maerowitz is a management consultant in the Financial Industries Section of Arthur D. Little, Inc. Previously, he was a research associate at the Federal Reserve Bank of Richmond. Mr. Maerowitz received a master's degree in management from Massachusetts Institute of Technology.

Ray E. Mauger, Jr. was employed for 27 years with the Savings Bank Life Insurance Fund, from which he retired in 1983 as senior vice-president of marketing. In this capacity he had overall responsibility for the development of SBLI's mass-media advertising, the marketing of new products, and the training of the more than 1,300 people who sell SBLI in New York State.

Jeffrey R. McCord is executive assistant to the chairman of the Securities Investor Protection Corporation (SIPC). He was previously a communications consultant to such organizations as Merrill Lynch and SIPC. He has served as a legislative aide to a U.S. senator and as an economic researcher for a major international bank in London.

Stuart A. McFarland is executive vice-president and chief financial officer of the Federal National Mortgage Association. Previously, he was president of the Ticor Mortgage Insurance Company.

Michele McNamara is assistant director of mortgage finance at the National Association of Home Builders (NAHB) and editor of *Mortgage Finance Update,* a monthly newsletter. Previously she was a staff writer in NAHB's Public Affairs Division and a reporter for the Whaley Eaton Newsletters. She has a master's in journalism from the University of California, Berkeley.

Stephen Meyerhardt is manager of public affairs for the U.S. Savings Bond Division, U.S. Department of the Treasury. He is a member of the National Association of Government Communicators.

Arthur M. Mikesell, a public-relations consultant in the banking area, was formerly associate director of information and marketing, and public-relations director of the National Association of Mutual Savings Banks. Prior to that, he was a public-relations officer with the American Bankers Association. Mr. Mikesell worked for ten years as a book and magazine editor and is the author of numerous magazine articles and one book.

Charles J. Mohr is chairman and chief executive officer of the Boston Stock Exchange. Formerly vice-president of system planning and development for the New York Stock Exchange, Mr. Mohr has an extensive background in trading surveillance, security regulation, financial analysis, policy development, strategic planning, and marketing. During his ten years with the NYSE, he helped design and launch the Intermarket Trading System and implement other national market system projects, along with developing new specialist-performance and stock-allocation procedures.

Mr. Mohr has served on various committees involving the Intermarket Trading System, the Securities Industry Association, the National Securities Trading Association, and the Boston Securities Traders Association. He received a master's in business administration in finance from the University of Vermont.

Mechlin D. Moore is president of the Insurance Information Institute, a trade association representing over 250 property/casualty-insurance companies. Previously he was senior vice-president of both public affairs and external affairs at United Airlines, president of the Downtown Seattle Development Association, director of information for the Urban Land Institute of Washington, D.C., director of urban renewal for the National Association of Real Estate Boards, and a reporter for the *Washington Post*. Mr. Moore is a graduate of Harvard University.

James L. Moorefield is president of the Health Insurance Association of America. HIAA represents more than 325 insurance companies, which are responsible for about 85% of the health insurance written by in-surance companies in the United States. Mr. Moorefield began his insurance career in 1953 as an attorney for the Paul Revere Life Insurance Company and joined HIAA in 1968 as vice-president and general counsel. He received an LL.B. degree from Virginia Law School.

Frank Morgan is vice-president, North American Division, for ContiCommodity Services, Inc., the international futures brokerage firm subsidiary of Continental Grain Company.

George M. Morvis is president of Financial Shares Corporation, a Chicago-based marketing, public-relations, and training consulting organization whose bank-client roster is spread across the United States. Previously he was executive secretary of the Illinois Bankers Association. He is a member of several professional associations and currently serves as president and member of the board of trustees of the Illinois Council on Economic Education. He is on the faculty of the Iowa School of Banking and the Midwest Banking Institute and has lectured and written extensively on the subjects of marketing and training. He received an M.B.A. in journalism from George Washington University.

Donald A. Moser is director of public relations and marketing support for Standard & Poor's Corporation. Prior to joining S&P, he was manager of publicity for McGraw-Hill, S&P's parent corporation. Mr. Moser has worked for newspapers in the Midwest and New York area and is a member of the Society of Professional Journalists.

Judah Munk is vice-president and manager of the Fresh Meadows, Queens, New York, office of Merrill Lynch, Pierce, Fenner & Smith, Inc. He has been registered with the New York Stock Exchange since 1960 and has lectured at Queens College in the area of investments and finance.

Craig A. Nalen is president and chief executive officer of Overseas Private Investment Corporation (OPIC). Previously, he was chairman and chief executive officer of STP Corporation and was a vice-president of General Mills. Mr. Nalen received an M.B.A. degree from Stanford University Graduate School of Business.

John M. Nash is president of the National Association of Corporate Directors. He is active in raising capital through securities and banking mechanisms, including equity funding, convertible debentures, venture capital, private placements, mergers and acquisitions, and the structuring of corporate and tax-exempt bond issues and tax shelters/limited partnerships. He has been called upon to solve financing problems in business, industry, state and local governments, and the marketing of real-estate projects. He has taught courses in corporate and municipal finance at the New York Institute of Finance, has served on a congressional committee to evaluate underwriters, and has appeared before other committees on behalf of the business community as an expert in tax-exempt securities.

Mr. Nash is a recognized author in the fields of finance and politics. His works include *The Tax Exempt Municipal Bond Guide for the Individual Investor, The World of Fixed Income, The Bondholders Newsletter, The Disclosure Digest,* and *The Corporate Directors Guide.* He has published *The Disclosure/ SEC Handbook* and the annual *Analysis of Shareholder Proposals* series, and is editor of *Directors Monthly* for the National Association of Corporate Directors. He is a columnist for the nation's oldest financial newspaper, the *Commercial and Financial Chronicle,* and publisher of *the Fixed Income Journal.* In 1968, Mr. Nash received the Investment Bankers Association of America's "Award of Excellence" for his proposed "Marshall Plan for the Cities."

Richard B. Niehoff is president of the Cincinnati Stock Exchange. He is also first vice-president and trustee of the Cincinnati Stock and Bond Club and exchange representative of the Consolidated Tape Association, Consolidated Quote Association, and Inter-Market Trading System. In addition, he is a trustee of the Contemporary Arts Center of Cincinnati. He was previously chairman of the Cincinnati Stock Exchange and associated with Thomson, McKinnon Securities, Inc.

Edward I. O'Brien is president of the Securities Industry Association (SIA). Previously, he had been associated with Bache & Company, Inc., for 19 years, most recently as chairman of the Executive Committee and as a director. Active in securities-industry affairs for many years, Mr. O'Brien served on SIA's Legislative Committee and is a former president of its Compliance and Legal Division as well as a former chairman of its Publicly Owned Firms Committee. Prior to joining Bache, Mr. O'Brien practiced law in New York. He holds an LL.B. degree from St. John's University School of Law.

Anthony C. Paddock is senior vice-president of Standard Research Consultants. He was previously a vice-president of the Chase Manhattan Bank, first as director of the Corporate Finance Division and later as administrator of the Multinational Corporate Finance Group, and an associate in the Investment Banking Division of Merrill Lynch, Pierce, Fenner & Smith. Mr. Paddock conducts a course in investment banking at New York University. He holds an M.B.A. from Columbia University and a J.D. degree from Harvard Law School.

Charles J. Parnow is employee communications editor at the Federal Reserve Bank of New York. Previously, he was on the public-information staff of the New York Fed, where he prepared booklets, comic books, posters, and filmstrips explaining money, banking, economics, and the Federal Reserve to students and the general public. A graduate of New York University's School of Commerce, Accounts and Finance, Mr. Parnow began his career at United Press International, where he was primarily responsible for covering the securities market. Between 1966 and 1970, he was assistant news bureau manager and head of listed Company Information Services.

James Parthemos is senior vice-president and director of research of the Federal Reserve Bank of Richmond. He joined the staff of the Reserve Bank in 1960 as an associate economist and the following year was named economist. He is a member of the American Economic Association and the Southern Economic Association. Mr. Parthemos received an M.A. degree from the University of South Carolina.

Alfred J. Patti is president of CM&M Futures, Inc., primary dealers in U.S. Treasury and federal-agency securities and money-market instruments. He was previously vice-president of operations and planning at Amex Commodities Exchange, Inc., and assistant vice-president, American Stock Exchange, New Products Planning Division. He holds an M.B.A. from St. John's University.

John J. Phalen, Jr., is chairman and chief executive officer of the New York Stock Exchange. He has served the exchange for more than 25 years and previously was president and chief operating officer. He is also chairman of the New York Futures Exchange.

Mr. Phalen is chairman of the board of trustees of Adelphi University, a member of the board of administration of Tulane University, a member of the board of trustees of New York Medical College, and a member of the board of advisers of the Center for Banking Law Studies at Boston University. Governor Mario Cuomo of New York appointed him a member of the State Temporary Commission on Banking, Insurance, and Financial Services.

Mr. Phalen is a director of the New York Heart

Association, for whose Heart Fund Campaigns in New York City he previously served as chairman. He is also a member of the executive committee of the New York Archdiocese Cardinal's Committee of the Laity.

Long active in educational, philanthropic, and community affairs, Mr. Phalen has twice served as Wall Street division chairman of the National Association of Christians and Jews, and is a recipient of its Brotherhood Award. He received the B'Nai B'Rith Youth Services' "Wall Street Man of the Year" award, the Stephen S. Wise Award of the American Jewish Congress, and the Good Scout Award of the Boy Scouts of America, Greater New York Council.

Mr. Phalen is a graduate of Adelphi University and a recipient of its Distinguished Alumni Award. He holds an honorary doctorate from Hamilton College.

Arthur S. Phillips is senior vice-president of the Home Insurance Company. He was formerly a vice-president of American International Group, Inc., where he was most recently in charge of global accounts for AIG companies.

Christopher Pitt is assistant director of legal and claims education of the American Institute for Property and Liability Underwriters and the Insurance Institute of America. Besides holding a professional certificate from the College of Insurance, Mr. Pitt has earned the CPCU designation from the American Institute and the Associate in Claims designation from the Insurance Institute of America.

Alan J. Pomerantz is a founding partner in the firm of Harvis, Pomerantz & Rosenbluth, a New York City law firm that specializes in commercial law. He is a member of the Volunteer Lawyers for the Arts and various bar associations. He has contributed articles to numerous publications about various aspects of the practice of law and has authored materials that are currently in use in college and law-school courses. He received his J.D. degree from the New York University School of Law.

Donna Pope is director of the United States Mint, appointed by President Ronald Reagan in May 1981. As director, she is responsible for the production of the nation's coinage and protection of silver and gold bullion reserves. A native Ohioan, Director Pope previously served six terms in the Ohio House of Representatives and was Ohio's co-chairman of the 1980 Reagan campaign.

Elizabeth Bean Qutb is staff vice-president of the Mortgage Finance Division of the National Associa-

tion of Home Builders (NAHB). She has been involved with promoting pension-fund investment in home mortgages, efforts to promote mortgage-backed securities, and developing industry policy on the secondary market.

Ms. Qutb came to NAHB from the Mortgage Bankers Association, where she was staff vice-president for government-agency relations. Prior to that, she was a marketing analyst and trading assistant with the Federal Home Loan Mortgage Corporation. Ms. Qutb was also a United States Foreign Service officer during the period 1964–72. She received her M.A. from George Washington University.

Harvey Rachlin is editor of *The Money Encyclopedia.* He won an ASCAP–Deems Taylor Award for excellence in music journalism for his volume *The Encyclopedia of the Music Business,* which was also named an "Outstanding Reference Book of the Year" by the American Library Association and is on the "Selected Bibliography for Musicians" of the Copyright Office of the Library of Congress. Mr Rachlin is also the author of *The Songwriter's Handbook* and of numerous magazine articles. He has taught business courses at the college level and has appeared on numerous radio and television shows, including *The Dinah Shore Show.*

Andrew Michael Rich is president of AMR Planning Services, Inc., on Long Island, a Registered Investment Advisor Corporation. He holds a Master of Science degree in taxation from Long Island University, a Certified Financial Planner designation from the College for Financial Planning in Denver, and lectures on financial planning at various colleges. He is the author of *How to Survive and Succeed in a Small Financial Planning Practice.*

Thomas E. Robinson is legal counsel for the National Association of Real Estate Investment Trusts, Inc. He was previously a staff attorney for the Department of Housing and Urban Development. Mr. Robinson holds an M.L.T. from Georgetown University Law Center and a J.D. from Suffolk University Law School.

Murray Rosen is associate professor at the College of Insurance in New York City and a practitioner of life and health insurance. He has served as a consultant on insurance to the U.S. Senate Subcommittee and the New York State Assembly Committee on Consumer Affairs. Mr. Rosen has contributed articles on insurance to professional journals and has appeared on radio in reference to consumerism on insurance. He lectures to professional and civic groups on financial planning. He is a Charter Life Underwriter and holds a Master of Science degree from New York University.

Richard A. Rossi is manager of public relations for Visa International. He was formerly an associate editor of *U.S. News & World Report* and an economics and business writer for Reuters Ltd. and United Press International.

Andrew L. Rothman is director of the Office of Public Affairs of the U.S. Securities and Exchange Commission. Previously he served as an aide to a U.S. senator and was a journalist covering principally politics and government. He received his M.B.A. from Loyola College.

Louis A. Russo is president of CEP Consultants, Inc., a Long Island consulting firm on pensions. He is a chartered financial consultant and is a member of the American Society of Pension Actuaries and the International Association of Financial Planners. He holds a master's degree from New York University.

Arthur Samansky is a special assistant in the public-information area of the Federal Reserve Bank of New York. In his post, Mr. Samansky serves as a press spokesman for the bank and heads the press- and community-relations staff. He has also written a number of booklets and books published by the Federal Reserve. Before joining the New York Fed, Mr. Samansky was a copy editor with AP–Dow Jones and a business and financial writer for the *World Journal Tribune* and its predecessor, the *World Telegram and Sun.* He is a member of several associations, including the New York Financial Writers' Association and the Society of Professional Journalists, and holds a master's degree from New York University.

James C. Sanders is administrator of the Small Business Administration. He was nominated for this position by President Reagan on February 4, 1982, and was confirmed for the post in March 1982. Previously, he was chairman and chief executive officer of Corroon & Black/Sanders & Sullivan, an international insurance firm.

Paul Schimmel is an attorney in private practice on Long Island. He holds a J.D. from Brooklyn Law School and a Master of Law degree in estate planning from the University of Miami School of Law.

Timothy A. Schlindwein is a partner in the investment-counseling firm of Stein, Roe & Farnham, a leading independent investment-counseling firm based in Chicago, Illinois. He manages the firm's fixed-income department and is vice-president and portfolio manager of SteinRoe Cash Reserves, Stein-Roe Government Reserves, and SteinRoe Bond Fund. His responsibilities also include managing major institutional fixed-income portfolios of public, private, and jointly administered retirement funds, college reserve and endowment funds, and life- and casualty-insurance-company portfolios. Previously Mr. Schlindwein was a trust investment officer at First National Bank of Chicago. He is a chartered investment counselor and a member of the Financial Analysts Society of Chicago. He holds an M.B.A. degree from the University of Chicago.

Kathleen A. Seebert is director of marketing for MidAmerican Commodity Exchange. She holds an M.B.A. from Northwestern University and an M.A. from the University of Notre Dame. She is a member of the Futures Industry Association and a registered commodity representative.

Steven A. Seiden has been a general partner of the investment firm of Herzfeld & Stern since 1966. Mr. Seiden serves on the Executive Committee of the firm and is a director and member of the Executive Committee of the Securities Industry Association (SIA). He has actively advocated and lobbied for better tax treatment of investors' capital gains by both the federal government and New York State.

Mr. Seiden is past chairman of SIA's New York district and is a member of the New York Stock Exchange Regulatory Policy Advisory Committee. He is also on the Policy Committee of the American Council for Capital Formation, a director of the Wall Street Tax Association, and on the editorial advisory board of the *Registered Representative* magazine.

Bernard M. Shavelson is marketing manager for Fidelity Brokerage Services, a division of the Fidelity Group. Prior to his employment with Fidelity, Mr. Shavelson was a registered representative for Paine Webber Co., DuPont Glore Forgon, and Shearson Hammill; a sales training director for Investors Planning Corp. of Boston; and the owner of an advertising agency.

Eugene J. Sherman is vice-president and economist of International Gold Corporation (Intergold), the marketing subsidiary of the Chamber of Mines of South Africa, the private-sector trade association of the country's mining interests. Mr. Sherman is a financial economist with extensive experience in domestic and international money markets. During his career he has observed the financial markets from a variety of perspectives—from the vantage point of a central bank, when he worked at the Federal Reserve Bank of New York; from the perspective of a commercial bank, when he was with the Bank of New York and Chase Manhattan; and from the viewpoint of economist and money manager when he was with Merrill Lynch. In addition, Mr. Sherman has been widely published in economic journals and the general-interest financial press, and is often quoted in the media as an authority on the economics of gold.

M. Alden Siegel is vice-president of convertible sales at the First Boston Corporation. He began his investment career in 1961 with Great American Insurance company as a portfolio manager and later worked at Kidder, Peabody as a block trader, general research salesperson, and specialist selling convertible securities. Mr. Siegel holds an M.B.A. from New York University.

Barrett Sinowitz is vice-president, investments, of Prudential-Bache Securities. Previously, he was a retail stockbroker with Bache, Halsey, Stuart, Shields, Cowen & Company. Prior to his work on Wall Street, Mr. Sinowitz was an international management consultant specializing in marketing management, finance, and business planning. He teaches personal financial planning and basic investing in the continuing-education division at the Cooper Union in New York City. Mr. Sinowitz received an M.B.A. in marketing and management from New York University Graduate School of Business Administration.

Martha E. Skoog is manager of the Department of Consumer Affairs of the Federal Reserve Bank of Philadelphia. She established the department in 1975 to resolve complaints, answer inquiries, and conduct an educational program. She also heads the Public Services Department, which conducts public relations for the bank. Ms. Skoog has authored numerous educational pamphlets for consumers.

Francis B. Smith is director of communications at the American Financial Services Association in Washington, D.C. In that position, she oversees the public-relations, publications, marketing, and membership programs of the trade association, which represents about 600 financial-services companies with 15,000 offices throughout the U.S.

Previously Ms. Smith was employed by the American Bankers Association and the Consumer Bankers Association, where she was vice-president and founding editor of the *Journal of Retail Banking.* She holds

an M.A. from the State University of New York at Buffalo.

Harley W. Snyder is president of the National Association of Realtors, the nation's largest trade association, representing more than 600,000 individuals involved in all phases of real estate. In a variety of other capacities, he has served the association for 27 years. At the state and local level, Mr. Snyder served as president of the Indiana Association of Realtors and president of the Valparaiso (Indiana) Board of Realtors. He was named Realtor of the Year at the state level and received the honor twice at the local level. He has held many committee memberships and chairmanships at both levels.

J. Roger Spjute is executive secretary of the Intermountain Stock Exchange and a full-time teacher for the Salt Lake Board of Education.

Charles N. Stabler is assistant managing editor of the *Wall Street Journal.* He was formerly banking editor, managing editor of the Pacific Coast edition, and manager of the Southeastern Bureau. He was a recipient of the Loeb Award (business and financial news) in 1967.

Carol A. Stone is associate economist at European American Bank in New York. Prior to that, she was a vice-president and senior economist at Merrill Lynch Economics, Inc., and specialized in financial market analysis. Ms. Stone is a member of several professional organizations. She holds an M.B.A. from Southern Methodist University, a Master of Philosophy in economics and international business from the Graduate School of Business Administration at New York University, and is currently writing her doctoral dissertation.

R. Bruce Swensen is an assistant professor of corporate finance and investments at Adelphi University, Garden City, New York. He has also held positions at Iona College, New Rochelle, New York; and at the State University of New York College at Old Westbury. Professor Swensen received his M.B.A. from New York University and is currently a doctoral student at that institution.

William H. Tankersley is president of the Council of Better Business Bureaus, Inc. Previously, he was vice-president of program practices of the CBS Television Network. Mr. Tankersley is a past member of the Television Code Review Board of the National Association of Broadcasters and of the Standards Committee of the American Advertising Federation. He has served on the U.S. Chamber of Commerce's Committee on Business Overview and is currently on the Committee on Marketing, Advertising and Distribution of the U.S. Council for International Business.

Paul A. Tattersall is president of the Minneapolis Grain Exchange. Previously, he was senior vice-president of the Minneapolis Star and Tribune Company. He has also held positions with the *Washington Post* and IBM Corporation. He received an M.B.A. from Columbia University Graduate School of Business.

R. William Taylor is president of the American Society of Association Executives (ASAE), a voluntary membership society of 10,000 executives who manage leading business, professional, technical, and industrial associations. Prior to becoming ASAE president, Mr. Taylor served for 13 years as chief staff executive of the Society of Manufacturing Engineers (SME). A 28-year veteran of association management, Mr. Taylor received ASAE's highest professional honor for the chief staff executives of associations—the Key Award—in 1976. He holds an M.S. from Ohio University.

Charles J. Terrana is vice-president and manager of the Bond Funds Trading Department of Merrill Lynch, Pierce, Fenner & Smith, Inc. For over 27 years he has worked in various capacities in the underwriting and trading of municipal and corporate fixed-income securities. His responsibilities included the pricing and marketing of competitive or negotiated municipal and corporate bond underwritings. In his present position, he is responsible for the management of bond fund security positions, which at times exceed $100 million and encompass over 750 different bond funds—including municipal, corporate, and government fixed-income securities funds, as well as equity funds.

Richard D. C. Trainer is an economist with the Federal Reserve Bank of New York. He was previously a professor of economics at various universities in the United States, and he is now an adjunct professor at the Graduate School of Business of Pace University. Dr. Trainer has written numerous articles in the areas of finance and economics for professional journals and consumer publications. He received a master's degree in economics from New York University and a Ph.D. in economics and law from the University of Notre Dame.

John Elting Treat is president of the New York Mer-

cantile Exchange. Prior to joining the exchange in 1981, Mr. Treat was responsible for energy policy in the White House as a member of the National Security Staff under President Carter and President Reagan. An economist, he has been directly involved in the formulation of national and international energy policy since the early 1970s. Mr. Treat held senior positions in the Federal Energy Administration and the Department of Energy, where he served as deputy assistant secretary for international affairs. He is the author of several publications and papers on international energy affairs and has been the recipient of numerous professional and educational awards. Mr. Treat received a master's degree from The Johns Hopkins School of Advanced International Studies.

James F. Tucker is vice-president/economist in the research department of the Federal Reserve Bank of Richmond and also the bank's community-affairs officer. In addition to these duties, Dr. Tucker serves as a lecturer in economics at Mary Washington College and is a member of the faculty at the Stonier Graduate School of Banking at Rutgers University. Dr. Tucker was president of Virginia State College from 1968 to 1970 and was professor of economics and director of the Center for Economic Education at Virginia Polytechnic Institute and State University from 1970 to 1974. Prior to 1970, he served as head of the Department of Business and Economics at West Virginia State College and North Carolina Central University. He also served as director of field operations in the Bureau of Works and Training Programs in the U.S. Department of Labor.

Dr. Tucker has contributed a number of articles and reviews to professional journals and is the author of three books: *Essentials of Economics, Current Economic Issues and Problems,* and *Anatomy of High-Earning Minority Banks, 1972–1975.* He is a member of the board of trustees at Howard University, a member of the board of directors of the Virginia Council for Economic Education, a member of the Virginia Public Building Authority, and a member of the board of directors of Richmond Renaissance, a city-sponsored organization seeking to promote economic growth. Dr. Tucker received M.A. degrees from Howard University and a Ph.D. in economics from the University of Pennsylvania.

Michael L. Unger is a financial economist and director of the International Division in the Office of Policy and Economic Research at the Federal Home Loan Bank Board, Washington, D.C. Previously, he was an international economist in the Office of the Secretary, U.S. Treasury Department. Mr. Unger holds graduate degrees in economics from the University of Toledo and Washington University and is a graduate of the Harvard Business School's Program for Management Development.

Gail Lutz Verley is a program analyst in the Insurance Division of the Federal Savings and Loan Insurance Corporation. She has a master's degree in public administration from American University.

W. N. Vernon III is executive vice-president and chief executive officer of the Board of Trade of Kansas City, Missouri, Inc. Previously, he was associate counsel of Campbell Taggart Bakeries. Mr. Vernon is a frequent speaker and writer on commodities and commodity-law subjects. He received his J.D. and LL.M. from Southern Methodist University School of Law.

Robert E. Waite, Jr., is vice-president for public affairs of the Export-Import Bank of the United States. Mr. Waite was previously associated with International Business Machines Corporation as manager for international associations, and has worked as an assistant to Senate Finance Committee Chairman Robert Dole (R-Kansas) and former senator Edward W. Brooke of the Banking, Housing, and Urban Affairs Committee.

Robert Waldron is New York director of the American Council of Life Insurance. He was previously a reporter, columnist, and editor for three New Jersey dailies, including the *Newark Star-Ledger,* and has also written for other publications, including *New York* and *American Heritage* magazines. As spokesman for ACLI, he has appeared in numerous broadcast settings, including the "Today Show" and "Good Morning America."

Elsie M. Watters is director of research of the Tax Foundation, Inc., in Washington, D.C., and the author of numerous articles on government finance and taxation. Prior to joining the Tax Foundation in 1962, she was an associate professor at the Tulane School of Business and held assignments in economic research at the University of Texas and Louisiana State University. Dr. Watters holds a Ph.D. from the University of Texas and master's degrees in business and economics from Louisiana State University.

John G. Weithers is chairman of the Midwest Stock Exchange. He has spent his entire business career with

the exchange: He was named vice-president in 1963, senior vice-president in 1967, executive vice-president in 1972, president in 1980, and chairman in 1983. He holds a master's degree in business administration from DePaul University.

Stan West is vice-president of business research of the New York Stock Exchange. He has been with the exchange since 1954. Previously, Mr. West was a senior researcher with the Tax Foundation and an editor with Prentice-Hall business services. He has also been a consultant and contributor to several encyclopedias. He is a member and has been an officer of numerous professional associations. Mr. West received his M.B.A. and J.D. degrees from New York University.

Eric A. Wiening is assistant director of curriculum for the American Institute for Property and Liability Underwriters, Inc., and Insurance Institute of America. He received the Chartered Property Casualty Underwriter (CPCU) designation from the American Institute for Property and Liability Underwriters and was designated an Associate in Risk Management (ARM) by the Insurance Institute of America. He is a member of the Society of CPCU and the Insurance Company Education Directors Society (ICEDS) and was a contributing editor for the text *Personal Lines Underwriting.*

Steven J. Wohl is a partner in the law firm of Perles & Albert, where he practices primarily in the field of estate planning and administration and related tax areas. He has been a lecturer and panel chairman at the Practising Law Institute and a faculty member at the New School for Social Research. He received his J.D. from Columbia Law School, where he was a Harlan Fiske Stone Scholar.

Shelia R. Wyse is vice-president of National Benefit Insurance Company, a division of American Can Company. She chairs the Disability Benefits Law Industry Advisory Committee and serves as publication coordinator of *Statutorystar,* a quarterly digest of state disability benefits, news, and commentary.

Matt Zachowski is director of marketing and communications for Commodity Exchange, Inc., where he has the prime responsibility for developing and administering the exchange's marketing and public-relations programs. Prior to joining COMEX, Mr. Zachowski was a metals analyst in the news department at E. F. Hutton & Company.

The Money Encyclopedia

Abstract of Title

See TITLE INSURANCE.

Accountant

See CERTIFIED PUBLIC ACCOUNTANT (CPA).

Actuary

The actuary is a mathematician who specializes in problems involving both money and uncertainty. Specifically, he or she is a professional whose training and experience is in evaluating the current financial implications of future contingent events. The actuary designs and manages insurance plans, and determines premiums and reserves to secure their ongoing solvency. The actuary does similar work with employee-benefit plans, self-insurance and social insurance schemes, and other programs involving fiscal risk.

Employment of Actuaries. Most actuaries are employed by insurance companies or by consulting firms that provide actuarial services. The approximate distribution of actuarial employment in the United States in 1983 was 55% for insurance companies, 40% for consulting firms, and 5% for other employers.

Actuarial Work. Actuaries tend to specialize, and generally refer to themselves as life, casualty, or pension actuaries. These shorthand descriptions are not mutually exclusive, however, nor fully descriptive. Thus, life actuaries often work on health insurance and sometimes on employee-benefit products. Casualty actuaries often work on property insurance and sometimes on health insurance. Pension actuaries generally do specialize in retirement plans, but some also work on other employee-benefit programs.

Nearly half of all American actuaries consider themselves to be *life* actuaries. Most are employed by life-insurance companies, with several of the largest insurers employing over 100 actuaries each. Some are employed by consulting firms, including a number of sole-proprietor individual consultants. The work of the actuary is central to the business of life insurance. He or she participates in the design of products to be sold (e.g., term life insurance intended to cover the declining balance of a mortgage), is responsible for pricing the product to be profitable yet competitive (e.g., the premium rate for the product may be $7.50 per $1,000 coverage at a given age), and must determine the company's liability after the policy has been sold and the premium received (e.g., the policy reserve may be $66.25 per $1,000 coverage at a given duration subsequent to sale). Life actuaries also spend a good deal of time evaluating the contingencies affecting life- and health-insurance products, such as mortality and morbidity rates. They also are heavily involved in corporate planning, expense analysis, and the preparation of financial statements. Most fully qualified life actuaries have management positions within their companies, and a disproportionately large number (relative to total employment) of life-insurance company presidents are actuaries.

About a third of all American actuaries consider themselves to be *pension* actuaries. The majority are employed by large consulting firms, with several of the largest employing over 100 actuaries each. These include insurance brokerage and accounting organizations as well as pure actuarial firms. A good number of pension actuaries are also employed by life-insurance companies; others work for small consulting firms or are self-employed. The pension actuary is usually involved in the design of employee-benefit programs, including retirement benefits. He or she is essential to the determination of the annual contribution to be made to the plan to cover future benefits promised to active employees, and to the determination of plan liabilities needed to ensure future benefit payments to retired (and active) employees. Pension actuaries rarely have management positions, except within their own consulting firms, but they often are key financial advisers in several areas (e.g., compensation, investments, etc.) of concern to company management.

More than a tenth of all American actuaries consider themselves to be *casualty* actuaries. Most are employed by property- and liability-insurance companies, but in 1983 none employed so many as 50 casualty actuaries. Some are employed by rating bureaus, and a small but increasing proportion are employed by consulting firms. The casualty actuary has not permeated his half of the insurance industry as much as the life actuary has done, but his part of the actuarial profession is expanding more rapidly than the other parts. Premium rates (e.g., $125 per year for bodily-injury liability insurance for a car) that were formerly developed by the rating bureaus are increasingly being developed by company or consulting casualty actuaries. Claim reserves (e.g., $125,000 to provide future medical and income-replacement benefits for an injured employee under workmen's compensation insurance) that were formerly estimated by nonactuarial staff are increasingly developed under the direction of a casualty actuary. Casualty actuaries also spend a good deal of time evaluating the contingencies affecting property- and liability-insurance costs, such as accident frequency and claim severity. They also are heavily involved in corporate planning, expense analysis, and the preparation of financial statements. An increasing proportion of fully qualified casualty actuaries have high management positions within their insurance companies, while others are key advisers to other providers (e.g., government insurance programs) and buyers (e.g., association insurance programs) of insurance.

A small proportion (under 10% in 1983) of actuaries are employed by other than insurance companies or consulting firms. Most of these work for government agencies. State insurance departments employ several dozen actuaries to assist in the regulation of the insurance industry. Federal agencies, such as the Internal Revenue Service and the Bureau of the Census, employ actuaries. The giant Social Security Administration employs a number of actuaries to help evaluate the future costs of benefits promised or proposed. Colleges and universities employ actuaries, generally involved in the education and training of prospective actuaries. Rating bureaus also employ several dozen actuaries, primarily in the property and liability lines of insurance. Other employers of small numbers of actuaries include major industrial corporations (generally to work on employee-benefit programs) and insurance-industry service organizations (such as trade associations).

In addition to the foregoing compilations of actively employed actuaries, there are actuaries who are retired. These are about one-tenth the numbers of active actuaries, and some of those retired accept occasional consulting assignments.

The work of the actuary thus is heavily concentrated in the fields of insurance and employee benefits. It can be seen also to revolve substantially around rates and reserves, at least in its technical manifestations. It therefore is fair to describe the profession as narrow and specialized, and it often is so described. At the same time, it also can be fairly asserted that actuaries are the dominant professionals in their fields (insurance and employee benefits), and that the actuarial profession has untapped potential well beyond those fields (such as in the evaluation of the future costs of government programs and in the pricing of products and services in private industry beyond insurance).

The Actuarial Core. Few actuaries spend all or even the majority of their time on technical work as such. Most are involved in management, at least to some extent, and in other nontechnical work, such as planning and communications. An actuary's day-to-day tasks may include, for example, running a department that evaluates applications for insurance, projecting company operations for a decade into the future, or appearing at a legislative hearing concerning unemployment-insurance financing. Nonetheless, the core of the profession is technical, and serves to define and unify the field as a unique and useful profession. That core was described above as being the evaluation of the financial implications of future contingent events. This brief statement of the essential elements of actuarial science may be described symbolically by the quantity QAV, where Q represents the probability of the contingent event; A represents the cost of the event, should it occur; and V is a factor reflective of the time value of money.

A good deal of actuarial training and effort is directed toward determining the probability (Q) that an uncertain event will or will not occur. Life and pension actuaries actually use the symbol q_x to represent the probability that a person age x will die during that year. Casualty actuaries deal equivalently with "claim frequency," such as the number of accidents expected in a given population during a year (which in turn is a function of the individual probabilities of accident within the population). The concept is central to actuarial work, extending to the probability that you will be hospitalized next year, that you will receive a raise before retirement, or that your ship will sink.

Equally important to basic actuarial work are the financial consequences of the future event. The actuary must estimate the cost (A) of the event if it indeed should come to pass. This cost is easiest to determine in the case of life insurance, where the death benefit is usually fixed at issue as the face amount of the policy. It becomes more complicated in the case of nonlife insurance, where the amount payable is usually less than the policy limit and is dealt with in terms of "claim severity." It is part of a lengthy formula for the pension actuary, who must determine the chance you will die before retirement (Q), the benefit payable when you retire (A), the chance you will die during retirement at a given age (Q), and any survivor benefit that may be payable (A). A good deal of actuarial work is directed toward analyzing the distribution of claims (or benefits) by size of loss.

However, even when it is known that an event will occur and that it will cost a given amount, recognition must still be given to the time value of money. This is usually done by means of discount factors (V), which reflect expected interest rates from now to the date of the future event.

The quantity QAV may be illustrated by a brief example. Consider the premium for a one-year life-insurance policy that pays $100 at the end of the year in the event of death. Suppose that the probability of death is 20% and that bond interest rates are 5%. Then Q is 20%, A is $100, V is 95%, and the premium (QAV) is $19 (Q times A times V).

This simplified presentation of actuarial science does not do justice to the many elaborations that have been devised to improve the analysis of actuarial problems. It does, however, roughly describe the common thread, the actuarial core, which serves to identify and unite the profession.

Statistics and Judgment. The dream of every actuary is to have a perfect data base, completely reliable and large enough to minimize statistical fluctuations, extending back over many years of stability, if not tranquillity, and filled to the brim with a wealth of information about probabilities and costs. Given such a treasure, he could fully realize his birthright as a mathematician, finding trends in the data and projecting them into a secure future. As a practical matter, however, the data he gets is usually far from perfect, even when he has the opportunity to participate in its design and collection. Furthermore, even if it were perfect, he still would have to use judgment as well as his training in statistics. This follows from the fact that the future is an uncertain and even volatile place, bearing much the same relationship to the past as the young adult does to his or her parents: reflective of them in both heredity and environment, yet at the same time independent and even willful. The actuary may call on others for their subjective evaluations, or may look for statistics beyond the data base that directly pertains to his assignment, but he ultimately must quantify his judgment and draw his conclusions. Actuarial analysis almost always involves both statistics and judgment, though the mix of the two varies greatly from one project to the next.

Licensing of Actuaries. Actuaries generally are not required to be licensed by the government to practice their profession; rather, they achieve their professional credentials by passing a series of examinations described below. Services are usually provided to an employer or client who is relatively sophisticated in comparison to the general public. There is an important exception to the free-practice rule, however, in the field of private pension plans: A federal license is required if one wishes to provide certain actuarial services in connection with retirement plans set up by private employers. The Joint Board on Enrollment of Actuaries (Joint Board) confers the status of Enrolled Actuary on those deemed to have met minimum standards of actuarial education and experience as applied to pension plans. There are other exceptions, generally resulting from the predominant regulation of the insurance industry at the state-government level. For example, an actuarial statement of opinion as to the adequacy of life-insurance and casualty-loss reserves is provided by a member of the American Academy of Actuaries (the Academy), or by another person acceptable to the insurance regulatory official of the state.

Training of Actuaries. A number of colleges and universities offer actuarial courses, and a few offer graduate courses and advanced degrees. Such courses generally deal with the mathematics of uncertainty (probability theory) and with the mathematics of finance (interest theory). They often also cover nonmathematical aspects of insurance and employee-benefit programs, such as law and accounting. The predominant training of actuaries, however, is by means of study courses and examinations given by two of the professional organizations: the Casualty Actuarial Society (property and liability and health insurance), and the Society of Actuaries (life and health insurance and employee benefits).

Actuarial Examinations. Fellowship in either the Casualty Actuarial Society (CAS) or the Society of Actuaries (SOA) is conferred on passing a set of ten examinations. The course of study prescribed by the societies is comprehensive, and is intended to cover actuarial science and many of the practical aspects of actuarial work thoroughly. Course topics include probability and statistics, compound interest, general economics, insurance accounting, insurance law, valuation of liabilities, marketing, and a number of others. The examinations are prepared and given by the societies, using volunteer members for the purpose. They are given twice each year, in various cities, and are considered to be quite difficult, usually requiring several hundred hours of home study per exam. Generally, more than half the students taking a given exam will fail, but there is no limit on the number of times an exam may be taken. There is also no discrimination on the basis of race, sex, or age since the exams are written and are graded anonymously. The examinations are an important qualifying and unifying force within the actuarial profession.

Continuing Education. The actuarial organizations generally do not require periodic requalification to retain membership. Continuing education is mostly by means of the actuarial literature and by attendance at professional meetings. The actuarial organizations all hold periodic meetings, and several publish newsletters and professional journals. These last include papers on actuarial topics, and comprise the following: the *Proceedings of the Casualty Actuarial Society,* the *Transactions of the Society of Actuaries,* the *Proceedings of the Conference of Actuaries in Public Practice ("Conference"),* and the *Journal of the American Academy of Actuaries.*

Professional Standards. Committees of the actuarial organizations are very active in establishing and revising standards of professional conduct and practice, and standards of qualification to provide actuarial services in a given area. Guides to professional conduct are set forth and distributed, with interpretive opinions and specific recommendations also made available. The close-knit nature of the actuarial community has played the major role in maintaining professional standards; expulsion and other severe disciplinary actions have been rare.

Actuarial Organizations. The Casualty Actuarial Society was established in 1914 as a result of the passage of workmen's compensation laws in the states. It subsequently expanded to cover all lines of property and liability insurance, as well as marine and health insurance. The CAS sponsors three exams jointly with the Society of Actuaries, plus four more exams leading to membership as an Associate, plus three more leading to membership as a Fellow. Nearly 10% of the membership is involved in the education and examination process. Meetings are held semiannually, with special-purpose seminars also held periodically. CAS headquarters are in New York City. There were in 1983 about 1,000 members, of whom about half were Fellows.

The Society of Actuaries resulted in 1949 from the merger of the Actuarial Society of America and the America Institute of Actuaries. Its province is those lines of insurance and employee benefits that cover mortality and morbidity (sickness and injury). The SOA requires five examinations for the student to become an Associate member, and five more for the

Associate to become a Fellow. Society offices are maintained in Chicago, and staff includes full-time professionals in public relations, education, and other areas. Meetings are held four times each year, and a number of continuing-education seminars are sponsored. There were in 1983 about 8,000 members of the Society of Actuaries, of whom about half were Fellows.

The Conference of Actuaries in Public Practice was established in 1950 to deal with the special problems of consulting actuaries and other actuaries in public practice (such as those in government). Fellowship in the Conference requires twelve years of experience as an actuary, including at least five in consulting, plus meeting certain educational requirements, such as having fellowship in the CAS or SOA. The Conference holds an annual meeting for its members, and cosponsors (with the Academy) an annual meeting for enrolled actuaries. Conference headquarters are in Chicago. There were in 1983 about 750 members, of whom about two-thirds were Fellows.

The American Academy of Actuaries was established in 1965 to seek federal licensing of actuaries and to represent qualified actuaries of all specialties. Unsuccessful in the former goal, the Academy has had increasing success in the latter. Founding organizations at inception included the CAS, the SOA, the Conference, and the Fraternal Actuarial Association (which disbanded in 1980). Individual actuaries not members of any of the founding organizations were admitted to Academy membership on meeting qualification standards set by the Academy until 1970. Admission to membership now requires three years of responsible actuarial experience plus membership in the CAS or SOA, or fellowship in the Conference or a recognized foreign actuarial organization, or status as an enrolled actuary. Academy headquarters are in Washington, with a staff that includes an executive director, general counsel, director of public information, and director of administration, among others. The Academy is particularly active at the federal level in matters involving actuarial science and the actuarial profession. The Academy holds an annual meeting, usually in conjunction with a meeting of one of the founding organizations. It also jointly sponsors (with the Conference) an annual meeting for enrolled actuaries, and jointly sponsors (with the CAS) an annual seminar on the subject of casualty-loss reserves. There were in 1983 about 7,000 members of the American Academy of Actuaries.

There are several dozen local and regional actuarial clubs across the country. Most hold meetings monthly or quarterly and are comprised of members of the Academy and the other actuarial organizations. There is also one special-purpose national actuarial organization, Actuaries in Regulation, whose members work for state regulatory agencies and are members of the CAS. Another national organization is the American Society of Pension Actuaries (ASPA), which was formed by persons who provide technical and other services in connection with smaller pension plans. Some members of ASPA are enrolled actuaries.

The Canadian Institute of Actuaries (CIA) was formed in 1965, successor to predecessor organizations dating back to 1907. Most Fellows of the CIA (and there are over 1,000) are also Fellows of the Society of Actuaries.

There are actuarial organizations in several dozen other countries around the world, from Mexico to Japan and from Turkey to South Africa. Most European countries have a national actuarial organization, including all five of the Scandinavian countries. The first of these was the Institute of Actuaries, established in England in 1848. The Faculty of Actuaries was established in Scotland in 1856.

The International Actuarial Association has about 5,000 members from more than 60 countries. Meetings are held every four years. The IAA contains a section devoted to casualty actuarial matters; ASTIN (actuarial studies in nonlife insurance) holds annual meetings. The International Association of Consulting Actuaries, with several hundred members in more than a dozen countries, holds biennial meetings.

There are a lot of actuarial organizations, considering the relatively small size of the profession. Efforts have been made to consolidate over the years, but, with one or two exceptions, these have not been successful. Concerted efforts at "reorganizing" the profession were made during the 1970s, but have been abandoned. There has been a persistent trend, however, toward increasing communication and cooperation among the various actuarial organizations.

Frederick W. Kilbourne

Adjustable-Rate Mortgage (ARM)

See HOME FINANCING, MORTGAGES.

Adjustable-Rate Preferred Stock

See PREFERRED STOCK.

Adjuster

A term mainly used in PROPERTY/CASUALTY INSURANCE for the person with the responsibility for investigating, evaluating, negotiating, and resolving claims made against an insurance company. (In life and health insurance, this is the job of the claims examiner.) The adjuster is the company's contact with the insured when a loss occurs. Job duties of the adjuster depend on the types of claims handled and the adjuster's employer.

To better understand the role of the adjuster, it is necessary to know some of the language of property-liability insurance. A loss is called a "first-party loss" when it occurs as a result of direct or indirect loss of property value from perils such as a windstorm or the obligation to pay medical bills in a no-fault state. Collision coverage on a car is another first-party coverage. The term derives from the fact that the insured is the first party to the insurance contract and the company is the second party.

Some policies agree to "pay on behalf of the insured." These policies are called "liability policies" or "third-party coverages," since a third party, the "claimant," is making a claim against the insured; the insurance company, if the act is covered, agrees to defend the insured and make payments on that person's behalf.

Some adjusters specialize in handling first-party claims, others in third-party or liability claims. Adjusters trained to handle either type of claim are called "multiple-line" or "multiline" adjusters.

On every claim and loss, adjusters must verify that insurance coverage exists, and, if coverage applies, adjusters determine the value of the case. Liability adjusters must also determine, based on the facts they develop in the file, which parties to an accident were "at fault," or, more precisely, who was legally responsible for an accident.

When the loss in a particular case is verified and, if necessary, the degree of liability, if any, of the insured is determined, the adjuster must explain his or her evaluation to the insured in a first-party case or the claimant in a third-party case. In a third-party case, the loss to the claimant is known as damages. The adjuster makes an offer based on liability and damages if the claim is meritorious, or denies the claim if it is not. The insured, or claimant, may give reasons why the figure is not correct. Through negotiation, a money value acceptable to both is reached in most cases. When both parties agree, the figure agreed upon is paid, and the claim is settled. In the event of disagreement, first-party coverages have built-in provisions for resolving problems. In the third-party situations, the claimant may sue the insured in court for a determination of liability and damages. The adjuster, working with an attorney hired by the company to represent the insured, will continue to attempt to resolve the claim. Most cases are settled before any lawsuit is necessary.

From the description of the adjuster's duties, one can see the need for knowledge of the policy coverages; the special languages of law-enforcement officers, contractors, attorneys, and doctors; of fact-finding and investigative skills; and skills in human relations, both in working with people to find out what happened and the extent of damage, and in explaining the adjuster's position and seeking acceptance of that position.

An adjuster can work for an insurance company, for a large national adjusting firm, or for an "independent" adjuster.

An inside adjuster handles claims by telephone. An outside adjuster meets with people face-to-face. Some companies call their adjusters "claims representatives." Whether or not there is face-to-face contact depends on company policy and may relate to the complexity of the claim and the nature of injuries sustained.

Several groups of companies have formed "adjustment bureaus" to handle losses shared by those companies, large losses, and losses in outlying areas. These bureaus developed into large national adjusting firms handling claims for companies and self-insureds for a fee.

In some regions of the country, individuals have started firms called "independent adjusters" offering similar services in those areas. These firms may specialize in first-party, third-party, or multiline adjustments.

A public adjuster is distinguished from the others in that he or she represents the insured in an adjustment for a fee or a percentage of the final settlement in first-party losses.

The designation AIC after an adjuster's name means Associate in Claims and demonstrates completion of a six-semester multiline college-level specialty program offered by the Insurance Institute of America to foster professionalism in insurance adjusting.

Christopher Pitt

Aid to Families with Dependent Children (AFDC)

Aid to Families with Dependent Children is a state-administered, federally regulated program of income support for families with dependent children. It is jointly financed by federal, state, and, in some states, local funds through formula grants to the states.

The purpose of the AFDC program is to protect dependent children in poor families where parents are either absent or lack the resources to provide for them. To realize its objective, AFDC provides cash assistance to families with dependent children who become financially deprived due to the death, disability, or absence of a parent. In about half the states, assistance is also provided to families in which a parent is unemployed. Payment to a family is related to a standard of need established by the state and takes into consideration income and resources available to the recipient. Treatment of similar recipients varies from state to state and many aspects of the AFDC program are either at state option (e.g., coverage of unemployed parents or pregnant women) or defined by the state (e.g., special needs).

The AFDC program is administered by the states and territories under supervision of the Social Security Administration. Basic categorical eligibility is set by federal law; broader coverage may be provided by individual states within the requirements of the law.

Role of the Federal Government. The federal government regulates and supervises the general AFDC program. It reimburses states for a share of payments to recipients. The federal share of overall AFDC costs is about 54%. The federal government also develops broad quality-control policies and procedures, and reviews and evaluates states' corrective actions when the quality-control system identifies erroneous payments.

Role of the States. The states are responsible for specific program legislation and regulation. They administer the AFDC program in accordance with state and federal laws and regulations. The states determine eligibility, set benefit levels, and make payments to the recipients. They are responsible for the integrity of the program, including opportunities for hearings, fraud investigation, and quality control.

Quality-Control System. The AFDC's quality-control system is a statistically valid case-review system that identifies payments to ineligible recipients, underpayments or overpayments to eligible recipients, denials of assistance to eligible recipients, denials of assistance to eligible applicants, and/or case closings of eligible recipients.

The states conduct the case reviews through home visits and collateral contracts; they develop, implement, and evaluate corrective actions. A federal agency conducts national semiannual subsample reviews of the state system's findings.

Quality-control results are used to determine state error rates and the level of federal funding under current law and regulation (e.g., a 4% error tolerance in 1982). The potential for reducing state (as well as federal) AFDC costs is an incentive for states to exercise improved quality control.

Program Operation. All 50 states, the District of Columbia, Puerto Rico, the Virgin Islands, and Guam participate in the AFDC program.

Basic Eligibility Benefits. For a family to be eligible for AFDC, it must include a child who is

- needy and under age 18, or, at state option, under age 19, if completing the last year of secondary school or equivalent level of vocational or technical training before turning 19;
- deprived of parental support or care by reason of the death, continued absence from the home, or physical or mental incapacity of a parent, or, at state option, the unemployment of a parent;
- living in the home of a parent or a specified relative;
- a resident of the state;
- a citizen or an alien lawfully admitted for permanent residence or otherwise permanently residing in the U.S. under color of law.

The state agency determines need, taking into consideration income and resources of any person included in the assistance unit.* The following are stipulations:

- The gross income of an assistance unit may not be in excess of 150% of the state's standard of need.
- Income of recipients is applied against the state's payment standard; and for those with earned income, the following disregards are applied: $75; up to $160 for child care per child per month and for the first four consecutive months, $30 and one-third of the remaining earned income.

Unless exempted, every individual, as a condition of eligibility, must register for manpower services, training, and employment. Exempted individuals are

- children under 16 or attending school full time;
- a parent providing personal care to a child under 6, or a person who cares for a sick or incapacitated family member;
- a person who is ill, incapacitated, or old;
- a person who lives outside a Work Incentive Program (WIN) area;
- the second parent in an AFDC-UP family (see below), if the other parent is registered;
- an individual working 30 or more hours per week.

An applicant or recipient must give the state agency his Social Security number. If he does not have one, he must apply for one.

An applicant or recipient must assign any rights to support from another person to the state agency and cooperate with the state in establishing paternity of the children. States must also have child-support programs in effect to pursue and collect support.

*The "assistance unit" is the group of individuals eligible for and receiving payments benefits from the AFDC program. Such individuals are the parents and all children under the age of 18, or 19, as stipulated above, and "essential persons," as defined by the state.

Aid to Families with Dependent Children—Unemployed Parents (AFDC-UP). This program functions to protect dependent children where there is an unemployed parent. To be eligible for assistance under AFDC-UP, the unemployed parent must

- be the principal earner—i.e., the parent who earned the greater amount of income in the 24-month period preceding the initial month of application for aid;
- not be a participant in a labor dispute;
- have been unemployed for 30 days;
- have a recent attachment to the work force (have received, or be qualified to receive, unemployment compensation in the year prior to application or have worked 6 of the 13 quarters—which may include participation in a Community Work Experience Program (CWEP) under Section 409 of Title 4A of the Social Security Act—in the period ending one year prior to application);
- not have refused a bona fide offer of training or employment without good cause;
- register for work or training; and
- not refuse to participate in a Work Incentive Program (WIN) or Community Work Experience Program (CWEP) without good cause.

Unemployment Defined. Unemployment is defined in regulations as working less than 100 hours a month or working more than 100 hours for a month at a job that is intermittent or of a temporary nature (i.e., worked less than 100 hours for the previous two months and is expected to work less than 100 hours in the following month).

History and Scope. AFDC-UP began in 1961 with 50,000 families in the program, compared to about 900,000 families that received regular AFDC assistance. Compared to regular AFDC, the AFDC-UP program has always been small. In 1982, 26 states, the District of Columbia, and Guam had AFDC-UP programs, with 200,000 families receiving AFDC-UP at a cost of about $563 million.

See MEDICAID.

Harvey Rachlin

All Savers Certificate

A fixed-rate, one-year certificate savings account available from October 1, 1981, through December 31, 1982, that permitted savers a once-in-a-lifetime exemption from federal income tax for interest earnings up to $1,000 for an individual, or $2,000 on a joint return. The account had minimums of $500 or less and paid interest at 70% of the most recent average investment yield on 52-week Treasury bills.

Mary Ann Irvine

American Bankers Association (ABA)

The national trade association for U.S. commercial banks, this group promotes the general welfare of the industry by keeping members aware of developments affecting them, providing education and training for personnel, and seeking improvements in bank management and service. Its broadly based program aims at one long-term goal: to enhance the ability of America's banks to serve the public.

About 92% of the nation's more than 14,400 banks are members of the association, which is headquartered in Washington, D.C. Each year more than 1,000 bankers volunteer their time to serve on ABA councils and committees. Although the ABA has a staff of more than 350 employees, the high level of member participation reflects the fact that bankers set and supervise the trade group's policies and activities.

The ABA sponsors an annual convention; national conferences; national schools, including the Stonier Graduate School of Banking at Rutgers University; regional seminars and other educational activities. The American Institute of Banking, the ABA's education arm, reaches more than 250,000 students annually.

In addition to its educational and informational services, the ABA represents the banking community before Congress and federal regulatory agencies.

The ABA's policy is made by the Banking Leadership Conference, a group of about 400 bankers who meet from three to eight times a year to discuss questions affecting the industry. With representatives from banks of all sizes across the country, this conference develops a consensus that reflects the interests of the entire banking community.

Although trade associations are widespread today, they were all but unknown when the ABA was formed in 1875. In fact, no more than three national associations predate the ABA.

On a cold and blustery January day, two St. Louis bankers, James T. Howenstein and Edward C. Breck, were walking home when they passed an auditorium where a woman's-suffrage meeting was in progress. Mr. Howenstein remarked that if women could come from all parts of the country in the interest of a common cause, there was no reason why bankers could not do the same. These casual words had far-reaching impact. In May he invited 17 representative banks to send delegates to an organization meeting, and in July 350 bankers from 32 states and territories convened in the Town Hall at Saratoga Springs, New York, to lay the foundation for the association.

With no models to follow, the ABA pioneered methods that are standard trade-group practices today, such as the national convention.

As banking has become increasingly complex, the dissemination of information to bankers and the general public has become a significant part of the ABA's operation. For example, in 1982 the group issued hundreds of publications on subjects ranging from bank marketing to bank operations. The ABA also publishes *Bankers News Weekly,* an industry newspaper.

Phil Battey

American Depository Receipt (ADR)

See COMMON STOCK.

American Stock Exchange

The American Stock Exchange, like other organized securities exchanges, provides an orderly, central securities marketplace for the trading of stock, bonds, options, gold coins, U.S. gold pieces, and other financial instruments.

The American Stock Exchange*—sometimes shortened to Amex—is housed in a limestone building on Trinity Place in New York City, not far from the southern tip of Manhattan Island, but the Amex traces its origin to the days when New York merchants began trading securities in the streets of lower Manhattan around 1790. By 1792, a group of brokers signed an agreement and decided to move indoors. But others remained outdoors, conducting a marketplace on the curbstones of New York's financial district for more than a century, exposed to the extremes of New York weather. These curbstone brokers and their Curb Market were the predecessors of today's American Stock Exchange.

As the nation pushed westward, the outdoor market helped finance turnpikes, canals, banks, shipping companies, and new factories. Though the outdoor market felt the effects of the Industrial Revolution and experienced great growth during the nineteenth century, the Curb reached its zenith and became one of New York's most popular visitors' attractions in the years prior to World War I.

Winter or summer, rain or snow, several hundred colorfully clad brokers filled the street each day. A broker received orders either by messenger or from a telephone clerk stationed in an office overlooking the street. Having received a buy or sell order, the clerk would lean from the window to relay the order to the broker below. Street noise made vocal communica-

*The name, American Stock Exchange, is an outgrowth of several changes. In a departure from informal trading, the market in 1908 was known as the New York Curb Agency, followed three years later by a change to the New York Curb Market Association. When the market moved indoors in 1921, the name was shortened to the New York Curb Market and later modified to the New York Curb Exchange. The present name was adopted in 1953.

tion virtually impossible, so the Curb brokers developed a hand-signal system—a one-hand version of the deaf sign language—to "talk" to their clerks at dazzling speed. The brightly colored hats and jackets were worn by the brokers to help their clerks spot them in the crowd.

In 1921 the Curbstone brokers moved indoors to their present site at 86 Trinity Place. The main floor—a vast, cavernous hall—stretches 63 feet from floor to ceiling. This huge, somewhat irregularly shaped room contains two levels (one is a balcony) and 30,000 square feet of trading-floor space, larger than the main arena of New York's Madison Square Garden. The lampposts and fire hydrants of the old outdoor market have been replaced by 21 ultramodern, highly automated trading posts, linked electronically to the Amex computer complex and surrounded by video display units that automatically show the last-sale price and the bid and asked quotations. Options, government securities, gold bullion coins, and U.S. gold pieces have joined the traditional stocks and bonds as investment vehicles being traded on the Amex. Investors from any state in the country can buy and sell stocks in minutes—anywhere there's a telephone.

For example, an investor in Texas wants to buy a stock listed on the Amex. First he calls his local broker and asks for a quote. The broker punches out the stock's symbol on an electronic desk unit (similar to a small portable TV with a keyboard attached) that is hooked into a computer complex in New York. The information on that stock flashes onto the screen instantly—last price . . . bid price . . . asked price. "Last" means the price at which the last sale of the stock was made. "Bid" is the highest price any buyer is now willing to pay for that stock. "Asked" is the lowest price at which a seller is now willing to sell. Stock prices are expressed in dollars and fractions of a dollar: ⅛ equals 12½ cents, ¼ equals 25 cents, ⅜ equals 37½ cents, and so on.

The market on the Amex is a two-way auction market, meaning that all buyers compete with each other, and all sellers compete with each other. The highest bid and the lowest offer give the current market.

The Texas investor instructs his broker to buy a hundred "at the market"—another way of saying "Buy the stock at the best possible price when the order reaches the trading floor." Most orders are relayed to the brokerage firm's booth overlooking the trading floor. Clerks then relay orders to the floor broker. In some cases, orders from brokerage firms can be electronically routed directly to trading posts.

Each stock listed on the Amex is assigned to one of the 21 trading posts. There a broker asks for a new quote from the specialist in the stock. The specialist gives the broker the most recent quote—e.g., 30⅛–30⅜, trading-floor language meaning "The current bid [buyer's price] for the stock was 30⅛. The current offer [seller's price] was 30⅜." He may take the offer and pay 30⅜, or he may try to get a better price by bidding 30¼. The other brokers gathered around the post—they are called "the trading crowd"—may sell to the bid by stating, "Sold!"

As noted, the buying broker came up in price and a selling broker came down in price. When bid and offer meet, a sale is made. Each broker has filled his customer's order at the best price at the time. No contract is signed; there's not even a handshake. A broker's word is his bond.

The two brokers then report the order to their respective booth clerks. The clerks in turn notify their main office order rooms. In the meantime, an Amex reporter records the sale on a card and gives it to a data clerk inside the post. The data clerk slips the card into an electronic reader. In a matter of seconds, the stock sale appears on the moving ticker on the trading floor and is displayed on thousands of automated quotation units in brokers' offices throughout the United States and foreign countries. As soon as the main office order rooms have been notified, they relay the news to their local offices. The local offices then call the buyer and seller to report the fact that their orders were executed and the price at which the stock was either bought or sold.

The buyer also receives written confirmation and must send payment for his purchase to the brokerage firm, usually within five business days. In the case of a typical sell order, unless the stock certificates are being held by the brokerage firm, the certificates must be surrendered in order to receive payment.

When a stock is listed on the Amex, it is assigned to a specialist on the trading floor. A specialist may trade in many different stocks, and it is the specialist's responsibility to help provide a continuous and orderly market in those issues assigned to them by the exchange. If there are no buyers, the specialist is expected to sell stock from his own inventory at a price near the last sale. Similarly, if a number of investors want to sell, and no one wants to buy, the specialist is expected to buy the stock at a price close to the last sale. In this capacity, the specialist acts as dealer or principal. However, the specialist also may act as an agent for other brokers who entrust to him customer orders that are "away" from the current selling price of the security. These orders, called "limit orders," are orders to buy below the market or sell above the market. Together, these orders make up what is called the "specialist book," which is highly confidential.

Acting as a broker's broker, the specialist keeps track of all the orders and prices during a day's trading. When the stock's price reaches the level that permits a limit order to be filled, the specialist will execute it and report back to the floor broker who left it with him.

The American Stock Exchange, under the direction of its board of governors, must provide the public with an open, fair, and orderly market. The Amex and other national securities exchanges in the United States have worked in partnership with their members and member firms to develop a system of self-regulation. Since 1934, when Congress passed the Securities Exchange Act, this system of self-regulation has itself been subject to the review of the SECURITIES AND EXCHANGE COMMISSION (SEC), an agency of the United States government.

The Amex keeps a record of *all* transactions, large or small, and its constitution and rules are designed to protect the interests of all investors whether they hold 10 or 10,000 shares or more. Two Amex regulatory groups, Stock Watch and Trading Analysis, carefully examine each day's trading.

Membership in the American Stock Exchange is classified into three primary categories—regular, options principal, and associate—providing traders with direct or indirect access to the exchange's trading floor. The 661 regular members may transact business in both equities and options; the 95 options-principal members may execute only principal transactions in options only; and the 143 associate members may transact business by wire through regular members.

Prices for regular memberships have ranged from a low of $650 to a high of $350,000. Options-principal memberships, instituted in 1975, have ranged from $10,000 to a high of $235,000. Stock trading volume on the Amex in 1983 exceeded 1 billion shares for the fifth consecutive year, while options trading on the Amex has reached new highs each year since 1975.

Approximately 950 issues of common and preferred stock and warrants trade on the American Stock Exchange, with close to 5 billion shares outstanding. These issues, in mid-1983, had a market value of some $87 billion. The approval of an application for an Amex listing is a matter solely within the discretion of the exchange. To assist interested companies, the Amex has established guidelines for evaluating listing candidates.

The minimum requirements for original listing of common stocks on the Amex are:

- *Shares publicly held:* 500,000, of which 150,000 must be in 100–1,000-share lots
- *Number of shareholders:* 1,000, including 800 holders of round lots, of which 500 must be holders of 100–1,000-share lots
- *Aggregate market value/price per share:* $3,000,000/ $5

These criteria are only a guide to consideration for listing. Each listing application is reviewed on its merits and is subject to specific action by the Amex.

A typical company on the Amex has median total assets of $45 million; median annual sales of $56 million; median net income of $2 million; and a price/earnings ratio of 12.

During the 1970s, after decades of a trading mix comprised only of stocks and bonds, the Amex introduced trading in put and call options on stocks, and odd-lot trading in government securities. The 1980s have given rise to the trading of options on U.S. Treasury notes and Treasury bills, as well as the American Gold Coin Exchange (AGCE), an Amex subsidiary trading the most popular one-ounce gold bullion coins and U.S. gold pieces. Even more recently, the Amex introduced options trading on stock indexes, namely on a Major Market Index (20 selected stocks listed on the New York Stock Exchange) and on the Amex Market Value Index (based on the issues listed on the American Stock Exchange).

The exchange simultaneously has initiated a wide range of ongoing corporate services for listed companies, opening up new channels of communication for reaching the investment community.

Through an expanding network of broker clubs, the Amex provides a forum for listed company managements to tell their corporate stories. The 17 domestic and 4 international Amex Clubs spread the news to financial communities throughout North America, Europe, and Asia.

Radio Amex, the exchange's broadcasting service, supplies up-to-the-minute financial news of the Amex marketplace to thousands of radio and television stations in the United States and Canada. In addition, Radio Amex provides stations with executive interviews on topical issues, in conjunction with Amex-sponsored events.

To provide listed companies an insight into leading issues and the people behind them, the Amex sponsors a series of conferences and seminars held throughout the United States and in Canada. The program includes a variety of topics ranging from briefings at the White House to regional question-and-answer sessions with leading economists and management experts.

Highlighting the Amex conference schedule is an annual conference held in Washington. Focusing on national and international issues that have an impact on creative growth companies, it features key administration, congressional, SEC, and Federal Reserve officials interacting with listed-company managements.

To further augment services to listed companies, the Amex annually invites top money managers and analysts from Europe, the Far East, and the Middle East to the United States to introduce company chief executive officers to new potential markets and over-seas investors.

Today, the traditions of the hardy curbstone brokers are carried forward by the Amex brokers, who are committed to the marketplace philosophy that success comes from providing better service more efficiently. These brokers are proud of their history and proud of their continuing contribution to our nation's economic life.

Robert J. Birnbaum

American Stock Exchange Market Value Index (AMVI)

The American Stock Exchange introduced its Amex Market Value Index on September 4, 1973, to provide investors with an improved perspective on current market performance. The new index replaced the old Price Change Index, which had been in effect since 1966.

The Amex Market Value Index measures the change in the aggregate market value of common shares, American Depository Receipts (ADR's), and warrants (market value is share price multiplied by the number of shares outstanding). By selecting an index based on market value—the key component of the new system—the Amex aligned itself more closely with other market-value indicators in the industry, such as those used by the New York Stock Exchange and Standard & Poor's.

In addition to the main index, 16 subsidiary market-value indexes, comprised of eight industrial and eight geographic groupings, also were introduced in 1973. Most Amex companies have been categorized in one of the industrial groupings, while all companies have been assigned to a geographic subindex based on the location of their corporate headquarters. The sub-indexes are shown in Table 1.

When the Amex Market Value Index was introduced in 1973, the AMVI and the subindexes all were assigned a starting level of 100.00. However, with the

AMVI in the first half of 1983 nearing the 500.00 level, the exchange on July 5, 1983, "split" the index two-for-one in order to make a pending new investment product—an option on the AMVI—attractive to institutional and individual investors. This new product began trading July 8, 1983. The action was similar to a successful corporation's splitting its stock to bring down the price, thus making the shares attractive to more potential investors.

Splitting, or halving, of the index did not affect the total market value of the Amex list. The index level now is measured against an adjusted base level of 50.00, and the index values disseminated by the exchange are one-half of what they would be if no split had been made. All historical records have been adjusted to reflect the change.

Robert J. Birnbaum

Amex

See AMERICAN STOCK EXCHANGE.

Amortization

The term given to the act of paying a sum of money gradually over a period of time or in installments. Installment payments of a debt to a creditor or an account, or periodic payments of an insurance premium, are examples of amortization. When the debt or premium is fully paid, it is said to be "amortized."

Amortization is sometimes used synonymously with the term *depreciation*. While the gradual reduction of the book value of some tangible asset "depreciates," such a reduction of the value of an intangible asset such as "goodwill" or a patent is often said to amortize.

In its most common usage, however, amortization is the paying off or liquidation of a sum of money or debt gradually over a period of time.

Samuel C. Hoyt

Analyst, Financial

See FINANCIAL ANALYST.

Annual Percentage Rate

This term means the ratio of a FINANCE CHARGE for the use of credit to the average amount of credit in use during the time period of a credit contract or agreement, expressed as a percentage rate per year. Under the federal Truth in Lending Act, such rates must be computed with great accuracy in accordance with the actuarial annuity method, United States Rule. By contrast, annual percentage rates disclosed under that law for open-end credit are less accurate because the

Table 1	
Industrial	*Geographic*
High technology	New England
Capital goods	Middle Atlantic
Consumer goods	North Central
Service	South Atlantic
Retail	South Central
Financial	Mountain
Natural resources	Pacific
Housing, construction, and land development	Foreign

annual percentage rate must be computed merely by multiplying the monthly rate or rates used by a creditor for computing the monthly finance charge by 12, the number of months in a year. Disclosure of annual percentage rates serves to improve consumer awareness of the cost of using credit, and also serves as an aid in shopping for credit.

Even when finance charges are expressed in dollars and cents by different sources of credit, they may not be comparable because of differences in the terms of the contracts or agreements. When annual percentage rates are disclosed in accordance with the requirements of the Truth in Lending Act, the rates disclosed are computed by uniform methods and serve to make the cost of credit from various sources more comparable for shopping purposes, just as "unit pricing"—that is, disclosure of the price per minimum unit of weight or volume—aids in comparison shopping for food and other items in grocery stores.

Prior to the Truth in Lending Act, creditors customarily disclosed add-on or discount rates per year or monthly, rates which they use to compute finance charges, but the rates disclosed were inadequate in shopping for credit. Today, creditors are required to disclose the annual percentage rates computed in accordance with the requirements of the Truth in Lending Act and are prohibited from disclosing other types of annual percentage rates to prevent possible creditor deceit or consumer confusion.

James A. Ambrose

Annuity

In its simplest form, an annuity is a series of payments over a period of time. You might arrange this yourself after winning a contest prize instead of taking a lump sum; or you could leave an inheritance to someone in your will to be paid in yearly installments. Usually, however, an annuity is a specific contract bought from a life-insurance company. (Occasionally, charities write annuities privately in return for a donation.) Although one can buy an annuity that pays income for only a chosen number of years, most annuities provide an income for life. Thus, it is logical that they are a product of life insurance companies, whose business is calculating rates for "mortality" and "life expectancy." With large enough numbers to begin with, a life-insurance company can predict very accurately how many people will die or live at a certain age each year. Since life insurance basically protects against dying too soon and annuities against living too long, some insurance experts think of them as separate and different. Most people, however, fail to see the distinction between "when we die" and "how long we live," and so the public usually considers an-

nuities a form of life insurance. For simplicity, we have done the same here.

Occasionally, people buy some types of annuities as short-term investments. Most of us, however, buy them for retirement income. You can do this long before you retire or wait until that time. Because the family, personal, and financial situation of each of us can vary considerably both now and at retirement, many different types of annuities have been developed over the years. You must choose among these, either at the time you buy the annuity or when income begins. After you buy an annuity, you are called the "annuitant."

Annuities can be categorized according to various characteristics, and the one you buy will combine several of these.

An annuity can be either *individual* or part of a *group* (like group life and health insurance). Group annuities are almost always used in qualified pension plans, and under most state laws you would find it difficult to join a group annuity plan for strictly personal reasons. So, although group annuities are somewhat cheaper than individual policies, most of us must buy individual-policy annuities for our personal retirement planning.

An annuity may be either *immediate* or *deferred.* All immediate annuities are purchased at the time income is to begin. A deferred annuity is bought some time before that, with income starting later. The time in between is called the "accumulation" or "deferral period." Interest on your deposits compounds tax-free during this period, an advantage Congress granted long ago to encourage people to save for retirement.

You may pay for your annuity with either a *single premium* or *annual premiums.* An immediate annuity is almost always bought with a single premium since few insurance companies would be willing to start your income without receiving all your premium. A deferred annuity can be either single- or annual-premium. Most are annual-premium (paid, if you wish, semiannually, quarterly, or monthly). However, there is an advantage to buying a single-premium, deferred annuity: You will compound much more tax-free interest by paying everything up front. Most annual-premium, deferred annuities today have what is called a "flexible premium": Although you will purchase the annuity with a particular premium in mind, you can pay more or less on each premium due date, as your finances permit. This is not only useful for a personal annuity, it is almost essential for an INDIVIDUAL RETIREMENT ACCOUNT (IRA) and a KEOGH PLAN.

You can buy *fixed-dollar* or *variable* annuities. The fixed-dollar annuity, where everything is spelled out in exact dollar amounts, is the traditional one. Both the *principal* (your deposits, less expenses) and a minimum interest rate are guaranteed. The insurance company invests your premium in "safe" things, such as bonds and mortgages, but will pay you more than the guaranteed interest rate if they earn it (which has been the case in recent years). You also know what you are going to receive at retirement as a minimum.

A variable annuity, on the other hand, guarantees you nothing. The insurance company invests your money in such things as common stock. Although some sellers give you a choice among several annuities with different kinds of investments, you are still gambling to a degree and will receive at retirement more or less than you might have expected. Variable annuities were developed as an answer to inflation (which can, indeed, destroy fixed-dollar annuities), because the stock market generally follows inflation or deflation. Unfortunately, this does not always hold true over a short period of time (the last decade, for example).

Some annuities permit you to change from fixed-dollar to variable and vice versa at will, at least during the accumulation period. You may also split your choice, either within the same annuity or by buying two. If your money is still variable when income begins (and you usually can switch here, too), the amount of each check you receive (usually monthly) will vary according to the then current value of the company's variable-annuity investments. It is quite possible with variable annuities to receive a larger retirement income, if the company's investments do well. Choose carefully, understanding that neither type provides an ideal solution.

Having made the above choices, you must then decide on your income option. There are a number of alternatives, and if you buy an immediate annuity, you have to pick one at the time of purchase. Deferred annuities, on the other hand, usually contain all the choices below and you don't have to decide until you are ready to receive income. Virtually all deferred annuities today also do not require you to pick the time of income (retirement age) when you buy and, in the area of annual-premium annuities, let you continue to make deposits as long as you wish. Following are your choices.

Nonlife. Here you pick a certain number of years of income payments (3, 8, 13, etc.). If you die, the unused principal is usually paid to your beneficiary. A nonlife annuity can be useful in a situation where you know you will be receiving additional income at some specific, future date. A clever idea, popular during recent times of high interest rates, is to use this option for only part of your annuity principal, telling the insurance company to keep the balance of your money in the meantime at high, tax-free interest so as to

equal the original, full principal again at the end of the chosen number of income years. If interest rates remain high, you can do this over and over again, thus leaving most of your principal to a beneficiary at your death. If interest rates drop, you can simply switch to one of the life-income options below (but you will now be older and therefore receive more income for your money). How well this idea works depends on interest rates and the amount of income you need. But it would pay you to remember to ask the insurance company to show you figures on this to compare with the life-income options.

Life. All of the life options listed below will pay you an income as long as you live, no matter how long. The only difference among them is how much, if anything, you want to leave to someone else when you die. The more you want to leave, the less income to you.

Straight Life (No Refund). There is no death benefit in this choice. No matter when you die, no one else will receive anything. However, it will pay you the highest income. It is useful if you have no close relatives or have taken care of your family in some other way.

Full-Refund Life (Installment Refund). The death benefit is determined by subtracting the total income you have received at the time of your death from the principal you started with when income began. The difference, if any, is paid to your beneficiary in a lump sum (Full Refund) or your income is continued to the beneficiary until the balance is used up (Installment Refund). Your principal is guaranteed.

Period Certain and Life. Here the death benefit is the continuation of your income to the beneficiary for the balance of an initial number of years that you pick (most commonly 5, 10, 15, or 20). Thus, if you choose a 20-year Certain and Life option and die after 5 years, the beneficiary will receive your income for 15 years.

Joint and Survivor Life. This popular option is the same as Straight Life (No Refund) except that the income is paid through two lifetimes. The amount of income is calculated on an actuarially combined life expectancy of two people (Joint), and when either dies, the income simply continues until the death of the other (Survivor). At that point, there is usually no death benefit for anyone else. Some companies permit you to add a Period Certain (see above) to this option so that if both annuitants die early, at least something will go to a beneficiary, but this will reduce the income to the annuitants.

The Joint and Survivor option is required by law in pension plans as a choice for workers who are married at retirement, because it is most commonly needed by married couples, particularly if both are in good health. It completely removes the uncertainties to a spouse that a beneficiary has in the other choices. Common variations of this option are to give the survivor only part of the income you both received—Joint and One-half, Two-thirds, or Three-quarters Survivor. These variations, which may seem logical when picked, will increase the income while both are alive but should be chosen with care because, if inflation occurs, the reduced income to the survivor may turn out to be inadequate many years later.

At the present time, women receive less annuity income than men on any option, because women live longer. Congress has considered changing this, as most pension plans have already done.

Most annuities have insurance-company expenses (called "loading") included in your premium. One of these is a sales fee. It can range from 2–3% for immediate annuities to 9–10% for single-premium, deferred annuities and 8% for annual-premium types. Some companies charge less, and a few offer "no load" deferred annuities, which have no sales charges but usually take back from you a "surrender charge" of up to 10% if you cash in the annuity in the early years of the accumulation period. What is really more important to you than sales fees are the premium you will pay, the interest your money will earn, and the income you will get at retirement.

It should be noted that virtually all life-insurance policies contain "settlement options," which include all the annuity options above. Settlement options are available to the beneficiaries for life-insurance death benefits and to the insureds for the cash values of permanent life insurance policies (at retirement, for example). Thus, both life insurance and annuities provide both nonlife and life income, and the public is therefore really not wrong in combining annuities with life insurance.

Harold C. Luckstone, Jr.

Apartment, Renting an

Before renting an apartment, you should be aware of the following considerations and responsibilities in order to make the best possible decisions about your new home.

Before the Hunt. There are several questions you need to ask yourself before you hop in the car with street maps and apartment ads.

1. How much living space do you need and want? What about storage space?

2. How much rent can you afford to pay? The long-standing rule of using one week's pay as a guide still applies: To live comfortably within your means, one week's take-home pay should cover your rent *and* re-

lated expenses such as water and telephone service. (Note: If you decide to rent in the city and own a car, you may have to rent garage or parking space. In large cities, this could add a substantial amount to your monthly living costs.)

3. Where do you want to live? The location should be convenient in terms of commuting time to work and access to shopping and other facilities or services you want.

4. What kinds of amenities do you want or need? Clubhouses, gyms, swimming pools, and tennis courts often mean you will pay more rent, so be sure you will really use these extras before you commit yourself. Similarly, units with dishwashers, balconies, and extra bathrooms will command higher rents as well.

5. Do you want to do your own decorating? Can you afford your own furniture? If so, do not waste your time or money on furnished apartments. On the other hand, a large apartment that is a bargain now could be very costly in the long run if you have to buy extra furniture to go in it.

Apartment Checklist. You have found an apartment in the right location and price range. Now it is time to look over the actual apartment and complex. Use the following checklist:

- Is the building itself attractive and well built? Does it look well maintained inside and out? Are hallways and corridors clean and well lit?
- What about security? Are there adequate locks on all doors? Is an intercom system or doorman provided for added protection against unwanted visitors?
- Is there extra storage space available? Where are the laundry facilities located? Trash-disposal areas?
- Does your mailbox lock? How many parking spaces are allowed for yourself and visitors? Are you charged extra for this?
- Try to see the actual apartment you will be renting. Is the floor plan convenient? Are the rooms large enough to accommodate you and your furniture?
- Are there enough windows and are they well located? What about electric outlets and telephone jacks? Are the walls soundproof?
- Do all the appliances work? Do doors and windows open and close properly? What about the plumbing—is it in working condition?
- Find out what routine maintenance is provided. Are blinds, curtains or drapes, and carpeting provided?
- Are there individual controls for heating and air conditioning?
- Last, but very important, ask about your neighbors. Are their life-styles compatible with yours?

The Credit Check. If the apartment and complex meet with your approval, the landlord will probably require a credit check before agreeing to rent to you. Most apartment owners will go to a credit-reporting agency to obtain a written report of your credit standing. (This may or may not include long-distance calls to previous landlords or employers.)

You may be charged anywhere from $15 to $60 for the credit check. It will not be refunded. Be prepared for this additional expense, especially if you're considering two or three different apartments.

When you are a prospective tenant, there are a few things to keep in mind when filling out the lease application. First of all, do not lie about your salary—that information will be verified in the credit check. It is also helpful to know the numbers of all your bank accounts and the addresses of your previous employers and landlords. You may be asked to give personal references as well.

The Fair Credit Reporting Act requires landlords to hold any information they receive about a person's credit standing in strict confidence. This information must be used only for a business transaction involving a prospective tenant.

Signing the Lease. Once your credit standing has been approved, it is time to consider your lease. This is a written agreement between you—the tenant—and your landlords. It is a very important document because it contains the key details of your occupancy as well as your basic rights as a tenant.

Be sure to read your lease carefully. Check to see that all blank spaces are filled in or crossed out. Because your lease serves as legal protection, even the small print is important to you. If you have any questions, talk with a lawyer.

The lease should answer many questions you may have and usually includes the following information:

- When you can move in.
- How long the lease is in effect.
- The amount of rent and when it is due. (Note: Many landlords charge a "late fee" when rent is overdue. Find out how much that charge is and when it goes into effect.)
- The description of the particular unit you are renting.
- The security deposit required, if any.
- Conditions for renewing the lease.
- Conditions under which you can sublease the apartment.
- What expenses you will pay and what expenses your landlord will pay—e.g., gas and electric, water, heat, etc.
- Conditions for raising the rent.

After the terms have been agreed upon and understood, both the renter and the leasing agent will sign the agreement. If you and a roommate both sign the lease and decide to evenly split the rent, be sure the lease spells out who is legally responsible to pay the full amount of rent should one of you default for any reason. If you're a young adult with little established credit, you may have a parent or other relative cosign the lease with you. Remember, this legally obligates that person to pay your rent should you default on payment.

Any verbal agreement made with your landlord should be written into your lease. For example, your landlord has no right to enter your apartment once you move in. Even in emergencies or to make repairs, he or she must get your permission to enter (if at all possible). Get this in writing to be safe.

Of course, your lease will require you to keep the property in good condition and leave it that way when you vacate. To protect yourself, go through the apartment with your landlord and list all damage already sustained on walls, fixtures, appliances, and floors. Give the landlord a copy of this list and keep a copy for yourself. That way, you will not be charged for damages you did not cause.

Find out what alterations or decorating you are allowed to do. Any alterations or decorations should be easily removed without damage to the apartment.

Find out what minor repairs you are responsible for and what the superintendent's duties are. Get the specifics. Is repainting provided? Who pays for cleaning rugs and carpeting? What about bug extermination and window washing?

Take a look at your cancellation clause. Are you required to give 30 to 60 days' notice before a move? What happens if you don't give notice within a specific time period? Is the lease automatically renewed on the same terms?

Check restrictions contained in your lease and have them stricken if your landlord says they do not apply. Are you allowed to have pets or children? What are the rules concerning parties or excessive noise? Extra roommates? How many parking spaces are you allowed?

The following points also deserve your attention:

1. *Your damage deposit.* This usually involves one month's rent. Find out the conditions under which your deposit will or will not be refunded. Will you be paid any interest on this deposit?

2. *Building security.* Does your landlord provide adequate locks and extra chains for your front door? Do both the front door and back door of the building have an intercom system that allows you to "buzz" open the door for legitimate guests?

3. *Insurance.* Who is responsible if the landlord's negligence causes you or your family bodily injury? What about the loss of your personal property? You may just play it safe and get your own renter's insurance to protect your belongings from theft, fire, or flood.

Clauses. A word of caution here regarding legal terms and clauses in some leases. Again, if you are confused or unsure about anything you see in the lease, consult a lawyer. You should be aware of clauses that (1) permit the landlord to show your apartment anytime he or she pleases to a prospective tenant, even before the usual few weeks or month before you are scheduled to vacate; (2) free the landlord from liability if injury or damage is sustained on the property even after you have repeatedly asked him or her to repair the cause of injury or damage—e.g., a broken handrail on the stairs or broken bathroom tile; (3) allow the landlord to evict you and literally throw your belongings on the street for violation of even a "fine point" in your lease.

After you have approved the lease and its contents, be sure both you and your landlord sign it and date it.

Moving. Be sure to check with the management or your landlord as to any particular moving restrictions or provisions.

Harley W. Snyder

Appreciation

The increase in value of an ASSET, particularly real property. When an asset's value increases over a period of time, the value (and/or the asset) is said to appreciate. The term is regularly used in the context of securities and commodities. Appreciation can also connote the actual sum that represents the difference between the appraisal value and the book value of fixed assets when the appraisal value has increased.

Samuel C. Hoyt

Arbitrage

The simultaneous purchase and sale of identical or equivalent investment instruments in order to profit from price differences.

Suppose an investor observes two different price quotes for the same stock at the same time; for example, a transaction might take place on a regional exchange at a price slightly higher or lower than a New York Stock Exchange transaction. If the investor is able to purchase the stock on one exchange at the lower price and simultaneously sell the stock on the other exchange at the higher price, he will earn an immediate profit equal to the difference in price, less any broker's commissions he must pay.

In the above example, the arbitrage profit results from the simultaneous purchase and sale of an identical security in two different markets. Transactions involving similar or equivalent investment instruments can also give rise to arbitrage opportunities. Consider the following example. XYZ Corporation common stock has a current market price of $50 per share. A

call option for one share of XYZ stock can be purchased for $4; the call option has an exercise price of $45. (This call option gives the investor the right to buy one share of XYZ stock for $45.) The following transaction will allow an investor to realize a $1 arbitrage profit (before deducting commissions): Purchase the call option for $4, then exercise the option to purchase a share of XYZ stock for $45, and sell the share for $50.

In both of the arbitrage transactions illustrated above, there are numerous obstacles to obtaining the profits indicated. First, any price discrepancies must exceed the commissions the investor would have to pay in order to complete the transactions. Second, the investor must have immediate access both to price quotations and to trading opportunities because small price changes can eliminate potential profit opportunities. Third, arbitrage profit opportunities tend to be eliminated very quickly by the actions of arbitragers.

This latter point is especially important to the investor because it is generally true that potential arbitrage profits are eliminated so rapidly that only professional traders are able to take advantage of such situations. In the first example described above, arbitragers will seek to purchase the security in the market where it is selling at the lower price, thus increasing demand and causing the price to rise in that market. Simultaneously, as these traders sell at the higher price in the other market, the additional supply of the security will tend to lower the price in that market. As a result, the arbitrage profit is quickly eliminated by these price changes. Similarly, in the second example, as investors purchase the call option and sell the stock, the price of the former will rise and the price of the latter will fall, eliminating the price discrepancy. Similar price changes will eliminate arbitrage opportunities involving other investment instruments, such as bonds, commodities, and foreign currencies.

The term *risk arbitrage* is used to describe a transaction in which an investor makes a purchase and/or short sale of the common stock of corporations that he anticipates will be involved in a merger or acquisition. Technically, the term *arbitrage* is incorrectly applied in this context, as will become apparent from the following discussion. In spite of this fact, such transactions are commonly referred to as "risk arbitrage" or simply "arbitrage."

The opportunity for risk-arbitrage profits typically arises when one corporation seeks to acquire another corporation by making a "tender offer" for the latter firm's stock. For example, Corporation A may announce a tender offer to purchase shares of Corporation B common stock directly from shareholders at a tender price of $65 per share. If the market price of Corporation B common stock is $50 per share, Corporation A might feel that a majority of Corporation B stockholders will be willing to "tender" their shares to Corporation A at the higher tender price. If Corporation A is able to acquire more than 50% of the outstanding shares of Corporation B common stock, and to overcome numerous legal and tactical obstacles that may be created by the management of Corporation B, the acquisition will be completed.

Given the potential increase in the value of Corporation B common stock, the risk arbitrager may be willing to purchase shares in this "target" company as soon as the tender offer is announced. Usually, when this announcement is made, the price of the target company's stock will rise significantly. However, since the price does not rise immediately to the tender price, there is a potential profit to be earned by the risk arbitrager if the acquisition is consummated. Because there is some uncertainty that the various obstacles to the acquisition will be overcome, there is substantial risk in purchasing Corporation B common stock for, say, $56 per share following the announcement of the tender offer. While there is a probability of a significant gain if the stock can be sold to Corporation A for $65, it is also possible that the stock price will decline to $50 or less if the acquisition is not completed.

Historically, it has often been true that the price of the acquiring company's stock declines when the acquisition is made. Therefore, a risk arbitrager, in addition to purchasing the target company's stock when the tender offer is announced, may also sell short the acquiring company's stock at that time. If the acquisition is completed, the arbitrager may be able to cover the short sale by purchasing the acquiring company's stock at a lower price and thus profit from the price change.

The fact that risk arbitrage is technically not arbitrage is apparent from the fact that an investor who purchases a share of a target company's stock does so with the expectation that he will sell the stock at a later date. He anticipates that if the acquisition is completed, the price of the share will rise. Similarly, when a risk arbitrager sells short the stock of the acquiring company, he expects that the price of the stock will decline, enabling him to cover the short sale at a lower price. Since in neither case is there a simultaneous purchase and sale of a security, the transactions are not arbitrage transactions in the strict sense of the term.

R. Bruce Swensen

Asset

A possession having present or future economic value to its owner. When listed on a balance sheet, assets are usually classified as "current," "fixed," and "intangible."

A current asset is cash or something that can be converted into cash quickly. However, some accounts receivable, a portion of which might not be collected until much later, can be classified as current assets if such a practice is common in a particular industry.

A fixed asset is a tangible asset that produces something of value, such as marketable products or services, for its owner. Land or buildings, which contribute to the production of products or services in that they are produced therein, are fixed assets. Equipment, machinery, and furnishings are other examples of fixed assets.

An intangible asset is something of economic value that is not cash or a physical object or place. An attribute such as goodwill (in its business sense), or a conceptual status, such as conferred by a copyright, patent, or trademark, could be classified as an intangible asset.

As asset ceases to be an asset if it stops being economically valuable to its owner. Some assets, such as machinery and equipment, lose value through depreciation. Others, such as stocks or securities, can increase in value or appreciate. Assets can be transferred or traded or used as security or collateral.

Samuel C. Hoyt

Asset-Based Financial Services

The asset-based financial services industry—consisting of commercial banks, large and diversified financial institutions, independent finance companies, factoring organizations, and financing subsidiaries of major industrial corporations—provides money to businesses through a variety of financing techniques. Two major components are *secured lending* and *factoring*.

Secured Lending. In secured lending, the lender provides funds that are backed by the borrower's assets. This collateral includes, singly or in combination, accounts receivable, inventories, and other assets, such as plant or equipment.

Accounts-Receivable Financing. As new invoices are billed by the client, they are assigned to the lender. Given satisfactory receivables quality, the lender generally immediately advances anywhere from 75% to 85% of the face amount of the receivables. The client buys more goods, sells them, and pledges the resulting receivables. The process is repeated continually. As receivable volume builds, extra loan availability is created. Loan repayment is made through receivable collections.

Example: Two young men start a wholesale electronics business with capital of $5,000. Assume they have no difficulty obtaining sales orders and getting supplies. They buy $5,000 worth of merchandise and sell it for $6,000. To be competitive, they give their customers normal credit terms of 30 days. But if they wait 30 days for collection of their cash, they're out of operation for that period. So they assign their receivables to an accounts-receivable financier, who advances 80% of the $6,000 and gives them a check for $4,800. They buy another supply of merchandise, sell it, pledge the receivables, and roll it over again. They continue this procedure and thus build their volume.

In secured lending, the customer controls his own borrowing. He draws funds only as needed—and in the amount needed—to pay bills, build inventory, take advantage of trade discounts, meet payroll, or for a variety of other corporate purposes. He pays interest only on the money used.

Inventory Financing. Inventories are also used as collateral by secured lenders, and the two types of assets are frequently used together. Inventory loans are not normally possible unless the lender has proper administrative control of the receivables. The reason for this is apparent. Repayment of the inventory loan is usually accomplished through sale of the merchandise. Hence the lien or security interest of the lender must follow the merchandise into the receivable, and into the proceeds of the receivable, or cash, which repays the original advance.

Inventory obviously is less liquid than receivables. Therefore inventory loans are treated more conservatively by secured lenders. Such conservatism is reflected in the evaluation of the liquidation value of the inventory, and the lower percentage of advance the lender is prepared to make. And finally, since the risk is substantially greater, the rate on an inventory loan is likely to be higher than that on a receivables loan.

Other Types of Loans. Companies within the asset-based financial services industry also offer a range of industrial financing services. Equipment leasing, for example, constitutes a financing outlet for acquisition of capital goods with a minimal cash investment. In other instances, companies engage in sale and lease-back arrangements, equipment-purchase loans, and time-sales financing for manufacturers.

Long- or intermediate-term secured financing (three to seven years) is also used frequently. Loans may be secured through a combination of plant, equipment, and real estate. Such programs often utilize accounts-receivable or inventory financing to boost working capital.

Factoring. Accounts-receivable financing (as explained above) is sometimes popularly but improperly labeled "factoring." The distinction between the two is important. Factoring involves the outright purchase of the receivables from the client and the factor's guarantee of the creditworthiness of the client's customer. If the client's customer is financially unable to pay the amount of the invoice, the factor absorbs the loss. There is no recourse to the client. It is, therefore, a form of credit insurance as well as a means of obtaining ready cash against receivables. Consequently, credit requirements are more stringent than those for accounts-receivable financing, and, since it is based on a statistical spread, the volume requirement is usually higher as well. In accounts-receivable financing, the receivables are assigned to the financer as security for the loan. The financer does not guarantee the credit of the client's customer.

Factoring developed in America's earliest days. During that period, large woolen mills in England shipped their merchandise in bulk to commission merchants or selling agents in America. These merchants sold the merchandise for the mill and guaranteed the credit of the customers. Obviously, the distant mill could obtain little or no credit information. Later, New England mills selling to the New York market used local factors to perform these functions. Over the years the selling and credit-guaranteeing functions were divorced. The mills developed their own sales forces, but the factors continued to guarantee the credit of the customers and to assume some moneylending functions.

Accounts-receivable financing arose early in the twentieth century to fill a need of certain undercapitalized businesses. The banks in that period were not equipped by theory, outlook, or technique to handle such financing. Hence, nonbank lending institutions, created with private capital, began to undertake such financing.

Accounts-receivable financing is a very flexible and adaptable form of financing. As sales volume increases, cash requirements rise; the attendant increase in receivables thus boosts the capital available to the borrower. If the cash requirement falls because volume is seasonally low, the receivables collections almost automatically repay the loan. It is, in this sense, a self-liquidating loan.

There are sharp differences in the mechanics of handling accounts-receivable financing and factoring. Since the factor is assuming the credit risk, he checks the credit of the client's customer prior to shipment. Furthermore, the factor usually insists that the invoice to the customer bear a legend indicating that payment be made directly to the factor. This procedure affords the factor tighter and more direct control of collections and claims for imperfect merchandise. In accounts-receivable financing, however, the customers pay the borrower. The borrower then remits the collections to the financer. The invoices and statements of the borrower do not bear any legend indicating the financing relationship.

Receivables financing and factoring make available more operating cash to an enterprise than can unsecured credit. Until the 1970s, accounts-receivable financing and factoring were undertaken primarily by nonbank lenders, who often had both factoring and accounts-receivable financing departments. Now many commercial banks have entered the asset-based financing and factoring fields. Such entry testifies to the economic justification and legitimacy of such relationships as well as to the increasing recognition and demand for such accommodation.

Rates. The rate for accounts-receivable financing or factoring is necessarily higher than unsecured bank rates since loan administration costs are higher. The collateral must be systematically processed, recorded, and controlled. Accounts receivable change daily. New shipments are made every day, and collections on prior receivables are affected daily. As a result, the collateral and the loan measured by the collateral are continuously revolving. Further, the secured lender must maintain complete and current records on the ever-changing receivables.

Yet the administration and revolving nature of the loan enables the secured lender to provide the additional accommodation required by the borrower. Regardless of size, the loan is measured by acceptable collateral. Thus, the secured lender can lend an amount far in excess of working capital. The loan may even exceed the borrower's net worth. Consequently, in most cases where the unsecured credit limit may be X thousand dollars, the amount available from a secured financer may be three, four or five times X thousand dollars. Since the borrower can usually improve his earnings substantially with the additional funds granted by the secured lender, the borrower is willing to pay a higher rate. Indeed in many cases, while the rate is higher, the actual cost is lower for secured credit.

The reasons for this apparent paradox are varied. Unsecured lending normally involves an agreed-upon annual rate computed for a 30-, 60-, or 90-day period, and the loan is discounted in advance. In addition, the unsecured lender requires the borrower to maintain a compensating bank balance of 15% or 20% of the amount borrowed. In receivables financing, the rate is computed on the daily loan balance and the borrower does not maintain any part of the loan on deposit with the lender. The ebb and flow of collections and advances can therefore result in a lesser cost per dollar in use.

Further, the increased availability of cash frequently enables the borrower to increase his volume and/or

earn discounts from his trade suppliers. The ready availability of extra cash also enables the company to make advantageous purchases of materials by paying in cash. All of these elements result in reduced costs per unit of sale, which offset the cost of the financing. Profits may therefore be greatly increased.

Factoring charges are usually based on an agreed-upon small percentage of sales volume, plus a borrowing rate for money utilized. This cost may be offset by any one or combination of the above-described elements. The elimination of credit losses, the cost of credit checking, and the bookkeeping expense (the factor maintains the receivables ledger) result in additional savings, which can increase the profits of the enterprise.

These administrative procedures also enable the lender or factor to keep the borrower's overall operation under close observation. Since the executives of the lender usually have had many years of experience in the problems of many types of businesses, such surveillance is frequently helpful to the borrower. These executives, of course, do not and cannot substitute for the operation's accountants and lawyers. They can, however, give considered, practical, and sound business advice to the borrower.

Leveraged Acquisition Financing. Leveraged acquisition may be defined as the purchase of a company, or a division thereof, primarily for cash provided principally by debt. This can be accomplished by using the assets of the purchased company as collateral for those loans, with debt servicing coming from the cash-generating capacity of the newly formed company.

The typical companies financed by a leveraged acquisition are firms where asset-based lending is most appropriate—manufacturers or distributors that are well established, have a consistent earnings record, and whose assets have a liquidation value equal to the purchase price plus ongoing financing needs. Typically, the company will not be a high-technology or capital-intensive one.

The buyer's cash contribution usually represents only a small portion of the purchase price, resulting in debt-to-equity ratios of four to one, ten to one, or even higher. The constraints on degree of leverage are limited only to the perception of future flow of cash in an assumed interest rate and economic environment, as well as the perceived liquidation value of the assets. Conservative lenders today are using 20%-plus interest-rate assumptions in determining whether a leveraged buy-out candidate meets the cash-flow test.

Typically, a leveraged buy-out is not an accounts-receivable deal only; it also frequently involves taking inventory and fixed assets. This is done because of the relatively large need caused by the purchase price.

Although the buyer puts up relatively little cash equity, he may very well contribute much in the way of expertise, time, and effort to the success of the new venture. In a leveraged buy-out, the lender is making a bet on the new owners and ultimate managers of an established enterprise, with all the risks attendant to such a wager. These transactions are complicated in that they are (1) a divestiture; (2) an acquisition; and (3) a financing—all rolled into one.

Size of Loans and Clients. The amount of credit that asset-based lenders extend depends on the lender, the borrower, the type of business, and, most of all, on the makeup and quality of the collateral.

If collateral is solid, the lender may advance funds well above the borrower's working capital (the difference between current assets and current liabilities). Generally, the loan will be several times a company's net worth. This policy of providing a disproportionate amount of funds relative to a company's capital contrasts markedly with unsecured financing. And additional infusions of asset-based funds often spell the difference between profitable growth or failure for undercapitalized companies.

Dollar amounts of asset-based loans cover a broad range. For the most part, asset-based lenders prefer a minimum loan of $100,000, though smaller lenders may initiate loans for $50,000 or less, particularly if the chances for future growth are good. At the other end of the loan spectrum, individual asset-based loans well up into the multimillions have been granted. With loans of this size, an asset-based lender will usually participate with other lenders, particularly local banks.

The asset-based financial services industry funnels money to companies with annual sales of as little as $250,000 or less up to giants with volume in excess of $100 million. The majority generally fall within the $1-million to $10-million annual sales sector. Such a range demonstrates the versatility of this financing technique. In other instances, "start-up" funds are provided to newly organized companies with nominal sales volume.

Asset-Based Financing Extras. Asset-based lenders also advise clients of changing market or money conditions within a particular industry; devise tailor-made financing plans; help clients to pinpoint their costs; alert clients to innovative products or ideas, without, of course, violating confidences; and provide credit information. Finally, secured lenders counsel clients on financial management, while taking care to avoid exercising control over management policies and decisions.

Leonard Machlis

Asset-Management Account

A personal money-management product that combines many different financial services into one all-purpose account. The first such product, called the Cash Management Account, was introduced by Merrill Lynch in 1977. Since that time, many full-service brokerage houses, banks, and mutual-fund companies have offered similar accounts to active investors. Asset-management accounts are also referred to as "central assets accounts," "CMA-type accounts," "sweep accounts," and "universal accounts."

Despite their many differences in features and price, all asset-management accounts are based on a single idea: the linking of brokerage services with a high-yielding investment vehicle, usually a money-market fund or a bank checking account. This linkage allows investors to earn market rates of return on idle cash balances, provides them with the convenience of a single integrated statement, and gives them the opportunity to borrow against marginable securities at a relatively low rate.

There are three common types of asset-management accounts—those that are based on

- a full-service brokerage account,
- a bank account, or
- a money-market fund.

Each of these alternatives is particularly well suited to a specific kind of investor.

Brokerage-Centered Accounts. Asset-management accounts are offered by all of the large, full-service brokerage firms. Although minimums can vary considerably, most offerings of this type require an initial investment of approximately $20,000 in cash and/or securities.

This version of the asset-management account has at its core a full-service brokerage account. That's a very significant fact, for two reasons. First, investors who open such an account at a full-service firm will be entering a relationship with a commissioned broker. Second, all of the securities trades they order will be performed at full-service rates, which include the cost of investment advice.

Because of their relatively high cost, brokerage-centered asset-management accounts are not well suited for people who trade infrequently or make their own investment decisions. They are most useful for investors who (1) trade often and (2) want and value a broker's advice.

Accounts Offered by Banks. The bank-sponsored asset-management account is built around a conventional checking or NOW account, with automatic "sweeps" into a high-yielding money-market fund.

Discount brokerage services typically comprise a third component of the account, with a variety of other features available depending on the diversity of the bank's product line and the preferences of its customers.

Asset-management accounts offered by banks usually have lower investment minimums than those of brokerage firms. They also offer a higher degree of safety, because the checking account has FDIC insurance.

This type of account is not appropriate for investors who are looking for the highest possible return on their money, or for those who need a broker's advice before trading in the brokerage portion of their account.

Bank programs are a good choice, on the other hand, for people who (1) value the insurance of the bank account, (2) don't need to maximize the yield on their cash, and (3) make their own buy and sell decisions.

Accounts Built Around Money-Market Funds. Fund-centered accounts were a new development in personal financial management in 1983. These accounts are built around a high-quality money-market fund. Other features include a discount brokerage account, a bank charge card, and a large selection of computer-based transaction services.

The money-market-fund–based asset-management account should appeal to people who consider themselves independent-minded investors. It's an economical way to obtain a wide range of financial services, and it offers an investment minimum that's much lower than those for most brokerage-sponsored accounts.

This type of account won't suit the needs of investors who like to have a broker make all their investment decisions, or those who only feel comfortable dealing directly with their bank. It could be exactly right, however, for those who (1) don't rely on a broker's advice and (2) want to maximize the return on their investment.

Samuel W. Bodman

Audit

An examination or investigation, usually by an independent third party. Almost any process, operation, contract, report, or action can be audited, but the term is used most commonly in connection with the examination of financial statements by a CERTIFIED PUBLIC ACCOUNTANT (CPA). Such a financial audit consists of an intense review of the internal controls and accounting records of the company being audited.

The SECURITIES AND EXCHANGE COMMISSION (SEC) requires that the financial statements of all publicly traded companies be audited annually, primarily as a protection for present and potential shareholders or investors. The results of the audit usually appear in the company's annual report in the form of financial statements, which include statements of revenue and expenses, statements of changes in fund balances or financial position, balance sheets, and supplementary notes. Affixed to these financial statements, and signed by the accounting firm conducting the audit, is an opinion as to whether the financial statements and related transactions fairly represent the company's financial position in light of generally accepted accounting principles.

Increasingly, banks and other credit-granting institutions require audits of credit seekers prior to granting loans.

While many different types of audits are conducted, the generic term has come to stand for the examination of the way something is done. A successful audit implies legitimacy and conformation to accepted standards or criteria on the part of the audited party, as well as independence on the part of the auditor.

Samuel C. Hoyt

Audit, IRS

While an audit is generally meant to be a verification of any financial account, many people think of their income tax when the word is mentioned. An audit certifies the activity within an account, such as income, expenses, and year-end balances, giving a concise picture of one's finances and the so-called bottom line. For that reason, businesses often rely on certified public accountants to prepare their audits for reporting purposes, and most nonprofit corporations are required by law to use an independent CPA to audit the books at the end of each year.

The utility and logic of an audit as a general practice in business should carry over to one's personal or business matters when and if the INTERNAL REVENUE SERVICE (IRS) audits one's tax return. The dread with which some taxpayers view a possible audit is largely unfounded, unless, or course, one has willfully or blatantly sought to avoid paying taxes. There is no need to imagine that a letter calling one to the local IRS office will automatically lead to a cell and a striped suit. Yet taxpayers, often mistakenly fearful of an audit, illogically will overpay on their taxes to avoid one.

The actual chances of being called for an IRS audit vary according to one's adjusted gross income, being higher for higher incomes, but nationally, there is about a 2% chance that a person's 1040 will be pulled for an audit. The chance of an audit is only slightly higher for business forms, and of course higher still for forms containing one or more particularly large deductions (medical, travel, office in home, etc.). The IRS maintains a staff of nearly 25,000 agents within their compliance division; but with over 100 million persons filing 1040 personal income-tax forms, the random audit is, by sheer necessity, a small risk.

Taxpayers may be audited only for forms filed within three years of a current tax year, except in certain instances of willful tax evasion. Auditors work with paper, and since the main function of the audit is to verify the amounts legally sworn to when one signed the tax form, it is necessary to keep all records and receipts for no less than three years—and if space allows, it is advisable to keep them longer. Moreover, the better organized one keeps one's books, records, filed checks, and receipts, the faster one can produce specific documents requested, thus helping to ensure a quick and favorable outcome of the audit.

It should be mentioned that the taxpayer is not obliged to appear in person, and is not usually called in for a "total audit." Rather, one or more specific items in the return may be selected for verification, and the taxpayer may send his or her accountant or the person who assisted in the preparation of the tax form. All one is required to bring are the documents pertaining to the item(s) specifically in question. Appearing at an audit in a panic, with a shopping bag of miscellany, can't do much to help either the taxpayer or the IRS auditor. In fact, it may unnecessarily provoke the audit of still more items on the return, and the audit will certainly go less smoothly.

The best defense or preparation for an audit, then, is ample documentation of each item in question. If one knows that one has declared three times the charitable deductions actually made in a tax year, one must be prepared to pay the price (back taxes and a steep rate of interest as a penalty). More likely, an informed taxpayer may be called in on such matters as documentation of large losses, or other unusually high deductions, and proving them in an audit should be no more than a matter of displaying checks and/or receipts—the IRS auditor may want both. Once the evidence is displayed, the matter should be satisfactorily disposed of. The IRS provides that one shall not be called in repetitively for audits, so that once a justification is made for deductions, or for any particular method of accounting, one usually has several years at least without concern that the same or similar deductions will be questioned.

All of this is to say that if the taxpayer is properly prepared and calm enough to be businesslike and, *if necessary,* persuasive, the results of an IRS audit need not be traumatic. After reviewing all the documentation and facts, the auditor may accept the form as filed or request that a change be made, or even find there has been an overpayment. In turn, the taxpayer

may accept the findings or turn to a number of alternatives for "appeal." As some issues, like the valuation and subsequent depreciation of property, may be interpretive, and other matters legalistic, there may be a need for further explanations and persuasive presentation of facts by the taxpayer. There is, of course, a clearly explained set of steps for formal appeal.

To summarize: The function of an audit is more logical than insidious. For all the tension surrounding the event, the facts are fairly simple. There is a very small chance that a mathematically correct, average tax form will be chosen at random for an audit. If a form does contain "deviant" deductions, the process of auditing them involves a straightforward evidentiary proceeding. Where possible, it would be wise to send a qualified representative.

David B. Axelrod

Autographs, Collecting of, for Investment

An autograph is anything that is handwritten (not necessarily a signature). Usually an autograph of value is much more than a mere signature or a trifling note. It may be an important document that provides a new interpretation of a famous battle; a vital clue for biographers of a great man or woman; a thought to change the course of history. When you invest in autographs, you are putting your cash into the preservation of culture. You may help to preserve mankind's intellectual heritage at the same time that you triple or quadruple your investment. As collectibles, autographs differ from stamps or coins because every autograph is different, and it requires considerable knowledge to be a successful collector. The collecting of autographs for investment is known as *philography.*

The History of Autograph Collecting. A popular hobby, even in ancient Rome, the collecting of autograph letters and documents of celebrities has during the past century developed into an exciting and very profitable form of investment. The great American composer Jerome Kern put nearly $100,000 into his collection of rare books and autographs. In 1928 he sold his collection for slightly more than a million dollars. It was more money than he'd ever possessed. His friends urged him to put his newfound wealth into the stock market. Kern followed their advice and within a year had lost every cent. Even during the Great Depression, when stocks plunged wildly, rare autographs, such as those of Lincoln and Washington, Dickens and Byron, Galileo and Pasteur, Beethoven and Wagner, held up well, and some fetched new record prices. Today, scores of knowledgeable collectors are making money out of handwritten history and literature by buying choice letters and documents of the great figures of the past. J. P. Morgan, Sr., was often ridiculed by his friends for paying "high" prices for rare autographs, but the prices he paid appear now to be ridiculously low. Franklin D. Roosevelt and John F. Kennedy were both autograph collectors, and neither one was known as being profligate with a dollar!

How to Obtain Rare Autographs. There are perhaps 20 reliable experts in America who are in the business of buying and selling rare old documents. Most of them issue priced catalogs. The intelligent collector who buys from reliable dealers and is willing to hold his purchases for a few years can not only participate in an exciting cultural pursuit but can double or triple his money. He can do even better if he wishes to present his collection to a college library or a historical society and take a tax deduction.

Buying at Auction. The purchase of autographs at auctions is an exhilarating pursuit and a great intellectual game. You can pick up incredible bargains. Make sure the auction house guarantees what it sells, however, as there are many forgeries and facsimiles on the market being sold by unscrupulous or inexperienced auctioneers. Investors who have very little money to spend and cannot afford the cost (often in the thousands of dollars) of choice and eagerly sought autographs can write directly to celebrities: Ask an interesting question and you may get an interesting handwritten reply. One collector wrote to Ronald Reagan, then governor of California, condemning Reagan's association with Frank Sinatra. Reagan's hand-penned reply, defending Sinatra's character, sold for $12,500 at the Charles Hamilton Galleries in New York, a world's record for the autograph of a living person, now in the *Guinness Book of World Records*. Less than ten years ago, it cost the original owner only a 15-cent stamp!

Which Autographs Are Sound Investments? If you want to go in for the blue chips, you can collect the traditional favorites.

Presidents. A complete collection of inexpensive examples of presidential autographs will today cost between $5,000 and $10,000. Such a collection might contain a routine document or note of Lincoln's ($1,200) and Washington's ($1,500) and very important letters of Coolidge's ($150) and Franklin D. Roosevelt's ($400). If you limit yourself to autographs signed while in office, you will encounter two rarities: William Henry Harrison, who died one month after taking the oath ($25,000); and James A. Garfield, who was shot four months after his inaugural ($3,500).

The autographs of both of these presidents are, however, very abundant during other periods of their lives.

Composers. This field has increasingly captured the fancy of collectors during the past three decades. Many noted composers—like Saint-Saëns, Gounod, Massenet, Offenbach, Friml, Romberg, Victor Herbert, and Cole Porter—are easily obtainable at modest prices. Berlioz, Wagner, Brahms, Verdi, and Gershwin run from a few hundred to several thousand for a fine letter or a brief musical excerpt signed. Priced very high, and an excellent investment, are letters and manuscripts of Beethoven, Mozart, and that superlative rarity, Bach.

Scientific Autographs. Much sought-after, and rocketing in value every year, are letters of Pasteur, Jenner, Edison, Fulton, Einstein, Freud, and other leaders in the world of science. Only a decade ago a fine Darwin letter could be picked up for $50 or $100. Today the identical letter, having proved a fine investment, would be a bargain at $1,500.

Royalty. Always a popular field are the documents and letters of British and French kings and queens. They increase dramatically in value over the years. For example, letters of Napoleon's that sold in 1960 for only $22 will today fetch around $500 each.

Authors. For less than $100, you can today buy letters of Longfellow, Holmes, Whittier, Sinclair Lewis, Dreiser, T. S. Eliot, Thackeray, and scores of other immortals. Anything by Hawthorne, Mark Twain, or Whitman will put a considerable dent in your purse. And for the most sought-after names—Emily Dickinson, Poe, and Herman Melville—expect to give your bank balance a severe jolt. It is these rarities, however, that have displayed the most vigorous increase in value during the past decade.

Other Popular Fields of Collecting. Other areas in philography that should appeal to the shrewd investor are African explorers (Stanley and Livingstone are not hard to obtain), astronauts, aviators, Western Americana, American Judaica, British authors, Civil War letters, Revolutionary War heroes, and signers of the Declaration of Independence. (Of the 56 signers, only Button Gwinnett of Georgia is really elusive and costly.) Also attractive are French authors, Napoleon and his marshals, and letters prior to 1850 with rare postal markings.

Franking Signatures. A free-franking signature is a signature written on an envelope or letter cover so that the letter can be sent without payment of postage. In the United States, all members of Congress and the Senate, as well as army officers, were and still are allowed to free-frank their mail. The last president to have the franking privilege was Ulysses S. Grant. Until recently, franks were regarded as little more than

Figure 1.
Example of autographs with their 1983 values.
a Standard Oil stock certificate signed by John D. Rockefeller, Sr. (value: $850);
b Fulton stock certificate (value: $850);
c check filled out and signed by George Washington (value: $4,000);
d bank note signed by Mormon leaders Joseph Smith and Sidney Rigdon (value: $600);
e Thomas A. Edison's prescription for success (value: $350);
f Henry Ford's signature (value: $200).

mere signatures, but every year now sees a dramatic increase in their value. Most prized are complete letter covers franked (signed) by Washington, Jefferson, Lincoln, John Hancock, and Benjamin Franklin. Letter covers franked by Henry Clay, John C. Calhoun, and Daniel Webster are abundant but eagerly sought. A free frank of Lincoln's signed as postmaster of New Salem, Illinois, would be valued at about $12,000 to $15,000 because of its rarity.

Black Leaders. The increase in value of letters of Martin Luther King, Jr., Booker T. Washington, and Frederick Douglass has been phenomenal in recent years. A fine handwritten letter of King's is worth almost as much as a comparable letter of Lincoln's—about $2,000. There appears to be no ceiling to the increasing values of prominent black leaders.

Nazis. If you like modern history, and violence intrigues you, the documents of Nazism, often flashy and ornate, make excellent investments. Hitler's signed papers are eagerly sought. Not many years ago, you could pick up a document authentically signed by the Führer for $15 or $20. Today you cannot find one for less than $500. Hitler's autograph is the most forged autograph of modern times. In spite of the war's devastation, Nazi autographs are plentiful. Documents signed by Himmler, Göring, Hess, Goebbels, Rommel (not a member of the Nazi party), and scores of other notorious leaders of the Third Reich are readily obtainable for a few hundred dollars. There may be a great financial future for these colorful documents of terror.

Feminist Leaders. Autographs of feminist leaders are another booming new field, highly recommended for investors who want a fast return. Only a few years ago Susan B. Anthony letters were selling for a dollar. Today these same letters are a bargain at $300.

Movie Stars. Undoubtedly the most spectacular increase in value of any autographs during recent years is in the field of motion pictures, especially signed photographs. In the late 1970s, inscribed photographs of such luminaries as Béla Lugosi and Boris Karloff were fetching $10. Today they bring upwards of $300. Recently, a souvenir script of *Gone with the Wind* inscribed by the producer, David O. Selznick, to one of the stars, Olivia de Havilland, sold at auction for $13,500. Consider that you can get a book of George Washington's, from his library and signed by him, for about $5,000 and you will at once see the importance of motion-picture stars to the modern philographer. It may be predicted that there will be dramatic increases in the values of motion-picture personalities. This newest and most exciting field of collecting, frowned upon by old-timers who live in the dustbins of the past, is certain to be the collecting area of the future.

Obsolete Stocks and Bonds. The collecting of obsolete stocks and bonds is known as *scripophily*. Only a few years ago disgruntled investors often papered their walls with obsolete stocks or unredeemable currency. Such a display would today be very costly, for many "worthless" old stocks and bank notes are now sought after by scripophiles. It is not uncommon for a certificate that has no redemption value to fetch a thousand dollars or more. The value of an obsolete stock or bank note is determined by the following factors: date of the certificate or banknote; its signer or signers; its subject or purpose; and beauty of ornamentation.

Like many new collectibles, obsolete stocks and bonds have yo-yoed erratically on the market. A few years ago (1978) they were almost unsellable. By 1980 many were fetching astronomical prices. In the spring of 1981, values plummeted, although still far above the level of 1978. Unlike other autographs, which appear unaffected by stock-market gyrations, obsolete stocks and bonds seem to follow the trend of the Dow-Jones.

Here are some categories of obsolete stocks that are eagerly sought by shrewd collector/investors:

Railroad Stocks and Bonds. These attractive old certificates, often bearing vignette engravings of early trains, mirror the westward movement of the United States. Except for very early railroad certificates (1820–60) or very rare stocks with small issues, early railroad stocks with beautiful ornamentation and in fine condition are available at $10 to $50 each.

Stocks for New Inventions. One of the most appealing of all scripophilic items are stock certificates that picture new inventions or improved products. Certificates personally signed by important inventors often fetch high prices, such as Thomas A. Edison ($500), Henry Ford ($1,500), Robert Fulton ($850). Stocks for bizarre inventions that never panned out make a fascinating assemblage. Automobile stocks, of which a most abundant supply exists, are very appealing. Early aircraft stocks fetch especially high prices, particularly when the aircraft itself is illustrated in a vignette on the stock.

Mining Stocks. Few stocks are so splashily pictorial as early mining stocks from California, Nevada, Arizona, and other western states. Stocks dated before 1870 are most desirable. Stocks issued after 1910 are seldom collected, because of their abundance.

Stocks Signed by Famous Persons. Only a few years ago, stock certificates signed by Henry Wells and William G. Fargo for the American Express Company sold for $15 each. Today they fetch $350 or more. In fact, less than ten years ago $15 was the price usually asked for mortgage bonds signed by General Santa Anna (Mexican general who captured the Alamo);

Cornelius Vanderbilt; John D. Rockefeller, Sr.; Jay Gould; and John Jacob Astor. These stocks have advanced dramatically in value and are certain to show a great increase in value in the future.

Rare Currency. Often regarded as the province of the numismatist, early currency is frequently sought by philographers (autograph collectors) and scripophilists. Consider that there are available scores of dramatic bank notes or financial documents bearing the signatures of Robert Morris, Haym Salomon, John Hart (signer of the Declaration of Independence), Joseph Smith and Brigham Young (Mormon leaders), Sam Houston—the list is almost without end. George Washington and John Hancock signed lottery tickets. Many, indeed most, of the early bank notes are in crisp, fresh condition and bear superb vignettes that make a brave and colorful display.

A final suggestion: Canceled checks of celebrated persons offer a unique opportunity to the discerning philographer. Many collectors specialize in presidential checks. For a few thousand dollars, you can pick up an original check, filled out and signed by Lincoln or Washington. Or, for $50 or $100, a check of Calvin Coolidge's or William McKinley's. This writer can conceive of no more dramatic a collection, certain to increase in value in the future as it has in the past, than an assemblage of presidential signatures on colorful checks of early American banks.

One thing is certain. Whoever gathers autographs for investment will not only add to his monetary wealth but will vastly increase his knowledge of the world's culture.

Charles Hamilton

Automated Clearinghouse (ACH)

A computerized clearing arrangement for settling balances between depository institutions arising from those payments sent or received electronically, instead of by paper check, on behalf of depositors. Examples of these payments include direct payroll deposits and Social Security payments. The automated clearinghouse is similar in concept to the clearing arrangements used by banks for settling balances arising from the paper check payments and receipts of their depositors.

The Federal Reserve operates 39 of the nation's 40 ACH's. The New York ACH is the one privately operated system, but it relies on the Federal Reserve bank of New York for delivery and settlement services (it does its own computer processing). In 1982 about 11,000 commercial banks and 3,000 thrift institutions were receiving electronic payments through the nation's ACH's; about 200 were initiating them for business and government accounts.

Depository institutions that make payments for business or government-agency depositors through an ACH convert the payment data to debit and credit items on a magnetic tape and deliver the tape, or the data itself by electronic transmission, to their local Federal Reserve office. There the debit and credit entries are posted by computer to other depositories' accounts for settlement. The Federal Reserve's computer generates its own magnetic tape of entries made, which is delivered to institutions whose depositors are receiving payments.

The ACH concept was developed in the early 1970s by a group of California banks who saw in ACH an operational response to the growing volume and increased costs of processing paper checks. For the most part, however, the Federal Reserve has played the major role in making ACH an alternative to paper-check collection, absorbing much of the developmental costs of establishing ACH processing facilities and providing guidance for regional associations of banks interested in organizing an ACH.

In 1982 there were 32 regional ACH associations in the United States. These associations are comprised of banks that have agreed to send and receive payments through an ACH in a given region of the country. ACH associations typically provide bank participants with a warranty for ACH transactions sent or received, market ACH services to corporations and the public, and are responsible for either processing ACH tapes directly or subcontracting the processing of entries to the Federal Reserve. The National Automated Clearing House Association (NACHA) is a nonprofit association of the 32 regional ACH associations. NACHA sets operating rules and standards for the exchange and settlement of ACH items between regions and for commercial ACH payments that are cleared and settled between ACH's.

In 1981 about 8,000 corporations used ACH's for making more than 60 million payments. However, government payments (160 million) accounted for about 75% of total ACH volume. In 1976 the federal government began an aggressive and successful program to convert its check-disbursement system into a direct-deposit electronic funds-transfer system. Today, ACH's handle a substantial share of the government's Social Security benefits and payroll, retirement, and revenue-sharing payments. Private-sector volume consists primarily of salary, wage, and preauthorized consumer payments for insurance premiums, mortgage-loan repayments, and other repetitive payments.

In the early 1970s, ACH payments were exchanged only between depositories located in the same region. In 1977 the Federal Reserve began to link the regional

ACH's into a national network, which became operational at the end of 1978. The regional ACH's are linked by the same telecommunications network used by the Federal Reserve to transmit interbank wire transfers of funds—the Fedwire.

U.S. bankers, on balance, did not actively promote ACH to depositors in the 1970s because they did not see ACH as providing them with significant marketing, competitive, or cost-saving advantages. For one, commercial use of ACH did not grow significantly in the 1970s, and there were substantial doubts throughout the decade whether a profitable private-sector market for ACH could be developed in the 1980s. For another, significant concerns related to ACH operations troubled many bankers. Corporations must submit payroll data to banks for ACH processing several days before payday, a schedule many corporations cannot or are unwilling to meet. Many corporations have also been reluctant to give up the substantial FLOAT associated with paychecks. In an ACH arrangement, the entire payroll is debited by the bank on payday. Under the paycheck-issued system, checks take several days to clear, giving rise to float that can be used by the corporation for daily investments in the money market.

The major thrust of the banking industry's promotion of ACH in the 1970s was to gain corporate acceptance of direct deposit. Little emphasis was placed on "selling" employees on direct deposit or convincing bank customers to use preauthorized bill-payment services. In a preauthorized payment program, consumers authorize their banks to make payments to a specific firm at a specific date each month or quarter, and the payments are made through automatic charges to their bank accounts. Public utilities and insurance companies were the most active promoters of this preauthorized payment service in the 1970s.

In 1981, when the Federal Reserve banks were required by the Monetary Control Act to price their services to bank users, the Federal Reserve instituted a subsidy for ACH service with prices set well below Federal Reserve costs. The subsidy was an effort to promote ACH services. Many bankers contended, however, that a subsidy price made it difficult, if not impossible, for the private sector to compete with the Federal Reserve in providing ACH and other electronic payment services, an intent of the Monetary Control Act. In 1982 the Federal Reserve announced its intention to phase out its ACH subsidy pricing by 1985.

David H. Friedman

Automated Teller Machines (ATM's)

Automated teller machines are computer-controlled terminals through which customers of financial insti-

tutions may make various kinds of transactions as they would through a bank teller. A recent innovation in personal banking services, they work like this: A customer fills out an application at the institution where he does his banking (assuming it has such a system). He is subsequently given a magnetically coded card and a personal identification number or code that permits only him to access the account on these machines. To use the ATM the customers insert their cards and operate push buttons as per instructions on the machine to find out their checking and savings-account balances (on the viewing screen); deposit money into their accounts; withdraw funds (usually limited amounts regardless of account balances); transfer funds from checking to savings and from savings to checking; and make payments on credit-card transactions, personal loans, and mortgages.

Many people find ATM's convenient to use because they can do their banking anytime and avoid long lines. Automated teller machines are located on the premises of financial institutions and in other places where they may be accessible 24 hours a day, every day of the week. ATM's are widely used by financial institutions, usually marketed and advertised under proprietary names.

Harvey Rachlin

Automobile, How to Purchase a New

Next to a new home, new cars are the biggest purchases most of us will ever make. Like any major purchase, there are many considerations: Which, among hundreds of makes, models, and available options, is the right car for you? How much can you afford to spend, considering down payment, trade-in allowance for your old car, interest rates, and the size of monthly payments? And are you familiar with new car warranties, service contracts, and other consumer-protection packages?

It all sounds very confusing, but it need not be. If a buyer shops with care, deals with reputable firms and products, and makes his or her choice based on good information and a sound personal evaluation, buying a new car can be what it is supposed to be—fun! The key is to approach a new car purchase one step at a time.

Fortunately, there is a wealth of information available to help consumers. Popular automotive magazines and consumer publications available at most public libraries rate new cars for performance, economy, comfort, and convenience. But one of the best, often overlooked, resources available to consumers is the franchised new-car dealer.

Franchised dealers are available to answer questions about any phase of an automobile purchase, including up-to-date technical engineering details, optional-equipment choices, and financing terms. And since repeat sales and word-of-mouth advertising depend on buyer satisfaction, it is in the dealer's best interest to help the buyer make the right selection and deal. It is also here that the consumer makes his own hands-on evaluation. He can sit in the cars, drive them, and examine every inch of them.

Before you go to a dealer showroom, however, you should answer two fundamental questions. First, what kind of car do you want and need? Second, how much can you afford to spend? Once you carefully answer these questions, your new-car purchase can be much easier.

What Kind of Car? This basic question is perhaps the most important one you will consider. Let's begin with the type of driving you do. Do you drive about 12,000 miles per year (average driver)? Do you drive more? Less? Are your trips on the highways or do you primarily drive around town? Answers to these questions help determine the style, size, fuel efficiency, and level of comfort necessary in your car.

You should also consider how many passengers you normally carry. Do you have a large family? Do other people car-pool with you? Are your passengers usually adults or children? How important is rear-seat size, accessibility, and comfort?

And how much cargo space do you need? Do you often carry golf clubs? Tools of your trade? Luggage? Do you frequently carry materials for household do-it-yourself projects? Will a sedan or hatchback model meet your needs, or do you need a station wagon?

Size Considerations. Today's automobiles are grouped by size into four broad categories: full-size, intermediate, compact, and subcompact.

A frequently heard distinction between the different types of automobiles is the size of their wheelbases (the distance between the front wheels and the back wheels measured from wheel center to wheel center). The wheelbase of a full-size car generally ranges from approximately 114 inches to 121 inches on some luxury models. By contrast, subcompact wheelbases range from 94 to 97 inches; intermediate models and compacts range between full-size and subcompact models.

Wheelbase size alone, however, doesn't give you all you need to make a choice on a car. You should consider interior room, too. In this case, the biggest difference is the rear seat. A full-size car can provide almost an additional foot of rear-seat legroom over a subcompact. In terms of rear-seat hip room, a full-size car tops the subcompact by as much as 18 inches; in rear-seat headroom, the full-size car has a 3-inch advantage.

Luggage space is yet another basic consideration. A full-size car frequently offers twice the luggage-carrying capacity of a subcompact. Subcompacts typically offer only 10 to 14 cubic feet of luggage space, while full-size cars offer 15 to 22 cubic feet. Remember, however, choosing a car for rear-seat room and trunk space alone might keep you from parking it in your garage, since full-size cars are often as much as one foot wider and four feet longer than subcompacts.

Style Considerations. Today's designers have brought many of the comforts and conveniences of full-size cars into compacts and subcompacts. Consider hatchbacks, for example. By adding a sloping door to the rear of a subcompact and designing a rear seat that folds flat, many subcompacts can be turned into mini–station wagons.

Even greater luggage-carrying capacity is available in the station wagon body style. Built on the same wheelbase as comparable sedans, station wagons often have more than five times the carrying capacity of sedans.

The number of side doors on a car is another style consideration. Two-door models are often sportier-looking and less expensive, but four-door models provide easier access for rear-seat passengers. Also, the doors on a four-door model are actually smaller and lighter, making them easier to open in crowded parking spaces. If rear-seat passengers are expected frequently, a four-door model might be desirable.

If passenger and cargo capacity are less important to you than performance and design, you may want to consider two- or four-passenger sports cars and convertibles.

Fuel Economy. Fuel economy continues to be one of the highest priorities of both buyers and automobile manufacturers, and all cars sold today are considerably more fuel-efficient than those of a decade ago. But generally speaking, the same rule applies today as it always has: The smaller the car, the greater the fuel economy. So your personal priorities in this area will have to be weighed against many other factors—size, style, comfort, hauling capacity, the amount of driving you do, etc.

In making this decision, fuel economy should be translated into transportation efficiency. Obviously, a car pool of four adults riding in a 17-mile-per-gallon (mpg) full size sedan is more fuel-efficient than if each of the four drove a 30-mpg subcompact.

All cars sold in the U.S. are tested by the Environmental Protection Agency (EPA) for mileage rating. EPA mileage figures are posted on every new car and are also available at new-car dealers, at libraries, and directly from the EPA.

EPA produces two mileage figures for each automobile: a highway mileage rating and an "estimated" city rating. The EPA recommends consumers use the "estimated" mileage for comparison purposes. Typical consumer gas mileage is likely to be lower than the EPA estimate because real driving conditions are difficult to duplicate in a laboratory test.

Engines. The trend today is toward smaller, more fuel-efficient engines. And, like cars, the larger the engine, or the greater the number of cylinders, the more fuel it consumes. Of course, larger engines provide greater power, so you will have to balance your desires for fuel economy and performance. Most manufacturers offer a wide choice of engines, however, and you should be able to find the right compromise. The best way to make your decision is to actually test-drive the cars at a franchised dealer.

You have probably heard talk of diesel engines. Diesels offer both advantages and disadvantages. They are generally more fuel-efficient than gasoline engines, but they offer somewhat less power and performance, and carry a premium price, sometimes as much as $700 or $800 more than gasoline engines. They also require more frequent oil changes, and fuel for diesels is not available at every service station. If you are interested in a diesel, talk with your dealer about it.

Optional Equipment. After you have considered size, style, and economic factors, give some thought to the optional equipment available. Keep in mind that a "base" model includes few popular options. The typical base model is equipped with the smallest possible engine, a manual transmission, a standard interior, and occasionally an AM radio. While that may satisfy some buyers, others may desire more comfort, convenience, and performance in their cars. It may be helpful to make a list of the options you feel you need, at a minimum, to make you happy, and a "wish list" of items you would like to have if you could afford them. This will help both you and the dealer make the right choices for you.

Worth noting, however, is the fact that resale value can be improved or diminished according to what options you select. For example, resale prices in the National Automobile Dealers Association (NADA) *Used Car Guide* usually itemize such add-ons as automatic transmission, power steering, and air conditioning. Other popular options can be power brakes, steel-belted radial tires, tinted windows, and a radio. All these are usually found on what manufacturers sometimes call a "normally equipped" model.

A second group of options is designed to add further comfort or convenience. Power windows, centrally operated door locks, power seat adjusters, sun roofs, stereo radios, and stereo tape players are examples of comfort-and-convenience options. Some increase resale value, while others have little effect. Consult a franchised dealer for details.

In recent years, a special group of "durability" options has become increasingly popular. This category

Table 1 **General Motors 1983 New-Car Options**
Body side stripe
Astroroof—electric sliding
Landau top
Long vinyl top
231 C.I.D. 2BBL V6
252 C.I.D. 4BBL V6
307 C.I.D. 4BBL V8
350 C.I.D. diesel V8
Automatic transmission
Air conditioner
Touch climate control air conditioner
Electric rear-window defogger
AM radio
AM/FM Radio
AM/FM stereo radio
8-track + AM/FM stereo
Cassette tape + AM/FM stereo
CB + AM/FM stereo
CB + 8-track + AM/FM stereo
CB + cassette + AM/FM stereo
Rear dual speakers
Automatic power antenna
Chrome plated wheels
Wire wheels (locking)
Styled aluminum wheels
Steel-belted whitewalls
Electric door locks
Automatic electric door locks
Electric trunk release
Electric fuel-cap lock
Electric seat back recliner (driver/passenger)
Power seat, 6-way (driver/passenger)
Power windows
Cruise control
Visor vanity mirror
Left remote-control mirror
Trip odometer
Low-fuel indicator
Dome reading lamp
Low washer-fluid indicator
2-speed windshield wiper with low-speed delay feature
Remote control mirror with illuminated thermometer (left)
Sport mirrors (left & right remote)
Door edge guards
Exterior molding package
Trunk compartment mat
Tilt steering wheel
Sport steering wheel
Grand touring suspension

includes undercoating, rustproofing, polymer paint sealants, and interior fabric protectors. Most of these are installed by the new-car dealer. Each is designed to protect the car from the effects of wear and tear, weather, road salt, and other hazards. By preserving the car longer, these protective options help increase resale value. Table 1 lists the new-car options of one major automobile manufacturer.

Resale Value. What will your new car be worth in three or four years? Unfortunately, there is no crystal ball to give us a reliable answer. Resale value depends on many factors, including unpredictable swings in consumer tastes and the supply and price of gasoline. The long-term trend toward smaller, more fuel-efficient cars will continue, but the recent rebirth of high-performance and luxury automobiles indicates that consumers want more than just miles per gallon. So buy for your own use today rather than betting on the car's future appeal to another owner.

Summarize Your Research. By now you should have a good idea of the kind of car that best suits you. List the several makes or models that meet all of your needs. Go to dealerships that sell those makes and take a firsthand look at the cars you've selected. Ask the salesmen to explain the cars' various features. Compare their features. Sit in the cars; check head, leg, and hip room in the front and back seats. Ask for a test drive to compare ride and handling characteristics. Try to include city and highway driving, as well as some country roads in your test drive to be certain that the car performs under varied driving conditions. If you are undecided about engines, transmissions, steering, or other options that directly affect performance and road handling, test-drive other vehicles so that you can try those various combinations.

If you are comparing dealership prices, be certain that you clearly understand what is included in each price. Do the cars have comparable sticker prices? Are their performance characteristics similar? Does the quoted price include additional dealer-installed options? Does it include applicable sales tax? Be certain that your comparison includes similar components.

Cost. The second fundamental question to address in buying your new car is what you have to spend. By answering this question before you "talk turkey," you'll save confusion and possible misunderstanding when you sit down with your salesman to talk price.

The new-car sales price typically includes three factors. One is your "down payment"—that is, the cash you actually take out of your bank account to buy the car. Another is the value of your trade-in vehicle. And the third is the amount financed, or the remainder of the purchase price after the down payment and the trade-in value are deducted.

Down Payment. The down payment is easy to figure out. It is based upon the amount of cash you want to put into the purchase of your new car. The fastest way to reduce monthly payments on the unpaid balance is to increase the amount of the down payment. However, you may have other investment or purchase demands on this money, so consider carefully whether you would be wiser to increase your down payment or to finance a greater portion of your purchase.

Trade-in Value. The true value of your trade-in will not be found in the newspaper or a used-car price guide. Those sources don't take into consideration the actual condition of your trade-in, its mileage, or its demand within your community. The best way to determine the value of your trade-in is to try to sell it. Speak to the used-car managers at several different auto dealerships. Tell them you're interested in selling your car for cash and ask what it's worth. It might be a good idea to have them jot that figure down on a business card for later reference.

Once you've taken this simple step, you've established the *actual cash value* of your trade-in—the amount either you or a dealer can receive by liquidating or selling the car in the wholesale automobile market. (The actual cash value will probably be less than the price similar models are selling for in your community.) You have the option, of course, of retailing your car, but most people find this a nuisance and elect to trade in the car as part of the new-car purchase.

Financing. Your homework is now complete. You know your automobile needs and what models and options are best. You've examined your personal finances and determined how much cash you can bring to the deal. You've had your present car appraised and have an idea of its actual cash value. You are now ready to discuss the terms of your new-car purchase.

If you finance part of the new car's purchase price, discuss all financing plans available to you with your dealer. New-car dealers offer competitive financing opportunities and some attractive terms. Dealers are also able to use contacts with many credit sources and know which lending institutions offer the best rates. As a consumer service, he may shop for a favorable interest rate for you. Since the money you borrow is the same no matter where you borrow it, it pays to shop around.

When comparing financing rates, be sure to compare rates that are followed by the letters *APR*. *APR* stands for ANNUAL PERCENTAGE RATE—a method of computing interest rates that has been standardized by the Federal Truth in Lending Act. Another important factor is the length of the loan.

The longer the repayment period you select, the more interest you pay and the more the loan costs. Repayment periods for new cars today commonly range from 36 to 48 months.

For example, financing $6,000 at an APR of 24% for 48 months would cost you $1,870 in interest. Financing the same loan amount at 16% for a shorter term of 36 months would cost only $1,594 in interest. So you can see that while your monthly payment might be higher, a shorter loan term could save you hundreds of dollars in interest.

On the other hand, one advantage of a longer loan term lies in smaller monthly installment payments. Since the finance charge and the total amount borrowed are divided among a greater number of payments, your monthly payment is smaller. A longer-term loan may be necessary in order to stay within your monthly budget. Your new-car dealer or financing source can help adjust the term of your loan to fit that budget.

You don't need to be an expert on finance to understand your new-car loan terms. Just remember that your finance charge is influenced by three things: the interest rate or APR, the amount financed, and the number of payments. Increase one and your finance charge increases; decrease either and your finance charge decreases.

When your finance contract is presented for your signature, read the terms carefully. Be certain that you understand your responsibilities under the agreement you are signing.

Service Contracts. Service contracts and mechanical insurance are both effective means of protecting yourself against unexpected major repair bills in the life of your new car. They work like your automobile collision insurance: If you have a mechanical breakdown during the covered period, the policy pays the cost of repairs, usually minus some predetermined deductible amount.

For example, the deductible amount of one very popular mechanical-breakdown insurance policy is $25. This means that if a policyholder's transmission breaks down and repair costs are $600, the policyholder pays $25 and the insurance company pays $575.

Like insurance, these programs charge a premium, which is paid at the time of new-car purchase. Sometimes it can be included in the new-car financing. Frequently these extend up to five years or 50,000 miles. Most policies cover the major mechanical parts of the car that carry the engine's power to the wheels; many also cover air-conditioners and electrical systems.

If you decide to include this kind of mechanical protection in your new-car deal, be certain that you fully understand what parts of your car are covered under the program and for how long. Be sure also that you understand your responsibilities for proper vehicle maintenance and operation and for partial payment or deductibles in the event that a repair is required under the contract.

Warranties. Another consideration in purchasing a new car is the warranty. Most new cars are protected against mechanical repairs by some type of manufacturer's warranty for the first 12 months or 12,000 miles. There is no additional charge for this new-car warranty. Basically, it is a promise by the car's manufacturer that the car is free of defects and that the company will bear, within certain limits, the cost of correcting defects that do appear.

Carefully examine the warranty documents for limitations in time and mileage, what parts are covered, and what your responsibilities for maintenance are during the warranty period.

Delivery. How long you have to wait before taking delivery of your new car varies. If you purchase a car that the dealer has in inventory, you can often arrange to drive away in your new car the same day. If the car you desire isn't in the dealer's inventory but is available from a nearby dealer, your dealer can usually arrange to get the car within a day or two. When the car is not available locally, or when you want a specific combination of options, the dealer may order your new car directly from the factory. This takes a bit longer, depending on the production schedule and demand for your model.

Although you don't pay for the car until it's delivered to you, the actual cash value of your trade-in may change during this period. Be sure to ask whether your trade-in will be reappraised before the delivery of your new car. This could affect the price you are paying.

Price. All consumers want to feel they received a "good deal" on their new car. They generally want to purchase the car for less than the amount stated on the window sticker. Whether or not this is possible depends on the demand for and supply of the particular model you are interested in. Many dealers depend on volume sales. They really want to sell you a car at a price you will be happy with. As a satisfied customer, you will likely buy another car from the same dealer, and you may recommend him to your friends and neighbors.

On the other hand, the retail new-car industry operates on relatively narrow price margins. If dealers intend to stay in business, they must make a profit on each car. So be realistic when buying a new car. Don't look for discounts the dealer cannot give.

Leasing—An Alternative. While most people still purchase their new cars, leasing is becoming an increasingly popular alternative—one you might want to explore before making your final decision to purchase. Leasing differs from purchasing in several ways.

First, your lease payments entitle you to the use of the car only. You are not buying the car but merely renting it over a specified term. The car is owned by the dealer or the company that leases the car to you.

While the required cash down payment for a lease is usually less, credit requirements are higher. You will need a solid credit history and a certain income level to meet the requirement of most lessors.

Four factors influence the size of the lease payment: the price the lessor paid the dealer for the car; the amount of mileage you plan to put on the car during the term of the lease; the "residual value," or how much the lessor expects the car to be worth at the end of the lease; and who bears the risk of any loss that may result from the sale of the car at the end of the lease.

In a closed-end lease, your responsibility ends with the last lease payment, assuming the car's condition at that time meets the lease requirements. A closed-end lease is similar to the lease you may have signed when you rented your first apartment.

Remember, in a leasing arrangement, you pay only for the difference between the price the lessor paid for the car and its residual value at the end of the lease, plus interest and other costs. Since your payments don't cover the full car price, a lease payment may be lower than the monthly payment on a car purchase. If you use your car for business purposes and deduct car expenses from your income tax, leasing can help simplify your tax preparation and maximize your deduction. Consult your tax accountant for these details.

An open-ended lease can reduce payments even further. With this type of lease, the lessor estimates the residual value or how much the car will be worth at the end of the lease period. You may be held responsible for paying at least part of the difference to the lessor if the returned car is judged to be worth less than the estimated residual value. By having you assume part of the risk of estimating the residual value, lessors reduce their costs and pass the savings on to you in the form of a lower payment. Your new-car dealer can consult with you on the details of leasing and whether it is right for you.

How to Get a Bargain or How to Get a Good Deal. The key to your satisfaction with any new-car purchase, or lease, is plenty of background work. A careful assessment of your driving needs will help you select a car that is right for you. A careful appraisal of the actual cash value of your used car and a determination of what down payment you can afford will allow you to negotiate your purchase from a position of knowledge.

If you enter a new car dealer's showroom well prepared, you will discover that the dealership is a source of valuable information and service to you. Dealers and consumers are not natural adversaries, despite widespread public misconceptions. Dealers know that customers will return if they are treated well and their questions are answered satisfactorily. And dealers value that return business.

As you discuss your purchase options with your dealer, don't hesitate to ask questions. Both you and the dealer know that you are not an expert on buying a new car. It is in the best interests of both of you to see that your questions are answered fully.

Harvey Rachlin

Automobile Insurance

In 1898, when Dr. Truman J. Martin of Buffalo, New York, bought the United States' first automobile-insurance policy, drivers were mainly worried about damage their noisy machines might cause by scaring horses. Barely 100 cars were on the streets then, coast to coast.

In 1981 there were more than 165.7 million registered vehicles and 148 million licensed drivers in the United States. American motorists covered an estimated 1.544 trillion miles in the year. Today's drivers encounter a degree of risk that could scarcely have been imagined at the turn of the century.

Based on 1981 data, some 18 million motor-vehicle accidents occur annually and result in 50,800 deaths and disabling injuries to 1.9 million people. The annual economic toll—in terms of medical expenses, property damage, lost wages, and the like—has been estimated at $40.6 billion a year. Without doubt, the automobile has proved to be the greatest threat of death or lawsuit in the average person's life.

Modern auto insurance is designed to protect against severe economic losses the auto can inflict in a matter of seconds. Most people today rank auto insurance as "very important" or "absolutely essential." It is the most widely purchased of all property-liability insurance.

Yet much confusion persists. People are puzzled about how premiums are established and how rates are figured, what coverages should be bought, and how to save money buying them. All this is discussed in this entry.

This is a guide to common auto-insurance coverages but should not be taken to represent the provisions of any particular policy.

The roots of the tort-liability system twist back through the lengthy history of English common law. They are fed by the ancient concepts of retribution or retaliation: Each person is responsible for his or her actions, and if an injury is caused through breach of a duty to others, the victim should be compensated at the cost of the person causing the injury.

Insurance That Pays for Injuries or Damage That You Cause. People buy liability insurance to pay for losses they may cause others to suffer. In practice, most forms of liability insurance are not payable directly to the insured. An insurance firm providing liability coverages pays for accidental damage you cause in operating a vehicle named in the policy, or while driving nonowned cars with owners' permission, or in pulling a trailer you own.

Liability coverage calls for the insurance firm to defend you in suits seeking damages after an auto accident, even if the suits are groundless, false, or fraudulent. The coverage may also pay for premiums on appeal bonds, bail-bond costs up to certain limits, investigation costs, court costs, and interest on judgments.

A policyholder selects limits for the *bodily injury* and *property damage* liability coverages. The bodily-injury limits apply in two situations: The first limit applies to injury per person for each accident; the second limit applies to the total that can be paid for the injuries of two or more persons for each accident. The remaining limit chosen by the policyholder applies to the property damage. For example, 50/100/25 means $50,000 per person bodily-injury limits, $100,000 per accident for bodily injury, and $25,000 limit for property-damage liability. Liability coverage is mandatory in more than half the states.

Insurance That Pays for Your Injuries or the Injuries of Your Passengers. *Uninsured-motorist* coverages are optional in some states and mandatory in others. This coverage provides insurance payable to you. If you are injured by an uninsured driver, who caused the accident, you collect for your injuries under the uninsured-motorist coverage. The uninsured-motorist coverage may provide for "pain and suffering" as well as medical coverages. It is important to note that the uninsured driver must be legally liable for the injury and that the uninsured-motorist coverage protects only in case of injury; it does not include property damage in most states.

The payment made to you under uninsured-motorist coverages may in some states be reduced by the amount you receive under workmen's compensation, disability insurance, or other auto medical coverages.

Under the *medical payments* coverage section, liability or fault is not a factor. The insurance firm pays for injuries up to certain limits that you select. These limits generally vary from $1,000 to $100,000 for each

person covered by your policy, which can include you or any guest passengers in your car. There is no limit on a "per accident" basis. The coverage pays for reasonable and necessary incurred expenses, which could include dental, surgical, X-ray, ambulance, hospital, professional nursing, eyeglasses, hearing aids, and orthopedic and prosthetic devices.

You or your resident relatives do not have to be in an insured car to collect under this section. Your child, for example, will have medical expenses paid for if hit by a car while riding a bicycle. If you are walking and are hit by a car, you may collect under the medical-payments coverage of your auto policy.

The *auto-death indemnity* section of a policy provides limited life-insurance protection in the event of a death that is a direct result of a vehicle accident. Payment is not contingent upon the establishment of negligence. However, the death must be caused by being hit by a car, trailer, or semitrailer, and must come within a year after the accident and during a period of continuous disability. Death by an intentional act of the insured is not covered. This section applies only to persons specifically named in the policy.

Some firms add a *dismemberment* coverage to the death-indemnity section. The dismemberment coverage pays a flat amount on a sliding schedule geared to the severity of the dismemberment.

The *disability income* section provides persons specifically named in the policy with a weekly income in the event of disability from an auto accident. The amount paid weekly is set forth in the policy. There may be no limit on the length of time or total amount of the payment. The payments may continue even if you receive a bodily-injury payment and even if you receive disability pay from your employer.

Insurance That Repairs Damage to Your Car. If your car is damaged in an accident, you collect for repairs under the *collision* coverage in your policy. Most insurers will not pay for repairs that surpass the actual cash value of the car, so its worth at the time of the accident usually constitutes a limit on the coverage.

Collision coverage is provided with "deductibles," generally ranging from $50 to $1,000. This means that you pay for any losses up to that level and that your insurance is effective only for the excess.

You can collect under your collision coverage regardless of who was at fault in the accident. However, if the other driver appears to have been at fault, your insurance company may seek reimbursement from that driver's insurer through a process called "subrogation." If successful, your company will then reimburse you for the amount of your deductible.

If you feel from the outset that the other driver was

at fault and you do not want, even temporarily, to pay the deductible for repairs under your collision coverage, you can file a claim with the other driver's insurance company in an effort to collect under the property-damage-liability coverage of the other driver's policy.

If your car is stolen, or is damaged (not including mechanical breakdown, wear and tear, rust damage, etc.) due to some cause other than collision, you may be reimbursed up to the car's cash value under your *comprehensive physical damage* coverage. This coverage may be offered without any deductible or it may be sold with deductibles ranging from $50 to $1,000.

The comprehensive coverage is broad in that it insures against glass breakage, fire, theft, larceny, flood, explosion, earthquake, windstorm, hail, water, malicious mischief, vandalism, riot, falling objects, or collision with a bird or animal. With some firms, it also includes insurance for sound systems that are built into places provided for them by the auto manufacturer. The section provides you with rental reimbursements, up to stated amounts and for stated lengths of time, after the total theft of your car.

Some insurers, for an additional premium, will endorse their policies for new or recent-vintage cars to provide collision and comprehensive coverages on a *replacement-cost* rather than an actual cash-value basis. This means that the adjustment for a car damaged beyond repair will be based on the cost of a new vehicle of the same size, body type, and equipment, rather than on the market value of the car prior to the loss. The insurer, however, usually retains the right to determine whether the car is repairable and, if so, to repair it. In most cases, coverage does not apply to fire, theft, or larceny. The conditions and scope of the coverages may vary among insurers.

If you borrow money to buy your car, the lending institution probably will insist that you carry collision and comprehensive coverage to protect their investment.

Other special coverages that may be available provide insurance for towing charges, coverage for stereo tapes in your car, coverage for installed or easily-removed stereo or sound systems and CB radios.

No-Fault Auto Insurance. In the late 1960s, there was a growing public discontent, shared by many auto-insurance companies, with the traditional legal methods of compensating injured victims of auto accidents. Although most auto-insurance policies did make available coverages to protect policyholders for medical expenses and other out-of-pocket losses, recovery of other major damages through liability coverages was generally dependent on the injured or deceased person's not having caused or contributed to the accident.

Determining who was legally at fault for an accident sometimes involved an expensive and time-consuming investigation on the part of insurers and the parties involved. In disputed cases where legal counsel represented the claimant and the insurance company, attorney fees and congested court dockets further increased expenses and delays. Inadequate liability-coverage limits in some instances (and an increasing number of negligent drivers who had no liability insurance at all) worked additional hardships on seriously injured accident victims.

No-Fault Insurance—The Concept. Reacting to the increasing problems in the existing legal system, legislatures in a number of states debated whether the no-fault concept (which in a somewhat different form had been operative for workmen's compensation insurance for many years) could be successfully applied to automobile insurance. The writings of researchers were widely read by lawmakers, insurance-industry leaders, the legal profession, and others.

The theory of no-fault is quite simple. Basically, the aim was to reduce the number of automobile-accident cases in the tort-liability system. The dollar savings resulting from this reduction in tort litigation (and the costs associated with it—including attorneys' fees), would be accumulated and used to pay the new and generous first-party no-fault benefits designed to compensate victims for essentially all of their actual economic loss. It was believed that if the nonserious cases could be removed from the tort system through the use of what has come to be known as a "threshold," the substantial overpayment of such claims settled pursuant to the nuisance theory (settlement was less expensive than defense in court) would be eliminated. This dollar savings would more than make up for the new costs of the required no-fault payments. Simply stated, the intended result of no-fault was to compensate most, if not all, accident victims for their economic loss, while allowing those who were seriously injured to pursue a cause of action in tort to receive compensation for pain and suffering—all without having to raise rates.

No-Fault Auto Insurance—Its Many Varieties. On January 1, 1971, Massachusetts become the first state to enact an auto no-fault law. In the next five years, 24 other states enacted some form of auto no-fault insurance legislation. However, of the total of 25 states, the laws of only 17 states included "threshold" limitations on the right to recover general damages; the other eight states legislated only that personal-injury protection (PIP) coverage be required or at least made available to protect a policyholder for actually incurred expenses up to specific per-person dollar limits. Three states included provisions in their laws for auto property-damage no-fault. Later Florida and Massachusetts rescinded those provisions, with only Michigan retaining this feature as of this writing.

The laws of many of the no-fault states were soon challenged in the courts, with various interest groups contending that the limitations on the right to claim and sue if necessary for "general damages" was a deprivation of a constitutional right. In general, the state supreme courts upheld the constitutionality of the no-fault laws. The exception was Illinois, where the law was struck down in 1972, largely on technical grounds.

Nevada repealed its no-fault law on January 1, 1980, due to the apparent failure of the concept in that state.

In spite of the fact that about half the states in the U.S. passed auto no-fault legislation in the relatively short span of a half-decade, many differences exist between the various state laws. Often the differences are the result of what individual legislatures regarded as the local needs of their own states.

For example, the scope of the personal-injury coverage varies widely, some states requiring only a few thousand dollars of first-party no-fault coverage, while other states—such as Michigan, New Jersey, and Pennsylvania—require unlimited medical-expense coverage and several thousands of dollars of coverage for wage losses and other expenses. The tort thresholds (used to remove cases from the tort system) also differ greatly between states.

No-Fault Insurance—The Dollar Threshold. The majority of states employ a dollar threshold—that is, individuals are prevented from suing in tort to recover for pain and suffering unless their medical expenses exceeded a certain dollar amount. The dollar threshold has failed in most states because it offers an inviting "target" at which the victim, his doctor, and his lawyer can take careful aim. All three have a substantial economic interest in witnessing the utilization of no-fault medical benefits to the extent necessary to cross the threshold: the victim because such gives him a chance at the "pot of gold" at the end of the tort-liability rainbow; his lawyer because he takes 30–50% of the "pot of gold" from the victim in the form of contingency fees; and the doctor because auto insurers pay the costs of medical services rendered to an auto-accident victim.

In addition, the effectiveness of dollar thresholds deteriorates over time since inflation is working to increase the average size of a claim. This increases the likelihood that a claim will exceed the dollar threshold.

Thus, dollar thresholds encourage overutilization of first-party (policyholder) benefits; and such overutilization, in turn, produces larger third-party, or tort-liability, judgments for pain and suffering, since pain-and-suffering awards are generally tied by way of a multiplier to the level of actual economic loss.

Ultimately, both first- and third-party costs increase beyond all expectation, and the public must simply be asked to pay higher auto-insurance rates to support either a tort system or a no-fault system.

No-Fault Insurance—The Disability Threshold. While the dollar threshold represents the predominant tort-restriction mechanism in effect in most no-fault states today, other approaches have been tried, including what is known as the "disability threshold." A disability threshold provides that a victim may not sue in tort unless he has been disabled (defined differently in various state plans) from the accident for a specific period of time. While perhaps a disability threshold is more difficult to abuse than a dollar threshold, it suffers from the same infirmities. That is because, again, it offers a target (a specific time period) to the victim, his doctor, and his lawyer. Moreover, it must be remembered that it is not economically painful for the victim, his doctor, and his lawyer. Moreover, it must be remembered that it is not economically painful for the victim, under a no-fault scheme, to remain disabled for a considerable period of time: He is being compensated at the same time for all his medical expenses as well as most, if not all, of his lost wages, and experiences little or no out-of-pocket loss while he waits long enough to qualify to pursue a cause of action in tort. Thus, the disability-threshold approach, while perhaps superior to the dollar threshold, still suffers from fundamental and fatal flaws.

No-Fault Insurance—The Verbal Threshold. The other major type of tort threshold is what has come to be known as the "verbal threshold." Here victims are allowed to sue in tort only if their injuries fit certain verbal descriptions of the types of injuries that should, as a matter of policy, render one eligible to seek to recover for pain and suffering in a cause of action in tort.

The verbal threshold was invented to cure the "target" problems inherent in a dollar threshold. It appears today that a verbal threshold holds out the best chance of meeting the original intent of no-fault, which is to compensate most victims for all of their economic loss without having to increase insurance rates substantially.

No-Fault Insurance—Multiple Recoveries. One other problem that has not been addressed by many legislatures is the opportunity for injured persons to realize multiple recoveries for the same expenses. This extends the invitation to profit from unnecessary medical treatment and overextended absence from work. When opportunities exist to duplicate an insurance recovery for the same expenses, the ultimate result is that higher premiums must be charged to cover such duplicate benefits.

No-Fault Insurance—Basic Idea Is Good. Legislatures in several major states have not enacted auto no-fault legislation, partly as a result of the lack of success of such laws in other states. The basic idea of auto no-fault insurance is good: The motoring public needs financial protection to cover the large expenses that can result from an auto accident, and it needs the protection as promptly as possible when expenses are incurred. Premium dollars should be returned as much as possible in the form of benefits to meet a victim's needs, and not be mitigated by costly investigations and attorney fees.

Improvement of existing state no-fault laws is entirely possible when legislators, insurers, the medical and legal professions, consumer organizations, and other interested groups objectively evaluate the results of such laws to date, and resolve to work for solutions based on carefully selected common goals.

A Federal No-Fault Plan? To the argument that federal no-fault standards are needed because the states haven't moved quickly enough to implement no-fault, proponents of state no-fault say that an objective historical evaluation of state experience produces convincing reasons why no-fault is not now in all 50 states.

First, there does not yet exist a proven design for no-fault automobile insurance that will work in every state.

Second, present results from no-fault states lead to the conclusion that the needs and problems differ so much from state to state that uniform national solutions are neither practical nor desirable.

Advocates of state laws say that they cannot voluntarily terminate the incomplete growth in the state-by-state no-fault learning process in favor of an essentially irreversible federal plan. Not even the strongest supporters of a federal no-fault plan can offer now any guarantee that the federal minimum standards are properly balanced for all the states, or that the major provisions will in fact operate as designed.

State-law advocates further point out that no-fault compensates more automobile-accident victims, compensates them more quickly, and can aid in returning victims to a truly useful life. These advocates fear, however, that if a rigid and irreversible federal plan is mandated too soon, in all 50 states, the high potential benefits of no-fault could be lost forever. For if the current guesses as to how best to balance no-fault are wrong, as most guesses have been to date in the states, the public may well forsake for good anything offered in the name of no-fault reform.

How and When to File a Claim. If your vehicle is involved in a mishap, here's what you'll need to know about insurance.

From a liability standpoint, you are on safest ground if you notify your insurance company promptly in the event of any auto accident. Indeed, your insurance policy may require it. An accident may appear inconsequential, particularly if damage is slight and no one is visibly injured, but assertions of serious injury may be made later, and you may be accused of being at fault. Under the tort-liability system, anyone with whom you're involved in an accident can file suit alleging your liability, regardless of what the evidence might seem to show.

Notifying your insurance company of an accident is not the same as filing a formal claim. A claim is a demand, under the terms of an insurance policy, for payment for loss from property damage or bodily injury. Filing a claim may consist of a "proof of loss" form being filled out by the insurance company. The company may ask for information on the time, date, place, and circumstances of the accident; the nature of the damage or injury; the expenses incurred; and the amount of reimbursement or reparation requested.

At the time you give notice of an accident, or soon after, your insurance company can advise you whether a claim is called for or allowed under the provisions of your policy and/or the circumstances of the accident.

Where a claim is filed will depend on the laws of your state, your insurance company, and the nature of the accident.

When you are seeking repairs on your car, you should file a claim with your insurance company if the cost exceeds the deductible amount specified in your policy. The company will pay the costs above your deductible depending on your policy coverage, or it will have the car repaired. If the cost of repair is less than your deductible limit and you feel the other driver was at fault, you should file a claim with the other driver's insurance company, depending on state law. Your insurer should be notified. Your insurer may pay the claim, minus the deductible, and collect as much as possible from the responsible driver or his or her insurer.

Some insurers now operate drive-in claim centers, where damage to your car can be assessed and a settlement made on the spot. If your claim is accepted, you will be issued a draft or check immediately for the appraised cost of repairs.

If you carry no-fault insurance, claims for losses from injuries you suffer in a accident should be filed directly with your insurer, regardless of who was to blame for the accident. The same is true if your policy carries medical-payment coverages.

If your costs from injuries surpass the no-fault threshold in your state and you believe the other driver caused the accident, you can file a bodily-injury claim with the other driver's insurance company.

If the other driver is not insured, you should notify

your own company of your losses, for payment under the uninsured-motorist clause in your insurance policy.

Notifying your insurance company as soon as is practical after an accident is essential to fully protect your interests. Under the terms of liability coverage, your insurer is obligated to pay justified claims against you and to defend you against any that are unjustified or questionable. Delays of a day, even of a few hours, may spell the difference between a weak defense and a strong one. As time passes, pertinent evidence often fades, witnesses disappear, physical items are moved or destroyed, memories get hazy, and victims may decide to exaggerate injuries or their pain and suffering.

Check Your Policy. It is important to follow the procedures and deadlines stated in your insurance policy regarding notifications and claims. An insurance policy is a "conditional contract": You must meet or comply with certain conditions obligated to you. If you do not, the company may legally deny responsibility.

How Much Auto Insurance to Buy? To comply with some state laws, you need to carry certain minimum liability coverages. But in light of today's medical costs and jury awards, you should consider buying coverage substantially above those limits. With auto liability insurance, the more coverage you buy, the less you generally have to pay in premiums per $1,000 coverage. Thus you may be able to add several hundred thousand dollars' worth of protection for a relatively minor increase in cost.

In determining how much insurance you should carry to protect your assets, talk to a tax accountant and attorney. An insurance agent can explain the scope of protection of the various coverages to help you decide both type and amount of coverage. A good rule is: Don't skimp. Insurance covering your car is important because of the potential of a huge judgment if you are negligent in an accident.

How to Save Money on Auto Insurance. Here are some tips that may help:

• *Consider increasing deductibles* on collision coverage or instituting a deductible on comprehensive coverages. By assuming more of the risk yourself, the portion of this premium computed from those coverages can go down substantially.

Example: by moving from a $100 deductible to a $500 deductible on collision coverage, a typical city owner of a Chevrolet Citation could cut collision premiums by about 45%, depending on his or her insurance company. By increasing the deductible for comprehensive coverage from full coverage to $250, the owner of a Mercury Marquis also may save 45% on that coverage.

If you drive an older car (i.e., a car more than five years old or worth less than $1,000), you may want to drop collision and comprehensive coverages entirely. If your older car is in a serious accident, it may not be worth repairing. The proceeds from insurance would be relatively small. However, remember that you will have to pay for damages to the car yourself under some circumstances if you do drop this coverage.

• *Inquire about price discounts* your insurance company may offer. There may be some you wouldn't expect. The types of discounts vary widely from company to company, from state to state, and in the amounts allowed for each discount. Generally the range is 10–25%. Some of the most common discounts are:

• *Good-driver programs,* which, typically, reward drivers whose record is free of moving traffic violations for 36 months and free of accidents and/or liability claims for 36 to 60 months. On the other hand, drivers who have had recent accidents and/or violations are surcharged to reflect the higher likelihood of future accident involvement.

• *Passive-restraint discount,* offered by many casualty insurance firms, for drivers of cars equipped with air cushions (air bags). A typical discount calls for a 30% reduction in the portion of insurance paying for injuries to the driver or passengers (medical payment in non–no-fault states and personal-injury protection in no-fault states). Studies have indicated that a substantial overall price reduction would be possible if air bags were available and installed now in all cars of the road.

• *Economy-car discount,* which offers a price reduction on liability coverages for drivers of small cars that meet certain criteria, because economy cars inflict less bodily harm and property damage on other people and cars in the event of an accident.

• *Multi-car discount.* If you own more than one car, consider insuring all of them with the same company. Many insurers offer multicar discounts if two or more cars are covered by the same company.

• *55-or-over-and-retired discount.* If you are 55 years of age or older and retired and you purchase a full complement of auto coverages (liability, medical, collision, comprehensive, and uninsured-motorist), there is one large insurer that will offer you lower rates. Retirees have demonstrated their expertise at driving and are better insurance risks. (Persons 55 and older and retired also qualify for lower homeowners' rates with this company.)

• *Families with a college student* more than 100 road miles from home may get a break on premiums, depending on the policy. An insurance firm often assumes the student will not have access to the car as often as when living at home, and reduces premiums accordingly.

- *Drive-to-work car pool.* Members of a car pool that rotates cars may be eligible for a discount, depending on the insurance company and the circumstances. Some insurers offer this discount on the grounds that a driver in a rotating pool uses his car less frequently in commuter traffic than does the motorist who drives to work alone.
- *Good-student discount,* for persons under 25 in the eleventh grade through college who maintain at least a B average, rank in the upper fifth of their class, and/or make the honor roll or dean's list.
- *Driver-training discount,* for persons under 21 who have graduated from an approved course meeting certain minimum standards of instruction. Because of the positive influence training has on driving style, such graduates tend to have fewer accidents than those who haven't had driver training. Driver training is so common nowadays, however, that many companies no longer offer separate discounts but automatically reflect the training into their customary rates.
- *Make and model experience program.* This program grew out of extensive analyses which revealed that within each standard classification grouping there are certain makes and models of cars for which losses had resulted that were significantly higher or lower than for the average car in that group.

Some cars are more easily damaged, more expensive to repair, and more tempting to thieves than other cars. Adjustments in physical-damage coverage rates were made to reflect these differences. Premium increases will also vary by make and model and to the degree such automobiles have worse experience than the average.

In applying this program, suppose that a person is shopping for a new car in a particular price range and has narrowed his choice down to three models—one qualifying for a premium decrease, one qualifying for an increase, and one for no change. This person would save insurance money by picking the model getting the premium reduction, and would lose money if he picked the model getting the premium increase.

- *Avoid payment fees,* if your insurance premiums are relatively low, by paying the amount due in a lump sum rather than in quarterly or monthly payments. The payment fee may be $1.50 or $2 per payment.

However, if your premiums are relatively high, you may want to put the amount for the premiums in a savings account, earn interest on the money, and then make quarterly or monthly payments if the interest earned exceeds the amount of the finance charge.

Remember to notify your insurer promptly of any changes of address of drivers on the policy.

- *Shop for insurance.* In most states, rates vary from company to company. Driver-car classification systems can vary from company to company; one company's rules may prove to be more favorable than those of other firms. Check an insurance company's financial soundness in *Best's Insurance Reports,* available at most libraries. In shopping, you can make comparisons by consulting at least three companies. Remember, though, that the least expensive is not always the best. A company's customer and claim services and solvency are equally important.

Regulation. Since the early 1500s in Europe, insurance practices have been considered a proper field for government supervision. Insurance inherently involves the public interest; and, through regulation, government seeks to promote the public health and welfare and, particularly, to safeguard policyholders and claimants. In this country, regulatory tasks have fallen primarily to the individual states. New Hampshire appointed the nation's first insurance commissioner in 1850, and New York nine years later became the first state to create an executive department devoted solely to insurance supervision. Now all states have some type of regulatory agency.

Specific powers differ form state to state, but generally regulators approve policy forms and clauses; monitor the financial status of insurance companies to ensure solvency; appoint rehabilitators or liquidators to run companies in trouble; and review rate changes. The rate-review function is the most visible of the efforts of the regulators.

Four systems of rate supervision for auto insurance are reflected in the various state laws:

- *Prior approval,* under which rate-change proposals must be filed with and approved by the state before they can be put into effect.
- *File and use,* where companies file notice of rate changes and the state reserves the right to review the new rates later.
- *Use and file,* in which companies may implement a rate change and afterward file a notice of the rate revision.
- *Open or competitive rating,* which allows companies to introduce new rates at will, on the theory that the marketplace will serve as a rate regulator. Under this system the regulatory agency would intervene only in cases of flagrant abuse, such as an attempt by one insurance company to drive others out of business and gain a monopoly by instituting untenably low rates.

Rate revisions may be filed with state insurance departments by independent companies or by rating organizations representing groups of insurance companies. Filings are generally accompanied by statistical data supporting the changes, or the filing may refer to previously submitted data. The state insurance commissioner or director then evaluates the revisions on the basis of at least these three criteria:

- Are the rate schedules sufficient to keep the company solvent and cover its probable losses?
- Are the rates free of unfair discrimination?
- Are the rates excessive?

(It is important to note the term *unfair discrimination*. Insurance classification systems by their nature are discriminatory. For example, frame houses are discriminated from those made of brick, and separate rates are charged for each group. The discrepancy in rates relates directly to the nature of the risk. Thus the rates cannot be unfairly discriminatory, which is a term of legal and regulatory definition generally requiring that classification systems be statistically supportable.)

If, in the commissioner's judgment, the rates fall within what has been called a "zone of reasonableness," the commissioner may allow the rates to go into effect as filed. If the rates do not meet with the commissioner's approval, he may ask for revisions of the rate schedule.

Financial-Responsibility Laws. Financial-responsibility laws require motorists to furnish evidence, either before or after an accident, of ability to pay for damages. If the driver cannot prove an ability to pay damages, the driver's license and auto registration may be suspended.

Acceptable proof may be a demonstration of financial worth or a showing of automobile-liability insurance coverage with specified minimum limits. Typical minimums are $10,000 per person and $20,000 per accident for bodily injury and $5,000 for property damage ("10/20/5" in insurance-industry shorthand), though some states require as much as 25/50/25.

Several types of financial-responsibility laws are on the books. One type provides that an uninsured motorist who loses a lawsuit and does not have adequate assets must supply evidence of financial responsibility for any future mishap in which he may be involved. The penalties for those who lack financial responsibility vary—in some states these drivers lose their licenses until the judgment is satisfied; in others a period of time must pass before a license is returned.

Many states have laws requiring that a driver prove he has sufficient assets or minimum auto insurance before an accident occurs.

In a few states and several Canadian provinces, the cars of uninsured motorists can be impounded after an accident and held until financial responsibility is established.

Compulsory Liability Insurance. Dissatisfaction with financial-responsibility laws has led some states to make automobile-liability insurance compulsory. These states may require evidence of minimum liability coverage for bodily injury and property damage before an automobile owner can register a vehicle. Those who do not own a car do not have to provide evidence of insurance in order to obtain a driver's license. Violating the law can bring a fine, imprisonment, and revocation of driver's license and car registration, depending on state law.

More than half the states require drivers to carry liability insurance.

Unsatisfied-Judgment Funds. As a supplement to financial-responsibility laws, a few states and several Canadian provinces operate unsatisfied-claim or -judgment funds to pay victims of automobile accidents when liability judgments against negligent motorists prove uncollectible. Depending on the state, both bodily-injury and property-damage claims may be honored. In some cases the fund will also cover injuries inflicted by hit-and-run drivers, without a judgment being entered. In no state will the fund compensate a victim who is an uninsured car owner.

Claimants must exhaust all other means of collecting a judgment before calling upon the fund. Even then, they may not necessarily collect the total amount due them. These funds assume liability only within a given range, usually above a minimum of $100 and below a maximum of $10,000 per person and $20,000 per accident.

Once a judgment is paid, the driver who caused the accident but cannot pay damages is indebted to the fund, and driving privileges are suspended until restitution with interest is made.

A certain proportion of money collected from vehicle registration fees may finance the funds, or insurers operating within the state may be assessed a prorated amount each year to support the fund.

Assigned-Claim Plans. Instead of unsatisfied-judgment funds, some states operate assigned-claims plans through which victims can be compensated for uncollectible judgments. Both systems share similarities. In assigned-claims-plan states, individual insurance companies are assigned, on a rotating basis, to investigate and satisfy the claims in question. The companies then are reimbursed from a fund financed by all companies doing business there.

How Costs Affect Prices. The majority of an auto-insurance company's costs go for paying claims for injuries connected with auto accidents and for losses or damages to cars. *More than anything else, rising* *auto-repair costs and medical costs have been responsible for the rise in insurance prices in recent years.* At times these costs have spiraled upward so persistently and in such big spurts that many insurance companies have been put in the position of playing "catch-up." They adjusted rates to cover increases in repair and medical costs and then, before the rates were fully effective, found that new rates were needed to counter new cost increases.

Increases in Consumer Price Index. According to the Consumer Price Index, the cost of the average hospital room leaped 233.8%, physicians' fees went up by 148.6%, and total medical-care services increased 156.2% during the period between January 1973 and December 1982.

On the other hand, auto-insurance premiums generally increased 106.9% in the same period.

Inflation and Auto Repairs. Inflation also has affected auto-repair prices dramatically. For example, prices of a combination of 11 most frequently damaged major parts for the 1976 Chevrolet Impala, Ford LTD, and Chrysler Newport were up 96% from December 1975 through October 1981 inclusive. Labor rates for car repairs in September 1982 ranged from $14.80 to $29.28 an hour, averaging $17.92.

At 1982 repair prices, damage to less than one-third of a car's parts can cost more to repair than the car is worth. Indeed, to replace all parts of a totally wrecked subcompact car that cost about $7,100 new in 1982 would have run more than $26,700 in parts and labor, according to the Alliance of American Insurers. No one would order that done, of course, but it illustrates why even minor crash damage is so expensive to fix. Repairing damage to 1% of that car's parts could cost more than $260, while repairs to 10% of the parts could cost more than $2,600. That's why drivers of average late-model cars are likely to be spending a large portion of their total insurance premiums for coverage against physical damage to the insured automobiles.

The Rating Process. Setting premiums for private-passenger-automobile insurance within any given state involves a number of projections designed to estimate an insurer's revenues and costs. These factors include number and type of policyholders; the coverages the policyholder will want; the estimated volume and severity of claims the policyholders may file and that may be filed against them; the administrative and marketing expenses of the insurer; and the trend in loss settlements. These factors must be calculated for the months the rate will be in effect on the basis of available evidence.

In making the projections, insurance-company actuaries consult scores of external information sources, including the Consumer Price Index, state motor vehicle department records, economic forecasts by banks and research institutions, political and economic evaluations, reports from car makers and the auto-repair industry, bulletins from the U.S. Department of Labor and Transportation, and so on. More important, however, is the intense examination of a company's own historical data, particularly the documented loss (claims-payout) experience. Using this data, the actuary can determine whether the present rate level in the state is likely to be adequate or inadequate in the future, and thus can make appropriate adjustments in the rate level.

Traditionally, the projections depend on a method called "trending"—that is, the rate of change that has most recently taken place in the various elements of the insurance product is extrapolated into the next period. Pricing experts use various analytical methods in making these projections.

Two Major Factors in Rate-Making. Two major factors involved in the rate-making eventually will pay: the *territorial rating* and the *classification.*

For insurance purposes, most states are divided into a number of territories. Each territory has its own loss-experience record.

Also, drivers are "class-rated" with other policyholders having certain similar characteristics, according to their statistical likelihood of incurring claims. These divisions recognize that not every driver or every car is an equal risk, and they attempt, as nearly as possible, to group cars and drivers subject to similar hazards.

To establish rates, an insurer first projects the total income it will need from premiums to cover claims and other costs in that state during the period the rates will be effective. An average rate is then determined for a particular coverage. This average, in turn, is adjusted up or down on the basis of relative risks for each rating territory and classification of car and driver.

Regulatory pressures and competitive considerations often cause insurance companies to implement a lower rate level than the statistics justify.

A main weakness of "trending" is its potential unreliability should fundamental changes occur, such as a sudden and unexpected spurt of inflation. In effect, an insurance company does not know for certain how accurate its rates are until a group of policies is sold at those rates and all the losses incurred on these policies are paid. When a company is unable to collect enough in premiums to cover the losses generated by the policies and the expenses incurred in servicing and writing the policies, the difference, if the company is to realize a profit, must be made up by investment income earned by the company. In general, insurance companies strive to have each "line" of insurance self-supporting.

Rate-making methods differ from company to company, depending on the individual firm and state laws. Where permitted by statute to do so, large insurance companies generally perform their own actuarial analysis. Smaller companies, however, may not have a broad enough statistical base to do this reliably and thus generally depend on "rating bureaus," which collect statistics from many cooperating companies and recommend rate plans for their members based on this data. In a few states, bureau membership is mandatory and only the bureau rates can be charged. Countrywide, however, insurers using bureau rates account for less than half the total premium volume.

Usually, bureaus and individual companies review rates at least once a year in each state. In times of sharp inflation, however, rate reviews may be instituted more often. Rates are changed only when there is sufficient evidence supporting the need for a rate-level change. Even so, auto-insurance premiums are revised more frequently than are the prices of most other kinds of insurance.

Classification Factors. When a person applies for an automobile-insurance policy, the insurance-company underwriters evaluate the information contained in the application to decide whether or not to insure the applicant. Some risks pose no problem to the underwriter; for example, a married 35-year-old with a clean accident-and-violation record would usually be acceptable to an underwriter. In fact, for these potentially "good" risks, the agent usually has the authority to provide coverage immediately. On the other hand, an applicant arrested twice for driving while under the influence of alcohol would probably be rejected by the underwriter. The premium charged this risk would likely be inadequate to cover the potential liability to the company.

Classification Aids Companies and Policyholders. Not all instances are as clear-cut as the two described above. For this reason, insurance companies have utilized the theory of classification of drivers by age, gender, marital status, mileage driven, use of car, and accident-and-violation history. This classification plan aids both insurance companies and policyholders. For example, policyholders with good driving records pay lower premium dollars under the above classification system than they would if there were no reflection of accident-and-violation history in the rate structure.

Distributes Costs More Equitably. The policyholders presenting the greater risk to the company (for example, those with accidents or violations on their record) pay higher premiums for coverage than do policyholders with clean records. Insurance companies are able to more equitably distribute the cost of insurance among its policyholders under a classification system, and charge a premium commensurate with expected loss costs.

It has been argued by some that the use of factors beyond a person's control in the rating process—such as age, sex, and marital status—should be eliminated. But statistical evidence proves that these classifications do predict, to a reliable degree, the future accident involvement of the class members. And no better method of classifying drivers according to the risk they present has been found and tested. Furthermore, polls indicate that people feel it would be unfair for everyone to pay the same price for auto insurance.

Why Prices Vary by Area. Some important risk factors are divorced from a person's driving ability. The physical environment in which a car is kept and driven is one of these. Environment involves such considerations as population density and shifts; traffic flow and congestion; safety and law-enforcement programs; the types and locations of employment centers; crime incidence; the judicial system; the propensity for area drivers to file lawsuits; climate and topography; the extent of on-street parking, and so on. These factors can vary markedly even from one part of a city to another, as well as from urban to rural areas within a single state. As environment changes, so do the hazards to which a car is exposed.

The evaluation of environment in setting a premium is called "territorial rating." For insurance purposes, a car is rated or classified according to the location in which it is normally garaged or parked overnight if it is kept on the street.

Location is a good predictor of potential insurance losses, because cars from a specific territory are likely to share an exposure to similar risks. Most driving is done relatively close to a car's garage or parking site. In fact, more than half of all auto trips are for distances of less than 5 miles, and more than 87% for less than 15 miles. Thus, on the average, a vast majority of a city dweller's driving will be done in the city, a suburbanite's in the suburbs, and a farmer's in the country.

As a group, urban drivers pay more for equivalent insurance coverage than do drivers in small towns or rural areas. The congested roadways traveled by urban drivers present a greater accident risk. More property-damage accidents, injuries, and fatalities occur per mile of urban roads compared to a mile of rural roads.

Moreover, repair costs, wages, hospital and other medical expenses, and jury awards may tend to be higher in metropolitan areas, so that accidents involving urban dwellers not only happen more frequently but also tend to be more costly per accident.

In addition, thefts and vandalism tend to be concentrated in the areas of highest population density.

When a car is involved in a mishap, regardless of where the incident occurs, any insurance loss is "charged back" to the car's home territory. In other words, if a suburbanite drives into the city and causes an accident with another suburbanite from a different rating territory, the accident is charged against the two suburban areas, not against the city, for rating purposes. This helps keep the loss experiences of "outside" drivers from unfairly driving up rates in territories other than their own.

It has been recognized over the years that the most equitable method of auto-insurance rating involves recognition of the statistically proven difference in risk between territories. In other words, each driver pays a fair price. Some insurance regulators have argued for the elimination of territory rating by insurance companies. This is an attempt to lessen the insurance-rate differential between different parts of a state. However, under this revised system, drivers in low-loss areas would be forced to subsidize the risks from the higher-loss territories.

Why Prices Vary by Driver. A driver's background is an important established criterion for estimating the likelihood of an accident. The more stable, mature, and responsible an individual is, the more careful and less aggressive he or she is likely to be behind the wheel. Statistical evidence suggests that stability strongly correlates with such factors as age, gender, marital status, and previous driving record. In establishing a premium, an insurance company weighs such factors in light of who will most often be driving the insured car ("primary operator"), who else regularly uses it, and what other licensed drivers who live in the same household will use the car.

Age a Reliable Predictor. Of the personal characteristics considered, age is perhaps the single most reliable predictor of insurance-loss potential. Generally, the more experienced the driver, the better the driving record, and experience correlates positively with age.

As a group, younger drivers—those under 25 generally, and in particular those under 21—are less experienced and more careless than the average driver in other age groups. The result is that they are involved in a vastly disproportionate number of both serious and nonserious auto accidents.

Reports from traffic authorities document that drivers under 25 are involved in accidents more than twice as often as drivers over 35. Thirty-three out of every 100 drivers under 20—or 1 in 3—are involved in accidents each year, while the rate among drivers

over 35 is 14 out of 100. All told, drivers under 25 represent 21.7% of the total driving population, yet they are involved in 36% of all auto accidents and traffic fatalities. For years, the leading cause of death among young men just finishing high school has been auto crashes; in fact, auto deaths for this group exceed the next five leading causes of death combined. Because they cost insurance companies more money than any other age group, younger drivers are charged higher rates for insurance.

Alcohol Heavily Involved. Drinking among accident-involved drivers is highest for ages 18 and 19, and declines steadily as age increases. Alcohol is heavily involved in accidents of all kinds and is a major contributing cause of highway deaths, injuries, and insurance losses.

Gender an Important Factor. Historically, a driver's gender also has been an important factor in insurance rates. Typically, younger females have paid lower rates than males, largely because their accident rate was lower by about 50%. Women used to do less night driving, less drinking, and less speeding than men.

The difference in accident rates seems to be narrowing, and the distinction between male and female driving patterns also appears to be gradually narrowing. Insurance companies, of course, react to these changes in loss patterns by revising classification rate factors.

Marital Status Is Significant. Marital status also has proved to be a good predictor of accident risk, possibly because marital status reflects one's stability and judgment and style of driving. Drivers under 25 get lower premiums from most companies if they are married. Indeed, many insurers classify married females of any age as adults, while a male who is the primary operator of the insured car and is also single may not get an adult classification until he reaches age 49.

Accident and Traffic-Violation Record. A driver's record of accidents and traffic violations is one indicator of accident risk. Some insurance companies surcharge the premiums of drivers having severe violations (such as drunk driving, vehicular homicide, and hit-and-run accidents) on their records during the previous three-years or "chargeable" accidents during the previous three to five years. Chargeable accidents generally are those involving liability claims above a set dollar limit and with the driver found to be at fault in the accident.

Why Prices Vary by Car Use. The purpose for which a car is used helps determine the hazards to which it will be exposed. For instance, a suburban businessman commuting to work every day at rush hour has a greater chance of being involved in an accident than does a housewife in a small town who uses her car for occasional short shopping trips.

Use categories vary with insurance companies, but typically cars are classified as being used primarily for (1) pleasure, (2) driving to work, (3) business, or (4) farming.

"Driving to work" usually includes any portion of the trip to or from the place of regular employment or train station, for example. "Business use" means that the car is customarily driven as an essential part of the driver's occupation, although not necessarily to and from a specific office. To be classified as "farm use," the car must be garaged on a farm or ranch and not driven to work or used for other farm or ranch business.

Cars driven for pleasure and in connection with farming usually have the lowest rates. Those driven to work or used for business purposes generally have higher rates.

Why Prices Vary by Miles Driven per Year, by Car Price, and by Age. Cars are also classified by some insurance companies according to the estimated total miles they are driven per year, because of statistical evidence that accident frequency tends to increase as road exposure increases.

The cost of repairing or replacing a particular car is considered in setting the premium for insurance to cover its potential theft or physical damage. There are vast differences in the values of cars. A new 1983 Chevrolet Chevette, for instance, lists for about $5,500, while a 1983 Cadillac Seville lists new for about $22,500. Replacing a fender on the Cadillac would cost more than replacing the same part on the Chevette.

At the beginning of each model year, all new cars are grouped by insurers into various price categories (the number of categories varying from one insurance company or rating bureau to another). A basic premium is then determined for each price group. In some cases, several closely related groups may be assigned the same premium.

The age of the car also becomes an important factor. Generally, older cars have a lower actual cash value so that age tends to diminish the possible amount of an insurance loss. Some insurers, consequently, have designated several distinct age categories into which a car might fit and the premium charged for older cars is less than that for newer cars.

Where most insurance companies are concerned, the combination of a car's price grouping and age ranking, along with deductibles, as well as territory and classification, determine the basic premium charged for physical-damage coverage. (Refer also to

"Make and Model Experience Program" under "How to Save Money on Auto Insurance," p. 38.)

Allstate News Bureau of Allstate
Insurance Company and Allstate
Life Insurance Company

Auto-Insurance Terms

disability threshold In no-fault states with the disability threshold, it provides that a victim may not sue in tort unless he has been disabled (defined differently in various state plans) from an accident for a specific period of time.

dollar threshold In no-fault insurance states with the dollar threshold, it prevents individuals from suing in tort to recover for pain and suffering unless their medical expenses exceed a certain dollar amount.

general damages Typically refers to awards for pain and suffering.

litigation The process of a lawsuit.

personal-injury protection (PIP) A no-fault insurance coverage that protects a policyholder for actually incurred expenses up to specific per-person dollar limits.

third party A person who files a liability-insurance claim.

threshold Used in no-fault insurance to remove nonserious cases from the tort system by establishing a point or "threshold" that must be met or exceeded to sue in tort. Seventeen of the 25 no-fault states have a threshold in their plan. There are three types of thresholds: the dollar threshold, the disability threshold, and the verbal threshold.

tort Any wrongful act, damage, or injury done willfully, negligently, or in circumstances involving strict liability, but not involving breach of contract, for which a civil lawsuit can be brought.

verbal threshold In no-fault states with the verbal threshold, victims are allowed to sue in tort only if their injuries meet certain verbal descriptions of the types of injuries that should, as a matter of policy, render one eligible to seek to recover for pain and suffering in a cause of action in tort.

Source: Allstate News Bureau of Allstate Insurance Company and Allstate Life Insurance Company.

Aviation Insurance

See INSURANCE.

·B·

Balance Sheet

A section of a company's or individual's financial statements; it usually lists assets on one side and liabilities on the other. The most common form of balance sheet is called an "account form." A newer format is known as a "report form."

Assets customarily listed on a balance sheet can include cash; marketable securities; investments; notes and mortgages receivable; inventories and other receivables, such as outstanding dues. Liabilities usually include accounts payable and loans and debts.

Samuel C. Hoyt

Balloon Mortgages

See HOME FINANCING, MORTGAGES.

Bank, How to Choose a

Choosing the right bank is as important as selecting any other professional service. Just as you would want an attorney who could handle most of your family legal matters, so do you want a financial institution that has made a serious commitment to meeting your present and future economic needs. You should get the most for your money and enjoy maximum control over your finances.

One Bank or Many? One result of the depression was that many people felt uneasy about banking at only one institution. It seemed better to lessen the risk of bank failure by establishing accounts at more than one bank. But today, with federal insurance on bank deposits up to $100,000, it is no longer necessary to diversify banking relationships for that reason.

These days, consumers should look for a bank that offers a "better deal" to those who bring all their banking business to that institution. By consolidating your money at certain banks, you will get a higher return in interest and service. Aside from the convenience, banking at only one place gives you the opportunity to have your money work for you in more ways than ever before. This total relationship can mean better rates on loans and mortgages, preferred treatment when credit is tight, and often interest-paying checking accounts with no charge. Look for the financial institution that offers convenience as well as the broadest variety of services at the best overall price.

This entry will discuss how to go about choosing a bank that fits your needs—the term *bank* used in a generic sense, referring to commercial banks and thrift institutions (savings and loan associations, savings banks, and credit unions).

As you consider consolidating your money at one institution, you should discuss with the officers of several banks the variety of accounts offered at each institution that will give you the best return on your money and answer your individual financial needs. For example, you may want to earn high interest in one account, cut taxes with another, and use the most convenient account for day-to-day transactions. A good banker will help you evaluate your financial goals and will develop a combination of savings investments that are practically tailor-made to meet those goals.

Profiting from a Partnership with Your Bank. In the past, getting preferential treatment from a bank was a somewhat "elitist" process. If you were lucky enough to be one of the bank's major accounts, then you were well taken care of—even the local bank president might extend extra service to you if he knew you or your family.

Today things are different. Banks are competing for your business, and superior technology allows them to offer better service to many more people at less cost than old-fashioned banking. It is always important, though, to keep abreast of your bank's products and services by reading its literature and meeting occasionally with a bank officer to make sure that the long-term relationship you have begun to establish is working to your best advantage. By taking those steps, you may learn about opportunities to earn even higher interest on your money—or about new services that may be appealing.

But most of all, use your bank and its services to gain the greatest possible control of your finances. For the best results, it's wise to first examine your financial goals before choosing a banking institution.

Examining Your Financial Needs and Goals You might examine your financial needs by asking yourself various questions and evaluating the answers in relation to your goals. Personal-goal-oriented questions might include the following:

- What is your current situation: Are you single, married, or divorced? How old are you? Are you young, saving for a first house and planning a family? Do you already have young children, and are you concerned about how you will pay for their education? Or do you have grown children and look toward retirement?
- What are your short-term financial goals (to pay off debts, begin a savings program, buy a new car, etc.)? You may have several.
- What are your long-term financial goals (to put the kids through college, save for retirement, buy a new home, etc.)? Again, there may be several.
- In your current situation, are tax savings important to you?
- How much money do you want to keep liquid (have quickly available to you)?
- Do you want your earned interest to be available monthly, or do you want it to remain in your savings account? (The young family saving for long-term goals will probably want the interest to accrue; the retired couple living on a fixed income will likely want the interest on savings to be paid to them monthly.)

You should also evaluate your current banking practices. Questions to ask include:

- How many checking and savings accounts do you have and where are they? Are they earning interest? How accessible is the money?
- Do you have a retirement plan other than the one your company offers?
- Do you have any of the following: A certificate of deposit (CD) or time-deposit account (if so, for what time period and earning what interest)? A money-market account? A NOW account? Other investments (are you pleased with their current rate of return)?

For further information on examining your financial needs and goals, *see* FINANCIAL PLANNING.

Deregulation For years, banks actively worked to change stringent government regulations that severely limited the amount of interest they could pay customers on their savings. Now, in the 1980s, we are finally beginning to see the benefits of deregulation emerge. Congress created the DEPOSITORY INSTITUTIONS DEREGULATION COMMITTEE (DIDC) to do away with all interest-rate ceilings on bank deposits by 1986. The first major steps toward deregulation took place in December 1982 and January 1983, when the DIDC ruled that banks could offer money-market rates to investors, thereby at last allowing banks to compete with money-market funds. This will, no doubt, soon be followed by removal of other restrictions, thus allowing banks to compete equally with all other financial institutions.

Investment Options and Financial Services. Banks offer a number of investment options and other financial services to their customers in addition to basic bank services. Some banks are more innovative than others. The kinds of investment services and other financial services offered and how they compare to others are important criteria in selecting a bank. For a discussion on these, *see* BANK INVESTMENT OPTIONS.

Personal Service and Convenience. Beyond rates and savings options, there's another important aspect to consider when choosing a bank—service.

It has been said that time is money. All too often, a major part of today's life-styles involves having to choose between the two: whether to incur additional costs to save time, or invest time to save money. If your bank is doing its job, it will help you save both.

How convenient is your bank? Are its branches and electronic self-service centers conveniently located? What are their hours? Do they meet your schedule or do you have to organize visits to meet theirs? Do you have to waste valuable time simply to cash a paycheck? Does the banking system make it easy for you to save? Some banks have an "auto-deduct" service, which will automatically transfer a set amount of your monthly deposits to a regular savings program.

Ask to see the type of statement you will receive if you become a customer. Are the statements clear, easy to read? Will you be getting separate statements for each account, or will your statement summarize all of your regular banking business for that period?

Does your branch have adequately trained staff to help sort out any problems or help you pick the right accounts for your financial goals? Are they ready and able to help you get control of your finances? Remember, in the long run, their time will save you money.

Keep up to Date. Finally, even after you have made your choice, you must keep current with new banking laws, regulations, and services to make sure your bank is best serving your needs and goals. The field of banking is now very dynamic.

For certain transactions, checks are becoming obsolete; more and more companies electronically deposit salaries directly to their employees' accounts rather than hand out paychecks, and many bills can be paid by phone. In fact, it is likely that much of our banking and even shopping will be done electronically from home—via combinations of telephones, home computers, and television sets.

Interactive cable, which permits two-way communication via television, is now being tested in a number of cities, and some banks are developing home-banking computers. Because of this new technology, branch banking, in the form we have known it, is already on its way to becoming an anachronism.

But banking is also changing in ways other than the simply mechanical. As the regulatory lid continues to be lifted from the industry, banks will be allowed to meet almost every consumer financial need. You will be able and encouraged to save, borrow, and invest your money all at one financial institution, as well as buy life insurance and purchase stocks.

The Eighties is an exciting period in the history of banking. Consumers who stay up to date on the latest developments can take advantage of the bank of the future—today.

Richard C. Kane

Bank Account

A fund held by a bank on behalf of a depositor, who may deposit money into it or withdraw money from it. To open and maintain a bank account, there is often a minimum deposit required. Money in savings accounts and some checking accounts earns INTEREST.

Harvey Rachlin

Bankbook

See PASSBOOK.

Bank Check

Either a check having no preprinted information on it concerning a specific account or a check drawn by a bank on its own account.

Phil Battey

Bank Credit Card

See CREDIT CARD.

Bank Discount

What a bank charges for discounting a promissory note (*see* NOTE) or bill of exchange.

Phil Battey

Bank Draft

An order written by a bank in one country against funds it keeps in an account at a bank in another country.

Phil Battey

Bankers' Acceptances

Bankers' acceptances are generally negotiable instruments drawn to finance the export, import, shipment, or storage of goods. They are termed "accepted" when a bank agrees to pay the draft at maturity.

These acceptances are drafts or bills of exchange—orders to pay a specified amount of money at a specified time. Drafts may be on individuals, businesses, or financial institutions. A banker's acceptance, however, must be drawn on and accepted by a bank.

Banks accept these drafts on behalf of their customers, who are obligated to pay the bank the amount financed on or before the maturity date. A bank may accept the draft for either the drawer or the holder.

Unlike a more traditional loan, however, an acceptance doesn't necessarily reduce a bank's lending capacity, because the bank can raise funds by selling the acceptance. The acceptance is nevertheless an outstanding liability of the bank and is subject to the reserve requirement, unless it is of a type eligible for discount by a Federal Reserve bank.

One common type of acceptance results from letters of credit in foreign trade transactions. For example, a U.S. firm importing goods from a foreign firm may ask a U.S. bank to issue a letter of credit on behalf of the importer to the foreign exporter. The letter authorizes the foreign exporter to draw a time draft upon the U.S. importer's bank in payment for the goods. When the goods have been shipped, the foreign exporter may discount the draft with the exporter's bank and receive immediate payment, rather than wait until maturity for payment.

The foreign exporter's bank forwards the draft and applicable shipping documents to the importer's bank in the U.S. for acceptance. The U.S. bank stamps the word *accepted* on the face of the draft along with an officer's signature, thus, making the draft a banker's acceptance. The importer's bank may discount the acceptance for the foreign bank, and the importer's bank will earn the difference between the discounted amount paid to the foreign bank and the face amount of the bill, plus the commission for originating the instrument. The importer's bank may then sell the acceptance it created in the open market to a dealer or investor and thus recoup the payment to the foreign bank.

Two significant terms used in reference to bankers' acceptances are *third-country acceptances* and *finance bills*. Third-country acceptances are created to finance both the shipment of goods between foreign nations and, to some extent, goods stored overseas. They principally reflect use of the U.S. acceptance market by Asian borrowers, especially Japanese importers and exporters.

Finance bills, which aren't related to specific transactions, are accepted by some banks as a means of extending short-term credit, presumably to provide working capital to the drawer of the draft. They can't be discounted or purchased by Reserve banks—for that reason they are also referred to as "ineligible acceptances"—and aren't counted in the survey of total outstanding acceptances reported monthly by the New York Fed. Member banks must maintain reserves against ineligible acceptances.

Maturities on bankers' acceptances at times extend to nine months, but more commonly range from 30 to 180 days. Maturities are usually arranged to cover the time required to ship and dispose of the goods being financed.

Although market rates for acceptances are low in relation to loan rates, they don't fully reflect the cost of acceptance financing to the borrower. The accepting bank charges a fee for the service. Thus, the cost to the borrower is the fee plus the discount on the acceptance.

The dealer market involves 10 to 15 large firms, most of which operate nationwide and also engage in buying and selling U.S. government securities. Most of these dealer firms are headquartered in New York City. Participants in this over-the-counter market, in addition to the dealers, are domestic and foreign accepting banks; Edge Act corporations; other financial and nonfinancial institutions; governmental units; individuals; and central banks, including the Federal Reserve.

Purchases of acceptances by the Federal Reserve may be for its own account or for foreign official correspondents, such as other central banks. Purchases for its own account are a supplemental method of conducting open market operations; ordinarily, the Fed purchases acceptances only under a repurchase agreement with dealers.

Arthur Samansky

Bank for International Settlements (BIS)

The Bank for International Settlements is a "bank" for CENTRAL BANKS. Almost all European central banks, as well as those of the United States, Canada, Japan, Australia, and South Africa, participate in, or are closely associated with, the various activities of the BIS.

Based in Basel, Switzerland, the BIS assists central banks in the investment of monetary reserves; provides a forum for international monetary cooperation; acts as agent or trustee in carrying out international loan agreements; and conducts extensive economic research.

In managing central banks' funds, the BIS engages in traditional types of investment. Funds not required for lending to other central banks are placed in world financial markets. The main forms of investment include deposits with commercial banks and purchases of short-term negotiable paper, including U.S. Treasury bills. These operations currently constitute a major portion of the bank's business.

The BIS also lends to other central banks some of the funds received as deposits from central banks. BIS credit transactions may take the form of swaps against gold; collateralized credits secured by gold or marketable short-term securities; credits against gold or currency deposits of the same amount and for the same duration held with the BIS; unsecured credits in the form of advances or deposits; and standby credits. Combinations of these and other types of credit also are used.

The BIS is a part of the FEDERAL RESERVE SYSTEM'S SWAP NETWORK. The bank isn't permitted, however, to make advances to governments or open certain types of accounts in their name. Real-estate transactions also are excluded.

In acting to further international cooperation, the BIS provides a forum for the governors of certain central banks, including the Federal Reserve, and representatives of international institutions to meet ten times a year at the BIS for discussions on current monetary policy. Since several central banks of Eastern European countries also are BIS members, the bank serves as a forum for contacts between East and West.

The BIS also organizes periodic meetings of experts to examine economic, monetary, and other questions of interest to central banks. It conducts studies in the field of domestic and external monetary theory and policy. It has responsibility for observation of the international financial markets, the establishment of a data bank for the central banks of the Group of Ten countries and Switzerland, and statistical coverage of international banking. The Group of Ten is composed of Belgium, Canada, France, Italy, Japan, the Netherlands, Sweden, the United Kingdom, the United States, and West Germany. Switzerland also participates.

In conducting banking operations, the BIS is required by its statutes to ensure conformity with the MONETARY POLICY of the central banks concerned.

The BIS has the legal form of a corporation as provided by its charter as an international organization originating from the 1930 Hague Agreement, and a board of directors is responsible for the bank's operations. The board of directors is comprised of the governors of the central banks of Belgium, France, West Germany, Italy, and the United Kingdom, as well as five representatives of finance, industry, or commerce appointed one each by the governors of those five central banks.

The statutes of the BIS provide that these ten directors may elect other persons as "co-opted" directors from among the governors of those member central banks that don't have a representative on the board. The governors of the central banks of the Netherlands, Sweden, and Switzerland are co-opted members, and have been on the board for many years. The 13-member board of directors elects the chairman of the bank from among the directors.

As an international organization, the BIS performs several trustee and depository functions for official groups. For example, the BIS provides the secretariat for the Committee of Governors of the European Community central banks and for the board of governors of the European Monetary Cooperation Fund (EMCF), as well as for their subcommittees and groups of experts, which prepare documents for the central bank governors.

Further, the bank acts as agent for the EMCF, carrying out the financial operations connected with the settlement of balances on behalf of the EC countries participating in the monetary union. Similarly, it has responsibility for the technical administration of the EC system of reciprocal short-term monetary support and for transfer payments in connection with EC borrowing operations.

Participation in the meetings at the BIS is reserved for representatives of central banks. The Federal Reserve is regularly represented at consultative meetings held in Basel. However, the U.S. doesn't sit on the board of directors. In addition, the Federal Reserve has never sought to exercise its rights of representation or of voting.

At its formation, participating central banks were given the option of subscribing for BIS shares or arranging for their subscription in their own countries. About 15% of BIS shares haven't been acquired by central banks and are currently owned by private shareholders.

The shares alloted to the U.S. were declined by the Federal Reserve and were subscribed to by several commercial banks. The shares were purchased during 1930 in the name of the First National Bank of the City of New York (now Citibank N.A.) by a syndicate consisting of J. P. Morgan and Company, First National Bank of Chicago, and the First National Bank of the City of New York. The BIS in 1930 designated the First National Bank of the City of New York to represent and vote by proxy the U.S. shares. Although all shares carry equal rights to participation in the bank's profit, private shareholders don't have voting rights or representation at the BIS general meeting.

Arthur Samansky

Bank Holding Company Act

See BANK HOLDING COMPANY.

Bank Holding Company

A company that controls at least one bank. Bank holding companies must register with the Federal Reserve Board, and their activities other than banking are restricted to those determined by the board to be closely related to banking. This restriction was designed to preserve the historic separation between banking and commerce in the United States as a way of avoiding an undue concentration of economic power. The restriction also grew out of concern that banks should not expose depositors' money to undue risk by investing even indirectly in equity securities of commercial enterprises, and that companies which controlled banks should not be in a position to give credit to commercial affiliates on preferential terms not available to competitors.

Under the Bank Holding Company Act, a company becomes a bank holding company when it owns or controls 25% of any class of voting securities of a bank (and may be deemed to have control in certain other circumstances). A bank is defined in the Bank Holding Company Act as an institution that receives demand deposits and makes commercial loans. By not making commercial loans, a bank may avoid being classified as a bank for purposes of the Bank Holding Company Act (and thus avoid the prohibitions on non-bank-related activities of affiliates). At the same time, it may remain a bank under other federal and state laws and may otherwise exercise the privileges of a bank.

Under the act, bank holding companies are generally confined to owning banks in a single state, except where the law of another state specifically allows the acquisition of its banks by out-of-state companies. Few states provide this permission, so the banks owned by a holding company are typically located in a single state. (A few bank holding companies own banks in more than one state under grandfather provisions, which were designed to avoid requiring divestiture of multistate operations formed prior to enactment of the act.) Some small bank holding companies own a single bank and have no nonbanking subsidiaries. These one-bank holding companies are formed to take advantage of favorable tax treatment. Some multibank holding companies are formed to avoid state restrictions on single banks having statewide branch systems. These multibank systems function in much the same way as multiple branches of the same bank. However, the primary benefits of the bank-holding-company structure are that it gives the banking organization the opportunity to engage in additional kinds of businesses on a broader geographic basis.

Using the bank-holding-company structure, a company can engage in financial businesses through non-bank subsidiaries when such businesses may not be permitted to a bank itself, and may do so nationwide, free of the geographic restrictions that otherwise apply to banks. The Federal Reserve Board has determined that bank holding companies may engage in a wide range of activities, including owning consumer finance companies, mortgage-banking firms, and leasing companies; acting as an insurance agent and insurance underwriter in certain circumstances; and providing some kinds of management, investment, and financial advisory services.

Bank-holding-company formations and acquisitions of additional banks must be approved by the Federal Reserve Board. In doing so, the board must consider the financial and managerial resources and future prospects of the company and the bank, the convenience and needs of the community, and any negative effects on competition. In assessing whether an individual bank holding company may engage in one of the permissible nonbank activities, the board must determine that the proposed activity can reasonably be expected to produce benefits to the public—such as greater convenience, increased competition, or gains in efficiency—that outweigh possible adverse affects, such as undue concentration of resources, decreased or unfair competition, conflicts of interest, or unsound banking practices.

At the end of 1982 there were approximately 4,500 bank holding companies that controlled banks with about 85% of the banking assets in the United States.
                                                Griffith L. Garwood

Bank Investment Options

Current investment options at today's banks include the following:

Money-Market Deposit Accounts: Government regulations dictate a minimum required balance in order to earn market rates. Six transfers including three checks a month from the account to third parties are permitted. Banks with automated teller machine (ATM) access for this account will permit unlimited electronic transfers. Unlike money-market mutual funds, the bank accounts are federally insured and at certain institutions the balance can work in conjunction with other account balances to eliminate check-

ing fees and offer other banking services that the funds can't provide. Each institution can price the account at its own discretion. (*See* MONEY MARKET DEPOSIT ACCOUNTS.)

Negotiable Order of Withdrawal (NOW) Account: This is an interest-bearing checking account paying by law (as of 1984) 5½% interest at thrifts and savings and loan institutions and 5¼% at commercial banks. Service fees vary, as do the rules for waiving them. The combination of a NOW account with a money-market account is often what many consumers need. (*See* NEGOTIABLE ORDER OF WITHDRAWAL (NOW) ACCOUNT.)

Super Negotiable Order of Withdrawal (NOW) Account: The second account regulators recently allowed banks to offer is commonly referred to as the Super NOW. However, many banks don't think it's really that "super." According to government rules, the interest payable on this checking account is unlimited with a minimum maintained balance. However, due to the transactional nature of the account, and the 12% reserve requirement (banks must hold 12 cents on every dollar deposited at no interest and notable to lend it out), banks cannot afford to price the account that favorably. The interest paid tends to be a little higher than a standard 5¼% NOW account, and there are higher fees. (*See* SUPER NEGOTIABLE ORDER OF WITHDRAWAL (NOW) ACCOUNT.)

Checking Accounts: For most of us, checking accounts are commonplace. So, too, are checking-account monthly service fees and sometimes per-check fees as well. But if you've shopped wisely, there is little need to pay either.

Some institutions now offer free checking if you maintain a minimum balance. They may require that the minimum balance be in the checking account itself, or credit your overall funds in any account in the bank (e.g., money you have in a CD or an IRA might contribute to your total balance).

Overdraft Checking Accounts: Overdraft checking accounts, which give you an automatic line of credit, are also of significance to consumers. If you have this service, which is known by a variety of names, you can write checks larger than the balance in your checking account and be confident that the bank will cover the check. Under these plans, the bank temporarily loans you the balance needed and you are charged an agreed-upon rate of interest for the time the money is outstanding. In an emergency, an overdraft account provides you with the security you may need to meet expenses without waiting for a deposited check to clear. (*See* OVERDRAFT CHECKING.)

Certificates of Deposit (CD's): When you buy a certificate of deposit, you agree to deposit a certain amount of money for a specific length of time. In return, you are paid an interest rate that is fixed when you open the CD.

When CD's first became available to consumers, the interest rates paid were extremely favorable, but there were two negatives: Large amounts of money (usually $10,000 or more) were required to purchase a CD, so small savers were still stuck at 5¼%; and if you needed the money before the term of the certificate had elapsed, you paid a stiff penalty. For that reason, most people who invested in CD's still found it necessary to keep their emergency savings in a low-yield savings account where the money was easily accessible.

But all that is changing, and the consumer is richer for it. Now not only can customers invest smaller sums of money in CD's—and still get high rates—but they also have access to their money at any time simply by writing a check.

Here's how the newer CD's work. You can take less than $10,000 (the minimum deposit is set by the bank) and invest it in a high-yield certificate. What if you need the money for an emergency? If you've shopped around, there should be no problem. Some banks now offer CD's with checks so you can easily withdraw funds as long as you maintain the specified minimum balance. The money to cover the check is actually a loan from the bank at an interest rate of as little as 1% per year and is automatically repaid out of the interest when the account matures.

This system also offers an interesting investment opportunity. Suppose you have $6,000 to invest in a six-month investment account, and for the first four months you're happy with your rate of return. Then, suddenly, interest rates shoot up. How to benefit? Withdraw $3,000 of your money (leaving the required minimum balance of $3,000 in the account) and reinvest the money in a new account paying the higher rate.

And if rates fall? Again, with the CD, you took advantage of a great investment opportunity. Because, unlike the rates on money-market funds, which fluctuate daily, rates at purchase are guaranteed for the term of the certificate. CD's are federally insured and are available for various time periods, each paying different interest rates. (*See* CERTIFICATES OF DEPOSIT.)

Shop Around. As you shop and compare bank programs, consider your own specific needs. If interest rates are high and you're saving for something you'd like to buy in a few years, you may want to lock your money into the high rate of a longer-term investment savings account. However, if this is your emergency savings and you're not sure exactly when you may need to dip into it, you're better off with a six-month

account or a new money-market account where your money is easily accessible.

When you compare investment offerings, be sure to look beyond rate to a certificate's yield. Because interest is compounded, the eventual yield—the interest you actually walk away with—is higher than the rate posted. And, of course, the longer the time period of the account, the greater the difference between rate and yield. At some banks, interest in various instruments may not be compounded, so you'll want to be sure to consider this point when comparison shopping.

Tax-Shelter Accounts. One way to save—and make—money is to cut your taxes.

All workers can make tax-deferred contributions to retirement savings via an INDIVIDUAL RETIREMENT ACCOUNT (IRA) or—for the self-employed—a KEOGH PLAN. Part-time workers can also contribute the maximum amount allowable even if it constitutes 100% of their earnings.

In short, even if you currently participate in a company retirement plan, you can still put away up to $2,000 per year and let the earnings accumulate tax-free until the age of 59½. Then, starting at that age, you can make withdrawals of any amount you wish and be taxed—when you are probably in a lower tax bracket than you are now—only on the amounts you withdraw each year. There is a penalty for early withdrawal except in cases of death or permanent disability.

If you are self-employed or have outside free-lance or consulting income in addition to your regular earnings, you are also eligible for a Keogh plan. Up to 15% of your annual income or $15,000, whichever is less, may be set aside, tax-deferred until withdrawal.

When you consider opening an IRA or Keogh plan, discuss with your banker which type of investment vehicle will pay the highest return. You'll have the choice of investing in instruments paying interest at a fixed rate (set at the time of deposit) or a variable rate (fluctuates according to the variations in an agreed-upon index), so you'll want to consider which will be most advantageous to you. As you decide on an institution for your IRA or Keogh, remember that bank deposits are insured. In other words, when you're ready to retire, you can be sure that your money will be there.

Also, investigate the services the institution offers with your tax shelter account. Does the institution have a staff of experts available to you? How often will you receive statements—quarterly or just annually? Even more important, do the large balances you will accumulate in such tax-shelter plans count toward other privileges and services, such as lower rates on loans? It's important to save for your future, but your money should also be working for you today.

If you have a young family, you might also want to explore another very simple tax shelter that allows money to be deposited in your child's name and saved for his or her education or other needs. Taxes on that money are avoided because they're based on your child's income, which is almost certainly a lot lower than yours.

Richard C. Kane

Bank Note

A promissory note issued by an authorized bank, payable in the specified amount on demand and acceptable as currency.

Harvey Rachlin

Bank Paper

A BANK NOTE; commercial paper (securities, bills of exchange) of such quality that a bank will accept it.

Harvey Rachlin

Bank Rate

The rate of discount established by a nation's central bank or banks.

Harvey Rachlin

Bankruptcy

Bankruptcy means insolvency, not paying debts. A bankruptcy proceeding is a Federal Court proceeding in which rights and obligations are adjusted in order to apportion the impact of the debtor's financial situation and to enable the debtor to resume an economic role in society. Although a debtor is any person having debt, the term usually refers to one who is the subject of a bankruptcy proceeding.

A bankruptcy proceeding is started by filing a petition with the bankruptcy court in the federal district where the debtor either lives, does business, or has substantial assets. A list, called "schedules," of all property and of all creditors must also be filed, together with answers to questions concerning financial affairs.

There are several types of bankruptcy proceedings. The most common are *personal bankruptcy, individual debt adjustment,* and *reorganization.* These three types of bankruptcy are examined in this entry.

Personal Bankruptcy. A personal bankruptcy involves a debtor not paying debts as they become due, a distribution of the debtor's nonexempt assets to creditors, and an economic fresh start by way of a discharge of indebtedness. A personal bankruptcy proceeding is also known as a Chapter 7 proceeding.

Under a Chapter 7 proceeding, the debtor generally appears in court on two occasions: once to be questioned by the court-appointed trustee, and another time to be counseled by the judge who grants a discharge of indebtedness. The trustee is appointed by the court on behalf of the creditors to convert the debtor's nonexempt assets into cash and make distribution to creditors. The trustee questions the debtor concerning the information contained in the schedules in order to determine the property to which the creditors may be entitled, and is empowered to bring legal proceedings in order to obtain it.

Understanding a personal bankruptcy proceeding requires an analysis of the following concepts.

Exemptions. Those assets that a debtor may keep free from claims of creditors. Each state fixes exemptions for its own residents. The Bankruptcy Code also fixes separate exemptions. Unless the debtor's state has passed a law restricting the debtor to the exclusive use of state exemptions, the debtor is free to choose either the state exemptions or the Federal Bankruptcy Code exemptions.

Exemptions generally include a limited interest in such necessary items as a homestead, automobile, clothing, household and personal effects, and tools of one's trade. Bankruptcy Code exemptions include a $7,500 homestead exemption for each debtor and provide that if the debtor does not have that great an interest in a homestead, the debtor may apply the unused portion of the homestead exemption toward anything else of value. For example, if the debtor owns a house worth $40,000 that has a $35,000 mortgage, the debtor has a $5,000 interest. If the debtor's state has not prohibited Bankruptcy Code exemptions for its residents, the debtor may elect those exemptions and apply $5,000 of the $7,500 exemption to save the house and have $2,500 of exemption left for anything else. (Of course, the debtor must keep making mortgage payments or the bank will take away the house.) In a majority of personal bankruptcies, all of the debtor's assets are exempt.

The debtor claims exemptions in the schedules. Exemptions are allowed as claimed unless a creditor or the trustee objects. Contested exemptions will be determined by the court.

Exemptions apply separately and fully to each debtor. Where a husband and wife file one joint petition, they are each entitled to a full set of exemptions; and, except where prohibited by their own state, each may make a separate election—one may choose the state and the other the Bankruptcy Code exemptions.

Discharge. A court order relieving a debtor from an obligation to repay debt. A discharge affects only claims, debts, liabilities, and obligations that exist on the date the petition is filed, even though the due date may be some time thereafter; it does not affect obligations that are first incurred after the petition is filed. For example, if in January the debtor takes a loan repayable in December, a June filing may discharge the debt. However, a loan first taken out in August will not be discharged.

A discharge will relieve only the debtor; it will not affect any other person also responsible, such as a co-maker, nor will the discharge by itself affect any lien on collateral. Certain conduct of the debtor may give a creditor or the trustee the right to object to and perhaps prevent the debtor's discharge. Some examples of such conduct are concealing property, lying to the trustee or in the schedules, disobeying a court order, or filing a second bankruptcy petition within six years.

Even though a discharge is granted, certain debts are not affected. Some examples of debts not affected by a discharge are most taxes (although ordinary income taxes may be discharged where a proper and timely return was filed at least two years before the petition); debts fraudulently or dishonestly incurred (such as money stolen or embezzled); debts owing to a creditor who neither knew of the bankruptcy nor was properly listed in the schedules in time to file a proof of claim; and most support obligations. Student loans are dischargeable only if they are not owed to a government agency or a nonprofit institution of higher learning, or if the student loan first became due at least five years before the bankruptcy or if payment would impose an undue hardship.

Reaffirmation. A legally binding agreement to repay an otherwise dischargeable obligation. A debtor may not want to discharge certain debts, such as loans from friends or relatives, or the bill of a trusted physician whose services are still needed. In order to preserve such debt, the debtor must enter into a new agreement, cancelable for 30 days, promising repayment. This new agreement must be approved by the court. If the debt is primarily for personal, family, or household purposes and is not secured by the debtor's real estate, reaffirmation will not be permitted unless the court is convinced either that reaffirmation is in the best interest of the debtor and will not impose an undue hardship, or that it was entered into as part of a good-faith settlement of certain specified types of litigation. In the absence of reaffirmation, the debtor may still choose to repay all or part of the discharged debt. Part payment will not affect discharge of the balance, nor will payment of one discharged debt affect the discharge of others.

Debtor's Rights. Special rights given by law only to debtors who file a bankruptcy petition and not available to others owing debt. These rights include *consumer redemption, freedom from governmental discrimination, automatic stay, lien avoidance,* and *examination of attorneys' fees.* A petition in bankruptcy may often be filed only to enable a debtor to take advantage of one of these special rights.

Consumer Redemption. The right of an individual debtor in bankruptcy to redeem from a creditor's lien consumer property that is exempt or has been abandoned by the trustee, by paying less than the full amount due. Consumer property is tangible property, other than real estate, that is intended primarily for personal, family, or household use. If the debtor bought the property on time, or used the property as collateral, the creditor has a lien upon the property that will not be affected merely by a discharge of the debt. The creditor may enforce this lien whether the property is still owned by the debtor or has been sold or turned over to any other person, including the trustee.

If the amount due on the lien is greater than the value of the property, there is no equity available to the creditors, and the trustee usually will obtain court permission to abandon the property. The debtor may want this property but may not have money to replace it. An individual debtor is given the right to redeem consumer property that is either exempt or that the trustee has abandoned, by paying to the creditor only its market value, even though a larger amount may be due. For example, the debtor may have purchased a bedroom set on time for $1,000. At the time the bankruptcy petition is filed, the furniture, due to normal use, wear, and deterioration, may be worth only $200. If the debtor has properly claimed the bedroom set as exempt, or if the trustee has abandoned it, the debtor may free the property from the lien by payment of the sum of only $200, even though the amount owing may have been the sum of $700 or $800. The debtor's personal obligation to repay the balance will normally be extinguished by the discharge.

Freedom from Governmental Discrimination. With a few rare exceptions, a debtor who files a bankruptcy petition may not be discriminated against with regard to licensing or employment by a government agency solely because of such filing. This prohibition does not apply to private persons. Thus, a state may not revoke or deny a driver's license for failing to pay a discharged judgment arising out of an automobile accident, but a private loan company is free to adopt a policy against lending money to anyone who has ever filed a bankruptcy petition.

Automatic Stay. A provision in the Bankruptcy Code. Immediately upon the filing of a bankruptcy petition, all creditors are automatically prohibited from proceeding against the debtor or the debtor's property with regard to obligations that arose before the petition was filed. Government agencies and taxing authorities are treated the same as other creditors, although they may exercise their legitimate police powers, and support obligations may be enforced out of exempt assets without violating this stay.

Action taken in violation of this stay is void, and if the creditor proceeded while knowing about the bankruptcy, the creditor may be fined or even jailed for contempt. For example, if a debtor files a bankruptcy petition just prior to a mortgage-foreclosure sale, the sale is void. If the person foreclosing actually knew that the bankruptcy petition had been filed and did not cancel the sale, a fine or jail sentence may be imposed.

The automatic stay expires if the court dismisses the case; when the case is closed; or at the time the debtor is granted or denied a discharge. Of course, once the debtor has obtained a discharge, a creditor may not proceed to collect a discharged debt, although it may enforce a valid lien upon the debtor's property and may also proceed to collect and enforce nondischargeable obligations. For example, if a bank has loaned money and taken a lien on the debtor's car as collateral, the bank cannot sue the debtor on the loan after the debtor has been discharged, but it may repossess the car, even if the car was declared exempt. If, however, the debtor had reaffirmed the loan to the bank, or if the debtor's obligation arose out of a theft or embezzlement, the obligation would not be affected by the discharge and the bank would then be free to sue the debtor.

Creditors who want to proceed before the stay expires must apply to the bankruptcy court and show a good reason. The court may consider some of the following situations as sufficient cause to grant permission for the creditor to proceed: a lawsuit against a debtor automobile operator who has sufficient insurance to cover the claim; foreclosure of a mortgage upon the debtor's house equal to or greater than the value of the house, especially where current payments on the mortgage are not being made; repossession of a car given as collateral for a loan where the car is inadequately maintained or insured.

In addition to the automatic stay, a debtor may ask the court to impose a discretionary stay in an appropriate case.

Lien Avoidance. A right given to debtors to have certain liens removed merely because of their filing a petition in bankruptcy. A *lien* is a property right given to one who does not own the property to have that property taken or sold to enforce payment of an obligation. There are many different types of liens. When a car is bought on time, the seller has a lien upon it (which is usually sold to a bank or finance company); when a borrower gets a mortgage on a house, the lender has a lien upon it; and in most states when a creditor sues a debtor and wins, the creditor obtains a judgment that becomes a lien upon the debtor's real estate. In each case, if the debtor does not pay, the creditor has the right to have the property sold to satisfy the debt.

Upon filing a petition in bankruptcy, the debtor acquires the right to ask the court to remove certain liens. Two classes of liens may be avoided, but only to the extent to which they interfere with the debtor's exemptions: (1) liens upon personal or household effects, items used for the production of the debtor's income, or professionally prescribed health aids, providing the liens are neither purchase-money nor possessory; and (2) judgment liens. A purchase-money lien is a lien that secures the purchase price of the item, such as something bought on time. A possessory lien is one that gives the creditor the right to hold the item, such as in a pawn shop.

Example: A creditor has a $10,000 judgment against a debtor who owns a $50,000 house with a $45,000 mortgage; since the debtor's interest—$5,000—is less than the homestead exemption, the entire judgment lien may be avoided. If the debtor had borrowed money from a bank and had given a lien upon all existing household furnishings, the debtor could avoid that lien; the debtor could not avoid a lien given to buy those furnishings, however. Some courts have held that where the creditor acquired the lien prior to November 6, 1978, the date when the Bankruptcy Code was signed into law, lien avoidance would be an unconstitutional taking of the creditor's property and have refused to permit it. Bankruptcy courts are not uniform on this point.

Lien avoidance is not automatic. If the debtor does not ask for it, the lien will remain valid and enforceable after the bankruptcy proceeding is over.

Examination of Attorneys' Fees. All fees paid or promised to the debtor's attorney by any person in connection with the bankruptcy proceeding within the year preceding the filing of the petition must be disclosed by the attorney to the court. To the extent that this fee exceeds what the court thinks is reasonable under the circumstances, it will order the agreement canceled or the excess repaid. If the excess was paid by the debtor out of nonexempt sources, it will be repaid to the trustee; otherwise it will be repaid to the person who had paid it.

Priorities and Payment of Claims. In order for a creditor to share in a distribution, a claim must be filed. The bankruptcy court gives all creditors notice of when this must be done. Filed claims are classified and are given a priority according to the class in which they are placed. Members of a class share proportionately, but no class receives anything unless and until all prior classes have been paid in full. The classes, in order of their priority, are (1) expenses incurred in administering the bankruptcy, such as fees for the attorney, for the trustee, or for the debtor; court, stenographic, and filing fees; or expenses of recovering, preserving, or selling assets; (2) in an involuntary case, claims arising out of the debtor's ordinary financial affairs after the case is started, up to the time when the court determines that the debtor is bankrupt; (3) claims of the debtor's employees for wages and benefits earned within 90 days before the petition was filed, up to a maximum of $2,000; (4) certain claims of employee benefit plans; (5) consumer claims for deposits given to the debtor up to $900 (6) certain tax claims; (7) timely filed general unsecured claims; (8) general unsecured claims filed late; (9) claims for certain penalties assessed against the debtor; and (10) interest that accrued after the filing of the petition. Any moneys remaining after the above distribution are then returned to the debtor.

Preference. A transfer of property of the debtor (usually money), on account of a past due obligation, which gives the creditor more than would be received in the debtor's bankruptcy distribution if the transfer had not been made. The trustee may set aside the preference and recover the property transferred if the debtor was insolvent when the transfer was made and if the transfer took place within the time provided by law. If the trustee does not recover the preference, where it was not voluntarily made, and provided that it was taken out of exempt property, it may be recovered by the debtor. All creditors, including governmental agencies and taxing authorities, are subject to this rule.

A transfer may be voluntary or involuntary; a debtor may willingly repay a loan or the tax collector may seize the debtor's bank account. If one week before filing the petition, the debtor makes payment for furniture purchased a year before, it may be a preference; if the debtor buys furniture one week before filing the petition and pays cash on delivery, it is not a preference since the payment was not on account of a previously owed obligation.

Some payments of old obligations leave the creditor no better off than does the bankruptcy distribution, and such transfers therefore are not preferences. Where the debtor owes $1,000 of federal priority taxes, and has nonexempt assets sufficient for the trustee to distribute $1,000 after payment of any priorities of the first five classes, any seizure of the debtor's $1,000 bank account by Internal Revenue just before the petition is filed is not a preference; even without the seizure, Internal Revenue would get its $1,000 as a priority distribution. But since state and federal taxes share the same priority, if the debtor also owed $500 in state taxes, the federal seizure would be a preference since Internal Revenue would now have to share the $1,000 distribution with the state taxing authority.

A preferential transfer made within 90 days before the filing of the petition may be recovered. If, however, the debtor and the creditor are closely related through blood, marriage, or business, or if the creditor is the debtor's lawyer, and if in addition the creditor had good reason to believe that the debtor was insolvent at the time of the transfer, the time period is increased to one year.

An individual whose debts exceed the value of nonexempt assets is considered insolvent.

Fraudulent Transfers. Certain transfers made by a debtor, or obligations incurred by a debtor that have either the purpose or the effect of hindering, delaying, or defrauding creditors. The Bankruptcy Code gives the trustee the right to set aside such transfers or obligations made within one year of the filing of the petition, and some states provide additional time. A transfer is fraudulent if it is made with actual intent to interfere with creditors' rights, such as transferring one's property to another or signing a fictitious note just before a lawsuit or just before bankruptcy; or selling or exchanging an asset for something of much less value if the debtor was, or was about to become, insolvent or unable to pay debts as they matured. Substantial gifts to close family members may inadvertently become fraudulent transfers if the giver is having trouble paying bills; if bankruptcy takes place shortly thereafter, the trustee may ultimately become the recipient of the gift.

Individual Debt Adjustment. A court-supervised arrangement for eligible debtors to repay all or part of their debts over a period of time during which creditors may not pursue the debtor. This is commonly referred to as a "Chapter 13 proceeding."

A Chapter 13 proceeding differs from a personal bankruptcy (Chapter 7 proceeding) in that the Chapter 13 contemplates at least a partial payback of indebtedness, while the Chapter 7 is concerned with a liquidation of assets. (Both, of course, seek a discharge of indebtedness.) The Chapter 13 debtor files with the court a petition and a statement setting forth a list of property and debts and a showing of family income and family expenses. The debtor then proposes a plan that sets forth the manner and the amount of debt repayment. In a Chapter 13 proceeding, the debtor does not lose any property.

Just as in a personal bankruptcy, the court appoints a trustee who will question the debtor in order to determine whether to recommend that the court confirm the debtor's plan.

Usually a Chapter 13 proceeding is filed instead of

a personal bankruptcy where (1) the debtor wants to repay all or a portion of existing indebtedness, or (2) the debtor has substantial nonexempt assets, which would be lost in a personal bankruptcy, or (3) the debtor wants to avoid discharge problems that would arise in a personal bankruptcy, or (4) the debtor wants to cure a default in, or modify the terms of, payment of an installment obligation. Understanding individual debt adjustment requires an analysis of the following concepts:

Codebtor Stay. In addition to the automatic stay imposed in every bankruptcy proceeding, creditors in a Chapter 13 proceeding are stayed from engaging in civil collection activities against individuals who are responsible for a consumer debt along with the debtor. (A consumer debt is one incurred primarily for personal, family, or household purposes.) A creditor may ask the court for relief from the codebtor stay if the creditor would be irreparably harmed, if the codebtor rather than the debtor is the one who actually received a consideration for the debt, or to the extent that the debtor's plan proposes not to pay a creditor. Example: Debtor borrows money for household expenses, and friend cosigns the note. Debtor files a Chapter 13 petition. The lender may not sue the cosigner. If the loan was for business purposes, however, it would not be a consumer loan and the stay would not apply. Even if it were a consumer loan, if the debtor's plan proposed repayment of only 75%, the creditor could ask the bankruptcy court for permission to sue the cosigner now for the remaining 25%; and if the friend had obtained the loan proceeds with the debtor acting only as comaker, the lender could ask the court for permission to sue the friend for the full amount.

Eligibility. Only an individual who has unsecured debts of under $100,000 and secured debts of under $350,000, and who has regular income sufficient to make the payments required by the debtor's own plan, may file a Chapter 13 proceeding, except that a stockbroker or commodity broker is not eligible. If a husband and wife file a joint petition, only one need have the requisite income. A debtor engaged in business may file a Chapter 13 proceeding if the other requirements are met.

The Plan. A proposal made by the debtor for partial or full debt repayment. After giving the trustee and creditors an opportunity to make objections, the court considers the plan and, if satisfied that it meets the requirements set forth below, will confirm it. Provisions of a confirmed plan are binding on the debtor and upon every creditor, whether or not the creditors consent to the plan.

The plan must submit as much of the debtor's future income as is required to meet the payments proposed in the plan under the supervision and control of the trustee. It must also provide for full payment of the first six priorities listed on page 54, unless the priority creditor is willing to waive this requirement in writing. The plan may also divide unsecured claims into classes, provided that all members of each class have similar interests and are treated equally. Example: The plan may provide "Unsecured Creditors shall be divided into two classes: Those whose claims are under $250 shall be paid in full; those whose claims are $250 or over shall be paid 75% of their claims." The plan may *not* contain the following provision: "Unsecured Creditors shall be divided into two classes: Those creditors who are related to the debtor by blood or marriage shall be paid in full; all others shall be paid 75% of their claims."

The plan may modify the rights of any creditor, secured or unsecured, except a creditor whose only security is the debtor's principal place of residence. Example: The debtor owes a balance of twelve payments secured by a lien on the debtor's automobile. The debtor may modify this obligation to provide for smaller monthly payments over a three-year period—provided that the present value of the smaller payments over the three-year period are at least equal to the present value of the larger payments over a twelve-month period originally contracted for, and provided that the creditor at all times remains adequately secured. The debtor may not so modify payments secured only by a mortgage on the house in which the debtor resides.

Normally the plan must provide for payments over a period of time not to exceed three (3) years. The court, however, may extend this period up to five (5) years if the debtor shows a good reason for the extension.

The plan may provide for the curing of any default by an immediate lump-sum payment; and if the last payment of the defaulted obligation would normally have been due after the final payment under the plan is due, then the default can be cured as part of the payments under the plan. Example: If the debtor's house or car payments are in arrears, the plan may provide for all of the past-due payments to be made up in one lump sum. This will preserve all of the debtor's original rights, such as a favorable interest rate. If the original term of the defaulted obligation extends beyond the plan's last payment, the arrears may be spread over the term of the plan so long as the creditor is given reasonable interest on the arrears and remains adequately secured. Defaults may be cured even after the entire obligation has been accelerated.

The plan usually treats secured and unsecured creditors differently. A secured creditor is one who has a lien on property of the debtor. If the value of the lien is less than the amount due, the creditor is secured to the extent of the value of the lien and unsecured as to the balance. To the extent that creditors are unsecured, the plan must offer them at least as much as they would have received if the debtor had filed a regular personal bankruptcy, plus interest on future payments. Secured creditors must be offered one of three alternatives: (1) a surrender of the security to the secured creditor, (2) the secured creditor retains the lien on the security and receives, over the term of the plan, payments whose present value is not less than the creditor's secured claim, or (3) any other provision that the secured creditor consents to.

The plan may also reject executory contracts. An executory contract is a contract in which both parties still have substantial obligations and where nonperformance by either would excuse performance by the other. The plan may cancel such a contract and excuse the debtor's obligation of future performance. The other party then has an unsecured claim for the actual damages sustained as a result of the cancellation and is treated the same as any other unsecured creditor.

Before the plan becomes binding, the court sends the debtor and all the creditors notice of the hearing, at which the debtor must be present and in which any creditor may participate. The court will then issue an order confirming the plan if the plan meets all of the requirements previously discussed, if the debtor has paid all of the required court fees, if the plan has been proposed in good faith, and if the court believes that the debtor will be able to comply with the plan and make all the required payments.

Payments required under the plan are made to the trustee, who then makes distribution to creditors who have filed claims. The court may order that a portion of the debtor's income be paid directly to the trustee for this purpose.

When the payments under the plan are completed, the court will order that, with only two exceptions, all of the debtor's debts provided for by the plan are discharged, whether they have been paid in full or only in part, unless the plan itself provides otherwise. The exceptions are (1) alimony, maintenance, and support obligations, and (2) payments on loan term obligations that have not yet become due.

Even if payments under the plan have not been completed, the debtor may obtain a hardship discharge if failure to make payments was for reasons not the fault of the debtor, and provided that creditors have actually received what they would have obtained if the debtor had filed a personal bankruptcy. A hardship discharge will not, however, discharge the debtor from an obligation that could not have been discharged in a personal bankruptcy.

Reorganization. A federal-court proceeding involving a debtor unable to continue full payment of debts as they become due, and operation of the debtor's business under supervision and court regulation until the business is liquidated or until its debts, capital structure, or both can be reorganized. Also referred to as a "Chapter 11 proceeding," it is used mostly by corporations, although available also to individuals, partnerships, and unincorporated businesses. A Chapter 11 proceeding filed by the debtor is a voluntary proceeding; one filed by creditors is an involuntary proceeding. To be eligible, the debtor must have either a domicile, residence, place of business, or property within the United States.

The primary purpose of a Chapter 11 proceeding is protection of the rights of creditors by rehabilitating an ailing business. The function of a business reorganization, as opposed to a liquidation, is to restructure the finances of that business so that it may continue to operate, to provide its employees with jobs, to pay its creditors, and eventually to produce a return for its stockholders. The theory is that the assets of a business are more valuable when they are used to provide a return in the business for which they were acquired than if they are liquidated in the open market, where they are often sold for nothing more than scrap. The return on assets that a business presently can produce may be inadequate to compensate those who have invested in it. Cash-flow problems may have created a situation that will result in crippling or even terminating a business if creditors are permitted to pursue their legal collection remedies. These creditors often will be better off if they are temporarily prevented from exercising their legal rights and if the business is enabled to extend or reduce its debts and eventually return to a viable condition. Chapter 11 recognizes that by preserving jobs and assets, reorganization of an insolvent debtor is often more efficient than liquidation. This is done by restraining creditor activity during a temporary period while a plan of reorganization is proposed, approved, and implemented.

Understanding a Chapter 11 proceeding requires an analysis of the following concepts.

Committees. Groups of representative creditors appointed by the court to speak for the interests of all creditors. After the filing of a Chapter 11 proceeding, the court will appoint a committee of the largest unsecured creditors willing to serve, and may also appoint additional committees of equity holders, such as owners of the debtor's stocks and bonds. These committees will be parties to most proceedings within the Chapter 11 in order to voice the position of the parties they represent. With court approval, they may employ attorneys, accountants, and other necessary professionals to assist them; the fees of such employees will be an administrative expense to be paid by the debtor.

Some of the customary activities of the creditors' committee are to consult with the debtor-in-possession, or the trustee (if one has been appointed) concerning the administration of the case; investigate the acts, conduct, financial condition, and business operations of the debtor, as well as the advisability of continuing such business, and any other matters relevant to the case or to the formulation of a plan; participate in the formulation of the plan; make recommendations to creditors voting on plans; collect, and file with the court, acceptances or rejections of a filed plan; request the appointment of a trustee or an examiner where appropriate; and generally to act in the best interest of creditors.

Debtor-in-Possession. A debtor that is permitted to remain in possession of its own assets and to transact its own business affairs under court supervision and control during a Chapter 11 proceeding. Upon the filing of a Chapter 11 petition, the debtor becomes a debtor-in-possession. The debtor-in-possession is in a fiduciary relationship to all of the creditors—that is, a relationship of trust and strict accountability. Any interested party, including the creditors' committee, may ask the court to discharge the debtor-in-possession and to appoint a trustee if it can show good cause, such as fraud, dishonesty, incompetence, or gross mismanagement. Once appointed, the trustee takes possession of the debtor's assets and conducts the debtor's business, and thereafter the debtor is no longer considered a debtor-in-possession. If the court feels that the facts do not warrant the appointment of a trustee, an examiner may be appointed to investigate the financial affairs and the management of the debtor's business and to report to the court. An examiner does not take over operation of the debtor's business.

Claims. Unlike a personal bankruptcy or a Chapter 13 proceeding, a creditor who is properly listed in the debtor's schedules need not file a proof of claim in order to share in the distribution of assets under the plan unless the creditor's claim is listed in the schedules as being disputed, contingent, or unliquidated. A disputed claim is one whose validity or amount the debtor denies; a contingent claim is an obligation that will arise only on the happening or nonhappening of an uncertain event (such as the debtor's loan guarantee where the borrower is still making payments); an unliquidated claim is one whose liability is admitted but whose amount cannot be determined without further proceedings (such as an automobile accident that requires either arbitration, a lawsuit, or an out-of-court settlement to establish the amount due). If the creditor does not agree with the way it was treated in the schedules, it may always file a claim. Payment of claims and priority of payment in Chapter 11 is the same as in a personal bankruptcy.

The Plan. A proposal containing provisions for the modification of the rights and the duties of the debtor and creditors, and a restructuring of the debtor's debts and capital. The confirmation of a plan is the goal of a Chapter 11 proceeding. In a voluntary case, the debtor may file a plan either with the petition or at any time thereafter, unless a trustee is appointed. The debtor is given a reasonable period of time during which only it may file a plan. Thereafter, any interested party may propose one. The plan may affect the rights of creditors in many different ways. For example, if the debtor had defaulted in making payments under an agreement with an automatic acceleration clause, the plan could provide for reinstatement of the original payment schedule; the plan might also change the maturity date, rate of interest, or other term of the debtor's outstanding securities; it may alter or modify the terms of a lien on the debtor's property and even authorize sale of encumbered property free of such lien; and it may provide that certain classes of claims be paid at a later date and even in a lesser amount than originally incurred—and that some classes of claims receive no payment at all. Before the plan becomes binding upon the creditors, however, it must be accepted and it must be confirmed by the court.

Acceptance of the Plan. Before the court may consider confirming the plan, it must be accepted by each class of claims or interests whose rights are impaired by it.

Generally, a creditor's rights are impaired if they are modified in any way unless the plan gives the creditor new rights of value equal to the rights it had before the Chapter 11 petition was filed.

After the plan has been filed, the debtor or the creditors' committee will contact the creditors to solicit their written acceptances. Before doing this, however, there must be a disclosure statement setting forth information about the debtor's financial condition sufficient to permit the exercise of informed judgment in evaluating the plan. This disclosure statement must be approved by the court and supplied to the holders of all claims or interests.

The holder of a claim is one who has a right to payment of a specific amount of money. The holder of an interest is one who has rights against the debtor other than payment of a specific amount—such as a stockholder, who has the right to vote for the election of the directors of a corporate debtor and to share in the distribution of the profits of a corporate debtor if and when they are earned and distributed.

Acceptance of a plan is accomplished by classes. Claims or interests are classified so that all members of a class have substantially similar interests. For example, a typical plan might provide: "Class A shall consist of all creditors having unsecured claims of $1,000 or less; Class B shall consist of all creditors having unsecured claims of more than $1,000; Class C shall consist of all creditors whose claims are secured by first mortgages on all of the debtor's real estate; Class D shall consist of the debtor's bondholders; and Class E shall consist of the debtor's stockholders.

Holders of claims or interests may either vote upon the plan or abstain. They vote by either accepting or rejecting it.

A plan is accepted by a class when at least as many members accept as reject, provided that the amount of claims held by the acceptors is at least twice the value of the amount of claims held by the rejecters. Neither the number of abstainers nor the amount of their claims is considered. As an example, consider the class consisting of A with a claim of $1,000, B with a claim of $10,000, C with a claim of $15,000, D with a claim of $25,000, and E with a claim of $1 million. If E rejects, there is no way for the class to accept; however, even if E accepts, any two of the others can prevent acceptance by voting for rejection. If E abstains, D can obtain class acceptance if A accepts and if either B or C also accept; however, with E abstaining, if D rejects there is no way for the class to accept.

Confirmation. In order for an accepted plan to become operative and binding upon all parties, it must be confirmed by the court. In order to confirm a plan, the court must determine the following:

1. that every class either has accepted the plan or is not impaired by it;

2. that each member of each class will receive under the plan at least as much as it would receive if the debtor were liquidated under Chapter 7; (This requirement may be waived for a particular class if each member of the class waives it by accepting the plan.)

3. that at least one class has actually accepted the plan; and

4. that the plan is fair and equitable with regard to each class.

Once confirmed, the plan is binding upon the debtor and all creditors, and all of the debtor's property is returned free of all liens and claims unless the plan provides otherwise. Normally the plan will provide that the debtor is to make certain specified payments, and that certain obligations and interests will survive consummation of the plan. Except as provided in the plan, confirmation wipes out all interests, claims, and liens against the debtor or its property except for the exceptions to discharge and dischargeability set forth in the preceding section, "Personal Bankruptcy."

Marvin A. Holland

Banks

Banks are a group of institutions that provide customers with a variety of financial services. Their major functions are the following:

- Loans and investments, the latter primarily in U.S. government securities. Loans are made to businesses and individuals and provide the bulk of banks' income.
- Transfer services that move money among individuals, businesses, and governments. Transfers are made through a variety of means, including checks, money orders, bank drafts, bankers' acceptances, and wire transfers.
- Depository services through which savings can be accumulated.

Banks also provide a number of other services to a greater or lesser degree, depending on the type of business they do. These include buying and selling foreign currency; collecting debts for customers; safekeeping, purchasing, and selling of corporate and government securities; and, in some cases, selling life insurance.

Banks in the United States are divided into two categories: COMMERCIAL BANKS and THRIFT INSTITUTIONS (SAVINGS AND LOAN ASSOCIATIONS, MUTUAL SAVINGS BANKS, and CREDIT UNIONS)—see Table 1. The distinction is based on how each lends money. Thrift institutions lend *existing* funds deposited by customers, effectively taking money in one window and lending it out through another. (Thrifts mainly lend money for home mortgages, although the Monetary Control Act of 1980 broadened their powers to allow them to handle certain banking transactions previously handled only by commercial banks.) Commercial banks lend by *creating* money through a process known as "fractional reserve accounting." This ability to create money is so important that it should be examined more closely here.

We know from personal experience that when we deposit money in our checking accounts, say our paychecks, we rarely draw it out again in one day; withdrawals are usually staggered over a period of days. Bankers have learned that they have to keep only a fraction of deposits on hand to meet these withdrawals. The rest provides the reserves to support loans.

When a commercial bank grants a loan, it doesn't give the borrower cash. Instead, the funds are added to a new or existing checking account. The loan is, in effect, the bank's promise to honor the checks you write on the new funds in your account.

How has the money been created? Suppose J. Jones comes to the bank for a $10,000 car loan. He swaps his promise to repay (an asset to the bank because it is worth $10,000) for $10,000 of checking-account money.

Table 1

Comparison of Commercial Banks and Thrifts

	Commercial Banks	Credit Unions	Savings Banks	Savings and Loan Associations
Ownership form:	Stock	Membership shares (one member, one vote)	Mutual or stock	Mutual or stock
Directed by:	Board of directors	Board of directors elected by and from membership	Board of trustees (mutual); board of directors (stock)	Board of directors
Basic form of accounts:	Time, transaction, certificate	Share (passbook), certificate, share draft (checking)	Savings, time, transaction	Regular, certificate accounts, checking accounts
Earnings:	Paid primarily as interest to depositors; also, paid as dividends to stockholders and retained as capital	Paid as dividends to members and sometimes as rebates on loans	Paid primarily as interest to savers; paid as dividends to stockholders	Paid primarily as interest to savers; paid as dividends to stockholders
How deposits are invested:	Commercial, agricultural, mortgage, and consumer loans; purchase of government securities	Primarily as consumer loans to individual members; some mortgage loans	Mortgage, commercial, and consumer loans; government obligations; bonds; stocks	Mainly as residential mortgage loans; other loans
State regulations	Vary from state to state	Vary from state to state	Vary from state to state	Vary from state to state
Chief federal regulators:	Federal Deposit Insurance Corporation; Comptroller of the Currency; Federal Reserve Board	National Credit Union Administration (NCUA)	FDIC (state-chartered); FHLBB (federally chartered)	Federal Home Loan Bank Board
Federal Insurer of Accounts:	Federal Deposit Insurance Corporation	National Credit Union Share Insurance Fund (administered by NCUA)	FDIC (most state-chartered); state insuring agencies; FSLIC (most federally chartered)	Federal Savings and Loan Insurance Corporation

Source: Phil Battey, Howard Cosgrove, Mary Ann Irvine, Arthur Mikesell

The banker simply writes in a deposit to the J. Jones account. With a stroke of the pen, J. Jones's account now contains $10,000.

On the books of the bank, it looks like this:

First National Bank

Assets	Liabilities
Loans $10,000 (J. Jones loan)	Demand deposits $10,000 (deposit to Jones)

When J. Jones spends the money, the amount in his demand-deposit account will decline. As he repays the loan, the value of the bank's asset will decline. Looked at in this way, you can also see that just as money can be created, it can also be destroyed.

Multiple Expansion The ability to create money in just one account is only part of the story. Let's look at J. Jones's loan a bit more extensively. Suppose Jones buys his car and gives the dealer, Max Cars, his check for $10,000. Max puts the check into his checking account at Second National Bank, then writes checks for $5,000 each to the Rubber Tire Company and Keen Advertising Agency. The tire company and the ad agency put their checks into their accounts at Third National Bank. Table 2 shows what the transactions would look like in terms of money flows.

You'll note that in each of the transactions we've made a notation about reserves. As explained earlier, bankers learned that since not all funds would be withdrawn on a given day, they needed to keep only a fraction of deposits on hand and could lend the rest. The fraction kept in reserve was determined in the early days by estimating the amount needed to meet withdrawals. Today, it is determined more scientifically and is a legal requirement aimed not so much at safety as at maintaining control over the amount of loans banks can make, an economic goal. In the U.S., the Federal Reserve Board decides how much banks must hold as a reserve.

Let's suppose that the reserve percentage is 10%. If we go back to the money flows shown in Table 2, you can easily calculate that when Second National Bank received the $10,000 deposit from Max Cars, it would have had to hold $1,000 in reserves and would have been able to create loans of $9,000. Suppose further that Second National loaned the $9,000 to a customer who spent it, and that the money ultimately moved to another bank (not an unusual occurrence, as you can see from the flow chart). That bank in turn would have to hold 10% in reserve ($900) and would be able to create loans of $8,100. Theoretically this cycle could continue until the banking system *as a whole* was able to create $90,000 in deposits through new loans.

Money creation, then, is a very powerful force in the economy and it's obvious why it must be controlled. The Federal Reserve system, the U.S. central bank, uses its ability to control the percentage of reserves a bank must hold to either stimulate or restrain the economy. For example, if the economy is in recession, the Federal Reserve may lower reserve requirements (allowing banks more lending capacity) to stimulate economic activity. If inflation is the problem and the economy must be restrained, the Fed may increase reserve requirements (curbing lending capacity).

Sources of Reserves. Except for short periods and relatively small amounts, there are only three important ways for reserve dollars to enter or leave our banking system. The most easily recognizable source is currency in circulation, the total of coin and paper money held by individuals, businesses, and banks, except for the Federal Reserve. When coin and paper money are deposited, banks gain reserves. When checks are written against these deposits, reserves decline.

Table 2

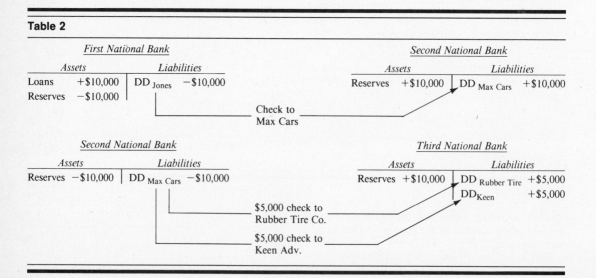

Another way is through changes in our international currency reserves. International currency reserves include gold and Special Drawing Rights (SDR's), international reserve assets first issued in the early 1970s by the INTERNATIONAL MONETARY FUND (IMF). When the Treasury buys gold from a foreign country, the payment is deposited in that country's account at the Federal Reserve. Since the country sold gold to get dollars to spend, the money will eventually flow into U.S. banks, increasing their reserves. When the Treasury sells gold, however, reserves flow out of the banking systems. This is because the payment is drawn from the foreign country's account at a U.S. bank. The Treasury deposits the country's check in its account at the Fed, which deducts the amount from the bank's account. Similarly, when the Treasury sells Special Drawing Rights to the Fed, reserves flow into the banking system, because the Treasury will eventually spend the funds it receives. When the Treasury redeems the SDR's, it draws funds from banks and pays the Fed, causing reserves to contract.

The third and most important means by which reserves are gained or lost is through the actions of the Federal Reserve. Largely by buying and selling U.S. government securities in the open market, the Fed can either add reserves (through a purchase) or reduce them (through a sale).

Multimillion-dollar transactions are made with securities dealers, who, like most people, maintain bank accounts into which they deposit the proceeds or from which they withdraw the money needed to make a purchase. These transactions, just like our deposits and withdrawals, increase or decrease bank reserves, but on a much faster and larger scale.

The Fed increases and decreases reserves in line with its analysis of the economy's needs—expanding reserves to speed economic expansion and reducing them to check inflation. All open-market operations are aimed strictly at policy goals. Some are undertaken simply to smooth ripples in the money supply. The Fed can also increase bank reserves by making temporary loans to offset sudden large reserve drains at individual banks.

Charles J. Parnow

Banks, History of U.S.

Banks were the outgrowth of the widening use of money. For example, a wider use of money in international trade required the use of foreign currencies, which in turn led to the need for foreign exchange, one of the functions of banks even today. Pinpointing the exact origins of banking is difficult from a historical perspective, since they seem to have evolved along the lines of need. The example cited typifies banks' growth with economic and financial needs.

The Babylonians and Assyrians performed various banking functions, such as foreign exchange, deposit holding, drafting of bills of exchange, and supplying instruments closely resembling our modern-day checks as early as the seventh and even the ninth century before the birth of Christ. The Greeks were early bankers, and they passed their knowledge on to the Romans.

No one really knows what happened during the Dark Ages, but the art and science of banking apparently survived and may even have spread, because we find historical references to banking in Germany, France, and Italy, to name a few, in the Middle Ages. Italy, apparently inheriting its banking tradition from the Romans, had banks that performed a variety of functions but were engaged in money changing primarily and, to a small degree, lending and the holding of deposits.

It's important to make some distinctions about the services that early banks performed. Deposits, for example, were made not for the primary goal of earning income. For the most part, people deposited funds to keep them safe from robbers.

Loans are another example. Until well after the Middle Ages, Christians were prohibited from making loans for interest because of biblical injunction, so the lending function fell largely to the Jewish community of the era. They made loans, but for the most part in much the same way that pawnbrokers do today: They loaned money largely against the security of items such as armor, jewels, or other easily liquidated property. (An interesting sidelight to the history of the lending function of the Jewish community is that during the Crusades it was not uncommon for the Christian lords to borrow the funds for their trips to the Holy Land from Jewish lenders and, upon returning, banish the Jews from their domain.)

Over the years, it has been assumed that the term *bank* derived from the tables or benches (*bancos*) upon which the Italian money lenders did their business. However, historians have disagreed sharply. The dissenters point out that the term probably derived from the German word *Banck,* which was used to describe a joint-stock company. Joint-stock companies were used in those days (about the mid- to late 1500s) to make public loans. The joint-stock companies would sell shares and raise funds to lend the government, which in turn would give the company the right to collect certain taxes. Of course, the amount of taxes would be larger than the amount loaned, thus giving the company its profit. The Italians called these loans *monte,* meaning a heap or mound of money. The Germans were very active in Italy during this part of the 1500s, and their word *Banck* probably became the popular term for this type of operation.

It's equally difficult to pinpoint just when banks moved into their next important phase, issuing their own currency and providing check services. However, England provides a good example of how it probably happened in most other locations.

In England, the goldsmiths had evolved into bankers of sorts when they began providing safekeeping services for people's money. It was not an unusual move, since the goldsmiths already had the strongrooms and guards to protect their valuables. However, the goldsmiths were confronted with a different problem—their apprentices, who at times borrowed small amounts from the unknowing goldsmiths and loaned it out for short periods for a little interest.

Of course, the goldsmiths tried to stop the practice, but they weren't always successful. After a time, they apparently adopted the philosophy of "If you can't beat them, join them," and began lending gold left with them for safekeeping. Depositors didn't mind, as long as they could get their gold. At some point, they, too, saw an opportunity for profit and began asking for a fee for allowing this practice.

The goldsmiths eventually began another practice—paying out amounts to third parties at the request of their customers. From that point it was a short jump to the practice of paying out to third parties on the customer's written request. Then, too, customers began using the receipts for the gold and silver on deposit at the goldsmith's to pay their bills, simply by writing instructions to the goldsmith on the back of the receipt. This was the beginning of our present-day system of checks.

Not long afterward, in the 1600s, banks took the next logical step—from checks to issuing their own notes. In all probability the reasoning went something like this: *If our customers can use their receipts for precious metal to pay their bills, why can't we do the same by using receipts for our own gold to make payments?*

It wasn't a great leap to the step after that: *If we can use these receipts to pay bills, and other people are doing the same, why not give customers these receipts instead of precious metals when we lend them money? They can use the receipts the same as money, and we get to keep the gold on hand.*

Thus began the practice of banks issuing their own "paper" money, something that would last until the late 1800s. It also began the practice of banks holding reserves. The reserves of gold and silver would be used to meet customer demands to exchange paper money for metal. Banks would continue to hold reserves for both conversion and "safety" reasons until roughly the middle of this century.

American Banking from the Revolutionary War Until Today. Banking has always played a central role in

this nation's political and economic history. At several points, money and banking issues became the most pressing public policy questions of the day.

Before American independence, modern banking simply did not exist in the colonies. Strict laws limited the amount of coins that could enter the colonies, and the need to import many of the necessities of daily life kept draining off what little coinage or precious metal was available. Faced with this shortage of hard cash, the colonists ran their economy by exchanging goods, a process known as "barter."

But the demand for money was so great that in 1690 Massachusetts issued its own paper money. The other colonies soon followed suit. Land banks also were established in several colonies. A group of farmers and merchants would gather together and pledge their property (inventory, land, stores, and homes) as security against paper money the bank would issue in the form of loans. Between land banks and colonial issues of paper money, the colonists managed to finance their daily lives for a while.

While the colonists found some salvation in these schemes, the British government found them a threat that undermined the authority of the crown and banished them. The paper money schemes were done away with by an order of Parliament; and in 1741 the Bubble Act, an antispeculation law, did away with the land banks.

The Revolutionary War gave new impetus to banks. The first formal bank in this country, the Pennsylvania Bank, was founded during the war to provide a means of financing the supplies needed by the Continental Army. It ceased to exist in late 1784.

Independence soon led to a banking debate that would last for the next 100 years—whether the federal government should sponsor a central bank to regulate the amount of money in the economy. Alexander Hamilton, the first secretary of the Treasury, persuaded Congress to create such an institution, the Bank of the United States, in 1781, over the vigorous objections of Thomas Jefferson and his supporters, who distrusted all banks.

The bank was chartered for 20 years. It was a private corporation. It issued its own notes backed by its holdings of silver and gold. It also held the government's deposits and helped market its securities. But it had another important, but indirect, economic function to perform: limiting the amount of paper money that *state-chartered* banks could issue.

Its opponents, who believed the bank had too much power over the nation's economy, succeeded in blocking its recharter, and it was allowed to close in 1811. During the War of 1812, however, the state-chartered banks couldn't manage the money supply effectively or help provide the financial support the government needed to fight the war, so in 1816 the pro-bank forces managed to get Congress to authorize a new bank.

If the first bank had raised a storm of controversy, the second bank raised even more furor. The nature of that controversy went right to the roots of democracy and involved far more than just the establishment of a financial institution.

An examination of the opposition to the second Bank of the United States has to begin with the population's attitude toward banks and paper money. The early Americans' experience with colonial paper money and, later, with the continentals issued by the Revolutionary Congress left them with a strong distrust of anything short of gold or silver. Many people who had accepted paper money during the Revolution lost out, and they were reluctant to fall into the trap again.

On top of that problem, there were also the regional differences that existed among the North, an increasingly industrialized area; the South, which was largely rural and agricultural; and the West, which was still largely unexplored but full of potential that attracted the more adventurous and speculative-minded citizens. All three regions were in need of the funds a bank could lend; however, they were not all of the same mind about investing in such a bank or about the possible lending policies the bank might adopt.

For example, the northeasterners and the westerners stood to benefit if the bank's lending policies were liberal. Southerners could also have benefited from loans, but saw little need for borrowing beyond what they were already getting from their own state banks. The South also saw the bank in terms of the government establishing an institution in which fortunes would be made through investments in the bank's shares. The southerners, whose borrowings and investments in land left them with little cash to buy bank shares, were angered by the idea that the northeasterners, who were generally better able to make such an investment, would benefit where they could not.

If you carry this viewpoint to its philosophical roots, the real nature of the argument comes down to the eternal and universal struggle between the *haves* and the *have nots.* On the one side you have those who have the money to invest, and on the other side those who don't and, by lack of opportunity, lose. You also have a situation in which the *haves,* by virtue of their ability to borrow, stand to gain, and the *have nots,* by their inability to borrow, stand to lose.

But above all there was the overwhelming argument that the bank, by the nature of its charter, would represent an overly powerful institution that could easily dominate the nation's financial structure and its economy. The key to this power lay in the bank's proposed ability to redeem its own notes in silver or gold. This is a major concept in understanding the opposition to the bank.

Let's start at the bottom. The bank's capitalization, about $35 million, made it the largest bank and corporation in the nation. It could issue virtually as much paper money as it wished, and these notes could be obtained by presenting either specie (gold or silver in bullion or coin form) or by presenting the notes of a state-chartered bank. The bank's notes were also redeemable in gold or silver on demand.

Looked at in skeleton form, the bank doesn't seem so menacing. But if you think in personal terms, the dangers become a bit more apparent. Suppose you wanted to go to Kentucky to buy some land. The state bank notes you held didn't travel very well in those days because they were sometimes discounted—accepted at less than face value at distant banks. So you would naturally go to the office of the Bank of the United States, the nation's largest bank, and exchange your state notes for Bank of the United States notes, which were acceptable virtually everywhere. The Bank of the United States could either hold your notes in its vaults or return them to your state bank and redeem them for silver or gold. State banks were also required, in most cases more by common sense than law, to hold enough specie to redeem notes presented daily.

As long as everything was going smoothly, the system worked well. However, when public confidence was shaken, the system faltered. If you became really panicked about the future of the economy, you would naturally present even your Bank of the U.S. notes and redeem them in specie. The Bank of the U.S., experiencing pressures on its specie reserves, would be forced to replenish them by cashing in state bank notes.

In a panic, state banks would also be experiencing pressure on their specie reserves and would be forced to begin calling in some or all of their loans in order to stay afloat. But in all likelihood—and as in fact often happened—borrowers wouldn't be able to pay off all or even part of their loans, particularly not in specie when it was in high demand. Usually, the state bank would be forced to close, wiping out its depositors and forcing its borrowers into bankruptcy.

The bank's structure also held the potential for intentional or unintentional abuses. Let's look at an example of the kind of power the bank had, and how it created its most forceful and powerful opponent.

The Second Bank of the United States was granted its charter in 1816. In 1819 its conservative policy in regard to redeeming state notes led to the downfall of a number of banks. Among them were several in the home state of Andrew Jackson. The pressure on the state banks and the subsequent pressure on Mr. Jackson caused him to lose a lot of money. His native suspicion of banks and paper money was reinforced.

Jackson became a lifelong foe of the Bank of the United States. The full story of his opposition to the bank is far too long and complex to go into here, but it is an exciting story and well worth pursuing through the history books. The battle between Jackson and the bank had all the elements of a major drama, with major personalities; political maneuvering; the bank alternately expanding and contracting the money supply; inflation; and, finally, panic. It's enough to say here that the bank's charter wasn't renewed, and it closed in 1836.

Prior to its closing, however, the bank followed a loose money policy that was sufficient to touch off a soaring speculative binge. But, like all speculative binges, the upward move in the economy had increasingly weaker underpinnings, and, finally, a crop failure that left farmers unable to repay merchants who extended credit, and left merchants without funds to repay their bank loans, brought the whole structure crashing down. The panic resulted in higher prices that cut off supplies of food and fuel to the poor. Starvation and turmoil spread. As the panic extended, depression set in and left the nation in chaos.

Although Americans had some bitter experiences with banks, it didn't mean banks were killed off. In the years preceding the Civil War, banks continued to operate. Some were very well run and gained the trust of their depositors and borrowers. However, not all banks were well run, or honest, for that matter. Although some states had already begun taking an activist role in terms of bank legislation, others had not. In some states, banks were allowed to operate with no restrictions at all. Of course, there were honest bankers in these states, trying to establish a legitimate business. But there were also a lot of sharp operators.

Some of these sharpies would grandiosely advertise the "vast" reserves they had backing their notes, even going as far as displaying large barrels of gold and silver coins in their front windows. Inches below those gold and silver coins, however, just low enough to avoid the keenest-eyed customer, the barrel was filled with nails or horseshoes. The banker's goal was to get customers to deposit their specie or exchange it for paper notes. The banker would be around for as long as it took him to collect what he felt he could get away with, and then he would disappear. The townspeople would be left with just paper souvenirs of the misplaced trust.

Other unscrupulous operators would open banks in remote wilderness areas, issue notes with no backing at all, and then exchange them for specie or valuables in a town some distance away. These "bankers" counted on the fact that the bank was so remote that no one would go there to change their paper notes into specie, at least not too soon. Because they located

their banks in areas so far into the wilderness that only the wildcats roamed there, they were called "wildcat bankers."

As it settled so much else, the Civil War was to settle the question of whether the federal government would have a measure of control over the banking system. When the war began, a number of problems with our money and banking system became apparent. One of the first of these was the need for a uniform currency. At that point the nation was beleaguered by a bewildering variety of state bank notes, some of which were widely acceptable but most of which were only acceptable in a very limited area.

One example of this limited acceptability can be found in the story of a rural farmer who, at one point during the war, came to Boston to make a major purchase. When the farmer presented his local bank notes, he aroused the suspicion of both the merchant and a surrounding crowd. The people thought the farmer was trying to swindle the merchant, and they began beating him before he could explain.

Another example can be found in the fact that, for a large part of the Civil War, coinage had disappeared. The coins, particularly the gold and silver, were being hoarded because they had become more valuable as metal than as coinage. Since issuing more coins would have led to more hoarding, the government did nothing, and the people gradually began using postage stamps as a substitute.

At the same time, the government was faced with the problem of paying its bills with specie while its supply of gold and silver was dwindling. At first the government issued "greenbacks," the first government-issued paper money since the Revolutionary War. The currency was issued by "fiat," meaning it was simply declared to be money.

The government's attempts to attract new specie to the Treasury were thwarted by an understandable reluctance to invest in government securities when there was no certainty the government would continue to exist—especially when the South was so strong at the beginning of the war. So a solution was needed that would provide a stronger banking system and also help the Treasury raise funds.

Fortunately, Treasury Secretary Salmon Chase saw the two problems as one and came up with the idea of the National Banking Act. The legislation provided for a new type of bank, a national bank, which would be chartered by the federal government. To become a national bank, a bank would have to have $50,000 in capital. Its reserve would be made up of government securities as well as cash.

In addition to giving them a government charter, the new banking act would allow the national banks to issue their own notes, a new uniform currency that would be used nationwide, in proportion to their holdings of government securities. As an added attraction, these new notes would be acceptable for payments on taxes or government loans or import duties. They would also be accepted at their full value by all other national banks.

Still, the bankers were reluctant, so Congress taxed state-bank-issued paper money and raised the tax in a series of steps until it became prohibitively expensive to issue paper money. State-issued bank notes disappeared and the number of federally chartered banks rose dramatically. The number of state-chartered banks declined for a time but then rose again as state legislatures enacted laws to encourage state-chartered banks. Thus, the U.S. has a "dual" system of state and federally chartered banks that is unique throughout the world.

This didn't mean that banking or the United States' financial system had smooth sailing. It was just the opposite, in fact: The nation suffered through a series of banking panics that created both chaos and suffering. The worst and last of these panics occurred in 1907, and while it didn't create a depression, as so many others had, largely because it occurred during a period of high prosperity, it did cause the failure of many banks and, for a time, the almost complete disappearance of money from circulation. Because the panic inspired hoarding of cash, there was such a shortage even of coinage that stores had to give out IOU's in lieu of change and even payrolls were delayed.

Convinced that something had to be done once and for all, Congress launched a detailed investigation into the causes of the panic, and began to find some interesting things.

First of all, they found that the banks had a practice of shipping their reserves to major money centers, such as New York and Chicago, where they could earn a return on them. A bank in Omaha, for example, might ship a large portion of its reserves to an institution such as the Knickerbocker Trust Company in New York City. The Knickerbocker Trust, a real institution of the time, would in turn lend these reserves out so they could earn a return, and, as long as there were no heavy withdrawals, both institutions could do very well for themselves.

However, as happened in the fall of 1907, demands for ready cash piled up in the banks of the Midwest. These banks wired the Knickerbocker Trust for their funds, and in the beginning some probably received them. But as the demands grew heavier, the Knickerbocker Trust's reserves were quickly drained. The bank tried to call in some of its loans, but generally without success since most of the loans were to businesses that used the funds for things like inventory

and expansion. The Knickerbocker Trust found itself in a bind. It wasn't broke, but it couldn't liquidate its assets quickly enough to meet the demands of the banks that wanted ready cash.

Finally the inevitable day came when a customer who wanted to withdraw cash had to be refused. Considering the era the nation had already gone through, it probably didn't take long for the word to get around, and soon a long line formed in front of the Knickerbocker Trust. The line, of course, attracted even more nervous customers, and soon a "run" was on. In short order, the Knickerbocker Trust had to close its doors, and then the panic really began. The banks that had their funds at the New York institution began running short of cash, and they also began experiencing "runs." People who had ready cash became very reluctant to part with it, and this only worsened conditions.

At this point, you can probably already guess two of the other major problems that Congress's investigation turned up. The first was that the practice of depositing reserves in other banks was highly dangerous. Should one or more of these "reserve-holding" banks experience trouble, the problem had the potential to spread.

The second problem was that when banks did experience runs, they had no place to turn. In fact, their attempts to call in loans only tended to aggravate an already difficult situation. It didn't take Congress long to realize that unless banks had a "lender of last resort" to turn to in times of trouble, financial panics would probably continue to occur.

After long and often heated debate, Congress finally approved a plan to avert another 1907-type panic. In 1913 it established the FEDERAL RESERVE SYSTEM, the nation's first central bank. The Federal Reserve system was designed to provide money that would expand and contract with the nation's money needs and to provide the much needed "lender of last resort."

Under the Federal Reserve Act of 1913, all of the nation's federally chartered banks would be required to join. State banks would join at their option. The act divided the nation into 12 Federal Reserve districts, each of which would have its own Federal Reserve bank. These banks would issue Federal Reserve notes in tune with the needs of the economy. They would work just as our checking accounts work today: When we have too much cash, we can deposit it into our checking account; when we have too little, we can withdraw. So, too, banks belonging to the Federal Reserve System would be able to deposit their reserves, usually in the form of excess cash, into their accounts at the Federal Reserve. This would provide a safe place for the reserves and at the same time permit excess cash to be withdrawn from the economy.

Banks would also be given the privilege of borrowing from the Federal Reserve banks when their reserves were under pressure. The act established requirements on the amount of reserves that banks would have to hold: stringent requirements to provide protection in times of trouble; easier requirements when the problem had passed.

But the nation's banks weren't completely safe yet. The stock-market crash of 1929 and the depression and bank failures of the 1930s would uncover still more flaws in the nation's financial system.

The years following World War I were boom times for America. The growth that began with the nation's entrance into the war continued and picked up pace. With most of Europe in rubble, the demand for U.S. farm products brought prosperity to even the most rural areas of the country. Demand for manufactured goods also was high, due not only to exports but also to expanded spendable income on the domestic scene. With the increase in manufactured goods, the demand for industrial goods moved upward. Credit also was easier than in the past, and consumer credit purchases were on the rise.

All things considered, America was in fine shape entering the 1920s. However, under the surface, problems were brewing.

Economists still debate the causes of the Great Depression that followed the 1929 stock-market crash. None cites any one specific cause, but they do cite several major contributing factors. Lets look at some.

In 1920, demand for American farm products was already beginning to soften, and farmers and merchants in rural areas of the country had difficulty in the fall of that year meeting their obligations. As a result, hundreds of banks failed. Later analysis of these bank failures showed that many of the nation's banks were undercapitalized and overextended. Some economists cite the rapid expansion of banks, particularly branch banking during the war years, as a contributing factor. These failures, as early as then, might have served as a warning of things to come. However, the warning went ignored, despite a depression in 1920.

The boom soon reasserted itself and the good times continued to roar. Worker productivity increased; wages, sales, and profits continued upward; and prosperity forever seemed certain. The brilliance of the economic outlook, of course, was reflected in the securities markets and in bankers' decisions on loans. The stock market soared, reaching one new height after another. Pursuing this market were hundreds of thousands of speculators who saw rising securities prices as the path to easy wealth. The path was made easier by their ability to purchase common stock on a 10% margin—meaning they only had to put 10%

down in cash and the remaining 90% was loaned on "margin," a form of credit used to purchase securities.

Let's look at a summary of some of the other factors that contributed to the depression.

- Demand for consumer goods came largely from the wealthy and the well-to-do, a group whose income derived largely from returns on investment in the form of rent, capital gains, interest, and dividends. With so much of consumer buying resting on this base, anything that tended to damp this group's income would damp overall purchases. Some economists also note that this market may have reached the saturation point and couldn't support any more buying.
- Foreign demand for American manufactured goods was also softening.
- Domestic demand in 1929 had already shown some signs of softening, but manufacturers either failed to spot the trend or ignored it in the general glow of prosperity. They continued to produce at the same pace, and inventories began to accumulate.
- America's corporate structure also had its problems. A variety of trusts and holding companies existed in which the dividends from the securities of one component were used to pay the dividends or interest on the securities of the others. One slip in projected earnings and ability to pay dividends or interest could topple the rest of the corporate structure.

All of these accumulated problems seemed to be waiting just beneath the surface for one event to coalesce them into a major disaster. The break came on October 29, 1929, when securities values fell sharply. As prices descended through one level after another, margin calls were triggered. Brokers put in frantic calls to customers, demanding either more cash to support the securities position or a sell order. Often the customers were warned that at the rate prices were falling, they could be sold out well before the cash could be presented.

Sales executed to cover margin positions put additional pressure on prices and tended to swell the downward move. Since many customers had purchased securities with only the bare minimum margin, they had little hope of supporting their position, and soon watched their dream of wealth disappear as the ticker tape announced the penetration of their margin-call level.

In the end, billions of dollars of values were wiped out; and millions of people, who the day before had looked forward to wealth, now faced poverty or, at best, mere survival. Securities used as collateral for loans became worthless overnight, and banks were left holding paper as an asset. As personal fortunes were wiped out, so, too, were the fortunes of some businesses whose futures were either directly or indirectly tied to those of the stock market.

Some banks, of course, were almost immediately affected, and, as with a stone cast into a pond, the initial ripple spread outward. As businesses failed, jobs were lost, income fell, people turned to banks to get their savings to live on, and some banks were overrun. By 1930, lost incomes, topped by already heavy inventories, forced more business closings and income losses.

While Congress and business debated what to do, bank and business failures continued. Some states were forced to declare "bank holidays," simply closing the banks to prevent runs from collapsing another institution and, in turn, causing the potential collapse of still others.

The pressure grew as the depression worsened and people's faith in their institutions deteriorated. In March of 1933, the situation had become so severe that the newly inaugurated president Franklin Roosevelt and an anxious Congress extended the bank holidays declared in many states. The goal of the closings was to allow time for federal and state examiners to determine the soundness of the institutions and to reopen those that had a chance of survival. The administration also hoped that by keeping people from overrunning banks for a while, some confidence could be restored and anxieties cooled.

The panic was indeed stemmed, and the situation gradually calmed. However, the depression was a long way from over, and the flaws uncovered in the banking system still had to be dealt with. In 1933 and again in 1935, Congress passed legislation aimed at strengthening both the banking system and the public's confidence in it. Among the most important moves was the establishment of deposit insurance, the elimination of the practice of allowing national banks to issue their own notes, and the prohibition against stock-market dealings by depository institutions.

During the late 1960s and throughout the 1970s, Federal Reserve member banks found the non-interest-bearing reserves they were required to hold too costly. State charters in many cases permitted banks to hold reserves in the form of interest-earning government securities, which were far more attractive. As a result, member banks began leaving the system to become state-chartered banks. As the system lost members, it lost control over increasingly larger amount of reserves, something the system saw as a threat to its ability to control the nation's money supply and, therefore, the economy.

In 1980 Congress passed the Monetary Control Act. Among the provisions of the act was a requirement that virtually all depository institutions, including state-chartered banks, be required to hold reserves at a Federal Reserve bank. The act also gave nonmember institutions access to Federal Reserve services, which were to be priced; provided for a gradual leveling of the differential between member and nonmember reserve requirements; and allowed nonmember banks access to the Fed's temporary loans to cover reserve-requirement deficiencies.

The act also granted thrift institutions the right to open Negotiable Order of Withdrawal (NOW) accounts, interest-bearing checking account–like service previously prohibited in most states; and permitted thrifts to compete in areas once previously handled only by commercial banks. However, the act further eliminated the interest-rate differential that had once helped thrifts attract more savings deposits than did commercial banks.

In all, the provisions of the Monetary Control Act tended to level out the differences that once existed between banks, in exchange for a strengthening of the Fed's powers. Just how this compromise will finally affect our banking system remains to be seen.

See also GARN–ST GERMAIN DEPOSITORY INSTITUTION DEREGULATION ACT OF 1982.

Charles J. Parnow

Banks for Cooperatives
See FARM CREDIT SYSTEM.

Bear Market

A period during which securities prices generally follow a downward trend. The term may be used to describe either a historical period of price declines or an anticipated decline in prices. While there may be some brief periods of price increases during a bear market, securities prices in general will decrease substantially for a period of several months or years.

The most significant bear market in the United States was the almost three-year decline in stock prices between 1929 and 1932. During this period the Dow Jones industrial average declined by almost 90%. Although bear markets since World War II have been significantly less severe, substantial declines of 20% or more are not uncommon. For example, between January 1973 and October 1974 both the Dow Jones industrial average and the New York Stock Exchange Composite Index declined by approximately 50%. Other recent declines in excess of 20% occurred between February and October 1966, during a two-and-one-half-year period between 1970 and 1973, and again between November 1980 and August 1982.

A "bear" (or one who is "bearish") is an investor who expects securities prices in general to decline during some future time period. An investor may also be a bear regarding the prospects for one particular security or for a group of securities, while not necessarily maintaining this opinion toward the stock market as a whole.

Although the term *bear market* is frequently applied to stock-market prices, it is also used to describe trends in the markets for other investment instruments, such as bonds and commodities.

See BULL MARKET.

R. Bruce Swensen

Better Business Bureau (BBB) System

The facilities of the nation's 150-plus Better Business Bureaus are available to the public at large. When you need factual information before making an important purchase, when you have a specific question or a complaint about a business or service, all you have to do is get in touch with your local Better Business Bureau.

BBB services are free. There are no charges, no strings attached. The business community supports the Better Business Bureau, which in turn provides consumers with the free service.

Millions of inquiries and complaints are received annually by all the BBB's combined. The more calls, the better, because it means so many more informed consumers who can expect and get their money's worth. The aims of the Better Business Bureaus are threefold:

• to protect the buying power of the consumer;
• to encourage honesty in business; and
• to inform the public on how to do business so the consumer can buy intelligently and gain maximum satisfaction.

The BBB helps you directly by
1. providing information about a company before you do business with it;
2. helping to resolve a complaint you might have against a firm, including a final step of arbitration in most areas;
3. providing you with good consumer information so you can make intelligent buying decisions; and
4. providing information on charitable organizations.

What the BBB Does Not Do. It does not give legal advice. It cannot help to breach or void contracts made without fraud or misrepresentation. It does not make collections of any kind, nor does it provide credit information. It does not act as a reference or give recommendations or endorsements. It does not appraise articles, pass judgment on prices charged for merchandise, or on quality of services or workman-

ship, or efficiency of operation of devices, or how long merchandise should wear or last.

Bureaus are private, self-regulatory agencies that seek the voluntary cooperation of business. When illegal practices are uncovered and the business refuses to cooperate with the bureaus, the matter is referred to an appropriate law-enforcement agency.

The Council of Better Business Bureaus. The CBBB was formed in 1970 by consolidating the former National Better Business Bureau and the Association of Better Business Bureaus International. The CBBB has a dual mission: to be an effective national self-regulatory force for business, and to demonstrate an active concern for consumers.

The CBBB's headquarters in Arlington, Virginia, coordinates the activities of member BBB's, issues advertising standards on the national level, administers the BBB arbitration program, disseminates information about charitable solicitations, and performs consumer-education and public-information functions. The CBBB's National Advertising Division (in New York) monitors and investigates complaints against national advertising.

William H. Tankersley

Big Board

See NEW YORK STOCK EXCHANGE (NYSE).

Block Trading

See COMMON STOCK.

Blue Chip

Refers to (1) the stock of a nationally known company that sells at a relatively high price because of the company's sound reputation and long record of earnings and paying dividends (also called a "blue-chip stock"); or (2) the company itself. The term comes from gambling, where blue chips are customarily accorded the highest value in casinos.

See COMMON STOCK.

Harvey Rachlin

Blue Cross and Blue Shield

The Blue Cross and Blue Shield organization is a nationwide network consisting of 68 Blue Cross Plans and 69 Blue Shield Plans. The Blue Cross Plans are nonprofit community-service organizations that contract with hospitals to provide services to Plan subscribers and their dependents, paid for by the Plans from membership fees paid in advance by the subscribers, or often by their employers. Blue Shield Plans are nonprofit community-service organizations that contract with physicians to provide medical services to Plan members, also from prepaid membership fees.

The Blue Cross and Blue Shield Plans are organized, managed, and financed locally, so the hospital and medical benefits they provide conform to local community hospital and medical practices and may thus vary somewhat from Plan to Plan. But a Plan member or dependent who is away from home can get whatever services his or her Plan membership provides, paid for by the Plans through an inter-Plan network arrangement.

Blue Cross and Blue Shield Plans are generally considered to be providing HEALTH INSURANCE, but they are different from health-insurance companies in two important respects. First, the Plans are nonprofit organizations, and they are regulated by state insurance departments, in some ways even more rigorously than the profit-making insurance companies are. The second, more important difference is that the insurance companies for the most part reimburse or indemnify their policyholders for the expenses of hospital and medical care, whereas Blue Cross and Blue Shield Plans usually pay hospitals and doctors directly. Plan members don't pay for the services their contracts include, though of course they must pay for services not included.

With so many Blue Cross and Blue Shield Plans, each offering several kinds of contracts for services that vary in accordance with community practices and the needs and wishes of the group, it is possible to make only a few general observations about what the Plans provide. Most often, Blue Cross Plans pay for a specified number of hospital days per contract year (120 days is a common figure), including semiprivate (two bed) room and general nursing service, medications, diagnostic services such as X-ray and laboratory, and special services such as operating room and intensive care. Blue Cross members should find out what their own Plans and their own contracts include, because they will be expected to pay for services that are not included.

They should also know what their Blue Shield Plan pays for: whether it is combined with the Blue Cross Plan in a single organization offering a single contract, as some are; or whether the Plans and contracts are separate, as is often the case. Either way, Plan members should know just what doctors' services are paid for, up to what limits. So-called surgical-medical coverage may include surgeons' fees, hospital visits, and the services of hospital anesthesiologists and other consultants who may be called in; "general medical service" contracts include office and home care. But there may be limits on these, leaving amounts the patient is expected to pay, and in some cases Blue Shield contracts call for payments to be made directly to the Plan member, who makes his own arrangement with the physicians.

Most Blue Cross and Blue Shield subscribers are enrolled in groups at their places of employment, and usually the employer pays all or part of the employee's subscription fee; in large corporations, this is commonly among the benefits negotiated in collective bargaining agreements. The corporation and the Plan may negotiate what the employer pays for the group as a whole, so there is no subscription fee or premium as such for the individual employee and his or her family. In smaller companies, employees themselves may pay for their families and for part of their own subscriptions, and have these costs deducted from their paychecks. The costs vary in different sections of the country, and from community to community in each region, and of course cost varies also according to the specific Plan coverage that is provided.

Enrollment in groups is an important means of spreading the risk to the insurer. Nobody knows when John Smith or a member of his family may become ill and require medical or hospital care, but the number of cases of illness in any year among a group of 1,000 employees and family members may be predicted with reasonable accuracy, and the cost of insuring against the expense of care can be estimated accordingly. Thus, the enrollment of individuals and small groups ("small" usually meaning 50 or fewer), who pay for their own subscriptions, is restricted to a specified period of a few days each year, and the rate charged is considerably higher than for large groups. The purpose of this is to protect against the likelihood that younger, healthy people may tend not to enroll, whereas those who are older and anticipate illness surely will. This "adverse selection," as it is called, results in individual membership rates as high as $90 a month for a single person and $200 or more for a family for Blue Cross and Blue Shield combined. In most areas, however, Blue Cross (hospital) and Blue Shield (medical) Plans, enrollments, and rates are separate rather than combined; prices vary by area and type of contract, but the cost for hospital coverage is usually several times the cost of the medical plan.

In 1983, Blue Cross and Blue Shield Plans were protecting more than 80 million members from the expenses of hospital and medical care. In addition, the Plans are the principal contractors administering the federal government's Medicare program for persons over age 65 and the Medicaid programs providing federal and state support of medical services for the poor and near-poor. Also, 1.6 million employees of the federal government and their families are enrolled in Blue Cross and Blue Shield Plans—for a total Blue Cross and Blue Shield constituency of more than 100 million. For all the subscribers and dependents in both the public and private programs, the Blue Cross and Blue Shield system paid a total of more than $60 billion for hospital and medical care in 1982, at a total cost for Plan operations of only $5 billion, or 7% of Plan revenues.

How did the Blue Cross and Blue Shield organization get to be larger than all but one or two of the nation's great corporations?

The first group hospitalization plan was organized in Dallas, Texas, in 1929, when Dr. Justin Ford Kimball, then vice-president of Baylor University, invited teachers in the Dallas public school system to contribute to a "prepayment fund" that would pay for the teachers' care at Baylor University Hospital. By the end of that year, 1,000 teachers had joined and were paying 50 cents a month to the fund. Hospital care at the time cost only $5 or $6 a day; and unlike today's patients, people in those days didn't go to the hospital unless they were seriously ill or had to have an operation. So the fund prospered, patients didn't have to worry about the cost, and the hospital didn't have to worry about collecting from patients who were hard up in the growing depression. Hospital people elsewhere heard about the idea, and soon similar group plans were under way in communities in California, New Jersey, New York, Minnesota, and Maryland— but with an important difference: What had been a one-group/one-hospital scheme at Baylor became multigroup/multihospital plans in the new communities, and soon the organizers were out soliciting employers to make it possible for their employees to join. The organizer in Minneapolis, Minnesota, introduced the idea of identifying the plan there with a blue cross; it caught on and was quickly adopted elsewhere.

At the time the Blue Cross Plans were getting started, county medical societies in the state of Washington were organized in "medical service bureaus" contracting with employers to care for employees in some of the mining, logging, and railroad communities of the Northwest. The idea was picked up by medical societies in California, Michigan, and Pennsylvania, and the concept of linking the medical society and group hospitalization or Blue Cross Plans bore fruit in 1939 with the first joint offering of a hospital-surgical plan to employees of the Ford Motor Company in Michigan. Details of services and rates were worked out with the assistance of the United Auto Workers, and the Michigan program became the pattern for health-insurance coverage for workers in many of the nation's major industries. To identify their separate status and still take advantage of their linkage with the Blue Cross Plans, the medical service plans started calling themselves Blue Shield Plans.

The separate status of Blue Cross and Blue Shield Plans still prevails in some communities, but in most places the linkage today is much stronger than it was in the beginning. In many cases, especially in the larger cities, the Blue Cross and Blue Shield Plans have merged into single corporations; in some places there are two corporations with separate boards of directors but with single executive and management staffs. In 1982 the national associations of Blue Cross and Blue Shield Plans, which had separate governing boards but a single executive and management staff, completed consolidation into the single Blue Cross and Blue Shield Association. The association is an information resource for the Plans, coordinates the administration of Medicare and large corporation groups having employees in many Plans throughout the country, and operates inter-Plan financial, claims, and information systems. Another important function of the association is monitoring Plan performance. Plans must conform to high standards having to do with governing structure, management, financial stability, and operating policies in order to continue their memberships in the association and their identity with Blue Cross and Blue Shield.

As just about everybody knows, the costs of hospital and medical care have been rising steeply for a number of years, and consequently the rates paid to doctors and hospitals by Blue Cross and Blue Shield Plans for service to Plan subscribers, and the rates charged for Plan membership, have had to rise with the costs. The reasons for the increases are complex and interrelated. The inflation in the national economy is foremost among them, but almost as important as inflation is the rapid introduction of new medical knowledge and the accompanying development of new medical technology. Hospitals, especially, are constantly adding new machines and equipment for diagnosing and treating illness, and the machines require highly skilled men and women whose salaries add to the upward cost spiral. Finally, the cost of hospital and medical care has increased because people visit doctors' offices and hospitals more often, and use more services, than was commonly done in the past. To some extent, the increase in utilization of services takes place because the new knowledge is there; there are more things to do because more is known about diseases and how to treat them. But to some extent more service is provided because Blue Cross and Blue Shield Plans, and insurance companies, pay most of the bills; the financial barriers to care have been largely removed.

The Blue Cross and Blue Shield organization is engaged in the effort to control costs, and in fact cost-containment programs are now a membership standard the Plans must meet to fulfill Blue Cross and Blue Shield Association requirements. There are many elements in the Plan programs. All the Blue Cross Plans, for example, have introduced new benefits, in addition to the standard benefit providing full payment for a specified number of days in a semiprivate hospital room and for required in-hospital services such as X-ray and laboratory examinations, operating-room and recovery-room fees, and special-treatment fees. The added benefits are designed to encourage subscribers and their physicians to seek care at the least expensive levels consistent with appropriate treatment. For instance, some services that the Plans paid for in the past only if the patient was admitted to a hospital are now paid for when the service is provided in a doctor's office or a hospital's outpatient department or emergency room. Some of the Blue Shield Plans now offer doctors incentives for performing operations in their offices or in ambulatory surgery units when the procedure is one for which hospitalization is considered unnecessary. These new outpatient benefits save all the costs of hospital rooms, meals, and nursing services. Moreover, the patient is fully safeguarded, and many doctors agree that recovery is speeded for the patient who resumes normal activity as soon as possible following surgery.

Another system of controls initiated by the Blue Cross and Blue Shield Association aims at limiting the use of services that are judged inappropriate and inefficient. This Medical Necessity Program was developed with the cooperation and assistance of leading medical specialty societies: it identified some services that were being performed routinely for all hospital patients but in many cases were not actually needed, some that were judged to be obsolete or ineffective, and some that were appropriate only under certain specified conditions. In each case, rules and guidelines were developed and issued to the Plans with the recommendation that payment for the services be limited as indicated. Substantial cost savings have resulted, and another effect has been to raise the level of cost-consciousness of physicians, hospitals, and Blue Cross–Blue Shield subscribers.

Still another series of experiments Blue Cross Plans have undertaken to save money and keep costs down has to do with the method of paying hospitals. The Plans have always negotiated special payment rates that recognize Blue Cross contributions to hospital financial stability, such as assured volumes of business, prompt payment, and elimination of losses on bad debts. Still, once the rates were agreed on, with pay-ment assured, the hospitals had no strong incentive to operate efficiently. So Plans have recently introduced methods that include such incentives, offering special awards for efficiency and productivity as measured by cost comparisons among hospitals, for example, or making payment on a per-case basis at "target" rates, with the hospital retaining what it can earn by keeping costs below the target, but losing when costs exceed it.

Many of the Plans are also offering employers and employees the opportunity to choose a new method of receiving and paying for medical and hospital services, the HEALTH-MAINTENANCE ORGANIZATION (HMO). Members of an HMO pay a fixed rate—usually about the same as the rate for Blue Cross and Blue Shield membership—that entitles them to all the medical and hospital services they may need, without limitation, as long as the services are provided by the HMO's designated doctors and hospitals. For a fixed annual fee per member (called a "capitation fee"), the HMO doctors and hospitals agree to provide all the services demanded by all the HMO members. Thus the doctors have incentives to treat HMO patients at the lowest possible cost, which means keeping them out of the hospital if care can be managed on an outpatient basis. As of 1983, Blue Cross and Blue Shield Plans operated 79 of nearly 300 HMO's available.

Another new form linking the delivery and financing of health-care services is selective contracting, or the preferred provider organization (PPO), which may be a Blue Cross or Blue Shield Plan, an insurance company, a group of hospitals or physicians, or an employer or employee group. In this method, the plan or PPO contracts with a hospital or hospital group and physician group to provide services for an agreed price, generally 10% to 20% less than the prevailing price for the same services. The hospitals and doctors offer the discount in consideration of the assured volume of services, the employer's or employees' premiums or fees are reduced accordingly, and the employees and families either are restricted to using the selected doctors and hospitals or may use others of their own choosing but pay for all or part of the services they receive themselves, as specified in the contract. The PPO has appealed to many employer and employee groups as a practical means of reducing the cost of their health insurance and health care; a 1983 survey reported 80 such groups either operating or in various stages of development, many of them by Blue Cross and Blue Shield Plans.

Another cost-saving activity of Blue Cross and Blue Shield Plans is their promotion of physical fitness and healthy habits of living in subscriber groups and in their communities generally. These activities of the Plans may range all the way from distributing simple health-education materials at places of employment explaining the importance of healthy diets, regular exercise, and moderation of bad health habits like smoking and drinking, to comprehensive health-promotion programs that include health assessment of employees, referral for treatment of those in need of care, and conducting classes for employees with special needs for dietary instruction, daily exercise sessions, and assistance with special problems such as stress, obesity, inability to quit smoking, and others. Even in the absence of specific data demonstrating that such programs will reduce expenditures for health insurance and health care, which may take years to prove, employers have been willing to spend substantial sums for employee health-promotion programs, convinced that the savings will be realized eventually and that meanwhile there will be returns in the form of reduced absenteeism and in many cases improved productivity, job performance, and employee morale.

How does one become a subscriber of a Blue Cross and Blue Shield Plan, and how does the Plan work when medical or hospital care is needed?

Most persons who are employed already have some form of health insurance. If your employer doesn't have any such benefit, you should talk to your fellow employees and see if you can persuade the company to make a group plan available. When this is being done, you can call the Blue Cross and Blue Shield Plan for your community and ask for information about the coverage; most Plans have some group program available to companies with as few as 25 employees, and you should be sure your employer considers Blue Cross and Blue Shield when a plan is being selected. If your group is too small or you are not employed, ask a Blue Cross or Blue Shield representative about the rates and benefits available for individuals, and find out when individual enrollment will be offered. If your company already has health insurance other than Blue Cross and Blue Shield, find out just what expenses your policy covers in the event of illness or injury. Compare these with the Blue Cross and Blue Shield Plan's rates and coverage, and be sure your employer knows about it if a change would be advantageous for the employees.

When you are a Blue Cross or Blue Shield Plan subscriber or family member and you are ill and need care, let the hospital or doctor's office know that you are covered. They will notify the Plan; and from that point on, the Plan and the providers of the services take over and handle all the details. You will be billed only for any services you may receive that are not included in your Plan membership. If you have any questions about what these are, ask the group leader or benefit manager at your place of employment, or the doctor's or hospital's business office, or a Blue Cross or Blue Shield representative, to explain them to you—and make certain you are getting all the services you are entitled to receive without paying.

Harvey Rachlin

Board of Governors of the Federal Reserve System

See FEDERAL RESERVE SYSTEM.

Boiler and Machinery Insurance

See INSURANCE.

Bonds

The last decade has been characterized by high and volatile interest rates. While this environment affected many traditional forms of investment, perhaps the greatest changes were recorded in the bond market. At various times during this period, bonds were viewed as approaching extinction. At other times they provided returns superior to any other financial asset. The movement of interest rates is shown in Figure 1, which follows the course of U.S. Treasury bond yields from 1973 through August 1983.

The market for bonds has become increasingly complex. This once basic security has been modified with many unique features. An understanding of bond investments in the 1980s can be achieved by building from a basic definition. Expanding from this definition's components, the interacting features of bond investments can be more fully appreciated.

A simple but generally accepted definition of a bond is as follows: A bond* is a contract of indebtedness issued by a governmental unit or a corporation which promises payment of a principal amount at a specified future date plus interest.

Contract of Indebtedness. The bond investment at its most elemental stage consists of a written contract that states the rights and duties of each party (borrower and lender) to this debt transaction. In contrast to the common-stock investor, who holds an ownership position and can participate in the growth (or lack thereof) of the stock issuer, the bond investor accepts some very specific terms. In return, the bond investor enjoys a superior position with respect to right of payment.

---

* For this discussion, the word *bond* will be used generically to describe a class of securities that includes bonds and notes. Notes generally are issues with a period ranging from one to ten years between initial offering date and final principal-payment date.

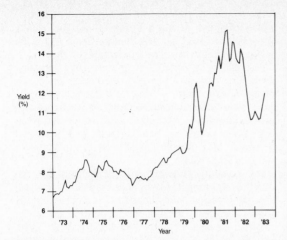

Figure 1. U.S. Treasury bond yields: a decade of volatility. (*Source:* Federal Reserve Release H.15.)

One bond type, the *convertible bond,* can provide investment characteristics of both bond and common-stock securities. The convertible bond gives the holder the right to exchange (convert) the bond for another security, usually a predetermined number of shares of common stock of the bond issuer. This type of bond may have a lower rate of interest than a bond without a conversion right (*see* CONVERTIBLE SECURITY).

Bonds have traditionally been issued as either *first-mortgage bonds* or *debentures.* First-mortgage bonds convey to the bondholder an interest in the real property of the issuer, a very secure position. The debenture, however, is secured only by the general credit of the issuer and any unpledged assets. While a first-mortgage bond may generally be viewed as more secure than a debenture, the actual importance of this distinction will depend on the issuer's overall debt burden, the amount of first-mortgage bonds versus debentures that the issuer has outstanding, and, most important, the issuer's ability to pay his debts on time.

The relative security of a bond can also be indicated by the terms *senior obligation* and *junior* or *subordinate obligation.* Senior bonds are entitled to payment of interest and principal prior to any payment on junior or subordinate bonds.

Government and Corporate Issuers. Bonds have been issued by a vast array of governmental units and corporations. A very visible issuer of bonds is the U.S. Treasury. United States TREASURY BONDS are available in maturities of from one to thirty years. (Issues sold with maturities of from one to ten years are called "notes.") These bonds are generally viewed

as being of the highest quality. U.S. Treasury bonds are fully negotiable and enjoy the most liquid market of all bonds. UNITED STATES SAVINGS BONDS are a form of investment designed for the individual investor. They are available in relatively small amounts but do not benefit from an active resale market.

Bonds are issued by several federal agencies. Some *federal-agency bonds* carry the full guarantee of the U.S. government, while others have an indirect or implied guarantee. Bonds issued in the United States by foreign governmental units and which are payable in U.S. dollars are called *Yankee bonds.*

Bonds issued by state or local governmental units are referred to as *municipal bonds.* These securities enjoy the unique feature of providing interest income that is exempt from federal income taxation. Municipal bonds are often purchased by banks, casualty-insurance companies, and higher-income individuals (*see* MUNICIPAL AND STATE SECURITIES).

Corporations of all types issue bonds. Utility companies often issue first-mortgage bonds, while industrial companies normally raise capital through debenture issues. Transportation companies finance specific equipment (e.g., airplanes or locomotives) with *collateral trust bonds.* This bond type can rely for payment not only on the general credit of the issuer but also on the specific equipment for which the bonds were issued.

Promise of Payment. An integral feature of the bond investment is the promise of a specific payment. The issuer's promise to pay must be viewed relative to his ability to pay. This ability to is usually referred to as the "credit quality" of the issuer. Most outstanding bonds have been assigned bond ratings by one or more of the RATING AGENCIES. The two most widely known rating agencies are MOODY'S INVESTORS SERVICE, INC., and STANDARD & POOR'S CORPORATION. These agencies rate bonds according to their assessment of the issuer's ability to pay. Table 1 lists the bond ratings from these two services.

The issuer's ability to pay should be reflected in the yield of the bond. Usually, an issuer with a lower level of ability to pay provides a higher yield than an issuer with higher ability. For this reason, bonds issued by corporations generally provide a higher yield than U.S. Treasury bonds. Many bonds are issued by very sound governmental units and corporations for which the probability of failure to meet the promise to pay is quite remote. The different yields of these issues are determined by the collective judgment of all bond investors as they meet as buyers or sellers in the bond market.

Principal Payment. The principal payment of a bond investment is also referred to as "par value" or "face

Table 1		
Bond Ratings		
Moody's	*Standard & Poor's*	*Investment Quality*
Aaa	AAA	Highest quality
Aa	AA	High quality
A	A	Upper-medium quality
Baa	BBB	Medium quality
Ba	BB	Various levels of
B	B	speculative quality
Caa	CCC	ranging from
Ca	CC	lowest speculation (Ba or BB) to highest speculation (Ca or CC)

Moody's assigns numerical modifiers (1, 2, 3) in the rating categories Aa through B to indicate securities ranging at the high, middle, or low range of the rating category. Standard & Poor's uses a plus ($+$) or minus ($-$) for modifying ratings in the categories AA through B to show relative standing within the category.

amount." Bonds are generally issued with the promise to pay a principal amount that is stated in multiples of $1,000. While a few examples exist of bonds with principal payments related to some index (e.g., inflation or the value of a precious metal), the majority of bonds promise a principal payment of nominal dollars in the future. Consequently, one of the risks in bond investing has been the impact of inflation on the return of a nominal principal amount.

A bond's principal payment or par value does not necessarily indicate the investor's purchase price. A bond whose purchase price equals the par value is referred to as a *par bond.* Bonds with purchase prices below par value are called *discount bonds;* those with prices above par value are *premium bonds.* Any bond with a purchase price other than par value has a component of yield in addition to interest payments, which the investor must measure in choosing among different bonds.

Specific Payment Dates. A simple but very important feature of the bond investment is the specified future date of principal payment. The period from purchase date to final principal-payment date is referred to as "term to maturity." Bonds are available in maturities ranging from one to forty years. The bond's term to maturity is important in many ways. Often the investor may be selecting a maturity date to match the date of a very specific future need (e.g.,

college tuition or retirement). The maturity of a bond is also important in that it will determine the relative importance of the final principal payment versus the payments of interest. The interaction of these variables is shown in Table 2. The maturity of a bond can also affect the degree to which the bond's price may change prior to maturity, due to a change in interest rates. This interaction of potential price change and term to maturity is relevant to the investor who wishes or needs to sell his bond prior to final maturity. Generally, the potential for price change increases as maturity lengthens.

The bond investment may have features that can alter the term to maturity by actions of either the issuer or the investor. Many bonds have call or refunding provisions giving the issuer the right to make the principal payment and retire the bond prior to maturity. While the issuer is often required to pay some amount in excess of par value for this right, the bond investor should be aware of this right as it could disrupt an investment program at an inopportune time. A bond may also be subject to a *sinking fund.* The sinking fund *requires* (versus the optional nature of a call or refund feature) that the issuer retire a percentage of the issue each year. The issuer can meet this requirement by buying bonds in the market from any investors who are willing to sell at the price the issuer has set. Alternatively, the issuer can retire a pro rata amount of each investor's holdings.

The investor may have the option to alter a bond's term to maturity through put or extension features. A *putable bond* gives the investor the right to demand accelerated payment of principal and retirement of the bond prior to stated maturity—a feature that would be attractive to the investor in a period of rising interest rates. An *extendable bond* gives the investor the right to extend payment of principal and retirement of the bond beyond maturity—which would be attractive to the investor in periods of declining interest rates.

Putable or extendable bonds may carry a cost for

Table 2				
Maturity Impact for 10% Bonds				
	(1)	*(2)*	*(3)*	*% Par*
	Par	*Total*	*Total*	*Value*
Maturity	*Value*	*+ Coupons*	*= Payments*	*(1) ÷ (3)*
One year	$1,000	$ 100	$1,100	91%
Five years	1,000	500	1,500	67
Ten years	1,000	1,000	2,000	50
Twenty years	1,000	2,000	3,000	33

their respective features. This cost is usually a lower current interest rate in the case of the putable bond and a lower future interest rate in the case of the extendable bond. The bond investor should consider the cost of these features relative to their value.

Interest Payment. Interest payments on bonds usually take the form of semiannual, fixed payments known as "coupons." A *coupon bond* has actual coupons attached to the bond certificate, which the investor must clip and submit to the proper agent for payment of interest. A *registered bond* provides for the automatic payment of interest to the investor whose name is registered (with the proper agent) as the owner of the certificate. A bond's interest-payment rate (or coupon rate) is usually stated in percentage form and is related to the bond's par value. For example, a 10%, $1,000-par-value bond with semiannual coupons would pay the investor $50 every six months.

Bonds can be purchased with coupon rates ranging from 2% to 20%. For fixed-coupon bonds, this range reflects the issuance of bonds at various levels of interest rates. When a bond's coupon rate is the only determinant of its price, the following comparisons are appropriate: If the 10%, $1,000-par-value bond noted above has a purchase price equal to the par value and a promise to pay the principal amount in one year, a 5%, $1,000-par-value bond of the same issuer will have a purchase price less than par value, and a 15% bond of that issuer will have a purchase price greater than par value. The exact purchase prices should be those from which a bond investor will have the same percentage amount of total return (coupons plus price change). This analysis is shown in Table 3.

Many new forms of interest payment have proliferated in the past decade. Periods of rising interest rates have inspired *floating-rate bonds.* These bonds have coupon rates that are adjusted periodically, from weekly to semiannually. The coupon rate is determined by a formula tied to some objective standard (e.g., 102% of the interest rate for three-month U.S. Treasury bills). Floating-rate bonds are appealing in periods of rising interest rates as they provide an increasing coupon rate. The purchase price of floating-rate bonds tends to remain closer to par value than the purchase price of fixed-coupon bonds as the coupon rate continuously reflects the general level of interest rates.

The *original-issue discount bond* is unique in that the bond is initially sold with a relatively low coupon rate and a purchase price at a substantial discount from par value. This discount (realized over the bond's term to maturity) plus the coupon payments is considered the total interest payment. The investor must be fully aware of this type of purchase-price discount as the appreciation from the original issue price to par value is ordinary income. For taxable bonds, the original-issue discount is subject to ordinary income taxes. For municipal bonds, this discount is exempt from federal income taxes.

The extreme version of the original-issue discount bond is the *zero-coupon bond.* As the name implies, a zero-coupon bond provides no periodic interest payments. The bond's return is derived solely from the difference between its purchase price, which is substantially below par value, and the payment of par value at final maturity. Original-issue discount and zero-coupon bonds are attractive to investors in periods of declining interest rates as the interest-payment return can be determined with certainty.

Interest-payment return is a combination of the actual coupon payments plus the process of reinvesting these payments. For the investor who spends the coupon payments, the process is not relevant. This process is extremely important over longer time periods for the investor who wishes to see his initial investment grow to a specific future amount. The reinvestment process is influenced by both the coupon payments and the rate at which the payments are reinvested, as shown in Table 4.

Table 3
Coupon Rates and Bond Prices, One-Year Maturity

	(1) Par Value		(2) Purchase Price		(3) Price Change		(4) Coupon Payment		(5) Dollar Return	Percentage Return (5) ÷ (2)
5% bond (discount bond)	$1,000	−	$ 955	=	$ 45	+	$ 50	=	$ 95	10%
10% bond (par bond)	1,000	−	1,000	=	0	+	100	=	100	10
15% bond (premium bond)	1,000	−	1,045	=	(45)	+	150	=	105	10

Table 4 Reinvestment Impact for Ten-Year $1,000 Bonds				
		Reinvestment Proceeds at Rates of		
Coupon Rate	Total Coupons	5%	10%	15%
5%	$ 500	$139	$327	$ 583
10%	1,000	277	653	1,165
15%	1,500	416	980	1,748

Bond Yields and Returns. The measure of bond return is generally referred to as "yield." Many yield measurements can be made, however, with varying degrees of importance for different investors.

Current yield is the simplest measure of bond return. This yield is the result of dividing a bond's interest payment by the purchase price. This measure is of particular importance to the investor who is spending the coupon payments. However, current yield does not describe properly the return from bonds whose purchase prices are significantly different from their par values.

Yield to maturity is the measure of bond return that gives consideration to both interest payments and price change resulting from the difference between purchase price and par value. Yield to maturity also assumes a reinvestment process with a reinvestment rate equal to the yield-to-maturity rate.

If bonds are subject to final payment at a time other than the stated maturity, or at a price other than par value, a yield calculation should include the foregoing factors if the probability of their occurrence is high.

After-tax yield calculations are essential for comparing alternative bond investments where income taxation is a factor. Applicable tax rates must be used for both ordinary income and capital gains. The investor must properly identify the two components as in the case of original-issue discount bonds.

Compound or *realized yield* recognizes interest payments, purchase price, reinvestment rates, final payment price, actual maturity, and tax rates in determining the investor's return from a bond investment. While the computation of this yield does require an investor's subjective inputs, this analysis provides the investor with a framework for testing the sensitivity of a bond return to these inputs and for comparing different bonds on an equal basis.

Summary. Bonds are among the most important financial assets the investor can choose to meet his in-

vestment objectives. Like other financial assets, the basic bond investment has a variety of features, all of which can have an impact on the investor's actual investment return. Some features lend themselves to exact quantitative analysis, while others are dependent upon the investor's own judgments. Additionally, the bond investment is subject to changes in the overall interest-rate environment. The bond investment provides relative certainty in some respects and relative uncertainty in others. As such, bonds, like other financial assets, have elements of risk as well as return. The proper assessment of expected return relative to anticipated risk will increase the likelihood that the investor's experience in bonds will be pleasurable and profitable.

Timothy A. Schlindwein

Bond Glossary

after-tax yield   a measure of bond return that includes the effect of tax rates for both ordinary income and capital gains.

bond   a contract of indebtedness issued by a governmental unit or a corporation and promising payment of a principal amount at a specified future date plus interest.

bond rating   an assessment of a bond issuer's ability to pay, published by one or more rating agencies.

call (refunding) provision   the right of the issuer to retire the bond issue prior to final maturity.

collateral trust bond   a bond secured by the general credit of the issuer and the specific property for which the bond is issued.

compound (realized) yield   a measure of bond return that considers interest payments, purchase price, reinvestment rates, final payment price, actual maturity, and taxation.

convertible bond   a bond that gives the holder the right to exchange (convert) the bond for another security, usually a predetermined number of shares of the bond issuer's common stock.

coupon (bearer) bond   a bond with coupons attached to the bond certificate; the holder must submit the coupons to the proper agent for the payment of interest.

coupon rate   the annual interest payments of a bond stated as a percentage of par value.

current yield   annual bond interest payments divided by purchase price.

debenture   a bond secured by the general credit of the issuer and any unpledged assets.

discount bond   a bond with a purchase price below par value.

federal-agency bond a bond issued by a federal agency and which may have a direct or indirect guarantee of payment by the U.S. government.

first-mortgage bond a bond that conveys to the holder an interest in the real property of the issuer.

floating-rate bond a bond whose coupon rate adjusts periodically according to a predetermined formula.

interest-payment return coupon payments plus the return from reinvesting those payments over the life of the bond.

junior (subordinate) obligation an obligation entitled to payment after any senior obligation payments.

municipal bond a bond issued by a state or local governmental unit, the interest payments of which are exempt from federal income taxation.

new-issue market the market for bonds that are issued (sold) to investors for the first time.

original-issue discount bond a bond issued at an original purchase price significantly below par value, the difference of which is considered interest income for tax purposes.

par bond a bond with a purchase price equal to par value.

par value the principal amount or face value of the bond, which is to be paid to the holder at maturity (usually multiples of $1,000).

premium bond a bond with a purchase price above par value.

purchase (market) price the price the investor pays for a bond either in the new-issue market or in the secondary market.

putable bond a bond that gives the holder the right to demand payment of par value and retirement of the bond prior to the stated maturity.

registered bond a bond that provides for the automatic payment of interest to the holder whose name is registered with the proper agent as the owner of the bond certificate.

secondary market the market for bonds that are bought and sold among investors from the time of initial issue to maturity.

senior obligation an obligation entitled to payment prior to junior or subordinate obligation payments.

sinking fund a fund included in some bond issues which requires the issuer to retire on a periodic basis a percentage of the bond issue prior to final maturity.

term to maturity the period from purchase date to final principal-payment date.

Yankee bond a bond issued in the United States by a foreign governmental unit and payable in U.S. dollars.

yield to maturity a measure of bond return that includes interest payments, price change resulting from the difference between purchase price and par value, and the reinvestment of interest payments at the yield-to-maturity rate.

zero-coupon bond a bond that provides no interest payments prior to maturity; the return on the bond results from the difference between purchase price and par value.

Source: Timothy A. Schlindwein

Book-Entry Procedure

The book-entry program of the Federal Reserve and United States Treasury has succeeded in steadily replacing paper U.S. government and federal-agency securities with computer entries at Reserve banks. By eliminating certificates, government and agency securities are better safeguarded and more rapidly transferred throughout the nation's depository institutions.

Depository institutions include member and nonmember commercial banks, mutual savings banks, savings and loan associations, credit unions, and foreign bank branches and agencies in the U.S.

Securities in book-entry form are less vulnerable to theft and loss, can't be counterfeited, and don't require counting or recording by certificate number. In addition, owners need not cut coupons to obtain interest payments or present certificates to redeem securities at maturity.

As of June 30, 1982, about $686 billion, or 95.2% of the total outstanding marketable government securities, and about $147.8 billion, or 99.9% of total outstanding federal-agency securities, were in computerized book-entry form.

The first steps toward modern securities clearance were taken in the 1920s when Treasury securities became transferable by telegraph wire within the Federal Reserve system. At that time, all transfers required specific approval by the Treasury's commissioner of the public debt. In time, these telegraphic securities transfers became known as CPD's.

Under the early CPD system, the sender of a security—usually a commercial bank—delivered certificates to the local Federal Reserve office. That office, as fiscal agent of the U.S., retired the securities and sent a telegram to another Reserve office located near the institution receiving the security. The Reserve office receiving the telegram issued identical physical securities to the bank to which they were being transferred, or they were deposited in that bank's safekeeping account at the Federal Reserve. Thus, the CPD arrangement required individual deliveries of paper securities to and pickups from Federal Reserve offices for each transfer transaction between the Federal Reserve and a financial institution.

The difficulties involved in making "street" deliveries of government securities to and from the Federal Reserve bank in New York City (and among the banks and dealers in the city) led to the establishment of New York's Government Securities Clearing Arrangement (GSCA) in 1965. At the end of 1977, when the need to settle transactions in physical securities was eliminated, the GSCA was disbanded. Under the GSCA, the Federal Reserve bank of New York and 12 of the largest New York City banks arranged to make transfers by Teletype message, debiting or crediting the bank's securities-clearing account on the books of the New York Fed.

Using this method, only one delivery of securities to or from each participating bank was necessary at the end of the day and only in the net amount due to or from that bank.

Banks participating in the former GSCA program, as well as 23 other banks in the New York district, several federal agencies, and two international organizations, now are linked to on-line communications facilities to a computer system at the New York Fed and, through that system, to each other. A similar electronic network connects all Reserve banks and branches in the U.S.

In 1968, another major step toward automating the government securities market was taken when federal regulation authorized the first book-entry procedures to eliminate paper representing a government obligation. Under book-entry procedures, securities are entered electronically on the records of a Reserve bank.

All marketable government securities held by depository institutions—whether owned by them or held on behalf of correspondent banks or other customers—are eligible for book-entry conversion and for transfer by wire.

As a result of the International Banking Act of 1978 and the Depository Institutions Deregulation and Monetary Control Act of 1980, U.S. branches and agencies of foreign banks and domestic depository institutions have access to book-entry conversion and wire transfer services at explicitly set prices. Thus, each participant in this New York wire network can make transfers for its own account, or for customer accounts, directly from communications terminals on its own premises to any other participant. Also, until recently transfers could be made through the New York Fed and the Reserve system's computer center at Culpeper, Virginia, to any member bank in the U.S. via its local Federal Reserve bank or branch.

In June 1982 the Federal Reserve initiated a new communications network, Federal Reserve Communication System-80, which provides for depository institutions a faster, more flexible system for the transfer of securities, funds, and other payments and data.

Earlier in 1982 the New York Fed began establishing a districtwide electronic funds and securities transfer and administrative message network to give depository institutions that have only a small volume of transfer activity on-line access to the Federal Reserve.

The dial-oriented terminal program expands the electronic network that links the New York Fed to depository institutions that have a larger volume of transfer activity.

Any eligible securities a depository institution purchases when originally sold—such as Treasury bills, notes, or bonds—can be issued directly in book-entry form.

Customers of depository institutions can use book-entry facilities. For example, if a brokerage firm purchases new Treasury securities at a Federal Reserve bank, it can instruct the Federal Reserve to deliver the purchased securities to the firm's commercial bank for its account. No physical securities are issued.

If, later, the brokerage firm needs physical Treasury notes or bonds and certain federal-agency securities for some purpose, it can obtain them. The firm instructs its commercial bank to obtain the paper securities from a Reserve bank. On instructions from the commercial bank, the Reserve bank issues the securities to the commercial bank, which in turn delivers them to or on behalf of the brokerage firm.

As part of the program to expand use of book-entry procedures, the Treasury began in December 1976 issuing 52-week Treasury bills in book-entry form only. At that time, the Treasury also began to establish direct book-entry accounts for any subscribers who elected not to deal through commercial banks. This service is provided at no cost to subscribers, who may present tenders and payments either through a Federal Reserve bank or directly to the Department of the Treasury in Washington, D.C.

Other bill maturities were phased in during 1977, and by September 1977 physical bills were virtually eliminated. Physical securities were issued to a limited class of holders required by law or regulation to hold securities in physical form. That practice ended in December 1978. The Treasury also plans to eventually cease issuance of physical notes and bonds.

Arthur Samansky

Book Value

See COMMON STOCK.

Boston Stock Exchange (BSE)

The Boston Stock Exchange is one of five regional exchanges located in the United States and can be found in the center of the Boston financial community at One Boston Place. As a participant in the National Market System, which electronically links all the nation's major exchanges, the Boston Stock Exchange provides all of the same services as the larger national exchanges. The exchange is an incorporated association of members that provides facilities for trading in the equity securities of over 800 national and international corporations.

In furnishing this public marketplace, the exchange plays no role in establishing the prices of the securities traded; it merely provides the means whereby competing buyers and sellers can come together, thus creating an auction-market setting, controlled by the laws of supply and demand.

To trade on the Boston Exchange, one must be a member. The current membership represents specialist firms, regional retail firms, and large national retail firms with offices throughout the country

The Boston Stock Exchange Clearing Corporation handles the settlement of trades made on the Boston floor and is linked with the National Clearing and Settlement System. Five days after a trade is executed, the transaction must be settled by the buyer receiving the stock and the seller receiving the proceeds of the sale. In order to provide more efficient service to its participants, the Clearing Corporation uses the fully computerized facilities of the National Securities Clearing Corporation and the Depository Trust Company in New York. By means of electronic bookkeeping entries, this system settles contracts and eliminates the costly need to physically deliver stock certificates. Further, the Clearing Corporation offers additional operational services whereby members can clear trades on a nationwide basis and interface with the Institutional Delivery System, as well as settle over-the-counter trades along with exchange trades. Similar services are also provided to the New England banking community.

The data-processing arm of the exchange is the Boston Stock Exchange Service Corporation. This subsidiary is responsible for providing a full range of services not only to the exchange complex but also to the specialist firms on the Boston floor. Moreover, the Service Corporation provides a complete brokerage bookkeeping and data-processing package to a number of exchange members.

History. The Boston Exchange was organized on October 13, 1834, and with the sole exception of the chaotic period between July 30 and December 10, 1914, which precipitated the beginning of World War I, it has continued its activities without interruption. The exchange grew as a result of the foresight of a group of 13 local men who realized the importance an organized securities market might play in the business and industrial development of New England and of the country as a whole. Membership in this voluntary association of brokers was expanded from 13 to 36 in 1847, and to 150 in 1879. Subsequently, by repurchase and retirement, authorized memberships were limited to 112, until 1968 when they were doubled to 224, the currently authorized limit.

Originally, trading was carried on in two daily sessions known as "call of the list," but since 1885 a continuous daily session has prevailed. The types of securities listed and traded then were principally those of New England–based banks, insurance companies, mills, canal projects, mining enterprises, and railroads. In 1888 the exchange inaugurated publication in the press of all transactions executed, and at that time 188 stock issues and 170 bond issues were listed and traded.

The depression of the 1930s and the creation of the Securities and Exchange Commission resulted in significant changes in the entire securities industry, and in exchange markets in particular. Seat prices, once as high as $30,000, fell to $1,200, and companies that could not or chose not to comply with the newly imposed disclosure requirements were delisted. Volume, which had been rather heavy during the late 1920s, dwindled to 25,000 shares a day.

Such was the state of the exchange until late 1965, which marked the appointment of the first full-time, nonmember president. Many constitutional and rule changes were approved, and the entire complexion of the exchange was altered to one of an innovative, vital, and competitive marketplace. In a further move, to effectively meet the challenge of the Eighties, the exchange named its first full-time chairman in 1981. Immediate emphasis was placed on enhancing the quality of their marketplace. To this end, innovative rules, policies, and procedures were developed and implemented, computer facilities were upgraded, and an active marketing plan was undertaken. As a result, the Boston Exchange enjoyed its largest volume ever in 1982 when over 111 million shares changed hands. Further, 1982 marked the first time that over a million shares were traded in one day on the Boston Stock Exchange, a volume that was accomplished on six different occasions.

The exchange was involved in an extensive effort in September of 1980 to relocate from 53 State Street, its headquarters since 1911, to One Boston Place. The newer, larger quarters offer increased efficiency and capacity within a modern office building. The exchange looks forward to providing continued responsive service to the New England financial community and investors throughout the world.

Membership. Currently, there are outstanding 189 memberships, commonly referred to as "seats," held by 185 members who have registered a total of 128 member firms. Of this number, 52 are also members of the New York Stock Exchange, and 76 are members of the Boston Stock Exchange only, or of the Boston Exchange and other regional exchanges. The membership of the BSE is comprised of specialists, regional retail firms, and national retail firms.

A specialist is a member of the exchange who is located on the trading floor. These members are required to maintain a continuous market in the shares of listed companies assigned to them. Some of these firms, in addition to acting as specialists, also provide floor brokerage services by which they execute orders for members who do not have representation on the floor.

The regional retail firms are usually Boston-only members, typically smaller, New England–centered firms that have as few as one or as many as 20 branch offices. They offer their customers the ability to purchase or sell securities listed on exchanges or traded over the counter. Many of these firms also offer their clients investment advice, research, mutual funds, and tax shelters, and they are traditionally the firms that underwrite and distribute the securities of local companies and municipalities.

The national retail firms are the large businesses that maintain multinational and international offices as well as being members of national and regional exchanges, and they engage in all phases of the securities business.

In recognition of the need of foreign broker/dealers to participate directly in the United States securities markets, the Boston Exchange, in 1968, was the first exchange in the country to furnish such membership. This step was a major industry development and encouraged foreign investors to trade in the securities of U.S. corporations. Currently, there are 17 foreign members of the BSE, representing Belgium, Germany, Italy, Japan, Switzerland, and the United Kingdom.

The Trading Floor. The center of much of the Boston Stock Exchange activity is the trading floor, where agents for buyers and sellers of securities meet to execute their customers' orders under the auction-market system, the traditional system for trading listed securities in the United States.

The trading floor consists of 72 posts where specialists maintain continuous markets in their assigned securities. Other agents on the floor act as floor brokers or agents for member firms that do not maintain their own representatives on the trading floor.

The latest tickers, news services, and electronic devices enable specialists to ascertain current market information on the securities in which they are interested, and enable them to carry out their obligation of maintaining fair and orderly markets. Moreover, a number of large national retail firms have placed elec-

tronic order-routing equipment on the floor to enable them to quickly get their orders to the Boston market.

A specialist's principal responsibility is to maintain a fair and orderly market in each stock assigned to him. In fulfilling this requirement, he executes customers' orders left with him by other members and, in the absence of immediate offsetting public interest, buys or sells shares for his own account. The specialist must maintain a ready market and supply and purchase shares on behalf of the public at prices that provide stability and continuity to the market. The only exception is where trading in a stock is halted momentarily for the dissemination of important news affecting a company or for a temporary order imbalance.

The exchange monitors a specialist's activities very closely to ensure not only compliance with exchange and Securities Commission rules but also that the quality of the marketplace is being maintained. Further, the specialist must be adequately capitalized at all times—an aspect that is also monitored daily. Moreover, the Boston Exchange has a unique program known as the Alternate Specialist System. This program permits other specialists, in addition to the primary specialist, to trade in listed securities in order to provide greater depth and liquidity to the exchange's markets.

In July 1978 the exchange floor became electronically linked through the Intermarket Trading System (ITS) with the trading floors of the American, Midwest, New York, Pacific, and Philadelphia Stock Exchanges, and in 1981 with the Cincinnati Exchange. Under the ITS, brokers with orders on any exchange can reach out to another participant exchange whose published quotations in a particular issue indicate a more favorable price for the order. Since all exchanges now make available continuously updated quotations on all issues in which a specialist has been assigned, it is possible for a broker to obtain an execution on his customer's order at the most favorable price available on any ITS participant exchange. Strategically placed terminals and support facilities on the trading floors of the participants make transcontinental access a reality within seconds.

The Boston Exchange took an important industry lead in 1982 when it increased the number of shares covered by its Guaranteed Execution Rule to an industry high of 1,099 shares. Simply stated, the Boston specialists will guarantee the execution of all agency orders up to 1,099 shares at the best price in the Intermarket Trading System. This development, coupled with faster response time on order confirmations and a greater commitment to market quality, enabled the exchange to almost double its average daily volume in less than a year.

The securities of over 700 major U.S. and foreign corporations are dually traded on the Boston Stock Exchange along with approximately 100 solely listed issues—securities that are listed only on the Boston Exchange. Slightly over 90% of the exchange's volume is derived from activities in dually traded issues (securities also traded on the New York and American Stock Exchanges), and the balance is from the BSE's solely listed issues.

Listing. Any publicly held company that meets the guidelines of the exchange is eligible for listing. Overall, most of the solely listed companies are growing corporations that someday may move into a larger national exchange. For example, American Telephone & Telegraph was first listed on the Boston Exchange before any other exchange. The makeup of the exchange's solely listed companies is indeed national as many of them are located outside of the New England area.

A listing on the BSE offers a number of benefits to a company, its stockholders, and the investing public. Probably the most important feature of a listing is the assignment of a permanent, well-capitalized specialist. As mentioned previously, a specialist is a member of the exchange whose function is to maintain a fair and orderly market in a company's stock. In addition, the specialist, unlike other dealers in the over-the-counter market, must always make a continuous two-sided market, and his bids and offers are required to bear an orderly and reasonable relationship to previous sales in the stock.

Another important benefit is that upon listing, a company's stock would automatically qualify for margin (buying on credit) under Federal Reserve regulations. Obviously, qualifying for margin gives shareholders more buying power as well as making the stock more attractive for bank-loan collateral. Further, it provides for a potentially broader shareholder base.

Once listed, a company gains greater visibility through quotations in newspapers and on national quote services. Moreover, trading in a company's stock is constantly reviewed by the exchange to ensure the quality of the marketplace and protection of the investing public.

Finally, listing no longer means severing sponsorship or interference with long-standing relationships enjoyed with a company's over-the-counter marketmakers. A Securities and Exchange Commission rule (19c-3) has eliminated all the restrictions on over-the-counter trading in securities listed on exchanges after April 26, 1979. In effect, the rule permits over-the-counter market-makers to continue their market-making activities in a stock even though it is listed on an exchange. By listing, a company will be merely adding another market-maker in the form of a well-capitalized, permanent specialist, thus creating a more competitive atmosphere for the price of the stock, which is an important benefit both to the company's shareholders and to potential investors.

Government of the Exchange. Under its constitution, the government of the exchange is vested in the board of governors, which is comprised of the chairman, vice-chairman, and 20 other governors who are elected by the membership. Three of the 20 are representatives of the public, and a fourth is a representative of a company whose securities are listed on the exchange. The balance of the board represents the different constituencies of the exchange community—namely, specialists, regional retail firms, and national retail firms. The chairman is the chief executive officer of the exchange.

Governors are elected for a two-year term, and the terms of half of the board members expire annually. The full board meets monthly, and an executive committee meets at least monthly. This committee is charged with the responsibility of making major policy recommendations to the board as well as reviewing strategic planning and the financial performance of the exchange.

The BSE is a self-regulatory entity. Its rules are designed to prevent fraudulent and manipulative acts and practices, to promote just and equitable principles of trade, and, in general, to protect investors and the public interest. To this end, the board of governors has appointed the Market Performance Committee to oversee the conduct of the membership, to administer the exchange's self-regulatory responsibilities, and to ensure the competitiveness and quality of the marketplace.

In addition, the Committee on Stock List administers exchange rules and policies as they pertain to listed companies and approves the original and additional listing of equity issues. Other important committees include the Traders Advisory Committee, the National Market Committee, the Arbitration Committee, and the Hearing Committee.

See STOCK EXCHANGES.

Charles J. Mohr

Bretton Woods System

See GOLD IN THE MONETARY SYSTEM.

Broker

See DISCOUNT BROKERAGE; FUTURES COMMISSION MERCHANT; STOCKBROKER.

Bullion

See GOLD.

Bull Market

A period during which securities prices generally follow an upward trend. The term may be used to describe either a historical period of price increases or an anticipated rise in prices. While there may be some brief periods of price declines during a bull market, security prices in general will increase substantially for a period of several months or years.

In recent years there have been several bull markets during which stock prices have increased substantially over a period of two to three years. For example, between May 1970 and January 1973 the New York Stock Exchange (NYSE) Composite Index rose by more than 70%. Other increases in excess of 60% also occurred between October 1974 and December 1976, and again between March 1978 and November 1980. One of the most dramatic bull markets of recent years began in August 1982. During the following ten months, both the NYSE Composite Index and the Dow Jones industrial average increased by more than 60%.

A "bull" (or an investor who is "bullish") is someone who anticipates a bull market, either for securities in general or for some specific stock or group of stocks. The term *bull market* is also appropriate to describe price changes in other markets, such as bond markets and commodity markets.

See BEAR MARKET.

R. Bruce Swensen

Bureau of Alcohol, Tobacco, and Firearms

See DEPARTMENT OF THE TREASURY.

Bureau of Engraving and Printing

See DEPARTMENT OF THE TREASURY.

Bureau of Government Financial Operations

See DEPARTMENT OF THE TREASURY.

Bureau of the Mint

The Mint of the United States and a national coinage system were provided for by an act of Congress approved on April 2, 1792. Mint operations were conducted at Philadelphia, then the nation's capital, with all activities directed by a superintendent appointed by the president. The Mint was made a statutory bureau of the Treasury Department in 1873, and a director was appointed by the president to oversee its operations from a newly established headquarters office in the Treasury Department in Washington, D.C.

Essentially a manufacturing organization, approximately 2,200 men and women are employed throughout the bureau in coinage-related operations, security and maintenance duties, and administrative and managerial functions. It is one of the few government bureaus earning substantial revenues, which are deposited to the General Fund of the Treasury. These moneys are derived principally from seigniorage on the coinage but come also from sales to the public of numismatic items. (*Seigniorage* is the term used to designate the difference between the face value of the coins and the cost of their manufacture, including metals.)

What the Mint manufactures is money. Its primary mission is to supply enough coins for the nation's commerce. The office of the Director of the Mint is located in the headquarters office in Washington, D.C. There is a network of six field installations. Those located in Philadelphia, Denver, San Francisco, and West Point, New York, implement the coinage functions, which include the shipping of finished coins to the 37 Federal Reserve banks and branches for distribution to the commercial banks.

In addition, the Mint manufactures and sells numismatic coins directly to the public, as well as bronze medals, many of which are duplicates of awards made by the Congress for distinguished or outstanding service to the country; special commemorative coin issues such as the silver half-dollars commemorating the 250th birthday anniversary of George Washington; and the silver dollars and $10 gold pieces produced to mark the 1984 Olympic Games at Los Angeles.

Smallest of the Mint facilities are the West Point Bullion Depository, housing a part of the government's gold and silver bullion, and the U.S. Bullion Depository at Fort Knox, Kentucky, where a major portion of the Treasury's gold reserves are held (*see* FORT KNOX). While not mints, both play important roles.

For instance, due to increased need for coins of all denominations, and particularly the anticipated demand for Bicentennial coins, Congress in 1973 authorized the secretary of the Treasury to utilize any facility of the Bureau of the Mint for coin production. The West Point Bullion Depository was selected as an auxiliary facility. Remodeled to accommodate 20 presses and provide the capability for riddling and upsetting blanks, striking coins, performing quality-control laboratory tests, and counting and bagging coins for storage or shipment, it has been producing 1-cent coins for circulation ever since. More interestingly, the special five-year gold-medallion program authorized by P. L. 95-630 and the production of the $10 gold coin for the 1984 Olympic Games at Los Angeles have been conducted there, with both the coins and medallions being stamped on commercially prepared blanks containing gold furnished by the U.S. government for this purpose.

Two Mint facilities are in San Francisco. The U.S. Assay Office, which manufactures proof coins for collectors as well as cents for circulation, also packages and ships the proof and other special coins and sets prepared for the collecting public. The Old San Francisco Mint, closed in 1937, was returned to bureau custody in 1972 under the cultural-enhancement program, and the building was completely restored to reflect the style of the time it was opened, in 1874. It houses a customer-services center for processing numismatic orders; administrative offices; and a two-level museum containing Mint and early California displays and memorabilia, and many objects of interest loaned by civic groups and individuals for public enjoyment. The San Francisco Museum is the largest of the exhibit and sales areas open to the public at each of the mints and the Treasury Exhibit Hall in Washington, D.C.

Donna Pope

Bureau of the Public Debt

See DEPARTMENT OF THE TREASURY.

Business-Interruption Insurance

See INSURANCE.

Business Organizations, Forms of

The law recognizes various distinct forms of doing business, each serving a particular purpose and each with its own organization and rules. Which form is right for a particular venture depends on many considerations.

One person just starting in business can set up shop as a *sole proprietor*. If the venture is successful, all of the profits are his, but if there is a loss or liability, this can be charged against the individual. The sole proprietor deals on his own credit and must finance his own venture.

If he and one or more other people pool their resources and engage in business, a *partnership* is formed, and the business becomes more complex. There must be an agreement between the partners that spells out their rights and duties to one another; and where before the sole proprietor could conduct his business as he saw fit, now he must consider his duty to his partner. What rights does each partner have? The partnership agreement should state these rights; if it does not, the law will.

Both the partnership and sole proprietorship have common advantages and disadvantages. The profits go directly to either the owner or the partners. However, suppose there are losses? Again, this is the responsibility of the proprietor or partners. Sometimes this can be an advantage in a tax sense, but some business enterprises involve a very high risk of liability. If there is a risk, the fact that a judgment creditor can reach the proprietor's or partners' personal assets should be considered (*see* BANKRUPTCY). Perhaps a form of doing business that limits liability should be employed.

Further, as a business grows, it may need financing beyond the means of either the sole proprietor or the partnership. A change to another form of business organization is indicated.

The *corporation* accomplishes both of these purposes. Chartered by the states, corporations provide a means of engaging in business without risk to a person's individual assets. Further, they provide, through the sale of stock, a means of finance and for the accumulation of capital. Other people are brought into the venture as investors.

The corporation involves an even more complex structure so that the rights of investors can be protected. Basically, the stockholders elect the directors who are responsible for running the business and who in turn name the officers who are in charge of day-to-day operations.

As for personal liability, individual assets of shareholders in small enterprises can be reached only where there is fraud or if the workers are not paid.

Some business forms are used for particular purposes. The *limited partnership* has some of the tax advantages of a partnership, coupled with the limitation of liability enjoyed by corporate shareholders. Thus, limited partnership shares can be sold that allow sharing of the profits and losses to the extent of the investment, but with no general liability. There are general partners who can be held generally liable.

Sometimes, instead of engaging in a general business, two or more individuals will get together to pool their resources to accomplish a particular purpose. A *joint venture* is formed—an organization that has many of the qualities of a partnership but is not the same.

The *business trust* is used where specific property can be turned over to trustees for use of the beneficiaries, and *joint-stock* companies are a cross between corporations and partnerships.

The various forms are set forth in more detail below.

Sole Proprietorship. This basic form of doing business involves one person who is the owner of the enterprise and is entitled to its rewards and is responsible for its liabilities. If more than one person is sharing the rewards and is responsible for the liabilities, another form of enterprise is involved. The sole proprietor supplies his or her own financing and deals only on his or her own credit. The business can be conducted in the owner's own name or in a trade name. Where the latter is used, there is usually a requirement that the trade name be on file with the county clerk of the county where the enterprise operates. This filing must disclose the true name of the owner and an address where he or she can be served with process.

The sole proprietor can hire employees and is responsible for providing them with a safe place to work. He or she is responsible for the actions of his or her employees and, if they are given authority or appear to have authority, may be bound by their agreements on his or her behalf. Further, if an employee commits a tort in the performance of assigned duties, the proprietor may be held liable. The proprietor is sued and may sue in his or her individual name—the usual form being: JOHN DOE, d/b/a DOE COMPANY (see DOING BUSINESS AS). A judgment against the sole proprietor may be enforced against his or her individual assets and is not limited to business assets. For this reason, while there can be sole proprietorships in any business, trade, or profession, other forms are usually employed for those enterprises where the risk of liability is high. This usual form is the corporation, which limits liability to the enterprise. An exception to this is the professional corporation, where individual liability continues.

Partnerships. Two or more persons may join together to conduct a business for profit. The essential ingredient of a partnership is an agreement whereby two or more persons pool their money and talents in an enterprise and share in the profits or losses. The business a partnership may engage in includes every trade, occupation, or profession.

Formation. The basis of the partnership is the agreement, or contract, whereby the persons involved set forth their rights and duties toward one another. No one person can become a member of a partnership without the consent of the others. A person has a right to select who will be his partners, and therefore a person who is not welcomed by all of the participants has no right to become a partner. The agreement should set forth the purpose for which the partnership is formed, which may be for any lawful business, trade, or profession. It follows that a partnership cannot be formed for an illegal purpose or for one contrary to

public policy. An agreement citing such a purpose may be held to be void. Usually the length of time, or term, that the partnership will be in existence is set forth. If it is not, the laws of most jurisdictions states that it is a partnership at will—that is, it exists until something is done to dissolve it.

The Contract. Although not always essential, a written agreement, carefully prepared, will often resolve future disputes between or among the partners. Partnerships can be formed by oral agreement. It should include the wishes of the participants as to the sharing of profits and losses, and should also include the priorities of distribution on the winding up of the partnership affairs. The contract of the parties controls and, like any agreement, to be valid must be supported by consideration. In this respect the consideration can be founded on one partner financing the business while the other devotes his time, skill, and knowledge to it.

Partnership Names. The partners usually adopt a name under which they conduct their business. The name can be fictitious, but in most jurisdictions there are limitations on this. A partnership cannot transact business in the name of a partner not interested in the firm; and where the designation "and company" is used, it must represent an actual partner. The reason for this is to protect the public. Further, most jurisdictions require that the partnership name and the names of the partners and the address of its place of business be on file with the county clerk of the county where the business is located. The partnership may be continued in the name of a deceased partner.

Partnership Assets. In forming a partnership, the members make contributions that will enable the enterprise to start in business. This and property subsequently added constitutes the partnership capital. Property acquired with partnership funds is partnership property unless a contrary intent is shown in the partnership agreement.

The partners do not, as a rule, have any individual rights to the specific assets of the firm. These belong to the enterprise and each partner's interest is his share of the surplus after the partnership debts are paid.

Partnership Rights. The partners in their agreement should set forth their duties and liabilities to one another. Generally, between partners a duty of trust and confidence exists, called a "fiduciary relation." They have no right to expel another partner from the firm; thus, unless the agreement so provides, a majority may not oust a minority. All partners have an equal right in the management and conduct of the business; where there are differences, the majority controls. They may agree to any distribution of the profits between themselves; where there is no agreement, each partner shares equally in the profits. They also share any losses equally, and each must contribute toward the same. They can, of course, agree otherwise. Each partner has a right to inspect the partnership books, which should be available at all reasonable times at the principal place of business. The books belong to all of the partners.

Partners' Responsibility to Each Other. The partnership relation is one of trust and confidence. There must be fair dealing between the partners. Each partner has a right to know all that the other partners know. There can be no false representations among them. There can be no self-dealing or secret profits as all profits belong to the firm. Each partner is authorized to transact the business of the firm and can bind the firm. While each can bind the firm, generally all partners must join in litigation. Thus, one partner cannot sue individually upon a partnership claim. Each of the partners is responsible for acts of the other partners just as a principal is responsible for the acts of his agent. Where a partner commits a tort, both he and the other partners can be sued, and can be held liable. They can also be sued for a wrong committed by an employee. A partnership does not have the advantage of a corporation, where liability is limited to the business entity. The partners are individually liable and their individual assets can be reached.

Death of a Partner. The partnership agreement should provide what happens in the event of the death of a partner. Where there is no agreement, the partnership laws of most jurisdictions provide that the partnership is dissolved. And on the dissolution, the partnership assets and property go to the surviving partners so that they may wind up the affairs of the firm. The representative of the dead partner has no legal interest in any of the assets; his only right is to be paid the value of the sale. He may not interfere with the surviving partners as long as they are closing up the business in good faith.

Dissolution of a Partnership. Ordinarily, partnerships are dissolved by mutual agreement of the partners. However, there are some dissolutions that work automatically. For instance, if the partnership agreement specifies a definite term and that term is reached; or if one of the partners goes into bankruptcy; or if a partner is expelled. Further, when a partner withdraws or a new one is admitted, the law provides that, in the absence of an agreement, the partnership be dissolved and a new one formed. A court has the power to dissolve a partnership.

Corporations. The advantages of limitation of liability and ease of finance make the corporation the most widely used form of doing business. Each state can and does create them, and the form has many uses, including public and quasi-public purposes. This discussion concerns only those corporations created for business purposes.

When a corporation is formed, an "artificial being" comes into existence and all business is done in the name of this being. For most purposes, this shields the individual stockholders or investors from liability. Only in extreme cases—usually involving fraud, illegality, or wrongdoing—will the courts disregard the corporate entity and "pierce the corporate veil" to reach the responsible individuals.

Incorporation. A business corporation is formed under the general laws of the incorporating state. While differences among states do exist, the usual method involves filing a certificate of incorporation with the designated department of the state. When the certificate is filed and the required fees and taxes are paid, the corporation comes into being. The certificate sets forth how long the corporation expects to be in business—the usual duration of corporate life being listed as "perpetual." The purpose for which the corporation is formed must be set forth, including the business in which it will engage. These purposes cover the wide spectrum of legitimate business purposes. Each corporation is authorized to issue stock, and the number and kind of shares it can issue must be set forth. There is also a requirement that an address where the corporation can be served with legal process must be set forth. The certificate will set forth the name under which the corporation is being formed and by which it will be known. Practically any name in the English language can be used; however, it can not conflict with a name already in use. The usual practice is to search the state's records to determine this before the certificate is filed, and it is wise for the incorporators to have several alternative names.

Bylaws. While the corporation comes into existence on the filing of the certificate of incorporation, exactly how it will function is set forth in the bylaws. These will include such things as where it will maintain its office, what its fiscal year will be, when its annual meeting will be held. Every corporation has a seal, and this is covered in the bylaws. The rights of the stockholders and the duties of the directors and officers are set forth at length. These are discussed in more detail below.

Shares and Shareholders. A corporation is initially funded by the stockholders. Perhaps an existing business will be transferred to it, in return for which stock will be issued at an agreed value. Or there may be a payment of cash in return for shares. In any event, the stock that is issued must be for a consideration, and the amounts paid in or the value of the property transferred to the corporation becomes its capital.

In return for his contribution, the shareholder receives a certificate, which is evidence of his holdings in the corporation. These holdings are registered on the corporate books, which must also set forth the consideration paid for the shares. The certificates and the shares they represent are freely transferable; the holder simply signs a power on the back side. When so transferred, the old share is presented to the corporation for cancellation and new shares are issued to the new owner. Often, restrictions are placed on the transferability of the shares; this can be done by noting the restriction on the face of the stock certificate.

The certificate of incorporation sets forth the types of shares a company may issue. The basic shares are common stock, which are usually issued without extraordinary rights and privileges; preferred shares, which have a preference in the distribution of dividends or assets upon dissolution. Shares can be authorized with either par value or without par value. Par-value shares have a predetermined value, representing the amount of money or property contributed by the stockholder for them. No-par-value shares do not have a fixed consideration.

The rights that a stockholder acquires when he purchases stock depend on the laws of the state of incorporation. Generally, the shareholder has a right to a share of the profits, paid in the form of dividends. Title to all corporate property is in the name of the corporation—the shareholders have no right to any specific property. If the corporation is dissolved, they do have a pro-rata right to share in what is left after payment of the business debts.

Annual and special stockholder meetings are held to determine basic corporate policy. Under the bylaws, a date for annual meetings is fixed, and special meetings may be called at the request of a specific number of shareholders. In any event, all who are entitled to attend and vote are required to be notified in writing of the meeting. The right to vote at meetings helps the shareholder protect his investment and his dividends. Unless the certificate of incorporation provides otherwise, every stockholder of record is entitled to one vote for every share of stock he holds. The main business of the stockholders is to elect the directors who will run the business.

Directors. The directors are responsible for the business of the corporation. They are elected by the stockholders, and their terms of office are usually stated to be until the next annual meeting. The number of directors is set forth in the bylaws, with reference to the law of the incorporating state. There may be a legal requirement for a minimum of three directors. However, as one-man corporations are permitted in some states, the laws of these states will usually specify a lesser number. The directors have an obligation to the corporation and to the stockholders to conduct the

business in good faith. If there is a neglect of duty or a waste of assets, this fiduciary relationship can make the directors personally liable for any loss.

Officers. While the directors are responsible for running the business, the day-to-day operation is in the hands of the officers. These are appointed by the board of directors and include the following:

The president, who is the general executive or administrator of the business and exercises such authority as the directors give him. He can bind the corporation within the scope of his authority.

The vice-president, who acts as the general executive in the absence of the president and performs such other duties as the directors give him.

The secretary, who keeps the records of the stockholder, director, and committee meetings, and usually has authority to speak on behalf of the corporation and to keep the corporate records.

The treasurer, who has custody of the corporate funds and securities and has charge of the financial dealings of the corporation.

The directors can also appoint assistant vice-presidents, secretaries, and treasurers to perform such duties as the board directs.

Finances. The initial financing of the corporation is through the purchase of its stock; from this the capital of the business is established. Generally a corporation also has the power to issue bonds, debentures, and notes, whether secured or unsecured. The corporation may sell its shares to the public through a national security exchange or on the over-the-counter market. A corporation doing this is referred to as a "public corporation" and has to comply with the blue-sky laws* of each state where it sells its shares, federal laws administered by the Securities and Exchange Commission, and the rules of the exchange where the shares are traded. These laws and rules are designed to protect the investing public. A nonpublic corporation with few stockholders is referred to as a "close corporation." As to these, there are some special provisions. For instance, in some jurisdictions the ten largest shareholders may be personally liable for wages, and salaries due to its laborers, servants, or employees. Further, in a close corporation there can be shareholder agreements as to how the corporation will be run, the election of directors, and the fixing of compensation.

When a corporation is formed, another taxpayer is created. Each state can and does tax them, and there is also liability for federal taxation unless the corporation wishes to and can qualify to be taxed as a partnership for income-tax purposes. This right is created

---

* "Blue-sky laws" are the state laws that regulate fraudulent stock transactions.

by filing an election on U.S. Treasury Form 2553 under Internal Revenue Code subchapter S. To qualify for subchapter S treatment, there must be fewer than 25 stockholders and only one class of stock; stockholders must be individuals, estates, or certain trusts, and cannot be affiliated with other corporations; and the shareholders may not be nonresident aliens.

Dissolution. The corporate existence continues until it is dissolved by either the courts or the state. Even though for all practical purposes it is out of business, some act is necessary to terminate its existence. On the consent of the state, the charter can be surrendered to the state that created it. It can be dissolved by action of the state if it fails to file corporate tax reports. A nonjudicial dissolution can be had if the holders of specified numbers of the voting shares approve (usually two-thirds). A certificate of dissolution is filed with the state, and after the state taxing authority has approved, the corporation is dissolved. However, it does not completely disappear, for it must then dispose of its assets and do all other things necessary to wind up its affairs.

A corporation may also be judicially dissolved. For instance, the attorney general of a state usually has authority to bring a court action where fraud, misrepresentation, or other illegality is involved. In certain instances, shareholders can petition a court for dissolution. Usually this is done where the corporate assets are not sufficient to discharge the liabilities or where there is a benefit to the shareholders in such dissolution. However, mere dissatisfaction with the way the business is being run will not give rise to a right to dissolution. Sometimes there is a deadlock between the directors on management policy, or among the shareholders as to the election of directors. Then usually the holders of one-half of the voting shares may petition for dissolution.

Limited Partnerships. A limited partnership combines features of the corporate and partnership forms of doing business. It is a creature of statute, being recognized and existing, in most states, under the Uniform Limited Partnership Act. It is a method of financing a venture and has certain tax advantages that make it useful for such things as oil and gas explorations and Broadway plays. It may carry on any business a regular partnership could conduct.

Formation. This enterprise starts with one or more persons who are the general partners and who are personally liable for all of the debts and obligations of the limited partnership. (Some states allow corporations to be general partners.) The general partners run the business. There are also limited partners, who contribute money or property to finance the enterprise but are not personally liable for the debts and obliga-

tions. The limited partner has been likened to a stockholder.

To have a limited partnership, there must be a written certificate executed by two or more persons and filed in the county where the principal office is to be, usually with the county clerk. This certificate must state the character of the business, where it is located, and the names and home addresses of the general and limited partners. It must state what each limited partner is to contribute, whether any additional contributions will be called for, and, if so, how much. The share of the profits or other income each limited partner will receive must be set forth. If the limited partner can assign his right, this must be set forth, as must the right to admit new limited partners. The certificate must also spell out the right of the general partner or partners, if given, to continue the business on the death, retirement, or insanity of a general partner. If a limited partner is to have a right to receive property other than cash in return for his contribution, this must be set forth.

Not only must the certificate be filed, but it will have to be published as well.

Conduct of the Business. The general partners have the exclusive management of the business. A general partner has the same rights, powers, and liabilities of a partner in a general partnership, with some exceptions. For instance, he can do no act in contravention of the certificate. He cannot bind a limited partner beyond the extent of his investment in the firm. He can do no act that would make it impossible to carry on the ordinary business of the partnership. He cannot confess a judgment against the firm. He cannot admit another general partner, and can admit a limited partner only if the certificate gives him that right.

Limited partners have no right to participate in the management of the business. The limited partner cannot be held liable for partnership debts, as a general partner can. However, if he does participate in the management of the firm, he may be held liable as a general partner. The limited partner does have the right to have the partnership books kept at the principal place of business and can inspect and copy any of them at any time. He has a right, on demand, to full and true information on all things affecting the partnership and can have a formal accounting when circumstances warrant. He has a right to receive a share of the profits.

Joint Venture. This is a form of business similar to, but not quite the same as, a partnership. Like a partnership, it is a combination of two or more persons to carry on an enterprise for profit. It differs in that the joint venture relates to a single transaction, while a partnership relates to a more general business. The members of the venture combine their property, money, skill, and knowledge in a specific undertaking, ordinarily for the purpose of profit.

The agreement between the coventurers governs, and no person can become a member of the venture unless all the other members agree. This element of agreement is essential to the establishment of a joint venture, and while a formal written agreement is certainly desirable and recommended, it is not essential to the creation of the relationship. This may actually be inferred from the conduct of the parties as to the joint enterprise, and it may be created orally.

Joint venturers are similar to partners in many respects. The venture is financed by their contributions. These contributions need not be equal, but each party must contribute either money, material, or service to the enterprise. The parties must have a community of interest in the project and equal authority in its management. They share profits and losses and they owe one another the same good faith as do partners. There can be no self-dealing during the venture, and any profits so realized belong to the venture. As to termination, a joint venture is subject to the same rules as a partnership.

Joint-Stock Companies. Joint-stock companies are a distinct class of association of individuals and have some features of both corporations and partnerships. They are not true corporations in that they come into existence by agreement and not by the power of the state. However, some statutes defining corporations include joint-stock companies, and thus they may have powers or privileges not enjoyed by individuals or partnerships. They do not have the full power of corporations. In fact, they were and, under some laws, are legally regarded as partnerships with some corporate powers. There are differences. For instance, in a joint-stock company there is no right to select one's associates as there is in a partnership. Further, death of a member does not dissolve a joint-stock company.

A joint-stock company is formed by the filing of a certificate with the secretary of state of the state where it will do business provided, of course, the laws of the state allow this form of association. The certificate is also filed in the county where the company will oper-ate. Usually a new certificate must be filed annually.

The stock of a joint-stock company is similar in nature to that of a corporation. This is usually represented by certificates setting forth the shareholders' rights. The rights of shareholders are sometimes said to be those of partners. However, there is no right to share in the operation of the company as a partner does. The certificates have the same transferability as corporate shares. The shareholders may also be liable as partners for the debts of the enterprise.

Business Trust. This form of business enterprise is also known as a "Massachusetts trust" or a "Common-law trust." The basic ingredient is that property is placed in the hands of trustees, who manage and deal with it for the use and benefit of beneficiaries. The form has been used to hold, manage, develop, and deal in real estate; for the liquidation of the business and assets of a corporation; and for the purchase and sale of securities for profit.

A business trust is created by a written instrument or declaration of trust. This will name the original trustees, fix their term of office, set forth their powers and duties, and state how their successors will be appointed. Title to the property conveyed to the trust is usually in the name of the trustees, to be held and managed for the benefit of the beneficiaries, who are shareholders. A characteristic feature of a business trust is the issuance of shareholders' certificates that evidence the shareholders' beneficial interest in the property and profits of the trust. The shares may be transferred, but the transferability generally depends on the terms of the trust instrument. Shares of business trusts have been listed and traded on stock exchanges.

C. Whitman Hobbs

Business Trust

See BUSINESS ORGANIZATIONS, FORMS OF.

Buydowns

See HOME FINANCING, MORTGAGES.

·C·

Call Provision

See PREFERRED STOCK.

Calls

See OPTION TRADING.

Capital

What most people refer to as "capital" is more correctly called "capital assets," which the INTERNAL REVENUE CODE takes great care to define. The term "capital assets" generally refers to wealth (property, money) from which a person, business, or corporation gains certain benefits. Hence, if a person had a great deal of "capital," it would mean that he had a large sum of money and/or property (real estate or personal) and that the person derived commensurate benefit from the capital.

The Internal Revenue Code, however, refers to "capital assets" as meaning "property held by the taxpayer (whether or not connected with his trade or business)," but the term does not include stock-in-trade or other property that would normally be regarded as inventory; property held primarily for sale to customers while doing ordinary business; depreciable or real property used in a trade or business; and at least three other categories, which are explained in section 1221 of the Code.

David B. Axelrod

Capital-Appreciation Bonds

Capital-appreciation bonds (CAB's) are a recent innovation in municipal bonds. They work very much like ZERO-COUPON BONDS in that they do not have a stated rate of interest. However, instead of having the value at maturity (face value) printed on the face of the bonds as zero-coupons do, capital-appreciation bonds have a par-value table printed on them to determine their redemption value at any given time. The basic difference between these bonds and zero-coupon

bonds is from the point of view of the issuer. It need not market an issue with a larger face value to receive the proceeds it needs at the time of financing.

Moore & Schley Cameron & Company

Capital Expense

The expenditure or investment of wealth or capital for the purpose of acquiring more property or for the improvement of one's present property. For tax purposes, capital expenses are not directly deductible from the gross income of one's business as ordinary and necessary business expenses, but instead are depreciable in keeping with a reasonable schedule based on the useful life of the property.

Capital expenses must have a useful life of one or more years, and may be incurred for the betterment of, or to increase the value of, one's property. Included in the category of capital expenditures are such costs as title insurance and legal fees when real estate is purchased, or legal fees and other specific start-up fees and costs when one establishes a business. For example, a mechanic who buys a garage and all the tools of his trade is "capitalizing" his business. If he subsequently fixes his lift or replaces any minor or normally "consumable" items, he will itemize those expenditures as business deductions. The first would be depreciable on his taxes over the life of the item; the consequent expenditures would be deducted dollar for dollar from his gross income in the year of the expenditure.

David B. Axelrod

Capital Gains/Capital Losses

Increases of wealth or capital assets are termed "capital gains" when they arise not from the normal ongoing business or trade of an individual but from a rise in the market value as reflected by the sale of an individual's property.

Capital losses would be any decreases in an individual's wealth or capital assets that, similarly, do not arise from the conduct of the individual's normal business or trade activities but from a lower market value as reflected when the property is sold, traded, or transferred.

Capital gains or losses can be divided into "short-term" and "long-term" or "net short- or long-term capital gains or losses." The actual period one must hold a gain before it is classified as long-term or short-term has fluctuated as the legislature tinkers with the tax laws from year to year. One might find, for example, that the Internal Revenue Code specifies as short-term any gain or loss from the sale or exchange of capital assets held for not more than six months; a long-term gain or loss would be one held for more than six months. As the span of time may vary, it is best to consult the Code, the Internal Revenue Service, or a qualified tax person. The "net" short- or long-term gains, simply stated, would be the excess of gains or losses after the year's totals are calculated and compared.

The tax rates vary for short- and long-term capital gains and for individual or business gains. The Internal Revenue Code provides that certain business transactions involving the exchange of stock for stock rather than the sale of stock outright, or a similar exchange of property for property rather than the sale of property outright, will not be governed by the usual laws for the short- or long-term gains. One should plan the sale or transfer to capital assets carefully so as to gain the best position when calculating taxes owed.

David B. Axelrod

Capital Stock

This term denotes all securities that represent ownership of a corporation. This includes COMMON STOCK and PREFERRED STOCK, since, technically, both of these securities represent ownership. However, for most practical purposes, only common stockholders are considered owners of a corporation. Common stockholders have the right to vote in corporate elections and the right to share in corporate profits. Since preferred stockholders do not have either of these rights, they are generally not thought of as owners of the firm. The term *capital stock* is used to distinguish common and preferred stock from debt securities, such as corporate bonds, but the characteristics of preferred stock are in fact significantly different from both common stock and bonds; hence, the classification of common and preferred stock as capital stock is not a useful distinction for the investor.

R. Bruce Swensen

Cash Flow

A term standing for the collection of income or revenue from services rendered or products sold and the expenses paid out to produce those services or products: in other words, the flow of funds into and out of a company. Cash flow results in a net income or net loss.

Samuel C. Hoyt

Cashier's Checks

A type of negotiable instrument drawn by a bank on itself, in contrast to a certified check, where the customer is the drawer. Banks use cashier's checks to pay out loans to customers, to pay suppliers, and for other types of payments. They may be sold to customers as a service. They are a direct obligation of the bank. They may also be called "official checks" or "treasurer's checks."

Phil Battey

Cash Letter

A transmittal document that accompanies cash items sent from one bank to another or to the Federal Reserve system in the CHECK CLEARING process. A cash item is any item that can be converted into cash immediately or that a bank accepts for immediate credit to a depositor's account: in other words, currency and checks. A cash letter is therefore functionally equivalent to a deposit slip. It itemizes each individual check in the shipment, showing the dollar amount, and is used for record-keeping.

Phil Battey

Cash Surrender Value

See LIFE INSURANCE.

Casualty Insurance

See PROPERTY-CASUALTY INSURANCE.

Cease and Desist Order

An administrative order issued by a federal financial-institution supervisory agency (the Federal Reserve Board, Office of the Comptroller of the Currency, Federal Deposit Insurance Corporation, or Federal Home Loan Bank Board) against a bank or other financial institution or its officers, directors, or employees, prohibiting any of them from engaging in an unsafe or unsound practice or violating a law or regulation. The process of issuing such an order, if the institution does not agree to it, includes the delivery of a notice of charges with an opportunity to contest the proposed order in a formal hearing and through review by the courts. Such orders may require that the institution both terminate the prohibited conduct and take affirmative steps to correct the conditions resulting from the unsafe, unsound, or illegal practice. A violation of a cease and desist order can subject the violator to a civil money fine of up to $1,000 per day for each violation.

Griffith L. Garwood

Central Assets Account

See ASSET-MANAGEMENT ACCOUNT.

Central Bank

A government entity that has the sole power to issue the nation's paper currency, serves as the lender of last resort (source of guaranteed liquidity) to banks and other institutions, acts as the government's bank, markets the government's debt, acts on behalf of the government to safeguard the value of the nation's money in international trade (usually by buying and selling the nation's money in foreign exchange markets), and seeks to control the growth of the nation's money supply to achieve national economic objectives.

Every nation in the world has a central bank; indeed, like a central government, it is one of the characteristics that define a country's "national sovereignty." While all central banks are different—in terms of structure, functions, and economic role—virtually all share the common characteristics cited above, which thus can serve as a broad working definition of *central bank.*

The FEDERAL RESERVE SYSTEM—the central bank of the United States—meets this definition of *central bank* but does so through a fundamentally different institutional structure and in a fundamentally different way from the world's other central banks.

First of all, the Federal Reserve has a quasi-governmental and decentralized structure that gives it a far greater degree of "independence" within the government than is true of most other central banks. This means that monetary policy can be, and is, established separately and independently from the policies of the president and the administration. Most of the world's central banks are more closely tied to the executive branch of their governments than is the Federal Reserve. Unlike the Federal Reserve, most are directly responsible to their government's Treasury Department.

Second, the Federal Reserve's administration of monetary policy and its use of monetary-policy tools are essentially oriented toward the "total" economy and toward broad national economic goals. Decisions on which sectors of the economy get money and credit and at what price (interest rate) are essentially decided in the marketplace and not by the central bank.

Other central banks more closely direct monetary policy toward specific sectors of the economy or industries in the economy and use monetary policy more directly to promote specific social and economic growth objectives. In some countries, particularly those where economic development is dependent on strong foreign trade, central banks often direct monetary policy toward strengthening export industries. Many foreign central banks also favor the agricultural or housing sectors of their nations' economies and lend money to government units for public projects or invest in private companies. Foreign central banks do this essentially by making loans directly to favored industries at interest rates well below prevailing market rates, or by making credit more freely available to favored firms than would be the case under prevailing market conditions.

On balance, other central banks are far more selective and direct in their use of monetary-policy tools and monetary-policy power than the Federal Reserve. The Bank of Mexico, for example, uses reserve-requirement powers over commercial banks to direct loans to specific industries and into low-income housing. The Bank of Japan lends money to specific companies to help achieve broad national growth objectives. The Bank of Italy uses its monetary-policy powers to prevent banks from lending money for purposes inconsistent with Italy's development efforts.

The Federal Reserve does not operate in these ways. It essentially relies on one major and general policy tool to achieve U.S. national economic goals. This tool is open-market operations, which is the Federal Reserve's buying and selling of U.S. government securities to increase or decrease bank reserves and the nation's money supply. The Federal Reserve's traditional "general" approach to monetary policy and use of the policy tools, and the Federal Reserve's fundamental reliance on the market to allocate money and credit, sets the Federal Reserve apart.

The nations of Europe have had central banks since before the beginnings of the Industrial Revolution. The Bank of Sweden and the Bank of England—two of the world's oldest central banks—were founded in the late 1600s. The United States, however, did not establish a central bank until 1913.

As a new nation, the United States was unable to reconcile itself to (1) government-issued paper currency, (2) a role for a central bank in the new economy, and (3) the application of federal power over money and banking matters.

The national debate on these issues split public and political opinion into two opposing positions—one in favor of central banking, championed by Alexander Hamilton; the other opposed, championed by Thomas Jefferson. Hamilton was an industrial visionary who believed that the future of the U.S. was in commercial and industrial development. He saw in the establishment of a central bank a crucial institution that would regulate the flow of money and credit necessary to finance the building of American industry and he argued for it. Jefferson and his followers argued against a central bank on constitutional grounds—that the federal government did not have the constitutional right to charter a central bank.

A First Bank of the U.S. was chartered for 20 years in 1791, but its charter was not renewed in 1811. A Second Bank of the U.S. was chartered in 1816, but its charter, too, was not renewed in 1836. Although the Supreme Court had ruled in 1819 that the Second Bank of the U.S. was constitutional (*McCulloch* v. *Maryland*), many opponents of the Second Bank—state-chartered banks, merchants, farmers, politicians—saw it as too powerful an institution for a market economy and a political democracy. Political opinion about central banking remained divided in the U.S., with no national consensus on the issue until December 1913, when President Wilson signed the Federal Reserve Act establishing a U.S. central bank.

David H. Friedman

Certificate of Title

In real-estate transactions, this term has two separate meanings.

In some parts of the country, the customary form of title evidence is a certificate prepared by an attorney after searching the public records and examining the legal effect of the matters found there. This is sometimes called a "certificate of title."

In the few parts of the country that have a land registration system, the public official who administers the system prepares a certificate showing the current status of registered ownership. This is sometimes called a "certificate of title." Ordinarily the original is in the official records, and duplicates may be issued to parties owning rights in the land.

See TITLE INSURANCE.

Hugh A. Brodkey

Certificates of Deposit (CD's)

Certificates of deposit—also called "time certificates of deposit" or "CD's"—are official receipts issued by a bank that state that a specified sum has been deposited for a specified period of time and at a specified rate of interest. Legally, they are similar to a promissory note. Outside of this general description, the terms of certificates of deposit vary widely and it is important to remember that they can be negotiable or nonnegotiable. If the CD is negotiable, the person or institution holding the CD can dispose of the right to

the funds it represents by merely transferring the certificate. In nonnegotiable form, holders cannot readily transfer their rights to the instruments before maturity. In virtually all cases, CD's issued by financial institutions are insured by the federal government up to $100,000.

On CD's with maturities of 32 days or more, there is no government-mandated minimum deposit or interest-rate ceiling. The issuing financial institution sets the minimum deposit and interest on the account.

On certificates with a maturity of 7–31 days, there is a minimum deposit required by the government, but the issuing institution is allowed to set the interest rate it will pay.

Phil Battey

Certified Checks

Checks that are guaranteed by a bank for payment. A check is a claim to money; it is not legal tender. Legally, certification of a check transfers payment responsibility to the bank. By certification, a bank guarantees that sufficient funds have been set aside from the depositor's account to cover the amount of the check when payment is demanded. To certify a personal check, the customer presents it to the bank, which immediately transfers funds from the customer's account to a special account on its books. The bank places an official stamp on the check, along with the signature of a bank official. While banks are not required to certify checks, many do as a service to customers. The service usually carries a fee.

Phil Battey

Certified Public Accountant (CPA)

A certified public accountant is an individual who has been certified by a state board of accountancy to engage in the practice of accounting in that state or jurisdiction. (CPA's practice in the 50 states, the District of Columbia, the Virgin Islands, Puerto Rico, and Guam.)

To qualify to practice as a certified public accountant, a candidate must pass the Uniform CPA Examination, written and graded by the American Institute of Certified Public Accountants (AICPA). This is a comprehensive two-and-a-half-day examination given twice a year in every state and jurisdiction. Many states also have collegiate educational requirements that must be satisfied before the individual is eligible to take the Uniform CPA Examination. Some states require a certain amount of experience in the practice of accounting before CPA certification is granted.

CPA's are certified by the individual states and jurisdictions rather than by a national body. However, 192,000 CPA's are members of the American Institute of Certified Public Accountants, the largest professional organization of CPA's.

What distinguishes the CPA from an "accountant" is that the CPA has passed the Uniform CPA Examination and has been certified by a state board of accountancy. As of September 1983, CPA's were required to take continuing professional education in 42 states and the District of Columbia.* As licensed public accountants, CPA's audit financial statements of publicly traded companies.

The public practice of accounting is conducted by firms staffed by CPA's and other professionals. These firms can range in size from a single CPA, called a sole practitioner, to large international firms with thousands of professional staff members.

The expertise provided by certified public accountants in public practice can be classified into four distinct areas:

Accounting services: applying diverse accounting expertise in the areas of computerized accounting, cost and management systems, earnings projections, and other areas that help management run companies efficiently and cost-effectively.

Auditing: examining financial statements and issuing opinions on the fairness of those statements for companies traded publicly, and for many other companies as well. Audits are performed routinely for companies seeking credit from banks or other lending institutions. CPA's can also issue two other types of reports on financial statements: compilations and reviews.

Taxation: preparing income-tax returns and advising businesses and individuals concerning taxes to ensure that their tax liability is properly computed.

Management advisory services: assisting business owners and managers in the areas of planning, implementation, and control; finance and accounting; electronic data processing; operations (manufacturing and clerical); human resources; marketing; and management science. This assistance can come in the form of an engagement, in which an analytical approach and process is applied; or it can take the form of a consultation, which is based mostly on the CPA's existing personal knowledge of the client and his or her business. A consultation generally takes place in a shorter time frame that does an engagement.

Certified public accountants in industry, as opposed to those in the public practice of accounting, provide accounting and tax services for their companies, which are their employers. CPA's in education

and government are concerned respectively with teaching future CPA's and providing accounting and auditing services for federal, state, and local governmental units, which are their employers.

Increasingly, the certified public accountant is seen as a protector of the public interest regarding the manner in which business is conducted. In fact the word *audit* has come to stand for the examination of the way in which something is done. An audit carries the imprimatur of legitimacy on the part of the audited party and implies thoroughness and impartiality on the part of the auditor.

The accounting profession today is largely self-regulated. This self-regulation is accomplished and carried out chiefly through a joint ethics-enforcement program administered cooperatively by the individual state societies and the AICPA. Cases of noncompliance with the Code of Professional Ethics or professional standards are investigated. If the facts warrant, the case is brought before a trial board of peers. A guilty finding by the trial board can result in suspension from AICPA membership. The certification to practice as a CPA can be suspended by a state board of accountancy.

The cornerstones upon which the practice of the profession is technically based are Generally Accepted Accounting Principles and Generally Accepted Auditing Standards. The former are established by the Financial Accounting Standards Board, located in Stamford, Connecticut. The latter are determined by AICPA's Auditing Standards Board. Both are enforceable under the Code of Professional Ethics of the AICPA.

Accounting, an ancient profession dating from the time of the Phoenicians, is experiencing a growth today unprecedented in its history. Accounting as a major field of study in colleges and universities is at an all-time high. In 1981, 52,290 students graduated with bachelor's degrees in accounting, and it was projected that this number would grow at a rate of 3–4% annually through 1984. An additional 6,690 students graduated with master's degrees in accounting in 1981. This category was expected to grow at a slightly higher rate through 1984.

Some states are moving to require 150 hours of collegiate course study, with a concentration in accounting, to become a CPA. There is a concerted effort under way to upgrade the educational credentials of aspiring CPA's by making this a nationwide requirement.

The education of a certified public accountant continues even after the individual has received CPA certification. A total of 42 states and the District of Columbia, as of September 1983, required CPA's to take a certain number of hours of continuing professional

---

* In Illinois, CPA's renewing their licenses after October 1, 1984, have to fulfill an 80-hour continuing-professional-education requirement.

education to retain their certifications. The average required annually is 40 hours.

The accounting profession is now in the process of some rather dramatic changes. Until 1979, CPA's were prohibited from advertising their professional services or otherwise soliciting new clients. This ban was rescinded, primarily due to legal advice that such a ban was in violation of antitrust law.

Released from the ban and now free to obtain clients by advertising or other forms of solicitation so long as they are not false, misleading, or deceptive, CPA's are becoming more visible to the general public. Many now author financial advice columns in newspapers and magazines, particularly trade journals, or appear regularly on finance-related talk shows on radio and television. This latter activity increases markedly as the deadline for filing income-tax returns approaches.

Conversely, while CPA's are becoming more visible, the competition for new clients has also increased. This competition takes place not only between the large international accounting firms but also between large and small firms.

In general, companies with substantial revenues and expenditures and complicated tax situations enlist the services of a CPA firm. Many of these companies also have in-house accounting staffs, made up primarily of CPA's, which can do much of this work.

Smaller businesses utilize the services of CPA's for their general accounting and tax expertise, as do most individuals who engage them. Generally, individuals with large incomes, extensive income from investments, income from more than one source, and extensive interest and dividend income can benefit from engaging a CPA. By virtue of their certification, CPA's are automatically enrolled for practice before the Internal Revenue Service.

An additional area of work performed by CPA's for individuals is FINANCIAL PLANNING, which includes tax and estate planning, investment counseling, and insurance advice.

Certified public accountants typically charge their clients on an hourly basis. The fee can vary, depending on the CPA's level in his firm. If the work is performed by a staff accountant, the lowest position a CPA can hold in a firm, the fee is correspondingly lower than if the work is done by a senior, a manager, or a partner, the highest position.

There are a number of ways to locate a CPA firm. Most clients come to a CPA firm as a result of referrals from attorneys, bankers, or other business owners, particularly business owners engaged in a business similar to the searcher's. Additional sources are the respective state societies of CPA's, financial journals, or even the Yellow Pages. Certified public ac-

countants can be found in every city and many towns. There were approximately 300,000 certified public accountants in the United States in 1983, and the profession grows at an approximate rate of 10% annually. AICPA membership figures for 1983 show approximately 23,298 sole practitioners; 33,707 CPA's who are members of firms with two to nine partners; 14,375 members of firms with ten or more partners; 27,761 members in the 25 largest accounting firms. Additionally, 52.5% of the AICPA's membership consists of CPA's in public practice; 37.6% are members of business or industry; 3.2% are employed by government; and 2.5% are in the field of education.

Samuel C. Hoyt

Chapter 7, 11, 13

See BANKRUPTCY.

Charge Account

See CREDIT.

Charitable Lead Trusts

See TRUSTS.

Check

A check, in its most basic form, is nothing more than written instructions to a bank to transfer funds from an account to a specific, named party. All checks have the command "Pay to the order of..." written on them, as well as the name of the bank and the name of the writer of the check.

In 1983 there were more than 100 million checking accounts in the United States. The largest single user of checks is the federal government—it writes about 3% of all checks.

Some payment orders, such as traveler's checks, use the word *check* in their names, but they differ from a bank check in that the issuer, not the signer, is responsible for the funds that the check represents.

A bank check has an important quality: It is negotiable. This means that the right to the funds that the check represents can be transferred to another party. The process by which this transfer takes place is called an ENDORSEMENT. The person or business who accepts an endorsed check or other negotiable payment instrument is called a "holder." For the protection of everyone involved in the checking process, laws have been written to define exactly what a negotiable instrument is and to state the rights and responsibilities of endorser and holder of the instrument.

A technological innovation helps the banking industry to process today's enormous volume of checks efficiently: The strangely shaped numbers at the bottom of each check are printed in an ink that enables a machine to sort checks automatically. Still, one of the most frequently asked questions about checks concerns the time it takes for the funds a check represents to be transferred from bank to bank and from account to account, a process known as CHECK CLEARING. Although the banking industry and federal regulators have for years discussed establishing some sort of time standard for clearing checks, there is really no set answer today. If a person writes a check at a local store that does business with the same bank, the check might clear within 24 hours after it is deposited. On the other hand, if a person in New York sends a check to a business in California, it might take several days or weeks for the check to go through the clearing process. When a person deposits someone else's check in his or her account, many banks will credit the account but put a "hold" on the deposited funds; no withdrawals will be allowed against the deposited check until it has actually been cleared. This policy varies from bank to bank.

Phil Battey

Check Clearing

The process by which banks that receive deposited checks obtain payment from the banks on which the checks are drawn. It is estimated that Americans wrote about 35–40 billion checks in 1983 against 115 million accounts. These checks transferred more than $30 trillion.

The key element in the clearing process is the "settlement" (transfer of value) of balances, either (1) internal account balances, (2) balances between banks when checks are presented to a correspondent bank for collection, (3) balances among banks when checks are exchanged at a clearinghouse, or (4) balances among banks that have accounts at the Federal Reserve banks.

There are four basic ways that checks are cleared in the American banking system:

1. About 30% of all checks written are cleared internally—they are deposited in the banks on which they are drawn and are collected through internal adjustments on the banks' books. These checks, called "on-us" items, are either presented at tellers' windows by depositors who want to "cash" a check (exchange demand-deposit money for currency) or presented for deposit by account holders who have received them from people or businesses that also have accounts at the same bank (not unusual in small towns or in rural areas where only one or two banks may serve a given geographic area). Banks handle "on-us" checks as in-

ternal credit and debit adjustments; the check writer's account is reduced by the amount of the check and the depositor's account is credited with a like amount.

2. About 15% of all checks written are cleared through local clearinghouses or clearing arrangements. In a clearing arrangement, a number of banks in a given region that typically receive large numbers of deposited checks drawn on one another meet to exchange and collect payment for them. Banks present checks to a central point—a separate physical facility or a back office room of one of the banks in the arrangement. There, checks are physically exchanged among participants and, more important, collection is made by netting the amounts presented by each bank against one another.

3. About 25% of all checks are collected through correspondent banks. When a CORRESPONDENT BANK receives a check from a respondent bank, there are several different routes the check-collection process can take. If the check presented by the respondent is drawn on a bank that also maintains an account with the correspondent, collection involves simply the correspondent's transfer of deposit credit from one account to another account on its own books. If the presented check is drawn on a bank that does not have an account relationship with the correspondent, the respondent gets credit for the check to its account and the check is either sent to another correspondent bank, in which the original correspondent bank and the bank on which the check is drawn both have an account, or sent to a clearinghouse or a Reserve Bank.

4. About 30% of the nation's checks are cleared through the Federal Reserve. The Federal Reserve collects checks by transferring credit balances from one account on its books to another, in much the same way that individual banks collect "on-us" checks. For presenting and paying banks that have accounts at two different Federal Reserve banks, an extra step is involved in the collection process. Each Reserve bank has an "interdistrict settlement account" that it maintains on the books of an Interdistrict Settlement Fund established in Washington, D.C., to handle settlements among Reserve banks. A check presented to one Reserve bank drawn on a bank in another Federal Reserve district will result in a transfer of interdistrict settlement-account balances from one Reserve bank to another.

Before the establishment of the Federal Reserve banks in 1914, the check-collection process in the American banking system was inefficient and costly. Banks could collect local checks by presenting them over the counter to the banks on which they were drawn, or through local clearing arrangements, but collecting checks drawn on banks located in different parts of the country caused problems.

Exchange Charges. Banks on which checks were drawn would impose an "exchange charge" on checks presented for payment by out-of-town banks. The charge was necessitated by the costs banks had to incur to ship gold or cash to pay for checks, the banking practice before the Federal Reserve.

Circuitous Routing. To avoid exchange charges, banks frequently sent checks on long, circuitous collection routes across the country. Circuitous routing magnified the risk banks incurred in collecting checks if those checks were not properly forwarded or were lost in transit. Final payment took an exceedingly long time, and there was no direct way for banks to return dishonored items. The cross-country collection process was costly to the banking system as well as the public.

Nonpar Checking. Exchange charges for nonlocal checks effectively meant that checks were credited to depositors' accounts at less than par (face) value. Because of this practice, nonlocal checks were often not accepted in commercial dealings, and business firms developed the standard of requiring bills to be paid either in currency or with a local check.

Uncollected Funds as Reserves. Correspondent banks receiving deposits of checks from respondents for collection developed the practice of crediting their respondents' accounts immediately, even though the checks could not be collected for a number of days. Since these accounts made up a substantial portion of banks' legal reserves, the result was that reserves, designed to assure bank safety and liquidity, were being held largely in uncollected funds.

Maintaining Compensating Balances for the Purpose of Collecting Checks at Par. In an attempt to receive full face value for deposited checks, banks often fragmented their reserve deposits across the country in the form of many different correspondent-account balances in different banking regions. The practice was damaging to banks' liquidity and grew exceedingly costly as check usage proliferated.

The centralization of bank reserves at the 12 Federal Reserve banks in 1914 provided the banking system, for the first time, with an efficient mechanism for clearing checks between the nation's geographic regions. By the 1920s the Federal Reserve had also established a nationwide wire-transfer settlement system to effect interregional collections without requiring the physical transfer of gold or currency. However, the Federal Reserve would only accept checks and make fund transfers by wire at face value. The Federal Reserve's refusal to accept nonpar items and

its elimination of the "transportation costs" of transferring funds for interregional settlement (through the establishment of the wire-transfer network) ended exchange charges for checks by the early 1920s in most of the country. In 1982, the Federal Reserve processed more than 15 billion checks through a network of 12 regional Federal Reserve banks, their 25 branches, and 12 off-premises regional check-processing centers located across the country in strategic suburban locations where transportation time in collecting checks is minimized.

David H. Friedman

Checking System of the United States

The system of checking accounts serves as a practical means for people to exchange money. It enables one to deposit money into a central source and pay for goods or services from this fund with written orders, or checks, making it unnecessary for people to carry hard cash, particularly large sums. Checking accounts are a basic component of the economic system of the United States and many other developed countries throughout the world. They are utilized by both individuals and businesses.

While the value of checking accounts is easily understood, the system by which checks and money flow is somewhat complicated. Since most checks in everyday practice are drawn on accounts outside the areas of the banks in which they are deposited, it is necessary to maintain a uniform system throughout the country under which checks can be processed accurately and efficiently. This entry examines the system whereby checks and the funds they represent ("demand deposits") move in the United States. (Detailed information on the process by which banks obtain payment on deposited checks can be found in the entry CHECK CLEARING.)

Paying by check is actually a matter of "dollar-switching"—subtracting funds from one account and adding them to another. Such transactions involve a payment circuit comprised of commercial banks and Federal Reserve centers. The FEDERAL RESERVE SYSTEM is divided into 12 Federal Reserve districts, each having a Federal Reserve bank and branches serving particular areas within districts. Local banks have "demand accounts" with the Federal Reserve Center in their district. These centers serve as check-clearing and collection banks for their members, and in essence are a national clearing mechanism. Thus, local banks can clear checks payable out of town through the area's Federal Reserve bank. Billions of checks amounting to trillions of dollars are handled annually by the Federal Reserve system.

People use checks every day to pay for a multitude

of things. It is a simple process to write a check; but once it is cashed or deposited, it sets a lot of wheels in motion (see Figure 1). The transaction process is generally as follows:

1. The person having a checking account with a commercial bank gives the check to a party. (The person giving the check is the *payer,* the receiver is the *payee.*)

2. The payee deposits the check in his account at his local bank.

3. The local bank deposits the check for credit on its account at its district Federal Reserve bank.

4. The district Federal Reserve bank sends the check to the Federal Reserve bank in the district serving the area in which the payer's bank conducts business (moneys are transferred through an "interdistrict settlement fund"—see below). The check will remain at the first Federal Reserve bank if it is in the district serving the bank on which the check is drawn.

5. The Federal Reserve bank that receives the check forwards it to the payer's local bank, where a bookkeeper (most often, today, a computer) deducts the amount of the check from the account of the payer.

6. The payer's bank authorizes its Federal Reserve

Center to deduct the amount of the check from its "demand account" with the Reserve bank.

7. The Federal Reserve bank pays the Federal Reserve bank in the district of the payee's local bank by crediting its share in the "interdistrict settlement fund."

8. The Federal Reserve bank credits the deposit account of the payee's bank.

9. The bank credits the payee's account.

10. The payer's bank sends the canceled check back to the payer along with other canceled checks on a periodic basis, usually monthly. (A canceled check may serve as a receipt for payment.)

Local banks have accounts with FEDERAL RESERVE BANKS, or with CORRESPONDENT BANKS, or both. When there is a transaction at a Reserve or correspondent bank, the sending bank's deposit account is credited and the receiving bank's account is credited-reduced by the amount written on the check.

There are numerous daily transactions between Federal Reserve banks. They pay each other using an "interdistrict settlement fund" maintained in Washington, D.C. Reserve banks and the interdistrict settlement fund are linked via an electronic communica-

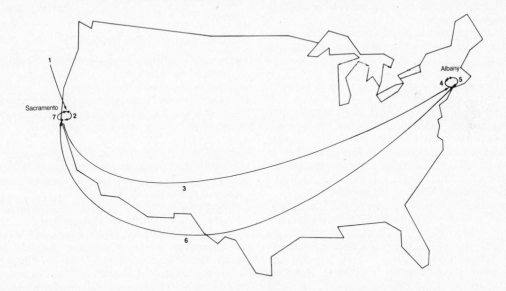

Figure 1. Route of a check. Mrs. Henderson, an Albany, New York, resident, buys a painting from an art dealer in San Francisco, paying with a check. (1) The art dealer deposits the check in his account at a Sacramento bank. (2) The Sacramento bank deposits the check in its account at the Federal Reserve Bank of San Francisco. (3) The Federal Reserve Bank of San Francisco sends the check to the Federal Reserve Bank of New York for collection. (4) The FRB of New York forwards the check to the Albany bank, which debits the amount from Mrs. Henderson's account. (5) The Albany bank authorizes the FRB of New York to deduct the amount of the check from its account. (6) The FRB of New York pays the FRB of San Francisco from its interdistrict settlement fund. (7) The FRB of San Francisco credits the Sacramento bank account, and the Sacramento bank credits the art dealer's account. (*Source:* Federal Reserve Bank of Minneapolis.)

tions system. For daily transactions, the electronic system settles net balances between the Federal Reserve banks.

Processing Operations at Federal Reserve Banks. On a single business day, more than 100 million checks may be written in the United States. It is thus necessary for the Federal Reserve system, through which about 40% of these checks are circuited, to maintain a system capable of collecting these checks quickly and transferring funds accurately.

A Federal Reserve bank works in the following way: Each day, bundles of checks arrive at the Federal Reserve Center from banks. These banks have accounts with the center and their accounts are credited accordingly. In each bundle are various packages of checks. Attached to each package is a tape listing the amount of each check. A bank will also send a "cash letter" listing the total of all packages. This is verified at the center, and the amounts will be credited to depositing banks' accounts.

The Federal Reserve Center has high-speed electronic machines that process the checks at a rate of over 60,000 checks per hour. Printed along the bottom of the checks are characters in magnetic ink, each of which has a special meaning and can be "read" by the electronic machines.

To illustrate the meaning of the digits that appear on the bottom of a check, let us look at the following example:

⑈0213 0217⑈ 1235⑈ 06831⑈ 0122 ⑈0000010850⑈

The first group of four digits, 0213, is the check-routing symbol. Specifically, the first two numbers signify the bank's Federal Reserve district number; the third number designates the Federal Reserve office (head office or branch) or a special collection arrangement; and the fourth digit represents the bank's state or a special collection arrangement.

The second group of four digits, 0217, designates the bank's identification number. The next digit, 8, is called the "check digit." This digit, combined with the first eight digits, verifies the routing numbers' accuracy and computer processing.

The third group of digits, 1235 06831, is the account number of the individual payer. The next group, 0122, designates the payer's individual check number. The last group of digits is the dollar amount encoded by the receiving bank. In this case, the check was in the amount of $108.50, encoded as 0000010850.

In the upper right-hand corner of a check, there are digits in the form of a numerator and denominator. For example, $\frac{50-217}{213}$. The numerator is the bank's identification number and the denominator is the check routing symbol. This fraction is used when hand-processing is necessary. While these digits are encoded in magnetic ink across the bottom of the check, the first two digits in the numerator are not. The nonencoded digits represent the city, state, or other territorial designations needed for hand-processing.

The electronic machines into which checks are fed perform various functions. They "read," itemize, record, and endorse the checks, then sort them into compartments that represent either single banks or groups of banks. Checks that are torn, folded, bear incorrect coding, or lack magnetic symbols may be rejected by the machines and are processed by hand. At the completion of this procedure, the machine's tabulations are cross-checked with the "cash letter" sent by the depositing bank. After verification, the checks are packaged and sent to the next step in the chain. Some checks passing through the Federal Reserve clearing operation are returned to the depositing bank, such as those improperly endorsed or drawn on accounts with insufficient funds. Because of the multitude of checks written, some Reserve banks and branches are supplemented by regional check-processing centers that facilitate check clearance.

Charles J. Parnow

Chicago Board of Trade (CBOT)

The world's oldest and largest COMMODITY-FUTURES EXCHANGE, on which wheat, corn, oats, soybeans, soybean oil, soybean meal, silver, gold, Treasury bonds, options on Treasury bonds, GNMAs, ten-year Treasury notes, unleaded regular gasoline, heating oil, crude oil, and other commodities are traded.

History. The Chicago Board of Trade was established in 1848 by 82 Chicago merchants responding to the need for a self-regulated marketplace amid the chaotic marketing conditions of the time.

From its beginnings as a small agricultural commodity exchange in the 1800s, the Chicago Board of Trade has become an electronic, sophisticated, and innovative commercial institution reflecting economic conditions throughout the nation and around the world. In just a short time during the 1800s, Chicago had become the hub of America's grain-marketing system. The newly invented telegraph was making its debut in the young frontier town, linking the area's booming grain trade with markets across the nation and around the world. Wheat would soon be arriving by rail from the hinterlands and would be stored in the first steam-powered bulk elevator. The city's elevators, rail yards, warehouses, and port facilities provided a steadily expanding number of farmers with a central marketplace where they could receive higher prices for their wagonloads of grain.

However, the city was without a central trading facility, and farmers had to go from merchant to merchant seeking the best price for their crops. At harvest time, too much grain arrived, more than could be stored or shipped. Prices dropped drastically, and what could not be sold was towed out into Lake Michigan and dumped. But by spring, existing supplies could not meet demand, causing prices to skyrocket. At the same time, standard grades and weights were nonexistent.

The merchants who founded the Chicago Board of Trade realized that their livelihood depended on a large, liquid, year-round central market with standardized practices for buyers and sellers. While they did not want to control prices, they did want a single location where buyers and sellers could arrive at a fair price based on current supply-and-demand factors.

When the exchange was formed in 1848, considerable time was taken with organizational details, such as establishing uniform grain grades and inspection systems that conformed to weights and measures utilized elsewhere in the commercial world.

The objectives set forth in the 1848 Chicago Board of Trade constitution still hold true today: "To maintain a commercial exchange; to promote uniformity in the customs and usages of merchants; to inculcate principles of justice and equity to trade; to facilitate the speedy adjustment of business disputes; to acquire and disseminate valuable commercial and economic information; and generally to secure to its members the benefits of cooperation in the furtherance of their legitimate pursuits."

In the early 1850s, the French government purchased large quantities of wheat in Chicago, the first time in the city's history that European buyers had come to the Midwest rather than to New York for grain. It established a trend that still continues because much of Chicago's expanding international banking activity today centers on grain-purchase transactions. Today, many countries with nationalized grain production and/or supply systems use the exchange to determine reliable prices and to hedge their import and export commitments.

Around 1870, futures contracts (standardized, transferable agreements enforced by the exchange) were introduced to facilitate and complement cash trade and forward contracts, the latter tailored agreements between specific buyers and sellers.

Shortly after the end of the Civil War, the first transatlantic cable revolutionized communications to and from Chicago. A cable could be sent from Chicago to London in the unheard-of time of three hours. Today, the exchange is one of the most intricate communications networks in the world, with a system that allows price and order information to move between the trading floor and any spot on earth in seconds.

In 1893, during the Columbian Exposition, the board opened its galleries to the public for the first time. Since then, tens of thousands of people have come to its Visitors' Center each year to watch an open and free marketplace in action.

During World War II, the government imposed price controls on grains. As a result, there was very little trading activity in the pits until after the war was over. Once the controls were lifted, the Board's worldwide influence resumed and grew steadily during the fifties and sixties.

The innovative spirit of the exchange continued to manifest itself when, in 1975, the Chicago Board of Trade introduced INTEREST-RATE FUTURES. The introduction of these contracts firmly established the commercial importance of financial futures.

The first interest-rate-futures contract was based on GOVERNMENT NATIONAL MORTGAGE ASSOCIATION (GNMA) certificates—mortgage-backed instruments guaranteed by the federal government—which began trading in 1975. The success of this contract led to the creation of several innovative financial instruments, including the exchange's U.S Treasury bond futures in 1977. The T-bond contract has been so successful that by 1981 it was the most active commodity on all U.S. exchanges, with volume at more than 13.9 million contracts for that year and 16.7 million in 1982.

By recognizing that money is also a commodity whose value changes and is expressed in fluctuating interest rates, the exchange identified the need to provide hedging opportunities to the world's financial community. Since 1975, interest-rate futures have grown to become approximately 40% of the board's total volume.

The CBT continues to expand its product line with new investment and risk-management vehicles, including long-term Treasury notes, options on financial and agricultural futures, stock-index futures, a complex of energy futures (gasoline, heating oil, and crude oil), and one-kilo gold futures.

Trading and Hand Signals. Commodity-futures contracts are traded on octagonal wooden risers known as "pits." The pits themselves are raised platforms with descending steps on the inside. This shape permits all buyers and sellers to see each other. Traders stand in designated areas in the pit according to the delivery month in which they wish to trade. Buyers and sellers are not separated, because a trader may buy or sell at any time.

Trading is conducted through a public auction system between members, employing a combination of hand signals and open, competitive outcry. Trading is permitted only between the opening and closing bells for each commodity during the specified trading hours.

A trader with his palm facing inward wishes to buy; one with his palm outward wishes to sell. Each finger held vertically on that hand indicates quantity. Then, by extending fingers in a horizontal position, a trader expresses the price at which he wishes to buy or sell.

The trading floor, in addition to being the scene of trading, is an information center for all aspects of the trade. Several tickers on the trading floor bring a constant flow of current news, including weather conditions in pertinent crop-growing regions in the U.S. and worldwide and market reports from other commodity exchanges.

Route of an Order. Futures orders originating outside of the exchange are received on the trading floor via telephone and Teletype by exchange members and member firms. To handle the thousands of calls coming from companies and individuals, batteries of telephone stations are located on the periphery of the trading floor. When an order is received at a phone station, it is time-stamped, then rushed by a messenger, or "runner," to a broker in a trading pit, where the order is executed.

As each order is filled, brokers report price changes to price reporters in the raised "pulpits" overlooking each pit. Board of Trade employees in the pulpits relay price changes as they occur to central quotation computers. The computers transmit the price information onto electronic price boards facing the trading floor and around the world via information services. Completed orders are picked up by the runners and returned to the telephone desks, where they are time-stamped again and customers notified that their orders have been filled.

Membership. The Chicago Board of Trade is a private membership organization. It has 1,402 full members who are eligible to trade any of the futures contracts offered. Each person qualifies for membership on his or her merits under board regulations. Currently, there are about 600 associate members who are eligible to trade financial instruments, gold, and plywood contracts. In addition, there are a number of limited members who are eligible to trade specific contracts in the following areas: government-instruments contracts; index, debt, and energy futures; and commodity-options contracts.

The Agricultural and Associated Market of the CBT is a classification only, whereas the other three represent classifications for which trading privileges can be purchased or leased. These four groups represent the basic classifications of Chicago Board of Trade contracts.

A membership is sold to an applicant through a "bid-and-ask" system, but only when one is available for sale. Each applicant must meet certain financial requirements, be sponsored by two members, and be approved by the exchange's board of directors. Prices vary, depending upon demand and supply.

The association is self-governing, with a board of directors, including an elected chairman, vice-chairman, fifteen member directors, three public directors, and the appointed, paid president of the exchange, who is also chief executive officer. The exchange is administered by an executive staff headed by the president. A staff of over 400 carries out the daily administrative work.

There are approximately 50 member committees responsible for policymaking for all phases of exchange activity. These committees include Arbitration; Business Conduct; Cash Grain; Commodity Options; Computer and Telecommunications; Customer Relations; Education; Energy; Executive; Feed Grain Contract; Finance and Exchange Oversight; Financial Instruments; Floor; Floor Conduct; Floor Governors; Forest Products; GNMA-CDR Origination; Long-Range Planning; Margin; Market Report and Quotations; Memberships; Member Relations; Member Services; Metals; New Products; Nominating; Public Relations and Marketing; Real Estate; Rules; Soybean; Soybean Meal; Soybean Oil; Statistics; Transportation; Warehouse, Weighing and Custodian; and Wheat.

CBT Clearing Corporation. Throughout the trading day, each trader turns endorsed orders of completed trades over to a clearing firm, one of approximately 100 clearing member firms of the Board of Trade Clearing Corporation. A separate entity from the Chicago Board of Trade, the Clearing Corporation settles the accounts of each member firm at the end of the trading day, balancing quantities of commodities bought with those sold. By Chicago Board of Trade rule, all members of the exchange must clear their trades on the day the trades are made.

Traders are financially responsible to their clearing firms, and the Clearing Corporation in turn guarantees performance of all contracts traded and cleared. For each trade made between a buyer and a seller, the Clearing Corporation legally substitutes itself as the buyer to every seller and the seller to every buyer. By thus guaranteeing each transaction, no customer has ever lost a cent due to a default on a futures contract bought or sold on the Chicago Board of Trade since the Board of Trade Clearing Corporation was founded in 1925.

The Clearing Corporation settles its accounts daily.

As prices change, causing variations in the value of all outstanding futures contracts, the Clearing Corporation collects from those who have lost money as a result of price changes and credits and funds immediately to the accounts of those who have gained as a result of price changes. Thus, before each day's trading begins, all of the previous day's losses have been collected and all gains have been paid or credited.

Thomas R. Donovan

Chicago Board Options Exchange (CBOE)

The Chicago Board Options Exchange is the world's largest options exchange and the nation's only exclusive marketplace for trading listed stock options, options on U.S. Treasury bonds, and options on Standard & Poor's stock indexes.

The CBOE lists securities that are traded in much the same manner as stocks. An option is a contract granting the holder (buyer) the right to buy or sell 100 shares of a given stock at a specified price for a specified period of time. The CBOE evolved to meet the need of investors for a regulated public marketplace to buy and sell options. This gave investors a new investment tool designed to transfer risk, provide leverage, hedge against market movements, gain additional yield on equity investments, and meet a variety of other investment objectives.

The exchange is an independent, membership corporation registered as a national securities exchange with the U.S. Securities and Exchange Commission. More than 55% of all listed stock-option trading in the U.S. takes place on the CBOE floor, making it the leading options marketplace.

Origin and Development. Created after four years of research and development by the Chicago Board of Trade, today the CBOE is a legally separate and independent corporation.

On April 26, 1973, the CBOE opened trading as the world's first and only exchange established expressly for trading stock options. This created a central, regulated marketplace for trading, at standardized prices, option contracts that until that time were traded with difficulty in the over-the-counter market by very few investors.

When the exchange opened, 284 members, including 121 firms, traded calls on 16 listed stocks. CBOE membership in 1983 was made up of more than 1,700, including nearly 700 firms. Members traded calls and puts on 145 of the most widely held, actively traded U.S. stocks, as well as on U.S. Treasury bonds and on Standard & Poor's stock indexes.

The CBOE follows the rules and regulations of the Securities and Exchange Commission, the Options Clearing Corporation (OCC), and its own stringent regulations. The OCC was created by the CBOE to guarantee integrity in every option contract by serving as the opposite party to each trade. Now owned jointly by all exchanges trading options, the OCC ensures that the writers of option contracts fulfill their financial obligations to buyers through collection of adequate margins and through contractual obligations of OCC clearing members.

In 1982 the exchange opened the world market for options on interest-rate instruments when it began trading options on U.S. Treasury bonds. The following year CBOE began trading options on the Standard & Poor's stock indexes, thus creating the first market-index option that was a security, trading directly off the market with no intervening future position.

Understanding Options. Understanding options begins with calls and puts. A call option is the right to *purchase* and a put the right to *sell* 100 shares of a specific common stock at a specified price at any time during the life of the option, which can be as long as nine months. This does not mean that for every call there is a put and for every put, a call. Calls and puts are not opposite sides of the same transaction. A call option and a put option involve totally separate transactions with the OCC.

Common stocks on which options are traded on the CBOE include such well-known companies as AT&T, Teledyne, IBM, Xerox, Honeywell, and Eastman Kodak.

Underlying Security	Exercise Price	Expiration Month/Premium			Close
		Jan.	Apr.	July[3]	
XYZ[1]	60[2]	1¼	4	6[4]	60¼[5]
XYZ	p60	¾	2½	4¼	60¼

Note: Superscript numbers refer to the following text.

Option quotations similar to the one in the accompanying table appear regularly in many financial publications and daily newspapers that report securities prices. The letter *p* following the underlying security's name denotes a put. Quotations without *p* are calls. The components of an option are shown in the table as follows:

1. *The Underlying Security.* This is the common stock. Here, an XYZ call is the option to buy 100 shares of XYZ Company common stock.

2. *The Exercise Price.* The exercise or strike price in this instance is $60 per share, the price at which the call-option buyer may exercise his right to purchase the stock from the option writer.

3. *The Expiration Month.* This is the month in which the option expires. All CBOE options expire

quarterly on cycles beginning in January, February, or March. In the example shown, XYZ Company put and call options were currently being traded with expirations in January, April, and July.

4. *The Premium.* This is the money the buyer pays to acquire an option. Since option contracts are for 100 shares of stock, the total call premium for the XYZ option is $125 for the January expiration, $400 for the April expiration, and $600 for the July expiration. The option premium is kept by the writer of the option whether the option is exercised or not.

5. *The Close.* The underlying stock's closing price.

Three major factors influence option premiums. The first factor is the current market price of the underlying stock in relation to the exercise price of the option. Call-option premiums increase as stock prices increase. The opposite is true of put options, which increase in value as stock prices decrease.

The second factor is the length of time remaining until expiration. The longer the time remaining until expiration, the higher the premium—reflecting the greater opportunity for change in the price of underlying stock. Puts and calls are "wasting assets": As expiration approaches, their value decreases.

The third factor influencing option premiums is the volatility of the underlying stock. The more volatile the price of the stock, the higher the option premium. Increased volatility means that the stock price is more subject to fluctuation. Therefore, a higher probability exists that an option will end up in the money. Since a static stock's price doesn't move much, it won't approach the exercise price, will end up out of the money, and will hence be worthless.

For further information, *see* OPTION TRADING.

The Option Marketplace. Options traded on the CBOE share many similarities with securities traded on other exchanges. Options are listed securities. Orders to buy and sell options are handled through brokers in the same way as orders to buy and sell stocks. Listed option orders are executed on the trading floor of a national, regulated exchange where all trading is conducted in the open, competitive manner of an auction market.

Still another similarity is the opportunity to follow price movements, trading volume, and other pertinent information minute by minute or day by day. The buyer or writer of an option, like the buyer or seller of stock, can learn almost instantly the price at which his order has been executed and its movements afterward.

While options and common stocks are similar, there are important differences. Most important, an option is simply a contract involving a buyer and a seller. Thus, unlike shares of common stock, there is

no fixed number of options. The number of options depends solely upon the number that buyers wish to buy and sellers wish to write.

Another difference between common stocks and options is that normally there are no certificates evidencing ownership of options. Instead, buyers' and sellers' positions are indicated on printed statements prepared by their respective brokerage firms. Certificateless trading—a major CBOE innovation—sharply reduces paper work and delays.

Finally, an option differs from common stock in that the option is a "wasting asset." The closer it gets to expiration, the less "time value" it has, since there's less time remaining for it to become profitable. If an option is not sold and not worth exercising at expiration, it becomes worthless and the holder loses the entire amount paid for it.

How the Floor Operates. When the CBOE initiated trading in listed options, a nontraditional system of procedures was instituted on the trading floor. In other securities exchanges, a single specialist is assigned to a specific security. Specialists have both a broker and dealer function; they handle orders from the public as well as trade for their own accounts. The CBOE system separates these functions: Persons handling public orders may not trade for themselves in the same security. A description of the floor personnel's responsibilities and functions will illustrate the CBOE system:

Order Book Official (OBO). Each OBO is assigned to a post where specific classes of options are traded. The OBO's are responsible for the recording and execution of all public orders given to them. They may not trade for themselves. OBO's are exchange employees and may accept only public orders.

The OBO's also are in charge of the trading crowd around their posts. They must maintain a fair and orderly market in the classes of options for which they assume responsibility. CBOE rules require that bids and offers be made by public outcry. Highest bids and lowest offers have priority. If two or more bids (or offers) represent this best price, priority is determined by the sequence in which the bids (or offers) were made.

The OBO must display the highest bid and lowest offer that appear in the book.

Floor Broker. Because floor brokers execute orders from the public, they act only as agents. A brokerage fee is charged for each order executed. Floor brokers also may function as market-makers, but they can act in only one of these capacities in any particular class on any given day. The floor broker receives written orders as they come to the brokerage houses' booths (by wire or by telephone). It is then the floor broker's responsibility to execute those orders.

Market-Maker. The market-makers are responsible for making markets in their assigned classes. They perform a dealer function. Market-makers trade only for their own accounts, at their own risk, for their own profit. Each market-maker competes with every other market-maker assigned to the same class of options. There are an average of 20 market-makers per stock group. However, more than 50 market-makers may be present in very active classes of options.

The Rise of Other Markets. The opening of the CBOE in 1973 gave birth to the market in listed stock options. Today there is growing investor awareness of options as a stabilizing market influence during periods of economic uncertainty. Options provide investors with a mechanism to help them meet their day-to-day financial objectives.

In 1982 the CBOE set a daily-volume record by trading 666,457 contracts. Participation by institutions is increasing; this is indicated by the rise of block trades—trades in volumes of 100 or more contracts (of 100 shares each).

Exchanges now offer options on futures, commodities, indexes, industry groups, and interest rates. The introduction of new products plus the growth of equity options are making heavier demands upon the Chicago Board Options Exchange, which, as the first, largest, and only exclusive options marketplace, has consistently grown to meet these demands.

See also STOCK EXCHANGES.

Walter E. Auch

Chicago Mercantile Exchange, International Monetary Market and Index and Option Market

A COMMODITY-FUTURES EXCHANGE on which live hogs, frozen pork bellies, live cattle, feeder cattle, Treasury bills (90-day), deutsche marks, Mexican pesos, British pounds, Canadian dollars, French francs, Swiss francs, Japanese yen, gold, Eurodollars, certificates of deposit, S&P's 500 stock index, S&P 500 options, S&P 100 futures, and lumber are traded.

History. In 1874 the Chicago Produce Exchange was founded as a contract market for trading butter and eggs. By 1898, when the population of Chicago was about 1.70 million, a group broke away from the Produce Exchange to form the Chicago Butter and Egg Board. The board was formed by merchants in this well-developed industry who felt the need for a central marketplace to help determine the prices for the raw materials needed in their business.

The objectives of the Butter and Egg Board, as stated in its bylaws, were "1. the establishment of daily market quotations on butter, eggs and other products; 2. the provision of general information regarding the market for such commodities; 3. the location of a convenient place to buy and sell commodities; and 4. the machinery to quickly adjust business disputes among its members."

While the egg and butter contracts proved popular, members of the Butter and Egg Board in 1919 formed committees to gather data about futures trading in other commodities in order to expand their markets. Grain, cotton, and other commodities were considered as possible new candidates to be traded.

With expansion into futures on the horizon, the Butter and Egg Board changed its name to the Chicago Mercantile Exchange (CME), and on December 1, 1919, opening day for the new exchange, three "cars," or futures contracts, were traded in a 45-minute period. None of the traders on the floor that day envisioned that by 1981 a typical day's trading would see nearly 100,000 contracts change hands, and nearly 125,000 daily in the first half of 1982.

To accompany the new exchange, a clearinghouse was formed to set up and process the futures transactions. This department, which is the heart of any modern exchange, acts as the central point where all buy and sell transactions for the day are matched, margin payments are monitored, and daily profits are dispersed and losses collected.

Early trading on the CME continued on a sporadic basis during the next two decades as new contracts were introduced and national economic developments affected the commodity markets. Volume during this period was unpredictable, with activity reaching a high of 93,946 contracts in 1942 and moving to a low in 1932 when 50,428 contracts changed hands.

Modernization and Expansion. Prior to World War II, the CME began trading cheese (1929), potatoes (January 12, 1931), hides (1938), and onions (September 8, 1942). But the advent of wartime price controls froze the cash market and made futures trading unnecessary. The introduction of government price-support policies after the war and the application of new technologies that developed during the war prompted exchange members to begin researching new contracts. Their hope was to find an expanding industry that would make use of futures in its economic planning. Still concentrating on agricultural commodities, the CME added turkeys (October 1, 1945), apples (1948), frozen eggs (1960), and shrimps (1964) to the list of futures contracts, and volume built to the credible level of 485,824 contracts traded in 1961.

Simple statistics, though, often do not tell the entire story. Somewhere during the decade 1950–60, a favorable attitude toward modernization moved over the exchange. It may have begun with the traders themselves, the backbone of any exchange, who actually execute the trades and often risk their own capital. Perhaps industry recognition of these markets added the needed liquidity and ensured a stable order flow. Or it might be attributed to great or small economic events that provided the necessary market conditions for the development of futures markets.

Regardless, futures markets clearly reached a new level of maturity at the beginning of the sixties. On September 18, 1961, a new futures contract based on frozen slabs of uncured, unsliced bacon, or pork bellies, began trading. After a slow start and despite its name, the contract eventually became one of the most successful futures contracts traded in the world, with over 24 million contracts traded in its first 20 years. This eventually pointed the exchange in the direction of developing three other key contracts based on meats.

The modernization of the exchange pushed for creative applications of new ideas. Traditionally, all commodities contracts were written on storable, perishable items. The reason for this can be traced to the original function of commodities, which was to provide a supply and a price of an agricultural item at some future date, regardless of the harvest season. Potatoes, onions, grains, and, with the advent of refrigeration, pork bellies all met this criterion. All elements of the markets—traders, the exchange, and industry participants—felt comfortable with these kinds of items.

So it was with some trepidation that this pattern was broken in 1964 when the first nonperishable commodity was introduced for trading: live cattle. Industry resistance was certainly present. One large user of futures markets remarked that he would not trade a commodity that could "kick back." More seriously, other futures-market users raised questions concerning delivery, grading, and location of the available supply. All of these questions were reasonable and were thoroughly researched beforehand.

First, delivery—which is an option any holder of a "long" futures contract has—was made into a direct, distinct process. Initially three delivery points were written into the contract: Chicago, Sioux City, and Omaha. Second, strict limits were set on the allowable weight of the delivered load of live cattle to guard against weight loss in transit. The quality of the animals, as to temperament, health, and gross physical condition, was also accounted for in the contract. In short, the use of a live animal as the basis for a futures contract was closely supervised by employees of the CME as well as U.S. Department of Agriculture inspectors, who did the actual grading of the animals.

Because live cattle served as such a watershed in agricultural-commodities history, being the transition point from storable to live commodities, the CME quickly began to research other possibilities in the livestock area. By 1966 live hogs were listed as the second nonstorable commodity available for trading, and they were followed in 1971 by feeder cattle.

It took ten years—from 1961 to 1971—for the CME to forge its dominance in the livestock and meat commodity area. This dominance can be measured in a number of different ways, from the qualitative innovation in the listing of the contracts themselves, to volume figures and the price of membership sales.

From 1964, after pork bellies became accepted in the marketplace, until 1973, when the four livestock contracts were listed, annual trading volume increased 31 times—from 250,000 contracts traded in 1964 to more than 6 million in 1973. A record volume for the exchange—which was to be broken many times afterward—was achieved in 1977 when 7.88 million contracts changed hands. In 1981 a record of over 24.5 million contracts traded.

Another decade of innovation began in 1972 with the start of trading in foreign currencies. To fully understand why this was considered a radical departure from the past, one must understand that prior to this the majority of commodity trading was limited to agricultural products.

However, as the world became increasingly complex, interdependent, and technological, money started to be considered a volatile commodity. Its price fluctuated constantly, creating additional business risks, which, unlike other risks, could not be covered by any hedging or insurance policy. Hence, it was a likely candidate for futures.

But before contracts based on money could begin trading, a number of other events had to prepare the marketplace for their introduction. In 1971 the Bretton Woods Agreement collapsed. This agreement, signed by President Harry Truman and representatives of most Western nations in 1945, established a narrow band of fluctuation between other currencies and the U.S. dollar. In the absence of this agreement, foreign currencies would begin to move more widely against the U.S. dollar. The Smithsonian Agreement of late 1971 widened the band of fluctuation, but, with some currencies already floating, that pact soon fell into disuse.

This convergence of events created the needed elements for a viable futures contract based on foreign currencies. But the marketplace still needed to be developed, user resistance overcome, and the integrity of the marketplace established.

With these obstacles in front of them, the International Monetary Market (IMM) began trading seven foreign currencies on May 16, 1972. Volume built slowly, but tripled during its first full year of trading, 1973.

From foreign currencies, the IMM expanded into gold bullion on December 31, 1974. This became possible when ownership of the precious metal by U.S. citizens was legalized. Bullion dealers, institutional traders, and the general public quickly entered this market.

The growing credibility of the IMM also spawned a new genre of contracts based on interest-rate instruments (*see* INTEREST-RATE FUTURES). In January 1976, 90-day U.S. Treasury bill futures started trading. This immediately afforded streamlined interest-rate risk protection to a wide range of money managers. Treasury bills would eventually become the most successful contract in the CME's history.

The exchange soon developed other short-term interest-rate contracts and introduced domestic certificates of deposit (July 1981) and Eurodollar time deposits (December 1981). All of these short-term instruments allowed easy arbitrage between the contracts while this centralized marketplace complemented activities in the interbank cash market. (*Arbitrage* is defined as the simultaneous purchase or sale of a security in order to profit from the price discrepancies.)

The acceptance of these contracts and the development of a cash settlement price for Eurodollars paved the way for the most recent new group of contracts: stock-index futures. In April 1982 a futures contract based on the Standard & Poor's 500 stock index, a widely recognized economic indicator, began trading. The contract would track the upward and downward movement of the actual index. At expiration, the contract would converge with the cash index (as closely as its five-point minimum fluctuation would allow). Settlement would be in cash, as opposed to the traditional physical delivery.

This contract also opened the futures markets to a tremendous potential audience. Current estimates show there are about 35 million participants in the stock market versus the 200,000 or so who use futures. This contract afforded new opportunities for small investors while allowing large stock-portfolio holders an easy and efficient means of hedging equity portfolio movements.

The next new vista is options on futures contracts. This area, now in its infancy, will offer users more limited risk exposure. In combination with other investment strategies, an almost unlimited menu of financial-management alternatives will develop. The CME planned to trade options on its S&P futures contract starting in late 1982.

Membership. CME members are individuals who purchase the right to trade a certain group of commodities in one of the exchange's two divisions: the International Monetary Market (which trades financial futures, gold, and foreign currencies); the Index and Options Market (which trades stock-index futures, options on futures, and lumber); or the Chicago Mercantile Exchange itself (which can trade agricultural, forest-product, and any other contracts listed in its two divisions).

The price for each membership category varies according to market conditions. Memberships, or seats, are traded openly, with qualified persons making bids for available seats. Bids and offers are posted daily and are available from the CME Membership Department.

The success of the individual membership divisions is reflected in the price of seats. As the accompanying chart shows, prices rose from $3,000 in 1964 to $380,000 in 1980. Supply, demand, and general market conditions are incorporated in these prices.

To provide the needed members to trade an expanding list of contracts, the exchange has gone through four membership expansions in its 63-year history. The original trading body prior to 1972 comprised 500 Chicago Mercantile Exchange members who were free to trade any listed commodity on the exchange. In 1972 the CME initiated the second major milestone in futures trading when futures contracts on foreign currencies began trading. The original list of foreign-currency futures included the Italian lira, Japanese yen, Canadian dollar, Mexican peso, British pound, deutsche mark, and Swiss franc. The Dutch guilder was added in 1973 and the French franc in 1974. The lira was delisted in 1974 because Italy's two-tiered system discouraged futures trading.

This concept attracted the attention of organizations that traditionally had skirted commodities because trading had no direct hedging application for them. They were financial institutions—banks, insurance companies, arbitragers, import-export firms, and multinational corporations. Because this was a complete departure from the traditional area of agricultural commodities, the CME formed an entirely new division to handle the influx of orders for this new generation of contracts. Currently, there are more than 725 IMM members.

There are also nearly 1,500 members eligible to trade on the Index and Option Market (IOM) division. They trade contracts based on stock-index futures, options on futures contracts, and lumber. This

Table 1
Chicago Mercantile Exchange: Membership Seat Sales, 1941–81*

	Sales	
	High	Low
1941	$ 800	$ 375
1942	600	225
1943	350	250
1944	1,500	450
1945	2,350	1,200
1946	3,000	2,350
1947	3,600	3,000
1948	3,900	3,000
1949	3,100	2,000
1950	2,800	1,800
1951	3,000	1,750
1952	3,000	2,350
1953	4,000	2,600
1954	4,600	2,700
1955	7,000	4,650
1956	6,300	5,250
1957	5,900	4,000
1958	5,250	3,500
1959	4,000	3,000
1960	4,500	3,000
1961	6,500	4,550
1962	5,000	4,025
1963	4,200	3,000
1964	5,500	3,000
1965	16,000	5,500
1966	16,000	12,000
1967	31,000	14,500
1968	38,000	21,500
1969	90,000	35,000
1970	85,000	44,000
1971	70,000	54,000
1972	100,000	75,000
1973	125,000	70,000
1974	124,000	75,000
1975	129,500	76,500
1976	165,000	125,000
1977	160,000	126,000
1978	255,000	150,000
1979	300,000	235,000
1980	380,000	225,000
1981*	320,000	250,000

* First half

turkeys. The AMM first began trading on February 3, 1976. Its distinct agricultural bent in contracts that had limited success meant it would eventually be replaced by a new genre of commodities that showed more growth potential. These were contracts in the IOM division, and 124 members out of 150 converted to IOM memberships.

Organizational Structure. Trading-floor activity often belies the fact that this is an extremely well organized business. Each order follows a distinct flow, and each trader is screened by member firms and the exchange itself before he or she can begin trading.

The casual visitor who comes to see floor activity is often dazzled by the gestures, colors, and motion. But behind this is the exchange itself. The CME, like most other futures markets in the world, provides the physical location (floor space, communication facilities, etc.), collects and disseminates information about the markets, and establishes and enforces rules for daily trading activity. The CME itself is the umbrella organization that encompasses its member firms. Its rules and guidelines underlie almost all the member firms' business activities.

The exchange itself, however, is nonprofit. Its prime income source is the clearing fees charged for each buy and sell transaction. These are collected from member firms. The fee is slight (about 25 cents per trade), so it is easy to see why the key concern of the exchange is to keep volume growing by developing and marketing contracts that offer wide applications to all users.

Unique to the Chicago Mercantile Exchange, however, are a number of financial safeguards designed to protect customers. During its entire history, the CME has never had a member's financial insolvency affect the stability of the CME. No clearing member of the CME has ever defaulted.

To guarantee that this record remains unblemished, the exchange has forged the cornerstone of its financial integrity, a trust fund with assets of over $23 million as of December 31, 1981. This fund is maintained by contributions derived from exchange operations.

Behind this fund is a list of additional safeguards: security deposits from the member clearing firms; margin deposits from a defaulting clearing firm and its assets; surplus funds of the CME and other capital assessments. All of the exchange's assets (in excess of $295 million as of December 31, 1981) can be used in the event of a major default.

This is only for catastrophic situations. Normal daily procedures provide sufficient monitoring to keep daily trading running smoothly. For instance, at the close of each trading day, the clearing, or ac-

division, formed in December 1981 and Activated in April 1982, replaced the Associate Mercantile Market (AMM) division. The AMM division allowed its members to trade contracts in lumber, stud lumber, potatoes, milo (yellow sorghum), butter, and frozen counting, process begins. Since the CME operates on a "no-debt" system, each account is settled daily—that is, "marked to market." Profits or losses are thus restricted to one day's market exposure.

The starting point for this no-debt system is the settlement price, or closing price, for the day. During the last 30 seconds or one minute of trading (depending on the commodity), the average of the prices is calculated for each contract in each delivery month. This determines the settlement price, Once established, it is used to calculate changes in the basic positions of all accounts. This is done by the member firms, as well as by the exchange clearinghouse, so all customer and member-firm accounts are adjusted daily. If either falls below the specified financial standards, additional funds are required. Conversely, any profit can be taken on a daily basis, if desired.

Another important part of this process is the role of the clearinghouse. Because of the safeguards mentioned earlier, and the need for quick settlement of all accounts, the clearinghouse stands between each buyer and seller to guarantee the trade. Essentially, this means the clearinghouse becomes the buyer for all sellers, and the seller for all buyers.

As a further safeguard, limits on daily price movements either up or down exist to reduce the market exposure of all commodities. Expanded limits go into effect after two consecutive days of maximum movements in the same direction.

Charles B. Epstein

Child Nutrition Programs

See SOCIAL WELFARE.

Child-Support Enforcement

See SOCIAL WELFARE.

Cincinnati Stock Exchange (CSE)

The Cincinnati Stock Exchange is a registered national securities exchange. As early as 1858 there was a stock exchange in the Queen City, which met every Wednesday and Saturday at 83-85 Walnut Street; but it did not survive the Civil War. The current exchange was organized by 12 brokers on March 11, 1885, and has been operating on every business day since. A permanent constitution was adopted on February 16, 1886. The original site was 29 West Third Street; today the exchange offices are in the Dixie Terminal Building. Incorporated as a nonprofit corporation on March 31, 1887, the Cincinnati Stock Exchange provides services for its members and for customers of its members. Among these services are the provision of rooms and facilities for the convenient transaction of the member brokers'/dealers' business, the promotion of equitable trading, the regulation of the quality of listed securities, the requiring of ample capital and insurance for members, and the maintenance of commercial honor and integrity.

When the Securities and Exchange Act became effective in 1934, the Cincinnati Stock Exchange was registered with the Securities and Exchange commission (SEC) as a national securities exchange. The SEC became the regulatory body of the exchange, and under its supervision the exchange was required to adopt rules to enforce compliance with the rules and regulations of the Securities and Exchange Act of 1934.

The Cincinnati Stock Exchange is governed by a board of trustees consisting of nine members elected for three-year terms. All administrative and floor-trading functions are performed by paid employees.

Trading. In the early years of the exchange, there were two "calls" each day: one in the morning and one in the afternoon. The chairman or "caller" called the name of each listed issue, at which time interested broker/dealers called out their bids and offerings, thus constituting an auction market. Sales as well as highest bid and lowest offering prices were recorded for each day.

In January 1902 a third session was held at noon. Noon sessions were suspended in the summer months and terminated in February 1903. During the busy markets of the 1920s, the morning session was continued until all trading was completed. In 1930 the exchange held two sessions a day; but with the advent of unlisted trading in many New York Stock Exchange issues, hours of trading were changed to conform with those on the New York Exchange. In 1952, Saturday trading was eliminated and trading hours extended.

Automated Auction-Market Trading. Since 1976, the exchange has operated the National Securities Trading System (NSTS), the nation's only automated auction market for the trading of listed securities. This system, which originally operated under experimental status granted by the Securities and Exchange Commission, was made permanent by the SEC on December 9, 1982.

The NSTS is a visible auction system. Agency orders and market makers' bids and offers can be directly entered into the system by Cincinnati Stock Exchange member broker/dealers. Bids and offers reposited in the NSTS are disseminated nationally through the consolidated Quote System. The NSTS is interfaced with the Intermarket Trading system, thus linking it with all other major exchanges.

In contrast to audible auction markets, NSTS places the participant directly in the trading arena. When like-priced bids and offers meet, an automatic execution occurs, based on price/time priority. Unlike manual systems, there is no variable time lag between the time the bid or offer is initiated by the broker/dealer and the time it is accepted and filled by the system. Executions are made instantly and locked in because there is no physical handling of an order between entry and execution.

Once a transaction is executed, the results are instantly displayed to the buyer and seller on their terminals. The Cincinnati Stock Exchange simultaneously reports the transaction to the Consolidated Tape. Hard-copy reports are printed and a precise record of the transaction is automatically recorded on computer tape, leaving a comprehensive audit trail of the transaction. The system also contains a composite limit order book.*

The SEC's September 1982 report, *Operation of the Cincinnati Stock Exchange National Securities Trading System 1978–1982,* indicated that 80% of the NSTS executions equaled the primary market quotations and 20% were executed at better prices, between the bid and asked quotations. Although the major portion of Cincinnati Stock Exchange transactions are executed through the NSTS, the exchange still maintains an auction market on its trading floor.

Membership. Original memberships sold for $50 in 1885. By 1929, during the great bull market, the price had reached a peak of $38,500. The value of memberships declined rapidly after 1929. Decreased trading volume, government regulation of security markets, and the depression of the 1930s had their effect. By 1936 the price had fallen to $2,050. After this low ebb, prices of seats rose in value to over $20,000. In 1965, membership certificates were split three-for-one, and in 1971 two-for-one.

Besides full membership, the Cincinnati Stock Exchange has tried variants to promote use of the exchange. In 1946 the exchange authorized the sale of "limited memberships." They sold for $1,000 and carried full trading privileges, but had no resale value and no equity in the assets of the exchange. This class of membership has since been eliminated.

In 1972 "access membership" was initiated. Membership of this category requires that a broker/dealer be registered with the SEC, be a member of the NASD, and maintain a minimum net capital of $25,000. Access membership may be renewed annually.

* A limit order is a priced order outside of the then-current market. If the current market is, say, $10–$11 and someone wants to limit his buying at $9, the order to buy at $9 will be executed only when the offer is reduced to $9.

Listings. Corporations desiring to list their securities on the Cincinnati Stock Exchange must be approved by the board of trustees. Information concerning organizational structure, distribution of stock financial reports, dividends, changes in corporate officials and stock-transfer agencies, and other pertinent corporate information must be provided. All corporations listing securities on the Cincinnati Stock Exchange must be registered with the Securities and Exchange Commission and at all times be in compliance with SEC regulations.

Stocks of some of the nation's larger corporations were originally listed on the Cincinnati Stock Exchange. This group includes Armco, Inc. (American Rolling Mill Company, listed 9/20/05); Champion International Corporation (Champion Coated Paper Company, listed 6/30/06); Cincinnati Gas & Electric Company (Cincinnati Gas Light & Coke Company, listed 3/13/85); Cincinnati Milacron, Inc. (Cincinnati Milling Machining Company, listed 9/28/06); Columbia Gas System (Columbia Gas & Electric Company, listed 5/28/07); Eagle-Picher Industries, Inc. (Eagle-Picher Lead Company, listed 10/15/24); Kroger Company (Kroger Grocery & Baking Company, listed 4/30/02); McGraw-Edison Company (American Laundry Machinery Company, listed 12/10/15); Mead Corporation (Mead Pulp & Paper Company, listed 11/4/26); Procter & Gamble Company (listed 4/26/01).

In 1940 the Cincinnati Stock Exchange began applying to the Securities and Exchange Commission for the privilege of trading stocks not fully listed on its exchange. These issues were fully traded on other exchanges. Since that time, the SEC has granted the exchange unlisted trading privileges in over 500 issues.

See STOCK EXCHANGES.

Richard B. Niehoff

Classified Common Stock

See COMMON STOCK.

Clearinghouse

A central site where banks in one locality present checks drawn on one another for collection. A clearinghouse acts not only as a central collection site where checks can be exchanged among payer and payee banks but also as a central accounting site where each participating bank's balances can be adjusted on a net basis to reflect the difference between the value of checks paid and the value of checks collected to and from other banks in the collection arrangement.

In 1982 there were more than 1,000 clearinghouses

in the United States. Historically, groups of banks in a given geographic area have found that collecting checks through a local clearinghouse is more efficient and less costly than collecting checks directly through each area bank against which deposited checks have been written. For direct collection to be quick and efficient, the payer and payee banks must have account balances at one another's institution, a practice that can be an exceedingly costly use of funds in a geographic area with more than two or three banks. Adding to the expense is that the checks themselves must be transported to the banks against which they are drawn. In forming a local clearinghouse, participating banks need keep only one clearing-account balance against which net credit or debit postings are made, and they can minimize transportation expenses by transporting all their area checks to one central site where they can be exchanged.

David H. Friedman

Clearing House Interbank Payments System (CHIPS)

The Clearing House Interbank Payments system is a computerized network for transfer of international dollar payments, linking about 100 depository institutions that have offices or subsidiaries in New York City.

Currently, about 70,000 interbank transfers valued at $185 billion are made daily through the network. The transfers represent about 90% of all interbank transfers relating to international dollar payments.

Until late spring 1970, most international dollar payments were made by official bank checks. At that time, the New York Clearing House Association (a group of the largest New York City banks) organized CHIPS for eight Federal Reserve member commercial banks that also were members of the Clearing House. The system eventually was expanded to include other commercial banks, Edge corporations, United States agencies and branches of foreign banks, Article XII investment companies, and private banks.

Until recently, in the CHIPS arrangement, final settlement, or the actual movement of balances at the Federal Reserve, occurred on the morning after the transfers. Next-day settlement was acceptable until volume rose substantially, and the Clearing House and CHIPS participants became increasingly concerned about overnight and over-weekend risks.

On October 1, 1981, a major change was made, enabling same-day settlement through a special account at the Federal Reserve bank of New York. Under an agreement signed in August 1981, the New York Fed established a settlement account for CHIPS-settling participants into which debit settlement payments are

sent and from which credit settlement payments are disbursed. Settlement is made at the close of each business day by CHIPS-settling participants sending and receiving Fedwire transfers through the settlement account. Fedwire is the U.S. central bank's electronic funds-and-securities-transfer network.

The New York Fed isn't required to provide financial assistance to ensure completion of the settlement. Settlement is completed when all settling participants owing funds have made payments to the special account and funds have been transferred from the special account to CHIPS-settling participants due funds.

In a typical transaction, suppose a London bank wants to transfer $1 million from its account at a New York correspondent bank "A" to an account at another bank, which maintains a correspondent relationship with New York correspondent bank "B." Banks "A" and "B" are both CHIPS participants.

Bank "A" receives the London bank's transfer message by telex or through the SWIFT system. SWIFT, the Society for Worldwide Interbank Financial Telecommunications, is a private electronic message transfer system to which some depository institutions and central banks belong.

Bank "A" verifies the London bank's message and enters the message into its CHIPS terminal, providing the identifying codes for the sending and receiving banks, the identity of the account at bank "B" that will receive the funds, and the amount. The message is then stored in the CHIPS central computer.

As soon as bank "A" approves and releases the "stored" transaction, the message is transmitted from the CHIPS computer to bank "B." The CHIPS computer also makes a permanent record of the transaction and makes appropriate debits and credits in the CHIPS account of banks "A" and "B." When bank "B" receives its credit message, it notifies the receiving bank, which, in turn, notifies its customer.

Immediately following the closing of the CHIPS network at 4:30 P.M. (eastern time), the CHIPS computer produces a settlement report showing the net debit or credit position of each participant. A separate settlement report shows the net position of each settling participant. The net position of a nonsettling participant is netted into the position of its correspondent settling participant.

Each settling participant has a set period to determine whether it will settle the net position of its participant respondents. After that time, if no settling participant refuses to settle, the settling participants with net debit positions have until 5:45 P.M. (eastern time) to transfer their debit amounts through Fedwire to the CHIPS settlement account on the books of the New York Fed.

When this procedure has been accomplished, the

Clearing House, acting on the New York Fed's behalf, transfers those funds via Fedwire out of the settlement account to those settling participants with net creditor positions. The process usually is completed by 6:00 P.M. (eastern time). Fedwire transfers of funds are final and irrevocable when the recipient receives or is advised of the transfer.

Arthur Samansky

Clifford Trust

See ESTATE PLANNING; TRUSTS.

Closed-End Investment Company

See MUTUAL FUND.

Closing Fees

Those costs incurred between a buyer and seller in a real-estate sale or mortgage. In the case of the buyer, closing fees typically are the expenses of the sale (or loan refinancing) that are paid in addition to the actual purchase price of the real estate. In the seller's case, they are expenses that must be deducted from the actual proceeds of the sale, such as the seller's attorneys' fees or brokerage commission.

Some closing fees are a direct result of legal requirements, while others result simply from local customs and requirements. The closing costs in real-estate transactions may include attorneys' fees; title-clearing and title-insurance fees; recording fees; brokerage commissions; transfer taxes; insurance costs; appraisal and inspection reports; and one-time loan fees, such as points and loan-origination fees.

Harley W. Snyder

Coffee, Sugar & Cocoa Exchange, Inc. (CSCE)

A COMMODITY-FUTURES EXCHANGE on which coffee, sugar, and cocoa futures, as well as options on sugar futures, are traded.

History. For over 100 years, the Coffee, Sugar & Cocoa Exchange's markets have provided a unique mechanism through which the various segments of the coffee, sugar, and cocoa industries can transfer, or reduce, the risks associated with the price volatility inherent in these commodities. In more recent years, futures markets have assumed an even broader economic role and have increasingly become a part of the financial portfolios of a number of individual investors and financial institutions.

Futures markets were born out of the simple danger of forward trading, where maturing contracts had to be redeemed by delivery of physical goods. Broken agreements, lack of available stocks, or oversupply could spell ruin for individuals or sometimes whole sectors of a particular trade, as occurred during the great New York coffee crash of 1880. In 1880, chaos reigned in the coffee trade in New York. Supplies of coffee mounted in the hands of importers and could not be sold—except at great sacrifice.

How did this situation come about? The answer lay in the unrelenting law of supply and demand. As a result of the new plantings in Brazil, Mexico, and other Latin-American countries, production and stocks of coffee had risen substantially during the previous two decades. This development had apparently been ignored by the market. The belated recognition of the large oversupply of coffee caused the bottom to drop out of the market, and importers were literally left "holding the bag."

A group of young, forward-looking coffee merchants recognized that measures were needed to prevent still another such disaster. New methods were called for that would permit all segments of the trade to protect themselves, and the public, from the consequences of a collapse of the market.

The Chicago Board of Trade and the New York Cotton Exchange were already in existence. They were successfully demonstrating that futures trading on commodity exchanges could and did move large crops with a minimum of risk to growers, merchants, processors, and consumers. It was reasoned that if exchanges acted as stabilizers for these domestic products, why not for imported coffee?

Within two years, on March 7, 1882, the Coffee Exchange of the City of New York opened its doors, establishing the first orderly market for the trading of coffee futures. The new exchange provided uniform operating procedures, fixed standards for grades of coffee, and a recognized court of arbitration. It also became a price-discovery forum where pertinent data about every transaction during the day was broadcast inside and outside the exchange. This mechanism helped to stabilize prices and to protect the industry and consumers alike.

World War I led to the closing of the raw-sugar exchanges in Hamburg and London in 1914, depriving the world's sugar trade of its leading markets. The Coffee Exchange acted immediately to meet this challenge, expanding its facilities and launching a contract for sugar futures in New York. This contract quickly proved its utility to the sugar industry, and on October 1, 1916, the exchange changed its name to the New York Coffee and Sugar Exchange. A few years later, on October 1, 1925, the New York Cocoa Exchange was founded, establishing the world's first marketplace for cocoa-futures trading. In September 1979, the New York Cocoa Exchange merged with the New York Coffee and Sugar Exchange, giving us today's Coffee, Sugar & Cocoa Exchange, Inc.

In October 1982 the exchange introduced options trading on its world sugar-futures contract, the first of its new products efforts. An options contract gives the holder the right, but not the obligation, to buy ("call") or sell ("put") one sugar-futures contract at a stated price at any time from the day of purchase to the expiration of the option. The cost of the option—the premium—is determined by the same type of competitive auction-market process used for trading futures contracts.

Options trading broadens the exchange's trading base by providing existing users of the futures markets with new trading opportunities and by offering new hedging and speculative strategies to a broad spectrum of additional market participants.

Who Trades Futures on the Coffee, Sugar & Cocoa Exchange? In the early years of its history, the exchange was largely trade-oriented, but heightened price volatility in all three markets in recent years has attracted a large number of new participants on both the hedging and speculative sides. The resulting volume increases have highlighted the exchange's ability to service the needs of a broad group of diverse interests.

The exchange membership is drawn from a wide spectrum of market participants. On the floor of the exchange, these diverse interests are represented by floor traders and floor brokers. Off the floor, traders are normally classified as "commercials" and "speculators."

Floor traders, or "locals," are independent, professional traders who trade primarily for their own accounts. Their ability to trade virtually instantaneously permits them to seek small profits on a large volume of transactions. This involvement, in turn, significantly enhances market liquidity to the benefit of all market participants.

Floor brokers execute orders on behalf of others, whether commercial firms or retail customers. Such orders are received either directly or via the major brokerage houses. Brokerage firms, also called "futures commission merchants" (FCM's), provide access to the markets for hedgers not wanting to buy their own seats on the exchange and for members of the general public who wish to speculate in coffee, sugar, or cocoa futures.

Commercial interests—growers, exporters, importers, processors, and manufacturers—use the futures markets to hedge their positions in the physical market, selling futures to reduce the risk of price decline on inventory, and buying to reduce the risk of price increases for commodities employed in processing and manufacturing finished goods. Large commercial firms frequently employ their own floor brokers to execute their orders on the trading floor, but may also utilize independent floor brokers, depending on the size and nature of their market involvement.

Speculators, whether professional traders or individuals placing orders through an FCM, seek to profit by anticipating fluctuating prices. By assuming the price risk that the hedger is unwilling to bear, speculators provide liquidity to the market and thus play a crucial role in its efficient operation.

The Mechanics of Futures Trading. While seemingly complex in nature, futures trading is really a rather straightforward system of matching buyers with sellers in a competitive trading environment. The process begins as orders to buy and sell futures contracts are transmitted from around the world to the trading floor of the exchange via Teletype, telex, or telephone.

A clerk at a communications booth on the floor will record each telephone order on a trading slip by the type of commodity being traded, the number of contracts, the delivery month, and the requested method of execution—such as at the prevailing market price, at a specified price, or at the discretion of the floor broker. The slips are then time-stamped to indicate the sequence in which the orders were received. On telexed or Teletyped orders, this information is recorded automatically.

Orders are executed according to the customers' instructions by open outcry among floor brokers and locals at the ring. Brokers also use a system of hand signals developed to assist in communicating over the din on the exchange floor. Exchange clerks stationed around the ring transmit price changes to recording clerks, who enter the details into the exchange's data-and-communications system. The price-reporting system is designed to display prices instantly on electronic wallboards on the trading floor while they are simultaneously transmitted around the world.

Once a trade is completed, the broker records the details of the transaction on a trading card. These cards are used as the foundation of the record-keeping system for business done on the exchange. Confirmation of each trade is immediately relayed back to the telephone clerk, who reports the details of the transaction to the originating customer. This entire process, from order entry to price display to confirmation, generally takes just a few minutes.

The details of every trade executed by members in the course of a day must be submitted to the Coffee, Sugar & Cocoa Clearing Corporation. The Clearing Corporation then verifies that there is a match of bought and sold contracts. Once matching trades have been cleared, the Clearing Corporation assumes the role of buyer to every seller, and seller to every buyer, removing the requirement that every contract must result in the delivery of physical goods. Instead, exchange contracts are offsettable instruments that may be bought and sold without the need for actual delivery or further reference to the original opposite party.

Since futures contracts are generally employed as a substitute for the actual delivery of current or anticipated physical commodities, only a small percentage of contracts usually mature for delivery; the remainder are closed out by an equal and opposite transaction. How does it work in practice? Suppose a merchant buys a large quantity of raw cane sugar. The price of sugar may fall substantially before he can sell it to his customers. To protect himself, he sells futures contracts on the exchange in a quantity equivalent to the sugar in his inventory and with a delivery date matching that of his own expected sugar sales.

Since cash and futures prices tend to move in the same direction at the same time, the merchant's futures contracts will minimize the risk of price fluctuation. If the price of sugar falls before he is ready to sell, the loss he sustains on his inventory should be reasonably offset by his profit when he comes to buy back the futures he sold—at a correspondingly lower price. Through the use of the futures market, the merchant will, in effect, have locked in his profit in the resale of his sugar.

It is important to note that if the price of sugar rises in the time between the merchant's order and sale, he will have foregone some potential profits. Thus, he effectively trades off his opportunity to make profits on his cash positions for protection against possible loss.

While the minimization of price risk is a principal advantage of futures-market hedging, other advantages include the expansion of credit and the reduction of operating costs. Financial institutions tend to lend larger sums of money to producers whose inventories are hedged. This in turn may permit the producer to expand operations and increase profits. In addition, a firm making use of forward-pricing hedges often reduces its operating expenses because its finances need not be tied up in storage costs.

Management. Governing the Coffee, Sugar & Cocoa Exchange is a board of managers, elected by their fellow members to serve in an unpaid capacity for a two-year term. There are a number of committees that deliberate on particular questions and make recommendations to the board. The board is composed of a balance of futures commission merchants, commercial interests, and floor traders, as well as representatives of the public.

The day-to-day running of the exchange is the responsibility of a professional management team, headed by the exchange president. In the self-regulatory framework of commodity markets, this team plays a vital role. Reporting to the president are legal, compliance, operations, economic-research, marketing, planning, and administrative staffs. Their tasks include monitoring of trading to assure smooth order execution and compliance with exchange rules; design of new contracts and modification of those currently being traded; monitoring the financial soundness of member firms; and writing rules that respond to the rapidly changing business and regulatory environment in futures markets.

Bennett J. Corn

Coinage Operations

See MINTING OF COINS.

Coinsurance or Copayment, Health Insurance

The percentage of health expenses paid by the insured, after the insured has paid the deductible amount. Typical copayments are 80–20, with the insurance company paying 80% of COVERED MEDICAL EXPENSES and the insured paying 20%.

See also HEALTH INSURANCE; DEDUCTIBLE, HEALTH INSURANCE.

James L. Moorefield

Collection Agency

A business whose objective is to collect money due the various clients (customers) that it serves. The agency may be a corporation, an individual, or may use an assumed name. Collection agencies vary in the scope of their activities and the types of accounts they handle. Some agencies represent businesses—from the largest corporations to the smallest—collecting accounts against other businesses. This is known as a commercial account (a business vs. another business). Other agencies collect accounts from consumers. This is a retail account (a business or individual vs. a consumer or individual). Depending on its size, competence, and reputation, an agency can collect any claim for services rendered (doctor and hospital bills, etc.) or goods sold and delivered (department-store and Visa–MasterCard purchases, oil deliveries, etc.) anywhere in the country or free world, either by itself or via the use of corresponding agencies or attorneys, wherever the delinquent account (debtor) may be located or have relocated to. Enlisting the help of an attorney or another agency in the debtor's immediate area is known as "forwarding the account."

The sooner a delinquent account is assigned to a collection agency, the better the chances for recovery. The problem here is that credit grantors, the agency's clients, have their own time frames as to when they turn over accounts for collection. To save the costs of outside collection services, some of the larger companies have their own collection departments that first try to collect delinquent accounts themselves. In many cases, they are successful. The question is, what does it cost them to run an internal collection department, and, in the long run, are they really saving money? Many other businesses and individuals also try to collect their own accounts in various ways (via letters, telephone calls, personal calls, past-due notices, etc.), which again is costly, and then, if unsuccessful, they refer the accounts to collection agencies. These internal efforts can buy time for a delinquent account to either pay up or file bankruptcy; give rise to disputes; and enable the debtor to move (skip) or go out of business.

This is when creditors look to collection agencies to perform the "miracles" and collect the money due. Ideally, the delinquent account should have been turned over for collection at the 60- to 90-day past-due period; this would have been sufficient time for the creditor to try to collect the account, and for the debtor to pay up or discuss the situation with the creditor. Naturally, each delinquent account is unique and must be evaluated before it is placed in collection. If an account has a pattern of paying each 90 to 100 days, then it should not be placed for collection with an agency before that period has elapsed, unless there is a known financial problem that would cause immediate concern to the creditor.

When an account is assigned to a collection agency, it is immediately acknowledged via a letter to the creditor telling him "we received the account and are proceeding with collection efforts." Some agencies call the account as a first step. Others send out a first collection notice, to be followed by additional collection notices, never making any personal contact via telephone or door-to-door follow-up. Other agencies use a combination of both procedures. One common fact is that each successive letter sent out is stronger and more serious than the previous one.

If the debtor does not respond by either paying the collection agency or calling to discuss the past-due account, then, depending on the agency and the service it renders, the balance due, and the creditor's willingness, the account may be forwarded to an attorney to commence suit. Many full-service collection agencies (see below) have their own legal departments, and they continue to try to effect collection before having their retainer attorney actually file suit. Collection agencies themselves cannot threaten suit or commence suit in their own names. They can recommend to their clients that suit be filed, and may even recommend an attorney to use, but the ultimate decision rests with the creditor himself.

There are state and city laws designed to protect consumer debtors from collection-agency harassment and from certain tactics used by some agencies in trying to collect the various claims they are assigned. These laws vary from state to state and city to city. Many states require collection agencies to be both licensed and bonded; others just licensed *or* bonded; and others, neither. Probably the single most important law enacted was the Federal Fair Debt Collection Practices Act, commonly referred to as "PL 95-109," which went into effect March 20, 1978, and which most states, cities, and municipalities have adopted in one form or another in the laws they created. PL 95-109 was designed to protect consumers by prohibiting abusive practices by debt collectors.

Full-Service Collection Agencies. A full-service collection agency is one that handles an account from the time it is turned over for collection, all the way through litigation and, it is hoped, collection. Many agencies are only letter-writing agencies, and when the letters fail to collect, the account is closed and returned to the creditor, who will either write off the account or turn it over to another collection agency, or attorney, for further collection attempts.

Phillip J. Bayer

Commercial Auto Insurance

See INSURANCE.

Commercial Banks

While there are many types of financial service companies in the United States, an institution called a "commercial bank" lies at the heart of the financial system. Both business in particular and the economy in general rely on commercial banks to provide money and credit.

Banking Is a Business. Because many commercial banks (also referred to simply as BANKS) use the word *state* or *national* in their names, some people conclude that they are a part of the government. This conclusion is mistaken. State banks are chartered—

granted a license to operate—by state authorities, and national banks are chartered by federal authorities. In operation, however, banks are a business just like supermarkets or hotels. Owned by private investors, they provide services that customers demand and try to earn a profit. Originally, commercial banks were established to meet the needs of business, but this distinction has become a little less clear today because they also serve the needs of the general public.

Modern commercial banks perform a wide variety of services—from maintaining safe-deposit facilities and selling traveler's checks to managing inheritances and handling international transactions for corporations. Their basic function, however, remains essentially what it was when the Bank of North America opened in 1782.

A bank deals in money. It acquires money from its depositors and lends it to borrowers.

Depositors generally earn INTEREST when they leave money with the bank. Borrowers, on the other hand, pay interest when the bank lends its depositors' money to them.

The difference between the interest paid to depositors and the interest received from borrowers is called a "spread" in the jargon of banking. It is the source of a bank's primary income. As a business, banking is a balancing act.

Commercial Banks Compared to Other Financial Institutions. Commercial banks, of course, compete with other institutions in the financial-services industry. Although many people speak of these other institutions as "banks," there are significant differences between a true commercial bank and these other institutions. In general, commercial banks offer a wider range of services than do the other institutions.

In addition to commercial banks, there are four types of institutions that accept deposits: savings and loan associations, mutual savings banks, credit unions, and industrial banks.

SAVINGS AND LOAN ASSOCIATIONS were originally chartered to provide money for home construction. Although they do other types of business today, they still concentrate their lending in residential mortgages. Some associations are stock corporations, but most are owned by their depositors, who receive dividends from the association's profits. This form of ownership is called a "mutual" association.

The mutual SAVINGS BANK was the historical predecessor of savings and loan associations. As of mid-1982, more than 400 of these institutions operated in 17 states. Most of their loans are made for residential mortgages. The *mutual* in their names indicates they, also, are owned by their depositors.

CREDIT UNIONS are nonprofit savings institutions

owned by their depositors, who must have a relationship called a "common bond." This common bond can be a shared ethnic heritage or employer. Most credit-union loans are used to finance consumer purchases and home improvements.

Industrial banks, originally established to promote the virtues of saving among workers in a specific industry, operate in 15 states. Most of their lending is for consumer purchases.

Nondepository institutions in the financial-services industry include mortgage companies, consumer finance companies, life-insurance companies, and money-market mutual funds. Although accounts in money-market mutual funds fall outside the legal definition of *deposit*, the funds accept money in the same way banks do.

On the basis of size alone, commercial banks are the most important group of financial intermediaries in the United States. For example, at one point in 1982, commercial banks held about $1,250 billion in deposits, compared to about $530 billion for savings and loan associations; about $154 billion for savings banks; and about $73 billion for credit unions.

Size, however, does not tell the whole story.

Because all other businesses need money, and generally credit, to operate, they use banks to make payments and as a source of funds. In a modern economy, banking services are as necessary to business as capital, labor, and raw materials.

Sources of Funds. Before banks can lend, they must take money in. There are several sources of funds on which banks can draw. By far the most important are deposits by customers. Individuals are not the only kind of bank customer; businesses, nonprofit organizations, and government agencies also deposit funds in banks, as do other types of financial institutions.

In addition to deposits, banks can also borrow money from the FEDERAL RESERVE SYSTEM—the United States' central bank—and from each other. As corporations, they can also issue stock and other forms of securities.

The *certificate of deposit* is a major source of bank funds. These certificates are receipts sold in exchange for a sum of money that is left at the bank for a specific period of time, called a "maturity." They are therefore called "time deposits" in the language of banking. At the end of the maturity period, the holder may present the certificate to the bank for payment of the principal (the money deposited) and the interest the deposit has earned.

Another important source of funds is the *transaction deposit*, a deposit on which checks or other orders for payment may be drawn. The traditional transaction deposit is the checking account, which bankers call a "demand deposit" because the bank will pay a check on demand. It does not bear interest. In the last few years, the government has allowed banks to establish a transaction account that does pay interest and on which checks may be drawn. It is called a negotiable order of withdrawal (NOW) account.

A third source of funds is the regular *savings account,* usually referred to as the "passbook account." Legally, banks can require the depositor to give prior notice before withdrawing any of the deposit. In practice, this notice is hardly ever required.

Loans. Lending banks can take many different forms. Most of the assets in the banking system are invested in loans to persons or businesses, but about 15% of the total is invested in securities issued by governments or government-related agencies.

Loans to businesses—*commercial and industrial loans*—are the largest single category of loans on most banks' books. Historically, about half of the loans made by banks are to other businesses.

The picture is far different, however, in the nation's farm belt, where *agricultural loans* dominate the average bank's lending. In recent years, banks have generally carried about a quarter of the nation's farm debt. About two-thirds of the nation's farmers borrow money each year to pay expenses or to buy farm equipment.

Historically, banks have also written about a quarter of the residential mortgages in this country. In recent years, banking's share of this market has been growing.

Banks were not involved in customer lending— loans to individuals—until the 1930s; but after World War II, bank participation in this field grew greatly. *Consumer loans*—primarily for the purchase of expensive durable goods, such as automobiles and appliances—are usually repaid in monthly installments. In recent years, banks have held more than half of all installment credit to consumers.

Bank Services. The president of one of America's largest corporations has estimated that commercial banks offer more than 155 services to their customers. Many of these services, especially to businesses, are highly technical, involving the latest computer and telecommunications technology. Most people, however, would say that the basic service banks offer is the checking account and its interest-yielding counterparts (*see* CHECK; NEGOTIABLE ORDER OF WITHDRAWAL (NOW) ACCOUNT: OVERDRAFT CHECKING; SUPER NEGOTIABLE ORDER OF WITHDRAWAL (NOW) ACCOUNTS).

Another important service banks provide in offering credit to customers without requiring them to make a personal appearance is the bank card. The most common bank cards are MasterCard and Visa. When a person uses a bank card—for example, in purchasing an appliance—the merchant is reimbursed by the bank. In effect, the bank has paid the bill and has loaned the purchaser the money. Most customers do not pay their bank-card bills immediately when they receive them and are charged interest on the outstanding balance.

To offer customers convenience and efficient service 24 hours a day, many banks have established AUTOMATED TELLER MACHINES (ATM's). Customers can use an automated teller machine to obtain cash, transfer funds from one account to another, repay loans, and request information on their accounts.

All these services to consumers involve transactions where money changes hands. However, banks offer consumers other types of services, too.

For example, banks must protect the assets—cash and securities—they keep on hand. When people think of a bank, in their minds they see the vault where these assets are stored. Banks extend this security and protection to their customers in the form of safe-deposit facilities in the vault, typically a SAFE-DEPOSIT BOX, for the storage of valuables such as jewelry. While these boxes are rented for a fee, the rentals usually do not generate profits for a bank.

In addition to payments, credit, and security services, many banks offer customers another type of traditional banking service: *trust management.* Banks manage property for the benefit of someone else. The goal may be to build up a fund for a child's education, a customer's retirement security, or for a charity. On a wider front, banks act as trustees for pension funds.

A reasonable detailed description of all the services that banks offer businesses would fill a book. An increasingly important example is cash-management services. These services generally involve informing depositors of how much of their funds are available at any one time for short-term (perhaps overnight), investments and what the investment options are. Although these services were originally oriented toward large, nationwide business customers, banks have increasingly marketed them to smaller companies, too.

Banking's contributions to the housing market extend far beyond mortgages. The industry is also a major source of credit for home construction, home improvement, and mobile-home loans. Banks also hold billions of dollars in government securities issued to finance mortgage and community investment programs.

Government Securities. Banks make purchases of securities issued by federal, state, and local governments. When a government sells a security—usually called a "*bond*"—to a bank, it is in effect taking out a loan. The bond itself is simply the promise that the government issuer will repay the bank at a specified date. Because banks invest in these securities, governments can be confident of finding a market for them. Everyone benefits from this arrangement, because a government's only source of income other than borrowing is taxation.

The Structure and Regulation of Banking. As of January 1983, there were approximately 14,700 banks in the United States. But because many banks have branches, there were more than 53,000 banking offices open for business. The size and structure of banks varied greatly according to the region of the country and the state in which they were located. The vast majority of banks had assets of less than $100 million; the largest had assets of more than $100 billion. The Middle West, for example, was dotted with thousands of smaller banks servicing the needs of local farmers; while in New York City, giant institutions have grown to operate in the world's major money market. The size and variation of the American banking system is far different from systems in most other major countries, where a comparatively few institutions operate on a regional or nationwide scale.

Market forces and government regulation determined the structure of the U.S. system. Both the states and the federal government have rights and responsibilities in chartering, supervising, and examining commercial banks, a setup commonly referred to as the "dual-banking system." The individual bank decides whether it wants a state or a federal charter. The states, however, have supreme jurisdiction over whether both state- and federally chartered banks can branch—that is, establish more than one banking office—within their boundaries. Many banks are supervised by both state and federal regulators.

Because of branching restrictions, banks may be classified into unit, branch, and group types. In unit-banking states, banks are limited to providing services at a single office. In branch-banking states, a single bank can conduct operations at two or more offices, with the branches controlled from one location, the head office. Group banking exists where two or more legally separate banks are controlled by the same owner or owners.

On the federal level alone, five regulators have direct supervision over banks: (1) the office of the comptroller of the currency charters and supervises national banks. Created in 1863, it is a part of the U.S. Treasury; (2) the FEDERAL DEPOSIT INSURANCE CORPORATION insures bank accounts for up to $100,000 in the event of bank failure; it has a great deal of regulatory authority over virtually all the state-chartered banks that it insures. All national banks are required to carry FDIC insurance; (3) the FEDERAL RESERVE SYSTEM has direct regulatory authority over bank holding companies. A bank holding company is a corporation that owns or controls one or more banks and generally operates other businesses that are closely related to banking. The majority of all banks are part of bank holding companies; (4) a panel of regulators called the DEPOSITORY INSTITUTIONS DEREGULATION COMMITTEE, created in 1980, has been charged with gradually eliminating interest-rate ceilings on deposits; (5) another panel of regulators, the Federal Financial Institutions Examination Council, tries to make the examination methods used by the different federal regulators more consistent.

From this list alone, it is easy to see why bankers sometimes say that banking is the country's most regulated industry.

Banking as an Economic Function. Banking's importance does not rest solely upon its role as a business; the system as a whole has an important economic function: It creates money. The Federal Reserve system, the nation's CENTRAL BANK, influences the growth of money in the United States by governing the amount of money the banking system creates. Money is anything that can be used to buy goods and services. While most people probably think of money as the coins and paper bills that they use to make small purchases, another form of money, the check, plays a more important part in the nation's economic life. More than 80% of all the purchases made in this country are by check, not by the coins and paper bills that bankers and economists call "currency." A check is money because it can be used as if it were currency. Through the use of checks and similar orders for the payment of funds, banks offer an efficient, convenient, and safe means of settling debts and other transactions.

When bankers, economists, and government officials refer to the money supply, they are using a shorthand term to describe currency and funds in transaction accounts that can be used as money. The Fed influences the level of this MONEY SUPPLY to encourage economic activity and discourage inflation, a process known as MONETARY POLICY. The Fed describes the basic supply of money as "M-1." Over the last few years, this mysterious M has appeared more and more often in newspaper and television news reports on the economy. However, an explanation of what this M represents takes the mystery out of it.

M-1 is simply the amount of currency in circulation at any one time and the funds that people keep in accounts at depository institutions that they can withdraw on demand through a check, a NOW check, or any other similar order of payment.

The banking system as a whole can increase or "create" funds in those accounts through a process known as "the multiplier effect of lending."

By law, a certain amount of the deposits that banks take in must be set aside as "reserves." The money that remains, after a reasonable amount is subtracted for expenses, is available for loans.

Let's assume that all commercial banks set aside 20% of their deposits in reserves. A bank receiving a $100 deposit thus sets aside $20. It then lends the remaining $80 to another customer, who uses it to purchase a calculator from an electronics store. The store then deposits the $80 in its bank, Bank B. After setting aside 20%—or $16—as its reserve, Bank B lends the remaining $64 to a customer who uses it to pay a creditor. The creditor deposits the $64 in its bank, Bank C. Bank C retains $12.80 to meet its reserve requirement and lends out the remaining $51.20. And so on.

With repeated loans and deposits, the original $100 will have grown to $500 before it is consumed by borrowers, assuming none of the funds leak out of the system into coffee cans buried in backyards. Borrowers, then, were able to buy $400 in additional goods and services from the $100 original deposit. It is not magic—it is merely mathematics. Of course, the process can work in reverse (*see* BANKS).

The Fed uses three techniques to influence the lending process to govern the money supply: reserve requirements, open-market operations, and the discount rate.

By 1988 the Fed will set the reserve requirements for all the depository institutions in the country.

When the Fed wants to reduce the supply of money to make loans, it raises the reserve requirement, thus reducing the amount of money available for lending. When it wants to increase the money supply, it lowers the reserve requirement.

Open-market operations are the most important and most frequently used monetary-policy technique. Just like any other large investor, the Fed buys and sells securities, usually issued by the U.S. government, in the open market. When the Fed buys securities, the money it uses to pay for them is put into the money supply. The payment is ultimately deposited in a commercial bank and the multiplier effect begins. When the Fed sells securities, the money the buyer uses to purchase them is simply kept by the Fed and withdrawn from the money available to banks to make loans.

The discount rate is the simplest of the Fed's three monetary-policy techniques, but it is also the least important. The discount rate is the interest rate that depository institutions pay to borrow money from the Fed. By raising or lowering the discount rate, the Fed influences the level of money available for lending

and also other interest rates that banks charge.

See also AMERICAN BANKERS ASSOCIATION; COMMERCIAL BANKS, ORGANIZATION AND STRUCTURE OF.

Phil Battey

Commercial Banks, Organization and Structure of

As a business, a bank has complete discretion over the form of its organization. Because there are approximately 14,700 banks in the United States, organizations vary widely. There are, however, common elements that many banks share.

Perhaps the best description of a bank's organizational structure is functional: the separating of tasks into individual assignments and then the grouping of those assignments together in units or departments to meet the institution's objectives. In short, it is a pattern of task and authority relationships. The structure may evolve in reaction to management's needs over many years or it may be the result of planning.

One element all banks have in common is the board of directors, the management body that sets the direction for the bank. While it is not directly involved with the day-to-day operation of the bank, the board selects the top management that oversees these operations. However, the legal responsibility for the effective functioning of the bank rests with the board. It establishes the bank's mission and formulates policy—that is, formal guidelines that govern management's actions, especially in the areas of lending, investment, and trust activities. Bank stockholders are responsible for selecting board members, whose other duties vary considerably from bank to bank.

Once a bank has established its mission and formulated policies to achieve it, it designs an organizational structure as a means to meet its objectives. Although there are exceptions, jobs and authority are generally grouped—by output or by function—into departments, with the president of the bank responsible for the departments' operations.

The output grouping may be along the lines of customers served. For example, the marketing department may be divided into corporate services (those directed at businesses) and retail services (those directed at individual consumers). Groupings may also be made according to product lines or location.

The most widespread grouping, however, is by function. In practice, this procedure becomes complicated, but a simple example of the organization of a small bank will illustrate this concept.

The hypothetical small bank has five vice-presidents reporting to the president. They are responsible for loans, investments, trusts, marketing, and operations. The loan department has four divisions—commercial loans, consumer loans, real-estate loans, and agricultural loans—and each division has its own staff, headed by a staff manager. The other departments are similarly divided by function.

By contrast, the 1982 corporate directory of a large bank based in New York City listed 201 officers with the rank of vice-president or higher heading divisions that ranged from agribusiness financing to corporate portfolio management.

Of course, the departmentalization in banking results in a highly specialized work force. For example, clerks handle the enormous amount of behind-the-scenes paper work generated by banks and account for nearly two-thirds of the 1.5 million people employed in the industry. The individual clerk, however, may handle only a single task, such as mortgage-loan bookkeeping. Because banking is a diverse industry, job titles, and the areas of responsibility they reflect, are not standard from bank to bank.

See COMMERCIAL BANKS.

Phil Battey

Commercial Credit Insurance

See INSURANCE.

Commercial Multiple-Line Policies

See INSURANCE.

Commercial Paper

Commercial paper is a short-term, unsecured promissory note sold by a financial or nonfinancial organization as an alternative to borrowing from a bank or other institution. The paper is usually sold to other companies that invest in short-term money-market instruments.

Because commercial-paper maturities don't exceed nine months and proceeds are used only for current transactions, the notes are exempt from registration as securities with the United States Securities and Exchange Commission.

Currently more than 800 companies in the United States regularly issue commercial paper. Financial companies comprise the largest group of commercial-paper issuers, accounting for more than 70% of commercial paper outstanding as of mid-1980. Financial-company paper is issued by firms in commercial, savings, and mortgage banking; sales, personal, and mortgage financing; factoring, finance leasing, and other business lending; insurance underwriting; and other investment activities.

Bank-related paper is a specific type of financial-company paper. It is issued by bank holding companies, nonbank subsidiaries of the holding company,

and nonbank subsidiaries of the bank. Bank-related paper accounted for about 25% of the financial-company paper component in mid-1980. Such paper is an obligation of the parent company or nonbank subsidiary and isn't an obligation of the bank. Likewise, bank-related paper isn't insured by the FEDERAL DEPOSIT INSURANCE CORPORATION.

The second group of commercial-paper issuers are nonfinancial firms, such as manufacturers, corporations, public utilities, industrial concerns, and service industries. Nonfinancial-company paper accounted for about 30% of the total paper outstanding at mid-1980.

There are two methods of marketing commercial paper: The issuer can sell the paper directly to the buyer, or sell the paper to a dealer firm, which then resells the paper in the market.

The dealer market for commercial paper involves large securities firms that operate internationally. Most of these firms also are dealers in U.S. government securities. Direct issuers of commercial paper are usually financial companies that have frequent and sizable borrowing needs and find it more economical to place paper without the use of an intermediary.

On average, direct issuers save the dealers' fee of one-eighth of a percentage point, or $125,000 on a $100-million offering. This saving compensates over time for the cost of maintaining a permanent sales staff to market the paper. In addition, direct placers often have greater flexibility in adjusting amounts, interest rates, and maturities of issues to suit the needs of investors with whom they have continuing relationships. Dealer-placed paper is usually issued by nonfinancial companies and smaller financial companies. The size and frequency of the borrowings usually don't warrant maintenance of a sales staff by the issuer.

Interest rates on commercial paper often are lower than bank lending rates, and the differential, when large enough, provides an advantage that makes issuing commercial paper an attractive alternative to bank credit. Daily interest rates, on a discount basis, on dealer-placed and directly placed paper with maturities of 30 days to 120 days are published weekly by the Federal Reserve Bank of New York. When sold at a discount, the purchaser pays less than the face amount for the paper. The yield is the difference between the purchase price and the face amount.

The rates for dealer and directly placed prime commercial paper, published by the New York Fed, are the unweighted arithmetic average of reported offering rates—the rates at which dealers or issuers are willing to sell. The rates are reported daily by five direct issuers and six major dealers for paper of corporations with "Aa" bond ratings. Before averaging, fractions are rounded to two decimal places.

Bond ratings are frequently assigned by STANDARD & POOR'S CORPORATION or MOODY'S INVESTORS SERVICE, INC. The ratings are based on current information about the corporation's creditworthiness. Aa-rated bonds have a very strong capacity to pay interest and repay principal.

The most often cited rate on commercial paper reported by the New York Fed is the 90-day dealer-placed commercial paper rate, which is published weekly by the Federal Reserve's board of governors in the *Weekly Summary of Banking and Credit Measures.* This rate generally is a five-day statement-week average of the daily figures. A four-day average is used for a holiday week. The statement week is Thursday through Wednesday.

Commercial paper has maturities ranging from 5 days to 270 days, but most commonly is issued for 30 days to 90 days. Paper is usually issued in denominations of $100,000 or more. Some companies do issue paper in denominations of $25,000 and $50,000 from 30 days to 270 days.

Three organizations currently rate commercial paper. However, as noted, interest rates for commercial paper reflect bond ratings, while the quality of the paper reflects the bond ratings and other factors.

Standard & Poor's and Moody's each rate more than 800 issuers. Fitch Investors Service Corporation rates more than 60 issuers. Standard & Poor's assigns ratings A-1, A-2, or A-3; Moody's uses P-1, P-2, or P-3; and Fitch uses F-1, F-2, or F-3. The rating services assign the highest-quality paper a "1" rating and the lowest quality a "3" rating. Ratings are reviewed frequently and are determined by the issuer's financial performance, bank lines of credit, and timeliness of repayment.

Investors in the commercial-paper market include private pension funds, government units, bank trust departments, foreign banks, and investment companies. There is little secondary market activity in commercial paper, primarily because issuers can closely match the maturity of the paper to the borrower's needs. If the investor needs ready cash, the dealer or issuer will usually buy back the paper prior to maturity.

Arthur Samansky

Commodity

This term generally refers to any article of trade, but in reference to FUTURES MARKETS "commodities" may be defined as goods, articles, services, rights, and interests in which contracts for future delivery may be traded. There are FUTURES CONTRACTS for many dif-

ferent types of commodities, ranging from precious metals, grains, feeds, oilseeds, meat, food, fiber, petroleum, and wood to United States Treasury bills, bonds, and notes, GNMA certificates of deposit, commercial paper, Swiss francs, British pounds, Canadian dollars, Japanese yen, and EURODOLLARS. Contracts are bought or sold on a COMMODITY-FUTURES EXCHANGE; as of 1983, there were about 45 different contracts being traded.

Principal users of the commodity markets fall into two categories: speculators and hedgers. The interplay of these two market participants provides much of the dynamism that characterizes pit activity, and the various strategies they employ have proven complementary to both the overall growth in trading volume and fluid market movements.

Hedgers take futures-market positions to offset existing positions in the cash or physical market. For instance, a gold-coin dealer or cattle rancher already has an inventory of these items; an adverse price movement can reduce the value of those goods. By taking an equal and opposite position in the futures market, hedgers limit their price exposure. This "insurance policy" works like this:

The holder of gold coins foresees a decrease in the price of gold. Not wanting to liquidate his inventory, he sells a futures contract. The result of this strategy, called a "short hedge," will be that any decrease in the value of the gold coins will be offset by profits from the futures "short." Offsetting positions also can be used if the coin dealer expects prices to rise and he expects to have to buy more gold. The overall goal of any hedger is to limit his exposure to price fluctuations.

Speculators are individuals who attempt to profit from price fluctuations. Unlike hedgers, they do not have a position in the cash market and therefore seek to turn their opinion of the market's direction into a purely profitable position by employing venture capital. Speculators also have different time considerations from other market users and, by taking market positions that often are quickly liquidated, provide those small incremental price moves that make for an orderly market.

Individuals and institutions enter into the futures market through commodity brokerage firms. Such a firm will help determine the client's goals, assist in setting up a strategy, establish the needed financial accounts, and do the trading.

The traditional appeal of futures markets for individuals has been leverage. For instance, speculators can control markets with as little as 1% to 10% of the value of the underlying futures contract; thus a $100,000 U.S. Treasury bond futures contract can be controlled for a margin of $2,000 (2%) or a 5,000 bushel soybean futures contract valued at $45,000 can be controlled for $3,600 (8%). This leverage enables futures-market users to gain tremendous profits or suffer large losses.

Participants in the futures markets should have some familiarity with the commodities they trade and the contract specifications. The contract, which is written by the futures exchange where the commodity is traded, provides the firm commitment to make or take delivery of a specific quality and quantity of the commodity during a specific time period in the future. The exchange also sets minimum margin requirements for its member firms.

The delivery of commodities has often been the subject of misunderstanding. Physical delivery is rare, involving less than 5% of all contracts traded. And despite the notion that thousands of bushels of grain will be suddenly dumped on one's doorstep, delivery is preceded by numerous announcements and statements of intent. Physical delivery is not the prime intent of the futures markets.

Choosing a commodity is of more concern to speculators than to hedgers. By definition, hedgers must take a position in futures opposite to positions they already have. Speculators are not tied to such restrictions; they can choose any commodity. As a general rule of thumb, hedgers and speculators gravitate toward liquid markets where there are quick, incremental price movements. This allows quick entry and exit from any position.

Because of the clearing procedure for futures, it is unnecessary for the buyer or seller of a contract to know his counterpart. This anonymity should not be misunderstood for lack of responsibility; each member firm is responsible for overseeing the financial integrity of its customers' positions, and a well-established, foolproof system is employed by the nation's exchanges to protect against customer and member-firm financial failure. In the case of the clearinghouses of some major exchanges, the exchange itself intervenes as the buyer; in this instance the exchange guarantees each trade, so it becomes immaterial who holds the opposite position.

Because of the high leverage and quick price movements, futures have a higher risk than many other investments. This risk provides greater opportunity for profit and loss. Commodity price fluctuations can be tied to any number of factors, just as they can in the credit and stock markets. Each is susceptible to systematic or marketwide risk, and each also has commodity-specific exposure. For instance, in trading Japanese yen futures, factors that enter into the market are general market expectations; relative economic conditions of Japan; political and government

influences; relationship of spot and forward rates; interest-rate parity; technical trading factors; and local floor activity. Any one of these factors can precipitate a major price move. And because of the convergence of these factors in the trading pit, price movements are extremely quick.

Once someone has entered into a futures-market position, he will be subject to daily market accounting. Prices are "marked" to market—that is, each net position is reconciled daily, and losses or profits are posted. If a futures trader has a loss, the commodity brokerage firm then looks at the customer's margin account. However, unlike the stock market, a futures margin acts as a good-faith deposit or performance bond.

If a customer's net cash position falls below the stipulated minimum maintenance margin level, the commodity firm may ask him to deposit more cash or collateral, usually in the form of Treasury bills. Factors affecting the size of the minimum margin level stipulated by a commodity firm are (1) the financial condition of the trader, (2) whether the account is for hedging or speculating, (3) which commodity is being traded, (4) past experience, and (5) which contract month is traded.

Anyone using the futures markets should be aware of maintenance margin calls. Failure to meet a call can result in the brokerage house closing out your position. Check with your broker to determine their procedure for this crucial aspect of the market. Some houses allow a grace period of up to three days, provided no new positions are initiated; other firms are not so generous.

As a general rule of thumb, speculators should consider the money used in futures trading as expendable income—risk capital—whose loss will not materially affect their life-styles. The minimum amount for opening a futures account varies among brokerage houses; some will open accounts for $2,500, others recommend $10,000 to $25,000 (see FUTURES COMMISSION MERCHANT).

Aside from the capital needed to open the account and meet margin requirements, the other costs involved in trading futures are usually restricted to commissions. As in the stock market, there is a complete range of brokerage houses—from full-service houses supplying research and individual counseling and charging commissions of over $100 per round turn (buy and sell), to discount brokerage houses charging round-turn commissions of $18 on some commodities.

In choosing a brokerage house, customers first should determine how much advice they need to trade the markets. If the trader has a solid level of understanding and knowledge of the individual commodity, a discount broker may be the best approach. Individuals requiring more guidance can employ a full service operation, but they should also be aware of the higher costs.

Few aspects of investing are as important as choosing the right broker. As in any investment, the futures trader must feel comfortable and confident with the firm and his broker. Aside from this important emotional aspect, users of these markets should also check their brokerage houses' financial status. Traders should also understand how the markets operate.

All of this preliminary work must be done so the commodity trader achieves his desired goal. When that goal is not achieved, he must identify the reason why, and where the fault lies. If it is with the brokerage house, he can pursue his complaint to determine whether compensation is justified.

Because futures markets are more organized and heavily regulated today than in the past, widespread commodity fraud is on the decrease. Unfortunately, certain instances do occur, however. To protect customers, the government, the commodity industry, and the exchanges themselves have erected a number of safeguards.

At the exchange level, clearing member firms must submit to frequent financial audits to guarantee their creditworthiness. Additionally, various exchange departments can investigate member firms' activities. All futures commission merchants (FCM's) must meet minimum financial requirements set by the Commodity Futures Trading Commission (CFTC), the federal agency that oversees the industry. An industry surveillance group, the National Futures Association, also has been formed to oversee industry activities and prevent commodity frauds.

As a quick rule of thumb, however, market users can detect potential frauds if they follow some basic procedures. Beware of excessive claims about unlimited upside profits. If the claims seem exaggerated, examine the performance numbers, talk to former customers, and see if the numbers were audited. Reputable firms also will be members of the nation's 12 commodity exchanges. Check to see if they are members in good standing and for how long. Each exchange has a legal and compliance department that can be helpful.

At the firm level, ask to see annual reports, and ask if the company is a clearing member of an exchange. Clearing members have more stringent financial requirements than nonclearing firms. Ask industry people about the company's reputation and the quality of its brokers and floor personnel. Also ask about the firm's back-office operation. This is where customer accounts are audited and nonmatching trades reconciled. It is often considered the key to a successful commodity-trading operation.

Futures trading has tremendous advantages for institutions and individuals when used in a well-defined program. And when the proper match of strategy, commodity firm, and trading capital is obtained, these markets can supplement any financial endeavor.

H. Phillip Becker

Commodities Glossary

actuals   the physical or cash commodities, as distinguished from commodity-futures contracts.

adverse move   occurs when a buyer's (long) position goes down and a seller's (short) position goes up.

approved delivery facility   any stockyard, mill, store, warehouse, plant, or elevator that is authorized by the exchange for delivery of exchange contracts.

arbitrage   simultaneous purchase of cash commodities or futures in one market against the sale of cash commodities or futures in the same or a different market, to profit from a discrepancy in prices.

at the market   type of order in which the customer states how many contracts of a given delivery month he wishes to buy or sell. The customer does not specify the price at which he wants to initiate the transaction but simply wants it placed as soon as possible at the best possible price.

backwardization   means that futures prices are trading at a discount to spot prices.

basis   the difference between a cash price at the specific location and the price of a particular futures contract.

bearish and bullish   when market conditions suggest lower prices, and prices are trending lower, a *bear* market is in existence. Conversely, with higher prices forecast and prices moving upward, the situation is termed *bullish*.

bid   an expression of a desire to buy a specific quantity of a commodity at a stated price.

break   a rapid and sharp price decline.

broker   a registered representative, either an account executive or floor broker, who is given the responsibility for the acceptance and/or execution of an order.

bucketing   the illegal practice of accepting orders to buy or sell without executing such orders, and the illegal use of the customer's principal—margin deposit—without disclosing the fact of such use.

buy-in   a purchase that will offset a previous short sale. Covers or liquidates a short position.

buy on close   to buy at the end of the trading session at a price within the closing range of prices.

buy on opening   to buy at the beginning of the trading session at a price within the opening range of prices.

carrying charge   the cost to store and insure a physical commodity over a period of time; also involves an interest charge and other incidental costs in ownership.

cash commodity   The actual physical commodity.

CFTC   Commodity Futures Trading Commission

clearing   matching the trading cards of the buyers and sellers with all their required information. Clearing is done by the exchange's clearinghouse on a daily basis.

clearing member   a firm that assumes the position of buyer and seller and, through the clearinghouse (an exchange department), guarantees the proper execution and payment of the trade. The clearing member is qualified to clear trades through the clearinghouse.

clearinghouse   a department of the exchange, through which all trades on the exchange are cleared and adjusted.

close   a period of time at the end of the trading sessions at which all orders are filled within the closing range.

commission   the fee paid for buying and selling commodities in a futures or cash market.

contract month   the month in which a futures contract may be satisfied by making or accepting delivery.

day order   an order that expires on the close of trading if not filled during that day.

default   a common term, but in commodity futures it normally means the inability of a firm or an individual to meet margin requirements.

delivery   the tender of the actual commodity in fulfillment of a short position in futures during the period specified by the futures contract.

delivery notice   a notice that must be presented by the seller to the clearinghouse. The clearinghouse then assigns the notice, and the subsequent delivery instrument, to the longest-standing buyer on record.

differentials   the premiums paid for grades better than the basis grade, and the discounts allowed for grades lower than the basis grade.

discount   the price difference between futures of different delivery months—"July at a discount to May" indicating that the price of the July future is lower than that of the May future.

discretionary account   an account for which buy and sell orders can be placed by a broker or other person without the consent of the account owner for each such individual order, a blanket agreement having been initially granted by the account owner for such action.

elasticity   the phenomenon of price change creating an increase or decrease in the consumption of a commodity; describes the interaction of supply and demand.

favorable   opposite of *adverse move.*

fill or kill   an order that has to be executed upon receipt by the broker or automatically canceled. Once the broker receives the order, he or she must try to fill the order at the price specified or at a better price. If filling the order is impossible, the broker reports an "unable" to the customer along with the latest quote, and automatically cancels the order.

first-notice day   the first day that notices of intentions to deliver actual commodities against futures contracts can be made.

floor trader   an exchange member who fills orders for his own account by being personally present on the floor. Usually called a "local."

forward contract   a contract calling for the delivery of a commodity sometime in the future; not to be confused with futures contracts, which are traded on regulated futures exchanges.

free on board (FOB)   means all costs of delivery, inspection, and elevation or loading of commodities on board a carrier have been paid.

futures   a term used to designate all contracts covering the sale of commodities for future delivery on a commodities exchange.

futures commission merchants   individuals, associations, partnerships, corporations, and trusts that solicit or accept orders from customers for the purchase or sale of any commodity for future delivery on or subject to the rules of any contract market and that accept payment from or extend credit to those whose orders are accepted. Their income is generated by the commission charged their customers. (Also called "commission houses.")

GTC   "Good Till Canceled"—an order instruction to the broker to keep the order open until either executed or canceled.

hedging   taking a position in a futures market opposite to a position held in the cash market to minimize the risk of financial loss from an adverse price change; a purchase or sale of futures as a temporary substitute for a cash transaction that will occur later. A hedger buys or sells a futures contract to reduce the risk of loss through price variation. A *short* hedger sells a futures contract to protect against the possible decline in the actual commodity owned by him. A *long* hedger purchases a futures contract to protect against the possible increase in value of an actual commodity needed to be purchased in the future.

inverted market when the cash price and nearby futures prices exceed distant futures prices, due to inadequate supplies of a commodity.

last trading day the final day on which trading may occur for a particular delivery month. After the last trading day, any remaining commitment must be settled by delivery.

limit the maximum price advance or decline from the previous day's settlement price permitted for a contract in one trading session by the rules of the exchange.

limit order an order to buy or sell only at a specified price or better.

liquid market an active market that permits easy entry and exit of a position.

long a long position is established by owning the actual commodity unhedged or by purchasing futures.

margin the amount of money or collateral deposited by a client with his broker, or by a broker with the clearinghouse, for the purpose of insuring the broker or clearinghouse against loss on open futures contracts. The margin is not a part payment on a purchase. (1) *Original* or *initial margin* is the total amount of margin per contract required by the broker when a futures position is opened. (2) *Maintenance margin* is a sum that must be maintained on deposit at all times. If a customer's equity in any futures position drops to or under the level because of adverse price action, the broker must issue a *margin call* to restore the customer's equity.

margin call a request from a clearinghouse to a clearing member, or from a brokerage firm to a customer, to bring margin deposits up to a required minimum level.

market order an order to buy or sell at the best possible price at the time the order reaches the floor.

maturity expiration of a contract.

nearby the nearest active trading month of a commodity futures market.

offer an indication of a willingness to sell at a certain price, as opposed to a *bid*.

offset execute an opposite transaction, thereby liquidating an existing position.

open a brief period of time, at the start of trading, at which all orders are executed within the opening range.

open interest the total number of futures contracts entered into during a specified period of time that have not been liquidated either by offsetting futures transactions or by actual delivery.

overnights persons who establish a position in the market and retain it into the second day or beyond.

p and s a purchase-and-sales statement sent by a broker to his client showing both the purchase and sale of a contract that has been closed out.

pit the area on the trading floor where trading in futures contracts is conducted. Also called the "ring."

position an interest in the market in the form of an open commitment either long or short.

pyramiding the practice of using accrued paper profits to margin additional trades.

range the difference between the high and low prices of a future during any given period.

regulated commodities those commodities over which the Commodity Futures Trading Commission has regulatory supervision for the purpose of seeing that commodity trading is conducted in the public's interest.

reporting limit sizes of positions set by the CFTC at or above which commodity traders and brokers who carry their accounts must make daily reports as to the size of the position by commodity, delivery month, and whether the position is speculative or a hedge.

retender to sell a futures contract to replace a delivery notice just received, thus returning the delivery notice to the clearinghouse for reissuance to another *long*.

round lot one futures contract. (In wheat futures, one round lot equals 5,000 bushels.)

round turn establishing and later closing a position in the market. Brokerage fees are based on a round turn.

sample grade the lower grade that can be put on a grain and still allow it to be called a specific grain (i.e., sample grade wheat is still wheat).

scalper a speculator operating from the trading floor who provides the market with liquidity by buying and selling.

settlement price the daily final market price at which a commodity-futures-exchange clearinghouse clears all trades and settles all accounts between clearing members for each contract month. Settlement prices are used to determine margin calls.

short selling selling a futures contract with the idea of purchasing it at a lower price at a later date because the speculator expects the market to decline. For example: The speculator sells a March Minneapolis spring wheat at $4.05 per bushel in December, and then repurchases that March Minneapolis wheat at $3.86 in January. Until the time in January that he repurchased this contact, his market position was known as a short position.

speculative transaction taking a position in the market in the hope of a favorable price move for profit and with no intention of making delivery of the commodity or financial instrument.

spot price   the price quoted for the actual commodity; same as *cash commodity.*

spread   assuming opposite positions in two or more futures contracts in the hope of profiting through changes in those price relationships.

straddle   a synonym for *spread.*

switch   offsetting a position in one delivery month of a commodity and simultaneous initiation of a similar position in another delivery month of the same commodity.

tender   the act of giving notice to the clearinghouse of intention to initiate delivery of the physical commodity in satisfaction of the futures contract.

ticker tape   a continuous paper tape transmission of commodity (or security) prices, volume, and other trading and market information; it operates on private wires leased by the exchanges.

trade register   trade data submitted by a clearing firm for each trade-confirmation card that is cleared; that data is reproduced on the trade register. Included in this report are open positions, settlement variation for all open positions, and transactions that cleared that day.

volume   the number of purchases and sales of a commodity made during a specified period of time.

warehouse receipt   a document evidencing possession by a warehouse (licensed by the U.S. or a specific state) of the commodity named in the receipt. Warehouse receipts, to be tenderable on futures contracts, must be negotiable receipts covering commodities in warehouses recognized for delivery purposes by the exchange on which such futures contracts are traded.

wash sales   a fictitious transaction that gives the appearance that purchases and sales have been made, usually not resulting in a change in the trader's market position.

wrong   a position that is unfavorable.

Source: Understanding Commodity Futures Trading (Minneapolis Grain Exchange) and contributors from commodity-futures exchanges.

Commodity-Brokerage Firm

See FUTURES COMMISSION MERCHANT.

Commodity Exchange, Inc. (COMEX)

A COMMODITY-FUTURES EXCHANGE trading gold, silver, and copper futures, and options on gold futures.

History. The product of a 1933 merger of four older commodity-futures marketplaces, COMEX traces its actual origins to the beginning of the New York Metal Exchange, incorporated in 1883. That entity gave way to the National Metal Exchange, which eventually joined with the Rubber Exchange of New York, the National Raw Silk Exchange, and the New York Hide Exchange. These four exchanges combined to form COMEX, which opened for business on July 5, 1933, with trading in six commodities: copper, hides, rubber, silk, silver, and tin. Contracts with a total value of more than $730 million traded in its first year. As the nation worked its way out of the depths of the Great Depression, COMEX attracted new members and recorded increasing trading volume annually.

However, the outbreak of World War II had serious repercussions for the young exchange. All commodities traded on COMEX were included on the government's list of strategic and critical materials. At first they were subject to price ceilings, allocations, and various other governmental controls. Eventually, futures trading in all commodities was suspended for four and a half years.

Trading resumed on a full-time basis in 1947 and gained steadily until the early 1950s, when operations were again suspended in most commodities for the duration of the Korean conflict. By 1954, trading had been reinstated in all suspended commodities. Volume growth continued for the balance of the decade, which ended with the best year in the exchange's history: 132,308 contracts traded in 1959, representing a value of $1.7 billion.

On June 12, 1963, trading in silver futures resumed after a 29-year hiatus following the nationalization of the metal on August 9, 1934. This, along with an improved economic picture, resulted in substantial volume increases during the next few years as COMEX established several trading records. By the end of the 1960s, the exchange had assumed a major role in both the domestic and international marketplace.

However, it was in the 1970s that COMEX experienced major growth. Everything from trading volume to the price of a membership seat virtually exploded during the decade. In 1970, volume on the exchange was just over 900,000 contracts. Nine years later it totaled nearly 13 million, and 1 out of every 6 futures contracts executed in the United States was traded on COMEX (compared to 1 in 45 some 12 years earlier). A COMEX membership, which could be purchased for as little as $7,500 in 1970, changed hands for a record $350,000 in the fall of 1980. Annual trading volume reached an unprecedented high of 17,341,025 contracts in 1982.

COMEX Contracts. Every contract for a specific commodity, such as COMEX silver, is identical. This standardization, coupled with the protections afforded by the COMEX Clearing Association, permits traders to establish positions in the open market without concern for the identity of the opposite party to the transaction.

In choosing its contract markets, COMEX has long been mindful of two objectives: to serve the evolving needs of industry to manage price risks while successfully attracting risk capital in order to provide liquidity. Best exemplifying COMEX's success in accomplishing these dual objectives is the exchange's gold contract, which began trading on December 31, 1974. Since that time, the COMEX contract has become the most active gold-futures contract in the world.

Exchange-traded options were recently introduced by the futures industry. Approved generically by the Commodity Futures Trading Commission in September 1981, futures options began trading in October 1982 under a three-year pilot program. On October 4, 1982, COMEX took the first step toward establishing its own options marketplace with the opening of trading in COMEX options on gold futures.

Matt Zachowski

Commodity-Futures Exchange

The buying and selling of goods for future delivery is a practice as old as commerce itself. However, it was not until the transportation and communications advances surrounding the Industrial Revolution that America's need for organized, specialized commodities markets became apparent. In 1848 the Chicago Board of Trade was established as this country's first organized market for commodity trading. In 1981 U.S. futures exchanges traded nearly 100 million FU-TURES CONTRACTS representing a financial value of almost $2 trillion.

A *futures exchange* is a centralized marketplace where contracts for the future delivery of various commodities are bought and sold through a competitive auction process.

Futures markets serve distinct groups called "hedgers" and "speculators," only a small percentage of which actually make or take delivery of the underlying physical commodity. Essentially, the futures market enables a business to protect itself against the financial risks associated with price fluctuations in the cash market by transferring that risk to speculators, who are willing to assume it. While the primary economic role of a futures exchange is to provide a marketplace for commercial hedging activity, the participation of speculators adds to the breadth and depth of the market, permitting traders to establish and close out market positions quickly and efficiently without an undue effect on prices.

Table 1 lists the U. S. futures exchanges and the commodities traded on them as of the early 1980s.

(Information on each of the commodity-futures exchanges can be found in this book under headings of their respective names.)

Hedging Futures exchanges provide an important risk-management tool for various commercial interests—including those who produce, process, market, or use the commodities traded on world exchanges. Through the hedging process, a business can get a form of price insurance that allows it to focus on commercial objectives without the constant threat of sustaining losses as a result of market volatility. In pure form, a hedge involves establishing a position in the futures market that is equal and opposite to a position held in the physical commodity. In other words, those who own a commodity can offset the risk of price decline by selling futures contracts; and those who will need a commodity in the future can offset the risk of uncontrollable price increases by purchasing futures contracts ahead of time. In either case, the aim

---

Table 1
Commodities Traded by Exchange

Exchange/Commodity	Contract Unit
Chicago Board of Trade (CBOT)	
Wheat	5,000 bu.
Corn	5,000 bu.
Oats	5,000 bu.
Soybeans	5,000 bu.
Soybean oil	60,000 lbs.
Soybean meal	100 tons
Iced broilers	30,000 lbs.
Plywood	76,032 sq. ft.
Western plywood	76,032 sq. ft.
Silver (old)	5,000 oz.
Silver (new)	1,000 oz.
Gold	100 oz.
U.S. T-bonds	$ 100,000
Com. paper loan (90-day)	$ 1,000,000
Com. paper loan (30-day)	$ 3,000,000
U.S. T-notes (4–6 yrs.)	$ 100,000
GNMA mortgages (CDR)	$ 100,000
GNMA mortgages (CD)	$ 100,000
Domestic CD (90-day)	$ 1,000,000
U.S. T-notes (6.5–10 yrs.)[1]	$ 100,000
MidAmerica Commodity Exchange (MACE)	
Wheat	1,000 bu.
Corn	1,000 bu.
Oats	1,000 bu.
Soybeans	1,000 bu.
Live hogs	15,000 lbs.

(cont)

Table 1 *(cont)*
Commodities Traded by Exchange

Exchange/Commodity	Contract Unit
Live cattle	20,000 lbs.
Silver	1,000 oz.
Gold	33.2 oz.
U.S. T-bonds	$ 50,000
U.S. T-bills[2]	$ 500,000

Kansas City Board of Trade (KCBT)

Wheat	5,000 bu.
Grain sorghum	280,000 lbs.
Value line index[3]	$ 500 × Index

Minneapolis Grain Exchange (MGE)

Wheat	5,000 bu.
Sunflower seeds	100,000 lbs.

Chicago Mercantile Exchange (CME)
and International Monetary Market/Index
and Option Market (IMM) (IOM)

Feeder cattle	42,000 lbs.
Live hogs	30,000 lbs.
Pork bellies, frozen	38,000 lbs.
Live cattle	40,000 lbs.
Broilers, fresh, frozen	30,000 lbs.
Russet potatoes	80,000 lbs.
Shell eggs	22,500 doz.
Lumber	100,000 bd. ft.
Stud lumber	100,000 bd. ft.
Plywood	152,064 sq. ft.
U.S. silver coins	$ 5,000
Gold	100 tr. oz.
Canadian dollars	100,000
French franc	250,000
Swiss franc	125,000
Dutch guilder	125,000
Deutsche mark	125,000
Mexican peso	1,000,000
British pound sterling	25,000
Japanese yen	12,500,000
U.S. T-bills (90-day)	$ 1,000,000
U.S. T-bills (1-yr.)	$ 250,000
U.S. T-notes (4-yr.)	$ 100,000
Domestic CD (90-day)	$ 1,000,000
Eurodollar (3-month)[4]	$ 1,000,000
S&P 500 Index[5]	$ 500 × Index

New York Mercantile Exchange (NYME)

Imported lean beef	36,000 lb.
Round white potatoes	50,000 lb.
Palladium	100 tr. oz.
Platinum	50 tr. oz.
U.S. silver coins	$ 10,000

Table 1 *(cont)*
Commodities Traded by Exchange

Exchange/Commodity	Contract Unit
No. 2 heating oil, NY	42,000 U.S. gals.
No. 2 heating oil, Gulf	42,000 U.S. gals.
Leaded reg. gasoline, NY[6]	42,000 U.S. gals.
Leaded reg. gasoline, Gulf[7]	42,000 U.S. gals.

New York Cotton Exchange and Associates (NYCE)

Orange juice, frozen con.	15,000 lbs.
Cotton no. 2	50,000 lbs.
Propane gas	100,000 gals.

Coffee, Sugar & Cocoa Exchange (CSCE)

Coffee "C"	$ 37,500 lbs.
Sugar no. 11	112,000 lbs.
Sugar no. 12	112,000 lbs.
Cocoa	10 metric tons

Commodity Exchange, Inc. (COMEX)

Zinc	60,000 lbs.
Silver	5,000 tr. oz.
Copper	25,000 lbs.
Gold	100 tr. oz.
U.S. T-bills (90-day)	$ 1,000,000
GNMA mortgages (CD)	$ 100,000
U.S. T-notes (2-yr.)	$ 100,000

New York Futures Exchange (NYFE)

U.S. T-bills (90-day)	$ 1,000,000
U.S. T-bonds	100,000
Domestic CD (90-day)	1,000,000
British pound	25,000
Canadian dollar	100,000
Deutsche mark	125,000
Japanese yen	12,500,000
Swiss franc	125,000
NYSE composite index[8]	$ 500 × Index

New Orleans Commodity Exchange (NOCE)[9]

Rice, milled	120,000 lbs.
Rice, rough	200,000 lbs.
Cotton	50,000 lbs.
Soybeans[10]	5,000 bu.

Source: This table first appeared in the 1982 *Annual Report* of the Commodities Futures Trading Commission (CFTC).
[1] Trading began May 3, 1982.
[2] Trading began April 2, 1982.
[3] Trading began February 24, 1982.
[4] Trading began December 9, 1981.
[5] Trading began April 21, 1982.
[6] Trading began October 5, 1982.
[7] Trading began December 14, 1981.
[8] Trading began May 6, 1982.
[9] The New Orleans Commodity Exchange discontinued in June 1983.
[10] Data were supplied by the Futures Industry Association, Inc.

is to establish a position in the futures market that would show a gain when a change in the cash-market price would produce a loss, or vice versa. In this way, the hedger can establish a future economic result at today's price. In order to reduce the financial effects of adverse price changes, the hedger willingly forgoes the possible profits that might accompany favorable movements in commodity prices. Although every hedge by definition is applied against a corresponding position in physicals, it is not a substitute for later cash-market activity. Like speculative positions, hedges are generally closed out or "lifted" sometime before contract expiration.

Speculation In contrast to the hedger, who seeks to avoid risk, the speculator tries to predict commodity-price movements before they occur, and thereby profit from price volatility. Speculators make decisions to buy or sell based on their evaluations of a commodity's supply-demand fundamentals, as well as general market tone and price trends. Unlike the hedger, who seeks merely to "lock in" a certain economic result, the speculator thrives on the uncertainty frequently associated with commodity-price fluctuations. Like an investor in registered securities, the commodity speculator's main concern is the probable direction of the market. Thus, he will purchase FUTURES CONTRACTS when he believes that the price of a commodity will increase, and sell contracts when he thinks that prices will decline. Often this involves taking the opposite side of trades offered by those who are hedging, although it is not always the case.

In most every case, however, speculators avoid becoming involved in the physical delivery process. Instead, they execute equal and opposite transactions before each contract matures. The difference between the original purchase or sale price of each contract and the price of the offsetting transactions represents the realized profit or loss.

Delivery The seller of a futures contract (short position) has the obligation to deliver the underlying commodity during that contract's expiration month. The obligation to deliver remains binding on the seller until an offsetting transaction removes that obligation. Similarly, the owner of a futures contract to buy a commodity (long position) may be notified during the contract's month of expiration that delivery will be forthcoming. If a long position remains open after trading ceases, delivery of the actual commodity will occur according to the terms of the particular contract.

However, futures markets are generally not used for delivery even by those who are hedging. The standardized grades, amounts, and fineness of gold, for example, preclude many hedgers from taking delivery because of variance from their individual needs. It is the *potential* for delivery that causes the price of a futures contract to approach the cash-market value of the commodity as the contract nears expiration. This movement of futures prices toward cash-market prices is known as "convergence."

Operations Futures exchanges are nonprofit membership organizations (similar to the stock exchanges) whose primary function is to provide an organized mechanism for the buying and selling of futures contracts in an open, competitive marketplace. The exchange itself does not directly buy or sell futures contracts; rather, it provides the facilities for trading futures contracts within established regulations designed to provide standard and equitable treatment for all market participants. Purchases and sales of all futures contracts are made according to standardized terms and conditions.

Exchange policy is established by an elected governing board headed by a chairman. The board of governors delegates administrative and operational responsibilities to a president, who oversees a highly skilled professional staff. The varied responsibilities of the exchange staff include supervision of trading facilities; auditing records of exchange members; dissemination of daily trading results; market surveillance; and new contract development.

The nation's commodity exchanges are regulated by the COMMODITY FUTURES TRADING COMMISSION (CFTC). The CFTC is an independent, full-time government agency, established in 1975 to administer the provisions of the Commodity Exchange Act, which subjects all commodity-futures trading to federal oversight and restricts trading to contract markets designated and licensed by the commission.

Membership. Exchange members make up a cross section of the diverse types of market participants who trade commodity-futures contracts. These individuals and firms are commonly divided into three primary categories: floor brokers and traders; trade houses; and commission houses.

Floor brokers and traders are individuals who have qualified for membership in the exchange and have also passed examinations, both written and verbal, to obtain the privilege of executing orders on the trading floor. A floor broker executes orders for others and essentially acts in the capacity of an agent. A floor trader, on the other hand, will buy and sell contracts for his own account, thereby contributing to market liquidity. Since floor brokers handle customer business, they are required to be registered with the CFTC.

Table 2
Futures Volume by Exchange, 1981*

Rank	Exchange	Contracts	%
1	Chicago Board of Trade	49,085,763	49.82
2	Chicago Mercantile Exchange	24,527,020	24.89
3	Commodity Exchange, Inc.	13,292,049	13.49
4	Coffee, Sugar & Cocoa Exchange	3,562,613	3.62
5	MidAmerica Commodity Exchange	2,588,540	2.63
6	New York Cotton Exchange	1,802,891	1.83
7	New York Mercantile Exchange	1,781,407	1.81
8	Kansas City Board of Trade	1,181,884	1.20
9	Minneapolis Grain Exchange	372,624	.38
10	New York Futures Exchange	290,585	.29
11	New Orleans Commodity Exchange†	35,995	.04
		98,522,371	100.00

*This table was compiled by the Futures Industry Association (FIA).
†The New Orleans Commodity Exchange discontinued in June 1983.

A *trade house* is a firm whose primary business involves the actual commodity for which futures contracts are traded on the exchange. The trade house generally engages in hedging activity and should be distinguished from the *commission house,* which accepts orders from individual speculators and carries their accounts. Commission houses must also register with the CFTC, as must any firm's employees who solicit customer business or handle funds.

These parties—each representing different interests but all sharing a common purpose—are brought together in a competitive auction market, thus allowing free and open price discovery in all the commodities traded. The broad-based membership of an exchange is fully represented on its ruling board of governors, providing a decision-making process that is exposed to diverse points of view on every issue. Moreover, the exchange also benefits from the presence of outside governors, who are not actively involved in commodities and thus can offer additional perspectives.

How Trades Are Made. Although uninitiated visitors to the trading floor often feel they are witnessing unleashed pandemonium, futures exchanges nonetheless provide an orderly and logically structured trading forum. All transactions take place in specific trading areas, or "rings," each designated for the trading of a particular commodity. Trades result from the meeting of a bid and an offer by open outcry in a competitive auction, with each member attempting to complete a transaction at the best possible price. Prices change when bids are raised or offers are lowered, reflecting changes in supply and demand for futures contracts. Thus, futures trading is a very dynamic process through which floor brokers and traders act as competing auctioneers, and trading ebbs and flows as buyers and sellers move into and out of the marketplace.

On a major futures exchange, the activities of floor traders account for a significant percentage of transaction volume. Like dealers in the cash market, these "locals," as they are called in industry parlance, seek to take advantage of temporary aberrations in price relationships. Thus, the floor trader is a unique type of market participant—neither a hedger nor a speculator in the traditional sense but providing critical liquidity to the marketplace. Floor traders continuously "make a market" in a contract by simultaneously offering to buy futures and sell them at a favorable differential in price.

As futures prices change, they are recorded instantly by floor reporters, who transmit the information through a computerized communications system. Trading data—including the high, low, and last three price changes—are posted on large electronic display boards near the trading rings. Additional information on each trade is available on computerized visual screens located at several vantage points around the exchange. Trading data is made public via the exchange's ticker system, which reports price changes as they occur and sends a daily summary of market activity to national and international financial media. This communications network thus provides a continuous flow of information concerning trading activity during the hours of the business day.

The Clearing System. All futures contracts are backed by a sophisticated clearing system that assures performance on all contracts traded. Generally, the "clearing association" is a separate corporation composed of exchange members with substantial capital who have agreed to honor the contract obligations of other exchange members.

Every trade executed on a futures exchange must be recorded on the books of a member of the exchange's clearing association at the end of each business day. All clearing members are required to deposit surety deposits called "margin" with the clearing association, based on the number of contracts cleared. The margin deposits, as well as the guarantee funds and surplus reserves of the association, are available against default by any clearing member. The initial margin requirements and daily adjustments to these good-faith deposits ensure complete credit security for all transactions completed on the exchange. As a result of these protective arrangements, futures-contract traders have never incurred a loss as a result of a clearing member's failure to meet its financial obligations.

Conclusion. The futures markets, particularly those specializing in commodities of international scope, have played a major role in the world's economy and have had a significant impact on standards of living throughout the world. As one of the most important areas of investment in America today, the futures markets have substantially expanded decision-making opportunities in virtually all areas of business. Many industries have come to realize the potential that commodity-futures trading offers in combating price uncertainty and increasing competitive position. In addition, speculators have discovered exciting new markets for trading based on their anticipations of price volatility.

Matt Zachowski

Commodity-Futures Price Tables, How to Read

Price is the key statistic generated by futures markets, although the volume of trade and the number of outstanding contracts (open interest) also are important. Prices are available from a variety of sources, such as the daily newspapers. Many papers also report volume and open interest.

The policies of the wire services and of newspapers vary, so this entry will describe price tables in general terms, from which the reader can select those that apply to any publication's system of reporting.

Column Designations. Across the top of most price listings will be some combination of these words or their abbreviations:

Open: the price or range of prices for the day's first trades, registered during the period designated as the opening of the market or the opening call. Many publications print only a single price for the market open or close regardless of whether there is a range with trades at several prices. For exchanges with split opens or closes, a commission house or exchange will be the accurate price source.

High: the highest price at which the commodity sold during the day.

Low: the lowest price at which the commodity sold during the day.

Close: the price or range of prices at which the commodity sold during the brief period designated as the market close or on the closing call.

Settlement price: Some tables report settlement price rather than closing price. In commodity mar-

kets, every trade is "marked to the market" each day—in other words, the gain or loss from that day's trading is computed and posted or charged to each trader's account. If a market closes on a range of prices, a "settlement price" is determined and used for the computation. The settlement price is a figure determined by formula from within the closing range, or it is the closing price if there is a single price. For some publications or markets, *settlement price* is used as a column heading; other tabulations use a small *s* to designate the settlement price. (See GNMA's, below.)

Yield, yield close, yield settlement, yield change, or some combination of like words may appear for the financial instruments. These columns translate the futures quotations and gain or loss into the annual return on the face value of the futures contract.

Season or lifetime high-low: the highest and lowest prices recorded for each contract maturity from the first day it was traded to the present.

Open interest: The outstanding contracts are reported in different ways, and the custom of each publication must be studied to determine the data that apply. Some publications show the open interest for each maturity month of each contract; others show the open interest for all maturities combined, plus the amount of increase or decrease from the last previous report; and some do not report this number.

Volume: Shortly after the market closes, some exchanges report the number of contracts traded on that day. Some report an estimate, and also a final figure for the previous session.

Commodities/Exchanges/Prices. Most publications identify each commodity, the exchange on which it is traded, the size of the contract, and the way in which prices are quoted. Following is a key to what the price numbers mean. (Some tables do not include decimal points.)

Grains on domestic markets: Cents per bushel 607½ = 607½ cents or $6.07½ per bushel.

Grains, Winnipeg: Dollars per metric ton (2,204.62 pounds). 75.60 = $75.60 Canadian dollars per ton.

Soybean meal: Dollars per ton (2,000 pounds). 162.30 = $162.30 per ton.

Broilers, cattle, cocoa, coffee, copper, cotton, hogs, orange juice, pork bellies, potatoes, soybean oil, sugar: Cents per pound. (The final two digits in all prices are hundredths of a cent, usually called a "point.") Soybean oil: 21.25 = 21¼¢ per pound. Coffee: 179.25 = $1.79¼ per pound, or 179¼¢. (*Note:* The minimum change for broilers, cattle, hogs, and pork bellies is $.00025 or 25/1000 of a cent. In these prices, therefore, a final digit of 2 or 7 is read as though it were followed by a 5. Cattle: 41.12 = 42 125/1000¢ per pound, or 42⅛¢. Pork bellies: 69.50 = 69 50/100¢ or 69½¢ per pound.)

Foreign currencies: Usually reported as American dollars per unit of foreign money. 1.9830 = $1.98 30/100 (one dollar 98 and 30/100¢) for one British pound sterling. Japanese yen are cents per yen: .5445 = $.005445 per yen; a yen is worth 5,445/10,000¢ or just over a half cent.

GNMA's, Treasury notes and bonds: Percentage of par. Minimum change may be 1/32 of 1%, equal to $31.25 per contract, or 1/64 of 1%, equal to $15.625 per contract. 96-00 = .96 x $100,000 = $96,000. 96-09 = .96 9/32 x $100,000 = $96,281.25.

Treasury bills, commercial paper: The quote is an index rate computed by subtracting the annual discount rate from 100. Minimum change is .01 percent or $100 per contract per year (360 days); $25 for 90 days. 94.03 = 5.97% yield (100 − 94.03) times $1,000,000 divided by 4 = $14,925. $1,000,000 minus $14,925 = $985,075, the 90-day T-bill price. 94.00 = 6% or $15,000 yield.

Silver: Cents per troy ounce. 472.50 = four hundred seventy-two and a half cents ($4.72 50/100) per troy ounce.

Silver coins: Dollars per bag. 3310 = $3,310 per bag of silver coins.

Platinum, gold: Dollars per troy ounce. 160.20 = $160.20 per ounce of gold.

Eggs: Cents per dozen. 47.75 = 47¾ cents per dozen.

Lumber: Dollars per 1,000 board feet. 207.10 = $207.10 per 1,000 board feet.

Plywood: Dollars per 1,000 square feet. 211.00 = $211 per 1,000 square feet.

Contract Maturities. In virtually all commodity price tables, the left-hand vertical column will be a series of months. These designate the maturities at which time deliveries are made or taken unless the contract has been offset by an opposite transaction. It is normal that commodities will be traded for at least a year into the future, and some commodities will have prices extending for more than two years.

Example 1 deals with contracts for live cattle traded in 40,000-pound units with prices quoted in cents per pound. For the October delivery, the market opened on a single price of 56.37¢ (56 375/1000¢) per pound and closed on a range with trades at 56.05 and 56.15, and probably at each 2½¢ in between.

The highest price registered in this session was 56.50¢, the lowest was 55.85¢, and the market closed .75 to .85 points higher than the close of the previous session.

During the time October has been trading, its high price has been 59.30¢ and the low was 38.50¢.

On this day an estimated 28,982 contracts were traded. Confirmed volume for the previous session is 23,084 contracts. Also, at the end of the previous session there were 94,540 outstanding contracts, down 38 from the session before that.

Example 2 shows October 1978 as the nearby future; during October, that maturity will also be called the "spot" month. Trading takes place for 13 different maturities stretching to June 1981—the most "distant" or "deferred" maturity.

These columns vary from the previous example by showing a settlement price and a yield, as well as the change to the settlement and yield. The far-right column shows the outstanding contracts (open interest) for each maturity as of the previous trading session. The bottom line shows the estimated volume, actual prior day's volume, open interest for *all* maturities, and the net change in open interest from that of the previous day.

There was no trade in either the nearby October or December maturity, but a settlement price was computed for accounting purposes. Since these were not actual transactions some publications might key the figures with an *n* to show they have been computed and are "nominal." In the distant June price series, the high has been keyed with an *a* to signify an asking price; the low with a *b* to signify a bid price. In neither case was there a transaction at that price.

Seasonal crops, such as grains, have price patterns

| Example 1
Cattle, Live—40,000 Pounds; Cents per Pound | | | | | Life of Contract | |
	Open	High	Low	Close	Change	High	Low
Oct.	56.37	56.50	55.85	56.05–56.15	+.75 to .85	59.30	38.50
Est. vol. 28,982; prev. vol. 23,084; open int. 94,540, −38							

Example 2
GNMA ($100,000 Principal) 32nds of 100%

	Open	High	Low	Settle	Chg.	Settle Yield	Yield Chg.	Open Interest
Oct.	—	—	—	91-07	+3	9.225	−.014	1
Nov.	—	—	—	91-05	+7	9.234	−.034	1
Dec.	91-04	91-12	90-31	91-09	+6	9.215	−.029	5,993
Mar.79	91-04	91-11	90-31	91-08s	+4	9.220	−.019	5,678
June	91-05	91-11	91-00	91-09	+5	9.215	−.019	5,683
Sept.	91-03	91-12	91-03	91-09	+5	9.215	−.029	3,763
Dec.	91-02	91-14	91-00	91-12	+7	9.225	−.038	4,236
Mar.80	91-01	91-09	91-01	91-07	+6	9.234	−.029	3,817
June	91-00	91-07	91-00	91-05	+6	9.234	−.029	3,899
Sept.	90-29	91-06	90-29	91-05	+5	9.244	−.025	4,306
Dec.	90-26	91-04	90-25	91-03	+6	9.259	−.029	3,767
Mar.81	90-21	91-02	90-23	91-00	+6	9.283	−.029	2,245
June	90-23	91-02a	90-23b	90-27	+6	9.283	−.029	419

Est. vol. 1,823; prev. vol. 3,636; open int. 43,808, +219.

Example 3
Corn

	Open	High	Low	Close	Change	Season's High	Low
Dec.	219¼	220½	219	219½-220	+1 to 1½	278¾	190¼
Mar.78	224¼	225¾	223¾	225½-¾	+2 to 2¼	283¾	195¼
May	226	228	226	227¾-228	+2¼ to 2½	286¾	203¼
July	227¾	228½	226¾	228¼-½	+2 to 2¼	272	205¾
Sept.	224¼	225¼	223½	225-225¼	+2¼ to 2½	237¾	209½
Dec.	224¼	225¾	223½	225-225¾	+1½ to 2¼	237½	220¼

Example 4
Platinum

	Open	High	Low	Close	Prev. Settle	Life of Contract High	Low
Jan.	322.70	323.50	322.70	322.70	312.70	321.50	160.90
Apr.	325.60	325.70	323.50	323.70	315.70	325.70	174.30
July	328.00	329.10	325.70	329.10	319.10	329.10	216.50
Oct.	332.00	332.30	329.00	332.30	322.30	332.30	230.00
Jan.	335.80	335.80	335.80	335.80	325.80	335.80	236.00
Apr.	337.00	339.30	337.00	339.30	329.30	339.30	278.80

Estimated vol. 2,757; prev. vol. 966; open int. 8,242, −85.

that may reflect the cost of storing the commodity, but the price must readjust at each harvest.

In Example 3, for corn, December is the first futures pricing of the new harvest. The market tends to pay for storage through the following September, although the price during September also may be affected by the supply-demand situation of the oncoming harvest. Closing prices are used when calculating carrying charges.

Other commodities, such as platinum (Example 4), have successively higher prices, usually called "contango," that also are said to represent storage and/or interest costs. There is no seasonality.

Some commodities—such as cattle, currency, and financial instruments—have no seasonality and the supply-demand factors for one month have little relation to the next. Others, like pork bellies, tend to have some seasonality since hog slaughter normally is lower from July to October so stocks are drawn from storage during those months.

Commodity Futures Trading Commission.

Commodity Futures Trading Commission (CFTC)

The Commodity Futures Trading Commission, created by Congress in 1974, is the federal regulator and overseer of the trading of commodity-futures contracts and commodity options contracts on U.S. futures exchanges. The agency's mission includes monitoring futures markets to detect and prevent commodity-price distortions and market manipulations, and protecting the rights of customers who use the markets for either commercial or investment purposes.

Futures contracts are commitments to buy or sell commodities at a specified time and place in the future. Hence the name "futures contract." The price is established when the contract is made in open auction on a CFTC-regulated and -authorized commodity-futures exchange.

Only a small percentage of futures trading actually leads to delivery of a commodity, for a contract may and usually does change hands or is liquidated before the delivery date. Market participants fall into two categories:

- *Commercial hedgers,* who use futures to minimize price risks inherent in their marketing operations by shifting that risk to speculators, and
- *Speculators,* who accept that risk through venture capital in the hope of profiting from price changes.

Futures prices are an indication of the direction of commodities prices based on current market conditions. Both hedgers and speculators purchase futures

contracts with only a small margin payment.

Futures contracts for agricultural commodities have been traded in the U.S. for more than 100 years, and have been under federal regulation since the 1920s. In the law that established the CFTC, however, Congress, in order to meet a need for regulation of futures trading in a broader array of commodities, expanded the definition of *commodity* to include not only agricultural products but "all other goods and articles, except onions . . . and all services, rights and interests in which contracts for future delivery are presently or in the future dealt in. . . ."

Under the law, the CFTC is responsible for regulating exchange trading of futures and options contracts for a variety of foreign currencies, financial instruments such as Treasury bills and bonds and industrial materials, as well as coffee and sugar. As of late 1983, only futures trading was permitted in domestic agricultural products, although the CFTC was in the process of adopting rules for the trading of options in these commodities. Many producers, wholesalers, assemblers, and processors of commodities buy and sell futures or permitted contracts in commodities related to their business. They do so to stretch marketing periods, to protect inventory values, and to establish firm prices for their products. Such commercial use of the markets for business purposes is called "hedging," and differs from the market use by speculators, who seek a profit from changing commodity prices.

Futures and options contracts may be bought and sold legally only through public outcry on exchanges licensed by the commission. There are also some contracts similar to futures for which the exchanges do not serve as a marketplace. The offer and sale of any such contracts is subject to CFTC regulation. The CFTC does not regulate cash commodity transactions.

The CFTC approves all exchange rules and may direct a futures or options contract market to change its rules or practices. U.S. commodity exchanges complement federal regulation with extensive rules and regulations of their own for the conduct of their markets—rules involving brokerage, clearance of trades, orders and spreads, trade records, position limits, price limits, the dissemination of quotations, disciplinary actions against members, floor trading practices, and standards of business conduct.

Before an exchange is permitted to trade a futures or options contract in a specific commodity, it must satisfy the commission that the contract will serve some economic purpose, and that trading in it will not be contrary to the public interest. The contract must reflect normal market flow and commercial trading practices in the actual commodity. The commission may, in an emergency and at its own discretion, order an exchange to take specific action to maintain or restore an orderly market in any futures contract that is being traded, an emergency power granted by Congress and upheld in federal court.

Companies and individuals who wish to handle customer funds for the purpose of buying or selling futures or options contracts, or to engage in the business of offering futures-trading advice, must apply for registration with the commission and undergo a background check that the CFTC conducts in cooperation with other federal agencies. The commission's basic customer-protection rules also require that customer funds be placed in bank accounts separate from those a firm maintains for its own use, and that customer accounts be marked to current market value at the closing of trading each day.

Organization. The Commodity Futures Trading Commission Act of 1974 provides for five CFTC commissioners—the commission—appointed by the president with the advice and consent of the Senate, to serve staggered five-year terms. No more than three commissioners may belong to the same political party. One of the commissioners is designated by the president to serve as commission chairman. The chairman presides over commission meetings and oversees management of the agency. In addition, the chairman's staff has direct responsibility for the agency's public-information and governmental-relations programs.

Major policy decisions and commission actions—such as approval of contract-market designations, adoption of agency rules and regulations, and the authorization of enforcement actions—must be approved by a majority vote of the commissioners. As a rule, commission meetings are open to the public. The time, dates, and subjects for discussion may be obtained from the CFTC secretariat.

The CFTC monitors markets closely by maintaining, in addition to its headquarters office in Washington, regional or subregional offices in cities that have a futures exchange—New York, Chicago, Kansas City, and Minneapolis. The commission also maintains an office in San Francisco.

The commission has five major operating units: the Divisions of Enforcement, Economics and Education, and Trading and Markets, and the Office of the Executive Director and the General Counsel.

The Division of Economics and Education reviews proposed futures or options contracts to determine whether their trade would serve a valid economic purpose, and it analyzes the economic ramifications of commission policies and regulations. The division also monitors trading on all contract markets to detect actual or potential manipulations, congestion, and price distortion; conducts or sponsors long-term research on the functioning of markets; and develops materials and programs explaining the CFTC and its responsibilities.

The Division of Trading and Markets drafts and revises the commission's contract-market and customer-protection regulations. It reviews the terms and conditions of proposed contracts for conformity with commercial practices and public-interest considerations, and monitors exchange-rule enforcement. It also registers industry professionals and audits commodity-futures brokerage houses and clearing associations for conformity with commission financial regulations.

The Division of Enforcement investigates alleged violations of the Commodity Exchange Act and CFTC regulations and, when it finds violations, may, at the direction of the commission, file complaints in the agency's administrative courts, or in the U.S. district courts. Alleged criminal violations of the Commodity Exchange Act, or violations of other federal laws that involve commodity-futures or options trading, may be referred to the Justice Department for prosecution.

The Office of the General Counsel acts as legal adviser to the commission; represents the commission before the United States Circuit Court of Appeals and, with the solicitor general, before the United States Supreme Court in cases involving review of remedial sanctions ordered by the commission as a result of its own administrative proceedings; and appeals from district-court decisions in commission injunctive and subpoena-enforcement actions. It defends the commission, its members, and staff acting in their official capacities, in suits brought in district courts to challenge commission regulations or to enjoin commission investigative or other regulatory activities, and it acts as commission counsel in resulting appeals.

The Office of the Executive Director is responsible for overseeing the administration of commission programs. It develops an agency budget for commission consideration; provides necessary agency services, supplies, and equipment; and handles personnel matters. The office includes Complaints, Hearings, and Appeals; Operations and Budget; Personnel and Administrative Services sections; and an Audit and Evaluation staff. The Hearings section consists of the administrative-law judges who preside over enforcement proceedings brought by the commission as well as reparations cases.

Commodity Futures Trading Commission

Commodity Money Managers

Professionals who manage funds for investors in the futures markets are broken down into two broad categories: Commodity trading advisers (CTA's) and commodity pool operators (CPO's). Each of these is regulated by both the COMMODITY FUTURES TRADING COMMISSION (CFTC), a federal government entity, and the National Futures Association, an industry self-regulatory body similar to the National Association of Securities Dealers.

Commodity Trading Advisers. Industry statistics indicate that eight out of ten people who participate in the futures markets lose money each year. Research indicates that this occurs because the average investor lacks capital, is emotional once a position is instituted, and lacks a plan defining profit objectives and limiting losses. Advisers say they can overcome these difficulties by using an unemotional trading plan with enough capital to diversify into a broad spectrum of commodities. Advisers use two basic approaches to the futures market: the fundamental approach and the technical approach.

Fundamental Approach. The fundamentalists believe they can predict market directions by analyzing the facts and statistics relevant to that market. This analysis will give the fundamentalist an idea of the supply of and demand for a particular commodity. If they felt that supply and demand were in equilibrium, they would not anticipate any price movement. If, however, they saw an imbalance developing, they would buy or sell that particular product. The successful trader is not necessarily the one who interprets the facts correctly, but the one who can gauge how the trading public will react to the facts, and take an appropriate position.

Technical Approach. The technicians believe they can predict the future direction of the market based on a study of high, low, and closing prices; volume; and open interest. The technician would say that any facts that will affect market movement will be reflected in various price charts—thus, analysis of these charts holds the key to market direction. A major premise in this theory is that the nature of the market movement is not random but predictable, based on repeating chart patterns. Edwards and Magee, in their book *Technical Analysis of Stock Trends,* sum it up well when they say:

> Of course, the statistics which the fundamentalists study play a part in the supply-demand equation—that is freely admitted. But there are many other factors affecting it. The market price reflects not only the differing value opinions of many orthodox security appraisers but also all the hopes and fears and guesses and moods, rational and irrational, of hundreds of potential buyers and sellers, as well as their needs and their resources—in total, factors which defy analysis and for which no statistics are obtainable, but which are nevertheless all synthesized, weighed and finally expressed in the one precise figure at which a buyer and seller get together and make a deal (through their agents, their respective stock brokers). This is the only figure that counts.
>
> Moreover, the technician claims with complete justification that the bulk of the statistics which the fundamentalists study are past history, already out of date and sterile, because the market is not interested in the past or even in the present! It is constantly looking ahead; attempting to discount future developments, weighing and balancing all the estimates and guesses of hundreds of investors who look into the future from different points of view and through glasses of many different hues. In brief, the going price as established by the market itself comprehends all the fundamental information which the statistical analyst can hope to learn (plus some which is perhaps secret from him, known only to a few insiders) and much else besides of equal or even greater importance.[*]

How They Work. When a person decides to open an account with a commodity trading adviser, the first thing he must do is look for an adviser with a trading philosophy compatible with his. This includes a meeting of the minds on the questions of acceptable risk and profit levels and which approach to the market (fundamental or technical) is best. This done, the investor should ask the adviser for a risk-disclosure document in the format required by the Commodity Futures Trading Commission. The adviser, by law, is required to provide this document and disclose the following information:

1. The adviser's background, including business offices, principals, a description of the trading program, and whether or not a client is free to choose his own commodity broker.

2. The actual performance of the trading adviser and each of his principals for their own accounts.

3. The actual performance of all accounts directed by the trading adviser and his principals for the last three years.

4. The latter two points of information must be in the following format:

[*] Robert D. Edwards and John Magee, *Technical Analysis of Stock Trends* (Boston: John Magee, Inc., 1966), pp. 5–6.

Mon.-yr.	Beg. asset	Net value	Additions & withdrawals	Net perf. for period	End net asset value	Period % return	Number of units

The data must be shown on at least a quarterly basis and the accounts can be shown singly or composited. If there are differences in the way the accounts were managed, these differences must be described.

5. A complete explanation of how the adviser will charge fees.

6. A complete description of any actual or potential conflicts of interest the adviser might have either with his principals or with the broker.

7. If there are no conflicts, this must be clearly stated.

8. The adviser must state whether he plans to trade for his own account and whether his clients can inspect the records of his trades.

9. If there have been any criminal or civil actions against the adviser or his principals in the last five years, this must be disclosed.

This document cannot be more than six (6) months old and must be presented to each client.

In reviewing the track record in the risk-disclosure document, there are several key guidelines the investor can use. These include profitability; the largest erosion of capital that the adviser subjected the client to during any period; commission charges in the track record vs. what the client will actually be charged; average rate of return over an extended period of time; total dollars under management; and length of time the adviser has been in business.

Once the investor has determined which adviser he wants to use, he will open an account at a commodity-brokerage firm. Key factors to consider in the selection of the broker are commission charges; whether the broker is currently working with the adviser; and the percent of the client's money on deposit with the broker that the client will earn Treasury-bill interest on. The broker has an obligation to notify the client each time the adviser makes a trade for him and to send a monthly summary of the activity that occurred in the account. The adviser takes a limited power of attorney to trade the account. He will phone the brokerage with the orders he feels are appropriate after utilizing his trading technique. For his services, the adviser will charge a fee that is broken down into two parts: (1) *the incentive fee,* which is a percent of the profits, normally between 10% and 15%, charged on an annual basis but billed monthly or quarterly, and (2) *the management fee,* which is charged whether or not the client makes money and is usually an annual 4% to 6% of the assets the adviser is managing; this fee, again, can be charged either monthly or quarterly.

There are other ways of operating that an adviser might choose. The first is by publishing a newsletter. The adviser takes no control over the client's account but leaves it up to him to pick and choose the trades, and the only cost is the subscription to the letter.

With the advances in telecommunications in the last few years, we have seen a new format for the dissemination of newsletters, via Teletype or computer communications. The investor gains in that he can put in an order within minutes after the adviser recommends taking a position. Often the adviser will charge a premium for this service.

Before using a service like this, the client should go to the trouble of verifying the track record of the adviser. This would include looking at the prices the adviser claims he got for particular trades and verifying them against the actual prices for the day to make sure they were realistic. The prospective client should also be aware of a factor known as "slippage." This is the difference between the price at which an order was placed and the price at which it was actually filled. This difference can have a significant impact on profitability.

Commodity Pool Operators. A commodity pool operator is a person or entity that runs a trust, syndicate, limited partnership, or similar form of enterprise for the purpose of trading commodity interests. These are normally limited partnerships, with the pool operator acting as general partner. They are considered the mutual funds of the commodity industry. In the last eight years, this has become an extremely popular investment vehicle that has experienced explosive growth. The total assets under management have gone from virtually nothing in 1976 to over $600 million today.

These pools or funds offer the investor several advantages over individually managed accounts. First of all, the investor can participate in these groups for a smaller total investment, normally $5,000, whereas an individually managed account may require as much as $50,000. This allows a broader spectrum of the public to participate, and also gives the investor with a larger amount of capital the opportunity to put money in several different pools, which could be managed by different commodity trading advisers using different systems and thus gaining the advantage of diversification.

Limited liability is another key benefit of the commodity pool. The investor's risk is no greater than the amount of capital he puts in. In an individual account, the investor, because of the leverage available in the futures markets, can lose more money than he initially puts into the account. Many pools offer further protection by incorporating a 50% dissolution clause. Let's say the initial value of a unit was $1,000. If there were a dissolution clause operating when the value of a unit reached $500, the fund would stop trading and the investor would get about half of his money back.

There are several factors the investor should evaluate before deciding on a limited partnership. These include:

1. The adviser's track record, using the steps discussed earlier.

2. The costs to get involved in the pool—i.e., front-end loads, legal expenses, and accounting expenses.

3. Whether commodity commissions charged to the fund will be negotiated below retail rates. The theory is that because of the large account size represented by the pool, the brokerage firm should be willing to charge less per trade, thereby saving the client money.

4. The amount of Treasury-bill interest on margin accounts that flows back to the pool. This is also a negotiated item and can help offset the management costs to the investor.

5. The pro forma track record versus the actual. By comparing these two, the investor can see how he would have fared under the actual operating conditions of the fund.

6. The procedure for redeeming his units; whether they receive any annual profit payout; how transferable units are; and the tax implications of being in the fund.

The commodity pool operator is required, by the Commodity Futures Trading Commission, to give the prospective investor the information necessary to make judgments on the above items. In addition, the commodity pool operator must provide regular financial statements to his investors and an audited annual report.

The accompanying chart and outline summarizes the operation and guidelines for evaluating a commodity pool operation.

1. *Partnership structure:* In the U.S., virtually all pools are organized as limited partnerships to take advantage of flow-through taxation. Figure 1 shows a typical structure. In most of the funds, the following parameters exist: (a) an 8–10% front-end sales charge; (b) $50–$60 round-turn commission charge; (c)

70–80% of T-bill interest going back to fund after repayment to general partner of all start-up expenses; (d) 1½–2%-per-year administrative charge; (e) management fees vary, but generally they will not allow a fee that can go up if the adviser churns (i.e., generates commissions excessively); (f) commissions going to another entity than the adviser.

2. *CFTC and NFA registrations:* Since these will be the same, one discussion can cover both. A risk-disclosure document is required. This must include the following items: (a) name, address, phone number, form of organization, and where books and records of adviser will be kept; (b) name of each principal; (c) description of trading program; (d) if client is required to carry account at a broker, that broker must be named; if no requirement, that must be stated; (e) five-year business background of adviser and his principals; (f) the performance record, not more than three months old, including material differences between accounts if composite of all accounts, and how composite was arrived at; (g) a description of all fees; (h) a description of any conflicts of interest; If there are none, this must be stated; (i) it must be disclosed if adviser is going to trade for his own account and, if he is, whether the investor can see the results; (j) any criminal actions in the last five years; (k) the prescribed statements (standard wording).

Summary. Over the last decade there has been a tremendous growth in the futures industry. For the average investor, this is considered a high-risk investment. The growth of the managed-money portion of the industry, commodity pool operators, and commodity trading advisers has been just as spectacular. The major reason for this is that managed money provides the investor with an opportunity to participate in the futures markets on a conservative basis with a defined set of risks.

Robert L. Isaacson

Commodity Supplemental Food Program

See SOCIAL WELFARE.

Commodity Trading Advisers

See COMMODITY MONEY MANAGERS.

Commodity Trading Pools

See COMMODITY MONEY MANAGERS.

Common Stock

Common stock is a security that represents an ownership interest in a corporation. An individual who

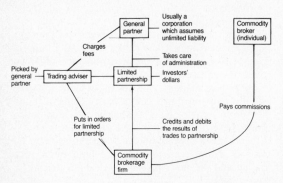

Figure 1.

owns shares of the common stock of the General Motors Corporation, for example, is referred to as a "stockholder" or "shareholder" of the corporation, which means that he is a part owner of the General Motors Corporation. Therefore, the terms *stockholder, shareholder,* and *owner* can be used interchangeably in describing an individual who owns shares of common stock.

Each stockholder's portion of the corporation is determined by dividing the number of shares of common stock he owns by the total number of shares owned by all stockholders. The divisor in this calculation is referred to as the "number of shares outstanding."

Example: Suppose that 100 individuals each own 1,000 shares of the hypothetical Big Apple Corporation. Each of these individuals owns 1% of the corporation, since each owns 1,000 of the 100,000 shares outstanding. Or, if Ms. Jones owns 90,000 of the 100,000 shares outstanding, while Mr. Smith owns 10,000 shares, then they are owners of 90% and 10% of the corporation, respectively.

The process by which ownership of a corporation comes to be shared among numerous owners can be illustrated by examining the Big Apple Corporation in further detail. Suppose that Jones is the founder of the corporation and that she has invested $800,000 of her savings in order to build a manufacturing plant to produce large business computers. Jones has presumably determined that there is sufficient demand for these computers, and that she has sufficient expertise in the design, manufacture, and marketing of computers so that she can profitably produce and market this product. However, she requires additional financing to ensure the success of the venture. She is able to convince Smith that an investment of $200,000 on his part, in exchange for 10% ownership of the corporation, will be financially rewarding to him. Jones decides to issue 90,000 shares of common stock to herself and 10,000 shares to Smith. Jones is now a 90% owner, and Smith, as promised, is a 10% owner. At this point, it would make no difference to either owner whether 100,000 shares or 10 shares were issued. In the latter case, Jones would own nine shares and Smith would own one share. Any number of shares could be issued, provided that Jones owns 90% of the shares and Smith owns 10%.

It is important to note here that Smith has contributed 20% of the corporation's financing in exchange for 10% ownership. While both parties are aware of the apparent discrepancy, this fact is not relevant for either of them. If Jones and Smith are both satisfied by the arrangement, there is no reason that there must be a direct relationship between the amount invested by each owner and the portion of the firm each owns.

Rights of Stockholders. Regardless of the size of the corporation or the number of shares a stockholder owns, the stockholder's most significant rights are essentially the same. These rights fall generally into two categories: the right to participate in corporate decisions and the right to share in the profits of the corporation. The relative importance of these rights to the owners will vary substantially from one corporation to another, and even among owners of the same corporation. However, it is these rights that represent the motivation for ownership of a corporation, and that therefore give a share of common stock its value.

Technically, stockholders also have the right to share in the proceeds from the sale of the firm's assets if the corporation is dissolved. However, since this right is very rarely significant to the owners of a corporation, the following discussion will deal only with the other two rights mentioned above.

Voting Rights. A stockholder has one vote in corporate decisions for each share of common stock he owns. The significance of these voting rights will vary with the size of the corporation and the portion of the corporation that a stockholder owns. While the owners of a small corporation would tend to be involved in the day-to-day operations of the firm, this is clearly not possible for a corporation with thousands of owners. Therefore, the kinds of decisions in which stockholders participate vary substantially between small and large corporations. Furthermore, an individual who owns a small fraction of a corporation will generally have little or no influence on the decision-making process, regardless of the size of the corporation.

Example: As the owner of 90,000 shares of the Big Apple Corporation, Jones is entitled to 90,000 votes in corporate decisions; while Smith, who owns 10,000 shares, has 10,000 votes. With only 10% of the votes, Smith will not be able to play a significant role in the decision-making process. If, for example, the owners must decide whether to expand the firm's production capacity, Jones's 90,000 votes will enable her to make the decision unilaterally, regardless of whether Smith concurs. Therefore, it is clear that voting rights were not relevant for Smith when he decided to purchase 10% ownership of the corporation. On the other hand, the 90,000 votes to which Jones is entitled are essential to her ability to make corporate decisions. By purchasing 10% ownership of the firm, Smith is expressing his confidence in Jones's decision-making ability, because it is her expertise that will determine, to a great extent, the degree to which the firm is successful in the manufacture and sale of its product.

In the above example, Jones exercises direct control over corporate decisions. Such direct involvement is extremely rare for a large corporation with thousands of shareholders. While the decision to expand capacity or develop a new product, for example, is extremely important to the owners of the firm, it is not the kind of decision that can be made directly by a large number of owners. Therefore, the right to make such decisions must be delegated by the owners to full-time managers acting in the best interests of the stockholders. In such a situation, the stockholders elect the members of the board of directors, who in turn select the firm's managers. The managers make the day-to-day operating decisions. Thus, the first important aspect of the stockholder's voting rights in a large corporation is the right to elect the members of the board of directors.

In addition to their indirect participation in managerial decisions, stockholders also participate directly in certain decisions affecting the purpose or structure of the corporation. Decisions in which shareholders vote directly are determined by the corporation's charter and the laws of the state in which the firm is incorporated. Examples of such matters include a merger with another company or a change in the nature of the firm's business.

Claim on Profits. For the vast majority of individuals who own stock in American corporations, voting rights do not add significantly to the value of a share; rather, it is the right to share corporate profits that most often provides the motivation to hold common stock, and therefore gives common stock its value. A stockholder who owns 10% of a corporation's outstanding shares of common stock has a claim on 10% of the corporation's profits.

Example: Smith owns 10,000 shares, or 10%, of the Big Apple Corporation's 100,000 shares of common stock outstanding. He anticipates that the corporation's net profit, after payment of all expenses and corporate income taxes, will be $500,000 per year. Therefore, Smith has a claim on $50,000, or 10%, of the firm's annual profit.

In the above example, the stockholder is said to have a claim on $50,000 of the firm's annual profit. This signifies that all, or part, of the $50,000 may be distributed to him in the form of dividends and that any remainder will be reinvested in the corporation on his behalf. This reinvestment might be used for expansion of the firm's productive capacity, development of a new product line, or modernization of the existing facility. A new and rapidly growing company might choose to pay no dividends in order to expand its capacity to meet a rapidly growing demand for its product. The expectation is that if shareholders are willing to forgo current dividends, they will be rewarded in the future when the company realizes even larger profits, from which larger dividends can be paid. For this reason, many so-called growth stocks pay small dividends even though the company has experienced relatively high levels of profitability.

Example: Suppose the Big Apple Corporation has a net profit of $500,000 for the year 1983. If the owners decide that $400,000 should be retained for the purpose of reinvestment and, therefore, that $100,000 should be paid as dividends,

then Jones and Smith will receive dividend payments of $90,000 and $10,000, respectively. That is, since Jones owns 90% of the corporation, she will receive 90% of the total dividends paid; while Smith, who owns 10% of the corporation, receives 10% of the dividends.

Per-Share Data. Since most people invest in common stock for profits, rather than for voting rights, it's important to know how to determine whether a particular stock is an attractive investment. An investor must consider the cost of the stock and the anticipated earnings and dividends to which he is entitled. These factors can be evaluated either on an aggregate basis or on a per-share basis. Investors find the latter approach far more convenient.

In order to evaluate an investment in 100 shares of IBM stock on an aggregate basis, an investor should compare the total amount he will pay to acquire the shares with the total return he anticipates from this investment. The major components of the return are the total amount of earnings and dividends he expects to realize from owning 100 shares. On a per-share basis, the investor would analyze the cost, earnings, and dividends for one share of IBM stock. If, on the basis of this evaluation, he finds that this share of stock is an attractive investment, then, since all shares of IBM stock are identical, an investment in 100 shares is also attractive.

Price per Share. One of the reasons why stockholders find it more convenient to evaluate their investment in common stock on a per-share rather than an aggregate basis is the availability of per-share data in the financial press. The major daily newspapers always report price-per-share data. An individual who is considering purchasing 100 shares of Exxon Corporation common stock can easily determine that the current price of one share is, for example, $30 and that his total investment would be $3,000. Furthermore, if, after he makes the purchase, he finds that the price of Exxon stock rises to $32, he can quickly calculate that his gain of $2 per share times the 100 shares he owns represents a total gain of $200.

Example: Smith invested $200,000 in the Big Apple Corporation in exchange for ownership of 10% of the corporation. This 10% ownership is represented by the 10,000 shares of common stock issued to him, out of a total of 100,000 shares outstanding. The price Smith paid for his common stock was $20 per share ($200,000 investment/10,000 shares). If the company had chosen to issue a total of 1,000 shares, Smith's 10% ownership would have entitled him to 100 shares at a price of $2,000 per share ($200,000 investment/100 shares). In each of these situations, Smith's ownership rights are the same: He has invested $200,000, and he has a claim on 10% of the firm's earnings and dividends. The only differences are the number of shares he owns and the price of each share.

While the stockholder's ownership rights are dependent only on the percentage of the corporation he owns, this does not mean that stockholders are indifferent regarding the total number of shares issued by the corporation. Their concern with the number of shares outstanding, and hence the price per share, stems from the fact that the stockholder generally anticipates selling his shares at some future date. He may reasonably expect that the marketability of his shares will depend on the price per share. For this reason, an owner may prefer that the corporation issue a large number of shares with a relatively low price per share.

Example: Suppose that when Smith purchased 10% of the common stock of the Big Apple Corporation for $200,000, he had a choice regarding the number of shares that the corporation would issue. If the firm issued 100,000 shares, he would receive 10,000 shares at a price of $20 per share; if 1,000 shares were issued, his ownership interest would be represented by 100 shares at $2,000 per share.

Smith would most likely find the former alternative more desirable. Even if he does not currently foresee selling his shares, he can anticipate that, should he desire to do so, he might find it easier to sell 10,000 shares at $20 per share, rather than 100 shares at $2,000 per share. Since he can sell his shares to whomever he wishes, it is not necessary that he find a single buyer for his holdings. Theoretically, he could sell each one of his 10,000 shares to a different buyer.

While this is unlikely to happen, it does provide the stockholder with greater flexibility if he owns the larger number of shares with a lower per-share value. Under these circumstances, he has the option to sell portions of his ownership interest to investors with as little as $20 to invest. If he owned 100 shares, he would have to find individuals willing to invest a minimum of $2,000, which would reduce the marketability of his stock. It is for this reason that the vast majority of common stocks listed on the New York Stock Exchange, for example, have prices in the range of $10 to $70 per share.

Earnings per Share. A corporation's earnings per share can be calculated, as the term clearly implies, by dividing the firm's total earnings by the total number of shares outstanding. As is the case with the price-per-share data discussed previously, earnings-per-share information is both readily available to the stockholder and convenient to use in analyzing an investment in common stock. When a stockholder evaluates his claim on the corporation's earnings, he will find that earnings-per-share figures are generally presented as part of the firm's financial statements and often in the financial press as well. Furthermore, since earnings per share are a much smaller quantity than total earnings, the shareholder will be able to perform the relevant calculations more easily.

Example: Smith owns 10,000 shares of common stock of the Big Apple Corporation and he anticipates that the firm's net profit will be $500,000 per year. He can use either of two equivalent approaches to evaluate his claim on the earnings

of the corporation. First, since his 10,000 shares represent 10% of the 100,000 shares outstanding, he has a claim on 10% of the firm's earnings: 10% of $500,000 equals $50,000. Alternatively, he can multiply the firm's earnings per share by the number of shares he owns. Earnings per share for the Big Apple Corporation equal $5 ($500,000 total earnings/100,000 shares outstanding). Smith's claim on the corporation's earnings is therefore equal to $50,000 ($5 earnings per share × 10,000 shares).

While both approaches can be applied relatively easily in the above example, this is not likely to be the case for the typical shareholder in a large corporation. The first calculation requires that the shareholder determine the percentage of the corporation that he owns. An investor who owns 100 shares of a corporation with millions of shares outstanding will find this approach extremely cumbersome because he owns a very small fraction of 1% of the company. On the other hand, since earnings-per-share data are often readily available to the stockholder from other sources, he can easily multiply earnings per share by the number of shares he owns to determine his claim on the firm's earnings.

Dividends per Share. The relationship between a corporation's total earnings and earnings per share is perfectly analogous to the relationship between the total dividend payments made by the firm and dividends per share. Total dividends divided by the number of shares outstanding equals dividends per share. For an individual shareholder, the total dividend payment he receives is equal to the firm's dividends per share times the number of shares he owns.

Example: The Big Apple Corporation will retain for reinvestment $400,000 of the firm's $500,000 net profit for 1983. Therefore, total dividend payments will be $100,000 and dividends per share will be $1 ($100,000 total dividends/100,000 shares outstanding). Smith owns 10,000 shares and will therefore receive $10,000 in dividends ($1 dividends per share × 10,000 shares).

Evaluation of Common-Stock Investments. In evaluating investment opportunities, the interest rate, or yield, is often the appropriate criterion for identifying the most desirable investments. In order to calculate the anticipated yield for a particular investment, it is necessary to know the dollar amount of the return that the investor will receive. A bank selling a 30-month certificate of deposit, for example, informs the investor of both the dollar amount he will receive at the end of two and one-half years and the annual interest rate he will earn on this investment. Since the amount the investor will receive is known with certainty, it is possible for the bank, or the investor, to determine the yield; there is no disagreement regarding this calculation. This yield can then be compared to the yields of other investment alternatives in order to identify the preferred investments.

Although the procedure described above is the appropriate technique for evaluating many kinds of investments, it cannot be easily applied to common stock. When an investor purchases a share of common stock, he knows the price he must pay to purchase the stock, but he does not know with certainty the return he will receive in the future. In order to predict the return, it is necessary to make two interrelated forecasts. First, the investor will forecast the firm's anticipated net profits, so that he can determine anticipated earnings per share and the individual investor's claim on the corporation's profits. Second, since not all of the firm's profits will be paid to stockholders as dividends, he must then predict when, and in what form, the stockholder will receive his share of the firm's profits. Both of these aspects of the forecasting process can be extremely complicated.

The first aspect of this procedure, predicting the firm's net profit, usually requires the investor to forecast total sales revenue and expenses, since net profit is the differene between revenue and expenses. Making such forecasts is at best somewhat difficult due to the large number of factors that must be analyzed. For example, a large manufacturer such as the General Electric Company produces hundreds of products. In order to predict General Electric's 1984 net profit, the investor must forecast the total sales of all of these products as well as the total cost of producing them. Clearly, given the complexity of this problem, it is possible that each investor might evaluate these factors differently and hence their forecasts could vary greatly.

Most forecasts that investment analysts are required to prepare are even more complicated than forecasting next year's earnings for a large and financially stable company like General Electric. There are two reasons for this added complexity. First, since stockholders often expect to hold their common stock for several years, it is necessary to forecast earnings several years into the future. This is much more difficult than making a one-year forecast, because there is more uncertainty about events further into the future. Second, an investor might want to consider an investment in the common stock of a new and growing company, and forecasting the profitability of such a firm is very difficult. A new company attempting to market a new product may be extremely successful if the product is accepted by consumers, but it is also possible that the enterprise will never be profitable at all. Thus, while it is important for the investor to predict a firm's earnings in order to determine the return he will receive, it is usually very difficult to make accurate forecasts.

Assuming that the investor is able to make a reasonably accurate forecast of, for example, General Electric's future profitability, he can then determine the firm's anticipated earnings per share and the claim on profits that would be associated with ownership of, say, 100 shares of General Electric stock. However, since part or all of the firm's earnings may be retained for the purpose of reinvestment in the corporation, it is still not a simple matter for the stockholder to determine the return he will receive on his investment.

Thus, the second aspect of the forecasting process requires the investor to predict the manner in which he will share in the firm's earnings. The uncertainty regarding this prediction arises from two sources: First, the shareholder does not know how the firm's earnings in any particular year will be divided between dividend payments and retained earnings; and, second, he does not know how successful the firm will be in generating future profits from its reinvestment of current earnings. Thus, for many corporations, the investor will find it difficult to predict both the firm's future earnings and the manner in which the stockholder will share in those earnings. As a result, it is often impossible to make an accurate forecast of the anticipated yield for an investment in common stock.

Example: The Big Apple Corporation manufactures large business computers. Smith, who owns 10,000 shares of Big Apple common stock, has predicted that the firm's 1984 net profit will be $500,000. Since the corporation has 100,000 shares of stock outstanding, earnings per share will be $5 ($500,000 net profit/100,000 shares outstanding) and Smith will have a claim on $50,000 of this profit ($5 earnings per share × 10,000 shares). While Smith is confident that this forecast is reasonably accurate, he also knows that Jones, who owns the other 90,000 shares, is considering expanding the firm's product line to include personal computers. To accomplish this expansion, $400,000 of the firm's 1984 earnings would have to be reinvested for the purpose of developing and manufacturing the new product. However, Smith is unsure whether Jones will decide to develop the new product—and if she does, he is not certain whether the new product line will be profitable. Thus, in spite of his confidence in his forecast of 1984 earnings, Smith does not know what his dividend payment will be in 1984 and he cannot accurately predict earnings for 1985 and beyond.

While not all common-stock investments involve the degree of uncertainty illustrated in the above example, it is generally agreed that evaluation of common-stock investments is very difficult. An investor would like to be able to determine the anticipated yield of an investment in common stock so that he can compare one stock with another, or stocks, in general, with other kinds of investments. However, the difficulties indicated above often force investors to resort to techniques that can at best be considered estimates of the rate of return one would earn by purchasing a share of stock. The dividend yield and the earnings yield are examples of this approach. A third procedure, closely related to the earnings yield, is based on the price/earnings ratio.

Dividend Yield. Theoretically, the dividend yield should be determined by dividing anticipated dividends per share by current price per share. This value should be useful to the investor in evaluating an investment in common stock. As a practical matter, however, the investor must be very careful in interpreting the dividend yield.

Example: Suppose that Smith has predicted that 1984 earnings for the Big Apple Corporation will be $500,000 and that $100,000 of this sum will be distributed as dividends. As previously calculated, earnings and dividends per share will be $5 and $1, respectively. If Smith purchases a share for $20, the dividend yield will be 5% ($1 dividend per share/$20 price per share)). The theoretical significance of this figure is that if dividends continue to be $1 per share for the foreseeable future, the rate of return on Smith's investment will be 5%. Practically speaking, however, he is unlikely to believe that dividends will remain constant. It is not clear whether dividends per share will increase or decrease, but, assuming that dividends do not remain constant, the actual yield on his investment will not be 5%; it could be either more or less than this figure.

The above example indicates that in applying the dividend yield, the investor must be aware of the fact that his forecast of next year's dividends does not necessarily apply to subsequent years. In order to interpret the dividend yield found in the daily newspaper listing of New York Stock Exchange transactions, he must extend this conclusion one step further. This dividend-yield calculation is based not on next year's dividends per share but rather on the current year's dividends per share. Therefore, if the investor expects a change in dividends from the current year to next year, or in any succeeding year, this published dividend yield must be interpreted accordingly.

Earnings Yield. The use of earnings per share, instead of dividends per share, to estimate the yield on a common-stock investment is based on the premise that the true return on a common-stock investment is earnings rather than dividends. Even though the shareholder receives directly only that part of the firm's earnings which is paid as dividends, the portion retained for reinvestment should produce a net benefit for the stockholder. If the firm retains a dollar that could have been paid to the stockholder, this is in the stockholder's best interests only if the ultimate benefit to the stockholder from the reinvestment is perceived by the stockholder to be worth more than one dollar. Under this interpretation, the earnings yield is a reasonable, and perhaps conservative, measure of the rate of return. But although this interpretation is theoretically valid, in practical application the stockholder encounters difficulties comparable to those involving the dividend yield.

Example: Smith's predictions of 1984 earnings and dividends for the Big Apple Corporation are $500,000 and $100,000, respectively; thus his per-share forecasts of earnings and dividends are $5 and $1, respectively. Since the price per share is $20, the anticipated earnings yield is 25% ($5 earnings per share/$20 price per share). The $400,000 difference between earnings and dividends is being reinvested in the firm on the stockholders' behalf. On a per-share basis, the $4 of retained earnings should be reinvested in the firm only if it produces a benefit for the stockholder, in terms of future increases in earnings and dividends, that the stockholder feels is worth more than a current dividend of $4. Assuming this is so, then the stockholder assesses his return to be at least the full $5 earnings per share, and the earnings yield of 25% is a conservative estimate of the rate of return.

As is the case for the dividend yield, a yield calculation of this form is technically correct only if the return—either the dividends or earnings per share—is expected to remain constant. There is no reason to assume, in general, that this will be true for an investment in common stock; and therefore the earnings yield, like the dividend yield, must be interpreted carefully in practical applications.

Price/Earnings Ratio. The reciprocal of the earnings yield is called the "price/earnings ratio": price per share divided by earnings per share. Although the price/earnings ratio, or P/E ratio, receives more attention in the financial press than does the earnings yield, the interpretation and application of the latter is easier to understand. In fact, the P/E ratio, as a technique for evaluating common stock, is for the most part merely a reinterpretation of the earnings yield.

Assume, for the purposes of this discussion, that the difficulties mentioned earlier regarding practical application of the earnings yield can be resolved so that the earnings yield can be considered the appropriate rate-of-return calculation for an investment in common stock. Therefore, an investor can compare the earnings yield he has calculated for U.S. Steel common stock, for example, with the yield available on other investments in order to decide whether U.S. Steel stock is an attractive investment. If he finds that the earnings yield on U.S. Steel is higher than the yields available on comparable investments, he will conclude that U.S. Steel is an acceptable investment; otherwise, he will choose one of the comparable investments with a higher yield. Here, the yield for these comparable investments, which might be other common stocks, establishes the minimum yield he will accept if he is to invest in U.S. Steel common stock.

If, instead of establishing a minimum acceptable earnings yield, the investor used the P/E ratio to evaluate the investment in U.S. Steel, he would then determine the maximum acceptable P/E ratio for U.S. Steel. Regardless of which evaluation technique he uses, he will arrive at the same conclusion as to whether he should invest in U.S. Steel.

Example: Smith has determined that the earnings yield on the Big Apple Corporation is 25% ($5 earnings per share/$20 price per share). If he had found that the earnings yield for comparable stocks was approximately 20%, he would conclude that Big Apple common stock is an attractive investment. In fact, he would be willing to pay any price up to $25 per share for Big Apple stock. At this price, the earnings yield would be 20% ($5 earnings per share/$25 price per share). At any price higher than $25, the earnings yield for Big Apple stock would be less than his required 20%, and the investment would therefore be unacceptable.

A convenient way to summarize these relationships is provided by the P/E ratio. When the investor specifies that he requires a yield of 20%, he is stating that the price of a share of stock must be five times earnings per share. A price per share equal to five times earnings is the same as earnings equal to one-fifth (or 20%) of the price per share. Having established his required P/E ratio to be five, Smith multiplies this figure by the anticipated earnings per share of $5. The result, $25, is the maximum price he is willing to pay for a share of Big Apple Corporation common stock. If he can obtain a share for $25 (or less), he will make the purchase, because his yield will be 20% (or more). If, on the other hand, he has to pay more than $25 per share, the yield will be less than the required 20% and he will therefore not purchase the stock. Therefore, the P/E ratio of five, which is the reciprocal of the required 20% earnings yield, establishes the maximum price he is willing to pay for a share of stock.

Since the price/earnings ratio is simply the reciprocal of the earnings yield, the same difficulties encountered in applying the yield as an evaluation technique also exist for the P/E ratio. Specifically, it must be emphasized that the relevant earnings-per-share figure in both calculations is the anticipated, rather than the current or past, earnings per share. For example, the P/E ratio that appears in the daily newspaper listing of New York Stock Exchange transactions is calculated by dividing the current price per share by the firm's most recent earnings per share. It is important for the investor to be aware of the common misinterpretation of this "current" P/E ratio as an indicator of whether a particular share of common stock is "undervalued" or "overvalued."

For instance, a share of common stock with a P/E ratio of 20 (and an earnings yield equal to 5%) might be referred to as "overvalued" by an investment analyst who feels that a price equal to 20 times the share's earnings is excessive. However, it is essential for the investor to keep in mind the fact that a current P/E ratio of 20 might have no bearing on the value of a share if it is anticipated that the earnings per share will increase substantially in the near future. An investor might be willing to pay $40 per share for common stock with earnings of $2 per share during the past year if he expects that next year, and in the foreseeable future, the firm's earnings will be $5 per share. In this case, the relevant P/E ratio, based on the anticipated earnings, is 8 ($40 price per share/$5 anticipated earnings per share), rather than the figure of 20 ($40 price per share/$2 current earnings per share), which might appear in the daily newspaper.

Dividend Policies. The above discussion indicates that the investor must deal with a high degree of uncertainty in evaluating an investment in common stock. Not only must he attempt to forecast the firm's earnings, but he must also predict the manner in which he will receive his share of those earnings. Part of the firm's profits will be reinvested in the corporation on the stockholders' behalf, and the remainder will be paid to stockholders in the form of dividends. In order for the investor to be able to forecast the return he will receive from an investment in common stock, it is helpful for him to understand how the distribution of profits between retained earnings and dividends is determined.

In the earlier description of the earnings yield, this distribution was presented in a manner indicating that the amount of the firm's dividends is treated as a residual—that is, the firm determines the amount of its earnings that can be profitably reinvested, and any remainder is paid as dividends to the stockholders. While this procedure is theoretically valid, numerous complications are encountered in applying this approach.

Example: Jones, who owns 90% of the Big Apple Corporation's common stock, must decide what portion of the firm's 1984 net profits should be retained for reinvestment and what portion should be paid as dividends. She is considering retaining $400,000 for the purpose of developing a new product line, which would leave $100,000 to be paid to the owners. On a per-share basis, earnings and dividends would be $5 and $1, respectively, with $4 per share retained for reinvestment.

Using the residual approach described above, this decision would be justified if the reinvestment of $4 per share produces increases in future earnings and dividends worth more than the $4 current dividend that could have been paid with this money. If the development of the new product line produces future benefits that the current stockholders perceive to be worth $5, for example, then they have benefited from the reinvestment. This does not mean that 1985 earnings will increase by $5; rather, it means that the owners of the firm would be willing to pay as much as $5 in exchange for the future benefits they will receive in 1985 and beyond. Since they are paying only $4 for these benefits, by forgoing the opportunity to receive $4 in dividends, they are receiving benefits worth $1 more than their cost.

While there are many difficulties in applying this residual approach to the dividend decision, two of the most important complications relate to the so-called information content of dividends and the uncertainty of future benefits to be derived from reinvestment of earnings.

Dividends are said to have "information content" because for many stockholders the major involvement—and in some cases the only direct involvement—with the corporation is the receipt of the dividend check; thus the only significant information used in their evaluation of the corporation's performance is the size of the dividend. A decline in the firm's dividends per share is often interpreted as an indication of mismanagement, regardless of the reason for the decline.

While such a judgment is perhaps justified if the reduced dividend payment results from a decline in profitability, it is clearly inappropriate if the firm increases the portion of earnings it retains in order to take advantage of profitable reinvestment opportunities. However, in the latter case, the board of directors may find it difficult to convince shareholders of the advisability of the residual approach to the dividend decision. Some stockholders are not familiar with information published in the firm's annual report to the shareholders describing the firm's plans for the future. They are, however, aware of the change in their dividend payments.

In order to avoid the potential misinterpretation in such a situation, many corporations adopt as one of their objectives the maintenance of future dividends at or above current levels, even if this results in dividend payments that are not consistent with the residual approach. For example, a corporation with little or no earnings during a recession might choose to maintain dividends at the same level as the previous year, even if this means borrowing money to finance the payment of the dividends. Or, a firm with one year of extraordinarily high earnings might retain a large portion of its earnings so as to avoid raising stockholders' expectations regarding future dividends.

The second major complication encountered in applying the residual approach to the dividend decision stems from differences of opinion regarding the relative value of current dividends as opposed to future benefits resulting from reinvestment of retained earnings. Shareholders may disagree, for example, about the likelihood or the size of future earnings increases resulting from reinvestment of retained earnings. As a result of this uncertainty, a conservative investor might prefer a known current dividend payment to a less certain, although perhaps more valuable, benefit

to be derived at some time in the future. Those who believe that the residual approach is still appropriate under these circumstances argue that even a stockholder who prefers a current return will be better off if earnings are retained for reinvestment in profitable opportunities.

Example: Smith owns 10,000 shares of Big Apple Corporation common stock with a price per share of $20, and he has a claim on earnings of $5 per share. Hence, his total claim on earnings is $50,000 ($5 earnings per share × 10,000 shares). Smith prefers that all of the firm's earnings be paid as dividends, so that he will receive $50,000. Jones, on the other hand, who owns the remaining 90,000 shares outstanding, intends to retain $400,000 ($4 per share) for reinvestment in the development of a new product line. Although Jones can make this decision unilaterally, she would prefer that Smith concur, so she will attempt to convince him that her decision is in his best interests.

Suppose Jones believes that reinvestment of the $4 per share will produce future benefits worth $5 to her; in other words, she would be willing to forgo as much as $5 of current income in order to receive these future increases in earnings and dividends. Since she has to forgo only $4 of current dividends, she prefers to reinvest $4 to develop the new product. Smith agrees that, under normal circumstances, he would evaluate this information similarly, but, due to unusual personal circumstances, he has a strong preference for current, rather than future, income. Given these facts, Jones can convince Smith that it is to his advantage to reinvest $4 per share, as long as he can sell some of his 10,000 shares to obtain current income.

If all of the firm's earnings are paid as dividends, Smith will receive $50,000 in dividends ($5 dividends per share × 10,000 shares) and he will own 10,000 shares worth $200,000 ($20 per share × 10,000 shares). Alternatively, if he receives a $10,000 dividend payment ($1 dividends per share × 10,000 shares), while the remaining $40,000 is reinvested, the value of his shares will increase to $250,000. This results from the fact that $4 of retained earnings produces future benefits worth $5 per share, which, in addition to the already established $20 value of a share, makes each of his shares worth $25. Thus, the total value of his shares is $250,000 ($25 value per share × 10,000 shares). If Smith desires $50,000 of income, he can supplement his $10,000 dividend payment by selling 1,600 of his shares for $40,000 ($25 price per share × 1,600 shares). Although he will now have only 8,400 shares left, these remaining shares are worth $210,000 ($25 value per share × 8,400 shares).

Therefore, the alternative favored by Jones would provide Smith with $50,000 of current income ($10,000 dividend payment + $40,000 proceeds from sale of 1,600 shares) and leave him with common stock worth $210,000. Payment of all earnings as dividends, the choice Smith originally preferred, would provide $50,000 of current income, but the value of his 10,000 shares would be $200,000. Thus, in spite of Smith's preference for current income, retention of most of the firm's earnings is the more desirable choice for him.

The above example illustrates that the residual approach to the dividend decision is in all stockholders' best interests, in spite of differences in preferences for current income, as long as two conditions exist: first, that stockholders can sell their shares; and, second, that existing, as well as potential, stockholders are in accord regarding the future benefits produced by reinvestment of earnings.

The first of these conditions applies to owners of common stock in large corporations, such as those listed on the New York and American Stock Exchanges. The holders of such stock can always find buyers for their shares. However, owners of small corporations may have difficulty finding buyers for their common stock, because there is generally no organized market for these shares.

The second condition mentioned above reintroduces the fact that different investors will evaluate a firm's prospects differently. Even a stockholder in a large corporation may not be able to find a prospective purchaser who believes that the value of the shares has increased as a result of the firm's reinvestment of retained earnings. In this situation, he will not be able to realize current income from the sale of some of his shares, as described in the above example. Therefore, the shareholder in either a large or a small corporation may be unable to sell his shares at a price that reflects the increased value he may have expected to realize. A shareholder in such a position, and who desires current income, might prefer that the firm pay current dividends rather than reinvest earnings.

The conclusion at this point is that there are often conflicting objectives involved in establishing a firm's dividend policy. While the residual approach to dividend policy is theoretically valid, it may produce a dividend pattern that is inappropriate because of the "information content" of dividends. Similarly, investors who prefer current income to future earnings and dividends may find that their objectives are not met by a firm that determines its dividend payments as the residual of the retained-earnings decision. How can these inconsistencies be resolved? To a great extent, the answer to this question depends on the pattern of the firm's earnings over time. In fact, the relationship between a firm's earnings pattern and its dividend policy is generally thought to be so consistent that certain terminology has developed to categorize many common stocks according to these characteristics. Hence, the terms *blue-chip stock, growth stock,* and *cyclical stock* identify a firm's earnings history and dividend policy.

Blue-Chip Stocks. A blue-chip stock is a common stock representing ownership of a major company with a long history of profitability and constant or increasing dividends, and with the financial strength to endure substantial economic downturns without significant effects on its dominant position in its in-

dustry or its profitability and ability to pay dividends. Firms such as Exxon, IBM, Eastman Kodak, Du Pont, and Sears are considered blue-chip. Although these firms may experience declines in earnings, or possibly even losses, during a recession, they are sufficiently large and stable that they are not usually vulnerable to any significant deterioration of their financial strength.

Blue-chip companies often adopt two objectives in formulating their dividend policy. First, in recognition of the information content of dividends, blue-chip stocks typically maintain dividends per share at a level that equals or exceeds the previous year's dividends. Second, since a company in this category often has opportunities for expansion, some portion of earnings will be retained for reinvestment. In order to meet the first of these objectives, it is possible that during a recession, when earnings are low, the company will be forced to pay all of its earnings as dividends, or even to borrow to finance the payment of dividends. However, this would occur infrequently, and it would be anticipated that profits would increase substantially following the recession, enabling the firm to reinvest a portion of earnings as well as increase dividend payments.

Since the term *blue chip* does not denote any specific quantifiable qualifications, it is clear that there is no consensus regarding what common stocks are classified as blue-chip stocks. Some stocks—perhaps 200 or so—are obviously blue-chip. However, since there is no absolute criterion regarding company size or consistency of earnings or dividends, it becomes a subjective matter as to what firms, or even how many firms, can be regarded as blue-chip.

Furthermore, even for those firms that are clearly regarded as blue-chip, there is no guaranty that past performance and current size will assure the investor of profitability and dividend growth in the future. Chrysler Corporation common stock would certainly have been considered blue-chip 15 years ago, but would not have been included in this category in recent years. Similarly, International Harvester has undoubtedly lost its blue-chip classification. The firm suffered losses totaling approximately $2 billion during the years 1981 and 1982, including the second-largest loss ever recorded by an American corporation: $1.6 billion in 1982, which is second only to Chrysler's $1.7-billion loss in 1980.

While examples like Chrysler and International Harvester are the exception rather than the rule, they do serve to emphasize the subjectivity and uncertainty inherent in any attempt to classify a stock as "blue-chip."

Growth Stocks. Growth stocks are stocks of corporations whose earnings have demonstrated relatively rapid growth in the past, in comparison with the growth of the economy, and are expected to continue to grow at above-average rates in the future. In order to maintain this increase in earnings, these companies must typically reinvest a large portion of earnings in order to expand production capacity. Without this expanded capacity, the large increase in sales that generates the growth in earnings would not be attainable. Since most, if not all, of earnings are retained, dividend payments are small relative to earnings. Stockholders are content with the high retention of earnings and low dividend payment because they expect that the rapid growth in earnings will result in exceptionally high dividend payments in the future. It is generally not necessary, however, for the owner of a growth stock to anticipate holding the stock for 10 or 15 years, until these large dividend payments are made, in order to realize a return on his investment. As it becomes apparent that the company's earnings are growing at an exceptional rate, the value of a share will increase rapidly and the stockholder can realize his return by selling his shares at a price higher than his purchase price.

These characteristics of a growth stock are clearly illustrated by the case of Wang Laboratories, a computer manufacturer that experienced an extremely high rate of growth in earnings between 1972 and 1982. During this period, Wang's earnings per share increased from $0.08 to $1.76 for an annual growth rate of greater than 36%. By comparison, the average growth rate in earnings for the 40 largest manufacturers of office equipment during the same time period was approximately 9%, and the average rate of growth in earnings for all corporations was approximately 10%. By any criterion, Wang would be considered a growth stock during this period.

During this ten-year period, Wang Laboratories has reinvested most of its earnings and has paid dividends equal to less than 10% of earnings. An investor could have purchased a share of Wang common stock for approximately $1.00 as recently as 1975, when earnings per share were $0.08 and dividends per share were less than $0.01. In 1978, as investors were becoming aware of the potential profitability of the company, the price of a share had risen as high as $8.00, even though dividends were still only $0.01 per share, and earnings had risen to $0.35 per share. An investor who had purchased a share for $1.00 in 1975 would have received only $0.04 in dividends between 1975 and 1978, but he could have earned an extremely high rate of return by selling the share for $8.00 in 1978. The individual who bought the share for $8.00 would have done so with the expectation that earnings would continue to increase rapidly, that dividends would eventually be increased substantial-ly, and that the price of a share would rise as well. In 1983 Wang continues to grow rapidly, dividends are still very low ($0.10 per share), and the price of a share of stock exceeds $40.00.

Cyclical Stocks. The common stock of companies whose earnings fluctuate with the business cycle are referred to as "cyclical stocks." These companies have relatively low, or even negative, earnings per share when the economy is in a recession, but earnings increase dramatically during the recovery phase of the business cycle. The basic manufacturing industries—such as steel, machinery, and automobile manufacturing—have historically been regarded as cyclical industries. General Motors, for example, is clearly a cyclical stock, although General Motors would be classified as a blue chip-stock as well, due to its size and long history of profitability and dividend payments. Since automobile sales decline sharply during a recession, GM's earnings display a strong cyclical pattern. The firm's dividends per share are also substantially lower during a recession than during periods of high profitability. General Motors has adopted a policy of paying "extra" dividends in addition to "regular" dividends when earnings are high. This approach is designed to remind stockholders that they should not expect dividends per share to be maintained at the higher level during a period of declining automobile sales. In other words, General Motors attempts to negate the "information content" associated with declining dividends by dividing the higher dividend payment into two parts: The extra dividend is the result of exceptionally high profitability, which cannot be expected to continue indefinitely; while the regular dividend represents the payment the stockholder can expect to receive even when sales and earnings decline.

Income Stocks. An income stock is a common stock with relatively constant earnings and dividends per share and a high dividend yield in comparison to other common stocks. The constant earnings usually result from the fact that the corporation has a stable market for its product. Since there are no significant opportunities for expansion of this market, only a small fraction of earnings will be retained for reinvestment. Therefore, dividends will be both constant and relatively high, because dividends are a large portion of the relatively constant earnings.

A typical example of an income stock is the common stock of a local electric utility company in an area with a stable population. There is little potential for expansion of sales in such a situation. Therefore, there is no incentive to retain a substantial portion of earnings, and a large percentage of earnings will be paid as dividends to the stockholders. Furthermore, since the utility is regulated, rates will be adjusted by the regulatory authority to reflect increases in costs of production or changes in demand for electricity, thus increasing the likelihood that earnings will remain constant.

Alternatives to Cash Dividends

Stock Dividends. A stock dividend is a distribution of additional shares of common stock to existing stockholders in proportion to their current holdings. For example, a 10% stock dividend would entitle each stockholder to receive one new share of common stock for each ten shares he currently owns. A firm that intends to retain all of its earnings for reinvestment might choose to issue a stock dividend as an alternative to cash dividends. Since a stock dividend does not change the shareholder's basic rights, it will generally not change the value of his holdings.

Example: The Big Apple Corporation has 100,000 shares outstanding; Jones owns 90,000 shares and Smith owns 10,000. The firm's earnings are $500,000 in 1983, so that earnings per share equal $5 ($500,000 earnings/100,000 shares outstanding). The firm will retain $400,000 and pay dividends of $100,000, or $1 per share ($100,000 total dividends/100,000 shares outstanding). Since Smith owns 10,000 shares, he has a claim on $50,000 of the firm's earnings ($5 earnings per share × 100,000 shares) and he will receive $10,000 in dividends ($1 dividends per share × 10,000 shares). Furthermore, he is entitled to 10% of the votes in corporate elections.

Suppose the Big Apple Corporation issues a 25% stock dividend. Jones will receive 22,500 additional shares (25% of 90,000 shares) and Smith will receive 2,500 additional shares (25% of 10,000 shares) so that they will now own 112,500 and 12,500 shares, respectively, of the 125,000 shares outstanding. Earnings per share will decrease to $4 ($500,000 earnings/125,000 shares outstanding), and dividends per share will become $0.80 ($100,000 total dividends/125,000 shares outstanding). However, Smith's claim on earnings will still be $50,000 ($4 earnings per share × 12,500 shares) and he will still receive $10,000 in dividends ($0.80 dividends per share × 12,500 shares). Also, he still has 10% of the corporation's votes (12,500 shares/125,000 shares outstanding). In other words, since he still has 10% of the shares outstanding, his claim on earnings, his dividend payment, and his voting rights will remain unchanged. Therefore, the stock dividend does not change the value of his holdings.

The above illustration demonstrates the fact that, theoretically, a stock dividend does not have any value to the shareholder. In spite of this conclusion, some investors and corporate managers believe that, under certain circumstances, stockholders may derive some benefit from the payment of stock dividends. For example, the management of a growth company may wish to retain all of the firm's earnings for reinvestment. It is sometimes argued that, in this situation, payment of a stock dividend conveys information to investors regarding management's ex-

pectations that earnings will grow rapidly in the future. The argument for this position is based on the fact that stockholders will receive some tangible evidence of the firm's profitability, in the form of the stock dividend, even though no cash dividend is paid. If existing and potential shareholders interpret this as evidence of current and future profitability, the total value of a stockholder's shares might increase. The issuance of the stock dividend does not change either the firm's current earnings or its prospects for earnings growth, but it might convince investment analysts that the firm does, in fact, have excellent growth potential.

Stock Splits. While there are some technical differences between a stock split and a stock dividend, there is no practical difference between the two. For example, a three-for-two stock split and a 50% stock dividend both leave a shareholder with three shares of common stock in place of two. As is the case for a stock dividend, the shareholder theoretically does not receive any benefit from a stock split.

A change in the number of shares a stockholder owns is usually considered a stock split when the number of new shares issued is large relative to the number of existing shares. For example, a two-for-one or three-for-one stock split will result in the shareholder's owning two or three times as many shares as he originally held. On the other hand, smaller distributions of stock, such as one or two new shares for every ten shares held, are referred to as "stock dividends."

As described previously, one of the reasons for a stock dividend is to convey information to investors. A stock split, on the other hand, is often used to lower the price of a share of stock to make it more attractive to smaller investors. For instance, a share that has a value of $200 might be split four-for-one, theoretically resulting in four $50 shares in place of each $200 share. The anticipated result of such a split is that the lower price per share will make the stock more accessible to smaller investors, and that this increased marketability will increase its value above the theoretical $50 per share.

Stock Repurchase. A firm that intends to distribute earnings to its stockholders will normally do this by declaring a cash dividend. However, under certain circumstances, earnings can also be distributed by stock repurchase—that is, the firm can use earnings to purchase some of the shares outstanding from existing stockholders. The stock repurchased is referred to as "treasury stock."

A stock repurchase is sometimes used by a firm that has few profitable reinvestment opportunities and large earnings to be distributed to stockholders. In this situation, if large dividend payments were made, stockholders might expect these payments to continue in the future. In order to avoid this expectation, which perhaps cannot be met by the company, stockholders might be offered the opportunity to sell their shares at a price higher than they could otherwise obtain. Those who take advantage of this offer clearly feel they are deriving a benefit; if they did not feel that it was beneficial to sell their shares at the offered price, they would not do so. Those who choose not to sell their shares will also benefit from the stock repurchase, because there will be fewer shares outstanding. The remaining stockholders will thus own a larger share of the corporation and have a larger claim on future earnings and dividends than they would have had without the repurchase.

Primary and Secondary Markets. The initial sale of a share of common stock by the issuing corporation to an investor is referred to as a "primary market transaction." Any subsequent sale of the share, by one investor to another, is a "secondary market transaction." While the primary and secondary markets have important effects on each other, there are substantial differences in the manner in which these markets function and the purposes they serve.

Primary Markets. When a small corporation is formed by a group of investors, these individuals, who become the owners of the corporation, might view their investment as a direct purchase, by them, of the assets required to commence the operation of the business. (Turn back to the first example, which describes the formation of the Big Apple Corporation.) Technically, however, this process should be regarded as two separate transactions. First, the investors purchase shares of common stock from the corporation. Then the proceeds of this sale enable the corporation, which is a legal entity separate from its individual owners, to purchase the required assets. The first of these two transactions is a primary market transaction because it is the initial sale of the common stock to the investors. Should any of the original owners of the corporation choose to sell his shares at a later date, this subsequent sale would be a secondary market transaction. These classifications allow investors to identify the differences between these two kinds of transactions, but the terminology does not imply that the transactions must occur in any particular location.

Any sale of a security by the issuing corporation to an investor is a primary market transaction. As described above, this term applies to the sale of common stock at the time when a corporation is formed. Similarly, if the corporation sells, or issues, additional shares at a later date, this is also a primary market transaction. Whenever the shares are issued, the purpose of the sale is basically the same: The proceeds from the sale of common stock are used to finance the purchase of assets, either the assets required to commence the operation of the business, or assets necessary for expansion or modernization of existing facilities. The shares that are sold to new owners are indistinguishable from those shares issued to the original owners, and therefore confer on new stockholders the same rights as those of the original stockholders.

Many large corporations regularly sell large numbers of shares of common stock. These new issues are usually in the form of a public offering—that is, these shares are offered to the general public at a specified price, and anyone willing to purchase a share at this price may do so. For the individual investor, the decision whether to purchase the shares depends on the return, in the form of earnings and dividends, that the investor anticipates receiving. Here, the investor would consider the anticipated earnings yield, for example, in order to determine whether the stock represents an attractive investment.

The mechanism for this public offering requires the services of a middleman between the issuing corporation and the investor. The middleman is referred to as an "investment banker." The investment-banking firm, or a group of such firms, purchases the shares of common stock from the issuing corporation with the intention of selling the shares at a slightly higher price to the general public. Theoretically, the issuing corporation could make the sale directly to the public, but, like any middleman, the investment banker has valuable experience and expertise. His knowledge of securities markets and the channels for the sale of securities to investors makes his services vital to the issuing corporation.

The investment-banking firm does not simply purchase the common stock from the corporation. Prior to the sale, the investment banker and the corporate management hold extensive discussions on such matters as the amount of financing required, the number of shares to be sold, and the price at which the shares should be sold. Since the investment banker is involved with the securities markets on a daily basis, he is able to provide valuable advice to the corporation.

Once the decision to sell the securities has been made by the issuing corporation, in consultation with the investment banker, the investment banker will usually "underwrite" the issue. This is the process whereby the investment-banking firm buys the securities from the issuing corporation and then sells them to the public. Often the sale to the public will take only a few days, or even a few hours, if the investment banker has been correct in his evaluation of investor demand for these shares. If the investment banker is unable to sell the shares at a higher price than he paid to the issuer, he will suffer a substantial loss. This entire transaction, from the issuing corporation to the investor, is considered the primary market transaction.

A small, relatively unknown corporation issuing new shares of common stock generally does not have access to the services of an investment banker because of the lack of public familiarity with the firm. since there is no receptive market for the securities, the investment banker will not underwrite the issue. Therefore, a small corporation must find potential investors through informal means, usually involving personal contacts.

Another form of primary market transaction is a "rights offering." Here, existing stockholders are offered the opportunity to purchase new shares of common stock in proportion to their existing holdings. For example, a firm with 1 million shares outstanding might offer its stockholders the opportunity to purchase one new share for each ten shares currently owned. In some cases, this rights offering is required, either by state law or by the corporate charter, as an alternative to a public offering. The rights offering protects existing stockholders against the possibility that they will suffer a reduction in their proportionate ownership of the corporation if a new issue of stock is sold to the general public. In other words, a stockholder who owns 10% of a corporation will experience a substantial diminution, or "dilution," of his voting rights and his claim on earnings if a large number of shares are sold to the public.

Secondary Markets. While any sale of stock subsequent to its original issue is a secondary market transaction, the best-known and most significant secondary markets are the organized exchanges. By far the largest of these is the New York Stock Exchange, where the common stock of approximately 1,500 of the largest corporations in the United States is bought and sold by investors. An individual seeking to buy or sell a share of stock listed on the exchange could attempt to arrange the transaction through his own personal contacts. However, the large number of investors who use the facilities of the exchange ensures that the individual will obtain the best price available if he completes his transaction at the exchange. Similarly, the American Stock Exchange provides the best opportunity for the purchase or sale of the several hundred stocks listed on that exchange.

The exchanges—including several smaller regional exchanges in addition to the two major exchanges—provide a formal mechanism for investors to complete their secondary market transactions. However, the common stock of many smaller companies, and even some fairly large companies, is not listed on any of the exchanges. Many of these securities can be traded through a network of securities dealers who comprise the over-the-counter market. The exchanges and

the over-the-counter market together include the vast majority of all secondary market transactions. However, the common stock of very small corporations cannot be traded in either of these markets. For a stock to be listed on an exchange, it must meet formal requirements with respect to size. Although there are no formal requirements for over-the-counter trading, securities dealers will not be interested in securities involving little or no potential for generating a sufficient number of transactions to be profitable for them. Hence, a stockholder seeking to sell shares in such a company must find a buyer on his own.

An individual investor is far more likely to purchase a share of common stock in the secondary market than in the primary market. However, the techniques the investor employs to evaluate a common-stock investment are the same regardless of the market in which the transaction takes place. In order to decide whether a particular stock is an attractive investment, the investor attempts to determine the return he will receive in relation to the price he must pay for a share. He might attempt to determine the anticipated earnings yield, for example, so that he can compare a particular common stock with other stocks.

Investors are constantly evaluating and reevaluating a firm's prospects in order to obtain the best possible returns. As conditions in the economy, or in a specific industry, change over time, a stock may become more or less attractive to a particular investor, or to investors in general. These changes in conditions and reevaluations lead to changes in the price investors are willing to pay for a stock. If most investors feel that a particular company's prospects for future profitability are improving, then the price they are willing to pay for shares in that company will increase. Thus, it is these changes in conditions and in investors' analyses of the conditions that result in increases or decreases in stock prices in the secondary market.

Although the primary and secondary markets are distinct markets, they clearly have important effects upon each other. If investors as a whole find that a firm's prospects for future profitability are improving, this consensus will be reflected in the stock price on the secondary market. Corporate management can use this price rise as an indication that a new issue of stock in the primary market can also be sold at a higher price per share. This means that fewer shares will have to be issued to obtain a given amount of financing. If the firm issues fewer shares than it might otherwise have had to issue, then existing stockholders will have to share future profits with fewer owners, and each stockholder will earn a larger share of profits. Since the stockholders are the owners of the company, this is clearly a favorable outcome.

In the above illustration, the secondary market provides a guide to corporate management for its pricing of a new issue of stock in the primary market. While this is an important relationship between primary and secondary markets, even more significant is the fact that, to a great extent, a firm's ability to sell shares in the primary market depends on the existence of the secondary market. An investor would be much more reluctant to purchase a share of stock in the primary market if he knew it would be difficult to find a buyer in the secondary market when he decided to sell the stock. In other words, the existence of well-developed secondary markets substantially increases the ability of corporations to obtain financing in the primary markets.

See CAPITAL STOCK; PREFERRED STOCK.

R. Bruce Swensen

Common Stock Glossary

American depository receipt (ADR) a document, representing ownership of shares of stock of a foreign corporation, which is traded in American securities markets. The actual shares are held by a foreign bank, acting as an agent for an American bank that issues the ADR in accordance with procedures administered by the Securities and Exchange Commission. The investor who owns the ADR is entitled to all the rights associated with ownership of shares of the foreign corporation.

block trading transactions involving large blocks of at least 10,000 shares of stock that are bought and sold by institutional investors.

book value the value of a firm, or of an individual asset, according to the firm's accounting records. For an individual asset, such as real property, equipment, or inventory, the book value is generally based on the acquisition cost of the asset; this figure may be adjusted according to standard accounting procedures to reflect changes in the value of the asset. The book value, or net worth, of a firm is equal to the total book value of all assets minus the firm's liabilities. (The par value of all outstanding preferred stock is considered a liability in this context.) The book value is also referred to as the firm's "equity." Book value per share is equal to the firm's total book value divided by the number of shares of common stock outstanding.

classified common stock two or more classes of common stock, issued by the same corporation, with different voting rights and/or claims on dividends. For example, a privately held corporation might issue class A common stock to the general public while the original owners of the corporation retain ownership of class B common stock. Holders of class A stock have reduced voting rights, or even no voting rights at all, but they are entitled to larger dividend payments than the owners of class B stock; the latter stockholders have full voting rights. In this way the original owners can attract investors while continuing to maintain control of the corporation.

day order a specification by an investor that a special order to buy or sell a security (e.g., a limit order or stop order) is effective for one day. If the order is not executed by the end of the trading day, it automatically expires. An investor may also specify that such special orders are effective for longer periods, such as a week or a month, or even indefinitely, as in the case of an "open" or "GTC" ("good-till-canceled") order.

dollar averaging an investment strategy whereby an investor periodically allocates a fixed dollar amount to the purchase of a particular common stock. This approach results in the acquisition of a large number of shares when the price of the stock is relatively low and a smaller number of shares when the price is high. For example, suppose that an investor decides to purchase $300 of XYZ Corporation common stock each month. If the price of the stock is $10, $30, and $20 respectively at the end of three consecutive months, he will purchase 30 shares, 10 shares, and 15 shares respectively. The average price paid for the 55 shares is $16.36 ($900/55 shares), which is substantially lower than the $20 average price the investor would pay if he purchased a constant number of shares each month.

ex-dividend a purchase of stock without the right to receive a recently declared dividend. An investor who purchases a share of stock on or after the ex-dividend date is not entitled to receive the dividends scheduled to be paid during the current quarter. When the board of directors of a corporation declares a quarterly dividend, it establishes the amount of the dividend, the payment date, and the record date. The payment date is the date on which the dividend check is mailed to stockholders. Dividend payments are made to all stockholders of record as of the record date, which is several weeks prior to the payment date. In order to allow time to complete a transaction and notify the corporation of a transfer of stock ownership, the ex-dividend date is four days prior to the record date. A transfer of stock ownership prior to the ex-dividend date is considered to be "cum dividends" or "dividends on" since the new owner of the stock will receive the dividend payment.

limit order an order placed by an investor with his broker to buy or sell a security at a price that equals or exceeds a specified limit. A limit order to sell specifies the lowest price at which the investor will sell his security. A limit order to buy specifies the highest price the investor will pay to purchase a security.

margin stocks   stocks that can be purchased on margin. Stocks listed on an exchange are generally eligible for margin trading, although, under exceptional circumstances, an exchange may decide that a particular stock or group of stocks should not be purchased on margin. The board of governors of the Federal Reserve system has the authority to classify individual over-the-counter stocks as margin stocks if they meet certain criteria regarding company size and trading activity.

market order   an order placed by an investor with his broker to buy or sell a security at the best price currently available in the market. A broker is obligated to execute, as soon as possible, a market order to buy at the lowest price obtainable and a market order to sell at the highest price obtainable.

most-active stocks   the stocks with the largest number of shares traded during a given time period in a particular market. For example, the "most-active list" for the New York Stock Exchange, which is published in major daily newspapers, enumerates the 15 stocks with the largest number of shares traded each day.

par value, common stock   a figure specified by the issuing firm but having little or no significance to the stockholder, although theoretically the stockholder could be liable to the firm's creditors for the difference between a share's par value and the purchase price of the stock if the latter is less than the former. For this reason, and also because some state taxes are based on par value, a corporation will specify a very low par value relative to the price of a share of common stock. Some common stock is issued without a par value and is referred to as "no-par stock."

penny stock   a common stock selling for less than $1 per share. Such stocks often represent ownership of mining companies and are highly speculative.

price quotation (or "price quote")   information regarding the current purchase and/or selling price of a security. A price quotation may take either of two forms. First, the quote might indicate the price at which the most recent transaction in the security was consummated. Price quotes such as those found in daily newspapers for stocks listed on the New York Stock Exchange take this form; the "closing price" for a particular stock is the price at which the last transaction of the day took place. The second form of price quotation is illustrated by the "bid" and "asked" prices for securities traded in the over-the-counter markets. The bid and asked prices for a particular security are the prices at which a dealer is willing to purchase or sell that security.

Therefore, to the investor, the bid price is the price at which he can sell the security to the dealer, and the asked price is the price he would pay to purchase the security from the dealer.

prospectus   information regarding a new issue of securities; the prospectus is provided to prospective investors in accordance with the requirements of the Securities Act of 1933, as administered by the Securities and Exchange Commission (SEC). A corporation must file a registration statement with the SEC and receive the commission's approval prior to making a public offering of common stock, preferred stock, or debt securities with a maturity exceeding 270 days. The registration contains extensive financial and legal information about the issuing firm and the proposed security offering. The prospectus is part of the registration statement and contains information that enables a prospective investor to evaluate the security.

proxy   a temporary transfer of voting rights by a common stockholder to another party. This transfer is generally valid only for a specific occasion. For example, the management of a corporation typically solicits proxies from stockholders prior to the annual stockholders' meeting. The proxies allow the management to cast these votes in electing members of the board of directors or in other matters requiring stockholder approval at the annual meeting. Stockholders who are satisfied with the performance of the existing management and board of directors are generally willing to transfer their voting rights to management. However, dissident stockholders sometimes solicit proxies from other stockholders in an attempt to replace existing board members and management. When a group of dissident stockholders wages such a "proxy battle," it must register with the Securities and Exchange Commission, which administers the procedures for soliciting proxies.

rating, common stock   a rating, based on earnings and dividend history, indicating the quality of a common stock issue. A stock with a history of stable or steadily rising earnings and dividends is considered a high-quality security, although such a rating does not necessarily indicate that such patterns will continue in the future or that the stock is an attractive investment. Both Moody's Investors Service, Inc., and Standard & Poor's Corporation rate common stock issues.

regular-way delivery   the usual procedure for completing a stock-exchange transaction, which requires that the buyer deliver cash and the seller deliver stock certificates by the fifth business day after the transaction has taken place.

round lot   a quantity of shares (usually 100) that is considered the customary unit for transactions involving that particular security. Securities with exceptionally low prices often trade in round lots larger than 100 shares (e.g., 500 shares) and securities with exceptionally high prices trade in round lots smaller than 100 shares (e.g., 50 shares). An "odd lot" is any quantity of shares fewer than a round-lot transaction.

secondary distribution a block-trading procedure whereby an institution sells a very large block of stock to a group of investment firms that then sells the stock to the general public. The investment firms are usually members of the New York Stock Exchange. The sale to the public is generally at a fixed price and usually takes place after the close of the exchange.

short interest the number of shares of a particular stock that have been sold short, but not covered, as of a given date. The short interest is considered an important market indicator by many technical analysts because it represents an eventual source of demand for the security; stock borrowed for a short sale must ultimately be purchased in the market in order to return the security to the lender.

short sale the sale of a security by an investor who has borrowed the security for this purpose. The short seller borrows the security with the intention of later "covering" the short sale—that is, he will return to the lender, at a later date, an identical security that he will purchase in the market. For example, an investor who expects a particular common stock to decline in value can borrow a share of stock, sell the share at the current price, and, assuming that the price declines, purchase a share at a lower price in order to return it to the lender. The short seller's profit will be the difference between the higher price at which he sold the borrowed share and the lower price at which he later purchases a share. If, however, the market price of the stock rises, the short seller's loss will be the difference between his selling price and the higher purchase price. The lending of shares of common stock for this purpose is usually arranged by the brokerage firm with whom the investor has his account.

specialist a member of a stock exchange who is responsible for maintaining an orderly and continuous market in a specified security (or group of securities). In fulfilling this responsibility, the specialist is required to (1) buy the security for his own account when there is insufficient demand for the security, and sell the security from his own holdings when there is an insufficient supply of the security; and (2) keep a "book" of special orders (e.g., limit orders) placed by other exchange members, which he executes when the specified price is reached.

stock certificate a certificate indicating ownership of capital stock. The certificate specifies the name of the issuing corporation, the name of the stockholder, the number of shares issued to the stockholder, the par value of the stock, and the kind of stock represented (common stock, preferred stock, classified stock, etc.). Additional information on the preferred-stock certificate indicates the dividend rate and whether the dividends are cumulative or noncumulative.

stock-market indicator (or "market average") an average or index based on a sample of stock prices, used to measure the overall price performance of a particular segment of the market for common stocks. The most widely known, and also the least representative, market indicator is the Dow Jones industrial average (DJIA). The DJIA is based on the stock prices of 30 of the largest corporations in the United States. These stocks are all listed on the New York Stock Exchange (NYSE). A more representative market indicator is the Standard & Poor's 500 Index, which is an index of the prices of the common stocks of 500 large corporations listed on the NYSE. The New York Stock Exchange Composite Index and the American Stock Exchange Market Value Index are indicators based on the prices of all stocks listed on the respective exchanges. Other indicators measure price levels for segments of the NYSE (e.g., the Dow Jones public-utility average or the New York Stock Exchange Transportation Index).

stop order an order placed by an investor with his broker to buy or sell a security if the market price of the security reaches a specified value. A stop order to sell specifies that if the market price of the security declines to a specified value, the broker will sell the investor's security at the highest price obtainable in the market. If the market price declines rapidly, it is possible that the actual selling price will be substantially below the price specified in the stop order. A stop order to sell is often used to preserve a profit on a security whose price has risen substantially, or to limit a potential loss on a security that might decline in price. A stop order to buy specifies that if the market price of the security rises to a specified value, the broker will purchase the security at the lowest price obtainable in the market. If the market price rises rapidly, it is possible that the actual purchase price will be substantially above the price specified in the stop order. A stop order to buy is often used in conjunction with a short sale of a security in order to limit the losses incurred when the price of the security rises.

Source: R. Bruce Swensen

Compound Interest

See DAILY COMPOUNDING; INTEREST RATES, CALCULATION OF.

Comptroller of the Currency

See DEPARTMENT OF THE TREASURY.

Condominium

A single unit in a multiunit building or complex of buildings that is individually owned. In addition to the single unit, each condominium owner holds an undivided share of common areas and facilities of the building or complex—land, foundation, central-heating and plumbing systems, hallways and entranceways, roof, and usually any recreational facilities.

Although the concept of condominiums can be traced to ancient Rome, the condominium form of ownership did not appear in the United States until 1958, when condominiums came to the continental United States via Puerto Rico. Section 234 of the National Housing Act of 1961 first authorized FHA mortgage insurance for condominium homes, and each of the 50 states has adopted statutes specifically allowing condominium ownership.

Since the 1960s, the American real-estate industry has shown great ingenuity in adapting the condominium form of ownership to a wide array of development projects. "Condos" can take many forms, ranging from detached single-family homes to high-rise commercial and industrial properties. Condominiums are located in the heart of metropolitan areas as well as in suburban and resort areas. A condominium may be used as a permanent home, a vacation home, an apartment, an office, warehouse space, or as an investment property.

Advantages. Some of the advantages of owning a condominium are as follows:

Cost. While not all condominiums are in the lower price range, they often can be less expensive than comparable single-family homes, and they frequently serve as a transition from renting to owning.

Location. Because all owners share in the cost of the land, some projects offer buyers a choice location they could not afford on their own.

Amenities. Many condominium projects offer owners amenities (such as swimming pools and golf courses) that most single-family homes don't have and in many cases can't have.

Tax and investment benefits. As with single-family homes, mortgage interest and property taxes can be deducted from income taxes. And, like single-family dwellings, condominium units often appreciate in value, providing owners with a hedge against inflation.

Security. Condos can provide a general feeling of security, and some complexes feature paid security guards as well.

Minimum maintenance. Individual owners are responsible only for the maintenance of their unit. Yard work, pool maintenance, and the day-to-day operation of the complex often are handled by a manager or a professional management company and paid for by assessments of owners.

Group activities. Group ownership presents opportunities to meet new people socially and encourages group activities.

Disadvantages. Some of the disadvantages of owning a condominium are as follows:

Reduced privacy. Because people live closer together, often sharing at least one common wall and other common elements, some may feel a lack of privacy or quiet.

Rules and regulations. Owners must abide by the wishes of the majority in a condominium association. Pets may not be allowed; the number of guests permitted may be limited; pool hours may not be convenient.

Responsibilities of a Condominium Owner. A condominium owner's responsibilities are similar to those of a single-family-home owner. Condo units may be mortgaged in the same way as single-family homes, and they are assessed for real-estate-tax purposes the same as single-family homes because they are considered individual parcels of real estate.

An additional responsibility of the condominium owner is payment of a monthly maintenance fee to cover all costs of maintaining and managing the condominium. Condo-unit owners frequently hire a professional management company to oversee management functions.

Legal documents. It is also imperative that the prospective condominium owner become thoroughly familiar with legal documents that to a great extent will govern his life as a condominium owner. Two basic documents that must be examined carefully are the declaration of condominium, or master deed, and the bylaws of the association.

Declaration. In legal terms the declaration of condominium describes the scope of the project, dimensions of and equipment located in each unit, common elements, limited common elements, easements by any parties, an explanation of the undivided interests of the unit owners, provision for assessments, and a management-agency agreement.

Bylaws. Usually attached to the master deed as an exhibit, these contain information about the administration and maintenance of the complex.

Among other things, the bylaws contain detailed information on the owners' association and how it works; further information on assessments; details on use and sale restriction, if any; and all insurance policies covering common elements.

Two other documents should be examined carefully as well. They are the management agreement and the recreational-facilities agreement.

Considerations When Shopping for a Condominium.

Think about your present life-style. Will a condominium suit the way you are used to living? Check out the life-styles of people in the complex. Will their style be compatible with yours?

Is the condominium complex convenient to work, schools, shopping, public transportation, hospitals, and churches? Depending on your particular situation, some of these items will loom more important on your list than others.

Is the complex well designed? Are the recreational facilities adequate for the number of people who live in the complex? If recreational facilities are promised but not yet built, make sure the developer has the necessary permits and that you are prepared for any special assessment that may be levied. Is there enough parking, and is that included as a common element or a separate expense item? Check to see if sewage and garbage disposal are adequate for present and future needs.

Make sure you know what you are buying. Read your contract carefully and check the builder's reputation. Be sure the management fee includes everything. You may later be assessed for use of swimming pools or parking spaces.

Get specifics on maintenance. What are your maintenance responsibilities? Will the builder pay full maintenance costs and assessments attributable to uncompleted or unsold units, or will this expense be added to your costs?

Look around. Are the grounds well maintained? Are the hallways clean? Are recreational facilities in good shape? Deficiencies may be indications of inadequate management.

Check zoning around the project and find out what restrictions are imposed in connection with resale of the unit. Find out whether the developer is retaining the right to manage the project and whether residents can fire him, should they find cause.

Inspect your housing unit if you can, or a model if one is completed. Inside the unit, look for signs of quality construction. Look for sound, smooth walls; firm floors; and professional painting and finishing work. Check to be sure the layout fits your needs.

Conversions.

An apartment complex that has been converted to condominiums presents some special considerations. Aside from the physical condition of the building, inquire about the heating, cooling, and electrical systems. What has been restored or will be? Some condo-conversion sponsors provide engineering reports on the condition and estimated remaining useful life of the building's components, plus the replacement costs. You should inquire about the estimated annual operating expenses after conversion. This is what your monthly assessment will be based on.

Talk to the tenants. Are they buying? Will the building be professionally managed and maintained? What improvements are being made to make the building more conducive to long-term occupancy? If professional managers are employed, what type of experience do they have?

Moving into a Condominium.

While condos offer the combined advantages of apartment living and traditional single-family-home ownership, you may find the actual move a little more complicated than you expected.

Remember to obey your condominium association's specific rules and regulations. This will mean more paper work and perhaps some additional fees. Owners may be assessed a moving fee in the form of a nonrefundable moving-damage deposit. Also, you may have to rent or reserve use of the elevator if you're moving into a high-rise building.

Check into exactly when you are allowed to move in. Some associations will not let you move on weekends. Most people try to get in on the first or last day of the month, especially in May and October. If you can, try to move in toward the middle of the month to avoid the peak period.

By taking time to learn everything you can about your condominium in advance, you will be much more likely to avoid unpleasant surprises and assure yourself of happiness later. Condominium ownership offers the best combination for achieving life-styles sought by confirmed city dwellers who seek tax shelters, older couples who seek maintenance-free living, suburbanites who rent apartments and would prefer the privacy of a single-family dwelling, or single-family-home owners who desire the advantages of common recreational facilities.

See CO-OP (COOPERATIVE OWNERSHIP).

Harley W. Snyder

Condominium and Cooperative Financing

See HOME FINANCING, MORTGAGES.

Consolidated Income Statement

A financial statement resulting from the consolidation or joining of the separate income statements of more than one business group, company, or individual. There is almost always some economic or business association between groups, companies, or individuals represented in a consolidated income statement.

Samuel C. Hoyt

Consumer

This term is usually used to designate any living person who uses any of the products or services that comprise any part of the GROSS NATIONAL PRODUCT (GNP) under methods used for its calculation by the U.S. Department of Commerce. More literally, it refers to one who "consumes" products and services—as opposed to a *producer,* who is a participant in the output of any product or service. With the exception of retirees and other unemployed persons, nearly everyone is both a producer and a consumer.

For purposes of the federal Truth in Lending Act, *consumer* means a credit-card holder or a natural person* to whom consumer credit or a consumer lease is offered, and it includes a natural person acting as a comaker, endorser, guarantor, surety, or similar person who may be obligated to repay the extension of credit or the lease obligation.

James A. Ambrose

Consumer Credit Protection Act

See CONSUMER-CREDIT REGULATION.

Consumer-Credit Regulation

Consumer credit is a very competitive field, yet one of the most heavily regulated areas of business. Congress and the state legislatures have enacted a massive body of laws and regulations to provide a wide range of consumer protection in the use of credit for personal, family, and household purposes, both with respect to borrowing money and buying on sales credit.

Consumer credit has been extended in the U.S. since colonial days, when consumer protection consisted solely of general usury laws, which set a single, maximum rate of interest that a creditor could legally charge. Today, nearly every aspect of a consumer-credit transaction is regulated by either state or federal law, and sometimes even by both. These laws are so numerous, often comprehensive, and sometimes even confusing for consumers that they may at times be

self-defeating in their goal of providing protection. Further, these laws and regulations are always in a state of flux as legislative bodies and regulatory agencies either revise them or add to the total body of them.

Getting information on some specific law or regulation, or a portion of one, often is not a simple matter. Even if a consumer consults an attorney, there may be delay and expense for the client because few attorneys specialize in consumer-credit law and they thus must engage in legal research. Consumer protection is usually stronger at the federal level, and information about federal laws and regulations is easier to get.

For information or complaints that relate to federal law, contact the Division of Consumer and Community Affairs, Federal Reserve System, Twentieth Street and Constitution Avenue, NW, Washington, D.C. 20551, or any of the 12 member banks of that system. If your inquiry or complaint relates to sales credit, you may wish to direct your contact to the Division of Credit Practices, Bureau of Consumer Protection, Federal Trade Commission, Pennsylvania Avenue at Sixth Street, Washington, D.C. 20580. If your correspondence should have been addressed elsewhere, these agencies will refer it to the proper federal regulatory agency.

If you have an inquiry about a state credit law or a complaint about a potential violation of one, finding the right address for your correspondence, either to get a reply or for referral to another state office, may require some effort on your part. The laws, and the state agencies responsible for administrating and enforcing them, vary substantially from state to state. Depending on the nature of your correspondence, the correct address for it may be your state banking commissioner, administrator of consumer credit, secretary of state, attorney general, or perhaps some other state official. For information on correct addresses, contact your closest local bar association, consumer-protection organization, or legal reference library, or consult an attorney.

Table 1 is but a brief itemization and general summary of the federal laws on consumer credit. As stated, these laws and regulations are numerous, comprehensive, complicated, and constantly changing. Thus discussion of them here must necessarily be limited and general, or it would soon be incorrect.

James A. Ambrose

Consumer-Credit Regulators

The board of governors of the FEDERAL RESERVE SYSTEM is charged with writing most of the consumer-credit regulations enforced by 12 different federal agencies.

One group of these regulators consists of the 12

*Under the Truth in Lending Act, there is a distinction between a "person" and a "natural person." A "person" can be an organization; a "natural person" is a human being, and not merely a legal entity.

Table 1
Federal Laws Directly Regulating Consumer Credit

Year	Name	Summary
1968	Consumer Credit Protection Act	Originally covered only the Truth in Lending Act, restriction of garnishment, and prohibition of loan sharking, but amended many times to include each of the following statutes, but not the FTC Trade Regulation Rule.
1968	Truth in Lending Act, as amended through 1980 and implemented by Regulation Z	This law requires disclosure of all the most important aspects of a consumer credit contract, especially the finance charge and annual percentage rate, and it provides a broad range of consumer protection. It also regulates the issuance of credit cards and prohibits the fraudulent use of them, in addition to limiting the liability of a consumer if a credit card is lost or stolen and illegally used thereafter.
1971	Fair Credit Reporting Act	This law is intended to protect personal privacy in the collection, dissemination, and use of information about individuals for credit, employment, or insurance; to insure accuracy in the collection and dissemination of such information; and to provide for disclosure of such information and a system for its correction when accuracy is disputed.
1974	Fair Credit Billing Act, as implemented by Regulation Z	Requires initial and periodic disclosure to consumers of their rights under it. Established a system for credit-card users to challenge billing errors and for resolution of errors and disputes with card issuers affecting a cardholder's obligation to pay.
1974	Equal Credit Opportunity Act, as amended in 1976 and implemented by Regulation B	This law is intended to provide equal access to consumer credit for all creditworthy persons, and to protect applicants for all kinds of credit against discrimination based on sex, marital status, age, race, religion, national origin, income from any public assistance program, or good-faith exercise of any right under the Consumer Credit Protection Act.
1976	Consumer Leasing Act, as implemented by Regulation M	This law requires disclosures and provides protection in consumer leasing of automobiles and other personal property. Since such leasing is an alternative to consumer credit use, its provisions parallel those of the Truth in Lending Act.
1977	Fair Debt Collection Practices Act	Regulates the collection of delinquent consumer debts by collection agencies and other third parties, but exempts attorneys and creditors in collection of debts under their own contracts. It prohibits harsh, abusive, unfair, and deceptive practices by bill collectors by mail, telephone, or in person.

In addition to the foregoing laws, regulation of consumer credit is indirectly affected by the following federal laws: Home Mortgage Disclosure Act (1975), Community Reinvestment Act (1978), and Electronic Fund Transfer Act (1978).

Because consumer credit has been regulated by both state common law and statutes, every state has a comprehensive set of consumer-credit laws that are similar to those in other states but may vary widely with respect to what is required of creditors or prohibited. Some states have laws paralleling the federal credit statutes.

One area of federal law that is not covered through an enactment by Congress is the Federal Trade Commission Trade Regulation Rule on Preservation of Consumers' Claims and Defenses, which preempted state statutes and common law on what is known as the "holder-in-due-course doctrine." The FTC rule gives the consumer the same claims and defenses against a subsequent creditor as the consumer had against the original seller/creditor, if a retail credit contract or agreement is transferred at any time to any third party, and it requires that a specific notice of such consumer rights be included in any such contract or agreement for open-end or closed-end credit. The rule regulates cash lenders only to prevent evasion by sellers. (Although a trade-regulation rule is not a law or statute, it has the full legal effect of one.)

Federal Reserve banks, each having responsibility in its district for the lending practices of state-chartered commercial banks that are members of the Federal Reserve System.

The role of the CENTRAL BANK as consumer-credit "rule-maker" was established in 1968 by the United States Congress in the Truth in Lending Act. Previously, consumer-credit regulation was the responsibility of individual states. Examination of state member commercial banks is the primary enforcement procedure used by the Reserve banks to assure compliance with the consumer-protection regulations.

Specially trained examiners review accepted and rejected consumer-loan files (including mortgages), application forms, savings and checking account operations, and other aspects of consumer business. Reserve banks' internal complaint files also are reviewed to see if problems are indicated in any area of a member bank's operations. After examination, a member bank is judged in compliance or agrees to establish procedures to avoid future violations. When necessary, follow-up examinations are made. Since lack of familiarity with the regulations is often a major cause of violation, Federal Reserve experts meet with bankers to discuss forms, procedures, policies and problems.

Reserve banks, such as the New York Fed, also investigate alleged violations against state member banks reported by consumers. Complaints against other lenders are sent to the appropriate regulatory agency. When a complaint is received by the New York Fed's consumer-affairs staff, it is acknowledged by letter and, in most cases, the state member bank is asked for comments. The bank's response is reviewed by the consumer-affairs staff and, if necessary, by legal, examining, or board personnel. The consumer is then advised of the results of the investigation. All Reserve banks and other agencies charged with enforcement duties have similar procedures.

- The *Comptroller of the Currency* is responsible for enforcing consumer-credit laws for commercial banks with national charters. The agency conducts consumer-credit-compliance examinations and investigates consumer allegations against national banks.
- The *Federal Deposit Insurance Corporation* enforces consumer-credit laws for insured banks that aren't Federal Reserve members. It has a separate compliance-examinations program. The FDIC also conducts inquiries to determine the merits of all discrimination complaints.
- The *Federal Home Loan Bank Board* enforces regulations for federally chartered savings and loan associations. In addition to regular examinations to determine compliance, it investigates consumer complaints.
- The *National Credit Union Administration* is the enforcement agency for federally chartered credit unions. Its enforcement activities, like those of the other financial regulatory agencies, include examiner training, specialized examination procedures, and, if a violation is discovered, follow-up with credit-union officials. The NCUA also conducts field investigations of written consumer complaints and institutes corrective action.
- The *Federal Trade Commission* enforces requirements of the Consumer Credit Protection Act appli-

cable to retailers, finance companies, and other lenders not subject to the jurisdiction of any other agency. Potential violators are identified through several sources, including consumer complaints, consumer and civil-rights organizations, and other enforcement agencies. When there is evidence of a violation, an informal inquiry is made and, if necessary, a full investigation.

- The *Civil Aeronautics Board,* the enforcement agency for domestic and foreign air carriers, monitors industry practices through consumer complaints. Enforcement measures include contacting the carrier or supplying information to the consumer.
- The *Interstate Commerce Commission* is the enforcement agency for regulated common carriers.
- The *U.S. Department of Agriculture* has within it several agencies with responsibilities under various consumer-credit laws. One subagency is the Packers and Stockyards Administration. The agency's monitoring is handled on a complaints-received basis. Another subagency is the Farmers Home Administration, itself a lender. It operates under the enforcement authority of the FTC, and is primarily concerned with farm loans. Complaints against the Farmers Home Administration itself concerning the denial of loans are handled by the USDA's Office of Equal Opportunity.
- The *Small Business Administration* is the enforcement agency for small business investment companies for the purposes of the equal-credit-opportunity regulation and, through a letter of understanding with the FTC, other recipients of SBA assistance. Those businesses subject to SBA review are monitored for compliance, subject to on-site reviews.
- The *Securities and Exchange Commission* is the enforcement agency for securities brokers and dealers for the purpose of the equal-credit-opportunity regulation.
- The *Farm Credit Administration* enforces the requirements of the consumer-credit laws pertaining to federal land banks and federal land-bank associations, federal intermediate credit banks, and production credit associations. The FCA's enforcement activities include examinations conducted every 12 to 18 months.
- The *banking departments of individual states* continue to play a role in certain aspects of consumer-credit regulation, such as the determination of usury ceilings. They, too, provide consumer assistance within their areas of responsibility.

Arthur Samansky

Consumer Finance Companies

Consumer finance companies specialize in providing loans to consumers and small businesses. The organizational structure of finance companies may be that of a corporation, partnership, or proprietorship. Finance companies provide loans both directly and indirectly. They make direct loans to consumers and also purchase installment contracts from dealers and retailers so that they can offer their customers financing for the purchase of durable goods.

Types of Companies. Finance companies range from large, diversified corporations with branch offices throughout the U.S. and in other countries, to small, one-office operations serving a local community. Some finance companies are owned by major corporations, insurance firms, bank holding companies, and other enterprises. Other large finance companies, independently owned, may themselves own banks, savings and loan associations, or industrial banks. Smaller finance companies are generally independently owned.

Finance companies used to be differentiated as consumer finance and sales finance companies. The former were companies whose primary business was making personal loans to consumers, while the latter were those whose major business was purchasing installment sales contracts from dealers and retailers. However, this no longer holds true, as most larger companies now offer a mix of direct and indirect lending.

Major Business. Finance companies offer a wide range of financial services to consumers and small businesses: personal loans, on an installment or single-payment basis and either secured or unsecured; second-mortgage loans; automobile and mobile-home loans; home-improvement loans; dealer and retailer sales financing. In addition, some companies offer open-end credit or revolving credit through major credit cards, and some offer "loan by mail" and special "executive loan" programs.

The services provided by finance companies to consumers are principally delivered through small offices in convenient locations, where customers receive personalized services. Some larger companies provide access to a preapproved line of credit by use of a card that gives access to an automatic teller machine. Some companies may also offer loans by mail to a preselected group—for example, teachers, lawyers, homeowners.

Large finance-company subsidiaries of automobile manufacturers provide financing for their parent companies' dealers. The auto dealers thus can offer credit to purchasers.

As noted earlier, companies also provide sales financing for retailers, so that they can offer credit to their customers. Usually, such merchandisers are selling durable goods, such as appliances. Although in many cases these loans are only marginally profitable (because of their relatively small size), they can be useful in identifying "good payers" as potential future customers.

Finance companies hold the second-largest share of consumer credit, next to commercial banks. As of the end of February 1983, they held 27% of the consumer credit outstanding, or $93.86 billion of the total $341.55 billion outstanding. About one-half of the finance-company total was automobile credit, followed by nearly one-third in personal loans. Research shows that over the past five years secured personal loans (automotive credit and second mortgages) by finance companies grew rapidly, while unsecured personal loans actually declined.

Characteristics of Borrowers. Data on finance-company borrowers also indicate changes over the past five years. Generally, finance-company borrowers now are older, in higher income categories, and have a different mix of occupations than was the case several years ago.

Certain information about the finance-company customers has been compiled by the American Financial Services Association. At the end of 1981, data showed that of the personal-loan borrowers at finance companies (exclusive of second-mortgage borrowers), over one-half (51%) had monthly incomes of $1,000 to $2,000. The greatest percentage (37.5%) were in the 25–34 age category, with 23.3% age 35–44, and 15.9% age 45–54. Data on the occupations of finance-company borrowers showed that the largest percentage (28.6%) were in the "operatives, laborers, etc." category, followed by "service workers" (11.5%) and "craftsmen, foremen, etc." (11.3%).

Demographics on second-mortgage-loan borrowers at finance companies reveal some important differences in comparison to other personal-loan borrowers. Second-mortgage borrowers at finance companies generally were older and had higher incomes than other personal-loan borrowers. Of the second-mortgage borrowers, 45.8% had monthly incomes of over $2,000, and 56.4% were 35–54 years of age.

Regulation of Finance Companies. Although consumer finance companies are principally regulated at the state level, they are subject to state and federal statutes applying to corporations, partnerships, and proprietorships. Federal consumer-protection laws and regulations relating to consumer credit also require compliance by finance companies. The major federal consumer-protection law affecting finance companies is the Truth in Lending Act, which requires uniform disclosure of terms and conditions of credit agreements.

In each state in which a company operates, finance

companies are licensed and supervised by a state agency—in most cases, a division of the state banking department. In nearly all states, the state agency examines the licensees annually. The states set the interest rates that can be charged on various types of loans. These usury laws establish the permissible interest-rate ceilings and also include consumer-protection provisions. In recent years, many states have raised or eliminated their ceilings and now allow market forces to operate.

Most state laws regulating consumer finance companies' loan rates were based on the Uniform Small Loan Law, which was drafted as a model act in 1916 and has gone through numerous revisions. In several states, consumer credit is regulated by the Uniform Consumer Credit Code (UCCC), which replaced those specific states' laws relating to consumer credit, and includes strong consumer-protection provisions.

History of Finance Companies. As the country became more industrialized in the last decades of the nineteenth century, workers increasingly moved to urban areas and became dependent on wages rather than farming for their subsistence. They also sometimes found it necessary to borrow small amounts to pay for emergency expenses. However, during this period and the first decade of the twentieth century, legitimate options for borrowing did not exist for wage earners. Most credit was extended on the basis of collateral or assets, rather than a borrower's future earnings. In addition, illegal loan sharks were lending to wage earners at extremely high rates of interest. Research funded by the Russell Sage Foundation during that period showed that there was an economic need for legitimate lenders, under strict supervision, to meet the financing needs of borrowers while earning an adequate rate of return on small loans.

The Uniform Small Loan Law, mentioned earlier, had as its main purpose to attract capital to the business of making small loans by allowing an adequate return while safeguarding the interests of small-loan borrowers.

Source of Funds. Finance companies principally procure their funds to lend from the money market. The majority of their funds comes from the issuance of commercial paper (unsecured promissory notes) and from long-term borrowing from commercial banks. Thus, they pay market rates for their funds and compete in the fund market with other types of businesses.

Trends. Consumer finance companies traditionally specialized in small personal loans of several hundred dollars. However, over the past few decades the average loan size has increased significantly. For example, in 1965 the average size of a loan made by finance companies was $558; by 1980 the average size had increased to $2,102. This increase occurred for several reasons. Chief among these is the fact that the costs of administering a small loan (taking applications, credit checking, accounting, statements, etc.) are considerable, which means that the yield on a small loan hardly covers its costs. Also, a sharp rise in prices has meant that consumer demand for small loans has dropped.

Finance companies historically had been characterized as charging higher rates of interest than other lenders, and lending to higher-risk borrowers. However, because of market developments and financial deregulations, finance companies today are competitive with other lenders, in terms of both rates and customers. Since finance companies used to specialize in small, unsecured loans, their rates generally were higher. The average cost per dollar of a loan is much higher for small loans than for large loans, because the administrative costs of a loan are roughly the same regardless of loan size. Also, as most small personal loans are unsecured, the risk of default is greater. Both of these factors—size of loan and risk—largely explain the historically higher rates charged by finance companies.

Traditionally, also, finance-company customers were from lower income groups than customers of other institutional lenders. Many customers also were new entries into the credit market and younger people without previous credit histories. All of these factors generally would portend a higher risk.

These characterizations of finance companies, however, are changing dramatically. Many finance companies are emphasizing larger loans, particularly those secured by equity in a home. Many are also offering services to appeal to higher income groups, such as large lines of credit secured by a borrower's equity in his home. In addition, there is greater rate parity on consumer loans between finance companies and depository institutions. Depository institutions competing in consumer lending used to have a stable and cheap source of funds—their customer deposits. Since they were restrained from offering market rates on these deposits and were largely immune to rate competition, their funding was inexpensive in comparison to finance companies. Now, with the deregulation of interest rates on deposits, such institutions are paying market rates for their funds, as finance companies have traditionally. Thus, they are also charging market rates on the funds they deploy for consumer loans.

Summary. Finance companies provide a broad spectrum of lending services to consumers and small businesses. Over the past several years, they have increasingly been attracting borrowers from higher income groups than they historically had served. Also, their rates charged for consumer loans today are often competitive with other lenders, as a result of deregulation of deposit interest rates.

Frances B. Smith

Consumer Laws, Banking

The FEDERAL DEPOSIT INSURANCE CORPORATION (FDIC), as directed by Congress, has established a Consumer Affairs Unit to receive and take appropriate action on complaints relating to unfair and deceptive practices by banks. This office has jurisdiction over state-chartered banks that are not members of the FEDERAL RESERVE SYSTEM and it will enforce compliance with regulations defining such unfair or deceptive acts or practices.

If a person has a complaint arising under any of the consumer-protection acts administered by the FDIC and has been unable to resolve the problem directly with the bank involved, he or she should advise the Consumer Affairs Unit or apply to the nearest regional office of the FDIC.

Sometimes the FDIC cannot be of assistance to bank customers. If, for example, a problem with a bank is essentially a personal dispute, the FDIC has no authority to resolve it. However, if the FDIC finds that a complaint or inquiry pertains to a matter outside its jurisdiction, it will refer the communication to the authority that can be helpful, or it may suggest an alternative course of action.

Some of the major consumer laws protecting bank customers and administered by the FDIC are shown in Table 1 (pages 159–162).

Federal Deposit Insurance Corporation

Consumer Leasing Act

See CONSUMER-CREDIT REGULATION.

Consumer Price Index (CPI)

The consumer price index is a special weighted average of prices of a "market basket" of goods and services that people buy for day-to-day living. Food, clothing, shelter, transportation fares, doctors' fees, cosmetics, and school books are among the items in the index. The Bureau of Labor Statistics (BLS) of the U.S. Department of Labor collects prices monthly on 400 items in 83 urban areas around the country to

Table 1
Major Consumer Laws Administered by the FDIC

Statute	Citation	Summary
Bank Holding Company Act Amendments of 1970	As amended by Title VIII of the Financial Institutions Regulatory and Interest Rate Control Act of 1978 (12 U.S.C. 1972)	In part, generally prohibit insured nonmember banks from requiring customers to obtain a service in exchange for credit or other services offered by the bank, and restrict insured nonmember banks from making certain loans to insiders of correspondent banks.
Bank Merger Act of 1966	12 U.S.C. 1828(c)	Requires FDIC approval for any merger in which the resulting bank is an FDIC-insured bank that is not a member of the Federal Reserve system ("insured nonmember bank") or in which an FDIC-insured bank acquires the assets of a noninsured institution. The FDIC is generally prohibited from approving mergers or acquisitions that may substantially lessen competition.
Bank Protection Act of 1968	12 U.S.C. 1881	Authorizes the federal financial institutions supervisory agencies to issue rules establishing minimum security measures for the institutions they regulate.

(cont)

Table 1   *(cont)*
Major Consumer Laws Administered by the FDIC

Statute	Citation	Summary
Bank Secrecy Act	Public Law 91-508	Requires FDIC-insured banks to maintain certain records on banking transactions and to report to the Department of the Treasury certain transactions in U.S. currency.
Bank Service Corporation Act	12 U.S.C. 1861	Authorizes certain banks to invest in corporations that provide services for banks, such as check sorting, interest computation, or electronic data processing, and subjects companies that provide such bank services to regulation and examination by the federal banking agencies
Change in Bank Control Act of 1978	Title VI of the Financial Institutions Regulatory and Interest Rate Control Act of 1978 (12 U.S.C. 1817[j])	Prohibits the change in control of FDIC-insured nonmember banks without first giving notice of the proposed change to the FDIC and permitting the FDIC to disapprove any proposed change.
Community Reinvestment Act of 1977	Title VIII of the Housing and Community Development Act of 1977 (12 U.S.C. 2901)	Directs the FDIC to take into account a bank's record of meeting the credit needs of the communities it serves, including low- and moderate-income neighborhoods, when the FDIC considers an application by a bank for deposit insurance; the establishment or relocation of a branch; a merger; a consolidation; or the acquision of the assets of another financial institution.
Garn-St Germain Depository Institutions Act of 1982	12 U.S.C. 226	Contains seven titles that change many aspects of banking and bank supervision. It gives greater powers to the FDIC, the FSLIC, and the NCUA to assist troubled institutions. It grants authority to federal thrift institutions to accept demand accounts and make commercial loans. It preempts due-on-sale prohibitions in certain circumstances, and makes numerous other technical changes in existing banking laws and regulations. It also authorizes the creation of an insured account for financial institutions that is the equivalent of money-market mutual funds.
Depository Institutions Management Interlocks Act	Title II of the Financial Institutions Regulatory and Interest Rate Control Act of 1978 (12 U.S.C. 3201)	Places prohibitions on certain interlocking directorate and employment relationships among financial institutions.
Electronic Fund Transfer Act	Title IX of the Consumer Credit Protection Act (15 U.S.C. 1693)	Provides rights, liabilities, and responsibilities of participants in electronic fund-transfer systems, with specific provisions on individual consumer rights.

Table 1 *(cont)*
Major Consumer Laws Administered by the FDIC

Statute	*Citation*	*Summary*
Equal Credit Opportunity Act	Title VII of the Consumer Credit Protection Act (15 U.S.C. 1691)	Prohibits discrimination against any applicant for credit because of race, color, religion, national origin, sex, marital status, or age.
Fair Credit Billing Act	15 U.S.C. 1666	Prohibits certain unfair and inaccurate billing and credit-card practices. It prevents banks and other institutions that issue credit cards from offsetting an unpaid credit-card bill against a customer's checking or savings account unless a court order has been obtained. The act also requires prompt correction of billing errors involving credit or charge accounts.
Fair Credit Reporting Act	Title VI of the Consumer Credit Protection Act (15 U.S.C. 1681)	Protects consumers against the circulation of inaccurate or obsolete information and ensures that consumer reporting agencies adopt fair and equitable procedures for obtaining, maintaining, and giving out information about consumers. The act requires creditors to disclose when information in a credit report from a consumer reporting agency or from a third party contributes to a denial or an increase in the cost of consumer credit. It also requires the establishment of procedures to keep credit information accurate, relevant, and confidential.
Fair Debt Collection Practices Act	Title VIII of the Consumer Credit Protection Act (15 U.S.C. 1692)	Protects consumers from unfair, harassing, and deceptive debt-collection practices.
Fair Housing Act	Title VIII of the Civil Rights Act of 1968 (42 U.S.C. 3601)	Prohibits conduct that has the purpose or effect of discriminating because of race, color, religion, sex, or national origin in the making of a loan for the purpose of purchasing, constructing, repairing, improving, or maintaining a dwelling.
Federal Deposit Insurance Act of 1950	12 U.S.C. 1811	Sets forth the powers of the FDIC. It includes the procedures by which a bank qualifies for deposit insurance, the maximum extent to which deposits are insured, and the procedures to be followed by the FDIC in supervising banks and enforcing its regulations.
Federal Reserve Act	12 U.S.C. 221	Includes restrictions on lending by insured nonmember banks to their insiders and restrictions on loans by insured nonmember banks to their affiliates.

(cont)

Table 1 *(cont)*
Major Consumer Laws Administered by the FDIC

Statute	*Citation*	*Summary*
Flood Disaster Protection Act of 1973	Public Law 93-234	Requires the federal financial institutions supervisory agencies to issue regulations requiring flood insurance for certain loans secured by property located in designated special flood-hazard areas.
Home Mortgage Disclosure Act of 1975	12 U.S.C. 2801	Requires any institution located in a Standard Metropolitan Statistical Area which makes loans secured by residential real property to disclose information on its mortgage-lending activities and to make such information available to the public. The act exempts institutions with assets of $10 million or less; also, the Federal Reserve is empowered to exempt institutions in states that have mortgage disclosure laws substantially similar to the federal statute.
International Banking Act of 1978	12 U.S.C. 3101	Provides for the federal supervision of foreign banks operating in the U.S. It requires a foreign bank to obtain federal deposit insurance for U.S. branches whenever the branches accept deposits of less than $100,000, unless the branches are determined not to be engaged in domestic retail operations. The FDIC has primary federal supervisory responsibility for FDIC-insured state-chartered branches of foreign banks.
Real Estate Settlement Procedures Act of 1974	12 U.S.C. 2601	Requires that consumers be provided in a timely manner with specified information on the nature and cost of settlement on a real-estate purchase.
Securities Exchange Act of 1934	15 U.S.C. 78a	Is a comprehensive statute regulating transactions in securities. Each federal financial institution supervisory agency is given primary authority to regulate certain securities transactions of institutions under its supervision.
Truth in Lending Act	Title I of the Consumer Credit Protection Act (15 U.S.C. 1601)	Requires certain disclosures of the terms of consumer credit for personal, family, household, and agricultural purposes, and regulates consumer-credit advertising so that individuals may compare the cost of credit among different financial institutions.

Source: Federal Deposit Insurance Corporation.

compute the CPI, probably the best known gauge of inflation and often called "the cost of living."

These prices are gathered from very large samples: 18,000 tenants and 18,000 homeowners give information on rent and housing expenses, including property taxes (property and sales taxes directly related to consumer purchases are included in the index). Other prices are collected from 24,000 businesses, mostly through personal visits of BLS personnel. This extensive sampling is designed to ensure the statistical accuracy of the index; the samples are so large that indexes for 28 individual cities also show small enough sampling errors to meet accuracy standards and are published either monthly or bimonthly by the BLS.

Consumer-Expenditure Surveys and Index Weights.

Currently, the index has a base period of 1967. Prices in other periods are divided by the 1967 prices and the ratios are then multiplied by 100 to arrive at indexes for individual items. These indexes are combined in a weighted total to get the overall CPI level. The items included in the index and their weights are determined through detailed surveys of thousands of consumers, asking them how they use their incomes. There have been five such surveys since the original one in 1919, the most recent in 1972.

The index was originally used mainly as a guide for wage negotiations, so the first consumer-expenditure surveys polled only blue-collar and clerical workers. The wide acceptance of the CPI as a general measure of inflation led the Labor Department to broaden the most recent survey to include a sampling of all urban consumers. The original, wage-earner-based CPI is called "CPI-W" and is still used to adjust wages in many collective-bargaining agreements; it is also the index used for adjusting Social Security benefits and other government retirement and welfare benefits. The all-urban index, called "CPI-U," is more widely used by economists and other analysts as the basic indicator of price change. Despite the distinction in the two indexes, they tend to move together. In December 1982, for instance, the CPI-W was 292.0 and the CPI-U was 292.4. Although they differ little, both are reported by the BLS and each has a separate use, so both have been described here.

Table 1 shows the current relative importance of the major categories and selected items in the CPI-U.

The Revised Housing Category.

The housing category in the CPI-U was redefined at the beginning of 1983, and its weight was lowered from almost 46% to the 38% shown in the table (weights of other components were raised commensurately). The homeownership category formerly included the cost of buying a

Table 1
The CPI-U

Category	Relative Importance
All items	100.000
Food and beverages	20.069
Housing:	37.721
Renters' costs	6.932
Homeowners' costs	13.881
Maintenance and repairs	0.526
Fuel and utilities	8.377
Household furnishing and operation	8.005
Apparel and upkeep	5.205
Transportation:	21.791
New and used cars	7.562
Motor fuel	6.191
Public transportation	1.541
Medical care	5.995
Entertainment	4.206
Other goods and services	5.014
Tobacco	1.387
Personal care	1.857
Education expenses	1.770

Source: U.S. Department of Labor.

house as an expense just like other living expenses—that is, it included the current price of a new house along with the current level of mortgage and financing charges. The wide swings in interest rates over the past few years meant that movements in the CPI were often dominated by mortgage-rate changes. However, only a small portion of homeowners pay current mortgage rates; the vast majority of people have been paying on their homes for some years. Moreover, the purchase of a house is really an investment, rather than a current expense.

On the basis of these considerations, the BLS altered the category: Housing is now treated as an investment, with homeowners viewed as charging themselves monthly rent (similar to the treatment in the gross national product). This rental equivalence measure constitutes nearly all of the "homeowners' costs" item; it includes some expenses for maintenance and appliances in addition to rent. So far, this housing definition applies only to the CPI-U; the CPI-W is scheduled to be modified in 1985. Thus, if mortgage rates move sharply in either direction, the two CPI's would diverge.

The CPI and the Purchasing Power of the Dollar.

Inflation over the past several years has been quite rapid, and the CPI helps to quantify this. For instance, in December 1982 the CPI-U stood at 292.4, meaning prices were 2.924 times what they had averaged in 1967, or an *increase* of 192.4%, which amounted to 8.6% per year. Put another way, items that cost $10.00 in 1967 cost $29.24 at the end of 1982. This inflation of the price index translates into an erosion of the purchasing power of money. One dollar in 1967 had eroded to only 34.2 cents by the end of 1982.

Carol A. Stone

Consumer Product Safety Commission (CPSC)

An independent regulatory agency of the federal government, the CPSC's purpose is to protect the public from unreasonable risks of injury associated with consumer products. The commission works with industry representatives to improve the safety of their products and has the authority to set standards relating to their safety. The CPSC has jurisdiction over 10,000 consumer products, but does not handle food, drugs, automobiles, warranties, or repairs. Five safety laws are administered by the CPSC: the Consumer Product Safety Act, the Federal Hazardous Substances Act, the Flammable Fabrics Act, the Poison Prevention Packaging Act, and the Refrigerator Safety Act. Created by the Consumer Product Safety Act of 1972, the CPSC began operating on May 14, 1973. It is directed by five commissioners who are appointed by the U.S. president with the advice and consent of the Senate.

Harvey Rachlin

Conventional Mortgage-Backed Bonds

See CONVENTIONAL MORTGAGE-BACKED SECURITIES.

Conventional Mortgage-Backed Securities

As a means of raising funds in the capital markets, SECONDARY MORTGAGE MARKET institutions issue mortgage-backed securities to provide funds for housing finance. *Conventional* mortgage-backed securities are issued against mortgage loans that are not insured or guaranteed by the federal government.

Mortgage loans have historically represented the largest single use of funds raised in the capital markets each year. In recent years, only government borrowing has used more. As traditional sources of mortgage credit became inadequate to satisfy demand, the secondary mortgage market was developed to make more funds available by attracting capital-market investors. The two major types of conventional mortgage-backed securities sold to investors are mortgage pass-through securities and mortgage-backed bonds.

Mortgage Pass-Through Securities. The GOVERN-MENT NATIONAL MORTGAGE ASSOCIATION issued the first mortgage pass-through security in 1970. "Ginnie Maes," as they are called, represent ownership interests in pools of FHA-insured and VA-guaranteed loans. They carry the backing of the full faith and credit of the federal government.

Conventional mortgage pass-through securities were first introduced in 1971 by the FEDERAL HOME LOAN MORTGAGE CORPORATION ("Freddie Mac"). They are known as Mortgage Participation Certificates or, more commonly, Freddie Mac PC's. They represent interests in loans purchased in whole or in part by Freddie Mac.

In 1981 the FEDERAL NATIONAL MORTGAGE ASSOCIATION ("Fannie Mae") began a conventional mortgage pass-through security program. Formerly, it financed the loans it purchased by selling corporate debt, holding in portfolio the loans it purchased.

Though Freddie Mac and Fannie Mae account for the vast majority of conventional mortgage pass-through securities outstanding, SAVINGS AND LOAN ASSOCIATIONS, mutual SAVINGS BANKS, COMMERCIAL BANKS, and mortgage-insurance companies conduct mortgage pass-through programs on a smaller scale.

Generally, conventional pass-throughs are formed by the issuer purchasing from lenders loans on residential properties. The loans are grouped together into "pools" against which the securities are issued. As many as several hundred loans could comprise a single pool. The loans may include fixed-rate, adjustable-rate, or other types of instruments and are made on single-family or multifamily properties.

The securities, sold to investors usually in $25,000 minimum denominations, represent undivided interests in the underlying pool of loans. Monthly payments of principal and interest made by the borrower to the lender are "passed through" to the issuer and on to the investor.

To insure that the securities are a safe investment, issuers examine the loans they purchase, making sure the lenders have adhered to prudent underwriting guidelines. Criteria have been established as to the borrower's creditworthiness and ability to make payments, the value of the real estate being financed, and ratio of loan amount to appraised value. In addition the securities carry the issuer's guarantee as to the payment of principal and interest.

Conventional mortgage pass-through securities are extremely liquid and marketable, with many nationwide investment bankers trading them on a daily basis (*see* INVESTMENT BANKING).

The yield, safety, and liquidity of conventional mortgage-backed securities make them a far more attractive investment than individual loans themselves.

As a result, many nontraditional mortgage investors—such as pension funds, insurance companies, trusts, and credit unions—buy them. In addition, savings and loan associations, mutual savings banks, and commercial banks are large investors, taking advantage of the increased financial flexibility of holding the securities rather than the loans themselves.

Pass-throughs are considered a relatively recent financial innovation, and many investors are still hesitant to invest in them, for several reasons. Mortgages seldom generate a continuous, even cash flow over the full payment schedule determined at the time of origination. Properties are sold or refinanced, causing the actual payments on a mortgage pool and security to vary. The common prepayment assumption is 12 years for securities backed by 30-year fixed-rate loans, but the performance of any given security cannot be predicted with certainty. Some investors prefer the predictable cash flow offered by corporate and government debt instruments and dislike the monthly bookkeeping associated with most mortgage securities.

Mortgage-Backed Bonds. Mortgage-backed bonds more closely resemble standard corporate or government debt than pass-through securities. Interest on most mortgage-backed bonds is paid semiannually and is not dependent on the cash flow from the underlying pool of mortgage loans. At maturity, typically five to ten years from the date of issue, the entire principal amount is repaid.

These bonds are a step further removed from the mortgages backing them than is the case with pass-throughs. Rather than receiving an ownership interest in a pool of loans, the investor holds a debt obligation of the issuing savings and loan association, savings bank, or commercial bank, *collateralized* by a pool of loans. Typically, the value of the pledged loans is 150% or more of the amount of the bond issue. The unpaid principal amount of the loans is periodically revalued, taking into account the level of prevailing interest rates and the amount of borrower repayment. Using mortgage loans as collateral for bonds allows even small thrift institutions to obtain bond ratings comparable with the highest-grade corporate issues.

Mortgage-backed bonds are usually sold in public offerings through investment bankers, but are sometimes placed privately. The primary investors in these bonds are pension funds, trusts, and insurance companies.

Federal Home Loan Mortgage Corporation

Conventional Mortgage Pass-Through Securities

See CONVENTIONAL MORTGAGE-BACKED SECURITIES.

Convertible Preferred Stock

See PREFERRED STOCK.

Convertible Security

A fixed-income investment that is exchangeable for common stock. Having characteristics of both equity and debt-type investments, the convertible security often provides an attractive avenue for participating in the success of a company while protecting against intermittent downside moves in equity prices.

There are basically two forms of convertibles: the convertible debenture and the convertible preferred.

Because explanation of convertible securities involves reference to basic terminology used by investors, our study of the subject will be much clearer if we define these concepts first. The values shown in Table 1, using the hypothetical PRS Company, will help illustrate our explanations.

Concepts to know (with examples from Table 1) include:

Conversion value: market of common times conversion rate ($40 \times 20.83 = 83.32$)

Point premium: market of convertible debt minus conversion value ($102 - 83.32 = 18.68$)

Percent premium: point premium divided by conversion value ($18.68 \div 83.32 = 22.4\%$)

Current yield differential: current yield on convertible debentures ($\$120 \div 1020 = 11.8\%$) minus current yield on common ($\$2.00 \div 40 = 5\%$) ($11.8 - 5.0 = 6.8\%$)

Quick break-even calculation: percent premium divided by yield differential ($22.4\% \div 6.8\% = 3.29$ years)—sometimes referred to as "payback period."

Table 1
PRS Company

Maturity date—12% debentures	Fixed	1/1/2002
Conversion price of debentures	Fixed	$48.00
Conversion rate (1,000 ÷ 48)	Fixed	20.83 shrs.
Coupon or interest rate of conversion	Fixed	12% ($120)
Current call price	Declines yearly to 100	109.00
Current market on PRS 12% debentures	Variable	102.00
Current market of PRS common	Variable	$40.00
Yearly dividend/share on common	Variable	$2.00

Although most of the features of convertibles will apply to both debentures and preferreds, let's begin our study with facts about convertible debentures. They are almost always issued by corporations in $1,000 denominations. At the time of issuance, the debenture's indenture usually will fix all the critical features of the security for the rest of its existence. For instance, the *conversion rate* (the number of shares into which the bond is convertible) is determined by dividing $1,000 par value by the *conversion price,* which is established from negotiations between the dominant buyers, the underwriting broker, and the issuing company's management.

Once you have the conversion price, you can determine the conversion rate. To calculate *conversion value* (what the convertible debenture would be worth if immediately converted into common), you multiply the current market price of the common stock by the conversion rate. (This value is sometimes referred to as *parity*.)

A word of caution is appropriate here: Common practice is to quote and trade convertible bonds in terms of percentage rather than actual full values—i.e., the market of 102 is really $1,020, and conversion value of 83.32 is really $833.20. The 12% coupon is really $120.

To help evaluate whether a convertible security is attractive or overvalued, it is necessary to determine the *premium* the issue is selling for *over conversion value*. This is expressed in terms of either points or percent. A high premium over conversion value usually indicates that the yield on the convertible security will also have to be high. A low premium indicates either a low current yield on the convertible, a small yield advantage, or vulnerability to call. Traders tend to express premium in terms of points, while longer-term investors utilize the more relevant percentage method.

The *break-even calculation* is to convertibles as the price earnings ratio is to common stocks. It is a method of measuring the relative attractiveness of these securities. Although there are several methods of calculating break-even, the most widely used is the simple percentage method. Once you have derived the *percentage premium* over conversion value of the convertible, you just divide that number by the current *yield differential* between the convertible and the common. This concept is most important to the equity-substitute investor. New issues have recently been coming out with a break-even period of two to three years, down from five years in the mid-Seventies.

Almost all convertible debentures have *call prices* (prices at which the issuing companies can redeem them), usually par value plus the coupon (100 + 12 or 112) for the first year, then scaling down to 100 in ten years. Recently investors have been demanding

and getting call protection on new issues for a period approximating the quick break-even time. This interval will help insure the investor against losing the premium he paid when the bond was issued. The noncall feature allows the investor to receive the increased income he paid the premium for, even if the common should appreciate substantially shortly after the bond is issued by the corporation. Thus, the call provision is a major factor to consider when evaluating a convertible.

During 1982 a new form of call feature was introduced. This has become known as "provisional call protection." What this means is that if a company's common stock runs up sharply and is now selling at 140–150% of the conversion price, the issuing company can call the issue at the call price even though it might be well before the stated noncall date. From the investors' viewpoint, this innovation has effectively negated the value of the noncall feature in a bull market.

A large percentage of convertible debentures have a *sinking fund* provision. It usually becomes active in the tenth year and will retire between 60% to 100% of the issue by maturity. In many cases the sinking fund is allowed to credit against their obligation any bonds converted by holders. The sinking fund is a definite plus feature for any bonds issued about ten years ago and now selling at 90 or lower.

Under ordinary circumstances, convertible debentures have semiannual *coupon-payment dates.* Interest is accrued on a 360-day basis and the purchaser pays the seller interest to the settlement date. Certain so-called Eurobond issues—convertibles issued by European subsidiaries of U.S. companies in Europe, convertible into the parent company's stock—may pay interest only once a year.

If a holder wishes to convert his debenture into common stock, it becomes critical to study the interest-payment date and its proximity to the current date—because in almost every case when a bond is converted, the holder loses any interest due from the last coupon payment. Hence, in our theoretical company's case, if a holder of the 12s of 2002 found the conversion value of the bonds to be 129½ and decided to convert them on June 15 of any year, he would be forfeiting all the accrued interest from January 1 to June 15, or 5½ points ($55) per bond. Were he able to wait till July 1, he would get not only his 20.83 shares per bond but the entire $60 coupon. This point is quite important to consider when evaluating issues selling well above call price with a fair amount of accrued interest.

Because companies issue convertible bonds with the expectation of *forcing conversion* into common stock as soon as practicable, the investor must constantly be considering this eventuality. There are two ways this objective is usually achieved. The first is to get the issue's conversion value up to about 125% of call price (in the case of PRS Company, 109 × 1.25 = 136+). At this level investment bankers (underwriters) are usually willing to form a group and guarantee the issuer that all bonds when called will be converted into common either by the holder or by the underwriting group, which will purchase and convert from anyone unwilling to convert directly. The cushion between 136 and 109 allows the common to drop rather drastically before there is any chance holders will opt to receive $109 in cash versus converting into stock worth more.

The second method of enticing holders of convertible issues to convert into common is to raise the dividend on the common to a level where the income received from converting into common exceeds the income from the convertible by about 10%. In the case of PRS Company, the dividend on the common would have to go to about $6.40 per share versus $2.00 currently before there is enough incentive to convert into common for the increased income. ($6.40 × 20.83 = $133.33 versus $120.)

Other, less frequently found features encountered when looking at convertible bonds are step-up or step-down conversion terms, expiration of conversion privilege before maturity, put features, and other exotic variations of what has already been discussed here.

Convertible Exchangeable Preferred Stock. Convertible exchangeable preferred stock has two distinctive features: (1) The holder can convert the security into the common stock of the company at any time, at a price determined at the offering, and (2) the corporation can exchange the convertible preferred for convertible subordinated debentures after a specified period of time. In the event of such an exchange, the coupon rate of the convertible subordinated debentures will be the equivalent of the dividend rate on the preferred stock. Similarly, the convertible subordinated debentures will allow conversion into the same number of shares of common stock at an equivalent dollar amount of the convertible preferred stock.

Due to differential tax treatment of dividends and interest to both the issuer and the investor, an exchangeable feature might allow a company to raise capital under more favorable terms. If a company is not currently a taxpayer and does not expect to be for the next few years, the fact that dividends on preferred stock are not tax-deductible does not affect the after-tax cost of funds. However, when the company's profitability improves and tax-loss carry-forwards are depleted, the after-tax cost of interest (paid at the same rate as the dividend) on the debentures would be less (1−tax rate) than the dividends paid on the

preferred stock. An exchangeable preferred allows the company to exchange the preferred stock for subordinated debentures and thus make its "interest" payments tax-deductible.

An issuer can achieve better terms on preferred stock than on debentures since the corporate investor is allowed an 85% deduction on dividends for income purposes, and is therefore willing to accept a lower pretax yield. In addition, the issuer has the balance-sheet benefits of preferred stock until the preferred is exchangeable for debentures.

Convertible exchangeable debentures were offered on the public market for the first time in December 1982 by Martin Marietta. Boise Cascade followed with a $100-million offering in January 1983.

About three-quarters of convertible debentures are listed on the New York Stock Exchange, but trading in the over-the-counter market represents about 90% of the volume. Prices listed in the paper are usually close to the levels at which trades are occurring, but the volume listed is really only a token of what is taking place off the exchange.

Having explored the convertible debenture at length, we now turn to convertible preferreds and find that many of the concepts studied before apply exactly the same way to preferreds.

The biggest differences from the standpoint of basics are (1) that almost all preferreds are listed on the exchanges and practically all volume is in fact shown in the paper; and (2) that preferreds are quoted and traded in real dollar terms, not percents as is done with bonds. Preferreds usually pay quarterly dividends; and because of the 85% intercorporate dividend-exclusion feature of the INTERNAL REVENUE CODE, preferreds are more appealing to corporations and insurance companies. The tax law also allows a company taking over another corporation to issue convertible preferred or common on a tax-free basis as compensation for the securities of the acquired company. Convertible debentures don't qualify for

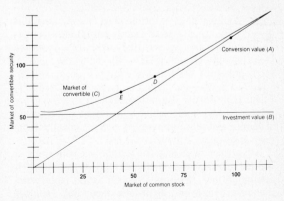

Figure 1.

this tax-free exchange. Many issues of the preferreds that are outstanding today were created for just this purpose.

Figure 1 may help explain how convertibles take on the properties of either debt or equity.

In this hypothetical example, as the convertible goes over 100 and the stock over 50, it becomes evident that the issue gets very close to conversion value and the two will eventually coincide. As the common stock goes down under 30, the convertible approaches investment value (where it would sell as a straight bond or preferred) and further deterioration in the common-stock price has much less influence on the behavior of the convertible. The convertible will tend to bottom out at a price approximating investment value unless investors sense bankruptcy is near.

Between points E and D on the graph, it is hard to characterize whether investment or equity values are more dominant.

Who might be attracted to convertibles, and why? Although there are many categories of investors that use convertibles, the two most definable investors for this type of security are the fixed-income-substitute buyer and equity-substitute buyer. The fixed-income-substitute buyer purchases convertibles when the yield, either current or to maturity, is close to the yield he could get on a straight debt issue of the same issuer or a similarly rated company. This buyer is naturally willing to pay a much higher premium over conversion value than the equity-substitute buyer because of the high yield factor. An example of a fixed-income-substitute issue might be a convertible bond selling at a 13% yield to maturity, with a 50% premium over conversion value. The buyers of such a bond are relatively insensitive to the length of break-even time—often insurance companies, older individuals, or any investor who believes that the equity markets are vulnerable to decline but is not quite willing to be completely out of equity participation.

The equity-substitute buyer is seldom willing to pay a large premium over conversion value. He is constantly looking for the short break-even issues. To this buyer, current yield advantage is paramount. An example of this type of security might be a preferred stock having a current yield of 8% versus the yield on the common of 4%, with a premium over conversion value of 3–5%—i.e., about a one-year break-even. Most likely to use equity-substitute convertibles are investors who trade actively, performance-oriented accounts, and those who generally don't take the long-term investment approach.

It has been said that convertible securities are of limited liquidity and often underperform versus their common stock. Like any generalization, this statement can be proven true or false depending upon the timing of the investment decision.

The first question an investor should ask is "Do I really like the fundamentals and outlook for this company?" If the answer is yes, the decision to utilize the convertible instead of the common can be studied. Never purchase attractive convertible securities just because they look cheap versus the common. Execution of convertible-securities purchases and sales requires extreme patience and discipline. An investor should establish a maximum price he will pay and a maximum premium level. If the market will not allow execution of the convertible program at these determined levels, then it is best to use the common and await a more opportune time to swap out of the common into the convertible. On the sell side of a trade, one may often have to sacrifice some part of the normal premium to liquidate a position, but this lower premium is worth taking versus waiting for the correct premium at much lower levels.

The total value of outstanding convertible preferreds and debentures is approximately $45 billion—about two-thirds bonds and one-third preferreds. Individual issue sizes range from $400 million of U.S. Steel 5¾'s down to $100,000 of several small companies.

There are over 46 issues of convertible debentures with par values of $100 million or more. Preferred stocks are led by the $450-million market value of Penn Central $5.27 preferred and United Technologies $2.55.

There are several publications that give the investor most of the necessary facts to analyze convertible investments. *Value Line Convertibles,* a weekly publication by Value Line, is probably the most widely used source of information. Moody's monthly *Bond Record* and Standard & Poor's *Stock Guide* will provide sufficient facts to assist those not subscribing to *Value Line.* Some of the larger brokerage houses provide customers with their in-house convertible publications.

The answer to who should use convertible securities, and when, will vary according to the investor's needs and restrictions. Many institutional investors are not allowed to own a security that does not pay a dividend. Using the convertible of such a company is one way of circumventing this restriction, especially when you feel this company's outlook is extremely promising. If you are limited to a certain percent of your portfolio in commons, using convertible securities will allow greater equity exposure, but they will be classified as fixed-income-type investments.

For an individual these securities can provide substantially more income than the common, and will still provide some of the appreciation, if a company is successful. The active investor who can negotiate low commission rates will find a strategy of swapping back and forth between convertible and common to

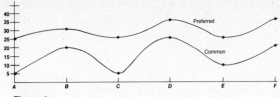

Figure 2.

Table 2

A	Sell preferred 100	@ 25		2,500
	Buy common 500	@ 5		2,500
B	Sell common 500	@ 20		10,000
	Buy preferred 333	@ 30		10,000
C	Sell preferred 333	@ 25		8,333
	Buy common 1,665	@ 5		8,333
D	Sell common 1,665	@ 25		41,630
	Buy preferred 1,189	@ 35		41,630
E	Sell 1,189 preferred	@ 25		29,720
	Buy 2,972 common	@ 10		29,720
F	Sell 2,972 common	@ 20		59,440
	Buy 1,698 preferred	@ 35		59,440

Performance:
Just owning 100 preferred A to F: $2,500 to $3,500
Just owning 500 common A to F: $2,500 to $10,000
Swapping points A to F: $2,500 to $59,440

be the most rewarding. Figure 2 may help to illustrate such a program.

At point A in this graph, the convertible is sold and common bought. The spread was about 5 versus 25. If the common runs up to 20, as at point B, the convertible might advance to 30, so a reversal of the previous trade is undertaken. If the common subsequently declines to 5, as at point C, the convertible will also come down, but by quite a bit less. Table 2 shows what will result from these swaps over a longer period, disregarding commission costs.

To say the least, we have assumed utopian executions, no tax consequences, and net trading prices. However, if such a program were even one-third as successful, a holder would benefit tremendously as opposed to having just held the common or preferred.

Trading convertibles is not as easy as it may appear. The number of firms equipped to proficiently handle customer convertible trades is limited. Close supervision of orders is most important, and many retail houses are not willing to accommodate this procedure. An active trader will probably be able to negotiate substantial commission discounts. The larger the investment, the easier it will be to lower costs. And the closer an investor follows the market, the more successful his results will probably be in using convertibles.

The most desirable convertible security to own is one that is issued by a company you like, that has a very low premium over conversion value, a decent yield advantage over the common stock, and is close to investment value. Find this and then everything should take care of itself.

M. Alden Siegel

Co-Op (Cooperative Ownership)

A cooperative is a form of real-estate ownership where a buyer purchases shares in a corporation, partnership, or trust that holds title to a building. Those shares entitle the buyer to live in one of the building units. Essentially, a co-op owner is a shareholder in a corporation whose main asset is a building. Instead of receiving stock in the corporation, the owner is allowed to occupy a specific unit in the structure by way of a proprietary lease. Since the buyer occupies under lease and does not own the unit outright, he does not acquire his own individual mortgage, but assumes a proportionate share of the blanket mortgage that finances the entire building. However, the owner's interest in the co-op is still treated as personal property.

Each unit owner is required to pay his or her pro-rata share of the corporation's expenses, including mortgage charges, real-estate taxes, maintenance, payroll, and so on. The owner is allowed a tax advantage on his or her share of taxes and interest charges as long as 80% of the cooperative's income is derived from "co-op" tenant/owner rentals.

There are differences between co-op and condominium ownership. In a CONDOMINIUM, each unit is individually owned and an owner's voting power in the condominium association is relative to the size or value of the owner's unit and the percentage of common interest. In a co-op, the corporation owns the actual building. The co-op tenant holds a proprietary lease, a corresponding number of shares in the corporation, and is usually allowed only one vote per unit.

Co-op tenants, under proprietary lease, are more restricted in the use of their units than condominium owners. Since they buy their individual units, condo owners can usually resell them at a later time to any qualified buyer they wish. In contrast, co-op owners must obtain approval from the co-op's board of directors before actually selling or leasing their units to other individuals.

There are different financial responsibilities as well. While condominium owners do have individual mortgages on their units (if they have not paid in cash), they do not have any legal responsibilities for the mortgage on their building as a whole. Also, since condominium owners get their own financing and hold responsibility for their individual property-tax assessments, they are not responsible for any default on another's mortgage or property taxes. However, in a co-op arrangement, when a tenant/shareholder (owner) does not pay his or her mortgage or tax payments, the other shareholders are responsible. If they do not cure the default, the entire building can be sold for taxes or foreclosed under the blanket mortgage. This liability on the part of all the owners is one drawback of the cooperative ownership of real estate. For protection, many co-ops charge an additional monthly fee to set up a reserve fund to cover the property taxes.

There are three basic co-op arrangements. In *market-resale co-ops,* shares are purchased and sold at whatever prices the market will bear. In *par-resale co-ops,* shares are bought and sold at a fixed price regardless of inflation. In *controlled-resale* or *limited-equity co-ops,* the amount of appreciation allowed per share is tied to the federal consumer price index or some other barometer, thereby ensuring that resale prices remain affordable.

Harley W. Snyder

Corporate Bond Investments

See UNIT INVESTMENT TRUSTS.

Corporate Bonds

Corporations have borrowed money for decades to finance a variety of activities. A primary debt vehicle for raising money to meet longer-term needs has been the corporate bond. While the issuers of corporate bonds are often household names, the features of individual issues and the mechanics of the market for corporate bonds are often less familiar. A review of the basic features of corporate bonds and their market can provide the foundation for investment in this dynamic vehicle.

Corporate Bond Issuers. Corporations have issued a significant volume of bonds on a regular basis over many years. At year-end 1982, in excess of $500 billion of corporate bonds were outstanding, representing more than 10% of all public and private debt in the U.S. economy. Bonds are issued by many types of corporations, as shown in Figure 1. The average size of a corporate bond issue is often several million dollars. Consequently, corporate bonds are generally issued by larger corporations: airlines, electric utilities, food companies, oil companies, railroads, telephone companies. Corporate bonds have been issued by many recognizable names: AT&T, Burlington Northern, Commonwealth Edison, Exxon, General Electric, IBM, Procter & Gamble, United Airlines.

Corporate Bond Investors. The investors in corpo-

Figure 1. Issuers of corporate bonds (estimated average annual distribution, 1978–82).

Figure 2. Investors in corporate bonds (estimated outstanding, as of year-end 1982).

rate bonds are as varied as the issuers of these investments. Figure 2 shows the broad distribution of corporate-bond investors. While the direct participation of the individual investor is relatively small, indirect participation through the other categories is quite large. Corporations investing in corporate bonds are dominated by insurance companies, particularly life-insurance companies that are investing the premiums received from their individual policyholders. Public and private pension funds are by far the largest institutional investors in corporate bonds as they seek to provide retirement income for many individuals.

The dominance of the corporate bond market by larger corporate and institutional investors reflects the investment characteristics of corporate bonds. This dominance in turn influences the structure of corporate bonds themselves and their market.

The interest income from corporate bonds is subject to ordinary income taxes at the federal, state, and local levels. The dominance of the corporate bond market by certain institutional and corporate investors is understandable in that these investors are either exempt from income taxes or subject to very low tax rates. Consequently, the individual investor subject to higher income-tax rates will often choose municipal bonds rather than corporate bonds.

The generally larger size of issuer and investor has resulted in a market for corporate bonds that requires a higher commitment of capital than that needed for investment in other securities. While individual corporate bonds are generally available in multiples of $1,000, round-lot transactions are in multiples of $100,000.

Corporate Bond Markets. Corporate bonds are available in two general marketplaces: the primary (new-issue) market and the secondary market. The initial offering of a corporate bond is transacted in the primary or new-issue market. Corporate bonds are generally offered to investors by a securities dealer or dealers. In a public offering, any investor can purchase corporate bonds through an initial offering. During the initial offering period, which can last from five to ten business days, investors will pay the same price for a specific bond issue. Corporate bonds can also be offered on a private or direct-placement basis. In this type of offering, the issuer may offer the bonds either through a securities dealer or through direct contact with investors. The investors in direct placements are generally larger corporate and institutional investors.

From the time of initial offering to the time of final payment, corporate bonds can be purchased and sold in the secondary market. Corporate bonds traded in this market are generally issues that were initially sold in a public offering in the primary market. Issues sold on a direct-placement basis do not benefit from an active secondary market.

While many bonds are listed and traded on national securities exchanges, the overwhelming majority of secondary corporate-bond transactions are conducted in an over-the-counter market. A corporate bond can trade both on an exchange and over-the-counter. Consequently, the reported price on an exchange may not be representative of all secondary transaction prices. In the over-the-counter market, securities dealers buy and sell corporate bonds among all types of investors. Corporate-bond transactions on the national exchanges are subject to a commission schedule. In the over-the-counter market, the cost of transactions is the difference between the price paid to the seller (bid price) and the price paid by the buyer (offered price). The difference between bid and offered prices is fully negotiable and subject to a variety of market conditions.

Corporate Bond Features. Corporate bonds are available with a vast assortment of investment features. Bonds can be purchased with high coupon rates or with no coupon rates; with a one-year term to maturity or a 40-year term to maturity; with call, sinking fund, put, or extension provisions; with conversion features that permit exchange of the bond for other securities. The interaction of these investment features has an important influence on the performance characteristics of a corporate bond over the period from initial offering to actual maturity.

The primary source of information with respect to the many features of an individual corporate bond is the prospectus. This document is prepared and made available to the investor at the time of an issue's initial offering. The SECURITIES AND EXCHANGE COMMISSION (SEC) regulates both the contents of the prospectus and its distribution. While prospectuses are often not readily available for corporate bonds that are transacted in the secondary market, investors can obtain information from other sources. Moody's Investors Service, Inc., and Standard & Poor's Corporation publish documents that can be purchased by any investor. These documents usually summarize the key features of a corporate bond. In addition, many securities dealers who participate in the corporate bond markets prepare documents describing bond features.

Corporate Bond Quality. An investor in a corporate bond relies on the promise of the issuing corporation to make some specific future payments. The ability of the corporation to make these payments is referred to as the "credit quality" of the corporation. Most outstanding corporate bonds have been assigned ratings by one or more of the rating agencies. A bond rating reflects the rating agency's assessment of the issuing corporation's ability to meet its obligations.

The quality of an individual corporate bond also reflects the position of the bond relative to other debt the corporation has issued. First-mortgage bonds generally benefit from a more secure position than debentures. Senior debentures are more secure than junior debentures. Subordinated debentures are less secure than straight debentures. The primary source of information for determining the relative position of a corporate bond is the *indenture.* This often lengthy legal document describes in detail the rights and obligations of the bondholder and the issuing corporation. The rating agencies will consider these factors in assigning a bond rating.

Corporate Bond Investing. Corporate bonds are an appropriate investment for many portfolios. To benefit fully from this vehicle, the investor should undertake a rather thorough analysis of a corporate bond's investment features and quality. Having acquired this knowledge, the investor should compare the yield available from this bond to the yield available from alternative bonds (corporate, federal-government, or municipal). The relevant measure of yield should be selected, whether current yield, yield to maturity, after-tax yield, or compound yield. The investor can choose from a large selection of bonds at any time. These bonds will have different investment features and will be offered at different prices and yields. While some features have direct implications (e.g., lower-quality bonds should provide higher yields than higher-quality bonds), the actual differences in prices and yields reflect the values assigned by investors to these features. In many respects, these values are the result of subjective judgments or opinions.

The mechanics of investing in corporate bonds have been simplified somewhat in recent years. Corporate bonds are generally issued in registered form, which ensures direct payment of interest and final principal to the registered bondholder. Many corporate bonds are now handled through central depositories, which reduce the cost and risks of handling the actual certificates. The investor can also minimize not only the mechanics of investing in corporate bonds but also the required analysis of individual issues by investing in bond mutual funds. These mutual funds generally offer participation in a diversified portfolio of corporate bond issues that are selected by a professional adviser.

Whether investing in corporate stocks or corporate bonds, the investor should determine his particular investment requirements with respect to both objectives and time frame. The suitability of an investment in corporate bonds and the degree of emphasis to be placed on individual bond features and quality can then be determined. This foundation will help assure success in corporate-bond investment.

Timothy A. Schlindwein

Corporations

See BUSINESS ORGANIZATIONS, FORMS OF.

Correspondent Bank

A bank that holds account balances of other, smaller banks and provides services to those banks, such as check collection, primarily through those accounts.

The American banking system is characterized by extensive correspondent banking relationships. Before the establishment of the Federal Reserve banks in 1914, small respondent banks relied on correspondents as depositories for their reserve funds and for check-collection services, primarily for deposited checks that were drawn on banks in other regions. After 1914, most respondent banks continued to rely on correspondents for check collection rather than dealing with the Federal Reserve directly. Until 1980, direct access to Federal Reserve check-collection service was limited to commercial banks that were members of the Federal Reserve system. Membership in

the Federal Reserve meant adherence to Federal Reserve reserve requirements, which were more costly—in terms of holding assets as non-interest-earning reserves—than those the states imposed on nonmember commercial banks. For this reason, most of the nation's smaller state-chartered banks (about 10,000 in 1982) were not members of the Federal Reserve system.

Over the decades, correspondent banks generally offered their respondents more liberal check-deposit deadlines than the Reserve banks, which meant quicker credit on presented checks than the credit granted by the Reserve banks. Correspondent banks also provided check-sorting and check-encoding services. Many banks that were members of the Federal Reserve used correspondents for check-collection service even though that meant maintaining a clearing account at a correspondent as well as a non-interest-earning reserve-account balance at the Federal Reserve, which could have been used for check-clearing purposes.

Today, most correspondent banks provide their respondents with a broad range of banking and payment services, including:

- Loan participations
- Backup lines of credit for respondents' customers
- Issuing of respondent banks' dividend checks to stockholders
- Maintenance of dividend reinvestment programs for respondents' stockholders
- Investment advice
- Analysis of respondent banks' operating problems.

Respondent banks typically pay for correspondent services either through direct charges or, implicitly, by being required to maintain a minimum account balance with the correspondent.

David H. Friedman

Cosigner

A person who endorses the signature of another, as for a loan or mortgage. Such person assumes equal liability.

Harvey Rachlin

Council of Economic Advisers

A council that advises the United States president on a wide range of domestic and international economic policy issues. Its members—a chairman, two council members, and a professional staff, consisting of economists, statisticians, and others—deal with such issues as federal credit programs; alternatives to federal regulation; federal housing programs; and economic statistics. The Employment Act of 1946, as amended, provides the statutory base for its activities.

Harvey Rachlin

Counterfeit Money

Most industries focus their research programs on finding easier ways to manufacture their products, but security printers are constantly concerned with developing more difficult and more intricate methods. Genuine currency is distinctive because it is made through a detailed process with special paper and ink. The complicated and careful procedures not only make the currency durable, but also provide protection against counterfeiters.

The most persistent problem for counterfeiters, even with the latest technological knowledge, is the unique style of the artist transmitted in the engraving process to each note. United States currency notes are printed by the engraved intaglio steel plate method, and each feature of the design—portrait, lettering, scrollwork, and the lacy geometric patterns—is done by an artist expert in his particular field. No photography enters into the creation of an engraved note, so that a camera can only picture a note and not make an actual duplication of it. A counterfeiter knows that a perfect counterfeit—one that would fool an expert—is practically impossible, so he must adopt a more modest objective. He tends to rely on his camera to produce work that will deceive an inattentive person.

Specially made paper is another important protection against counterfeiters. Its quality is far higher than paper generally available to the public and presents a difficult problem to would-be wrongdoers. Money paper has a particular feel, strength, a good appearance, and printability; it should have long life.

Can you spot a counterfeit? Perhaps the following suggestions, from the U.S. Secret Service, will show you how it is done.

1. *Study* genuine currency. Look closely at the workmanship of the features.

2. *Paper* used for genuine notes is very high quality. Small red and blue threads are in it, but may not be visible if the bill is badly worn or dirty. Counterfeit paper may feel different, or may be whiter than genuine paper. Threads may be imitated by fine red and blue lines made by a pen.

3. *Rubbing* a bill on a piece of paper is *not* a good test. Ink can be rubbed off genuine as well as counterfeit notes.

4. *Consult* an experienced money-handler if in doubt—a bank teller, for example.

5. *If you get a counterfeit bill,* (*a*) write your name and the date on the back of it, so you can identify it later; (*b*) write down all the details about how you got it: *who* gave it to you? *where* did you get it? *when* did you get it? (*c*) contact the nearest U.S. Secret Service office, the local police, a commercial bank, or any Federal Reserve bank.

Anyone convicted of passing a counterfeit may be fined as much as $5,000 or imprisoned for up to 15 years, or both.

Duane Kline

Coupon Stripping

Coupon stripping is a process in which securities are created by separating the individual coupon payments of a bond from the principal amount due at maturity. Each piece (coupon or principal) can then be sold as an individual investment, which takes the form of a zero-coupon bond (*see* ZERO-COUPON BONDS).

Coupon stripping generally involves U.S. Treasury issues, since the coupons from these issues can be physically detached from the principal payment. Several brokers have created pools consisting of stripped U.S. Treasury issues that are placed in custodianship with a bank. These pools have been given a variety of "feline" acronyms, such as TIGR, CAT, and LION. Certificates are sold that represent specific interests (ownership) in these pools.

Investments created through coupon stripping can be purchased through several major brokerage firms. Some issues are traded on the New York Stock Exchange.

These investments are of the highest quality, as they are, in fact, obligations of the U.S. Treasury. They also provide the investor with flexibility, since cash flows can be matched to actual cash needs, and their rate of return is assured if the investment is held to the actual payment date. However, they provide no actual income prior to the final payment date, and the market for resale may be less active than the market for unstripped (regular) U.S. Treasury issues.

Timothy A. Schlindwein

Covered Medical Expenses

Expenses for which a HEALTH INSURANCE policy will provide benefits. Expenses that are *not* covered include the deductible (*see* DEDUCTIBLE, HEALTH INSURANCE) amount and treatment for a PREEXISTING CONDITION, which may be subject to a policy exclusion or a waiting period. Typically, health-insurance policies will not provide benefits for medical procedures considered experimental or purely cosmetic, nor will they cover the cost of a telephone or rental television receiver in a hospital room.

James L. Moorefield

Credit

This term usually means the provision by a creditor of goods, services, or money to a person or legal entity for repayment at a later date, and sometimes means the forbearance of a previously existing debt, such as in a refinancing. A creditor is any person or legal entity to whom a debt is owed, whether a debt has arisen through the use of credit or from taxes, a legal suit, or other source. *Credit granter* is a generic term for any person or legal entity that extends credit, which consists of myriad forms, classes, and types.

For instance, commercial credit is commonly extended for use for business purposes. Consumer credit, by contrast, is any kind of credit extended for personal, family, or household purposes. It is extended by many types of credit *granters,* including unlicensed or unchartered sources, such as retailers and other vendors who provide sales credit, as well as by credit *grantors,* who are lenders licensed or chartered by governments to provide cash for consumer credit purposes. One of the primary characteristics of consumer credit is that it is extended to applicants on the basis of a promise to pay out of future income.

Credit makes it possible for consumers to have what they want when they want it and to pay for it in full in one payment or in installments, a series of partial payments, out of future income. People use it to fulfill every kind of human need from the cradle to the grave, from the obstetrician to the mortician. It is so prevalent in American society and available in so many different ways that some people will erroneously say that they never use credit. Some of them are simply unaware of it, and others seem to think they are using credit only when they repay in installments.

Consumer credit makes a constructive contribution to the overall economy of our nation and others by facilitating mass production, mass distribution, and mass consumption. It makes it possible for us to have, enjoy, and benefit from an ever-increasing range of goods and services that improve our standard of living, which we could not afford if we all had to pay cash on delivery for what we want or need. All of its many forms can be classed either as open-end credit, such as charge accounts, by which we buy convenience goods and services (known as "nondurables"), or as closed-end credit, such as the traditional installment credit, by which we buy automobiles and other "big ticket" items (known as "durables").

Service credit is a type of open-end credit that nearly every adult individual or family uses. It is extended by utility companies, doctors and other health-care sources, and many other credit granters who provide goods or services over a period of usually a month, and send a single itemized bill or statement for all charges once a month.

Charge accounts, offered by department stores and other retailers to the vast majority of Americans today, once were available only to the rich, but are now available to nearly anyone with a good credit reputation and the capacity to repay out of future wages, salary, or other reliable income. The original form of such accounts, known as the "monthly charge" or "30-day account," is still common, and may or may not involve the use of a credit card, but most frequently does.

But credit cards are most commonly issued in connection with what is known as "option credit" or "revolving accounts." Under them, a replenishing line of credit is extended to a customer, who has the option of paying in full on billing or paying at his or her option on an installment basis each month at or above a minimum amount required by the creditor, for from five months to as long as two years, with the line of credit being replenished as the customer repays for past purchases.

Some stores sometimes offer so-called budget accounts for persons of limited means. These accounts offer a continuous line of open-end credit that is small to moderate and is usually paid in regular fixed installments.

Today, about 85% of American individuals or families have credit-card charge accounts with retailers, banks, oil companies, travel and entertainment credit granters, and others. Since most people who use credit cards often have several, more than 550 million credit cards are reliably estimated to be in use, either regularly or at least sporadically to meet day-to-day needs and special or seasonal ones.

Like 30-day charge accounts, traditional installment sales credit is one of the oldest, yet most common, forms of retail credit. Usually this type of credit is used to buy a car, furniture, home appliance or other relatively expensive item, or an expensive service such as travel, a vacation, or education. Installment sales credit involves a single purchase or a series of purchases made at one time, a down payment or trade-in, fixed monthly installment payments, a fixed initial balance to be repaid, and a term of from 12 to 60 months for total repayment.

So-called scrip or coupon credit plans may be either charge-account credit or installment sales credit, depending on whether the customer owes the total value of the scrip or coupons issued by the creditor at the outset or as used, with replenishment on repayment for what has been used. Customers of these plans are aided in their budgeting by strictly limiting their maximum credit usage with the issuer of the scrip or coupons, which are used like money to make purchases on credit.

Personal loans are a form of installment cash credit in which money is supplied by the creditor to a customer for a specific purpose or for use in any manner the borrower may choose, and it is available these days either as open-end or closed-end credit. Often the money is paid to a third party on behalf of the borrower for a large purchase or other specific purpose. Bank credit cards, as well as others issued by third parties, can be used both to obtain goods and services and to borrow cash money.

For statistical and other purposes, consumer credit can be classified as short-term, intermediate-term, and long-term. Service credit and 30-day accounts are short-term credit. Revolving charge accounts, installment sales credit, and personal loans or other types of credit that can be repaid in more than 30 days but not more than 5 years are intermediate credit. But home-mortgage credit, including first and second mortgages, which must be paid in from 5 years to 30 or even 40 years, is classified as long-term credit. Home-mortgage credit can be cash credit to buy a home or other real property, or sales credit for the same purpose.

Consumer credit can also be classified as either secured credit or unsecured credit, depending on whether the written contract or agreement gives the credit granter the right to repossess or take over ownership personal or real property in the event that the debtor defaults in repayment of the debt.

Credit is never really "free," even though goods and services may be offered to customers at the same price for cash or credit. The cost of credit may be included in the price of goods or services, such as in 30-day accounts, or it may be a separate, specific finance charge, as is always the case with personal loans or home-mortgage credit.

The cost of credit is usually referred to as a finance charge, interest, or time-price differential, depending on the type of credit used and the laws under which the credit is extended. For the creditor, there are always some costs involved in making credit available to customers or borrowers. The creditor has the cost of financing the credit extended to customers; the costs of opening, controlling, and collecting each account; losses from customers who default; and other overhead expenses.

Retailers and other vendors offer consumer credit primarily to sell goods and services and to make a profit therefrom, even when the cost of credit is quoted as a cost separate from the price of the goods or services. Lenders, on the other hand, can make a profit and stay in business only from the finance charges paid by their customers. This charge is commonly called "interest," but, strictly speaking, interest is only the cost of "renting" money, whereas a "finance charge" involves all the costs of extending credit to customers, which they pay for the privilege of credit. For instance, you pay a part of the cost of a creditor's losses from the bad debts of others because the credit granter must recover these costs from "good-paying" customers in order to make a profit from total operations and stay in business.

Consumer credit makes it possible for those who use it to buy with greater flexibility and timeliness than they could with cash. Whether the cost of credit is included in the price of goods or services or as a separate charge, both cash customers and credit customers benefit from its use because volume sales create lower prices and a higher standard of living for everyone. Cash customers sometimes do subsidize the use of credit by others, but generally they do not, because they can buy cheaper than they would be able to if others did not buy on credit, especially when the credit seller offers the same price as is offered by those who sell for cash only.

James A. Ambrose

Credit Glossary

balance The amount that still remains to be paid in a credit transaction.

budget The systematic handling of money in terms of what is earned, what is saved, and what is spent.

capacity The ability of an individual to pay what he owes, measured in terms of how long he has worked, what he earns, and how permanent his employment seems to be.

capital The financial position of the individual, measured in terms of money and property.

charge account The privilege of using credit in making purchases in a retail store.

collateral Something tangible and of monetary worth which serves as a pledge that credit payments will be made.

collection The process of follow-up to make sure that payments are made as promised on any credit agreement.

conditional sales contract Any contract which provides that the seller retain title to goods sold and delivered to the purchaser until full payment has been made.

consolidation of bills The borrowing of a lump sum of money for the payment of past-due bills; the money that is borrowed is then repaid in installments.

consumer finance company A business firm whose

chief activity is to make cash installment loans to individuals or families.

credit analyst   An expert who determines by examining a person's present and past activities whether the person has earned credit.

credit application   The first step in establishing your credit record; a series of questions concerning your personal and work history.

credit investigation   The verification of the information you have provided in your credit application.

credit record   A complete and permanent record of your credit performance.

credit risk   A gauge of how well you will meet your credit responsibilities.

declining balance   A balance that decreases in the amount owed with each payment; the service charge is often computed on the declining balance.

discount   To deduct the service charge before giving the borrower the money in a personal loan.

distribution   The transmitting of goods and services from producer to consumer.

down payment   The initial sum of cash usually required in an installment purchase.

durable goods   Commodities used by the consumer over an extended period of time and frequently referred to as "hard goods." (Example: automobiles, televisions, radios, etc.)

financial institution   Any business organization engaged in the exchange of money for present or future use, including credit; for example, banks and finance companies.

future income   Earnings or other income that seem to be reasonably certain for some time to come.

hard goods   See *durable goods.*

installment credit   The use of credit that permits payment of specified amounts at stated intervals over a period of time.

mass production   The manufacture of large quantities of goods at the same time, resulting in low unit costs.

money management   The comprehensive financial planning of a household, taking into consideration income and expenditures, immediate and future needs.

open account   A charge account that permits credit purchase without down payment or service charge, and which is payable in full in 30 days.

option account   A charge account in which the consumer may choose either to pay at the end of 30 days or to spread payments over a longer period of time. If he chooses to spread his payments beyond 30 days, he pays a service charge.

outstanding   The amount a consumer owes on a credit transaction.

overhead   The expenses associated with the operation of any type of business: rent, utilities, salaries, etc.

pawnbroker   A person who will lend a small amount of cash, provided an item of personal property of requisite value is left in his possession as security.

personal loan   A cash sum lent directly to an individual to help him meet a personal expense; usually repaid in installments.

producer   Anyone directly or indirectly involved in growing, processing, or manufacturing goods or in making services available.

refinance   To reschedule a series of payments due on an installment contract so that the individual payments are smaller and are extended over a longer period of time.

repossession   Reclaiming by the legal owner of durable goods purchased on an installment contract, for which payment is long past due.

revolving credit   A type of charge account in which a limit is set on the amount that can be owed, and which requires a specified amount to be paid monthly.

sales finance company   A financial institution that extends installment sales credit.

service credit   A form of consumer credit used in payment of services from utility companies and for professional services.

small loan   A term sometimes used to designate a personal cash loan.

soft goods   Commodities that are used up by the consumer within a relatively short period of time; in contrast to "hard" or durable goods.

teen-age account   A limited amount of revolving credit some retail establishments make available to young adults, primarily to give them direct experience in money management.

terms   The conditions that apply to an installment sales credit transaction, including down payment, amount of periodic payments, length of contract.

title   Legal ownership.

trade-in   A used item of durable goods that is often accepted as part or all of the down payment in the installment-credit purchase of a new item.

Source: International Consumer Credit Association.

Credit Bureau

A clearinghouse of factual consumer credit information used by businesses extending credit to determine the CREDITWORTHINESS of consumers.

"Buy now, pay later" has become so popular in the

United States that virtually any product or service can be purchased on credit if the consumer can qualify for it. Companies that offer goods and services on credit are generally referred to as "credit granters," and it is these credit granters that commonly use the information in credit-bureau files to make credit-granting decisions.

The credit bureau neither recommends nor decides who qualifies for credit. The credit-granting decision is made only by the credit granter.

The information contained in a consumer's credit-bureau record is objective data that summarizes the consumer's bill-paying habits. This information does not include anything about a consumer's life-style, morals, personal habits, or any other subjective information that has no direct affect on the individual's bill-paying habits.

The information in consumer credit records comes generally from three sources. Some of it comes from the consumer as the result of a credit application, such as name, address, former address, spouse's name, employer, former employer, etc. Some of it comes from public records reflecting legal actions that might affect a consumer's ability to meet fiscal obligations, such as bankruptcy, court judgments, etc. But the "heart" of a credit report is the listing or historical record the consumer has established with his creditors over a period of time. These data come directly and regularly from credit granters to the credit bureau for a comparatively constant and updated flow of bill-paying information.

Most, though not all, credit granters regularly report consumer bill-paying records to the credit bureau. This exchange of information through the clearinghouse of the credit bureau has made it possible for large numbers of business and professional firms to make reasonable credit-granting decisions and thus to make credit available to most consumers.

If a consumer's bill-paying record is acceptable to a credit granter, it is not uncommon for him to be granted credit even though other information, such as place of employment or most recent address, is not current. However, when a consumer applies for a large loan, home mortgage, or a certain type of charge card, the credit granter usually will require the consumer to provide updated information about income, employment, address, etc., and will ask the credit bureau to verify these data. When that occurs, the new, updated information will be entered in the consumer's credit record at the credit bureau and will be available to other credit granters as needed.

Fair Credit Reporting Act. The Fair Credit Reporting Act of 1971 (FCRA) was passed by Congress to establish minimum and uniform standards for the protection of consumer privacy, to allow consumer access to credit-bureau records, and to provide consumers with a measure of control over the accuracy of information maintained in credit-bureau files.

Associated Credit Bureaus, Inc., the credit-reporting industry's trade association, had already established policies similar to those in the act, but the Fair Credit Reporting Act provided a legal mandate that required all credit bureaus to live up to these standards, even those bureaus that were not members of the trade association.

Among the most significant provisions of the act are those that allow consumers access to their credit records and the right to have them corrected.

A consumer has the right to review his credit record anytime. Arrangements for this review can be made by telephone or in person. The credit bureau can make a nominal charge for this unless the consumer was denied credit within the previous 30 days and the denial was based even partly on credit-bureau data.

If, in reviewing his credit record, a consumer finds what he believes to be an error, the credit bureau must reinvestigate without charge. If the information proves to be in error, it will be deleted. The consumer can then request that credit granters that have recently received this information be provided with the corrected or revised data. Occasionally, a consumer challenges the accuracy of a particular item of information that the credit granter insists is correct. In that case, the law allows the consumer to enter a brief statement disputing that particular item, and the bureau must then report the dispute to any other credit granter receiving future credit reports.

The FCRA limits the time in which adverse information may be reported on an individual. Except for bankruptcy, which can be reported for up to ten years, adverse information about a consumer can be reported for only seven years. Positive information may be reported indefinitely.

Although the act does not require credit bureaus to provide consumers with written copies of credit reports, many credit bureaus do so, and the trade association had endorsed this practice for its members.

The FCRA specifies the permissible purposes for a credit report and limits access to credit reports for the protection of consumer privacy. Only businesses that meet the law's criteria may purchase reports from the credit bureau, which maintains many of its own procedures for protecting consumer privacy and the integrity of credit information.

The FCRA also strictly limits government access to consumer credit reports. Generally, government agencies may obtain only identifying information from a credit report, such as name, address, former address, place of employment. Under certain circumstances, government access to a credit report may be allowed when a government agency is considering a consumer for credit, a special license, a security clearance, for employment or insurance, or for account review or collection purposes.

Private-sector businesses can obtain credit reports only for legitimate reasons, such as credit granting, review, or collection of an account, or for employment considerations or insurance purposes.

Obtaining a credit report from a credit bureau for purposes other than those specified by law is punishable by imprisonment, fine, or both.

Equal Credit Opportunity. A federal law called the Equal Credit Opportunity Act was passed by Congress in the mid-1970s to assure that consumers would be considered for credit only on the basis of their creditworthiness and not be judged on the basis of race, age, sex, or marital status.

One of the major purposes of this act is to assist married women in establishing their own credit histories. At one time, a shared or joint account used by both a husband and wife was generally listed in credit-bureau records under the husband's name. This law requires that a shared or joint account be listed for both spouses.

It is up to the consumer to make certain that credit granters are aware that an account is shared or joint and that credit granters report this fact to the credit bureau. Otherwise, the credit bureau has no way to know unless the credit granter reports the account in both names.

The law also allows a woman to have a joint account with her husband carried in any legal name she desires, but it should be consistent with all other accounts in her name.

If a woman is divorced or widowed, then the credit record she established with her husband in joint or shared accounts will become a part of her own credit history. This, of course, can include both good and poor credit history. She must also be aware that credit granters will want to be assured of sufficient income to accommodate any future credit she applies for if the previous credit was based primarily on income generated by her husband. All other considerations aside, the law says income or the capacity to pay as agreed must be the prime consideration in the granting of credit.

Credit Denial. Credit granters deny applications for a wide variety of reasons. Each credit granter has its own standards or criteria for granting credit, and these criteria not only may differ from one credit

granter to another, but may also differ when general or local economic conditions undergo major changes. Any given credit granter may be more liberal in its credit-granting policies when economic times are good, and more conservative when they are bad.

When a consumer is denied credit, the law requires the credit granter to give the consumer the name and address of the credit bureau from which it obtained any information used in making that decision. The consumer can then review his or her credit record at the credit bureau, as stated previously, at no charge within 30 days.

This review may indicate some obvious reason for the credit granter's denial, such as a long-overdue balance. It may also show that there is some adverse information on file that the consumer does not believe is correct. If so, the credit bureau will reverify it and correct it if it proves erroneous. The bureau will also notify the credit granter if the information proves erroneous and if the consumer asks that the credit granter be notified. That way, the credit granter may have the opportunity to reconsider the application.

If a review of the credit record indicates no obvious reason for the denial based on the consumer's credit-paying history, this could mean that the credit application was denied for other reasons.

Federal law provides that credit denials be made in writing to consumers. The credit granter may provide one or more specific reasons for the denial with the notice that credit has been denied. If the reasons are not provided with the denial notice, then the credit granter is required to inform the consumer that he or she has a right to request these specific reasons.

Finally, it should be noted that a credit denial is not recorded at the credit bureau. In other words, the credit granter does not report to the credit bureau that it considered an individual for credit and decided not to grant credit to that consumer.

For further information, *see* CREDIT DENIAL.

Credit Rating. The term *credit rating* is one that most people are familiar with. But, interestingly enough, it has no relation to the information maintained in today's credit-bureau records.

At one time, many years ago, before credit was so widely used, consumers were classified in rather inexact terms, such as *slow pay, fast pay,* and so forth. But as credit became more common, it became obvious to the industry that such terms were both inappropriate and insufficient to describe the activity of an increasingly diverse population base.

The credit industry, led by Associated Credit Bureaus, Inc., then devised a system of simple numbers, from 1 through 9, to indicate the general manner of payment of consumer accounts. A 1 indicated that an individual normally paid his account within 30 days; a 2 indicated payment within 60 days; and so forth through 9, which indicated a "bad debt." At no time did the credit bureau assign such numbers to consumer accounts—the numbers were assigned only by credit granters.

This system, termed the "common language of credit," served the industry and the consumer public well for a time. But as extending credit became more complex and as credit granters developed more sophisticated and individualized internal systems and controls, it became obvious that even the "common language" system could not meet the requirements of credit granters and the needs of consumers. Therefore, during the 1970s, Associated Credit Bureaus, in consultation with the nation's credit granters, developed a system of credit reporting based strictly on the historical record. As the "common language" system is phased out, the historical-method system, which the industry calls "Crediscope," has come into more general use.

The Crediscope system is a model of simplicity and objectivity. Each account for each consumer shows clearly and simply whether the account has been past due or paid on time over a given period of months. If there is any past-due amount recorded, the history indicates if and how many times it has been past due 30 days, 60 days, 90 days, or more. There is no numerical value assigned, even by the credit granter that reported the account to the bureau. As in earlier types of credit reports, the Crediscope system also shows the date and method of reporting, date the account was opened, date of last payment, highest or last contract, balance owed, type, and terms.

The Crediscope system helps eliminate the notion that an account will be, in effect, summarized by the use of a single digit or symbol. If the use of such single-digit or numerical-symbol evaluation ever contributed to the concept of the term *credit rating,* then it is safe to say that the term *credit rating* is no longer relevant.

See Figure 1 (page 180).

D. Barry Connelly

Credit Card

A plastic card, issued by a bank or other financial institution, that permits the holder access to a line of CREDIT that may be used to purchase goods or services or to obtain cash. Repayment of the balance may be required in full after 30 days or may be made in installments.

History. Credit cards came into widespread use in the United States in the mid-1960s when hundreds of banks across the country began issuing them to their customers. However, the history of credit cards in America dates back to the early 1900s when Western Union issued a simple metal plate to a selected number of its patrons. Holders of these plates were assured of prompt, courteous attention, as well as the convenience of deferred payment. Within a few years several hotels, department stores, oil companies, and railroads were also issuing "metal money" to preferred customers.

The first travel and entertainment card was introduced in 1950 by Diners Club. This card provided travelers with a convenient payment device for use at hotels, restaurants, airlines, etc. The following year Franklin National Bank in New York issued the first actual bank credit card—a card that could be used by bank customers at a wide variety of local merchants. Within two years, nearly 100 other banks had entered the field.

While the cards provided a useful service to both cardholders and merchants, the problem was that acceptance of each bank's card was limited to a relatively small geographic area. In the mid-1960s, therefore, banks began linking their card programs. In 1965 the Bank of America began licensing other banks in the U.S. and eventually abroad to issue cards bearing the BankAmericard name and/or the distinctive blue, white and gold bands. Now a bank customer could use his Blue, White and Gold card even when he traveled out of state. The following year, groups of banks in the Midwest and on the East Coast formed card associations to accomplish the same thing. Out of these two movements were born the present Visa and MasterCard systems.

In 1970 the Bank of America transferred administration of the Blue, White and Gold card program to a new company, National BankAmericard, Inc., a membership corporation owned and operated by the former Bank of America licensees. In March 1977 the new company formally changed its name to Visa.

MasterCard, formerly Master Charge, evolved from a merger of a number of major regional bank-card associations, including the Western States BankCard Association, which owned the name Master Charge, and Interbank, an association of 14 eastern banks.

By 1983 approximately 100 million Americans carried Visa or MasterCard or both. Both systems are also international, with a combined total of more than 170 million cards outstanding. The reason two large systems grew out of many smaller ones was the need to provide cardholders with payment devices that would be accepted all over the world, just as were the major travel and entertainment cards, American Express, Diners Club, and Carte Blanche.

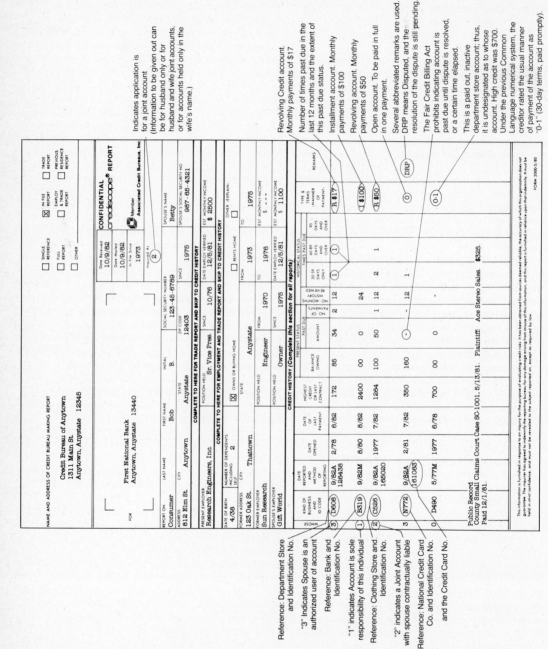

Figure 1. Sample credit report. (*Source:* Associated Credit Bureaus, Inc.)

Structure. Both Visa and MasterCard are membership organizations, jointly owned by member financial institutions. Visa is headquartered in San Francisco, California, and MasterCard is headquartered in New York.

Neither organization actually issues cards. Cards are issued by member institutions to their own customers. That's why virtually all Visa cards and MasterCards bear the names and logos of commercial banks, savings and loan associations, savings banks, or credit unions. It is the member that establishes credit policies, credit limits, interest rates, billing practices, etc. It is also the member financial institution that contracts with merchants to accept one or both cards. The merchants pay a fee to their bank, averaging about 2.5% of each transaction.

The two card organizations administer the card programs on a worldwide basis. One of their most important functions is to provide a sophisticated computer telecommunications and processing network so that cardholder purchases can be authorized and members can settle accounts among themselves (see below). The two organizations also actively develop new products, provide marketing support for members, establish and enforce operating rules, and settle disputes among members.

Anatomy of a Card Purchase. Operationally, the two systems are similar. So, with the Visa system as an example, let's examine a typical purchase, using a cardholder from California with a card issued by a California bank making a purchase in Chicago from a merchant who has a contract with a Chicago bank.

The cardholder purchases a $100 jacket and presents his card to the clerk for payment. Because the purchase exceeds a specified amount called the "floor limit," the clerk must have the purchase authorized by the bank that issued the card. The clerk calls the Chicago bank's processing center and gives the cardholder number and the amount of the purchase to an operator who is sitting at a computer terminal. The operator feeds the information into a computer and it is transmitted over phone lines to a Visa operations center on the West Coast. If the California bank is still open or provides 24-hour service, the request for authorization is automatically switched to the bank. There the purchase is approved and a message is sent back over the same route to the Chicago merchant. The entire process takes only a few seconds.

Once the purchase is approved, the clerk places the card in an imprinter, which prints the cardholder's name and account number on a sales draft, which the cardholder signs. One copy of the draft is given to the cardholder, and the transaction is complete. The mer-

chant keeps one copy for his records and turns one copy back to his bank.

When the bank receives the draft, it credits the merchant's account with the amount of the purchase less a small fee. The information on the sales draft is then entered onto a computer tape and later transmitted to a Visa operations center where accounts are settled between the California and Chicago banks. The system would operate essentially the same way if the cardholder used his card in New York, London, Cairo, Singapore, Sydney, or anywhere else in the world.

Types of Credit Cards. There are basically two types of credit cards—secured and unsecured.

Secured credit cards are issued by a variety of institutions, many of which are savings and loan associations. They normally carry a line of credit that is equal to or represents some fraction of an amount of money the customer has on deposit with the institution. If the customer fails to pay his bill, the institution may withdraw funds from his account to cover the amount owed.

The overwhelming majority of credit cards issued in the U.S. are of the *unsecured* variety. Essentially, the financial institution grants the customer a credit line that typically ranges from $1,000 to $3,500. The cardholder need not pledge any assets to obtain this type of credit card.

In recent years a large number of financial institutions have begun offering premium Visa or MasterCard credit cards to their higher-income customers. (Although requirements vary widely from one institution to another, normally to qualify for such a card the customer must have an annual income of $30,000 or more.) These cards carry a minimum spending limit of $5,000 and offer holders many other travel-related services as well.

Other Products. Over the years, both organizations and their members have developed other kinds of cards.

Debit Cards. A debit or "deposit-access" card works very much like a credit card. The major difference is that rather than giving the cardholder access to a line of credit, it gives access to the value of assets already owned by the cardholder. Typically, at the point of sale, the card electronically transmits funds that the customer has on deposit in a checking or savings account to the seller's account. However, there are cards that also transmit funds held in a money-market fund or the value of funds held in stocks, bonds, equity in home mortgages, life-insurance policies, or other assets.

In the Visa system, these cards look exactly like

credit cards. MasterCard debit cards normally bear the logo MasterCard II on the front. In either case they work at the point of sale exactly like credit cards. Merchants follow the same procedures and the authorization and settlement process is the same.

The major difference from the cardholder's point of view is that instead of getting a bill at the end of the month that he can elect to pay in total or in installments, funds are deducted directly from his checking or other deposit account. In this respect debit cards function like plastic checks.

Most debit cards linked to checking accounts have an overdraft line of credit attached so that cardholders don't have to worry about having a transaction turned down because they are out of funds. However, it is up to the financial institution to decide whether to grant such a line of credit.

ATM Cards. From 1971 to 1983, banks installed about 40,000 AUTOMATED TELLER MACHINES (ATM's) that customers may use to obtain cash or make other routine banking transactions both during and after banking hours. Although often Visa cards and Master-Cards can be used to obtain cash from these machines, most banks also issue special plastic cards to give access to ATM's. Approximately 70 million Americans carried such cards by 1983. Right now such cards are usable only in ATM's, but Visa recently announced a new program that will enable financial institutions to place a new Visa service mark on these cards so that their customers can use them at merchants around the world who have special electronic terminals that can be linked into the Visa authorization network.

Why Get a Card? There are a variety of reasons why people obtain credit or debit cards. Among the most important are the following:

Economic identification: The main function of a credit or debit card is to identify a buyer to a seller, and a seller to a buyer. If a customer has a credit or debit card, the merchant has some assurance that the individual is able to pay for the goods or services he is purchasing. Indeed, it is very difficult to obtain some services, such as automobile rentals, unless you have a card.

Money management: A great many people use their credit cards as a tool to manage their monthly finances. They charge a number of purchases during the month, and when the bill comes in from their bank, they need only write one check to cover the entire amount. This practice is far more common than most people realize. Indeed, fully 50% of the dollar amount charged on Visa cards, for example, is paid off in full each month. The rest is paid in installments.

Convenience and safety: The cards also provide consumers with a convenient method of making purchases. A consumer who carries a card has less need to carry large amounts of cash or a checkbook. If cash is lost or stolen, it is gone forever. If a card is lost or stolen, the consumer has substantially more protection (see below). Having a card also allows a consumer to take advantage of special sales or to make a large purchase that he or she would otherwise have to defer. In addition, consumers have a great deal of flexibility when it comes to repayment of credit-card balances. One can choose to repay the entire balance immediately, or over several months, or over many months or even years. In general, consumers have demonstrated that they are careful and prudent in the use of credit cards and they do not overextend themselves. Nearly 97% of the charges made on credit cards are paid back on time.

How to Get a Card. As noted earlier, Visa and MasterCard are issued by financial institutions that are members of those two systems. To obtain a card, you normally must apply to a financial institution. Banks are no longer permitted to send unsolicited credit cards through the mail. Some banks do market cards through the mail, but to obtain one, the consumer must specifically request it. When you apply for a card, you are asked to fill out a credit application. After your credit has been checked, the financial institution decides whether to issue the card and assigns a credit limit.

To obtain the travel and entertainment cards—American Express, Diners Club, Carte Blanche—the consumer applies directly to the company.

Interest Charges. The amount of interest a financial institution may charge on credit-card purchases is governed by state law. Although there are some exceptions, banks typically charge 18–20% annually on that portion of a cardholder's bill that is not paid within 25 or 30 days after the statement date. If the consumer pays his bill in full within that time, he incurs no finance charge. Finance charges, however, are usually levied on cash advances from the date the cash advance was made. Most banks also charge an annual fee of from $10 to $20 for each card in those states that permit annual fees. Premium card fees typically range from $25 to $50.

Travel and entertainment cards are really charge cards and the holder is expected to pay his bill in full each month. There are some purchases, however, on which consumers may elect to defer payment, such as airline tickets. In that case the card company levies a finance charge much the same as a bank.

Consumer Protection. Federal laws protect consumers against unauthorized use of their credit and debit cards. The most important aspect of these laws is that they limit the consumer's liability to $50 in the event that his credit card is lost, stolen, or used without proper authorization.

In the case of a debit card, the same $50 maximum applies, but only if the cardholder reports the loss of the card to the issuer within two business days after discovering the loss. If the cardholder allows more than two days to elapse before notifying the issuer, he could be liable for up to $500 in losses. The consumer can be liable for unlimited losses if he fails to notify the issuer within 60 days after an unauthorized transaction first appears on his statement.

The law also gives the consumer the right to contest unauthorized charges and provides legal protection in disputes with merchants.

Richard A. Rossi

Credit Denial

This term usually means rejection of a credit application by a credit granter, but sometimes means refusal to extend the type or amount of credit requested when the creditor in the ordinary course of business extends such credit or such amounts of credit. It does not mean termination of a charge account or other open-end line of credit because of delinquency or default in repayment, nor is there a denial of credit when authorization of an over-limit charge purchase for a customer is refused.

Consumer-credit granters have the right to deny credit to anyone for any reason, except by reason of discrimination prohibited by the Equal Credit Opportunity Act, federal civil-rights laws, or state antidiscrimination laws. The ECOA itself prohibits discrimination in both commercial and consumer credit on the basis of sex, marital status, age, race, religion, national origin, or receipt of public-assistance benefits. This law is implemented by Regulation B, issued by the Federal Reserve Board, which sets out "ground rules" for creditors with respect to what types of credit conduct are forbidden. Discrimination in home-mortgage credit is prohibited by not only the ECOA but also certain federal civil-rights laws. The state laws, where antidiscrimination measures have been enacted, generally parallel the ECOA and federal civil-rights laws, but may be less enforceable.

Under the ECOA and Regulation B, a creditor is required to act on an application for credit within a reasonable time limit. If the application is denied, the creditor is obligated to notify the applicant within a time limit and to either give the consumer the reasons for the denial or tell the person where and how to have the reasons disclosed. Such disclosure is intended to prevent unlawful discrimination against an applicant, to educate that individual with regard to credit deficiencies, and to give the individual an opportunity to protest a credit denial that may be based on error.

Under the ECOA, an applicant who has been denied credit has the right to sue for civil liability penalties if the creditor has violated the law. In addition, a consumer who has been denied credit may file a complaint with the federal agency responsible for "policing" that creditor's compliance with the law. In giving notice to a rejected applicant, a creditor is obligated by the law to provide a notice that briefly sets forth ECOA rights and identifies the appropriate federal agency to contact for more information or to register complaints.

Credit denials are sometimes based wholly or in part on information that a creditor has obtained about the applicant from a CREDIT BUREAU, which is one of the consumer reporting agencies regulated by the federal Fair Credit Reporting Act or a similar, but more protective, state law. When an applicant is rejected for such cause, the creditor is obligated under these laws to give notice of this to the applicant and to provide the name and address of the credit bureau or other type of consumer reporting agency that provided the information.

The Fair Credit Reporting Act and similar state laws are intended to protect consumer privacy in the dissemination of information from reporting agencies such as credit bureaus. These laws set forth procedures by which credit-report information must be disclosed in full to a consumer and by which the consumer can challenge errors and not only get them corrected but also get a statement inserted in future credit reports to tell the consumer's side with respect to disputed accounts with creditors.

The Fair Credit Reporting Act not only protects personal privacy but also requires that consumer reporting agencies maintain reasonable procedures to ensure the accuracy of both objective and subjective information they compile about consumers and disseminate to creditors, employers, and insurance sources. This law also establishes eligibility to obtain credit information and consumer reports. It is enforced through the Federal Trade Commission and authorization of civil suits.

In most cases when an application for credit is rejected, the consumer is aware of the reason(s) before legally required disclosures have been made. But that will not be the case if the rejection is based on mistaken identity of the applicant, erroneous credit information supplied by a third party, or some other such reason. When a rejection is based on information received from a third party that is not a consumer reporting agency, under the Fair Credit Reporting Act the creditor is required to give written notice of that fact to the consumer, as is the case when the information came from a credit bureau or other consumer reporting agency. The creditor is not obligated to specifically identify the source of the information, but must indicate the nature of the information involved in the credit rejection and the type of creditor or other third party from which the information was obtained.

As is the case when a consumer is the victim of a billing error, a person who is rejected for credit should act promptly if he or she has reason to believe the denial of credit was unjustified. Credit is a privilege that creditors have the right to deny for any reason not prohibited by law. But they are in business to extend credit, not to reject applicants, so when a consumer requests reconsideration of an application for reasons that are not frivolous, even when the possibility of violation of law is not involved, creditors are usually willing to give reconsideration, but may sometimes require reapplication in connection with it.

Sometimes when credit is denied wholly or in part on the basis of a credit report, disclosure by a credit bureau will not reveal the reasons(s) for the denial. That is why is is important for a consumer to get from the creditor—and understand—the reason(s) for denial. If nothing else is accomplished, at least the consumer will be helped to a better understanding of the meaning of creditworthiness as it applies to requests for credit.

It is important for consumers to be aware of their rights and the obligations of creditors under various laws, but it is equally important for rejected credit applicants to realize that consumer credit is a highly competitive business where credit is offered by many sources. The rejection of an applicant by one creditor is a rejection by only one source, which may not be repeated if an application is filed with a competitor, especially when the applicant is a borderline risk or perhaps does not have the best kind of a credit history. Every creditor sets individual standards for creditworthiness. Some simply have easier policies than others, and some creditors are in business to serve higher-risk applicants.

James A. Ambrose

Credit Granter

See CREDIT.

Credit, How to Obtain

Consumer credit is usually made available whenever it is applied for or requested by a person with a good credit history who has the willingness and ability to repay as agreed. Ordinarily, it is denied only for just cause. The applicant may not have used credit sufficiently to develop a reliably good credit history, or may be asking for credit of the wrong type or in too great an amount, or may already have a debt burden that should not be enlarged, or some other problem that would lead a creditor to deny credit. What you can do if you are denied credit is discussed in the entry CREDIT DENIAL. This section is intended to deal primarily with the establishment of credit.

At the outset it should be clearly understood that credit is not a right, but rather a privilege that one must earn and that, after it has been obtained, should be safeguarded by paying as agreed so the privilege will be available in the future as personal or family needs arise. By contrast, a consumer-credit granter has the right to deny credit to anyone for many reasons, so long as rejection of an applicant does not involve discrimination prohibited by the Equal Credit Opportunity Act, federal civil-rights laws, or state antidiscrimination statutes.

Consumers should begin establishing credit as soon as they reach majority and have the legal right to contract for debts. Upon marriage, both men and women should continue to maintain separate credit histories for credit identification throughout their lives, because every marriage eventually terminates through the death of a spouse, divorce, or legal separation. Failure to maintain separate credit histories will not always eventually result in trouble getting credit, but it frequently happens.

Instead of viewing consumer credit as a personal or family financial-management tool, some people view the use of credit as a necessary evil; they pay cash for goods and services even when it would be better to use credit, and then they have more difficulty getting credit when it is a necessity than they otherwise would have.

When a young person reaches adulthood, his or her first goal should be regular employment and the establishment of a savings and/or checking account, unless the individual has already done so. This is a good beginning in establishing what are known in trade jargon as "character and capacity," always the most important factors leading to a favorable credit decision.

When a person who has not previously established and maintained a credit history begins to seek credit, he or she should first seek out credit sources of the right kind and inquire about policy with regard to persons who do not have established credit. Then an application for credit should be filed following an appropriate course of action, which may be filing with some other creditor.

Beginners will usually find it easier to get credit

from retailers than from cash lenders. First of all, retailers have easier credit policies because their aims are to sell merchandise and to create repeat business. Many would like to establish a lasting or even lifelong relationship with customers and they still want the cash business of those to whom they may not be willing to extend credit. So they are very considerate of all credit applicants and want to retain their goodwill even if they must deny credit. They usually will readily grant credit to a beginner and sometimes even to minors.

Cash lenders usually incur greater risk of problems in repayment than retailers because their extensions of credit usually involve larger amounts and because the use of credit by their customers is far less discretionary and often arises from financial distress. Consequently, they prefer to deal with people who have established and maintained at least some extended credit history by which they can adequately judge creditworthiness. But banks, other financial institutions, and finance companies need a broad base of customers to stay in business, want repeat business, and recognize that young people provide a very desirable base for future business, when both their credit needs and income will be greater.

When a person establishing credit cannot meet the creditworthiness standards of a creditor on his or her own merit, that person very often can obtain credit from the same source by getting a parent, relative, or other person in good financial standing to be a guarantor or COSIGNER. When repayment has been made, the person to whom the credit was extended is the person who has paid as agreed, thus establishing the beginning of a credit history that can be used to obtain additional credit.

Once established, credit will usually continue to be available unless application is made to the wrong type of source or for an excessive amount, or some other logical reason. It is always best to apply for new credit at sources you have previously used, because repeat business is particularly welcomed and processing is quicker and easier.

Credit is granted to consumers on the basis of a promise to pay out of future income. Denials frequently occur because applicants want more credit than they can repay with reasonable money management. Repayment usually comes from your disposable income (your "take-home" pay) and from your discretionary income, which is the amount of your income that is not already committed for repayment of other debts and to provide the day-to-day necessities of life for you and your family, if you have dependents whom you are supporting. Any applicant who has 15% or less of disposable income committed to repayment of consumer credit is usually regarded by

credit executives as lightly to moderately burdened. Applicants who have more than 25% committed are usually regarded as overburdened.

The weight of debt burdens in the midrange between 15% and 25% depends on individual characteristics of debtors, particularly their willingness to make sacrifices to repay if they should get into financial difficulty. Character, as evidenced by an individual's credit history, may be the deciding factor in whether credit will be extended or denied. Banks and other sources of cash credit, therefore, are sometimes willing to make "character loans" to applicants whose situations are such that they would not ordinarily qualify for credit.

It is always best to be frank and truthful in applying for credit; to seek the advice and counsel of creditors on the use of credit; and to follow that advice and, if you run into problems in repaying, seek aid from your creditors before you have become delinquent or are in default.

Obtaining credit is only the first step in its long-term use, which should be a mutually beneficial relationship based on trust.

James A. Ambrose

Credit Life Insurance

See LIFE INSURANCE.

Credit Line

This is a term used in connection with the extension of open-end credit plans to denote the maximum amount, or credit limit, that the creditor is willing to extend to an individual customer in the ordinary course of business.

In the bank-credit-card field, it is customary for a credit line or credit limit to be assigned to each credit-card account. The credit limit is either one that has been agreed on by both parties, one applied for by the customer and approved by the card issuer, or one assigned unilaterally by the issuer, based on evaluation of the creditworthiness of the account holder. Usually, to have a line of credit increased, you must request it, stating the credit limit you would prefer.

This process of setting account limits is also used by other open-end consumer-credit granters, but retailers usually set a credit limit for each account at the time an account is opened and then increase or decrease that limit, based on the history of use and payment of the account, with adjustments made from time to time, as appropriate.

When a retail charge-account customer makes small charges that exceed the assigned credit limit and pays as agreed, this indicates that the customer needs a higher credit limit and can handle repayment. If the customer wishes to make a larger purchase through a charge account, and the amount of the purchase exceeds a "floor limit"—an automatically approved amount—the purchase must be specifically approved by contact between the salesclerk and an "authorizer," a person who can approve or disapprove the sale on credit through quick access to information on the current status and past history of the account.

Some bank credit-card issuers are very strict about holding to the credit limits assigned to accounts, and sometimes revoke credit cards of persons who break their rules about exceeding credit limits. This is because they have less capability than retailers to control the use of accounts on an up-to-the-minute basis.

James A. Ambrose

Credit Rating

See CREDIT BUREAU.

Credit-Scoring Systems

When a person applies for consumer CREDIT, the creditor can evaluate the applicant's CREDITWORTHI-NESS by two different methods: judgmental evaluation or credit scoring. In the judgmental evaluation, an employee of the creditor will examine the application and other information obtained (credit-bureau reports, etc.) and draw on his personal experience to evaluate the applicant's creditworthiness. The other method, credit scoring, uses a numerical formula to evaluate creditworthiness.

The credit-scoring system assigns points to the information contained in the credit application. Some credit-scoring systems also assign points to the information contained in credit-bureau reports. For instance, a renter might receive 30 points and a homeowner 65 points for their housing status; a person with an annual income of $12,000 might receive 32 points while one with an income of $28,000 might receive 72 points; and people with poor payment histories in the credit bureau might lose 95 points while those with good payment histories might receive 67 points. Approximately 8 to 20 items are assigned points, and the total of the points is used to predict creditworthiness: The higher the total, the more creditworthy.

The creditor then sets a cutoff score that is the minimum acceptable score for receiving credit. In selecting the cutoff score, the creditor will often consider the approval rate, the predicted credit-loss rate, and sometimes the profitability of accounts with different levels of creditworthiness. Changes in the creditor's willingness to take risks and changes in the economics

of the credit product will cause the creditor to change cutoff scores.

Often the information contained in the application is scored first and credit-bureau reports are obtained for only those passing the first score cutoff. The credit-bureau information and the application information are then scored together, and those final scores are compared to a second score cutoff. Those passing the second cutoff are accepted for credit. In a few instances, those scoring very high on the first score are approved without obtaining credit-bureau reports.

The credit-scoring system is most often used as a management tool. In many instances, creditors also subject the application and credit-bureau report to a judgmental review and sometimes overrule the credit-scoring recommendation.

Usage. Credit-scoring systems are widely accepted and used today, with approximately 20–30% of all consumer credit applications being evaluated by such systems. Credit-scoring systems were first developed in the late 1950s, but they did not become widespread until the 1970s. Many large creditors (banks, retailers, finance companies, and oil companies) utilize credit scoring. These creditors believe that credit-scoring systems offer several advantages over judgmental systems—such as more accurate measurement of creditworthiness, better control over approval rates and credit losses, more efficient and less expensive evaluation of creditworthiness, and more consistency in their evaluations.

Credit-scoring systems have their limitations: They make mistakes just as judgmental systems do, and cost money to develop and utilize. Overall, however, most creditors believe that scoring systems allow a higher approval rate of applicants and a lower credit-loss rate than judgmental systems.

Legal Issues. Credit-scoring systems are regulated by Regulation B and its amendment, which implement the Equal Credit Opportunity Act. Regulation B defines both credit scoring and judgmental systems. It also provides general guidelines for the development of credit-scoring systems. Neither credit-scoring systems nor judgmental systems may consider the prohibited characteristics (sex, marital status, race, color, religion, national origin, receipt of income from public-assistance programs, and good-faith exercise of rights under the Consumer Credit Protection Act) in evaluating creditworthiness. Credit-scoring systems may assign points to the ages of applicants provided that elderly applicants (62 years and older) receive at least as many points for age as younger applicants. The judgmental process cannot directly consider the applicant's age. When an applicant is denied credit by a creditor utilizing credit scoring, the reasons provided by the creditor must relate to items actually scored by the credit-scoring system.

Development. These systems are developed by analyzing samples of the creditor's past applicants who turned out to be good payers, bad payers, and rejected applicants. Typical sample sizes are 1,500 good payers, 1,500 bad payers, and 1,500 rejected applicants. Statistical analysis programs utilize computers to determine the differences in characteristics of the good and bad payers. For instance, a creditor might find that 40% of the bad payers owned a home, while 68% of the good payers owned a home. Homeownership would thus be considered individually predictive of creditworthiness. Approximately 40 to 60 characteristics are examined. All characteristics that are individually predictive are analyzed simultaneously by the computer programs and points assigned to those characteristics that are predictive within the entire scoring system.

Each credit-scoring system is unique to the creditor. The characteristics that are predictive and the points assigned to the characteristics will differ with each system. Larger creditors often utilize several different systems for different credit products and different geographic areas.

Additional Uses. Scoring systems very similar to credit-scoring systems are also being utilized to aid consumer creditors in the areas of collections, solicitations, credit-line control, and purchase authorizations. In business credit, such models are starting to be used in commercial leasing, small business loans, and accounts-receivable factoring.

Gary G. Chandler

Credit Union National Association, Inc. (CUNA)

The national trade association for U.S. CREDIT UNIONS.

Credit unions have applied the basic principles of cooperation and self-help, which they follow in their own operations, to the state and national trade groups that serve their needs. Thus they have built large, full-service trade associations designed to meet as many of their business and financial needs as possible from within the credit-union movement.

The dominant national credit-union trade group is the Credit Union National Association, Inc. CUNA is a federation of the 52 state credit-union leagues. About 92% of the 20,000-plus credit unions in the U.S. are affiliated with their state leagues, and thus with CUNA.

Leagues have the primary responsibility for organizing new credit unions, carrying out state governmental-relations functions, conducting statewide advertising and public-relations programs, and performing many other services. In many of these areas, leagues cooperate closely with CUNA.

CUNA was formed by the leagues in 1934, shortly after the passage of the Federal Credit Union Act. Its principal job then, as now, was to promote the growth and development of credit unions throughout the U.S. It also provides a number of services typical of any trade association, such as legal counsel, economic and consumer research, lobbying, political action committee functions, political and legislative education, human-resource development, magazines and newsletters, public relations, and a national advertising program. In addition, CUNA has several affiliated corporations that provide a wide range of business and financial services required by credit unions. For example:

- The CUNA Service Group (CSG) develops and markets financial services, such as share drafts, credit cards, electronic fund-transfer systems, Individual Retirement Accounts, and other services. CSG concentrates primarily on those services that can be more efficiently developed on a national level than by individual credit unions. CSG also provides marketing and advertising materials and promotional items; forms; custom printing; and many other services for credit unions. A national data-processing and telecommunications network is currently under development to link the various parts of the credit-union movement. Most state credit-union leagues maintain service corporations that provide many of the same types of services to credit unions in cooperation with CSG. Common leadership structure and management link CUNA and the CUNA Service Group, as well as the U.S. Central Credit Union.
- The U.S. Central Credit Union is the central banking facility for the entire credit-union movement. With more than $7 billion in assets, it ranks among the largest financial institutions in the nation. It is owned and controlled by the credit union-movement and operates through a network of 42 corporate credit unions. The corporates act as regional or statewide correspondent financial institutions serving only credit unions. U.S. Central and the corporate credit unions are chartered by either the state or federal government and are democratically controlled by their members.
- The CUNA Mutual Insurance Group consists of five corporations providing all types of insurance services to credit unions and their members. As a

mutual company, CUNA Mutual is owned and controlled by the credit unions it serves. CUNA Mutual is the nation's largest provider of credit life insurance; more than 90% of U.S. credit unions use CUNA Mutual's insurance services.

- Other affiliated organizations provide retirement services, professional development, entry into the secondary mortgage market, national electronic fund-switching, and other services.

While credit unions remain free of purchase services from outside suppliers, in practice they turn to the leagues, CUNA, and their affiliated organizations for most of their needs. The reason for this all-encompassing structure lies in the fact that most credit unions are small, with less than $1 million in assets.

This national structure is controlled by the credit unions it serves. CUNA's 350-member board of directors is elected annually by credit-union representatives from each state. The board meets once a year to elect officers, approve a budget, and conduct other business. Board members also serve on various policy-review committees throughout the year. In addition, a smaller Executive Committee is elected on a regional basis to act between annual meetings.

Howard Cosgrove

Credit Unions

A credit union is a not-for-profit cooperative financial institution, owned and democratically controlled by its members.

Credit unions originally were created to provide a safe place for "average" people to save, and to give people a ready source of consumer credit at reasonable interest rates. That was in the days when banks were primarily concerned with their business customers and savings and loan associations concentrated only on home mortgages. There were few other legitimate sources of credit for the person of average financial means. Things have changed in the half-century since the Federal Credit Union Act authorized the creation of credit unions anywhere in the U.S. People today have many other sources for consumer loans and other financial services.

Credit unions have changed, too. Many have expanded their services to include transaction accounts (share drafts), savings certificates, credit cards, money orders, traveler's checks, mortgage loans, Individual Retirement Accounts, and money-market accounts.

But the basic structure and purpose of a credit union have remained the same. Credit-union leaders still consider themselves part of a "movement," not an industry. And they still consider the purpose of their organizations to be service, not profit. The spirit of mutual assistance is evident in the fact that more than half of all credit unions offer some kind of financial counseling to their members.

History. Credit unions started in 1848 in Germany as a means of financial self-help for farmers and small tradesmen whose only alternative source of credit was local moneylenders, who often charged usurious interest rates.

The original credit unions were based on six fundamental principles of cooperative organization, called the "Rochdale Principles" after an early cooperative organization in England. Modern credit unions still incorporate these basic principles:

1. Membership is restricted to a specific group of people.
2. Within that group, membership is open to all persons equally.
3. The members are the sole owners of the credit union.
4. The credit union is democratically controlled. Members elect the board of directors, officers, and committee members from among themselves.
5. Each member has one vote, regardless of how much money he or she has in the credit union.
6. All profits are returned to the members in the form of dividends on savings, rebates on loans, or improved services.

Structure. Members elect from among themselves a board of directors, a credit committee, and a supervisory committee. Other committees, such as an education committee, may also be formed. In nearly all credit unions, elections are held annually at a membership meeting, with no proxy voting.

The directors choose the officers from among their number. Directors, officers, and committee members serve without pay. The only exception is the treasurer. In smaller credit unions, the treasurer usually is the operating officer, working either full-time or part-time. In larger credit unions, the treasurer may serve as the full-time manager.

Membership. There were about 19,600 credit unions in the U.S. at the end of June 1983, with nearly 48 million members, $85.3 billion in savings, $52.4 billion in loans, and $95 billion in assets. The number of credit unions has fallen consistently since reaching a peak of 23,700 in 1970. The decline chiefly reflects a trend toward the merging of smaller credit unions into larger, more efficient units.

Since 1970, however, membership has more than doubled. Today, one adult in five is a credit-union member. Nearly 7% of the adult population now consider a credit union their primary financial institution—that is, the place where they do most of their financial business. Only 4% said the same in 1977.

The Common Bond. Every credit union's charter—whether state or federal—defines the group that may be served. This is referred to by credit unions as a "common bond." Anyone who shares the common bond may become a credit-union member by opening a share (savings) account for as little as $5.

More than 78% of U.S. credit unions are based on an occupational common bond—that is, the group served by the credit union works for a common employer or closely related employers.

About 17% have a common bond of association—such as membership in a church, labor union, or professional group—and 4% have community charters permitting them to serve a specific community or neighborhood.

Most early U.S. credit unions had community charters, as do nearly all credit unions elsewhere in the world. It was during the 1920s and 1930s that the occupational bond came to prevail in the U.S., because of the relative ease of organizing credit unions based on employment. That situation is now changing, as many credit unions seek community charters either because of plant closings or layoffs, or to achieve greater economies of scale. Many credit unions also are expanding by altering their charters to take in additional groups of members.

Since the first U.S. credit union opened its doors in 1909, credit unions have concentrated on paying members a fair return on savings and providing loans for productive purposes at reasonable rates. At the end of 1982, credit unions held 5.5% of consumer savings on deposit at financial institutions.*

Deregulation Expands Services. While consumer loans and regular savings plans are still at the heart of credit-union services, recent legislation and deregulation have given federally chartered credit unions the right to offer many new services, including savings accounts for any term and at any interest rate. State-chartered credit unions in the majority of states have been granted similar powers, through either legislation or regulation. The result has been a trend away from regular share (savings) accounts, which usually pay in the neighborhood of 6.5%, and toward higher-interest certificate and money market type accounts.

Insurance and Regulation. More than 99% of credit-union savings are covered by share insurance, in most cases to a limit of $100,000 per account. Federal insurance, through the NATIONAL CREDIT UNION ADMINISTRATION (NCUA), covered 82.9% of credit-union savings at the end of 1982. Another 16.4% was insured by state insurance plans or private plans approved by state regulators. Share insurance is mandatory for all federally chartered credit unions and for state-chartered credit unions in all but four states.

In addition to the strength and stability represented by the various share-insurance plans, credit unions are also examined regularly by state or federal regulators. About 60% of credit unions have federal charters and fall under the jurisdiction of the NCUA. The remaining 40% are state-chartered and are regulated by state agencies. Four states and the District of Columbia have only federal credit unions.

Loans. Credit unions traditionally have been known for offering loans at no more than 12%. In fact, that figure was written into the Federal Credit Union Act in 1934. However, inflation in recent years has ended that long tradition.

Congress raised the legal limit on loan interest rates for federally chartered credit unions to 15% in March 1980, and granted the NCUA the right to raise that limit for specified periods of time if prevailing high interest rates required it. The NCUA has since used that authority to establish a temporary maximum of 21% for federal credit unions.* Conditions vary for state-chartered credit unions, but most states permit credit unions to charge up to 21%. Few charge the maximum, however. The majority of credit-union loans in 1982 were in the 15–18% range. The mean loan rate for all credit unions rose from 13.5% in December 1980 to approximately 16% in December 1982.

Most loans are relatively small, averaging about $2,500, and short-term, for such things as autos, vacations, household appliances, and education. This has enabled credit unions to rapidly adjust their loan portfolios to account for changes in market interest rates. The average time remaining on all loans in July 1982 was 16.4 months. Credit unions held 13.8% of all consumer credit at the end of 1982, and 17.3% of all automobile loans.

National Network. Credit unions as a rule are small. As of mid-1983, about 60% had less than $1 million in assets, and 13% had less than $100,000 in assets. Only 1.2% had assets exceeding $50 million. However, due to the cooperative nature of the credit-union movement, even small credit unions can enjoy significant economies of scale.

*Financial institutions included are commercial banks, savings and loan associations, mutual savings banks, open-end mutual funds, U.S. savings bonds, and credit unions.

*In May 1983 NCUA voted to extend the 21% limit until November 1984. At that time it could be renewed at 21% or revised. If it is not renewed or revised, the maximum would revert to 15%.

State and national trade associations for credit unions are very active in providing operating assistance, professional training, financial services, advertising, and other assistance. More than 90% of credit unions are members of the 52 state credit-union leagues, and, through the leagues, the CREDIT UNION NATIONAL ASSOCIATION (CUNA).

Service corporations affiliated with the trade associations at the state and national levels offer operational forms and marketing materials designed only for credit-union use. They also develop and market financial products and services such as share drafts, credit-card programs, automated-teller-machine networks, Individual Retirement Account programs, and investment options that permit even small credit unions to offer sophisticated financial services without heavy development or administrative expenses.

Entry into the SECONDARY MORTGAGE MARKET is provided through the CUNA Mortgage Corporation, which was established to package and resell credit-union mortgage loans. (Federal credit unions didn't receive full freedom to offer mortgages until 1978.) Most credit unions offer life savings insurance and credit life insurance at no cost to members.

Corporate Credit Unions. As of 1983, approximately 17,500 credit unions were also members of the corporate credit-union network. This cooperatively owned and operated network of 42 "corporate" credit unions—credit unions for credit unions—acts as the central banking system for the movement, offering both short- and long-term loans, market-rate investments, and correspondent banking services, all at a lower cost than credit unions could obtain from banks or savings and loan institutions.

At the center of this network is the U.S. Central Credit Union. With more than $9 billion in assets as of July 1983, U.S. Central ranks among the largest and safest financial institutions in the country. In 1982 it obtained the highest ratings possible on its first commercial-paper offering from both Standard & Poor's and Moody's rating services.

Taken as a whole, the national financial and support system serving credit unions constitutes a highly organized and complete system of support designed to provide efficiency of scale while allowing complete local autonomy. This support system will become more important to the movement as deregulation and competition increase the varieties of financial services demanded by consumers.

Howard Cosgrove

Creditworthiness

This word has emerged from the trade jargon of the consumer-credit industry to denote that a potential credit applicant has a good past history of repayment, would not become overburdened in taking on new debt, and appears to be both willing and able to repay any additional credit that may be extended. It is derived from another trade-jargon term, *creditworthy,* which means worthy of credit.

If you are deemed generally creditworthy, that does not mean you will always get credit on application, although people with very good credit histories are usually accepted and those who lack creditworthiness are usually rejected. Your creditworthiness will often depend on the type and amount of credit that you want. Each creditor sets individual standards of creditworthiness, intended to limit, but not totally eliminate, collection problems and bad debts arising from default in repayment. These standards are derived from past experience in dealing with customers who have turned out to be good or bad credit risks; such people usually have certain characteristics in common and can be identified from information in a credit application, especially when it is confirmed and/or augmented through a credit report from a credit bureau.

No creditor has an infallible method of evaluating creditworthiness. Formerly, all consumer-credit granters extended or denied credit on the basis of subjective evaluation of applicants by persons whose experience and skill in making such judgments varied substantially. Such subjective evaluation of creditworthiness is still the most common method used to decide who will or will not get credit. So it may happen that a person who is truly creditworthy is turned down, or that a person who lacks creditworthiness is given credit, especially in borderline cases.

Credit applications are designed to obtain information for record-keeping purposes and for the evaluation of an applicant's creditworthiness, based on what credit granters call "character, capacity, collateral, and conditions." So when you fill out a credit application, do it as truthfully, accurately, and completely as you reasonably can while still keeping it brief.

Character generally relates to an applicant's willingness to repay, as shown by past use of consumer credit, stability of residence and employment, and other data that identify a person as a good credit risk.

Capacity relates to an applicant's source of income and the amount of it that can be relied on for repayment of the credit. Character and capacity are the two most important factors considered in evaluating creditworthiness.

Collateral is property that may be pledged by an applicant to assure repayment of credit. The applicant's creditworthiness is enhanced because the creditor's risk in extending credit is reduced: If the consumer defaults in repayment, the creditor can recover all or part of what is owed by repossession, replevin, seizure, or the voluntary surrender of the property pledged. Usually, when a car, furniture, or other expensive item is purchased on credit, the creditor takes a security interest in what is purchased, which serves as collateral. However, in cash loans, creditors may require that previously owned property be pledged as collateral.

Conditions refers to current or future economic conditions that have a bearing on an applicant's ability to repay. Certain conditions affect an applicant's prospects for future employment or for increases or decreases in earnings from wages, salary, or other sources of income. For instance, if a strike or layoff is likely in an applicant's future, his or her creditworthiness may be diminished.

As stated earlier, the majority of consumer-credit granters still rely on subjective evaluation of applicants in making credit decisions. But very large retailers, finance companies, and other creditors who have a large base of credit customers use a more reliable, scientific, and objective means of evaluating creditworthiness, called "credit scoring" or "point scoring." In such a system, "weights" or "points" are assigned for each characteristic covered by application information. The total of the weights or points comprises the applicant's credit score, which will fall above or below a cutoff point, which is the minimum score an applicant must achieve to be granted credit. The development of such a system is complicated and expensive, and the system is usually valid only for the creditor for whom it was developed and requires revision from time to time to continue to be reliable and valid. But even the best and most scientific credit-scoring system is not infallible, so that the use of the system will result in some good risks being declined and some bad ones accepted.

Creditors who evaluate credit applicants subjectively must also revise their standards of creditworthiness from time to time. Credit policies change with general economic conditions and in accordance with the creditor's desire to increase or decrease the volume of credit business being done.

Creditors make use of a range of credit information that has proven reliable in evaluating applicants as credit risks. But both commercial- and consumer-credit granters are forbidden under the federal Equal Credit Opportunity Act from considering sex, marital status, age, race, religion, national origin, or income received from any public assistance program, either at all or adversely, in determining the creditworthiness of applicants.

The availability of credit is the most valuable financial asset of most consumers, and if you have a job or other source of steady income and a good credit history, you can generally expect to be approved for credit whenever you apply.

James A. Ambrose

Crime Insurance

See INSURANCE.

Currency, How It Gets into Circulation

At mid-1981 about $138 billion of U.S. paper currency and coin was held by the public, primarily as a result of demands by the public to hold cash. A substantial portion of pocket cash is obtained by cashing checks, personal or payroll, which turn checkbook dollars into paper currency and coin.

Public demands vary by the day of the week, the week of the month, and the season of the year. For example, during the Christmas season, people prefer to hold more paper currency as they travel from store to store looking for "that" gift. The periods around other holidays from Labor Day to Independence Day produce a similar high demand for pocket cash, although far less than that near Christmas.

Depository institutions are the first to feel the impact of the public's demand for cash. Thus, to meet the needs of the public, the institutions turn to their regional Reserve banks for coin and currency when their own vaults don't have enough, or when they don't have enough of the requested denominations. In this sense, Reserve banks serve as bulk handlers of cash.

As a result of the International Banking Act of 1978 and the Depository Institutions Deregulation and Monetary Control Act of 1980, all depository institutions in the United States became eligible to use Federal Reserve services. The MCA also requires Federal Reserve banks to charge institutions explicit prices for CENTRAL BANK services.

Depository institutions include member and nonmember COMMERCIAL BANKS, mutual SAVINGS BANKS, SAVINGS AND LOAN ASSOCIATIONS, CREDIT UNIONS, Edge Act and Agreement corporations, and foreign bank branches and agencies in the United States.

Some depository institutions also provide currency to other depository institutions through correspondent arrangements. When some institutions need currency or coin, they contact their correspondent, which has an account at the Federal Reserve. Institutions have accounts at the local Reserve bank similar to accounts the public has at depository institutions. The account-holding institution then provides the "customer depository institution" with the necessary currency or coin and charges the customer institution's account.

Much of the cash at a Reserve bank has been deposited by depository institutions when they had more currency or coin than needed to satisfy their customers. When excess currency and coin are sent to the Reserve bank, the accounts of the depositing institutions are credited. Ideally, only excess fit and unfit currency should be deposited at Reserve banks (*see* CURRENCY PROCESSING AND DESTRUCTION).

Some cash services aren't charged since providing currency is a government function and Reserve banks are charged with the responsibility. However, Reserve banks now charge for paper currency and coin transportation services. Coin or currency ordered by an institution from the Reserve bank is transported by armored car or registered mail. Coin also is shipped by mail. The institution's account is charged for the amount ordered.

Often, currency sent to depository institutions is new. The notes are claims upon the assets of the issuing Reserve bank and liabilities of the U.S. government. About one of every four notes paid out by Reserve banks is new. New inventory is carefully managed by Reserve banks to minimize note-printing costs, which ultimately are borne by the public. Currently each note costs about 2 cents to produce.

In addition, the law requires each Reserve bank to transfer to its Federal Reserve agent, (a representative of the board of governors of the system at each Reserve bank) collateral equal to at least 100% of the value of the currency being issued. The bulk of that collateral is in the form of U.S. government securities owned by the Federal Reserve system. The remainder of the collateral is comprised of gold certificates, special drawing rights, or other "eligible" paper, such as bills of exchange or promissory notes. Also included are foreign government or agency securities acquired by the Federal Reserve.

Regardless of how currency moves into circulation, the process starts with order requests by the Federal Reserve. Each summer, on the basis of recommendations of the currency departments at the 12 Reserve banks, orders are placed with the comptroller of the currency, a part of the U.S. Treasury.

The comptroller, after reviewing requests, passes them to the Bureau of Engraving and Printing, another Treasury arm, which produces the appropriate denominations with the seal of the ordering Reserve bank. The uncirculated Reserve notes are shipped under guard to the ordering Reserve bank.

The procedures involved in circulating new coin are similar to those for new currency. The supply of coin is governed primarily by demand, as well as production capacity. Currently, coins are made in West Point, New York; Philadelphia; Denver; and San Francisco, under the control of the director of the

Mint, also a unit of the Treasury.

Like paper currency, coin is shipped to the Reserve banks and through those institutions to depository institutions and on to the public. Unlike paper currency, Reserve banks receive coin at face value from the Treasury since they aren't considered claims upon the assets of Reserve banks, but are issued by the U.S. government.

Federal Reserve banks arrange in advance for shipments of new coin from the U.S. Mint for the coming year in amounts and on a time schedule to maintain inventories at required levels. Under this arrangement, the Mint can schedule its production of coin efficiently and, at the same time, Reserve banks can provide coin as required to meet business demands. There are occasions when coin shortages arise, such as when the Mint's production capabilities can't generate sufficient coins to meet strong demand. Federal Reserve banks are required to adhere to the advance shipping schedules. Except in emergencies, there is no provision for obtaining additional coin.

In essence, Reserve banks maintain inventories of coin at levels that permit them to fill orders from depository institutions to meet business demands. Inventory levels are based on historical demand patterns with additional provision for normal growth in demand.

Arthur Samansky

Currency Processing and Destruction

Responsibility for maintaining physical quality of circulating United States paper currency is shared by the Federal Reserve banks and the U.S. Treasury Department.

Each day, millions of dollars of deposits in Reserve banks, made by depository institutions, are carefully scrutinized. Worn or mutilated notes are removed from circulation and destroyed. Only Reserve banks and their branches, and in certain cases the Treasury, are permitted to destroy currency. Thus, only that currency sent to the Reserve banks by depository institutions can be destroyed if it doesn't meet fitness standards. Counterfeit notes that are detected are forwarded to the Secret Service, a part of the Treasury.

Since 1966, the Reserve banks have been authorized by the secretary of the Treasury to destroy FEDERAL RESERVE NOTES, which now account for nearly 100% of all paper currency in circulation.

Between the mid-1960s and mid-1981, about $123 billion in folding money was deemed unfit for circulation and was destroyed. In 1981 alone, more than 3.5 billion notes, with a face value of almost $25 billion and weighing about 3,000 tons, were destroyed by the 12 Reserve banks and their 25 branches.

The Reserve banks destroy all denominations of paper currency except gold certificates issued prior to 1934 and old currency issues. These notes are destroyed in conjunction with the Treasury. At the New York Reserve Bank, about $20 million in paper currency is daily destroyed under strictly controlled and highly secure procedures.

Since mid-1981, the New York Fed has almost exclusively used high-speed equipment to electronically sort and count fit currency, and detect and destroy unfit currency. Nearly 2 billion notes were processed in 1981 by the New York Reserve Bank.

High-speed machines inspect up to 60,000 notes per hour, four times the number processed per hour by medium-speed machines. In that medium-speed system, unfit notes were moved to an incinerator where temperatures up to 1,800° Fahrenheit reduced the currency to a whitish ash similar to talcum powder. The New York Fed ceased burning currency in July 1981.

The current currency-destruction process starts in the receiving area of the New York Fed, as depository institutions make deliveries in large canvas bags of paper currency for deposit in their accounts. The currency is moved quickly to the currency-processing-verification section. There, bags of currency are opened under high security and personnel count the bundles of currency, each containing 10 packages of 100 notes of the same denomination, to confirm that the number of bundles matches the number on the bag's tag. In addition, these personnel separate the bundles by denomination.

The currency is then moved under security to a vault area, where it is held temporarily before being moved under dual control to the sorting and counting area for final processing. Once in the processing room, the high-speed-equipment operators remove paper straps around each package—which identify the depository institution—and insert computer-readable cards in front of each package. That card tells the computer how many notes to count.

Prior to loading the first stack of currency into the reader-sorter, the computer is programmed to count a specific denomination. The equipment is then tested to ensure it is functioning properly. The currency, in stacks of up to 10,000 notes, is loaded onto a shelf on the side of the machine and the notes are automatically fed into the sorter. As the currency moves through, the denomination of each note is confirmed

and each note counted, and the currency is checked for fitness based upon light reflectivity (the dirtier the note, the less light reflected) and genuineness (based upon magnetic qualities within each note).

Fit notes are automatically directed into one of two pockets in the machine, where, in packages of 100 notes, they are restrapped by the machine. Questionable notes, such as those considered by the computer to be possible counterfeits or another denomination, are directed into another pocket and examined by hand. About 50 to 60 counterfeit notes are detected daily by the New York Fed.

Unfit currency is directed to the far end of the sorter, where stainless-steel blades cut the notes lengthwise into one-eighth-inch strips. The strips are sent by vacuum tube to a disposal area several floors below. After shreds from each reader-sorter (which count different denominations) are mixed, the strips are compressed by machine into 400-pound bales. Currently, a private contractor picks up the bales and discards them at designated landfills. This method of disposal is less expensive than other means.

Some Reserve banks, under Treasury rules, sell shredded currency to businesses. However, Treasury rules sharply limit the uses to which such currency can be put. Among those uses forbidden are for printing or for making food containers.

Arthur Samansky

Cusip Number

The code on a security that indicates the issuing company and the class and type of the security. The number is assigned by the Committee on Uniform Security Identification Procedures in order to facilitate security transactions. It is advisable to record the cusip number, because if the certificate is lost, stolen, or destroyed, the number will support a claim and perhaps expedite replacement.

R. Bruce Swenson

Custodian Account

A savings account controlled by a custodian, rather than by the party to whom the funds belong. The account remains in the custodian's care until the funds are distributed. A custodian ordinarily does not hold legal title.

Mary Ann Irvine

·D·

Daily Compounding

This means that INTEREST is computed and paid on both the principal and the unpaid interest added to it. Thus one earns interest on the interest every day. The interest earned is called "compound interest."

See INTEREST RATES, CALCULATION OF; SIMPLE INTEREST.

Harvey Rachlin

Day Order

See COMMON STOCK.

Debit Card

See CREDIT CARD.

Deductible, Health Insurance

An initial amount of health expenses that the insured pays out of pocket annually before benefits begin. Typical deductibles are $100 to $200 or more; in individual policies, the higher the deductible, the lower the premium paid by the insured.

See HEALTH INSURANCE.

James L. Moorefield

Deductibles (Property/Casualty Insurance)

Most auto and homeowners insurance policies have deductibles—the dollar amount of loss the policyholder agrees to absorb in case of a fire, accident, or other covered peril.

Deductibles are provided in amounts such as $100, $250, and $500. Insurance companies charge lower premiums when policyholders choose higher deductibles. The reason: They don't have to handle as many small claims, which often cost as much to investigate and adjust as the bigger ones.

Savings on premiums can be considerable, the actual dollar amounts varying from city to city and from company to company. Generally, the higher the deductible, the greater the premium savings.

Among commercial insurance policyholders, deductibles also are commonly known as "retentions." Commercial customers often "retain"—or self-insure—substantial portions of their risks.

Mechlin D. Moore

Deductions, Tax

Under the INTERNAL REVENUE CODE, the term *deductions* usually means business expenses that may be used to reduce one's gross income to a net taxable amount. The Code states that "there shall be allowed as a deduction all ordinary and necessary expenses paid or incurred during the taxable year in carrying on any trade or business."

In determining whether an expenditure is in part or wholly an allowable deduction, the key words are *ordinary and necessary* for *trade or business*. As long as one is actually pursuing a profit, it is reasonable to say that business is being done or a trade engaged in. If one ordinarily does business over lunch—a working lunch like a lunch with a client—the expense of the meal would be deductible. If, however, one goes to the most expensive restaurant and orders the most expensive dinner, that may not be ordinary and it certainly may not be necessary for the successful transaction of business, and the deduction or a part of it may be disallowed. If one must travel, a car and other travel expenses are a necessary part of doing business and are ordinarily deductible.

It is most important to document deductions by keeping accurate records of the amounts expended (the expenses must be paid, not just incurred); the nature of the business at the time of each expenditure; and the time, place, and date. Whenever possible, receipts or suitable written documentation should be obtained and kept for no less than three years.

David B. Axelrod

Deed

A document by which rights in real property are transferred. The deed must identify a grantor (the person conveying the rights), a grantee (the person receiving the rights), a statement as to the consideration being given to the grantor, a description of the real property involved, words of grant, and the signature of the grantor. If the rights being conveyed are less than the full rights of ownership, this must be described. In most states, the statement of consideration is general and does not have to reflect the exact consideration. The selection of the words of grant, however, can make an important difference in the legal effect, and deeds are sometimes classified on this basis, as follows:

Quit claim deed. This deed does not say that it is conveying the land but merely the *grantor's interest* in the land. Whatever the grantor owns will be conveyed, but the grantor makes no warranty (i.e., no convenant or promise) as to exactly what interest is being conveyed.

Deed of bargain and sale. Sometimes called a "deed without covenants" because it states that it is conveying the land but makes no warranties or covenants concerning the title.

Warranty deed (or general warranty deed). This not only conveys what the grantor owns but includes several warranties or promises on the part of the grantor. These warranties may be spelled out or may be legally implied by the use of certain words, such as a statement that the grantor "conveys and warrants" the land. The exact effect depends on the law of the particular state. The typical warranties are that the grantor owns the property; that there are no legal claims or restrictions against the property (other than those specifically stated in the deed); and that the grantee will not be evicted or disturbed by anyone having a better title or claim. If the grantee is harmed because the title is not as warranted, the grantee has a right to sue the grantor for damages.

Special warranty deed. Sometimes called a "grant deed" or "deed of bargain and sale with Covenant," this deed includes only limited warranties—usually that the *grantor* has done nothing to change the ownership or to create claims against the property. It does not warrant that the grantor is actually the owner or that no such claims were created by others.

See TITLE INSURANCE.

Hugh A. Brodkey

Delinquency

In the field of consumer credit, this term is used to denote failure to pay as agreed. Generally, most creditors do not regard a customer as delinquent unless if payment is not received by the due date or before the date after which a late charge will be imposed. In providing information on credit customers to credit bureaus, credit granters report customers' payment habits in a uniform manner so that a creditor can use a credit report to determine a customer's usual manner of payment to current or former creditors.

Every credit contract and agreement calls for the debtor to pay as agreed, and such contracts will usually specify when a customer who is delinquent will be in default and therefore subject to exercise of a creditor's legal rights and remedies to compel payment or otherwise recover the outstanding balance of the debt.

James A. Ambrose

Demand Deposit

A deposit or account that is either (1) payable on demand; (2) issued with an original maturity of less than 14 days; or (3) holding funds for which the bank does not require the depositor to give at least 14 days' written notice of intent to withdraw the funds.

A demand deposit allows the holder of the account to make payments by writing checks against the deposit or to withdraw cash from the bank on demand by presenting a check drawn on the account. Since 1933, when the federal government prohibited the payment of interest on demand deposits, these deposits have been non-interest-earning. In 1982 the American public held $235 billion in demand deposits at commercial banks and thrift institutions.

David H. Friedman

Department of Agriculture

An executive branch of the U.S. government whose responsibilities include improving farm income, expanding overseas markets for farm products, assuring consumers of an adequate food supply at reasonable prices, and providing food assistance to those in need. Its agencies include the Farmers Home Administration (FmHA) and the FOOD AND NUTRITION SERVICE (FNS).

Harvey Rachlin

Department of Health and Human Services (HHS)

An executive branch of the U.S. government concerned with the general welfare of the public. It is comprised of an Office of the Secretary and five operating divisions: the Social Security Administration, the Health Care Financing Administration, the Public Health Service, the Office of Community Services, and the Office of Human Development Services. Among the programs directed by these operating division are MEDICARE and MEDICAID (Health Care Financing Administration) and SOCIAL SECURITY, SUPPLEMENTAL SECURITY INCOME, and AID TO FAMILIES WITH DEPENDENT CHILDREN (Social Security Administration). The Department of Health, Education, and

Welfare was created on April 11, 1953, and redesignated the Department of Health and Human Services by the Department of Education Organization Act, approved October 17, 1979.

Harvey Rachlin

Department of Housing and Urban Development (HUD)

An executive department of the U.S. government responsible for administering programs concerned with housing needs, fair housing opportunities, and improving and developing communities in the United States.

Programs. To carry out its objectives the Department of Housing and Urban Development administers numerous programs, including the following: mortgage-insurance programs that help low- and moderate-income families to become homeowners; a rental-subsidy program to help lower-income families obtain decent, safe, and sanitary housing; administration of the law that prohibits discrimination in housing on the basis of race, color, religion, sex, and national origin; programs that aid sound community development, neighborhood rehabilitation, and the preservation of U.S. urban centers from blight and decay. HUD also protects the home buyer in the marketplace and fosters programs that stimulate and guide the housing industry to provide not only housing but a suitable living environment. Within HUD is the GOVERNMENT NATIONAL MORTGAGE ASSOCIATION (GNMA).

HUD was established by the Department of Housing and Urban Development Act of September 9, 1965, which became effective on November 9, 1965. It replaced the Housing and Home Finance Agency, which was created in 1947.

Harvey Rachlin

Department of Labor

An executive department of the U.S. government established by Congress to "foster, promote and develop the welfare of the wage earners of the United States, to improve their working conditions and to advance their opportunities for profitable employment." Among its many activities and responsibilities, the Department of Labor develops standards for health and safety and inspects workplaces to see that these standards are met; establishes a minimum wage and overtime rates after 40 hours a week; protects the employment and pension rights of wage earners; enforces labor laws that protect workers; prohibits discrimination (for any reason except incompetence); provides

job training; administers workmen's compensation programs for job injuries and deaths of federal employees, longshoremen, coal miners who are victims of black lung disease, and certain other groups; promulgates guidelines for state unemployment-insurance programs; and disseminates statistics about laborers and the economy by collecting, analyzing, and publishing information about workers, occupational outlook, working conditions, wages, prices, productivity, and economic growth.

The U.S. Department of Labor was created in 1913 by Congress and included the Bureau of Labor Statistics, the Bureau of Immigration and Naturalization, and the Children's Bureau.

Harvey Rachlin

Department of the Treasury

An executive department of the U.S. government having the following basic types of functions: to formulate and recommend economic, financial, tax, and fiscal policies; to serve as financial agent for the federal government; to enforce the law; and to manufacture coins and currency. Specifically, its responsibilities include collecting taxes; controlling the making of U.S. paper money, coins, and government bonds, notes, and certificates; handling the collection of all revenue paid to the government and paying all its bills, and supervising the operation of national banks.

The Treasury Department was created by an act of Congress approved on September 2, 1789. Its duties have been expanded over the years by subsequent acts and it is now composed of the secretary of the Treasury and various offices and bureaus directed by the secretary. The functions and responsibilities of these are summarized in Table 1.

Harvey Rachlin

Deposit Ceiling Rates of Interest

Limits imposed by federal law and regulations on the rates of interest that financial institutions can pay depositors.

The idea that restrictions should be placed on the rates that financial institutions can pay on deposits initially grew out of a belief that excessive rate competition among commercial banks contributed to the instability of the banking system in the 1920s and especially during the early years of the Great Depression. As a result, in the Banking Acts of 1933 and 1935, the Federal Reserve Board and the Federal Deposit Insurance Corporation were authorized to set ceilings on the rates that could be paid by banks on time and savings accounts, and the payment of interest on demand deposits (checking accounts) was prohibited. In

Table 1
Department of the Treasury

Office or Bureau	Overview
Secretary of the Treasury	Advises President on domestic and international financial, economic, and tax policy, manages public debt, oversees activities of Treasury Department, and reports to Congress on nation's finances
Bureau of Alcohol, Tobacco and Firearms	Administers regulations and enforces laws regarding production, use, and distribution of firearms, explosives, alcohol, and tobacco products, and collects taxes on these commodities
Bureau of Engraving and Printing	Designs, engraves, and prints U.S. paper currency; Treasury securities; and postage, revenue, and certain customs stamps
Bureau of Government Financial Operations	Responsible for various fiscal activities including maintaining records of government spending and receipts and disbursing public monies, including issuance of monthly payments to beneficiaries under major Federal benefit programs and issuance of U.S. savings bonds under Federal Payroll Savings Plan
Bureau of the Mint	Makes U.S. coins and medals (in four major plants—Denver, Philadelphia, San Francisco, and West Point, N.Y.)
Bureau of the Public Debt	Administers country's debts, receiving, storing, issuing, and redeeming government securities
Federal Law Enforcement Training Center	An interagency facility that trains federal law agents from 48 federal law enforcement organizations
Internal Revenue Service	Collects personal and corporate income taxes
Office of the Comptroller of the Currency	As administrator of national banks, Comptroller promulgates rules and regulations governing their operation and is responsible for supervising and maintaining sound national banking system
Office of Revenue Sharing	Controls the sharing of federal funds with state and local governments
United States Customs Service	Assesses and collects customs duty and excise tax on imported merchandise, enforces customs and related laws, prevents entry into U.S. of narcotics and illegal drugs, and assists other government agencies in enforcing laws and regulations that apply to international trade
United States Savings Bond Division	Promotes sale and retention of U.S. savings bonds
United States Secret Service	Protects against counterfeiting by enforcing laws relating to coins, currency, and securities of the U.S. and foreign governments; protects President and members of immediate family, Vice President and family, former Presidents and wives or widows and minor children until they reach 16 years of age, and visiting heads of foreign government or state.

1966 this same authority was granted to the Federal Home Loan Bank Board to set interest ceilings for most savings and loan associations. Until recently, federal credit unions were likewise restricted in the rates that could be paid to their "shareholders." Such ceilings are often referred to as "Regulation Q" ceilings, the name of the Federal Reserve Board regulation.

Over the years, doubt began to be cast on the validity of the original assumption that rate regulation was needed to prevent destructive rate competition among depository institutions. However, during the same period new policy reasons emerged to support the continuation of rate ceilings. For one, they became an important tool of monetary policy: Rate ceilings could help to restrain the amount of funds in the banking system (and thereby help to restrain bank credit) during a period of tight money; when market rates exceeded deposit rate ceilings, deposit growth would be curtailed. Second, ceiling differentials that allowed thrift institutions to pay somewhat higher rates than banks could encourage savings to flow into thrifts, whose primary function was to finance housing. Ceilings could thus be used to channel deposit flows to support the national goal of promoting affordable housing.

However, in periods of high interest rates, ceilings prompted large scale "disintermediation" as borrowers removed funds from depository institutions and placed them in market instruments free of rate ceilings, such as Treasury securities or money-market funds. Moreover, the effect of ceilings in limiting rates paid on deposits had often been to subsidize borrowers at the expense of savers—for example, retired persons who depend upon interest on deposits as an important source of income.

National policy has now shifted toward the removal of deposit rate ceilings. Federal credit unions are now free to pay whatever rate the institution wishes. The Depository Institutions Deregulation Act of 1980 provides for the elimination of bank and thrift-institution deposit ceilings on time and savings accounts as soon as economic conditions permit, but no later than March 31, 1986. The responsibility for setting the timetable for elimination of deposit interest-rate ceilings resides in a governmental body called the DEPOSITORY INSTITUTIONS DEREGULATION COMMITTEE (DIDC). The phasing out of ceilings is designed to permit depository institutions to pay market rates of interest on an increasing proportion of their deposits, thereby easing the transition to an environment of market rate competition for deposits.

Griffith L. Garwood

Depository Institutions Deregulation Committee (DIDC)

A six-member committee of financial regulators established by Congress in 1980 to phase out interest-rate ceilings on time and savings deposits by 1986. The Depository Institutions Deregulation Committee was created by the Depository Institutions Deregulation and Monetary Control Act of 1980, enacted on March 31, 1980. Title II of that act empowered the DIDC to regulate interest-rate ceilings on time and savings deposits at commercial banks, mutual savings banks, and savings and loan associations. Prior to the act, this authority had been delegated by Congress to the Federal Reserve Board of Governors, the Federal Deposit Insurance Corporation (FDIC), and the Federal Home Loan Bank Board (FHLBB) for depository institutions under their respective jurisdictions.

Members of the committee are the secretary of the Treasury and the chairmen of the Federal Reserve Board, FDIC, FHLBB, and the National Credit Union Administration Board. The comptroller of the currency serves as a nonvoting member of the committee.

The committee's responsibility under the Monetary Control Act is to provide for an orderly phase-out of interest-rate ceilings over a six-year period (1986). These ceilings—often referred to as "Regulation Q" ceilings for the Federal Reserve's implementing regulation on banks—impose maximum limits on the interest rates that banks and thrift institutions can pay on time and savings deposits. Since 1966, thrift institutions have been allowed under Regulation Q to pay a somewhat higher interest rate on time and savings deposits than commercial banks. This interest-rate differential—one-quarter of a percentage point in 1982—is to remain in effect throughout the six-year phase-out period. At the end of that period (1986), the differential, as well as all ceiling limits, is to be ended. In 1986 all authority granted the DIDC expires and the committee is to be disbanded.

Several of the committee's early actions in deregulating interest rates were controversial. In June 1981 the DIDC adopted a schedule for the gradual phase-out of interest ceilings, beginning with longer-term accounts. However, one month later the U.S. district court of the District of Columbia nullified the schedule. In September 1981 the committee voted to increase the ceiling on passbook savings accounts by one-half of a percentage point, effective November 1, 1981. However, in October 1981 the committee indefinitely postponed the scheduled increase. In March 1982 the DIDC adopted a new schedule for the gradual phase-out of interest ceilings, beginning with accounts with maturities of three and a half years or longer.

Under the procedural rules established in the Monetary Control Act, the committee must meet at least once every three months in sessions open to the public. The committee's actions are decided by majority vote. The federal financial regulatory agencies are charged with implementing regulations issued by the committee.

David H. Friedman

Depository Trust Company (DTC)

See STOCK EXCHANGES.

Depreciation

Often a company has to buy an item of property for use in its business, and the property is used up or wears out as time passes by. A typewriter, for example, will not last forever; after a reasonable period of time, it will have to be replaced. In order to give effect to the wear and tear of that property, the tax laws have created the concept of depreciation.

Basically, *depreciation* is a deduction of a portion of the cost of property used in a trade or business to give effect to the wear and tear, or loss of use over a period of time. For example, X Company purchases a typewriter for $1,000. The typewriter is used by the company for its business. Let's assume that the typewriter will be in use for five years before it will be replaced. Theoretically, the wear and tear or loss of the typewriter will be 20% per year. Because of depreciation rules, the company will be able to deduct 20% of the value of that typewriter after one year, or $200, as an expense against its other income. In the second year, the company will again deduct $200, and will be able to do so for the five years until the entire cost of the typewriter is deducted or "written off."

Generally, any *tangible item of property that has a limited useful life and is used in a trade or business* is depreciable. Buildings; machinery; automobiles; livestock acquired for work, breeding, or dairy purposes; patents; license agreements; franchises; and copyrighted material are examples of depreciable or "wasting" assets. All of these assets have limited useful lives and will have to be replaced if the business is to continue exactly the same. Inventory held by a business for sale, although appearing to be a tangible asset with a limited useful life, is not depreciable, nor are depletable natural resources. These are treated differently for tax purposes. Land is not depreciable either; it lasts forever and will never be "lost" or need replacement like a car or machine.

Depreciation is obviously a very important aspect of tax planning. Accordingly, the tax treatment of depreciation is often changed by government fiscal policy as a method of controlling or emphasizing certain aspects of business. The government has created a system of fast depreciation that it often uses to encourage certain types of investments. Called the Accelerated Cost Recovery System, or ACRS, it permits you to take the major portion of an asset's depreciation in earlier years. For example, the government could permit the depreciation of our typewriter by allowing a $400 deduction (instead of a $200 deduction) in the first year, a $300 deduction in the second year, a $200 deduction in the third year, a $75 deduction in the fourth year, and a $25 deduction in the fifth year. The total depreciation is still $1,000 over five years, but by taking the deductions earlier, the business will have the use of the money sooner, and the government will get its taxes later.

A second way the government can manipulate depreciation is by controlling the period of time over which an asset may be depreciated. For example, the government could pass a law allowing office equipment to be depreciated over three years. Therefore, the business would deduct $333 of the typewriter's cost in the first year, second year, and third year, even though the typewriter actually will last for five years. Although the total depreciation over the life of the

typewriter is the same ($1,000), the business would get back the cost of the typewriter in three years and not five.

There is one major wrinkle with respect to depreciation. At the end of five years, the typewriter will still have some value; someone will probably pay something for that typewriter regardless of its condition. This is called its "salvage value." Let's assume that the typewriter will have a salvage value of $100 at the end of five years. The typewriter will not actually waste away to nothing, but to $100. Accordingly, our business will be able to depreciate only $900 of the typewriter's cost over the life of the typewriter, since the residual or salvage value is not lost, and therefore cannot be depreciated.

Alan J. Pomerantz

Disability Income Insurance

This is a type of HEALTH INSURANCE that provides a replacement income should a person become sick or injured and unable to work.

There are a large number of disability income-protection programs—both government and private. A basic understanding of the nature and purpose of the various types of programs is necessary in examining one's present disability protection to determine if it is adequate to meet personal needs during a disability.

Employer's Benefits. Determining what benefits an employer provides in case of a disabling illness or injury is the first goal. Many, but not all, employers provide this protection for their employees through group disability income-insurance plans. The typical disability policy will provide a percentage of predisability income for a stated period of time and under specified circumstances outlined in the contract. In most cases, the employer pays all or part of the cost of this insurance.

The levels of protection provided by group disability plans vary considerably. An employee with such group coverage should confer with his or her personnel or union office to learn exactly what benefits are provided. If disability is due to an accident, how long must the worker wait before benefits begin? How long is the wait if the disability is due to an illness? Benefits sometimes begin sooner for an accident—often the first day. It is also important to determine how long the benefits will continue during a disability.

There are two basic forms of this coverage. *Short-term disability insurance* typically provides benefits for 13, 26, or 52 weeks, but the benefit period may run as long as two years. This type of coverage is more common than is *long-term disability insurance,* which offers benefit periods from two years to age 65, or longer if employed, but most frequently five years or longer.

Social Security. Most salaried workers in the U.S. participate in the federal government's SOCIAL SECURITY program for disabled people, which is separate from the Social Security retirement program. Benefits are determined by a person's salary and years covered under Social Security. Key features of this program are as follows:

- Benefits are tax-free.
- Benefits for permanent or indefinite-term disabilities begin with the sixth month.
- After 24 months of benefits, the recipient also qualifies for MEDICARE, which helps pay medical bills.
- Dependents can also qualify for certain benefits.

Social Security benefits are very important in calculating an individual's insurance needs. To determine the extent of these benefits, write to the Social Security office listed in your telephone directory.

Other Benefits. If an accident or illness occurred at an employee's job or resulted from some aspect of employment, the disabled employee may be entitled to WORKERS' COMPENSATION benefits under a state-administered program. The extent of these benefits is also determined by earnings and work history and can vary considerably. Other benefits may be available to residents of California, Hawaii, New Jersey, New York, Rhode Island, and Puerto Rico, which have "cash sickness programs" that provide income replacement to people disabled due to nonoccupational injury or illness. These benefits also vary considerably among the states.

Other possible sources of disability income are:

- Veterans Administration pension disability benefits
- Civil Service disability benefits for government workers
- State vocational rehabilitation benefits
- State welfare payments to low-income people
- Aid to Families with Dependent Children (AFDC)
- Group union disability benefits
- Auto insurance that provides benefits for disability from traffic accidents
- Special private insurance programs—such as credit disability insurance, which pays monthly loan or mortgage payments during a disability

The availability and extent of these programs vary widely in different parts of the country. But because it is possible to have access to many of them, it is wise to find out if you qualify for these various programs.

Will Benefits Fill Income Need? Once you have de-termined what your potential benefits would be under the various programs, add them together. If the sum of potential disability benefits—particularly from your employer's plan and, after five months, Social Security—equals your after-tax income, you are probably well protected against a disability. But, again, the waiting period before benefits begin and the length of the benefit period should be considered in calculating the extent of personal protection. If the total benefits, including Social Security, do not add up to enough to support your family during a disability, you may want to consider buying individual disability insurance.

Individual Coverage Purchased by the Consumer. Most individual disability policies require that the worker be totally disabled before benefits begin. Benefits for partial disability are sometimes provided, but most often only if the partial disability follows a period of total disability from the same cause. There are different definitions of what constitutes a disability; an agent should be asked to explain what *disability* means in the policy offered. In some cases, the insured is considered disabled only if he or she is unable to work at his or her *own* occupation. Other policies define *disability* as the inability to work at *any* occupation for which the insured is reasonably qualified by education, training, or experience. The distinction is significant.

Benefits are tax-free or generally subject to limited taxation. All state and federal programs, such as Social Security and workers' compensation, provide tax-free benefits, except for some tax limitations on state "cash sickness programs." Disability programs provided by a union or employer, for which the employee does not pay, are subject to tax but are most likely eligible for an annual exception of $5,200. Benefits from policies paid for solely by the employee are tax-free.

A person seeking individual coverage can choose a policy in which the benefit payments start anywhere from the first day to six months or more after the onset of disability. The longer the wait, the lower the premium cost. A consumer can choose a policy in which the benefits will be paid for as little as one year or as long as to age 65, or beyond. The shorter the benefit period, the lower the premium.

It is unrealistic to expect to insure oneself for replacement of full salary. Most insurers will limit benefits from all sources to no more than 60% or 70% of gross salary. The reasoning is that a disabled person does not need full income replacement, because the disability-benefit payments are not taxed. Also, a disabled person is saving on transportation, clothing, and other work-related expenses.

The insurance agent offering an individual policy should explain its "renewability," or the conditions of extending the policy beyond its expiration date. Guaranteed renewable policies (*see* GUARANTEED RENEWABLE, HEALTH OR DISABILITY INSURANCE) offer protection as long as the insured works, or to a specified age, providing the premiums are paid, no matter how poor the health of the insured may become. "Optionally renewable" policies are extendable at the discretion of the insurer. Prices of policies depend in part on the extent of renewability granted.

James L. Moorefield

Discount-Borrowing Surcharges

On several occasions since early 1980, the Federal Reserve has imposed a surcharge on certain borrowings by depository institutions from the DISCOUNT WINDOW. A 3% surcharge was applied from March 17, 1980, through May 7 to short-term adjustment credit borrowings of depository institutions with deposits of $500 million or more, borrowing in two consecutive weeks, or in five or more weeks in a calendar quarter.

After May 7 the surcharge was discontinued until November 17, 1980, when a 2% surcharge was introduced. On December 5, 1980, that surcharge was increased to 3%, and on May 5, 1981, raised to 4%. The surcharge was reduced to 3% on September 22, 1981, and to 2% on October 12, 1981.

On October 1, 1981, the formula for applying the surcharge was changed to a moving 13-week period, from a calendar quarter. The surcharge was eliminated on November 17, 1981.

The March 1980 imposition of a surcharge—the first since the 1920s—was part of a broader series of steps by the CENTRAL BANK to restrain money-supply growth and reduce inflation. These steps were taken in concert with the U.S. government's credit-restraint program.

The surcharge was designed to discourage frequent use of the discount window; encourage banks with access to the money market to adjust loans and investments more promptly to changing market conditions; and facilitate the ability of the Federal Reserve to achieve longer-run bank-credit and money-supply objectives.

To ensure that discount-window borrowings are appropriate, borrowing institutions are asked to provide general background on liquidity needs and the reasons for the request to use the window at the time of each request. Reserve Bank lending officers review changes in the key weekly financial-statement items of the institution, as well as the overall pattern of the institution's discount-window use.

Frequency of borrowing is an important criterion in reviewing use of the window to determine if credit is used for short-term adjustment needs, the primary purpose of the lending service. Frequency of borrowing refers to the number of reserve weeks during which an institution borrows. In monitoring the overall frequency record, discount officers consider the number of consecutive weeks in which an institution borrows, as well as borrowing over moving periods of 13 weeks and longer.

A borrower with a high frequency record normally would be contacted to determine the underlying cause for borrowing and to discuss plans for reducing reliance on the window for an extended period. The amounts borrowed also are reviewed in relation to the level of the depository institution's domestic deposits and required reserves.

Discussions with an institution also can arise if there is an appearance of an artificial pattern of borrowing, such as a pattern of weekend borrowings or of borrowing every other week. Such patterns would be more likely to be considered inappropriate.

Guidelines covering the availability of credit vary with the size of the institution. Generally, smaller institutions are granted greater access to adjustment credit than are larger institutions, which have access to more alternative funding resources.

Arthur Samansky

Discount Brokerage

The servicing of customer requests to buy and sell securities without offering or charging for investment advice.

Brokers trading on the nation's security markets buy and sell stocks, bonds, and options. In return for these services, customers pay brokers a commission. Prior to the mid-1970's, the New York Stock Exchange—the nation's leading stock market—had a fixed minimum commission rate. No member firm could charge less for its services than any other member firm. In practice, all firms charged the same rates. Under this structure, investors paid a single charge for order entry and execution, securities clearing, and the advice of a broker (salesperson), whether or not the customer required that advice.

In 1975 the SECURITIES AND EXCHANGE COMMISSION (SEC) required the NYSE to abolish its minimum-fee policy. This opened the door to discount brokerage on the New York Stock Exchange, and many brokerage firms were established to pioneer the idea of the discount commission rate.

The Discount Concept. Today discount brokers offer individual investors full trading services in stocks, bonds, and options at fees which are as much as 75%

less than the typical commissions of most full-cost firms. Discount firms are able to charge less because they do not maintain large sales and research staffs. In the usual full-cost brokerage firm, 30% to 40% of the commission may be paid to the account executive for advice that, in many cases, customers simply do not need or want.

Clients of discount brokers make their own investment decisions. A representative merely takes the order and transmits it to the marketplace to be executed. This is the crucial difference between a discount and a nondiscount broker: the former is paid to buy and sell stocks and the latter provides an advisory service. An account executive of a full-cost firm is a salesperson paid by commission; the more the customer buys and sells, the more the salesperson makes. Representatives of a discount brokerage firm are salaried; they have no incentive to encourage customers to make portfolio changes.

Nondiscount firms help clients manage their investments. Large research staffs provide opinions and recommendations on securities, which the salespeople then may recommend to their clients. The cost of this research is built into the commission rates. Since independent investors do not look to a broker for advice about which securities to trade or when, they are the investors who benefit from using a discount broker.

The Discount Commission Schedule. Three factors influence the typical discount commission rate in all cash and margin transactions:

1. A savings of up to 75% or 85% of the fees charged by most full-cost firms
2. A maximum charge per 100 shares or per option contract
3. A minimum charge of about $20 per transaction

The savings, the maximum charge, and the minimum charge are all based on the size of the order—that is, the number and value of the securities traded.

Discount commission schedules are structured in various ways. For example, a firm might tie its commission rate to the dollar amount of the transaction. For a stock transaction under $5,000, the rate might be $28 plus .008 of the dollar amount; for $5,001 to $15,000, it would be $28 plus .006 of the dollar amount; and so on, with a lowering of the rate until the $50,000-and-over transaction, when it would be $28 plus .0033 of the dollar amount. The maximum charge might be 40 cents per share on the first 100 shares, 30 cents per share from 101 to 500 shares, and 20 cents per share thereafter. The minimum charge might be 2 cents per share.

Discount Commission Savings. The maximum charge per 100 shares or per option contract usually decreases as the number of shares or options goes up. Thus, the percentage of savings on the transaction usually increases as the size of the order goes up.

Typical savings over rates charged by full-service firms might be, on 100 shares at 40, $30–$40 versus from $75 to $81 charged by the full-service firms; on 300 shares at 30, $60–$85 versus from $165 to $175; and on 1,000 shares at 20, $95–$125 versus $350–$385. Other comparisons might pit the discount broker's commissions against the full-commission broker's prices: $30–$40 versus $70–$75 on 5 options at $2; $50–$60 versus $130–$140 on 10 options at $3; $90–$115 versus $210–$225 on 15 at $8; and $70–$80 versus $220–$230 on 25 at $2.

Full-service, nondiscount brokerage firms today negotiate their commission charges to active accounts. While institutional investors benefit from such negotiations, most individual investors do not. Studies show that commissions charged by most nondiscount brokerage firms are currently over 20% higher than they were under the old fixed commission rate.

Dollar savings with discount firms can range from small amounts on small trades such as the purchase or sale of 100 shares at $10 per share ($37.00 NYSE rate versus $20 at one discount house) to very substantial savings on large orders—for example, $1,467 on 3,000 shares at $100 per share ($1,842 versus $375). The savings can run even higher when discount-broker rates are compared with nondiscount-broker rates.

An investor who bought 500 shares at $40 would pay a discount firm $115 instead of the $300 or more that would go to a nondiscount firm. Repeating that trade or its equivalent each month for a year would save the investor at least $2,220—an extra 11% return on the original $20,000.

Savings for clients of discount brokers can average over 50% on stocks and 35% on options. Significantly, discount rates are the same for all investors, whether they trade every day or once a year.

In all important aspects, discount brokers offer services that parallel those found at full-cost firms. A discounter can handle every aspect of a security transaction, from execution of orders to processing of stock certificates and payments of funds. Like all brokers, they rely on extensive computer support in their trading. In fact, some of the most advanced computer systems in the industry are in use at discount firms. Terminals display quotes and monitor all issues and indices. The broker usually has computer access to extensive information about the client's account, including recent transactions, money balances, and security positions.

Questions about recent activity are readily answered. The account number is simply entered into a keyboard terminal, and a detailed history is displayed instantly on the screen:

- Executed price of a given transaction
- Dates of receipt or delivery by the firm of cash or securities
- Customer's debit or credit balance
- Status of any recently bought securities that are in the process of being registered in the client's name

This information is also summarized in written monthly statements, copies of which are kept on microfiche for quick retrieval. Many discount brokers provide monthly statments that are more detailed and understandable than their full-cost counterparts.

Market Information. Stock-market quotation equipment is also part of the discount broker's office. Each account representative can instantly call up quotes on individual securities and market indices on a computer screen—often the same one which displays information on customers' accounts.

The larger discount firms also have specialized departments to provide service in bonds, options, and over-the-counter stocks. Thus, swift and inexpensive trading services are provided on all markets. The only usual brokerage service not offered—and therefore not charged for—is investment advice.

Insurance. Like all brokers, discounters are members of the SECURITIES INVESTOR PROTECTION CORPORATION (SIPC), which protects a broker's clients in liquidation up to $500,000 (or up to $100,000 in cash). Some discount firms also purchase additional protection for their customers for several times the basic SIPC coverage.

Dividends and Interest. A discount broker might issue either a cumulative income check per month or a check for each dividend or interest payment as it comes due.

Standing Instructions. Customers may leave standing instructions with the broker either to transfer and deliver securities when each transaction is executed or to hold securities in the customer's account.

Securities that will be held for a long time are probably best transferred and delivered to the customer. This process normally takes from three to five weeks from date of purchase. Customers who buy and sell frequently usually leave securities in their accounts. This avoids the inconvenience of mailing securities back and forth. In most cases there is no charge for this service.

Types of Accounts. Discount companies offer various types of accounts: individual; joint tenants with rights of survivorship; tenants in common; uniform gifts to minors; trust; corporation; partnership; and estate. Authorizing another person to enter orders for one's account requires completion of a trading authorization to show who is to be given power of attorney.

Margin-Option Accounts. In addition to cash accounts, discount brokers might offer margin-option accounts to qualified customers. Certain option trades and all short sales must be conducted through a margin account. Of course, reduced commission rates also apply in these transactions.

Employee Benefit Plans and Estates. A discount broker might devise a benefit plan for publicly held companies and their employees that would enable employees to buy and sell the corporation's stock at reduced commission rates. A discounter also helps executors of estates and their attorneys in the transfer and sale of securities for estates.

Opening an Account. Most discounters advertise heavily in newspapers and magazines. Potential customers simply call (often an 800 toll-free number) to get an application form, which the customer can then complete and mail to the discount firm. The application is reviewed, and the customer is notified if it is accepted and of the account number so assigned. Normally there is no deposit or prepayment required. When the customer calls to place his or her first trade, the representative checks the computer screen to verify the account, and the customer is in business.

Placing an Order. A discounter can be reached through toll-free long-distance and local telephone numbers. A call to a discounter's office is taken by the first available account representative, unless the caller specifies a particular person.

Account representatives have passed qualifying examinations and are registered with the NEW YORK STOCK EXCHANGE (NYSE) and the NATIONAL ASSOCIATION OF SECURITIES DEALERS, INC. (NASD). The representative who answers the call is the one who places the order. Order executions are reported to the customer by the representative who is free when the reports are received.

To place an order, the customer simply gives his or her name and account number, the name of the security, and the quantity he or she wishes to buy or sell. The account representative gives the latest sale price and current bid and asked prices. Then the representative places the order at the market price or at a price specified by the caller.

The entire order is repeated to the customer. Moreover, telephone conversations are likely to be taped and kept in a confidential file for reference in discussing transactions.

Turnaround Time. Orders for exchange-listed securities are transmitted directly to the exchange floor by a computer-directed, automated order-entry system. Average turnaround time on market orders can be as little as three minutes. Some discount brokers employ their own floor brokers on the New York Stock Exchange and American Exchange; others utilize the services of specialized firms to handle their orders.

Confirming and Settling Trades. According to the Federal Reserve Board requirements, brokerage firms must settle trades on the fifth business day after the trade date. This settlement date is normally one calendar week after the trade date, except when there is a national holiday.

Securities buyers must pay for their purchases within five business days after the trade date. If payment is not received within that time, the broker must liquidate the securities and hold the buyer responsible for any loss that results. Customers receive written confirmations of all executed orders.

Moving Certificates. When a sell order is entered, the securities to be sold should be in the customer's immediate possession or in the broker's account. Stock or bond certificates are due in the broker's office by the settlement date (the fifth business day after the trade date). Funds due the customer are mailed on the settlement date if the securities in the broker's possession are properly endorsed and if all previously purchased securities have been paid for.

Securities sent to the broker should be endorsed to the broker. This makes them nonnegotiable by anyone but the broker. The certificates may be mailed by first-class or by certified or registered mail.

For the customer's protection, securities are often microfilmed upon receipt. For purchases, securities that have been registered in a customer's name might be microfilmed prior to delivery to the customer.

Going from One Broker to Another. Customers wishing to transfer their accounts to a discount broker should request a transfer form from the discounter. This form reflects the customer's security positions and money balance. The transfer form will be sent to the old broker, along with a copy of the customer's most recent monthly statement.

Recent Developments. At the beginning of 1982, not a single major bank in the U.S. offered discount brokerage service to its customers. Federal law prohibited banks from underwriting stock or bond issues. However, during the year the government began approving requests from banks and bank holding companies to establish or acquire discount brokerage services. By year-end, almost 500 commercial banks had announced plans to enter the business, and the number had increased to an estimated 1,000 by the end of 1983. There are more than 14,000 commercial banks in the U.S., and a great majority are expected to eventually offer this service. Major banks have entered the market by buying established discount firms. Smaller banks may easily access discount brokerage through these banks and through a number of firms who aggressively market their services to banks. Under these arrangements, banks may give the customer a choice between placing orders with the bank representative or directly with the discount broker. The discount house executes the transaction and allows the bank a rebate for a percentage of the commission charged.

Banks have added a new dimension to the discount market because of their new customer base and the confidence they generate due to their financial strength. Savings and loan associations are another factor in discount services. Through a cooperative undertaking, manned booths are set up in savings and loan branches throughout the country offering a combination of pure discount transactions and partial investment information.

By the end of 1983 it was estimated that 15% of public trades were processed through discount operations. Analysts observed that the discount customer tends to trade more frequently than the average investor.

Summary. The main characteristic of a discount customer is that he makes his own decisions and is not seeking advice from a broker in making transactions. He is also considered more likely to trade for short-term profits, and, therefore, he is more sensitive to the commission involved. In summary, the customer of a discount broker is mostly concerned with price, while the customer of a full-service firm is looking for a number of other services besides execution—for example, research, recommendations, and help with the myriad of questions that investors face.

According to a New York Stock Exchange survey, by the end of 1983 42 million Americans, or a total of 18.1% of the population, owned shares either directly or through mutual funds. The popularity of discount brokerage could conceivably attract new investors, who would then seek the services that only full-service investors provide.

A growing number of investors now use both full-service and discount brokers. The occasional investor who wants to invest in securities for the long term finds the guidance of a registered representative especially valuable. Despite its price advantages, discount brokerage is not for everyone.

Jim Bowman, George M. Morvis,
and Bernard M. Shavelson

Discount Rates

The Federal Reserve discount rates are the interest charges that borrowers—almost exclusively domestic banks, thrift and similar institutions, and United States branches and agencies of foreign banks—pay when obtaining loans from their local Reserve bank or branch.

The discount rates are one of three major tools used by the U.S. central banking system to conduct monetary policy, which is the influencing of the cost and availability of money and credit. The other major tools are reserve requirements, which are reserves certain institutions must keep against customer deposits; and open-market operations, the buying and selling primarily of U.S. government and federal-agency securities in the secondary market.

The discount rates are particularly important because they establish the costs of reserves borrowed from the central bank, and can, on occasion, be interpreted as a signal of a change in MONETARY POLICY. Of eligible depository institutions, typically only a small fraction borrows from the Federal Reserve in any one week. These borrowings also generally represent only a small part of the banking system's reserves.

Until March 31, 1980, generally only member commercial banks were eligible to borrow. As a result of the International Banking Act of 1978 and the Depository Institutions Deregulation and Monetary Control Act of 1980, all depository institutions, including U.S. branches and agencies of foreign banks, with transaction accounts or nonpersonal time deposits were given the same discount-window privileges as member banks.

Nevertheless, under normal circumstances, all institutions are expected to seek funds outside the Federal Reserve before applying for discount-window borrowings. Among those sources are credit programs of the FEDERAL HOME LOAN BANKS, for member savings and loan associations and mutual savings banks; or the Central Liquidity Facility of the NATIONAL CREDIT UNION ADMINISTRATION and credit-union centrals, for member credit unions.

Although the basic discount rate generally receives the widest public attention, there are two other Federal Reserve discount rates covering extended credit and emergency credit. Starting in September 1980, four types of credit became available to eligible depository institutions: short-term adjustment credit, and three types of extended credit (*see* DISCOUNT WINDOW). Interest on adjustment credit generally is at the basic rate, plus any surcharge that might be applied, depending upon the length and frequency of the borrowing. Advances for seasonal credit also are at the basic rate, plus any surcharge. The rate for other extended credit may be more than the basic rate, depending upon policy considerations and money-market conditions. In extraordinary circumstances, emergency credit is available for individuals, partnerships, and corporations, other than depository institutions, at a rate in excess of the highest discount rate in effect for depository institutions.

Previously, there were five types of credit available: short-term adjustment; seasonal; emergency; special for individuals, partnerships, and corporations; and special for foreign central banks, foreign governments, and monetary authorities. Interest rates for most of the borrowings were scaled upward from the basic rate covering short-term adjustment credit.

As part of the March 1980 credit-restraint program, the Federal Reserve instituted a surcharge on borrowings by large commercial banks to discourage frequent use of the discount window and speed bank adjustments in response to restraint on bank reserves. The law requires each discount rate to be set by the board of directors of each Reserve bank every 14 days, subject to review and determination by the board of governors of the FEDERAL RESERVE SYSTEM.

The board of governors of the Federal Reserve system doesn't initiate discount-rate changes, but acts on recommendations of Reserve bank directors. The board of governors has three options when it receives a recommendation: The governors may approve the rate, disapprove the rate, or make no decision. In either of the last two circumstances, the Reserve bank directors may continue to recommend a rate change. In addition, the board of governors may act on one petition or may wait until it has requests from several Reserve banks before acting. The board of governors also may act on any day to approve a rate.

With 20 exceptions from 1914 through August 1982, the basic discount rate has not been changed by one percentage point or more at one time by the Federal Reserve Bank of New York.

The exceptions were September 26, 1916, when the rate moved to 3% from the 4% established on February 18, 1915; January 23, 1920, to 6% from 4.75% on November 3, 1919; June 1, 1920, to 7% from 6%; August 9, 1929, to 6% from 5% on July 13, 1928; November 1, 1929, to 5% from 6%; October 9, 1931, to 2.5% from 1.5% on May 8, 1931; October 16, 1931, to 3.5% from 2.5%; March 3, 1933, to 3.5% from 2.5% on June 24, 1932; November 1, 1978, to 9.5% from 8.5%

on October 16, 1978; October 8, 1979, to 12% from 11% on September 19, 1979; 13% on February 15, 1980; 12% on May 30, 1980; 11% on June 13, 1980; 10% on July 28, 1980; 11% on September 26, 1980; November 17, 1980, to 12%; December 5, 1980, to 13%; May 5, 1981, to 14%; November 2, 1981, to 13%; and December 4, 1981, to 12%.

The lowest basic discount rate at the New York Fed was ½% effective October 30, 1942, through April 24, 1946. The highest rate was 14% from May 5, 1981, through November 1, 1981.

Historically, too, the basic discount rate generally has been changed infrequently in the course of a year. In only eight years through early March 1983 has the rate changed five times or more at the New York Fed: 1921, 1930, and 1958, five times each; 1971, six times; and 1973, 1978, 1980, and 1982, seven times each.

Uniformity of rates was generally maintained from the founding of the Reserve system in 1914 to the mid-1920s. Variations developed in subsequent years. Discount-rate uniformity returned to the system in recent times in the recognition that the rate reflected national credit policy rather than regional credit conditions.

Occasionally, because the separate Reserve bank boards of directors don't meet on the same day, rate differences occur for a few days. There have also been occasions when a particular Reserve bank has decided not to change its rates immediately to indicate its disagreement with the direction of monetary policy. However, the holdout Reserve bank typically has brought the rate into line quickly to avoid distorting national money and credit flows.

Since the early 1970s, the term *discount rate* has been somewhat of a misnomer, since virtually all loans made by Federal Reserve banks are in the form of advances rather than discounts. Until 1971, advances and discounts were on a discount basis at some Reserve banks; interest was deducted at the time of the loan. If a borrowing institution repaid the loan before maturity, the institution received a rebate.

Most Reserve banks computed the rebate at the rate at which the advance was made. Some Reserve banks computed the rebate at the rate prevailing at the time of the rebate, if the discount rate was less than at the time the advance was made. Since 1971, interest on advances has been computed on an accrual basis and paid at the time of loan repayment. Changes in the discount rate during the period are applied to all outstanding borrowings.

Interest on loans is computed for the borrowing period on a 365-day year. If the maturity date falls on a Sunday or holiday, the computation follows applicable state laws. In the New York district (New York

State, the 12 northern and central counties of New Jersey, and Fairfield County, Connecticut), the computation includes the Sunday or holiday. Advances in the New York district are granted so the maturity falls on a business day.

Arthur Samansky

Discount Window

Depository institutions with transaction accounts or nonpersonal time deposits are eligible to borrow at the discount window of a Federal Reserve bank (*see* FEDERAL RESERVE SYSTEM). A transaction account is a deposit against which a depositor may make withdrawals by a transferable instrument to pay a third party. Among these accounts are checking accounts, negotiable order of withdrawal accounts, savings deposits subject to automatic transfers, and credit-union share draft accounts. Nonpersonal time deposits are those of organizations rather than persons.

The basic type of credit available at the discount window is short-term adjustment credit. Such credit is available to domestic COMMERCIAL BANKS, mutual SAVINGS BANKS, SAVINGS AND LOAN ASSOCIATIONS, CREDIT UNIONS, and United States branches and agencies of foreign banks, to help them achieve an orderly adjustment to unexpected changes in their assets and liabilities, primarily increases in loans or declines in deposits. Through the use of discount-window credit, eligible institutions are given the time necessary to make internal adjustments to these changed circumstances. These institutions may appropriately look to the discount window for credit assistance when their funding needs can't be met in the money markets. Smaller institutions may borrow for longer periods.

Reserve bank credit is available after reasonable alternative sources of funds, including credit from special industry lenders, are used. Special industry lenders include the FEDERAL HOME LOAN BANKS, for member savings and loan associations and savings banks; and the NATIONAL CREDIT UNION ADMINISTRATION's Central Liquidity Facility and credit-union centrals, for member credit unions.

The Federal Reserve Act requires all advances at the discount window, including those for short-term adjustment purposes, to be secured. Most discount-window loans are secured by U.S. government and agency securities and short-term customer notes. Short-term adjustment credit is extended at the basic discount rate, plus any surcharge that may be imposed (*see* DISCOUNT RATES). Loans also may be secured by other forms of collateral, such as state and municipal securities, longer-term customer notes, and mortgage loans covering one- to four-family residences. Smaller country and regional banks generally use U.S. government and agency securities as collateral, while the larger money-market banks primarily use customer notes or residential mortgages.

The Reserve banks administer discount-window credit under provisions of the Federal Reserve Act and Regulation "A," which was amended effective September 1980 to reflect changes brought about by the International Banking Act of 1978 and the Depository Institutions Deregulation and Monetary Control Act of 1980.

The statutory and regulatory framework generally provides rather broad latitude to the Reserve banks for the exercise of judgment and discretion in the operation of the discount window. Thus, the window can be equitably administered in a manner responsive to the needs of individual institutions and the local and regional conditions affecting those institutions. In fulfilling this broad administrative responsibility, Federal Reserve banks consider, among other things, an institution's size, its access to the money markets and other sources of funds, the special circumstances facing the institution, and the geographic and economic environment in which the institution is operating.

The general practice at the New York Reserve Bank has been to limit maturities on adjustment-credit advances to not more than two weeks for smaller banks, to the end of the weekly reserve period for larger banks, and to overnight for the largest banks. Discount-window loans may generally be renewed beyond their initial maturity if institutions need the additional time to make adjustments in their assets and liabilities.

In addition to short-term adjustment credit, the provisions of the Federal Reserve Act and the amended Regulation "A" authorize the Federal Reserve banks to provide extended credit. Extended credit is provided through three programs designed to assist depository institutions in meeting longer-term needs for funds.

One program provides seasonal credit, for periods up to six months, to smaller depository institutions, which generally lack continuous access to market funds. A second program assists institutions that experience special difficulties arising from exceptional circumstances or practices involving only that institution. Assistance in these cases is provided only when funds aren't available from other sources.

In situations where more general liquidity strains affect a broad range of institutions—such as thrift institutions that emphasize longer-term, mortgage assets—credit may be provided to address the problems of the institutions being affected by the general situation.

In very unusual circumstances, a Reserve bank may, after consultation with the board of governors of the Federal Reserve system, advance credit to individuals, partnerships, and corporations that aren't depository institutions, if the Reserve bank determines credit isn't available from other sources and failure to obtain that credit would adversely affect the economy. This authority has been utilized rarely.

Arthur Samansky

Doing Business As (DBA)

Sometimes an individual or entity wishes to engage in a business activity under a business name other than the person's own name or the name of the company itself. Under these circumstances, the person may assume a business name and conduct a business under that name. Thus, the person would be known as "John Doe, doing business as Doe Booksellers."

Unlike a corporation, "doing business as" does not create a separate entity from the person or company that adopts it; it is merely the use of a promotional name or a name better suited for the actual business activities being conducted. In many states, the law requires that any entity or person assuming a fictitious name to conduct business must register that name by filing a certificate with the appropriate clerk's office in the county where the business is being conducted.

Alan J. Pomerantz

Dollar Averaging

See COMMON STOCK.

Dow Jones Averages

Statistical indicators of broad price fluctuations in the stock market. Published by Dow Jones & Company, Inc., which is also the publisher of the *Wall Street Journal*, these indexes are widely used to analyze and report on price trends in the market for industrial stocks, transportation companies, and public utilities, as well as the market as a whole.

The *Dow Jones industrial average (DJIA)*, first published on May 26, 1896, is the oldest continuous average of U.S. stock-market prices. It is composed of 30 major companies whose stock is held by many institutions and individuals. The *Dow Jones transportation average*, formerly the "railroad average," is composed of 20 transportation companies. The *utility average* includes 15 public utilities. A *composite average* of all 65 stocks also is published. All of the companies are listed on the NEW YORK STOCK EXCHANGE (NYSE).

Minute by minute, as stocks are bought and sold, some prices are rising while others are falling or holding steady. The Dow Jones average, especially the widely followed industrial average, is designed to reflect the broader, underlying price trend of the market as a whole.

Reading the Chart. The Dow Jones averages are usually presented in chart form. The one published by the *Wall Street Journal* shows the high, low, and close for each day's trading during the current week and the 12 preceding weeks. Each day's range is indicated by a vertical bar, with the top as the high and the bottom as the low, and a small dot that shows the closing average. Statistical material presented with the chart includes the hour-by-hour level of the averages each trading day, the closing level, and the change from the preceding day's close.

Dow Jones 65 Components. Thirty stocks used in the Dow Jones industrial average are Allied Corporation; Aluminum Company; American Brands; American Can; American Tel & Tel; Bethlehem Steel; Du-Pont; Eastman Kodak; Exxon; General Electric; General Foods; General Motors; Goodyear; Inco; IBM; International Harvester; International Paper; Manville Corporation; Merck; Minnesota M & M; Owens-Illinois; Procter & Gamble; Sears Roebuck; Standard Oil of California; Texaco; Union Carbide; United Technologies; U.S. Steel; Westinghouse Electric; and Woolworth.

The 20 transportation stocks used are American Airlines; Burlington Northern; Canadian Pacific; Carolina Freight; Consolidated Freight; CSX Corporation; Delta Airlines; Eastern Airlines; MoPac Corporation; Norfolk Southern; Northwest Air; Overnite Transp.; Pan Am; Rio Grande Ind.; Santa Fe Industries; Southern Pacific; Transway International; Trans World; UAL, Inc.; and Union Pacific.

The 15 utility stocks used are American Electric Power; Cleveland E. Ill.; Colum-Gas System; Commonwealth Edison; Consolidated Edison; Consolidated Natural Gas; Detroit Edison; Houston Ind.; Niagara Mohawk; Pacific G & E; Panhandle Eastern; People's Energy; Philadelphia Electric; Public Service E & G; and Southern Cal. Edison.*

How the Averages Are Used. The averages are generally used as a kind of shorthand answer to the question "How is the market today?" The answer is usually expressed in terms of the Dow Jones industrials, or "the Dow," as it is also known. "It's strong—up ten points" is a reference to the DJIA.

The averages also are used in technical analyses of market trends. Indeed, this was their original purpose. Technical analysts of the market, known as "techni-

*Components current as of year-end 1983.

cians," have developed a variety of theories to explain and possibly forecast broad movements of the market. They rely on statistical indicators and ratios rather than on so-called fundamental factors, such as trends in corporate profitability. One of the most widely known of the statistical techniques is the Dow theory, which is based on observations of the market by Charles H. Dow, a cofounder of Dow Jones & Company and the originator of the Dow industrial average.

Some analysts used ratios related to the averages. For example, the price/earnings ratio of the DJIA provides a multiple that reflects the value placed on earnings of the market as a whole. A similar ratio is the dividend yield of the DJIA.

Investors use the averages and these related ratios to compare particular stocks in which they may be interested to the market in general. For example, an increase in the price of a particular stock would be regarded as more favorable on a day when the DJIA fell than it would be if the entire market had moved up.

Strictly speaking, the so-called averages should be called "indexes" or "indicators." They aren't averages in the sense that the industrials, for example, represent the total of the prices of 30 stock issues, divided by 30. Thus, a ten-point rise or fall in the industrials doesn't mean a rise or fall of $10 per share. With the industrials at, for example, 1,000, a ten-point change would indicate a change of only 1% for the average share.

Calculation of the Averages. When the DJIA was initiated, the calculation of the average was simple arithmetic. The prices of the 30 stocks were totaled and divided by 30. If this method were still followed, distortions would be introduced that would make a current reading not comparable with readings of previous periods. The chief reason is that companies split their stocks when the price rises; for example, issuing one new share for each share currently outstanding—a two-for-one split. Similar distortions could occur through stock dividends or the substitution of a new stock in the average.

Here is an illustration: Take a three-stock average made up of one share in each of three companies—Blue Co., Green Co., and Black Co. If Blue is at $30 and Green is at $20 and Black is at $10, the total is $60 and the average is $20. Now, say Blue splits two-for-one. A Blue stockholder now has two certificates, each worth $15 (other things being equal), instead of one certificate worth $30. If the average were computed in the same way, it would be $15—$15 plus $20 plus $10, divided by 3. But the dollar value of all the outstanding shares hasn't changed at all.

There are various ways of dealing with this problem. The method used by Dow Jones is to change the divisor. In the illustration, the new divisor would be 2.25 instead of 3, giving an unchanged result of 20.

Over the years, stock splits and substitutions have reduced the divisor of the DJIA to less than 2, from the original 30. This is why the DJIA is much greater than the price of any individual share in its makeup. Also, this means that it is incorrect to speak of changes in the average in terms of dollars. The correct term is *points*.

Whenever a change is made in any of the divisors of the various Dow Jones averages, it is announced in the *Wall Street Journal* and on the Dow Jones News Service wire.

History. Charles Dow used averages in his reporting on the stock market in a newsletter published by Dow Jones from the time of its establishment as a company in 1882. But the first publication of an index of U.S. industrial stocks is dated as May 26, 1896. In 1916 the list was expanded to 20 industrials. The 30-stock index dates from October 1, 1928.

The transportation average, originally all railroads, was first published on October 26, 1896. Transportation companies of other kinds were first added on January 2, 1970. The utility average was first published in December 1929.

As of mid-July 1982, the all-time high of the DJIA was 1051.70, reached on January 11, 1973. The Dow also topped 1,000 during 1972, 1976, and 1981. The all-time low was 41.22, reached in the depths of the depression, July 1932. The predepression high was 381.70 in 1929.

Selection of the Components. Selection of the companies used in developing the averages is the responsibility of the editors of the *Wall Street Journal*. The issues are chosen from the 2,000 or so issues traded on the New York Stock Exchange as representative of the broad market and American industry. The Dow is often called a BLUE CHIP indicator because the companies making up the industrial average are large, well established, and widely owned by the public.

For the sake of continuity, changes are made infrequently. Most often a new issue is added to the list in order to replace one that has been merged into another company, but changes are also made from time to time in order to improve the representation of particular industries. The last major such change occurred in June 1979 when International Business Machines and Merck & Company were substituted for Chrysler Corporation and Esmark, Inc., in order to gain representation of the technology and health-care industries.

Further Information. Dow Jones & Company, the copyright owner of the averages, provides further information on them through the Educational Service Bureau, Dow Jones & Co., P.O. Box 300, Princeton, New Jersey 08540.

A daily chart of the averages is published in the *Wall Street Journal* and the statistics are widely available. A list of the companies in the various indexes and other statistical material is published each Monday in the *Journal*.

Charles N. Stabler

·E·

Economic Recovery Tax Act of 1981 (ERTA)

This major legislation was the largest tax reduction in U.S. history. It contained a number of important advantages for financial planning involving the unified tax (estates and personal gifts) and income tax, which the law has always treated separately. (Normally, estates and personal gifts are not subject to income tax.) Please remember we are referring here to gifts to your friends and family, not to charities, which is another matter entirely.

Estates and Gifts to Spouses. You may now leave on death (estate) or give while living (gifts) *unlimited* amounts to your spouse without any tax at all.

Estates and Gifts to Other Persons. The act did the following in this regard:

- Raised the unified-tax credit. Although gifts made and estates left to people other than your spouse are taxable under the unified tax, you receive a credit toward this tax, which ERTA raised to $62,800 in 1982, going up in steps to $192,800 in 1987. It is easier to understand this "tax credit" by relating it to the estate or gift amounts: $192,800 is the unified tax on $600,000 of assets; thus, by 1987 you will be able to give away while living or leave on death a total of $600,000 to people other than your spouse (children, for example) without tax.
- Raised the amounts of the annual gift exclusion. In addition to unlimited gifts to a spouse and the uni-fied-tax credit, everyone can also make tax-free personal gifts through the annual gift exclusion. Each year a single person can give up to $10,000 and a married couple $20,000 to each of as many persons as desired. People usually find this surprising, so let's repeat: $10,000/$20,000 to *each* recipient, *each* year, with *no limit* to the number of recipients. And, as mentioned before, people who receive the gifts do not pay income tax on them.

Other Provisions. The Economic Recovery Tax Act also did the following:

- Reduced the maximum unified-tax rate from 70% to 50%.
- Made all individuals below age 70½ who have earned income eligible for Individual Retirement Accounts (IRA's), even if they are also in qualified pension plans. (This applies to *both* husbands and wives.) The act also permits a tax-favored annual contribution of up to $2,000 or 100% or earned income, whichever is less, to an IRA, which is subtracted from your income for tax purposes. If your spouse does not work, you may contribute up to $2,250 each year.
- Made various personal-income-tax improvements, such as lowering rates for ordinary income and capital gains; giving married couples a special credit; indexing tax rates to inflation (1985); and creating the one-time All Savers Certificates. Since ERTA, Congress has discussed revising some of these, so you would be wise to check out current tax status.

Harold C. Luckstone, Jr.

Economist

The fundamental question of economics is how to use limited resources to meet unlimited wants. The answer tells which wants are satisfied and the degree of sacrifice necessary to achieve that satisfaction. This question can be asked in many kinds of situations, from how many children a family can afford to have, to how a nation can balance the conflicting goals of low inflation and low unemployment. Economists analyze these problems from many points of view and using many different methodologies. Demand for their analyses is growing, particularly in view of the rapidity of world events and the accompanying volatility of financial conditions and business institutions. The U.S. Department of Labor estimated that there were 160,000 people working as economists in America in 1981 and that this number will grow by almost 30% by 1990, compared with a total projected employment growth of just over 20%.

Economists in History. Early economists were philosophers and political thinkers, fairly removed from the workaday world. Adam Smith, for instance, taught moral philosophy at the University of Glasgow before he wrote *The Wealth of Nations.* In this famous economics classic, he advocated free trade and pure competition as ways to achieve the greatest economic well-being; and he introduced the concept of the invisible hand, whereby rational, economic man, if he acts to further his own welfare, will be led to act cooperatively with others to further the welfare of society as a whole.

These fundamental topics continued in the writings of Smith's successors, most notably David Ricardo and Thomas Malthus, but their conclusions had a different emphasis: that the frailty of humanity, along with population growth, would lead to a constant struggle for economic betterment. This conclusion inspired Karl Marx, a history scholar, to develop a theory of constant class struggle.

All these writers developed broad concepts of economic policy based largely on tenets of moral and social philosophy. Writing during the Industrial Revolution, they all believed the value of a product rested in the amount of the labor required for its manufacture—that is, price was a function solely of production cost.

Full-time economists first appeared about 1870. Several English and Austrian writers realized that consumer utility and demand were as important as cost in determining value and price. They began to apply calculus and other mathematical techniques to this more complete supply-and-demand system. Statistical and business-cycle analysis emerged early in the twentieth century, stimulated after the depression by Keynes's conclusion that government policy should be designed to help offset business cycles. It was then necessary to develop quantitative models of the economy in order to judge the kinds and extent of policy actions that might be used to try to diminish swings in economic activity.

What Do Economists Do Now? All these threads have come together in the 1980s, producing a wide range of both micro- and macroeconomic problems for economists to deal with, including such things as determining appropriate schedules of airline fares and assessing the best method for implementing monetary policy to forecast economic trends, including those of both airline fares and monetary-policy developments. Economists no longer do their work only in academic environments, although these remain important breeding grounds for new economic ideas.

An easy way to see the variety and significance of the work economists do is to look at the places where they are employed and the kinds of issues they deal with in each place.

Colleges and universities. Teaching economics has gained increasing importance as the complexity of the modern economy has made it necessary for ordinary citizens to understand how it functions. Economics professors also engage in research at the frontier of economic knowledge. Some of this research is quite abstract, but the ideas they develop may eventually become the basis for quite concrete applications. Rational expectations, for instance—the theory behind part of President Reagan's economic policy instituted in 1981—were first explored by professors as early as 1961.

Research institutions. Several nonprofit economic research institutes sponsor research, often in particular fields or applications. The Brookings Institution, for example, employs scholars who specialize in public policy problems, mostly fiscal policy. The National Bureau of Economic Research (NBER) also conducts research in many macroeconomic areas; it is best known for analysis of business cycles, including the determination of the dates of business-cycle peaks and troughs.

Governments. City, state, and federal governments employ thousands of economists. They study population trends; analyze local and national business conditions to facilitate budget projections; make fiscal and monetary policy recommendations; and analyze individual product markets and industries as background for regulatory and antitrust actions. They use all this information to design statistics for themselves and private economists to follow economic developments. (Although government economists are the biggest data gatherers, private economists also engage in this activity.)

Businesses, trade associations, and unions. Individual companies employ economists to help with corporate planning. They analyze the determinants of supply and demand for the company's products and forecast the costs the company must pay—for wages, raw materials, interest, and taxes—and the prices it can charge. Company economists and those of trade associations and unions also assess the impact of public-policy proposals and actions on their industries and may then advocate a particular outcome.

Banks and financial institutions. Economists at financial institutions assist in business planning; but because the product of this industry is money and its prices are interest rates, these economists concentrate on macroeconomic developments. Some of them conduct specialized analyses of day-to-day interest-rate movements and short-term Federal Reserve policy; they are called "money-market economists" or "Fed watchers." The work of all these financial economists is used by their own firms to formulate investment strategy. They also often publish their analyses in newsletters and reports circulated to the firms' customers and the media.

Consulting firms. Many companies either are too small to support their own economics department or they want to supplement theirs with outside resources such as special expertise or computer facilities. They then hire an economic consulting firm. Consulting firms range in size from one person operating from a home office to large computer-based organizations utilizing sizable econometric models and data bases and maintaining branches in several cities.

Carol A. Stone

Edge Act Corporations

Corporations, generally subsidiaries of banks, organized under the Federal Reserve Act for the purpose of engaging in international or foreign banking or similar activities. They are named for Senator Walter E. Edge, the sponsor of the 1919 legislation authorizing them. These corporations are designed primarily as a means of either conducting business abroad or financing international trade, particularly exports, in the United States. Although most banks themselves have authority to organize foreign branches and invest in foreign corporations abroad, they are generally restricted to engaging in the commercial banking business. Through Edge Act corporations, United States banks are able to compete more effectively with foreign financial institutions by conducting a wider range of financial activities than permitted to banks. Edge corporations can also function in the United States essentially as branches of their parent banks' international departments, but with the additional benefit of being able to operate in several states, unlike banks, which are generally restricted to branches in a single state.

These two functions of Edge Act corporations, the one foreign and the other domestic, are normally conducted in separate organizations. Edge corporations used as vehicles to make foreign investments are considered "nonbanking Edges." They are essentially holding companies that own the shares of foreign corporations. At the end of 1982, there were 50 nonbanking Edges with investments in hundreds of such companies abroad. These include foreign commercial, investment, and merchant banks; and finance, trust, consulting, and leasing companies. These financial activities include such nontraditional banking activities as the underwriting, distribution, and sale of corporate securities.

Edge corporations that operate within the United States are known as "banking Edges." These corporations may engage directly in any financial activities that the Federal Reserve Board determines are inci-

dental to international or foreign business. A major purpose is to assist U.S. exporters and importers with financing international trade. Permitted activities include foreign lending, trading in foreign currencies, acceptance financing, maintenance of certain deposits, financing of domestic transport and storage of imports and exports, and financing the production of goods for export. At the end of 1982, there were 81 banking Edges, several with branches in more than one state.

Griffith L. Garwood

Effective Annual Yield

See YIELD.

Electronic Fund Transfer (EFT) Systems

Systems that enable funds to be paid or transferred electronically through the use of electronic terminals, telephones, computers, magnetic tape, or other devices for transmitting data. These systems are made possible by recent advances in data processing and telecommunications, and they offer opportunities to provide payment services that are more convenient, secure, and efficient than paper-based payment systems using cash or checks. They can significantly reduce the costs of providing routine banking services, and provide financial institutions with a means of conducting business on an interstate basis where direct expansion beyond state lines is otherwise prohibited. Nearly all depository institutions receive electronically originated payments on behalf of their depositors through the U.S. Treasury's program of directly depositing recurring federal payments such as Social Security. At the end of 1982, over 76% of commercial and mutual savings banks, and 16% of all other depository institutions, were themselves providing some type of EFT services. These services take several different forms.

Automated Teller Machines (ATM's). AUTOMATED TELLER MACHINES may simply dispense cash, or they may be more complex and allow a customer to electronically perform a wide range of banking transactions. Such machines typically require the use of a plastic card, either a CREDIT CARD or a debit card. Although it looks like a credit card, a debit card is used to immediately obtain funds from a customer's existing deposit account, rather than causing a financial institution to advance funds, which later must be repaid by the cardholder. In addition to withdrawing funds, a customer using an ATM can often make deposits, transfer funds between accounts, and in many cases instruct the bank to make payments to third parties—for example, to a utility company. At the end of 1982, approximately 30,000 ATM's were in operation. Although most are owned by single institutions and provide access only to accounts held at that institution, in some localities several financial institutions may share in the ATM system, giving access to accounts at more than one institution through a single machine. Increasingly, individual bank ATM systems are being linked together in regional or national interchange networks, thereby providing electronic access to accounts over a wide geographic area.

Automated Clearinghouses (ACH's). AUTOMATED CLEARINGHOUSES are computerized facilities that provide the means for processing electronic payment instructions. ACH's receive payment instructions in computer-readable form, and sort these instructions in order to provide individual institutions with lists of either electronic "credits" (payments *into* individual accounts) or "debits" (payments *from* individual accounts). For example, rather than preparing individual payroll checks for employees, an employer may deliver to a depository institution a magnetic tape containing the names, account numbers, and pay amounts for each employee. The depository institution combines this pay information with similar payment information from other customers and sends it to the ACH. The ACH sorts the information and transfers funds from the employer's account at one institution to each institution identified on the tape, which in turn credits the individual employee's account. ACH's also process "debit" or withdrawal instructions—for example, where individuals have authorized mortgage or insurance payments to be made automatically from their accounts. The federal government is the biggest user of the ACH system in its "direct deposit" program.

Point-of-Sale (POS) terminals. These connect a merchant electronically with a financial institution. By use of a debit card, a customer can transfer funds directly from his account to the merchant's account in payment for goods or services. The merchant thus obtains immediate access to the funds (without, for example, waiting for a check to clear), and of course the customer's account is immediately reduced by the amount of the purchase. (*See* POINT-OF-SALE (POS) SYSTEMS.)

Home (Videotex) banking. Efforts are under way to develop systems that will enable customers to transact banking business electronically at home through "Videotex" hookups with financial institutions. Such systems will enable customers to view their accounts on display screens (in some cases on their own televisions) and to instruct the institutions to transfer funds between accounts or pay bills.

Large dollar electronic fund transfers between banks are made within the U.S. through two systems

known as FEDWIRE and Bank Wire, and internationally through the CLEARING HOUSE INTERBANK PAYMENTS SYSTEM (CHIPS) and the Society for Worldwide Interbank Financial Telecommunications (SWIFT). The Fedwire is a wire transfer network operated by the Federal Reserve system and used to transfer large dollar amounts—averaging over $2 million per transaction—between banks, for their own accounts or for customers. Bank Wire is a private alternative to Fedwire and likewise provides for large dollar transfers between banks. CHIPS processes international fund transfers for members and associates of the New York Clearing House Association. SWIFT delivers fund-transfer instructions, worldwide, through a telecommunication network linking 900 member banks in 39 countries.

Efforts are being made to automate portions of the check system through so-called check truncation—the conversion of the paper check to electronic payment information at some point during the check-handling process. For example, a bank receiving a paper check in deposit may hold the check and send the payment instruction electronically to the bank on which the check is drawn. The customer in turn receives a detailed list of the withdrawals from the account, rather than the canceled checks.

EFT systems are subject to a complex combination of federal and state laws. Some state laws restrict the use of ATM's by local institutions and prohibit out-of-state institutions from placing them within the state. The Federal Electronic Fund Transfer Act establishes rights and liabilities of consumers and financial institutions. Among other things, it requires disclosure of the terms and conditions of accounts subject to EFT activity, sets limits on customer liability for unauthorized transfers, requires periodic reporting of EFT activity, and provides that allegations of errors must be promptly investigated.

Griffith L. Garwood

Employee Retirement Income Security Act of 1974 (ERISA)

The Employee Retirement Income Security Act of 1974 was enacted on Labor Day to reform the nation's laws relating to private pensions. It deals with the protection of employee benefit rights and covers pension and welfare plans in the U.S.

ERISA does not cover government plans, certain church plans, or plans maintained solely to comply with workers' compensation, unemployment compensation, or disability-insurance laws. ERISA does not require any employer to establish a plan, but employers that do so must comply with ERISA's provisions relating to minimum funding, participation and vesting, fiduciary responsibility, tax qualification, and plan termination, among others.

ERISA contains four titles. Title I deals with employee benefit rights and is administered by the Labor Management Services Administration of the U.S. Department of Labor. Title II is administered by the Employee Plans Division of the Internal Revenue Service and deals with the tax qualification of employee benefit plans. Title III deals with the division of responsibility among the agencies and contains other miscellaneous provisions. Title IV deals with plan termination and plan insolvency insurance for defined benefit plans and is administered by the PENSION BENEFIT GUARANTY CORPORATION (PBGC).

Edwin M. Jones

Endorsement

An endorsement is the most frequently used means of transferring legal rights in negotiable instruments. Checks, drafts, notes, and certificates of deposit are considered negotiable (that is, commonly acceptable in lieu of legal tender) instruments if they meet four conditions. They must be in writing and signed by the maker or drawer. They must contain an unconditional order or promise to pay a specified sum of money. They must be payable on demand or at a specified time. They must be payable to a specified party or to anyone to whom that party has transferred rights or to the person in possession of the instrument.

There are four principal kinds of endorsements. A *blank endorsement* consists simply of the signature of the instrument's previous holder. A *special endorsement* is where the previous holder names the party and signs the instrument. A *restrictive endorsement* is where the holder, in addition to signing the instrument, identifies the purpose of the transfer and restricts its use—for example, endorsing a check "For Deposit Only." Finally, there is the *qualified endorsement*, which limits the endorser's liability to guarantee reimbursement if the instrument is later dishonored.

Phil Battey

Equity Income Unit Trusts

See UNIT INVESTMENT TRUSTS.

Estate Planning

Estate planning, in its broadest sense, is the means people use to accumulate and conserve property during their lifetimes and to distribute such property to the objects of their bounty both during their lifetimes and upon their deaths.

Throughout the processes of accumulation, conservation, and distribution, tax considerations and personal considerations are ever present, influencing to a limited or major extent what decisions ultimately are made. These considerations may or may not be in conflict with each other. For example, if one's personal consideration is to leave the greatest amount of money to one's favorite charity and this can be accomplished by full use of a tax deduction, such as the estate-tax charitable deduction, then both considerations work together to achieve the desired result. If, however, you wish to leave your brother most of your estate, to the exclusion of your spouse, your personal consideration for your brother is in conflict with the tax consideration for making full use of the unlimited marital deduction. In this type of situation, only the person whose property it is can decide which consideration is more important. It is the job of the estate-planning professional to put forth the options that may be taken and to explain all of the consequences, both tax and nontax, that are generated by the exercise of those options.

Most people, when they hear the term *estate planning,* immediately think of a will (*see* WILL). It is true that the will is the cornerstone of the distribution part of estate planning, as this is the document that speaks for you after you are gone. However, before property can be distributed according to your wishes at death, there must be property to be distributed. This is the accumulation element of the estate-planning process.

One's property consists of everything that one has the power of alienation (i.e., disposition) over, whether it be real, personal, tangible, or intangible. Property is accumulated in many different ways, most commonly from salary, business income, investment income, and inheritances. Life-insurance benefits are included in the broad category of inheritances.

As one accumulates property, the same tax considerations vs. personal considerations are at work, either harmoniously or in conflict. For example, for a young person, the job or profession is usually the main means of acquiring an estate. If he is receiving salary or is self-employed, he will face the choice of whether to contribute to a qualified retirement plan (an INDIVIDUAL RETIREMENT ACCOUNT or a KEOGH PLAN) or use that money for personal pleasures, such as an extra vacation or buying a new automobile. Once again, only the individual involved can make this choice, but he must be advised of the consequences of each action. Of course, if his personal goal is to have the greatest amount of money available to him at retirement and pay the least amount of present taxes, then the tax considerations and personal considerations will go hand in hand, and the choice of action will be an easy one.

Another consideration for the young person is whether he wants to, and how much he should, invest in life and disability insurance. People plan estates based on the systematic accumulation of assets. They then plan to distribute these assets to their loved ones years later, after the systematic accumulation is completed. The two most common roadblocks to this plan are death and disability. Both will stop the accumulation process in its tracks. However, one can plan for these contingencies by having adequate insurance coverage. LIFE INSURANCE is sometimes called the "instant estate." It provides for your loved ones what you would have wanted them to have if you had survived and systematically accumulated property pursuant to the accumulation part of your estate plan. It also provides for the current needs that would have been taken care of with current income.

DISABILITY INCOME INSURANCE may be even more important than life insurance in an estate-planning sense, in that it provides for the insured, as well as his family, in case of a disability that prevents the insured from earning money. While people generally can conceive of a premature death, be it by accident or otherwise, not many give much thought to what consequences accrue when one is disabled and unable to earn money and acquire an estate. To consider this possibility in one's early income-producing years is an essential element of total estate planning and should not be overlooked.

As one accumulates an estate, it is vital that it be conserved to the maximum extent within the realm of satisfying personal needs and desires (*see* FINANCIAL PLANNING). The greatest threat to the depletion of accumulated assets, other than a medical catastrophe, is taxes.

The effects of inflation and higher wages in the last ten to fifteen years has been evidenced to a great extent in the increased tax rates endured by all taxpayers. With our graduated tax-rate system, more and more of our income is earmarked to pay income taxes. If we are to conserve our estates, consideration must be given to minimizing the amounts that go to the tax collector.

As stated previously, an excellent means of deferring taxes, while at the same time providing for one's retirement, is by setting up and contributing to a tax-qualified retirement plan. This will reduce current taxes while providing for additional accumulation on a tax-deferred basis. While taxes ultimately must be paid when distributions are made, this will theoretically occur in the participant's retirement years, when he will be in a much lower tax bracket.

Another means of taking advantage of the law to reduce current tax liability is to set up what is commonly known as a Clifford Trust. This is generally established by a high-income taxpayer who wants to divert passive income to someone else while retaining the right to recover, at a later date, the underlying property that generated the income. The income beneficiary of such a trust is a person in a low income-tax bracket, usually an elderly parent or other relative.

For such a trust to be effective for the purpose created, it must last for at least ten years or the lifetime of the income beneficiary, whichever is shorter. The ten-year period is measured from the date on which property is delivered to the trustee and not the date the trust was executed, if that was a different date. At the end of the trust period, the underlying property of the trust reverts back to the granter. There are gift-tax considerations that must be looked into by the granter and his advisers before establishing this type of trust.

After one has accumulated property so that his estate has been established, the second basic phase of the estate-planning process must be addressed, that of estate distribution. Estate distribution can be during the lifetime of the individual or, more commonly, upon his death.

Where the size of an estate is beyond the reasonable lifetime needs of the individual, consideration should be given to making lifetime gifts. The benefits of such a gift-giving program can be personal as well as financial. The personal pleasure of giving to a loved one is a feeling most people can relate to. However, there are also basic income- and estate-tax benefits to be derived.

When one distributes income-producing property, quite obviously such income is no longer taxable to the granter. If he is in the 50% income-tax bracket and the beneficiary is in a substantially lower bracket, the amount of disposable income is greatly enhanced, and likely for one in greater need of such income.

When making gifts to individuals, gift-tax implications must be analyzed and addressed. A person may now give federal-gift-tax-free, $10,000 per year to each one of an unlimited number of people. If his spouse joins in the giving, this amount is increased to $20,000 per year per person.

The effect of such a program will be to decrease the estate of the gift giver upon his or her death. While the Economic Recovery Tax Act of 1981 substantially increased the amount of the unified credit, to $192,800 (the exemption equivalent of $600,000), to be phased in over a six-year period ending in 1987, the estate-tax consequences for those whose estates are above the exemption equivalent are substantial. For these people, the possibility of a gift-giving program almost *has* to be examined and seriously considered.

After accumulating property, and conserving it to the maximum extent consistent with personal needs and desires, and making the lifetime distributions one felt were appropriate, the individual must consider how his estate will be distributed upon his death.

The common conception is that a last will and testament distributes all the property one owns at death. This, however, is not the case in many instances.

The most common example of a will not controlling how property is distributed is where property is held jointly. Property so held automatically passes by operation of law to the surviving joint tenant at the moment of death. Even if the will provides for another disposition, this does not overcome the rights of the surviving joint tenant in that property. The surviving joint tenant is entitled to that property, subject only to possible tax levies thereon. This is true whether there is a valid will in existence or not. (*See* PROPERTY, FORMS OF CO-OWNERSHIP.)

Although joint tenancies are quite prevalent between husbands and wives, it is important for each spouse to have his and her own will to distribute their property in the case of a common accident or upon the subsequent death of the survivor. The individual will also distributes the property that is held solely in the name of one of the spouses.

If one dies without a will, the state in which the decedent was domiciled, or the state in which real property is located, dictates how that property is to be distributed. This, in many instances, may not be exactly how the decedent would have wanted it to be done.

In New York State, for example, if you die without a will, leaving a spouse and one child, your spouse would receive $4,000 plus one-half of your remaining estate. Your child, whether a minor or an adult, would be entitled to the other one-half. If you have more than one child, your spouse would receive only $4,000 plus one-third of your estate, with the balance being equally divided among your children.

Additionally, if any of your children is under 18 years of age at the time of your death, a legal guardian would have to be appointed by the court to manage that child's inheritance. Although this in all probability would be your spouse (if you died having a spouse), such an appointment would necessarily involve additional court costs, a bond possibly having to be posted, and court supervision over the child's money until he or she turns 18. If in the meantime this money is needed for the child's education, clothing, or other living costs, prior approval of the court would have to be obtained. The court would also require annual accountings from the guardian for receipts and expenditures. These are consequences that most decedents do not desire and which can be eliminated by a property drafted will appointing a guardian and providing that guardian with the requisite powers of distribution

commensurate with the size and complexity of the estate.

A proper will also provides for the guardian of the person and property of your minor children should you die without a spouse (or the other natural parent is deceased if you are divorced) or should both parents die in a common accident. In this instance, the court will not be forced to choose in a vacuum who would be best suited to provide the physical care of your children and to look after the financial security of their assets. These two functions do not have to be performed by the same person or persons, and generally it is the parents who will know who would be best suited for these important tasks. A parent's designation in a will as to who shall be the guardians of the person and the property of a minor child will not be absolutely binding upon the court. However, the court will go along with such an appointment unless there is a showing by a contestant that such an appointment will not be in the children's best interest. The appointment of a guardian for one's minor children is the primary reason why many young couples with small children, who do not have much of a monetary estate, have wills prepared. The importance of such a designation cannot be overemphasized.

For those with larger estates, a will with trust provisions in it allows for distributions to be made to children and/or grandchildren at specified ages chosen by the decedent. For example, if your estate is $150,000 and you have two children and no spouse, you may not feel that it would be in the children's best interests to be entitled to $75,000 each upon reaching the age of 18. Instead, a trust could be established in the will wherein stepped distribution dates could be set, such as one-third of the principal amount to be distributed to a child upon reaching age 22, one-half of the remaining principal to be distributed upon the child's reaching the age of 26, and the balance to be distributed upon the child's attaining the age of 30. The timing and percentages of the distributions are entirely up to you to decide, bearing in mind all the personal factors that you feel are relevant. If the factors change while you are alive, you are not bound to your prior determination; you merely execute a new will or possibly a codicil to your old will, setting a different distribution schedule.

In this type of trust, the trustee generally would have the discretion to provide your children with income and principal from their shares prior to a distribution date if a valid need arose, such as for education or a medical emergency. The trust itself could be set up to be as flexible or as rigid as you desire with regard to the trustee's discretionary powers of invasion. The trustee itself could be an individual or individuals, or a bank trust department, or any combination of the above. The important point to note is that it is the testator, with the advice of his advisers, who establishes the trust to suit his particular needs and desires and those of his beneficiaries.

Just as they were present in the accumulation and conservation stages of the estate-planning process, tax considerations are present in the distribution stage.

Because the 1981 tax act brought about major changes in the federal estate-tax law, the federal estate tax is not a significant factor for the great majority of people. By increasing the amount of the unified credit to an exemption equivalent of $600,00 (to be phased in stages) by 1987, and by establishing an unlimited marital deduction, most married couples with estates of less than $1,200,000 will have to do relatively minimal federal-estate-tax planning.

Basically, if a trust is set up by one spouse for the benefit of the other, with the principal of the trust being an amount that will completely use up the unified credit in the first estate, this amount of money (up to $600,000) will completely avoid federal estate taxation on both spouses' estates. The surviving spouse, as the beneficiary of the trust, would have certain restrictions as to the trust principal but could have an unlimited right to all other trust income.

The balance of the decedent's estate could be passed to the surviving spouse outright or in a marital-deduction trust, which would entitle the estate to a marital deduction for the full amount, thereby eliminating all federal estate tax in this first estate. The amount passed outright or in a marital trust would have to be included in the gross estate of the surviving spouse, who would have the benefit of his or her unified credit of up to $600,000.

For estates in excess of the total of the spouse's unified credits, decisions must be made as to how much property should go into the marital share. For example, in a $3-million estate of the first spouse, assuming a $600,000 unified credit, if the marital share is allocated the excess over the credit, or $2,400,000, there will be a substantial federal estate tax in the subsequent estate. By possibly allocating more to the second trust, there will be some tax in the first estate, but much less tax in the second estate, due to graduated estate-tax rates. The merits of paying less combined tax by paying some in the first estate against the benefits of deferral must be explored and considered in every large estate.

The 1981 tax act has created a new concept in estate planning by permitting a Qualified Terminable Interest Property Trust (Q-TIP trust). In this type of trust, the executor makes a determination, after the death of the first spouse, as to how much property is to be applied for the marital deduction. In this way, the greatest tax benefits can be realized at the time of death based on factors known at that time and do not have to be estimated at the time the will is drawn. This, however, puts much more responsibility and pressure upon the executor who must make this decision.

A method of reducing the gross estate, for those estates that have to deal with the federal estate tax, is by possibly making use of the irrevocable life-insurance trust. Basically, when you own a policy on your own life or have certain rights of ownership in such a policy, the proceeds are includable in your gross estate upon your death. However, if all rights of ownership are properly transferred to an irrevocable trust, which is responsible for the payment of premiums, the proceeds can be excluded from the gross estate. If the policy was originally owned by the insured and transfer is made, there may be a gift-tax consequences on the transfer, and the transferrer must survive for three years after the transfer for the exclusion to be effective. If the trust itself obtains the policies, these gifts and survival problems do not exist.

The trust itself can be structured according to your desires, and the proceeds can also bypass estate taxation in a surviving spouse's estate if it is properly drafted and that is your desire.

While the federal tax laws have drastically changed over the past few years, the various state laws have not always mirrored the federal changes. When it comes to estate taxation, it is the federal statutes that must be looked at first if there is a possibility of having a taxable estate, as federal rates are substantially higher than state rates. However, in estates that are within the federal unified credit, the estate-tax laws of the state wherein the person is domiciled must be examined, as there may be state estate or inheritance taxes due where there are no federal estate taxes due.

As can be seen from this general treatment of estate planning, it is a many-faceted process that must be constantly reviewed as one passes through life. In different life stages, different aspects take on more or less significance. It is important for the individual, with the help of his advisers, to be aware of what options he has, both in life and at death, so that he may make the decisions that best reflect what he wants to accomplish.

Paul Schimmel

Eurodollars

Eurodollars are deposit liabilities denominated in United States dollars, of banks located outside the United States. (Dollar-denominated deposits at a bank located outside the United States are Eurodollars, even if the bank is affiliated with a bank whose home office is in the United States.) Eurodollar deposits may be owned by individuals, corporations, or governments from anywhere in the world. The term *Eurodollar* dates from an earlier period when the market was located primarily in Europe. Although the bulk of Eurodollar deposits is still held in Europe, today dollar-denominated deposits are held in such places as the Bahamas, Bahrain, Canada, the Cayman Islands, Hong Kong, Japan, Panama, and Singapore, as well as in European financial centers. Nevertheless, dollar-denominated deposits located anywhere in the world outside the United States are still referred to as "Eurodollars."

Banks in the Eurodollar market and banks located in the United States compete to attract dollar-denominated funds worldwide. Since the Eurodollar market is relatively free of regulation, banks in the Eurodollar market can operate on narrower margins or spreads between dollar borrowing and lending rates than can banks in the United States. This allows Eurodollar deposits to compete effectively with deposits issued by banks located in the United States. In short, the Eurodollar market has grown up as a means of separating the United States dollar from the country of jurisdiction or responsibility for that currency, the United States. It has done so largely to reduce the regulatory costs involved in dollar-denominated financial intermediation.

Incentives for Development of the Eurodollar Market. By accepting deposits and making loans denominated in United States dollars outside the United States, banks can avoid many U.S. banking regulations. In particular, banks located outside the United States are not required to keep non-interest-bearing reserves against Eurodollar deposits. These foreign banks hold balances with U.S. banks for clearing purposes only. Moreover, there is no required FEDERAL DEPOSIT INSURANCE CORPORATION (FDIC) insurance assessment associated with Eurodollar deposits. Virtually no restrictions exist for interest rates payable on Eurodollar deposits or charged on Eurodollar loans, and there are few restrictions on the types of assets allowed in portfolio.

In most Eurodollar financial centers, entry into Eurodollar banking is virtually free of regulatory impediments. In addition, banks intending to do Eurodollar business can set up in locations where tax rates are low. For example, Eurodollar deposits and loans negotiated in London or elsewhere are often booked in locations such as Nassau and the Cayman Islands to obtain more favorable tax treatment.

Foreign monetary authorities are generally reluctant to regulate Eurodollar business, because to do so would drive the business away, denying the host country income tax revenue, and jobs. Even if the

United States monetary authorities could induce a group of foreign countries to participate in a plan to regulate their Euromarkets, such a plan would be ineffective unless every country agreed not to host unregulated Eurodollar business. In practice, competition for this business has been fierce, so even if a consensus should develop in the United States to regulate Eurodollar business, it would be extremely difficult to impose regulations on the entire Eurodollar market.

Instruments of the Eurodollar Market. The overwhelming majority of money in the Eurodollar market is held in fixed-rate time deposits (TD's). The maturities of Eurodollar TD's range from overnight to several years, with most of the money held in the one-week to six-month maturity range. Eurodollar time deposits are intrinsically different from dollar deposits held at banks in the United States only in that the former are liabilities of financial institutions located outside the United States. The bulk of Eurodollar time deposits are interbank liabilities. They pay a rate of return that although fixed for the term of the deposit, is initially competitively determined.

From their introduction in 1966, the volume of negotiable Eurodollar certificates of deposit (CD's) outstanding reached roughly $50 billion at the beginning of 1980. Essentially, a Eurodollar CD is a negotiable receipt for a dollar deposit at a bank located outside the United States.

On average from 1974 to 1981, fixed-rate three-month Eurodollar CD's have yielded approximately 30 basis points below the three-month time deposit London Interbank Offer Rate (LIBOR). LIBOR is the rate at which major international banks are willing to offer term Eurodollar deposits to each other.

An active secondary market allows investors to sell Eurodollar CD's before the deposits mature. Secondary-market-makers' spreads for short-term fixed-rate CD's are usually 5 or 10 basis points.

Eurodollar CD's are issued by banks to "tap" the market for funds. Consequently, they have come to be called "Tap CD's." Such Tap CD's are commonly issued in denominations of from $250,000 to $5 million. Some large Eurodollar CD issues are marketed in several portions in order to satisfy investors with preferences for smaller instruments. These are known as "Tranche CD's." Tranche CD's are issued in aggregate amounts of $10 million to $30 million and offered to individual investors in $10,000 certificates with each certificate having the same interest rate, issue date, interest-payment dates, and maturity.

In recent years Eurodollar Floating Rate CD's (FRCD's) and Eurodollar Floating Rate Notes (FRN's) have come into use as means of protecting both borrower and lender against interest-rate risk.

Specifically, these "floaters" shift the burden of risk from the principal value of the paper to its coupon.

Eurodollar FRCD's and FRN's are both negotiable bearer paper. The coupon or interest rate on these instruments is reset periodically, typically every three or six months, at a small spread above the corresponding LIBOR. Eurodollar FRCD's yield, depending on maturity, between 1/8 and 1/4% over six-month LIBOR. They are an attractive alternative to placing six-month time deposits at the London Interbank Bid Rate. Eurodollar FRN issues have usually been brought to market with a margin of 1/8 to 1/4% over either the three- or six-month LIBOR or the mean of the London Interbank Bid and Offer Rates. To determine LIBOR for Eurodollar FRN's, the issuer chooses an agent bank who in turn polls three or four reference banks—generally, the London offices of major international banks. Rates are those prevailing at 11:00 A.M. London time two business days prior to the commencement of the next coupon period.

Eurodollar FRCD's have been issued in maturities of from one and a half to five years and are employed as an alternative to short-term money-market instruments. Eurodollar FRN's have been issued in maturities of from four to twenty years, with the majority of issues concentrated in the five- to seven-year range. Eurodollar FRN's tend to be seen as an alternative to straight fixed-interest bonds, but they can in principle be used like FRCD's. Eurodollar FRN's have been issued primarily, but not exclusively, by banks.

A secondary market exists in Eurodollar FRCD's and FRN's, although dealer spreads are quite large. Secondary-market-makers' spreads for FRCDs are normally 1/4% of principal value. The spread quoted on FRN's in the secondary market is generally 1/2% of principal value.

Interest-Rate Relationships Between Eurodollar Deposits and Deposits at Banks in the United States. Arbitrage keeps interest rates closely aligned between Eurodollar deposits and deposits with roughly comparable characteristics at banks located in the United States. This is illustrated in Figures 1 and 2. Figure 1 shows yields on federal funds and overnight Eurodollar deposits. Figure 2 shows yields on Eurodollar CD's and CD's issued by banks located in the United States.

The Relative Riskiness of Eurodollar Deposits and Dollar Deposits Held in the United States. There are three basic sources of risk associated with holding Eurodollars. The first concerns the chance that authorities where a Eurodollar deposit is held may interfere in the movement or repatriation of interest or principal of the deposit. But this risk factor does not neces-

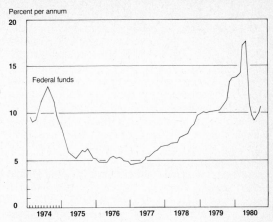

Percent per annum

Figure 1. Yields on federal funds and overnight Eurodollar deposits (monthly average). (*Source:* Morgan Guaranty Trust Company of New York, *World Financial Markets.*)

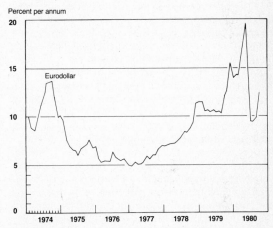

Percent per annum

Figure 2. Yields on United States and Eurodollar three-month certificates of deposit (at or near the first of the month). (*Source:* Salomon Brothers, *An Analytical Record of Yields and Yield Spreads,* part IV, table 2.)

sarily imply that Eurodollar deposits are riskier than dollar deposits held in the United States. The riskiness of a Eurodollar deposit relative to a dollar deposit held in the United States can depend on the deposit holder's residence. For United States residents, Eurodollars may appear riskier than domestic deposits because of the possibility that authorities in the foreign country where the deposit is located may interefere in the movement or repatriation of the interest or principal of the deposit. Foreign residents—Iranians, for example—may feel that the United States government is more likely to block their deposits than is the British government. Consequently, Iranians may perceive greater risk from potential government interference by holding dollar deposits in the United States than by holding Eurodollar deposits in London.

A second element of risk associated with Eurodollars concerns the potential for international jurisdictional legal disputes. For example, uncertainty surrounding interaction between United States and foreign legal systems compounds the difficulty in assessing the likelihood and timing of Eurodollar deposit payment in the event of a Eurodollar issuing bank's failure.

A third type of risk associated with holding Eurodollars concerns the relative soundness per se of foreign banks compared to banks located in the United States. Specifically, it has been argued that Eurodollars are absolutely riskier than deposits held in the United States because deposits held in the United States generally carry deposit insurance of some kind while Eurodollar deposits generally do not. In addition, it has been argued that in event of a financial crisis, banks located in the United States are more likely to be supported by the Federal Reserve system, whereas neither Federal Reserve support nor the support of foreign central banks for Eurodollar banking activities in their jurisdiction is certain.

A related factor compounding the three basic risk factors identified above is the greater cost of evaluating foreign investments compared with domestic investments. Acquiring information on the soundness of foreign banks is generally more costly than assessing the soundness of more-well-known domestic banks. This means that for a given level of expenditure on information acquisition, investors must generally accept more ignorance about the soundness of a foreign bank than a domestic bank.

Two comments on this argument are relevant here. First, the fact that it is more costly to evaluate foreign investments does not imply that Eurodollar deposits are inherently riskier than deposits held in the United States. If a depositor resides in the United States, the argument implies that a given expenditure on research will generally yield more information about the safety of deposits located in the United States than in the Eurodollar market. But if the depositor resides outside the United States, the reverse may be true.

Having said this, it must be pointed out that the amount of financial disclosure required by regulatory authorities abroad is generally not as great as in the United States. This fact may make it more difficult to evaluate the soundness of non-U.S. banks for any depositor, regardless of his residence.

Second, to a large extent assessing the safety of Eurodollar deposits relative to deposits in banks located in the United States is made easier by the fact that many banks in the Eurodollar market are affiliated with and bear the name of a bank whose home office is in the United States. For example, a London branch of a United States bank is as closely associated with its home office as a branch located in the United States.

However, foreign offices bearing the name of a United States bank, usually in a slightly altered form, have been set up as subsidiaries. Under most legal systems, a branch cannot fail unless its head office fails; but a subsidiary can fail even if its parent institution remains in business. Technically, a foreign office can bear the name of a United States bank in some form, and yet the parent institution may not be legally bound to stand fully behind the obligations of its foreign office. This suggests that a foreign office named after a parent United States bank may not be as sound as its namesake, although the parent bank unquestionably has great incentive to aid the foreign office in meeting its obligations in order to preserve confidence in the bank's name.

On the whole, it is difficult to assess the relative riskiness of Eurodollar deposits and dollar deposits held in the United States. Some factors affecting relative risk can be identified, but their importance is difficult to measure. What is more, perceived relative riskiness can depend on the residence of the depositor. The extent to which risk-related factors affect the interest-rate relationship between Eurodollar deposits and comparable deposits at banks in the United States remains unclear.

Summary. From the depositor's point of view, Eurodollar deposits are relatively close substitutes for dollar deposits at banks located in the United States. Eurodollar deposits are able to compete effectively with deposits offered by banks located in the United States because Eurodollar deposits are free of reserve requirements and most other regulatory burdens imposed by the United States monetary authorities on banks located in the United States. In fact, the tremendous growth of the Eurodollar market in the last two decades has been largely the result of efforts to move dollar financial intermediation outside the regulatory jurisdiction of U.S. monetary authorities.

Host countries have competed eagerly for Eurodollar business by promising relatively few regulations, low taxes, and other incentives to attract a portion of the Eurodollar banking industry. Financial intermediation in United States dollars is likely to continue to move abroad as long as incentives exist for it to do so. Since these incentives are not likely to disappear soon, the Eurodollar market's share of world dollar financial intermediation is likely to continue growing.

Marvin Goodfriend

European Monetary System (EMS)

In March 1979, nine European nations formally inaugurated the European Monetary System, a joint floating foreign exchange-rate arrangement aimed at maintaining stability among their currencies as well as against the European Currency Unit (ECU), a hypothetical currency. The arrangement's goals include moving Europe closer to monetary integration. The EMS may also contribute to greater stability in international monetary relations.

Eight of the nine nations are currently participating in the joint float arrangement: Belgium, Denmark, France, Ireland, Italy, Luxembourg, the Netherlands, and West Germany. Great Britain isn't participating in the exchange-rate system at this time. All the nations are members of the European Economic Community. Except for Ireland, whose currency had been pegged to British pound sterling, all were at times part of the European "joint float," or "snake," monetary arrangement that preceded the EMS.

As part of the EMS arrangement, all except one of the participating monetary authorities agreed to intervene during the European trading day in their national foreign exchange markets to maintain their currencies within a 2.25% margin of agreed-upon rates against the currency of any other member. It was agreed that Italy, because of prevailing economic conditions, would keep the lira within a 6% range of the other EMS currencies.

For existing "snake" members, the central rates prevailing at the initiation of the EMS were maintained. For new EMS members—France, Italy, and Ireland—the central rates were based on the currency relationships prevailing in the market on March 12, 1979, the day the EMS began.

If one EMS currency reaches the upper or lower limit of its range against another EMS currency, the nations whose currencies are involved must intervene in their exchange markets to keep the currencies within the rate band.

Thus, a nation whose currency reaches its upper limit against one or more of the other currencies must offer its own currency in unlimited amounts (potentially increasing the supply in the market) in exchange for the currency against which it is rising. Similarly, a nation whose currency reaches its lower limit must buy unlimited amounts of its currency (making it dearer) in exchange for the currency against which it has fallen. In addition, each participating government agreed to limit the fluctuation in its currency against a weighted average of the exchange rates of all member currencies, plus the British pound sterling. This weighted average is called the "ECU."

Specifically, the ECU, equivalent to $1.35 on March 12, 1979, is composed of 109 Italian lire, 83 West German pfennigs, 28.5 Dutch cents, 22 Danish ore, 14 Luxembourg centimes, 9 English pence, 3.5 Belgian francs, 1.2 French francs, and three-quarters of an Irish pence. These weights are based on the relative sizes of the economies of the participating nations.

If any currency moves beyond 75% of the agreed maximum divergence allowed against the ECU, that nation is expected either to take steps to bring its currency into line or to explain to the other members why, in its view, no action is appropriate. Apart from intervention, other steps the nation might take include adjusting interest rates or developing other economic policies aimed at eliminating conditions that led to the currency movement. These conditions include inflation, recession, and certain types of trade barriers.

A nation also may be required to revalue (officially increase the value of its currency against others) or devalue (officially lower the value of its currency against others).

Since Great Britain isn't participating in the joint floating arrangement, there isn't any obligation to correct any disparity between an EMS currency and the ECU if it is caused by a change in the rate of sterling.

Simultaneous with its central exchange-rate role, the ECU serves or may play a number of other roles. Currently, the ECU serves as the "currency" in which intervention debts will be settled among the eight EMS participating nations. Thus, if one nation borrows funds from another to support its currency—selling the foreign funds for its currency—the debt will be denominated in ECU.

As part of the agreement, a nation has several sources of finance for its intervention.

First, it may use its foreign exchange reserves.

Second, to satisfy its immediate intervention needs, it may borrow unlimited amounts of currencies from other participants for up to 45 days after the end of the month in which the funds are borrowed. Thus, if the funds are borrowed on the first day of a month with 31 days, the loan could have a maturity of 76 days. These loans can be extended three months from the maturity date, but the amount that can be rolled over is subject to a limit. A second three-month rollover is possible if it is mutually agreeable between the parties.

Third, a nation also may borrow from the other participants under a short-term credit facility for three months with extensions up to six months from the initial maturity date. The amount that can be borrowed under that facility is limited by the available pool of credit (currently 14 billion ECU) and the member's quota in the pool. The credit pool is maintained on the books of the European Monetary Cooperation Fund. The BANK FOR INTERNATIONAL SETTLEMENTS acts as agent for the EMCF.

Fourth, a nation may borrow under a medium-term credit facility. Two-year to five-year loans are available from the pool of funds (currently totaling 11 billion in ECU for this purpose) based on the nation's quota in the 14-billion ECU pool.

In the future, the ECU also may become a type of "international currency," with members of the EMS receiving ECU bookkeeping entries in return for gold and dollar reserves deposited with a European monetary fund. It also may eventually be used by nonmember central banks as a reserve asset similar to special drawing rights—a bookkeeping-entry reserve asset created in 1970 by the INTERNATIONAL MONETARY FUND (IMF) for use by governments in official balance-of-payments transactions.

Arthur Samansky

Exchange Stabilization Fund (ESF)

The Exchange Stabilization Fund of the United States Treasury is used to counter disorderly conditions in the foreign exchange market and to finance exchange-related, short-term credit arrangements with foreign governments.

Operations of the ESF normally are conducted through the Federal Reserve Bank of New York, which, as fiscal agent for the government and international arm of the Federal Reserve, acts for the Treasury and the FEDERAL RESERVE SYSTEM in foreign exchange matters.

Actions on behalf of the Treasury are made at the direction of the secretary of the Treasury, and those for the System at the direction of the Federal Open Market Committee—the top policymaking unit of the U.S. central banking system.

Through continuing consultations at many levels, Treasury and Federal Reserve positions are closely coordinated and often have been conducted jointly. The Reserve Bank is reimbursed by the Treasury for expenses incurred in carrying out Treasury actions.

Although it also is used to finance certain credit arrangements with foreign governments, it isn't used to provide foreign aid, to finance a specific trade transaction, or to support any fixed value of a currency.

In recent years the ESF has been used in connection with providing short-term credit to Mexico, Portugal, and the United Kingdom. In early 1978 a swap arrangement between the Treasury and the West German central bank—Bundesbank—was arranged using the ESF. That swap agreement isn't part of the Federal Reserve's SWAP NETWORK.

In the 1976 Mexican arrangements, the ESF and the Reserve's swap network were used to provide interim financing to the Bank of Mexico to offset disorderly exchange-market conditions for the peso, while the Mexican government negotiated with the INTERNATIONAL MONETARY FUND (IMF) to obtain medium-term financing for a new economic program. Stability in underlying domestic economic conditions is an important factor in bringing about exchange-rate stability.

The ESF also was used in February 1977 to extend short-term credit to the Bank of Portugal as part of a three-phase program of assistance involving short-term credit, drawings on the IMF, and a proposed medium-term multilateral credit facility to assist Portugal in stabilizing its economy.

Similarly, the ESF and the Reserve's swap network were used in June 1976 as part of a multilateral short-term credit package for the U.K. during a period of disorderly market conditions for the pound sterling and to accompany and reinforce an economic program of the British government implemented in 1977.

The ESF was established in 1934 by the Gold Reserve Act to enable the Treasury, at the direction of the president of the United States, to deal in gold, foreign exchange, and other credit instruments in an effort to stabilize the value of the dollar.

When the U.S. accepted the revised Articles of Agreement of the IMF, the U.S. Congress amended the Gold Act to delete references to "exchange stabilization." Instead, it was specified that the ESF is to be utilized as the secretary of the Treasury "may deem necessary, consistent with U.S. obligations in the IMF regarding orderly exchange arrangements and a stable system of exchange rates."

In addition to exchange-market operations and providing short-term credit needs, the ESF is used for holding and administering Special Drawing Rights (SDR's) allocated by the IMF or acquired by the U.S. and to pay for certain ESF-related administrative costs. SDR's are an international monetary reserve asset created in 1970 by the IMF for use between governments in official balance-of-payments transactions.

Initially, the ESF was funded by a U.S. congressional appropriation resulting from funds obtained through the devaluation of the dollar. Currently, it obtains funds from gains on operations and from interest earned on U.S. Treasury securities in which it temporarily invests idle balances. As of March 30, 1980, ESF assets totaled about $10.8 billion. About $3.7 billion was in SDR's.

Arthur Samansky

Ex-Dividend

See COMMON STOCK.

Executor

The person named in a will to manage the property and estate of a deceased person (a "decedent") is called an "executor" once the will has been admitted to PROBATE by the appropriate court. As executor, the person so appointed is in a trust or fiduciary position. His or her job is to take legal title to and possession of all property owned by the decedent or in which the decedent had an interest; to pay off all just debts and claims (and reject those that are improper); to retain attorneys, accountants, appraisers, and such other professionals as may be necessary to evaluate the decedent's estate and to prepare and file all necessary state or federal estate- or inheritance-tax returns, and pay the taxes shown due thereon; and, finally, after completing the foregoing, to pay all legacies and shares of the remaining property (called the "residuary estate") to the persons and in the amounts or proportions directed by the will.

The person designated as executor will frequently be a family member (such as a spouse, adult child, or sibling) or a close friend, business associate, or professional adviser such as an attorney, investment adviser, accountant, or banker. Sometimes, more than one person is named—two or three or even more can be appointed, since most states place no limit on the number that can be named. In the case of multiple appointments, each designee is referred to as a "coexecutor."

Regardless of how many appointments are made, their common denominator is usually that each nominee brings some special qualification to the position—either financial or business expertise or acumen, or a knowledge of the needs of the various beneficiaries, or a combination of the two.

In all cases, however, each appointee should be someone who is responsible and worthy of a high degree of trust, since the essence of the executor's function is the management of property solely for the benefit of another person or persons. An executor is bound by statute and by centuries of judicial precedents to act with complete loyalty to the beneficiaries and without any self-interest whatsoever. If an executor is motivated in a transaction by personal considerations, he may place himself in a so-called self-dealing situation and may be subject to removal from office merely upon proof of his inherent conflict of interest, even if no damages to the beneficiaries are proven. If in fact his self-interest has resulted in harm to the beneficiaries' financial interests, he can also be "surcharged"—that is, fined to the extent of the damages. Indeed, some courts have awarded punitive damages in this situation.

Moreover, the executor is required to act, to the fullest possible extent, in an impartial manner toward the estate's several beneficiaries. Frequently, one beneficiary may be most benefited by the executor's taking one course of action, while another beneficiary will urge a second path. This is often the case with respect to certain tax elections, or options. For instance, executors are required to file not only estate-tax (or death-tax) returns, but also income-tax returns with respect to income earned by the estate after the decedent's death. The tax law permits the executor to deduct various of the estate's expenses *either* on its estate-tax return *or* on its income-tax return, but not on both. The choice made by the executor will therefore affect different beneficiaries differently, depending on whether they are recipients of estate principal only, income only, or a combination of both. The executor must balance each beneficiary's viewpoint against the position of all other beneficiaries and then make whatever decision he sincerely believes to be in the best interests of all beneficiaries, taken collectively; he cannot show personal favoritism.

Finally, the executor must conform to state law in the manner in which he invests the estate's assets. Unless the will provides otherwise, no money can be retained after death or be newly invested in any vehicle unless it either (a) is listed as an approved fiduciary investment by the state law (so-called legal investments) or (b) falls within the general definition of the "prudent-man rule." That rule states that an executor shall invest funds only "in such securities as would be acquired by prudent men of discretion and intelligence in such matters who are seeking a reasonable income and preservation of their capital."

The will may give the executor a broader latitude for investment than either the "legals" list, or the prudent-man rule; it may, for instance, permit him to retain non-income-producing property that he received from the decedent upon the latter's death. However, it should be noted that many states do not permit a will to exonerate an executor, or give him immunity, with respect to acts or investments that ultimately turn out to have been negligent. In the long run, therefore, an executor is always charged with the responsibility of acting as prudently as possible under the circumstances, taking into account what leeway the will lawfully may give him.

As a result of the many and heavy duties of his office, an executor is ordinarily compensated for serving as such. Sometimes his compensation is precisely set by statute, and may run in a range of from 2% to 5% of the estate; if more than one person has been appointed, often each is entitled to a full and separate commission. Some states, rather than specifying the rate of compensation, just provide that executors are to be "reasonably" compensated—a phrase that has a way of winding up in the same percentage range as mentioned above.

However, it should be noted that most, and perhaps all, states permit testators to specify the terms and conditions of an executor's appointment, including his compensation. Thus, the will can provide the exact amount (or percent) an executor is to be paid as a commission—an amount or percent that may be less (or even more) than that otherwise provided by the state law. Similarly, if coexecutors have been designated, the will might, for example, provide that all share the commissions that one would be entitled to, if only one had been appointed; or perhaps the testator might stipulate that *no* commissions are to be paid. In any of these cases, the general rule is that if an executor accepts his appointment, he also accepts the compensation conditions set out by the testator in the will.

Steven J. Wohl

Export-Import Bank of the United States (Eximbank)

The Export-Import Bank of the United States is an independent government agency that aids in financing the overseas trade of the United States. Since its inception in 1934, Eximbank, as it is commonly called, has supported more than $110 billion in U.S. exports to more than 160 nations worldwide.

Eximbank was originally established by President Franklin D. Roosevelt. His February 2, 1934, executive order created the bank as a mechanism for financing trade with the USSR. However, due to disagreements regarding the settlement of the Soviet Union's World War I debt, the bank never played this role. A Second Export-Import Bank was therefore also established in 1934, to finance trade with all nations *except* the Soviet Union. The two were merged in 1936 by an act of Congress.

At the end of World War II, with much of Europe destroyed and in need of capital equipment to begin the rebuilding process, Eximbank was called upon to play a unique role. On July 31, 1945, the bank was reconstituted as a fully independent U.S. agency, given $3.5 billion in lending authority, and was charged with the responsibility of facilitating capital-goods exports. From 1945 until 1948, when the Marshall Plan became effective, Eximbank provided a credit "bridge" that allowed the nations of Europe to begin the recovery process. Today, with more than 70% of Exim's current credit and guarantee authority directed toward developing countries, Exim is again playing an important role in the world economy. The bank has been playing a key role in keeping trade flowing during a period of economic dislocation and uncertainty.

Eximbank receives no appropriations from the U.S. Congress and was originally capitalized with a $1-billion loan from the U.S. Treasury. The bank has repaid the loan, paid $1 billion in interest and dividends into the Treasury, and currently has more than $1 billion in reserves, which represent the accumulation of profits from loan activity. In fiscal year 1982, however, Eximbank recorded a loss of $160 million, the first in its history. This situation resulted from an unfavorable spread between the bank's cost of borrowing (from the Federal Financing Bank) and its interest rates charged on loan commitments. It is expected that this factor, coupled with an increase in claim activity resulting from the world economic recession, will produce a series of deficit years into the mid-1980s. In an effort to stem these losses, Bank Chairman William H. Draper III, in cooperation with the U.S. Treasury, successfully negotiated an agreement between the 22 member nations of the Organization for Economic Cooperation and Development (OECD) to establish the International Arrangement on Export Credits in July 1982. This arrangement set minimum interest rates for official, government-supported export financing at levels closer to actual market rates, thus reducing the subsidy factor by more than 50%.

Eximbank is directed by statute to (1) offer financing for U.S. exporters that is competitive with the financing provided by foreign export credit agencies to assist sales by their nations' exporters, (2) determine that the transactions supported have a reasonable assurance of repayment, (3) supplement, but not compete with, private sources of export financing, and (4) take into account the effect of its activities on small business, the domestic economy, and U.S. employment.

The Foreign Credit Insurance Association (FCIA), a New York–based group of 42 of the nation's leading private insurance companies, cooperates with Eximbank to cover repayment risks on short- and medium-term export credit transactions.

Eximbank is located in Washington, D.C., and has no branch offices. Its 334 employees include loan officers, country economists, engineers, legal staff, and policy analysts, who, working together as a team, process applications, which are considered by the bank's five-person board of directors on a case-by-case basis.

Among the major programs currently supported by the bank are Direct Loans and Guarantees; the Small Manufacturers' Discount Loan Program; the Medium Term Credit Program; the Commercial Bank Guarantee Program; the Export Credit Insurance Program; the Export Trading Company Loan Guarantee Program; and the Foreign Currency Guarantee Program.

Robert E. Waite, Jr.

·F·

Factoring

See ASSET-BASED FINANCIAL SERVICES.

Fair Credit Billing Act

See CONSUMER-CREDIT REGULATION.

Fair Credit Reporting Act

See CONSUMER-CREDIT REGULATION; CREDIT BUREAU.

Fair Debt Collection Practices Act

See CONSUMER-CREDIT REGULATION.

Fannie Mae

See FEDERAL NATIONAL MORTGAGE ASSOCIATION.

Farm Credit Administration (FCA)

The Farm Credit Administration is an independent agency within the executive branch of the U.S. government. The purpose of the FCA is to supervise, examine, and regulate the activities of the borrower-owned banks and associations of the FARM CREDIT SYSTEM. The Farm Credit Administration is composed of the Federal Farm Credit Board, the governor of the Farm Credit Administration, and other personnel. The FCA was established as an independent agency by an executive order of the president in 1933. In 1939 it was made part of the U.S. Department of Agriculture but was returned to independent status by the Farm Credit Act of 1953.

Harvey Rachlin

Farm Credit System

The cooperative Farm Credit System, composed of three parts—Federal Land banks and Federal Land bank associations; Federal Intermediate Credit banks and Production Credit associations; and the banks for cooperatives—functions to improve the income and well-being of American farmers and ranchers. Essentially, it works to carry out its purpose by providing sound and adequate credit and closely related services to them, their cooperatives, and selected farm-related businesses, and also to provide credit for rural homes, to producers and harvesters of aquatic products, and to associations of such producers.

Federal Land Banks. The 12 Federal Land banks (FLB's) make long-term mortgage loans secured by the equivalence of first liens on real estate through more than 450 Federal Land bank associations. Loans are made for a variety of agricultural and related purposes, including the purchases of farms, farmland, equipment, and livestock; refinancing existing mortgages and paying other debts; constructing and repairing buildings; and financing other farm, farm home, or family needs.

Federal Intermediate Credit Banks. The 12 Federal Intermediate Credit banks (FICB's) provide loans for the 400-plus Production Credit associations and discount the notes of farmers, ranchers, and commercial fishermen that are given to other institutions financing agricultural producers. Production Credit associations (PCA's) make short- and intermediate-term loans and provide closely related services to farmers, ranchers, rural homeowners, farm-related businesses, and commercial fishermen.

Banks for Cooperatives. The 12 district banks for cooperatives (BC's) make loans to agricultural and aquatic cooperatives. The Central Bank for Cooperatives (in Denver, Colorado) participates with the district BC's in loans that exceed their lending limits. All 13 banks operate on a cooperative basis and with other financing institutions in making loans. The banks of the Farm Credit System obtain their loan funds through the sale of securities in the nation's money markets.

Harvey Rachlin

Farm Insurance

See INSURANCE.

Federal Deposit Insurance Corporation (FDIC)

The Federal Deposit Insurance Corporation is an independent agency of the U.S. government. The basic function of the FDIC is to insure bank deposits. In the event an insured bank closes, the FDIC arranges a deposit assumption by a healthy institution or pays off depositors up to a certain amount. (This amount has increased gradually over the years and at this writing is $100,000.) Payment can be made in cash and usually begins within a few days after the date of the final closing.

The FDIC insures deposits of all types—checking accounts, time accounts, and savings accounts—held by individuals and businesses at banks. A depositor is covered for the basic amount ($100,000) at an insured bank for any account or combination of the aforementioned accounts. The FDIC also provides separate $100,000 insurance coverage to holders of Individual Retirement Accounts and Keogh Plan retirement accounts.

The Federal Deposit Insurance Act entitles certain types of banks to insurance benefits. The FDIC insures deposits in national and most state banks, including commercial and mutual savings banks. (Federal law requires all member banks of the FEDERAL RESERVE SYSTEM to have deposit insurance, and most state laws require state-chartered banks that are not members of the Federal Reserve system to carry deposit insurance.) Also insured are deposits in some U.S. branches of foreign banks. (Note: The FEDERAL SAVINGS AND LOAN INSURANCE CORPORATION insures deposits at savings and loan associations, and the NATIONAL CREDIT UNION ADMINISTRATION insures savings at credit unions.)

To be eligible for membership in the FDIC, a bank must meet certain standards in banking practices. Furthermore, approved members are regularly examined by federal and state agencies. Members pay semiannual insurance fees (based on a percentage of the volume of deposits). These assessments, which are invested in federal government securities, comprise the corporation's deposit-insurance fund. The FDIC is also permitted to borrow up to $3 billion at any one time from the U.S. Treasury, although it has never done so since its creation.

Insurance Coverage. A depositor may have funds in any of the various types of insured deposit accounts in the same bank. If they are owned in the same right and capacity, this does not increase the amount of insurance protection. For example, if a person has a checking and savings account at the same bank, both accounts together are insured up to $100,000. However, if a person has accounts in separate banks, each separate account in an insured bank carries a maximum insurance of $100,000.

If a person has both an individually owned account and a joint account in the same insured bank, each of his accounts is separately insured up to $100,000. With respect to the joint account, however, he must have a right of withdrawal on the same basis as the other co-owner(s).

An individual may have an interest in more than one joint account. In such a case, insurance coverage is considered in a twofold manner: (1) Any and all joint accounts owned by the same combination of individuals is insured up to the $100,000 maximum; and (2) an individual's interests in each joint account owned by different combinations of persons is collectively insured up to $100,000.

A practical situation may be as follows: Bob and Susan have a joint account containing $115,000; Bob also owns a joint account with Jim containing $60,000. What is the total insurable interest of each person?

Each separate joint account is insured up to $100,000. Thus, Bob and Susan's account has $15,000 that is uninsured. In a joint account, the amount of insurance protection is prorated equally; thus Bob and Susan each have an insurance interest of $50,000. For the joint account owned by Bob and Jim, each has an insurable interest up to $30,000. The total insurable interest Bob has in the two accounts is $80,000; Susan has an insurable interest of $50,000; and Jim $30,000. The two accounts, containing $175,000, carry a total insurance of $160,000.

Bank Failure. The FDIC acts immediately in the event a federally insured bank is closed by its chartering authority (the state or, in the case of a national bank, the comptroller of the currency). It frequently is able to arrange for another bank to take over the assets of the failed bank and assume its deposits (this is called "deposit assumption"). If this cannot be arranged, the FDIC pays off all depositors to the insured maximum as soon as possible, usually within a few days of a banks closure. Deposit amounts are usually treated the same as other general debts of the bank and their owners share pro rata in the bank's liquidated assets. In a deposit assumption, the FDIC takes over assets not wanted by the acquiring bank, such as bad loans and investments, and liquidates them.

History of Deposit Insurance. The need for a system of insurance to protect depositors from bank failure had been recognized in the United States long before its inception. As bank closings could leave depositors with heavy losses, the lack of an insurance system could result in lack of public confidence and have a disastrous effect on banking.

The first insurance plans were implemented by states, beginning in 1929. These plans, however, eventually failed. From the time of the Civil War to the end of World War I, thousands of banks in the United States closed. A few thousand more closed even during the prosperous decade of the 1920s. Attempts to establish deposit insurance on a national basis were made, unsuccessfully, between 1886 and 1933. Finally, the devastating depression of the early 1930s prompted Congress to fulfill the need for a national, uniform system of deposit insurance by passing the Banking Act of 1933, thereby creating the Federal Deposit Insurance Corporation. The FDIC officially opened on January 1, 1934.

The FDIC was formed to protect the public in case of bank failure, to restore public confidence in banks, and to maintain a sound banking system. The corporation first insured deposits up to a $2,500 maximum per deposit. This was increased to $5,000 on July 1, 1934; to $10,000 in 1950 by the Federal Deposit Insurance Act; to $15,000 on October 16, 1966; to $20,000 on December 23, 1969; to $40,000 on November 27, 1974; and to $100,000 on March 31, 1980. Since the corporation's inception, the overwhelming majority of banks in the United States (over 90%) have become insured.

Organization. The Federal Deposit Insurance Corporation is administered by a board of three directors. Two of the directors are designated by the U.S. president, the other is the current comptroller of the currency in the United States. The FDIC is subject to congressional oversight and reports to Congress annually on its operations; its chairman appears from time to time before congressional committees, at their request, to report on corporation matters. Responsibilities of FDIC are carried out by ten divisions and offices.

Harvey Rachlin

Federal Funds

The market for the most liquid of money-market instruments—federal funds—evolved as borrowers and lenders sought to exploit opportunities through trading in reserve deposit funds. Trading in federal funds began in the 1920s and involved only a few Federal Reserve member banks located in New York City. As of 1982 the market included over 14,000 commercial banks and a wide range of nonbank financial institutions. The characteristics of federal funds, as well as

the mechanics of their purchase and sale, reflect the needs of today's market participants.

What Are Federal Funds?* Federal funds are short-term loans of immediately available funds—i.e., funds that can be transferred or withdrawn during one business day. Such immediately available funds include deposits at Federal Reserve banks and collected liabilities of COMMERCIAL BANKS and other depository institutions. Federal funds are exempt from reserve requirements and the vast majority are unsecured. Most federal funds are "overnight money"—money lent out on one day and repaid the following morning. Loans of longer maturity, known as "term federal funds," are not uncommon, however.

The law requires, for purposes of monetary control, that all depository institutions maintain reserves as prescribed by the FEDERAL RESERVE SYSTEM. Federal Reserve Regulation D delineates specific classes of liabilities that are subject to Federal Reserve requirements. Commercial banks, thrift institutions, U.S. branches and agencies of foreign banks, and EDGE ACT CORPORATIONS must hold set percentages of these liabilities in a combination of vault cash and non-interest-earning reserve balances at a Federal Reserve bank. The cost of holding reserve balances, which yield no return, provides the incentive to depository institutions to minimize their holdings of excess reserves. The federal-funds market provides the primary avenue for doing so.

Ordinary banking activities give rise to variations in a bank's asset and liability holdings. These changes in the balance sheet result in corresponding fluctuations in a bank's reserve position. Consequently, on any given day some institutions hold reserves above their desired reserve position while others are below their desired position. An institution holding excess reserves can earn interest on its funds by loaning them to others in need of reserves. Such a transaction is considered a federal-funds purchase by the borrowing institution, and a federal-funds sale by the lending institution.

The Mechanics of Federal-Funds Transactions. Federal-funds transactions can be initiated by either a fund lender or a fund borrower. An institution wishing to sell (buy) federal funds locates a buyer (seller) either directly through an existing banking relationship or indirectly through a federal-funds broker located in New York City. Federal-funds brokers maintain frequent telephone contact with active buyers and sellers of federal funds. Brokers match federal-

*The term *federal funds* is occasionally used in a broader sense than that described in this article. Sometimes, members of the financial community will consider all funds that are immediately available and not subject to reserve requirements to be federal funds. Repurchase agreements, included under this broad definition, are excluded from this discussion.

funds purchase and sale orders in return for a commission on each completed transaction.

At the center of the federal-funds market are financial institutions that maintain reserve accounts at Federal Reserve banks. These institutions use the Federal Reserve communications system, or FED-WIRE, to carry out rapid transfer of funds nationwide. The Federal Reserve communications system links all Federal Reserve banks and branches. Private financial institutions and government agencies are able to gain access to the wire network either through direct (on-line) links to Federal Reserve computers or through telephone or telegraph (off-line) contact with their Federal Reserve bank.

When transfers are conducted within a Federal Reserve district, the institution transferring funds authorizes the district Federal Reserve bank to debit its reserve account and to credit the reserve account of the receiving institution. Interdistrict transactions are only slightly more complicated but are best clarified by an example. Suppose a thrift institution in Richmond (the Fifth Federal Reserve District) wishes to transfer funds to a bank in New York (the Second Federal Reserve District). The thrift initiates the transaction. The Federal Reserve Bank of Richmond debits the account of the thrift and credits the account of the Federal Reserve Bank of New York. Finally, the Federal Reserve Bank of New York debits its own account and credits the reserve account of the receiving commercial bank. This series of accounting entries is carried out instantaneously.

Overnight Federal Funds. In a typical federal-funds transaction, the lending institution with reserve funds in excess of its reserve requirements authorizes a transfer from its reserve account to the reserve account of the borrowing institution. The following day, the transaction is reversed. The borrower pays back the loan through a transfer of funds from its reserve account to the lender's reserve account in an amount equal to the value of the original loan plus an interest payment. The size of the interest payment is determined by market conditions at the time the loan is initiated.

Numerous institutions that buy and sell federal funds do not maintain accounts at the Federal Reserve. Instead, these institutions buy and sell funds through a CORRESPONDENT BANK. Correspondent banks will often agree to purchase on a continuing basis all federal funds that a respondent has available to sell. Typically, the respondent institution holds a demand-deposit account with the correspondent. To initiate a federal-funds sale, the respondent bank simply notifies the correspondent by telephone of its intentions. The correspondent purchases funds from the respondent by reclassifying the respondent's liability

from a demand deposit to federal funds purchased. Upon maturity of the contract, the respondent's demand-deposit account is credited for the total value of the loan plus an interest payment for use of the funds. The rate paid to respondents on federal funds is usually based on the nationwide effective federal-funds rate for the day.

Alternatives to Overnight Federal Funds. The different needs of participants in the federal-funds market, and the wide range of financial environments in which they operate, have resulted in the development of alternatives to overnight federal funds. These alternatives include term and continuing-contract federal funds. According to the results of a 1977 survey, approximately 7.5% of all federal-funds transactions have maturities longer than overnight. Banks contract for term federal funds when they foresee their borrowing needs lasting for several days and/or believe that the cost of overnight federal funds may rise in the immediate future. Like overnight federal funds, term federal funds are not subject to reserve requirements. For this reason, term federal funds are often preferred to other purchased liabilities of comparable maturity. The majority of term federal funds sold have maturities of 90 days or less, but term federal funds of much longer maturity are purchased occasionally.

Federal funds sold through a correspondent banking relationship are sometimes transacted under a continuing contract. Continuing-contract federal funds are overnight federal funds that are automatically renewed unless terminated by either the fund lender or borrower. In a typical continuing-contract arrangement, a correspondent will purchase overnight federal funds from a respondent institution. Unless notified by the respondent, the correspondent will continually roll over overnight federal funds, creating a longer-term instrument of open maturity. The interest payments on continuing-contract federal funds are computed from a formula based on each day's federal-funds quotations. The specific formula used varies from contract to contract.

Secured and Unsecured Federal Funds. Most federal-funds transactions are unsecured—i.e., the lender does not receive collateral to insure him against the risk of default by the borrower. In some cases, however, federal-funds transactions are secured. In a secured transaction, the purchaser places government securities in a custody account for the seller as collateral to support the loan. The purchaser retains title to the securities, however.* Upon completion of the

---

*The crucial difference between a secured federal-funds transaction and a repurchase agreement is that, in a federal-funds transaction, title to the security is not transferred. RP's are available to a wider range of market participants than federal funds.

federal-funds contract, custody of the securities is returned to the owner. Secured federal-funds transactions are sometimes requested by the lending institution, or encouraged by state regulations requiring collateralization of federal-funds sales.

Seth P. Maerowitz

Federal Home Loan Bank Board (FHLBB)

An independent agency of the executive branch of the federal government, the Federal Home Loan Bank Board is charged with promoting thrift and home ownership by regulating and supporting SAVINGS AND LOAN ASSOCIATIONS, as well as other thrift/housing finance institutions. The institutions regulated by the Bank Board have for many years been the nation's primary source of housing finance, particularly for one- to four-family residences.

Historical Development. During the depression, nearly a quarter-million families were losing their homes each year as a result of inability to meet their mortgage payments. In addition, due to the number of financial-institution failures (in 1930 there were over 2,000 commercial-bank and over 100 S&L failures), people were generally afraid to put what savings they had into thrift institutions since these deposits were not insured. Consequently, people were deprived of a safe and sound place to save, as well as being deprived of an opportunity to earn interest on their savings. Moreover, as a result of the lack of savings, thrift institutions had little money available for home financing. The FHLBB was therefore created by Congress to help rectify these problems.

The FHLBB first came into existence when the Federal Home Loan Bank Act was passed in July 1932. This act authorized the board to establish the Federal Home Loan Bank system. The primary purpose of this system is to provide savings and loan associations with a place to borrow funds. This is necessary in order to be certain that S&L's have adequate funds available to cover withdrawals, and also to enable them to continue lending during periods when there is a shortage of savings deposits. During 1982 the system advanced over $66 billion to member institutions.

In 1933, Congress, by the passage of the Home Owners Loan Act, authorized the board to grant federal charters to savings and loan associations. There were two reasons for this action: to create a system of financial institutions that enjoyed a greater degree of confidence by reason of being federally regulated; and to encourage the development of new thrift housing-finance institutions in previously neglected areas. By the end of 1981, there were over 1,900 such institutions. In addition, the act authorized the establishment

of the Home Owners Loan Corporation. This corporation, which went out of existence in 1953, enabled over 1 million Americans to keep their homes by arranging to have the mortgages refinanced.

Finally, in 1934, the third major piece of legislation affecting the board's mission was adopted: the National Housing Act Title IV of that act provided for the creation of the FEDERAL SAVINGS AND LOAN INSURANCE CORPORATION (FSLIC) and placed it under the direction of the Federal Home Loan Bank Board. The purpose of the FSLIC is to provide for insurance on deposits in thrift institutions. At the end of 1982, there were 3,343 FSLIC-insured savings and loan associations. During its 48 years of existence, not a single saver has lost any money in an insured account.

Over the past 50 years, the Bank Board has played an increasingly important role in the national economy due to the dramatic growth of the industry it regulates. For example, in 1945 the savings and loan industry had approximately $10 billion in total assets; in 1960, $60 billion; and in 1982, over $706 billion. Moreover, nearly 1 million Americans are customers of the industry as savers or borrowers. While the growth during this period is to a great extent the result of the unprecedented demand for housing finance and general economic prosperity, it also reflects the success of the board in achieving its legislative mandate to promote thrift and homeownership through the regulation and support of the savings and loan industry.

Organization. The FHLBB is directed by a bipartisan three-member board. The three members are nominated by the U.S. president and confirmed by the Senate for fixed four-year terms. The chairman of the board is appointed by the president. The board is responsible for the Federal Savings and Loan Insurance Corporation, the Federal Home Loan Bank System, and the FEDERAL HOME LOAN MORTGAGE CORPORATION. In addition, the Bank Board has 14 staff offices that provide it with a variety of technical services (legal, economic research, etc.). The largest staff office is the Office of Examinations and Supervision. This office, which has over 800 employees located throughout the United States, is responsible for conducting regularly scheduled examinations of savings and loan institutions and for initiating corrective measures when problems are detected.

The board's expenses are met through assessments on the regional Federal Home Loan banks, the FSLIC, and on S&L's for examinations. Consequently, the board uses no federal tax revenues. Congress, however, reviews the board's budget and annually sets limits on expenditures.

Responsibilities. In addition to supervising the activities of the Federal Home Loan Bank system and the

FSLIC, the Bank Board is also responsible for establishing policies and regulations affecting the operations of the savings and loan industry. The board's authority to regulate savings and loan associations is based upon the granting of federal charters, the granting of insurance of accounts, and by virtue of membership in the Federal Home Loan Bank system. The board's policies and regulations are intended to insure safe and sound operations, to protect the interests that the public has in those institutions, and to implement the various laws passed by Congress governing the activities of financial institutions. The board uses its examining force to determine if S&L's are operating in a safe and sound manner and in compliance with the board's regulations and policies. The Bank Board also has a special division of consumer affairs, which processes consumer complaints. In addition, there are supervisory agents in each district bank who are responsible for dealing with S&L problems.

Some examples of board regulations are (1) requirements for full disclosure of the terms and conditions of a loan or of a particular savings instrument, (2) requirements for lending on a nondiscriminatory basis, (3) restrictions on interstate branching, (4) restrictions on the types of lending and on the terms and conditions of loans, (5) restrictions on loans to employees or to members of the board of directors of the association; etc.

During the 1950s and 1960s, the number of regulatory restrictions on S&L operations gradually increased to the point where virtually every major decision area was covered by a regulation. However, starting in the early 1970s, the board began to deregulate the industry. Two major breakthroughs in this regard came in the early 1980s: The first was the Depository Institutions Deregulation and Monetary Control Act (DIDMCA) of 1980; and the second was the Depository Institutions Act (DIA) of 1982, also called the Garn-St Germain Act (*see* GARN-ST GERMAIN DEPOSITORY INSTITUTION DEREGULATION ACT OF 1982).

The major provisions of the DIDMCA established a process for eliminating all controls on interest rates that depository institutions (commercial banks, savings and loans, and credit unions) could pay on their deposits. Prior to this time, and especially from the mid-1960s onward, there were interest-rate controls on all federally regulated financial institutions. The DIDMCA required that all interest controls be lifted by 1986, leaving the determination of the exact schedule to a committee (called the DEPOSITORY INSTITUTIONS DEREGULATION COMMITTEE [DIDC]) made up of the heads of the financial regulatory agencies. However, during 1983 virtually all external regulatory controls on interest rates were effectively removed.

The Garn-St Germain Act substantially broadened the scope of savings institutions' asset powers. The act also directed the Depository Institutions Deregulation Committee to speed up the deregulation of interest rates on all insured deposit accounts, and directed the Bank Board to establish an emergency capital assistance program to aid savings institutions whose net worth was seriously eroded as a result of the 1981–82 record-high interest rates. The Bank Board implemented virtually all of the principal elements of this major legislation by mid-1983, thereby providing the thrift industry with the opportunity to compete aggressively with other institutions in the rapidly changing financial marketplace.

John M. Buckley, Jr.

Federal Home Loan Banks

A system of federally chartered, privately owned government corporations that provide reserve credit and other services for eligible THRIFT INSTITUTIONS that are engaged in long-term home-mortgage financing.

Historical Development. The Federal Home Loan Bank Act of 1932 established the Federal Home Loan Bank Board and charged it with the responsibility of setting up a permanent system of reserve credit banks for financial institutions that engage in home-mortgage financing. Congressional hearings on legislation to establish a central credit system for mortgage-lending institutions had been held as early as 1919. However, it wasn't until the Great Depression, starting in 1929, that the need for this system became apparent.

By the summer of 1932, unemployment, business failures, and the collapse of real-estate values had disrupted the usual home-financing process. Furthermore, loss of income and the inability to refinance mortgage loans led to numerous (over 250,000) foreclosures. The problem was further exacerbated by the fact that mortgage-lending institutions had to stand alone in meeting the needs of savers and borrowers.

Although the impetus for the Federal Home Loan Bank Act was the need for a means of combating the effects of the depression, Congress intended the system to be a permanent structure with continuing responsibilities.

On October 15, 1932, the 12 Federal Home Loan banks began operations, using the capital of slightly under $125 million provided by the U.S. Treasury. According to the act, this money was to be repaid by the banks when stock purchased by member institutions equaled the amount provided by the government. Final retirement of government-owned stock was completed on July 2, 1951. In 1982 the 12 banks had over $6.2 billion in capital stock outstanding and total assets of $80.2 billion.

Organization. The 12 Federal Home Loan banks are part of the Federal Home Loan Bank system. The FHL system consists of the Bank Board as the overall regulator, the 12 Federal Home Loan banks, and approximately 4,000 thrift and housing-finance institutions that are members of the individual banks.

Each Federal Home Loan bank is wholly owned by its member institutions and is responsive to its members' needs. A district bank is controlled by a board of directors consisting of at least 14 members, 8 of whom are elected by the stockholders and 6 of whom are appointed by the Bank Board. The banks are required to operate within the policies and regulations established by the Bank Board.

To be eligible for membership in the Federal Home Loan Bank System, the act requires that each applicant be duly organized under the laws of any state or of the United States, be subject to examination and regulation by any state or by the United States, and make long-term home-mortgage loans. Each applicant shall also be, in the judgment of the board, in sound financial condition, and the character of its management and its home-financing policy shall be consistent with sound and economical home financing.

The Bank Board establishes broad guidelines within which the district banks operate as decentralized entities. The directors of each bank are responsible for monitoring the bank's compliance with the system's regulations and policies, as well as with the Federal Home Loan Bank Act. In general, the directors adopt and review policies governing advances (loans to member thrift institutions), set parameters for interest rates on deposits and advances, and review various operating policies. Some specific actions taken by the directors are subject to Bank Board approval. These include adopting the bank's annual budget, setting a dividend rate, and selecting a president and other officers of the bank.

Active management of the bank is the bank president's responsibility. The president is responsible both to the bank's board of directors and to the Federal Home Loan Bank Board. He carries out the policies and objectives established by the board of directors and reports directly to them. In his responsibility to the Bank Board, the president is concerned with effective and efficient adoption and execution of federal laws and the policies, programs, objectives, and regulations of the Bank Board. He is also the Bank Board's principal supervisory agent for his district and, as such, assures that each member institution in his district complies with all applicable laws and Bank Board regulations.

Functions. The major function of the district banks is to lend funds in the form of advances to member institutions for savings withdrawals, seasonal needs, and expansion of mortgage lending.

In 1982 the banks had over $66 billion in advances outstanding. The banks also accept deposits of the members, supervise their members in accordance with Bank Board regulations, and provide services such as economic analyses and the safekeeping of securities. The primary source of funds for the banks is consolidated obligations in the form of bonds and discount notes that are the joint and several obligations of all 12 district banks. These are sold through the system's Office of Finance and a nationwide group of securities dealers and banks. All negotiations relating to the public offering and sale of consolidated Federal Home Loan Bank obligations are performed by the Office of Finance. These consolidated obligations are not obligations of the United States, nor do they carry any governmental guaranties.

In addition, the district banks take an active role in implementing many of the Bank Board's major programs. For example, since the late 1970s, each district bank has had a community investment officer. This individual has the overall responsibility for assisting the bank members in achieving the objectives of the Community Reinvestment Act—legislation designed to promote mortgage lending and investment in areas previously neglected. Also starting in 1981, most of the district banks have offered NOW-account processing services to their members.

The system's total net income from operations in 1982 was $962 million. The banks paid 1982 dividends to their member institutions totaling $791 million, or 12.6% of capital stock.

The 12 district banks are spread throughout the country (see Figure 1, page 232). Each bank district takes its name from the city in which the bank's main office is located. The banks vary widely in geographic size, number of members, and amount of assets. The San Francisco Bank is currently the largest, holding over 31% of the assets of the entire system.

John M. Buckley, Jr.

Federal Home Loan Mortgage Corporation

The Federal Home Loan Mortgage Corporation, known commonly as "Freddie Mac," was created by Congress in 1970 under Title III of the Emergency Home Finance Act. The corporation's purpose is to enhance the liquidity of mortgage investments and increase the availability of mortgage funds by developing and maintaining a national secondary market for conventional mortgage loans. A secondary market for government-backed mortgages (FHA-insured and

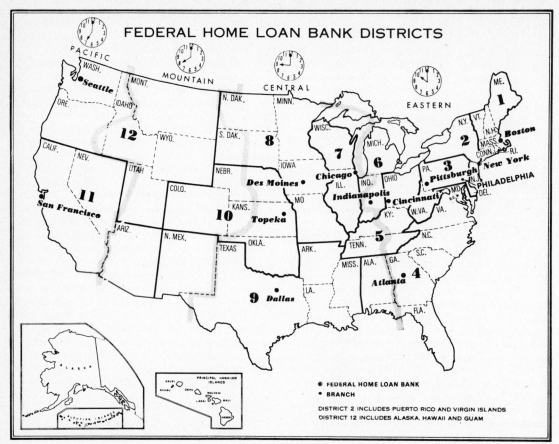

Figure 1.

VA-guaranteed) already existed, but there was no recognized market for conventional loans (without government backing).

Freddie Mac fulfills its congressional mandate by establishing and maintaining programs for the purchase and sale of mortgage loans secured by liens on residential properties. Most of these loans are purchased from SAVINGS AND LOAN ASSOCIATIONS, but other THRIFT INSTITUTIONS, COMMERCIAL BANKS, and MORTGAGE BANKING companies also sell to Freddie Mac. The programs are available to all lenders.

Freddie Mac buys from lenders single-family (one to four units) fixed-rate and adjustable-rate loans, multifamily (more than four units) fixed-rate loans, and home-improvement loans. Lenders may sell either whole loans or participations. (In a participation sale, the lender retains ownership of 5% to 50% of the loan.)

All of the loans sold to Freddie Mac must satisfy its prudent underwriting guidelines, which have become industry standards. These guidelines set standards for determining the creditworthiness of a borrower, set limits on the loan amount and the ratio of loan amount to property value, and establish other criteria to warrant that the loans purchased are of investment quality. To foster efficiency in the secondary-market process, Freddie Mac has standardized the forms used to originate loans.

Financing. Freddie Mac finances the loans it purchases by grouping them together into pools and selling to investors conventional mortgage pass-through securities called "mortgage participation certificates" (*see* CONVENTIONAL MORTGAGE-BACKED SECURITIES). Known as Freddie Mac PC's, they represent undivided ownership interests in pools of mortgages purchased wholly or in part by Freddie Mac. Borrowers' interest and principal payments are passed through from the lender to Freddie Mac, which passes them through to the investor, or holder of the PC. These investors include depository institutions, investment companies, individuals, and others.

Because PC's represent interests in investment-quality mortgage loans and carry Freddie Mac's unconditional guarantee as to the timely payment of interest and full collection of principal, they are regarded as a safe investment. Through July 1983 Freddie Mac had committed to sell over $69 billion in PC's. With a group of 13 INVESTMENT BANKING firms maintaining an active market, PC's are also extremely liquid—far more so than mortgage loans themselves.

While PC sales account for over two-thirds of the funds raised for mortgage purchases, Freddie Mac also issues short-term and long-term debt obligations, gives access to lines of credit, and has in the past sold guaranteed mortgage certificates (GMC's). Like PC's, GMC's represent interests in mortgages, but interest payments are made to investors semiannually, principal payments are made annually, and minimum annual principal-reduction schedules are predetermined. They were last sold in 1979. Freddie Mac periodically issues Collateralized Mortgage Obligations (CMO's), which are debt obligations secured by conventional mortgages. CMO's employ short-, intermediate-, and long-term maturities and provide long-term financing.

Mortgage Swaps. In 1981 the Guarantor program was introduced. It enables lenders to sell Mac mortgage loans to Freddie in return for PC's representing interests in the same loans. This "swap" activity gives savings and loans and other lenders increased financial-management flexibility and has been a boon to the industry. Lenders use PC's as collateral for various borrowing arrangements or sell them to investors.

As of July 31, 1983, Freddie Mac had committed to swap over $42 billion of PC's for mortgage loans.

Structure. The 12 FEDERAL HOME LOAN BANKS provided the initial $100 million of capital and remain Freddie Mac stockholders. In 1982 Congress authorized the public issuance of nonvoting preferred stock. The three presidentially appointed members of the FEDERAL HOME LOAN BANK BOARD, serving in separate capacities, function as Freddie Mac's board of directors.

Freddie Mac is headquartered in Washington, D.C., and operates regional offices in Atlanta, Chicago, Dallas, Los Angeles, and Arlington, Virginia. In addition, it maintains branch offices in Denver, San Francisco, and Seattle.

Federal Home Loan Mortgage Corporation

Federal Housing Administration (FHA)

The Federal Housing Administration, a part of the DEPARTMENT OF HOUSING AND URBAN DEVELOPMENT since 1965, insures mortgages on single-family homes; multifamily rentals, condominiums, and cooperative projects; land purchased for residential development; and nursing homes and intermediate-care facilities, group-practice medical facilities, and hospitals. HUD also insures loans for property improvement and the purchase of manufactured (mobile) homes.

The assistant secretary for housing also serves as the federal housing commissioner. In this capacity he directs the housing and mortgage-insurance programs of the department, which support the production, financing, and management of new or substantially rehabilitated housing, and the conservation and preservation of the existing housing stock.

Harvey Rachlin

Federal Intermediate Credit Banks

See FARM CREDIT SYSTEM.

Federal Land Banks

See FARM CREDIT SYSTEM.

Federal Law Enforcement Training Center

See DEPARTMENT OF THE TREASURY.

Federal National Mortgage Association (FNMA)

The Federal National Mortgage Association, also known as FNMA or "Fannie Mae," is the nation's largest single supplier of home-mortgage funds. In 1983, for instance, it provided the funding for about one in every seven mortgages originated in the United States. By purchasing mortgages from local lenders, Fannie Mae serves to replenish those institutions' supply of lendable funs.

Although currently a shareholder-owned NEW YORK STOCK EXCHANGE corporation, Fannie Mae was originally formed in 1938 by congressional action as a wholly owned government entity, and its business was primarily the purchase and resale of mortgages insured by the FEDERAL HOUSING ADMINISTRATION (FHA), and later mortgages guaranteed by the VETERANS ADMINISTRATION (VA). Under 1968 legislation, the company was partitioned into the GOVERNMENT NATIONAL MORTGAGE ASSOCIATION (GNMA), to remain a federal agency as a part of the DEPARTMENT OF HOUSING AND URBAN DEVELOPMENT, and Fannie Mae in its present state as a shareholder-owned and privately managed company. In 1972 Fannie Mae began purchasing conventional mortgages as well as those backed by the government. The corporation has since become the largest participant in the SECONDARY MORTGAGE MARKET, in which loans are bought and sold in order to increase the supply of funds for housing and to improve the distribution of investment capital available for financing housing throughout the country.

Fannie Mae purchase activities are financed principally from payments on mortgages it already owns and through the issuance of debentures and short-term discount notes. In addition to investing in mortgages for its own portfolio, the company began in 1981 to issue and guaranty mortgage pass-through securities to provide a means for others, such as pension funds, to invest in mortgages.

Fannie Mae's debt issues—its debentures and short-term notes—represent general obligations of the corporation; they are not guaranteed or insured by the federal government. Fannie Mae's debt, however, has been classified by the credit markets as having "agency status."

Fannie Mae's main sources of income include: return on mortgages it owns; and fees paid by lenders for loan commitments and for FNMA guaranteeing of mortgage-backed securities.

The Federal National Mortgage Association has a fifteen-member board of directors, ten elected by shareholders and five appointed by the president of the United States. Its headquarters are in Washington, D.C., and it operates five regional offices located in Atlanta, Dallas, Philadelphia, Chicago, and Los Angeles. Fannie Mae also maintains a fiscal office in New York City.

Fannie Mae as an Investor. As a major force in the secondary mortgage market, Fannie Mae serves several purposes. Through nationwide borrowing in the general financial market, the corporation taps many capital resources that might not otherwise be available for residential mortgage financing. And because Fannie Mae has access to the financial markets at all times, it provides funds to finance home loans even when other sources become cyclically more scarce.

Thus, Fannie Mae–approved lenders are assured a market—and a source of long-term funds—for mortgages they originate in their local markets. They often obtain commitments from Fannie Mae that it will purchase a specified dollar amount of mortgages in advance of actually originating the loans, so that they

know funds are available and at what interest rate.

Some mortgage lenders, like mortgage companies, have always relied on other investors, like Fannie Mae, to provide the long-term funding for loans they originate. Now, however, even other types of lenders are turning to the secondary market. Predominant among this latter group are SAVINGS AND LOAN ASSOCIATIONS, who traditionally used savings deposits to fund their mortgages. More recently, however, due to volatile interest rates and financial-institution deregulation, the cost of savings deposits has increased substantially and their availability has become less predictable. So the S & L's, which used to fund their own mortgages, are now often operating like mortgage companies, originating mortgages and selling them to Fannie Mae and others.

Changes in the economy and in financial institutions have also brought about changes in mortgages themselves. In part, these changes have come about in order to make home financing more affordable, despite high interest rates. In part, they have occurred because the traditional, fixed-rate mortgage became less attractive—and more risky—for lenders and investors.

In 1981 Fannie Mae began introducing an array of new and refined mortgage types, to assure a market and hence funds for the newer loans, as well as to address its own financial needs as an investor. In addition, it began to purchase innovative types of mortgages—designed by local lenders, builders, and others—on a case-by-case basis, providing in many cases the only available market for these new loans.

Mortgage-Backed Securities. In 1981 the Federal National Mortgage Association also introduced perhaps its most major innovation: the FNMA-guaranteed mortgage-backed security. These securities are expected to become a major source of funds for conventional home mortgages because they make mortgage investments attractive and easy for investors like pension funds, which do not usually invest directly in home loans.

Many investors are willing to buy mortgage-backed securities, but not individual mortgages, because the securities work much like bonds. The investor receives regular payments of principal and interest on the mortgages backing the securities, but the administrative work of actually collecting those payments and handling other loan-administration details is handled by someone else, usually the originating lenders.

Fannie Mae did not invent mortgage-backed securities, but it has made them available as a means of financing many more mortgages. GNMA first introduced the idea in the early 1970s, when it began guaranteeing securities backed by FHA and VA loans pooled by local lenders. These securities now provide financing for most new FHA and VA loans.

FNMA's securities were modeled after the successful GNMA's, but they are backed by conventional loans, which are the predominant kind of mortgages now originated. Local lenders originate the mortgages backing the securities, which Fannie Mae issues and guarantees. FNMA's guaranty assures investors they will receive 100% full and timely payment of the principal and interest due, whether or not those payments were actually collected from the homeowners. This guaranty, combined with FNMA's recognition as the standard-setter in mortgage underwriting and investing and as the second-largest presence in the capital markets (second only to the U.S. Treasury), makes securities backed by all kinds and sizes of lenders equally attractive, thus giving all lenders equal access to investor funds.

The Future of the Secondary Market. Mortgage lenders, mortgage instruments, and sources of funds for mortgages have all undergone tremendous changes, the result of change in the overall economy. Most participants and observers of the housing and mortgage industries believe the secondary market and, through it, capital-market investors will provide a primary source of funds for homeownership in the balance of the 1980s and beyond.

Stuart A. McFarland

Federal Open Market Committee

See FEDERAL RESERVE SYSTEM.

Federal Reserve, How It Is Audited

Federal Reserve banks and branches, like commercial depository institutions, are regularly audited and examined (*see* FINANCIAL INSTITUTION REGULATORS). Audits of Reserve banks and branches are conducted by a permanent internal audit staff at each Reserve bank. Each audit staff is headed by a general auditor, who reports directly to the board of directors of the Reserve bank rather than to bank management. This reporting relationship promotes the independence necessary for objective audits.

The scope and frequency of audits conducted in the Federal Reserve are determined by assessing the risk factors inherent in particular operations at each bank. A traditional audit primarily involves the verification of assets, liabilities, and items held in custody as reported in official bank records. In addition, the audits at Reserve banks usually include an evaluation of the

procedures and controls of each area.

At the Federal Reserve Bank of New York, this type of audit is performed by the auditing department, which has responsibility for such areas as cash, check, government bond, accounting, and the foreign areas. The department also prepares and certifies for bank examiners and public accountants information concerning the status of accounts maintained by the bank for depository institutions, and maintains, with two nonauditing departments, control of the bank's gold vault.

A second audit group at the New York Fed—the audit-analysis department—specializes in audits of the bank's electronic data-processing operations and of areas such as bank supervision and research and statistics.

In addition to the internal audit program conducted at each Reserve bank, annual examinations are conducted by a division of the Washington-based board of governors of the FEDERAL RESERVE SYSTEM, on a surprise basis. An examination primarily involves a review of financial records, as well as a physical count of selected assets, liabilities, and custodies. Evaluations also are made of operating procedures and management effectiveness.

Procedures used by the board's examiners are surveyed annually and appraised by a private certified public accounting firm. The board also is audited by its own staff, and examined by a private CPA firm.

And, too, except for certain activities, such as transactions for or with foreign central banks and communications concerning the conduct of monetary policy, including open-market operations, the Reserve banks and the board of governors are reviewed periodically by the General Accounting Office, which reports to the United States Congress.

Regular public reports are issued by the Reserve banks and the board of governors covering foreign exchange operations, domestic open-market operations, and monetary policy in general.

Arthur Samansky

Federal Reserve Bank

See FEDERAL RESERVE SYSTEM.

Federal Reserve Bank Directors, Role of

The 1913 Federal Reserve Act requires each Reserve bank to be supervised and controlled by a board of directors. Accordingly, each of the 12 Reserve banks has nine directors, who serve three-year terms and represent the interests of the district. Reserve bank branches have five to seven directors, who represent interests in the branch territory. Branch directors also serve as advisers to their Reserve bank's head office.

For purposes of representation and selection, Reserve bank directors are divided into three classes of three each. Class A directors are representative of the member COMMERCIAL BANKS in the district and are usually bankers. Class B directors and Class C directors are selected to represent the public, with particular consideration to the interests of agriculture, commerce, industry, services, labor, and consumers. Thus both the providers and the users of banking services in the district are represented on the bank's board. Class A and Class B directors are elected by district member banks, while Class C directors are appointed by the system's board of governors.

The chairperson and deputy chairperson of each nine-member board are selected by the board of governors from the C directors to serve one-year terms. These directors, who must be district residents for at least two years, are often educators, community leaders, lawyers, and retired business people.

Directors can't be members of the Congress. Further, Class B and Class C directors can't be officers, directors, or employees of any bank. Nor can Class C directors own stock in any bank. Additionally, since a Reserve bank directorship is a form of public service, directors are asked to limit other activities. All directors are also expected to avoid participation in partisan political activities.

In electing Class A and Class B directors, district member banks are grouped by capitalization into three size categories—small, medium, and large. Each group of banks elects one Class A and one Class B director.

Reserve bank branch directors aren't elected. The majority are appointed by the Reserve bank's head office directors; the remainder, by the board of governors. The chairperson is selected from those appointed by the board of governors.

Directorships of Reserve banks and branches generally are limited to one or two full terms to assure a greater number of people serving on the boards, representing a wider range of interests.

Although directorships aren't "full-time" jobs, the responsibilities of directors are broad, ranging from the general management of the Reserve bank, assigned by the Federal Reserve Act, to making monetary-policy recommendations.

Directors appoint the Reserve bank president—the chief executive officer—and the first vice-president—the chief administrative officer—to five-year terms, subject to approval by the board of governors. The Reserve bank directors also appoint all officers of the bank.

Directors at the New York Fed also appoint a member and alternate member to the Federal Open Market Committee—the top policymaking unit of the Reserve system. FOMC appointments by New York Fed directors have special significance, since the New York Fed representative to the FOMC, traditionally the bank president, is a permanent voting member of the committee and, by custom, serves as its vice-chairman. Directors also provide advice and counsel to the bank president for use during FOMC policy formulation.

Annually, too, directors appoint the district's representative to the Federal Advisory Council, which periodically confers with the board of governors on business conditions and makes recommendations on issues affecting the system.

Directors are responsible for each Reserve bank's expenditures and yearly budget. They also review the annual internal audit program of the Reserve bank. The Reserve banks also are audited by the board of governors, and the board of governors is audited by a private accounting firm, whose findings are submitted to Congress.

In addition to providing advice to the bank's FOMC representative, directors play a direct role in the formulation of monetary policy. Specifically, the Federal Reserve Act requires directors to meet every 14 days to set the bank's discount rate, subject to review by the board of governors. The discount rate is the interest rate that member commercial banks pay when borrowing from the Federal Reserve for temporary, emergency, or seasonal needs. By raising or lowering the rate, the system can influence the cost and availability of credit.

Overall, directors bring to the Reserve banks a broad range of experience in management techniques, community compensation practices, and technological developments that are important to the banks. That experience provides the bank with a wider range of expertise than normally would be available to a public institution.

Arthur Samansky

Federal Reserve Notes

Paper money of the United States issued for circulation as authorized by section 16 of the Federal Reserve Act. The notes are direct obligations of the U.S. government. They are also liabilities of the Federal Reserve banks and are secured, dollar for dollar, by Reserve bank assets designated by statute as eligible to be pledged as collateral. The notes are LEGAL TENDER for all debts, public and private, and are the mainstay of the United States currency system.

Federal Reserve notes originated with the enactment of the legislation that created the FEDERAL RE-

SERVE SYSTEM. The legislation, coauthored and introduced in the House by Congressman Carter Glass of Virginia, was approved by the Sixty-third Congress in second session and signed by President Woodrow Wilson on December 23, 1913. The first Federal Reserve notes were issued on November 16, 1914—opening day for the Federal Reserve banks.

The notes of 1914–28 measured 7.42 inches by 3.125 inches and were sometimes called "blanket" bills. Those old, large-size notes were issued in two series, 1914 and 1918, and in denominations of $5 to $10,000. Modern small-size notes date from 1929, a year that ushered in a new era in size and design for all United States currency. They range in denomination from $1 to $10,000, but are no longer printed or issued in denominations of over $100.

Federal Reserve assets acceptable as collateral initially consisted of notes, drafts, and bills of exchange accepted for rediscount by the Reserve banks. The list has since been expanded to include bills of exchange and BANKER'S ACCEPTANCES purchased by Reserve banks in the open market, gold certificates, U.S. government and federal-agency securities, and Special Drawing Right certificates.

Federal Reserve currency is printed by the U.S. Treasury Department's Bureau of Engraving and Printing in Washington, D.C. The quantities of each denomination are governed by printing orders placed annually by the board of governors of the Federal Reserve system with the comptroller of the currency. Finished notes, each overprinted with the seal and district number of the Reserve bank for which it was ordered, remain at the bureau until they are needed by the Reserve banks.

Billions of dollars in Federal Reserve notes are kept on hand by commercial banks and other depository institutions to meet the public's need for currency. Billions more are stored in cash department vaults at the Reserve banks, awaiting shipment to replenish vault cash at depository institutions and to replace old, worn-out notes.

The circulating supply of Federal Reserve notes, unlike that of pre–Federal Reserve paper money, adjusts readily to changes in the public's demand for cash. It may rise several billion dollars in the weeks leading up to Christmas, for example, and decline that much, or more, once the holiday season is over. The circular flow of Federal Reserve notes—from Reserve banks, to depository institutions, to the public, and back again—ensures that the amount in circulation at any given time is the amount that needs to be in circulation at that particular time. These characteristics of Federal Reserve currency attest to the achievement of the purpose for which Federal Reserve notes were added to the currency system: to provide an elastic currency, a currency responsive to, and adequate for, the needs of commerce, industry, and agriculture.

Doris E. Harless

Glossary

bill of exchange; draft; banker's acceptance   Short-term credit instruments. A *bill of exchange* is a written and signed order drawn by one party (the drawer) instructing a second (the drawee) to pay a specified sum of money to a third (the payee) on demand or on a specified future date. A *draft* has essentially the same characteristics as a bill of exchange, except that it may be made nonnegotiable and a bill of exchange may not. The two terms—*draft* and *bill of exchange*—are often used interchangeably. A bill of exchange, or draft, becomes an *acceptance* when the drawee formally acknowledges his obligation to honor the instrument, usually by stamping "Accepted" on its face. A *banker's acceptance* is a bill of exchange, or time draft, that has been accepted by a bank.

legal tender   Money a debtor is authorized by law to offer, and a creditor is required by law to accept, in payment of obligations expressed in terms of money.

rediscount   To discount a negotiable instrument a second time. To discount is to deduct the charge for use of money loaned on, or paid for, a negotiable instrument from the principal sum at the time the loan is made or the instrument is acquired.

Special Drawing Right (SDR)   A type of international money created by the International Monetary Fund and allocated to its member nations. SDR's can be used by a member nation with a balance-of-payments deficit to settle debts to another member nation or to the IMF. A transfer of SDR's is accomplished through an accounting entry, not through an exchange of actual money.

Federal Reserve Security Loans to Dealers

The Federal Reserve system's open-market account lends U. S. government securities to dealers with whom it does business. These loans enable the dealers to meet commitments to deliver specific securities to a third party, when another party is failing to meet a commitment to deliver those securities to the dealer on a timely basis (*see* REPORTING DEALERS; SYSTEM OPEN-MARKET ACCOUNT).

The inability to deliver a security on time is called a "fail." Fails occur from time to time in the government and other securities markets. The firm failing to deliver is penalized by having to pay the interest accruing on the "fail" securities to the buyer, even though the buyer isn't required to pay for the securities before they are delivered. The penalty occurs because the buyer pays the originally agreed-upon price and receives the late-delivered security with a greater amount of accrued interest.

The system's lending arrangement was established in November 1969 to help ensure the smooth functioning of the government-securities market. The authority to lend securities is reviewed annually by the Federal Open Market Committee, the top monetary policymaking unit of the system.

The borrowing firm makes its request to the system's trading desk at the Federal Reserve Bank of New York, or through its local Federal Reserve bank, certifying that the loan is to fill a contract to deliver and that the securities won't be used for a short sale. (A short sale involves the selling of a borrowed security, which the seller must eventually return.) In addition, the New York Fed's trading-desk officers must be reasonably assured the borrowing firm isn't able to obtain the necessary securities from another source.

The New York Fed lends securities to dealers for a maximum of five business days. Limits also are placed on the amount of securities that can be lent to any dealer: up to $50 million (face value) of a particular issue of U.S. Treasury bills; up to $10 million of any particular issue of Treasury notes and bonds; and a maximum of $150 million on all issues to any dealer.

The borrower must return a security of the same issue to the Federal Reserve. In return for the borrowed security, the dealer must pledge to the Federal Reserve other U.S. government securities in an amount with market value (including accrued interest) that exceeds the value of the borrowed securities plus accrued interest on the borrowed securities.

Interest paid by the dealer on the principal amount of the securities borrowed is calculated at an annual rate of 1 1/2%. If the borrowed securities aren't returned on time, the dealer is penalized by being charged an annual rate up to 6%.

Interest due from the Treasury on the securities lent by the Federal Reserve system is paid to the Federal Reserve, while interest on the collateral will be paid to the firm pledging the collateral.

The amount of securities lent at the close of the statement week (Wednesday) is reported in a footnote to the H.4.1 statistical report (*Factors Affecting Reserves of Depository Institutions and Condition Statement of Federal Reserve Banks*), issued weekly by the board of governors of the Federal Reserve system, as well as the weekly statement of condition of the New York Fed.

Lent securities remain in the total portfolio count of U.S. government securities held by the Federal Reserve system, since an identical security will be returned.

The collateral held for the lent securities is neither an asset nor a liability of the Federal Reserve system and thus isn't shown on any public statistical report. However, it is shown on internal reports as an item held in safekeeping in the name of the Federal Reserve. Neither the lending of the security nor the return of the security has any effect on reserves of depository institutions.

Arthur Samansky

Federal Reserve System

The Federal Reserve system is the CENTRAL BANK of the United States. Its main responsibility is to promote economic stability and growth by regulating the flow of money and credit. It is composed of 12 independent Reserve banks, each in an established Reserve district; a supervising board of governors in Washington, D.C.; the Federal Advisory Council; other system committees; and member banks.

In carrying out its objectives, the Federal Reserve performs a variety of functions, including:

• Managing the nation's money and credit
• Supervising banks and financial institutions such as bank holding companies
• Providing payment services to banks, such as check, wire-transfer, and automated clearinghouse services
• Acting as the government's banker in marketing its securities, paying its debts, and handling its international transactions
• Issuing coin and currency, including Federal Reserve notes, which make up virtually all of the nation's paper money
• Holding the reserves of commercial banks and depository institutions
• Providing short-term (discount) loans to banks temporarily short of reserves

Federal Reserve Banks. The Federal Reserve banks are the operating arms of the Federal Reserve system—the nation's central bank—and carry out its day-to-day policies and activities. To carry out these everyday operations, the United States has been divided into 12 Federal Reserve districts, each with a Federal Reserve bank (see below). By establishing regional arms, Congress intended that all parts of the nation would have access to the system and that local economic developments and needs would be represented in monetary policy.

Each Federal Reserve bank provides supervision and services for the banks in its district. Reserve banks distribute FEDERAL RESERVE NOTES, designated with each bank's name, district number, and letter; process checks and electronic transfers, government notes, bonds, savings bonds, and food coupons; supervise and examine the state-chartered member commercial banks and certain other depository institutions in their districts to ensure they are operating soundly and complying with federal rules and regulations; hold the cash reserves of depository institutions in their districts and make loans to them; and participate in setting monetary policy of the Federal Reserve system, in part by reporting on economic developments in their regions. (The Federal Reserve Bank of New York is unique in the system in that it also acts as the foreign exchange arm of both the system and the U.S. Treasury, provides account services to foreign governments, central banks, and international monetary institutions, and also executes monetary policy at the direction of the Federal Open Market Committee, the system's top policymaking body.)

As stated above, the country is divided into 12 Federal Reserve districts, each with a Federal Reserve bank. There are also 25 branches of these banks that serve particular areas within each district.

Reserve Bank Structure. Each Federal Reserve bank has a nine-member board of directors designed to provide representation from commerce, industry, agriculture, banking, and the public. Each member serves a three-year term. Six of the directors are elected by member banks (see below)—three stockholders (usually commercial bankers) of the member bank and three who represent the interests of producers, workers, and consumers. The remaining three directors, none of whom may have any banking affiliation

Figure 1. Federal Reserve System. Lines show boundaries of Federal Reserve Districts. Heavy circles show Federal Reserve Bank cities. Star shows Board of Governors of the Federal Reserve System. Light circles show Federal Reserve branches: Buffalo, Cincinnati, Pittsburgh, Baltimore, Charlotte, Birmingham, Jacksonville, Miami, Nashville, New Orleans, Detroit, Little Rock, Louisville, Memphis, Helena, Denver, Oklahoma City, Omaha, El Paso, Houston, San Antonio, Los Angeles, Portland, Salt Lake City, and Seattle.

either, are appointed by the board of governors in Washington, D.C. One of these three directors is appointed as the bank's chairman and Federal Reserve agent. The Federal Reserve agent's duty is to supervise the issuance of Federal Reserve notes and to account for the Reserve bank's assets backing those notes.

Directors are elected to three-year terms. The number of terms is usually limited to one or two to assure that a greater number of individuals, representing a wider range of views, can serve. Directors aren't full-time Reserve bank employees, but they do have broad responsibilities, ranging from general management to advising on monetary policy.

They appoint the president (chief executive officer) of the bank, as well as the bank's officers. They also make annual appointments to the Federal Advisory Council, which meets at least four times a year to discuss business and financial conditions and make recommendations.

Directors are responsible for budgets and expenditures and also review the bank's internal audit program. Directors also play a direct role in monetary policy. They are required to set the bank's discount rate—the interest rate charged depository institutions that borrow to overcome temporary reserve deficiencies—every two weeks. By raising and lowering the rate, the system influences the cost and availability of money and credit.

But it is in their advisory role that the directors play perhaps their most important role. By providing their evaluation of business and economic conditions and by giving their insights into local conditions, they help bring more information and depth to the policymaking process.

Table 1
Federal Reserve Banks

City	District Number	Letter Designation
Boston	1	A
New York	2	B
Philadelphia	3	C
Cleveland	4	D
Richmond	5	E
Atlanta	6	F
Chicago	7	G
St. Louis	8	H
Minneapolis	9	I
Kansas City	10	J
Dallas	11	K
San Francisco	12	L

Board of Governors. The board of governors is the Federal Reserve system's supervisory body. As such, it has various duties.

Its prime responsibility is the formulation of monetary policy. This policy is designed to promote the country's economic goals, and the board reports and accounts to the Congress. The board also establishes member-bank reserve requirements (the percentage of deposits that depository institutions must maintain with the Federal Reserve or as vault cash); issues rules regarding "discount" loans made by the Reserve banks to depository institutions; has the authority to set maximum interest rates on time and savings deposits of member banks; and sets margin requirements for the use of credit in national securities markets. Other duties include supervising and examining the activities of member banks, approving acquisitions by bank holding companies, approving the salaries of officers of Reserve banks, and establishing regulations that will implement federal consumer-credit laws.

The Federal Reserve Board is composed of seven governors appointed by the president, with the advice and consent of Congress. Terms of office are for 14 years. After serving a full term, a governor is ineligible for reappointment. A chairman and vice-chairman are named by the president; their terms are for four years and they may be reappointed.

Federal Open Market Committee (FOMC). The Federal Open Market Committee is the Federal Reserve system's top policymaking body. It establishes open-market policy and has sole authority over open-market operations. Open-market operations, which involve the purchase and sale of government securities in the open market, are the means through which the system conducts monetary policy—by determining the cost and availability of money and credit in the U.S. economy. Policy relating to the system's operations in the foreign exchange markets is also established by the FOMC.

The committee consists of the seven presidentially appointed governors of the Federal Reserve system (members of the Federal Reserve Board) and five Reserve bank presidents, one of whom—the president of the New York Reserve Bank—is a permanent member (because the New York Fed handles open-market operations for the committee). The four other presidents, who serve one-year terms, are selected in rotation from the following four regional clusters of Reserve banks:

1. Boston, Philadelphia, and Richmond
2. Cleveland and Chicago
3. Atlanta, St. Louis, and Dallas
4. Minneapolis, Kansas City, and San Francisco

There are no statutory rules on how the FOMC can organize itself, but by tradition the chairman of the board of governors serves as chairman of the committee, and the president of the New York Reserve Bank serves as vice-chairman.

The committee formally meets in Washington, D.C., every four to six weeks at the Federal Reserve Board. However, committee members routinely communicate with one another on an almost daily basis, and if economic or financial conditions warrant action between regular meetings, special meetings or meetings by phone are held.

At every formal meeting, the committee must vote on a course of action for monetary policy, essentially to tighten or to ease MONETARY POLICY or to maintain the status quo until the next meeting. Several times each year the committee also votes on establishing certain longer-run policy objectives and operational targets, specifically the target rate of growth for the money supply over the next 12 months.

The decisions of the committee are incorporated into a policy directive, which is forwarded to the Federal Reserve Bank of New York for implementation through the New York Reserve Bank's open-market trading desk. The Federal Reserve Bank of New York is the operating arm of the Federal Reserve system in implementing open-market operations and buys and sells government securities on behalf of the entire system.

The FOMC was not part of the original Federal Reserve Act of 1913. It was created by the Banking Acts of 1933 and 1935, which amended the Federal Reserve Act. However, it wasn't until the early 1950s, when the Treasury and the Federal Reserve agreed to allow prices and interest rates on government securities to be determined by trading in the U.S. money market, that open-market operations became the dominant device for implementing monetary policy.

Open-Market Desk. As stated above, the open-market desk buys and sells U.S. government securities to fulfill the goals set by the FOMC. Transactions are executed with about three dozen securities dealers, who can account for hundreds of millions of dollars in value daily. The effect on the economy is indirect. For example, if the Fed sells securities, the dealers draw down their bank accounts to pay for them. By drawing down their accounts, the dealers also draw down the reserves of their COMMERCIAL BANKS. If the BANKS lose excess reserves, their ability to create money through loans is reduced.

Conversely, if the system is encouraging economic growth, the trading desk would buy securities. The dealers deposit the funds they receive into their bank accounts, and the banks gain reserves and their ability to lend expands.

Federal Advisory Council. The Federal Reserve Act provides for this council to serve in an advisory capacity to the board of governors. The council consists of one representative from each of the 12 Federal Reserve districts. It meets four times a year in Washington and offers its view on monetary policy and other current developments of importance to the system.

Member Banks. These are depository institutions that are members of the Federal Reserve system. All national banks—that is, those holding charters from the federal government—must belong to the system. State-chartered commercial banks and mutual savings banks may join at their option.

Federal Reserve History. The creation of the Federal Reserve system, on December 23, 1913, was the culmination of a century-long search for the proper forum in which America could make its monetary decisions. The nation's first attempt to organize its decision-making machinery came in the 1790s when Alexander Hamilton convinced Congress to charter the Bank of the United States. The bank fulfilled many of the requirements of a central bank. It issued its own paper currency, based on its holdings of gold. It made loans to the public and handled the government's coins, payments, and tax collections. The bank was chartered for 20 years and performed fairly well. However, political opposition blocked renewal of its charter, and it closed.

A second Bank of the United States was chartered in 1816 when opposition was overcome by the need to finance the War of 1812 and by the financial instability plaguing the nation. The second bank was similar in structure and operations to the first. However, it, too, had political opponents and expired with its charter, in 1836.

From that point until the Civil War, America's monetary fate lay in the hands of a proliferation of state-chartered banks, which issued a bewildering assortment of notes with little or no regulation. In an attempt to help finance the Civil War, Congress passed the National Banking Act of 1863. Under the act, Congress would charter banks, and they would be able to issue a new federal currency, based on their holding of U.S. government bonds. Few state-chartered banks volunteered for the new national charter. However, Congress also proposed a tax on notes issued by state banks. The tax was gradually raised until notes issued by state banks were driven from circulation.

Through the remaining years of the nineteenth century and the opening years of the twentieth, the nation's monetary decisions were made by Congress in the political arena, where constituencies tended to pull decisions in a variety of directions and political clout tended to dominate monetary needs.

In the fall of 1907, the Knickerbocker Trust Company failed, touching off a nationwide bank panic, the third in roughly 20 years. Within a matter of days, money virtually disappeared from circulation. Banks found themselves in a highly vulnerable position: They were unable to keep up with the public's demands for cash, and, at the same time they were unable to recall loans or borrow against them to meet cash needs.

Spurred by the severity of the 1907 panic, Congress began searching for means to prevent further troubles. Based on a series of exhaustive investigations, they proposed establishing a central bank similar to European institutions and yet with uniquely American features aimed at defusing the political arguments of bigness and excess power that had defeated the first and second Banks of the United States.

Instead of one large central bank, this one would be made up of a series of smaller institutions. They would have a good deal of regional independence, but they would be supervised by a central body in Washington, D.C. The central bank would be responsible to Congress and subject to the checks and balances of the Constitution, such as presidential appointment with the advice and consent of Congress.

All federally chartered banks, those under federal control, were required to join. State-chartered banks could join at their option. All members would be required to hold a specific percentage of deposits as reserves at the Reserve Bank. Previously, banks held their reserves as interest-earning deposits at larger city banks, where they were lent out. As a result, when those reserves were needed to meet sudden demands for withdrawals, they couldn't be retrieved in time.

System members would also be entitled to borrow from Reserve banks in times of need, pledging customer notes as collateral. By acting as "lender of last resort," Reserve banks could provide the liquidity lacking in the 1907 panic.

Reserve banks would also issue their own notes, Federal Reserve bank notes, which would be issued to meet public demand and revert back to Reserve banks when no longer needed. This "elastic" currency would avoid the disappearance of currency as happened in the 1907 panic.

Since those beginnings, the Federal Reserve has changed with the times. In the 1920s the committee that oversaw the investment of Reserve Bank assets was formalized into the Federal Open Market Committee. In later years the function of Reserve system transactions was changed from managing assets to controlling the level of commercial bank reserves. Following the crash of 1929 and the bank runs of the 1930s, Congress enacted legislation aimed at correcting flaws in our banking system. The new legislation permitted banks to hold common stock, and broadened the Federal Reserve's powers to include controls over credit purchases of stock.

In 1951 the Federal Open Market Committee's powers were strengthened when an accord with the Treasury relieved the committee of the responsibility of supporting government bond prices. Relieved of this responsibility, the committee could focus its efforts on transactions aimed at affecting the economy.

The Monetary Control Act of 1980 produced far-reaching changes in the Reserve system. Prior to passage of the act, members were required to hold reserves at a Reserve bank or in vault cash, neither of which earned interest. Nonmembers, on the other hand, held reserves as specified by state laws, which tended to allow lower reserves to allow them to be held in the form of interest-earning government securities. This differential caused increasing numbers of banks to abandon system membership in the late 1960s and the 1970s. This outflow of banks gradually eroded the monetary base upon which the system's economy-controlling powers rested. In 1980, Congress voted a multiphase plan aimed at halting this erosion. Among the major provisions of the act were the following:

• All depository institutions, commercial banks, savings and loan associations, savings banks, and credit unions would have to hold reserves at a Reserve bank.
• Reserves of members were to be gradually scaled down and nonmembers' reserves scaled upward until they were equalized.
• Depository institutions would be permitted to offer negotiable order of withdrawal (NOW) accounts, interest-bearing accounts on which checks may be drawn.
• Depository institutions were given access to the Fed's discount window.
• Reserve banks would be required to provide access to their services to all depository institutions and to establish prices for those services.
• Interest-rate ceilings on bank deposits were to be phased out in an orderly fashion.

Charles J. Parnow

Federal Savings and Loan Insurance Corporation (FSLIC)

The Federal Savings and Loan Insurance Corporation is a permanent government entity created by the National Housing Act of 1934 with the responsibility of insuring the savings of account holders in SAVINGS AND LOAN ASSOCIATIONS.

Historical Development. During the early 1930s, the savings and loan industry became a victim of the pervasive depression that plunged the country into economic chaos. Defaults on mortgage loans surged as the unemployment rate reached unprecedented levels. Property used as collateral against loans declined in value, often falling below the amount of the loan. Because there was no insurance on savings accounts, depositors quickly withdrew their savings whenever they heard that an association was in trouble. As a result, inadequate funds were available to honor the heavy withdrawals, and associations were forced to close their doors. During this time approximately 1,700 institutions failed, causing losses to depositors of more than $200 million.

In 1933, after bank and thrift-institution failures and financial distress had culminated in the nationwide "bank holiday," Congress created the FEDERAL DEPOSIT INSURANCE CORPORATION (FDIC) to provide insurance for bank deposits. Similarly, in 1934, Congress passed the National Housing Act, which established the Federal Savings and Loan Insurance Corporation for the purpose of insuring the accounts of all federal associations, qualified state-chartered building and loans, savings and loans, homestead associations, and cooperative banks.

As a permanent instrument of the federal government, the FSLIC's actual operations were placed under the supervision and authority of the FEDERAL HOME LOAN BANK BOARD (FHLBB). Immediately after the National Housing Act was passed, the FHLBB organized the FSLIC and met as the first trustees to adopt bylaws and complete the organization of the corporation.

The original capital of the FSLIC, amounting to $100 million, was contributed in its entirety by the federal government, acting through another government agency, the Home Owner's Loan Corporation, which bought all the FSLIC stock. Ownership of the stock was subsequently transferred to the secretary of the Treasury. By applying 50% of its annual net income, the FSLIC began to retire the stock in the early 1950s and completed the repurchase in 1958. The corporation has been self-supporting since that time.

Insurance and Growth of the FSLIC Reserve Fund. From the end of the Great Depression through 1979, the involvement of the FSLIC in default-prevention activities was limited. As the insurer of deposits in a growing industry, the FSLIC usually enjoyed ample premium income and was involved in few assistance cases. After 1936, the FSLIC's total operating expense and case assistance never exceeded half of the total yearly income. This resulted in a steady growth of the insurance fund to the current figure of over $7 billion.

When the FSLIC was created, insurance of accounts was set at a $5,000 ceiling per savings account and an annual premium of one-quarter of 1% of insured savings was assessed against each FSLIC-insured institution. Amendments by Congress raised the coverage on savings accounts in 1950 to $10,000; in 1966 to $15,000; in 1969 to $20,000; in 1974 to $40,000, with special coverage of $100,000 for public-fund accounts; and in 1980 to $100,000 for all accounts including public-fund accounts.

Changes in the original premium assessed against insured institutions also occurred between 1935 and 1980. In 1935, legislation called for a reduction to one-eight of 1% of insured savings for the annual assessment; in 1950, this was reduced to one-twelfth of 1%. This reduction had a significant negative impact on the growth of the reserve fund relative to insured deposits. While the decade of the 1950s saw insured savings growing annually at 15% to 20%, the FSLIC ratio of reserve to insured liability annually declined, to 0.63% in 1959.

The FHLBB, increasingly concerned about this threat to the financial security that backed the industry, proposed legislation to Congress to correct the situation. In 1962, Congress called for an additional premium to be paid to the FSLIC. Under the statute, insured S & L's were required to make annual prepayments into a secondary reserve until the total FSLIC reserve equaled or exceeded 2% of the total amount of all FSLIC-insured accounts. Once this level was reached, each S & L received a pro rata share of the excess amount.

This distribution of the pro rata share was authorized, by Public Law 91-151, to continue until the total of the FSLIC reserves dropped below 1.6%. In 1969 the ratio had been reached, but by 1972 the ratio had declined to 1.564%. To eliminate the "stop-start" pattern of payments to the FSLIC, Congress changed the law in 1973 as follows:

1. All prepayments to the secondary reserve were discontinued.

2. Authority was given to the board for setting, within a range of 30–70%, the portion of the regular annual insurance premium to be paid in cash. The remainder would be charged to the insured institution's pro rata share of the secondary reserve, until the reserve was exhausted.

3. The ratio of FSLIC reserves to total savings was changed to 1.25% (down from 1.6%) before resumption of full cash payments.

In 1974 new legislation provided for the complete phasing out of the secondary reserve over a ten-year period beginning May 1975.

Additional Sources of Funds. The strength of the FSLIC is evidenced by its reserves. However, in addition to its own resources, the FSLIC has a substantial safety feature in the form of a loss reserve and surplus of its member associations. The FSLIC also has statutory authority for the use of three other sources of funds:

1. A credit line of $750 million with the U.S. Department of the Treasury.

2. The ability to require additional premium assessments (not to exceed one-eighth of 1% of the account balance and creditor obligations) of its insured members.

3. The ability to call upon insured associations to deposit up to 1% of their total withdrawable savings. The FSLIC has never had to use these three sources of funds.

Preserving the Strength of the FSLIC Reserve Fund. In maintaining the security of the insurance fund, the FSLIC has authority to apply several actions to preserve an association in danger of default. These actions are used to stabilize the failing association while maintaining the insurance fund. As described in section 406(f) of the National Housing Act, the FSLIC has broad flexibility to provide loans or contributions, or to acquire the assets or liabilities of the troubled institution, as long as the estimated cost of the action does not exceed the expense of liquidating the association.

From 1934 to 1979, the FSLIC provided assistance in only 124 cases. And in only 13 of these cases were the association's problems so severe that the association was closed and insurance payments made to insured depositors. Seven closings occurred during 1940 to 1941, and six cases took place between 1965 and 1971. During 1980 and 1981, the FSLIC gave assistance to 35 cases (11 in 1980, and 24 in 1981). The increase in the number of associations needing assistance is a direct effect of the economic constraints affecting the S & L industry. The assistance has significantly increased the number of mergers over the past five years.

Facilitating a merger or consolidating or acquiring the assets of an association following a default were options not available to the FSLIC until 1978. This authority came with the passage of the Financial Institutions Regulatory and Interest Rate Control Act of 1978. Then, in 1981, new options made available by the FHLBB, such as interstate mergers and acquisitions, contributed to the substantial decline in present value costs of default prevention. Additionally, the FSLIC developed an "income capital certificate" (ICC), which may be issued by an association in exchange for cash or cash-equivalent FSLIC notes. Although having some attributes of debt, the ICC also has substantive equity features that allow it to be treated as permanent equity capital for purposes of determining net worth.

Payment of Insurance. Today, cash payments representing the total account balance and default interest up to the maximum insured limit are made within four to five days after default. However, during the first eight years of the FSLIC, seven insured associations were placed in default and payment of insurance was conducted primarily through the transfer of individual accounts to other insured associations. Only six persons out of a total of 7,846 holders of insured claims in these seven cases received payment of insurance in cash. By transferring the account, the insured investor received an equal amount in the new association. On the other hand, the cash method provided 10% of the insured investment immediately, 45% in negotiable non-interest-bearing debentures due within one year from the date of default, and 45% in similar debenture due within three years from the date of default.

Gail Lutz Verley

Federal Trade Commission (FTC)

An independent law-enforcement agency of the U.S. government, responsible for promoting fair and free competition in interstate commerce by preventing unfair and deceptive business practices. The FTC has the authority to stop business practices that are anticompetitive or harmful to the public, provided that they fall within the legal scope of its statutes, are carried on interstate, and affect the public interest. The FTC may hold hearings on complaints of violations and issue cease and desist orders to discontinue such practices or apply to the federal courts to issue injunctions.

To articulate the legal obligations of the business community and to inform consumers of their legal recourse when they recognize unfair or deceptive business practices, the FTC periodically issues trade-regulation rules and industry guides, which define practices that violate the law. It also issues business advice, called "Advisory Opinions," to firms and individuals requesting it.

The FTC was created by the Federal Trade Commission Act on September 26, 1914. It is administered by five commissioners who are appointed by the president with the advice and consent of the Senate. Not more than three commissioners may be members of the same political party. A chairman, also designated by the president, is responsible for the administrative and personnel aspects of the FTC's operations.

Harvey Rachlin

Fedwire

The Federal Reserve's electronic communications network that is used to transfer reserve balances; government securities; and the administrative, supervisory, and monetary-policy communications of the Federal Reserve.

The nation's large banks use Fedwire to adjust their reserve positions on a daily basis by buying or selling reserve-account balances from or to one another. The network also allows banks to transfer U.S. government and federal-agency securities in book-entry form, and to transfer funds on behalf of customers. Transfers on behalf of customers, called "third-party payments," typically involve the purchase and sale of commercial paper, bonds, and securities, or the cash management operations of major corporations.

The Fedwire network interconnects all the Federal Reserve banks, branches, and off-premises regional check-processing centers (49 offices in all) through a computer system that in 1982 had its central switching center in Culpeper, Virginia. The Treasury and over 400 commercial banks are also tied directly into this network by direct computer-to-computer links. Thousands of other commercial banks originate and receive transactions over Fedwire, using terminals on their own premises linked to the Federal Reserve's computers. Eighty-five percent of all fund transfers processed by the Federal Reserve are handled in this manner, with all processing and accounting fully automated. Thousands of smaller banks transfer funds and securities over Fedwire by telephone and subsequent paper confirmation. In 1981 Fedwire handled 50 million transfers whose combined value exceeded $100 trillion (more than $300 billion per day).

The Federal Reserve "settles" wire-transfer transactions over Fedwire through the act of transfer itself. When a Fedwire transfer is made between banks, the Federal Reserve's computer debits the reserve account of the sending bank and credits the reserve account of the receiving bank in immediately available and final funds. These postings produce an immediate change in ownership and, like a cash payment, the transaction itself effects the settlement.

The book-entry-securities-transfer component of the Fedwire has enabled the federal government to replace virtually all U.S. government and federal-agency paper securities with computer entries at Reserve banks. In 1981 about 95% of all outstanding marketable government securities and virtually all federal-agency securities were in computerized book-entry form.

The Federal Reserve's securities-transfer system was developed in the 1920s when Treasury securities became transferable by telegraphic wire among the Federal Reserve banks. However, this early system still required subsequent physical exchange of securities. It was not until the late 1960s, when Treasury regulations authorized book-entry procedures, that wire transfer of securities came into its own in the nation's payments system. Under those procedures, securities could be registered and traded electronically on the records of a Reserve bank.

David H. Friedman

"Felines"

See COUPON STRIPPING.

Finance Charge

This term means the cost of obtaining and using consumer credit, stated as a dollar-and-cents amount. For purposes of the federal Truth in Lending Act, it includes any charge payable directly or indirectly by the consumer and imposed directly or indirectly by the creditor as an incident to or a condition of the extension of credit. It does not include any charge of a type payable in a comparable cash transaction. Credit contracts and other written credit agreements must state the finance charge, within tolerances for accuracy prescribed by the federal law, before the contract or agreement is consummated.

Examples of the components of a finance charge are interest, service charges for credit, time-price differentials, transaction or activity fees, and carrying charges, among other types of charges imposed for the use of credit.

Ordinarily, delinquency charges and late fees, charges for bad checks or overdrafts of checking accounts, membership fees for participation in a credit-card plan, certain fees and charges made or paid in connection with real-estate transactions, and legal fees are not components of a finance charge. Charges for credit-related insurance usually also are not part of the finance charge unless insurance, such as credit life insurance, is required by the creditor as a condition of credit.

When you use credit, you have a right granted by federal law to know exactly what you will have to pay for it, so that you can make comparisons among competing creditors and will be aided in shopping for credit, if you choose to do so.

James A. Ambrose

Financial Analyst

As related to the field of investment, the financial analyst is defined by the Financial Analysts Federation—the professional organization for securities analysts, portfolio managers, investment counselors, and pension-fund and other money managers—as "an individual who spends a substantial portion of time collecting, evaluating, or applying financial, economic, and statistical data, as appropriate, in the investment decision-making process." There are about 15,000 such analysts in the United States and Canada who belong to the 53 societies and chapters of the federation. Such analysts are employed primarily by broker/dealers, investment-banking firms, banks and trust companies, insurance companies, mutual and pension funds, and investment-management firms. Foundations, educational institutions, and in some instances corporations with substantial amounts of their own money to invest also employ financial analysts.

A major function of the analyst is to define the probable risk and potential return of a given investment under a variety of different circumstances. Analysts who are portfolio managers or investment counselors also help their clients to define their investment objectives (capital appreciation, current income, retirement income, tax relief, preservation of capital, or a combination of such objectives) and make a recommendation or develop several alternative recommendations about investments and investment selections that can help the client reach the defined goal.

Most financial analysts are primarily concerned with equity investments; they evaluate the relative attractiveness of the common stocks of different companies. To do this, analysts usually estimate future corporate earnings, both near-term and long-term. Analysts are frequently concerned with "earning power," which can be defined as the earnings from normal operations, excluding extraordinary or nonrecurring factors.

Earning power can change for many reasons, sometimes quickly, sometimes over a period of several years or a decade or more. Changes in earning power can be caused by changes in management (the death of a strong chief executive, or an overall change in management style, direction, or strategy); a change in the availability or cost of raw materials; a switch in consumer demand; competition within the industry, or the development of competing industries; the economy; changes in government policy, or political change. Analysts therefore need to monitor the factors that affect individual companies and industries as well as investment in general. They do so to keep their earnings estimates current so that they can provide timely, useful recommendations to their clients, whether institutions or individuals, about buying, selling, or holding particular investments or a selection of them (called a "portfolio").

Some financial analysts are primarily concerned with the evaluation of fixed-income investments, such as preferred stock and debt instruments. The latter are issued by governmental entities as well as corporations. While the techniques used are similar to those used in the analysis of common stocks, the emphasis is different. Fixed-income analysis is primarily concerned with evaluating the security of such investments and evaluating any possible risk of nonpayment.

Investment looks toward the future, but the information on which investment decisions are based come from the past and present. The analyst uses both quantitative information—a company's financial statements, statistical histories, etc.—and qualitative information—judgments about management ability; the clarity of management goals and strategy for achieving them; management understanding and coping with external forces (changes in market demand or supply, changes in international economics, etc.)—to formulate earnings estimates.

The analyst's sources of information include corporate annual and quarterly reports to stockholders; 10-K's and 10-Q's (annual and quarterly filings with the Securities and Exchange Commission); other filings with the SEC and with other federal, state, and local governments and agencies; fact books and statistical supplements prepared for professional investors; press releases; proxy statements and stockholder mailings; annual meeting summaries; major speech texts; field trips to corporate facilities; interviews with management; and corporate presentations to management and other investor groups.

Most analysts, and particularly those who function as portfolio managers (about a third of them do) or as investment counselors (about one in six does), try to pinpoint the best possible selection of stocks, bonds, cash, or cash equivalents that will be most likely to give a client the desired return on an investment. Of course, investors vary in their goals, and also in the period of time they have available for investment, their desired results (growth or income or a combination of both), and their tax status, as well as their ability or willingness to assume risk. Therefore, analysts need to be able to assess the earning power of a company not only as it stands alone but also in comparison with other companies in its industry, companies in other industries, and other potential investment instruments (government securities, such as Treasury bills, notes, and bonds, municipal bonds, etc.) so that a portfolio can be developed that is most likely to meet investor need.

Some analysts publish newsletters or reports that summarize their research. Such reports are available to clients and in some instances to the public.

An examination that leads to the designation "Chartered Financial Analyst" defines, in general, the experience and knowledge requirements of the financial analyst. To become a C.F.A., an analyst needs to pass three six-hour examinations within a seven-year period. The exams cover six major subjects: financial accounting; ethical and professional standards and security law and regulation; fixed-income securities analysis; equity securities analysis; economics; and portfolio management. The examinations are given in about 65 locations in the United States, Canada, and other nations. The Institute of Chartered Financial Analysts, in Charlottesville, Virginia, administers the examination program.

To enter the C.F.A. program, an analyst needs a bachelor's degree or its equivalent. In addition to passing the three examinations, an analyst must also have three years' experience in financial analysis as defined at the outset of this article.

By the end of 1983 approximately 7,400 analysts held the C.F.A. designation. Many more have passed the first or first and second of the examinations. Some 400 charters are awarded annually.

A recent survey of analysts employed in a research capacity by broker/dealers showed that a typical FAF member in that position had passed two qualifying examinations (the registered representative's exam or the New York Stock Exchange's supervisory analyst exam, or one or more of the C.F.A. exams) and had, in addition, an advanced degree and from ten to fifteen years' experience.

Analysts who are members of the Financial Analysts Federation are bound by a Code of Ethics and Standards of Professional Conduct that recognize the diversity of their employers and assignments and hold them accountable to provide "competent, objective, and trustworthy advice with regard to investments and financial management."

Mildred M. Hermann

Financial Futures

See INTEREST-RATE FUTURES.

Financial Institution Regulators

Depository institutions in the United States are regulated by a network of federal and state laws, and the administrative rules and regulations of several government and quasi-government departments and agencies. The broad objective of bank supervision and regulation is to protect depositors and assure the economy of an efficiently functioning banking system.

Depository institutions are COMMERCIAL BANKS, SAVINGS BANKS, SAVINGS AND LOAN ASSOCIATIONS, CREDIT UNIONS, foreign bank branches and agencies in the United States, and Edge Act and Agreement corporations (*see* EDGE ACT CORPORATIONS).

Commercial-bank regulators include the FEDERAL RESERVE SYSTEM, the comptroller of the currency, the FEDERAL DEPOSIT INSURANCE CORPORATION (FDIC), and the 50 state banking departments. Banks are subject to the supervision of these regulators according to the charters under which they operate. Hence, all commercial banks aren't under the jurisdiction of the same regulator, nor are most regulated by just one authority.

National banks are chartered and primarily regulated by the comptroller of the currency, who is an official of the U.S. Treasury Department. The comptroller rules on the domestic branching and merger activity of national banks and is also the primary examining agency. By law, nationally chartered banks must be members of the Federal Reserve system and, therefore, are also subject to Federal Reserve regulation. State-chartered banks have an option to join the Federal Reserve.

All national banks, as well as the great majority of state-chartered banks, are insured by the Federal Deposit Insurance Corporation, a quasi-governmental agency. Thus, these institutions also are subject to FDIC supervision and regulation, including rules on branching and mergers.

The Federal Reserve is responsible for supervision and regulation of all bank holding companies (companies that own one or more banks and that may engage in certain nonbank activities not permissible for banks) and state-chartered member banks. It also has authority to examine all national banks, although this authority is not exercised and the Federal Reserve relies on supervision by the comptroller of the currency.

State-chartered banks are primarily regulated by the banking authority of the issuing state. However, as noted, those that have chosen Federal Reserve membership are subject also to Fed supervision and the central bank's rules on branching, mergers, and other requirements.

Foreign bank branches and agencies in the United States generally are examined by state authorities.

Edge Act and Agreement corporations are examined by the Federal Reserve. Edge Act corporations, chartered by the board of governors of the Federal Reserve system, finance international commerce. Agreement corporations, chartered by state authorities, conduct operations under the same general practices as Edge Act corporations.

The various regulators also review the condition of overseas branches of a commercial bank in conjunction with the domestic examinations. These reviews may be conducted on site or may be based on branch-office records at a bank's head office.

In general, each commercial bank is examined annually by the primary federal and/or state regulators. In January 1981, the time between Federal Reserve examinations of trouble-free banks was widened to 18 months, and later to 24 months, provided a state examination is conducted in the interim.

In midyear 1981, the New York Fed and the New York State Banking Department began a program of alternate annual examinations of New York State–chartered Federal Reserve member commercial banks. Under the program, most state-chartered Federal Reserve member banks are divided into two comparable groups. In the first year, one group of banks is examined by the New York Fed and the other group by state authorities. The following year, examining teams switch groups. The New York Fed and New Jersey banking authorities started a similar program in 1982.

Similar arrangements exist or are being discussed between Reserve banks and states within other Reserve districts. And, too, similar arrangements exist between some states and certain other regulators.

The Justice Department, part of the executive branch of the U.S. government, is responsible for enforcing antitrust laws in connection with mergers and bank-holding-company acquisitions. The department also renders advisory opinions on merger proposals of both state and nationally chartered banks.

At the end of April 1981, there were 46 New York State–chartered Federal Reserve member banks, 10 New Jersey–chartered member banks, 139 nonmember state-chartered commercial banks, 171 nationally chartered commercial banks, 147 foreign bank branches and agencies, and 40 Edge Act and Agreement corporations in the New York (second) Federal Reserve district. The district encompasses New York State, 12 northern and central New Jersey counties, and Fairfield County, Connecticut. For examination and certain other purposes, the district also includes Puerto Rico and the Virgin Islands.

In addition to commercial banks, myriad other institutions provide financial services to the public. These institutions are supervised by a variety of regulatory agencies. The only exception is a few private banks, which some states allow to operate without supervision.

At the end of April 1981, there were nearly 260 savings and loan associations, about 140 savings banks, and about 1,800 credit unions in the New York Fed district. Depending upon the amount of various kinds of deposits held, these institutions, like member and nonmember commercial banks, must keep reserves with the Federal Reserve.

Savings banks that are state-chartered are supervised by state banking departments. However, savings banks may be insured by the FDIC. If they are, they also become subject to that agency's regulations. Savings banks chartered by the FEDERAL HOME LOAN BANK BOARD (FHLBB), a quasi-governmental agency, are subject to that regulator's rules.

Savings and loan associations are chartered by either the Federal Home Loan Bank Board or the local state banking department. Savings and loan associations, which are insured by the FEDERAL SAVINGS AND LOAN INSURANCE CORPORATION (FSLIC), are regulated by the Federal Home Loan Bank Board.

Credit unions may be licensed by the NATIONAL CREDIT UNION ADMINISTRATION, a government agency; or by a state banking department.

Securities brokers, dealers, underwriters, and investment companies are regulated by the Securities and Exchange Commission. Certain aspects of their business also are subject to Federal Reserve regulations dealing with securities credit transactions and purchasing or carrying margin stock.

Additionally, state laws deal with finance companies, mortgage banks, thrift and loan or Morris Plan (industrial) banks, issuers of MONEY ORDERS and TRAVELER'S CHECKS, and check cashers.

Arthur Samansky

Financial Institutions, Private

Financial organizations that function as intermediaries between economic units that have money to lend or invest (surplus units) and economic units that need to borrow (deficit units). Or, simply, financial organizations that function as receivers and suppliers of funds.

The group of private financial intermediaries is made up of COMMERCIAL BANKS and a number of nonbank institutions:

- Savings and Loan Associations
- Savings Banks
- Credit Unions
- Private Noninsured Pension Funds
- Life-Insurance Companies
- Property-Casualty Insurance Companies
- Investment Companies
- Real-Estate Investment Trusts
- Finance Companies

Distinguishing Characteristics. Commercial banks, as a group, are the largest in asset size and operationally the most diversified. Banks offer deposit, payment, loan, trust, and numerous other financial services, including international transfers of funds. Their customers include businesses and governments as well as individuals.

Savings and loan associations, saving banks, and credit unions are basically savings-oriented and are often spoken of as "thrift institutions," or simply "thrifts." The savings options and other services offered by these intermediaries are designed to appeal mainly to individuals. In the case of savings and loan associations and savings banks, "individuals" are people in general; in the case of credit unions, people with a common bond, such as the nature or place of employment. Credit unions, unlike other financial intermediaries, are nonprofit organizations.

Life-insurance companies, property-casualty insurance companies, and private noninsured pension funds are also frequently grouped because each of these types, too, has a like primary function: to market financial products that afford protection against financial loss, loss that may result, for example, from the disability or death of the head of a household, the destruction of property, or retirement from the work force. Sales of protection against such "hazards of living" are customarily contractual, often long-term, and to groups as well as to individuals.

Investment companies are corporations or trusts that pool funds of numerous, often small, investors and invest those funds in a wide variety of securities. Real-estate investment trusts, too, sell shares and pool and invest funds of individual and institutional investors. The activities of real-estate investment trusts are concentrated, as their name indicates, wholly in the real-estate sector.

Finance companies center their operations in the fields of consumer, retail, and wholesale finance. These companies are perhaps best known as sources of personal cash loans and of loans to finance purchases of durable goods, especially consumer durables.

Commercial banks and thrift institutions receive most of their funds in the form of deposit-type payments and are consequently called "depository institutions." Insurance and investment companies, pension funds, real-estate investment trusts, and finance companies receive most of their funds in the form of nondeposit-type payments and are consequently known as "nondepository institutions."

Sources and Uses of Funds. Sales of financial products (deposit and nondeposit claims) are principal sources of funds. Acquisitions of financial assets are principal uses of funds.

Financial products marketed by commercial banks and thrifts include those traditionally available from depository institutions—fixed-rate savings accounts, for example—plus others of more recent vintage authorized by the Depository Institutions Deregulation and Monetary Control Act of 1980 and the Garn–St Germain Depository Institutions Act of 1982. Market-rate certificates of deposit, for example, have recently been added to savings options, as have interest-bearing transaction accounts. Nondepository institutions differ more from one another than do depository institutions, and their offerings are consequently more diverse. Life and health insurance, property and personal-injury insurance, individual and group retirement accounts, and equity instruments are a representative sample of the financial products such institutions originate and market. Prominent among purchasers of claims issued by private financial intermediaries are households, nonprofit organizations, personal trusts, educational institutions, and nonfinancial businesses.

Asset acquisitions are predominant in the form of direct financial claims against nonfinancial sectors. Loans typically figure more prominently than other financial assets in portfolios of banks, thrifts, finance companies, and real-estate investment trusts; corporate securities, in the portfolios of life-insurance companies and pension funds; state and local government obligations, in the portfolios of property-casualty insurance companies. Outlets for funds favored by investment companies depend upon investment objectives and vary considerably from one type of company to another. Stock funds, for example, channel all funds not needed for liquidity into common stocks; money-market funds—a highly income-oriented type—buy only short-term money-market instruments. To say that an intermediary favors one use of funds over another is not to imply concentration of assets. Degree of diversification does vary, but a reasonably well-diversified portfolio is the rule rather than the exception. (See Table 1, page 250.)

Growth and Relative Importance. Development of the financial-services industry dates from the mid-1700s. The first domestically owned and operated fire-insurance company—the Philadelphia Contributorship for the Insurance of Houses from Loss by Fire—was founded in 1752. The first life-insurance company—the Corporation for the Relief of Poor and Distressed Presbyterian Ministers and of the Poor and Distressed Widows and Children of Presbyterian Ministers—was organized in 1759. The first permanently organized bank—the Bank of North America—was chartered in 1781.

Most of the principal financial intermediaries of the late 1900s were in existence by shortly after the turn of the century. The burgeoning of the financial-services industry, however, has been mainly a post-World War II phenomenon. Aggregate assets, less than $250 billion at year-end 1945, had topped $1,000 billion by 1967, $2,000 billion by 1974, $3,000 billion by 1978, $4,000 billion by 1981, and at last report were continuing to climb toward the $5,000-billion mark.

Commercial banks, with assets of close to $1,900 billion, are the largest segment of the financial-services industry. Savings and loan associations, with assets of between $725 billion and $750 billion, and life-insurance companies, with assets of just over $600 billion, rank far below commercial banks but far above other financial intermediaries. At the opposite end of the asset-size scale from savings and loan associations and life-insurance companies are credit unions, with assets of less than $100 billion, and real-estate investment trusts, with assets of less than $10 billion. The remaining institutions—private noninsured pension funds, property-casualty insurance companies, investment companies, finance companies, and savings banks—hold assets in the $200-billion to $400-billion range and thus occupy positions that cluster about midway between the two largest and the two smallest of the nonbank group.

A Force in the Financial System. Private financial intermediaries, as a group, provide a large share of the financial assets purchased by households, nonprofit organizations, and personal trusts. In 1982 that share was 80%. They advance a sizable portion of funds raised in credit markets by nonfinancial sectors. In 1982 that portion was 60%. They advance a smaller but not insignificant portion of funds raised in corporate equity markets. In 1982 that portion was 24%.

In each of the ten years from 1973 to 1982, deposit and nondeposit claims outstanding against private financial institutions made up one-half or more of all financial assets held by households, nonprofit organizations, and personal trusts. In each of those same ten years, debt claims held by private financial institutions against nonfinancial sectors represented three-fourths or more of the total outstanding; equity claims, one-fifth or more.

As these measures of relative importance attest, private financial institutions greatly enhance the mobility of funds and thus perform a role vital to the smooth functioning of the financial system and to the economic well-being of the nation.

An Industry in Transition. The financial-services industry has recently undergone, and continues to undergo, rapid structural and functional changes. Savings and loan associations convert to savings banks, and savings banks convert from mutual to stock form. Thrifts and banks offer deposit accounts that earn interest at market rates. Brokers provide investment options with transaction-account features. Insurance companies acquire broker/dealers. Department stores enter the insurance business. And the list goes on.

Changes are sweeping the industry, and uncertainties abound. Should deregulation be implemented as scheduled? . . . accelerated? . . . slowed? Should geo-

Table 1
Private Financial Institutions' Principal Sources and Uses of Funds

Financial Institutions	Principal Sources of Funds*	Principal Uses of Funds†
Depository institutions:		
Commercial banks	Demand deposits Checkable interest-bearing deposits Savings and time deposits	U.S. government securities and federal-agency obligations State and local government securities Commercial and industrial loans Consumer loans Real-estate loans
Savings and loan associations	Savings and time deposits Checkable interest-bearing deposits Federal Home Loan Bank advances	U.S. government securities and federal-agency obligations Municipal securities Bankers' acceptances Mortgage loans
Mutual savings banks	Savings and time deposits Checkable interest-bearing deposits	U.S. government securities and federal-agency obligations Corporate bonds Mortgage loans Mortgage-backed securities
Credit unions	Savings shares and deposits	U.S. government securities and federal-agency obligations Shares/deposits at other financial institutions Consumer and other loans to members
Nondepository Institutions:		
Life insurance companies	Premium receipts	Corporate bonds Corporate stocks Mortgage loans Policy loans
Property-casualty insurance companies	Premium receipts	U.S. government bonds State, municipal, and special revenue bonds Corporate stocks
Investment companies	Share sales	Municipal bonds Corporate bonds Corporate stocks Money market instruments
Pension funds‡	Employer contributions	U.S. government securities Corporate and other bonds Corporate stocks
Finance companies	Long-term debt instruments Commercial paper Bank borrowings	Consumer loans Business loans
Real-estate investment trusts	Share sales Commercial paper Bank borrowings Mortgages on owned property	Mortgage loans on completed properties Land and development loans Construction loans Acquisition of real property

*Other than earned income.
†Available for lending and investing.
‡Private noninsured.

graphic restrictions on the establishment of branch facilities be lifted? Should the legal definition of *bank* be changed? Should cross-industry acquisitions be checked? These questions and others of equal or greater import are subjects of debate in legislative and regulatory circles. The way in which they are answered will help to determine the course the reshaping of the financial-services industry will follow in the years to come.

Doris E. Harless

Financial Pages, How to Read

An important constituent of the financial pages of a newspaper are the quotation tables. A person with an astute and discriminating mind will be able to derive much from the various securities indexes given. For the uninitiated, however, the indexes may seem a bewildering jumble of numbers that take up substantial space. This entry will attempt to clarify this mass of data.

There are various important quotation tables that will be explained here, and these include the following:

- New York and American Stock Exchanges
- Over-the-counter stocks
- New York and American Exchange bond lists
- Options trading quotations
- U.S. government and government-agency bonds
- Commodity exchanges
- Municipal bonds
- Money market funds
- Mutual funds
- Foreign securities exchanges
- Foreign exchange tables
- Corporate earnings reports
- Daily dividend report

Stock Market Indexes. Of the many indexes watched by most investors, the most closely followed are the DOW JONES AVERAGES. The Dow Jones industrial average is composed of 30 major industrial corporations, including American Telephone & Telegraph (AT&T). There is also a Dow Jones transportation average, made up of 20 transportation stocks; a utility average, derived from 15 public-utility stocks; and a composite of all three.

For a more overall view of daily market activity, the Standard & Poor 500 Index—composed of 400 industrial, 20 transportation, 40 utility, and 40 financial stocks—is often used. The S&P Index is listed as the S&P 500 and, separately, as the 400 Industrial (*see* STANDARD & POOR'S CORPORATION). Other indexes include the New York Stock Exchange Composite; Industrial; Utility; Transportation; and Financial. The

American Stock Exchange offers a composite list, and the NASDAQ system provides a variety of indexes. The Value Line Index is still another widely followed. Finally, the Wilshire 5,000 Equity—composed of the dollar value of all domestic common stocks on the New York and American Stock Exchanges plus about 2,500 actively traded over-the-counter securities—attempts to provide another form of very broad index. The *Market Diary* provides information on the breadth of market activity, including how many issues were traded, with advances, declines, unchanged, and new highs and lows.

Figure 1 shows how the various averages might appear in your newspaper. From the tables you can see that the total issues traded on June 30, 1982, were 1,863, up slightly from the previous day. Advances outpaced declines, but the Dow Jones industrial index declined by 0.28, which amounted to a decline of 0.03%. Compared with the preceding year, 1981, the Dow had declined 16.09%, and since December 31, 1981, it had declined 63.07 points, or 7.21%. The transportation index shows the greatest decline, 15.70% since December 31, 1981; and the utility index the least—1.21%. For a list of the components of

MARKET DIARY

	Wed.	Tue.	Mon.	Fri.	Thu.	Wed.
Issues traded	1,863	1,846	1,843	1,811	1,849	1,875
Advances	801	689	879	468	772	1,036
Declines	602	702	511	902	660	426
Unchanged	460	446	453	441	417	413
New highs	29	26	26	13	29	23
New lows	40	55	43	60	35	55

DOW JONES CLOSING AVERAGES

	——Wednesday——			Yr. Ago	—Since—	
	1982	Change	%	1981	% Chg.	Dec. 31	%
Ind.	811.93	−0.28	−0.03	967.66	−16.09	−63.07	−7.21
Trn.	320.59	+2.32	+0.73	412.46	−0.45	−59.71	−15.70
Utl.	107.70	+0.74	+0.69	107.49	+0.20	−1.32	−1.21
Cmp.	316.64	+0.93	+0.29	375.37	−18.55	−31.16	−8.96

OTHER MARKET INDICATORS

		1982	—Change—		1981
N.Y.S.E.	Composite	63.02	−0.26	−0.41%	75.35
	Industrial	71.56	−0.47	−0.65%	87.03
	Utility	37.07	+0.15	+0.41%	38.65
	Transp.	53.62	+0.03	+0.06%	75.14
	Financial	63.09	+0.20	+0.32%	77.37
Am. Ex. Mkt. Val. Index		250.79	+0.57	+0.23%	371.88
Nasdaq OTC Composite		171.30	+0.77	+0.45%	214.63
	Industrial	196.33	+1.15	+0.59%	263.88
	Insurance	172.49	+1.03	+0.60%	198.45
	Banks	130.61	−0.18	−0.14%	138.32
Standard & Poor's 500		109.61	−0.60	−0.54%	129.77
	400 Industrial	122.42	+0.87	+0.71%	145.95
Value Line index		120.57	+0.26	+0.22%	153.76
Wilshire 5000 Equity		1,125.134	−0.884	−0.08%	1,391.395

Market value, in billions of dollars, of N.Y.S.E., Amex and actively traded OTC issues.

TRADING ACTIVITY

Volume of advancing stocks on N.Y.S.E., 28,190,000 shares; volume of declining stocks, 27,337,700. On American S.E., volume of advancing stocks, 1,528,400; volume of declining stocks, 1,128,700. Nasdaq volume of advancing stocks, 8,145,900; volume of declining stocks, 5,331,100.

Figure 1. Wednesday, June 30, 1982. (*Source: The Wall Street Journal.*)

the various Dow Jones averages, *see* DOW JONES AVERAGES.

New York and American Stock Exchanges—Stock Tables. Table 1 shows quotations for AT&T common stock, convertible preferred stock, and straight preferred stock as they would appear in your daily newspaper.

An explanation of the different elements of Table 1 follows:

52-week high: The highest price the security has been in the last 52 weeks ($61\frac{1}{2}$ for the common stock),

52-week low: The lowest price the security has been in the last 52 weeks ($52\frac{3}{4}$ for the common stock).

Stock: ATT—American Telephone & Telegraph—common stock where there is no qualifier. This means the company has no obligation to pay a fixed rate of dividend. The *pf* means preferred stock; it has a fixed rate of return and has "preference" over the common stock in dividend distribution or in the event of a bankruptcy or reorganization. Preferred stocks are either "convertible" into a set number of common shares or "straight" (nonconvertible). To identify one from the other, you will need a reference book such as *Standard & Poor's Monthly Stock Guide.* Each convertible preferred has its own provisions and should be inspected.

Div.: This is the *annual* dividend payable on each share of stock. For AT&T it is $5.40 per share per year or $1.35 quarterly. For the convertible preferred, it is $4.00 annually or $1.00 quarterly; and for the straight preferred, it is $3.64 annually or $.91 quarterly. Common-stock dividends can change according to the company's profits. Preferred dividends are viewed as fixed expenses and rarely change.

Yld. %: This is the return the current dividend is paying you based on the current price. For AT&T common stock, if you were to buy it at $52\frac{7}{8}$ per share, you could expect to receive $5.40 annually in dividends on each share, for a rate of return or yield of $5.40/52.875 \times 100 = 10.2\%$. Similar calculations can be performed to arrive at the convertible and straight preferred yields.

PE ratio: This is the stock price divided by its earnings per share for the past four quarters. It is used to compare one company with another—especially within the same industry. AT&T's PE of 6 means that if you divide its price ($52\frac{7}{8}$) by its earnings, you should have a ratio of 6:1. Therefore, AT&T earned about $8.75 per share for the past four quarters ($52\frac{7}{8}$)/6 = 8.75.

Sales hds.: This represents the trading volume for that day. Just add two zeros to the number printed. For AT&T common stock, the volume in hundreds was 6483. Adding two zeros, we get 648,300 as the number of shares traded that day. If a *z* comes before the volume number, it means that the number is the *actual* volume of shares traded.

High, low, and last: The highest price the security traded at that day; its lowest price that day; and the price at the last trade of the day.

Net chg.: The net difference between the last trade of that day and the last trade of the preceding day on which the stock was traded.

Over-the-Counter—NASDAQ National Market. Over-the-Counter stocks are traded on a telephone-and-computer-linked system making up a network of securities dealers. The dealers are all members of the NATIONAL ASSOCIATION OF SECURITIES DEALERS AUTOMATED QUOTATIONS (NASDAQ) system. Quotations are normally printed in three lists: the NASDAQ National Market; Over-the-Counter Quotations; and Additional or Supplemental O-T-C Quotes. Table 2 illustrates the form normally used for the largest list—Over-the-Counter Quotations.

An explanation of the different elements in Table 2 follows:

Stock: Pabst Brw is Pabst Brewing.

Div.: The annual dividend rate per share or $.40.

Sales in 100s: The trading volume for that business

Table 1										
52-Week				*Yld.*	*PE*	*Sales*				*Net*
High	*Low*	*Stock*	*Div.*	*%*	*Ratio*	*Hds.*	*High*	*Low*	*Last*	*Chg.*
Common stock:										
$61\frac{1}{2}$	$52\frac{3}{4}$	ATT	5.40	10.2	6	6483	$53\frac{1}{4}$	$52\frac{3}{4}$	$52\frac{7}{8}$	$-\frac{3}{8}$
Convertible preferred stock:										
$64\frac{1}{4}$	$56\frac{1}{8}$	ATT pf	4.00	7.1	—	11	$56\frac{1}{2}$	$56\frac{1}{8}$	$56\frac{1}{2}$	$-\frac{1}{2}$
Straight preferred stock:										
$33\frac{1}{2}$	$27\frac{1}{4}$	ATT pf	3.64	11.3	—	14	$32\frac{1}{8}$	$32\frac{1}{8}$	$32\frac{1}{8}$	—

Table 2

Stock & Div.		Sales in 100s	Bid	Asked	Bid Change
Pabst Brw	.40	2467	20⅞	21	+1⅛

day in 100s. That day 2,467 hundreds of shares traded, or a total of 246,700 shares.

Bid, asked: The highest bid price and the lowest asked price in the NASDAQ system as of 4:00 P.M., which coincides with the closing time of the New York Stock Exchange.

Bid change: The net change in the bid compared with the highest bid at the end of the previous business day.

Additional O-T-C Quotes concern the generally less active over-the-counter stocks. Only bid and asked prices are given, and they are for 2:00 P.M. Eastern Standard Time.

The NASDAQ National Market is a new quotation list with the same format as that of the New York and American Exchanges. It concerns a select group of heavily traded securities in which the public is interested and in which many securities dealers make markets. It is expected to grow as more sophisticated electronics are developed.

New York and American Exchange Bond Tables. Corporate bonds are traded on the New York and American Exchanges as well as over the counter. Normally, only the two exchanges provide listings; there is no central listing for the over-the-counter bond market. There are two basic types of corporate bonds: straight, paying a stated coupon or percent until maturity or until called; and convertible which pays a stated coupon but can be converted, usually into common stock, at set rates and within specific time periods. A new type of bond—zero-coupon—paying no interest at all but offered at a large initial discount to eventually mature at par or $1,000 has also come into the marketplace. Table 3 gives examples.

An explanation of the different elements in Table 3 follows:

Straight corporate bond:

Bonds: Here we have GMAC (General Motors Acceptance Corporation) 8% bonds maturing in the year 2007. The 8% coupon means that each bond will pay $80 per year interest at a $40 semiannual rate. The *s* after the 8 merely aids in reading the bond.

Cur. yld.: The current yield is approximately 14%, arrived at by dividing the 8% coupon by the current price of 56.

Vol.: The volume is the number of bonds traded that day—15 in this case.

High, low: The highest price—56⅝ (566.25)—and the lowest price—56 (560)—at which the bond traded that day.

Close: The final price—56 ($560)—for the last trade of that day.

Net chg.: The price change from the previous day the bond was traded— −¼ down $2.50 per bond.

Convertible corporate bond:

Bonds: Bk NY is Bank of New York 6¼% bonds maturing in 1994.

Cur. yld.: The current yield is not given, and *cv,* meaning convertible, is placed in the Cur. Yld. column. This means that the bond owner can convert the bond into a specified number of common-stock shares, usually at any time until its maturity in 1994. The bond may or may not have a call provision. You can, of course, calculate the current yield by dividing the coupon (6¼) by the latest price (101).

Zero-coupon bond:

Bonds: Bkam is BancAmerica zero-coupon (no interest is paid), maturing in 1987. There is no current yield because no interest is being paid. (*See* BONDS for a more complete description of zero-coupon bonds.)

U.S. Government Issues. The major U.S. government bond issues traded are Treasury bonds, notes, and bills. Bonds and notes are traded similarly to corporate bonds, while Treasury bills are traded on a discounted basis—that is, the amount of interest you receive on maturity is based on the discount from par value that you received on purchase. Treasury bills are issued in maturities of up to one year; notes from one to ten years; and bonds more than ten years. See Tables 4 and 5 for examples.

An explanation of the different elements in Table 4 follows:

Mat. date: This is the bill's maturity date—December 2, 1982.

Bid: The person buying is willing to pay (bid) at a

Table 3

Bonds	Cur. Yld:	Vol.	High	Low	Close	Net Chg.
Straight corporate bond:						
GMAC 8s07	14	15	56⅝	56	56	+¼
Convertible corporate bond:						
Bk NY 6¼494	cv	4	101	101	101	−6
Zero-coupon bond:						
Bkam 87s	—	16	52⅛	51½	51½	−⅝

Table 4
U.S. Treasury Bills

| Mat. Date | Discount | | Yield |
	Bid	Asked	
12-2-82	11.68	11.54	12.43

discount of 11.68% from par based on the portion of the year remaining to maturity.

Asked: The person selling is willing to sell at a discount of 11.54% from par based on the portion of the year remaining to maturity.

Yield: This is the annual rate of return to maturity based on the asked price. In this example, a person buying a Treasury bill at an 11.54% discount due 12/2/82 would be receiving an annualized rate of return of 12.43% for the portion of the year remaining to maturity.

An explanation of the different elements in Table 5 follows:

Rate: The coupon that the bond carries. Here 13⅜ means 13⅜% paid semiannually or $133.75 interest per $1,000 face-value bond paid in two semiannual installments of $66.875. The *s* is for pronunciation only.

Mat. date: This issue will mature in March 1985. The *n* means that the issue is a note and was originally issued for maturity one to ten years later. Bonds will not have the "n" designation and are originally issued for longer than ten years' maturity.

Bid: The note was last bid at 99¹²⁄₃₂s. The decimal in bid and asked represents 32nds. The number 99.12 = 99¹²⁄₃₂ = $993.75.

Asked: The note was last offered at 99.16 or $995.00.

Bid chg.: Bid chg. is the change in the bid from the previous business day. Here −.1 equals −¹⁄₃₂, or $3.13 per bond.

Yield: The yield to maturity based on the asked price.

Government-Agency and Miscellaneous Securities. Listed the same way as U.S. Treasury bonds and notes (decimals in 32nds). The lists vary from newspaper to newspaper but the more complete lists include the following:

- FNMA (Federal National Mortgage Association)
- FHLB (Federal Home Loan Bank)
- Bank for Co-Ops (Banks for Cooperatives)
- Federal Farm Credit (Farm Credit System Banks)

- GNMA Issues (Government National Mortgage Association)
- Intermediate Credit (Federal Intermediate Credit System)
- Inter-American Bank
- World Bank
- Federal Land Bank
- Asian Development Bank

Municipal Bonds. Not every newspaper prints lists of municipal (tax-exempt) bonds—perhaps because individual issues are not always traded daily and because there is no central marketplace; all transactions are done on the telephone. Securities dealers trade municipals from their portfolio inventories and will also list many of their municipals in the *Blue List,* a daily publication where offerings are posted. Some newspapers provide a list of tax-exempt revenue bonds issued by toll roads and other public authorities. Here is one example:

Agency	Coupon	Maturity	Bid	Asked	Chg.
Munic. Assist Cp NY	10¼s	'93	96	100	—

Here we have the Municipal Assistance Corporation of New York; the 10¼s or 10.25% coupon bonds maturing in 1993. They were bid for at 96 or $960 and offered at 100 or $1,000 for no change from the prior day's bid or asked prices.

Corporate Earnings Reports. Every day corporations are issuing earnings reports, usually for the latest quarter and the year to date. Corporate earnings reports will usually include figures for the comparable periods of the previous year. Table 6 gives one example.

Here we have CSX Corporation, a railroad holding company with interests in real estate and publishing. It is listed on the New York Stock Exchange (N). For the latest quarter, ending June 30, 1982, CSX reported revenues of $1,300,000,000, an increase of $100 million over last year's second quarter. Its net income rose dramatically from $37 million to $70 million,

Table 5
U.S. Treasury Bonds and Notes

Rate	Mat. Date	Bid	Asked	Bid Chg.	Yld.
13⅜s	1985 March	99.12	99.16	−.1	13.60

Table 6
Corporate Earnings Report—CSX Corp.(n)

Quarter June 30	1982	1981
Revenues	1,300,000,000	1,200,000,000
Net inc.	70,000,000	37,000,000
Shr. earns. Net inc.	1.67	.90
6 mos. Revenues	2,600,000,000	2,500,000,000
Net. inc.	118,000,000	125,000,000
Shr. earns. Net inc.	2.83	3.04

Table 7
Dividends Reported June 30, 1982

Company	Period	Amt.	Payable Date	Record Date
Regular:				
Cascade Natural Gas	Q	.28	8/15/82	7/16
Funds, REITS, investment cos.:				
AmerGenCapBdFd	M	h.06	7/30/82	6/30
Stock:				
NutriSystems, Inc.	Q	50%	8/6/82	7/15
Increased:		New	Old	
Long Island Lighting	Q	.50	.48½ 8/1/82	7/9
Reduced:		New	Old	
Ryan Homes, Inc.	Q	.25	.32½ 7/30/82	7/13

and per-share earnings increased from $.90 to $1.67. The six-month results indicate that the first quarter wasn't very good. The six-month figures show a $100-million revenue increase (all of which occurred in the second quarter). Net earnings for the half-year fell by $7 million, from $125 million to $118 million, indicating that the first quarter had earnings of $48 million down from $88 million. Earnings per share were down to $2.83 from $3.04. Of course, much detail would have to be researched from a more complete quarterly report and from descriptive statements from the company.

Daily Dividend Reports. Many newspapers report dividends declared by companies. Occasionally, where dividends have been raised or reduced, a small story will accompany the news. Table 7 shows a typical dividend report.

In Table 7 we see that Cascade Natural Gas is declaring its regular quarterly dividend of $.28 on its common stock, payable August 15, 1982, to shareholders of record on July 16. The American General Capital Bond Fund is declaring its monthly dividend of $.06 per share derived from its income earnings (h). NutriSystems is declaring a 50% stock dividend. One would have to find out specifically why NutriSystems chose to give a stock dividend rather than cash. Long Island Lighting has increased its dividend by 1½ cents quarterly. Ryan Homes, on the other hand, has slashed its dividend by about 20%.

Stock Options. A stock option gives the owner the right to buy or sell shares of a stock at a specified "strike" price for a specified period of time. An option to buy a stock is a "call." An option to sell a stock is a "put." When you buy an option, you pay a "premium." The person who "writes" or sells you the option pockets the premium money but must buy the 100 shares per option that he sold you if you "put" it to him at the agreed-upon strike price, or must sell 100 shares to you at the strike price if you exercise

your option and call the shares from him. Each option period expires on the third Saturday of the option month. Options are currently traded on the Chicago Board Option Exchange, American Stock Exchange, Pacific Stock Exchange, and Philadelphia Stock Exchange.

Table 8 shows a typical options table from the Chicago Board on June 1, 1982.

Table 8

Option & NY Close	Strike Price	Calls—Last			Puts—Last		
		Jun	Sep	Dec	Jun	Sep	Dec
GM	35	7⅞	8¾	9¼	¹⁄₁₆	⁵⁄₁₆	¾
42⅞	40	3⅜	4⅞	5⅞	³⁄₁₆	1¼	1¹⁵⁄₁₆
42⅞	45	⁷⁄₁₆	2	3¼	2¼	3¼	4¼
42⅞	50	¹⁄₁₆	⁹⁄₁₆	1⅜	6⅞	6⅝	r

The option shown in the table is for General Motors Corporation. The common stock closed at 42⅞ on June 1, 1982. The June 35 call closed at 7⅞ or $787.50 for the option to buy 100 shares of GM at a price of $35 per share. The June calls are on a par with the market price—in other words, if you paid 7⅞ for your call and exercised it at 35, you would have paid a total of 42⅞ per share or the same as the market price (excluding commissions). This usually happens as the options near their expiration date. In contrast, the September call is at 8¾, nearly a point more. It is trading at a higher premium because there are three more months than the June option and the stock price can possibly vary much more. The put option group shows the June option trading at 1/16 or $6.67. This option is nearly valueless as the stock is trading well above the strike price and there would be no profit in buying it at 42⅞ and "putting" it at 35. When an option is not traded at a particular strike price, an "r" footnote is given; and if the option isn't being offered, an "s" footnote is shown.

Money-Market Funds. One of the biggest new developments in the markets has been the growth of the money-market funds. Normally investing in short-term U.S. government securities, commercial paper, bank certificates of deposit, and the like, these funds provide the depositor with a high current yield based on prevailing rates. The depositor is provided with a daily dividend and liquidity—usually on a next-business-day basis—and many funds give free check-writing privileges, too. Each Friday the newspapers report the major funds' positions, showing their size (amount of money on deposit); average length of maturity that each fund is invested in; and the annual yield you would have received had you been in the fund for the past 7 days and for the past 30 days. Table 9 shows a sample entry from June 18, 1982.

The two Shearson/American Express funds shown in Table 9 represent a regular fund investing in all types of short-term instruments (Daily Dividend) and a second fund investing only in U.S. government and U.S. government-agency short-term securities. The table shows that on June 18, 1982, the Daily Dividend fund had $5,899,700,000 on deposit invested in instruments maturing on average in only 26 days. If your money was on deposit in this fund, you would have been earning at a rate of 13.6% for the past 7 days and 13.6% for the past 30 days. Very often the rates will vary for the 7- and 30-day periods as short-term interest rates can fluctuate widely. The second fund shown, Government and Agencies, had $1,204,700,000 on deposit, was invested out only 23 days, and had been paying 13.0% for both the past 7 and 30 days. Normally a U.S. government and/or

U.S. government-agency fund will pay at a lower rate than the general funds because government instruments are considered safer.

Commodities. Commodity-futures trading used to mean trading in contracts for grains and livestock only. Today, commodity-futures trading consists of grains and oilseeds; livestock and meat; food and fiber; metals and petroleum; wood; and financial futures. Newspaper listings for each category detail the contract size; where it is traded; how the price quotation is denominated; the different delivery months being traded; and how trading went that day.

Table 10 gives an example from "Grains and Oilseeds" for Wednesday, June 30, 1982. Table 11 gives another example—this one from the fast-growing financial-futures market.

An explanation of some of the elements in Table 10 follows:

Corn (CBT)—5,000 bu.; cents per bu.: The commodity item being traded is corn. "CBT" stands for Chicago Board Of Trade, where this particular contract is traded. "5,000 bu." is the contract size—5,000 bushels. "Cents per bu." is how each contract is priced.

Mar 83: A contract for corn to be delivered in March 1983. Trading in the contract opened at 283¾ or 283.75 cents per bushel. Its high was 284.75; low 282.00; and it closed (settled) at 283.25 for a net change of 2.75 cents per bushel. With 5,000 bushels per contract, this amounts to a decline of $137.50 per contract.

Lifetime high, low: This particular contract has had a high of 320¾ and a low of 282 since being traded.

Open interest: The number of contracts outstanding (11,799). When open interest declines, it means contracts are being closed out. When it increases, it means more are being initiated. Open interest is compiled at the end of each trading day and reported the following day.

Est. vol.: The line at the bottom of the contract includes estimated volume for that day (37,753), actual volume for the day before (42,109); total open interest

Table 9 Shearson/American Express				
Fund	*Assets ($ Million)*	*Av. Maturity (Days)*	*7-Day Av. Yield (%)*	*30-Day Av. Yield (%)*
Daily dividend	5,899.7	26	13.6	13.6
Govt. and agencies	1,204.7	23	13.0	13.0

Table 10
Futures Prices: Corn (CBT)—5,000 bu.; cents per bu.

						Lifetime		Open
	Open	High	Low	Settle	Change	High	Low	Interest*
July	266½	267¾	265½	265¾	−2	399	265½	16,573
Sept	266	266¾	264¾	264¼	−2	388½	264¾	28,579
Dec	270	270	267½	268½	−2½	345½	267½	47,175
Mar 83	283¾	284¾	282	283¼	−2¾	320¾	282	11,799
May	293½	294¾	291¾	292¾	−3¼	322½	291¾	4,705
July	300	301½	298½	299¾	−3½	316½	298½	1,518

Est. vol. 37,753; vol Tue 42,109; open int. 110,349, −1,324

*Open interest reflects previous trading day.

Table 11
Treasury Bonds (CBT): $100,000; pts. 32nds of 100%

						Yield		
	Open	High	Low	Settle	Chg.	Pct.	Chg.	Open Interest
Mar 83	61−04	61−12	60−31	61−09	+19	13.711	−.133	15,772

for all of the different contract months as of the day before (110,349), and the increase or decrease (−1,324) in open interest for the day before.

An explanation of some of the elements in Table 11 follows:

Mar 83: Treasury-bond contract due March 1983, face value $100,000. This is a contract to buy $100,000 face value of Treasury bonds with a maturity of 20 years and a coupon of 8%.

Open, high, low: The contract opened at 61-04 or 61 4/32 of a $1,000 point. The total is $61,000 plus 4/32 × $1,000 or $125 for a total of $61,125. Each 1/32 of a $1,000 point is called a "tick" and is worth $31.25.

Settle, chg.: The contract settled (closed) at 61-09 or $61,281.25 for a net change of +19 ticks or 19/32 equal to $593.75 per $100,000 contract.

Yield: The contract is being priced to yield 13.711% based on the remaining life of the Treasury bonds to maturity.

For further explanation, see COMMODITY FUTURES PRICE TABLES, HOW TO READ.

Cash-Commodity Prices. Many newspapers print lists of cash commodities. These prices are for immediate delivery of specific commodities. Table 12 illustrates the format.

Table 12
Cash Prices for Wednesday, June 30, 1982
(Quotations as of 4 P.M. Eastern Time)

	Wed	Tues	Yr. Ago
Corn no. 2 yellow cent-Ill. bu.	b 2.50	2.49	3.10½

The sample quote states that as of 4:00 P.M. Eastern Time on June 30, 1982, the bid was $2.50 per bushel of no. 2 yellow corn for delivery in Central Illinois. The price was $2.49 the day before and $3.105 a year ago.

Mutual Funds. Investment companies that pool the funds of many individual investors and manage the total moneys with stated investment objectives. Mutual funds are either open-ended (issuing and redeeming shares on a continuous basis) or closed-end (offering shares in a single public offering, the shares then being traded on an exchange or over the counter with market supply and demand determining the share price). Open-ended funds redeem their shares on a daily basis based upon the net asset value of all of their investments at the close of each day. These same funds offer their shares at either the same net asset value, wherein they are called "no-load funds," or at a fixed percentage charge (load) above the net asset value for the "load funds." Table 13 shows a sample from a newspaper.

Table 13
Mutual Funds, Wednesday, June 30, 1982*

	NAV	Offer Price	NAV Chg.
Loomis Sayles Funds:			
Cap. dev.	15.04	N.L.	+.09
Mutual	13.84	N.L.	+.03
Lord Abbett:			
Affiliated	7.08	7.63	—
Bond deb.	8.65	9.45	+.05
Devel gro.	15.87	17.34	−.01
Income	2.68	2.89	+.01

*Price ranges for investment companies, as quoted by the National Association of Securities Dealers. NAV stands for net asset value per share; the offering includes net asset value plus maximum sales charge, if any.

The table shows two different mutual-fund organizations: Loomis Sayles, which offers funds on a no-load basis; and Lord Abbett, offering shares on a load basis. Each fund would have to be contacted to learn of its investment objectives and past history. Prices of closed-end investment trusts, showing their discounts or premiums from net asset value, are normally published every Monday showing prices from the previous Friday.

See MUTUAL FUND.

Other Markets. Other markets may include regional exchanges in the United States, such as the PACIFIC STOCK EXCHANGE, MIDWEST STOCK EXCHANGE, BOSTON STOCK EXCHANGE, and PHILADELPHIA STOCK EXCHANGE. Tables may also include a small selection from the Toronto and Montreal Exchanges.

Foreign Securities—ADR's. Securities of foreign corporations traded in American depositary receipts (ADR's) representing ownership of securities physically deposited abroad are usually listed in the "Other Markets" section.

Foreign Securities. Overseas exchanges are frequently represented by condensed lists in the newspapers. The London Exchange may be printed with a repre-

sentative sampling of 40 to 50 securities, with the closing prices normally in the local currency. Other exchanges frequently printed include Tokyo, Frankfurt, Paris, Hong Kong, Milan, Brussels and Sydney as well as a group of South African Mines.

Foreign Exchange. Foreign exchange tables provide the exchange rates in two ways—as dollars per unit of foreign currency and as foreign currency per unit dollar. Table 14 provides an example.

Table 14
Foreign Exchange, Wednesday, June 30, 1982

Country	U.S. $ equiv.		Currency per U.S. $	
	Wed.	Tues.	Wed.	Tues.
Australia (dollar)	1.0216	1.0191	.9788	.9813
France (franc)	.1462	.1468	6.84	6.81
Mexico (peso)	.0212	.0208	47.07	48.04

The New York foreign exchange selling rates above apply to trading among banks in amounts of $1 million and more, as quoted at 3 P.M. Eastern Time by Bankers Trust Co. Retail transactions provide fewer units of foreign currency per dollar.

Barrett Sinowitz

Financial Planning

Financial planning is the development of a comprehensive personal financial program taking into consideration not only investments, taxes, insurance, and other financial matters, but also the personal goals, feelings, and attitudes of the individual. Thus successful financial planning involves more than simply shifting assets from one place to another; it also requires the implementation of products and ideas that the plan recommends. The professional person who plans another's financial future is known as a "financial planner."

Modern financial planning is a continuing process and does not offer quick final solutions to problems. Financial solutions must be well thought out and defined prior to implementation of products and ideas. In today's world, all the various components that make up financial planning are interrelated. Planning must take everything into consideration. For example, investments affect tax strategy, taxes affect cash flow, cash flow affects dollars available for insurance premiums. Accordingly, a financial plan is a complete program concerning one's financial life, usually written by a financial planner. Although individuals may write their own financial plans, it is most difficult to do, because of the need for objectivity.

Generally, a financial plan will cover the following areas:

A Review of Goals. A person's goals are the starting point for any financial planning. Sound financial planning targets in on your short- and long-term goals. What are your major financial problems? Where do you want to be in five years? How much money do you need to retire, or to provide for your children's college education? Is your goal to pay less taxes or to preserve the assets you already have, or both? Furthermore, in reviewing goals, financial planning should consider your outlook toward risk. Are you comfortable with a particular investment, or is another investment better even though it may pay less income? An individual's feelings are an integral part of financial planning; thus before any financial plan can be written, the planner must truly understand what these feelings are.

A Review of Income and Estate Taxes. No one likes to pay taxes, especially more than they really have to, and financial planners recognize this as a major priority of any financial planning. The objective of a skilled financial planner is to reduce income taxes as much as possible, depending, of course, on the client's beliefs, goals, and risk outlook. A planner may reduce income taxes through pensions, tax-sheltered and tax-deferred investments, trusts, interest-free loans, family gifts, tax-free corporate benefits, and tax planning of deductions. Financial planning strives to use the benefits of the income-tax laws as much as possible.

A financial plan should also review potential estate taxes (see ESTATE PLANNING). An estate tax is a tax levied at death upon an individual's estate. Although the majority of people are not subject to an estate tax, many persons unknowingly are, since an estate consists of more than just money. Tangible property such as real estate, jewelry, antiques, pensions, collectibles, securities, as well as the death benefit of life insurance are included in the estate. An individual may pass, without being subject to estate taxes, estate assets of $275,000 in 1983, $325,000 in 1984, $400,000 in 1985, $500,000 in 1986, and $600,000 in 1987 and later years. In planning for estate taxes, the combined estates of both spouses should be taken into consideration. One of the most popular ways to reduce the size of an estate, and thus reduce estate taxes, is through lifetime gifts to family members and others. The present law allows an individual to exclude $10,000 per donee per year from the gift tax. Other methods of reducing estate taxes are by trusts, bequests, transfer of ownership, etc. Financial planning seeks to mini-

mize the aggregate estate tax that a family would pay, maximizing the dollars left for beneficiaries, and to accomplish this within the objectives of the client.

A Review and Repositioning of Assets. The assets that an individual owns, such as stocks, bonds, mutual funds, bank accounts, real estate, property, businesses, etc., should be reviewed and repositioned according to his or her goals. Financial planning also redirects the accumulation of new assets in order to provide for future goals such as retirement, college education, or a home. For example, a financial plan may redirect taxable income into a pension plan, thereby lowering current taxes and providing taxable income in future years. The assets a person acquires should be a matter of personal preference. Assets should be acquired not only for the purpose of maximizing economic wealth, but to satisfy one's comfort level. A person seeking riskless investments should avoid investments that fluctuate in market price. A financial planner analyzes the desired level of risk and then suggests suitable investments that maximize the investment return and meet the individual's needs and goals.

A Review of Risk Management. Financial planning takes into account a person's risk-management program. Simply put, is there enough insurance to protect against the risk of death, disability, illness, destruction of property, or personal liability? Financial planning seeks to minimize one's risk through the purchase of insurance.

Most personal financial planning programs begin with a review of LIFE INSURANCE coverage, analyzing the need for additional or less insurance coverage and the cost of premiums. A financial program may use term insurance (pure low-cost coverage), whole-life (permanent insurance with cash value), or a combination of both. However, since there is a greater chance of permanent disability than of death, a good financial plan also reviews one's HEALTH INSURANCE coverage. There are basically two types of health insurance—medical-expense and disability income. Medical-expense coverage is for sickness and injury and partially covers the costs of hospitals and doctors. Disability income is for loss of income due to sickness or injury. A financial plan should also provide for adequate MAJOR MEDICAL PROTECTION in the event of a catastrophic illness. Protecting one's property is quite important, too. Financial planning analyzes the level of homeowner's or home renter's insurance as well as automobile coverage and general liability.

Financial planning, however, is more than just planning for the moment to provide an immediate solution to a current problem. It is an ongoing process that constantly changes because of other changes that take place. For example, the economy changes, the tax laws change, and, most important, people's goals frequently change. Financial planning therefore cannot be rigid; it must be able to accommodate change. As persons move through life, their situations change. They work hard. They make money. And they wish to preserve what they have worked very hard to achieve.

Furthermore, the planning itself is only one part of the task—it is a blueprint and no more. The next, equally vital step is implementation—putting the plan into action: purchasing the recommended insurance or investments; drafting a will or a trust; changing old habits. Whatever the recommendation may be, some action must take place for a financial plan to succeed.

Financial planning therefore has two separate stages—the planning stage and the action stage. Both are vital. And both must take place for a plan to work.

Andrew Michael Rich

Financial Services Company

A firm that offers customers a full range of innovative investment products and services, all available at one convenient location. These products might include mutual funds, securities, and insurance; services might include tax guidance and banking services. They are usually available both as individual components and as part of integrated financial packages known as "asset-management accounts."

Financial services companies are often referred to as "financial supermarkets" and "one-stop financial centers," because they provide a convenient way for customers to shop for and obtain a variety of services, all under one roof.

Financial services companies began to appear in 1981, with the rapid combination of some very large financial and nonfinancial organizations. The first such combination occurred in March 1981, when Prudential Insurance acquired the brokerage firm of Bache Halsey Stuart Shields. Shortly thereafter, Shearson Loeb Rhoades, another brokerage firm, merged with American Express, the credit-card company; Sears, Roebuck & Company bought Dean Witter Reynolds; and Bank of America purchased the discount broker Charles Schwab. Many other mergers and acquisitions have followed in recent years.

These consolidations have served to blur the functional distinctions between different providers of financial services. Brokerage houses have become cash managers and have begun issuing credit cards. Banks are offering their customers accounts in money-market funds, and many of them have entered the discount brokerage business as well. A credit-card company has gone into investment banking. So have an insurance company and an international commodity-trading firm. Before long, many people will be depositing their paychecks and making securities transactions at retail department stores.

Financial services companies are seeking to broaden their product lines in order to secure larger roles in their customers' financial lives. By offering customers a way to consolidate all their financial accounts, they hope to establish long-term, "cradle-to-grave" relationships with them. With this goal in mind, a financial services company might attract young investors with, for example, real-estate financing or mutual funds that have low investment minimums. Later, these people might become brokerage customers, or be interested in insurance or retirement products.

Convenience and flexibility are important to investors today. For this reason, financial services companies are committing substantial resources to the development of asset-management accounts. These accounts, which generally combine brokerage services, a money-market fund, a credit or debit card, and a variety of computer-based transaction services, can be individualized to meet customers' specific needs and preferences. New products and services can be plugged into the account as they are developed, or as changes in the investment environment make them more attractive.

The evolution of securities- and investment-management firms into financial services companies is closely linked to advances in technology. For the most part, these companies already had large customer bases and strong distribution networks. Technology has allowed them to develop sophisticated new products quickly, and to constantly improve the services they provide their customers.

These new services come in many forms. The ELECTRONIC FUND TRANSFER (EFT) SYSTEMS and AUTOMATED TELLER MACHINES (ATM's), for example, now enable customers to do most of their banking with a plastic card, at any number of convenient locations. Computerized telecommunications systems make it possible for investors to check on their account balances and monitor the performance of their holdings at any time of the day or night. Soon, customers will be able to handle all of their financial transactions from computer terminals in their homes and offices. In short, technology has made it just as convenient for customers to deal by telephone with financial services companies across the country as it used to be for them to walk down the street to their local bank or brokerage firm.

Technological developments have also made it possible for financial companies to provide specialized services to *each other* on a wholesale basis. The Fidelity Group, for example, has arrangements with over 400 banks to provide discount brokerage services to their customers. Fidelity handles order entry, processing, and record-keeping through its discount brokerage company, Fidelity Brokerage Services, Inc. Bank personnel assist customers in opening accounts and placing orders. This linkage provides benefits for all sides. Fidelity is able to quickly expand its brokerage services to a much larger market than it would be able to reach on its own. For the bank, the arrangement is a source of new income, as well as a way to provide an attractive new service to customers at a relatively low cost. The customer benefits by being able to obtain a wider range of services at one convenient location— in this case, at his or her bank.

Most observers expect such "networking" relationships to become very common in the future. As consumers become more sophisticated and demanding in their investment choices, financial companies will find it difficult to develop new products and services quickly enough—and very expensive to do so on their own. Thus, we may soon see a financial services industry made up of both huge financial conglomerates and small specialty firms, all linked together through networks of computers.

The creative process that began with the evolution of financial services companies can be expected to continue as better ways are found to respond to investors' changing needs. As financial services companies become more competitive with each other, they will develop an ever-wider variety of investment alternatives, and learn to provide state-of-the-art technology in exciting new ways.

Samuel W. Bodman

Fineness

See KARAT.

Fiscal Policy

Fiscal policy is the course of action pursued by the government that is designed to achieve society's economic-stability goals. The main purpose therefore is to counteract cyclical fluctuations in the economy— i.e., to alleviate price instability, unemployment, and sluggish economic growth. These are caused most frequently by fluctuating demand in the private sector of the economy. Consequently, the government may utilize its budgetary instruments—namely, taxes and spending—as compensatory measures in stabilizing the aggregate demand and hence the economy.

These compensatory measures are designed to fill gaps in aggregate demand. For example, a deflationary gap develops when economic activities are at a low level. Thus, government spending can be increased and/or taxes decreased in order to boost aggregate demand. Similarly, an inflationary gap develops when the economy is "overheating." In this case, the government spending can be decreased and/or taxes increased in order to lower aggregate demand. For this reason, fiscal policy is sometimes known as "fine tuning" by the government. It is fundamentally based on the Keynesian economic philosophy of demand management.

Short-Run Effectiveness. In the short run, the effectiveness of these compensatory measures depends on two factors. One is the magnitude of spending and tax changes; obviously the larger the compensatory changes, the faster the gaps disappear. The other is the degree of response by the private sector—namely, consumer demand and private investment demand. Three historical examples illustrate the way consumer demand has responded to tax policies.

The year of 1964 was a period of mild recession. The government decided that a pump-priming effect was needed. Therefore, personal income taxes were reduced by approximately $9 billion. The consumption expenditure responded greatly, increasing by about $30 billion in 1965. Thus, the tax policy was immensely successful as it achieved its intended result. However, subsequent tax policies were not that successful.

During 1968 the economy was overheating and Congress enacted a 10% rise in personal income tax, called a "surcharge." The intent was to depress consumer spending, but consumers did not respond; in fact, the consumption expenditure increased by an overwhelming $44 billion. While this figure was probably below what it would have been in the absence of the tax increase, the tax policy was not very successful in checking rapid growth of the consumption expenditure.

The 1975 tax policy was least successful—indeed, it was a failure. The 1974–75 period was characterized by a severe recession. Congress accordingly reduced personal income taxes by about $20 billion, but the consumption expenditure did not increase. Thus, the tax policy designed to boost the consumption expenditure failed completely.

Government-spending policy can also be ineffective. It may even create the opposite "crowding effect," which partially cancels the intended effect. The intended effect of increased government spending is to increase production, income, and employment by increasing aggregate demand. But as the government competes with the private sector for available funds, the market interest rate may increase and dampen entrepreneurial investment propensities by discouraging risk-taking inclinations. Thus, lowered private investment may partially offset higher government spending.

Long-Run Effectiveness. In the long run, the effectiveness of fiscal policy must be judged in terms of its ability to balance other economic considerations, such as tax burdens. Persistent efforts to stimulate our economy may involve continuous deficit spending—hence the fear of a continuously increasing tax rate. It can be shown, however, that this is not inevitably the case. As long as the rate of growth of national debt arising from the continuous deficit spending is not allowed to exceed the rate of growth of national income, the future tax rate may rise, but only up to a certain limit.

The state of New Jersey adopted a variation of this principle in its state and local budgets. The so-called cap law (chapter 68, PL 1976) prohibits the growth of state and local government budgets to approximately 5% of the previous budgets, even though some expenditures, such as fuel, are exempted. The more ominous trend is the recent clamor for a federal constitutional amendment mandating a balanced budget. If this amendment passes, notwithstanding several escape clauses, the effectiveness of fiscal policy may be further diminished.

There are those who condemn fiscal policy on the grounds that it is counterproductive. The so-called monetarists argue that the timing of fiscal policy is consistently wrong, accentuating the business cycle. For example, fiscal expansion is effected when the economy is actually on the upswing, adding unnecessary fuel to the already expanding economy. Similarly, fiscal restraint is effected when the economy is already on the downswing, creating a greater fall from the peak. Thus, they advocate monetary rather than fiscal policy.

This debate is academic if the real cause of economic instability is fluctuations not in aggregate demand but rather in supply of real resources. In this case, no amount of demand management can provide a cure for unstable economic conditions, and this in part explains the rise of supply-side economics.

Yet, fiscal policy of the supply-side economists, who are in the conservative camp, is in dilemma. The supply-side economists advocate lower taxes to boost the supply of goods and resources in order to reduce unemployment and inflation. However, such a policy can lead to substantial deficits in the short run, as these economists are reluctant to decrease military spending. The result is the necessity to increase taxes.

This about-face in tax policy actually occurred recently. In 1981, under the Economic Recovery Tax Act, personal income tax was to be gradually reduced by 23% over a three-year period. However, by 1982 other taxes had to be increased as the government faced the unpleasant prospect of an annual deficit in excess of $100 billion. Clearly, even the supply-side fiscal policy, as well as the Keynesian, is limited to its effectiveness.

Joseph Chorun

Fixed-Income Investments

See UNIT INVESTMENT TRUSTS.

Float

Float is checkbook money that, for a period of time, appears on the books of both the check writer and the check receiver due to a lag in the check-collection process (*see* REGIONAL CHECK-PROCESSING CENTERS [RCPC's]). The lag is caused by a number of factors and it results in various types of float.

Federal Reserve float is the addition to depository institutions' reserve accounts that arises unintentionally during the Federal Reserve's check-collection process.

The Federal Reserve credits the reserve accounts of depository institutions within two business days after they deposit checks, even though more time may be needed to process the checks and collect funds from the depository institution on which the checks are drawn. This crediting procedure sometimes results in addition to the reserves of some depository institutions before reserves are taken from other depository institutions. Thus, float is generated.

The check-collection cycle begins with the deposit of a check at a depository institution. If the check is drawn on that institution, the collection is completed internally. If the check is drawn on another depository institution, other steps are required before funds can be transferred from the depository institution upon which the check is drawn.

Checks may be sent by the depository institution receiving them as deposits directly to the depository institution on which they are drawn. In such cases, the two institutions settle directly with each other. Alternatively, checks may be sent to correspondent banks that provide clearing and collection services. Checks also may be cleared through a clearing association of which both depository institutions are members.

Checks that aren't handled through any of these arrangements are likely to be processed through the Federal Reserve's check-collection system.

The majority of checks cleared through a Reserve bank are processed by high-speed computer equipment. The depositing depository institution will receive credit, according to the Federal Reserve's published time schedules, ranging from the date the checks are received to a maximum of two business days later.

On the day credit is due, the depositing institution's reserve-account balance at the Reserve bank is increased; and on the day payment is made, the paying institution's reserve balance is reduced. Assuming the collection process goes smoothly, the day the credit is available for use by depositing institutions corresponds to the day payment is received.

However, a variety of factors may prevent the Reserve bank from obtaining payment from the depository institution on which checks are drawn on the day credit automatically is given.

Checks received in poor condition must be processed at Reserve offices on semiautomatic equipment, slowing the collection process. Or delays may occur due to unexpected volume or equipment malfunctions.

Another factor may be transportation. A Federal Reserve bank's time schedule for granting credit for checks is based on shipping times between Federal Reserve offices and depository institutions. However, transportation delays may arise from bad weather, strikes, or mechanical breakdowns. When checks don't reach their destination as scheduled, credit is given anyway. At that moment, float is created.

In addition, in certain circumstances, some depository institutions and the Federal Reserve Bank may be open, while other depository institutions in the same district are closed. In the New York Reserve district, for example, New York State and New Jersey banks sometimes are closed on different days to mark a holiday. The New York Fed gives credit as scheduled to depositing institutions that are open for checks drawn on the closed institution, but doesn't collect payment until the following business day. As a result, Federal Reserve float is created.

It should be noted that Federal Reserve float affects the monetary aggregate since it creates reserves in the overall banking system. Therefore, depending on monetary objectives, Federal Reserve open-market operations may have to be used to offset movements in float.

Another kind of float is commercial-bank float, which appears on the balance sheets of banks as "cash items in the process of collection." Cash items include checks, postal money orders, food coupons, and other items payable on demand.

Banks generally credit customer accounts when deposits are made, but don't allow customers to use those funds for a specified time to allow the banks to collect the funds. Since uncollected funds appear in

two accounts simultaneously (the check writer's and the check depositor's), float occurs.

Still another type of float, not involving the Federal Reserve, is mail float, which occurs when a corporation or a person writes a check and mails it. In many transactions, the writer of the check considers the payment made. However, float exists until the check is delivered to the recipient and deposited, which may be several days after the check is written. During this interval, the writer of the check continues to have use of the funds and, in this sense, float continues.

Arthur Samansky

Floating-Rate Preferred Stock

See PREFERRED STOCK.

Floating-Rate Tax-Free Bonds and Trusts

Floating-rate tax-free bonds have "floating" (rather than fixed-rate) coupons pegged to a recognized yield (usually the prime rate). Trusts are made up of tax-free industrial-development bonds (IDB's) secured by an irrevocable letter of credit from a major bank. Every bond in the portfolio has a floating rather than fixed coupon. Hence, when interest rates rise, the coupons on the bonds will rise; and when rates drop, the coupons will drop. The investor can always be assured of getting the most competitive tax-free income available and have his principal protected against wide swings in interest rates.

Moore & Schley Cameron & Company

Food Donations Program

See SOCIAL WELFARE.

Food and Nutrition Service (FNS)

The Food and Nutrition Service is the agency in the U.S. Department of Agriculture that is responsible for administering the department's food-assistance programs. These programs are designed to provide a more nutritious diet to low-income children and adults. The programs also encourage better eating patterns among all the nation's children, through such activities as school lunches. The Food and Nutrition Service, which is headquartered in Alexandria, Virginia, administers the programs together with state governments and local agencies.

Ordinarily, state departments of education have responsibility for food programs serving children in schools, child-care centers, and summer recreation centers. State departments of health, welfare, and agriculture usually have responsibility for programs providing food stamps or supplemental foods to families or individuals.

The programs administered by FNS include the food-stamp program; the food-distribution program; the supplemental food program for women, infants, and children (WIC); the school lunch and breakfast programs; the child-care food program; the summer food program; the food-distribution program on Indian reservations; and the commodity supplemental food program.

See FOOD STAMPS.

Virgil L. Conrad

Food Stamps

The food-stamp program is a nationwide assistance program that helps low-income households purchase the foods they need for good health. Families participating in the program get coupons, free of charge, which they exchange for food at authorized stores. The amount of food stamps a household receives depends on its size and income.

By law, eligibility for food stamps is based on federal rules that are the same everywhere in the country. However, the law makes state agencies and their local offices responsible for determining whether households are eligible. State agencies also issue food stamps.

In order to qualify for food stamps, a household must meet two income tests: First, its "gross income"* must be less than 130% of the federal poverty guidelines; and second, its "net income"† must fall at or below the federal poverty guidelines. In addition, household assets must fall below certain limits and household members must meet work-registration requirements. Only U.S. citizens, legally permanent aliens, and certain other aliens may qualify.

If a household member fails to register for work, the household will be disqualified from the program until the member registers. If a member fails to accept suitable employment without good cause, the household will be disqualified until the member accepts employment.

The food-stamp program has several special provisions to help the elderly and disabled apply for and receive food stamps: For example, the gross-income test does not apply to them; they are allowed to deduct certain medical expenses when determining net income; and they are allowed to deduct more shelter costs than other households.

To apply for food stamps, a family member contacts the local office of the Welfare Department. He or she then completes an application form and is interviewed by a representative of the department. The applicant should bring along papers showing home address; how many are in the family; how much income they have; and how much they are paying for rent, child care, and other expenses. Qualifying households get food stamps within 30 days of the day the office received their application. Families that need help immediately may be able to get food stamps within a few days.

The food-stamp program is operated by the FOOD AND NUTRITION SERVICE (FNS) of the U.S. Department of Agriculture. Under agreement with FNS, state public agencies administer the program through their local offices. FNS develops program policies and procedures and pays for 100% of food-stamp benefits and approximately 50% of state agencies' administrative costs.

The food-stamp program began as a pilot operation in 1961. Today, it operates nationwide. In 1982 it served an estimated 22 million individuals.

Virgil L. Conrad

Foreign Banks and the Federal Reserve

Most foreign bank branches and agencies operating in the United States are subject to various Federal Reserve regulations and are permitted direct access to FEDERAL RESERVE SYSTEM services, under the same rules and at the same prices as other depository institutions. These developments are primarily a result of the International Banking Act of 1978 and the Depository Institutions Deregulation and Monetary Control Act of 1980.

COMMERCIAL BANKS chartered in the U.S. and owned by foreign banks also are subject to some Federal Reserve rules and have access to services under the provisions of the IBA and MCA, as well as the Federal Reserve Act and the Bank Holding Company Act.

Foreign-owned banks and foreign branches and agencies have assumed an important position in the U.S. financial community. By the end of September 1981, 158 foreign banking organizations operated 186 branches, 182 agencies, and 49 banks chartered in the U.S. Those branches, agencies, and foreign-controlled banks chartered in the U.S. had close to $255 billion or about 14% of the total assets of all commercial banking institutions in the U.S. They had commercial and industrial loans of about $70 billion or about 19% of all commercial and industrial loans booked in the U.S. As of the end of September 1981, foreign

---

*Gross income is a household's total income before any allowable deductions have been made.
† Net income is gross income minus any allowable deductions. The allowable deductions for nonelderly (59 and under) and nondisabled households are as follows: an earned-income deduction; a standard deduction for all households; and a dependent care and shelter deduction. Additional deductions are allowed for the elderly and disabled.

branches and agencies alone had total assets of $182 billion, and total commercial and industrial loans of about $52 billion.

Foreign banks operate various types of offices in the U.S., such as agencies, branches, representative offices, investment companies, nonbank subsidiaries, and foreign-controlled banks chartered in the U.S.

As a result of the IBA, for the first time foreign banks were able to establish Edge Act banking subsidiaries in the U.S. EDGE ACT CORPORATIONS are chartered by the Federal Reserve to engage in international banking and financial operations. In addition, since early December 1981, foreign banks in the U.S. also have been able to operate international banking facilities.

Branches, agencies, and investment companies generally finance international transactions between businesses in the U.S. and their home nations. A number of foreign-owned branches, agencies, and banks also extend credit to U.S. firms and consumers. In some cases, foreign institutions operate a retail banking business in the U.S.

Foreign-owned branches, banks, and agencies in New York State may accept certain kinds of deposits, but investment companies can't. However, investment companies may hold "credit balances," which in several important ways are similar to deposits.

Domestically chartered commercial banks, whether owned by U.S. or foreign interests, may choose to become Federal Reserve members and, thus, own Federal Reserve stock. Although foreign bank branches and agencies don't own stock in Federal Reserve banks, they have access to many Reserve bank services. Likewise, they are subject to Federal Reserve requirements.

Specifically, as a result of the IBA, the Federal Reserve established reserve requirements for any U.S. branch or agency of a foreign bank whose parent organization has more than $1 billion in assets. Almost all foreign units in the U.S. are in that category. As part of the Monetary Control Act of 1980, all branches not yet covered were brought under Federal Reserve requirements.

In October 1979, the Federal Reserve established marginal reserve requirements against all increases in "managed liabilities" of member banks, Edge Act corporations, and, under the provisions of the IBA, U.S. agencies and branches of foreign banks. Those rules were eliminated in mid-1980.

Managed liabilities are large time deposits, Eurodollar borrowings, repurchase agreements against U.S. government and federal-agency securities, and federal fund borrowings from nonmember institutions.

The establishment of marginal reserve require-

ments was part of a program to gain better control over the expansion of money and bank credit; to help slow speculative excesses in financial, foreign exchange, and commodity markets; and to dampen inflation in the U.S.

As the Monetary Control Act was phased in, foreign bank branches and agencies that maintained basic reserve balances at the CENTRAL BANK became eligible to use Federal Reserve services, such as check clearing, ordering coin and paper currency, and transferring funds by wire through the central bank without an intermediary. They also were given the privilege of borrowing from the Federal Reserve DISCOUNT WINDOW.

Meanwhile, the IBA also authorized federal licensing of agencies and branches of foreign banks, and limited the extent to which foreign banks could open new offices in more than one state.

A foreign bank may operate with a federal license in one state and a state license in another state. Interstate expansion of a foreign bank's deposit-taking activities generally is limited to accepting deposits related to international business, except in its designated "home state." In its home state, the foreign banking unit's deposit-taking powers aren't restricted by the IBA. Until the law was enacted, foreign bank branches and agencies generally operated under state rules only.

General supervision of foreign banking units, as specified in the IBA, is divided among several regulators. The Federal Reserve has authority to conduct an on-site examination of any branch or agency of a foreign bank. Foreign banks with one or more U.S. branches, or agencies or investment companies, are treated like bank holding companies, although they aren't subject to the provisions concerning acquisition of bank shares. In addition, foreign bank holding companies continue to be regulated by the Federal Reserve.

On a day-to-day basis, foreign branches and agencies choosing a federal license will be supervised by the comptroller of the currency; those choosing a state license and insured by the FEDERAL DEPOSIT INSURANCE CORPORATION (FDIC) will be supervised by that agency and by the states in which the foreign bank operates; those licensed by a state, but not insured by the FDIC, will be supervised by state authorities and the Federal Reserve.

Arthur Samansky

Forged Check

A CHECK signed in the name of a real or fictitious person for fraudulent purposes.

Harvey Rachlin

Fort Knox

The United States Gold Bullion Depository in Fort Knox, Kentucky, is the primary gold vault for the United States gold reserves. Generally referred to as "Fort Knox" because of its proximity to the military reservation, the depository is under the control of the Bureau of the Mint, U.S. Treasury Department. At present, there are 147,342,260 fine troy ounces of gold stored in the depository's vault.

Opened in 1937, over 16,500 cubic feet of granite, 4,200 cubic yards of concrete, 750 tons of reinforcing steel, and 670 tons of structural steel were used in the building's construction. Within the building is a multilevel steel and concrete vault, divided into compartments. The vault door weighs nearly 30 tons. No one person is entrusted with the combination.

The building is equipped with the latest and most modern security devices. At each corner of the building are four guard boxes, and there are two sentry boxes at the entrance gate. In addition to the security force at the depository, the local military post provides additional protection.

The gold stored in the depository is in the form of standard Mint gold bars. They are somewhat smaller than an ordinary brick—their approximate dimensions are $7 \times 3\frac{5}{8} \times 1\frac{3}{4}$ inches. Each bar contains approximately 400 troy ounces of gold and has an avoirdupois weight of $27\frac{1}{2}$ pounds. During World War II, the depository was also used to store priceless historical documents, including the Declaration of Independence, the Constitution, three volumes of the Guttenberg Bible, and the Magna Carta. The rigid security of the depository and a continuous auditing program insure the safety of U.S. bullion reserves.

No visitors are permitted at the depository. This policy was put into effect when the depository was established and is rigidly enforced. In the filming of the James Bond film *Goldfinger,* the depository was filmed from outside the security fence. Interior and close-up filming was done on stages constructed by the film company.

Donna Pope

Freddie Mac

See FEDERAL HOME LOAN MORTGAGE CORPORATION.

Fringe Benefits

Sometimes called "perks" (short for *perquisites*—additions to regular pay or profits) or "employee benefits," these methods of compensating a worker are usually deductible by an employer and often not included in the gross income of the worker, making them highly desirable rewards for workers. A clear example of such a benefit would be payment by an employer of an employee's accident- or health-insurance plan, which is a deductible business expense to the employer and specifically excluded from calculations of the employee's gross income. Other examples of fringe benefits include other forms of insurance; pension plans; scholarships or tuition payments at schools or colleges; meals and lodging furnished for the convenience of the employer; certain Christmas gifts, like turkeys; and employee discount plans.

The laws regarding the administration of benefit plans are strict in their requirements that such plans generally be applied in nondiscriminatory fashion, applying, for instance, equally to officers, supervisors, and lower-paid employees alike. Those considering instituting a benefit plan should seek proper legal and/or tax advice to assure that they have selected a business structure that will allow the legal administration of the plan. Similarly, employees should be careful to list such benefits as cash bonuses and even certain meals and lodging as part of their gross taxable income. For example, in order for meals and lodging to be excluded from one's gross income, and from taxes, the meals and lodging must be furnished on the employer's premises and for the employer's convenience, and the lodging must be required as a condition of employment.

David B. Axelrod

Fundamental Analysis

A procedure for evaluating common-stock investments, based on the relationship between the market price of a firm's common stock and the firm's expected earnings and/or dividends per share. Fundamental analysts generally forecast a firm's earnings and dividends several years into the future so that they can determine the returns an investor can expect to realize from an investment in a particular common stock.

To predict a company's earnings, the fundamental analyst must evaluate the company's sales prospects. Often a firm's sales and profitability are heavily dependent upon the state of both the economy and the industry. Hence, the fundamental analyst must examine the current condition of the economy and attempt to predict the future level of overall economic activity (measured by, for example, the gross national product, the level of industrial production, and the unemployment rate), the rate of inflation (measured by the producer price index and the consumer price index), and interest rates. In cyclical industries, such as the automobile industry, sales and earnings are significantly affected by economic conditions; during a recession, automobile sales decline substantially, while sales are generally much higher during a growth phase of the business cycle. On the other hand, the health-care and food industries are examples of industries that are affected to a lesser degree by the overall condition of the economy.

Once the analyst has made what he feels is a reasonably accurate forecast for the economy and has also determined the relationship between the state of the economy and that of the specific industry, he then evaluates the position of an individual firm within the industry. If, for example, the firm is in an industry that is expected to achieve a relatively high level of sales in the future, the analyst must determine whether the firm can be expected to succeed in competing against other companies in the industry for a significant share of the market.

The fundamental analyst also examines the firm's costs, since earnings are equal to sales revenue minus costs. In addition, numerous other factors must be evaluated, including the capabilities of the firm's management, the effect of possible technological advances, the significance of government regulations, and the firm's relations with unions representing its employees.

The last step in the fundamental analyst's evaluation of a stock is the determination of whether the security is an attractive investment. Since the desirability of any investment depends on the relationship between the cost of the investment and the returns that will be received by the investor, the analyst generally compares the cost of a share of stock with the earnings and/or dividends per share. He must determine whether the anticipated return, in the form of earnings and dividends, is sufficient to warrant purchasing a share of stock. This decision is based on a comparison with alternative investment opportunities, which include not only other common stocks but also preferred stocks, bonds, and numerous other securities.

This comparison generally takes one of two forms. First, the analyst can calculate the rate of return, or yield, that he may expect to earn if he purchases the stock at the current market price and receives the returns indicated by his earnings forecasts. This yield can be compared to the anticipated rate of return for other investments available in the securities markets in order to determine the desirability of the stock under consideration. (This approach is illustrated by the dividend yield and the earnings yield discussed under COMMON STOCK.)

The second form of comparison between a common stock and other investment alternatives requires the fundamental analyst to determine the minimum rate of return he would find acceptable for the stock being considered. This required rate of return is determined by examining rates of return available for other investments, and is then used to calculate the price an investor would be willing to pay for a particular share of stock. This price is sometimes referred to as the "intrinsic value" of the security. If the market price is less than the intrinsic value, the investor will purchase the stock because he will earn a yield higher than the required rate of return. Conversely, if the market price exceeds the intrinsic value, he will not purchase the stock. Fundamental analysts often use the price/earnings ratio to calculate the intrinsic value of a stock.

R. Bruce Swensen

Futures Commission Merchant (FCM)

Also called a "commission house," "commodity brokerage firm," "futures brokerage firm," "wire house," "brokerage house." The Commodity Futures Trading Commission, the federal agency that regulates futures trading, defines futures commission merchants as "individuals, associations, partnerships, corporations, and trusts engaged in soliciting or in accepting orders for the purchase or sale of any commodity for future delivery on or subject to the rules of any contract market (exchange) and that, in or in connection with such solicitation or acceptance of such orders, accepts any money, securities, or property (or extends credit in lieu thereof) to margin, guarantee, or secure any trades or contracts that results or may result therefrom."

Essentially, then, a futures commission merchant (FCM) is a firm that transacts futures business on behalf of commercial and speculative traders.

There are over 400 FCM's, and they differ in size, composition, and business emphasis. Some are international investment firms that conduct business in all types of financial investments. The degree of emphasis they place on futures business varies, ranging from major to minor importance.

Some FCM's are futures-only firms, specializing exclusively in the futures markets. Firms in this category may be quite large and hold memberships on all major futures exchanges—doing business in all types of futures contracts. Or they may specialize in futures contracts traded on one particular exchange.

Another type of FCM does relatively little outside customer business. These firms are designed primarily to handle and clear the transactions of their member partners, who either trade on their own or act as order brokers for other FCM's.

Regardless of the name, size, or scope of the firm, the main function of the FCM is to represent the interests of those in the market who do not hold seats on the futures exchanges. In return, they receive commission income.

In addition to offering account executives, research services, accounting services, and order-execution capability, many FCM's offer various ways of getting involved in the futures markets. These may include a variety of commodity funds and managed accounts products. Often these products are tailored to the individual investor. Such programs offer professional management and, in some cases, limited liability. Information on funds and managed account programs, including track records, is available from many FCM's.

The most important contact that a customer has with his FCM is through his account executive. The account executive, or registered representative, guides the investor in taking market positions—or in selecting a commodity fund or a managed account compatible with the customer's financial objectives. He or she accepts and transmits orders, and reports the prices at which they were filled. The account executive also keeps the customer informed about market activity and is available to answer the customer's questions regarding trading situations and account status.

Even within the futures area, account executives have a variety of specialties. They may specialize in a particular market—currencies, for example, or grains. They may make trading decisions based on an individualized method of market analysis—one that uses computer-generated trading signals, for example—or they may rely on the recommendations of their firm's research department. They may concentrate on the area of commodity funds and managed accounts—where professional managers make trading decisions for the pooled accounts of many investors; or they may not handle business from individual investors at all, preferring to concentrate on "commercial" accounts—like banks or processors or exporters, or any number of other firms that use the futures market not as a means of making profits but as a risk-management tool.

The services provided by an FCM fall into three general categories. First, the FCM offers order execution. Because prices on the futures market are highly volatile, the speed with which an order is filled is often a critical consideration. To assure the fastest, most accurate order fills, many FCM's maintain extensive communication networks and skilled floor personnel.

When a customer order is received, it is relayed via telephone or wire to the FCM's order desk on the trading floor. From there it is taken by messenger to the appropriate broker in the trading area. There, using a system of open outcry and hand signals, the order is filled. Often the time elapsed from verbal order to pit execution is less than ten seconds. The customer is then notified that the order was filled, and at what price.

In selecting a brokerage firm, it is important to investigate the process by which an order is filled. Trading-floor capability and the method used to transmit orders are important considerations.

Second, the FCM acts as an agent for its customers. Futures exchanges set the minimum initial margin requirements for trading futures, and the maintenance margin levels, but individual FCM's may require margin in addition to that required by the exchange. The FCM is responsible for seeing to it that customers deposit the required margin money promptly and that, if necessary, customers deposit additional margin money.

Based on its customers' positions, the FCM makes deposits of margin money to the clearinghouse of the exchanges on which positions are carried. Those FCM's who are not members of the clearinghouses rely on other firms with clearing-member status to perform this function.

Unlike margin in the equity market, margin in the futures market is a kind of performance bond, designed to assure that the customer will perform against the futures contracts. On the FCM side, clearing margin guarantees the ability of the firm to perform against its clients' commodity-futures transactions.

In addition to handling margin, the FCM also performs accounting services, including written confirmation of all futures orders. Weekly purchase and sale (P&S) statements show the number of contracts bought or sold and margin deposit balances. A monthly statement shows all trading activity, net positions, margin balance, and commission fees. Customers can also receive complete, up-to-the-minute information on the status of their accounts by calling their account executives.

Third, the FCM provides information to its customers. This information takes many forms and varies widely among different firms. Many of the larger firms have research departments that specialize in analysis of the markets. Research analysts are responsible for one or more related markets—livestock, grains, financial futures, or currencies, for example. Often this information includes a market outlook and perhaps specific trade recommendations disseminated through weekly or daily market letters.

Of course, the customer's account executive is another source of information. He or she remains in close contact with trading-floor activity in order to relay news that may have an impact on a customer's trading decisions. Other market information provided by FCM's includes technical advisory services, such as computer software and various analysis packages.

Finally, FCM's share, with the exchanges and with the Commodity Futures Trading Commission, an important responsibility for protecting customers in the futures markets. They inform customers not only of the potential profit from futures trading but also of the possibility of losses. Checks and balances, carefully observed by the futures industry, help to make certain that customers are financially prepared to undertake the risks inherent in futures trading.

Frank Morgan

Futures Contracts

A futures contract is a firm and binding legal commitment to deliver or receive a specified quantity and grade of a COMMODITY during a specified month or on a specified day in the future, at a price determined by public auction on a COMMODITY-FUTURES EXCHANGE. All of the terms and conditions or specifications of the contract, with the exception of price, are standardized by the exchange on which it is traded following the approval of its membership.

As with all contracts, all of the participants have committed to perform their specified duties and obligations. The buyer of a futures contract, referred to as the "long," is assuming the responsibility to take delivery and make payment for the underlying commodity if the contract position remains open beyond the last day of trading. The seller of a futures contract, referred to as the "short," is assuming the responsibility to make delivery and receive payment if the contract position remains open beyond the last day of trading.

A futures contract that is outstanding is referred to as "open"—in other words, it has not been liquidated by an offsetting transaction on the exchange or fulfilled by delivery. In practice, most contracts are *offset* or *closed out* through a liquidating transaction prior to their expiration. Only a very small percentage of deliveries are actually ever made when compared to the total number of outstanding open contracts (net longs and shorts or *open-interest*). The amount of open interest on each business day is reported by the exchanges (*see* COMMODITY-FUTURES PRICE TABLES, HOW TO READ).

The guidelines of the COMMODITY FUTURES TRADING COMMISSION (CFTC) state that in order for a commodity to be eligible for futures trading on a regulated exchange, it must serve a useful economic function. It can only be justified if it serves the purpose of either (1) *price discovery,* or the reflection of the present judgments of different persons concerning the future value of a commodity; or (2) *hedging*—the taking of a position in futures that is opposite to a position held in the cash market to minimize the risk of financial loss from adverse price changes. Hedging is also the purchase or sale of futures as a temporary substitute for a later cash transaction. A special concern of the CFTC is that a futures market not be dominated primarily by speculators.

Alfred J. Patti

Futures Exchange

See COMMODITY-FUTURES EXCHANGE.

Futures Markets

Discussions of the economy and of our economic system inevitably make frequent use of the term *market.* Seldom, however, is an effort made to define the term—probably because it is not as simple as it may seem. Markets are not all the same; they differ significantly in a physical and geographic sense and also in terms of the economic purpose they serve. There are markets for automobiles and copper, for soybeans and corn, for doctors' and lawyers' services, for stocks and bonds, and even for money. In fact, for everything that is bought and sold, there exists some sort of market, a mechanism through which buyers and sellers stay in touch with one another in order to buy and sell a commodity, be it corn or gold or rare paintings.

Futures markets are no exception. There are many futures markets. Some are large; others quite small. Some are in the United States; others are in foreign countries. What they all have in common, however, is that they provide a specific place and a specific mechanism through which individuals and business firms can buy and sell FUTURES CONTRACTS. Thus, a descriptive definition of a futures market is that it is a mechanism used to buy and sell futures contracts.

In Chicago, for instance, one can buy and sell futures contracts on corn, soybeans, U.S. Treasury bills, and foreign currencies; in New York, one can buy and sell futures contracts on gold, silver, coffee, cocoa, and heating oil; and in London, Hong Kong, and other foreign countries, still other futures contracts on other commodities are bought and sold. In a locational sense, therefore, futures markets are easier to define than many markets: They exist in specific geographic locations—New York, Chicago, and so on.

In addition, futures contracts, by definition, can be bought and sold only on an organized futures exchange, which at present can exist only if properly designated as a contract market by some governmental entity—the COMMODITY FUTURES TRADING COM-

MISSION (CFTC) in the United States. Consequently, to understand what is meant by the term *futures market,* it is necessary to understand not only what a futures contract is but also what an organized futures exchange is.

A *futures contract* is an agreement between a seller and a buyer that obligates the seller (called a "short") to deliver to the buyer (called a "long") a specified quantity and grade of a certain commodity during a defined period in the future, *at a price that is agreed upon when the contract is first entered into.* A futures contract can be written on almost any kind of commodity (agricultural products, precious metals, heating oil), security (U.S. government bonds, Treasury bills), currency (French franc, German mark), or any combination thereof, such as stock indexes.

Organized futures exchanges play a key role by standardizing all futures contracts; the only contract term that the parties can negotiate or bargain about is the price of the contract. For example, a corn-futures contract may call for the delivery of 5,000 bushels of No. 2 grade corn during one of a number of specified future months, to be delivered in, say, Chicago according to predetermined delivery procedures. These terms are established by the organized futures exchange on which the futures contract is bought and sold; they are uniform and nonnegotiable and must be accepted by all parties.

In contrast, the price of a future contract varies continually. Its initial price and all subsequent prices are established by competitive bidding by brokers and floor traders at a designated location on the floor of an organized exchange (a trading pit). An important function of an organized futures exchange, therefore, is to provide a specific location where brokers and floor traders can interact with one another according to rules determined by the exchange in order to establish futures prices—an "auction market." Futures prices change from one moment to the next, according to the ebb and flow of the bids and offers made on the floor of the exchange. When a futures contract reaches its maturity date, it ceases to exist—it no longer has a price.

The brokers on the floor of an exchange buy and sell ("trade") both for themselves and for others, acting as agents for buyers and sellers who are not physically present on the floor. In this way the entire demand and supply of all buyers and sellers throughout the world (for, say, corn) is channeled to one or a few specific market locations—certain trading pits on the floors of particular organized futures exchanges. The price of a futures contract at any moment therefore reflects the total worldwide supply and demand for that contract at that moment.

Thus, an important economic function of futures markets is to establish prices for commodities that truly reflect overall market demand and supply for those commodities. They tell us, for example, the price of corn today, as well as what we would have to pay today to have corn delivered to us in one month, six months, or a year. These prices are the market's best guess or forecast about what the actual price of corn will be in one month, six months, or a year. These predictions help individuals and business firms make decisions about the future. This feature of futures markets is called its "price discovery" function.

The organized futures exchange is important for still another reason. Besides creating uniform and standardized futures contracts, and providing organized auction markets to which all demand and supply for such contracts is channeled, they also transform futures contracts into highly liquid financial instruments. While all futures contracts start out as bilateral transactions between two individuals or parties, they almost immediately become separate agreements between the respective buyers and sellers of the contract and the "clearing association" that is affiliated with the relevant organized exchange. Both the buyer's and the seller's obligations are to the clearing association, not to each other. Thus, as long as the clearing association is known and trusted by all buyers and sellers of futures contracts, there is no need for buyers and sellers to know one another.

The most important result of this institutional agreement is that it permits buyers and sellers of futures contracts to get out of their contractual obligations by "offset," rather than by having to make or take delivery of some commodity as actually specified in their contracts. In particular, to get out of his contract, the buyer (or "long") need only enter the market a second time to sell (or "short") the identical contract. He will then have equal but opposite obligations to the clearing association: The two contracts will cancel ("offset") one another, eliminating all of his obligations. Sellers ("shorts") can similarly offset their positions with corresponding "long" positions. In practice, about 95% of all futures contracts are extinguished in this manner. The practical impact of having "offset" is that it makes futures contracts more liquid and therefore more attractive to use.

Of course, it is highly likely that there will have been a change in the price of the futures contract between the buyer's (or seller's) first and second transactions, so that someone will have made money and someone will have lost money. In futures markets, what one party makes, the other loses. We can say that the party making money made a better forecast about what prices would be in the future than did the party who lost the money, He may have been better informed, or just luckier.

Some participants in futures markets are primarily interested in "hedging"—that is, insulating themselves from the risks associated with changes in the prices of the commodities for which futures contracts are traded. Others simply seek to profit from changes in futures prices (speculators). An example of the former is a farmer who is reasonably certain that he will have 100,000 bushels of wheat to sell at harvest time in three months and wants to be certain about how much it will earn him. He can do this by selling a futures contract for delivery of this amount of wheat in three months. He then knows precisely how much money he will receive for his wheat crop when it is ready three months from now. If before the three months are up the price of wheat falls, he will have avoided a monetary loss he would have suffered save for his futures contract; if the price of wheat goes up, however, he will not get the additional profit he otherwise would have. The ability to reduce risk through the holding of futures contracts is often called the "risk-transference" or "insurance" function of futures markets.

Speculators, in contrast, consciously expose themselves to the risks associated with changes in futures prices in an effort to profit from these changes. A speculator who buys a futures contract usually hopes to be able to offset it before it matures by selling an identical contract at a higher price than he paid. Similarly, a speculator who sells hopes to be able to offset by buying another contract at a lower price. The adage "buying cheap and selling dear" applies to trading futures contracts just as to other types of businesses.

Speculators are an essential component of futures markets: They willingly assume risks that others wish to shed; and through their trading activity, they create volume and liquidity in these markets, which lowers the cost of using futures markets to everyone, hedgers and speculators alike.

In recent years, futures markets have grown rapidly as uncertainty about the future has increased. With greater uncertainty has come greater risk, along with an increased need to hedge against these risks. But more uncertainty also has increased the opportunity for making speculative profits, and as a result has attracted more speculators. It is a happy congruence of our market system that the desire of speculators to bear risk has increased just at the time that the need of hedgers to avoid risk has expanded. We must all live with risk and uncertainty—futures markets just make it easier.

In summary, a functional definition of *futures markets* is that they are organized forums through which hedgers and speculators can interact for the purpose of sharing risks and for the purpose of establishing competitive prices on many different kinds of commodities.

Franklin R. Edwards

·G·

Garn-St Germain Depository Institution Deregulation Act of 1982

On October 15, 1982, President Reagan signed into law the Garn-St Germain Depository Institution Deregulation Act of 1982. This act has been described by the president as the most significant piece of financial legislation to be passed by the Congress in 50 years. Quite simply, what the act does is provide the legislative authority to foster the process of change in the financial-services community by broadening the asset powers of thrift institutions similar to those of commercial banks.

The Garn-St Germain Act is divided into eight major sections or titles, each dealing with a separate aspect of financial-system reform. Collectively, the purpose of the act is to revitalize the housing industry by strengthening the financial stability of home-mortgage-lending institutions and ensuring the availability of home-mortgage loans.

Title I of the act expands the type of financial aid that can be provided by the FEDERAL DEPOSIT INSURANCE CORPORATION (FDIC) and the FEDERAL SAVINGS AND LOAN INSURANCE CORPORATION (FSLIC) to federally insured depository institutions in need of assistance.

Title II provides capital assistance to depository institutions that have suffered earnings and capital losses primarily as a result of their mortgage-lending activities. To receive assistance, the institution must issue capital instruments called "net worth certificates," which are purchased by the FDIC or FSLIC with their promissory note. The promissory note is counted as part of the institution's net worth.

The third section of the act, Title III, provides for increased investment powers for federally chartered thrift institutions. Federal thrifts now have authority to invest in all types of government securities, as well as commercial, agricultural, and corporate loans, both domestically and internationally. Specific limits as a percent of assets exist for each category on nonresidential loans.

Title IV contains provisions relating to national and member banks of the Federal Reserve system. Many provisions of the existing banking laws are either revised or repealed by this section, thus increasing the lending limits and authority of member commercial banks.

Title V amends the Federal Credit Union Act in order to provide greater operating flexibility and lending authority for credit unions and the NATIONAL CREDIT UNION ADMINISTRATION (NCUA).

Title VI addresses the insurance activities of bank holding companies.

Title VII of the act covers a variety of matters, such as (1) truth in lending for student loans; (2) industrial-bank eligibility for FDIC insurance; (3) applicability of the International Bank Act of 1978 to securities; (4) Negotiable Order of Withdrawal (NOW) accounts for public funds; (5) the Federal National Mortgage Association (FNMA); (6) bank service corporations; (7) reserve-requirement phase-in; (8) the Neighborhood Reinvestment Corporation; and (9) a study of optional insurance of large deposits.

The last section, Title VIII, involves the offering of alternative mortgage instruments by non–federally chartered housing creditors.

The provisions of the Garn-St Germain Depository Institutions Deregulation Act of 1982, if fully implemented, will have a profound effect on the role and function of individual depository institutions. Concern exists that the act will have an adverse effect on the availability of mortgage credit as savings and loan associations become diversified lenders. Whether the act has the effect of diverting funds away from housing or of increasing the flow of funds to housing through more financially stable and diversified institutions will be seen as the changes authorized by this act are assimilated by the industry.

Michael L. Unger

General Assistance

Aid provided by states and localities to needy individuals and families who are not eligible for SUPPLEMENTAL SECURITY INCOME (SSI) or who are not receiving adequate help from SSI. General assistance (GA) programs do not receive any grants from the federal government. For persons temporarily or permanently unemployed and for those out of work who cannot obtain unemployment insurance or whose benefits are inadequate or exhausted, GA is often the only aid available. A number of states, however, will not provide such help if there is an employable person in the household, except in defined emergency situations.

Harvey Rachlin

General-Obligation Bond

See MUNICIPAL AND STATE SECURITIES.

Ginnie Mae

See GOVERNMENT NATIONAL MORTGAGE ASSOCIATION (GNMA).

Glass Insurance

See INSURANCE.

Gold

Gold has held a unique position for thousands of years as a metal prized for worship, for aesthetics, and for its value. The oldest known civilizations, Egypt and Mesopotamia, are both known to have used gold first as an object of worship and secondly as a store of value more than 6,000 years ago. Most of the great civilizations since then have used gold as a medium of exchange and as a store of value. These include the Chinese, the Minoans of Crete, the Mycenaeans, the city-states of Ancient Greece, the Persians, the Romans, the Byzantines, the Islamic and Ottoman empires, India, and the African kingdoms. The Aztecs and Incas used gold reverentially, and it played an important role in their cultures. However, they did not have the concepts of "medium of exchange" or "store of value." It is particularly noteworthy that, although the Eastern and Western Hemispheres did not know of each other's existence prior to the discoveries of Columbus, gold was highly regarded on both sides of the ocean. Clearly, the unique properties of gold make it ideal as a basis of value.

The history of gold coins is almost as long. Lydia, in 560 B.C., was the first known kingdom to strike a gold coin and issue coins regularly. This became the forerunner of more than 20,000 types of gold coins struck over the centuries by over 1,200 different cities and governments. In fact, the issuance of gold coins came to be recognized as a reflection of the stability of a government and the prosperity of a state, and the debasement of these coins was almost always a reflection of the deterioration of that society. People's recognition that coins were being debased led to a behavior pattern that later became known as Gresham's Law, which states simply that bad money drives good money out of circulation. If there are two or more qualities of money available, people will spend the less valuable money first and hold on to the more highly valued money. Gold and gold coins throughout history have been the more valued money that has been withheld from circulation in times of political unrest, inflation, and money debasement. In modern times, central banks and governments are the holders of the substantial reserves of gold, and rarely if ever do they make payments with it. At most, they use it for collateral against loans. Thus, in the broadest sense, gold retains its identity as money and as a store of value, and Gresham's Law is still at work.

Supply. Gold is in limited supply. In the past 10,000 years, only an estimated 90,000 tons have been extracted from the earth. One-third of that has been mined in South Africa in the last 90 years. All of the world's gold existing aboveground could be contained in a cube measuring 19 yards on each side.

The annual supply of gold on the world's markets is a combination of sales from new mine production and from existing stocks of bullion and fabricated gold. The main components that make up the total supply are non-Communist mine production, net trade with the Communist bloc, and net sales from official and private gold stocks.

Newly Mined Gold. South African gold-mine production consistently accounts for more than 70% of non-Communist mine production and 50% of the world's total. The other major producers in order of tons produced are the Soviet Union, Canada, Brazil, and the United States.

Unlike oil, for which exploration offers hope of sudden new discoveries, gold occurs only in specific geological areas, most of which have been thoroughly explored and exploited through the centuries. Prospecting and opening new mines is a time-consuming and expensive operation. High capitalization is required to finance mining at depths of up to 15,000 feet, using elaborate underground transportation, ventilation, rock support, and earthmoving equipment. Even if strong increases in demand were indicated, it is doubtful that gold supply could quickly respond. Total free-world gold production is expected to remain on a plateau of between 950 and 1,000 metric tons a year through the mid-1980s.

Purchases and Sales by "Official" Institutions. Bullion held and changes in official government reserves are important parts of the supply/demand picture.

While there has been a tendency in recent times for many nations to hold their gold reserves and often increase them, this gold potentially can be sold on the open market. In recent years, the INTERNATIONAL MONETARY FUND (IMF), the United States, and Canada have sold substantial amounts of gold at auctions in the gold markets and in coin and medallion forms. Altogether, monetary authorities of the non-Communist world own some 35,625 metric tons of gold (year-end 1981, estimated). The Soviet Union and China combined have another estimated 2,200 tons. Thus, close to 38,000 metric tons of gold are held by official institutions. This represents perhaps 40% of all the known gold ever mined and suggests the size and importance of the monetary reserves when estimates of future gold prices are considered. Clearly, official decisions regarding gold ownership have the potential to move the price dramatically.

Over a four-year program ending May 1980, the IMF sold one-sixth of its gold holdings at auctions and "restituted" another one-sixth to its members. The total came to 1,555 metric tons. During the same period—May 1978 through November 1979—the U.S. Treasury sold 491 metric tons at auctions. Despite these large supplies, the price of gold moved upward throughout the period.

Some countries, particularly in the third world, have been making regular purchases of gold in recent years. Such purchases may be offset to some extent if other countries follow Canada's recent example of reducing its gold holdings because they make up a large part of its total reserves.

A number of countries have made use of their gold reserves as collateral for international loans, among them South Africa, Italy, and Portugal.

Net Trade with the Communist Bloc. Communist-bloc countries, principally the Soviet Union, sharply reduced their sales of gold in 1979 and 1980, but increased them in 1981 and 1982. Estimates of Russian production range between 280 and 350 tons per annum. There is the possibility that the Russian stocks of gold have dipped to a minimum acceptable level because part of the sales of over 400 tons per year in the three-year period from 1976 to 1978 may have come from stocks. The Russians are believed to sell gold as a means of raising foreign exchange, and sell only as much as they must to meet their objective. The higher the price, the less gold they have to sell to raise a given amount of exchange.

Unlike Russia, which releases no statistical data about its gold-mining industry, China has released some information on its gold production. The Chinese gold-mining industry is broadly similar to that of Canada and the U.S. Total production is estimated to be in the range of 30 to 60 tons per annum. China

could probably add somewhat to this and, therefore, to the world supply in the years ahead.

Demand. Supply and demand are, of course, always in arithmetic balance. The variables are the price of gold and the ability of the various market segments to absorb the gold.

Over the period 1969 to 1972, the consumption of gold for fabrication purposes exceeded newly mined supplies, the difference being made up of sales from private gold hoardings. In 1973 and 1974, the rising price of gold adversely affected industrial consumption of the metal, but fabrication demand revived in the three years 1975 through 1978. In 1979 and 1980 higher gold prices again caused a price-elastic response (i.e., purchases were reduced as the price rose). In 1981, offtake for fabrication returned to normal. Over the period 1969 to 1981, on average about 70% of gold supplies were consumed for fabrication purposes.

Jewelry. The largest segment of the commercial or fabrication demand for gold has historically been karat jewelry. Western Europe and the Middle East have always provided strong markets. Significant demand also comes from North America and Japan. However, there is scarcely a part of the world where gold jewelry is not manufactured. Demand from the jewelry market can be price-elastic. When gold prices rose sharply in the 1972–74 period, shipments to jewelry manufacturers dropped. But in 1975, offtake for jewelry rebounded in spite of continued price increase for gold. Jewelry manufacture appears to be more sensitive to consumer spending patterns and real incomes than to prices. Further, the recognition of karat-gold jewelry as having a dual role as both adornment and a store of value seems to have come into play, particularly in the Middle East. Another important factor is discretionary income. For example, the International Gold Corporation in New York tested and found that almost all of the variations in jewelry purchases by consumers in the United States can be explained by changes in discretionary income.

Official Coins. Official coin production has accounted for a large and growing amount of gold usage in recent years. All indications point to even greater market acceptance and therefore to an expansion of production.

The South African Krugerrand, which contains exactly one troy ounce of gold, is by far the dominant coin in world markets. In 1980, the one-ounce Krugerrand was supplemented by a range of smaller, low-premium bullion coins. The United Kingdom has substantially increased coin production both in the fabrication of ordinary sovereigns and in the striking of proof sovereigns and gold coins for foreign countries. Demand for the Mexican gold coins has varied in a range of 20 to 46 tons in recent years.

The Royal Canadian Mint entered the bullion coin market on a large scale during 1979 with the introduction of the one-troy-ounce Maple Leaf. Production rose in 1980 but fell in 1981.

Electronics. Gold use in the manufacture of electronic components has been rising in recent years. Demand is mainly from the U.S., Japan, and West Germany. This is happening despite technological substitution aimed at reducing plated surfaces and thicknesses and the introduction of devices using no gold. The increased use can be attributed primarily to strong business demand, which has resulted in an increase in the volume of production large enough to more than offset the decline in gold use as a consequence of technical change.

Gold-price increases have added to incentives to seek alternative processes and use less gold. However, the development of this technology takes time. A combination of a business recession and the more efficient use of gold points to a short-term halt to the rising trend in consumption, but these negative effects could be offset by increased defense expenditure. Traditionally, defense applications in elecronics have required higher specifications, which are usually achieved by the use of gold.

Dentistry and Other Uses. Gold and gold-alloy restorations are unsurpassed in terms of effectiveness and service life in dentistry. This is one of the important industrial uses of gold. Others include the use of gold in industrial and decorative plating (excluding electronics); liquid gold used in ceramics; rolled gold (gold fill); and industrial and laboratory chemicals.

In this area the cost of gold is not a major component in the price of the final product, and gold-price increases in the context of inflation are of little consequence for consumer demand. On the other hand, the higher gold prices have led to some decline in its use to decorate glass and ceramics. In ophthalmic frames, gold-filled use seems to have ended and gold plate substituted. The main consuming countries in this sector are the U.S., Japan, and West Germany.

Gold-coated glass windows are currently being promoted as both an energy saver and a means of improving the appearance of buildings. These windows permit visible light to come through but not heat waves. Air-conditioning costs in summer can be reduced because the infrared radiation is reflected back into the outside air. During the winter, the window reflects indoor heat back into the building and saves energy in the reverse manner. Additional savings are made in capital costs because a building fitted with gold-coated glass requires smaller-capacity equipment for heating, ventilating, and air conditioning.

Medals, Medallions, and Fake Coins. The three main centers for this business are currently Saudi Arabia, Kuwait, and Syria. Fake-coin manufacture is a traditional industry in the area, and the designs range from copies of ancient Turkish coins right up to modern coinage, including the British sovereign. Quality of reproduction varies widely, but the gold content is usually up to the standard of the official version. In most instances the replicas are used as a convenient form of gold hoarding. In Yemen, for example, it is usual to have bracelets made up of some 20 to 30 replica sovereigns. Traditionally, the making of fake gold coins in the Middle East has been a specialty of the Syrians from Aleppo, and for many years the main centers were Aleppo, Damascus, and Beirut.

The five-year program for the production of gold medallions by the U.S. is going ahead with limited success. In each of the five years, about 31 tons of fine gold will be used to mint one-half-troy-ounce and one-troy-ounce gold medallions.

Net Private Bullion Purchases. The difference between the gold supply to the free market and gold use for fabrication is referred to as "net private bullion purchases."

Part of this residual is made up of gold that is physically transferred to the country of residence of its new owners. The remainder stays in the country where it was purchased, because the new owners prefer this arrangement. While large amounts of gold were taken by investors in 1973, 1974, 1977, 1979, and 1980, there was substantial dishoarding, or net sales, in 1970, 1972, 1981, and early 1982.

The Markets for Gold. There are many ways to participate in the gold market as either an investor or a speculator. There are bullion markets; markets for official and rare coins; futures; options, and shares of gold mines. When looked upon on a worldwide basis, trading is continuous. In fact, that is how the market for gold should be viewed, since social, political, economic, and natural phenomena can influence the price of gold at any time. Those price reactions are transmitted to all markets and are almost immediately reflected in gold prices anywhere in the world.

Market Basics. Gold bullion, referred to as a "good delivery gold," is gold refined to a purity of .995 or better, and is the medium most typically employed by investors. Gold of a purity of .9995 or better is proportionally more expensive because it requires a more costly electrolytic refining process. This is not necessary for investment purposes, although it is valuable for specialized uses, such as jewelry.

Gold bullion comes in various sizes, but for investment purposes the following are of relevance (all measures refer to troy ounces, although bars denominated in grams are also available): 400-ounce "good delivery bars," which are used primarily in international transactions between governments; 100-ounce bars, typically used in U.S. domestic transactions; smaller bars of 50 ounces, 1 kilo (32.15 ounces), ½ kilo (16.075 ounces), and 10 ounces; and wafers of 5 ounces, 1 ounce, ½ ounce, and various-size gram bars.

All gold bullion must be marked with a registered number, the degree of purity, and the name of a prescribed refinery or assay office responsible for certifying its purity.

The Bullion Markets. The most important markets for newly mined gold are in London and Zürich. Production from South Africa and the Communist bloc is largely shipped through Zürich. The London market absorbs a smaller proportion of South African production than Zürich, but exerts a strong influence on price setting. Smaller amounts of new gold reach New York, Frankfurt, and other European centers.

The London market is conducted by five member firms who meet twice daily for the purpose of "fixing" the gold price. Three Swiss banking companies maintain a market in Zürich known as the Gold Pool. In the U.S., cash prices for gold generally follow those made at the New York Commodity Exchange. Another major market is located in Hong Kong, where 194 Chinese members trade on the Hong Kong Gold and Silver Exchange Society.

Communication in the international gold markets is swift and constant, reporting price changes and information influencing supply and demand. Traders, dealers, and investors have access to a worldwide telecommunications network, as well as the daily reporting of print and broadcast media.

In London, twice a day, five days a week, the representatives of five precious-metals dealers gather to "fix" the local gold price. It is an exercise that serves to establish an equilibrium price at which supply and demand are balanced. The London "fix" serves as the benchmark for most commercial and investment transactions in the industrialized world. These prices are reported in the business sections of newspapers, by the wire services, and by most brokerage houses, or one can simply dial certain toll-free numbers provided by several precious-metals dealers in the U.S.

When buying gold for investment purposes, investors should bear a number of factors in mind. First, the smaller the size of a bar or wafer, the higher the premium over the gold content. An investor clearly wants the most favorable terms of purchase. Typically, therefore, he should invest in 400-ounce, 100-ounce, 50-ounce, and kilo (32.15-ounce) bars—or buy low-premium bullion coins. Second, buyers may have to bear the cost of assay, which normally runs from $75 to $100 per bar. This factor also argues against

investment in the smaller bars.

Gold bullion may be purchased from precious-metals dealers, precious-metals exchange companies, banks, and many brokerage offices. Prices will normally be based on the London "fix" or the New York cash market, but commissions, delivery, assay, storage, and insurance fees can vary from one dealer to another. The normal spread between bid and asked is .5–1%. Minimum-size initial orders are common— e.g., ten kilo bars, five 100- and 400-ounce bars. Volume discounts are available, but they vary, again increasing the importance of checking several sources.

Gold purchased for cash is available for delivery within a specific time period (usually two business days) after payment, or can be stored for a fee—e.g., 10 to 12 cents per ounce per month. Physical possession is not recommended, because of the threat of loss or robbery, or cost of assay. Those who take possession of their gold should store it in a bank safe-deposit box.

It is also possible to purchase gold bullion and bullion coins utilizing leverage. A number of precious-metals exchange companies will sell gold against a down payment—approximately 20–33.3% of the asked price—charging simple interest, billed quarterly, on the unpaid balance. Such contracts can run for very long periods and generally require that a minimum equity be maintained; calls for additional funds are made if the equity falls below the required minimum percent.

Many buyers of gold for investment purposes prefer not to take physical delivery. They will instead opt to purchase "gold certificates," "bullion certificates," "delivery orders," or "warehouse receipts" issued by certain banks, brokerage houses, and mutual funds. These are nontransferable certificates designated at warehouses in the U.S. or abroad, generally in states that do not levy sales taxes, thus avoiding an additional cost. Minimum amounts or dollar values are usually stipulated—for example, 10 ounces of gold, or $1,000 to $2,500 per initial investment, with as little as $100 permitted for subsequent purchases, depending on the issuing institution.

In 1979 a small number of U.S. banking institutions introduced "precious-metals passbook accounts." These are not unlike savings accounts, except that they involve purchases (additions) or sales (withdrawals) for customers' accounts of specific quantities of metal. Again, delivery is available if requested. In the case of both delivery orders and passbook accounts, commissions on purchases and sales vary slightly between different institutions, but all are on a downward-sliding scale depending on the increasing dollar value or amount involved. Assay costs are thereby not necessary. Costs of storage and insurance vary, but typically run about ½–1%. Arrangements for physical delivery are made upon request, normally requiring a few days' notice. A number of issuers offer certificates permitting delivery in designated foreign as well as domestic locations.

When investing in gold, as with any investment, it is very important to deal only with known and reputable brokers, banks, and dealers. The investor should check to ensure that the party effecting sales is capable of delivering precisely what it has sold, and to ascertain the conditions under which it stands ready to repurchase.

Gold Coins. There are two types of gold coins: numismatic coins and bullion coins. Numismatic coins derive their value from their condition and rarity, rather than from their gold content, which is normally only a fraction of their price. Their attraction for investment purposes can fluctuate for reasons quite divorced from the gold price. Furthermore, the spread between bid and asked is often substantial, which means that, unlike bullion, a considerable portion of an investment in numismatic coins could be lost upon resale. The same is true of gold medals, medallions, and similar works purchased for historical or artistic reasons. A subjective "fashion" or scarcity element enters into the price of these items. They are not homogeneous and therefore may or may not be readily marketable at a particular time and place. The higher the premium over bullion content, the greater the risk from a strictly investment standpoint.

Bullion coins, on the other hand, are sold and bought primarily for their gold content, although they may also have fashion appeal as jewelry. They command modest premiums over bullion value, usually on the order of 3–15%, and a large part of that may be recovered in the event of resale. Again, the higher the premium, the more diluted the risk. Nevertheless, some small premium over bars is justified by the attributes of bullion coins: their ready divisibility, convenience, portability, marketability, and the nonnecessity of assaying.

Most of the comments pertaining to investing in gold bullion also apply to bullion coins. They may normally be purchased at selected banks, coin dealers, gold and precious-metals dealers, brokerage firms, and jewelers. Volume discounts are generally available, but vary somewhat, as may commissions (there is generally a .5–1% spread between the bid and asked prices) and storage and insurance charges (typically, $1 per coin per year). For all these reasons, it is important to shop for the best price. Purchases are often subject to sales tax, so that use of "delivery orders" or warehouse receipts on coins stored in states where the coins are not subject to tax is a logical approach. For those wishing physical possession of the coins, storage in a bank safe-deposit box is a sensible precaution.

With the major exceptions of the Krugerrand and Maple Leaf, virtually all bullion coins are official restrikes—that is, newly minted copies of previously issued coins. The major exception is the Krugerrand, which is legal tender coin in South Africa and circulated in unlimited issue. It was first minted in 1967 in limited quantities, and in larger numbers starting in 1970. It was specifically designed for investment purposes. It contains precisely 1 ounce of pure gold, and its intrinsic value or face value is therefore instantly available by reference to the London gold "fix." Because of its convenience and universal recognition, and the fact that it generally commands the lowest premium over bullion content, it has emerged as far and away the largest-selling bullion coin in the world. In 1980 fractional Krugerrands were introduced. They are respectively the ½-, ¼-, and 1/10-ounce coins, containing exactly those amounts of pure gold. Canada launched the 1-ounce Maple Leaf coin in late 1979 for limited amounts. However, having enjoyed such success, legislation has since expanded the amount and duration of issue of new coins through 1990.

The principal bullion coins are as follows:

	Gold Content (Oz.)
Austrian 100 Crown	0.9802
Austrian 4 Ducat	0.4438
Canadian Maple Leaf	1.0000
Hungarian 100 Crown	0.9802
Mexican 50 Peso	1.2056
South African Krugerrand	1.0000

Futures. Gold-futures contracts represent commitments to buy or sell a designated amount of gold at a specified time in the future at a preagreed price. Contracts are generally actively traded, their prices arrived at by open competitive bidding, usually within prescribed fluctuation limits. Since the contracts can be purchased on margin, they provide a leverage participation in the investment medium. In brief, the mechanics of trading gold futures are similar to trading most other commodities.

There are five exchanges in the United States where gold futures are traded. Based on volume of gold contracts traded in 1979, 1980, and 1981, the two largest are the COMMODITY EXCHANGE, INC. (COMEX) and the International Monetary Market (IMM) of the CHICAGO MERCANTILE EXCHANGE. The others are the CHICAGO BOARD OF TRADE (CBOT), the NEW YORK MERCANTILE EXCHANGE (NYMEX), and the MIDAMERICA COMMODITY EXCHANGE (MACE). There are also gold-futures exchanges in Hong Kong, Singapore, Winnipeg, and Sydney, and others being developed in London and Tokyo.

There has been a dramatic increase in gold-trading activity on these exchanges, to the point where the U.S. market has clearly emerged as the leading gold volume trading center. As a result, market breadth and depth are considered excellent, providing good liquidity for all participants—producers and fabricators and speculators. All trades for each commodity are transacted during specified market hours at one location (the pit) via "open outcry." Floor members are required to undertake diligent execution. An array of orders may be left with the floor trader, such as market orders, stops, limit trades, and so on. These should be explored and understood before entering into futures trading.

As with any commodity, gold producers and users utilize the futures markets to hedge inventories or production against future price fluctuations. They can thus better assure their prices when calculating their cost and price structures for budget and planning purposes. When used under certain circumstances, futures contracts can be a means of stabilizing performance. An investor contemplating the use of the futures market should carefully define his objectives and familiarize himself with the appropriate techniques.

Speculators, on the other hand, seek trading profits arising out of market fluctuations. They provide basic liquidity to the market by putting up risk capital on the basis of their expectation of future market prices. As with any other commodity-futures market, a speculator will normally close his position before maturity by the offset feature of futures trading, whether to realize profits or to limit losses. In other words, the buyer (or seller) of a contract can either maintain his position and take possession (or deliver) upon maturity of the contract or offset the transaction before maturity by assuming a position equal and opposite to his original trade, involving the same delivery month and on the same exchange as his original contract. About 98% of gold-futures contracts are normally offset in this manner. A simple warehouse receipt obviates the need to take physical possession if the contract is not offset. In the latter case, of course, costs of storage and insurance must be involved.

The use of margin accounts—usually 5–15% of the principal amount involved and typically 10%—provides the opportunity for leverage. A change in price that affects the minimum equity of the position will bring forth a call for additional margin. Brokers will generally sell out customer positions that do not meet minimum margin requirements if these customers cannot quickly put up the additional margin. A common device used to overcome this possibility is to keep more than the minimum margin in the account. To limit losses, investors can place stop-loss orders, although these will not necessarily limit losses to the

intended amounts since it may be impossible to execute such orders at the price intended. Brokerage commission fees are charged on executing purchases and sales.

The exchanges, through their clearinghouses, have established financial safeguards designed to protect the integrity of the futures market against the domino effect of defaults by individual exchange members.

Investors can participate in the gold-futures market by opening an account with a brokerage firm or commodity dealer that is, or deals with, a member of a commodity exchange. Almost all brokerage firms are members of one or more commodity exchanges. The brokerage firm can help explain the complexities of futures trading. The risk of loss in trading commodity-futures contracts can be substantial. You should therefore consider whether such trading is suitable for money under your management.

Options. Yet another approach would be the purchase/sale of options—i.e., the right, but not the obligation, to buy or sell at a specified price by a certain date a specific quantity of metal of a designated fineness.

Commodity options offer a wide range of benefits. Depending upon the terms of the option, they offer potential for profit, with losses limited to the initial investment; there can be neither calls for further margin nor forced liquidations. Still another advantage is that commodity options are a versatile tool for investors. They have many uses—ranging from the very conservative to the very speculative. However, options do contain risk, and, as in the case of futures, the investor should carefully consider whether or not they are appropriate for his investment needs.

Commodity options can serve both the speculative and hedging needs of investors without requiring large margins, accepting unknown risks, or compelling continuous market attention typically associated with futures contracts. Because buying a commodity option gives the buyer the right to exercise it, the option enables him to take full advantage of a market move in his favor. However, because he's not obligated to exercise it, his risk is limited to the price paid to buy the option. Holders of gold can also grant gold options to commercial users, thereby earning a yield on their gold, particularly in cases where the option is not exercised.

Well-established brokerage firms that offer a breadth of services can assist investors with information on options. Be sure to ask for a disclosure document.

Gold Shares and Gold Funds. Gold investors can purchase equities of quoted gold-mining companies, thereby receiving a dividend income as well as an opportunity to participate in any appreciation in the price of the share. The choice of gold-mining shares outside of South Africa is limited, but they are to be found in Canada, the United States, and the Philippines.

As stated earlier, South Africa annually accounts for about 70% of non-Communist mine production. It possesses sophisticated and well-developed financial, capital, and equity markets. Foreign investors, traditionally in London and the continent of Europe, and in recent years increasingly in the United States, have actively invested in South Africa's gold-mining industry.

Many of South Africa's leading gold-mining shares are traded, if not actually quoted, on European and North American stock markets. This being the case, Americans can easily invest in South African shares merely by dealing directly through U.S. brokers. In this way investors need have no concern about settlement in South Africa and can remain safely outside of the country's dual currency system and, particularly, the mechanics of the Financial Rand, the investment currency used predominantly by overseas investors.

A small number of mutual funds and investment companies that have placed a large or predominant portion of their assets in gold-mining securities and/ or gold bullion, or related vehicles, are also available to investors. These have the advantage of providing the uninitiated with experienced management of gold assets.

All of the foregoing vehicles may be purchased through brokerage firms on a commission basis for effecting the securities transaction.

As with any security investment, the risk/reward ratio must be carefully weighed. On the one hand, mining costs are rising inexorably, and some mines are unprofitable below certain gold selling prices. There are also political, economic, mining, and currency risks. On the other hand, there are frequently very attractive current dividend returns and, for selected investment issues, the prospect of capital appreciation if the gold price rises.

Gold-Price Behavior. There is a general misunderstanding about the gold price. Many people will say that it is volatile and fluctuates widely. In fact, the gold price is usually rather stable. Simple inspection of a gold-price chart from 1968 forward, the period of free market, demonstrates that in most years the gold price moves little, and then only gradually. The exception to this was the period of late 1979 through mid-1981. Various tools normally applied to equities in modern portfolio theory have demonstrated statistically that the gold price varies less radically and by smaller amounts than do prices of stocks and bonds.

Another general misunderstanding is the belief that the gold markets are mysterious and cannot be understood in terms of conventional economic analysis. Recent research, however, has demonstrated that the gold markets are not mysterious, and can be understood by using the basic tools of economic analysis. The gold markets behave efficiently, analogous to other financial markets, and incorporate known information into the price with very short time lag. Rigorous analysis has established that the key factors that influence the gold price are (1) excess world liquidity, which is the rate of growth of the money supply worldwide plus Euro-currencies less the rate of growth of real economic activity of the same countries; (2) the U.S. dollar trade-weighted foreign exchange rate; (3) real economic growth of seven major industrialized countries; (4) real interest rates, which is the three-month Eurodollar rate less the consumer price index for industrialized countries for the trailing six months on an annualized basis; (5) unanticipated inflation, which is current world inflation rate minus a moving average for the prior 18 months; and (6) a measure a political tension.

This research has found that political tensions are important when an event occurs; but as the event recedes, so, too, does the gold price. Over long periods of time, the major influence on the gold price is the rate of growth of money supply in excess of what is required for normal economic growth. Real economic activity is also important because research has demonstrated that as incomes rise, the use for gold in jewelry and other purposes and the demand for gold for investment also rises. This demand elasticity is more powerful than the price elasticity. In other words, gold-price increases are not as strong a suppressant as similar percentage increases in overall economic activity.

Since the gold market has been permitted to find its own level, there have been two major gold-price cycles: a rise from the $35-to-$40-an-ounce rate to $200 by the end of 1974; a decline from the end of 1974 to September 1976, when the price fell to almost $100; another rise in price, which culminated in the extraordinary surges of January 1980, when the price reached a high of $875, and September 1980, when the price reached $720; followed by a decline through the first half of 1982, bringing the gold price into the low $300 range. A third upward cycle began at mid-year 1982 with two spikes of over $500 occurring in September 1982 and January–February 1983. Both surges were quickly reversed. But the basic uptrend from the low in June 1982 was clearly visible. Throughout the 1970s and early 1980s a widening circle of investors and speculators joined in and became conscious of gold as an alternative investment. The infrastructure of the markets also expanded to accommodate these people. Thus, gold has emerged as a major investment vehicle, both in physical terms and in markets for futures and options.

Gold Weights and Purity

Weights. The weight of gold is customarily measured in either troy ounces or metric units.

0.47 oz. troy	=	1 baht (Thailand)
1 oz. troy	=	31.10 grams
1.2 oz. troy	=	1 tael (Hong Kong)
3.75 oz. troy	=	10 tolas (Indian subcontinent)
32.15 oz. troy	=	1 kilo
100 oz. troy	=	3.11 kilos (COMEX contract)
32,150 oz. troy	=	1 metric ton

Purity. The purity of gold is described by its "fineness" (parts per 1,000) or by the KARAT scale.

Fine Gold		Karats
1,000	=	24
995		(London good delivery)
916	=	22
750	=	18
583.3	=	14
417.7	=	10 (legal minimum for karat gold jewelry in U.S.)
375	=	9
333.3	=	8

Eugene J. Sherman

Gold in the Monetary System

Gold has all the basic requisites of money: It is scarce; it is indestructible; it cannot be manufactured; it is recognizable; it is measurable to minute fineness; it can be easily divided into finite amounts; and it is portable. Its dual role as both money and a means of adornment has contributed to its desirability; after all, even if people were to reject gold as a form of money, it would still be widely used for jewelry and other decorative purposes. For all of these reasons, it has served as a store of value. In more recent times, it has also been found to have numerous uses in electronics, dentistry, heat shields, and other things.

The history of gold as money was touched upon in the opening paragraphs of the entry on GOLD. This entry will explore the role of gold in the monetary system in modern times.

The Gold Standard. The gold standard had its heyday in the three or four decades before World War I. It was pioneered by Britain, the world's leading industrial power for most of the nineteenth century, and was adopted by an increasing number of countries that had economic ties with the British. By 1870, all the world's leading trading nations were linked to gold. Prior to the evolution of the gold standard, there was no formal, widely accepted international financial system, but rather a plethora of settlement arrangements, which, among other things, included silver as a means of payment.

The gold standard was based on two rules: Gold had to be convertible into the currency of a country on the standard, either bullion or freely circulating coin; and participating countries were obligated to allow the free import and export of gold. Ideally, if these rules were observed, the gold standard worked with splendid precision and served as an equilibrating force in economic adjustments. Under the gold standard, a currency's value was stated in terms of a fixed amount of gold and was convertible from paper into gold by anyone on demand. It was a rigid system that presupposed approximate balance among countries in international payments, assumed that there would be accommodating adjustments for periods of imbalance, and required final settlement in gold.

As the currency of a country on the standard was defined in terms of a fixed content of gold, this meant that the exchange rate between currencies was also fixed. Thus, before 1914 the pound sterling was equal to 4.866 U.S. dollars, a rate derived by relating the gold content of the British pound (113 grams) to that of the American dollar (23.22 grams).

As an example, let us suppose that because of especially heavy British imports from the U.S. there was a shortage of American currency available to British merchants. As a result, the rate of the dollar against sterling would appreciate until it reached what was called the "gold export point"—i.e. $4.827 to the pound. At that level it was economic to export gold from London to New York, allowing for transport and insurance charges. This differential was necessary as gold transfers were required for the purchase of dollars or their equivalent with which British importers could pay American exporters. In the reverse case, there would be a shortage of sterling bills of exchange available for purchase by American merchants, so that sterling would appreciate against the dollar. In this case, the gold import point would be $4.890 to the pound, and gold would be shipped from New York to London.

One-way gold flows could not continue indefinitely, as there were corrective mechanisms that reversed the process. In the short run, a deficit country could expect its interest rates to rise because of reduced domestic liquidity as a result of less gold in the country. The higher interest rates would encourage an inflow of foreign funds. As a supplementary measure, the CENTRAL BANK could raise the discount rate if the liquidity shortage was not by itself sufficient to attract overseas short-term capital. Over the long run, adjustments would take place through a combination of reduced investment and consumption in the deficit country because of higher interest rates, and lower prices resulting from reduced liquidity. All of this would make for a stronger balance of trade by curbing imports and encouraging exports. By the same token, surplus countries, which by definition would be receiving gold, would find their positions eroded by rising prices and greater domestic investment and consumption resulting from lower interest rates. Also, the residents of a country in balance-of-payments surplus would tend to spend more than those of a deficit country, some of which consumption would be devoted to imports, so that there would be a natural tendency for equilibrium to be restored. The gold standard also regulated the amount of notes on issue through a complex of laws and regulations.

A number of countries followed the British example with small modifications and adopted the gold standard, among them Germany, France, Belgium, Switzerland, Italy, Greece, Norway, Sweden, and, somewhat later, Austria-Hungary, Russia, and Japan. By the outbreak of World War I, virtually all major countries were on the system.

In the United States, the Resumption Act required that paper money the Treasury had issued be made redeemable in coin on demand. Since the Treasury complied with this act by redeeming in gold coin, the country effectively adopted the gold standard with the return to convertibility in 1879. In 1900 the Gold Standard Act formally recognized the de facto gold standard.

There were strong forces making for the unity of theory and practice. The free movement of gold was essential for equilibrating balance-of-payments distortions between different countries; otherwise, the international character of the standard would have been destroyed. In practice, this was made possible because the pre-1914 gold standard was in effect a sterling standard. Most countries kept their currencies stable in terms of sterling; the alternative would have been a failure to attract British investment and difficulties in financing their trade with London. Sterling was the key currency, particularly for international transactions on both current and capital account. Britain had deficits with Europe and the United States and surpluses with the new countries. Britain was a long-term investor in the latter group, which made possible their payments for British goods.

But the gold standard did not work entirely according to classical theory. The movements of exports and imports between deficit and surplus countries on the gold standard were supposed to diverge, but in fact there was a high degree of parallelism in the movements of these trade flows. Also, export prices in a number of countries moved together over time, although more-frequent divergencies would have been expected in terms of the classical theory. Furthermore, while adjustment was supposed to have been facilitated for deficit countries by price flexibility downward, in practice prices did not decline in response to payments disequilibria as readily as the theoretical model suggested. In fact, substantial price changes were largely in response to variations in the flow of new gold to monetary stocks.

The exhaustion of old mines, discovery of new ones, and breakthroughs in mining and refining technologies produced significant changes in the cost of producing gold during the nineteenth century. Since the monetary price of gold was fixed, the resulting changes in the rate of gold production generated similar fluctuations in the growth of money supplies of countries on the gold standard.

The world's monetary gold stock increased only 1.4% a year from 1916 to 1948. The annual growth of monetary gold stocks then jumped to 6.2% from 1849 to 1873, fell back to 1.4% from 1874 to 1892, and recovered to 3.6% from 1893 to 1913. The jump in 1849 largely reflected the discovery of gold in California.

The use of both paper currency and demand deposits increased markedly during those years. Paper money and demand deposits probably accounted for less than a third of the U.S. money supply in the first part of the nineteenth century, but possibly for as much as nine-tenths by 1913. And the monetary gold stock—gold coins and gold reserves of the Treasury—declined sharply relative to the nation's money supply over the corresponding period.

If, as under a true gold standard, gold was to be the sole regulator of the rate of monetary expansion, monetary gold should have maintained a constant ratio to the money supply. But if this had happened during the nineteenth century, prices in the United States and other countries would have fallen severely, instead of remaining relatively stable.

The discipline of gold was consistent with relatively stable prices only because it was not fully operative during a period of gold shortage. The monetary price of gold was too low to call forth production of monetary gold in proportion to the growth in economic activity. If demand deposits and paper money had not been substituted for gold, there would have been a severe deflation.

In addition to the mutually beneficial nature of the pre-1914 gold standard, there were other factors that contributed to its success. First, and perhaps most important, the world economy was growing rapidly. Changes in demand, reflected in price changes, did not therefore lead automatically to widespread unemployment and lower profits. Because of the international economy's dynamism and flexibility, necessary adjustments could readily be made by industrial-structure alterations that did not give rise to deflationary tendencies.

Second, the rules of the game were not as invariably observed as the common view of the gold standard would have it. In principle, central banks had little discretion in implementing their discount policies: If there was a deficit, interest rates were raised; if there was a surplus, they were lowered. It followed that the domestic situation would be entirely dependent on the state of the balance of payments. In practice, central banks, including the Bank of England, were aware of the need to achieve external balance without excessive restrictions on domestic activity. Interest rates were therefore often allowed to decline so as to counteract the deflationary effects of gold outflows.

A third reason why the system worked smoothly was the growth of a multilateral settlements network. This provided a variety of ways to offset payments between countries and thus considerably reduced the need for gold in international transactions.

To sum up, the smooth working of the international gold standard before 1914 is not a myth, but its success was very closely bound up with historically transient factors, particularly the predominance of Britain in the international economy and rapid economic growth and international expansion. Sterling was increasingly used as a supplement to gold in settling global economic transactions. Indeed, it is difficult to see how the international monetary system could have functioned smoothly had this not been so, as it would otherwise have been heavily dependent on such accidental factors as the discovery of gold and its rate of production.

The Gold-Exchange Standard. The international gold standard broke down under the strains of World War I. Belligerent countries generally sought to get gold coins out of circulation and into official hands and to prevent the exportation of gold abroad. Neutral governments frequently suspended the free coinage of gold and ceased to buy gold freely at the official price so as to avoid importing inflation.

Partly because of the severe inflation experienced in many countries during the war, popular sentiment favored restoration of the international gold standard. The United States was the first to return to the gold standard, in 1919, with the removal of its embargo on gold exports, and by 1927 the number of countries on a gold standard was larger than ever before. But the restored international gold standard bore only a superficial resemblance to the previous one.

Once again, central banks bought and sold gold at fixed prices, and gold was allowed to move freely internationally. But with the exception of the United States, most countries operated on a gold-bullion standard, rather than a gold-coin standard. These countries redeemed their money in gold bars of large denomination only, and some—like Great Britain and the Netherlands—restricted gold sales to people wanting it for export or industrial uses only. By reducing the amount of gold used in domestic circulation, these measures made more gold available for international payments. Without such measures, gold would have tended to be in short supply.

Of even more significance was the widespread adoption of a gold-exchange standard for international reserves. To economize further on gold, central banks began to hold a significant proportion of their reserves in the form of financial investments in London and, to a lesser extent, in New York and Paris. Because these reserves could be withdrawn anytime, and especially because the gold reserves of Great Britain were not large, this system contained the seeds of its own destruction.

Another problem with the restored gold standard was that the new gold parities did not adequately reflect the different degrees of inflation after 1914. Of particular significance, because of its role as a reserve currency, was the overvaluation of the British pound sterling. To reassert its financial leadership and to attempt to restore prices to prewar levels, Britain returned to gold in 1925 at the prewar parity for the pound sterling. But because many other countries had devalued their currencies from prewar parities, Britain's trade balance became depressed, and the pound sterling was at or near the gold-export point most of the time. However, the losses of gold, and consequent monetary deflation in the British economy, did not reduce wages and prices enough.

Finally, in 1931, a series of continental bank failures led to heavy withdrawals from the London money market, forcing the Bank of England to announce that its gold reserves had fallen to the point where it could no longer maintain the gold standard. The pound sterling was allowed to float downward, creating losses for the central banks that held their reserves in London. Pressure then shifted to other countries, forcing most of them off the gold standard also.

The depression brought an important modification to the gold standard of the United States. In 1933, apparently as a temporary measure for alleviating the banking panic of that year, the Roosevelt administration prohibited private holdings of gold coin, gold bullion, and gold certificates. But in 1934 the Gold Reserve Act gave the government permanent title to all monetary gold and allowed gold certificates to be held only by Federal Reserve Banks. This put the United States on a limited gold-bullion standard, under which redemption in gold was restricted to dollars held by foreign central banks and licensed private users.

Also under this act, President Roosevelt devalued the dollar by increasing the monetary price of gold from $20.67, as established in 1834, to $35 an ounce. The devaluation of the dollar was not undertaken for the purpose of defending the country's balance of payments, but rather in the belief that it would raise the dollar price of exports and thus help stimulate prosperity. This assumed that demand and market share would not be affected by the higher prices.

One effect, however, was to overvalue the currencies of the few countries that were still on gold—notably France. These countries had earlier repudiated the gold-exchange standard and decided to depend on gold as the only reliable international reserve. But the deflationary effects stemming from its overvalued exchange rate prompted France to devalue the franc 25% in 1936 and to float it in 1937. When the French franc was once again pegged in 1938, it was to the pound sterling rather than gold.

The limited gold-bullion standard could have been the basis for complete regulation of the money supplied by gold if that had been desired. In this system, when the U.S. Treasury bought gold, the cash balances to pay for it were created by issuing gold certificates to Federal Reserve banks. The total amount of credit that Reserve banks could create was in turn limited by law to a multiple of their holding of gold certificates. Each dollar of Federal Reserve credit generated several dollars of money in circulation. So, if the Federal Reserve had varied its credit creation in proportion to gold flows, the effect would have been to make the money supply vary in proportion to the monetary-gold stock of the Treasury.

In practice, such gold-backing requirements did not significantly limit the operations of most central banks during the interwar period. For instance, in the 1920s, the amount of gold certificates held by Reserve banks was nearly twice the amount legally required, giving the Federal Reserve system considerable leeway in its money-creating powers.

Some central banks were constrained, however, by the effects of their operations on the balance of payments and, hence, on their limited gold stocks. For example, because of a precarious balance-of-payments position, the Bank of England did not allow money and credit to expand as much as would otherwise have been desirable for the domestic economy. The balance-of-payments constraints were asymmetrical. The United States and France both experienced large gold inflows in the 1920s, which, under the rules of the gold standard, should have led to expanded money supplies. But rather than allow such expansions to inflate their economies, these countries neutralized the monetary effects of gold inflows.

The attempted restoration of the gold standard in the 1920s did not meet the test of consistency. Exchange rates were pegged on an ad hoc basis following the upheavals of the war, but hoped-for price adjustments in countries with payments deficits were too slow in coming, and the looser ties between money and gold allowed countries to follow more independent monetary policies than before. Also, international reserves varied in a haphazard manner as central banks substituted more or less reserve currencies for gold.

Though the worldwide depression subjected it to abnormal stress, the system was basically fragile. Gold parities were adopted without a complete acceptance of the other rules of the gold-standard game, and therefore could not have been permanently viable.

The Bretton Woods System. Growing out of discussions among the major powers during World War II was a new international monetary organization, formally created at a 1944 conference at Bretton Woods, New Hampshire, and called the International Monetary Fund. The purpose of the fund was to reestablish a fixed exchange-rate system, with gold as the primary reserve asset. At the same time, rigidities and inconsistencies of the previous gold-exchange standard were to be avoided.

Member countries were obligated to declare fixed parities for their currencies in terms of gold, or, alternatively, the gold content of the U.S. dollar in 1944. Thus, these parities were unequivocally expressed in gold. But other countries were not required to join the United States in making their currencies convertible to gold for foreign central banks. The requirement of maintaining a fixed parity for a currency could also be fulfilled by stabilizing its dollar value within plus or minus 1% of parity through central bank intervention in the foreign exchange market.

The U.S. Treasury continued to buy and sell gold at $35 an ounce in transactions with foreign central banks and licensed users. But foreign countries that had been on the gold standard before World War II did not return to it. Even though their citizens could, in many cases, freely hold gold, no currency other than the U.S. dollar was again made convertible to gold.

Thus, the Bretton Woods system restored a gold-exchange standard, with the United States assuming

Britain's earlier role as the main reserve-currency country. Because of vast inflows of gold during the 1930s, the United States was in a better position to assume this role than Britain had been before.

An important implication of the use of dollars as a reserve currency was that the total supply of international reserves varied with the payments position of the United States. When the United States ran a payments deficit, other countries were obligated to purchase the excess supply of dollars in the foreign exchange market to maintain the exchange values of their currencies at parity. If these dollars were converted to gold, the total amount of international reserves did not change, but the process increased foreign reserves at the expenses of U.S. reserves. However, to the extent that foreign countries were satisfied with holding inflows of reserves in dollars, there was an increase in reserves abroad but no decrease in the gold reserves of the United States. Similarly, as long as no gold changed hands, a payment surplus for the United States produced a decline in total international reserves.

A problem with the gold-exchange standard of the 1920s had been that exchange rates were fixed in terms of gold parities but monetary policies of central banks were not harmonized sufficiently to ensure that fixed rates could be easily maintained. So, under the Bretton Woods system, member countries were allowed to change the par values of their currencies in case of a fundamental disequilibrium.

Although this term was not defined in the "Articles of Agreement," it seemed to mean that internal economic stability should not be unduly sacrificed to achieve a balance in international payments. Nevertheless, it was widely believed that national monetary policies could be harmonized enough so that the need for changes in par values would be infrequent. In actual practice, this basic assumption was the flaw that led to the system's demise. Lacking a mandatory and automatic adjustment mechanism, the system took on an inflationary bias that became more pronounced over time. Moreover, since the process was "sanctioned" by international agreement, it became immutable.

To facilitate the financing of temporary and reversible swings in a country's payments position, a new credit facility was established. Each member country paid into the IMF an amount of gold plus its own currency equal to a quota that was roughly proportionate to its economic size. Countries with temporary payments deficits could obtain foreign exchange from the IMF's pool of funds by purchasing it with their own currencies. Later, they would sell an equivalent amount of foreign exchange back to the fund. Interest on credits extended in this manner was normally paid in gold. Countries could automatically purchase foreign exchange in an amount equal to the gold they had deposited with the fund. Further drawings were conditional on the fund's being satisfied that the countries' economic policies were consistent with an improved balance in their international payments.

Although quotas have been increased from time to time, credits extended by the IMF have in fact constituted only a small proportion of total international reserves. Gold and the U.S. dollar—and to a much lesser extent the British pound sterling—have been far more important.

By allowing a degree of flexibility in exchange rates, the Bretton Woods system was supposed to discourage exchange controls. But maladjustments inherited from the war were so great that most currencies did not become freely exchangeable for one another at near their official parities until 1958. Although reappearance of the prewar dollar shortage had been expected, this did not materialize. Marshall Plan aid and very substantial devaluations of foreign currencies against the dollar in 1949 had helped restore the competitive positions of war-torn countries relatively quickly.

The Search for an Alternative. Dollar liabilities of the United States to foreign official institutions exceeded U.S. gold holdings for the first time in 1964. A run on the U.S. gold stock then became conceivable, but was not likely so long as U.S. payments deficits could be corrected. The fund agreement did not require that the gold value of the dollar remain fixed, but the special position of the dollar as a reserve currency made it difficult for U.S. officials to contemplate a dollar devaluation in terms of gold. Also, the economic importance of the United States made it difficult for them to devalue the dollar without triggering sympathetic devaluations by other countries, leading to uncertain results.

Actually, it was not clear that U.S. payments deficits ought to be eliminated before something was done about the shortage of monetary gold. The Bretton Woods system needed the international reserves being created by U.S. deficits, because world production of gold barely exceeded private demand. But if the United States continued to run payment deficits, its position as the world's banker would deteriorate. Further deficits would increase its dollar liabilities and reduce its holdings of gold, leading to weakened confidence in its ability to maintain convertibility of the dollar to gold.

On the other hand, if the United States restored confidence in the dollar by taking steps to curb its payments deficits, an important source of international reserves would be cut off. If this happened, the expansion of international reserves would tend to lag behind the growth of international trade and payments, making it more likely that countries would resort to tariffs, exchange controls, or deflationary policies for balancing their international payments.

A devaluation of all currencies by the same amount would have maintained exchange rates exactly as before, but would also have increased the value of gold reserves. The difficulty with this idea was that a large increase in the price of gold might generate such large increases in gold production and reserves as to encourage inflationary monetary policies. But only a small increase could generate expectations of further increases, which might swell private hoarding of gold and decrease its availability to central banks. In addition, a higher gold price would have penalized the countries that had, in good faith, held most of their reserves in dollar or pound-sterling balances.

In 1967 the members of the IMF agreed to the creation of a new international reserve asset—called Special Drawing Rights (SDR's)—to supplement dollars and gold. These bookkeeping entries in the accounts of the fund were allocated to participating members in proportion to their membership quotas and have been used to settle payment imbalances between members.

Special Drawing Rights were to be similar to gold in that they would be generally acceptable as a reserve asset without being a legal debt. They were called "paper gold," and initially their value was defined in terms of gold and they had a gold-value guarantee. However, their establishment did not prevent a breakdown of the Bretton Woods system as a result of overly rigid exchange rates.

Steps were taken to insulate the gold stocks of central banks from the effects of the gold shortage. To keep the market price of gold from being bid up above the official price of $35 an ounce, the major central banks stood ready to feed gold into the London market—i.e., the "Gold Pool" arrangement. But by 1968, speculative buying of gold had so depleted the stocks of central banks that this practice was abandoned. Instead, the free-market price of gold was allowed to find its own level.

Also in that year, an act of Congress eliminated the requirement that the Federal Reserve hold gold certificates equal to at least 25% of the value of Federal Reserve notes, thereby freeing all Treasury gold for international use. A similar reserve requirement against other Federal Reserve liabilities had been dropped in 1965.

By the time of the first allocation of SDR's in 1970, the U.S. payments position had worsened, rather than improved. The U.S. trade balance, which had been in surplus by over $6 billion in 1964, registered surpluses of less than $1 billion in 1968 and 1969 and fell into deficit by over $2 billion in 1971. The deterioration was due partly to rising inflation in the United States and partly to more rapid productivity increases abroad.

Countries with payments surpluses might have revalued their currencies upward in the light of the fundamental disequilibrium that had occurred, but they were reluctant to revalue because of the resulting impact on employment in their export industries. Moreover, they did not seem willing to accept a devaluation of the U.S. dollar without countering with some devaluations of their own, at least partially nullifying its effects.

A basic weakness of the Bretton Woods system was that the responsibility for adjustment was unclear. A multilateral agreement was needed on a new structure of exchange rates, acceptable to all countries. To private holders of dollars, however, a depreciation of the dollar, one way or another, was inevitable. And the resulting massive outflow of dollars in the summer of 1971 induced the United States to suspend convertibility, as Britain had done 40 years before.

In December 1971, parties at an international conference at the Smithsonian Institution agreed to a new structure of exchange rates. But the attempted return to a fixed parity system was unsuccessful. The reserves of central banks amounted to less than half of the short-term funds that could be switched from one currency to another. Moreover, even when reserves of central banks could be used to defend fixed parities, the cost in terms of economic stability had become too high. Central banks of countries with payments surpluses, by buying foreign exchange to maintain their currencies at parity, injected new money into their economies. And the resulting inflation was not easily offset by other means. In early 1973, after another bout of massive speculative flows of money into surplus countries, the major central banks decided to allow their currencies to float, rather than try to defend the Smithsonian parities or negotiate a new structure of rates.

Meanwhile, as monetary officials struggled to regain control over the monetary system, they began to look upon the role of gold in the system as an encumbrance. Accordingly, from 1968 onward, a determined attempt was made to demonetize gold. In March of that year, the two-tier system for gold transactions mentioned above was established. In 1971 the United States ended the gold convertibility of its currency, and in March 1973 the link was severed altogether. When floating exchange rates became widespread, the IMF made a determined attempt to reduce the role of gold by changing the provisions relating to it in the fund's "Articles of Agreement."

With the ratification of the new provisions in April 1978, gold ceased to be the common denominator of par values of member countries; obligatory gold payments to the IMF were abolished; one-sixth of the IMF's gold reserves were restituted to members; and the IMF sold another one-sixth of its official gold reserves in the private market through regular auctions, with the proceeds used to help its poorer members finance their large payments deficits. In sum, the IMF reduced its holdings by 1,555 metric tons in the four-year period ending May 1980. In addition, final settlement among central banks in gold ended. At the same time, the U.S. Treasury conducted a series of gold auctions from May 1978 to November 1979 during which it sold 491 metric tons.

In the spring of 1978, the managing director of the IMF proposed the creation of a "substitution account." This was intended to allow official dollar holders to hold, or substitute, SDR's for dollars. The purpose was to reduce the temptation to sell dollars on foreign exchange markets at a time when the dollar was already weakening. The problem was that the SDR still maintained a high weighting of dollars and no one was willing to accept the exchange risk for the differential between dollars and substituted SDR's. Thus, if a central bank held dollars and the dollars went down relative to other currencies, it lost value in its own currency terms. Alternatively, if it exchanged dollars for SDR's and the dollar declined, so, too, would the SDR, based on the dollar's weighting. Although the central bank might lose less in the SDR's, it would lose anyway. Meanwhile, it would earn less on its holdings of SDR's, owing to the interest-rate formula, than it would if it held dollars and invested in interest-yielding dollar-denominated money-market instruments.

From the U.S. point of view, one country's balance-of-payments deficit was another country's surplus, and both had an obligation to move their balances to zero, so that the adjustment process and burden should have been mutually shared. Therefore, the U.S. was not willing to assume the full foreign-exchange risk. The problem of making the "substitution account" sufficiently attractive to provide a substitute asset of international liquidity to the dollar and other hard currencies is still "being considered" within the IMF, but progress, if any, in this direction is expected to be slow.

In summary, like the gold-exchange standard of the 1920s, the Bretton Woods system suffered from basic inconsistencies. Because exchange-rate adjustment was made only in cases of fundamental disequilibrium, private speculation could anticipate coming devaluations or revaluations, setting the stage for an international monetary crisis. The fund agreement did not establish a procedure for making timely and frequent adjustments of exchange rate, but instead assumed that exchange adjustment would be rare because of a hoped-for harmonization of national monetary policies. Yet there was no mechanism to coordinate national monetary policies, as had automatically occurred under the nineteenth-century gold standard.

There was a similar lack of consistency in the rules regarding gold. Gold was to be the primary international reserve asset, and its price was fixed because of the uncertainties and inequities involved in changing it. But there was no assurance that there would be enough gold production at a fixed price. When a gold shortage arose, dollars and SDR's had to be substituted for gold in international reserves. The price of gold was not permitted to rise, as this would imply a devaluation of the dollar.

Moreover, since the dollar was convertible to gold for foreign central banks, the United States could not continue to feed it into the private market to keep its price there at the official level of $35 an ounce. Instead, there had to be a separation of the private-market price from the official price. But central banks became unwilling to trade gold at the official price when the market was telling them it was really worth much more. The resulting immobilization of gold suggested that a rethinking of its role in the international monetary system was badly needed.

A Multicurrency Reserve System. In the absence of a single alternative financial unit that could be acceptable worldwide as a specie such as gold, the international financial system has evolved a multicurrency reserve system. This is necessary since an interdependent world economy requires an acceptable medium of exchange and a store of value.

The dollar is still the most widely held and widely used currency. The share of dollars in proportion to all currencies in central bank foreign-exchange holdings in recent years has been in excess of 70%. However, excluding the major industrial countries and the largest oil-producing nations, the proportion of dollars held by other nations is much lower, perhaps 50–60%. Among the industrialized countries and large OPEC members, a part—and probably a large part—of the explanation for so large a proportion of dollar holdings is the absence of viable alternatives of substantial size. The large dollar holdings of those countries are also the result of accumulation arising out of persistent U.S. balance-of-payments deficits and some of those countries' dollar-support operations. Among the countries with a smaller proportion in dollars, diversification of currency holdings is probably more feasible, primarily because the amounts involved are not nearly so large.

The main impulse toward a multicurrency reserve system comes from the fact that, in a world of floating exchange rates, diversification of currency holdings reduces risk. For a central bank, ownership of a diversified portfolio of foreign exchange means less risk than ownership of a dollar portfolio. The measure of risk is variability. The variability of a diversified portfolio, with respect to any currency that is floating, is bound to be less than the variability of any one floating currency, including the dollar. The principle is the same as the diversification of an investment portfolio of common stocks. The risk of even the most promising single stock is higher than that of a diversified portfolio, and so is the risk of even the strongest single currency, making allowance for total return in that currency, compared with other currencies, rather than expectations of appreciation alone.

Of course, this does not mean that all central bankers would tend to prefer the same kind of diversification among currencies. The precise composition of a diversified portfolio will differ for different banks. This in turn would often be dependent on the country's trade relations, and on the currencies in which its foreign debt, if any, is denominated.

The most serious liability of a multicurrency reserve system is switches among currencies constituting the system. Shifts between sterling and gold, sterling and dollars, and dollars and gold in the past have plagued the international monetary community even when the amounts that could or did move were relatively moderate and fixed exchange rates limited some of the consequences of such shifts. Today, with large international reserves lodged in floating currencies, the potentially destabilizing effects of switching could be even greater.

In an effort to further expand world liquidity and achieve greater use of its form of international reserves, the IMF has ambitious plans for the SDR. In the meetings held in September 1980, the fund approved a plan to allow countries to borrow up to 600% of their quota over three years, virtually tripling the existing credit range. Prior to this, countries were permitted to borrow 200% over two years, and in those cases the IMF exacted stringent commitments of sound fiscal, monetary, and international financial policies. The new extended borrowings will be with much less severe strictures. As a result, instead of serving as a barrier to inflation, as was the case prior to this step, the IMF now seems ready to become part of the inflationary process. In short, these borrowings will be used to finance balance-of-payments and na-tional deficits, with strong potential inflationary consequences. Clearly, the SDR's will proliferate. The IMF plans to borrow in international markets to raise the funds to meet member countries' borrowing requirements. This development is likely to provide central banks with renewed incentive to diversify reserves.

The Reemergence of Gold in the Monetary System. There is a growing body of evidence that gold is reemerging as a monetary asset. Each bit of evidence by itself is significant; but even more important is the fact that, when seen together, a clear pattern begins to come into focus.

First, over the past few years, parallel to the evolution of a multicurrency system, a growing number of official institutions have started to look upon gold as an integral and mobile part of their reserve holdings. A large number of central banks have restated their gold holdings at current market prices, using different formulas. Indeed, many of these would have shown losses on the foreign-exchange component of their reserves had they not done so. Some 50–60% of total world central bank reserves are held in gold. Obviously, the proportion changes as the value of the dollar varies in relation to other reserve currencies and as the gold price varies.

Second, in the EUROPEAN MONETARY SYSTEM (EMS), which came into operation in March 1979, gold plays a vital role. It helps support the European Currency Units (ECU's) that now form a substantial part of member countries' convertible currency reserves. In exchange for depositing 20% of their gold and dollar reserves in a central pool, members receive holdings of ECU's which are used for central-bank settlements within the EEC. Currently, some 2,722 metric tons of gold are held as part of the pooled reserves of the European monetary system.

Third, as mentioned earlier, the IMF discontinued its gold sales in May 1980. There is now greater acceptance of the view that its gold reserve is a valuable asset that enhances its credit standing in the international financial markets. This should make its anticipated borrowings relatively inexpensive. In the extreme, the IMF may use gold to collateralize loans, but IMF officials see no near-term need for that recourse.

Fourth, over the course of 1980 and 1981, a number of central banks accumulated large amounts of gold. In 1980 this included South Africa and Russia, the major producers, both of which held back some of their production. Some of the accumulation by other countries was through restitution from the IMF, while other accumulations were through outright purchases.

Some countries accumulated smaller amounts in the late 1970s, but the cumulative amount of all countries in 1980 was considerable, at 230 metric tons, and was even greater in 1981, at 276 metric tons. There was a reduction in net accumulations to 98 metric tons in 1982, owing to liquidations forced on some central banks due to problems in servicing their international debts. This was partly offset by some U.S. and Canadian liquidations for coin and medallion sales. Obviously, a growing number of central banks are diversifying reserves into gold and in the process adding to their gold holdings.

Fifth, gold has been gaining acceptance as collateral in international lending. There have been a number of instances of this, particularly by official institutions, and with growing frequency in recent years.

Perhaps most important, in terms of both total holdings and supplies to world markets, is the United States. While the secretary of the Treasury retains the right to sell additional amounts of gold if such transactions might help to maintain an "acceptable" level for the U.S. dollar against other currencies, give valuable assistance to the management of the balance-of-payments position, or help to control inflation, none has been sold at auction or in world markets since the last gold auction in November 1979. Of course, the Treasury has its program of medallion sales, but these account for only about 1 million ounces of gold per annum at most, and sales have not met expectations. Future decisions of the United States regarding its gold reserves will be important influences on both its market value and its use as a monetary asset.

U.S. Gold Commission. The U.S. Congress created the Gold Study Commission to review and make recommendations regarding the role that U.S. official holdings of gold should play in the domestic monetary system and the international financial community.

The report of the commission recommended essentially no important changes in the role of gold in the U.S. or international financial system. The majority concluded that under present circumstances restoring a gold standard does not appear to be a fruitful method of dealing with the continuing problem of inflation. The commission acknowledged that no precise level for gold stock is necessarily right, and recommended that the Treasury retain the right to conduct sales of gold at its discretion, provided adequate levels are maintained for contingencies. In fact, the proceedings of the commission, even more than the wording of the final report, revealed a strong sense that gold should be maintained as a valuable asset. The commission also recommended that the Treasury and the Federal Reserve conduct studies as to possible realistic revaluation of gold in current market terms, provided that such revaluation, if any, not be used to help finance the federal deficit.

In fact the only departure from prior practice was a recommendation by the commission that the Treasury issue a gold bullion coin of specified weight, without dollar denomination or legal-tender status, to be manufactured from its existing stock of gold and to be sold at a small markup over the market value of the gold content. The commission further recommended that Congress implement the proposal and exempt the coin from capital-gains taxes and from state and local taxes. The exemptions from the various taxes are perhaps the most controversial aspect of the commission's recommendations. There is no assurance that Congress will accept these recommendations, or act on any of the proposals made by the commission.

Eugene J. Sherman

Government National Mortgage Association (GNMA)

A federal agency within the DEPARTMENT OF HOUSING AND URBAN DEVELOPMENT (HUD) that guarantees privately issued securities backed by pools of federally insured mortgages.

History and Organization. The Government National Mortgage Association (also known as "GNMA" or "Ginnie Mae") was created in 1968 through amendment to Title III of the National Housing Act. Under the provisions of the Housing and Urban Development Act of 1968, the FEDERAL NATIONAL MORTGAGE ASSOCIATION (FNMA), originally established in 1938, was rechartered as a private corporation to provide secondary-market support for the private residential-mortgage market, and GNMA was established as a government corporation within the Department of Housing and Urban Development to administer mortgage-support programs that could not be carried out in the private market.

Though in form a corporation (thus having corporate officers, such as a president), GNMA functions as an office within HUD and is, by law, subject to the overall direction of the secretary of HUD. The president of GNMA ranks as an assistant secretary, and GNMA's budget is part of the budget of the United States.

For several years, GNMA engaged in so-called tandem mortgage-purchase programs that provided deep subsidies to multifamily construction projects. While those programs are still authorized, the administration has asked that no further funds be appropriated for them. Activity is limited to selling the portfolio of mortgages accumulated in the course of the programs.

GNMA's best-known and most important ongoing activity is its mortgage-backed-securities (MBS) program, which is the subject of the remainder of this entry.

MBS: Concept. The purpose of the MBS program is to increase the availability of mortgage credit for federally underwritten mortgages by attracting new sources of funds for the mortgage market and increasing liquidity in the SECONDARY MORTGAGE MARKET.

Through the MBS program, GNMA guarantees privately issued securities (popularly known as "Ginnie Maes") backed by pools of mortgages. Holders of the securities (the investors) receive a "pass-through" of the principal and interest payments on the pool of mortgages, less amounts to cover servicing costs and certain GNMA fees. Under the "modified" pass-through approach, if borrowers fail to make timely payments on the mortgages, the securities issuers must nevertheless make timely payments to the registered holder, using their own resources. The GNMA guaranty assures that the registered holder of the security certificate will receive *timely* payments of scheduled monthly principal and interest, as well as certain prepayments and early recoveries of principal on the underlying mortgages.

It is important to remember that GNMA does not loan the funds for the underlying mortgages, nor does it issue the securities. GNMA's function is limited to acting as a surety for the performance of the security issuer, while the underlying mortgages are insured by other government agencies. The funds are ultimately raised by sale of the securities in the private capital market.

MBS: Economic and Legal Basis. The MBS program provides a means for channeling funds from the nation's securities markets into the housing market. The U.S. government's full-faith-and-credit guaranty of securities makes them widely accepted in those sectors of the capital markets that otherwise would not be likely to supply funds to the mortgage market. The funds raised through the securities issued are used to make residential and other mortgage loans. Through this process, the program serves to increase the overall supply of credit available for housing and helps to assure that this credit is available at reasonable interest rates.

Statutory authority for the MBS program is provided in Section 306(g) of the National Housing Act. It authorizes GNMA to guarantee the timely payment of principal and interest on securities that are based on and backed by a trust or pool composed of mortgages that are insured or guaranteed by the FEDERAL HOUSING ADMINISTRATION (FHA), the Farmers Home Administration (FmHA), or the VETERANS ADMINISTRATION (VA).

As previously stated, GNMA's guaranty of mortgage-backed securities is backed by the full faith and credit of the United States. Besides having reserves that could be liquidated if needed, GNMA has the statutory right to borrow without limit from the U.S. Treasury, if this should ever be necessary in order to make payments to security holders.

Commitment authority is granted to GNMA by a congressional appropriation. This is not a grant of funds from the Treasury, but merely a limit to the aggregate amount of new securities that GNMA can guarantee in any given year. In the 1984 fiscal year, this limit was set at $68.25 billion.

As of the end of fiscal 1983, the MBS program had helped finance about 5 million housing units. Over $180 billion in securities had been issued, and more than $150 billion of the aggregate principal balances was still outstanding. There were more than 70,000 GNMA mortgage pools in existence. More than a thousand firms are approved as GNMA issuers, and the securities are marketed by about 90 securities dealers. The majority of the issuers are mortgage bankers (*see* MORTGAGE BANKING), though many SAVINGS AND LOAN ASSOCIATIONS, COMMERCIAL BANKS, and other financial institutions have also been approved as issuers.

MBS: Program Mechanics. In order to become an approved issuer of GNMA securities, a firm must be in the business of originating or servicing mortgage loans. It must be an FHA-approved mortgagee in good standing, and have a net worth that assures GNMA of the firm's financial capacity to pay security holders when mortgagors (homeowners) fail to make their mortgage payments on time.

The process of Ginnie Mae security issuance begins when a prospective issuer applies to GNMA for approval, at the same time asking for a commitment of guaranty authority from GNMA. Once approved as an issuer, the firm can get subsequent commitments of guaranty authority under a modified process, and its ongoing performance and capacity are monitored to assure continuing compliance.

With the commitment in hand, the issuer proceeds to originate or acquire mortgage loans and to package a "pool" of mortgages. The pool must aggregate at least $1 million in original principal amounts. Except in the new GNMA II pools, described below, all the loans in a single pool will bear the same interest rate. Typically, the issuer also makes arrangements with a securities dealer to market the mortgage-backed securities when they become available. Arrangements are made for an independent custodian to maintain actual possession of the mortgages and other documents during the life of the securities. A custodian is also appointed to hold principal and interest, and tax and insurance funds as they come in from homeowners, pending their distribution to security holders.

As part of the packaging of the pool, the issuer executes documents assigning all the mortgages to GNMA. These documents are deposited with the custodian and are not recorded unless there is a default and GNMA must take possession of the pool. This rarely happens. Defaulted payments have amounted to a very small fraction of 1% of payments due under the program. Though billions of dollars are passed through every year, only $10 million has had to be written off over the life of the MBS program.

When the pool of mortgages is assembled, the issuer submits to GNMA all the documents needed for final approval of the securities issuance. GNMA's policy is to complete its review of the documents and effect the delivery of securities within 20 calendar days. Under the GNMA II program, the processing is delegated to the central paying agent (which will be explained in detail later), thus providing the issuer with "one-stop" service.

Upon approval of the pool documents, GNMA will instruct its transfer agent (presently Chemical Bank, in New York City) to actually prepare and deliver the certificates in accordance with instructions (i.e., the names and addresses of the holders) provided by the issuer. With the timely delivery of the certificates assured, the issuer can make firm plans for the sale of the certificates to investors (holders).

Each certificate in a new pool, when first issued, must represent at least $25,000 in original principal amount. This is an undivided interest in the underlying mortgages—i.e., the holder does not own any particular mortgage or other part of the pool, but is entitled to a pro rata portion of all the proceeds of the pool.

Every month, the security holder receives a check from the issuer for a share of the principal and interest payments that were scheduled to be made (whether or not they were acutally made by the mortgagors), and a pro rata share of any prepayments of principal, or recoveries (in the event of foreclosure or assignment). He also receives an accounting that shows the remaining share of principal balance represented by the holder's certificate, and a breakdown of how much of the check is for principal and how much for interest.

MBS: Certificate Size and Coupon Rate. Obviously, as a pool ages, the principal balance outstanding declines, and so each certificate represents a smaller bal-

ance. It is therefore possible for a GNMA certificate actually to be worth less than the original minimum amount of $25,000. Most certificates, however, are very large. The average size is about $500,000.

As noted before, all the loans in a single pool have the same rate of interest (except for the GNMA II pools described later). But the interest rate on the Ginnie Mae security is always one-half percentage point less than the rate on the underlying mortgages. Because one full percentage point is equal to 100 "basis points," the interest paid to the holder is 50 basis points less than the mortgagor pays to the servicer. Of these 50 basis points, 6 are passed on to GNMA as a fee for its guaranty. Out of these funds, GNMA pays all its expenses and invests the remainder in Treasury securities as a reserve in the event of defaults by issuers. This reserve does not secure the mortgages themselves, which are separately insured against default by the FHA, VA, or FmHA.

MBS: Trading of Certificates. Critical to the acceptance of Ginnie Maes has been their liquidity—i.e., the ability of holders to sell them on short notice in an active market. The standardization of the Ginnie Maes contributes to this, as, of course, does the federal guaranty. Every Ginnie Mae certificate is exactly like all others, except for the principal balance and the interest rate.

Liquidity of Ginnie Maes would be impaired if a prospective buyer could not determine, independently of the seller's information, what remaining principal balance there was in back of the certificate. GNMA has contracted with a private firm to provide on a monthly basis a listing of "pool factors." A pool factor is simply the proportion of the original principal balance remaining in any specified pool. With a telephone call, a prospective buyer who has the number of the pool in which he is interested can find out the factor for that pool and thus establish what a certificate of any given original amount still represents in principal balance. Given the principal balance remaining, and taking into consideration the interest rate paid, the buyer is able to calculate the appropriate price to pay for the certificate.

Of course, like any capital instrument that has a fixed rate or coupon, a Ginnie Mae will rise in price as interest rates decline, and drop when rates increase. But the exact price, or its movement, may be influenced by expectations of whether the pool underlying the certificate may prepay rapidly. For example, it should be noted that the mortgagors, or homeowners, in effect are able to call the Ginnie Maes by paying off their mortgages. In a time when current rates for new mortgages are greatly below the rates on some Ginnie Maes, there would be a danger that many homeowners who have mortgages in the pools behind those certificates would pay off their loans in order to refinance at the lower available rates. When they pay off, they do so at par. Hence, a high-coupon Ginnie Mae (one with a rate above current new mortgage rates) should not be expected to move above par as well as a Treasury bond, for example, of similar rate and maturity.

There are other influences on the prepayment experiences of individual pools, and there is a good deal of research by securities firms devoted to tracing these pools and forecasting future prepayments. In the securities industry, it is assumed as a standard that a Ginnie Mae pool has a life of 12 years. Obviously, a pool priced on the assumption that the mortgages will pay off at par in 12 years is a bargain if in fact they pay off in 6.

MBS: GNMA II and Other New Developments. Beginning in August 1983, GNMA started a new securities program in addition to its original program. The new program, called GNMA II, uses a central-paying-agent system. Under this arrangement, all funds collected from homeowners go to a single agent. This agent issues a single check to each security holder, no matter how many certificates a holder owns. This is a convenience to trustees, in particular, who in some cases hold as many as a thousand or more certificates.

Also, the new program permits loan rates to be mixed in a pool, within a range of one percentage point. This gives the loan originator a lot more flexibility in putting together a package of loans. In turn, these features permit the establishment of multi-issuer, or "jumbo" pools.

Jumbo pools incorporate mortgages originated from a number of different issuers in a given month, thus mixing loans from different issuers from different geographic areas. Every certificate is issued on the basis of that entire aggregate, no matter who the individual issuer is. Hence, when an issuer delivers the necessary documents to GNMA's agent showing a certain amount of aggregate original-principal balance in the mortgages, he then has a right to sell that same amount in certificates. But the certificates he sells do not represent solely the mortgages he delivered, but a pro rata share of all that are in that pool.

By thus combining billions of dollars' worth of mortgages every month, these pools eliminate much of the special prepayment experience that otherwise occurs in particular small pools. There will still be a tendency for refinancing payoffs to occur when rates fall drastically, but that, and other influences on prepayment, will be spread over many pools and certificates, instead of being concentrated.

Ginnie Maes are being modified in other ways. GNMA now permits pools to have any maturity or mix of maturities, provided that proper disclosure is made to buyers. Some firms have issued pools with 15-year maturities, which are more attractive to both homebuyers and investors. Securities firms have formed mutual funds to invest in Ginnie Maes, and participations in these have sometimes been made available for initial amounts as low as $1,000. There are also Ginnie Mae pools of graduated-payment loans, and the securities based on these loans have the same graduated-payment features.

Louis C. Gasper

Government National Mortgage Association Investments

See UNIT INVESTMENT TRUSTS.

Government Securities Investments

See UNIT INVESTMENT TRUSTS.

Graduated-Payment Adjustable-Rate Mortgage (GPARM)

See HOME FINANCING, MORTGAGES.

Graduated-Payment Mortgage (GPM)

See HOME FINANCING, MORTGAGES.

Grandfathered Activities

Activities that are normally impermissible for companies subject to the Bank Holding Company Act, but that are nevertheless allowed for certain companies because of when the activities were begun.

Bank holding companies are generally prohibited from engaging in nonbank activities unless those activities have been determined by the Federal Reserve Board to be closely related to banking. Under the original Bank Holding Company Act of 1956, which applied to multibank holding companies, and the 1970 amendments, which extended the act to one-bank holding companies, companies with existing impermissible nonbank activities that had been started within a certain time period were generally given two years, in the case of the 1956 Act, or ten years, in the case of the 1970 amendments, to divest such activities. In other words, these companies were accorded two-year or ten-year "grandfather" privileges for these activities to minimize disruption of their business. However, bank holding companies that became covered by the act in 1970, and would also have been covered on June 30, 1968, if the 1970 amendments had been in effect then, were permitted to continue indefinitely any nonbank activities that they had conducted since June 30, 1968. These otherwise impermissible activities were thus indefinitely "grandfathered" and exempted from the prohibitions that generally apply under the act.

The Federal Reserve Board is authorized to terminate a company's grandfather rights if it determines that this is necessary to prevent undue concentration of resources, decreased or unfair competition, conflicts of interest, or unsound banking practices.

Griffith L. Garwood

Gross National Product (GNP)

Gross national product is the market value of the goods and services produced in a nation during a particular period (a quarter or a year). It is the broadest measure of economic activity and gives rise to statements such as "The U.S. economy grew by 2% in 1981," meaning that GNP, adjusted for inflation, expanded by 2% that year. GNP data are compiled quarterly and updated each month by the U.S. Department of Commerce and are the key items in a detailed array of data called the "national income and product accounts."

These data are calculated from the myriad of other economic information collected by the Commerce Department from its own sources, from other government sources, and from private sources. Monthly surveys of businesses—manufacturers, wholesalers, and retailers—conducted by the Census Bureau, the Labor Department's monthly labor market and price surveys, and IRS income-tax statistics are among the background data used in counting up GNP.

GNP describes the output of the economy valued at current market prices. In 1982 this total was $3,059,300,000,000, referred to as GNP in "nominal terms" or in "current dollars." It is also helpful to translate this into volume. This is done by dividing today's prices by those of a base period (currently, 1972 is used), making a price index. Then current-dollar GNP is divided by the price index, yielding GNP in "real terms" or in "1972 dollars." In 1982 the price index, known as the "implicit price deflator," was 207.15 (1972 = 100), making real GNP $1,476,900,000,000. The implicit price deflator is thus a broad measure of inflation, much broader than the CONSUMER PRICE INDEX (CPI), because it covers all sectors of the economy, not just consumers. Inflation by this measure averaged 7.6% a year from 1972 to 1982; CPI inflation was 8.7% annually.

The Components of GNP. GNP is most often thought of in terms of the amounts spent for goods and services by various groups in the economy. Table 1 shows this basic breakdown in both nominal and

Table 1
Gross National Product

| | 1982 ($ Billions) | | % of |
	Nominal	Real	Total*
Total GNP	3059.3	1476.9	100.0
Personal consumption expenditures	1971.1	956.9	63.3
Durable goods	242.7	138.8	9.6
Nondurable goods	762.1	365.0	24.2
Services	966.3	453.1	29.5
Gross private domestic investment	420.3	196.9	15.0
Nonresidential fixed investment	348.1	165.7	11.3
Producers' durable equipment	206.5	112.6	7.9
Structures	141.5	53.1	3.3
Residential structures	96.2	40.3	3.4
Inventory change	−23.8	−9.2	0.2
Net Exports	20.5	31.8	2.5
Exports	350.8	148.1	10.0
Less: imports	330.3	116.3	7.5
Government purchases	647.4	291.3	19.2
Federal	257.9	116.4	7.3
National defense	178.6	78.6	4.8
Nondefense	79.3	37.8	2.4
State and local governments	389.4	174.9	11.9

* In real terms, average 1978–82.
Source: U.S. Department of Commerce.

real terms for 1982 (the data are given in billions of dollars).

Consumer spending is by far the largest category. Consumers buy durable goods, which include automobiles, furniture, appliances, and other items that should last three years or more. Nondurable goods include shorter-lived items such as food, fuel, clothes, drugs, and cosmetics. Services consist of rent, utilities, medical care, travel, and other intangible items.

Businesses' spending is listed in the investment category. Businesses buy equipment and buildings. The full purchase value of these items is included in GNP, which is the reason it is called "gross" national product. As capital assets wear out or become obsolete, their value depreciates, offsetting at least partially the value of new investment. In an alternative national-product definition, the Commerce Department calculates depreciation, which is subtracted from GNP, yielding "net national product." (Depreciation is an important cost of doing business, and this subtraction will be used later to derive profit measures.) Two other technical, but significant points about the business-investment category. First, items purchased by businesses to use in production are not in GNP, which includes only the value of the final products when they are sold (including materials and supplies would be double-counting). An exception is those items and products held in inventory. The net addition to inventories in a particular period is part of GNP. Second, housing is part of investment. Homeowners are defined as businesses that invest in houses. (The rental value of houses is estimated by the Commerce Department and included among consumer expenditures on services.)

The net of sales to and purchases from foreigners is described by net exports, which include both merchandise trade and service items (foreign travel, freight, etc.).

Finally, for the government sector, it's important to remember that GNP contains only purchases of goods and services. Therefore, the federal-government category looks small compared with total federal outlays (which were about $760 billion in 1982). Defense outlays are mostly for goods and services, so they are close to the total budget amounts. But for nondefense programs, the program outlays themselves—Social Security benefits, for example—are not purchases, so they're not in GNP; the administrative expenses of running the program are, however.

Income: The Other Side of GNP. The revenues generated by the spending in GNP become the income of those people and firms producing GNP: Workers get wages, salaries, and fringe benefits; farmers and other businesses earn profits; landlords collect rent; and investors receive interest. To see the relative importance of these kinds of income, begin again with total GNP, subtract depreciation to get NNP, then take away sales and property taxes and some other small adjustments to arrive at national income, as shown in Table 2.

Definitions of these kinds of income are fairly straightforward except for profits (including proprietors' income). Profits in GNP are those generated out of current operations. Thus they exclude paper profits resulting from the effects of inflation on inventories, while an adjustment is included because, for tax purposes, companies use accelerated depreciation, which is greater than actual economic depreciation. For corporations, those adjustments are added back to reach what is called here "book profits," which, after income taxes, correspond to the earnings reported to stockholders by companies.

Table 2 shows that wages are about half of GNP, while after-tax profits have been just over 5% in the last five years. In comparison, net interest income is

Table 2
GNP and National Income

	1982 ($ Billions)	% of Total*
Total GNP	3059.3	100.0
Less: Depreciation	356.4	11.0
Net national product	2702.9	89.0
Less: Sales and property taxes	258.8	8.3
Other adjustments	6.8	0.2
National income	2437.3	80.5
Employee compensation	1856.5	60.4
Wages and salaries	1560.6	51.1
Supplements and fringes	295.8	9.3
Rental income of persons	34.1	1.2
Net interest	264.9	7.3
Proprietors' income	120.3	4.6
Farm	19.0	0.9
Nonfarm	101.3	3.7
Corporate profits	161.5	7.0
"Book profits"	175.6	8.6
Profits taxes	58.1	3.0
Profits after taxes	117.5	5.6
Dividends	70.3	2.2
Retained earnings	47.3	3.4

* Average, 1978–82.
Source: U.S. Department of Commerce.

more that 7% (and with 1982's high interest rates, it reached almost 9% of GNP in that single year).

What's Not in GNP. GNP is the broadest measure of economic activity, but it does not include every transaction that takes place. Some kinds of transactions are excluded because they don't represent new production, the very essence of gross national *product*. Thus, neither purely financial transactions nor trading in secondhand items are part of GNP. And capital gains also do not contribute.

There is some controversy over some other exclusions from GNP. Its definition contains the term *market value*. Thus, nonmarket activities are excluded even if they clearly have economic worth. The value of housework is a good example: If someone is hired to do it, it can be included; but if a member of the household performs it, there is no addition to GNP. Hobbies similarly are excluded, even though the resulting homemade articles may have value. Finally, another key ingredient for inclusion in GNP is public knowledge of transactions. Therefore, informal barter arrangements, or transactions involving money but done in secret—perhaps to avoid taxes—are omitted from GNP. This ignorance of the so-called under-

Table 3
GNP Around the World

	U.S. Dollar Value in 1981 ($ Billions)	Real Growth (%)		
		Average 1960–73	Average 1974–81	1982*
Total	11,725	5.2	2.9	0.2
Developed countries	7,020	5.1	2.7	−0.5
United States	2,926	4.1	2.7	−1.8
Canada	280	5.6	2.6	−5.0
Japan	1,150	10.4	4.4	2.5
European community	2,420	4.7	1.9	0.3
France	577	5.8	2.5	1.5
West Germany	687	4.7	2.2	−1.3
Italy	299	5.2	2.1	0.8
United Kingdom	502	3.1	0.9	0.5
Other developed countries	245	5.1	1.9	n.a.
Developing countries	1,965	5.8	4.4	0.8
Oil-exporting countries	540	—	3.7	1.2
Others	1,425	—	4.6	0.7
Communist countries	2,740	5.2	2.7	1.4
USSR	1,587	5.2	2.3	1.6
Eastern Europe	671	4.1	1.8	−0.7
China	328	6.5	5.9	5.0

*Preliminary; n.a. = not available.

Note: All categories include countries not shown separately.

Source: U.S. Council of Economic Advisers.

ground economy may mean GNP understates economic activity.

On the other hand, failure to account for some items may mean GNP overstates activity, especially if it is taken to be equivalent to economic welfare. GNP data do not separately indicate pollution or urban congestion or other discomforts of modern life, so their negative value cannot be eliminated. These flaws, however, detract only a little from the widespread acceptance of GNP as the best measure of the overall economic well-being of a country.

Economic Growth in the U.S. and Abroad. In 1981, GNP for all the world's economies totaled $11.7 trillion, according to the U.S. Council of Economic Advisers (CEA). Table 3 contains the CEA's data for the major areas of the world. U.S. GNP was about 25% of the world total and about of the same magnitude as the totals for all of Western Europe and for the Communist countries.

Growth rates for real GNP for several periods since 1960 are also shown in this table. They show a widespread slowdown in economic growth since 1974, related to the energy crises and inflation that have plagued those years. According to these data, total world GNP has expanded just over half as much on average in these later years as from 1960 through 1973. The slowdown has been greatest in Europe, where growth has been reduced by 60%. The U.S. has fared somewhat better, with a 35% reduction. Developing countries had experienced only a modest slowing, but the more recent economic contraction, shown in the table by an outright decline in GNP in 1982 for the developed countries, may lead to a dramatic slowing for the developing countries in the near future.

The Uses of GNP. These GNP data and comparisons, both across countries and in different time periods, have several uses. They show the pace and pattern of economic activity. Divided by population size, they show relative standards of living. The combined spending and income accounts can be used to trace the effects of a change in one sector, such as an increase in defense spending or a decline in consumer demand for cars, through the economy. The shifting mix of GNP spending and income components allows analysis of the changing structure of the economy. Planners and policymakers can use all these tools—and especially their interactive nature—to design strategies for increasing growth or meeting other goals to improve living standards at the macroeconomic level, or to increase the profitability of an individual company by knowing how changes in its level of sales relate to changes in income and in spending in the overall economy.

Carol A. Stone

Group Term Life Insurance

See LIFE INSURANCE.

Growing-Equity Mortgage

See HOME FINANCING, MORTGAGES.

Guaranteed Renewable, Health or Disability Insurance

A health- or disability-insurance policy guaranteed to provide coverage up to a certain age (or as long as the insured is working, in the case of disability coverage) providing the premiums are paid; the insurer cannot raise the premiums to one consumer unless it raises the premiums for all other insured persons in a particular class, such as everyone in a certain state who has the same kind of policy. Some health policies are guaranteed renewable for life.

Renewable at Company Option. This means that the insurance company reserves the right to stop providing coverage for an individual. However, benefits cannot be cut off in the midst of an illness or disability.

See DISABILITY INCOME INSURANCE; HEALTH INSURANCE.

James L. Moorefield

Guaranteed Stock

See PREFERRED STOCK.

·H·

Health Insurance

A type of insurance that reimburses individuals or families for health-care costs or provides replacement income when a person is unable to work due to illness or injury. It can be provided to groups, such as employee groups as a job benefit, or it can be individually purchased by individuals and families. At the end of 1981, more than 186 million Americans—some 85% of the civilian noninstitutional population—were protected by one or more forms of private health insurance. This included nearly 172 million persons under 65—nearly nine out of ten persons in this age group. More than 14 million persons—six out of ten of the 65-and-older population—held private health insurance to supplement MEDICARE (*see* MEDIGAP).

Private health-insurance coverage is made available in various forms by several types of insurers. These include insurance companies, hospital and medical service plans like BLUE CROSS AND BLUE SHIELD, group medical plans operating on a prepayment basis such as HEALTH-MAINTENANCE ORGANIZATIONS (HMO's), and others.

Health insurance offered by the nation's 1,000 commercial health-insurance companies can be divided into two basic categories: medical-expense insurance and DISABILITY INCOME INSURANCE. Medical-expense insurance is a "reimbursement" type of coverage providing broad benefits that can cover virtually all kinds of expenses connected with hospital and medical care and related services. Disability insurance provides periodic payments to replace income lost when the insured is unable to work due to illness or injury.

Basic Protection. In general, coverages for the costs of hospital care and surgery and physicians' services are called "basic protection."

Hospital-expense insurance generally provides specific benefits for daily hospital room and board and usual hospital services and supplies during confinement. The maximum benefit for miscellaneous expenses is frequently a specified dollar amount, which may be expressed as a multiple of the daily room-and-board benefit.

Room-and-board benefits are usually stated in one of two ways. One is reimbursement for the actual room-and-board charge up to a specified maximum amount per day for hospital confinement. The other provides a service-type benefit (e.g., Blue Cross/Blue Shield) that equals the semiprivate-room-and-board charge of the hospital. Persons covered for hospital expense by insurance companies include those who have only HOSPITAL INCOME INSURANCE. This type of coverage, issued to individuals and not groups, provides a stipulated daily cash payment during hospitalization. At year-end 1981, 186 million persons were covered by hospital-expense insurance.

Generally, hospital-expense insurance is sold in combination with *surgical-expense insurance* so as to provide benefits for surgical operations and for inpatient doctors' visits. In such cases, the policy is called a "hospital- and surgical-expense policy" or "hospital-surgical coverage." Surgical-expense coverage provides benefits for the cost of surgical procedures performed as a result of an accident or sickness. Payment for administration of an anesthetic for a covered surgical procedure is often included. Benefits under this form of insurance might be paid according to a schedule of surgical procedures, with the policy listing the maximum benefit for each type of operation covered. But an increasing number of insurance plans now offer surgical benefits for the physician's fee up to the "reasonable and customary" charge in the region for the procedure performed. In this case, no surgical schedules are included in the policy. At the end of 1981, over 175 million persons had protection against the costs of surgery.

Physician's-expense insurance provides benefits to help pay a physician's fees for nonsurgical care in a hospital, home, or doctor's office. There are usually maximum benefits for specific services that sometimes include diagnostic X-ray and laboratory expenses. Nearly 167 million Americans have this type of coverage.

Major Medical Protection. Major-medical-expense insurance provides broad and substantial protection for large and unpredictable medical costs. It covers a wide range of medical charges with few internal limits on hospital-room rates or specific medical procedures and a high overall MAXIMUM BENEFIT. There are two typical types of major medical plans: One supplements the *basic protection* insurance program; the other provides comprehensive protection by integrating basic-protection coverage and extended health-care benefits. Typically, major-medical policies provide coverage for hospital care; physicians' treatment and specialists' consultation and care in hospital, home, or doctor's office; prescription drugs; private-duty nursing; medical-care services in the home; psychiatric care; diagnostic X-ray and laboratory procedures; therapeutic X-ray and radium therapy; physiotherapy; anesthesia; prosthetic devices; and rehabilitation services.

To help assure wise and appropriate use of health-care services, major-medical policies include both deductible and coinsurance provisions. The deductible is the amount the insured person must pay each year before the benefits begin. A typical group-plan deductible is $100 to $200, meaning benefits begin after the insured person has paid the first $100 or $200 in medical costs incurred that year. Family coverage usually has a somewhat higher deductible. The coinsurance (or copayment) provision defines the percentage of the covered expenses to be paid by the insurance company after the deductible. The typical coinsurance factor is 80-20 (the insurance company pays 80% of the covered benefits; the insured person pays 20%), although coverage for mental-health benefits, such as outpatient psychiatric care or alcohol- and drug-abuse treatment, often is less extensive. A typical copayment for mental-health care is 50-50.

A relatively new approach further limits the insured person's share of the total cost by providing a "stop-loss" feature. This specifies that after the insured person's own (out-of-pocket) costs have reached a stated annual amount (often $1,500), the insurance company will pay 100% of all further COVERED MEDICAL EXPENSES. Typical major-medical policies provide a maximum benefit that ranges from $50,000 to $1 million or, in many cases, no limit. The number of people with private major-medical coverage totals 155 million—three out of four persons under age 65.

Two Types of Coverage: Group and Individual. Most people with health insurance are covered by *group insurance,* typically provided through their employer or union and considered a basic "job benefit." To the insured person, group health insurance has the following advantages over *individual insurance:*

• It is economical because many people can be insured under a single contract, with savings in sales, administrative, and claims costs.

• The group-contract holder—the employer, union, or association—usually pays a part or all of the premium.

• The health of the insured person is generally not a factor in eligibility; the insurance company is concerned with evaluating the overall health status of the group, not the individual, in determining costs and eligibility. However, for very small groups (perhaps ten or less employees), some individual selection factors may be used.

• The individual's coverage cannot be canceled, unless he or she leaves the job (or other insured group) or the group plan itself is terminated.

In addition to employee and union groups, group coverage is also available through professional, fraternal, and other associations, and welfare or employee benefit groups.

Most commonly, the policyholder (employer, union, or association) and the insurance company jointly administer the group plan. For example, the employer's personnel office may receive and process claims for employee health-insurance benefits. This helps keep down costs to the insurance company and thus reduce premium costs, whether paid by employer or employee, or shared. A government study published in 1981 shows that in firms with employee health-benefit plans, the average share of the total annual premium paid by the employer was 80.4%.

Individual and family policies are designed to accommodate two fundamental needs. First, they offer protection for people not employed in a group and for those whose employers do not provide group coverage, or for those unable to obtain group coverage through association or other membership. In addition, these policies can provide supplementary coverage when the health-insurance needs of an individual (and family) are not fully met under a group plan. These policies can be fitted to individual requirements because they offer a wide range of coverages and benefits at varying premium levels.

Individual plans differ from group plans in several important ways. Under group insurance, the level of benefits is fixed by the terms of the plan. Under an individual policy, the applicant selects the policy desired, and each person or family is enrolled separately. Age, health status of the insured, and other factors are considered in determining coverage and premiums (cost of coverage).

Supplementing Group Insurance. Group health plans vary widely from group to group, and members of group plans often have no idea of the extent to which they are protected. Instead of waiting until they or someone in their family suffers a major illness or accident, employees and others relying on group health coverage should ask some simple questions to determine the extent of their coverage. An employer's personnel department is a good place to ask these questions; often an explanatory booklet on health benefits is provided.

Some questions to ask about the comprehensiveness of group coverage:

• What hospital and medical services does the group policy cover? Does it cover related hospital expenses, such as X-ray service? Does it cover doctors' services outside the hospital?
• What are the deductible and coinsurance amounts?
• What members of the family are covered?
• What are the maximum benefit limits in terms of dollar amount and length of time?
• What is the waiting period (the length of time from date of employment until coverage becomes effective)?
• Are there any exclusions (i.e., specific conditions or circumstances listed in the policy for which the policy will not provide payments)?
• What provisions have been made against loss of income when the insured is unable to work due to illness or injury (i.e., disability income insurance)?
• How do these benefits compare with the level of health-care costs in the local area?

A careful review of existing health-insurance coverage—before actual need arises—will help indentify gaps in protection and provide an opportunity to fill those gaps with supplemental individual coverage. The indication that group coverage needs supplementing would be its failure to provide benefits for the major portion of potential medical-care bills—mainly hospital, doctors', and surgical charges. If, for example, an employee's group policy will pay only about half of the current hospital-room rate in the area, the employee should consider looking for an individual health policy covering most of the difference. Also, if the group plan will cover only a minor portion of the going rate for surgical procedures in the area, supplemental individual coverage should be considered. Or, if the group policy's maximum major-medical benefit is only $100,000, consideration should be given to buying supplemental coverage to increase that maximum to at least $250,000. "Piggyback" policies can be purchased that pick up when group benefits stop because of a limited maximum.

In shopping for an individual health policy, price (premium cost) should be an important factor, but not the only factor. Policies with different companies are not identical, and this variation affects costs. Even similar policies from different companies may vary in cost, depending on the exact extent of benefits and the companies' past claims experience. Savings can be realized by selecting policies that feature higher deduct-

ibles; the higher the deductible on a major policy, the lower the premium. Generally, an individual insurance contract goes into effect only after an application has been completed, signed by the applicant, and accepted by the insurance company.

Some Tips on Health Coverage. People who pay premiums directly, on individual coverage, should try to arrange to make the payments annually, rather than quarterly or monthly. It is less expensive.

Policies should be delivered within 30 days of application. If not, the applicant should contact the insurance company to find out—in writing—why. If requested, an insurer must tell an applicant why coverage was denied.

A "free look" provision allows consumers ten days after delivery of a policy to look it over and obtain a refund, if they so decide.

Carrying duplicate coverage is wasteful and expensive. Also, most group policies now contain a "coordination of benefits" clause limiting total benefits to 100% of charges. For example, if husband and wife both have insurance through separate job plans, the total benefits paid by both insurers for the family's hospital and doctors' bills cannot exceed the actual bills.

Most mail-order health-insurance policies should be considered supplements to basic protection—not primary insurance. Many mail-order policies are hospital income insurance, providing daily cash payments while the insured is hospitalized. Find out how many days the insured must be in the hospital before these payments start.

Cancer insurance and other "dread disease" coverage are limited types of insurance, paying only for costs connected to one disease. They are *not* substitutes for comprehensive protection. Before even considering this type of coverage, consumers should be sure they have a policy that protects against all kinds of illnesses and accidents.

Individual insurance policies should be kept up-to-date. Some adjust better to inflation than others. Benefit levels should be reviewed annually.

To resolve further questions about group insurance, ask the employer, union, or association providing the coverage. For questions about individual coverage, ask the insurance agent or contact the company directly. To lodge complaints, contact the state insurance department or insurance commissioner, listed in the phone directory under the name of the state. Many insurance commissioners have free WATS long-distance telephone lines for resolving consumer complaints.

Filing for Benefits. The first step in filing for health-insurance benefits, whether under an individual or a group policy, is to notify the insurance company that an expense has been incurred. This notice should be given within 20 days after the first doctor's visit or other claim basis, or as soon as reasonably possible. In turn, claim forms must be supplied by the insurer within 15 days of the notice. The forms seek, first, basic facts such as the identity of the patient, whether the policy is in force, whether the loss is covered, and what restrictions may apply. Second, the forms request necessary medical information. Standardized forms for hospital, surgical, and medical expenses have been developed to speed payment of claims. Hospital-expense forms, completed by the hospital, itemize room-and-board charges and specific other charges, such as lab fees. An attending physician's statement is required, describing the diagnosis, nature and dates of treatment, and charges incurred. In many group policies, claims are received by the employer's personnel department.

Under individual policies, information is needed to determine whether a PREEXISTING CONDITION is involved, which might not be covered by the policy. This is not required under a group plan, where preexisting conditions are not a disqualifying factor. The claim forms also may provide for assignment of benefits directly to the hospital or physician. The forms state that the individual is responsible for charges not covered under the policy.

Benefits Meeting Special Needs. The objective of health insurance is to provide financial protection against sickness and injury for as many people as possible. To accomplish this, it is necessary to classify the insured person by degree of *risk* so that no one is asked to pay a premium that is not reasonably related to the risk being insured. As is true with all forms of insurance, health insurance deals in averages. Therefore, the person to be insured under an individual health policy must meet certain average health standards—he or she must be an "average" risk to be charged the normal or standard premium. That is why a physical examination is often required in applying for individual health coverage.

Many people who are not average risks—because of poor health history, existing illness, or chronic health problems—may still be insured under certain circumstances. The insuring of people with existing health problems may be handled in several ways:

- Payment of benefits for the condition named may be excluded entirely, so that the insurance covers all other conditions and is issued at a standard rate.
- The policy may be amended to provide a longer waiting period at a standard premium. In this event, regular policy benefits would be payable.
- The premium may be increased to compensate for

the greater degree to risk, with regular benefits payable.

Dental-expense insurance is a relatively new type of coverage that helps pay for normal dental care as well as damage caused by accidents. The fastest-growing form of health insurance, it is generally available today through insurance companies, prepayment plans, or plans sponsored by state dental associations. Under these programs, virtually all forms of dental care are covered. Following the pattern of major-medical coverages, there is frequently a deductible amount and a 20–50% coinsurance payment share assumed by the individual. There may be a maximum benefit, and a common feature of some plans is a schedule of benefits for specified dental procedures.

Some group health plans now are also providing benefits for *eye care.*

Coverage for People out of Work. Since most people's health insurance is provided as a job-related benefit, that protection will terminate if an employee loses a job, either by being laid off or by resigning. An employee who is leaving a job should determine how long, if at all, health benefits will continue. Some plans provide coverage for 30 days after termination.

Second, before leaving the payroll, the employee should determine whether he or she has a *conversion privilege.* This provision allows a departing employee to convert group coverage to individual coverage provided by the same insurance company. When converting to individual coverage, the benefits will most likely be reduced, and the insured ex-worker will now have to pay the full premium, since no employer is involved. The advantage of conversion, however, is that coverage cannot be denied, regardless of the health condition of the insured, and no medical exam is required.

There is a deadline for applying for conversion and the employee should determine how soon after termination such an application must be made. Many group insurance plans also offer the conversion privilege to a divorced person who had been dependent upon the former spouse's group plan for health coverage. Again, there is a deadline for applying for the conversion, but coverage cannot be denied due to poor health.

James L. Moorefield

Health-Maintenance Organizations (HMO's)

Organizations that provide a wide range of comprehensive health-care services, physicians, and facilities for a specified group at a fixed annual or monthly payment payable in advance. Sometimes called "prepaid health care," health-maintenance organizations operate on the principle that emphasis on preventive health procedures can save money by keeping people healthier. HMO's can be sponsored by the government, medical schools, hospitals, employers, labor unions, consumer groups, insurance companies, and hospital-medical plans. Some HMO's accept MEDICARE enrollees.

James L. Moorefield

Hedging (Commodities)

See COMMODITY-FUTURES EXCHANGE.

Home Financing, Mortgages

Few home buyers have the resources to purchase a home outright. Most finance their homes with mortgages, a type of loan that pledges the home to the lender (mortgagee) should the borrower (mortgagor) fail to make payments on time. With some exceptions, a down payment of at least 5% is required to assure that the borrower has a stake in repaying the loan.

A homeowner may have more than one mortgage on a single property. Often, after a part of the first mortgage has been repaid, a homeowner will borrow against the equity in the home to finance renovations, a child's education, or a business venture.

The second loan is called, not suprisingly, a "second mortgage." Generally, the first and second mortgage together may not exceed a certain percentage of the home's value. In the event of foreclosure, or transfer of title (i.e., sale of the property), the first mortgage takes precedence over the second and must be repaid before any funds may be assigned to the second.

If a home buyer is assuming a mortgage from a previous owner, or using a loan program with maximum loan limits, a second mortgage may be used to cover the gap between the sales price and the first mortgage and down payment.

Sources of Mortgage Loans. Following are all possible sources of mortgage loans.

Thrift institutions. These include savings and loan associations, building and loan associations, and mutual savings banks. Thrifts are the predominant source of mortgage money.

Mortgage bankers. Listed under "Mortgage Lending" in the Yellow Pages, these institutions are not really banks but originate mortgage loans for resale to investors. Traditionally, mortgage bankers have specialized in FHA/VA loans, but most now offer a full range of mortgage programs.

Banks. Although not generally associated with mortgage lending, many banks are becoming increasingly active in this field.

Credit unions. Some of the larger credit unions also offer mortgage loans to their members.

Housing-finance agencies. Many state and local governments provide below-market mortgage money through their housing-finance agencies. The money for mortgages is usually raised through the sale of tax-exempt bonds. Since investors do not pay federal income taxes on the income received from the bonds, they will accept a lower return than they would on a taxable investment; and this in turn enables the housing-finance agency to make mortgage money available at a lower rate. Because these loans are targeted to low- and moderate-income buyers, there will be a limit on both the buyer's household income and the value of the home.*

Builders. Home builders often make financing arrangements for prospective buyers. Often the builder will have a commitment from a lender to provide a certain type of financing. The buyer is not obligated to accept the builder's financing package, but the buyer may find that other concessions—such as the builder's payment of closing costs—are included in the package.

Home seller. The owner of an existing home may be interested in providing financing for the purchaser. Seller financing can be very attractive, but there are many intricacies involved with this type of financing. Both the buyer and the seller should have a competent real-estate lawyer or financial expert examine the contract and loan agreement before signing.

Types of Mortgage Loans. Most mortgage loans fall into one of three main categories: those insured by the FEDERAL HOUSING ADMINISTRATION (FHA); those guaranteed by the VETERANS ADMINISTRATION (VA), and conventional loans—that is, those involving no government backing.

FHA insurance was established in 1934 to make low-down-payment loans acceptable to lenders who had been accustomed to 40–50% down payments. The FHA assured the lender that he will be compensated for his losses should the buyer fail to make monthly payments. The most widely used program is FHA Section 203(b). Legislation was recently passed that would allow a down payment of 3% on homes up to $50,000. Regulations implementing this change were expected in mid-1984. Homes above $50,000 require a down payment of 3% on the first $25,000 of the home's value and 5% on the remainder.

Until recently, the FHA rate was set by the FHA commissioner. Now the interest rate is subject to agreement between the lender and the borrower. The interest rate sometimes lags behind the rates required

---

* Legislative authority for these bonds expired on December 31, 1983. As of early 1984, legislation was pending that would reinstate this authority.

by the investors who ultimately buy these loans, so additional discount points may be required to make up the difference. A point is equal to 1% of the loan amount. For an interest rate that is one percentage point below market, approximately six discount points will be required. Points may be paid by the buyer or seller.

FHA loans are subject to a maximum limit that varies according to the location of the property and ranges from a base of $67,500 to a high of $90,000 in certain high-cost areas. The limit for Alaska and Hawaii is $135,000. FHA loans may be assumed by subsequent buyers.

The VA loan-guarantee program, established at the end of World War II, works somewhat differently. The VA guarantees 60% of the loan, or $27,500, whichever is lower, for veterans with full eligibility and the ability to repay. No-down-payment loans are available, but for practical purposes VA loans may not exceed $135,000 if they are to be sold to investors through the secondary market.

Eligible borrowers include veterans who served in the armed forces on active duty for at least 90 days during specified periods of war or 181 days during peacetime. Also included are the unmarried surviving spouses of those killed in action, or of those who died from a service-related disability, or of those listed as missing-in-action.

To use this program, borrowers must obtain a "certificate of eligibility" from the VA. The back of this certificate will state the amount of the guarantee the veteran is entitled to. The veteran may use the entitlement more than once, because it is restored when a loan is repaid.

VA loans may be assumed by subsequent buyers. If the buyer is a veteran who substitutes his or her own entitlement, the seller will have full benefits restored. If the buyer is not a veteran, the seller may still have partial entitlement, if the full entitlement was not used for the purchase of the first home or if benefits were increased in the meantime.

The interest rate is set by the Veterans Administration and traditionally tracks the FHA rate. Just as with FHA loans, points may be required if the VA interest rate does not match the market rate.

The Farmers Home Administration (FmHA) offers a direct loan program for low- and moderate-income households in rural areas with populations below 20,000. Homes must be modest in size, design, and cost. The FmHA sets income limits based on median incomes for the area. Moderate-income families pay a market rate. Interest-rate subsidies may be available for low-income buyers.

Conventional loans are those that involve no government guarantee or insurance. These loans once required a 20% down payment. However, with private mortgage insurance developed in the late 1950s, down payments as low as 5% or 10% are possible.

Qualifying for a Mortgage Loan. In determining whether a borrower qualifies for a mortgage loan, a lender will consider the borrower's credit history and income as well as the borrower's additional monthly obligation (car payments, child support, etc.). For conventional loans sold to investors, monthly payments for principal, interest, taxes, and insurance usually cannot exceed 28% of the borrower's gross monthly income. These monthly housing payments plus other debts with a remaining term of 11 months or more cannot exceed 36% of gross monthly income.

FHA underwriting guidelines are traditionally more liberal. Monthly housing payments may not exceed 38% of the borrower's net monthly income. It is important to know, however, that the FHA subtracts federal income taxes from the borrower's income and includes monthly utilities in calculating housing expenses. Moreover, all monthly obligations with a remaining term of seven months or more are included in the 53% limit on housing expenses and other debts.

The VA calculates the borrower's ability to pay on a case-by-case basis.

Underwriting guidelines leave room for interpretation. Many lenders will consider more liberal or conservative requirements if personal circumstances warrant.

Table 1 gives a ballpark estimate of the mortgage a typical home buyer could afford at different interest rates. The figures are based on principal and interest equaling 25% of gross income. They do not include taxes, insurance, and condominium or homeowners association fees, which vary from area to area. All of these expenses are included in the 28% limit for conventional loans. These expenses plus utilities are included in the 38% limit for FHA loans. Buyers in high-cost areas may require slightly higher incomes than those shown in this table.

Buyers who find that their incomes fall short of the amounts listed here may find that they will qualify under one of the alternative mortgage options listed later in this section. This is because underwriting is based on initial monthly payments. Several mortgage types allow for lower monthly payments in the early years of the loan.

Table 2 shows the monthly payments for principal and interest on loans of $30,000 to $100,000 at various interest rates. The table does not include property taxes, insurance, and condominium fees. However, a sales agent or a loan officer should be able to assist the buyer in determining the total monthly payment required.

Mortgage Instruments. There are many kinds of

Table 1
Estimate the Mortgage You Can Afford

Interest Rate	Annual Income						
	$20,000	$25,000	$30,000	$35,000	$40,000	$45,000	$50,000
10%	47,480	59,349	71,219	83,089	94,959	106,829	118,699
11%	43,753	54,691	65,629	76,567	87,505	98,443	109,382
12%	40,503	50,635	60,761	70,888	81,015	91,142	101,269
13%	37,667	47,083	56,500	65,916	75,333	84,750	94,166
14%	35,166	43,957	52,748	61,540	70,331	79,122	87,914
15%	32,953	41,191	49,429	57,667	65,905	74,143	82,381
16%	30,985	38,731	46,477	54,223	61,969	69,715	77,461

Example: If your income is $35,000 and the interest rate is 14%, you could qualify for a $61,540 mortgage.
Source: NAHB

Table 2
Monthly Mortgage Payments

Mortgage Amounts	Interest Rates				
	10%	11%	12%	13%	14%
$ 30,000	$263	$286	$ 308	$ 331	$ 355
35,000	307	333	360	387	414
40,000	351	381	411	442	474
45,000	395	429	462	497	533
50,000	439	476	514	553	592
55,000	483	524	565	608	651
60,000	527	571	617	663	711
65,000	570	619	668	718	770
70,000	614	667	720	774	829
75,000	658	714	771	829	888
80,000	702	762	822	884	948
85,000	746	809	874	940	1,007
90,000	790	857	925	995	1,066
95,000	834	905	977	1,050	1,125
100,000	878	952	1,028	1,106	1,185

Based on 30-year, fixed-rate mortgage.

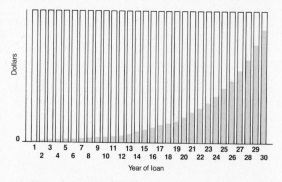

Figure 1. Level payment mortgage—fixed interest rate. (Dark area = principal; light area = interest.) (*Source:* Home Mortgage Access Corporation.)

mortgages available. Following is a description of each.

Fixed-Rate, Fixed-Payment Mortgage. Generations of Americans are familiar with the long-term, fixed-rate mortgage. Traditionally these loans have run for 25 or 30 years, with the interest rate and basic monthly payment remaining the same for the life of the loan. As shown in Figure 1, interest accounts for the lion's share of monthly payments during the early years of the loan, with contributions to principal increasing gradually. All of the interest paid on a mortgage is tax-deductible.

15-Year, Fixed-Rate Mortgage. Many of today's home buyers are too young to remember, but the 30-year mortgage is a relatively recent development, phased in over three decades spanning the 1930s through the 1950s. In the days when mortgages typically ran for 15 or 20 years and mortgage interest rates were 4–5%, the housing industry pushed for longer loan maturities to help more buyers qualify for loans. But as interest rates rise, the advantage of stretching out payments diminishes. The difference between monthly payments of principal and interest on a 30-year and a 15-year $50,000 mortgage drops from $110.95 at an 8% rate to $73.43 at a 14% rate (see Table 3).

With a 15-year loan, the monthly payment is higher, and a larger percentage is applied to the principal. Therefore, the homeowner accumulates equity in the home more rapidly and total interest payments over the life of the loan are much lower (see Figure 2). It is necessary for the buyer to keep in mind, however,

Table 3 Monthly Payment Comparison, $50,000 Loan				
Term	8%	10%	12%	14%
30-year	$366.88	$438.79	$514.31	$592.44
15-year	477.83	537.30	600.08	665.87
Diff.	110.95	98.51	85.77	73.43

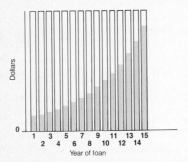

Figure 2. 15-year, fixed-rate mortgage. (Dark area = principal; light area = interest.) (*Source:* Home Mortgage Access Corporation.)

that because less interest is paid, tax deductions will also be lower.

Adjustable-Rate Mortgage (ARM). Also called a variable-rate mortgage (VRM), a renegotiated-rate mortgage (RRM), or an adjustable mortgage loan (AML), an ARM is usually a 30-year loan with an interest rate that rises or falls at regular intervals along with changes in a specific index used to measure the cost of money. The most commonly used indexes are those that track Treasury securities.

The ARM became common during the last bout of high interest rates when lenders suffered heavy losses on large holdings of fixed-rate mortgages that carried interest rates far below the rates they needed to pay consumers in order to attract deposits. Losses were so severe during this period that many thrifts were forced to merge with healthier institutions. The ARM was intended to shift most of the interest-rate risk inherent in long-term lending from the lender to the borrower.

The interest rate on an ARM may be adjusted at intervals ranging anywhere from six months to five years.

Because these loans involve less interest-rate risk for the lender, they may carry a lower interest rate than the 30-year, fixed-rate loan. Which type of loan is the more desirable depends on the buyer's circumstances. A buyer on a fixed income might be willing to

accept a higher interest rate in exchange for the certainty of fixed monthly payments, while a buyer with a solid financial foundation or someone who moves every few years might be willing to take a chance on higher interest rates in the future in exchange for lower rates now.

For buyers at the upper end of the market—those who will need a loan that exceeds $108,300—an adjustable-rate mortgage may be easier to obtain. This is because lenders find it more difficult to sell these larger loans and must, therefore, hold them in their portfolios.

Graduated-Payment Mortgage (GPM). A GPM is a fixed-interest-rate mortgage that allows buyers to qualify for a mortgage with a lower income by providing lower monthly payments in the early years of the loan. The lower payments are possible because a part of the interest is deferred until later years. GPM's are usually 30-year loans.

The most popular plan calls for monthly payments to increase at a rate of 7.5% each year for the first five years. Thereafter, payments remain fixed for the life of the loan. Both the FHA and the VA offer graduated-payment plans.

Because GPM's involve deferred interest, the buyer will ultimately pay more for the loan, but the lower initial payments allow many young buyers to purchase homes earlier than they could otherwise. These loans usually carry a slightly higher interest rate than the fixed-rate mortgage.

Graduated-Payment Adjustable-Rate Mortgage (GPARM). The GPARM is a hybrid combining the features of the graduated-payment mortgage and the adjustable-rate mortgage. As with the GPM, payments start out at a lower level and increase gradually for a number of years. The difference is that the interest rate will be adjusted periodically, usually every three or five years. With most GPARM plans, it is only with the last step of the graduated payments that the buyer is faced with an adjustment in the interest rate. In some cases, the buyer has the option of extending the graduated payments for one more period should the last step of the graduated payments coincide with an increase in the interest rate. These loans may involve a slightly higher interest rate than an ARM because they are viewed as involving greater risk to the lender.

Buydowns. Monthly payments may also be reduced by the use of a buydown—an up-front payment of part of the interest on the loan. This payment may be made by the builder or seller of the home, by the buyer, or by a parent or employer. A permanent buydown will result in lower monthly payments for the life of the loan, while a temporary buydown usually applies to the first one to five years of the loan. One of the most common buydown plans reduces the monthly payments by three percentage points the first year, two points the second year, and one point the third.

Land Leases. Another method used to make homeownership more affordable in the early years of the loan is to buy the home and lease the lot it is sitting on. At present this type of financing in available in only a few areas of the country. Land leases usually require a lower down payment since only the home and not the land is financed. Generally the land lease runs for a longer term than the mortgage, and in most cases the homeowner will have the option of buying the land after a certain initial period. One point to remember: Since the rental payment involves no interest, it is not tax-deductible.

Balloon Mortgage. This is a short- or intermediate-term loan that is called due after a number of years— usually three, five, ten, or fifteen. Monthly payments are usually based on a 25-to-30 year AMORTIZATION schedule, with most of the payment going to interest. The unpaid principal balance of the loan is due in one lump sum at the end of the specified period, hence the term *balloon.*

Growing-Equity Mortgage.* A growing-equity loan requires regular increases in monthly payments, usually on the order of 3–5% per year. But the interest rate is fixed, and all increases in monthly payments go toward reducing the principal balance of the loan. Increase may occur for a specified number of years or for the life of the loan. As a result, the growing-equity loan is paid off much earlier, usually sometime between the twelfth and nineteenth years. Qualifying income may be slightly lower than for a 15-year mortgage, and initial tax deductions somewhat greater, because the initial monthly payment is based on a 25-to-30-year amortization schedule.

Shared-Appreciation Mortgage (SAM). With a shared-appreciation mortgage, the lender usually gives the borrower a lower interest rate in the early years of the loan in return for a share in the appreciation of the home, payable either at the time the home is sold or at a specified time five to ten years into the loan, whichever comes first. These loans have met with only limited lender acceptance.

Shared-Equity Mortgage (SEM). The shared-equity mortgage brings together an investor with a buyer who cannot quite afford to purchase a home on his or her own. The investor may provide part or all of the down payment, or a portion of the monthly payments, or both. There are a variety of different plans, but generally the investor receives a proportionate share in the equity of the property, including any ap-

preciation. Usually the agreement runs for three to five years. Theoretically, by that time either the home buyer will be able to buy out the investor's share, or the buyer's share of the proceeds from the sale of the home will be sufficient for a down payment on a new home.

If the owner/occupant pays a fair-market rent on the investor's share of the property, the investor may be entitled to a tax deduction for depreciation. Both are eligible for tax deductions for any interest they pay. One drawback of an SEM is that each partner is to some extent dependent on the other. However, SEM's can provide a good method for relatives to assist each other in buying a home. All parties should seek expert legal and tax counsel before entering into an equity-sharing arrangement.

Take-back. This is a loan provided by the seller. It may be used in many different ways. The seller may be looking at the investment value of a mortgage and offer to lend the buyer the entire amount needed to finance the home. When interest rates are high, many sellers will take this route, often accepting below-market interest rates to facilitate a quick sale. Many seller take-backs are balloon loans, with monthly payments based on a 25- or 30-year amortization schedule and the balance due after a few years. A seller who has an assumable loan may be willing to take back a loan to cover the difference between the principal balance on the original loan and the purchaser's down payment. If a lender is involved in any part of the financing, some down payment will be required. With any seller financing, an expert in real-estate law should be consulted.

Wraparound (Wrap). If a home carries an assumable mortgage that is insufficient to finance a sale without a very large down payment, a buyer may be able to arrange a wraparound mortgage. A wraparound packages the original loan with a new one, and the buyer makes one monthly payment for the total financing package to the lender who originated the new loan. For instance, if the home is worth $100,000 and the principal remaining on the old loan is $50,000, the buyer may be able to assume the loan and arrange a new loan to cover a portion of the remaining $50,000. Some downpayment will be required. For practical purposes, the interest rate on the wraparound loan would be a blend between the rate on the assumed loan and the current market rate.

Reverse-Annuity Mortgage (RAM). A RAM is a loan that permits older homeowners to draw on the equity in their homes during their retirement years. Instead of receiving the loan in one lump sum, the borrower receives monthly payments over a period of several years. At the end of this period, the borrower begins to repay the loan based on a 30-year amortiza-

---

*These loans are not referred to here by their obvious acronym, GEM, because GEM is a service mark owned by GEM Savings in Dayton, Ohio.

tion schedule. The loan must be repaid if the home is sold or the owner dies. Lenders have been reluctant to offer these loans, largely because of the uncertainty surrounding a borrower's ability to repay the loan in later years.

Costs. The interest rate is the most obvious cost of a mortgage loan. But the lowest interest rate isn't necessarily the best buy. Other points to consider include the following:

1. How large a down payment is required?

2. Are there any origination fees? One percent of the mortgage amount is typical, but these fees may run higher. A buyer may decide the extra money is worth it—for instance, if the extra fee guarantees a fixed-rate mortgage as opposed to an adjustable-rate loan.

3. What other fees will be charged for application, appraisal, credit report, document preparation, etc.? All lenders must provide good-faith estimates in advance.

4. Will the buyer have to pay points? (A point equals 1% of the mortgage amount.) Points are often required with FHA or VA loans if the interest rate lags behind rates required by investors. For an interest rate 1% below market, an investor requires about six points. If the seller is paying the points, the selling price of the home may be raised accordingly.

5. Will mortgage insurance be required? Private mortgage insurance may be paid for in one of two ways: by a single up-front payment or by an annual fee based on the declining balance of the loan. The buyer may be able to drop the private insurance once equity in the home reaches a certain level.

A good way to compare the cost of two different financing packages is to ask for the "annual percentage rate." The annual percentage rate, or APR, factors most financing costs into the interest rate. The APR won't, of course, include any points that may have been included in the sales price of the home. Here, again, the buyer may be willing to settle for a slightly higher APR in exchange for a lower down payment or for a different type of mortgage loan.

Shopping for a Mortgage Loan. Following are some points to keep in mind for buyers seeking mortgage loans.

1. Buyers should contact as many lenders as possible, including SAVINGS AND LOAN ASSOCIATIONS, SAVINGS BANKS, COMMERCIAL BANKS, and mortgage bankers. Because lenders now sell many of the mortgages they originate to investors, financing packages may vary significantly from lender to lender.

2. For each loan considered, buyers should compare both the monthly payments required and the ANNUAL PERCENTAGE RATE (APR).

3. Buyers should ask the lender or builder how soon they must close on a loan to obtain the quoted rate. Sometimes the rate will be good for a specified period, such as 60 days. Sometimes buyers are quoted a floating rate that changes from day to day.

4. What are the relative advantages of each loan type: lower monthly payments in the early years, fixed interest rate, lower interest rate, lower fees?

5. Is the loan callable—that is, can the lender demand full repayment for any other reason other than failure to make monthly payments on time? If the loan is callable, is refinancing allowed or guaranteed?

6. Is the interest rate fixed or will it be adjusted at regular intervals? If the interest rate can be adjusted, how often will this occur and are any increases in payments likely to be affordable? Is there a cap on how much either the interest rate or the payments may change at any one time?

7. Will the loan be assumable for future buyers? If the home has been previously occupied, can the buyer assume the current owner's loan? Buyers should exercise caution in assuming mortgages, because recent changes in the law have strictly limited the assumability or mortgages, and if the mortgage assumption is outside the law, the borrower could lose the home.

Condominium and Cooperative Financing. CONDOMINIUM financing works very much like the financing of a single-family home. The purchaser buys a clearly defined housing unit and obtains a mortgage loan just as with a single-family home. Often the developer will arrange in advance with a lender to provide mortgage loans to the purchasers of newly built or converted condominiums. A purchaser is free to seek other financing, but some lenders may require that a certain percentage of the units in a condominium project be sold before they will originate a mortgage loan for an individual purchaser.

FHA loans, including graduated-payment mortgages, are available on individual condominium units under Section 234(c) of the National Housing Act, but mortgage limits may be slightly lower than those for loans obtained on single-family homes. The FHA will insure mortgages only in condominium projects that meet one of the following criteria:

1. The project contains 11 or fewer units.

2. The mortgage on the entire project is covered by FHA insurance.

3. The project is at least one year old.

VA loans are also available on condominium units, provided that the VA has approved the project for sale to veterans and that 70% of the units have been sold to people who intend to occupy their units.

In addition to monthly mortgage payments, the condominium owner will have to pay a monthly fee to the condominium owners' association to cover maintenance, insurance, taxes, etc. Purchasers of newly built or converted condominium units should find out when control of common elements will pass from the developer to the condo owners' association. They should also find out the extent of their liability if the developer fails to complete or defaults on a loan on common elements such as recreational facilities.

If a condominium project contains more than one building, the development may be done in phases, with some units completed and sold before others. Buyers should be aware of their liabilities should the developer be unable to complete the project. This information should be contained in the condominium documents.

Cooperative financing has typically been more complicated. The purchaser in a cooperative does not buy an individual unit; he or she buys a share in a corporation that owns the entire property. Membership in the cooperative carries with it the exclusive right to occupy a particular unit and a voice in the operation of the co-op.

There are two basic forms of financing. In some cases, there will be a project or blanket mortgage covering the entire project. If the mortgage is insured by the FHA, it may cover as much as 98–100% of the property value. Members would not require their own financing; rather, each would make a single monthly payment to the cooperative corporation to cover his or her share of the project mortgage, as well as operating costs.

A second method of buying into a cooperative involves both an underlying or blanket mortgage obtained by the corporation and a share loan to the individual seeking to occupy a unit. The share loan is not a mortgage per se, but a personal loan secured by the stock in the corporation and an occupancy agreement or proprietary lease. A buyer using this type of financing would make two monthly payments—one to the cooperative corporation to cover the underlying mortgage and operating expenses, and one to the lender to cover the share loan.

Except in New York City, where this type of financing is common, lenders have been reluctant to offer share loans, because they cannot claim a specific piece of property if the borrower defaults. This situation should improve, however, because states are beginning to pass laws allowing loans on cooperatives to be treated as real-estate rather than consumer loans. Moreover, private mortgage-insurance companies have been willing to insure loans to co-op purchasers, further reducing the risk to the lender. The lender will, however, usually require the cooperative corporation to sign a recognition agreement honoring its claim to the co-op shares should the borrower fail to repay the loan.

Until share loans become more common, resales may be difficult. In some cases, the cooperative has the right of first refusal and must be offered the opportunity to buy back the shares before the unit may be offered to outsiders. Usually, co-op members may rent out their units for one year.

Shareholders in the co-op will be given several documents, including (1) an information bulletin spelling out all rights and responsibilities; (2) a subscription agreement similar to an agreement to buy stock; and (3) an occupancy agreement, which is a form of lease that usually runs for three to five years, subject to renewal at the member's option provided he or she has complied with the agreement.

Cooperatives may rent units to nonmembers of the co-op. However, the cooperative corporation may not obtain more than 20% of its income from nonmembers if it wishes to maintain the exemption from federal income taxes usually given this type of corporation.

Equity. Equity represents the difference between the value of property and the amount owed on a loan backed by that property. Equity includes any appreciation or any drop in the property's value.

Underwriting Guidelines. Underwriting guidelines are those factors a lender considers in deciding the size and type of loan a borrower could reasonably be expected to repay. They include such things as the borrower's income and expenses, previous credit history, and stability of employment.

Michele McNamara and Elizabeth Bean Qutb

Home, Purchasing a

Purchasing a home is probably the single most important investment an American makes. Before considering the process by which one purchases a home, the decision to buy a home must be made.

There are advantages and disadvantages to buying a home. Advantages are as follows:

- *Tax benefits.* Certain expenses arising from home ownership are deductible from one's income tax. They are (1) interest on mortgage, (2) real estate taxes paid to municipalities, and (3) certain structural improvements.
- *Ownership.* A home has historically been an appreciating asset. It usually can be sold at a price greater than that paid for it.
- *Esthetic.* Ownership allows one to modify the living

space in any way; this would be strictly prohibited in a lease situation.

The disadvantages of owning a house are as follows:

- *Maintenance.* When the roof blows off in an apartment or rental unit, it is usually the landlord's problem. In a home, the expense is incurred by the homeowner.
- *Additional expense.* The monthly carrying charges on a home are usually greater than the monthly carrying charges on an apartment. (Experts tend to believe, however, that the tax benefits make the actual cost of homeownership somewhat less than indicated.)
- *Nonliquidity.* Real estate is a nonliquid asset—it must be sold to be converted into cash. The forced sale of real estate can reduce the selling price. Moreover, investments of equivalent cash may produce a higher yield than the purchase of a home.

While these are not all the advantages and disadvantages of owning a home, they are prime examples of the basic differences.

Let us assume that John and Mary Jones, after weighing the advantages and disadvantages of owning a home, have made the decision to buy. The decision having been made, their next consideration is "Can we afford it?" The corollary of this question is "If we can afford it, should we pay all cash or should we finance?" When considering whether John and Mary Jones can afford to buy a house, we must first look at their financial position.

All transactions for the purchase of a home, with the exception of certain types of mortgage financing (*see* MORTGAGES), require an amount of cash to be deposited toward the purchase price. Throughout the United States, the amount of the purchase price the buyer must put in as cash can vary between 20% and 30%. Therefore, if John and Mary Jones are looking to purchase a house at $100,000, and they don't have $100,000 and wish some sort of mortgage financing, they will need anywhere from $20,000 to $30,000 cash. This is called "equity."

John and Mary Jones must also consider their income. A rule of thumb used to be that one week's net salary should equal one month's principal, interest, and tax payment on the mortgage. This rule came about when interest rates ran to a maximum ceiling of about 8½–9%. Today's interest rates are much higher. Therefore, a person should either acquire a smaller mortgage or live on a less disposable income.

The monthly carrying charges of a house are as follows:

1. Principal and interest
2. One-twelfth the total tax bill
3. One-twelfth the insurance premium on the property
4. Heat
5. Electricity
6. Water

Today's energy costs make the fuel costs for both heating and electricity run higher than before. John and Mary Jones should plan on spending more than one week's salary to carry the house. Many mortgage companies today expect that an individual will spend up to two weeks of his disposable income in carrying the house.

The tax advantages of owning a house reduce the income-tax bill of the homeowner. They can be used to reduce the weekly withholding and increase the effective weekly take-home pay. Of course, this is a consideration only if John and Mary Jones do not wish to get a big rebate when they file their income tax in April.

Assume the Joneses have the $20,000 to $30,000 necessary to put down toward the purchase of a $100,000 home. Assume further that they can carry the maximum $80,000 mortgage, and that they can carry a house whose tax bill runs approximately $1,500 a year. The next step is to find a house that will fit their budget.

John and Mary Jones are about to embark upon the process of purchasing a home—a process that can be divided into three basic steps: (1) finding and deciding on a house, (2) contracting for the purchase of the house, (3) closing title to the house. While these steps sound simple, they are complicated in their execution.

Finding and Deciding on a House. Finding a house is a process of discovering the greatest value for your budget. John and Mary Jones wish to buy the closest thing they can find to their dream house: a house in a good neighborhood, a neighborhood with all major conveniences and with a good record for high resale value. But as life is a compromise, purchasing a home is also.

John and Mary Jones may find that their ideal house—a split-level with a swimming pool, located in the best part of town, near all railroads, buses, major parkways, shopping centers, and entertainment areas, with an annual appreciation of 15%—sells for $350,000. Therefore, they are unable to afford it. They must then search out geographic areas similar in nature, and be willing to compromise on the various elements they want in their dream house. It may be necessary to buy a house similar in size but in a less desirable or not-so-convenient location, with a lower appreciation rate. Or they may compromise somewhat on construction. While a relatively newer home, with modern conveniences, is more salable than an older home, John and Mary may have to settle for a home that is not quite as desirable as what they see in magazines. In this case, as long as it is in an area where homes have good resale value, they can rest assured that the investment will stand. This is a valid assumption and a valid decision in buying a house.

Under all circumstances the prudent buyer, after deciding on a house, has it inspected by a professional. A professional engineer or construction company will, for a fee, inspect a home on behalf of a buyer. Unless the buyer is familiar with the forms of construction, condition of construction, or types of construction, he should not undertake this himself. It is best to know, before going to contract, what shape a house is in. A house that seems well constructed on the outside is not necessarily the same on the inside. If John and Mary Jones are going to put down $20,000 to $30,000, you can be sure they want the best house for their money.

How do they go about finding a house that suits them? There are two ways. First, after deciding what geographic area they wish to concentrate in, they can check the local newspapers for private listings of homes in that area and call the owners to make an appointment. They would deal directly with the homeowner. All offers to purchase would be made to the homeowner, and all negotiations handled directly with the homeowner.

The other approach is to see a REAL-ESTATE AGENT. A real-estate agent is a professional, acquainted with the business of real estate in his area, and as such may be able to direct John and Mary to better neighborhoods and houses than they would have seen through advertisements. A real-estate agent is also more likely to know the availability of financing and the relative resale values in the neighborhood. However, a real-estate agent receives a fee for his or her services, in the form of a commission paid by the seller at closing. This commission is a percentage of the purchase price, and the seller may build this commission into the price when listing the property for sale. If so, John and Mary will actually be paying the commission, while the seller receives his predetermined net proceeds from the sale.

A home buyer does have the option of building a home rather than buying an existing one. Existing homes are usually older homes—used homes—and buying a used home is like buying a used car. You may get something with a little more charm, but it may have its problems. The older the home, the more expensive the problems, and the buyer should be ready to face this expense.

Buying a new home or having a home built for you also has its problems. A new home that is not custom-built for a specific buyer is usually built on speculation by the builder. In order to compete with the sale prices of used homes in the neighborhood, the builder will save in the construction where he can. This does not mean that the house is constructed in violation of the area's building codes. But building codes are meant to establish *minimum* standards for construction in a municipality, and a home that conforms to these standards thus conforms to the minimum. In order to be competitive, a builder must, in the face of escalating material costs, come as close to the minimum as he can. However, the buyer is getting new construction, which carries with it certain guarantees—on appliances, roof, and other portions of the home. In addition, if the builder has not completed the new home when the buyer sees it, certain custom alterations can be made at less cost than renovation of a used home.

If the buyer has the house custom-built, it will be done to his specifications. This is more expensive than purchasing a new home from a speculative builder or buying a used home. A custom-built home requires an architect or general contractor to carry out the construction. And as most banks will not give mortgage loans on vacant land, it is necessary for the buyer to buy the land on which the house is to be situated before he can acquire financing to build it. The advantages of a custom-built house are very simple. The house is built to the buyer's specifications. These will be as good or as bad as he wishes to pay for. A person has complete control over a custom-built house.

Let us assume that John and Mary Jones have made the decision to buy a used house through a real-estate agent. Let us also assume that they have found the house they wish to buy. In addition to the $20,000 or $30,000 down payment on their $100,000 home, there will be *closing costs*—expenses paid to the bank, the state, and the title company for closing the transaction. With this in mind, John and Mary must now proceed to contract for the house.

Contract for Sale. No matter what area of the country a person buys a house in, the buyer and seller enter into a *real-estate contract*. This agreement establishes the various legal rights of the parties. As it is a legal document, a person may want to consult an attorney before signing. In certain states it is the role of the attorney to negotiate the terms of the contract by representing either buyer or seller at contract signing. In these states it is the custom for the parties to sit down and discuss the terms before signing the papers. In other states contracts are drawn by real-estate agents under standard forms approved throughout the state. Under no circumstances should a party sign an agreement to purchase a home without understanding it. Consult an attorney. A real-estate contract is a binding obligation, and unexcused failure to satisfy this obligation may subject a party to legal penalties that can be expensive.

The real-estate contract contains the terms and conditions that both parties must fulfill in order for the closing to take place. A real-estate contract of the type that John and Mary Jones would enter into usually stipulates that the contract is conditioned upon the buyer's obtaining a mortgage. In the event that John and Mary Jones do not receive a mortgage, they are not obligated to complete the purchase.

It is usual for the buyer to put a down payment with the signing of the contract. This is an amount of money, given to a third party, agreed upon by everyone, to be held in escrow until closing. The money is to ensure that the buyer will have a vested interest in fulfilling all the terms and conditions of the contract. It makes the contract less of a gamble for the seller. In some states this amount can be as high as 10–20% of the selling price.

The contract sets the conditions upon which the buyer must accept title to the house. The terms and conditions of the contract are subject to state law requirements, therefore the law of the state in which a person buys a house will be controlling.

Most states follow the rule that, absent contrary provisions in the contract, a buyer is entitled to *marketable title*—that is, title free and clear of all encumbrances. As most homes do not have marketable title, a real estate contract will state what encumbrances the buyer will accept the property being subject to— which is to say that the buyer will have to accept title with certain encumbrances affecting it. Some of these encumbrances are *restrictive covenants, zoning ordinances,* and *easements.*

The buyer will very rarely have to take title that a TITLE-INSURANCE company does not wish to insure. Title-insurance companies ensure that no one, other than the first mortgagee, will have a better interest in the house than the titleholder has. Title-insurance companies base their decision to insure on an abstract of title—a written report prepared by a title-company employee or agent, showing the sequence of deeds vesting title in the hands of the seller. In addition, an abstract will show all outstanding judgments, liens, easements, restrictive covenants, or any filed encumbrance affecting the title to a parcel of real property. It is the buyer's obligation and expense to order a title policy. Usually this is done by the buyer's attorney, the real-estate agent, or the escrow agent who has set up the contract. If the seller cannot deliver insurable or marketable title, the buyer has the right to cancel the contract.

Let us assume that John and Mary Jones have gone to contract for the purchase of their $100,000 home. The contract is subject to their acquiring an $80,000 mortgage, and also subject to their getting clear title to the property from the seller.

The next step for the Joneses is to acquire the necessary mortgage financing for their home. This is done by making applications to banks and/or mortgage companies. Mortgage companies can sometimes offer different financing from that offered by banks, but historically they have been slightly more expensive in their closing costs. In today's changing market, the distinction between the two is becoming blurred and of less importance.

Once a mortgage commitment has been obtained and a title report has been ordered, it is time to set up a closing date.

Closing of Title. The procedure by which the title to real estate is transferred from buyer to seller is called the "closing." The seller's obligations pertaining to ownership of the house cease on the date of closing, and the purchaser's obligations begin.

The entire closing process involves the exchange of certain documents and the apportionment of certain costs between buyer and seller.

Prior to actual closing and subsequent to the signing of the sales contract, there are certain details that must be attended to. Table 1 is a list of these details and the party primarily responsible for them.

Prior to closing, John and Mary Jones would have had all the items in the above chart handled and prepared by their attorney, the bank's attorney, or the seller's attorney. If the Joneses were closing in a state where escrow closing processes are used, all of these matters would have been handled and cleared through the escrow agent. A short explanation of these items follows.

Survey. A document that specifically identifies the property and all of the structures located thereon. It shows whether or not there are any encroachments on the property—that is, buildings or structures that are partially on the property but do not belong to the property. An example is the next-door neighbor's fence that is six inches over the property line. Encroachments must always be corrected by the seller prior to the closing. A survey inspection is a physical inspection by a title-company representative in which he compares the structures, as they presently exist, to an existing survey. This should be done a short time prior to closing to reveal any changes in the property from the date of survey.

Title Search and Report. A written compilation of all liens, assessments, deed restrictions, and other encumbrances of record that may affect the seller's title.

Report or Document Prepared for Closing	Buyer	Seller	Lender
Table 1			
1. Survey	X		X
2. Inspection	X		X
3. Title search and report	X		X
4. RESPA disclosure			X
5. Encumbrances accepted by the buyer	X		X
6. Encumbrances to be removed by seller		X	
7. Instruments			
(a) Abstract of title or preliminary title report		X	
(b) Deed	X		X
(c) Mortgage or trust deed	X		X
(d) Promissory note or bond	X		X
(e) Title insurance policy or certificate of title	X		X

The seller's title is always subject to limitations and it is the seller's obligation to remove these limitations prior to closing unless the buyer has agreed in the sales contract to accept these at closing. The lender is directly concerned with all items relating to title. In placing a first mortgage on the property, the lender wishes to ensure that this mortgage is in fact a true first mortgage, and that there are no other interests of any other party affecting this first-lien position.

RESPA. All closings where a lending institution makes a first mortgage loan on a one-family home involve RESPA disclosure. RESPA stands for the Real Estate Settlement Procedures Acts. It is an obligation at closing that the buyer and seller are given a document containing full disclosure of all the actual expenses and actual costs. This document lists expenses involved in the closing and specifies who is responsible for them. At the final moment of the closing, it is the obligation of the lending institution to present one of these forms to both buyer and seller. It is a little more difficult to understand than an attorney's closing form, but it is a good idea where a closing is out of escrow.

Instruments. The following documents are instruments of the sale and purchase.

Deed. It is the obligation of the seller to prepare a deed. The deed is the document that transfers title from the seller to the buyer. Once the deed has been delivered to the buyer, the buyer has the obligation to have it recorded so that he will have the protection of the recording statute, informing the whole world that he owns the property.

Mortgage or Trust Deed, and Promissory Note or Bond. These documents evidence the buyer's obligation to the lender for the moneys used for closing, and it is the buyer's responsibility to have them recorded. The seller may be obligated to remove an encumbrance of an outstanding mortgage. Therefore, certain mortgage-satisfaction pieces may be present at the closing.

Closing Costs. There are certain expenses incurred by buyer and seller at the closing. The buyer will pay the following expenses:

1. *Title search and report, and title insurance.* This runs approximately $200 to $300 on a $45,000 home. John and Mary Jones's title charges would run approximately $750. A survey for the buyer would cost $175 to $250, depending upon land size.

2. *Attorney fees.* Attorney fees vary across the United States, ranging from a flat charge of $150 to 1% of the purchase price.

3. *Loan-related charges and fees.* The following are the major costs of mortgage financing. (*a*) *Lender's service charge.* "Points" (*see* MORTGAGES), usually from 2% to 4½% of the mortgage amount. (*b*) *Appraisal fee.* The charge for the lender's appraisal of the property to make a loan-to-value determination. The charge runs approximately $100 to $150. (*c*) *Prepaid interest.* The simple interest computed on the money from the date of closing until the end of the month. The buyer should remember that the first full mortgage payment will not come until the first full day of the second full month following closing. (*d*) *Hazard insurance.* The lender will require that the borrower have in force and effect on the date of closing fire insurance sufficient to cover the mortgage. The cost of fire insurance varies, depending on the carrier and the type of coverage the borrower buys. (*e*) *Tax escrow amounts.* Most if not all mortgages provide that the monthly payment to the lender will include one-twelfth of the annual property-tax bill. This is to insure that the taxes will be paid by the lender on behalf of the borrower when they are due. Lenders do not lend money for the purposes of paying taxes; they merely escrow for them. Therefore, there must be sufficient money in an escrow account to pay the taxes as due. (*f*) *Recording fees.* The buyer pays the fees for the recording of the deed and recording of the mortgage. These fees may total $15 to $50, depending on the municipality. (*g*) *Taxes.* Some states levy a tax on a mortgage, based on a percentage of the mortgage value. When purchasing a home, the buyer should check the mortgage-tax regulations in the area where he is buying.

The seller's closing costs are much more limited. They are as follows:

1. *Real-estate agent's fee.* Usually a percentage of

the purchase price, anywhere from 2% to 7%.

2. *Real-estate transfer tax.* States charge a tax for the sale of real estate. This can run anywhere from $100 to a percentage of the selling price.

3. *Legal costs.* The legal costs to the seller are usually approximately the same as the legal costs to the buyer.

The final expenses at closing are the adjustments between the buyer and the seller. Buyer and seller will adjust all costs that are assessed on an annual basis, either prepaid or outstanding as of the date of closing. For example, if the seller has prepaid the property taxes for a period of 12 months and the closing takes place 6 months into the year, it shall be the buyer's obligation to repay the seller for the portion of taxes from the date of closing to the close of the tax year.

Adjustments between the parties are also made to cover fuel charges, electric charges, sewer charges, and any other items attributable to the house.

Table 2 shows a closing statement that contains all of these items. It is an example of a closing in the state of New York, but John and Mary Jones will pay closing costs similar to these in the purchase of their home anywhere they decided to buy.

Douglas R. Hoffmann

Homeowners Insurance

A wide range of insurance coverages, normally written as a package, to protect individuals against financial loss from exposures associated with residential living.

With the exception of automobile insurance, there is probably no form of property-casualty insurance carried by more people. The possibility of damage to or destruction of personal property faces everyone. Homeowners policies, though they differ widely in price and in extent of coverage, all provide protection for six essential areas: the home; other structures on the premises; home contents (furniture, clothing, etc.); additional expenses if the policyholder and family must leave their home due to loss from an insured peril; personal liability; and medical payments to others.

The range of periods covered is very broad, including fire, windstorm, smoke, theft, vandalism and malicious mischief, water damage, glass breakage, and collapse. In fact, the only perils generally excluded from homeowners policies are those whose very nature makes them impractical to insure against: flood, earthquake, war, intentional loss, neglect, power interruption, government ordinance, and nuclear accident. Even some of those perils may in certain cases by covered by special insurance arrangements, as we shall see.

Until the mid-1950s, it was necessary to buy a number of separate insurance coverages to be sure of com-

---

Table 2
Sample Closing Statement

PREMISES: 2629 Chase Street, Wantagh, New York
SELLER: John Doe
PURCHASER: John Jones and Mary Jones
DATE OF CLOSING: January 26, 1982
PLACE OF CLOSING: Bayside Federal Savings & Loan Association
PRESENT AT CLOSING: John Jones and Mary Jones—
Purchaser
Robert Richmond, Esq.—
Atty. for Purchaser
John Doe—Seller
Jack Smith—Atty. for Seller
Jim Brown—For Title Company
Ann Conlin—For the Bank
Mary Courtenay—For Agent

ALL ADJUSTMENTS AS OF JANUARY 26, 1982

CREDITS DUE SELLER:

Purchase price	$74,990.00
Total credits due seller	$74,990.00

LESS CREDITS DUE PURCHASER:

Down payment	$ 6,288.00
1st mortgage balance	$60,000.00
Taxes	$ 251.21
Total credits due purchaser	$66,539.62

NET DUE SELLER AT CLOSING: $8,450.38

PURCHASE PRICE PAID AS FOLLOWS:

By cash:	$74,900.00
By check:	8,450.38

DISBURSEMENTS OF PURCHASER AT CLOSING:

Mortgage tax	$ 425.00
Recording mortgage	36.00
Recording deed	14.00
Title policy (mortgage)	563.00
Tax escrow	790.00
Commitment fee	1,500.00
Credit report	25.00
Appraisal fee	150.00
PMI	324.00
Interest 1/26–2/1	152.08
Bank legal fee	275.00
Legal fee	400.00
Insurance	313.00
Total disbursements	$4,967.08

Respectfully Submitted,

Robert Richmond, Esq.
Atty. at Law
2000 Banks Ave.
Seaford, New York
516-623-1111

Dated: Seaford, New York
February 3, 1982

plete personal-property and liability protection. Though most homeowners bought fire and extended coverage (windstorm, vandalism, and certain additional perils), many overlooked or ignored other forms of protection. To encourage people to safeguard their assets more adequately, insurers developed homeowners "package" policies offering adequate coverage against a variety of perils at a cost lower than the combined costs of individual policies.

Variations in policy provisions and endorsements do occur among companies; thus, to determine coverage in any specific case, the individual policy must be reviewed. Generally, however, companies offer a series of basic coverage forms that adhere closely to the categories established by the Insurance Services Office, a national advisory rating organization: HO-1 through HO-6 and HO-8. Since different insurance companies call their homeowners coverage forms by different names, there is room for further confusion. But the variations in basic forms are likely to be in the direction of more rather than less coverage. Therefore, the clearest approach to an analysis of homeowners insurance is by way of the basic coverages, proceeding from them to optional coverages, amounts, and pricing—and always keeping in mind that we are describing general conditions; the consideration of an individual program of insurance should include consultation with a company, broker, agent, or financial adviser.

Property Coverages. A discussion of different policies follows (see Table 1).

HO-1 (the Basic Policy). This is being phased out of insurance-company use, due to limited demand, but it is a logical starting point for outlining homeowners coverage, since it was the original basic package policy. It covers 11 specified perils: fire or lightning; loss of property removed from premises endangered by fire or other perils; windstorm or hail; explosion; riot or civil commotion; aircraft; vehicles; smoke; vandalism and malicious mischief; theft; and breakage of glass constituting part of the building.

HO-2 (the Broad Form). This adds seven other perils: falling objects; weight of ice, snow, or sleet; collapse of building(s) or parts thereof; bursting of steam or hot-water appliances and heating systems; leaks from plumbing, heating, or air-conditioning systems; freezing of plumbing and heating systems; and sudden, accidental injury from currents to electrical appliances. As is apparent, this form considerably extends the provisions of HO-1. What's more, it does so for a relatively modest additional premium, which is why HO-2 has all but supplanted HO-1.

HO-3 (Special Policy). For the homeowner who wants the broadest coverage available for dwelling and other structures, but does not want to pay for equally broad coverage on personal property. This special form gives the same "all-risk" protection as does the comprehensive form (see HO-5, below) to dwelling and other structures, but limits protection of personal property to the 18 perils in the broad form (HO-2). Because it provides the most protection for a moderate premium, HO-3 has become the policy of choice for most homeowners.

HO-4 (Renter's Policy). Also known as the *tenant's policy* or *contents broad form,* this is intended for those who rent an apartment or house or own a cooperative apartment. Household contents and personal belongings are insured against all the perils in HO-2. The landlord or cooperative association is responsible for insuring the building(s). Note: The renter's policy *does* cover additional living expenses.

HO-5 (Comprehensive Policy). Covers all perils except a few that are specifically excluded—chiefly, flood, earthquake, war, and nuclear accident. Designed for homeowners who desire the maximum coverage despite a significantly higher cost, HO-5 is an expensive luxury for most people.

HO-6 (Condominium Unit-Owner's Policy). Available to unit owners who want to insure their personal property or any additions and alterations not covered through the condominium association, which normally covers buildings, structure, and liability. Coverage is basically the same as HO-4.

HO-8 (Older-Home Insurance). Essentially a "no-frills" form for houses whose market value is substantially less than replacement cost. The policy contemplates returning property to serviceable condition, though not necessarily using the same materials that went into the original structure. HO-8 covers the same perils as HO-1, but restricts insurance against loss by theft to a maximum of $1,000.

Mobile-Home-Owner's Policy. A recent addition to traditional homeowners forms, this policy is available to the growing numbers of people who own and occupy mobile homes, providing the home is at least 10 feet by 40 feet. The coverage can be written to afford essentially the same protection as the homeowners broad-form policy (HO-2). However, because of the difference in construction and the greater vulnerability of mobile homes to wind damage, premiums are substantially higher than for similar coverage on a conventional house.

Additional Coverages. Repair of property doesn't tell the whole story when a house is damaged or destroyed. Insurers have added six related exposures to the homeowners policies (the last of these applies also to renter's, condominium, and mobile-home policies).

1. *Debris removal.* Insurers will pay the reasonable expense of removing damaged property.

Table 1
Perils Against Which Properties Are Insured

Perils	Basic (HO-1)	Broad (HO-2)	Special (HO-3)	Renter's (HO-4)	Compre-hensive (HO-5)	Condo-minium (HO-6)	Older-Home (HO-8)
1. Fire or lightning.	*	*	†	‡	*	‡	*
2. Loss of property removed from premises endangered by fire or other perils.§	*	*	†	‡	*	‡	*
3. Windstorm or hail.	*	*	†	‡	*	‡	*
4. Explosion.	*	*	†	‡	*	‡	*
5. Riot or civil commotion.	*	*	†	‡	*	‡	*
6. Aircraft.	*	*	†	‡	*	‡	*
7. Vehicles.	*	*	†	‡	*	‡	*
8. Smoke.	*	*	†	‡	*	‡	*
9. Vandalism and malicious mischief.	*	*	†	‡	*	‡	*
10. Theft.	*	*	†	‡	*	‡	*
11. Breakage of glass constituting a part of the building.	*	*	†	‡	*	‡	*
12. Falling objects.		*	†	‡	*	‡	
13. Weight of ice, snow, sleet.		*	†	‡	*	‡	
14. Collapse of building(s) or any part thereof.		*	†	‡	*	‡	
15. Sudden and accidental tearing asunder, cracking, burning, or bulging of a steam or hot water heating system or of appliances for heating water.		*	†	‡	*	‡	
16. Accidental discharge, leakage or overflow of water or steam from within a plumbing, heating or air-conditioning system or domestic appliance.		*	†	‡	*	‡	
17. Freezing of plumbing, heating and air-conditioning systems and domestic appliances.		*	†	‡	*	‡	
18. Sudden and accidental injury from artificially generated currents to electrical appliances, devices, fixtures and wiring (TV and radio tubes not included).		*	†	‡	*	‡	
All perils except flood, earthquake, war, nuclear accident and others specified in your policy. Check your policy for a complete listing of perils excluded.				†	*		

* Dwelling and personal property.
† Dwelling only.
‡ Personal property only.
§ Included as a peril in traditional forms of the homeowners policy; as an additional coverage in the simplified (HO-76) policies.
Source: Insurance Information Institute.

2. *Reasonable repairs.* When temporary repairs are needed to protect property from further damage, insurers will pay for the additional expense.

3. *Trees, shrubs, and other plants.* For certain covered perils (not including windstorm), insurers will pay up to $500 for individual trees, shrubs, and plants, or up to an overall maximum of 5% of the insurance limit on the dwelling. Lawns are also covered.

4. *Fire department service charge.* When property owners must pay for fire department service, they may be reimbursed up to $250.

5. *Property removal.* When property is rescued from

a dwelling, it is protected against direct loss from any cause for up to 30 days.

6. *Credit card, forgery, and counterfeit money.* If policyholders lose their credit cards and others charge purchases to their accounts, insurers will reimburse policyholders up to $500. The same limit holds true for check forgery and for loss resulting from acceptance in good faith of counterfeit money.

Endorsements. A great variety of endorsements may be added to homeowners policies for an additional premium. The two mentioned here answer needs often overlooked but likely to be felt by the largest number of homeowners, and will serve to illustrate the ways in which protection can be expanded.

Personal-Articles Floater. Though homeowners policies do cover such "unscheduled" personal belongings as furniture, clothing, appliances, and other possessions, they strictly limit coverage of such valuables as money and securities, jewelry, furs, silverware, goldware, pewterware, art, antiques, and other collectibles. When this property is more valuable than the limits set, it may be insured on an "all-risk" basis by purchasing a "personal-articles floater," either as a separate coverage or by endorsement to the basic policy. The term *floater* means that the coverage applies wherever the property is located at the time of loss, so the coverage may be said to "float" with the property.

Mortgage Extra-Expense-Coverage Endorsement. This is available from a small number of insurers to cover three basic areas of additional expense encountered by the homeowner who has a low-interest mortgage and suffers total loss of the insured premises:

- Legal expenses incurred to maintain an existing mortgage or renegotiate a new one.
- Mortgage-maintenance expenses when the insured is required to retain an existing mortgage until the dwelling is rebuilt.
- Mortgage-renegotiation expenses if the insured must renegotiate an existing favorable mortgage at higher interest rates.

Simplified Homeowners Policies. In recent years the insurance business has developed policies that are easier to read than those couched in the aggressively legal language of more traditional forms. The HO-76 program, so named because it was introduced in 1976, offers simplified versions of policies HO-1 through HO-6 and has been accepted by the majority of insurance companies as the format under which their policies are drafted. These "easy read" policies, as they are often called, are briefer overall—some contain as many as 5,000 fewer words—but they convey equivalent information.

For example, wording in a traditional homeowners policy reads: "In Consideration of the Provisions and Stipulations Herein or Added Hereto and of the Premium Above Specified, this Company, for the term shown above at noon (Standard Time) to expiration date shown above at noon (Standard Time) at location of property involved, to an amount . . ." In the new policy, this reads: "We will provide the insurance described in this policy in return for the premium and compliance with all applicable provisions of this policy."

Some minor changes in coverages are included in these revised policies, primarily to reflect the effect of inflation; but rating and price structures remain unchanged.

Volcanic-Eruption Insurance. The need for this coverage was not uppermost in most people's minds until the series of eruptions from Mount St. Helens in Washington State, starting May 18, 1980—a catastrophe that resulted in millions of dollars of property damage.

In the aftermath of these eruptions, there was some confusion regarding insurance coverage. Traditional homeowners policies specifically exclude volcanic eruption, but the simplified HO-76 series of homeowners policies unintentionally failed to respond to this peril. The great majority of damage claims in the blast area were covered by insurers as "explosions," a category of risk included in both types of policy.

The upshot was that the Washington insurance commissioner promulgated a rule, effective July 1, 1981, that homeowners and dwelling fire policies "that provide coverage for damage resulting from volcanic eruptions" spell out precisely how the coverage applies. The industry has since responded by clarifying the exclusion of volcanic eruption and offering a "buy-back" option.

Floods and Earthquakes. As we have noted, homeowners policies do not cover damage from these causes. But persons who live in earthquake or flood areas can buy separate property insurance, subject to deductibles, against these hazards.

A program of the Federal Insurance Administration makes flood insurance available in many areas. Since the coverage is attractive only to people living in those areas, it is not economically feasible for insurers to provide it. To qualify for flood insurance, property must be located in one of several thousand communities that have agreed to implement land-use controls to limit damage from future flooding. Property owners can find out whether the coverage is available where they live by contacting any insurance agent or broker.

Earthquake insurance normally is written as an addition to a fire, homeowners, or other property-insurance policy. Earthquakes strike most often in the Pacific Coast area, so more than half of all earthquake endorsements are purchased in California. But since many states are vulnerable to this hazard, there is a sufficient spread of risk to allow private insurers to provide this coverage for an additional premium.

Property-Insurance Plans. In many states, property insurance is made available through special plans for high-risk properties or those in coastal areas vulnerable to windstorm damage.

About half the states have property-insurance programs known as FAIR Plans (the acronym stands for Free Access to Insurance Requirements). They were established after Congress passed the Housing and Urban Development Act of 1968, which offered federal riot reinsurance to those states that set up such property-insurance pools. In 1981 there were FAIR Plans in 26 states, the District of Columbia, and Puerto Rico.

These plans are supported by insurers who write property coverages in the states in question. To qualify for federal riot reinsurance, any plan must provide insurance on inner-city properties at rates no higher than those of the voluntary market. As a result, many of the plans have steadily sustained losses. New York and a few other states have set rates high enough to make the plans more nearly self-sustaining, rather than satisfying the requirement for federal riot reinsurance.

All FAIR Plans offer fire insurance and extended coverage on residences and commercial properties. Several now offer homeowners as well. Counterparts to these pools are the *beach and windstorm plans* operated by property insurers in seven states along the Atlantic and Gulf coasts: Alabama, Florida, Louisiana, Mississippi, the Carolinas, and Texas. These assure availability of coverage for damage from hurricanes or other windstorms.

Liability Coverages. All forms of the homeowners policy include coverages for potential liability, and this protection applies not only to the policyholder but to all family members who actually live in the home. These coverages include the following:

Personal Liability. This is designed to protect a homeowner against a claim or lawsuit that could be financially devastating. For instance, suppose a visitor approaching the house slips on ice in the driveway, suffers a back injury that results in partial paralysis, and eventually sues for $100,000 or more. Or suppose sparks from a backyard grill set fire to the house next door, causing substantial damage, and the owner files a claim. If the parties involved agree the policyholder is legally liable for the damage or injury, or a court so rules, the insurance company will pay the damage assessed, up to the limits of the policy. In the event of a lawsuit, the insurer will pay the legal

costs of defense, whether or not the policyholder finally is held to be legally responsible.

All homeowners policies automatically provide the minimum liability limit of $25,000, but larger amounts may be purchased. The coverage applies not only to accidents occurring on or in the immediate vicinity of the homeowner's property, but also to those occurring elsewhere (so long as they are not business-related) if they are caused by the policyholder, a family member, or a pet.

Medical Payments. This coverage is intended to avoid the costly and burdensome process of deciding legal liability when there is an accident resulting in a minor injury to another that is inexpensive to treat. The medical-payments section of every homeowners policy provides payment of bills without regard to fault when injuries to others occur on the policyholder's premises. It also covers injuries caused elsewhere by the policyholder, a family member, or pet. The basic amount of the protection is $500; again, larger amounts may be purchased. Both this and the personal-liability coverages apply even to small boats—and to golf carts when they are being used for golfing.

Supplementary Coverage. This is for minor damage accidentally caused by the homeowner or someone in his or her family to another person's property. This coverage applies regardless of who is at fault—and, indeed, when the question of fault doesn't even arise. Damage by children under 13 is covered even when caused intentionally, because such damage is considered to be accidental. The maximum amount an insurance company will pay under supplementary coverage is $250.

Workers' Compensation. Ordinarily considered a coverage for business and industry, this is also available to homeowners and renters who employ part-time or full-time domestic help. New Hampshire and New Jersey require that every policy issued for private individuals for comprehensive personal liability—and that means homeowners and renter's policies—include workers' compensation insurance for household employees. In California, any homeowner who employs domestic workers full-time or part-time must carry workers' compensation coverage.

Amounts of Coverage. The question of insurance to value is crucial in purchasing and maintaining homeowners insurance protection. This has become truer than ever as inflation pushes the value of housing up practically from one month to the next. A house built for $50,000 in 1974 would cost $100,000 to build today, and it is quite possible for a homeowner inadvertently to be carrying insurance that would not reimburse the full value of loss or damage to property. Indeed, the Insurance Information Institute reports that studies have shown many thousands of homeowners are underinsured because they haven't kept pace with inflation by increasing the amount of their coverage.

Why is this oversight unusually critical in the case of homeowners insurance? Because in order to recover the full cost of partial loss or damage under a homeowners policy, the owner must have the dwelling insured for at least 80% of its replacement value. If a home has a replacement value of $100,000 and the owner carries $80,000 worth of coverage, everything's fine. A loss of $10,000 to, for instance, the kitchen, would be paid by the insurer, minus the deductible, to cover repairs. If, on the other hand, the house were insured for less than $80,000, the payment for a partial loss would be reduced in one of two ways. With coverage of only $60,000, the owner would stand to collect either 60/80 (three-fourths) of the $10,000 loss ($7,500) or the *actual cash value* (replacement cost less depreciation), whichever is more. Of course, should there be a total loss, the insurer will pay only the amount of coverage—$60,000 in this case, $80,000 if the house is insured for 80% of replacement cost.

The market value of a house is not a safe or accurate guide to the appropriate amount of coverage. Homeowners should consult their agents or brokers for guidance in establishing replacement value. Many insurance companies make available, through agents and brokers, a capsule guide to replacement cost. A typical example is a brochure that provides simple tables where the homeowner can list the construction units and half-units in a dwelling , figure cost per construction unit, and apply a geographic multiplier to arrive at an estimate of what it would cost to rebuild a dwelling.

Some such index is indispensable, for the amount of coverage on the house becomes the basis for establishing the amounts of coverage that are automatically assigned to other structures on a property, as well as to personal property and additional living expenses. Other structures are insured for 10% of the amount covering the dwelling; personal property for 50%; additional living expenses for 20% (10% under the basic policy, HO-1); and trees, shrubs, and plants for 5%, subject to the maximum of $500 per item.

The Insurance Information Institute gives a detailed example. If a house with an $80,000 replacement value were insured to full value under a broadform homeowners policy (HO-2), other structures would be covered for $8,000; unscheduled personal property for $40,000; additional living expenses for $16,000; and trees, shrubs, and plants for $4,000. If the same house were insured for 80% of replacement value, or $64,000, the equivalent amounts would be

$6,400, $32,000, $12,800, and $3,200. In both cases, personal liability would be covered for $25,000 per occurrence; medical payments to others for $500 per person injured; and damage to the property of others for $250 per occurrence. In the first two categories, and for unscheduled personal property, larger amounts may be purchased. These amounts would be the same under the basic form (HO-1), the special form (HO-3), and the comprehensive form (HO-5), except that additional living expenses under HO-1 are covered only up to 10% of the dwelling amount.

Insurance to Value. Some insurance companies automatically increase homeowners coverage each year, using an index that reflects the rate of inflation, unless the policyholder objects. Also widely available to homeowners is an *inflation-guard endorsement,* which periodically raises the amount of protection under a homeowners policy. One such endorsement, for example, automatically increases coverage every three months at the rate of 1% of the original coverage amount.

Three things must be emphasized. First, homeowners coverage should be purchased and maintained at a rate equal to at least 80% of the dwelling's value. Second, policyholders should make and keep an inventory of household furnishings and personal belongings to help decide how much insurance to buy, and for use in the event of a loss. This inventory, with photographs or video records of important items and receipts for major purchases, should be stored in a safe place away from home. Finally, the homeowner or tenant should seek the assistance of a qualified insurance company, agent, or broker to be certain that the appropriate kinds of homeowners insurance are purchased and in the right amounts.

Cost of Coverage. Many factors help determine the cost of homeowners insurance; here again the assistance of a knowledgeable insurance counselor is essential. Among the factors affecting homeowners premiums are rate differentials, both within and between companies; state; territory (reflecting the loss experience on similar dwellings in a given area); construction; protection class (based on distance to and capability of fire department[s] and availability of water); policy forms; deductibles; and, of course, the amount of coverage. Some of these are so technical as to be beyond the scope of this discussion. There are, however, cost-related policy elements of which every homeowner should be aware.

Deductibles and Credits. HO-76 homeowners policies are written with a flat $100 deductible applying to all property losses except credit cards. But HO-8 may have a special $250 deductible for losses under the theft peril.

Other policies vary. In many states the "disappearing" $50 deductible is used ($100 in HO-5), and may be changed to a flat deductible by endorsement. Theoretically, the property owner who wants a policy with no deductible at all can have it for an additional premium. Because of the high cost to insurers of settling smaller claims, that premium is apt to be substantial.

Flat deductibles, which apply to all losses under the policy, may be increased to $250, $500, or more by endorsement. Obviously, property owners who know they can absorb a deductible greater than that included in the policy are wise to do so, for this will lower the cost of their homeowners insurance by a considerable amount.

A form of discount offered by several insurance companies is the *new-house credit,* which offers advantageous terms to policyholders living in homes built recently. Usually, the credits are on a sliding scale. For instance, an insurance company may extend a 15% discount to homes built within the past two years, 12% to houses between two and three years old, and so on, down to 2% for houses ten years old, after which the discount disappears.

Many insurers offer *protective-device credits* to homes with burglar or fire alarms, smoke detectors, sprinkler systems, or other safety features.

Example of Coverage Range. Because of the many variables that must be considered, it is really not possible to speak in terms of a "typical" homeowners premium. All we can do is take an example of one of the more common homeowners coverages and show the range of premiums that would be charged (as of January 1, 1982) by 14 of the largest property insurers for an average amount of insurance on such a policy. The policy in question has an amount of $75,000 written under HO-3 on a frame-construction house, with a $100 deductible, $100,000 of comprehensive personal-liability protection, and $1,000 in medical-payments and extended theft coverage.

In San Francisco the annual premium for such a policy would range from $233 to $271, depending on the insurer chosen. In San Jose the range would be from $194 to $287. Some other locations, with lowest and highest premiums calculated for the same 14 insurers: Alabama, $319 to $368; Arizona, $219 to $294; Colorado, $188 to $254; Connecticut, $288 to $316; Massachusetts, $426 to $486; Syracuse, New York, $315 to $349; Jericho, New York, $328 to $468; South Carolina, $314 to $357; Virginia, $186 to $271.

Insurance companies continue to update and adjust homeowners rates and coverages. That process, together with the range of coverage prices we have indicated, emphasizes once again the wisdom of seeking expert financial guidance when considering the purchase of homeowners insurance.

Arthur S. Phillips

Hospital Income Insurance

A type of HEALTH INSURANCE that has limited benefits but wide uses. Benefits are paid only when the insured is hospitalized, but the payments are in cash, directly to the insured, and are made in addition to any benefits from other group or individual health-insurance policies. These policies are available through insurance agents or directly from insurance companies through the mail. They require periodic updating because their benefits are in fixed dollars, while health-care costs are increasing. Hospital income policies contain a waiting period before they become effective if the insured is ill, or recently has been ill. It is important to determine the "elimination period" or how long the insured must be hospitalized before benefit payments start, keeping in mind that the average length of hospitalization is 7.6 days.

James L. Moorefield

·I·

Income Statement

The recapitulation or listing of a company's or individual's revenues and expenses over a specific period of time. The resulting comparison between income and expenses results in a "net income" (or "net loss") for that particular period of time in question. Can also be called an "earnings statement," "operating statement," or "profit-and-loss statement."

Samuel C. Hoyt

Income Tax, History of U.S.

The income tax—or, more specifically, a direct tax on one's income—is a relatively new invention in the United States. While it was Ben Franklin who popularized the remark "Nothing is certain but death and taxes," the colonists were busy, as we know, dumping tea in Boston Harbor to protest even specific taxes. They would have nothing to do with an income tax! Americans have cut their teeth on such appealing slogans as "Taxation without representation is tyranny!" Hence, Americans tend to remember any leader who imposed high taxes as a tyrant, and any country that forced tribute as tryannical. In the United States, it seems that the fabric of our free economy is all the more colorfully embroidered with sentiments against taxation.

Indeed, any form of direct income taxation was anathema to the Founding Fathers, who allowed only for specific excises and tariffs. Customs, duties, and excises, not personal or income taxes, constituted the major source of income for the new government at least until the Civil War. Even the assessment of excise taxes was met with substantial resistance and rebellion. The colonial distaste for taxes on such staples as sugar and tea so influenced those drafting the Articles of Confederation that they failed in many ways to give the federal government sufficient power to tax. The Constitution forbid the assessment of any direct tax on income, but excise taxes on whiskey and tobacco, as lucrative as they first appeared, proved not enough to fund the growing federal government. Several times in the early years, the Congress endeavored

to pass more direct tax measures, but it remained for the nation to reach a real crisis before such measures would be tolerated.

If Lincoln is remembered for freeing the slaves, it must also be noted that he shifted their burden, more or less equitably, to all the citizens of the United States of America, for it was the Civil War, and his Revenue Act of July 1, 1862, that established the Office of the Commissioner of the Internal Revenue in the Department of the Treasury, and brought the enabling legislation for the collection of a net income tax (*see* INTERNAL REVENUE SERVICE, HISTORY OF THE). That office has functioned continuously since then, together with collection districts that were immediately established. By the start of 1863, 4,000 people were already employed for the collection of the new taxes. The collectors, or "Revenuers," as they were called, pursued individuals who resisted the net income tax, and collected the excise taxes on whiskey and other "manufactures." The *Handbook of The U.S. Tax Law,* the first commercially published taxpayers' advice book and manual, published in 1863, notes:

A party is permitted to swear as to the amount of his income liable to assessment, and the amount thus sworn to is received as the sum upon which the duties are to be assessed and collected . . . [or, he] may be permitted to declare, under oath or affirmation, that he is not possessed of an income of $600 liable to assessment. . . . He is then exempt. Of course, this does not preclude the assistant assessor from ascertaining the truth of such an affidavit, and he is at liberty to take measures for verifying it.

Thus the "audit" system was first initiated, and the Revenuers, working on a piecework basis, patrolled the hills for illegal stills and untaxed whiskey, or applied their cynical eye to the declarations of income made by the citizenry throughout at least the northern states of America. Taxes, by the way, were due then on May 1 for earnings totaled on December 31 of the previous year. It was common for people to stay up all of the night before, on April 30, sweating over their taxes!

Several challenges to the income tax were made in the courts during and after the Civil War. The proportion of federal income derived from income tax grew to well over 50% during the Civil War. With such a successful tax, the enabling legislation was extended from its original term of four years through 1872, when anti-income-tax sentiment forced its repeal. The Revenuers continued to operate, under the Office of the Commissioner of Internal Revenue, but specifically as collectors of manufacturing taxes on items from awnings to umbrellas, and licenses from circuses to theaters, with a careful definition of each item or enterprise requiring the payment of "duty" or acquisition of a "license." A law reviving the income tax was struck down as unconstitutional in 1895, in the case of *Pollock* v. *Farmers Loan & Trust Co.,* amid strong arguments that the direct tax of income was communistic and socialistic.

It was not until 1909 that an amendment to the Constitution was passed by Congress that would allow the government to impose a direct tax on the income of each individual, but it was not ratified by the necessary three-fourths of the states. On February 25, 1913, the Sixteenth Amendment was ratified, providing that "Congress shall have power to lay and collect taxes on incomes from whatever sources derived, without apportionment among the several states, and without regard to any census or enumeration." Within a short time that year, the income-tax laws were instituted and have remained in force continuously since.

It is important to understand, in the history of taxation in America, that the tax laws, in principle, have remained the same from their inception, as have attitudes toward taxes at the most official and public levels. Justices of the Supreme Court have declared that no person should pay a penny more in taxes than he or she legally owes. Needless to say, the people agreed!

The same laws and codes apply to the rich and poor. With little exception, the same deductions and inclusions are applicable to businesses big and small. While three-fourths of the federal budget now comes from direct income taxes, a survey done in 1979, by the Advisory Commission on Intergovernmental Relations, indicated that only one in four Americans believed that they "got the most out of the federal government per dollar, as compared to state or local taxes." Most people preferred to pay local property tax, a state or even federal sales tax, rather than an income tax. However, of the many kinds of taxes that have been tried, the income tax has become the most entrenched form of taxation, worldwide.

David B. Axelrod

Individual Account

A savings or checking account owned and controlled by one individual.

Mary Ann Irvine

Individual Retirement Account (IRA)

An Individual Retirement Account is a TAX-DEFERRED investment plan that allows any wage earner (and spouse) to save a portion of income for retirement or to legally shelter income from taxation. In other words, an investor can accumulate funds for retirement by making tax-deductible payments to the plan. The earnings (interest) of the IRA are not taxed until they are distributed.

Individual Retirement Accounts may be the single most important tax break ever made available to the average American. Anyone who earns a paycheck is eligible. This includes, of course, all those millions who do what most people in the work force do—work full-time for one employer. It doesn't matter if that employer is a giant corporation or a small service company, a federal or local public body, a trade association or a labor union.

It also doesn't matter whether you are covered by an existing retirement program or not; or, conversely, if you fail to qualify for the one at the place where you work; or if your company does not offer one at all. If you receive earned income, you are eligible.

Nor do you need to be a full-timer. Part-time workers, casual workers, moonlighters, students who put in a few hours a week at a gas station—all can take advantage of the opportunity. Even those already retired from their jobs are eligible if they continue to do some paid work.

The fact is that the United States Congress decided that just about everyone who gets a paycheck should have the opportunity to set aside money in his or her own retirement plan, and get some pretty healthy tax benefits in doing so.

Until 1982, IRA's were restricted to people who were not already covered by some other retirement program. For them, IRA's were extremely attractive, and indeed by the beginning of 1982 some 5 million people had opened accounts worth about $25 billion. The IRA program offered these people the chance to build up funds of their own to help meet living costs in those years ahead when their paychecks would stop and be replaced by Social Security and precious little else.

So important was this concept of self-help, however, that those concerned with problems of retirement began to realize that IRA's just for those not already covered by retirement plans at work were unduly limited. After all, they argued, inflation eats away at all retirement funds, and we all worry about keeping our heads above water when our earnings stop. Through this kind of thinking, the boundaries placed on IRA's were dramatically loosened. The upshot was that from January 1, 1982, the new near-universal individual retirement programs came into effect.

The tax break is twofold. First, all contributions to an Individual Retirement Account—up to the maximum of $2,000 a year—are immediately tax-deductible. This means that you deduct from your tax return the full amount of whatever you put into your IRA. Let's say, for example, you elect to contribute the $2,000-a-year maximum. Let's say also that you are in the 40% tax bracket. The net effect is that your federal tax for that year will be reduced by $800 (40% of $2,000). Every year you make a contribution of that size; and for as long as you are in the 40% tax range, your Federal income tax will be $800 less than it would otherwise be.

Obviously, the higher your tax bracket, the more you save. But even at 30%, your taxes would go down $600 if you contributed $2,000. Similarly, the tax saving will be lower if your contribution is less. At $1,000, for example, someone in the 40% tax bracket would save $400 a year.

However, your full contribution—$1,000, $2,000, whatever—goes into your Individual Retirement Account. There it can immediately begin building toward your retirement fund. To put it another way: You'll have invested, say, $2,000, but—if you are in the 40% tax bracket—it will have cost you only $1,200.

We now come to the second tax benefit: All money in an IRA accumulates free of taxes as long as it stays there. This means that it can grow and compound without annually having a hefty slice taken off for current taxes, as would be the case with any ordinary taxable investment. The result is that your pool of money can grow much more rapidly.

Again, let's take a hypothetical example. Assume you put your money into an investment that on average produces a rate of return of 12% a year. Assume, too, that you invest $2,000 a year. In an investment on which you pay ordinary income tax at 40%, the growth would be substantial: After 20 years you would have as much as $89,838. But look at the same investment in an IRA. Because you are not paying taxes year in and year out, the money grows even faster. In 20 years you would have no less than $161,397.

Even this, however, does not exhaust the full impact of the tax break. Suppose you did not put the $2,000 into an IRA. In that case you would have to pay normal taxes on it. The result—in the 40% tax bracket—would have reduced what you had available to invest to $1,200; the rest would have gone to the tax man. To follow this example through, therefore, $1,200 invested at 12% for 10 years would give you $17,942. In 20 years you'd have $53,903, and in 30 years $125,976. A comparable IRA investment—in which you invest $2,000 a year—would produce $39,309 in 10 years, $161,397 in 20 years, and no

less than $540,585 in 30 years.

Of course, you will have to pay taxes on your IRA investment sometime. But this is a retirement fund, and normally you would not start taking that money out until you did retire. When people stop working, their income usually drops very sharply—on average by about 50%. That immediately puts them in a lower tax bracket, and so the amount they are likely to pay in taxes is reduced significantly. This is why the Economic Recovery Tax Act, which sets the requirements for IRA's, stipulates that you pay only normal income taxes if you start to take your money out between ages 59½ and 70½.

You should know that if you take anything out before 59½, you will pay a penalty—10% on the amount withdrawn—and then the sum withdrawn will be taxed with the rest of your income. Also, you have to start taking your money out by the time you are 70½, or again you will be penalized—and at that time you must take it out in amounts related to average life expectancy. There are detailed rules about this, but any institution offering an IRA can provide them to you. For most people, these are all reasonable conditions.

Setting up an IRA is usually easy—just some forms to fill in. Costs for most types of IRA's are quite modest, but that should be checked before you make your choice.

You can contribute to an IRA individually or through a payroll-deduction program. In the latter case, your employer simply deducts money from your paycheck in whatever amount you have decided and puts it directly into an investment that you yourself have chosen. There is no clear indication yet how many employers are offering this service, but a May 1982 check by the Investment Company Institute showed that well over 50 of the Fortune 500 corporations—that is to say, the largest corporations in the United States—were in fact doing so, with mutual funds as one option. Many hundreds of other leading companies and institutions have also indicated that they were starting these programs.

As to contributions, you can put away up to $2,000 a year—but no more—into an IRA, provided you earn that much a year. For those few people who earn less than this—generally part-time workers—the maximum is 100% of anything they earn. But these are just maximum amounts—you can put in whatever amount you wish up to those levels. You can also vary the amount year by year, depending on what you can afford, and you can skip some years entirely if you wish.

The maximum amounts are those for an individual. If you are married and both of you work, you can both set up an IRA to a maximum of $2,000 each a year. If only one of you works, there is a "spousal" account, and in this case the total for the two of you would be $2,250 a year.

You can put money into an Individual Retirement Account up until the time you file your tax return for that year. If you're like most people, that's April 15 of the following year. So to take out an IRA for 1984, the last date for you would be April 15, 1985. If you get a tax-return extension, you have until that date to make contributions to your Individual Retirement Account for the previous year. The timing will depend on your own circumstances.

If you invest late in the year, you have the advantage of being able to determine more clearly how much you can afford. On the other hand, you will have missed an opportunity that could be valuable: If you make your contributions near the beginning of the tax year, any earnings on your investment will be growing tax-free all that extra time.

More basically, the earlier in your life you start investing in an IRA, the more likely it is that you will build up adequate funds. You will need to put three times as much away when you are 55 as you would have done at 35 to reach the same goal at 65.

But later is better than not at all. For example, even if you did not start an IRA until you were 60½, by contributing $2,000 a year, and assuming you get a 12% rate of return, you would still have $39,309 by the time you had to start taking your money out at 70½.

You have a lot of flexibility in deciding how to invest your money. A wide range of financial institutions will open an IRA for you, and each of them has special features. BANKS, CREDIT UNIONS, and SAVINGS AND LOAN ASSOCIATIONS offer CERTIFICATES OF DEPOSIT (CD's) that give current rates of interest and run for different periods. Sometimes the interest rate is fixed, sometimes it varies with different market conditions. These deposits are insured. One disadvantage is that if you want to change your investment before the certificate matures, you could face that extra penalty for early withdrawal that you hear so much about. More particularly, they do not offer any possibility for capital appreciation, which is one of the things that many people consider in preparing for retirement.

Insurance companies offer annuities, which are contracts guaranteeing regular payments upon retirement, based on life expectancy. Different companies have quite different plans, so you'll need to do some digging.

Stockbrokers offer a wide range of investments, like common stocks or bonds, in what are called "self-directed" accounts. Going this way gives you a degree of flexibility that is difficult to match elsewhere, but more of the decision-making on what and when to buy and sell will be on your shoulders. A degree of sophistication therefore is called for—and, of course, if you do make frequent changes, commission costs could eat into your capital.

Mutual funds, because they come in such a variety, offer a similar degree of flexibility, but because they are run by professional money managers, you do not need to be an investment expert to take advantage of changing conditions. Mutual funds do not guarantee any particular rate of return, but they do go all the way from just about the most conservative investments around—money-market funds that invest in the very short-term securities of the government, the leading banks, and top-rated corporations—to investments in the common stocks of every kind of corporation.

So with an IRA you have plenty of choice. Moreover, you can split your contributions into any number of different accounts so long as the total does not exceed the $2,000-a-year maximum. You can also switch from one investment into another once a year, or, if you follow some cumbersome procedures, more often. The main exception to this is with a family of mutual funds, where you can change from one fund to another within the same management group just about as often as you wish. The freedom to switch from one type of investment to another is obviously important as it gives you the opportunity to take advantage of different economic conditions and any changes in your own situation. For example, when you are a good many years away from retirement, you may think it worthwhile to take some calculated risks in the stock market to try to build up your capital more quickly. You have time on your side to ride out the inevitable ups and downs in prices. As you approach retirement, you will probably want to move some of your money, perhaps all, into an investment with more stability, albeit less expectation of growth. At that stage you could quite easily get out of your stocks, or a common-stock mutual fund, and into, say, a bank CD or a money-market fund.

You also have plenty of freedom in drawing on your IRA when the time comes. You can, if you wish, take it all out at once. Of course, this would sharply increase the amount you pay in taxes that year, so most people will probably want to make withdrawals over a period of time in order to supplement retirement income. That, too, should present no problem. Many financial institutions have experience in tailoring withdrawal programs to suit whatever needs their investors have. Again, this is something for you to ask about.

There is one special lump-sum payment that may come your way, and often with little warning. Many people do get single payments from retirement programs—if you leave your firm or if it simply terminates its retirement program, or if you are the surviving spouse of someone who was covered by a retirement plan, or if you become disabled. In all these cases, you could get a lump-sum payment—and, not much later, a tax demand based on it.

There is now a way to avoid this tax, however, and that is by putting the money into an IRA. You have to do this within 60 days, but once you have done so, you neither pay taxes then nor on any earnings the investment makes until you start withdrawals—as with any other IRA. The amount of money that can be put into this type of IRA is not subject to any limit and could be quite a large sum. You can have a normal IRA running alongside this special investment, which is known as a "roll-over" IRA.

No one can predict what any investment will do in the future; nor can anyone tell what will happen to inflation, Social Security, or the general economic health of the country. Even the level of your own future salary is uncertain. Obviously, then, it is not possible to predict what your IRA will be worth in real terms when you retire. But there are some clues for the long haul. For example, it is true that common stocks go up and down, but over the years the trend has been strongly up. So, over the long run, the last 30 years, in fact—a period long enough to include every type of economic condition except a Great Depression—mutual funds that invest in common stocks have produced an average rate of return of around 9% a year. That includes the reinvestment of all dividends and capital gains. It also covers the good and bad years, the better- and worse-performing funds, and is net of all expenses. For those years, this was well ahead of the rise in the cost of living. In more recent times, inflation has been at a painfully high level and aspirations have risen to compensate for this erosion of purchasing power. For the five years through June 1982, the common-stock mutual-fund average was 10.4% a year.

But high interest rates resulting from inflation have also provided an opportunity for other types of investments. And so in the 12 months (through May 1982) analyzed in the latest survey of investments by Salomon Brothers, the investment bankers, bonds were a best buy—up 11.4%. An investment in a pool of bonds therefore could have helped stave off some of the disturbing effects of high inflation.

The money market was even more rewarding. Money-market funds, for example, produced a better rate of return than any of the groups in the Salomon survey—something over 15%. As the cost of living went up 6.6% in that period, this was clearly an attractive hedge and a way of building up funds toward retirement at minimal risk.

All this adds up to a flexibility that allows you to prepare for retirement in a more realistic way than was possible before. With the choices now open, you do not have to simply wait out the bad times. Instead, you can have an appropriate response to a wide variety of personal circumstances and economic conditions.

See KEOGH PLANS.

Reginald F. D. Green

Industrial Life Insurance

See LIFE INSURANCE.

Inflation

Inflation is an economic condition characterized by a sustained rise in most prices. Classically, it is referred to as "too much money chasing too few goods."

Economists divide inflation into two types: demand-pull inflation, in which the demand for goods and services raises prices; and cost-push inflation, in which the cost of producing goods and services forces producers to raise prices to maintain profit margins. In either case, the cause is the application of too much money. The process of inflation is easier to understand if you view money as a claim on goods and services. Each dollar is like a claim check for a portion of the goods and services produced by the economy.

Sources of Money. The money fueling the engine of inflation comes from two major sources—government and commercial banks (*see* BANKS; FEDERAL RESERVE SYSTEM). Governments feed money into the economy through their purchases of goods and services and through transfer payments, such as government pensions, Social Security, and welfare payments. Ordinarily, government purchases of goods and services can be absorbed by our market system. However, the vastness of government purchases can push an economy already straining to meet private demand over the edge and into inflation.

Wars are a typical example of those times when government demand for goods and services creates inflation. Throughout our national history, wars—from the Revolution to Vietnam—have been major contributors to inflation. In fact, our recent inflation largely reflects the Johnson administration's decision in 1965–66 to provide both the "guns" for the Vietnam conflict and the "butter" for sweeping domestic social programs. Transfer payments pump money directly into the economy, giving individuals the funds to place additional demands on the economy.

Commercial banks contribute to inflation by creating money through their lending and investing. This money-creation process finances demands that ordinarily couldn't be exercised without the proceeds of loans.

The Federal Reserve System's policy decisions regarding the level of reserves in the nation's banks affect banks' ability to create money. So, indirectly, the Federal Reserve System may contribute to inflation, or deflation, as it struggles to try to provide the right amount of money to balance the economy between inflation and recession.

Picture our economy as an auction in which people can exercise their claims to the economy's output of goods and services. Of course, some individuals have more claims to use than others, and they will, naturally, claim more of the economy's output. Our market system is geared to handle that type of situation. Output is aimed at meeting an anticipated demand. However, as well as our market system meets demands placed on it, output isn't unlimited. We have only a given amount of the factors of production (land, labor and capital, machines, etc.). Only so much can be devoted to producing a given good or service in relation to other goods and services, or in producing a given total of goods and services.

Demands. Given these conditions, picture the imbalance that would occur if everyone's claims were increased by, say, 10% in number over a relatively short period of time. The immediate result would be the using up of the available goods and services. After a time, buyers would begin bidding against each other to obtain what they wanted. While individuals and businesses account for the bulk of demand, governments—federal, state, and local—are also a source.

As the supply of goods and services is eroded by demand, producers struggle to keep up with demand. They begin bidding higher for the resources they need—labor, raw materials, and plants and equipment. As they tap these scarce resources, the prices of the resources are bid higher. In addition, they may resort to overtime, increasing their costs further. In the end, producers are forced to raise prices. Labor costs can rise again as less-skilled workers are pressed into service from a tightening labor market.

Other Effects. Inflation doesn't just mean rising prices—its effects go much deeper. The effects on business are often misunderstood. Inflation artificially bloats profits, partly because accounting practices don't allow enough to be set aside for things like replacing worn-out machinery. On top of this, business must pay higher taxes on illusory profits. Furthermore, businesses also face scaled-up labor demands to provide a wage increase as well as catch up on past and future wage losses to inflation.

Inflation also takes a toll on business planning. Anticipating future material and labor costs in an inflationary environment becomes increasingly difficult as prices continue upward. Forecasting demand and anticipating the need for future plant and equipment also are thwarted.

Purchasing raw materials, for example, can be troublesome. In a high-demand economy, do you purchase just what you need, or overbuy to beat an expected price increase or short supply? If you, and others, overbuy, will this create a self-fulfilling prophecy?

To some degree, the impact of inflation on business planning reflects an "inflationary psychology." This mental fixation is perhaps best seen in consumer behavior. For example, as prices rise and dollars buy less, some individuals may decide to spend more of their incomes and save less, and even withdraw savings and spend them. Some will make major purchases sooner than anticipated to beat price increases. Others will buy more than they need, contributing to the price spiral. Still others will borrow and spend in anticipation of repaying their loans with dollars further cheapened by inflation.

As inflation continues, real goods take on more value in relation to money, and savings may be directed into less-productive investments, such as gold, diamonds, or art. Investment turns to speculation.

Inflation strains financial markets. Banks face increasingly stronger loan demands, and interest rates rise. At some point, some borrowers will be priced out of the market or find that funds aren't available. Business borrowing to support inventories or accounts receivable may be difficult to arrange.

Within this framework, business decisions become distorted by the uncertainty of returns. Inventories are over- or understocked; productivity-increasing changes planned for plant and equipment are delayed or abandoned; research and development are stalled.

As inflation progresses, it becomes like a merry-go-round driven by too much money. The longer it turns, the faster it goes. On this merry-go-round are three horses—rising costs, distortions, and expectations. There are no free rides on this merry-go-round; worse yet, each ride is more expensive. The merry-go-round can be slowed and eventually stopped, but each anti-inflation strategy has its difficulties.

Controls. Historically, one of the first anti-inflation solutions seized upon is wage-price controls. It's usually the most obvious choice because it attacks the symptom of inflation that seems to hurt the most—prices. However, controls contain flaws that aren't always immediately obvious.

In a complex economy such as ours, the big question is which of all the millions of prices should be controlled. Besides the political problems this would raise, there also are economic difficulties. If you freeze the price of chickens and allow the price of chicken feed to rise, farmers will soon reach the point where it costs more to raise chickens than they can get in return. In short order, chicken will disappear from our diets.

In industry, a freeze in auto prices without a similar freeze in steel prices will soon cut off car production. As for wage freezes, workers faced with these can't easily decide to stop providing their services or switch to better-paying jobs, but they certainly can resort to such tactics as union rule-book slowdowns, more sick days, and just plain "goldbricking."

A similar proposal, called "indexing," would tie all wages and prices to an index of consumer prices, such as the consumer price index. As the index rose, so would all wages and prices, including contractual agreements, such as insurance premiums, mortgage interest rates, and rents. Critics of indexing attack the fact that while both wages and prices move in lock-step, indexing doesn't go after inflation's root causes, nor does it avoid inflation's subsequent effects of rising expectations and inflation's distortion. Instead, they claim, indexing merely validates the existence of a pernicious inflation, supercharges inflationary expectations, and magnifies distortions to come.

Fiscal Policy. Another solution is the use of FISCAL POLICY—the government's budgetary and taxing controls. In short, government would cut spending and raise taxes, both of which would remove money—and thus demand—from the economy.

The solution sounds ideal, but it has some drawbacks. First, not all government spending programs can be cut that easily. Many are established under laws that make it virtually impossible to eliminate and extremely difficult to stunt spending by cutting funding. Attacking the establishment of new programs is easier in terms of legislation, but evokes political repercussions most lawmakers don't want to face.

Even in terms of slashing current expenditures, such as defense programs, most lawmakers don't want to face the ire of constituents thrown out of work because of the closing of an army base or a defense plant. A tax increase would definitely cool demand by cutting people's spendable income, but its unpopularity often holds it in check.

On the other hand, a tax cut for business or upper income brackets would produce the incentives needed to boost investment plant and equipment that would increase output and expand employment. However, such a proposal is often greeted as "feeding the rich from the tables of the poor."

Monetary Policy. MONETARY POLICY seeks to influence the excessive growth of money and credit during inflationary periods and restrain private demand, the largest source of inflationary pressure. By using its three monetary tools (open-market operations, reserve requirements, and discount-rate policy) the Federal Reserve seeks to control spendable income by affecting the amount of loans created by commercial banks.

For example, a business seeking a loan to expand inventories might find its plans cut short because it can't get a loan, or because interest rates are higher than it can pay. This change in plans in turn will help to reduce overall demands on the economy. Multiply the impact of this situation by the millions of individuals and businesses seeking loans, and you'll have some idea of how potent monetary policy can be.

But monetary policy also has its drawbacks. First, because it's indirect, its effects don't show up immediately and prices can continue upward even after demand slackens. This delayed reaction can cause considerable debate over the effectiveness of monetary policy, and cause an anti-inflationary policy to be abandoned just as its effects are about to be felt.

At the same time, monetary policy must walk a tightrope between cutting back inflation and causing recession. Monetary policy, of course, does have an effect on employment, but the Federal Reserve carefully tries to minimize this side effect.

About the only certainty that can be attributed to the various solutions to inflation is that none are simple, painless, or quick.

Charles J. Parnow

Installment Account

This is usually a traditional form of retail CREDIT for the purchase of "big-ticket," more costly items, primarily durable goods and services that most consumers either cannot afford to purchase with cash or prefer to buy on credit to avoid depleting any savings they may have. Such an account is usually opened through an individual contract or agreement for a single purchase or a series of purchases made at one time, such as items of furniture. Down payments or trade-ins are often involved in opening such accounts. Credit is extended for a fixed period of time, and repayment is made in part each month in equal amounts, except perhaps for the first and/or last payment, which may be larger. The cost of credit is usually separate from the cost of the goods or services purchased, although it is sometimes combined with or buried in the purchase price.

James A. Ambrose

Installment Loan, Early Repayment of an

Money borrowed from a lending institution (such as a

bank, consumer finance company, or savings and loan association) is repaid with interest by a specified date in a number of equal installments. Sometimes in the course of repayment a person may wish to repay the entire loan early, not only to eliminate the debt but to avoid paying the balance of the interest due. Early repayment of a loan is advantageous, but the borrower may be disappointed to learn, after asking the creditor about the balance due, that the payoff figure is higher than anticipated.

It is a common misconception that all of the equal installments used to repay a loan contain the same amount of interest. Thus, a person might believe that if he repays a loan in six months instead of twelve, he will pay only one-half the total interest. However, the methods used by lending institutions to calculate the sum necessary to repay a loan in full at any point earlier than originally scheduled do not bear this out.

Lenders use several different methods to determine the amount of interest to be paid by a borrower at any point in a loan. The most widely used, reflected in a number of state lending laws, is based on a mathematical formula known as "the Rule of 78s" or "the Sum of the Digits." The Rule is a practical way to calculate the portion of the total interest charge that does not have to be paid when a loan is paid off early. The formula rests on the idea that the interest amount should be higher in the beginning of the loan period, when the borrower has more money available, than in the latter part.

There are various factors that affect the final payoff figure of a loan when it is paid off early. The most important is the original time to maturity. Other factors are variances in the payment schedule and the lag between the date of computation and the date of payment. A creditor is required by the Truth in Lending Act to disclose whether or not any portion of the finance charge will be rebated if the debt is paid in full before maturity. A borrower should find and carefully read the prepayment terms of a loan agreement before signing, and ask questions if anything is unclear.

The Rule of 78s. As stated above, the interest due each month on an installment loan is greater in the beginning and less as the debt is reduced. The interest in each installment is the fraction of the number of months remaining in which the borrower must make payments divided by the sum of the digits of the number of months in the installment plan. In a 12-month installment plan, the sum of the numbers 1 through 12 is 78 ($1 + 2 + 3 + 4 + 5 + 6 + 7 + 8 + 9 + 10 + 11 + 12 = 78$). There is a formula used to calculate the total of all numbers in a series:

$$\frac{N \times (N + 1)}{2}$$

The letter N represents the number of payments. For a 12-month loan, where $N = 12$, we have:

$$\frac{12 \times (12 + 1)}{2} = 6 \times 13 = 78$$

Thus, in a 12-installment loan, the borrower in the first month pays 12/78s of the total interest; in the second installment, he pays 11/78s of the interest; and so forth until in the last installment he pays 1/78 of the total interest.

Example: John Doe borrows $6,000 from a bank to purchase a car, with the total interest to be $450. If the total amount to be repaid, $6,450, is divided into 24 equal installments of $268.75, then (a) what is the interest paid per installment; and (b) how much interest will he save if the loan is paid off with the twelfth payment?

The amount of interest per installment is calculated using the rule of 78s:

$$\frac{24 \times (24 + 1)}{2} = 12 \times 25 = 300$$

Consequently, with the first payment, John Doe pays 24 parts of the total interest, or 24/300; with the second installment, he pays 23/300 and so forth. These fractions times the total interest give the amount of

Table 1

Payment Number	Interest Paid per Installment	Reduction of Debt	Total Payment
1	$36.00	$232.75	$268.75
2	34.50	234.25	268.75
3	33.00	235.75	268.75
4	31.50	237.25	268.75
5	30.00	238.75	268.75
6	28.50	240.25	268.75
7	27.00	241.75	268.75
8	25.50	243.25	268.75
9	24.00	244.75	268.75
10	22.50	246.25	268.75
11	21.00	247.75	268.75
12	19.50	249.25	268.75
13	18.00	250.75	268.75
14	16.50	252.25	268.75
15	15.00	253.75	268.75
16	13.50	255.25	268.75
17	12.00	256.75	268.75
18	10.50	258.25	268.75
19	9.00	259.75	268.75
20	7.50	261.25	268.75
21	6.00	262.75	268.75
22	4.50	264.25	268.75
23	3.00	265.75	268.75
24	1.50	267.25	268.75

interest due for each installment. For example, the interest in the first payment is 24/300 of $450 or $36. The interest due for the second payment is 23/300×$450 or $34.50. This can be viewed in table form (see Table 1).

If the loan is paid off with the twelfth payment, the interest to be rebated is determined in the following way:

First, the "digits" in the remaining 12 installments are added to find out how many parts will be rebated:

$$\frac{12 \times (12 + 1)}{2} = 6 \times 13 = 78$$

This shows that the borrower will have 78 parts of the total interest rebated; 78/300 of $450 equals $117. John Doe doesn't save one-half the interest (which would be $225) by paying back the loan in one-half the time—that is, in 12 months instead of 24. The quicker the loan is paid off, however, the greater the portion of interest he saves.

Martha E. Skoog

Insurance

Simply described, insurance is protection against risk.

Our society could hardly function without insurance. There would be so much uncertainty, so much exposure to sudden, unexpected, and possibly catastrophic loss, that it would be difficult for anyone to plan with confidence for the future.

By sharing the risk—transferring a major portion of it from individuals and companies to a professional insurer—insurance aims to reduce financial uncertainty and make losses manageable. The receipt of a known fee—an insurance premium—enables the insurer to assume the risk of a large loss in return for a promise to pay in the event of such a loss.

The insurance product is a contract, known as a "policy," which legally binds the seller (the insurer) and the buyer (the policyholder) to certain obligations. Insurers are obligated to pay for losses should a specific event covered by the policy occur. Policyholders pay a premium for the financial protection the policy provides.

The insurance buyer has a choice of agents or brokers, who often live or work nearby. It's the agent's job to advise the purchaser, to issue or arrange for issuance of the policy, and to provide follow-up service as needed.

Although many people think of insurance as one giant industry, the two principal segments—life insurers and property-casualty insurers—market entirely different products, although often the same agents or brokers handle both kinds. Still other companies sell accident and health insurance exclusively, although many life insurers and property-casualty companies also compete in the accident and health market.

Insurers are capitalized and operate in a variety of ways. The principal categories of companies are:

Capital stock companies, which are owned by stockholders whose invested funds enable a company to begin operations and enlarge its capacity to serve the insuring public. A stockholder-elected board of directors, together with officers elected by the board, makes and oversees the implementation of policies aimed at fulfilling the company's responsibilities to the public it serves and achieving a profit.

Mutual companies, which are owned by their customers or policyholders. The policyholders elect members of the board of directors, who in turn appoint officers to operate the company. The policyholder's financial "investment" is in the form of the premium he or she pays for insurance coverage. It shouldn't be compared with the investment of a stockholder, whose aim is to achieve dividends or a profit. In some cases, depending on operating results, a mutual company may return a payment to its customers in the form of a policyholder's dividend.

Insurance underwriting is a decision-making process: The underwriter must evaluate each application for coverage and decide whether to accept or reject it. A primary function of the underwriting department is to promote the company's growth by proper risk selection to achieve an acceptable balance of risks properly priced for each line of insurance.

The monitoring of insurance companies' financial condition continues as a primary responsibility of regulators to assure that companies remain solvent and thus able to meet their obligations to policyholders. While their powers vary from state to state, regulators generally are charged with licensing and monitoring insurance companies, approving the form and conditions of policies, and reviewing rate changes to ascertain that customers are not overcharged or unfairly discriminated against and that rate levels are adequate to maintain a company's solvency.

Invariably, consumers will have questions: where and how to shop for insurance, what kinds of protection are afforded by their policies, and what to do if they have an insurance-related problem.

The first step is to find the right agent, broker, or company representative, perhaps by consulting a friend or neighbor, or even the telephone book. Agents and brokers can answer questions about the insurance policies they sell, and they serve as a liaison between the insurance company and the consumer.

Many state insurance departments have personnel whose responsibilities include working directly with consumers who have complaints or differences of opinion with their insurers.

Table 1 categorizes the various types of insurance for the many types of risks, and Table 2 (pages 328– 334) lists and briefly explains the types of insurance policies and coverages. Further explanation of some of these can be found in their respective entries.

Mechlin D. Moore

Table 1
Types of Risk and Insurance

Types of Risk	*Corresponding Types of Insurance*
Personal risks (loss of life, health, or personal income)	*Personal insurance*
Risk of premature death	Private insurance:
Risk of dependent old age	Life insurance
Risk of accident or sickness	Annuities
Risk of unemployment	Health insurance
	Social insurance:
	Old-age, survivors', disability, and health insurance
	Workers' compensation
	Nonoccupational disability insurance
	Unemployment compensation
	Medicare
	Other forms of social insurance
Property risks (loss of property values or loss of income from, or use of, property)	*Property insurance*
Direct physical loss of or damage to one's property	Direct-damage coverages:
	Fire and allied-lines insurance
	Automobile material-damage insurance
	Ocean and inland marine insurance
	Aviation physical-damage (hull) insurance
Consequential loss arising out of damage to property:	Consequential-loss coverages:
Time element losses:	Time-element coverages:
Losses due to interruption of business	Business-interruption insurance
Loss of income from rents, etc.	Rent insurance
Non-time element losses	Coverages not involving a time element
Loss of one's property due to dishonesty or deficiency of others	Crime coverages, bonds, etc.:
	Fidelity bonding
	Surety bonding
	Burglary, robbery, and theft insurance
	Credit insurance
	Title insurance
Liability risks (loss due to legal responsibility for specific acts or failure to act)	*Liability insurance*
Bodily injury to others	Bodily-injury liability insurance:
	Automobile liability insurance
	Aviation liability insurance
	General public liability insurance, etc.
Damage to property of others	Property-damage liability insurance:
	Automobile liability insurance
	Aviation liability insurance
	General public liability insurance, etc.
Damage to reputation of others	"Personal injury" liability insurance:
	Libel
	Slander
	Defamation of character

Source: General Principles of Insurance and Property Loss Adjusting Course Guide, Insurance Institute of America.

Table 2

Type	Brief Description
Automobile insurance	Automobile insurance is the most widely purchased of all property-liability coverages. Following are 10 basic types of auto-insurance coverage.
Bodily-injury insurance	Pays up to limits of liability for all damages the person insured is legally obligated to pay because of accidental bodily injury to any other person arising out of the insured person's ownership, maintenance, or use of his car.
Property-damage liability	Pays up to limits of liability for all damages the person insured is legally obligated to pay because of accidental damage to or destruction of property of any other person arising out of the insured person's ownership, maintenance, or use of his insured car.
Uninsured motorist	Pays the policyholder and any passengers in his car for losses sustained by reason of bodily injury, sickness, disease, or death caused by the owner or operator of an uninsured automobile, or a "hit-and-run" driver.
Underinsured motorist	Coverage is intended to cover losses unpaid because sufficient bodily-injury liability limits are not available from the policy of an at-fault person. How and under what circumstances the coverage becomes operative varies in different states. In some states, your incurred damages must exceed the limits available. In other states, your own underinsured coverage limits *and* your damages both must exceed the liability coverage available from the at-fault person's bodily-injury policy.
Medical payments	Coverage in non-"no-fault" states that pays, without regard to fault, the reasonable and necessary medical expenses incurred by the policyholder, resident family members, and guests in the policyholder's car. Medical expenses are covered only if they arise from bodily injuries sustained in an automobile accident, or from injury to the policyholder or resident family members by a vehicle while walking, riding in another car, or riding a bicycle.

Table 2 *(cont)*

Type	Brief Description
Personal-injury protection	Coverage in "no-fault" states that usually pays for medical expenses; loss of income; death and/or disability; and loss of services incurred as a result of an automobile accident. Coverage varies according to state law so that no two states have identical coverages.
Auto death indemnity	Provides limited life-insurance protection to insured persons specifically named in the policy in the event of a death that is a direct result of a vehicle accident. Payment is not contingent upon the establishment of negligence, but death by an intentional act of the insured is not covered.
Auto disability income	Provides persons specifically named in the policy with the weekly benefit shown in the policy in the event of continuous total disability as a direct result of bodily injury, sickness, or infection caused by an auto accident.
Collision	Pays for damage to the policyholder's car as a result of a collision with another vehicle or another object, or by upset of the insured car. Collision coverage is provided with "deductibles," generally ranging from $50 to $1,000. This means that you pay for any losses up to that level, and your insurance pays for the excess. Most insurers will not pay for repairs that surpass the actual cash value of the car, so its worth at the time of the accident usually constitutes a limit on the coverage.
Comprehensive	Covers losses due to theft or from damage to the insured auto due to some cause other than collision. The coverage usually insures against fire, glass breakage, vandalism, falling objects, explosion, earthquake, hail, windstorm, flood, or collision with an animal.
Specialty coverages	(1) *Recreational-vehicle insurance.* Provides package coverage for vehicles designed primarily for off-road use and not subject to registration—for example, dune buggies, all terrain vehicles, etc., as long as they are not used on public

Table 2   *(cont)*

Type	Brief Description
	roads. If used on roads or highways, or if subject to motor-vehicle registration in a given state, coverage is available under an automobile policy. (2) *Motor-home insurance.* Provides essentially the same coverage as a homeowners policy, with only a few modifications as needed to reflect the difference in the structures. Some companies rate mobile-home policies in the same manner as homeowners, while others use a technique similar to automobile-insurance rating, which adjusts rates based on the increasing age of the unit.
Aviation insurance	Commercial aircraft insurance covers both physical damage and liability suits resulting from use or ownership of aircraft. The market for aviation insurance includes commercial passenger and cargo airlines as well as business firms that use their own aircraft. Individual airplane owners, operators of flight schools, aircraft manufacturers, and charter services are also eligible for coverage.
Boiler and machinery insurance	A specialized line of coverage for power-producing equipment in business and industry. Generally, coverage is afforded against losses resulting from the breakdown of mechanical, electrical, and pressure equipment ranging from boilers to refrigeration systems, engines, compressors, pumps, motors, transformers, and other machinery that generates, converts, or uses power.
Business-interruption insurance	There are numerous versions of business-interruption insurance that can provide protection for a business that is forced into a total or a partial shutdown because of damage inflicted by a fire, a severe storm, or some other peril. This insurance can reimburse the business for lost income and for continuing expenses such as payroll, mortgage or rent payments, and continuing utility expenses.
Commercial auto insurance	Covers the loss of or damage to commercial vehicles used by businesses and the legal liability

Table 2   *(cont)*

Type	Brief Description
	associated with the operation of these vehicles. There are three main classifications of business automobiles for insurance purposes: (1) private passenger automobiles owned by businesses; (2) trucks; and (3) public conveyance vehicles, which include any type of vehicle used to carry passengers.
Commercial credit insurance	Protects manufacturers and wholesalers from credit losses by providing reimbursement for lost payments due to insolvency or default.
Commercial multiple-line policies	The term *multiple-line* is used to describe an insurance policy that combines more than one of the traditional lines, or types, of insurance. Even though multiple-line policies are often called "multiperil policies," the terms are not synonymous. Any policy that covers certain properties from more than one peril, such as fire, windstorm, theft, etc., is a multiperil policy. Multiple-line policies are multiperil packages that include both property and liability coverages against a wide range of perils. There are many commercial multiple-line policies on the market, each with a common purpose—to cover the major property and liability exposures faced by a business, organization, or group of businesses. These policies are designed to meet virtually all insurance needs of businesses. (For some specialized operations, unusual hazards may be covered separately or by endorsement to one of these package policies.)
Disability income insurance	See *Health insurance.*
Farm insurance	A traditional family-owned farm contains much property—such as barns, sheds, farm equipment and machinery, hay and grain—not covered by the standard homeowners policy. Under the farmowners/ranchowners policy, three types of coverage for the farmer's home and nonbusiness property are available: basic, broad, and tenant's coverages. A package policy may have options for

Table 2   *(cont)*

Type	Brief Description
	covering "farm personal" property, including equipment and livestock but excluding farm buildings. Liability coverage also is included in the farmowners/ ranchowners package (FR-9).
Basic coverage (FR-1)	Covers the farmer's house and all personal property as well as additional living expenses or loss of rental income should the home be uninhabitable because of damage caused by an insured peril. The perils covered by this policy are fire, theft, windstorm or hail, explosion, riot or civil commotion, aircraft, vehicles, smoke, vandalism and malicious mischief, and damage to personal property resulting from the overturn of a vehicle.
Broad coverage (FR-2)	This policy insures the farmhouse and nonbusiness personal property against the same perils listed in the broad form of the homeowners policy (see p. 331).
Tenants broad coverage (FR-4)	Protects tenants of farms and farmhouses against the same perils as the FR-2 policy, but only for the personal property kept at the location—property not used for business purposes.
Scheduled farm personal property (FR-6)	Protects property usual to the operation of a farm, including hay, grain, fertilizers, machinery, farm vehicles and equipment, farm records, and even livestock.
Blanket coverage [unscheduled farm property] (FR-7)	This coverage "blankets," for insurance purposes, most farm personal property on the farmer's premises. The blanket coverage applies to goats, horses, mules, and donkeys (other animals and poultry are not included). Certain crop yields—such as tobacco, cotton, vegetables, and fruit—are not covered.
Farm buildings (FR-8)	Barns and other farm structures, including dwellings other than the main farmhouse, are covered under the FR-8 section of a farmowners package policy.
Liability (FR-9)	The liability coverage provided in the farmowners/ranchowners package, FR-9, is similar to that offered under the homeowners policy except that it also applies to

Table 2   *(cont)*

Type	Brief Description
	the liability resulting from the farmer's business operation. Thus, it would cover a claim by a person who was injured on the farm, whether in the farmhouse, in the cattle barn, or in the open.
Crop-hail insurance	Provides protection against potential financial ruin due to damage to crops by certain perils (a variety of crop-hail policies are available, each with its own set of coverages and exclusions). Perils may include fire, lightning, hail and wind (if accompanied by hail that destroys at least 5% of the crop), insects, excessive moisture, and drought.
Fire insurance	Provides money to cover damages resulting from fire, lightning, and smoke.
Glass insurance	Comprehensive glass insurance can provide protection for windows, mirrors, art glass, structural glass, leaded glass, etc. Glass insurance does not cover damage caused by war, nuclear energy, or fire. Scratches and surface chippage are not considered breakage—the damage must penetrate the entire thickness of the glass.
Health insurance	Insurance that reimburses individuals or families for health-care costs or provides replacement income when a person is unable to work due to illness or injury. Private health insurance, insurance issued by nongovernment agencies, is made available in various forms by several types of insurers. These include companies, hospital and medical service plans, group medical plans available on a prepayment basis, and others. Health-insurance coverage is of two basic types: medical expense insurance and disability income insurance.
Medical expense insurance	A "reimbursement" type of coverage that provides broad benefits that can cover virtually all kinds of expenses connected with hospital and medical care and related services. Medical expense insurance is of the following types:
Blue Cross/ Blue Shield	Nonprofit membership plans offering individual and group

Table 2   *(cont)*

Type	Brief Description
	health- insurance coverage in an area confined to one state or other regions. Blue Cross plans provide hospital-care benefits on essentially a "service-type" basis, meaning the organization through a separate contract with member hospitals for covered services to the injured. Blue Shield plans provide benefits for surgical and medical services performed by a physician. The typical Blue Shield services plan provides benefits similar to those under the hospital surgical policies issued by insurance companies.
Major-medical insurance	Protection against extraordinary medical expenses that otherwise would create serious financial hardship. This policy provides for payment of a percentage of all covered medical expenses incurred in excess of the deductible up to the amount of the maximum benefits for the plan selected. Characterized by large benefit maximums ranging up to $250,000 or no limit, the insurance, above an initial deductible, reimburses the major part of all charges for hospital, doctor, private nurses, medical appliances, prescribed out-of-hospital treatment, drugs, and medicines. The insured person as coinsurer pays the remainder.
Cash indemnity program	Compensation of the value of a loss. Used loosely to refer to health-insurance benefits paid in cash rather than in terms of health-insurance service.
Group insurance	Insurance with an employer or other entity that covers a group of persons identified as individuals by reference to their relationship to the entity.
Medicare	A federal government program providing medical insurance for the aged, created by the 1965 amendments to the Social Security Act, and operated under the provisions of the act.
Disability income insurance	A form of health insurance that provides periodic payments to replace income when an insured person is unable to work as a result of illness, injury, or disease.
Home insurance	Insures homeowners and renters

Table 2   *(cont)*

Type	Brief Description
	against damage to homes or property. Insurance coverages for the home, its contents, and the homeowner's or tenant's liability to others usually are combined into a single package (homeowners) policy, although separate policies are available for fire, theft, and other perils. There are various forms of the homeowners policy.
Homeowners policies (HO-1, HO-2, HO-5)	HO-1, the basic homeowners policy, provides coverage against 11 perils; HO-2, the broad form, covers 7 additional perils; and HO-5, the comprehensive form, covers all perils except a few specifically excluded (see chart on p. 313).
Special policy (HO-3)	Provides the same "all-risk" coverage for a homeowner's dwelling and other structures on the property as does the comprehensive form (HO-5), while limiting coverage of personal property to the various perils included in the broad form (HO-2).
Renter's policy (HO-4)	HO-4, the tenant's policy or contents broad form, is designed for those who rent an apartment or house or own a cooperative apartment. It insures household contents and personal belongings against all of the perils included in the broad form (HO-2), as well as the policyholder's liability to others. Coverage for the house or building is the responsibility of the landlord or cooperative association.
Condominium unit-owner's policy (HO-6)	A condominium association usually buys the insurance to cover the condominium's property (building and structures) and liability. However, a special condominium unit-owner's policy (HO-6) is available for unit owners who wish to insure their personal property or to cover any additions or alterations that are not insured by the association's policy.
Older-home insurance (HO-8)	This policy allows owners of older homes to carry lower limits of insurance by returning the property to serviceable condition in case of damage, but not necessarily with the use of materials of the same kind and quality as the original.

Table 2 *(cont)*

Type	Brief Description
Mobile-home owner's policy	A special policy for persons who own and occupy a mobile home that is at least 10 by 40 feet long. Provides basically the same coverages as the homeowners broad-form policy (HO-2).
Insurance against crime	Various forms of insurance are available to businesses to help protect against losses caused by thieves. Theft policies cover both the missing goods and the damaged property. Generally, theft policies cover two types of crimes—burglary and robbery, but other crimes can be covered by endorsement to a policy if protection against them is not included in the basic policy. Some of these crimes are forgery, embezzlement, misappropriation, willful obstruction, willful misapplication, and mysterious disappearance.
Kidnap and ransom insurance	Kidnap and ransom insurance reimburses a policyholder for any ransom or extortion payments up to a certain limit (usually in the millions of dollars).
Life insurance	Insurance on a person's life providing a specific sum of money to be paid to the individual or group designated in the policy as the beneficiary upon death of the insured or to the insured should he live to a certain age. There are different types of life-insurance policies having various benefits.
Term insurance	Provides the insured with coverage for a "term" of one or more years. Premium payments are made during the term of the policy. The beneficiary receives death benefits (face of the policy) only if the insured dies within the specified term. Most term insurance policies are "renewable" (at higher premiums for one or more additional terms) and "convertible" (into a whole-life or endowment policy).
Whole-life insurance	Provides the insured with coverage for life. Premiums are paid as long as the insured owns the policy. Death benefits are paid to the beneficiary any time the insured dies. Premiums remain the same throughout life, but are higher than

Table 2 *(cont)*

Type	Brief Description
	those initially paid for the same amount of term insurance.
Endowment insurance	Provides for the payment of a sum or income to the insured if he lives to a certain date ("maturity date"). If the insured dies before this date, the death benefit is paid to the beneficiary. Endowment insurance enables the policyholder to receive the face of the policy if he lives to a certain age, but premiums and cash values are higher than for the same amount of whole-life insurance.
Annuity	A contract written by an insurance company providing for one or two persons (the annuitant[s]) to make a lump-sum payment to the company, in return for which the policy promises to pay income for life. Payments are typically made monthly and begin at a specified age. The primary advantage of the annuity is that the annuitant(s) cannot outlive the income. If an annuitant dies prior to the commencement of payments, the death benefit is usually the greater of the premiums paid, or the cash value of the policy.
Life insurance for members of the armed services	Since 1965, all armed-service personnel have been covered by Servicemen's Group Life Insurance (SGLI) unless they elect to refuse it. It is term insurance, the current maximum amount is $35,000, and the premium is deducted from paychecks (the amount of insurance is chosen by the individual). After separation from the service, the veteran can continue this group insurance for five years, when it will terminate unless converted to an individual policy of permanent, cash-value type. SGLI is administered by Prudential with many other participating companies. Prior to 1965, the government itself provided life insurance to ser-vicepersons during or right after wars. In 1919 the first of these, U.S. Government Life Insurance (USGLI), appeared. Little of this insurance remains in force. It was followed in 1940 by National Service Life Insurance (NSLI), and

Table 2 *(cont)*

Type	Brief Description
	then by a free $10,000 policy in 1950 that was exchangeable on separation for an NSLI policy (until 1956). These were term insurance but convertible to permanent plans. In 1971 disabled veterans became entitled to up to $40,000 in mortgage-protection life insurance. A major benefit to armed-service personnel occurred in 1956 when Social Security coverage was extended to them.
Marine insurance	The term *marine insurance* is a general one, encompassing two more widely used insurance types: ocean marine, which covers property whose mode of transportation is by waterways; and inland marine, which covers transportation-related or transportable property on land. There are two basic types of ocean marine property coverages: insurance for the boat or vessel (hull insurance) and insurance for cargo. Inland marine provides financial protection against perils to almost anything transportable: for example, artificial turf in sports stadiums; white mice used in the space program; the beryllium nose cone of a moon rocket; a submarine (a small one) being shipped on a flatbed trailer; even corpses.
Medicare	A federal health-insurance program covering most people 65 years of age or older and certain disabled younger people.
Mortgage insurance, private	Protects lending institutions from financial loss in the event of borrower default on a mortgage note.
Nuclear insurance	Insurance against losses resulting from nuclear accidents is provided by special insurance pools created by property- and liability-insurance companies. These pools have the resources to insure risks of a size that would be beyond the financial capabilities of any one insurance company. The pools provide both liability and property coverages. The liability coverage protects the operators of nuclear facilities and their suppliers from legal responsibilities they may incur as a

Table 2 *(cont)*

Type	Brief Description
	result of bodily injury or property damage resulting from a nuclear accident. Property insurance covers damage (up to $300 million) to the property of nuclear-facility operators on an "all-risk" basis.
Product-liability insurance	Protects the maker or distributor of a product in the event he or she is held liable for compensation to a user, consumer, or other person who suffers injury or loss arising from the use of that product.
Professional liability insurance	Protects individuals and organizations whose services are expected to meet consistently high standards because of their status as professional practitioners from the consequences of their failure to use due care and the high degree of skill expected of a professional. Medical malpractice, the subject of widespread public attention, is only one of many professional liability coverages. Under the general heading of "professional liability," insurers use two categories to classify professionals: malpractice liability, which technically applies to those professionals whose services include touching of the body; and errors and omissions (E & O) coverage, for those professionals whose services usually do not involve touching of the body.
Public liability insurance	Public liabilities refer to legal obligations that if neglected or broken could require that the business or business owner pay monetary damages to another party. Some of these obligations arise from the ownership and maintenance of a premises; the conduct of a business or an operation; the manufacture, distribution, or selling of products; completed operations; work done by independent contractors or subcontractors; and liabilities assumed by contract. Broad liability protection is available through a comprehensive package policy or through one of several specialized packages of coverages. There are also policies with coverages limited to specific types of public liabilities.

Table 2   *(cont)*

Type	Brief Description
Railroad social insurance	Provides social insurance nationally for employees of railroads, railroad associations, and railway labor organizations.
Serviceman's insurance	See *Life insurance.*
Statutory disability benefits	Statutory requirements of five states (New York, California, New Jersey, Rhode Island, Hawaii) and Puerto Rico to provide benefits for employees totally unable to work as a result of nonoccupational injury or sickness.
Social Security	An insurance program of the federal government providing a continuing income when family earnings are reduced or stop because of retirement, disability, or death. Administered by the Social Security Administration.
Suretyship	Surety bonds, issued by a surety company in exchange for a premium, guarantee to one party that another will perform specified acts—often within a stated period. Surety companies have carried to completion all manner of private and public works—buildings, roads, canals, railways, waterworks, dams, ships, and utility projects.
Surplus and excess line insurance	The term *surplus lines* has come to be applied to any insurance coverage that is unattainable through a company licensed in the applicant's state and is obtained through a market outside the state. (The term *excess lines* has come to mean virtually the same thing as *surplus lines.*)
Title insurance	Protects purchasers of real estate against losses resulting from previously existing defects in a title, such as unsatisfactory liens and mortgages, forgeries, misrepresentation, or invalid wills. The policy covers only defects that existed when it was issued—not those that might occur later. The policy is in force as long as the policyholder and his or her heirs maintain ownership. The insurer also agrees to defend the policyholder against lawsuits involving the title.
Unemployment insurance	Cash benefits to regularly employed members of the labor force who

Table 2   *(cont)*

Type	Brief Description
	become involuntarily unemployed and who are able and willing to accept suitable jobs.
Workers' compensation insurance	Insurance purchased by an employer to cover occupational injury and illness. All the states and Puerto Rico, the U.S. Virgin Islands, American Samoa, and Guam have workers' compensation laws.

Sources: Allstate News Bureau of Allstate Insurance Company and Allstate Life Insurance Company; Hugh A. Brodkey; Insurance Information Institute; Harold C. Luckstone, Jr.; James L. Moorefield; Arthur S. Phillips; Robert Waldron; Sheila R. Wyse.

Insurance Trusts

See TRUSTS.

Interest

Interest is simply money paid for the use of money.

When you deposit money with a bank, it uses the funds for loans and other types of investments. Except for demand deposits (*see* DEMAND DEPOSIT), the bank will pay you interest for the use of your funds.

When you borrow money from a bank, it charges you interest for the use of the funds.

Interest rates on loans are set by market forces. However, monetary policy conducted by the Federal Reserve (*see* FEDERAL RESERVE SYSTEM) influences these market forces, and thus the level of interest rates.

Interest can be computed in two ways. *Simple interest* is a flat percentage of the principal and is usually calculated on an annual basis. *Compound interest* is a percentage of the sum of the principal plus any successive interest increments added to the principal. The easiest way to think of compound interest is as interest on interest as well as on the principal.

Phil Battey

Interest-Rate Futures

Interest-rate futures contracts are standardized agreements to buy or sell a specified quantity and grade of a designated financial instrument on a specified future date at a price that has been determined by public auction, through the facilities of a regulated commodity exchange. The terms of the contract are set by the exchange, and the exchange clearinghouse system guarantees performances on each contract.

Interest-rate futures, more specifically, refer to futures contracts on fixed-income securities: for example, U.S. Treasury bonds and bills, and certificates of deposits. They are often referred to as "financial futures," which, in the broader context, would also include foreign currencies.

The markets in interest-rate futures have grown and flourished since their inception in 1975 because the underlying instrument, or "commodity," exhibits characteristics similar to those of the more traditional physical commodities—that is, money or the price of money (interest) is affected by time, and the supply, demand, and price equation. In a free market environment, the uncertainties of supply of and demand for money create significant price risks for persons and institutions who depend on the ability of the money and credit markets to meet their capital or investment needs.

As shown in Figures 1 and 2, the rate for government and corporate debt was relatively stable up through the 1950s and into the early 1960s. The rate

of change was such that there was almost no significant short-term risk and very little long-term risk involved in the money and credit markets. Since the mid-to-late 1960s, these risks have been greatly magnified for both long- and short-term debt securities.

History of Interest-Rate Futures. The CHICAGO BOARD OF TRADE (CBOT) is credited with introducing the first interest-rate-futures contract, on GOVERNMENT NATIONAL MORTGAGE ASSOCIATION (GNMA) certificates in October 1975. This was shortly followed by futures on 90-day U.S. Treasury bills on the International Monetary Market (IMM) of the CHICAGO MERCANTILE EXCHANGE in January 1976. The third and presently most successful contract, Treasury-bond futures, was introduced on the CBOT in August 1977. For more information on this and the history of futures trading in general, consult these and the other entries on the commodities exchanges in this book.

The Exchange System. Futures trading on organized exchanges effectively removed the "caveat emptor" risk from agricultural forward-contracting transactions. In more than 100 years of futures trading, there has been only one recorded instance of a futures-contract default that caused a loss to a buyer or seller. This sole instance involved a potato-futures contract on the New York Mercantile Exchange in 1977.

This legacy of safety has carried through to the financial-futures markets. Despite the increasing volatility of the money market since interest-rate futures trading began in 1975, no user of these markets has ever experienced a loss due to the failure of a buyer or a seller to make good on his delivery commitment. This is due both to the strict surveillance of the futures markets by the exchanges and government regulators and to the insurance function of the exchange clearing corporations, which make good on any defaults by contracting parties.

This safety record does not hold true in the cash and interbank forward markets where defaults, in both foreign currency and delayed-delivery fixed-income security transactions, have caused significant losses and even bank failures and corporate bankruptcies in past years.

The functions of futures exchanges are to provide marketplaces for the purchase and sale of futures contracts. Underlying this function are the operation of a trading floor and the providing of facilities to clear the trades made on the floor of the exchange.

An extremely important element of the functioning of a futures exchange is guaranteeing the performance of every trade made on the exchange floor. This is accomplished by the "clearinghouse" of each ex-

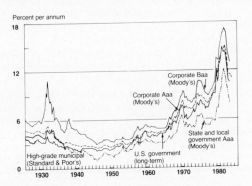

Figure 1. Long-term bond yields (quarterly averages).

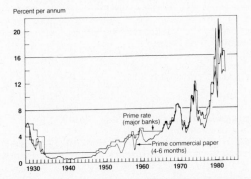

Figure 2. Short-term interest rates: business borrowing (prime rate, effective date of change; prime paper, quarterly averages).

change taking the opposite side of every trade by the process of substitution.

After all trades executed by open outcry on the floor are submitted to and accepted by the clearinghouse, it assumes the position of seller to every buyer, and buyer to every seller. Thus, the identities of the parties who have taken the other side of their trades are of no consequence to customers, since the exchange clearinghouse guarantees the performance of every trade. The exchanges, however, do not deal directly with customers; they officially conduct business only with their clearing members, who in turn handle business with public customers.

The exchanges impose margins on their clearing members, and the clearing members in turn impose margins on their customers. Their customer margins, which in fact are security deposits to cover any initial loss that may result from price movements, flow directly to the clearinghouse at the close of business each day.

Another important safety feature is the segregation of customer funds. The rules of the COMMODITY FUTURES TRADING COMMISSION (CFTC), the government agency that regulates the commodity industry, require that all customer moneys, securities, and equities must be maintained in a separate, segregated bank account and not be commingled with the funds of the broker or FUTURES COMMISSION MERCHANT (FCM). This provides protection of all customer money should a financial failure occur. The exchanges and the CFTC maintain audit and compliance staffs that monitor the compliance of all clearing members and FCM's with segregation and minimum-financial-integrity requirements.

While clearinghouse requirements and systems may differ from exchange to exchange, their purpose is to assure that each exchange has a high degree of financial security.

Interest-Rate-Futures Contracts. To fully grasp the information that follows in this section, it will be helpful to review the economic nature and functions of futures contracts in general. (Readers so inclined should also consult the entry on FUTURES CONTRACTS.)

The growth, maturity, acceptance, and success of interest-rate futures all arise from the principle that interest rates—the cost of money—behave in the same fashion as the prices of other commodities, and that certain kinds of institutions that may be adversely affected by volatile interest rates need a hedging mechanism to transfer such risks. Conversely, with risk comes opportunity for those with the capital to accept such in the hope of realizing profits.

These risk-takers, both speculators and arbitragers, have combined with the growing number of hedgers (risk-avoiders) to make interest-rate futures the leading and dominant force in the commodity markets during the late 1970s and early 1980s.

The statistics in Table 1 chart the growth of the first three and most active interest-rate-futures contracts available. This table takes into account only three contracts. When ten-year U.S. Treasury notes (CBT—881,325), domestic certificates of deposit (IMM—1,566,327), and Eurodollar time deposits (IMM—323,619) are added to the 1982 figures, volume rises to 28.2 million contracts or 25% of all commodity contracts traded on U.S. exchanges.

Since their inception in 1975, the markets for interest-rate futures have gone through various phases of expansion and consolidation. For example, at one point in 1980, fourteen interest-rate-futures contracts were traded on no fewer than four separate exchanges. In October of 1979, there were three 90-day treasury-bill contracts on three separate exchanges, three GNMA contracts on two exchanges, and two Treasury-bond contracts on two exchanges. Despite this proliferation and competition, the markets grew and the original three interest-rate futures (CBOT GNMA's, IMM 90-day bills, and CBOT T-Bonds) remained the sole primary markets.

With maturity came the markets' ability to absorb additional contracts to help fill in the yield curve (ten-year Treasury-note futures—CBOT) as well as the spectrum of non-Treasury short-term money-market debt (90-day domestic CD's and Eurodollar deposits—IMM). Tables 2 and 3 present a summary of the contract specifications for the six actively traded interest-rate futures.

Table 1

Trading Volume of Most Active Interest-Rate-Futures Contracts, 1978–82 (Millions of Contracts)

	1978	1979	1980	1981	1982
Treasury-bond futures (CBOT)	.56	2.1	6.5	13.9	16.7
Treasury-bill futures (IMM)	.77	1.9	3.3	5.6	6.6
GNMA (CDR's CBOT)	.95	1.4	2.3	2.3	2.1
Total	2.28	5.4	12.1	21.8	25.4
Total contracts all commodities	58.5	76.0	92.1	98.5	112.4
Interest-rate futures as % of all	3.9%	7.1%	13.1%	22%	23%

Source: Futures Industry Association.

Table 2
Short-Term Interest-Rate Futures

Contract Specifications	90-Day U.S. Treasury Bill	Three-Month Domestic Certificate of Deposit	Three-Month Eurodollar Time Deposit
Trading Unit	$1,000,000	$1,000,000	$1,000,000
Deliverable grade	1. Treasury bills with 91 days to maturity	1. "No-name" CD's. Deliverable banks announced 2 business days before 15th day of delivery month. Deliverable CD's determined by polling of dealers. 2. CD's must mature between 16th and last day of the month, 3 months after delivery month. 3. Deliverable maturity range approx. 2½ to 3½ months. 4. CD's with no more than 185 days accrued interest. 5. Variable-rate and discount CD's are deliverable if and when yields are equivalent to "no-name" run.	1. Cash settlement
Months traded	Mar., June, Sept., Dec.	Mar., June, Sept., Dec.	Mar., June, Sept., Dec., and spot month
Price quotation	IMM Index 100.00 bank discount rate—e.g., 9.50 would be quoted as 90.50	IMM Index 100.00 yield	IMM Index 100.00 yield
Minimum fluctuation	.01 (1 basis pt.) ($25/pt.)	.01(1 basis pt.) ($25/pt.)	.01 (1 basis pt.) ($25/pt.)
Daily price limit	.60 (60 basis pts.) ($1,500)	.80 (80 basis pts.) ($2,000)	1.00 (100 basis pts.) ($2,500) no spot month limit
Initial margins*	$2,500	$2,500	$2,500
Hours of trading (CST)	8:00 A.M.–2:00 P.M.	7:30 A.M.–2:00 P.M.	7:30 A.M.–2:00 P.M.
Delivery date	1st day of delivery month when a 13-week bill is issued and a 1-year bill has 13 weeks remaining	15th through last day of month	Last day of trading
Last day of trading	Day before the first delivery day	Last business day before last delivery day	2nd London business day before 3rd Wednesday

*Approximate amounts. Initial margins can be changed from time to time by the exchanges.

The Instruments

United States Treasury Bills. Short-term debt instruments issued by the U.S. Treasury through the Federal Reserve Bank. They are issued to help the Treasury manage its short-term cash position. Treasury bills are issued in book-entry form only—that is, there are no physical certificates, only entries within the computer records of the Federal Reserve Bank. They are sold at a discount and redeemed for face value at maturity.

Three-month and six-month bills are sold weekly through public auctions conducted by the Federal Reserve banks. Auctions are normally announced on Thursdays and held the following Monday with "de-

Table 3
Long-Term Interest-Rate Futures

Contract Specifications	CDR GNMA	U.S. Treasury Bonds	Treasury-Note Futures 6½ to 10 Yrs.
Trading unit	$100,000 principal balance of GNMA 8% coupon or equivalent	U.S. Treasury bonds, $100,000 face value	U.S. Treasury notes with $100,000 face value
Deliverable grade	Modified pass-through mortgage-backed certificates guaranteed by GNMA, with coupons of an equivalent principal balance based on an 8% coupon yielding 7.96% at par. Based on the assumption of a 30-year certificate prepaid in the 12th year.	U.S. Treasury bonds maturing at least 15 years from date of delivery if not callable; if callable, not so for at least 15 years from 1st day of delivery month. Based on 8% coupon and conversion factor.	U.S. Treasury notes. Maturity no less than 6½ years and not more than 10 years from date of delivery. Based on 8% coupon and conversion factor.
Months traded	Mar., June, Sept., Dec.	Mar., June, Sept., Dec.	Mar., June, Sept., Dec.
Price quotation	Percentage of par—e.g., 70-01 (70$\frac{1}{32}$)	Percentage of par—e.g., 76-01 (76$\frac{1}{32}$)	Percentage of par—e.g., 85-01 (85$\frac{1}{32}$)
Minimum fluctuation	$\frac{1}{32}$ of a point ($31.25 per contract)	$\frac{1}{32}$ of a point ($31.25 per contract)	$\frac{1}{32}$ of a point ($31.25 per contract)
Daily price limit	$\frac{64}{32}$ ($2,000 per contract) above or below the previous day's settlement price	$\frac{64}{32}$ ($2,000 per contract) above or below the previous day's settlement price	$\frac{64}{32}$ ($2,000 per contract) above or below the previous day's settlement price
Initial margin*	$2,000 per contract	$2,000 per contract	$2,000 per contract
Hours of trading (CST)	8:00 A.M.–2:00 P.M.	8:00 A.M.–2:00 P.M.	8:00 A.M.–2:00 P.M.
Delivery date	Any business day of the delivery month	Any business day of the delivery month	Any business day of the delivery month
Last day of trading	The business day prior to the last 7 business days of the delivery month	The business day prior to the last 7 business days of the delivery month	The business day prior to the last 7 business days of the delivery month

*Approximate amounts. Initial margins can be changed from time to time by the exchanges.

livery" or settlement occurring on the Thursday following the auction. One-year Treasury bills are auctioned and issued every four weeks.

As noted above, Treasury bills do not carry a coupon but are quoted in terms of their discount from par. At maturity the bill is redeemed at par with the difference from cost representing the investor's return. The formula for calculating price from bank discount rate is as follows:

$$\$1,000,000 - \frac{(\$1,000,000 \times \text{days to maturity} \times \text{discount})}{360}$$
$$= \$price/million$$

Example: A new three-month Treasury bill with 91 days remaining quoted at 7.75% discount would represent:

$$\$1,000,000 - \frac{(\$1,000,000 \times 91 \times .0775)}{360} = \text{Price}$$

$$\$1,000,000 - \frac{\text{Discount}}{(\$19,590.28)} = \text{Price}$$
$$\$980,409.72 = \text{Price}$$

The actual rate of return based on a 365-day year, also referred to as the "bond equivalent yield" (BEY), will be higher than the discount rate. It is calculated as follows:

$$\text{BEY} = \frac{\text{Discount}}{\text{Price}} \times \frac{365}{\text{Days held}}$$
$$\text{BEY} = \frac{19,590.28}{980,409.72} \times \frac{365}{91}$$
$$\text{BEY} = .01998 \times 4.010989$$
$$\text{BEY} = 8.13\%$$

Domestic Certificates of Deposit. Domestic certificates of deposit (CD's) are negotiable receipts or liabilities from a bank for deposit of funds for a specialized period of time at a specified rate of interest. CD's are issued at par, usually in multiples of $1 million, with the CD yield determining the interest paid on the principal amount at maturity.

Since their creation in 1961 by Citibank, money-center banks have come to rely heavily on the sale of CD's as a source of funding. Volume in this instrument has grown from approximately $1 billion outstanding shortly after the instrument's creation to upwards of $100 billion and more at times during recent years. The growth in popularity of CD's as both a mechanism and money-market funding investment has been fostered by the development of the secondary market, where CD's are actively traded among dealers and investors following their primary issuance by the bank.

The 100 largest commercial banks in the U.S., with deposits in excess of $1 billion, account for about 90% of all large-denomination CD's issued.

CD's were originally designed to attract corporate capital into the bank liability portfolio. Today, corporations hold close to two-thirds of all the large domestic CD's issued. CD's are popular with corporate portfolios because they usually offer higher yields than other short-term investments, such as U.S. Treasury bills. There is also more flexibility in matching maturity dates, enabling corporate inflows from maturing certificates to be closely matched to anticipated outflows. Finally, the availability of a secondary market provides a convenient mechanism for the liquidation of these investments prior to maturity, if necessary.

Unlike Treasury bills, however, CD's are the obligation of banks and not the government, so an implied credit risk does exist—thus the higher yield of the CD. As money-market and credit conditions tighten, these risks are perceived to increase, and normally yields of CD's will rise relative to Treasury bills.

Because of the coupon/yield features of CD's, the pricing of CD's differs from that of Treasury bills. Table 4 presents one method of calculating the price of an outstanding CD.

Eurodollar Time Deposits. Eurodollar time deposits are dollar-denominated funds deposited in banks outside of the United States. They originated in Europe in the 1950s.

The great majority of Eurodollar activity is handled by the London branches of U.S. commercial banks and other banking institutions in London. Most of the deposits are large sums—usually $½–1 million, with larger amounts quite common. The deposits are made by big domestic and multinational corporations, foreign central banks, and other official institutions, U.S. banks, and wealthy individuals. While most of the maturities of these deposits are less than six months, some have fixed terms extending to five years.

Table 4
Pricing of Domestic CD

$$P = 1,000,000 \times \frac{360 + L_1R_1}{360 + L_2R_2} - R_1 \frac{L_1 - L_2}{360}$$

$$S = P \times \frac{360 + (L_1R_1)}{360 + (L_2R_2)}$$

$$I = P \times R_1 \frac{L_1 - L_2}{360}$$

$$Q = S - I$$

Where:
S = Settlement value of a delivery unit
L_1 = Original life of CD
L_2 = Remaining life of CD
R_1 = Coupon rate of CD
R_2 = Yield to maturity (bank discount rate)* of CD
P = Par value
I = Accrued interest
Q = Principal value of a delivery unit

* Bank discount rate is equal to the settlement price subtracted from 100.00%.

Eurodollars compete with domestic banking instruments because they are free from Reserve requirements and most other U.S. regulatory restrictions. Eurodollars are subject to two types of risk. Unlike T-bills, but as in CD's, they are affected by credit risk based on the strength and overall soundness of the banks involved. They are also subject to "sovereign risk," which relates to the country under whose regulations particular banks operate. Most banks will be restricted to specified total amounts of deposits placed with institutions in any one country. These are also referred to as "sovereign lines."

As the Eurodollar cash market has grown over the last three decades, banks have used it extensively in making loans to corporate borrowers as well as in managing their own trading positions. Corporations have increasingly used Eurodollar borrowing as an additional source of funds.

United States Treasury Notes and Bonds. U.S. Treasury notes and bonds are debt instruments issued by the Treasury to fund its intermediate and long-term credit needs. They are backed by the full faith and credit of the U.S. government. They are coupon instruments paying interest semiannually until maturity, at which time the full principal and the final interest coupon is paid to the holder.

U.S. Treasury bonds (maturities at original issuance of more than ten years) may also be callable prior to maturity (usually five years) at the option of the Treasury. They are usually issued in minimum denominations of $1,000, but generally trade in the secondary dealer market in round-lot amounts of $1 million.

U.S. Treasury notes (maturities of ten years or less at original issuance) are not callable. They are auctioned by the Treasury in regular cycles, depending on maturity. Maturities of less than four years are issued in minimum denominations of $5,000.

In addition to the regular cycles for the various maturity note auctions, the Treasury conducts regular quarterly refundings to refinance, add to, or pay down maturing issues due on the fifteenth of February, May, August, and November. The standard refunding package consists of three issues of 3–3½-year notes, 10-year notes, and 30-year bonds.

Like Treasury bills, notes and bonds are supported by a broad and liquid secondary market composed of some 30 to 40 bank and nonbank primary dealers that report to the Federal Reserve Bank of New York and act as primary distributors for new Treasury debt offerings.

Treasury notes and bonds are broadly distributed among various classes of institutional and individual investors, both foreign and domestic, including foreign governments and central banks.

The bond's and note's coupon rate, callability (if applicable), and maturity all determine the conditions of the future stream of income, which, together with the price paid, determines the instrument's yield to maturity.

The GNMA* Mortgage-Backed Pass-Through Security. Trading in GNMA interest-rate futures is conducted in modified pass-through, mortgage-backed certificates guaranteed by the GOVERNMENT NATIONAL MORTGAGE ASSOCIATION (GNMA). These certificates—GNMA's—are issued exclusively by FHA/VA-approved financial entities such as mortgage bankers and thrift institutions and represent a pro rata share of a pool or package of FHA†-insured or VA‡-guaranteed mortgages. The issuer of the certificate collects the fixed monthly payments of principal and interest on all mortgages in the pool and passes these sums, plus any prepayments and proceeds from foreclosures, through to the GNMA certificate holder —the investor.

Timely payment of principal and interest to the certificate holder is guaranteed by GNMA and backed by

the full faith and credit of the U.S. government.

All the mortgages in the single pool are required to be of the same type in terms of interest rate, dwelling class, and maturity. The minimum amount of a pool is $1 million for single-family-home mortgages and certificates are issued in multiples of $5,000 face value with a minimum of $25,000. The certificates are fully and freely transferable and assignable.

The interest rate stated on the face of the GNMA certificate is the interest rate of the FHA/VA mortgages in the pool less 0.50%, which represents the issuer's servicing fee and the GNMA guarantee fee—e.g., an FHA/VA rate of 11½% produces GNMA certificates with a coupon rate of 11%.

Although the original maturity of the mortgages backing GNMA certificates is usually 30 years, yields are quoted on the basis of a 12-year maturity due to FHA actuarial experience of prepayment patterns.

These particular instruments were selected as the underlying securities for interest-rate-futures contracts for several reasons. For one thing, GNMA certificates represent an excellent proxy for the hedging of various mortgage securities in addition to the actual GNMA issuances of mortgage bankers and thrift institutions. The mortgage market is also one of the largest sectors of the debt market, so there is an economic need among the participants in that market to protect themselves against adverse price movements.

Additionally, and also applicable to U.S. Treasury securities and futures on those securities, is the fact that large deliverable supplies of these issues are outstanding and continually being issued into the market, thereby minimizing the potential for manipulation and "squeezes at delivery time." Finally, the fact that four of the six security groupings are backed by U.S. government guarantees means that virtually no credit risk exists for these securities, making them a more valid barometer of interest-rate sensitivity.

CD's and Eurodollar deposits are not backed by the full faith and credit of the government but are the credit risks of private corporations. The deliverable supplies of CD's are those of the ten largest commercial banks in the United States; therefore the credit risks, while real, are negligible. How negligible is determined by the marketplace. Since Eurodollar futures are settled in cash, there are no problems of deliverable supply.

The Futures Markets. Participants in traditional futures markets are loosely divided into hedgers, speculators, and arbitragers.

Hedgers seek to transfer risks assumed or about to be assumed in the cash market by taking an equal and opposite position in the futures market. For example, a corporate money manager concerned with a possible

---

* "GNMA" refers to certificates fully described in the standard prospectus form HUD 1717.
† FHA—Federal Housing Administration—is a division of the U.S. Department of Housing and Urban Development (HUD). It insures residential mortgage loans under standards that it sets.
‡ VA—Veterans Administration—guarantees home loans made to veterans.

rise in short-term bank lending rates can sell T-bill futures contracts in an amount equal to his short-term borrowings. If the bank raises its lending rates while the loans are outstanding, the gains in the futures positions should approximately offset the increased interest cost.

Conversely, a corporate money manager who expects a future cash flow on which he wishes to assure himself of present high interest rates may purchase T-bill or CD futures contracts in the amount and for the period of the anticipated cash flow. If interest rates fall, the increased value of the futures positions will offset the lower interest earned in investing the cash flow.

Speculators, on the other hand, are those who have capital and are willing to assume risks in anticipation of gains. They buy or sell futures contracts for profit, based on their perception of future interest-rate changes. The speculator is essential to the marketplace since a risk-transfer market requires participation by those willing to assume risk. Hedgers with offsetting risk positions provide some of the essential liquidity; but the speculator, through his willingness to accept risk in a timely manner, thereby meeting the needs of the hedger, is a necessary market participant.

Arbitrage is a trading strategy that takes advantage of value dislocation between futures and cash markets or between two futures contracts. The arbitrager hopes to profit from such perceived value differences. In doing so, he performs an essential market function of keeping prices of various financial instruments and futures contracts in a proper relationship.

Hedging. Understanding hedging must begin with an application of "basis." In all commodities, including interest-rate futures, *basis* is defined as the difference between cash-market prices and futures-market prices (see Table 5).

A parallel exists between cash and futures markets, with futures markets largely reflecting cash-market transactions plus expectations for the future—e.g., accrued interest and financing costs (net cost of carry). Similar basis relationships also exist between cash and futures markets in different but related commodities (e.g., GNMA to T-bond), offering opportunities for "cross-hedging." Historically, prices in cash and

futures markets in any commodity tend to converge as contracts near delivery, although they are subject to short-term aberrations resulting in "basis risk."

When a cross-hedge must be executed between a futures contract and a different underlying cash instrument—e.g., T-bill or CD futures and banker's acceptances, or T-bond futures and corporate bonds—the correlation of price movements between these instruments must be factored into the basis. For example, a position of $1 million in corporate bonds may be hedged with a position of more than ten $100,000 futures contracts. Maturity of the cash issue to be hedged will also be a factor. If 90-day CD futures were being used to hedge 180-day cash CD's, the hedger should sell twice as many futures to make up doubling of the maturity period.

If the difference between the cash and futures markets maintained a constant relationship, the hedger could effect a perfect risk transfer, a perfect hedge. Thus, any transaction in the cash market could be fully protected from adverse market moves by an equal and opposite transaction in the futures market.

Unfortunately, this is often not the case. Although the relationships between cash and futures markets tend to be close, they are not perfect; thus a given hedge, no matter how well executed, usually still includes some risk. Accordingly, basis risk must be taken into account in planning a hedge program.

Table 6 demonstrates how the basis relationship may affect the efficiency of a hedge. In the example, a bank is planning to issue (sell) 90-day CD's in the open market. To hedge this transaction—that is, protect the bank against a rise in short-term rates—90-day CD futures can be sold immediately in an amount equal to the number of cash CD's to be sold. The transaction is an example of an imperfect hedge because the bank's cash-market expense increase by 100 basis points, whereby the futures gain from being short was only 90 basis points. An unfavorable change in the basis cost the bank 10 basis points per million for 90 days. Had no hedge been in effect, the bank would have realized a full increase in cost of 100 basis points in their CD program.

Table 6 is an example of a *short hedge:* the sale of futures today in anticipation of, or as a substitution for, the sale of a "cash" instrument in the future.

A *long hedge* is the purchase of futures today to protect against a possible decline in rates (and rise in price) prior to one's investment in the actual securities in the future. For example, in three months a portfolio manager expects to receive $1 million for investment. Yields on long-term bonds are presently attractive at 10½%. For fear that an easing of credit conditions might cause long-term bond yields to decline (and prices to rise) three months from now, the

---

Table 5
Relationship of Cash to Futures

Cash 91-day T-bill	7.75
March '83 T-bill future	92.50 (7.50)
Basis is "25" under.	

Table 6
Liability-Management Hedge

CD—Cash		Basis	CD—Futures Market
Bank plans to issue $10 million of 90-day CD's.			Bank sells $10 million of 90-day CD futures at 9.50% or (IMM Index):
Current 90-day rate is:	9.00%	.50	90.50
Bank issues 90-day CD's at:	10.00%	.40	Bank buys 90-day CD futures at 10.40% or: 89.60
Borrowing-rate increase:	1.00%		Futures gain: .90
Basis change		−10	

manager could execute a long hedge through the use of Treasury-bond futures, as executed in Table 7.

The long hedge shown in this table, while not perfect, was clearly effective. Also, notice that while the cash market for 10 3/8s moved 32/32, futures moved only 24/32. The sale of three additional contracts served to equalize the difference in yield values of a 1/32 between the 8% futures and 10 3/8% cash. This is referred to as "weighting the hedge."

Speculating in Interest-Rate Futures. The most fundamental speculative strategy for a trader expecting interest rates to decline, and, conversely, the price of fixed-income securities to rise, is to simply purchase or take a long position in a particular month of a given interest-rate-futures contract. A trader expecting rising rates and lower prices would take the opposite position—that is, he would establish a short position by selling interest-rate futures. Profits from such trades would be realized by entering offsetting transactions.

Spreading is another trading technique. Intramarket spreading (Table 8) involves the simultaneous purchase and sale of two different contract months of the *same* interest-rate-futures contracts in order to benefit from anticipated changes in the price relationships between these different contract months. A variation of such a spread would be an intermarket spread (Table 9) whereby a simultaneous purchase and sale of two *different* interest-rate futures for the same contract month is executed to benefit from anticipated price-relationship changes.

If a trader anticipates that interest rates will decline, with financing costs declining even more so, a *bull spread* may be purchased. This involves buying a nearby interest-rate-futures contract and selling a deferred contract—the expectation being that the nearby will increase at a higher rate than the deferred. The normal trading convention for buying or selling a spread is determined by the action taken in the nearby month. If the opposite scenario from that depicted

Table 7
Long Treasury-Bond Hedge

Cash Market	Futures
Wants to lock in 10½% yields on $1 million in long-term Treasury bonds today when the 10⅜ of 2012 are trading at about 99.00.	Buy 13 T-bond futures contracts at 76.16. (Because of the factor delivery system of the CBOT contract, which is a nominal 8% contract, it is necessary to buy more than ten $100,000 contracts in order to effect comparable dollar value against a 10⅜% issue maturing in 2012.
If, three months later, prices rose a full point on the 10½ of 2012 to 100 (par), the yields would have declined to 10⅜%, and cost increased by $10,000.	Assuming the basis to 10⅜% bonds remained constant, had futures risen to 77.8 for 13 contracts, the profit would have been 24/32 or $9,750 (24 × 31.25 × 13).
Loss = $10,000	Gain = $9,750

above was anticipated, the trader would execute a *bear spread:* He would sell the spread by going short on the nearby contract and long on the deferred.

During periods of tight money-market conditions, normally accompanied by rising interest rates, the yields on bank certificates of deposit will normally rise relative to those of T-bills. Likewise domestic CD rates may not rise as much as Eurodollar deposit rates. To take advantage of such anticipated events, traders would execute intermarket spreads by buying or taking long positions in T-bill futures, and selling or taking short positions in CD's or Euro Deposit futures, or both on an equally weighted basis. While a rising rate environment should cause prices for all

Table 8
Intramarket Spread

Trade:

Buy 1 June T-bond @	$80^{16}/_{32}$
Sell 1 September T-bond @	$80^{2}/_{32}$
Spread	$+ ^{14}/_{32}$

Cost of financing bond positions declines, and positive carry from a growing spread between bond yields and financing costs should cause spreads to widen. Anticipating these events, a bull spread position was executed.

Result:

Sell 1 June T-bond @	$81^{4}/_{32}$
Buy 1 September T-bond @	$80^{12}/_{32}$
Spread	$+ ^{24}/_{32}$
Profit	$= ^{10}/_{32}$
	$= \$312.50$

Table 9
Intermarket Spread

Trade:

Buy 1 March T-bill @	90.00	(10.00%)
Sell 1 March CD @	89.50	(10.50%)
Spread +.50		

If the Federal Reserve raises the discount rate and money tightens, perceived risk should cause CD rates to rise further than T-bills.

Result:

Sell 1 March T-bill @	89.00	(11.00%)
Buy 1 March CD @	88.25	(11.75%)
Spread +.75		

T-bill loss	=	100 basis points
CD gain	=	125 basis points
Profit	=	25 basis points @ $25 each
	=	$625

three of these contracts to decline, the expectation of increased credit risk for CD's and/or Eurodollars is greater than that of the long T-bill position, thereby resulting in a net profit on the trade.

Many speculators who trade interest-rate futures, as well as other commodities, employ a tool known as *technical analysis,* which is a study of the past price behavior of futures as a technique for forecasting future price movements. Technical analysis involves the use of different types of charts to depict past price patterns, as well as statistical analysis of price data to construct such charts as moving averages, oscillators, etc.

Traders will also use technical analysis together with *fundamental analysis* to determine their forecast of future price movements. Fundamental analysis is, simply put, the study of the interaction of potential supply and demand for a commodity. With respect to interest-rate futures, fundamental analysis looks at the supply of and demand for money. These are integrally related to the state of the economy and to the fiscal and monetary policies of the government, which can be monitored through the many regular statistical releases of the Federal Reserve and various government agencies.

Arbitrage. ARBITRAGE was defined earlier as the simultaneous purchase and sale of the same or equivalent security in order to profit from price discrepancies. It refers to the purchase of undervalued securities and sale of overvalued securities based on either historical price or yield spreads. Such transactions are equivalent to spread trades described in the previous section on speculating. There is also "closed-end" arbitrage, which differs from spreading in that it "locks in" a profit from small price differentials between the cash and future markets.

The typical cash/futures long arbitrage will involve three stages:

1. The purchase of a deliverable underlying security
2. Financing of the cash instrument until the delivery date in futures
3. The sale of an equivalent amount of corresponding futures contracts

The strategy is that the cost of purchasing the security (including any accrued interest) plus the cost of financing that security to the delivery date (arbitrage is highly leveraged and no securities are purchased for outright cash; they are financed through REPURCHASE AGREEMENTS (RP's) by banks and dealers at competitive market rates) will be more than offset by the proceeds generated from the actual delivery of the cash instrument on delivery date plus accrued interest earned during the holding period of the transaction. When price discrepancies or aberrations appear between cash and futures to make such a transaction profitable, arbitragers will immediately bring them back into line by bidding up the cost of the "cheap" cash security and offering down the price of "expensive futures."

Treasury-Bill-Futures Arbitrage. In the following example, the June 23, 1983, Treasury bill is deliverable against the March 1983 T-bill-futures contract on the IMM. If a trader can buy the June 23 bill on February 1, 1983, finance it until March 23, 1983 (the delivery date), and sell one (1) March T-bill-futures contract and lock in a profit, a successful arbitrage would be accomplished.

Assume:

1. June 23, 1983, 141-day T-bill bought
   @ 7.60% =   970,233.40
2. Financing cost for 50 days 2/2/83 to
   3/23/83   @ 7.90% =   10,539.14
3. Cost of capital at assumed rate of 8.25% =   394.29

   Total costs = $981,166.83

4. Proceeds from sale and delivery of
   March 1 T-bill futures @ 92.65   7.35% = $981,420.90

   Net profit (loss) $ 254.07

Formulation

---

1. Using T-bill pricing formula on p. 338

2. $.99 \times \text{cost of bill} \times \dfrac{50}{360} \times .0790 = \text{(financing cost)}$

3. Initial margin on trade is $2,500, which must be maintained until delivery (50 days). Also, only 99% of total cost can usually be financed. An opportunity cost for use of these funds (i.e., margin + 1% haircut) should be imputed (e.g., Fed Funds rate).

   $9{,}702.33 + 2500 \times \dfrac{141}{360} \times .0825 = \text{(cost of capital)}$

4. Proceeds from sale of futures are based on price at which futures were sold (same calculation formula as step 1). Price at which delivery is actually made will be *settlement* price of futures on the last day of trading. The gain or loss between these two prices would have been either credited or debited to the trader in the form of daily variation margin during the time the position was held open.

The above trade is an example of profitable T-bill-futures arbitrage, also referred to as a "cash-and-carry" arbitrage. It is the type of trade that can be monitored and executed most effectively by cash-market participants with quick access to open financing lines as well as futures execution. The interest-rate-futures markets have become too efficient for opportunities such as this one to exist very long before being arbitraged back into line.

Tax Implications. In recent years, the tax rules of commodity futures have been subjected to continual and substantial change. Due to the rapidity of these changes and the complexity of the tax rules in this area, readers should consult their own tax advisers for the tax implications of their individual transactions.

The tax consequences of dealing in interest-rate futures vary, depending on whether the investor's transactions are viewed for tax purposes as a hedge or an investment. Profits or losses from hedging transactions are treated as ordinary income or ordinary loss, and are fully taxable or fully deductible for federal income-tax purposes in the same manner as other business income and business losses.

The term *hedging transaction* is not defined in the INTERNAL REVENUE CODE; its meaning has been developed through a long line of court cases spanning several decades. In general, it means a transaction designed to offset a loss that a businessman might incur on inventory that he holds for sale to customers as part of his regular business activities. For example, a government-bond dealer, who sells government bonds, might hedge his inventory of governments by shorting interest-rate-futures contracts.

Taxpayers who buy and sell interest-rate futures for speculative profit are treated as investors for federal income-tax purposes and realize capital gain or loss on their transactions. Capital gains are divided into two categories: short-term and long-term. Short-term capital gains are fully taxable, but only 40% of a long-term capital gain is taxable. Since the maximum federal tax bracket is 50%, the maximum federal tax on one dollar of long-term capital gain is 20 cents ($1 \times 40\% = .40 \times 50\% = .20$).

A short-term capital gain is a gain from the sale of a capital asset held for one year or less. If the capital asset was held more than one year, it is treated as a long-term-capital-gain transaction.

The ECONOMIC RECOVERY TAX ACT OF 1981 (ERTA) created a special holding-period rule for commodity-futures contracts. Under the terms of the act, all gains and losses incurred by investors in commodity-futures contracts are treated as 60% long-term and 40% short-term regardless of the period of time that the contract was held by the investor. For example, if an investor earned a $1,000 profit from an interest-rate-futures contract that was purchased and sold during the same day, $600 of the profit would be treated as long-term capital gain and $400 would be treated as short-term capital gain.

The same 60-40 rule applies to losses incurred on commodity-futures contracts, including interest-rate futures. Furthermore, it does not matter whether the gain or loss was incurred on a long position or on a short sale. If an investor has only commodity-futures transactions in his account, the maximum tax rate payable on any profits would be 32%.

Special rules apply to capital losses and also to certain offsetting positions ("spreads" or "straddles") in which an investor maintains concurrent long or short positions in certain debt obligations while simultaneously holding offsetting short or long positions in interest-rate futures.

Alfred J. Patti

Interest Rates, Calculation of

Simple Interest. Simple interest is the dollar cost of borrowing (or the dollar return from lending) money. This cost or return is based on three elements: the amount borrowed or lent, which is called the *principal;* the *rate of interest;* and the amount of *time* for which the principal is borrowed or lent.

The following formula may be used to find simple interest:

Interest = Principal × Rate of Interest × Time, or
$$I = P \times R \times T$$

Interest Rate R. As the term implies, an interest rate is a *ratio* or fraction of two numbers. For example, an interest rate of 12%—12 per cent or centum— means 12 divided by 100. (Per centum is Latin meaning "for every one hundred.") Interest rates can also be written in decimal form. Since two decimal places are the same as the "%" sign, 12% becomes 0.12, which is read as twelve one-hundredths. If it is to be used correctly in *any* interest formula, the interest rate must be stated as a fraction or a decimal. For example, multiplying $5,250 by 13½% does not make sense; but $5,250 multiplied by 13.5 ÷ 100 or 0.135 does.

The federal consumer Truth in Lending Law requires that interest rates on consumer loans be stated in annual percentage rate (APR) terms. In this form, the interest rate becomes a useful indicator of the true cost of credit on a yearly basis. In addition, the law requires the lender to disclose the total finance charge on the loan.

Amount of Time T. The amount of time for which simple interest is calculated is usually stated in years. If less than a year, time may be expressed as a fraction of days per year—that is, as days/year. The term *year* in the denominator may take one of three values: a 360-day year, normally used by bankers; a standard 365-day calendar year; or a 366-day leap year. Also, the amount of time may be written in months per 12-month period. For example, 3 months is 3/12 or 1/4 of a year.

Example. Suppose an individual borrows $1,000 at 12% simple annual interest and repays it in one lump sum at the end of one year. To find the interest on the loan, use the simple interest formula:

$$I = \$1,000 \times 0.12 \times 1$$
$$= \$120$$

Now, suppose the loan is for *two* years and the borrower is required to repay the loan (principal *and* interest) at the *end* of two years. What will be the interest charge?

• Over the first year, the borrower has the full use of the $1,000 principal and therefore incurs an interest

obligation of $120 or $1,000 × 0.12 × 1. This first year's interest expense, however, is payable at the *end* of the second year.

• Over the second and last year of the loan, the borrower again has full use of $1,000, for which another $120 interest obligation is incurred and due at the end of the second year.

At the end of two full years, the borrower must repay the two years' interest ($120 + $120 = $240) in addition to the original amount borrowed ($1,000). In other words, the borrower has to pay interest *only* on the amount borrowed and *not* on any accumulated interest charges. This is the essence of *simple* interest.

Summary. To calculate the total amount of a simple-interest loan that is due to a lender at the end of two years, the following formula may be used:

Total loan repayment (or future amount due)
= principal + interest charges on the principal only
= $P + I$, or
= $P + (P \times R \times T)$
= $1,000 + ($1,000 × 0.12 × 2)
= $1,000 + $240
= $1,240

With some manipulation of this total loan-repayment formula, a shorthand expression for simple interest can be obtained:

Total loan repayment = $P(1 + R \times T)$

While this formula looks difficult, try the problem to see how easy it really is.

Problem. What is the interest cost *and* the total amount due on a six-month loan of $1,500 at 13.2% simple annual interest?

Answer. $P = \$1,500$; $R = 0.132$ or 13.2/100; and $T = 6$ months ÷ 12 months or ½ year. The amount due on the loan consists of principal plus the half-year's interest on the principal:

Total loan repayment = $1,500 (1 + 0.132 × ½)
= $1,500 (1 + 0.066) = $1,500
(1.066)
= $1,599

Note: While the simple *annual* interest rate is 13.2 %, the amount of interest charged for *half* the year is 6.6% or ½ of 13.2% of the principal.

Since the total amount due is $1,599 and the amount borrowed is $1,500, the difference of $99 ($1,599 − $1,500) is the total amount of simple interest on the six-month loan.

Compound Interest. Unlike simple interest, compound interest is the amount paid or earned on the original principal *plus* the accumulated interest. With interest compounding, the more periods for which interest is calculated, the more rapidly the amount of interest on interest *and* interest on principal builds.

Compounding annually means that there is only *one* period annually when interest is calculated. On a *one-year* loan, interest charges are identical whether figured on a simple or on an annual compound basis. However, a new interest formula—based on the simple-interest formula—must be used if there is annual compounding for more than a year or with more than one compound period per year.

Multiple-Year Annual Compounding. Let's illustrate multiple-year annual compounding.

Suppose a borrower takes a two-year loan of $1,000 at 12% per year, compounded annually. While not due until the loan's maturity, interest charges accrue on the principal *and* interest at the end of each year or annual compound period. In this example, the nature of annual compounding requires the borrower to pay interest at the end of the *second* year on the *first* year's accumulated interest on principal. In addition, the borrower is obligated to pay 12% interest on the principal for each of the two annual compound periods.

What is the amount (principal and compound interest) the borrower must repay at the end of two years? Figure 1 helps with the answer.

Summary. The total amount of interest consists of the following:

a. Interest of $1,000 for the first year or period	$120.00
b. Interest on $1,000 for the second year or period	$120.00
c. Interest on the first year's or period's interest of $120 for second year or period	$ 14.40
Total	$254.40

Adding the total amount of interest to the original sum borrowed gives the amount of the loan that must be repaid at the *end* of two years:

$$I + P = \$254.40 + \$1,000 = \$1,254.40$$

Compare this result of compounding annually for two years with simple interest. On a two-year, $1,000 loan at 12% *simple* annual interest, the amount of interest is $240: $I = P \times R \times T = \$1,000 \times 0.12 \times 2$. This sum is $14.40 *less* than the result found with *annual compounding*. The difference, of course, is attributable to paying interest on interest—which is what compounding is all about.

Compound Formula. A compact formula which describes compound interest calculations is:

$F = P (1 + R)^T$, in which
 F is the total future repayment value of a loan (principal *plus* the total accumulated or compound interest);
 P is the principal;
 R is the rate of interest per year or annual percentage rate; and
 T is time in years.

Now, use the compound-interest formula to answer the following problem.

Problem. What is the total amount of interest that must be paid on a $3,000 loan for six years at 10% per year, compounded annually?

Answer. First, find the *lump-sum* amount that must be repaid (F) at the end of six years:

$$F = \$3,000 (1 + 0.10)^6$$
$$= \$3,000 (1.10)^6$$

The factor $(1.10)^6$ can be obtained easily using pencil and paper, a calculator, or a compound-interest-rate table. (Compound rate tables will be explained later.)

Using paper and pencil, $(1.10)^6$ equals the following: $(1.10) \times (1.10) \times (1.10) \times (1.10) \times (1.10) \times (1.10)$ or 1.771561. Now, place this result in the compound-interest formula:

$$F = \$3,000 \times 1.771561$$
$$= \$5,314.68$$

Subtracting the principal (P) from the total amount due (F) equals the total amount of accumulated compound interest on the loan:

$$I = F - P$$
$$= \$5,314.68 - \$3,000$$
$$= \$2,314.68$$

Multiple Compound Periods per Year. So far, we have been discussing *annual* compounding—with

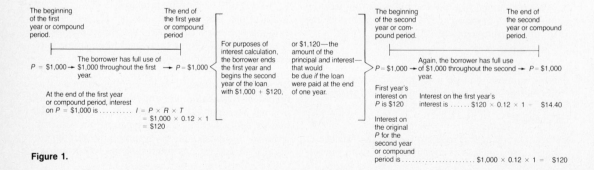

Figure 1.

each year consisting of *one* compound period. For multiple-period compounding, each year is divided into a corresponding number of equal periods. For example, compounding *semi*annually means that there are *two* compound periods per year; compounding *quarterly* means there are *four* compound periods per year; compounding *monthly* means there are *twelve* compound periods per year; and compounding *daily* means there are *three hundred and sixty* compound periods per year.

What is important in multiple-period compounding is the *total* number of compound periods for which the principal is borrowed or lent. For example, with a five-year loan compounded *monthly,* there are 60 periods (5 years × 12 months or compound periods per year) for which interest will be calculated on interest and principal.

Before the compound-interest formula can be used for *multiple*-period compounding, two important adjustments must be made:

- First, adjust the *annual* interest rate (*R*) to reflect the number of compound periods per year. For example, a 10% annual rate of interest, compounded quarterly, works out to 2½% (10% ÷ 4) per quarter.
- Second, adjust the time factor (*T*), which is measured in years, to reflect the *total* number of compound periods. For example, a loan for three years compounded monthly works out to 36 compound periods (3 years × 12 compound periods per year) over the length of the loan.

Note: The method of calculation just described assumes that the borrower has *full* use of the principal over the length of the loan. Rather than making periodic payments, the borrower is obligated to repay the loan in one lump sum when due. Problems where the borrower does not have full use of the principal and must make periodic payments on the loan are taken up later in the section "Consumer Borrowing: Mortgages and Installment Credit."

Problem. What is the total amount that must be repaid on a $2,500, three-year loan at 18% per year, compounded monthly?

Answer. The total amount of compound interest on this loan is $1,772.85 or $4,272.85 − $2,500.

$$F = \$2,500 \ (1 + {}^{0.18}\!/_{12})^{3 \text{ years} \times 12 \text{ compound periods/year}}$$
$$= \$2,500 \ (1 + 0.015)^{36}$$
$$= \$2,500 \ (1.70914)$$
$$= \$4,272.85$$

As you can see, the solution to this problem is complicated. A calculator or a compound-interest table can help make interest calculations more manageable, as we will now see.

Using Compound-Interest Tables. Tables have been constructed to ease the arithmetic manipulations in calculating compound interest. Turn to Table 1. Various annual percentage rates are shown along the top of the table; time, measured in periods, is shown down the side. The figures in the body of the table state the total amount (principal *and* interest) that will be repaid (earned) on a $1 loan, at various interest rates and time periods. For example, the total amount of principal and interest on a $1 loan at 12% per year, compounded *annually* (i.e., one period per year) for five years, is found as follows: Read across the top of the table to the column labeled "12%"; then read down that column until it lines up with the row labeled "5 periods." (Remember, with *annual* compounding, there is exactly *one* period per year.) The figure given by the intersection of the interest-rate column and the time-period row is $1.762. Subtracting the amount of the loan from the total amount due gives the amount of compound interest expense over five years: $1.762 − $1.00 = $0.762.

The table is easily adaptable for sums greater than $1. For example, the amount of principal and interest due on a five-year, 12% annually compounded loan of $1,500—which is 1,500 times greater than the $1 amount for which the table has been constructed—is found by multiplying $1.762 (the figure at the intersection of the "12%" column and the "5 period" row) by 1,500. The total amount due is $2,643. Subtracting the amount of the loan from the amount due yields the total compound-interest expense of the loan: $2,643 − $1,500 = $1,143.

Suppose the compounding period is other than annually. With the two minor adjustments for multiple-period compounding mentioned above, the same compound-interest table can be used.

Example. What is the amount due on a six-year, $1 loan at 18% per year, compounded *semiannually?* The 18% rate is stated in *annual* terms. Since there are two periods per year with semiannual compounding, the per-period or half-year interest rate is 9% (18% per year divided by 2 periods per year). In addition, measured in compound periods, the length of the loan is 12 periods (6 years × 2 periods per year). Now, to find the amount due, read across the top of the compound-interest table to "9%"; then read down to "12 periods." The result is $2.813. The total compound-interest expense is $1.813 (the total amount due—$2.813—minus the total amount borrowed—$1).

Problem. How much interest will be paid on a $2,000 loan at 12% per year, compounded monthly, with a lump-sum payment at the end of four years?

Answer. With 12 compound periods per year, the annual interest rate of 12% becomes 1% per compound period; the four-year loan contains 48 monthly periods. And $2,000 is 2,000 times greater than the $1 value on which the table is constructed. The total

Table 1
Compound-Interest-Rate Table

NUMBER OF PERIODS	1.00%	1.50%	2.00%	2.50%	3.00%	3.50%	4.00%	4.50%	5.00%	6.00%	7.00%	8.00%	9.00%	10.00%	12.00%	14.00%	16.00%	18.00%
							(FUTURE VALUE OF $1—PRINCIPAL PLUS ACCUMULATED INTEREST)											
1	1.010	1.015	1.020	1.025	1.030	1.035	1.040	1.045	1.050	1.060	1.070	1.080	1.090	1.100	1.120	1.140	1.160	1.180
2	1.020	1.030	1.040	1.051	1.061	1.071	1.082	1.092	1.103	1.124	1.145	1.166	1.188	1.210	1.254	1.300	1.346	1.392
3	1.030	1.046	1.061	1.077	1.093	1.109	1.125	1.141	1.158	1.191	1.225	1.260	1.295	1.331	1.405	1.482	1.561	1.643
4	1.041	1.061	1.082	1.104	1.126	1.148	1.170	1.193	1.216	1.262	1.311	1.360	1.412	1.464	1.574	1.689	1.811	1.939
5	1.051	1.077	1.104	1.131	1.159	1.188	1.217	1.246	1.276	1.338	1.403	1.469	1.539	1.611	1.762	1.925	2.100	2.288
6	1.062	1.093	1.126	1.160	1.194	1.229	1.265	1.302	1.340	1.419	1.501	1.587	1.677	1.772	1.974	2.195	2.436	2.700
7	1.072	1.110	1.149	1.189	1.230	1.272	1.316	1.361	1.407	1.504	1.606	1.714	1.828	1.949	2.211	2.502	2.826	3.185
8	1.083	1.126	1.172	1.218	1.267	1.317	1.369	1.422	1.477	1.594	1.718	1.851	1.993	2.144	2.476	2.853	3.278	3.759
9	1.094	1.143	1.195	1.249	1.305	1.363	1.423	1.486	1.551	1.689	1.838	1.999	2.172	2.358	2.773	3.252	3.803	4.435
10	1.105	1.161	1.219	1.280	1.344	1.411	1.480	1.553	1.629	1.791	1.967	2.159	2.367	2.594	3.106	3.707	4.411	5.234
11	1.116	1.178	1.243	1.312	1.384	1.460	1.539	1.623	1.710	1.898	2.105	2.332	2.580	2.853	3.479	4.226	5.117	6.176
12	1.127	1.196	1.268	1.345	1.426	1.511	1.601	1.696	1.796	2.012	2.252	2.518	2.813	3.138	3.896	4.818	5.936	7.288
14	1.149	1.232	1.319	1.413	1.513	1.619	1.732	1.852	1.980	2.261	2.579	2.937	3.342	3.797	4.887	6.261	7.988	10.147
16	1.173	1.269	1.373	1.485	1.605	1.734	1.873	2.022	2.183	2.540	2.952	3.426	3.970	4.595	6.130	8.137	10.748	14.129
18	1.196	1.307	1.428	1.560	1.702	1.857	2.026	2.208	2.407	2.854	3.380	3.996	4.717	5.560	7.690	10.575	14.463	19.673
20	1.220	1.347	1.486	1.639	1.806	1.990	2.191	2.412	2.653	3.207	3.870	4.661	5.604	6.727	9.646	13.743	19.461	27.393
22	1.245	1.388	1.546	1.722	1.916	2.132	2.370	2.634	2.925	3.604	4.430	5.437	6.659	8.140	12.100	17.861	26.186	38.142
24	1.270	1.430	1.608	1.809	2.033	2.283	2.563	2.876	3.225	4.049	5.072	6.341	7.911	9.850	15.179	23.212	35.236	53.109
26	1.295	1.473	1.673	1.900	2.157	2.446	2.772	3.141	3.556	4.549	5.807	7.396	9.399	11.918	19.040	30.167	47.414	73.949
28	1.321	1.517	1.741	1.996	2.288	2.620	2.999	3.430	3.920	5.112	6.649	8.627	11.167	14.421	23.884	39.204	63.800	102.967
30	1.348	1.563	1.811	2.098	2.427	2.807	3.243	3.745	4.322	5.743	7.612	10.063	13.268	17.449	29.960	50.950	85.850	143.371
32	1.375	1.610	1.884	2.204	2.575	3.007	3.508	4.090	4.765	6.453	8.715	11.737	15.763	21.114	37.582	66.215	115.520	199.629
34	1.403	1.659	1.961	2.315	2.732	3.221	3.794	4.466	5.253	7.251	9.978	13.690	18.728	25.548	47.143	86.053	155.443	277.964
36	1.431	1.709	2.040	2.433	2.898	3.450	4.104	4.877	5.792	8.147	11.424	15.968	22.251	30.913	59.136	111.834	209.164	387.037
38	1.460	1.761	2.122	2.556	3.075	3.696	4.439	5.326	6.385	9.154	13.079	18.625	26.437	37.404	74.180	145.340	281.452	538.910
40	1.489	1.814	2.208	2.685	3.262	3.959	4.801	5.816	7.040	10.286	14.974	21.725	31.409	45.259	93.051	188.884	378.721	750.378
42	1.519	1.869	2.297	2.821	3.461	4.241	5.193	6.352	7.762	11.557	17.144	25.339	37.318	54.764	116.723	245.473	509.607	1044.827
44	1.549	1.925	2.390	2.964	3.671	4.543	5.617	6.936	8.557	12.985	19.628	29.556	44.337	66.264	146.418	319.017	685.727	1454.817
46	1.580	1.984	2.487	3.114	3.895	4.867	6.075	7.574	9.434	14.590	22.473	34.474	52.677	80.180	183.666	414.594	922.715	2025.687
48	1.612	2.043	2.587	3.271	4.132	5.214	6.571	8.271	10.401	16.394	25.729	40.211	62.585	97.017	230.391	538.807	1241.605	2820.567
50	1.645	2.105	2.692	3.437	4.384	5.585	7.107	9.033	11.467	18.420	29.457	46.902	74.357	117.391	289.002	700.233	1670.704	3927.357
52	1.678	2.169	2.800	3.611	4.651	5.983	7.687	9.864	12.643	20.697	33.725	54.706	88.344	142.043	362.524	910.023	2248.099	5468.452
54	1.711	2.234	2.913	3.794	4.934	6.409	8.314	10.771	13.939	23.255	38.612	63.809	104.962	171.872	454.751	1182.666	3025.042	7614.272
56	1.746	2.302	3.031	3.986	5.235	6.865	8.992	11.763	15.367	26.129	44.207	74.427	124.705	207.965	570.439	1536.992	4070.497	10602.113
58	1.781	2.372	3.154	4.188	5.553	7.354	9.726	12.845	16.943	29.359	50.613	86.812	148.162	251.638	715.559	1997.475	5477.260	14762.381
60	1.817	2.443	3.281	4.400	5.892	7.878	10.520	14.027	18.679	32.998	57.946	101.257	176.031	304.482	897.597	2595.919	7370.201	20555.140

amount due is found by locating the amount-due factor at the intersection of the "1%" column and the "48 period" row and multiplying the result by 2,000:

$$\$1.612 \times 2,000 = \$3,224$$

Subtracting the amount of the loan yields the total interest charges over the term of the loan:

$$\$3,224 - \$2,000 = \$1,224$$

Daily Compounding. Some financial institutions pay interest on deposits, compounded on a daily basis. Under daily compounding, each year for which interest is calculated is *normally* divided into 360 equal parts or compound periods.

Both a formula and a table can be used to find what a bank deposit will grow to with daily compounding. Using the basic compound-interest formula discussed above, two modifications must be made: Divide the annual interest rate by 360—the number of daily compound periods each year—and multiply the number of years (T) by the number of *calendar* days each year:

$$F = P \left(1 + \frac{R}{360}\right)^{T \times 365}$$

Alternatively, a daily compounding table (Table 2) can be used in the same manner in which we used Table 1.

Problem. What will a $500 savings deposit grow to in six years at 5½% per year, compounded daily? Compare this result with quarterly compounding.

Answer.

Daily compounding

$$F = \$500 \left(1 + \frac{.055}{360}\right)^{6 \times 365}$$
$$= \$500 \, (1.000152778)^{2190}$$
$$= \$500 \, (1.397322433)$$
$$= \$698.66$$

Quarterly compounding

$$F = \$500 \left(1 + \frac{.055}{4}\right)^{6 \times 4}$$
$$= \$500 \, (1.01375)^{24}$$
$$= \$500 \, (1.387844515)$$
$$= \$693.92$$

Daily compounding results in $4.74 more in accumulated interest than quarterly compounding.

The same daily-compounding result can be found by using Table 2. The intersection of the "5½%" column and the "six year" row is $1.3973 per $1 deposit. Since the size of the deposit is 500 times greater than the $1 value for which the table has been constructed, the $500 deposit will grow to $698.65 or 500 × $1.3973. (Comparing answers using the daily-compounding formula and Table 2, a small discrepancy may result due to rounding.)

Table 2
Interest-Rate Table for Daily Compounding (360-Day Basis Year)

NUMBER OF YEARS	ANNUAL PERCENTAGE RATE												
	5.00%	5.25%	5.50%	5.75%	6.00%	6.25%	6.50%	6.75%	7.00%	7.25%	7.50%	7.75%	8.00%
(WHAT A $1 DEPOSIT WILL GROW TO IN THE FUTURE)													
1	1.0520	1.0547	1.0573	1.0600	1.0627	1.0654	1.0681	1.0708	1.0735	1.0763	1.0790	1.0817	1.0845
2	1.1067	1.1123	1.1180	1.1237	1.1294	1.1351	1.1409	1.1467	1.1525	1.1584	1.1642	1.1702	1.1761
3	1.1642	1.1731	1.1821	1.1911	1.2002	1.2094	1.2186	1.2279	1.2373	1.2467	1.2562	1.2658	1.2755
4	1.2248	1.2373	1.2499	1.2626	1.2755	1.2885	1.3016	1.3149	1.3282	1.3418	1.3555	1.3693	1.3832
5	1.2885	1.3049	1.3215	1.3384	1.3555	1.3727	1.3903	1.4080	1.4259	1.4441	1.4625	1.4812	1.5001
6	1.3555	1.3762	1.3973	1.4187	1.4405	1.4625	1.4850	1.5077	1.5308	1.5543	1.5781	1.6022	1.6268
7	1.4259	1.4515	1.4774	1.5039	1.5308	1.5582	1.5861	1.6145	1.6434	1.6728	1.7027	1.7332	1.7642
8	1.5001	1.5308	1.5622	1.5942	1.6268	1.6601	1.6941	1.7288	1.7642	1.8004	1.8373	1.8749	1.9133
9	1.5781	1.6145	1.6518	1.6899	1.7288	1.7687	1.8095	1.8513	1.8940	1.9377	1.9824	2.0281	2.0749
10	1.6602	1.7028	1.7465	1.7913	1.8373	1.8844	1.9328	1.9824	2.0333	2.0855	2.1390	2.1939	2.2502
15	2.1391	2.2219	2.3080	2.3975	2.4904	2.5868	2.6871	2.7912	2.8993	3.0117	3.1284	3.2496	3.3755
20	2.7561	2.8994	3.0502	3.2087	3.3756	3.5511	3.7357	3.9299	4.1343	4.3492	4.5753	4.8132	5.0634
25	3.5512	3.7834	4.0309	4.2946	4.5755	4.8747	5.1936	5.5333	5.8952	6.2807	6.6915	7.1292	7.5955
30	4.5756	4.9370	5.3270	5.7478	6.2019	6.6918	7.2204	7.7907	8.4061	9.0701	9.7866	10.5596	11.3937

	ANNUAL PERCENTAGE RATE												
	8.25%	8.50%	8.75%	9.00%	9.25%	9.50%	9.75%	10.00%	10.25%	10.50%	11.00%	12.00%	13.00%
(WHAT A $1 DEPOSIT WILL GROW TO IN THE FUTURE)													
1	1.0872	1.0900	1.0928	1.0955	1.0983	1.1011	1.1039	1.1067	1.1095	1.1123	1.1180	1.1294	1.1409
2	1.1821	1.1881	1.1941	1.2002	1.2063	1.2124	1.2186	1.2248	1.2310	1.2372	1.2498	1.2754	1.3016
3	1.2852	1.2950	1.3049	1.3148	1.3249	1.3350	1.3452	1.3554	1.3658	1.3762	1.3973	1.4404	1.4849
4	1.3973	1.4115	1.4259	1.4404	1.4551	1.4699	1.4849	1.5001	1.5153	1.5308	1.5621	1.6268	1.6941
5	1.5192	1.5386	1.5582	1.5781	1.5982	1.6186	1.6392	1.6601	1.6813	1.7027	1.7464	1.8372	1.9327
6	1.6517	1.6770	1.7027	1.7288	1.7553	1.7822	1.8095	1.8372	1.8654	1.8939	1.9524	2.0748	2.2049
7	1.7958	1.8279	1.8607	1.8940	1.9279	1.9624	1.9975	2.0332	2.0696	2.1067	2.1827	2.3432	2.5155
8	1.9525	1.9924	2.0333	2.0749	2.1174	2.1607	2.2050	2.2502	2.2962	2.3433	2.4402	2.6463	2.8698
9	2.1228	2.1718	2.2219	2.2731	2.3255	2.3792	2.4341	2.4902	2.5477	2.6064	2.7281	2.9886	3.2741
10	2.3080	2.3672	2.4279	2.4903	2.5542	2.6197	2.6870	2.7559	2.8266	2.8992	3.0499	3.3752	3.7353
15	3.5062	3.6421	3.7832	3.9298	4.0820	4.2402	4.4044	4.5751	4.7523	4.9364	5.3263	6.2009	7.2191
20	5.3267	5.6036	5.8949	6.2014	6.5238	6.8629	7.2197	7.5950	7.9899	8.4053	9.3019	11.3922	13.9522
25	8.0922	8.6215	9.1854	9.7861	10.4261	11.1080	11.8345	12.6085	13.4331	14.3116	16.2447	20.9295	26.9651
30	12.2937	13.2648	14.3125	15.4430	16.6628	17.9790	19.3990	20.9313	22.5845	24.3683	28.3697	38.4513	52.1150

Interest-Rate Applications. Now, let's turn from the general discussion of interest rates to some practical applications. Many individuals are confused and uncertain about the meaning and calculation of interest rates on Treasury investments and consumer credit loans. Shorthand methods using formulas and tables will be used to show how to calculate the effective interest rate or investment yield on Treasury securities and the monthly payments on consumer installment loans.

Interest Rates on Treasury Securities. The federal government may need to borrow money to bridge the gap between expenditures and income. This borrowing is done at least weekly when the Treasury, with the Federal Reserve acting as its banker, sells Treasury bills to investors. Treasury bills are short-term government IOU's with maturities of three months, six months, and one year. Longer-term securities—Treasury notes and bonds—are sold less frequently. Knowing the actual, annual interest return or investment yield is crucial to an investor's decision whether to purchase Treasury securities or alternative investments.

Three-Month (91-Day) Bills. Bills are sold at a discount rather than at face or par value. Explicit interest is not paid; instead, the investor's dollar return is measured by the difference between the bill's par or maturity value and the discount price paid. Since the investor purchases the bills at a discount, calculation of the interest return is based on the total amount paid (and not on the face value), given the assumption the bill is held to maturity. The result is called the *effective* or *investment* yield.

While it appears unmanageable, calculating the effective yield using the following formula is fairly simple. Even though the bill is held for a period of less than one year, the calculation results in an *annualized* return, thus allowing comparisons with other investments.

$$\text{Effective or investment yield to maturity} = \frac{(\$100 - \$P) \times 365}{\$P \times 91 \text{ days}}$$

(use 366 days in the numerator for leap years)

P is the purchase price that the investor pays the Treasury for each $100 of the bill's face value. Bills are sold in minimum denominations of $10,000. With an auction price of $96.562 per $100 of face value, an investor purchasing a $10,000 bill would pay $9,656.20 ($96.562 per $100 times 100 since there are one hundred $100 in $10,000). At maturity, the investor will receive the face value, a full $10,000, or a gain of $343.80 ($10,000 − $9,656.20).

Now, find the effective annual yield or return from a $9,656.20, three-month (91-day) investment:

$$\text{Effective yield} = \frac{(\$100 - \$96.562) \times 365}{\$96.562 \times 91}$$

$$= \frac{\$3.438 \times 365}{\$96.562 \times 91}$$

$$= \frac{\$1,254.87}{\$8,787.142}$$

$$= .1428 \text{ or } 14.28\%$$

While 14.28% is the *annualized* or effective rate of return, the three-month or quarter-year return earned if the bill is held until maturity is 3.57% or 14.28% ÷ 4 quarters.

Note: The annualized or investment yield is not a compound rate; it is found by using the basics of simple annual interest, discussed earlier.

Six-Month (182-Day) Bills. Essentially, the same logic used to determine the effective return on a three-month bill applies to a one-half-year (182 day) Treasury bill.

If the Treasury's auction price is $93.336 per $100, an investor must pay $9,333.60 for a $10,000 bill. If held for the full 182 days until it matures, there is a gain of $666.40 ($10,000 − $9,333.60). As before, what an investor may want to know is not the dollar gain but the annual rate of return from purchasing the six-month bill and holding it to maturity. The effective yield to maturity of this six-month bill is:

$$R = \frac{(\$100 - \$P) \times 365}{\$P \times 182} \qquad = \frac{(\$100 - \$93.336) \times 365}{\$93.336 \times 182}$$

$$= \frac{\$6.664 \times 365}{\$93.336 \times 182}$$

$$= \frac{\$2,432.36}{\$16,987.152}$$

$$= .14318 \text{ or } 14.32\%$$

Since 14.32% is the *annual* return, the six-month or half-year equivalent is 7.16% or 14.32% ÷ 2.

One-Year Bills. Finding the effective yield to maturity for a one-year T-bill is a bit more involved than for the three- and six-month Treasury securities (see Table 2a). The following formula may be used:

$$R = \frac{\sqrt{B^2 - (4 \times A \times C)} - B}{2 \times A}$$

Note: The square-root symbol—"$\sqrt{\ }$"—is not as difficult as it appears. The square root of a number, say 100, is a value that if multiplied by itself produces that number. The value is 10, since 10 × 10 is 100.

What is the value of $\sqrt{9^2 - (16 \times 2)}$? Answer: 7. (Since the value of $9^2 = 9 \times 9 = 81$ and 16 × 2 =

32, then $\sqrt{81 - 32} = \sqrt{49}$; the square root of 49 is 7, since 7 multiplied by itself is 49).

In the above formula, the terms are defined as follows:

- *A* is the ratio of the total number of days (*D*) between the bill's issue and maturity dates and two times the number of days in the year (*Y*) following the issue date, minus 0.25. In other words,

$$A = \frac{D}{2 \times Y} - 0.25$$

- *B* is the ratio of the total number of days (*D*) between the bill's issue and maturity dates and the number of days in the year (*Y*) following the issue date. In other words,

$$B = \frac{D}{Y}$$

- *C* is the ratio of the bill's purchase price ($P) per $100 minus $100 and the purchase price. In other words,

$$C = \frac{\$P - \$100}{\$P}$$

Example. An example may help clarify the mechanics of using this formula. A T-bill issued January 2, 1981, and maturing December 31, 1981, had an issue price of $87.825 per $100. The effective yield, assuming the bill was held to maturity, would be determined by using the following value for the formula:
D is 363 days;
Y is 365 days (had 1981 been a leap year, the value of *Y* would have been 366 days); and
P is $87.825.

Now plug these values into the formula:

$$R = \frac{\left[\sqrt{\left(\frac{363}{365}\right)^2 - \left[4 \times \left(\frac{363}{2 \times 365} - 0.25\right) \times \frac{87.825 - 100}{87.825}\right]} \right] - \frac{363}{365}}{2 \times \left[\frac{363}{2 \times 365} - 0.25\right]}$$

$$= \frac{\left[\sqrt{0.98907 - [4 \times 0.24726 \times (-0.13863)]}\right] - 0.99452}{0.4945}$$

$$= \frac{\left[\sqrt{0.98907 + 0.13711}\right] - 0.99452}{0.4945}$$

$$= \frac{\left[\sqrt{1.12618}\right] - 0.99452}{0.4945}$$

$$= \frac{1.06122 - 0.99452}{0.4945} = \frac{0.0667}{0.4945}$$

$$= 0.1349 \text{ or } 13.49\%$$

Notes and Bonds. Instead of borrowing funds for a year or less, the Treasury may decide to obtain funds

Table 2a
One-Year Bills

Computing the yield for a T-bill with more than six months to maturity is more involved than for three- and six-month bills. The complexity arises because it is customary to state the yield on a basis directly comparable to the quoted yields on coupon securities. The coupon-equivalent yield (also called a "bond-equivalent yield") reflects the opportunity for the reinvestment of the semi-annual coupon paid holders of interest-paying securities (i.e., notes and bonds). The coupon-equivalent yield is calculated as if interest were compounded six months from maturity. It is less than the investment yield.

The derivation of the equation given on p. 350 is straightforward (symbols are defined on p. 350.)

$$\frac{P\left(D-\frac{Y}{2}\right)R}{Y}$$ equals the interest that would be earned at six months from maturity;

$$P\left[1+\left(D-\frac{Y}{2}\right)\left(\frac{R}{Y}\right)\right]$$ equals the principal plus the interest earned at six months from maturity; and

$$\left(\frac{R}{2}\right)$$ is the interest rate for the remaining six months:

$$P\left[1+\frac{\left(D-\frac{Y}{2}\right)}{Y}(R)\right]\left[1+\frac{R}{2}\right]=100$$

$$1+\frac{\left(D-\frac{Y}{2}\right)}{Y}(R)+\left(\frac{R}{2}\right)+\frac{R^2}{2Y}\left(D-\frac{Y}{2}\right)=\frac{100}{P}$$

$$\left(\frac{1}{2Y}\right)\left(D-\frac{Y}{2}\right)(R^2)+\left[\left(D-\frac{Y}{2}\right)\left(\frac{1}{Y}\right)+\frac{1}{2}\right](R)+1-\frac{100}{P}=0$$

$$\left(\frac{1}{2Y}\right)\left(D-\frac{Y}{2}\right)(R^2)+\left[\frac{D}{Y}-\frac{1}{2}+\frac{1}{2}\right]R+\left(\frac{P-100}{P}\right)=0$$

$$\left(\frac{D}{2Y}-0.25\right)R^2+\left(\frac{D}{Y}\right)R+\left(\frac{P-100}{P}\right)=0$$

which is a quadratic equation of the general form: $ax^2+bx+c=0$

where $A=\frac{D}{2Y}-0.25$ The solution to such an equation is given by:

$$B=\frac{D}{Y}$$ $$R=\frac{\sqrt{B^2-4\times A\times C}-B}{2\times A}$$

$$C=\frac{P-100}{P}$$

$$x=R$$

Table 2a *(cont)*
One-Year Bills

Notes and Bonds
The published yields for Treasury notes and bonds are generally yields to maturity that are only approximated by the annualized investment yield present on pages 350–352. The calculation of yields to maturity can be a laborious task without a computer or an electronic calculator, since the yields assume that the interest earned (the coupon payments) are reinvested at the same interest rate until the bonds mature. Precise yields to maturity can be found in published bond tables.

for a longer period by selling notes or bonds. These securities pay the investor a fixed annual return or *coupon* (which is paid twice a year) in addition to the face or par value, if held to maturity.

Treasury notes and bonds may be sold either at a discount or at a premium. When sold at a discount, the investor pays less than face value. For example, a newly issued bond or note with a purchase price of $95 means the investor receives a discount of $5 per $100 of face value. A security with a face value of $1,000, then, would cost $950.

When a bond or note is sold by the Treasury at a premium, the investor pays a price greater than face value. For example, if the purchase price of a new bond or note were $110, the investor would pay $1,100 for each $1,000 of par or face value.

The actual price paid—whether a discount or a premium—determines the true rate of return or investment yield on the note or bond, as it does on an other financial investment. If the security is purchased at a premium or at a discount, the return will be different from the fixed annual coupon rate the investor is legally entitled to receive.

The following formulas may be used to calculate the approximate annualized investment yield of a bond or note if held to maturity: (*a*) investment yield if the security is bought at a *discount:*

$$R=\frac{\text{coupon rate}+\left[\frac{\text{amount of the discount}}{\text{number of years to maturity}}\right]}{\frac{\text{security par or face value}+\text{purchase price}}{2}}$$

(*b*) investment yield if the security is bought at a *premium:*

$$R=\frac{\text{coupon rate}-\left[\frac{\text{amount of the discount}}{\text{number of years to maturity}}\right]}{\frac{\text{security par or face value}+\text{purchase price}}{2}}$$

Note: The difference between the two is that the discount formula takes a *plus* sign, while the premium formula has a *minus* sign in the numerator.

Example. Suppose the Treasury auctions a two-year note that has a coupon rate of 8½% of the par or face value. The coupon is payable semiannually. (The annual total dollar value of the coupon is $8.50 per $100 of par value; semiannual payments are one-half the annual coupon or $4.25 per $100 of par value.) Also, assume that the original price of this note is $99.802 per $100 par value—i.e., there is a discount of $0.198 per $100 ($100 − $99.802). What is the investment yield? To find it, use the discount formula:

$$R = \frac{8.5 + \left[\frac{\$0.198}{2}\right]}{\frac{\$100 + \$99.802}{2}}$$

$$= \frac{8.5 + \$0.099}{\$99.901}$$

$$= \frac{8.599}{\$99.901}$$

$$= .0861 \text{ or } 8.61\%$$

Note: The coupon rate is written into the formula without the "%" sign.

If the number of years to maturity is stated in years and months—e.g., four years and one month—convert the month into a fraction of a year. In other words, one month is 1/12 of a year—or, in its decimal equivalent, 0.0833 years. Four years and one month, then, can be written as 4.0833 years.

Problem. What is the investment yield of a 20-year, 1-month Treasury bond issued at a price of $99.407 and with an annual coupon of 11.75%, payable semiannually?

Answer.

$$R = \frac{11.75 + \left[\frac{\$0.593}{20.0833}\right]}{\frac{\$100 + \$99.407}{2}}$$

$$= \frac{11.75 + 0.02953}{99.7035}$$

$$= \frac{11.77953}{99.7035}$$

$$= .1181 \text{ or } 11.81\%$$

In the preceding sections on Treasury bills, notes, and bonds, the investment yield was calculated on the assumption that an investor purchased a *newly* issued security and held it until maturity. Such a purchase is done in the *primary* securities market. Rather than holding a security to maturity, an investor may decide to sell it to another investor. This is done in the *secondary* securities market. The above formulas can be adapted to evaluate the investment yield of government securities traded in secondary markets, but that step does not add to the basics of interest-rate calcula-

tion. For additional information, consult published bond-value handbooks.

Consumer Borrowing: Mortgages and Installment Credit. Most home buyers are unable to pay the full purchase price of a home. After making a down payment, the balance of the purchase price is financed by borrowing with a mortgage from a bank or thrift institution. Let us examine the conventional or fixed-interest-rate mortgage even though there are a number of different types of mortgage loans now being made.

Under a fixed-rate mortgage, the borrower promises to pay a *fixed* monthly amount over the length of the loan. The monthly payment is applied to reduce the principal and pay interest on the total amount borrowed. Over the initial years of the loan, most of the monthly payment is used to pay interest; the rest slowly reduces the principal. As the loan approaches maturity, more of the monthly payment is used to pay off the principal than to pay interest.

The following formula may be used to compute the total *monthly* payment (principal and interest) on a conventional mortgage loan:

Monthly payment = loan ×
$$\frac{\text{monthly interest rate} \times (1 + \text{monthly interest rate})^{T \times 12}}{(1 + \text{monthly interest rate})^{T \times 12} - 1}$$

Note: Because the monthly mortgage payment is sought, both the *annual* interest rate and the total length of the loan must be adjusted by 12 (months).

Problem. On a 30-year mortgage loan for $60,000 at a 12% *annual* rate of interest, what is the total monthly payment (MP)?

Answer. Plug the numbers into the formula:

$$MP = \$60,000 \times \frac{\frac{0.12}{12} \times \left(1 + \frac{0.12}{12}\right)^{30 \times 12}}{\left(1 + \frac{0.12}{12}\right)^{30 \times 12} - 1}$$

$$= \$60,000 \times \frac{(0.01) \times (1 + 0.01)^{360}}{(1 + 0.01)^{360} - 1}$$

$$= \$60,000 \times \frac{(0.01) \times (35.9496)}{(35.9496) - 1}$$

$$= \$60,000 \times \frac{0.359496}{34.9496}$$

$$= \$60,000 \times 0.010286$$

$$= \$617.17$$

Using Tables. Finding the monthly payment on a mortgage or consumer installment loan may become rather involved when problems must be solved manually. Fortunately, the task can be eased with the use of tables.

The steps required in using a mortgage- or installment-loan table are similar to those with a compound-rate table. See Table 3. *Annual* percentage rates are measured across the top of the table; the number of monthly payment periods is measured down the side. The numbers in the body of the table represent the total finance charge per $100 of the amount financed.

Example. Find the total finance charge on a 30-year, $60,000 loan at a 10.5% annual interest rate. Turn to the table and locate the finance charge per $100 financed, which is at the intersection of the "10.5%" column and the "360 payments" row (30 years × 12 periods per year = 360 payments). The intersection number is $229.31 per $100 financed. However, the amount financed is 600 times greater than the value for which the table has been constructed ($60,000 ÷ $100 = 600). To find the total finance charge on the $60,000 loan, multiply $229.31 by 600. The answer is $137,586.

The total amount the borrower must repay is obtained by adding the total finance charge and the amount financed: $137,586 + $60,000 = $197,586. To find the monthly payment on this $60,000 mortgage, simply divide the total amount that must be repaid by the number of payment periods of the loan:

$$\text{Monthly payment} = \frac{\text{total finance charge} + \text{total amount of loan}}{\text{total loan periods in the loan}}$$

$$= \frac{\$137,586 + \$60,000}{360}$$

$$= \frac{\$197,586}{360}$$

$$= \$548.85$$

Problem. A consumer wants to buy a $7,500 automobile financed with the *lowest* possible monthly payment. After visiting three lending institutions, the consumer learns that each offers a different loan package:

• A: a three-year loan may be obtained at an 18% annual rate;
• B: a two-year loan at an 18% annual rate; and
• C: a two-year loan at an annual rate of 16%.

Which loan will produce the *lowest* monthly payment? Let's work through each case.

Lending Institution A. With 12 payment periods per year, this three-year loan will require 36 monthly payments. The total finance charge per $100 of the

Table 3
Annual Percentage Rate Table for Monthly Payment Plans

NUMBER OF PAYMENTS	10.00%	10.50%	11.00%	11.50%	12.00%	12.50%	13.00%	13.50%	14.00%	14.50%	15.00%	15.50%	16.00%	16.50%	17.00%	17.50%	18.00%
						(FINANCE CHARGE PER $100 OF AMOUNT FINANCED)											
1	0.83	0.87	0.92	0.96	1.00	1.04	1.08	1.12	1.17	1.21	1.25	1.29	1.33	1.37	1.42	1.46	1.50
2	1.25	1.31	1.38	1.44	1.50	1.57	1.63	1.69	1.75	1.82	1.88	1.94	2.00	2.07	2.13	2.19	2.26
3	1.67	1.76	1.84	1.92	2.01	2.09	2.17	2.26	2.34	2.43	2.51	2.59	2.68	2.76	2.85	2.93	3.01
4	2.09	2.20	2.30	2.41	2.51	2.62	2.72	2.83	2.93	3.04	3.14	3.25	3.36	3.46	3.57	3.67	3.78
5	2.51	2.64	2.77	2.89	3.02	3.15	3.27	3.40	3.53	3.65	3.78	3.91	4.04	4.16	4.29	4.42	4.54
6	2.94	3.08	3.23	3.38	3.53	3.68	3.83	3.97	4.12	4.27	4.42	4.57	4.72	4.87	5.02	5.17	5.32
7	3.36	3.53	3.70	3.87	4.04	4.21	4.38	4.55	4.72	4.89	5.06	5.23	5.40	5.58	5.75	5.92	6.09
8	3.79	3.98	4.17	4.36	4.55	4.74	4.94	5.13	5.32	5.51	5.71	5.90	6.09	6.29	6.48	6.67	6.87
9	4.21	4.43	4.64	4.85	5.07	5.28	5.49	5.71	5.92	6.14	6.35	6.57	6.78	7.00	7.22	7.43	7.65
10	4.64	4.88	5.11	5.35	5.58	5.82	6.05	6.29	6.53	6.77	7.00	7.24	7.48	7.72	7.96	8.19	8.43
11	5.07	5.33	5.58	5.84	6.10	6.36	6.62	6.88	7.14	7.40	7.66	7.92	8.18	8.44	8.70	8.96	9.22
12	5.50	5.78	6.06	6.34	6.62	6.90	7.18	7.46	7.74	8.03	8.31	8.59	8.88	9.16	9.45	9.73	10.02
18	8.10	8.52	8.93	9.35	9.77	10.19	10.61	11.03	11.45	11.87	12.29	12.72	13.14	13.57	13.99	14.42	14.85
24	10.75	11.30	11.86	12.42	12.98	13.54	14.10	14.66	15.23	15.80	16.37	16.94	17.51	18.09	18.66	19.24	19.82
30	13.43	14.13	14.83	15.54	16.24	16.95	17.66	18.38	19.10	19.81	20.54	21.26	21.99	22.72	23.45	24.18	24.92
36	16.16	17.01	17.86	18.71	19.57	20.43	21.30	22.17	23.04	23.92	24.80	25.68	26.57	27.46	28.35	29.25	30.15
42	18.93	19.93	20.93	21.94	22.96	23.98	25.00	26.03	27.06	28.10	29.15	30.19	31.25	32.31	33.37	34.44	35.51
48	21.74	22.90	24.06	25.23	26.40	27.58	28.77	29.97	31.17	32.37	33.59	34.81	36.03	37.27	38.50	39.75	41.00
54	24.59	25.91	27.23	28.56	29.91	31.25	32.61	33.98	35.35	36.73	38.12	39.52	40.92	42.33	43.75	45.18	46.62
60	27.48	28.96	30.45	31.96	33.47	34.99	36.52	38.06	39.61	41.17	42.74	44.32	45.91	47.51	49.12	50.73	52.36
66	30.41	32.06	33.73	35.40	37.09	38.78	40.49	42.21	43.95	45.69	47.45	49.22	51.00	52.79	54.59	56.40	58.23
72	33.39	35.21	37.05	38.90	40.76	42.64	44.53	46.44	48.36	50.30	52.24	54.21	56.18	58.17	60.17	62.19	64.22
78	36.40	38.40	40.41	42.45	44.49	46.56	48.64	50.74	52.85	54.98	57.13	59.29	61.46	63.66	65.86	68.09	70.32
84	39.45	41.63	43.83	46.05	48.28	50.54	52.81	55.11	57.42	59.75	62.09	64.46	66.84	69.24	71.66	74.10	76.55
90	42.54	44.91	47.29	49.70	52.13	54.58	57.05	59.54	62.05	64.59	67.14	69.72	72.31	74.93	77.56	80.22	82.89
96	45.67	48.22	50.80	53.40	56.03	58.68	61.35	64.05	66.77	69.51	72.28	75.06	77.88	80.71	83.57	86.44	89.34
102	48.84	51.59	54.36	57.16	59.98	62.83	65.71	68.62	71.55	74.51	77.49	80.50	83.53	86.59	89.67	92.78	95.91
108	52.05	54.99	57.96	60.96	63.99	67.05	70.14	73.26	76.40	79.58	82.78	86.01	89.27	92.56	95.87	99.21	102.57
114	55.30	58.43	61.61	64.81	68.05	71.32	74.63	77.96	81.33	84.73	88.15	91.61	95.10	98.62	102.17	105.74	109.35
120	58.58	61.92	65.30	68.71	72.17	75.65	79.17	82.73	86.32	89.94	93.60	97.29	101.02	104.77	108.56	112.37	116.22
180	93.43	98.97	104.59	110.27	116.03	121.85	127.74	133.70	139.71	145.79	151.93	158.12	164.37	170.67	177.02	183.42	189.88
240	131.61	139.61	147.73	155.94	164.26	172.67	181.18	189.77	198.44	207.20	216.03	224.93	233.90	242.94	252.03	261.19	270.39
300	172.61	183.25	194.03	204.94	215.97	227.11	238.35	249.69	261.13	272.65	284.25	295.92	307.67	319.47	331.34	343.26	355.23
360	215.93	229.31	242.84	256.50	270.30	284.21	298.23	312.35	326.55	340.84	355.20	369.63	384.11	398.65	413.24	427.88	442.55

amount financed is $30.15, found from the table at the intersection of the "18%" column and the "36 payments" row. The actual amount financed— $7,500—is 75 times greater than the amount on which the table is based. The total finance charge on the automobile is:

$$75 \times \$30.15 = \$2,261.25$$

The monthly payment is:

$$\frac{\$2,261.25 + \$7,500}{36} = \$271.15 \text{ (after rounding)}$$

Lending Institution B. With 24 monthly payments at 18%, the total finance charge is $19.82 per $100 of the amount financed. Since the total amount financed is 75 times greater than the amount on which the table is based, the total finance charge is:

$$75 \times \$19.82 = \$1,486.50$$

The monthly payment is:

$$\frac{\$1,486.50 + \$7,500}{24} = \$374.44 \text{ (after rounding)}$$

Lending Institution C. With 24 monthly payments and an annual rate of 16%, the total finance charge is $17.51 per $100 of the amount financed. The total finance charge is:

$$75 \times \$17.51 = \$1,313.25$$

The monthly payment is:

$$\frac{\$1,313.25 + \$7,500}{24} = \$367.22 \text{ (after rounding)}$$

Summary. A wise borrower should know how the length of a loan and the annual interest rate affect both the monthly payment and total finance charges. Creditors are required by federal law to provide this information before consumers become contractually obligated. This enables consumers to shop for the credit plan that best fits their needs. Table 4 summarizes the three credit plans.

At a given interest rate, shortening the length of a loan will increase the monthly payment but reduce the borrower's total finance charges. With a given loan term, borrowing at a lower interest rate will reduce both the monthly payment and total finance charges. Of course, borrowing less will result in lower monthly payments and total finance charges.

Richard D. C. Trainer

Intermountain Stock Exchange (ISE)

The Intermountain Stock Exchange, formally known as the Salt Lake Stock and Mining Exchange, was founded in 1895. The name was changed on May 19, 1972, because it was felt that the term *intermountain*

Table 4
Three Credit Plans

Lender	Annual Percentage Rate	Length of Loan	Monthly Payment (After Rounding)	Total Finance Charge* (Based on Table 3)
A	18%	36 months	$271.15	$2,261.25
B	18%	24 months	$374.44	$1,486.50
C	16%	24 months	$367.22	$1,313.25

*Due to rounding out the amount of the monthly payment, the total finance charge may be slightly different.

gave it a broader scope of influence and interest than the name Salt Lake Stock and Mining Exchange.

The Intermountain Stock Exchange is the oldest and largest mining exchange that uses the "call" or auction system in setting the market price. Under the system, the executive secretary calls out a stock and brokers respond with bids to buy or sell, which then establishes the stock's price.

Located in Salt Lake City, Utah, the Intermountain Stock Exchange is administered by a five-man board of governors, with one acting as president and another as vice-president. In 1983 the exchange had 25 members, with 32 active stocks listed. The exchange is virtually a one-man operation—the executive secretary takes care of all activities that the exchange is responsible for, including typing and printing a daily quote sheet.

With the ruling of April 1, 1976, allowing any stock to be traded over the counter, the trading activity on the ISE has dropped dramatically. In 1982, ISE traded a total of 1,813,032 shares, with a market value of $820,493.18.

J. Roger Spjute

Internal Revenue Code

The Internal Revenue Code (Title 26 of the United States Code) is the set of rules and regulations governing the collection of taxes in the United States. Approved by Congress on February 10, 1939, the code contained all United States statutes that were in force on January 2, 1939, relating exclusively to taxation of revenues generated within the United States. Although there were prior laws aimed at raising revenues within the United States, these pertained mainly to taxation on the sales of spirits, tobacco, and beer. The 1939 code was the first actual compilation of all prior laws with very few changes or enactments of new legislation.

Between 1939 and 1954, over 200 internal-revenue statutes were enacted, including 14 major revenue acts. Accordingly, in 1954, Congress determined to revise the code. The 1954 enactment is basically the Internal Revenue Code as currently exists.

The code is divided into seven major areas, or "subtitles." They are as follows:

1. Income taxes
2. Estate and gift taxes
3. Employment taxes
4. Miscellaneous excise taxes
5. Alcohol, tobacco, and other excise taxes
6. Procedures and administration
7. The joint committee on internal revenue taxation

These subtitles deal with the following general areas of taxation:

1. *Income taxes.* Subtitle A defines those transactions that will be deemed subject to tax under the law; defines the taxpayer; sets forth the tax rates; and imposes certain obligations to withhold tax at the source of the income.

2. *Estate and gift taxes.* Under the code, dying and giving may be taxable events. The estate tax section defines the property owned by a deceased individual that will be subject to tax, and sets the amount of that tax. The gift tax section imposes a tax on certain gifts—that is, transactions whereby one entity gives something of value to another without consideration or without the recipient having to do anything to earn it.

3. *Employment taxes.* This section sets forth the withholding-tax system for employees and the federal unemployment tax system.

4. *Miscellaneous excise taxes.* This subtitle imposes certain taxes on retailers, manufacturers, services, documentary stamps, wagering, imports, and other taxes which the government feels is necessary to regulate the tax activities.

5. *Alcohol, tobacco, and other excise taxes.* Subtitle E imposes taxes on the manufacturing of spirits, wine, and beer; the manufacturing and sale of tobacco and tobacco-related products; and on guns and other firearms.

6. *Procedure and administration.* This subtitle sets forth the nature and information necessary for tax returns, the time and place of paying taxes, and the method of collecting the taxes. It also establishes interest on taxes, penalties, and details crimes related to tax obligations.

7. *The joint committee on internal revenue taxation.* This subtitle establishes a committee to research, review, and study the Code.

Alan J. Pomerantz

Internal Revenue Service (IRS)

A division of the DEPARTMENT OF THE TREASURY responsible for administering and enforcing the internal-revenue laws and related statutes (except those relating to firearms, explosives, alcohol, and tobacco). It assesses and collects annually individual income tax; corporate income tax; employment taxes; and excise, estate, and gift taxes.

To maximize voluntary compliance with the tax laws and regulations, the Internal Revenue Service communicates requirements of the law to the public, informing the public of its rights and responsibilities and taking enforcement actions necessary for fair tax administration.

Organization. There are three organizational levels of the IRS: the national office, in Washington, D.C., which supervises the field organization and develops programs for the administration of the internal-revenue laws; regional offices, which oversee the operations of the district offices and service centers; 60 district offices, whose various functions include assisting taxpayers, determining tax liabilities by examination of tax returns, collecting delinquent returns and taxes, and investigating criminal and civil violations of internal-revenue laws (except those regulations administered and enforced by the Bureau of Alcohol, Tobacco, and Firearms); and ten service centers, which process and verify tax returns and assess tax refunds.

Harvey Rachlin

Internal Revenue Service, History of the

The INTERNAL REVENUE SERVICE (IRS), from a historical perspective, may be reviewed by highlighting four major dates: 1862, 1913, 1954, and 1961. The Revenue Act of July 1, 1862, precipitated by the Civil War, established the Office of the Commissioner of Internal Revenue within the Treasury Department. From that time on, the IRS has functioned much as it does today, as the collection and enforcement agency for the government, charged primarily with administration of the income tax. Until July 1, 1972, the Bureau of Alcohol, Tobacco, and Firearms was a division of the IRS. In fact, the early IRS agents, referred to as "Revenuers," were more famous for their pursuit of illegal whiskey than for their piecework enforcement of the new personal income tax. When Abraham Lincoln appointed George S. Boutwell the first commissioner, Boutwell hired 4,000 Revenuers to work on the commission. They were charged with verifying the declarations of individual citizens to assure that they paid their taxes. When the law authorizing a direct tax on personal income was repealed in 1872, the Revenuers concentrated on their other functions, inspecting factories and enforcing manufacturing taxes, licenses, and other excises.

The personal income tax was not restored until February 25, 1913, with the passing of the Sixteenth Amendment. Within the year, the Bureau of Internal Revenue (the name for the IRS until 1954) was established. Between 1872 and 1913, without a direct income tax, 90% of the internal revenues collected in the United States were from such levies as a tax on opium and taxes on whiskey. By 1925, internal revenues outweighed all other taxes by the vast proportion of $3.2 billion to $464 million. With the increasing importance of the Bureau of Internal Revenue, the number of its employees had already risen to 15,800. The bureau also instituted an Intelligence Division to fight tax fraud.

In 1954, in part because of its tremendous growth of staff and revenues collected, and also in response to accusations of internal inefficiency and corruption, the BIR was reorganized by Congress and replaced by our present Internal Revenue Service (IRS). It was decided to emphasize the word *service* so that the public would perceive the agency as less threatening and its employees would remember their role as advisers to taxpayers, functioning to facilitate the payment of any taxes owed.

More recently, the IRS added a new dimension to its intrastructure, reflective of the ever-increasing revenues it collects and innovations of the new technology. The IRS National Computer Center was opened in 1961, and the Data Center in 1966. Located in Martinsburg, West Virginia (70 miles from Washington, D.C.), and in Detroit, respectively, the centers employ a vast computer network and storage system keeping a master file of all taxpayers and tax information.

David B. Axelrod

International Bank for Reconstruction and Development

See WORLD BANK.

International Banking Facilities (IBF's)

International banking facilities enable depository institutions in the United States to offer deposit and loan services to foreign residents and institutions free of FEDERAL RESERVE SYSTEM reserve requirements and interest-rate regulations, as well as some state and local taxes on income.

IBF's permit U.S. banks to use their domestic U.S. offices to offer foreign customers deposit and loan ser-

vices that formerly could be provided competitively only by foreign offices.

Among depository institutions that may establish an IBF are U.S. commercial banks, Edge corporations, foreign commercial banks through branches and agencies in the U.S., and mutual savings banks.

Despite the use of terms such as *international banking facilities, international banking zones, international banking branches,* and the *Yankee dollar market,* which convey a meaning of special offices in separate locations, activities of IBF's can be conducted by institutions from existing quarters. However, IBF transactions must be maintained on separate books or ledgers of the institution.

IBF's are expected to enable institutions operating in the U.S. to compete more effectively for foreign-source deposit and loan business in the Eurocurrency markets abroad. Institutions that operate IBF's will be able to reduce the cost of foreign-source funds as a result of exemption from CENTRAL BANK reserve requirements imposed by the Federal Reserve. Also, IBF's can offer the short-term deposit maturities that are widely employed in foreign markets.

IBF's may offer foreign nonbank residents large-denomination time deposits subject to a minimum notice of two business days before withdrawal. Foreign banking firms and official institutions may place overnight funds with IBF's. Foreign corporations that are subsidiaries of U.S. companies must acknowledge in writing the Federal Reserve Board's policy that funds deposited in, or borrowed from, an IBF must be used only to support the non-U.S. operations of IBF's. An IBF may pay interest free of restrictions imposed by Federal Reserve regulation Q. The nonbank deposits at an IBF must be at least $100,000. Likewise, minimum withdrawals are set at $100,000.

IBF's also may extend credit to foreign residents, other IBF's, or the U.S. offices of the IBF parent—subject to Eurocurrency reserve requirements—and may transact business in foreign currency.

IBF operations are under the jurisdiction of the Federal Reserve and other federal and state regulators. However, the Federal Reserve's regulations don't give depository institutions any additional banking powers. An institution is subject to restrictions established by its chartering or licensing authority or by its primary supervisor concerning the types of activities in which its IBF can engage.

U.S. regulators currently examine the foreign operations of U.S. banks through the U.S. head offices of the institutions, and regularly conduct on-site examinations of selected branches and subsidiaries abroad.

The IBF concept was formally proposed in July 1978 to the Federal Reserve Board of Governors by the New York Clearing House Association. On June

18, 1981, the board of governors approved establishment of IBF's beginning December 3, giving state legislatures time to revise tax and banking laws. By late January 1982, more than 225 depository institutions had opened IBF's, or informed the Federal Reserve of an intention to open IBF's. By the end of March 1982, more than 300 institutions had opened or planned to open IBF's.

Under Federal Reserve regulations, IBF's can be operated in any state. Some states, including New York, have revised laws to facilitate IBF's. The revised New York State laws exempt from state and local taxes net income, over a base, derived from an IBF. However, those earnings are subject to federal taxes.

Arthur Samansky

International Development Association

See WORLD BANK.

International Finance Corporation

See WORLD BANK.

International Monetary Fund (IMF)

The International Monetary Fund was established at the Bretton Woods Monetary and Financial Conference, toward the end of World War II, by countries seeking to avoid a repetition of the destructive competition in trade and exchange rates of the 1930s, which had worsened the depression throughout the world. Nearly 50 countries joined together in 1944 to try to promote international monetary cooperation and foster expanded international trade under the aegis of the IMF.

The IMF provides a permanent international monetary forum where countries can work to coordinate their economic and financial policies. The IMF is concerned not only with the problems of individual countries but also with the functioning of the international monetary system. It focuses as well on fostering policies and strategies through which its members can work together to ensure a stable world financial system and sustainable economic growth. In early 1983 the IMF had 146 members, accounting for about four-fifths of total world production and 90% of world trade.

To achieve its purposes, the IMF has both regulatory and financing functions. In joining the IMF, countries agree to abide by a code of economic conduct. They agree to cooperate with the IMF and with each other to assure orderly exchange arrangements, promote exchange-rate stability, and avoid exchange

and payments restrictions that would jeopardize national and international prosperity. The IMF monitors member countries' compliance with these obligations. Member countries are free to choose the form of their exchange arrangements, but the IMF is required to exercise surveillance over the exchange-rate policies and over the international monetary system.

Since the existence of a code of conduct alone cannot prevent payments imbalances, the IMF maintains a large pool of currencies from which to help finance the temporary imbalances of its members. This financial assistance—provided temporarily and usually subject to economic policy conditions—affords member countries greater latitude in correcting their payments imbalances without having to resort to trade and payments restrictions. Members are required to repay the IMF in relatively short periods of time, and the revolving nature of its resources is thus preserved.

Each IMF member is assigned a quota expressed in Special Drawing Rights (SDR's) and related to the size of its economy. The subscription of each member is equal to its quota; 75% is paid in the member's own currency and the balance in SDR's and/or in the currencies of other members prescribed by the IMF. As of January 31, 1982, the total pool of members' currencies amounted to $55.5 billion.

Quotas have been increased periodically since the IMF's creation to enable it to fulfill its role in the continually evolving monetary system. To date, seven "general reviews" of IMF quotas have been completed, as well as a special review in 1958–59. The Seventh Review, adopted in 1978, increased quotas by 50%. Under the Eighth Review, agreement has recently been reached on a proposal to increase total quotas by 47.5% to approximately $99 billion. In most cases, however, legislatures of member governments must approve the required funds.

The policy adjustments that countries make in connection with the use of IMF resources support their creditworthiness and thereby facilitate their access to credit from other official sources and from private financial markets. As a result, total capital inflows resulting from an adjustment program designed in collaboration with the IMF may be much greater than that provided directly by the IMF. The IMF also offers technical assistance in various fields to help members improve their economic management.

Since the IMF is responsible for the international payments system, it is particularly concerned with global liquidity—that is, with the level and the composition of the reserves that member nations have available for meeting their trade and payments needs. In 1969 the IMF was given the responsibility for creating Special Drawing Rights (SDR's). The SDR is a worldwide reserve asset established by international agreement, and the IMF's long-term objective is to encourage its development as the principal international reserve asset. The IMF has periodically allocated SDR's to its members in proportion to their quotas, as a supplement to their reserves. To date, approximately 21.4 billion SDR's have been allocated.

From its inception until the early 1970s, the IMF has presided over a system of exchange rates based on stable par values defined in terms of gold and the U.S. dollar—a system that collapsed in the face of growing imbalances in the world economy. Since March 1973, the international monetary system has been characterized by generalized floating of currencies of major trading industrial countries, with most other countries pegging their currencies to one of these, to the SDR, or to some other basket of currencies. The more recent period has also been marked by sluggish economic growth and stagnant trade. The efforts of the IMF have thus been focused on encouraging and assisting the adjustment process of developing- and industrial-country members, with the aim of restoring conditions for stable noninflationary economic growth and the expansion of international trade.

David M. Cheney

International Monetary Market

See CHICAGO MERCANTILE EXCHANGE, INTERNATIONAL MONEY MARKET AND INDEX AND OPTION MARKET.

International Trade Commission

An independent agency of the United States government; its purpose is to contribute to the development of U.S. international trade policy in a manner that is soundly based and as equitable as possible to all concerned. It attempts to achieve its objective by conducting factual and objective research on factors relating to U.S. foreign trade and its effect on domestic production, employment, and consumption; and the competitiveness of U.S. products. Through public hearings and other avenues, it receives the views of interested parties from public and private sectors and considers and evaluates these in formulating and rendering technical assistance and recommendations to the president and Congress. Its advice forms a basis for economic policy decisions on U.S. international trade.

Harvey Rachlin

Interstate Banking

The practice of establishing commercial bank offices in more than one state to accept deposits from customers. With an exception for 12 bank holding companies, federal law in effect prevents this practice.

Historically, the issue of interstate banking has been tied to state policies on branching (*see* COMMERCIAL BANKS). The federal government has generally deferred to the states on branching questions. Ironically, however, federal prohibitions on interstate banking began with an exception: an effort to expand the branching authority of national banks.

The federal government has chartered national banks since 1863. Until the 1920s, national banks were prohibited from operating more than one office where they could offer a full range of banking services. Many states, however, allowed state-chartered banks to operate more than one office, leaving national banks at a competitive disadvantage. As a result, national banks began to convert to state charters.

In an effort to lessen this disadvantage, Congress passed the McFadden Act of 1927. This law permitted national banks to operate branches within the limits of the cities where the banks were located if the state law allowed state-chartered counterparts this freedom. Then, in the Banking Act of 1933, Congress allowed national banks to branch to the extent that states allowed state-chartered banks to branch. For example, if the state allowed a state-chartered bank to establish branches in the county where the head office was located, a national bank could branch throughout the county, too. If state-chartered banks were allowed to branch throughout the state, so, too, could national banks. A result of these laws, however, was that all national banks were restrained by the branching laws of the states. In effect, banks were prohibited from crossing state lines to accept deposits unless expressly permitted to do so.

Bank holding companies—corporations established to hold stock in legally separate banks—originally fell outside this prohibition. Congress, however, curtailed interstate banking by holding companies by passing the Bank Holding Company Act of 1956. That law prohibited the acquisition of a bank in any but a holding company's home state unless explicitly authorized by state law. Twelve holding companies that then held banks in more than one state were exempted from the prohibition.

Until Congress passed the International Banking Act of 1978, foreign banks could establish offices to accept deposits in more than one state. The law, in effect, brought foreign banks under the interstate restrictions imposed on domestic banks. Existing operations were exempted, but the law limited further foreign bank expansion to one state in which the banks were already operating. Foreign banks entering the U.S. after passage of the law were limited to accepting deposits in one state.

The International Banking Act also requested that the Carter administration prepare a report on whether existing restraints on interstate banking should be eased or eliminated. Long delayed by political considerations, the report recommended the gradual easing of legal restraints on interstate bank mergers, acquisitions, and other banking activities, so that banks would be allowed to accept deposits at offices in more than one state. No action has been taken on the recommendations.

Within the banking industry, there is wide disagreement as to whether changes in the laws are needed.

Deposit-taking is only one side of the banking business; the other side is lending. There are no federal prohibitions on interstate lending.

Furthermore, Congress amended the Bank Holding Company Act in 1970 to make clear that there were no geographic limits on nonbanking subsidiaries of those corporations. Thus, subsidiaries of bank holding companies, such as mortgage companies and personal finance companies, can operate in more than one state. As the 1980s opened, individual states began to approve legislation to allow out-of-state banks to cross state lines under limited circumstances.

Phil Battey

Investing

In the broadest sense, *investing* means committing capital with the expectation of a profit. It is useful, however, to define it more narrowly by distinguishing between investing and speculating. Investing, as used here, is committing capital to a productive venture with the anticipation of profit from a share of the venture (dividends) or an agreed-upon fixed return (interest). Speculation is the attempt to make a profit from the predicting of shorter-term changes in the price of some asset. Investments may be active, as in the case of someone starting a business or buying and managing real estate; or passive, in which case the investor commits the funds but someone else decides on the specific employment of them.

Investment Decision-Making. Deciding on a general type of investment, and then which specific investments are best, requires an understanding of the investor's situation and the specific characteristics of the investment. Investors must analyze their own situations in terms of income, cash requirements, and net worth over the years, and from this establish a suitable level of risk for themselves. They must also determine the appropriate time horizon—short, intermediate, or long-term.

After evaluation of the individual situation is completed, the characteristics of available investment alternatives must be evaluated in order to find the ideal match between individual needs and investment choices. The evaluation should proceed from general

investment areas to specific investments within areas. For example, investors should first decide how much, if any, of their assets should be committed to bonds, stocks, real estate, and bank accounts, and then concentrate on which bonds, stocks, real estate, or type of bank account to choose. The essential characteristics to consider in evaluating different investments are yield, risk, duration, liquidity, and tax treatment.

Yield. Return from an investment may come in the form of capital appreciation; profit distribution; interest; or a combination of these. The total yield is the increase in the value of the investment, usually stated as a percent of the invested capital per year. After-tax yield is the percent return remaining after appropriate taxes have been paid. After-tax yield is the appropriate criterion for investment decision-making. Some investments are free from taxation, others have lower tax rates than ordinary income, and some defer the payment of tax until the future. The deferment of tax is a partial tax reduction because the deferred amount earns yield up to the time it has to be paid. The term *real yield* is sometimes used to refer to the yield after the inflation rate has been subtracted. The impact of taxes and inflation is extremely important in the evaluation of yield. As the high inflation of 1980–82 subsided, the yields on low-risk investments went from 15% to 8%, and in early 1983 it was common to hear people complaining that their yields were terrible. Assume a 30% tax bracket and the situation with 15% yields and 15% inflation goes like this: 15% gross yield, 10.5% after-tax yield, −4.5% real yield. In early 1983, with 5% inflation, the situation is: 8% gross yield, 5.6% after-tax yield, +.6% real yield. Which is better?

Risk. There are two general ways to define *risk*. In a nontechnical way, it can be defined as the probability that at different points in time an investment, with all of its cumulative yields, will be worth less than when it was made. A refinement would be to say "less in real dollars" to allow for inflationary loss. Risk can also be measured by statistical tools. When this is done, the expected or long-term average yield of the investment is plotted over time and then the degree to which actual yield varies from average yield is measured mathematically, usually by the standard deviation of returns. There are special risk measures for specific types of investments. Beta is used for common stocks and measures the riskiness of an individual stock relative to the stock market as a whole. The market as a whole has a beta of 1.00, so a stock with a beta of 1.50 is considered 1½ times as risky as the average stock. Bonds are given ratings based on the probability of default on principal or interest. The risk of a real-estate investment may be based on coverage of the annual expenses.

The defining of *risk* in terms of the variation in the

value of an investment over time points out that investments sometimes called "risk-free" are not risk-free; they are only free of default risk. To illustrate this important distinction, a 20-year government bond can be examined. A T-bond is guaranteed by the government and cannot default on principal or interest. However, as investors who held bonds into periods of inflation know, you may purchase a T-bond at $100 and shortly thereafter find that if you have to sell, you will receive only $80. This is risk. The only risk-free investment is one that is free from default risk and variation in value due to interest-rate variation. T-bills are virtually risk-free, although their market value can vary a little over their short life.

The Risk-Yield Relationship. What every investor would like is high yields and low risk. Unfortunately, in an efficient economic system like ours, there is a direct and pervasive relationship between the risk and the yield of investments. The higher the yield, the higher the risk, and vice versa.

Yield is paid for two reasons. First, some yield is necessary to compensate the investor for inflation—to adjust for the difference between real and nominal value. Second, yield is paid for risk-taking. This would lead to the conclusion that if there is no risk, an investment would have only enough yield to compensate for inflation over the long run. In fact, the yield for T-bills over the last 50 years is just below the inflation rate. No real yield. The payment by an efficient economic system for risk-taking, however, is only for necessary risk.

Necessary and Unnecessary Risk. Necessary risk will be rewarded over the long term by higher yields, but the system will not pay higher yields for unnecessary risk. One obvious type of unnecessary risk comes from bad decision-making—paying more than one should (accepting too low a yield for the risk) for an investment. This is akin to not negotiating or not shopping around when buying a car or a home. This type of unnecessary risk can be avoided by evaluating investment choices.

A less obvious type of unnecessary risk is the additional risk that comes from not diversifying. A well-diversified portfolio of common stocks, for example, will have from one-third to two-thirds less risk than the average risk of the individual stocks. The stock market assumes that rational investors diversify, and the yield paid is for the risk remaining after diversification.

An example of the value of diversification should emphasize this point. A gambling casino expects to win on 53 percent of the plays of the dice, which adds up to a handsome profit over time. If they allowed a player to bet the casino's entire net worth on a single roll, they would have a 47 percent chance of going bankrupt. That would be highly risky, so they limit each bet to a small percentage of net worth. Over a million rolls, their chance of going bankrupt becomes virtually nil.

Since the individual investments within the market tend to move together, not all risk can be diversified away, but the yields paid assume that necessary (unsystematic) risk has been diversified away and that only necessary (systematic) risk remains.

Since various investment markets are reasonably, not perfectly, efficient, the level of necessary risk will to a large extent determine the yield. The task of the individual investor then becomes one of determining the maximum level of risk that can reasonably be assumed and investing in portfolios of those investments that provide the highest yields for that level of risk. Additional reduction of risk can be achieved by diversifying among different investment areas: some stocks, some interest-rate instruments, some real estate, etc. In assessing risk level, it is the overall risk of all investments that is important. A combination of very risky and no-risk investments can be used to match the risk level of medium-risk investments. Many people believe that because institutions are so risk-averse, the higher-risk investments pay a yield higher than the risk justifies. If this is true, then a portfolio composed of T-bills and growth stocks might pay a higher yield than a portfolio of blue-chip stocks with the same overall risk level.

Time Horizon. The period over which individuals are investing and over which they will evaluate success will affect the level of risk and the yields they can achieve. Many investments that are highly risky in the short term are not as risky in the long term. The investor planning to profit in a year cannot have the same view as one investing for retirement 20 years in the future. The risk level of investments tends to go down over the long run. Most risk is short-term risk. Using the earlier example, the T-bond buyer whose $100 had shrunk to $80 in a short time should not have purchased long-term bonds if the money was needed in the short term.

The stock market can be used as an illustration. While stocks are extremely risky over a term less than an economic cycle (three to five years), they are not extremely risky in the longer term. If investors had bought a diversified portfolio (S&P 500) of common stocks each morning and sold it the next morning for the last 50 years, they would have had a loss a little less than half the time (excluding transaction cost). If they had purchased the same portfolio each year and sold it at year-end, they would have had a loss less than a third of the time. A holding period of five years would have provided a loss 3 times in 46, or less than 7% of the time. Over the past 50 years, if the holding period was eight years, there would never have been a loss. The example could adjust for inflation, but illustrates the point that the time period of an investment is important in assessing the risk level.

Liquidity. The liquidity of an investment relates to whether you can withdraw the invested funds on demand. It is different from the time duration of the investment. Thirty-year T-bonds are long-term, but there is an active secondary market and they can be sold at any time—though not necessarily at the price paid. On the other hand, some real-estate partnerships have no provision for selling out an interest, and some bank accounts can be drawn on before maturity only if a penalty is paid. If the investment can be used as collateral for a loan in the event of necessity, the problems of liquidity are somewhat reduced.

General Categories of Investment. Investments can generally be categorized as *equity* or *debt,* although there are some investments that are a combination. Equity investments entitle the investor to participate in the profit (or loss) of the enterprise invested in. The profits may be distributed regularly (dividends) or reinvested in the enterprise (capital appreciation). The best-known passive equity investments are common stock and partnership interests. Partnership interests are unwieldy for larger enterprises, but they avoid double taxation and so are still common, particularly in real-estate and tax-shelter investments. Real-estate holdings are equity-type investments if the enterprise is involved in the development or rental of property, not just in mortgages.

Debt instruments are investments where the yield is at a set level and paid either by appreciation or interest payments. Debt instruments have a fixed term by which time all invested capital is returned. The most common type of debt instruments are banker's acceptances; certificates of deposit; corporate bonds; commercial paper; mortgages; government bonds, bills, and notes; and the various kinds of bank accounts. The specific classification depends on who is issuing the debt, the terms of repayment, the nature of the debt agreement, and the collateral behind the obligation. While preferred stock is not legally a debt instrument, it behaves like and is similar to a bond with an infinite term.

Investments that combine the features of equity and debt include convertible bonds, convertible preferreds, and participating preferreds.

The specifics of each investment area have not been discussed, but it should be clear from this discussion that investing is complex and should be approached as a business venture. To achieve investing success, the investor must study investing and investments or find a competent and trustworthy adviser.

While an individual may invest in all of the investments mentioned above, it is sometimes advisable to pool investment funds with other investors and have them professionally managed. This is achieved through investments in mutual funds or limited partnership shares. The tax laws permit pooling of funds without double taxation on profits for many classes of investments, and these funds will be corporations or trusts. Where this pass-through privilege is not permitted, mutual funds will be limited partnerships to avoid double taxation. There are funds that invest in most of the investments discussed and various combinations of them. Virtually all funds will have annual management and administrative fees. In addition, load mutual funds and most partnership interests will have an initial sales charge. No-load funds do not charge a sales fee. As in the case of individual investing, the individual must decide on the appropriate areas for investment and choose the mutual funds on this basis. The specific investments in each area are then made by the fund adviser.

See Table 1, pages 362–375.

James B. Cloonan

Investment Banking

Every growing business, regardless of its size, requires funds for use in the expansion of its operations. These funds may be internally generated or may come from external sources. In general, *investment banking* is the intermediary function between businesses, municipal corporations, and other *users* of capital and *providers* of capital. Over the past 30 years, this intermediary activity has broadened to include such related activities as leasing, intermediary work in mergers and acquisitions, and financial advisory services. (Because of a peculiarity in our regulatory framework, banks that take deposits from the general public are excluded from the traditional definition of investment bankers.)

This entry will cover the various strands of investment-banking activity related to the financing needs of corporate and other borrowers; the regulatory environment (which is a major element in determining the shape of investment banking); and, briefly, the history of investment banking (which explains the role of individual firms in the marketplace today).

History. Until the early part of the nineteenth century, commercial establishments in the United States were for the most part so small and of such a local nature that external financing was done through local merchants and one's neighbors. With the opening of the West in the 1840s, the demand for capital from other than local sources rose dramatically and new mechanisms were developed to meet this need. This was particularly true in the case of the railroads, which

(Text continued on page 375.)

Table 1
Investments

Type	Definition	Where Purchased or Account Is Open	Why One Would or Would Not Want to Invest	
			Advantages	*Disadvantages*
Annuity	Provides income for life or for a certain number of years to the purchaser. It is most frequently used to provide retirement income.	Life-insurance companies and occasionally charitable institutions (often in return for a gift).	In the case of deferred annuities, if waiver of premium is available, the plan is self-completing in the event of total disability. Annuity investments are safe and usually have a minimum guaranteed rate of interest. In the case of variable annuities, a higher but fluctuating rate of interest may be paid. The cash value of most deferred annuities can be borrowed by the policyholder at usually low interest rates. May provide income that cannot be outlived.	For some annuities, life-insurance company's costs of sales, marketing, etc., are reflected in service charge or lower returns. Some annuities carry a very low rate of interest.
Asset-management account	A financial service that draws together, into a single account, a variety of investment and transaction services. The most common components of these accounts are brokerage services (e.g., execution of orders to buy securities, investment advice, custody of securities, and collection of dividends due), a money-market fund, and a debit or credit card. All transactions in each of these services are recorded on an integrated monthly statement.	Commercial banks. Full-cost brokerage houses. Discount brokerage houses. Insurance companies. Mutual-fund companies.	Centralizes all of your investment and banking activities in a single account. Simplifies record-keeping. Reduces the work involved in managing your money. Gives you market rates of return on idle cash balances. Offers margin loans at a competitive rate. Allows you to make purchases based on the value of assets in your brokerage account.	High initial investment ($20,000 is typical). If a money-market fund is part of the account, the fund may not be federally insured. Annual fees can be high ($100 or more). If account is established with a full-cost broker, the broker may call you to solicit unwanted activity in the brokerage part of your account.
Bankers' acceptances	Negotiable time drafts drawn primarily to finance the import, export, transfer, or storage of goods and	Commercial banks. Brokerage firms.	Safe, short-term investments because they are: backed by the credit of borrowing company;	Early demand for money would probably incur a penalty. Probably not covered by deposit insurance.

Table 1 *(cont)*
Investments

| Type | Definition | Where Purchased or Account Is Open | Why One Would or Would Not Want to Invest | |
			Advantages	Disadvantages
	are termed "accepted" when a bank guarantees payment at maturity.		collateralized by goods being shipped, or stored; guaranteed by bank. Yields generally higher than those on deposits.	Riskier than bank certificates. Have to first run a credit check on the bank involved. Usually when bought in denominations of less than $100,000 a fee is charged.
Bond-anticipation notes	Notes secured by a pledge to issue bonds or notes in the future to finance a specific project or projects, the proceeds of which would be used to retire the BAN's.	Municipal dealers. Brokerage firms. Commercial banks.	See *Tax-exempt notes.*	See *Tax-exempt notes.*
Certificate of deposit	Receipt sold in exchange for a sum of money that is left at a bank for a period of time ranging from days to several years. At the end of the period, the bank pays deposit plus interest.	Commercial banks. Credit unions. Savings banks. Savings and loan associations. Brokerage firms.	Insured by the Federal government. Allow depositor to "lock in" yield for stated time. Higher rate of return than passbook savings account. No risk to principal.	Penalty for early withdrawal of funds. Loss of liquidity.
Commercial paper	Short-term, unsecured promissory notes generally sold by large corporations on a discount basis to institutions and other corporations.	Brokerage firms. Corporations. Financial conglomerates. Bank holding companies.	Yields generally higher than on deposits of similar maturity. Unsecured promissory notes generally backed by the credit of the borrowing company.	Not collateralized by any assets of the issuing company. Riskier than bank deposit or market instruments.
Common stock	A security that represents an ownership interest in a corporation.	Brokerage firms. Subsidiary firms of bank holding companies, savings banks, and savings and loan associations. Financial-services companies.	Equity investment representing ownership of a company. Potential for relatively high rates of return due to prospects for sharing in corporate profits and capital appreciation. Allows for participation in management through right to vote for board of directors.	Subject to market risk. Not insured or collateralized. Value of stock fluctuates on a day-to-day basis. Owner incurs brokerage fee when buying and selling.
Corporate bonds	Debt obligations generally issued by larger domestic corporations. The maturities of corporate	Brokerage firms. Corporations.	Pay holder a fixed investment return over a relatively long period of time. Not subject to day-to-	Riskier than government bonds of similar maturity. Require physical storage and in many

Table 1 *(cont)*
Investments

Type	Definition	Where Purchased or Account Is Open	Why One Would or Would Not Want to Invest — Advantages	Disadvantages
	bonds range from 1 year to 30 years. The interest income is subject to ordinary income taxes at the federal, state, and local levels.		day fluctuations in investment return or in value if bond is held to maturity. Could safely control capital loss if held to maturity. Broad diversification of issuers.	instances forwarding of "coupons" to bank to obtain investment return. May be subject to early redemption.
Coupon stripping	Coupon stripping is a process whose end result is an investment vehicle. It is the creation of a zero-coupon issue by physically separating a bond's coupon payments from its principal payment.	Brokerage firms on the New York Stock Exchange.	High quality. Flexibility. Assured return.	No income prior to maturity. Limited marketability.
Eurodollars	Any dollar-denominated deposits on the books of banking offices outside the United States. (These deposits need not be on the books of European banks.)	Eurodollar deposits can be obtained on behalf of a customer through commercial banks, mutual funds, savings and loan associations, and savings banks, if the institution does international business.	Yields on the whole are generally higher than comparable instruments held in the United States. Deposits not subject to Federal Reserve Regulation Q interest-rate ceilings. There may be tax advantages on the earnings of Eurodollars.	More information (e.g., on the mechanics of making the deposit and on the credit-worthiness of the depository institution) is needed to make a Eurodollar deposit than to make a comparable deposit in the United States. The cost of maintaining a Eurodollar deposit is higher than the cost of maintaining a comparable account in the United States (because it's abroad). Not as liquid as other deposit investments. Minimum-deposit requirements may be too high for the small investor. Large minimum deposits make this primarily a corporate investment.
Futures	Goods, articles, rights, services, and interests in which contracts for future delivery may be traded.	On a registered exchange through a licensed futures commission merchant.	Potential to accumulate a large position (several contracts) on a small investment.	Extremely speculative. Investor can lose more than his initial margin deposit. The commodity

Table 1 *(cont)*
Investments

Type	Definition	Where Purchased or Account Is Open	Why One Would or Would Not Want to Invest	
			Advantages	*Disadvantages*
			High potential return based on the use of leverage. Brokerage commissions are low. Commodity transactions are taxed at a favorable rate as compared to other forms of investments. Commodity markets have a high degree of liquidity.	markets are extremely volatile. Not a passive investment (one must continually monitor the market to be able to make rational trading decisions). Sometimes difficult to find a competent broker.
Individual Retirement Account	A long-term or tax-advantaged account that allows an individual to accumulate retirement funds. Account earnings and new funds deposited, up to specified limits, are exempt from income tax until they are withdrawn.	Mutual-fund companies. Savings and loan associations. Savings banks. Brokerage firms. Commercial banks. Credit unions. Insurance companies.	Contributions up to 100% of compensation to a maximum of $2,000/year are fully tax-deductible. Account can grow untaxed; no taxes are paid until withdrawals begin—normally after retirement, when most people are in a lower tax bracket. Everybody who works for a living can have an IRA, even if they are already covered by a corporate pension or profit-sharing plan. Can contribute up to a maximum of $2,250 if a working individual has a nonworking spouse.	Withdrawals made before age 59½ are generally subject to death and disability income taxes and a 10% penalty.
Keogh plan	A retirement plan for self-employed individuals and their employees. Plan earnings and new funds deposited, up to specified limits, are exempt from income tax until they are withdrawn.	Mutual fund companies. Savings and loan associations. Savings banks. Brokerage firms. Commercial banks. Credit unions. Insurance companies.	Contributions up to a maximum of 15% of compensation, but not in excess of $30,000, may be deducted each year. Plan assets can grow untaxed until withdrawals begin. Any self-employed person can have a Keogh plan. Keogh plan holders can also have IRA's.	Rules can be complicated, particularly for Keogh plan owners with employees. Withdrawals before retirement can be penalized.
Life insurance	Insurance on the life of a person requiring the	Life-insurance companies via licensed agents.	Self-completing in the event of death.	Life-insurance company's cost of

Table 1 *(cont)*
Investments

Type	Definition	Where Purchased or Account Is Open	Why One Would or Would Not Want to Invest — Advantages	Disadvantages
	insured to pay regular premiums during his lifetime, or a specified period thereof, and guaranteeing a stipulated amount of money to a designated beneficiary upon the death of the insured or to the insured should he live beyond a certain age.		If disability waiver of premium is used, the plan is also self-completing in the event of total disability. Insurance company investments have high safety. Most policies have a guaranteed rate of interest. In the case of variable life insurance and some so-called universal life policies, a higher but fluctuating rate of interest may be paid. The cash value of most life-insurance policies can be borrowed by the policyholder at usually low interest rates.	sales, marketing, promotion, etc., are reflected in service charge or lower returns. Insurance-company investments are very conservative and tend to produce low yields.
Money-market deposit account	Market-rate, federally insured investment accounts that allow limited third-party transactions.	Commercial banks. Savings and loan associations. Savings banks.	No federal regulation of interest-rate yields—banks set their own yield. Insured by the federal government. Allows holder to earn interest on checking account balances. No withdrawal penalty. Funds can be withdrawn by "check," transfer, or in person.	Minimum-balance requirement. Limitation on number of check transactions. Transaction charges and account-maintenance fees.
Money-market mutual fund	Puts the pooled money of many investors in a variety of short-term money market securities issued by the federal government, "blue-chip" corporations, and leading banks. Initial minimum investments usually start at $1,000 or less. Some funds have no minimum.	Mutual-fund companies. Brokerage firms. Insurance companies. Financial planners.	Offers just about the highest short-term interest rates available to the ordinary investor. Professional managers invest in highest-quality money-market instruments. Wide diversification of investment—individuals can invest in obligations	Not insured except in limited cases. Provides income but not the possibility of capital growth. Money-market funds may not provide some of the services available at banks or thrifts.

Table 1 *(cont)*
Investments

| Type | Definition | Where Purchased or Account Is Open | Why One Would or Would Not Want to Invest | |
			Advantages	Disadvantages
	MMF's offer checkwriting.		otherwise unaffordable. Provides a checking-account feature. Check payments can be made from accounts. No withdrawal penalty; funds can be withdrawn by check (no limit on number of checks). Typical minimum investment is $1,000 or less.	
Mortgage-backed bond	An obligation of the issuer secured by a mortgage loan or pool of mortgages.	Securities dealers, mainly.	Bonds can be actively managed to give investors considerable certainty as to maturity and cash-flow. Some have been issued under the umbrella of an implied federal guaranty (e.g., Freddie Mac's collateralized mortgage obligations).	Investors do not own mortgages, must rely on creditworthiness of the issuing institution.
Mortgage-backed security	A security representing an ownership share of a pool of mortgage loans on which the security holder receives a prorated share of monthly payments of principal and interest on the underlying loans.	Securities dealers and sometimes the issuing institution itself.	The security represents actual ownership of the underlying mortgages. Many come under the umbrella of an implied (Freddie Mac and Fanny Mae) or explicit (Ginnie Mae) federal guarantee. Both bonds and securities offer: increased marketability over whole loan investment; elimination of the need for investors to originate, underwrite, or service the underlying mortgages; reduced risk due to diversification in a pool of mortgages. Favorable yields compared to other investments.	Uncertain cash flow and monthly maturity.

Table 1 *(cont)*
Investments

Type	Definition	Where Purchased or Account Is Open	Why One Would or Would Not Want to Invest — Advantages	Disadvantages
Municipal bond	A legal, contractual obligation between an authorized political subdivision (e.g., state, county, city, school district) and the investor, promising to pay specific amounts of money on specific dates.	Investment-banking firms. Commercial banks. Brokerage firms.	The interest received is exempt from federal income taxes. In many cases the interest is also exempt from state and local taxes in the state of origin. Safety record: excellent repayment record on high-quality bonds (A-rated or better); tax-exempt bonds as a class are considered second only in safety to obligations of the U.S. government. For maximum-tax-bracket investors, usually better than equivalent-grade corporate bonds on an after-tax basis. Provides for diversification of portfolios, spreading risk. Huge number of issues, maturities, etc., to fit different investor needs.	Fluctuation in interest rates. As rates change, either up or down, so generally does the principal value of outstanding bonds. Some more obscure local issues may also have secondary-market problems. Interest return is lower than on taxable bonds, so may not be best return or instrument for low-tax-bracket investor. Must deal through specialized dealer firm. Market risk resulting from changes in credit quality. Prices may decline if inflation increases.
General obligation bonds	Bonds issued by various political subdivisions (i.e., states or local governments) that are to be repaid, principal and interest, from limited or unlimited ad valorem taxes on all the taxable property in the particular subdivision.	Investment-banking firms. Commercial banks. Brokerage firms.	Unlimited taxing power backing most GO's gives the issuer added flexibility in finding resources to pay interest and principal even during periods of budgetary stress.	Yields are usually lower than those available on revenue bonds of similar rating and maturity. Credit ratings of many major GO issuers have declined as a result of recent budgetary problems. Poor secondary-market liquidity for more obscure issues.
Revenue bonds	Bonds issued and paid from a specific income source—e.g., electric revenues, toll highways, water revenues, etc.	Investment-banking firms. Brokerage firms.	Yields tend to be higher than those available on GO's of similar rating and maturity. Specific revenue source *may* be easier to analyze than the backing on GO's.	Long maturities on many revenue bonds are not suitable for all investors. Narrow revenue base for some revenue bonds *may* be less secure than GO's of the same municipality.

Table 1 *(cont)*
Investments

Type	Definition	Where Purchased or Account Is Open	Why One Would or Would Not Want to Invest	
			Advantages	*Disadvantages*
			Credit quality may fluctuate less widely over time for certain types of revenue bonds. Excellent liquidity for long-term, large-size revenue bonds called "dollar bonds."	Complex legal structure may be difficult to understand or analyze. Some issues are subject to extraordinary redemption at par.
Special-tax bonds	Bonds issued by state or local agencies, secured by the receipts from a specific tax. Common types include excise tax, gasoline tax, extraction tax on mineral resources such as coal, and sales tax. Usually, the proceeds from the bond sale are used for a specific purpose—highway construction, airport construction, urban redevelopment, etc.	Investment-banking firms. Commercial banks. Brokerage firms.	Revenue stream easy to analyze. Often, legal requirements in the offering documents ("bond resolution") stipulate a high ratio of taxes available to annual debt service on outstanding bonds ("coverage").	Tax receipts may be sensitive to economic fluctuations or decline.
Mutual funds	Pools the money of many shareholders and invests in a variety of securities; there are funds that invest solely in stocks, bonds, and money-market certificates, and funds that invest in various combinations of these securities.	Mutual-fund companies. Brokerage firms. Insurance companies. Financial planners.	Allows the purchaser to obtain a broadly diversified portfolio of securities at a relatively low cost; broad diversification reduces risk. Long-term rates of return have been among the very best. Relatively low fees. Professional management. "Switching" privilege from one type of fund to another. Wide selection—there's a fund available to match almost anyone's needs and/or interests. Minimum initial investments vary enough so that almost anyone can afford to get in.	Broad diversification of investments tends to keep return on portfolio lower than specialized investments in the stock and/or bond markets. Not federally insured. The values of stocks and bonds (and therefore equity and bond funds) do go up and down. Yield will be reduced by the annual management fees and any sales charges.

Table 1 *(cont)*
Investments

Type	Definition	Where Purchased or Account Is Open	Why One Would or Would Not Want to Invest — Advantages	Disadvantages
NOW account	A savings account that allows checklike drafts (negotiable orders of withdrawal) to be drawn against the interest-bearing account.	Commercial banks. Savings banks. Savings and loan associations.	Funds on deposit earn interest and can be withdrawn on order. One monthly statement shows all account activity plus interest earned.	Interest earned on money in the account only if a minimum balance is maintained.
Options (puts/calls)	The right to buy (call) or sell (put) a fixed amount of a given stock at a specified price within a limited period of time.	Brokerage firms. Brokerage divisions of commercial banks.	Large amount of leverage—you can indirectly have participation in price movements of large amount of shares without investing a great deal of money. Limited risk—what you invest in option is all that is at risk. Inexpensive way to speculate. If you *write* options, you can create additional income for your portfolio.	Can lose your entire investment in set period of time. If you write a call, you may have your stock called away from you.
Preferred stocks	Stock sold by corporations, with a fixed dividend. Preferred stock has a priority in claims over common stock if the company is liquidated.	Brokerage firms. Subsidiary firms of bank holding companies, savings banks, and savings and loan associations. Financial-services companies.	Receive preference over common stock in distribution of dividends or, if the company is liquidated, assets. With a fixed dividend, the investor knows in advance what return he will receive. Not subject to large day-to-day fluctuations.	Investor will receive a lower return than for common stock of same company because of the reduced risk. For individual investors, risk/yield ratio generally poorer than bonds.
Real estate	Investment in land and buildings.	Owner of deed (transaction often conducted through real-estate broker).	Capital appreciation has tended to outpace inflation. Represents a tangible asset (as opposed to a paper asset). No risk of default or bankruptcy of issuer.	Illiquid and immobile. Costs incurred in buying and selling, as well as taxes. Return predicated solely on capital appreciation.
Real Estate Investment Trusts (REIT's)	A business trust or corporation that operates by purchasing or financing primary real estate projects such as office	Brokers.	Capital appreciation. Liquidity. Limited use as a tax shelter. Centralized management. Limited liability for shareholders.	Brokerage fees incurred in buying and selling.

Table 1 *(cont)*
Investments

| Type | Definition | Where Purchased or Account Is Open | Why One Would or Would Not Want to Invest | |
			Advantages	Disadvantages
	buildings, shopping centers, hotels, apartment buildings, condominiums, industrial buildings, and warehouses. REIT's are sold in the form of securities, most of which are traded on major national or regional stock exchanges. REIT's and public offerings of their securities are regulated by the Securities and Exchange Commission and the various state securities regulators.			
Repurchase agreement ("repo")	The sale by a financial institution of an interest in a security at a set price with the agreement that the institution will repurchase the interest in the security at a specified time at a specified price that includes interest. A retail repurchase agreement is neither a savings account nor a deposit.	Brokerage firms. Commercial banks.	Short-term investment that allows holder to lock into a relatively high return by buying securities from dealer with an agreement that they will be replaced in a day or two at a predetermined rate.	Not a deposit, therefore not insured. Generally requires an ongoing relationship with bank or dealer. Cannot be done in small increments. Complex, requires time for management, and generally appropriate for portfolios approaching a million dollars.
Revenue-anticipation notes	Notes secured by a pledge of a specific future revenue source, such as state revenue-sharing payments, water-system revenues, etc.	Municipal dealers. Brokerage firms. Commercial banks.	See *Tax-exempt notes.*	See *Tax-exempt notes.*
Savings account	An account in which funds deposited earn interest. In practice, financial institutions allow the withdrawal of funds at any time without notice.	Commercial banks. Credit unions. Savings banks. Savings and loan associations.	Federally insured. Safety of principal. Guaranteed yield. Accessibility. Can provide collateral for low-interest loan.	Federal interest-rate ceiling. Some financial institutions, in effect, require a minimum balance.
Super NOW account	A market-rate, federally insured transaction account. A minimum balance is	Commercial banks. Savings banks. Savings and loan associations.	No government-set interest-rate ceilings as long as a minimum is maintained.	If the balance falls below the minimum, an interest-rate ceiling will apply on the

Table 1 *(cont)*
Investments

Type	Definition	Where Purchased or Account Is Open	Why One Would or Would Not Want to Invest	
			Advantages	*Disadvantages*
	required; if the balance falls below the minimum, an interest-rate ceiling will apply on the balance until it returns to the minimum.		There are no limits on the number of personal transfers on this account.	balance until it returns to the minimum. Financial institutions probably charge fees for transactions written on these accounts. Yield not necessarily market-rate; rate set by financial institution— may be adjusted at any time.
Tax-anticipation notes	Notes secured by a pledge of a specific future tax (e.g., all ad valorem taxes collected by the issuer prior to the maturity date).	Municipal dealers. Brokerage firms. Commercial banks.	See *Tax-exempt notes.*	See *Tax-exempt notes.*
Tax-exempt notes	Municipal securities, usually of 1-year or shorter maturity. They are generally divided into 3 categories: bond-anticipation notes; revenue-anticipation notes; and tax-anticipation notes.	Municipal dealers. Brokerage firms. Commercial banks.	Notes are normally rather stable in value. The holder gets all the interest and principal at maturity. No need to cut coupons. For bond-anticipation notes, yields may be somewhat higher than on other types of notes.	The investor in notes is limited in maturity choice. Locked in to some extent if rates change and one wishes to lengthen maturity to increase yields. For bond-anticipation notes, credit risks may be greater than on other types of notes, since repayment is dependent upon the issuer's ability to access the market for the amount needed to retire the bonds.
Tax shelter	A security representing a direct participation in a business or venture that is structured for both tax and economic purposes, the most common organizational form being the limited partnership. Tax shelters span the investment spectrum from real estate, to oil and gas equipment leasing, to the more esoteric areas of venture capital.	Brokerage firms. Financial planners. Many CPA's, attorneys, and insurance companies.	Tax benefits. Direct ownership. Not subject to the vagaries of the stock market. Professional management. Limited liability.	Illiquid. Long-term investments. Limited say in management.

Table 1 *(cont)*
Investments

Type	Definition	Where Purchased or Account Is Open	*Why One Would or Would Not Want to Invest* Advantages	Disadvantages
Treasury bills	Short-term securities of the United States Treasury with maturities of 13 weeks, 26 weeks, and 52 weeks, respectively. Sold in minimum amounts of $10,000 and in multiples of $5,000 above the minimum.	Federal Reserve Banks. Branches of Federal Reserve Banks. Bureau of Public Debt, U.S. Treasury Department. Brokerage firms. Commercial banks.	Safety (backed by the full faith and credit of the U.S. government). Salability. Interest earned is exempt from state and local taxes. No physical storage problems because issued in "book-entry" form. Book-entry securities protect against loss, theft, and counterfeiting. Can be purchased without a service charge at Federal Reserve Banks and the Bureau of Public Debt, U.S. Treasury Department.	Minimum investment requirement of $10,000. The purchaser does not know the yield at the time the security is purchased. If purchased through a bank or dealer there may be a service charge.
Treasury bonds	Long-term securities of the United States Treasury with maturities of more than 10 years. Minimum is usually $1,000.	Federal Reserve Banks. Branches of Federal Reserve Banks. Bureau of Public Debt, U.S. Treasury Department. Brokerage firms. Commercial banks.	Safety (backed by the full faith and credit of the U.S. government). Salability. Interest earned is exempt from state and local income taxes. Can be purchased without a service charge at Federal Reserve Banks and the Bureau of Public Debt, U.S. Treasury Department.	There is risk due to interest-rate fluctuations. If purchased through a bank or dealer there may be a service charge.
Treasury notes	Medium-term securities of the United States Treasury maturing not less than one year and not more than 10. Minimum on notes of less than 4 years is usually $5,000; above that, $1,000.	Federal Reserve Banks. Branches of Federal Reserve Banks. Bureau of Public Debt, U.S. Treasury Department. Brokerage firms. Commercial banks.	Safety (backed by the full faith and credit of the U.S. government). Interest earned is exempt from state and local income taxes. Salability. Can be purchased without a service charge at Federal Reserve Banks and the Bureau of Public Debt, U.S. Treasury Department.	Some interest rate risk. If purchased through a bank or dealer there may be a service charge.

Table 1 *(cont)*
Investments

Type	Definition	Where Purchased or Account Is Open	Why One Would or Would Not Want to Invest	
			Advantages	*Disadvantages*
Unit investment trust	A fixed portfolio of securities that is assembled by an underwriter sponsor and then offered in units to the investor.	Through the sponsor (the firm that organizes the trust) or general securities dealer.	Diversification: There are usually a number of different issues in the trust. Professional selection: Most components of a tax-free fund are from the top 4 ratings by Moodys or Standard & Poor's. The individual investor thus does not have to make various choices himself. Resale: In most cases the investor may redeem his units without a redemption charge. The sponsor quotes bid prices on a daily basis. Available in small denominations for a smaller investor.	Unit trusts are not suitable for all investors. Most of them are in a maturity range of 25–30 years. New issues of unit investment trusts are normally priced close to par and would not appeal to the individual investor seeking deeply discounted bonds. May yield less than a like portfolio created by the investor from individual bond purchases. Portfolio is not managed. Long maturity structure may result in high market volatility. Must be held 5 years to realize maximum return.
United States savings bonds	A nonmarketable obligation of the U.S. Treasury aimed at small savers and investors.	Commercial banks. Savings banks. Savings and loan associations. Federal Reserve banks and branches. U.S. Treasury Department.	U.S. government obligation with guaranteed principal and interest. If held 5 years, they return 85% of average yield on 5-year Treasury marketable securities on as little as $25. If held 5 years, minimum guaranteed rate of 7.5%. Exempt from state and local income taxes; federal tax may be deferred until time of redemption or maturity, if desired. Registered; can be replaced if lost, stolen, or destroyed. Can be purchased as part of payroll savings plan offered by many employers, as well as at financial institutions. Liquid after 6-month holding period; can be redeemed at most financial institutions.	Less-than-market interest. Interest return determined by government policy rather than by direct market forces. No liquidity in first 6 months.

Table 1 *(cont)*
Investments

Type	Definition	Where Purchased or Account Is Open	Why One Would or Would Not Want to Invest Advantages	Disadvantages
Warrant	A certificate giving the holder the right to purchase securities at a stipulated price within a specified time limit or perpetually.	Brokerage firms. Brokerage divisions of commercial banks.	Inexpensive way to have access to shares of stock without investing a larger sum of money for the primary shares. If primary shares go up in price, the warrant usually will also. Then you can exercise your warrant according to its terms or simply sell it in the marketplace.	If warrant expires, you can lose all your investment.

Sources: Phil Battey; William J. Beahan; Samuel W. Bodman; Randy Cepuch; Vance Clark; James B. Cloonan; George D. Friedlander; David H. Friedman; David M. Geliebter; Marvin Goodfriend; Reginald F. D. Green; Robert L. Isaacson; Harold C. Luckstone, Jr.; Stephen Meyerhardt; Edward I. O'Brien; Charles J. Parnow; Harvey Rachlin; Timothy A. Schlindwein; Barrett Sinowitz; R. Bruce Swensen; James F. Tucker.

required huge amounts of capital. For the first time, foreign investors—particularly from the United Kingdom—were enticed to invest funds in the booming railroad industry. Specialized promoters and dealers appeared, to act as intermediaries between investors across the Atlantic and the new railroad systems. With the growth of worldwide demand for U.S. cotton and other agricultural commodities, a network of commodity brokers appeared in the major southern cities, such as New Orleans and Memphis. These commodity brokers acted as intermediaries between the local produce agent and users of the commodities, located in the North and in England. Many well-known U.S. investment-banking firms can trace their beginnings to these two types of intermediary activities.

The tremendous industrial expansion immediately following the Civil War led to a dramatic increase in the need for putting the users of capital—corporations—in touch with the providers of capital, who for the most part were commercial banks taking deposits from the general public. By the 1880s the large corporate commercial banking structure in the United States had already taken a recognizable form, and a major function of the commercial banks was the intermediary function described above. The three strands of American investment banking were in place by 1900: the international merchant bankers; the traders in commodities (who had found that financial expertise was a necessary ingredient in their basic business); and the large commercial banks (whose loans were a source of vital lifeblood for the

burgeoning manufacturing corporations). In the years before World War I, investment banking as we know it today had crystallized. The rise of the private investment-banking houses, such as Lehman Brothers, Goldman Sachs, and Dillon, Read, was matched by the growth of the commercial banking houses, such as J. P. Morgan (which became Morgan Stanley & Company), the forerunner of the First Boston Corporation, and other major banking houses.

Major developments were to take place after World War I. The "turbulent Twenties" showed for the first time that middle-class Americans could be enticed into the securities markets. The speculative boom that culminated in the 1929 crash saw a tremendous development in the sophistication and complexity of investment banking, but it also allowed many practices to spring up that were clearly detrimental to both individual investors and the economy in general. After the 1929 debacle and the onset of the Great Depression, the federal government felt that the securities industry must be regulated to protect the individual investor. The resulting federal regulation was much more comprehensive and detailed than the state "blue sky" laws already on the books.

After a detailed investigation by Congress, major legislation was passed in Washington creating the Securities and Exchange Commission to regulate the investment-banking business. The four major acts passed in the 1930s created a framework for investment-banking firms that would not change for 40 years. The Securities Act of 1933 spelled out the fundamental information that had to be disclosed by an issuer of new securities, as well as the obligations of an underwriter during a public offering. The Securities Exchange Act of 1934 set out specific guidelines for the regulation of the stock exchanges so that the individual investor would have a fair opportunity to buy and sell securities on the open market. The third act was the Glass-Steagall Act of 1936, which prohibited commercial banks from underwriting publicly offered securities. As a result of this act, the investment-banking arms of the major commercial banks were spun off. The last major piece of regulation was the Trust Indenture Act of 1939, which set up mechanisms to protect the holders of corporate bonds.

Although the Great Depression and the aftermath of World War II held back growth in investment-banking activity until the 1950s, the following 20 years saw enormous growth in the investment-banking community and in the U.S. economy, which needed to recycle capital after a long period of quiescence. As the securities industry enticed more middle-class Americans to invest in stocks, the securities firms that had large branch-office networks connected by wire (the "wire houses") grew rapidly. For the first time, these firms had so many customers who wanted to buy securities that they started to rival the old-line investment-banking houses.

Although the 1950s and 1960s may be seen as a Golden Age of investment banking, the 1970s and early 1980s were a period of enormous change in the investment-banking world. The booming stock market of the late 1960s took a nose dive at the beginning of the next decade. This, combined with the enormous expansion of the securities industry during the 1960s, resulted in bankruptcies or forced mergers of many respected investment-banking houses in the 1970s. By the end of the 1970s, five major firms, with great prestige and capital bases, increasingly dominated the investment-banking community. One was a traditional old-line investment-banking firm with many long-established relationships with corporate clients. Another firm, because of its expertise and very large capital position, was a major factor in the trading of corporate bonds. A third firm was the largest securities firm in the world, with 9,000 salespeople and hundreds of branches in the U.S. and abroad.

However, as the investment-banking industry sorted its problems out during the late 1970s, the financial world was changing in a way that affected investment banking very sharply. For the first time in a decade, it appeared that investment banking was an attractive industry for other financial institutions to have a stake in. As a result, a number of major investment bankers were acquired by other companies. The acquirers included a very large insurance company,

the largest retailer in the United States, and a large financial conglomerate. As the 1980s progressed, investment banking no longer was a separate, clearly defined activity in the larger financial arena. It was losing its identity and becoming merely another service—albeit an expensive and complex activity—that was offered by a number of financial "supermarkets."

Public Offerings. The historical backbone of investment banking has been its role in helping a corporation offer its securities—both debt and equity—in the public market. Generally, before securities may be offered for sale to the public, a registration statement must be filed with the SECURITIES AND EXCHANGE COMMISSION (SEC) disclosing various kinds of information. Before the actual sale can take place, the registration statement must be declared effective by the SEC.

There are a number of stages in the public-offering mechanism. From the standpoint of an investment-banking firm, these stages are as follows:

1. Helping the corporate issuer decide the type, amount, and timing of the offering. The investment banker's involvement in this stage depends on whether he has an established relationship with the issuer. If there has been an established relationship, the company's financial managers typically will ask the investment banker for advice as to the size of the issue that is marketable, the type of security that should be offered—common stock, preferred stock, straight debt, or a convertible security—and whether market conditions are expected to be attractive at the time of the offering. One of the primary ingredients of successful investment banking is a knowledge of what is happening in the various securities markets and how potential investors will regard the proposed transaction.

If there is not a preexisting relationship, the company may have already reached a decision as to the type and timing of the offering. It usually will interview a number of potential investment-banking firms and choose the one that it feels best meets its particular needs for that offering. Factors such as the size of the corporation and whether it wishes to have national or regional distribution of its securities will play a part in its choice of an investment banker.

2. The second stage is preparing the registration statement and filing it with the SEC. The registration statement describes the securities being offered and the company's operations and sets forth the company's financial history and position. Although it is the responsibility of the company's management, the underwriter and its counsel are actively involved in helping to draft the document. The document must follow a detailed form set forth by the SEC, must con-

tain all material facts, and must not misstate or omit material information. Yet it must also be a selling document. The underwriter wants the registration statement to set forth the attractive aspects of the offering as clearly as possible in order to stimulate investor interest. Gathering the information and putting it into written form is an expensive and time-consuming operation, particularly if this is the first registration statement the company has prepared.

While the registration statement is being prepared and filed with the SEC, the managing underwriter is responsible for organizing a *syndicate,* a group of underwriters (i.e., brokerage houses) who will help sell the securities. The syndicate is chosen by the managing underwriter with guidance from the company so that the securities will be offered to the proper type of investor and the underwriting risk will be spread among several underwriting firms. Invitations are sent out to the potential members of the syndicate during the waiting period that follows filing of the preliminary prospectus with the SEC. Normally, the underwriters will accept the invitation after examining the preliminary prospectus.

3. After the SEC examiners have reviewed the preliminary registration statement and have made comments regarding changes to the company and the managing underwriter, the offering can be priced. If the offering is of securities that already have a public market, the offering will be priced at a slight discount from the current market price. This is because the relatively large size of the new offering tends to depress the market price, and the discount will encourage investors to buy the security.

The offering is usually priced the night before the securities are to be offered; and early on the morning of the offering, a final amendment to the preliminary prospectus is filed with the SEC in Washington. The SEC gives its final approval at that point and the securities are offered on the public market. Just before that occurs, however, the managing underwriter signs a contract with the issuing corporation binding it to buy the securities at a fixed price (hence the underwriting risk), and in turn the members of the underwriting syndicate sign a contract with the managing underwriter that sets forth their underwriting responsibilities for the offering.

The transaction closes seven business days later, when the underwriters pay the company the agreed sum for the securities less the underwriting discount, which is the fee for the underwriting risks involved and the cost of selling the securities through the sales staff of the various brokerage houses that are syndicate members. This kind of underwriting is called a "firm underwriting," firm in that the company can plan on receiving a definite amount of money regard-

less of whether the public buys the securities. The underwriters take the risk that they will be unable to sell the securities at the price agreed upon with the company. Another form of underwriting, used for emerging and small companies, is "best efforts" underwriting. This does not guarantee the issuer a fixed sum of money but rather depends on the best efforts of the underwriter to sell securities when and if it is possible.

The underwriting offers these advantages to the syndicate members and the managing underwriter: It provides securities that can be offered to the firm's brokerage customers by its salesmen, which enhances the volume done by the brokerage side of the business. (The underwriting discount includes the cost of compensating its salespeople for selling the securities to their customers.) For the managing underwriter, there is an additional fee for undertaking the expensive and time-consuming role required in the "due diligence" process—investigating the issuing company and assessing its prospects. The managing underwriter also will be able to retain for its own selling organization a larger percentage of the securities being offered.

The managing underwriter, after the offering, must make an orderly market (if there wasn't one before) so that people who wish to sell the securities they bought on the offering can do so at a reasonable price. This is important from the standpoint of the issuer in order to retain the confidence of the investment community, which demands liquidity for securities.

Private Placements. After public offerings, the second major area of investment banking is the private-placement market. In the 50 years since the SEC was formed by Congress, it has been gradually recognized that the registration process mandated for public offerings is a highly time-consuming and expensive proposition, particularly for smaller and medium-size companies. Furthermore, because of the time required to prepare a registration statement, in many cases the market for the securities changes adversely, causing companies to be unable to offer their new securities successfully. As a result, in the last 20 years there has been enormous growth in private placements. This in effect is a financing that is exempt from the registration requirement of a true public offering. The exemption is usually based on the limited number of potential purchasers involved and/or their financial sophistication. A private placement is a sale of securities, but not to the public.

From the standpoint of the investment-banking community, there are two distinct forms of private placements. One is the direct offering to a limited number of offerees of debt of substantial corporations to large life-insurance companies, pension funds, and other institutional investors. This type of offering to sophisticated institutional investors represents a very major part of the money involved in the private-placement market, and has several advantages.

One advantage is that the information disclosed to potential investors can be kept confidential. (Remember that a registration statement must adhere to the SEC's detailed disclosure requirements.) Second, the issuer has much more freedom in the information permitted to be put into the private-placement memorandum, including detailed projections of the company's future operations. Historically, registration statements have not allowed the use of prospective information on the company's operations except in very controlled and general terms. Third, the terms of a private placement are negotiated with the individual investing group, a relatively small number of parties. Thus, for complex or unusual financings, a private placement is much more convenient than a public offering. Finally, the private-placement market, because of the sophistication of institutional investors, allows more speculative offerings than are possible in the public market. Since the underwriter is not risking his capital and is not spending time preparing a registration statement, the cost to the issuing company of the underwriting spread is considerably less.

The buyers of corporate-debt private placements are predominantly the top 15 or 20 life-insurance companies in the United States. If the corporate debt is of investment quality, governmental and corporate pension funds also are significant buyers of private placements. For this reason the investment banker's role in a private placement is considerably different from that in a public offering. The investment banker is an agent for the issuing company, and is therefore not risking his own capital. Nor is he involved in preparation of the SEC registration statement. His knowledge—who the buyers are in a private-placement market, their pecuniary needs, and their pricing thoughts—is the expertise that the investment banker brings to the private-placement transaction. Knowing what institution is interested in what sort of offering, and being able to set the price at a level that is attractive, are key elements in a successful transaction.

The pricing of a debt offering in the private-placement market traditionally was higher than in a public offering because the takers of the private placement had no public market in which to sell their securities if they wished to liquidate all or part of their positions. However, the tremendous growth of the private-placement financing alternative has made the costs of this route often very comparable to a similar transaction in the public market. As a result, the importance of public offerings to the investment-banking community has been reduced considerably.

A second and very different type of private placement is the equity placement. The SEC has recently recodified its rules regarding exempt private placements for smaller issuers into Regulation D. In effect this redefines what a sophisticated investor is and sets new limits on the amount of money that a smaller corporation can raise without being subjected to the rigors of a registration statement. Although this is a growing area for smaller companies who wish to offer ownership participation in various forms to individual sophisticated investors, this sort of financing is still a very small part of the total efforts of the U.S. investment banking community.

Finally, it should be noted that the SEC has moved to relieve the largest BLUE CHIP corporations of the time-consuming constraints of the normal registration-statement procedure. By issuing Rule 415, the SEC has recently allowed the largest corporations, who have very high creditworthiness, to issue securities from time to time through a "shelf registration." This allows an issuer who is regularly in the capital markets to prepare a registration statement and then issue securities as it wishes over a period of time. Making it no longer necessary to prepare a registration statement for each new offering has created considerable concern in the investment-banking community because the investment banker's role in helping the company prepare a registration statement will be very greatly reduced, as will his compensation and his close relationship with the issuer. This rule seems to be another step in easing the burdens of the registration-statement framework, which has been largely unchanged since its adoption in the 1930s.

Tax-Exempt Securities. The third major segment of the capital market in the United States involves tax-exempt securities. Because many tax-exempt securities are issued by local municipal governments, they are also called "municipal bonds" (see MUNICIPAL AND STATE SECURITIES). This market is enormous, with approximately 1.5 million issues available. In 1981 the total amount of offerings in this market was *$47.7 billion.*

The tax-exempt market in the United States is in many ways unique in the world. Because the Constitution of the United States specifically exempted securities issued by state and local governments from the federal government's taxing power, there is no federal income tax payable on such securities. As a result there is a considerable difference in interest yields between tax-exempt securities and corporate issues, which are taxed by the federal government (securities issued by the federal government are subject to federal taxes, so are not part of the municipal market). This two-tier market as far as bond yields are concerned makes the municipal market quite different from the corporate-debt market. Furthermore, SEC rules and regulations do not normally extend to securities issued by governmental bodies. Therefore, the regulatory framework discussed above for corporate issues is not applicable in the tax-exempt marketplace.

There are three general types of tax-exempt securities: general obligation (GO) bonds, revenue bonds, and specialized bonds.

- *General obligation bonds* depend for their creditworthiness on the general tax-revenue-raising ability of the local government, and therefore on the ability of the inhabitants of the governmental area to support the issue through taxes. Ultimately, creditworthiness depends on estimates of future tax-revenue flows.
- Payment of interest and principal on *revenue bonds* depends on the flow of revenue coming from a specific source. Examples include toll bridges and tunnels, airports, and toll highways, which generate their own revenues from users and do not depend on the general taxing authority of the local government. Revenue bonds may also be supported by special tax assessments allocated to support these issues.
- *Specialized tax-exempt bonds* are peculiar creatures of the tax laws. They often straddle the line between tax-exempt securities and corporate obligations. One example is industrial-revenue bonds, which are issued by government agencies for the benefit of profit-making corporations. Another example is pollution-control bonds. These bonds are also issued by local governmental units in order to enable profit-making corporations to acquire, at lower cost, equipment that will reduce air and water pollution. These bonds fall on the line between traditional municipal securities and CORPORATE BONDS.

Specialized and Creative Financing Techniques. The investment-banking community structures and distributes various forms of financing that fall outside the three traditional categories of the U.S. capital market described above. These so-called specialized financial techniques have arisen over the last 10 or 15 years and are increasingly important as a means of financing corporations. One major form of specialized financing is the industrial-revenue bond (IRB), of which pollution-control bonds are a subcategory. In essence, this is a form of financing that enables a profit-making company to use the benefits of the lower interest costs available in the tax-exempt securities markets. There are three parties to a transaction involving industrial-revenue bonds. The corporation that is to use the plant or equipment involved guarantees payment of interest and principal of the bond. It enters into a sale-and-leaseback arrangement with the bond issuer—a local government body or specialized agency. (This governmental entity, which claims to have the power to issue tax-exempt securities, must receive a legal opinion from bond counsel, who in effect says to the buyers that the bonds are indeed tax-exempt securities.) The third party to the transaction is the bond buyer. The underwriter can offer the bond in a public offering, or in a private placement to institutions, local banks, and wealthy individuals.

This vehicle has engendered abuses in certain profit-making corporations' ability to use a tax-free security for their own benefit. As a result, the Internal Revenue Service (IRS) has set out very specific rules limiting the amount and timing of these offerings. Nonetheless, this type of financing has greatly increased over the years as a way of stimulating corporations to locate businesses in economically depressed areas at a relatively low cost in order to create job opportunities. Because of criticism from the standpoint of tax fairness, the regulations concerning IRBs have been gradually tightened over the years.

A subset of the industrial-revenue bond market are bonds issued to finance pollution-control activities. Unlike the concept of promoting general economic development through the issuance of local IRBs, the exception for pollution-control financing is to encourage corporations to take steps to maintain or improve the environment. The IRS stringently defines what eligible pollution-control facilities are and has rules to make sure that the installation of such facilities does not give the issuing corporation an economic benefit.

Another extremely important specialized financing technique, one that has grown enormously in the 1970s, is tax-based leasing, which involves complex techniques that retain the use of productive equipment while transferring the benefits of ownership to investors. Here again the investment-banking community has been in the forefront. In highly simplified form, tax-based leasing splits the *use* of productive property (such as an airplane) from the *ownership* of the property.

A typical leveraged lease transaction would be as follows: An investor who needs to shelter his income stream buys a piece of productive equipment. The resulting ownership enables him to depreciate the equipment and receive valuable investment tax credits. He will typically borrow much of the purchase price of the equipment from financial institutions. The third party to the transaction is the user, in this case an operating airline. The airline may have decided that it is unable to use the depreciation and investment tax credit profitably but needs the new equipment to carry on its business. It will lease the aircraft for a fixed number of years, obligating itself to make payments (to the investor/owner) that will *(a)* cover the interest and principal payments to the financial institutions that have put up the purchase price, and *(b)* provide a sufficient return to the investor/owner for his risk of ownership. This risk includes the possibility that the airline might become unable to make the lease payments. This transaction enables the airline to enjoy the use of necessary productive property without making a major capital outlay all at once; enables the owner to receive the benefits of depreciation and investment tax credit without putting up a major part of the purchase price; and enables financial institutions to make a loan secured by a valuable piece of equipment.

The development of tax-based leverage leasing has been spectacular over the last decade, and the major investment-banking firms are involved in structuring these complicated transactions as well as identifying the sources of financing and ownership necessary to put together such leases. For their efforts, the investment bankers are paid a fee related to the size and complexity of the transaction.

In 1982, however, a major change in the tax laws threw the leasing industry into a state of turmoil because of the tax uncertainties created in such transactions. The advantages of leasing make it inconceivable that this confusion will not be gradually cleared up; but until that happens, a serious cloud remains as to the impact of these transactions.

Another area of specialized financing is the use of guarantees or loans by various departments of the federal government to help for-profit corporations. The federal government over the last ten years has developed a variety of programs designed to encourage economic development for specific purposes or for particular geographic areas. These programs provide for-profit corporations with guarantees of financings obtained from private financial institutions. The investment-banking community often acted as intermediaries between government agencies and corporations who could participate in programs to benefit underpopulated rural areas, inner-city ghettos, or struggling industries. Such programs grew rapidly in the 1970s. Recently, however, with the cutback in federal spending, this aspect of specialized financing has declined substantially.

The Merger and Acquisition Industry. In the decade of the 1970s, a major development took place in the investment-banking community: the enormous increase in resources and profits from the merger and acquisition business. The M&A business now represents a very significant portion of the profits generated by the investment community as a whole. This is probably the most publicized activity of investment banking in the early 1980s.

Investment bankers traditionally have been heavily involved in putting together companies. Many of these transactions have taken place on a friendly basis with direct negotiations between the managements of the companies involved. Today, however, it is unusual for a medium-size or larger company to negotiate a merger without engaging the services of an investment banker. The investment banker's role in a friendly merger is somewhat different than in the case of the adverse tender offer, which is discussed below.

The history of merger and acquisition activity in the United States from the turn of the century on shows a pattern of cycles. High points of merger activity have generally coincided with the tops of economic cycles. There were many mergers in the period 1900 to 1905. Another major burst of activity was the late 1920s, when the stock market boomed. There was a significantly increased amount of merger activity in the late 1960s, when the Dow Jones industrial average reached 1,000. The collapse of the stock market in the early 1970s and the sharp rise in interest rates stifled the merger and acquisition business until the end of the decade. The early 1980s has shown another peak of activity, particularly for mergers involving two huge companies. In 1981 the total dollar value paid was $83 billion as compared with only $11.8 billion in 1975. The Du Pont–Conoco merger in 1981, the largest up to that time, was valued at approximately $8 billion.

Another aspect of M&A activity was the rise in the mid-1970s of contested takeovers of public companies. For the first time, managements of conservative companies would seriously consider buying the stock of public companies without the approval of their managements. Until then it was rare for a large company to even consider making an adverse tender offer. This change in attitude was fueled by the realization that inflation had made the replacement of plant and other assets more expensive than buying companies in a depressed stock market.

The change in management style in this area was paralleled by a very significant change in the investment-banking community. The major investment-banking houses have all increased the size of staff that spends time solely in merger and acquisition activity. Because of the large overhead that these professionals represent, investment bankers increasingly have tended not only to represent their investment-banking clients during the actual merger negotiations but also to actively seek out possible mergers for their clients and sell corporate managements on the potential of such mergers. It is a moot question whether this selling effort has caused the tremendous rise in adverse tender offers. (By the beginning of 1982, adverse merger activity had dropped significantly because of a weak economy, high interest rates, and an erratic stock market.)

The investment banker, if asked by a good client, will conduct a search for potential merger candidates in given industries. Through use of extensive computer programs, the banker also will provide voluminous comparisons of various potential candidate companies' operating histories and financial condition, including stock-price information, in order to make an acceptable offer. In many cases the investment banker will arrange the introduction of clients to one another and will actively participate in the negotiation process. At the same time, the investment banker will advise the buying company as to methods of financing the acquisition and ensuring that existing and potential investors in the stocks involved are fully aware of the benefits of the proposed merger. Finally, the investment banker is often the key element in deciding what an equitable price is for the merger. It is the investment-banking firm's knowledge of the market and of what price action can be expected of the stocks in question that is instrumental in ensuring that the merger is successfully structured.

The role of the investment banker in an adverse tender offer differs, depending on whether he is representing the attacker or the defender. As mentioned previously, investment bankers are increasingly feeding their clients ideas for potential takeover candidates. When a corporation decides to make an "attack" on another company, the investment banker devises ways of overcoming the other side's defenses, and he will have arranged ahead of time for financing necessary for the takeover. The banker will be a major factor in setting the price to be offered to the stockholders of the target company and providing stock-market intelligence to the attacker if the initial bid appears to be too low. He also acts as the soliciting agent for the stock that is turned in by the public stockholders upon receipt of the tender offer. This mechanical function is very important to maximize the number of shares of the target company's stock that will be taken under the control of the investment banker's client.

On the other side—helping a client defend against a takeover—the investment banker's roles include performing financial analyses showing that the merger terms are "grossly" unfair and issuing an expert opinion to that effect to be used as ammunition by his client. At the same time, the investment banker will search for a "white knight"—another company that might be more palatable to the target company. Finally, the investment banker will work with his client to devise ways of making the company's record and prospects appear so financially attractive that few stockholders will tender their shares to the opposition. All of these activities must be carried out under great time pressure, without regard to weekends, holidays, or vacations. For this the investment banker's fees are very sizable.

Because of the conflicts of interests and great confidentiality surrounding this activity, many investment-banking houses have separated their merger and acquisition activity from their other corporate finance functions.

However, the stock-in-trade of an investment banker is a continuing detailed knowledge of the marketplace for securities and how to apply this knowledge to the activity in question. It is for this reason that the investment banker's fees are often well earned. Although the merger and acquisition business would seem far removed from a public offering or a private placement, it does represent another form of growth for corporations and falls historically within investment-banking activities. The investment bankers clearly are the dominant force in the merger and acquisition business, although many smaller acquisitions are carried out through other types of intermediaries—or without any intermediary at all.

Real-Estate Financing. A significant area of financing expertise is in real estate. Not all investment bankers are involved in the real-estate industry, but a number of major investment bankers have sizable real-estate financing departments or subsidiaries. This is another area of diversification away from the underwriting activities that used to represent the classic investment-banking business.

The role of an investment-banking firm in the real-estate market falls into two categories. The first is using its corporate finance expertise to find sources of capital for major, complicated real-estate projects while representing the owner or developer of the project. The investment banker's role, besides introducing the sources of capital to the real-estate developer, encompasses structuring the financing within the constraints of the marketplace.

The second area is investing at times the investment-banking firm's own funds in the equity portion of real-estate financings, a quite different function from corporate financings. Commercial banks provide the short-term construction financing, while the investment banker's role is usually restricted to identifying and negotiating with the provider of the "long-term takeout"—i.e., permanent mortgage financing. The investment banker often also will line up additional sources of ownership funds, sometimes committing its own capital. Occasionally, these financing sources are tapped through a public offering, but—

particularly in a high-interest-rate environment—both equity and long-term financing tend to come from institutions via private placements.

The enthusiasm of the investment-banking community for involvement in the real-estate markets, at least for large, complicated projects, ebbs and flows with the state of the economy and the stock market and the attractiveness of the real-estate markets. Because of the sharp differences between corporate finance and real estate, both in ways of doing business and in looking at credit risks, not all investment-banking houses have pursued this activity. Nonetheless, real estate is an important part of the spectrum of activities that a number of major and regional investment bankers offer to their clients.

Recent Developments in Investment Banking and a Look at the Future. In reviewing the history of investment banking in the United States, it can be seen that this industry has always been subject to rapid change because it is a direct reflection of what is happening in the securities markets. Agility, intelligence, and inventiveness are required for success in this business.

Another element, however, has become increasingly important for success in investment banking. Since the early 1970s, particularly since the abolition of fixed commission rates in 1975, investment-banking firms have become more and more dependent on having sufficiently large amounts of capital not only to develop their channels of securities distribution but also to make markets in securities where they must take large positions for resale. This need for capital and the volatile nature of the securities markets caused a large number of well-known investment-banking houses to merge in the 1970s. Yet there always has been a place for the small, specialized, expert investment banker.

A second wave of mergers took place in the early 1980s. A number of financial institutions and other industrial corporations have perceived investment banking as an industry that would have great potential in the turbulent economic environment that has been predicted for the 1980s. The acquisition of Shearson, Hayden, Stone by American Express, Dean

Witter by Sears, Roebuck, and Bache & Company by the Prudential Life Insurance Company all are outstanding examples of this trend.

A related development in investment banking is the breaking down of the traditional boundaries between the various parts of the financial and capital markets in the United States. The commercial banks are pushing hard to have the Glass-Steagall Act repealed so that they can enter the more attractive parts of the investment-banking business. Conversely, the investment-banking community has expanded its range of products, including the lightly regulated money-market funds, so as to compete directly with commercial banks. Other types of financial institutions, the life-insurance companies, and quasi-financial companies such as American Express and Sears, Roebuck are also developing a very broad range of services that include investment-banking products with other types of financial activity. This development has been accelerated by the investment of increasing amounts of non-U.S. capital in the investment-banking community.

In summary, the investment-banking community is in a state of great change, with the large investment-banking houses offering an increasingly wide range of services in order to stay in business. This trend is also being felt by the regional investment-banking houses, a number of which have also been acquired by financial conglomerates in the last few years. The outlook for the investment-banking industry is that during this decade it will gradually become an organic part of a much larger financial marketplace. Its former arcane expertise will be made much more broadly available to corporate managers—and, indeed, to the general public. It promises to be a very different business from what it was as late as 1970.

Anthony C. Paddock

Investment Savings Account

A savings account where each unit of savings placed in the account is represented by a certificate. Usually earnings are distributed to the holder, not credited to the account.

Mary Ann Irvine

·J·

Joint Account

A savings or checking account owned by two or more persons who have equal rights to and control of the account with the right of survivorship. Deposits and withdrawals may be made by any of the parties. Joint accounts are commonly held by spouses. If one owner dies, the survivor(s) maintain all rights to the account.

Mary Ann Irvine

Joint-Tenancy Ownership

See PROPERTY, FORMS OF CO-OWNERSHIP.

Joint Venture

See BUSINESS ORGANIZATIONS, FORMS OF.

·K·

Kansas City Board of Trade (KCBT)

A COMMODITY-FUTURES EXCHANGE on which wheat and stock-index futures are traded.

The KCBT is today the world's center of trade for hard red winter wheat and the largest market in the world for trading hard-winter-wheat futures. Prices established in Kansas City serve as world prices for wheat and play a vital role in the movement of food and grains worldwide.

The membership of the Kansas City Board of Trade has grown over the years to include the major grain-exporting companies of the world, large regional grain cooperatives, grain elevators, millers, bakers, and large financial and brokerage houses. The KCBT was incorporated in 1973.

More than 1.5 million contracts valued at almost $7.5 million changed hands on the KCBT trading floor during 1982—1 million contracts for futures on hard winter wheat and 500,000 for futures on the stock market, as measured by the Value Line Composite Index.

Why Futures? The set of prices for each variety reflects a distinct and dynamic pattern of supply and demand; economic conditions that influence consumption patterns; the weather in different parts of the world; and other such factors. Supply-and-demand fundamentals change frequently and unexpectedly, causing wheat prices to sometimes change dramatically. The volatility of prices creates sizable risk for anyone owning or controlling inventories of wheat—growers, elevator managers, exporters, millers, and bakers. Their businesses, and profits, depend on the ability to sell wheat inventories at prices higher than what they paid to produce or procure the crop.

The trading of wheat futures at the KCBT allows those with wheat inventories to "insure" the value of those inventories. In an organized futures market, the inventory holder promises to buy or sell an agreed-upon quantity of wheat for a specified price at a specified date. Contracts are traded in a futures "pit," and prices are agreed to by open outcry as at an auction.

The Speculator. Commercial grain-trading interests are not the only participants in the fast-moving wheat-futures market. Obviously, markets could not work efficiently if participants were only commercial users attempting to transfer the risk of inventory price changes. Because futures markets are markets for risk transfer, and commercial users are seeking to transfer risk, "liquid" futures markets require the active involvement of speculators—those willing to accept risk.

Futures markets provide unique opportunities for aggressive investors with adequate risk capital. Large leverage, the controlling of a contract valued in late 1982 at about $19,000 (5,000 bushels at $3.80 per bushel) for a $750 investment, allows a trader to realize the benefit of a full price movement on the contract.

Each contract comprises a 5,000-bushel commitment to deliver U.S. Grade No. 2 hard red winter wheat in March, May, July, September, or December. Prices per bushel fluctuate in minimums of one-quarter of a cent equal to $12.50 in contract value. Trading hours are from 9:30 A.M. to 1:15 P.M. (Kansas City time) each day.

History. As early as 1850, there were strong indications that Kansas City would develop into one of the world's centers for grain and livestock trade. The West was growing. Railroads sprawled across the country, and Kansas City developed into a major commercial and transportation hub. More and more people populated Kansas City and the fertile farm regions surrounding the town. The need for a center of trade grew, and in 1856 local civic leaders organized the first Kansas City Board of Trade.

That first Kansas City Board of Trade was not the grain-marketing and financial center that the name today implies. It acted merely as a gathering place for those who had products or service to sell and those needing to buy such products or services.

The Civil War abruptly ended the initial growth of the marketplace, and in about 1870 the exchange was reorganized as the Commercial Club of Kansas City.

By the early 1870s, the trading of grain began to dominate the varied business transactions at the exchange.

The birth of futures trading as it is known today occurred in June 1876 when the first "grain call" was inaugurated at the Kansas City trading center. The "grain call" took place at certain hours of the day under rules and regulations approved by the Kansas City Board of Trade.

The KCBT's specialization in the trade of hard-winter-wheat futures contracts developed naturally after the mid-1870s, when the seeds were sown for the evolution of the Great Plains into the breadbasket of the world. During this period, large-scale immigration of Russian Mennonites to this country brought new farming practices to large parts of Kansas and to a lesser extent Nebraska and the Dakotas. The Mennonites brought seed wheat called "turkey red" from the Crimea.

Turkey red was a hardy winter wheat well adapted to Kansas soils and climate. Early Kansas farmers had tried to raise wheat crops from seeds brought from the eastern U.S., largely with poor results. The hard wheat, turkey red, survived the cold winters and more arid conditions of the plains. Soft wheat, brought from the East, could not thrive under such adverse conditions.

Turkey red today is the parent stock for virtually all of the hard red winter wheat grown in the U.S. Its introduction has made Kansas the largest wheat-producing state in the U.S. and one of the largest producing regions in the world. Hard winter wheat has become a standard bread wheat in this country and around the world.

Hard winter wheat, while only one of five varieties grown and marketed in the U.S., is perhaps the most important farm commodity in the world of commerce. U.S. farmers have grown more than 2 billion bushels of wheat annually in recent years, and 50–60% of that is hard red winter.

Soft red winter wheat, traded at the Chicago Board of Trade, accounts for about 18% of normal production; hard red spring, traded in Minneapolis, accounts for about 13%; western soft white, about 14%; and durum, 5%.

Fifty to 70% of all U.S. wheat is exported every year, and half or more of that is hard red winter. Flour milled from hard winter wheat is the dominant ingredient of the world's bread; hard wheat is the only variety purchased by the USSR.

Futures trading in hard winter wheat expanded sharply in Kansas City during the years following the first big Russian grain purchase in 1972. About 6 billion bushels' worth of wheat futures have been traded in each of the last several years. Since the Russian grain purchase, hard-winter-wheat prices have exhibited volatility and an independent course of movement. The price relationship between hard red winter and soft red winter and between hard red and other varieties is closely monitored by commercial grain traders the world over.

Market Growth in Recent Years. The volume of trading at the Kansas City Board of Trade and in hard-winter-wheat futures has exploded in recent years. In 1972, when the U.S. reestablished trade with the Soviet Union and People's Republic of China, a record 1.5 billion bushels' worth of futures were traded. The total volume in 1980 of 6.2 billion bushels was almost ten times the average volume for the 25 years preceding 1972. This dramatic increase in futures trading is attributable to growing export markets for U.S. grain and unprecedented production by U.S. farmers, who now enjoy disease-resistant and weather-hardy varieties.

Through the futures-trading facilities of the KCBT, the movement of grain from farmer to consumer is accelerated rapidly and economically. Returns to growers may be increased by as much as 10 to 25 cents per bushel, perhaps more, by the existence and use of future markets. The hedging operations made possible by futures permit the financing of grain handling and milling with enormous savings in credit requirements alone.

How Futures Markets Work. Excitement in the trading pit on the floor of the KCBT conveys a sense of pandemonium and confusion because futures trading is a fast-moving business that requires traders to act aggressively to fill the orders of their customers. The rules and bylaws of the KCBT apply in each transaction. Millions of bushels are traded daily in the pit by oral agreement—no contracts are signed. These oral contracts are as legally binding as any other commercial agreement.

Each trade must be reported to the Grain Clearing Company, a wholly owned subsidiary of the KCBT, within one hour after the close of trading. The Clearing Company matches each contract reported by any seller to each reported by any buyer.

The clearinghouse acts as intermediary for all trades—acting as buyer to all sellers, and seller to all buyers. Margins for both buyers and sellers remain on deposit with the clearinghouse until outstanding contracts are closed out by offsetting transactions or until delivery of the required commodity is made. This interposition of the clearinghouse facilitates trading, transfers of contract positions, and settlement.

More important, however, is the substitution of the financial strength of the clearinghouse for that of the buyer and seller. The financial strength of the individual on the opposite side of a trade executed in the pit does not concern traders. The creditworthiness of the clearinghouse and its members guarantees the validity of "open" contracts.

In turn, the financial viability of the clearing company is carefully safeguarded. Although there are more than 200 exchange members, only 50 firms have been approved to clear transactions directly with the clearing company.

To achieve clearing membership status, firms must meet high standards of business integrity and financial strength. Nonclearing members settle their transactions as "customers" through the accounts of qualified clearing members. All trades are settled daily.

Stock-Index Futures. The history of the Kansas City Board of Trade is inextricably linked to the growth and evolution of this nation's agricultural markets and the burgeoning worldwide demand for food. But in 1977 the KCBT took steps to meet the risk-transfer needs of another large segment of the nation's business community—those who hold inventories of common stock.

After more than four years of research, planning, and effort by the KCBT, the CFTC in February 1982 approved the introduction on the exchange of trading in futures based on movements of the stock market as reflected by a stock index. This was the first stock-index futures contract—a concept which subsequently has been adopted by other exchanges, and which has grown to be one of the leading types of all futures contracts. The Value Line Composite Average of the performance of 1,700 stocks was quickly accepted as a way to manage the risk of common-stock ownership.

From February through December 1982, more than 500,000 contracts traded in the new instrument. Trading in Value Line futures quickly outpaced that of any newly introduced futures contract before it.

Value Line futures were designed to allow investors to hedge against risk resulting from fluctuations in the overall stock market. Diversification can protect against loss from a single stock or narrow group of stocks, but cannot protect from losses tied to the "market." Value Line futures for the first time allowed investors to guard against a general downturn of the stock market—market breaks that before had eroded the value of even well-managed and well-diversified stock portfolios.

As with wheat futures, a trade in Value Line futures constitutes an agreement by two parties to make or take delivery of funds equal to the value of the Value Line index at the end of a specified month in the future (March, June, September, and December). The price is determined freely by bid and offer via public outcry on the trading floor in such a manner as to be available to all members at the same time.

Small and large investors alike have benefited from the use of Value Line stock-index futures to protect the value of stocks during periods of bear markets, to protect the value of stock "inventories" between purchase and sale by an underwriter, and to improve the timing of stock acquisitions. Many investors have also used Value Line futures to speculate on the general movement of the market. During bullish circumstances of late 1982, a high-risk investor could have purchased Value Line futures for an initial investment of $6,500 and profited as the overall market rose without buying or selling shares of individual stocks. That $6,500 investment could have controlled a contract worth $80,000 at the time.

For instance, the stock market as measured by the Value Line was at 110.00 in early August. By mid-December the market had risen to 160.00. Because each 1.00 in Value Line futures equals $500, an investor who purchased Value Line futures at 110.00 and sold the futures at 160.00 would have profited 50.00 points or $25,000 on an initial investment of $6,500.

As with wheat, Value Line futures prices vary in response to changes in underlying factors of supply and demand that affect the overall economy. The anticipated performance of the economy, expectations of stock-market direction, ideas about inflation, the general level of interest rates and corporate profits, consumer behavior patterns, and pertinent national and international political and economic developments all play a role in the "price discovery" process for stock-index futures. The Value Line futures contract for the first time provided investors—from managers of large institutional portfolios to relatively small investors in common stock—with an appropriate tool to manage market risk.

Other Products. In 1983 the KCBT began trading in Value Line options and in Mini-Value futures contracts (one-fifth the size of the regular Value Line contract). However, neither of these contracts attracted extensive trading volume at the outset.

Government of the KCBT. The Kansas City Board of Trade is a federally designated contract market. It operates under provisions of the Commodity Exchange Act and its activities are supervised by the COMMODITY FUTURES TRADING COMMISSION (CFTC).

As of January 1984 the KCBT had approximately 300 members representing about 100 firms engaged in all branches of the agricultural and financial industries. Its membership comprises public and private elevator operators, futures commission merchants, flour and feed manufacturers, and other processors, exporters, futures traders, brokerage firms, and speculators.

The members and firms are governed by a strict code of rules maintained to ensure fairness and integrity of all commercial transactions. The corporation's officers include the president, first vice-president, and second vice-president elected from the membership to serve a term of one year. There are 14 directors on the board of directors, who serve two-year terms. Twelve are elected from the membership and two are appointed to represent the interests of nonmembers.

An executive vice-president acts as the chief executive officer and works to implement the policies of the members as determined by member committees and the board of directors. The executive vice-president and secretary also administers the professional staff of the corporation, keeps a journal of proceedings, maintains records and historical data, and is responsible for the property of the corporation. Several departments operate under his guidance, including the Marketing Department, the Transportation Department, the Department of Audits and Investigations, the Department of Public Affairs, the Operations Department, and the Grain Market Review, the daily news and statistical paper of the exchange.

W. N. Vernon III

Karat

Gold in its pure state is usually considered too soft for general use, including use in jewelry. By mixing, or alloying, it with other materials, its hardness can be increased and its color modified. The various measures of gold content are referred to in terms of karat or fineness, or in terms of percentage.

The word *karat* (and *carat,* the unit of weight used to measure gems) derives from the Italian *carato,* the Arabic word *qirat,* or the Greek *keration,* all meaning "the fruit of the carob tree." The seeds of the fruit were once used to balance the scales in weighing gems and gold in the bazaars of ancient times. The various measures are as follows: 100 percent means 100% gold; fineness means that 100% gold would be marked 1,000; karats are measured in 24 parts so that the equivalent pure gold would be 24-karat. Table 1 shows various measures in equivalents.

In the U.S., 10K is the legal minimum accepted standard of gold karatage, with 14K the most popular. In France and Italy, 18K is the lowest permissible standard to be called "gold." England accepts 9K, while in some countries 8K is the legal minimum standard.

Eugene J. Sherman

Table 1

	European System		Karat System	
% Gold	Gold Present	Mark on Jewelry	Gold Present	Mark on Jewelry
100.0	1,000 parts fine	999	24 karats	24K
91.7	917 parts fine	917	22 karats	22K
75.0	750 parts fine	750	18 karats	18K
58.5	585 parts fine	585	14 karats	14K
41.6	416 parts fine	416	10 karats	10K
37.5	375 parts fine	375	9 karats	9K
33.3	333 parts fine	333	8 karats	8K

Keogh Plans

Corporate retirement plans can be wonderful things—but they're meaningless to the millions of small business owners, doctors, dentists, lawyers, artists, writers, and others who work for themselves and don't incorporate their businesses.

Fortunately, self-employed people can build their own retirement funds, by investing up to $30,000 a year or 25% of income (whichever is less) in Keogh plans—retirement savings programs for the self-employed, which offer tax benefits.

Named for Congressman Eugene J. Keogh (N.Y.), who spent more than ten years shepherding the legislation through Congress, Keogh plans were formally created by the Self-Employed Individuals Tax Retirement Act of 1962, an amendment to the Internal Revenue Code. When Keogh plans first became effective, in 1963, the annual contribution ceiling was $1,250, or 10% of income (whichever was less). But in the two decades since, Congress has raised the limit several times—most recently with the Tax Equity and Fiscal Responsibility Act of 1982, which mandated the current ceilings effective as of plan years beginning on or after January 1, 1984. The new law also provides for cost-of-living adjustments to the $30,000 ceiling, beginning in 1986.

Although the amount one can contribute has been changed on several occasions, the basic premise behind Keogh plans has remained the same: Given sizable tax breaks as an incentive, self-employed people will build retirement funds for themselves and their employees. The tax breaks are sizable, indeed.

Two Tax Breaks. First, every penny contributed to a Keogh plan—up to the annual maximum—is fully deductible on that year's federal tax return. That means a person in the 50% tax bracket who puts $30,000 in a Keogh plan saves $15,000 that year in taxes. Partial or total deductions are allowed on taxes in some states as well, cutting annual liability still further.

The second break is on earnings. In an ordinary investment, earnings are taxable each and every year. Not so in a Keogh plan, where both contributions and earnings grow untaxed until withdrawals begin—normally at retirement.

Because taxes are deferred, Keogh-plan accounts can grow much faster than ordinary investments. A self-employed person in the 40% tax bracket, for example, would end up with about $250,000 if he or she put $3,000 every year for 30 years into an ordinary, taxable investment paying 10% annually. The same contributions to a Keogh plan paying an identical rate of return would grow to more than $540,000.

Actually, the difference would probably be even greater, as it would be necessary to pay taxes first on any money set aside for the ordinary investment. (A person in the 30% bracket, for example, would really need to have $7,143 available—$2,143 for the tax man—to be able to put $5,000 in a taxable investment. For someone with only $5,000 to invest, taxes would leave just $3,500. That amount, placed each year for 30 years in an investment paying 10% a year, would bring about $353,000—only about one-third as much as a comparable Keogh-plan investment.)

For those who have the money to contribute the full $30,000 each year, the potential returns are mind-boggling. By putting $30,000 every year for 30 years into a Keogh plan paying 10% annually, it's possible to end up with more than $5.4 million! And for those with even more money, the law allows nondeductible voluntary contributions amounting to as much as 10% of earned income. Although such additional contributions aren't tax-deductible, they do grow untaxed with the rest of the investment until withdrawals begin.

Some self-employed people may wish to defer taxes on more than the $30,000 Keogh-plan ceiling; they can put as much as an additional $2,000 a year into the plan as a Voluntary Deductible Employee Contribution (VDEC), or they can invest up to $2,000 in an INDIVIDUAL RETIREMENT ACCOUNT (IRA).

For those at the other end of the income spectrum, there's no minimum contribution required for Keogh plans, except in some cases involving Keogh-plan owners with employees. In fact, it's possible to skip years altogether, depending on the terms of the plan. Even small investments can grow to large sums, through compounding. Annual investments of $250 every year for 30 years in a Keogh plan paying 10% annually would grow to more than $45,000, for example.

Similar to Corporate Retirement Plans. Corporate retirement plans are defined-contribution plans (which provide for fixed annual contributions) or defined-benefit plans (which provide for fixed benefits at retirement). Similarly, Keogh plans can be one or the other.

The 1982 tax law created a parity between the permissible contributions and/or benefits offered in a Keogh plan or a corporate plan. (The $30,000 ceiling refers to the maximum contribution for a defined-contribution plan. In a defined-benefit plan, the actual ceiling is a maximum annual benefit of $90,000, assuming a retirement age of 62. Benefits are reduced actuarially for persons who retire before that age, but only to a maximum of $75,000 annually for benefits commencing between the ages of 55 and 62. After 1985, the maximum for both defined-contribution and defined-benefit plans will be adjusted to reflect cost-of-living increases.) Not incidentally, it also removed the incentive for doctors, lawyers, ballplayers, musicians, and the like to form "personal corporations" for tax advantages.

Under the new law, Keogh plans are now usually "top-heavy" plans—defined as those under which 60% or more of accrued benefits are provided for "key employees." (A key employee is an officer, a 5% owner, a 1% owner with compensation in excess of $150,000, or any employee who owns one of the ten largest interests in the business.)

For self-employed people with no employees, the Keogh plan rules are relatively simple. It gets trickier for those with employees, and a consultation with an attorney or financial adviser might be prudent. In most instances, any financial institution offering Keogh plans can help complete the initial paper work.

Contribution Rules. Generally, contributions can be made to top-heavy Keogh plans for as long as the participant continues to work. Any employee who must be covered by a retirement plan under the general discrimination standards established in the Employee Retirement Income Security Act (ERISA) must be included in a Keogh plan. (Such employees must be fully vested, in top-heavy plans, either within three years or at a rate of 20% each year after the second year, up to 100% in six years.)

Contributions for all persons covered by a plan must generally be equal, in terms of percentage of compensation, across the board. However, a plan may be integrated with Social Security benefits so that employer contribution levels will be coordinated with Social Security benefits.

Minimum contributions must generally be made for all nonkey employees covered under a top-heavy

Keogh plan. The amounts required depend on whether the plan is structured as a defined-contribution or a defined-benefit plan.

In the case of a defined-contribution plan, the minimum required contribution for covered persons is not less than 3% of compensation—not including Social Security or amounts placed in salary-reduction programs.

In the case of a defined-benefit plan, each nonkey employee under the top-heavy plan must accrue a minimum benefit that is not less than 2% of the person's average annual compensation multiplied by his or her years of service with the employer, up to ten years. (Certain years of service need not be taken into account.) Benefits provided upon retirement by Social Security cannot be considered a part of this minimum benefit, which must be provided through employer contributions.

If a self-employed individual maintains both a defined-benefit and a defined-contribution plan, certain other restrictions apply. If, for example, accumulated benefits for the self-employed person or key employee exceed 90% of the benefits for all employees in the plans, additional contributions must be made on behalf of the nonkey employees. For defined-benefit plans, the extra contribution must be an additional accrual equal to 1% of average annual compensation multiplied by the number of years of service, or 1% more than is required for a top-heavy plan. For defined-contribution plans, the extra contribution must equal 1% of compensation, thereby increasing the minimum contribution rate from 3% to 4% per year.

Withdrawal Rules. Withdrawals (also called distributions) from top-heavy Keogh plans by key employees must begin by age 70½. Withdrawals by nonkey employees are often more flexible and vary according to the specific plans.

Normal income taxes are paid on any Keogh-plan withdrawals. It's expected that most people won't start taking money out until they retire, and by then they'll probably be in lower tax brackets and won't pay as much.

If the plan provides for lump-sum withdrawals, it's often quite possible to get favorable tax treatment, such as averaging the tax liability over ten years, rather than the five years permitted through regular income averaging. Any withdrawals from a top-heavy plan by key employees made before age 59½—except in cases of disability or death—are subject not only to normal income taxes but to a special 10% penalty as well. Nonkey employees can begin withdrawals at whatever retirement age is specified in the plan. If a Keogh plan is funded through profit-sharing, it's

sometimes possible to take money out before retirement, for reasons of hardship.

Withdrawals by key and nonkey employees must be made in a manner that should use up the money within the participant's expected life-span, according to actuarial estimates. If the participant dies, all withdrawals from his or her account must be made within five years—unless withdrawals have already begun on a schedule that will exhaust the account by the end of the joint life expectancy of the participant and the spouse (another actuarial determination).

It is possible for employees (but not the self-employed individual) to borrow against vested benefits in a Keogh plan without having the loan considered a withdrawal—provided any individual loan does not exceed $10,000 and the total loans outstanding from a plan do not exceed half the vested balance or $50,000 (whichever is less). All such loans from Keogh plans must be repaid within five years, except those used to buy or repair the principal residence of the participant or a close family member.

Plans That Aren't Top-Heavy. A small number of Keogh plans may not be top-heavy. A large law firm with a considerable number of nonkey employees enjoying relatively large benefits, for example, might well not meet the top-heavy criteria. For those Keogh plans that are not top-heavy, the rules for contributions and withdrawals will differ to some extent, but all contributions on behalf of plan participants must be based on the same percentage of salary, across the board.

Plan Investment Options. Keogh plans can be opened at any time of year, but all contributions for any year must be made by the time tax returns are filed for that tax year.

Mutual funds, banks, savings and loans associations, insurance companies, and brokerage houses are among the financial institutions offering Keogh plans. It's perfectly legitimate to have Keogh-plan accounts with more than one institution at a time—provided the total contribution to *all* such accounts does not exceed the annual maximum allowable.

All or part of a Keogh-plan investment can be moved from one institution to another at any time, under the law, but there may be charges assessed for doing so by the financial institutions involved. (Special penalties may apply in some circumstances—early redemptions of bank or savings and loan certificates of deposit, for example.)

Costs for setting up and maintaining a Keogh plan will vary from institution to institution, and each of the financial institutions that handle Keogh-plan investments offers distinct features. Comparison shopping may thus prove quite valuable.

Banks, savings and loans, and most credit unions offer the security of insured deposits up to $100,000. While all three types of institutions offer fixed interest rates—usually in the form of certificates of deposit—some also offer variable-rate certificates. But there are limitations on investments with these institutions. They offer no opportunity for capital growth, and can "lock" the depositor into fixed rates over long periods. (And, of course, early redemptions of certificates of deposit are subject to those special penalties referred to earlier.)

Brokerage houses can help set up a Keogh plan in a wide range of investments, from common stocks and bonds to money-market funds. Mostly these are "self-directed" accounts—which means the investors themselves attend to the specifics, deciding when and what to buy and sell, within Keogh-plan rules. (The rules do forbid investments in anything requiring leverage—for example, some kinds of real-estate deals—or in precious metals or collectibles.) Self-directed accounts require a bit of investment sophistication and considerable discipline. Frequent changes in investments can be expensive.

Insurance companies offer fixed annuities, which are contracts guaranteeing fixed payouts for life after retirement. Although actual interest rates are currently running far higher, interest-rate guarantees on fixed annuities are usually relatively low. Variable annuities are also available, offering higher potential payouts (depending on results of the company's investments), but without guarantees. Deposits with insurance companies are not insured.

Mutual funds offer a diversified investment with a very good past performance record and the flexibility to adapt profitably to virtually any changes in the economic climate. They pool the money of many people and invest in a wide range of financial issues—giving individuals the chance to own a diversity of stocks, bonds, and money-market instruments they could not have afforded on their own.

Of course, there's no guarantee of future rates of return from mutual-fund investments—stock values and interest rates do go up and down—and they're not insured. But there are funds to match just about anyone's leanings—financial, philosophical, or other—and returns over the years have generally been superior. Historically, mutual funds have proven to be the most popular choice for Keogh-plan investors.

Randy Cepuch

Krugerrand

See GOLD.

·L·

Land Leases

See HOME FINANCING, MORTGAGES.

Late Charge

This is usually an amount of money, regulated by state law, that is charged by a creditor in open-end or closed-end credit for failure to make a payment within a specified deadline, most commonly a date five days beyond the regular due date. Such a late charge, fee, or penalty is not a finance charge under the federal Truth in Lending Act, although that law regulates disclosure of such charges and penalties for delinquency.

James A. Ambrose

Leasing an Automobile

See AUTOMOBILE, HOW TO PURCHASE A NEW.

Legal Tender

Legal tender is the term used to denote the acceptability of United States coins and currency as money of the United States at their stated values for use in payment of debts incurred in the purchase of goods and services and for meeting other financial obligations.

During the early years of the Republic, a considerable quantity of foreign coins circulated in the United States. These were made legal tender by the act of February 9, 1793, at rates proportional to their gold or silver content. Although this act was suspended for several years and was amended from time to time, final provision for the retirement of foreign coins from circulation and repeal of their legal-tender qualities was not made until the passage of the act of February 21, 1857.

While foreign coins do circulate from time to time near the borders of this country, they are not legal tender in the United States, and consequently no one may be required to accept them in satisfaction of any debt. Their circulation in those areas is based upon a mutual understanding between shopkeepers and consumers of their acceptability at face value in the purchase of merchandise or in other business transactions.

The restrictions on private gold ownership were terminated effectively December 31, 1974, pursuant to Public Law 93-373. Accordingly, U.S. gold coins lawfully and legally issued may be used as money and, when so used, must be accepted and redeemed at face value on the same basis as any other legal tender. It should be remembered, however, that they may have a value different from their face value for numismatic or bullion purposes.

Donna Pope

Lender of Last Resort

The FEDERAL RESERVE SYSTEM is termed the "lender of last resort" because, as the nation's central bank, it stands ready to be the ultimate provider of credit to the financial system. Through its DISCOUNT WINDOW, the Federal Reserve system makes loans to help financial institutions meet short-term liquidity needs that can arise from unexpected events, such as sudden deposit withdrawals. The Federal Reserve also provides credit to assist smaller institutions in meeting seasonal credit needs. In addition, it is authorized to extend credit in unusual circumstances to financial institutions experiencing longer-term liquidity problems arising from changes in money-market conditions, and to individual institutions and others whose financial condition has been adversely affected by exceptional circumstances or practices. In short, the Federal Reserve stands ready to provide a source of liquidity when other sources are unavailable, and to do so in substantial amounts. It can finance such lending by selling part of its large holdings of securities, or, should the situation warrant, by "creating" additional money.

Griffith L. Garwood

Leverage

The magnification of rates of return that results from investing borrowed funds, in addition to one's own funds, in a particular security. For example, borrowing from a broker a portion of the funds required to purchase a share of common stock (i.e., "buying on margin") magnifies both the favorable and unfavorable rates of return that can be realized on the investment.

Suppose an investor purchases a share of common stock for $100. If the price of the share increases to $120, the investor will earn a 20% rate of return ($20 price increase/$100 investment). On the other hand, if the price declines to $95, he will experience a 5% loss ($5 price decline/$100 investment). Both of these figures would be magnified if the investor were to invest $100 of his own funds and borrow $100 from his broker at a 10% interest rate in order to purchase two shares of common stock. If the price of a share increased to $120, the investor would have a $30 gain ($20 per share price increase × 2 shares, less $10 interest). His rate of return on his $100 investment would be 30% ($30 gain/$100 investment), compared to the 20% rate of return he would have earned if he purchased one share using only his own money. If, however, the price per share declined to $95 after he had purchased two shares on margin, his loss would be $20 ($5 per share price decline × 2 shares, and $10 interest), or 20% of his $100 investment. Therefore, just as the favorable outcome is magnified by leverage (from 20% to 30%), the unfavorable outcome is also magnified (from a 5% loss to a 20% loss).

R. Bruce Swensen

Liability

A debt—something owed by one person or business entity to another party. Most liabilities are paid, or satisfied, in cash, although they can also be satisfied through performance of a service or delivery of a product.

A person assumes a liability when something is purchased on credit, or when a contract to perform a particular service or produce a particular product is concluded.

The side of a balance sheet that lists net worth and obligations is called the "liability" side.

Samuel C. Hoyt

Life and Health Insurance, How to Purchase

Approximately 86% of Americans are covered by life insurance and 85% are covered by health insurance, mostly through their employers. About 50% of the life-insurance coverage is through employer-sponsored group plans over which the individual has no control as to amount and type of policy. This discussion will be limited to the purchase of personal life insurance and personal health insurance.

Life Insurance. What is a life-insurance policy? A LIFE INSURANCE policy is a contract between a life-insurance company and an individual in which the company promises to pay a stipulated amount of money, called the "face amount," at the death of the insured individual, and the insured promises to pay the premium as stated in the policy.

There are four basic types of life-insurance policies: term, whole-life, endowment, and annuity.

Term insurance insures a person for a stated period of time such as one year, five years, or ten years, or to a specified age, such as 65. The premium increases by a stated amount for each new period. For example, a five-year term policy for $10,000 at age 35—male—will have an initial premium of $35. Every five years the premium will increase for another five-year interval until the stated expiration date of the policy, usually age 65 or 70. The term policy is usually renewable and convertible. "Renewable" means that the insured may continue the policy at the end of the time period specified in the policy for an additional period without having to provide evidence of insurability to the company. "Evidence of insurability" refers to the health, occupation, and moral requirements of the insurance company. "Convertible" means that the insured may convert the term policy to a permanent type of policy such as "whole-life" without evidence of insurability. Term insurance serves temporary financial needs, such as family income until the children are grown, money to pay off a debt such as a home mortgage or a personal loan, money for a child's education, or any other temporary need. Term insurance is initially low in cost but increases substantially in later years.

Whole-life insurance insures you for your entire lifetime—in other words, until you die. (For insurance purposes, life ceases at age 100.) Other important features of a whole-life policy are that the premium remains level and the policy builds cash values, which the insured may receive by terminating the policy or may use as collateral for a loan from the company. The whole-life policy also contains two additional "nonforfeiture benefits"—namely, the insured's contractual right to select a reduced paid-up policy or extended term insurance. The policy contains a table of nonforfeiture benefits mandated by state insurance laws. The advantages of a whole-life policy are that you are insured for your lifetime, you know the exact premium you will pay, and you have flexibility due to the nonforfeiture benefits mentioned above.

Endowment policies may be considered a combination of term insurance and a savings plan. If death occurs during the term period, the face amount is payable to the beneficiary. If the insured lives to the maturity date (the end of the term), the face amount is payable to the insured. Endowment policies emphasize the savings element. They were popular in the past as a means of saving money combined with life insurance. However, due to inflation, the purchases of endowments have substantially decreased.

Annuity policies may be considered the opposite of a life-insurance policy. This policy promises to pay one or two persons monthly income for life, commencing at a specified age. In other words, the income is payable to the annuitant or to two annuitants for as long as they live or one continues to live. The primary advantage of the annuity is that the annuitant(s) cannot outlive the accumulated capital. If the named annuitant(s) dies prior to the commencement of payments, the death benefit is usually the greater of the premiums paid on the cash value stated in the policy. Annuities are an excellent method of guaranteeing retirement benefits. Payments may be a fixed amount or a variable amount determined by some index.

How to Determine Which Type of Policy Is Best for You. In deciding which type of policy is best for you, the following factors must be considered.

1. What are your financial objectives for your dependents if you die?

2. What are your financial objectives for your retirement?

3. Are your financial objectives short-, medium-, or long-range?

4. How much can you afford and how much are you willing to spend or save for life insurance?

5. Will your heirs need money to pay estate taxes at your death? Estate taxes are imposed by the federal government and some states on the property you leave to your heirs at your death.

Here are some typical examples:

• John Jones is 38. His wife, Mary, is 33. They have two children, ages 8 and 5. John earns $25,000 a year and owns a house with a $70,000 mortgage. His most important financial objective is economic security for his family. His company provides $40,000 of group life insurance, and Social Security will pay approximately $1,000 per month to his family as survivorship benefits until the children reach age 18 (benefits are reduced after the first child reaches 18, and benefits cease to Mary when the younger child reaches age 16). John Jones may purchase renewable and convertible term insurance to meet his financial objectives—namely, final expenses, mortgage repayments, family income, and education funds. The premium for the term insurance will be within his budget. In the future, John may convert all or part of the term insurance to whole-life (permanent insurance) to provide a widow's benefit after the children are grown and to supplement his company pension.

• Charles Wilson is a self-employed professional earning $100,000 a year. He is age 50 and wants to provide a reasonable standard of living for his wife, Anna, age 48, for as long as she lives. Charles Wilson should purchase a whole-life policy to achieve his financial objectives. He can afford the premium, and the need is permanent.

• Edith Brown is a well-known singer. She is single, with no dependents, and her main concern is providing for her retirement. An annuity policy would suit her financial objectives.

• Elmer Black, age 60, is an industrialist with an estate of $4 million. His financial objective is to provide money to pay estate taxes at his death and again at the death of his wife, Carol, age 57, regardless of the sequence of death, and thereby leave his estate intact to his children. Whole-life insurance policies on each life will solve this problem. A third party should own the policies so that the proceeds will be excluded from the estates.

Determining which policy or combination of policies is best for you requires an analysis of your financial objectives. The simplest approach is to list your financial needs and consider them as liabilities. Then list your assets, such as group life insurance, company pension, personal life insurance, savings and other liquid (ready cash) assets. Any difference would be made up by life insurance.

Health Insurance. HEALTH INSURANCE policies pay for medical expenses and provide income in the event of disability. Most Americans have some form of group medical insurance through their employers or unions. For those who are self-employed, medical insurance is available from insurance companies and organizations such as BLUE CROSS AND BLUE SHIELD, and HEALTH-MAINTENANCE ORGANIZATIONS (HMO's), available in certain areas. Everyone realizes the importance of hospitalization insurance and major-medical insurance. The most important factor in purchasing this insurance is to determine what coverage you require and how much of a medical bill you can pay from your own pocket (self-insure). Here are some typical examples:

• Fred Brown, age 36, is married and has three children. He is a self-employed carpenter earning $25,000 a year. His main concern is how he would pay for medical bills. The solution is the purchase of a basic hospitalization and surgery policy and a major-medical policy.

• Joan Henry, age 40, is a widow with two children. She is a free-lance clothing designer and earns

$75,000 per year. She is not concerned with relatively small medical bills but with bills in excess of $2,000. She can purchase a major-medical policy with a $2,000 deductible, which means that she will not be insured for any medical bills less than $2,000.

DISABILITY INCOME INSURANCE replaces a part of your income if you are disabled through accident or sickness. All of us who are covered by SOCIAL SECURITY have disability insurance as a Social Security benefit if the disability lasts five months or longer and we meet the definition of *disability*. Other state laws mandate workmen's compensation insurance in case we are disabled by a job-related cause. A few states mandate disability benefits if we are disabled by a nonoccupational cause. Many employers provide group disability insurance to their employees.

It has been advised that a wage earner or self-employed individual insure 50% to 60% of income in the event of a disability. Again, the procedure is to determine your income needs (liabilities) and your sources of income (assets) in the event of your disability, such as employer group benefits, Social Security benefits, any guaranteed income such as interest, and individual disability insurance. An individual disability policy is purchased to cover the difference.

There are basically three types of individual disability policies.

1. *Optionally renewable.* The company reserves the right to refuse to renew your policy on the anniversary date or may raise your premium. This type of policy is usually not recommended.

2. *Guaranteed renewable.* The company must renew your policy and may raise your premium, but only by class (all insureds in your classification).

3. *Noncancelable.* The company must renew your policy and cannot increase the premium.

Of the three policies mentioned, the noncancelable offers the most beneficial guarantees.

The definition of *total disability* is most important. When are you considered totally disabled? Each company has its own definition and it is important to understand the definition of disability by requesting a specimen policy for your review.

The "waiting period" is similar to a deductible in a major-medical policy—that is, monthly payments commence after you have been disabled for the waiting period. (Some companies use the words *elimination period.*) This period may be one week, one month, or as long as one year, depending on your financial situation. The amount of disability income is usually limited to 50–60% of your income since the disability-income payments are income-tax-free. You may select a payment period from one year to age 65, or, in some cases, lifetime. Certain restrictive provisions—such as Relation to Earnings, Change of Occupation, Hospital or House Confinement—may limit your right to collect payments. The premium is based on the above-mentioned factors.

How to Choose an Agency and Company. The question of how to choose an agency and company may be asked in reference to the purchase of any important product or service, be it a car, house, medical care. Insurance combines both a product (the policy) and the service and expertise of a professional (the agent). Insurance is an intangible and represents future promises upon which the purchaser is basing his family's and his own financial security. It is usually too late to make retroactive changes after the fact. Therefore, utmost care must be used in selecting the insurance agent and company.

Where do we begin our search? First of all, let us define certain common terms.

A *full-time agent* represents one life- and/or health-insurance company. Most full-time agents have a contract with one company and derive substantial benefits from their companies, such as office space, a pension, and other important employee benefits. It is to their advantage to recommend their company's products.

An *independent agent* (sometimes referred to as a "broker") represents many companies and is not obligated to give any company all of his business.

Both full-time agents and independent agents are compensated by commissions.

In reference to life- and health-insurance companies, there are two major divisions: *mutual companies* and *stock companies.* The primary difference is ownership and the resulting distribution of profits (or surplus). A mutual company is owned by the policyholders, who share in the surplus of the company and thereby receive dividends, since they own participating policies. A stock company is owned by stockholders, who are investors. Stock companies issue nonparticipating life-insurance policies. However, some stock companies may also issue participating policies similar to mutual companies. These stock companies are called *mixed companies.*

Savings banks in New York, Connecticut, and Massachusetts sell life insurance (*see* SAVINGS BANK LIFE INSURANCE [SBLI]). However, there is a relatively low limit of life insurance permitted per individual. For example, in New York State the maximum total face amount allowed is $30,000. Savings banks do not solicit outside of the bank, and their in-house representatives are salaried employees.

Some fraternal organizations that have been in existence for many years offer life insurance to their members and are regulated in the same manner as other life-insurance companies.

There are a number of sources and checkpoints to follow in selecting an agent. Inquire as to the credentials of any agent.

1. Is he a neighbor or friend? Was he referred to you, or did you contact him from an ad or directory?

2. Is he a full-time agent or an independent agent?

3. Is he a Chartered Life Underwriter (CLU)? This professional designation signifies that he has successfully passed ten examinations in life and health insurance and related subjects. There are many agents who do not have this designation but are nonetheless competent.

4. Are you comfortable with this person? Do you feel that there is a rapport and mutual respect and that he has attempted to solve your life- and/or health-insurance needs by clearly analyzing your problem and giving you a written proposal of his plan?

5. Does he have your interest at heart or is he pushing for a fast sale? Beware of the high-pressure salesperson who demands that you buy immediately.

6. What is his reputation in the community?

7. How long has he been in the insurance business? Everyone has to start somewhere, but the attrition of new life agents is very high and future service is most important.

8. Beware of the sales presentation made by two salesmen who work together. This is a favorite tactic of high-pressure selling.

9. Remember that the agent is paid a commission. Certain policies pay much higher yearly commissions than others. For example, the first year's commission for the same face amount on whole-life is many times that of term insurance. A competent professional agent will recommend the best plan for you and seek referrals from you. The high-pressure agent will attempt to sell the policy that pays the highest commission.

All agents must be licensed by the state insurance department of the states in which they sell insurance.

Some states require that the agent present a written proposal or "disclosure statement" to you when you purchase a policy, giving the salient benefits and costs of the policy.

Beware of any agent who recommends that you terminate existing life- and/or health-insurance policies and purchase new policies. In the majority of cases, replacement is to your detriment. Many states require that the agent complete replacement and disclosure forms to be given to you that effectively compare the existing and proposed policies. There may be some instances where replacing existing insurance may be to your advantage, but only in the minority of cases.

How do you select a company?

1. Make certain the company is licensed in your state.

2. Ask the agent for a current financial report on the company. This will give you some idea of the company's size, age, and financial status.

3. Some state insurance departments (such as New York's) issue consumer shopping guides. Request this information from your state insurance department. Your local library may have a source book entitled *Best's Insurance Reports,* which analyzes most of the life-insurance companies in the United States.

4. Do not compare companies on cost alone. Most of the prominent life-insurance companies are within a reasonable price range of each other.

5. Certain companies are known for their fair treatment of policyholders in that they will extend any new benefit provisions or lower premiums to existing policyholders.

6. Ask for a specimen policy. A reputable agent will give you one. In reference to medical-expense policies, review terms such as maximum dollar amounts, deductibles, coinsurance, covered expenses, exclusions, the company's right to cancel your policy or increase premiums, age termination, dollar amount paid for room and board and surgical and medical procedures, coordination with other insurance, and other important terms. In reference to disability-insurance policies, review terms such as the company's right to cancel, to renew, to increase your premiums; the definition of *disability;* the effect of other insurance; the elimination period; exclusions; the stated amount of monthly benefits; the duration of payments; and restrictive provisions, such as change of occupation or relation to earnings at the time of claim.

The Contract. If you decide to buy any type of life or health policy, you must clearly understand that you are making a contract. You are required by law to be truthful in your answers to the agent's questions and the physician's questions (if a physical examination is required). The agent will request a premium payment from you when you sign the application. If you give your check or cash to the agent, he is required by the state insurance laws to give you a conditional receipt. There have been many court cases relating to the effective date of an insurance policy. The typical conditional receipt states the date on which the life or medical insurance goes into effect. The agent does not have "binding power," as is the case in property- and liability-insurance coverage. It is vital that you read and understand the conditional receipt.

Some states have laws giving the insured a specified number of days to examine his policy—a so-called free look. The insured has the right to return the policy to the company within that period and receive a full premium refund. Some states require that this "free look" right be printed on the policy or attached to it. Be sure you are aware of this right and take the time to read your policy. Most buyers assume that the policy is written in highly technical language above their comprehension. Many states have laws requiring that policies be written in simplified terms that can be understood by the average person. Don't be afraid to read your policy or, better still, the specimen policy you requested.

Policy provisions explain your rights and the insurer's rights as established by your state insurance laws. There are certain important provisions that the buyer should understand. These are:

1. *The entire contract.* This means that the policy and an attached photostat of your application constitute the entire contract. Representations (statements) you made to the agent (and physician) are available for you to see on the application. It is these facts that the insurance company has used in deciding to issue the policy to you.

2. *The incontestability provision.* Most of us are familiar with the legal term *statute of limitations.* That is what is meant by the "incontestability provision." The legality of the policy cannot be challenged by the insurance company after two years (or earlier if stated) from the date of issue, regardless of any misrepresentations you may have made in the application.

3. *The grace period.* The grace period is an extension of time to you for payment of the premium beyond the due date. It is usually 31 days.

4. *Nonforfeiture benefits (life insurance).* If you have purchased a permanent plan (whole-life, endowment, annuity), you are entitled to certain benefits if you decide to stop paying premiums. These dollar-amount benefits are listed in a chart in the policy.

5. *Change of beneficiary.* You may change your beneficiary at any time if you are the owner of the policy.

6. *Assignment.* You may assign the rights in your policy to another party—for example, to guarantee a loan.

7. *Change of plan.* You have the right to change from one life-insurance plan to another by meeting certain company requirements.

There are other general provisions required by state insurance law, but the above-mentioned provisions are the most important ones.

Contract Riders. Life-insurance policies may have additional benefits added to the basic policy. The important and often used benefits are included by an attachment to the policy called a "rider." These are:

1. *Accidental death benefit.* If death is due to an accident, an additional amount of money, usually a multiple of the face amount, is payable. However, death must occur within a specified time (usually 90 days and caused by accident). This rider is commonly referred to as a "double indemnity." However, multiples of the face amount, other than one times, may be purchased. The advisability of purchasing this rider is debatable. You should not determine your life insurance needs based on dying accidentally. The additional cost may be better spent purchasing additional life insurance. (For special events that expose you to a greater risk of accident, such as vacation or business travel, you can purchase special accident coverage as a separate policy.)

2. *Disability waiver of premium.* This rider guarantees that you will not be required to pay the premium for your policy if you are disabled as defined in the rider. The definition includes total and permanent disability. Check your policy rider for the exact definition. The Disability Waiver of Premium is very important to the average insured, since most of us pay insurance premiums from our earned income.

Tax Considerations. The tax treatment of life insurance is divided into two areas: income tax and estate tax.

The premiums for personal life insurance are not tax-deductible, which means you are paying for your personal life insurance with an after-tax dollar. Dividends received by the holder of a participating policy are considered by the Internal Revenue Code as a return of an overpayment of premium and are not taxable as income. Interest earned on the accumulated dividends (dividends left at interest with the company) is taxable. The lump-sum payment to your beneficiary at your death is income-tax-free.

Life-insurance proceeds are included in the estate of the decedent if the decedent owned the policy at the date of death or transferred the ownership within three years prior to the date of death. Because the federal estate-tax law allows an unlimited marital deduction, the proceeds from a life-insurance policy naming the spouse as beneficiary would escape federal estate taxes.

Personal medical- and disability-insurance premiums are not tax-deductible. Payments received for reimbursement of medical expenses not in excess of the medical bills are tax-free. Disability income received on a personal disability policy are income-tax-free.

Summary. In purchasing life and health insurance, it is most important that you not lose sight of the forest because of the trees. Determine your life- and health-insurance needs as objectively as possible. Use common sense in selecting an agent and company. There are many competent, honest agents and many reputable companies. Check the costs of comparable policies on the basis of benefits and indexes. Make a decision and act on it. Review your life- and health-insurance needs periodically as your circumstances change.

Murray Rosen

Life Insurance

Insurance that pays a stated amount of cash benefit upon the death of the insured. It is bought most often to replace income lost to a family when a breadwinner dies; or to provide for the survivor years of a spouse. It also has business uses. Traditionally, there have been two popular kinds of life insurance: term (temporary insurance) and whole-life (permanent insurance).

Term insurance is issued for a specified period of time—one year, five, ten, or twenty years, or up to a certain age, such as "Term to 65." It is usually renewable for additional periods of time, but is not often issued or renewed beyond age 70. It also may be converted to permanent insurance. *Whole-life insurance* is issued, as its name suggests, for the whole of the insured's life.

Both term and whole-life insurance are usually paid for in installments, called "premiums." The premium-paying basis can be annual, semiannual, quarterly, or monthly. Term-insurance premiums are closely linked to the death rates of each age group and they rise with each renewal. Whole-life-insurance premiums are level throughout life—higher than term premiums for the same amount of insurance early in life, but surpassed by term-insurance rates as time goes on and death rates climb. This leveling of the premium is designed to enable people to afford life insurance throughout life by developing a continually rising reserve. The reserve supports the premium in later life, when it would be otherwise insufficient to meet death claims. The reserve is also an equity for the policyholder, who may borrow against it. Should the policy be dropped, the reserve can be claimed as a "cash surrender value."

A third type of traditional policy, not much used in recent years, is the *endowment.* This policy insures its owner for a stated amount. After a specified number of years, it provides cash benefits in the face amount and expires. However, if the policyholder should die before that time, the full amount of insurance is paid to a beneficiary.

A fourth kind of life-insurance policy, annuities, is treated in a separate entry (*see* ANNUITY) because it is actually the exact reverse of life insurance. With life insurance you pay a periodic installment and, should

death occur, the beneficiary receives a lump sum. With an annuity, you make (or accumulate) a lump-sum payment and in return the policy will pay a periodic income for as long as you live—no matter how long that may be. In short, you are insured against outliving your income.

All life-insurance policies are legally enforceable contracts. All contain a number of standard features, spelled out in three major sections of the policy—the summary, the details, and the application.

The summary is usually contained on the first page of a policy. It tells its owner how much he or she is insured for; describes the kind of insurance it is—whole-life, term, endowment, or a variant of those three; states the premium and the premium-paying basis; and states whether the policy is on a participating basis or a guaranteed-cost basis.

With a participating policy, the insured shares in the experience of the insuring company. Premiums are somewhat higher initially than guaranteed-cost policies. At the end of each year, the company measures its actual cost of insuring each class of policyholder against premiums contributed by that class and refunds to the policyholder the difference between its estimated costs and its actual costs. That refund is called a "dividend." The policyholder, in turn, has a number of different options in disposing of the dividend. The dividend options are to take them as cash; use them automatically to reduce premiums; leave them as interest with the company; use them to buy more life insurance.

The details of the life-insurance policy spell out the company's and the policyholder's obligations in about 15 major clauses. Briefly, they cover the following:

The due date. This is the date on which the policyholder must pay the premium.

The grace period. If the policyholder misses the due date, he or she will have about a month to pay the premium without penalty.

Lapse. If the due date and the grace period go by without a premium payment, the policy expires. Often, however, a policy will have continuing value. Policyholders are cautioned never to destroy a policy without checking this out with the issuing company.

Reinstatement. If a policyholder can show continuing good health, the company will restore the policy to full effect with the payment of the overdue premium, plus interest. A policy can usually be reinstated up to five years after it lapses.

Nonforfeiture. These are rights and values that cannot be lost, even if a policy lapses. Whole-life, endowments, and their variations have these values. Term policies usually don't.

Surrender value. A nonforfeiture value. If you give up the policy completely, the portion of the company reserve represented by the policy will be returned in cash. A table in the policy will provide these values for each policy year per thousand dollars of insurance. Surrender value is also sometimes called "cash value."

Loan value. Closely akin to cash value. It's the amount a policyholder may borrow against his policy from the company. In policies issued prior to 1981, the rate of interest was stated in the policy. After 1981, the rate in most states was linked to the current market rate for average corporate borrowing. (*See* "Borrowing on Life Insurance," below.)

Extended term. This is another nonforfeiture value. If a policy lapses and is not surrendered for cash, in the absence of any instructions from the policyholder, the insurer of the policy will be extended at term (lower) rates as long as the cash value will pay for it. A table in the policy describes the length of time cash values will last if used this way.

Reduced paid up. Another nonforfeiture value. It's the amount of permanent life insurance the cash value will purchase without further payment of premium.

Death proceeds. The sum of money payable to the beneficiary. Usually it is the face amount stated on the front of the policy, but it could be more or less. More, for example, if dividends had either been used to buy more insurance or left on deposit with the company; less if part or all of a cash value had been borrowed.

Incontestability. After a policy has been in force for a stated period of time—usually two years—the company loses the right to challenge statements made in the application. Prior to that time, a misstatement of health condition, or occupation, for example, can result in cancellation of the insurance and return of premium.

Suicide. If a policyholder dies by suicide within a specified period—usually two years—the company will not pay the benefit, only return premiums, plus interest. After the specified period, the policy will pay the death proceeds even for suicide.

Age clause. If the age of the policyholder was misstated, the company will pay an adjusted benefit upon death. The benefit will be lower if the age was understated; higher if overstated.

Policy rights. The policyholder is the owner of the policy, and the policyholder alone can make the allowable changes in it or make the allowable option choices unless these rights are expressly assigned to someone else by the policyholder.

Beneficiary options. The policyholder may choose one or several beneficiaries. One or more contingent beneficiaries may also be chosen in the event a primary beneficiary dies before the policyholder.

Settlement options. The most common option is a lump-sum payment of the death proceeds to the bene-ficiary or beneficiaries. There are other options, however. The beneficiary may leave the proceeds with the company at interest until he or she chooses to draw it. Alternatively, the beneficiary may elect any of several income options—including lifetime income, income of a specified amount until both principal and interest are exhausted, or income for a specified period of time.

Life-insurance policies may also have a number of additions attached to them, called "riders." The most common of these are accidental-death benefits and waivers of premium, in the event of disability.

Accidental-death benefits are sometimes called "double-indemnity riders," since often the accidental-death benefit will double the face amount of the policy. The cost of such a rider is fairly low compared with the cost of the policy itself. Disability waivers are designed to enable those who have suffered a permanent disability to retain their insurance. In the event of disability, as defined in the rider, the company will assume the cost of the insurance for as long as the disability lasts.

Another election policyholders may make is the automatic policy loan. This election costs nothing. In the event a premium is unpaid, the company is authorized to make an automatic loan from cash value to prevent the policy from lapsing. The loan may be paid back at any time.

For most people, life insurance is an essential part of FINANCIAL PLANNING. Nearly nine out of ten U.S. families own it, and usually it is accumulated and altered throughout life as individual circumstances change.

Term life insurance is usually bought by younger people to provide for the high family and debt obligations of early adulthood in the event of untimely death. This kind of life insurance is inexpensive at younger ages since, in effect, the buyers are sharing the unlikely risk of early death. For example, the chances of a 30-year-old man dying at age 30 are only about 11 out of 10,000. This means that if the company insures 10,000 30-year-old men, it need provide from their premiums only 11 benefits.

Term-life-insurance rates rise fairly slowly through the decade of the thirties, moderately through the forties; more swiftly through the fifties, and very rapidly through the decade of the sixties. After the sixties, term-insurance rates are beyond the reach of most people of those years.

Whole-life insurance was designed to solve this dilemma of life insurance becoming unaffordable just when its benefits are needed—as years advance and death becomes more likely. Starting at, say, age 30, its rates are about five times higher than term insurance issued in like circumstances. But the premium remains level from the date of issue, and an equity—or cash value—begins to build up. Sometime around the mid-fifties, the person who bought term insurance and renewed it periodically will be paying higher rates than the person who bought whole-life insurance. By the mid-sixties, that rate will be nearly twice as high as the continually level premium of the whole-life policy. By the mid-seventies, when average life expectancy will have been reached, the term rate will be three times as high.

The need for life insurance varies with circumstances throughout life. Often the highest amounts are needed early in adult life, when the means to pay for it are usually under the most pressure. Typically, however, these are temporary needs: the dependency years of children; the unfunded mortgage liabilities of early homeownership; high debt loads for furniture, an auto; the dependency of a child-rearing spouse. All represent high liabilities before any assets have been built.

Term life insurance was designed for precisely these circumstances. At rates of $1.50 per thousand of insurance for a male age 30, a $150 annual premium will purchase $100,000 of term insurance that year. By age 40, that amount of insurance will still be priced low, typically at about $300, but starting to climb more rapidly.

Estate needs start to emerge about this time. Children will be leaving the home within the next decade, and their dependency years and educational needs will have been seen to. Home mortgages are being paid down. An end can be seen of term-insurance needs. But permanent insurance needs may become more visible. The life-expectancy statistics are illuminating. Males at age 65 have an average life expectancy of 14 years; females at age 65 live four years longer. If both spouses are the same age, the odds are that the wife will outlive the husband by four years. These are the dependency years that permanent life insurance is designed for.

Other permanent life-insurance needs for families are a need for final expenses—medical, burial, readjustment funds; and a need for liquid assets to conserve other, less liquid assets from the demands of state inheritance taxes, from creditors, and from untimely sales for estate division. Stocks, bonds, and real estate, for example, could form a sizable part of an estate. If they must be sold to satisfy estate demands, they might not fetch their proper value. Life insurance is frequently used to conserve such assets against forced sale.

Combinations and Variations. Most life insurance available to individuals other than term and whole-life are variations on or combinations of those two traditional types, although some recent innovations go beyond mere variations on traditional themes (*see* "Newer Types of Life Insurance," below).

One combination policy links the amount of whole-life insurance with a multiple of term insurance in a single policy to provide a measure of permanent insurance along with a much higher level of temporary insurance for the dependent family. Such a policy typically will combine $10,000 of whole-life insurance upon the head of the household, plus $50,000 of term insurance. Another type of combination policy links permanent insurance on the head of household with a smaller amount of term insurance for a dependent spouse and still smaller amounts of term insurance to age 21 on as many children as are in the family—all for a single premium.

There are several variations on term insurance:

Declining-balance term has a level premium throughout the period of coverage, but the benefit declines each year—slowly at first, then more quickly as time goes on. Such decreasing term insurance is useful in covering a declining debt, such as a mortgage; or a shrinking obligation, such as the dependency years of children. Frequently such a policy will be designed to provide a specific monthly income should the policyholder die at any time during the term.

Modified term insurance is a type of policy that, after a specific period, converts automatically to whole-life insurance.

Revertible term insurance is very low-cost, based upon the superior health of the buyer. At each renewal period, however, the buyer is required to meet specified standards of physical condition, otherwise the premium "reverts" to a higher rate.

Deposit term insurance enjoyed a period of popularity several years back. The buyer paid a very high first-year premium for a ten-year renewable term policy, premiums for the ensuing years were more in line with other term-insurance costs. At the end of the tenth year, the policyholder was refunded a dividend usually equal to twice the additional cost of the first-year premium.

Whole-life insurance also has its variations:

Modified whole-life has an initial low premium for its first ten years; then, typically, the premium will double, but still be lower than the buyer would pay if he or she were to purchase straight whole-life insurance at the then-attained age. This kind of policy is designed for younger families that want to start a permanent program but are not yet able to afford the higher initial premiums of straight whole-life.

Paid-up whole-life has a shortened premium-paying period to relieve the buyer of paying premiums later in life. Some typical paid-up policies are ten- or twenty-payment whole-life; or whole-life paid up at 65.

Single-premium whole-life, as its name implies, means putting down a lump-sum premium at one time and never paying another premium. Older people who want to assure a tax-free benefit to a spouse or an heir are the most frequent users of this kind of variation on whole-life.

Other Kinds of Life Insurance. Types of life insurance other than the more popular kinds bought by individuals are group term life insurance, credit life insurance, and industrial life insurance.

Group term life insurance is most often made available through employer-employee groups. Other types of groups are also eligible for it, such as professional groups, but employer group term is the most common type. Life insurance is made available either in a common amount to all, or in amounts based on a fraction of or a multiple of salary. Often the employer pays all or part of the premium. This kind of insurance usually terminates when the individual either leaves the job or retires. In recent years, some employers have extended group life-insurance benefits into retirement, usually in reduced amounts. Employer group term life insurance is convertible upon termination of employment to whole-life insurance without the need to prove insurability. This is often a valuable option, particularly if an individual's health is poor.

Credit life insurance is also issued on a group basis, through lending institutions. The creditor is named as the beneficiary and the debt is automatically extinguished by the insurance in the event the borrower dies. Credit life insurance is usually made available for financial "big-ticket" items such as cars, boats, and large appliances. If an individual is young and healthy, it is worthwhile shopping the cost of individual term insurance to cover such debts. Group credit-insurance rates are often higher than those available in the individual marketplace.

Industrial life insurance is so named because it emerged early in the Industrial Revolution of the last century. Essentially, it is whole-life insurance bought to provide for final expenses. It is sold in amounts of less than $1,000 and typically it is paid for with small weekly premiums—often collected by a home service agent. Popular among working people up through World War II, it has been largely supplanted by the more common higher-benefit term and whole-life policies, which replace income and provide for survivorship.

Newer Types of Life Insurance. A number of new kinds of life insurance began to appear in the marketplace as interest rates grew volatile and buyers sought to hedge their long-term asset accumulations against virulent inflation.

Variable life insurance is a kind of permanent insurance whose death benefits and cash-value accumulations can rise, based on the performance of an underlying fund of common stock. Traditional whole-life insurance is funded largely with a portfolio of bonds, mortgages, and real estate, although the portfolio will also include some common stock and other equities. With variable life insurance, the benefit is guaranteed never to fall below the initial amount. If the underlying stock fund performs well, however, the benefit will increase.

Universal life insurance is a package of term insurance and an accumulation fund, based largely on short-term debt issues. Typically, such a policy will accumulate the first $1,000 of cash value at a guaranteed interest rate of 4%. Accumulations above $1,000 will earn interest at rates close to those available in the current market, which at this writing were in the neighborhood of 10–11%. The owner of such a policy also has the option of deciding how much or how little insurance is to be carried, how much or how little is to be accumulated in the accumulation fund. In addition, the policyholder may decide to use part of the accumulation fund to pay premiums on the underlying term-insurance policy.

Variable life II is not available on the market as of this writing, but innovators are talking of a policy that will combine the flexibility of universal life with the longer-term funding of variable life. Such a policy would permit the underlying insurance to vary upward and downward and would enable the policyholder to make some broad investment decisions about the accumulation fund. For example, a policyholder could decide whether he wanted the funds to go into a money-market type of account; into a bond fund; or into one of several types of stock or equity funds. Additionally, a policyholder might be allowed to switch back and forth among different types of funding among different types of investments.

These types of policies are different from traditional life insurance in that the policyholder is assuming more of the investment risk traditionally assumed by the insurance company. In return for assuming the risk, however, the policyholder is being offered the prospect of higher accumulations of long-term assets.

Different from this type of policy, but an innovation nevertheless, is *adjustable life insurance*. This policy allows the policyholder to raise or lower the amount of insurance and vary the kind of insurance between whole-life and term, as life's circumstances change.

Borrowing on Life Insurance. Life insurance that builds a cash value—such as whole-life or endowment life insurance—is a ready source of credit. The cash value of such a policy may be borrowed against, often at very attractive rates.

Cash-value life insurance bought prior to the 1970s, for example, carried interest rates as low as 5%. In the 1970s, as interest rates began to climb precipitously, insurance companies sought from their state regulators the authority to raise the rates on newly issued policies. As a result, policies issued beginning in 1974 began to carry rates of up to 8%.

As the market rate for borrowing continued to climb, insurers sought a more flexible solution to keeping the loan provision of their policies current with the market. In 1980, legislation was sought enabling insurers to link the interest rate they charged for loans to an index more closely reflecting whatever the market rate might be. Many states have since adopted this approach. The index that insurers are using is Moody's Index for Seasoned Corporate Bonds. It produces an interest rate slightly below the so-called prime rate that banks charge their best corporate customers. Because the rate is linked to an index, the cost of borrowing on life insurance issued since adoption of this practice will vary over the life of the loan.

Borrowing on one's life insurance is a contractual right. That means a policyholder need not give a reason for borrowing; nor may the company refuse a loan. If, however, the loan is still outstanding at death, the company will deduct it from death proceeds, along with any unpaid interest. Furthermore, studies show that policies that have been fully borrowed against are twice as likely to lapse as those that have not been borrowed on.

Claims. Collecting the death benefit on a life-insurance policy is quick and simple. It's the final step in the life-insurance contract, and companies carry it out with little delay. A 1981 industry survey of the 20 largest life-insurance companies in the U.S. showed that 75% of all claims are processed within five working days; 39.6% in three to five working days; and 43.9 % in fewer than three working days.

Usually, the beneficiary need only notify the insurance company that death has occurred and produce the policy. If the benefit is relatively small and the claim is valid, the benefit check can be picked up at the company office. A claim is valid if the insurance-company claims examiner can determine that the policy was in force at the time of death (this is easily checked in company records), and that the death actually occurred. A death certificate or a statement from a physician certifying the death is usually sufficient proof. In cases where the insured person has been missing for a long time without a reasonable explanation and a diligent search proves fruitless, the laws in

many states allow for a legal presumption of death so that the beneficiary can claim the death benefit.

A claim can be denied for several reasons. A claim is not valid, for example, if the policy was not in force at the time of death, or if the death resulted from suicide during the "suicide period"—usually up to two years from the date of issue of the policy. If the suicide occurs after the two-year period, the claim is valid.

A claim can also be denied if there was misrepresentation or fraud in the application for the policy. However, misrepresentation is "incontestable" after a period of two years from the date of issue, and can't thereafter be used to deny a claim.

Beneficiaries who murder the insured person will ordinarily not receive the proceeds; the insurance will go to the estate of the insured or to a contingent beneficiary. Laws in each state differ on this question.

If a policy has been lost and a death occurs, the beneficiary must sign a lost-policy certificate so that the claim can be processed. The American Council of Life Insurance, the industry's trade association, provides a lost-policy search service free of charge to policyholders. Some 150 companies participate in the service.

Sometimes, the insured person's age has been misstated on the policy. In such instances the benefit paid will be the amount that would have been purchased by the premiums had the age been accurately stated. Most insurance companies check birth, baptismal, or Bible records to determine correct age if a question about it comes up.

For the most part, the validity of claims is seldom challenged. Industry estimates place the challenge rate at less than two-tenths of 1%.

See also LIFE AND HEALTH INSURANCE. HOW TO PURCHASE.

Robert Waldron

Limit Order

See COMMON STOCK.

Liquidate

To convert into cash, such as assets and securities; to settle an obligation or debt; to conclude or close the affairs of a business concern by determining the liabilities and applying the assets to the obligations or debts.

Harvey Rachlin

Loans

Individuals borrow money or use credit for a variety of purposes. Credit allows consumers to invest in homes, automobiles, and education, which offer real returns over time. Consumers' credit dollars are in many cases buying things that continue to have worth long after they are paid for. Through use of credit, many consumers have been able to improve their standard of living by purchasing goods and services they need in the present and paying for them in the future.

Consumer loans are available from a wide variety of sources, including commercial banks, consumer finance companies, savings and loan associations, credit unions, savings banks, and industrial banks.

Lenders are regulated at both the state and federal level. Within each state, there are state-chartered or state-licensed institutions, as well as those with charters from federal regulatory agencies. Which type of charter or license an institution has determines to a large extent at which level—state or federal—the institution is mainly regulated.

The maximum interest rates that can be charged on consumer loans are set by the states in which the lenders do business. In recent years, many states have raised these limits—called "usury ceilings"—or have eliminated them, which results in competition and market forces setting the rates. Within a state, there are different rates for different types and sizes of loans.

Shopping around for the best rate on a loan has become easier for consumers since the federal Truth in Lending Act (1968). This act requires all types of creditors to disclose to consumers the finance charge (the dollar cost of credit) and the annual percentage rate (the percentage cost over a year).

Types of Consumer Credit. The major categories of consumer credit are noninstallment or single-payment loans and installment loans. As of June 1983, noninstallment credit outstanding totaled $87.8 billion, while installment credit totaled $353 billion.

In the installment-loan category, there are two main types of loans: open-end and closed-end. Open-end credit is also called "revolving credit." This means that there is a line of credit that a consumer can use at his discretion up to a prescribed limit. Repayments are also made at the borrower's discretion, as long as an agreed-upon minimum payment is made when due. The most common examples of open-end or revolving credit are bank credit cards and retailers' credit cards.

Closed-end loans are for a specific amount for a definite period of time, with a specified number of payments to be made. Most large extensions of credit, such as for an automobile purchase, are closed-end loans.

Loans can also be categorized as secured or unse-

cured. A secured loan is backed by collateral—that is, an item of value that serves as security for the loan and is claimed by the creditor if the borrower does not repay the loan. An unsecured loan, on the other hand, does not have collateral to back up the loan in case of default.

Below are listed some common types of loans to consumers:

Mortgage loans finance the purchase of a house or other property, and the property acts as security for the loan. They may be offered on a fixed-rate or a variable-rate basis and are available from institutions such as savings and loan associations, commercial banks, savings banks, credit unions, mortgage lenders, government agencies, and sometimes from the seller of the property. A down payment is required, and the interest rate may be set at the time the loan is made or may fluctuate according to an index.

Second mortgages, or home equity loans, are loans that are secured by a borrower's equity in a home—that is, the interest held by a property owner after subtracting the balance of any debt on the property. Generally, second mortgages are given in amounts up to 80% of equity. Such loans have shorter terms than standard home mortgages and occasionally have balloon payments (a final lump-sum payment) due at the end of the term of the loan.

Home-improvement loans are to finance additions to and renovation or repair of a dwelling. Generally such loans are on an installment basis. Larger loans may be secured by a second mortgage on the home or by other assets of the borrower.

Education loans are loans to parents offered by an institution to finance a child's education—generally higher education. Education loans guaranteed by the government are also available to students. Loans guaranteed by the federal government may have a maximum income level as a qualification. Such loans may be available from commercial banks, savings and loan associations, savings banks, and credit unions.

Mobile-home loans finance the purchase of a dwelling that is not permanently fixed on a site. The mobile home serves as collateral for the loan, which is usually an installment loan for a period of several years.

Automobile loans are usually installment loans, with the automobile serving as collateral. The maximum term of the loan is usually three years, though some lenders offer four-year terms. Automobile loans are available from a variety of lending sources, including automobile manufacturers' finance subsidiaries, which finance auto loans for their dealers.

Personal loans are granted on the basis of a borrower's capacity to repay the loan and previous credit history. This type of loan, not secured by collateral, usually has a term of one to five years and is sometimes called a "cash loan," since the funds are not earmarked for a particular purpose.

Consolidation loans are used to repay other debts of a borrower to several creditors. The amount of the loan allows the borrower to pay off the other debts in full. The term of the loan is usually longer than those of the previous loans, and the monthly payments are less than the total monthly payments of the previous debts.

Checking overdraft loans or *share draft loans* are tied to a special type of checking account in which the institution allows the account holder to overdraw the account up to an agreed-upon amount. The amount overdrawn is treated as a revolving loan and carries a finance charge.

Bank credit cards are issued by banks or other financial institutions that belong to one or more national card systems. In many cases an annual fee is required for use of the card. The type of credit is revolving or open-end credit. Cardholders can use the cards for goods or services at any retailer, restaurant, or other merchant that accepts the card.

Travel and entertainment cards are prestige cards that allow the user to buy goods and services at participating merchants. An annual fee is required. Usually, bills are payable when due, but some T&E cards have extended-payment features.

Besides these major types of loans, credit is used for a variety of other purposes involving the purchase of goods or services.

Types of Lending Institutions. The principal consumer installment lenders are commercial banks (which hold the largest share of the market), followed by finance companies, credit unions, retailers, savings and loan associations, gasoline companies, and mutual savings banks.

COMMERCIAL BANKS, besides their major business of commercial lending, provide a wide variety of consumer loans. They may be either state or federally chartered. Generally, banks offer personal loans, both secured and unsecured; first and second mortgages; home-improvement loans; education loans; consolidation loans; checking overdraft loans; bank credit cards; and other special types of loans. Some banks may offer certain types of loans only to their depositors. Banks also engage in sales financing (see below).

CONSUMER FINANCE COMPANIES have as their major business the extension of credit to consumers, both directly to consumers and indirectly, through dealers and retailers. Finance companies are licensed and regulated by the states in which they operate. They usually offer both secured and unsecured personal loans, second mortgages, home-improvement

loans, mobile-home and auto loans, and consolidation loans. Some companies offer "loan by mail" programs. Finance companies also engage in sales financing by the purchase of installment sales contracts from dealers or retailers. This allows retail establishments to extend credit to their customers and sell the contracts to a finance company, to which the customer makes the payments.

CREDIT UNIONS also offer a variety of consumer loans. Credit unions are state- or federally chartered membership organizations whose members must share a common bond in order to belong—for example, employment by a particular company. Credit unions usually offer first and second mortgages, education loans, home-improvement loans, consolidation loans, and secured and unsecured personal loans. Many also offer credit cards to their members.

SAVINGS AND LOAN ASSOCIATIONS historically have been major providers of home mortgages, but in recent years they have been allowed to offer other types of consumer loans. They can be state- or federally chartered. Savings and loans offer first and second mortgages, education loans, home-improvement loans, and personal loans. Many also offer credit cards. Mutual savings banks (which differ from S&L's in their type of ownership) generally offer the same types of consumer loans.

Retailers vary in the types of CREDIT they extend. Large department stores may accept certain credit cards issued by other institutions. However, in such cases, they are not extending the credit themselves; the customer will pay the CREDIT CARD issuer. Some retailers offer their own store card, which may have a dollar limit on use and operate similarly to bank credit cards. Retailers may also provide other types of credit—for example, 30-day, 60-day, or 90-day credit plans. Smaller retailers may offer customers credit through retail installment contracts that they then sell to financial institutions, such as finance companies.

Gasoline companies offer credit cards so that customers can purchase gasoline and other goods at their dealers. Some gasoline cards can be used to purchase goods or services at other businesses. The credit extended is revolving credit.

Historically, interest rates have varied considerably among different types of lenders, with banks and credit unions usually offering the lowest rates and finance companies asking the higher rates. This, however, is no longer generally true, for a variety of reasons. Chief among these is the cost of funds that financial institutions use for lending. Depository institutions' (banks, savings and loans, and others) major source of funds for lending is their deposits. Before deregulation of deposit interest rates, which occurred in 1982, depository institutions were restricted in the interest rates they could pay their depositors. Now these institutions pay market rates on deposit accounts; thus, the cost of their funds is higher. Consumer finance companies, as nondepositories, traditionally have paid market rates for their funds, which they procure principally from bank loans and issuance of commercial paper. As a result of other institutions' higher costs of funds, loan rates among various types of lenders are much more comparable.

Frances B. Smith

Lower-Income Rental Assistance

See SOCIAL WELFARE.

Low Income Energy Assistance Program

See SOCIAL WELFARE.

·M·

M-1, M-2

See MONEY SUPPLY.

Major-Medical Protection

See HEALTH INSURANCE.

Margin Stocks

See COMMON STOCK.

Margin Trading (or "Buying on Margin")

A purchase of securities that is partially financed by borrowing from a brokerage house, using the purchased securities as collateral for the loan. The board of governors of the FEDERAL RESERVE SYSTEM has the authority to establish the initial margin requirement. This requirement is the percentage of the purchase price of a security that the investor must pay in cash; the remainder can be borrowed from the investor's broker. Currently, the margin for stock purchases is set at 50% of the price of the stock. The securities exchanges and individual brokerage houses sometimes impose more stringent initial margin requirements than those imposed by the Federal Reserve Board.

Exchanges and brokers also determine the *maintenance margin*. The maintenance margin becomes significant to the investor if the security he has purchased declines in value. Under this circumstance, the investor's equity in the security (i.e., the difference between the value of the security and the amount borrowed to finance its purchase) has declined. The maintenance-margin requirement specifies that the equity must exceed a certain percentage of the value of the security. Since the maintenance margin is generally less than the initial margin, the value of the security can decline somewhat without violating the maintenance-margin requirement. However, if the value of the security should decline to the point where the requirement is not satisfied, the investor is subject to a "margin call"—that is, he must either repay enough of the loan so that the requirement is satisfied, or sell the security in order to repay the loan.

R. Bruce Swensen

Marine Insurance

See INSURANCE.

Marital-Deduction Trusts

See TRUSTS.

Market Order

See PREFERRED STOCK.

Maximum Benefit, Health Insurance

The total maximum amount of benefits a health-insurance policy will pay. Typically, lifetime maximum benefits under major-medical policies range from $50,000 to $250,000, although many such policies now provide maximums of $1 million or more. Major-medical plans offering unlimited benefits are becoming common.

James L. Moorefield

Medicaid

Medicaid is a federally supported, state-run program that helps pay medical bills for certain groups of needy people: members of families with dependent children; some other children; the aged (65 or older); the blind; and the disabled. In 1983, Medicaid funds supplied by federal, state, and local taxes paid medical bills for about 21.7 million eligible people.

Medicaid is available in every state and in the District of Columbia, Puerto Rico, Guam, the northern Marianas, and the Virgin Islands. Since each state may decide for itself who is eligible for coverage and what services it will cover (within federal rules), Medicaid is a rather complicated program that varies from state to state. (See Table 1, pages 408–409.)

Medicaid should not be confused with MEDICARE, which is a federal health-insurance plan that covers most people 65 and older, as well as some younger, disabled people.

This entry describes Medicaid in some detail: who is eligible; what services must be covered by all states and what are optional; how the program is financed and care paid for; and a brief history and background. Because space does not permit a description of each state's Medicaid program, a chart summing up the "optional services" each offers is provided.

Eligibility for Medicaid. Congress authorized Medicaid in 1965 to help certain needy people pay their medical bills. Over the nearly two decades since then, the definition of *needy* has been changed and expanded. Here are the categories of people who may now be eligible for Medicaid under federal law:

Categorically Needy People. People who are getting or are eligible for public financial assistance, such as:

Members of needy families who receive cash assistance from the AID TO FAMILIES WITH DEPENDENT CHILDREN (AFDC) program. These people are eligible in all states. Also eligible are those under 21 who would qualify for AFDC except for age or school-attendance requirements.

Needy persons who are aged, blind, or disabled. In some states, this applies only to people receiving cash benefits from the SUPPLEMENTAL SECURITY INCOME (SSI) program because of age, blindness, or disability. In other states, they may also be people who meet certain state standards for disability, income, and resources that are stricter than federal SSI standards.

People in medical institutions who have sufficient income to meet their needs, but if living in the community would be eligible for cash welfare assistance.

People who receive approved state payments that supplement SSI benefits, so long as their income is not above a specified level.

People who would be eligible for AFDC, SSI, or state supplementary payments, but have not applied for them.

People who would be eligible for AFDC, but whose state program is not as liberal as the law allows (such as families with unemployed fathers); certain people (not themselves eligible for AFDC) who are caring for AFDC-eligible young people under 21; young people who meet Medicaid income limits but live independently and are not considered dependent children; and people who receive child-care services through an agency, but, if they had to pay for such services, would meet income requirements.

Medically Needy People. In 34 states, the medically needy (those whose income is too high for Medicaid but who have large medical bills and who otherwise qualify) are eligible. In other words, this is an individual—aged, blind, or disabled, or a member of a family with dependent children—who has sufficient income for ordinary living expenses, but not enough to cover medical bills.

In general, Medicaid income standards are linked to those of the two assistance programs, AFDC and SSI. Each state sets an income level that represents the minimum cost of basic necessities, adjusted for size of family. Owning a house or car of reasonable value and limited amounts of other property usually does not affect eligibility for Medicaid.

In 1979 approximately two-thirds of all Medicaid beneficiaries were eligible because they were members of families with dependent children. The remaining one-third were aged, blind, or disabled. The accompanying chart shows in which states Medicaid covers the categorically needy only or the medically needy as well.

Services Provided by Medicaid. By law, Medicaid states must offer certain basic services to all categorically needy persons (those eligible for AFDC and SSI): physician, hospital, and skilled nursing-home care; health screenings and follow-up treatment for children; laboratory and X-ray services; home health care; and family planning and rural health-clinic services.

In addition, states *may* include such optional services as dental care, eyeglasses, clinic services, prescribed drugs, care in an intermediate-care facility, and services by optometrists, podiatrists, and chiropractors. A state may choose to provide some or all of these services to only the categorically needy or to the medically needy as well. Both required and optional services are described in more detail below.

Basic services. A state Medicaid program *must* provide the following services throughout the state to all categorically needy persons:

Physicians' services provided by or under the personal supervision of a licensed practitioner of medicine or osteopathy.

Inpatient services in a hospital (other than an institution for tuberculosis or mental disease), including items and services ordinarily furnished by the hospital for the care and treatment of inpatients, under the direction of a physician or dentist. The hospital must be licensed or formally approved as a hospital by an officially designated state standard-setting authority and either qualified to participate under Medicare or meeting such requirements.

Outpatient hospital services, including preventive, diagnostic, therapeutic, rehabilitative, or palliative items or services furnished by or under the direction of a physician or dentist. The hospital must meet the same requirements as for inpatient services.

Rural health-clinic services in certified clinics, provided by a physician, physician assistant, nurse practitioner, nurse midwife, or other specialized nurse practitioner.

Other laboratory and X-ray services ordered by a physician or other licensed practitioner and provided by or under the direction of a physician or other licensed practitioner in an office or similar facility. The laboratory must be qualified to participate under Medicare or meet requirements for such participation.

Services in a skilled nursing facility (SNF) (other than an institution for tuberculosis or mental disease) for individuals age 21 or older. The services must be ordered by and under the direction of a physician, and the facility qualified for participation in Medicaid. For all eligible individuals entitled to skilled nursing-facility services, the state must also provide home health services.

Early and periodic screening, diagnosis, and treatment (EPSDT) for children up to age 21 for physical or mental defects or chronic health conditions.

Family-planning services and supplies for eligible individuals of childbearing age who desire them.

Optional Services. There are certain medical services that a state may decide to cover and for which the federal Medicaid program will help pay. For instance, nearly all states cover the following:

- Prescription drugs
- Prosthetic devices
- Intermediate-care-facility services for physically ill or mentally retarded persons who are not in an institution for TB or mental diseases
- Emergency hospital services
- Skilled nursing-facility services for persons under 21 years of age
- Clinic services to an outpatient by or under the direction of a physician or dentist in an outpatient facility that is not part of a hospital

In addition, *some* states cover under Medicaid *some* of the following optional services: care by licensed chiropractors (with limitations), optometrists, and podiatrists; home health-care services, equipment, and supplies usually provided by a licensed home health agency or, if such is not available, by a registered professional nurse or licensed practical nurse under a doctor's supervision; private-duty nursing (with certain limitations); dental care; dentures; and physical and occupational therapy.

Other optional services a state may cover are services for individuals with speech, hearing, and language disorders; orthopedic shoes; eyeglasses; other diagnostic, screening, preventive, and rehabilitative services; inpatient hospital, skilled nursing facility, or intermediate-care-facility services to persons age 65 or over in institutions for tuberculosis or mental disease; inpatient psychiatric hospital services for persons 21 and under; Christian Science sanatoriums and nursing services; and personal-care services in the home.

Some qualifications: States that cover the medically needy must see that they receive all required services. If the state covers inpatient hospital or SNF services to the medically needy, it must also cover physicians' services to them while in those facilities. Finally, if SNF services are covered, persons entitled to them must also be covered for home health care.

No state provides all the optional services listed, but all Medicaid states provide some. The decision as to what services a state will provide its needy residents under Medicaid and whether it will limit their use is normally made by the state legislature, just as the overall coverage the program provides throughout the country and the amount of federal funds to support them are decided by the Congress. For example, nearly all states pay for prescription drugs, but most states place some kind of restriction on drugs covered.

All Medicaid services must be medically necessary (provided or prescribed by a physician or in certain cases an optometrist, podiatrist, or dentist) and must be provided in accordance with any state laws that apply—for example, those concerning medical practice and licensing.

Medicaid has special provisions aimed at improving the quality of long-term care for the elderly in nursing homes, mental hospitals, and other health-care facilities. Also, it promotes noninstitutional care in the community for persons who are chronically ill, disabled, or aged, but wish to live at home.

In most states, a person who is eligible for both Medicaid and Medicare will have his or her premium for Medicare part B (medical insurance) paid by the Medicaid program. In addition, Medicaid may pay for certain medical costs Medicare does not cover, such as prescription drugs and long-term care.

Who Pays the Costs of Medicaid? In general, the costs of Medicaid services to the needy are paid partly by the federal government from its general revenues and partly by the state. In certain states and certain cases, funds also come from local government. In addition, if a Medicaid recipient is also covered by Medicare or other health-insurance plans, these must pay before Medicaid will pay.

Who decides how much of Medicaid costs the federal government will pay? Its share depends on the state's ability to pay: The lower the per capita income in the state, the larger the share the federal government covers, with a maximum of 83% and a mini-

Table 1
Optional Medicaid Services by State

	Who Is Eligible	Podiatrists' Services	Optometrists' Services	Chiropractors' Services	Other Practitioners' Services	Private Duty Nursing	Clinic Services	Dental Services	Physical Therapy	Occupational Therapy	Speech, Hearing and Language Disorder	Prescribed Drugs	Dentures	Prosthetic Devices	Eyeglasses
Alabama	•		•									•		•	•
Alaska	•		•				•				•				•
Arizona	†											†	†	†	
Arkansas	+		+	+	+		+					+		+	+
California	+	+	+	+	+		+	+	+	+	+	+	+	+	+
Colorado	•	•					•					•		•	
Connecticut	+	+	+	+	+	+	+	+	+	+	+	+	+	+	+
Delaware	•	•			•		•					•		•	
D.C.	+	+	+		+			+				+		+	+
Florida	•		•		•			•				•		•	
Georgia	•	•			•		•					•		•	
Guam	+		+				+				•	+			
Hawaii	+	+	+		+		+	+	+	+	+	+	+	+	+
Idaho	•	•	•	•			•		•			•			
Illinois	+	+	+	+	+	+	+	+	+	+	+	+	+	+	+
Indiana	•	•	•	•	•		•	•	•	•	•	•	•	•	•
Iowa	•	•	•	•	•		•	•	•	•	•	•	•	•	•
Kansas	+	+	+	+	+	+	+	+	+	+	+	+	+	+	+
Kentucky	+		+				+		+	+	+	+		+	
Louisiana	+		+				+					+		+	
Maine	+	+		+	•		+		+	+	+	+		+	
Maryland	+	+	+				+		+			+	+	+	+
Massachusetts	+	+	+		+	+	+	+	+	+	+	+	+	+	+
Michigan	+	+	+	+	+		+	+	+	+	+	+	+	+	+
Minnesota	+	+	+	+	+	+	+	+	+	+	+	+	+	+	+
Mississippi	•											•			
Missouri	•	•	•				•	•	•	•		•	•	•	•
Montana	+	+	+		+	+	+	+	+	+	+	+	+	+	+
Nebraska	+	+	+	+	+	+	+	+	+			+	+	+	+
Nevada	•	•	•	•	•	•	•	•	•	•	•	•	•	•	•
New Hampshire	+	+	+	+	+	+	+	+	+	+	+	+		+	+
New Jersey	•	•	•	•	•		•	•	•	•	•	•	•	•	•
New Mexico	•	•	•		•	•	•	•	•	•	•	•	•	•	•
New York	+	+	+		+	+	+	+	+	+	+	+	+	+	+
North Carolina	+	+	+	+			+	+				+	+		+
North Dakota	+	+	+	+		+	+	+	+	+		+	+	+	+
N. Mariana Island	+		+				+	+	+			+	+	+	+
Ohio	•	•	•	•	•		•	•	•	•	•	•		•	•
Oklahoma	+	+					+					+		+	
Oregon	•	•	•	•	•		•	•				•	•	•	•
Pennsylvania	+	•	+	+			+	•				•	•	•	
Puerto Rico	+				+		+	+	+	+	+	+			
Rhode Island	+	+	+				+					+	+	+	+
South Carolina	•	•		•								•		•	
South Dakota	•		•				•	•		•		•	•	•	
Tennessee	+						+					+			
Texas	•	•	•	•	•							•		•	•
Utah	+	+	+		+	+	+	+	+		+	+	+	+	+
Vermont	+	+					+					+	+		
Virgin Islands	+						+	+	+	+	+	+	+	+	+
Virginia	+	+	+				+		+	+	+	+			+
Washington	+	+	+		+		+		+	+	•	+	+	+	+
West Virginia	+	+	+	+	+	+	+	+			+	+	+	+	+
Wisconsin	+	+	+	+	+	+	+	+	+	+	+	+	+	+	+
Wyoming	•						•	•		•				•	

Symbols: • Categorically needy (people receiving federally supported financial assistance—AFDC or SSI)
+ Categorically needy and medically needy (people eligible for medical, but not financial assistance)
† Arizona instituted a statewide Medicaid program with federal funding in 1982. The program covers most of the medical services that are mandatory in other states and relatively few optional services.

Diagnostic Services	Screening Services	Preventive Services	Rehabilitative Services	Services for Age 65 or Older in TB Institutions			Services for Age 65 or Older in Mental Inst.			Intermediate Care Facility Services	ICF for Mentally Retarded	Inpatient Psychiatric Service for Under Age 22	Christian Science Nurses	Christian Science Sanitoria	SNF for Under Age 21	Emergency Hospital Services	Personal Care Services
				A. Inpatient Hospital Services	B. SNF Services	C. ICF Services	A. Inpatient Hospital Services	B. SNF Services	C. ICF Services								
				•				•	•	•	•	•			•	•	
							•			•	•	•			•	•	
			+	+	•	•	+	•	•	•	•	+			•	+	•
+	+	+	+	+	+	+	+	+	+	+	+	+	+	+	+	+	
							•		•	•	•	•			•	•	
+	+	+	+				+			•	•	+		+	+		
•							•								•	•	
+		+	+	+			+			+	+	+			+	+	+
			•		•		•			•	•	•		•		•	
				•	•	•	•	•	•	•	•	•			•		
+	+	+	+							+	+				+	+	
			•							•					•	•	
+		+	+	+	+	+	+	+	+	+	+	+			+	+	
•		•	•				•			•	•	•	•		•		
•	•	•					•			•	•	•			•		
			+	+	+	+	+	+	+	+	+	+			+	+	+
			+				+	+	+	+	+	+			+	+	
			+	•			•	•	•	•	•	•			•	+	
+	+	+	+				+	+	•	+	+	+	+	+	+	•	
			+				+		+	+	+				+		+
+	+	+	+				+	+	+	+	+		+	+	+	+	+
+							+	+	+	+	+	+			+	+	+
+	+	+	+	+	+	+	+	+	+	+	+	+			+	+	+
			•				•			•	•	•			•	•	
			•				•			•	•	•			•		
+	+	+	+				+	+	+	+	+	+			+	+	+
							+	+	+	+	+	+			+	+	+
		•					•	•	•	•	•	•			•	•	
+	+	+	+				+			•	•	•	+	+	+	•	+
•	•	•	•				•			•	•	•			•	•	
			•							•	•	•			•		
+	+	+	+	+	+	+	+	•	+	+	+	+			+	+	+
+	+	+	+	+			+			+	+	+			+		
+	+	+	+				+			+	+	+			+	+	
				+	+		+	+				+			•	+	
							•			•	•	•			•		
			+				+			+	+	+					+
•		•	•				•	•	•	•	•	•		•	•	•	•
							+	+	+	+	+	+			+	+	
+	+	+	+	+			+								+		
							+			•	•				+		
			•							•	•	•			•	•	
							•	•		•	•	•			•	•	•
			+	+	+	+	+	+	+	+	+	+			•		
		•		•						•	•	•		•			
							+	+	+	+	+	+			+	+	
							+			+	+	+			+	+	
				+			+	+	+	+	+			+	+	+	
•		+	+	+	+	+	+	+	+	+	+	+			+	+	
										+	+				+	+	
+	+	+	+				+			+	+	+	+	+	+	+	+
			•							•					•		

Note: This chart contains the most recent information compiled by the Health Care Financing Administration on *optional* Medicaid services, but the following should be noted: (1) Definitions and limitations may vary from state to state; (2) recent changes in federal law modified eligibility for services to the *medically needy;* and (3) in addition to services listed above, some states now cover home- and community-based services that help eligible individuals remain in their own homes instead of being admitted to a hospital or nursing home. Current information on Medicaid eligibility and services in a particular state can be obtained from that state's Medicaid agency or the local welfare office.

Source: Health Care Financing Administration.

mum of 50%. No state receives the maximum; Mississippi is paid the highest share at 77.5%, while 17 states receive the minimum.

For certain Medicaid-covered services and costs, the federal government pays an even higher percentage: 100% for inspectors of SNF's, 90% for family-planning services or for development of computerized systems to process Medicaid data; and 75% to run data systems. But in contrast, some state Medicaid programs offer certain health-care services for which no matching federal funds are provided.

About one-third of the states require the beneficiary to pay some of the cost of the services he or she receives under Medicaid. Requiring some Medicaid patients to share in the costs is mainly to encourage them to be careful in the use of medical care and not use services needlessly. Medicaid also takes special steps to be sure that doctors, hospitals, and other providers of care are not wasteful or fraudulent with Medicaid funds.

Also, all state programs require Medicaid patients in long-term-care institutions to contribute their "excess" income (usually any above $25 per month for personal needs) to the cost of their care.

In 1979, well over one-third (37.4%) of Medicaid expenditures went for recipients age 65 and over. A large part of this was spent for long-term care, which has become an increasingly important item in the Medicaid budget. New York and California were the states spending the largest number of Medicaid dollars; they also had the greatest number of recipients.

For all services to Medicaid beneficiaries, the state makes direct payment to the doctor, hospital, or other provider of care. The provider must accept this as payment in full and may not bill the patient any additional amount (except in the one-third of all states where a small copayment by the patient is required by state law).

In 1979 Medicaid paid out over $20 million in federal, state, and local funds for some 21.5 million recipients. This averages $950 per recipient for the year.

Background and Administration of Medicaid. The Medicaid program, established in 1965 under Title XIX of the Social Security Act, grew out of previous medical-assistance programs established by the various states, usually as part of their welfare programs, which received some federal funding. In 1970, the first year that all states took part in the program, Medicaid provided benefits to about 14.5 million persons, a figure that jumped to 19.6 million in 1973, and to an estimated 22.2 million in 1983.

At the federal level, Medicaid was first administered by the Social and Rehabilitation Service of the Department of Health, Education, and Welfare. In 1977 the Health Care Financing Administration (now under the Department of Health and Human Services) was created to administer both Medicaid and Medicare.

In each state, the Medicaid program is generally managed by one of the state agencies, usually the public health or the public welfare department, with assistance from a state advisory committee of physicians and representatives of the other health professions and of consumer groups.

Nearly nine out of ten Medicaid programs use computerized information systems to keep track of claims, payments, and other information on the programs. These systems also help the states control Medicaid fraud and abuse, which waste taxpayer dollars and can mean less money for people who need care.

Individuals seeking more information about Medicaid in their own states may contact their local welfare office or their state public health or public welfare department. Overall information on the federal Medicaid program can be obtained from the Health Care Financing Administration, 330 Independence Avenue, S.W., Washington, D.C. 20201.

The only state whose state legislators had not previously voted to join the Medicaid program, Arizona, has recently developed a modified form of Medicaid, which will operate with federal funds as a "demonstration program."

Today, the Medicaid program is working to hold down costs to the federal and state governments, while still seeking to make sure that poor people get the health services they need. Without Medicaid, millions of Americans might suffer health problems because of their inability to pay for care.

In the long run, Medicaid saves money—for individuals, families, and the government—by helping to detect and treat disease early, especially in children from low-income families. It also helps improve the quality of life for many elderly or disabled persons who might have to enter institutions if it were not for the Medicaid-covered home health services they receive.

Virginia T. Douglas

Medicare

Medicare is federal HEALTH INSURANCE that covers most people 65 years of age or older. It also covers certain disabled younger people—those who have been receiving Social Security disability benefits for 24 months and kidney patients needing continuing dialysis or a kidney transplant.

Medicare should not be confused with MEDICAID. Medicare is federal insurance for the elderly and disabled, while Medicaid is a federal/state assistance program for needy and low-income people. Some people, however, qualify for both programs.

There are two parts to the Medicare program:

- Part A, hospital insurance, helps pay for care provided patients in a hospital or skilled nursing facility and for health care at home;
- Part B, medical insurance, helps pay for doctors' services, outpatient hospital services, and other medical services and supplies that are medically necessary but not covered by Part A. Medical insurance also pays for certain home health services.

In this article, we will discuss who is eligible for Medicare, what health services parts A and B cover, how payment is made for services, how claims are submitted, and examine some of the background.

Who Is Eligible for Medicare? Medicare enrolls only individuals who are eligible under the Medicare law, passed in 1965 by the U.S. Congress and later amended. Generally, individuals eligible to receive Social Security or railroad retirement benefits are eligible for Medicare at age 65. They need not retire, however, to enroll in Medicare. If they retire earlier, they must wait until age 65 to qualify for Medicare and usually will be enrolled automatically. At the time they are enrolled in Part A, individuals may also enroll in Medicare Part B upon payment of the monthly premium ($14.60 in 1984). For enrollees who also qualify for Medicaid, most state Medicaid programs pay the Part B premium.

People who refuse Part B then may sign up for it later, during the general enrollment period (January 1 through March 31 each year). (But for each year an eligible individual declined to enroll, the Part B premium charged him or her goes up 10 percent.) For 65-and-older enrollees, hospital-insurance protection lasts as long as they live. Their medical-insurance protection ceases only if they stop paying premiums or voluntarily cancel it.

Also eligible for Medicare enrollment are individuals who, although under 65, meet one of the following two conditions:

- Are entitled to Social Security disability payments for at least two years. Protection ends if the individual recovers from the disability before age 65. If disability benefits stop because the beneficiary is working, but he or she has not recovered from the disability, Medicare protection may continue for up to 36 months after the monthly benefits stop. Enrollment in Part B is optional.
- Need continuing dialysis for permanent kidney failure or are preparing to receive a kidney transplant.

The protection ends 12 months after maintenance dialysis stops or 36 months after the patient receives a kidney transplant. Again, enrollment in Part B is up to the individual.

Certain individuals who are 65 or over, but not eligible in their own right to Social Security benefits, can obtain Medicare coverage. An example is the person who did not work in employment covered by Social Security, but whose spouse worked long enough to be eligible for Social Security retirement. For these persons, Medicare eligibility lasts as long as their eligibility for benefits lasts.

Finally, individuals 65 or over and not eligible for Social Security benefits either on their own or their spouses' work records may enroll in Medicare and pay a monthly premium ($155 in 1984). They must enroll in and pay premiums for both parts A and B. They can later cancel Part A and keep Part B, but not the other way around.

Anyone already enrolled under Medicare should check with a Social Security office before canceling either part, to avoid mistakenly losing valuable benefits or having to pay a higher premium.

An individual enrolled in Medicare is given a Medicare card, showing the date protection started; whether protected by Part A, Part B, or both; and the Medicare claim number. When seeking care, the beneficiary shows this card to the doctor, hospital, or other provider of service.

What Services Does Medicare Cover—and Where? Medicare pays for many health-care services. By law, however, it does *not* cover *custodial* care, or care not *reasonable and necessary* for diagnosing or treating an illness or injury. Also, Medicare usually pays only for care provided by a hospital or other facility approved for participation in the program.

Custodial care primarily meets personal needs and can be provided by persons without professional skills or training. Thus, Medicare does not pay for help in walking, getting in and out of bed, bathing, dressing, eating, and taking medicine.

Here are some examples of care that Medicare considers not reasonable and necessary and does not cover: if a beneficiary's stay in a hospital or skilled nursing facility is longer than needed; if a doctor places the beneficiary in such a facility when the care could be provided elsewhere; if the beneficiary sees a doctor or other practitioner more often than is the usual medical practice in the area and there are no medical complications requiring this; or if services and supplies not generally accepted by the health community as being reasonable or necessary for treatment (such as acupuncture and histamine therapy) are provided.

It is for the patient's protection that Medicare usually pays only for care provided by a health-care organization or professional *approved* for participation in the program. Such providers must meet licensing requirements of state or local health authorities, and other Medicare requirements concerning the quality of care. Also, approved providers may not discriminate against patients because of race, color, or national origin.

Does Medicare cover nursing-home care? Yes—and no. A "nursing home," to many people, means a *skilled nursing facility,* which Medicare defines as a specially qualified facility staffed and equipped to provide skilled nursing care, physical therapy, or rehabilitation services. This care is covered. In some nursing homes, only certain sections provide skilled nursing care for Medicare-covered patients; other sections provide a lower level of care, called "intermediate care." Also, a "nursing home" may provide *only* intermediate care, which is not covered by Medicare. ("Skilled" and "intermediate" do not refer to the *quality* of care but to the *level.*) Further information appears later in this entry.

In addition to physicians, hospitals, and skilled nursing facilities, other providers of care that receive Medicare payments include home health agencies; independent diagnostic laboratories; organizations providing X-ray, physical-therapy, and speech-pathology services; ambulance firms; chiropractors; independent physical therapists; facilities providing kidney dialysis and transplant services; and rural health clinics.

Recently, some prepaid health plans or HEALTH MAINTENANCE ORGANIZATIONS (HMO's) have begun to participate in Medicare and provide all covered services. Each month, Medicare contracts to pay such an HMO for most of the cost of care for its Medicare-eligible enrollees. The enrollee pays a small monthly premium to cover the cost of deductibles and coinsurance for which he or she is responsible. Some HMO's offer, for an added premium, additional benefits beyond those covered by Medicare. To participate, the Medicare beneficiary must continue to pay his or her monthly Part B premium, live in the area served by the HMO, and agree to follow the HMO's rules. HMO's attract people who like the convenience of centralized care, the fixed monthly payment for out-of-pocket costs, and the availability of preventive care (although Medicare may not cover this). Either the HMO or the local Social Security office can provide information on such an arrangement.

Hospital Insurance. Medicare hospital insurance (Part A) pays for most (but not all) of a beneficiary's inpatient hospital care, medically necessary inpatient care in a skilled nursing facility after a hospital stay, and home health care. Inpatient care must have been prescribed by a doctor, the patient must require the kind of care that can be provided only in a hospital, and the hospital must participate in Medicare. In the few cases where the hospital stay or part of a stay is reviewed and disapproved by an appointed health-care team, Medicare will not pay for it.

Use of services under hospital insurance is measured by *benefit periods.* The first benefit period starts when the beneficiary first enters a hospital, and ends when the patient has been out of the hospital (or other facility primarily providing skilled nursing or rehabilitation services) for 60 days in a row. Benefit periods are renewable, and there is no limit to the number an enrollee may have.

Hospital insurance can help pay for up to 90 days of medically necessary inpatient hospital care in each benefit period. During days 1–60 of the benefit period, hospital insurance pays for all covered services except a deductible amount (for 1984, $356). For days 61–90, hospital insurance pays for all covered services above $89 a day (1984), for which the hospital may charge the patient. Covered are a semiprivate room; all meals; regular nursing services; lab tests and X-rays billed by the hospital; anesthesia and other operating- and recovery-room costs; rehabilitation services; and hospital-furnished drugs and blood transfusions. Medicare does not, however, cover the first three pints of whole blood or units of packed red cells in each benefit period. The patient may choose to either pay the nonreplacement fee or have the blood replaced by another person or a blood-assurance plan.

In case of an illness requiring a hospital stay of more than 90 days, Medicare provides reserve days—an extra 60 hospital days. For each reserve day used, hospital insurance pays for all covered services over $178 a day (1984). Unlike benefit periods, the 60 reserve days are not renewable.

Hospital insurance does not cover doctors' services (covered under Part B); private-duty nurses; personal convenience items that the patient requests, such as a television or telephone; or extra charges for a private room, unless medically necessary.

Care in a hospital not approved for participation in Medicare is covered only if the patient is admitted for emergency treatment and that hospital is the closest one equipped to handle the emergency. An "emergency" is a situation where treatment is immediately necessary to prevent death or serious impairment to health. Medicare generally does not pay for hospital or medical services outside the United States, except in certain circumstances when a Canadian or Mexican hospital is closer than a U.S. facility, or under certain emergency situations.

Medicare covers care in a Christian Science sanatorium, if operated or certified by the First Church of Christ Scientist.

Medicare does not cover *long-term care* in a nursing home, but does cover inpatient care in a participating *skilled nursing facility* when the following conditions exist:

• The patient was in a hospital at least three days in a row (not counting day of discharge) before transfer to the nursing facility.
• The patient still requires daily skilled nursing or rehabilitation services that, practically speaking, can only be provided in such a facility.
• The care is required for the condition that was treated in the hospital.
• The patient is admitted to the facility within a short time (generally 30 days) after leaving the hospital.
• A doctor certifies need for and the patient receives skilled nursing or rehabilitation services daily.
• The facility's utilization review committee or a professional review organization does not disapprove the stay.

Hospital insurance helps pay for up to 100 days of skilled nursing care in a benefit period. Such care may be provided only by or under the supervision of licensed nursing personnel, and may include physical and speech therapy. A patient who leaves a skilled nursing facility, but is readmitted within 30 days, need not have a new three-day stay in the hospital to be covered, as long as a portion of the 100-day benefit is left. In each benefit period, hospital insurance pays for all covered services in the skilled nursing facility for the first 20 days; for days 21 through 100, there is a deductible of $44.50 a day (1984), for which the patient may be charged. Doctors' services at the facility are not covered (Medicare medical insurance helps pay for these). As with inpatient hospital care, private-duty nurses, personal convenience items, and extra charges for a private room (unless medically necessary) are not covered.

For a three-year period starting November 1, 1983, Congress authorized Medicare to cover hospice care for terminally ill beneficiaries whose life expectancy is six months or less. These beneficiaries can choose to receive hospice care instead of certain other Medicare benefits. Hospice care may cover nursing care, physical or occupational therapy, speech/language pathology, certain outpatient drugs, homemaker/home health aide and medical social services, short-term inpatient care (including respite care), and counseling.

Medical Insurance. Medicare Part B—medical insurance—helps pay for doctors' services, outpatient hospital care, outpatient physical-therapy and speech-pathology services, home health care, and other health services and supplies not covered by Medicare hospital insurance.

The basic payment rule is: The patient pays for the first $75 in *approved charges* for Medicare-covered services each calendar year; then Medicare pays 80% of approved charges for covered services for the rest of the year. Payment is not based on what a doctor or other provider currently charges, but on what the Medicare law defines as *approved charges,* which may be less than the actual charges for which the patient is billed.

Here is how the approved charge is decided. Medicare determines what each doctor or supplier in a specific locality customarily charged for a service or supply during the previous year. It then determines an amount—called the *prevailing charge*—that is high enough to cover the *customary charge* for that service or supply in three out of four claims the previous year. Then, for each patient's claim, Medicare pays 80% of (1) the actual amount billed, (2) the customary charge, or (3) the prevailing charge—whichever is lower.

Each July, Medicare increases its customary- and prevailing-charge figures, but limits the increases for doctors' services by relating their fee increases to actual increases in costs of maintaining their practices and to raises in general earning levels. Medicare does this to try to control the increases in costs of medical care, while still paying doctors and other providers fairly.

Assignment is an important concept to Medicare Part B beneficiaries. A doctor or supplier who accepts assignment of the medical-insurance payment agrees that his or her total charge for the covered services will be the charge approved by Medicare. Doctors and suppliers need not accept assignment, but many do, particularly for patients who have difficulty meeting medical expenses. The assignment method of payment is used only if both patient and doctor agree to it. When a doctor accepts assignment, he or she may charge the patient only for any part of the $75 deductible not yet met, the 20% coinsurance portion of the bill, and any services not covered by Medicare.

If the assignment method is *not* used, the doctor or other supplier bills the patient, who pays the bill directly and sends Medicare a claim for reimbursement. Such a doctor's bill may be for more or less than Medicare's approved charge, but Medicare reimburses the patient only the 80% of the approved charge after the deductible is met. Regardless of whether assignment is used or not, Medicare pays only the approved charge under law.

Following is a discussion of the services medical insurance covers:

Doctors' Services. Medical insurance helps pay for covered doctors' services in the office, the home, a hospital, a skilled nursing facility, or elsewhere in the U.S. Covered services include medical and surgical services (including anesthesia), diagnostic tests and procedures that are part of the treatment, and other services ordinarily furnished in the doctor's office as part of the treatment and included in the bill. The latter include X-rays, blood transfusions, medical supplies, drugs and biologicals that cannot be self-administered, physical therapy, speech-pathology services, and services of the doctor's office nurse.

But some doctor's services are *not* covered, such as routine physical examinations or foot care, eye or hearing examinations done for prescribing or fitting eyeglasses or hearing aids, immunizations (except pneumonia vaccinations or immunizations needed because of an injury or immediate risk of infection), and cosmetic surgery (unless needed because of accidental injury or to improve the functioning of a malformed part of the body).

All surgery involves some risk, and many conditions can be treated equally well without it. If a doctor recommends elective surgery, the Medicare program encourages the patient to get a *second opinion* before deciding on the operation. Medicare medical insurance pays for a second medical opinion by another doctor in the same way it pays for other doctors' services. A patient either may ask his or her own doctor to be referred to another doctor for a second opinion, or may call Medicare's "hot line" (Second Opinion Referral Center) for the names and phone numbers of doctors in the area who provide second opinions. The toll-free number is 800-638-6833 (in Maryland, 1-800-492-6603).

For certain medical services, Medicare applies special conditions. For outpatient treatment of mental illness, the maximum that medical insurance can pay toward doctors' services is $250 per year (less if charges for these services are used to meet part or all of the $75 deductible). For chiropractors' services (by a licensed, Medicare-certified practitioner), only manual manipulation of the spine to correct a subluxation that can be demonstrated by X-ray is covered (no other diagnostic or therapeutic service by a chiropractor is covered). For foot care by a licensed podiatrist, medical insurance helps pay for any covered services, including removal of plantar warts and, for patients with medical conditions affecting the lower limbs (such as severe diabetes), routine foot care. Not covered are such services as hygiene care; treatment for flat feet; or removal of corns, calluses, and most warts. Optometrists' services are generally not covered, except for examination related to the condition of aphakia (absence of the natural lens of the eye).

Dental care is covered only if it involves surgery of the jaw or related structures, setting fractures of the jaw or facial bones, or services that would be covered when provided by a physician. Not covered are filling, removal, replacement, or treatment of teeth; root-canal therapy; surgery for impacted teeth; or other surgical procedures involving the teeth or structures directly supporting the teeth.

Outpatient Hospital Services. Hospital insurance covers specified services provided outpatients by a participating hospital for diagnosis or treatment of an illness or injury. Such covered services include services in an emergency room or outpatient clinic; laboratory tests, X-rays, and other radiology services billed by the hospital; medical supplies such as splints and casts, drugs and biologicals that cannot be self-administered; and outpatient blood transfusions.

Not covered are routine physical examinations and related tests, eye or ear examinations to prescribe or fit eyeglasses or hearing aids, immunizations (except pneumonia vaccinations or immunizations required because of an injury or immediate risk of infection), and routine foot care.

The hospital usually files the claim for medical-insurance payment, which is 80% of the approved amount for the covered services received after subtraction of the deductible (or any unpaid part of the deductible). The patient is charged for any balance. (If the total charge for services received is less than $75, the hospital may bill the patient, who then files a claim with Medicare for reimbursement.)

For certain kinds of outpatient care, special conditions apply to coverage of approved charges. Physical therapy and speech-pathology services are covered in the doctor's office, from an independent physical therapist, or in a hospital outpatient department. For independent laboratory services, the laboratory must be certified by Medicare for the services received (the prescribing doctor can usually tell the patient if the services will be covered).

Ambulance transportation is covered if the ambulance, equipment, and personnel meet Medicare requirements and if transportation in any other vehicle could endanger the patient's health. (Medicare covers such transportation from the scene of an accident to a hospital, from home to a hospital or skilled nursing facility or back to home, and between hospitals and skilled nursing facilities, but not between home and a doctor's office.)

Prosthetic devices are covered if needed to substitute for an internal body organ, including heart pacemakers, corrective lenses after a cataract operation, colostomy or ileostomy bags and certain related supplies, and breast prostheses and surgical brassieres after a mastectomy, as well as artificial limbs and eyes, and arm, leg, back, and neck braces. (Orthopedic shoes are covered only if part of leg braces and included in the orthopedist's charge; dental plates and other dental devices are not covered.)

Purchase or rental of durable medical equipment—such as oxygen equipment, wheelchairs, home dialysis systems, and other medically necessary equipment prescribed for home use—is covered. In the case of purchase, Medicare usually makes monthly payments until its share of the approved purchase price is paid or the equipment is no longer medically necessary, whichever comes first; but if the equipment will be needed for a long time, Medicare may pay its share in a lump sum.

Medical supplies, such as surgical dressings, splints, and casts, are covered; but common first-aid supplies, such as adhesive tape and antiseptics, are not. Approved charges for preadmission diagnostic testing received in a hospital's outpatient department or doctor's office within seven days before admission as a hospital inpatient are covered in full, as are approved charges for pneumococcal (pneumonia) vaccine (no deductible applies to this service). For blood transfusions, nonreplacement fees charged for the first three pints or units of blood or blood components received in each calendar year are not covered.

Medical insurance can cover part-time skilled health care (including physical or speech therapy) for a patient confined to the home (but not to a nursing home or rehabilitation facility) for treatment of illness or injury. An unlimited number of visits is covered. But Medicare does not pay for general household services, home-delivered meals or meal preparation, shopping, help in bathing or dressing, or other home-care services intended mainly to assist the patient in meeting personal, family, or domestic needs. Occupational therapy, part-time services of home health aides, medical social services, and medical supplies and services provided by the agency are covered, but only if the patient also needs part-time skilled nursing care or physical or speech therapy.

Submitting Claims. When a participating hospital or other facility provides services to a patient under *Part A* of Medicare, the patient need not submit a claim. A Medicare *intermediary* pays Medicare's share of the costs directly to the facility that provided the care, but sends the patient a notice that explains the decision made on the claim and what services Medicare paid for. (An intermediary is a private firm, usually an insurance company, that handles Part A claims for the program.)

To submit a claim for covered services under *Part B* of Medicare, if the doctor or supplier is willing to accept the assignment method of payment, the provider submits the claim form to Medicare. If assignment is not used, the patient submits the claim form

to Medicare, attached to an itemized bill. Medicare provides the forms, information on submitting them, and even a folder for the patient to keep records of claims together. Some time limits are set for submitting claims, but the patient always has at least 15 months.

The claim should be submitted to the Medicare *carrier* for the state in which the services were received (not the Social Security office). A carrier is a private insurance organization that handles Medicare Part B claims from doctors and other suppliers. The addresses of all Medicare carriers and areas they serve are listed in *Your Medicare Handbook,* a booklet that explains the Medicare program and is available from any Social Security office.

If the enrollee disagrees with Medicare's decision on the amount paid or whether a service is covered, he or she can ask for a review of the case (under Part A) or appeal the decision (Part B). The appeal process includes a formal hearing by Medicare and, for hospital insurance claims over $1,000, possible federal court appeal.

Because Medicare does not cover all of an individual's health-care expenses, some enrollees also buy private insurance coverage that supplements their Medicare protection and pays additional amounts on claims. Medicare is not directly involved in such coverage, but provides information on it by means of a free booklet, *Guide to Health Insurance for People with Medicare,* available from any Social Security office.

Some Background on Medicare. In 1982, Americans spent some $322 billion on health care—an average of $1,361 for every American and nearly 10.5% of the gross national product. Of the total cost, Medicare paid $51 billion. In 1967, Medicare's first full year of operation, its bill was only $3.4 billion. Medicare was signed into law on July 30, 1965, after some 30 years of controversy and debate throughout the nation and in the Congress. It provided aged beneficiaries with basic hospital insurance financed through Social Security taxes, plus supplementary medical insurance available for a small monthly premium.

Since then, Congress has expanded Medicare coverage to cover the permanently disabled and persons with end-stage renal disease. This expansion of coverage, along with dramatic growth in America's population of elderly people and rapid increases in the price of health care—much greater than that of living costs generally—has contributed to Medicare's average rise in costs of 20% annually.

When created, Medicare was administered by the Social Security Administration. Its companion program for low-income Americans, Medicaid, was ad-

ministered at the federal level by the Social and Rehabilitation Service. In 1977 the Health Care Financing
Administration was created under the Department of
Health and Human Services to administer both programs and to oversee payments for the health care of
one out of every five Americans. But Social Security
offices still handle enrollment in Medicare and provide information on it.

In 1983, nearly 30 million people were enrolled in
the Medicare hospital-insurance program, including
about 95% of the nation's aged population. Nearly all
of these beneficiaries also were enrolled voluntarily in
Part B, the medical-insurance program. Every month,
about 180,000 persons become entitled to Medicare.
The average reimbursement per person served in the
Medicare program in 1979 was $1,663. Medicare's fo-
cus on acute care services, required by law, is shown
by the fact that 67.8% of its total dollars went toward
inpatient hospital care in 1979.

Medicare benefits and the costs of administering
the program are paid from two separate trust funds.
Money in the hospital-insurance trust fund comes primarily from a tax on current earnings from employment covered under the Social Security Act, while
money in the medical-insurance trust fund comes
from premiums paid by persons enrolled in the program (or paid on their behalf) and from general revenues of the federal government. Medicare's rapidly
increasing costs have threatened the future of the program, requiring action by the Congress to protect the
health-care benefits now enjoyed by America's elderly
and the disabled.

See also MEDIGAP.

Virginia T. Douglas

Medigap

Private insurance to supplement MEDICARE. Medicare
was never meant to be an all-inclusive health-insurance program; it was designed as a federal program to
relieve people age 65 and older of a part of the costs
associated with hospitalization, surgery, and lengthy
periods of recovery. So while Medicare pays a part of
older people's health-care expenses (recently about
38% on average), the remaining part (62%) must still
be paid by the individual. And as government cutbacks continue and Medicare deductibles rise, the
portion of the total health-care bill borne by many
people covered by Medicare is increasing, as are
health costs in general. Thus, the need for private
health insurance to supplement Medicare is also increasing. Because private insurance to supplement
Medicare is intended to fill the gaps in Medicare, it is
often called "Medigap" coverage.

Closing the Gaps, Before Age 65. People approaching retirement should examine their *group health-
insurance* plan where they work, or group plans
possibly held through a professional or fraternal organization. Many group plans continue some coverage
after a member becomes eligible for Medicare, with
some employers paying part or all of the costs. Federal
law was changed in 1982 to require employers offering a group plan to continue providing benefits to employees who work past age 65 and so request.

If the benefits of the group plan fill many of the
gaps in Medicare, and if continued coverage is offered, the insured should definitely continue group
health insurance when he or she becomes eligible for
Medicare. Group coverage is less expensive than that
offered to individuals. A retired person may find it
advantageous to continue a group plan even if it
doesn't fill all the Medicare gaps, and purchase an
individual plan for those gaps that remain.

Individual health-insurance coverage should be examined before a person reaches 65. If an existing individual *major-medical policy* is guaranteed renewable
for life, it can extend the range of Medicare for the
insured. The insured should check with the insurance
company to determine what benefits are available after age 65. The benefits may decrease at age 65 so as
not to duplicate Medicare, but premiums also would
decrease. Continuing such a policy avoids gaps in
coverage that would be caused by purchasing another
individual policy after age 65 because of the new policy's "waiting period" during which a prior health
problem is not covered.

An existing HOSPITAL INCOME INSURANCE policy
can be useful in filling small gaps in coverage, if coverage can be extended beyond age 65.

Closing the Gaps, After Age 65. People who have no
existing private health insurance when they become
eligible for Medicare can choose from several types of
policies to supplement this program.

The *hospital income policy* pays cash benefits daily
when the insured is hospitalized. Because Medicare
covers most of the cost of up to two months of hospitalization, some people use these cash benefits to
build a reserve to cover future out-of-pocket expenses.
These policies deliver cash, and it is up to the insured
to pay the out-of-pocket costs to the doctors and hospitals as they arise. Hospital income policies are available either through agents or directly from insurance
companies by mail. Like any product that offers many
choices, these policies require care in matching the
plan to needs. They also require periodic updating because their benefits are in fixed dollars and health-
care costs are rising. These policies typically contain a

waiting period before they become effective if the insured is ill, or has been ill recently.

Supplementary Medicare policies usually pay a high proportion of health expenditures Medicare doesn't cover. These expenditures may include deductible or copayment amounts not covered by Medicare, or they may include other health services not covered by Medicare, such as out-of-hospital prescription drugs, medical appliances, and equipment. Often these policies, in effect, extend the number of hospital days covered under Medicare, and they may also pay the co-payments in a skilled nursing home. Recently, federal standards were established for policies called "Medicare supplements" to establish a minimum level of approved benefits at reasonable cost. The standards are voluntary, meaning policies with less-extensive benefits may still be sold, but they cannot be cited or advertised as meeting the "federal standards." Subsequently, most of the states reviewed their own regulations to ensure that they are as strict or stricter than the federal standards. A consumer considering Medicare-supplement coverage should ask the agent or the company whether the policy meets federal minimum standards or those of the state in which it is offered.

Retirement associations offer supplementary insurance. Membership fees in these associations are nominal and, in addition to offering insurance, they provide other programs of interest to older people, such as mail-order prescription drugs at reduced rates. Typically, the insurance plans they offer permit enrollment regardless of previous health history and have relatively short waiting periods for preexisting conditions.

James L. Moorefield

Member Bank

See FEDERAL RESERVE SYSTEM.

MidAmerica Commodity Exchange

A COMMODITY-FUTURES EXCHANGE on which wheat, oats, corn, soybeans, cattle, hogs, U.S. Treasury bonds, U.S. Treasury bills, gold, silver, the British pound, the deutsche mark, the Swiss franc, the Japanese yen, the Canadian dollar, and refined sugar are traded.

The MidAmerica Commodity Exchange offers commodity-futures contracts in smaller-size units. These contracts, known as "MiniContracts," make the commodity markets more accessible to more people interested in participating in the futures market.

The majority of MidAmerica's contracts are small-er versions of similar futures contracts traded on other futures-exchange floors. For example, the size of a corn contract at MidAmerica is 1,000 bushels of corn, in contrast to the Chicago Board of Trade contract of 5,000 bushels. MidAmerica silver is one-fifth the size of the contract offered at the commodity exchange in New York, and U.S Treasury bills at MidAmerica are one-half the size of the International Monetary Market contract offered at the Chicago Mercantile Exchange.

There are probably many potential traders who would like to give the futures markets a try but who are reluctant to, or simply cannot commit $20,000 or more to a first-time experience. This point is verifiable. A few years ago, a government study estimated that more than 62% of commodity traders had less than $5,000 in futures trading-account equity. Taking economic factors over the last several years into consideration, and assuming that the figure is now $10,000, a trading account of this size would still be limited to trading one, or possibly two, of the larger contracts in order to retain sufficient margin capital in the event of an adverse price move.

With MiniContracts, this same account could be used to trade a diversified commodity portfolio, spreading the same risk capital across several different commodities. Considering the fast-moving pace of commodity prices, MiniContract diversification makes even more sense. Commodity-futures trading can indeed be risky; but by trading in a number of different, smaller contracts, the risk factor can be better managed.

The strategy behind MiniContracts has served the exchange well. Yet recently, MidAmerica has adopted a more aggressive policy, branching out with its first unique contract in domestic refined-sugar futures. To commercial sugar-market participants, this new contract represents a risk-management tool, one designed specifically to help the refined-sugar industry cope with potentially volatile price fluctuations. To the investor, it represents another vehicle in which to participate in order to realize a potential profit.

The Changer Market. Because of MidAmerica's MiniContract size, the exchange has become recognized as the nation's only "derivative" marketplace, since its prices are largely derived from the "primary" futures-contract markets—like the Chicago Board of Trade or the Chicago Mercantile Exchange—where the larger-size contracts are traded. MidAmerica's floor traders rely on the prices shown on the quotation systems of the primary markets to help determine MidAmerica's own prices. Generally, MiniContracts move in parallel with the primary market, and only a nominal price differential exists at any one point in time.

One reason why prices are so close is because of MidAmerica's rules providing for a unique species of trader called the "changer." The changer's function is to enable members of MidAmerica, who are not members of one of the other exchanges, to execute trades on those exchanges. In a function similar to that of an arbitrager, the changer conducts intermarket spreading with a primary exchange market. This creates a direct link to the pricing mechanisms of the primary market and keeps MidAmerica's MiniContract market in alignment.

If a MidAmerica member believes he can obtain a better price through a primary market, he may give an order to a changer's representative stationed in the trading pit. Using a direct telephone line, the changer's representative calls the order to the floor of the changed (primary) market. A written, time-stamped order is prepared and run into the pit for execution. When filled, the order is returned to the desk, time-stamped, and reported immediately by phone to the changer's representative in the MidAmerica pit.

The changer market allows the MidAmerica floor trader greater flexibility to execute a commodity trade at the best price available. As a general rule, however, most trading at MidAmerica does not involve the changer. In many instances, MidAmerica makes its own market in similitude to the primary market. The combined activity both in MidAmerica's own pit and through the changer market provides MidAmerica's members and customers with a liquid commodity-futures marketplace.

Exchange History. The MidAmerica Commodity Exchange began as a grain-contract market in Chicago more than 100 years ago. Back in the 1870s, a handful of men would assemble each day at the corner of LaSalle and Washington Streets—then just an open field—to trade grain contracts. This marked the humble beginnings of what was then called "Pudd's Exchange." Records for those early years are scant, but it is known that by 1880 Pudd's Exchange was incorporated as the Chicago Open Board of Trade. Open Board members moved indoors to trade 1,000-bushel lots of wheat, corn, oats, barley, and rye.

The third commodity exchange in the United States, the Open Board in 1974 changed its name to the MidAmerica Commodity Exchange. In 1983 a total of 1,205 floor traders owned memberships on the exchange, including representatives of 25 brokerage firms.

Kathleen A. Seebert

Midwest Stock Exchange (MSE)

The Midwest Stock Exchange was organized as the Chicago Stock Exchange, and opened for trading on May 15, 1882.

The initial list of securities that were traded consisted of 134 items, of which 82 were bonds and 52 stocks. Because communications had not evolved into the sophisticated systems known today, the early trading concentrated on regional issues, including such companies as Chicago Gas Light & Coke Company (now Peoples Gas); Atchison, Topeka & Santa Fe Railroad; Illinois Central Railroad; First National Bank of Chicago; and Chicago & North Western Railroad, along with other railroad companies that sprang up as Chicago became the rail center of the United States.

As time went by and the marketplace evolved, the emphasis on trading shifted from bonds to stocks, and it was speculation in newly issued local securities that prompted the early growth of the Chicago Stock Exchange. These local securities included the utilities, meat-packing companies, and railroads.

In the 1880s, the old Chicago Gas Light & Coke Company merged with its rivals, and the first known case of dual listing came about when the newly issued stock was quoted on both the New York and Chicago Stock Exchanges. Chicago remained the center of interest, and orders from the East Coast poured into the local brokers.

The practice of dual listing grew over the decades with improved communication, and soon most of the stocks traded on the Chicago Exchange were also traded on the New York Stock Exchange.

As the years passed and the market for securities expanded after World War II, the Chicago Stock Exchange in 1949 merged with the stock exchanges of St. Louis, Cleveland, and Minneapolis–St. Paul to form the Midwest Stock Exchange. A decade later the New Orleans Stock Exchange became part of the Midwest.

From the small list of stocks and bonds originally listed for trading, the Midwest Stock Exchange has grown to the point where approximately 1,800 securities in January 1984 were available for trading.

The growth of the Midwest Stock Exchange is attributable to many factors, one of which is that the exchange has been an effective and efficient marketplace and an innovator of new services to the securities industry. In addition, the urging from the U.S. Congress and the Securities and Exchange Commission for a national market system allowing for more effective competition between exchange centers has added to the growth of the Midwest.

The innovations brought about by the MSE covered both electronic sophistication and also encompassed concepts of industry structure.

In late 1969, exchange officials saw the upcoming need by member firms to raise capital in amounts necessary to cover costs of new systems and programs and to ensure that the capital was permanent for the continuity of the firms. In January 1970 the exchange was the first to submit and implement rule changes that allowed MSE member firms to be publicly owned, or to be owned wholly or in part by a parent firm.

Investment in new technology is part of the exchange's plan for handling the increased trading volumes expected throughout the 1980s. In the surveillance area, the MSE has developed the latest in market-information-retrieval equipment, allowing exchange officials to check trades and trading patterns on an up-to-the-second basis to ensure fairness in markets. A new generation of surveillance equipment is now being developed as the MSE remains in the forefront of improvement of sophisticated electronic equipment for the securities industry. The Midwest Stock Exchange anticipates that its current average daily trading volume of 4.4 million shares could more than double within the next few years. This, coupled with rapid changes in the securities industry, will continue to create a need for new methods of operations, and the Midwest Stock Exchange, with its tradition of innovation, is preparing to respond to this challenge as it has in the past, with a wide variety of services.

As the Midwest Stock Exchange enters its second 100 years, the exchange is further refining the function of the members on its trading floor. In addition to the traditional specialist and floor broker, a new type of member function is taking shape—that of the independent market-maker. Although the system is new, it is believed that the advantage of this type of member will eventually result in the infusion of more capital and add depth to the marketplace.

The Midwest Stock Exchange has been involved in the major advances in recent years in the national market system—including the Consolidated Reporting Tape; order routing to all exchanges; timely quotations effectively displayed; and the creation in the late 1970s of the Intermarket Trading System (ITS), which electronically links all of the stock exchanges in the United States.

The Midwest Stock Exchange, Inc., has three operating subsidiaries: the Midwest Clearing Corporation, the Midwest Securities Trust Company, and the Mortgage Backed Securities Clearing Corporation.

The Midwest Clearing Corporation is fully equipped to compare, record, and provide settlements for trades originating from numerous securities mar-

kets. The Clearing Corporation and the Midwest Securities Trust Company combine to offer a full network of securities-transaction services, and, interfaced with clearing and depository agencies nationally, they effectively produce a National Securities Clearance and Settlement System that is truly national in nature.

In 1971 the Midwest Clearing Corporation provided an especially important innovation to the industry by establishing the Continuous Net Settlement System, in which member firms have positions in securities with the clearing center, much as retail customers have with the member firms.

The Midwest Securities Trust Company provides depository services to the financial-services industry. The subsidiary was formed as efforts were made by the industry to develop central depositories and eventually move to the point of certificate immobilization.

The Mortgage Backed Securities Clearing Corporation was formed in 1979 to service that industry. Today, it is the only organization offering trade comparison—recording, margin, and settlement on a balance order basis—to this industry. MBSCC settles approximately 1,300 trades with a settlement value approaching $1.5 billion each month.

Membership Qualifications. An individual member may function either as a cospecialist, floor broker or registered floor trader on the equity floor, or as a partner in a member firm or an officer in a member corporation.

The active principals and branch-office managers of a member organization have adequate experience in and knowledge of the securities business to comply with the rules and policies of the exchange and to properly serve the public.

An individual applicant for membership or nominee has a liquid net worth of at least $10,000 over and above the cost of the membership; and if he is not a partner or an officer of a member organization that is subject to certain rules, he will maintain a liquid net worth in such amount.

The prime requisite for listing on the Midwest Stock Exchange is the quality of the corporation. Its products and services must enjoy public acceptance and good reputation. Its management must operate the company in the public interest. Its securities must also meet the technical requirements of an auction market.

The following requirements must be met in order for the exchange to entertain an application for listing:

1. The company must have at least $2 million in net tangible assets.

2. It must be actively engaged in business and have been so operating for at least three consecutive years.

3. It shall have outstanding 250,000 or more shares of the common or preferred stock to be listed, exclusive of the holdings of officers, directors, controlling stockholders, and other concentrated or family holdings.

4. Experience has shown that outstanding shares should be owned by approximately 1,000 stockholders if the stock sells at less than $15 per share. In the price range of $15 to $50, it is advisable to have 1,500 holders; from $50 to $100, 2,500; and above $100, in excess of 3,000 shareholders. These amounts should be weighed in light of type of issue, current activity over the counter, and in consideration of near-future secondary distributions, stock splits, and/or new underwritings.

5. It shall maintain stock-transfer and registrar facilities acceptable to the exchange, which may be an independent bank or trust company acting as both transfer agent and registrar for any listed security other than its own stock.

6. Its certificates of stock shall have a steel engraved border prepared by an approved bank-note company. The face of the certificate may be engraved or surface-printed.

7. The exchange must be satisfied (*a*) as to the adequacy of the company's working capital; (*b*) that the management enjoys a reputation of good character, competence, and integrity; (*c*) as to its ability to show net earnings of at least $100,000 annually; and (*d*) that the company has agreed to publish periodic reports.

The exchange reserves the right to delist the securities of any corporation—subject to Securities and Exchange Commission rules—that engages in practices not in the public interest, or whose assets have been depleted to the extent that the company can no longer operate as a going concern, or whose securities have become so closely held that it is no longer feasible to maintain a reasonable market in the issue. Furthermore, the exchange reserves the right to delist the securities of any corporation that has drastically changed its corporate structure and/or its type of operation.

Issues normally will be considered for delisting if the company fails to maintain a net worth that is the greater of (a) 150% of the prior year's consolidated net loss or (b) $500,000, or when the volume of trading declines to a level that will not support a listed market in the judgment of the exchange and its Committee on Floor Procedure.

See also STOCK EXCHANGES.

John G. Weithers

Minneapolis Grain Exchange (MGE)

A COMMODITY-FUTURES EXCHANGE on which spring wheat and sunflower futures contracts are traded.

The Minneapolis Grain Exchange, a nonprofit organization, is a grain terminal market. The exchange does not buy or sell grain; it records the price after the buyer and seller have agreed on a transaction. It provides a centralized gathering place for buyers and sellers of grain—merchants, processors, shippers, farmers, elevator operators, brokers—all of whom are assured of equal consideration. The members of the exchange buy and sell grain.

In addition to serving as an effective marketing link between producer and consumer, the exchange gathers information pertinent to grain marketing and transportation and provides objective third-party services for members, such as grain weighing and obtaining grain samples for grading by state-licensed inspectors.

The Minneapolis Grain Exchange is designated a contract market by the COMMODITY FUTURES TRADING COMMISSION (CFTC). Like other commodity markets, it is regulated by the Commodity Exchange Act of 1936, as amended in 1974, and by a set of self-imposed rules and regulations. Exchange rules are regularly reviewed and revised to reflect changes in the marketing process. A method of arbitration is provided to settle disputes.

The Minneapolis Grain Exchange was organized in October 1881, and in 1982 had 420 members. It is governed by a board of directors, and various committees composed of exchange members skilled in particular aspects of the grain business help direct this commodity market. Membership in the exchange may be purchased by any person of legal age with a record of personal integrity.

The Minneapolis Grain Exchange provides a place for three types of markets:

1. A cash or "spot" market, for the immediate transfer of grain.

2. A cash call or "to arrive" market, where buyers and sellers arrange for certain quantities and qualities of grain to arrive at a specified location on a specified date.

3. A futures market—the only market in the world trading in spring wheat futures.

Cash Spot. At the tables reserved for the trading of cash grains, samples of wheat, barley, oats, rye, flax, corn, sunflower seeds, and soybeans are inspected by prospective buyers. The samples (many of them fresh from railcars awaiting destination orders at country elevators across four states) are felt, sniffed, sifted, eyed, and even nibbled to ascertain elements of quality. Each sample already carries with it a USDA-approved analysis of weight, moisture, protein, and other factors bearing on its market value. Volume records are not kept in the cash market, but the exchange estimates that about 1 million bushels of grain are traded each day, making this the world's largest cash grain market.

Cash Call. The cash call market acts as a "bridge" between the spot market and the futures market. It provides agribusiness an efficient marketplace for large grain transactions. Pricing efficiency results when the commodity is exposed to a wide variety of buyers and sellers and then trades at a fair market price. Operational efficiency results when the commodity travels by the most efficient method from the producer to the consumer, arriving at an optimum time.

Futures Contracts. Each futures contract calls for a specified amount and grade of product. For example: A person buying a March spring-wheat contract at 4.05 is accepting a legal obligation, now, to take delivery of 5,000 bushels of U.S. No. 2 spring wheat with 13.5% protein, the contract to be delivered during the month of March, for which the buyer will pay $4.05 per bushel. Futures enable grain to enter the market year-round, smoothing the seasonal supply and price cycles.

The average trader does not take delivery of a futures contract, since he normally will close out his position before the contract matures. As a matter of fact, a survey conducted by a leading exchange has estimated that less than 3% of the contracts traded are settled by actual delivery.

Perhaps the single unique feature of doing business at the exchange, compared to other types of business centers, is that the thousands of contracts negotiated there each day are done so on the word of the traders—without written agreements. The writing of the transactions comes later. This is why the regulations state that membership is open to persons of legal age who have a reputation for fair and honest dealings. Membership includes producers (farmers), processors, elevator operators, merchandisers, and speculators.

The Minneapolis Grain Exchange is dedicated to its basic objective of providing an open marketplace for commodity trading, and is looking forward to doing it for as long as the need exists to move grains—food—off the farms and to the processors and ultimately the consumers in an orderly and equitable manner.

See also FUTURES CONTRACTS.

Paul A. Tattersall

Minor's Trusts

See TRUSTS.

Minting of Coins

A mint is an industrial plant of a very special type: It is a factory for the purpose of turning out new coins. You'd like to make your own? Well, that is not possible, for this particular industry is a government monopoly. The right to manufacture U.S. coins is vested only with the government, and those who would do so on their own are breaking the law.

Engraving Division. The Engraving Division, headquarters of the U.S. BUREAU OF THE MINT's chief sculptor-engraver and staff of artists, is a highly specialized office, offering services performed at no other U.S. Mint facility. The chief sculptor-engraver holds a unique position, the only one of its kind in the country. The engraver has total responsibility for the staff, planning and coordinating the activities of the Engraving Division. This includes creating original designs and sketches; preparing wax and plaster models to scale for coins, medals, insignia, and special awards; and the engraving of all master dies.

Services performed by the Engraving Division also include the preparation of sketches and dies for foreign coinage, and sketches, dies, and counsel for those private sponsors who have been authorized by the Congress to have commemorative medals struck by the United States Mint.

All working dies used by the Bureau of the Mint, including those dies used in the Mint's special coinage and medals programs, are manufactured in the Die Manufacturing Division of the Philadelphia Mint. Mint marks are hand-stamped on the dies at the Philadelphia Mint prior to shipment to the field facilities.

Preparation of Working Dies from the Original Design. The sculptor-engraver prepares a Plastilene (modeling wax) model in bas-relief from the approved sketch of the design for a coin, keeping in mind the depth of relief suitable for coining. This model is generally made three to twelve times larger than the size of the finished coin.

A plaster-of-paris negative is cast from the wax model. After suitable refining and touching up of the detail, a plaster positive is made from this negative. The plaster positive or a photograph is then submitted for comment to the director of the Mint and the Commission of Fine Arts. It is submitted to the secretary of the Treasury for final approval.

When final approval is received, a second negative is prepared, from which a copper electrotype, or galvano, is made. To do this, a negative plaster cast is thoroughly dried and then coated with hot beeswax and powdered copper. A conductor is attached and the treated model suspended in an electroplating tank, where copper is deposited on the negative model to a thickness of approximately one-sixteenth of an inch. This requires about three days in the plating tank. The resulting copper shell, or galvano, is separated from the plaster, trimmed, and all defects eliminated. The shell is backed with lead to give it more strength.

The completed galvano is then mounted on a transfer engraving machine. This machine reduces the design on the galvano while cutting it with a fine tracing device into a soft tool-steel blank directly to the size of the finished coin, producing a positive replica, or hub.

The hub is then heat-treated to harden it and is used in a hydraulic press to prepare a master die. The master die, in turn, is hardened, and by this cold forging process a working hub is used to produce working dies. The original hub is carefully stored in a safe place to ensure against loss.

The Manufacturing Process. One-cent blanks are purchased commercially, and already have an upset edge. The stamping process is the same as for the nickel.

United States five-cent coins are made from cupronickel—an alloy containing 75% copper and 25% nickel. Strip purchased commercially is fed into high-speed punch presses that cut planchets or blanks of the proper diameter. The cupronickel planchets are softened by annealing in a special type of furnace. Then, cleaned and dried, they are put through an edge-rolling operation that produces a raised rim. With a single stroke, the coining press stamps the designs of both the obverse (front) and reverse (back) dies on the planchet.

The dime, quarter, half-dollar, and dollar are manufactured from coinage strips composed of three layers of metal bonded together and rolled to the required thickness. This is called "cladding." The face is 75% copper and 25% nickel and the core is pure copper, which is visible on the edges of the coins. All clad material is purchased from outside manufacturers. The manufacturing processes are the same as for the five-cent piece. The edges of the dimes, quarters, half-dollars, and dollars are reeded during the stamping operation.

Coin Distribution. All denominations are inspected, then counted and bagged preparatory to shipment. Coins produced for circulation are shipped by the mints only to the Federal Reserve banks for distribution to commercial banks. Huge tractor-trailer trucks—some measuring 55 feet in length and 13½ feet in height—transport the coins to the Federal Reserve banks. Dimes, quarters, and half-dollars are sacked $1,000 per bag for each denomination; nickels are sacked $200 per bag, and cents $50 per bag. The Anthony dollar is shipped $2,000 to the bag. The Philadelphia Mint formerly made all canvas bags used to ship coins. Now all are purchased from commercial suppliers.

Coin Designs. What goes on United States coins is to a great extent controlled by law. For instance, law requires an impression emblematic of liberty, with an inscription of the word *liberty,* the year of the coinage, the inscriptions *United States of America,* and *E Pluribus Unum,* a designation of the value of the coin, and the motto *In God we trust.* The figure or representation of an eagle is also required on the quarter, half-dollar, and dollar coins, but not on the dime, nickel, and cent. Coins issued for special events—such as the bicentennial of American independence, the George Washington commemorative half-dollar, or the Olympic coin program—are authorized by the Congress, and the legislation usually allows a wider latitude in the selection of the design elements.

No change may be made in the design of any United States coin more often than once in 25 years without legislative authority of the Congress. However, there is no provision that a design must be changed upon the expiration of that period.

The director of the Mint recommends what designs shall appear on coins. However, the design elements may also be detailed in specific legislation. In selecting the artist, sometimes a number of sculptors are invited to compete. On other occasions national competitions, some open to all, have been held. Also, through the years Mint sculptors have prepared the designs. The components of the design may be prescribed, or the artists may be permitted to submit designs of their own choosing. Designs are reviewed by the Commission of Fine Arts for artistic merit, and they are submitted to the secretary of the Treasury, who has the responsibility for final approval. All details of execution and manufacture are handled by the director of the Mint.

Mint Marks. In the beginning, with only the Philadelphia Mint in operation, identification of coinage was unnecessary. Mint marks, or the absence of them, were initiated with the advent of the branch mints to identify each manufacturing unit and serve as a quality control, assuring that correct standards of production were observed. Coinage dies used by the mints are manufactured at the Philadelphia Mint and supplied to the field facilities. Mint marks are hand-stamped on them prior to shipment. Because of its secondary position in any coin design, it has been the custom to make the mint marks as inconspicuous as possible. See Tables 1 and 2 for a list of mint marks.

Coin Content. Today, five denominations of coins are being manufactured for circulation: the cent, nickel, dime, quarter, and half-dollar.

The traditional 90% silver coinage was gradually phased out and cupronickel-clad coinage introduced when the Coinage Act of 1965 removed all silver from the dime and quarter and reduced the silver content of the half-dollar to 40%. P. L. 91-607, approved December 31, 1970, removed the remaining silver from the half-dollar and, in providing for the resumption of dollar coinage, directed that both denominations produced for circulation be cupronickel-clad metal. A special provision authorized a separate striking for collector purposes in 40% silver-clad metal of the then newly adopted dollar design bearing the likeness of the late President Dwight David Eisenhower and a design emblematic of the symbolic eagle of *Apollo II* landing on the moon.

P. L. 95-447, approved October 10, 1978, further amended the Coinage Act of 1965 to provide for changes in the design, weight, and size of the $1 coin. Beginning in January 1979, the likeness of Susan B. Anthony replaced the Eisenhower likeness on the obverse, but the *Apollo II* moon landing was retained on the reverse. Sized between the half-dollar and the quarter, it was designed to save in the cost of dollar-bill production and help the circulation of the little-used dollar coin. With a stock on hand of approximately 510 million, coinage was suspended in March 1980 because inventories were more than adequate to meet the needs of business. While there is a continuing demand for dollar notes, there is very little for the dollar coin. The Treasury Department will, of course, continue to provide the nation with a method of exchange that is favored by the public.

To effect every possible savings in government spending, the decision was made to replace the traditional 95% copper cent with a copper-plated zinc coin. Production of the new composition commenced early

Table 2
Special Coins and Sets

	1¢	5¢	10¢	25¢	50¢	$1.00
Regular proof sets	S	S	S	S	S	
Bicentennial silver proof and uncirculated sets				S	S	S
George Washington 1982 silver proof half dollar					S	
George Washington 1982 silver uncirculated half dollar					D	
1983 and 1984 Olympic silver proof dollars						S
1983 and 1984 Olympic silver uncirculated dollars						P-D-S
1984 Olympic proof and uncirculated $10 gold coins produced at West Point. Mint mark W.						

Table 1
Current Mint Marks

Institution	1¢	5¢	10¢	25¢	50¢	$1.00
Philadelphia	No mark	P	P	P	P	
Denver	D	D	D	D	D	
San Francisco	No mark	—	—	—	—	
West Point*	No mark	—	—	—	—	—

(Philadelphia, Denver, San Francisco, and West Point entries bracketed as "General Circulation")

Note: Former mints—C (Charlotte, North Carolina, 1838–1861), CC (Carson City, Nevada, 1870–1893), D (Dahlonega, Georgia, 1838–1861), O (New Orleans, Louisiana, 1838–1909).

*No mint mark used on West Point and San Francisco coins for general circulation to assure that the limited quantities produced at these facilities will not be withdrawn by collectors or investors.

Table 3
Composition of Current Coins

1 cent: 97.6% zinc and 2.4% copper.
5 cents: 75% copper and 25% nickel alloy.

The dime, quarter, and half-dollar are clad metal, or bonded, coins. The outside layers are composed of a 75% copper and 25% nickel alloy. The core contains pure copper. The outer layers are bonded to the core, and represent one-third of the total thickness of the coin. If the coins were to be melted, the composition would be 91.66% copper and 8.33% nickel.

The new small-size dollar authorized by P. L. 95-447, approved October 10, 1978, is also cupronickel-clad, 75% copper and 25% nickel on the outside with a pure copper core. If melted, it would contain 87.5% copper and 12.5% nickel.

in 1982 and conversion was fully implemented by the end of the year. Both types are circulating simultaneously. They are identical in size, shape, color, and design, but the copper-plated zinc cent is somewhat lighter, having a standard weight of 2.50 grams as opposed to the 3.11-gram standard weight of the copper cent. The outer surface of the planchet or blank, including the edge, is barrel-electroplated with copper. This modification will reduce metal costs by $25 million a year. (See Table 3.)

How Money Gets into Circulation. The nation's coinage requirements have been increasing steadily over the past years. From a total production of 2,802,241,716 pieces in 1960, the amount of coin needed increased to 19,458,707,386 pieces in 1982. As an operating bureau of the Department of the Treasury, the Mint is responsible for producing coins in quantities sufficient to fill these needs. The Mint performs this function by producing and issuing coins to the 37 Federal Reserve banks and branches, which in turn distribute available coin supplies to commercial banks.

To achieve a smooth flow, it is necessary that the techniques for estimating coin demand be continually reviewed and revised. As indicated, the supply of our coins is governed by the needs of business. In planning production and scheduling shipments, the Mint uses historic seasonal trends, such as Christmas, and long-range economic indicators to determine how much should be manufactured. Since experience has shown that forecasting the demand cannot be done with absolute accuracy, estimates must include an amount sufficient to provide an inventory that would absorb any deviations that might occur.

The mints ship coin for circulation only to the Federal Reserve banks and branches. There, it is stored until needed to fill orders from the commercial banks, whose responsibility it is to supply businesses and the public. The Reserve banks fill commercial-bank orders from their vault stocks of both new and circulated coin. However, new coin is generally paid out only when stocks of circulated coin are exhausted. Coin orders are filled without regard to date or mint mark. If a commercial bank has excess cash on hand, the coin may be returned to the Federal Reserve banks. Here, it is sorted for fitness. Badly worn or bent coins are returned to the Bureau of the Mint for recoinage. According to Federal Reserve sources, nearly 20 billion coins valued at well over $2 billion pass through their coin-processing units each year. Foreign and counterfeit coins are removed as the coins are processed.

Coin shipments from the Federal Reserve banks are made by armored car, registered mail, or express. The Mint ships one-cent and five-cent coins to the Federal Reserve banks by common carrier. Dimes, quarters, and halves are transported by armored carrier (*see* CURRENCY, HOW IT GETS INTO CIRCULATION).

Medals. The Mint's national medal program commenced in 1860, but medals were produced prior to that time as Congress bestowed awards upon war heroes and in commemoration of special events.

Today, about 300 bronze medals are offered for sale by the Mint under general authority granted to the Mint by the Congress in 1873, and by special legislation from time to time. The John Wayne Medal, mandated by Public Law 96-15, approved May 26, 1979, is an example. The Congress authorized a gold medal to be presented posthumously to the Wayne family. It also directed the Mint to manufacture bronze duplicates for sale to the public.

A special Mint project embraces the production of a five-year series of one-ounce and half-ounce gold medallions authorized by the American Arts Gold Medallion Act of November 10, 1978. The designs are specified in the legislation. The medallions are being marketed commercially by J. Aron & Company. The medallions are not coin of the realm, have no legal-tender properties, and are not intended to be used in lieu of money.

Commemorative Coins. A special commemorative-coin program was carried on from 1892 through 1954. Prior to the World's Fair in Chicago in 1892, private groups approached the Congress for permission to have commemorative coins produced to sell as fundraisers to defray Fair expenses. The idea caught on, and until 1954 many different varieties honoring distinguished persons and marking state and national events were authorized for production at the United States mints. The sponsoring organizations sold them under conditions and at prices determined by them. However, because of abuses that plagued the commercial sales of these limited-edition pieces, counterfeiting problems, and public confusion due to the multiplicity of designs, congressional hearings ensued that resulted in legislation terminating the practice.

The George Washington silver half-dollar authorized by P. L. 97-104, approved December 23, 1981, and issued in 1982 to commemorate Washington's 250th birthday anniversary, was the first commemorative coin to be struck since 1954. The coins were produced and sold by the United States Mint.

Foreign Coinage. Many countries do not have their own minting facilities and the United States performs this function for them on a reimbursable basis, provided the service does not interfere with the required coinage of the United States. Congress granted this authority by act in January 29, 1874, and the first order executed was for the government of Venezuela, in 1876.

Donna Pope

Monetary Control Act of 1980

See FEDERAL RESERVE SYSTEM.

Monetary Policy

The Federal Reserve's actions to influence the cost of money (interest rates) and the availability of money (the growth rate of the money supply) as a means of promoting full employment, economic growth, price stability, and balance in trade and payments flows between the U.S. and the rest of the world.

COMMERCIAL BANKS are the principal conduits through which the FEDERAL RESERVE SYSTEM transmits monetary policy to the economy, because commercial banks create demand-deposit money through their lending. Demand-deposit money is a key component of all money measures whose growth the Federal Reserve seeks to control. The task of controlling bank lending and money-supply growth, however, is exceedingly difficult and complex.

The pace at which banks make loans is dependent on their "reserves." All banking is based on the principle of "fractional reserves"—that some fraction of a bank's assets must be kept in liquid form to meet demand claims from depositors' checks that are presented for collection by other banks, or from depositors withdrawing cash. Only cash assets in excess of this fraction can be used as a base to support new loans. The modern application of reserve requirements by central banks as a monetary-policy control device is rooted in this fundamental banking principle.

The more reserves a bank has, the greater its potential for making new loans and investments. The less reserves it has, or, more precisely, the closer its reserves are to its liquidity margin or to its legal reserve requirements, the smaller its potential for expanding loans and investments. To the Federal Reserve, controlling the growth of bank reserves is the means for controlling the growth of the MONEY SUPPLY.

If the economy is experiencing inflation (rising prices), the Federal Reserve will seek to restrain bank lending by pursuing a "tight" (restrictive) monetary policy, providing banks with reserves at a relatively slow rate. Such a policy will typically lead to a slow rate of money-supply growth and to rising interest rates. If the economy is in a recession (declining output), the Federal Reserve will seek to stimulate banks to lend more by pursuing an "easy" (expansive) monetary policy, providing banks with reserves at a relatively fast rate. Such a policy will typically lead to a fast rate of money-supply growth and to falling interest rates.

The Federal Reserve can alter the quantity of reserves available, and the pace at which reserves are provided to banks, by using either (or a combination) of three policy devices:

1. *Reserve requirements.* The Federal Reserve can change the reserve-requirement percentages it specifies banks must hold against designated deposit liabilities. If it raises reserve requirements, for example, banks have to come up with more required reserves. "Excess" reserves available in the banking system would be immediately reduced as banks earmarked some or all of those reserves to meet the new higher requirements. The Federal Reserve could also change the rules on what bank assets constitute "legal reserves." Currently, only vault cash and deposits at Reserve banks are acceptable. However, if the Federal Reserve allowed any other asset to be used as well, such as government securities, the total amount of "reserves" available in the banking system would immediately expand. Finally, the Federal Reserve could change the base against which banks must keep reserves by including or excluding types of deposits from its list of bank liabilities against which reserves must be maintained.

2. *Discount rate.* The Federal Reserve can raise or lower the interest rate it charges depositories that borrow from it, as a means of discouraging banks from borrowing reserves, or encouraging such borrowing. It can also change the rules under which banks can obtain loans of reserves, and in so doing effectively make more or less reserves available to banks through the DISCOUNT WINDOW.

3. *Open-market operations.* The Federal Reserve can buy or sell government securities in the open market. When the Federal Reserve buys, banks' reserves and the nation's money supply increase because the Federal Reserve pays with checks drawn on itself. When those checks are collected, banks' reserve accounts are increased, as are the private demand-deposit accounts of the securities sellers. Since these checks were not collected against any other private banks, the Federal Reserve's purchase does not "redistribute" reserves and money, but actually creates new reserves and demand deposits.

When the Federal Reserve sells securities, bank reserves and money supply decline. Private purchasers—government-securities dealer firms—pay with checks drawn on their banks. When the Federal Reserve collects these checks, it reduces the reserve accounts of the banks on which the checks were drawn just as the banks reduce the demand-deposit balances of their dealer depositors. Since these reserves and deposits do not get transferred into other commercial banks, as they would in a private transaction, but are retained by the Federal Reserve, the effect is a reduction in bank reserves and money supply.

While the Federal Reserve has the power to use these three devices, it relies on open-market operations as its basic device for controlling reserves.

Monetary Policy Decision-Making. The 12-member Federal Open Market Committee (FOMC) is the monetary policy decision-making body of the Federal Reserve, the entity that effectively determines the cost and availability of money and credit in the U.S. economy. A discussion of the committee is found under FEDERAL RESERVE SYSTEM.

Implementing Monetary Policy. The effect of a Federal Reserve open-market purchase is to increase bank reserves and money supply immediately. However, there are also powerful secondary effects. Banks whose deposits have increased by virtue of dealers' sales of securities to the Federal Reserve find that they have to keep somewhat more required reserves against the dealers' new funds but have a significant margin of excess reserves against which new loans can be made.

Since excess reserves are not earning assets, banks with excess reserves will seek to turn them into income-generating assets by making loans or investing in government securities. The recipients of these bank loans (or investments) take their newly created money and spend it in the economy, and these funds get deposited by others in banks throughout the country. The total of deposits in the banking system increases. Required reserves increase by a fraction, but excess reserves appear in many different banks. This leads to still more bank lending and an expansion in the money supply several times greater than the amount of the Federal Reserve's initial open-market purchase that started the process.

When the Federal Reserve sells from its $130 billion portfolio (1982), the initial impact of the sale is a reduction in the excess reserves of those banks whose depositors purchased the securities. Indeed, if some of those banks had no excess reserves, they would be plunged into a temporary reserve deficiency as the checks of their depositors were collected by the Federal Reserve in payment for the securities sold. Banks in that predicament will seek to obtain the reserves they need to meet reserve requirements by selling government securities they maintain in their own portfolios, borrowing from other banks (federal funds), borrowing from Federal Reserve, calling in loans, or making some other adjustment in their assets or liabilities.

Banks that simply lose excess reserves may not have to make such extensive adjustments immediately. However, most banks commit themselves to borrowers well in advance of the dates the loans are due to be granted. Those commitments are typically based on a bank's projection of its reserve and deposit growth. If the reserves don't materialize, then to honor those commitments banks must go through the same asset or liability adjustments as banks with reserve deficiencies.

An individual bank can meet a reserve deficiency by adjusting its assets or liabilities. However, it is impossible for the banking system as a whole to meet a reserve deficiency if the total of all reserves available to banks is less than the amount needed by all banks to meet reserve requirements. No combination of asset and liability adjustments by banks will create new reserves. At best, a given bank can transfer its reserve deficiency to another bank, or a group of smaller banks can redistribute their reserve deficiencies to one or two large money-market banks. But, on balance, the banking system will still hold the same amount of reserves as before.

If the intent of monetary policy in effecting such a reserve deficiency is to reduce the money supply, then, within days, the money supply would indeed decline as bank loans were repaid and no new loans were made. It's only when the total deposit base of the banking system declines that the available reserves will equal the amount needed to meet reserve requirements.

In practice, the Federal Reserve rarely, if ever, uses its open-market operations in such a blunt way when it wants to restrain bank lending and money-supply growth. Rather, it implements restraint in a gradual and more subtle way, reducing the rate at which it supplies reserves, not the level. As expansion of reserves begins to slow against strong demand for reserves by banks to make loans, the cost of reserves begins to rise. The increased cost of reserves means that banks will have to charge a higher interest rate on loans. Some banks will begin to see a falloff in loan demand from customers who are unwilling to pay higher interest rates for borrowed funds.

Monetary Policy and the Economy. Monetary restraint invariably leads to higher interest rates, which can have a dampening effect on the nation's financial markets and on industries, such as housing, that are dependent on credit availability. Monetary restraint can also slow the economy's growth and help generate higher levels of unemployment. However, in a period of inflation, monetary restraint is essential for restoring noninflationary, balanced economic growth.

The inflation of the 1970s posed a profound challenge to U.S. monetary policy. Consumers, businesses, and banks had developed deep-rooted inflationary expectations, and these expectations established themselves in spending, borrowing, and lending attitudes and practices that added to the economy's inflationary momentum. Unemployment reached record highs in key sectors of the economy, and productivity and business investment spending remained exceedingly low. In the 1970s the U.S. economy demonstrated an unhealthy dependency on imported oil, which made the economy susceptible to price "shocks" from abroad. This added to inflation and impaired economic growth. Some of the nation's key industries, like the auto industry, lost much of their competitiveness to foreign industry. By the late 1970s, widespread consumer and business skepticism began to develop about the ability of U.S. monetary policy to stop inflation.

The Federal Reserve's policies came under substantial public and governmental scrutiny in 1981 as a new administration and a new Congress initiated a fundamental reappraisal of and redirection for the conduct of U.S. economic policy. What emerged was a recognition that (1) because the problem of inflation developed over many years, its solution cannot be achieved quickly; and (2) while monetary restraint is absolutely essential for stopping inflation, the effectiveness of monetary policy depends on how well government spending and tax policy (FISCAL POLICY) and government regulations complement monetary restraint.

David H. Friedman

Money

Money is perhaps man's most useful discovery, next to fire. Through the device of money, a system of exchange for goods and services in society is effected. But *money* is not an easily defined term, because its definition lies more in what it does than what it is. To grasp fully the significance of money, a look at the roles it plays will be helpful.

It is interesting that the use of money in various forms has occurred in different and widely separated cultures throughout the world. It appeared in the Hebraic-Egyptian world described in the Bible and the Greco-Latin world in forms very similar to those we know today. But it also appeared in many primitive cultures separated by thousands of miles and hundreds of years of development. For example, the Yap Islanders evolved a money made of brightly colored feathers stitched neatly into bands; and, closer to home, the American Indian tribes had evolved wampum, strings of beads, as their money. The early American colonists readily adopted the Indian wampum to fill the gap in their money-short economy

until a few greedy individuals learned to counterfeit the wampum and destroyed its value, and thus its usefulness.

If one approaches the concept of money logically, one has to ask why money seemed to appear somewhat spontaneously in so many different, far-flung locations and cultures. The answer that comes readily to mind is really quite simple. Money probably evolved out of man's experience in trying to exchange values—buy and sell—under various systems of barter.

Barter. Let's suppose for a few moments that you had no money but did have a small supply of various commodities to trade. Let's also suppose you desperately needed a jack handle to repair a flat tire.

If you took your supply of commodities—say, a carton of cigarettes, a gallon of gasoline, five pounds of jelly beans, and a fishing rod—to your neighbor who had a jack handle, he might be willing to trade the jack handle for one or more of your commodities. Then again, he might not.

Just for argument's sake, let's say your neighbor had the only jack handle within 100 miles and wouldn't lend it to you for an hour, much less part with it permanently, for less than ten pounds of pot roast. Luckily, you know someone who has some extra pot roast, but he won't part with it for less than four bottles of Burgundy.

You can readily see how, under barter, you could spend considerable time and effort simply trying to match your wants with those of your neighbors. And that transaction was for only *one* rather specific item. Consider the difficulties involved in trying to barter for the everyday items of survival.

Frustration = Money. You can now easily see how money came into use and how its functions—the qualities that make an item money—were established.

The first and most important quality money must possess is fairly obvious: It must be something that is widely acceptable, something many people will accept in exchange for something else. Wide acceptability also implies that the item must have some value. It can be valuable because it is valuable in and of itself, such as gold or diamonds. It may also be valuable because it is useful, such as salt or cattle. Value, in turn, implies a certain degree of scarcity. Only a limited quantity is available. Surprisingly, while we today consider precious metals and gems valuable primarily because of their scarcity, they were also prized by the ancients because of their usefulness both as decorative items and as special items to be used in religious worship.

If the item designated as money is widely acceptable, it becomes a medium of *exchange*. You accept it in exchange for what you have because you're confident another person will accept it in exchange for something you want. Given that confidence, you can progress to a more sophisticated level on the economic ladder—being able to exchange an item of no inherent value for a given value in return.

If an item is widely acceptable for a period of time, the value of other items begins to settle into a pattern in which similar items take on similar, and relative, values. Thus, bread will sell at one price, and cake or pastry at another. As this happens, money takes on its second function, as a standard of value. In this way, such diverse items as a pound of fish, a bushel of wheat, 12 ears of corn, and 10 pounds of nails, can all be equal in value to, say, 50 fishhooks. A later refinement in the history of money was the development of the concept of *fractional value*. This allowed people to exchange, say 1½ bushels of corn for 3½ pounds of fish. Every time we buy an item for $1.90 and receive 10 cents change from $2, we are practicing the *fractional value* aspect of money.

Money's last function may seem somewhat simplistic in terms of primitive societies, but in our modern society it takes on monumental importance. To work well, money must also serve *as a store of value*. In short, you must be able to hold money for later use. Ice cream might make a good money outdoors in Antarctica, but in Miami, without refrigerators, it would be worthless.

Throughout history we've tried a variety of items as money, only to find that in the end they were poor stores of value. Even gold, which we prize so highly, has at times failed as a store of value. The reason is simple and yet complex. It's all involved in another economic condition, known as INFLATION.

While the reason is simply stated, the concept is not that easily explained. Basically, inflation occurs when the amount of money available for purchasing goods and services exceeds the amount of goods and services that can be purchased. If you consider money as a ticket that allows you to buy a given amount of goods and services, and the supply of what you can buy is limited, it stands to reason that the more you buy, the lower the supply gets. At some point the supply will reach the level where sellers will demand more tickets, or claims, for each unit you try to buy.

Inflation has been experienced again and again by almost every civilization. For example, Alexander the Great conquered so much territory, and took so much booty from the conquered, that he reduced the value of money in what was then the known world by one-third.

A perhaps more recognizable example occurred in colonial Virginia. At that time tobacco was the prime crop. Because the colonists lacked money, but had a valuable commodity, they decided to use tobacco leaves as their money. One use for this "tobacco money" was to pay the salaries of local ministers. Things went well until the colonists had a bumper crop of tobacco. Their prime market, London, became so saturated that the value of the crop dropped sharply. Tobacco became substantially cheaper. A hundred pounds was suddenly worth what 50 pounds had been worth in buying power the year before. The ministers, who had signed a contract for 50 pounds of tobacco, now found their salaries cut in half, and sued.

The outcome of the suit is irrelevant in relation to its cause. Clearly, money, in both examples, failed in its most important function. Further examples could fill volumes, but the major point is that at times money has failed so badly as a *store of value* that it's become enormously cheapened or disappeared as a medium of exchange for a time.

From Precious to Paper. The shift from precious metals to paper began in medieval Europe. Precious metals became too risky to hold and too heavy to transport, so the wealthy began to leave their precious metals with goldsmiths, who had the ability to protect it.

Gradually, a system evolved whereby transfers of money to another party or parties could be made by letter of instruction. A short while later, these letters of instruction were used to settle payments between third, fourth, fifth, and sixth parties. The letters, representing value held by the goldsmith, began to represent value in themselves, because they were used in place of the value of gold held by the goldsmith and could be exchanged for precious metal at any time.

This period in money's evolution gave us three important consequences. First, money was no longer directly tied to something of intrinsic value. Second, the goldsmiths became bankers, intermediaries, holding and transferring value. Third, the ability to transfer value by slips of paper set the stage for the development of the most important form of money used today—checks.

The Long Haul. The intermediate functions performed by the goldsmiths were just a first step. Over the next few years, further refinements were added.

For a few hundred years, banks issued paper money. Since these notes could be redeemed in silver or gold, the banks' ability to issue notes was limited by their holdings of precious metal. As the Western world moved into the twentieth century, however, economists and governments began to recognize the essential truth that the value of money was directly related to what it could buy, rather than its backing in previous metals.

The Modern World. Today, the value of money reflects its ability to buy goods and services. Governments have devised statistical measures that reflect how much of a given basket of goods and services their money can purchase. Thus, money has come full circle from the time when it was worth what it could acquire, through the period when its value reflected its intrinsic worth, back to a measurement of what it could accomplish.

Charles J. Parnow

Money Market

Economic units, such as financial institutions, other business firms, governmental units, and even individuals, find, as a rule, that their inflow of cash receipts does not coincide exactly with their cash disbursements. The typical economic unit finds that on some days its cash holdings build up because receipts exceed outlays. On other days, it might experience a sharp reduction in cash balances because spending outstrips cash inflow.

One of the most important reasons for holding cash reserves is to bridge the gap between receipts and outlays and to ensure that a planned stream of expenditures can be maintained somewhat independently of cash inflow. There are, of course, other reasons for holding reserves. In particular, depository institutions must meet legal reserve requirements.*

Maintenance of cash reserves involves cost, either in the form of interest paid on borrowed balances or in the form of interest forgone on nonborrowed balances that have not been lent out. For many economic units, especially large firms, these costs can be significant, particularly in periods of high interest rates. To minimize such costs, economic units usually seek to keep their cash holdings at a minimum consistent with their working capital needs and, in the case of depository institutions, with their reserve requirements. This may be done by holding low-risk and highly marketable income-bearing assets instead of cash and by maintaining access to the market for short-term credit. The institution of the "money market" has evolved to meet the needs of such economic units. The term *money market* applies not to one but rather to a group of markets. In the early part of the United States' financial history, the term was frequently used in a narrow sense to denote the market for call loans to securities brokers and dealers. At other times in the past, it has been employed broadly to

* As a result of the Depository Institutions Deregulation and Monetary Control Act of 1980, all depository institutions must meet federal reserve requirements on reservable liabilities, i.e., transaction accounts and nonpersonal time deposits. These requirements are prescribed in Regulation D of the Federal Reserve System.

embrace some long-term as well as short-term markets. In current usage, the term *money market* generally refers to the markets for short-term credit instruments such as Treasury bills, commercial paper, bankers' acceptances, negotiable certificates of deposit (CD's), loans to securities dealers, repurchase agreements, and federal funds.

In general, money-market instruments are issued by obligors of the highest credit rating, and are characterized by a high degree of safety of principal. Maturities may be as long as one year but usually are of 90 days or less, and sometimes span only a few days or even one day. The market for money-market instruments is extremely broad and on a given day it can absorb a large volume of transactions with relatively little effect on yields. The market is also highly efficient and allows quick, convenient, and low-cost trading in virtually any volume. Unlike organized securities or commodities markets, the money market has no specific location. Like other important financial markets in this country, its center is in New York, but it is primarily a "telephone" market and is easily accessible from all parts of the nation as well as foreign financial centers. No economic unit is ever more than a telephone call away from the money market.

At the center of the money market are numerous "money-market banks," including the large banks in New York and other important financial centers; about 34 government-securities dealers, some of which are large banks; a dozen-odd commercial-paper dealers; a few bankers' acceptance dealers; and a number of money brokers who specialize in finding short-term funds for money-market borrowers and placing such funds for money-market tenders. The most important money-market brokers are the major federal-funds brokers in New York.

Market Participants. Apart from the groups that provide the basic trading machinery, money-market participants usually enter the market either to raise short-term funds or to convert cash surpluses into highly liquid interest-bearing investments. Funds may be raised by borrowing outright, by selling holdings of money-market instruments, or by issuing new instruments. The issue and sale of new money-market instruments is, of course, a form of borrowing.

Generally, money-market rates are below the prime lending rates of the large money-market banks. Consequently, borrowers who have the ability to do so find it advantageous to tap the money market directly rather than obtaining funds through banking intermediaries. The U.S. Treasury, many commercial banks, large sales finance companies, and well-known nonfinancial corporations of the highest credit standing borrow regularly in the money market by issuing their own short-term debt obligations. Short-term loans to government-securities dealers, loans of reserves among depository institutions, and Federal Reserve DISCOUNT WINDOW loans to depository institutions are also money-market instruments, although they do not give rise to negotiable paper.

Suppliers of funds in the market are those who buy money-market instruments or make very short-term loans. Potentially, these include all those economic units that can realize a significant gain through arranging to meet future cash requirements by holding interest-bearing liquid assets in place of nonearning cash balances. The major participants on this side of the market are commercial banks, state and local governments, large nonfinancial businesses, nonbank financial institutions, and foreign bank and nonbank businesses. In recent years individuals have also become a significant supplier of funds to the money market, both indirectly through investment in short-term investment pools, such as money-market mutual funds, and directly through the purchase of Treasury bills and short-term federal-agency securities.

By far the most important market participant is the FEDERAL RESERVE SYSTEM. Through the Open Market Trading Desk at the New York Federal Reserve Bank, which executes the directives of the Federal Open Market Committee, the System is in the market on a virtually continuous basis, either as a buyer or as a seller, depending on financial conditions and monetary-policy objectives. The System's purpose in entering the market is quite different from that of other participants, however. As noted in greater detail below, the Federal Reserve buys and sells in certain parts of the money market not with the objective of managing its own cash position more efficiently but rather to supply or withdraw bank reserves in order to achieve its monetary-policy objectives. In addition, the Federal Reserve enters the market as an agent, sometimes as a buyer and sometimes as a seller, for the accounts of foreign official institutions and for the U.S. Treasury. Overall, the operations of the Federal Reserve dwarf those of any other money-market participant.

Interrelation and Size of the Various Market Sectors. While the various money-market instruments have their individual differences, they nonetheless are close substitutes for each other in many investment portfolios. For this reason the rates of return on the various instruments tend to fluctuate closely together. For short periods of time, the rate of return on a particular instrument may diverge from the rest or "get out of line," but this sets in motion forces that tend to pull the rates back together. For example, a large supply of new commercial paper may produce a rapid run-up of commercial-paper rates, resulting in a relatively large spread between these rates and rates on CD's. Sophisticated traders note the abnormal differential and shift funds from CD's into commercial paper, causing CD rates to rise and commercial-paper rates to fall. In this way, a more "normal" or usual rate relation is restored. This process, known as "interest arbitrage," ensures general conformity of all money-market rates to major interest-rate movements.

A measure of the relative dimensions of the various money-market sectors may be obtained from data, shown in Table 1, on amounts outstanding and trading volume. The table illustrates that short-term Treasury issues constitute the backbone of the money market's stock-in-trade. The volume outstanding of short-term Treasury issues is the largest among the money-market instruments and the daily average volume of transactions is exceeded only by that of federal

---

Table 1
Selected Money-Market Instruments: Volume Outstanding and Volume of Trading, December 1980 ($ millions)

	Volume Outstanding	Volume of Transactions (daily average)
U.S. government securities:		
Treasury bills	216,104	13,751*
Other, 1 year or less	81,281	466*
Federal agencies, within 1 year	31,637†	1,285*
Negotiable certificates of deposit	116,374	2,472*
Bankers' acceptances	54,744	
Commercial paper placed through dealers	56,985	
Directly placed commercial paper of financial companies	68,083	
Federal funds and repurchase agreements		82,753‡

* Figures include only transactions of U.S. government security dealers reporting to the Federal Reserve Bank of New York (average of five weeks ending in December).

† Federally sponsored agency debt with an original maturity of one year or less as of December 1979.

‡ Gross funds purchased in federal funds and repurchase agreements (one day and continuing contract) by banks with assets of $1 billion or more on December 31, 1977 (average of five weeks ending in December).

Sources: Federal Reserve Bulletin, "Dealer Transactions in U.S. Government and Agency Securities and Negotiable Certificates of Deposit," Federal Reserve Bank of New York; various federally sponsored credit agencies.

funds and repurchase agreements. Commercial paper and negotiable CD's rank next-highest in terms of amount outstanding.

The Market's Significance. The money market provides an important source of short-term funds for many borrowers. In addition, since there is a continuous flow of loan funds through the market, it is possible for borrowers, through successive "roll-overs," or renewals of loans, to raise funds on a more or less continuous basis and in this fashion to finance not only their immediate cash requirements but also working capital and some long-term capital needs as well. By bringing together quickly and conveniently those units with cash surpluses and those with cash deficits, the market promotes a more intensive use of the cash balances held in the economy.

The market is especially important to COMMERCIAL BANKS in managing their money positions. Banks in the aggregate are large-scale buyers and sellers of most money-market instruments, especially federal funds. The money market permits a more intensive use of bank reserves and enhances the ability of the commercial banking system to allocate funds efficiently. By allowing banks to operate with lower excess reserves, it also makes the banking system more sensitive to central-bank policy actions.*

Finally, the money market is an eminently free and competitive market, and the yields on money market instruments react instantaneously to changes in supply and demand. As a result, the behavior of the market provides the most immediate indication of the current relationship between credit supplies and credit demands.

The Federal Reserve and the Money Market. The Federal Reserve System influences the money market not only through open-market operations but also through the discount windows of the 12 Federal Reserve banks. Commercial banks may borrow short-term from the Federal Reserve to meet temporary liquidity needs and to cover reserve deficiencies as an alternative to selling money-market securities or borrowing federal funds. Similarly, banks with cash or reserve surpluses can repay outstanding borrowings at the Federal Reserve rather than invest the surpluses in money-market instruments.

Reserve adjustments made by individual institutions using the discount window differ in one important respect from alternative adjustment techniques. Trading in such instruments as federal funds, negotia-

ble certificates of deposit, and Treasury bills among commercial banks or between banks and their customers involves no net creation of new bank reserves; rather, existing reserves are simply shifted about within the banking system. On the other hand, net borrowings or repayments at the discount window result in a net change in Federal Reserve credit outstanding, and consequently they affect the volume of bank reserves. Thus, the choice by individual institutions between using the discount window or alternative means of reserve adjustment may influence the supply of money and credit in the economy. Decisions to use the discount window or raise funds elsewhere in the money market depend importantly upon the relation of the Federal Reserve's discount rate to yields on money-market investments and on the legal and administrative arrangements surrounding use of the discount window. Both sets of factors are determined primarily by Federal Reserve actions.

The daily operations of the Federal Open Market Trading Desk occupy a central role in the money market. For many years the Desk has conducted transactions in U.S. government securities and in bankers' acceptances, and in December 1966 it was authorized to conduct operations in federal-agency issues also. The Federal Reserve enters the market frequently either to provide new depository-institution reserves through purchases or to withdraw reserves through sales. To a large extent, Federal Reserve operations are undertaken to compensate for changes in other factors that affect the volume of reserves, such as float, Treasury balances, and currency in circulation. Such operations are undertaken primarily to ensure the smooth technical functioning of the market mechanism. But the operations of the greatest importance from the standpoint of the economy are those undertaken by the Federal Reserve to achieve its policy objectives. Since the early 1970s, these objectives have centered on achieving targeted growth rates of the money supply. Thus, in addition to its other functions, the money market serves as the mechanism for implementing the Federal Reserve's objectives.

James Parthemos

Money-Market Deposit Accounts

Market-rate, federally insured investment accounts that allow limited third-party transactions.

In legislation signed into law in October 1982, Congress called on federal regulators to authorize a new account that would be "directly equivalent to and competitive with" money-market mutual funds. The money-market deposit account and the SUPER NEGOTIABLE ORDER OF WITHDRAWAL (NOW) ACCOUNT were the regulators' response to this order.

---

*As the phase-in of required reserves for nonbank depository institutions, mandated by the Depository Institutions Deregulation and Monetary Control Act of 1980, progresses, it is likely that these institutions will also become active in the market for reserve funds.

Money-market deposit accounts require a minimum deposit.* The customer must maintain a minimum balance in the account to receive market yields. If the monthly average balance on the account drops below the minimum, the bank is required to drop the interest rate. However, as long as the minimum deposit is maintained, there is no interest-rate ceiling required by law on the account—banks are free to offer any interest rate they choose.

There are limits on the transaction capabilities of this account, but the limits allow for substantial liquidity. Federal regulations permit no more than six transfers on the account each month, and only three of these can be checks or other payment orders to third parties. However, cash withdrawals from these accounts are unlimited.

The important aspect to remember about these accounts is that they are investments that allow limited access to funds.

To open a money-market deposit account, simply go to the "New Accounts" desk at your bank.

Phil Battey

Money-Market Fund

See MONEY-MARKET MUTUAL FUNDS.

Money-Market Mutual Funds

Money-market mutual funds have won swift and widespread acceptance in the United States. Individuals and corporations alike have flocked to these investment vehicles, which offer attractive yields, liquidity, safety, stability, and convenience. By the fall of 1983, some 300 money-market funds existed, with total assets around $160 billion and well over 12 million shareholder accounts. Before examining the types, benefits, and uses of the money-market mutual funds, it might be helpful to look at how the money market operates.

The Money Market. If you have the notion that the "money market" is located in the heart of a great financial center, then you will be frustrated in your efforts to find it. It simply doesn't exist in any central place, like a stock exchange. The "money market" exists throughout the country and extends even to such financial centers as London and the Bahamas. Participants include large corporations, banks, the federal government, and local governments.

When large corporations, banks, and governments need cash for a very short period of time, they borrow

it in the "money market" by issuing money-market instruments. In return, other large corporations, banks, institutions, and very wealthy individuals purchase these instruments. Generally, the instruments pay attractive interest rates because the amounts are very large, the maturities are very short, and the instruments are backed only by the good name and reputation of the borrower.

The money market is made up of a variety of securities. Of particular importance are the following:

Treasury bills. Short-term obligations of the United States government. They are sold at a discount (an amount less than the $10,000 face value paid at maturity; the difference between the discount price and the face value reflecting yield) through competitive biddings. Currently, 91-day and 182-day bills are offered at a regular weekly auction, while offering of 52-week bills are made on a monthly basis.

Certificates of deposit. Sold to the public by commercial banks and savings and loans for money deposited for a minimum time period—14 days, 91 days, 6 months, 30 months, etc.—with a specified fixed rate of return regulated by the Federal Reserve. Usually if the amount of the certificate is $100,000 or less, it is guaranteed by an agency of the federal government. Rates for certificates over $100,000 may be negotiated.

Commercial paper. Unsecured IOU's issued to the public by large corporations and institutions to finance their short-term business needs—usually in amounts of $100,000 or more for up to 9 months.

Bankers' acceptances. Drafts issued and sold by banks with a promise to pay at maturity—usually 180 days or less. They are traded at a discount in amounts of $25,000 to $1 million or more.

Repurchase agreements (repos). Short-term transaction agreements initiated by securities dealers and banks who hold inventories of Treasury bills, notes, and bonds well in excess of capital—requiring them to borrow to finance securities inventory. Therefore, a repurchase agreement represents the temporary sale of these securities to investors holding surplus cash, with the agreement to buy them back at some future date—often the next day.

Eurodollar certificates of deposit. Short-term obligations of large U.S. or foreign commercial banks, payable outside the United States. The minimum is usually $1 million with a maturity of 14 days or longer.

Government-agency obligations. Short-term securities issued by a U.S. government agency and sometimes backed/guaranteed by the U.S. Treasury or the right of the agency to borrow from the U.S. Treasury.

As indicated above, most money-market instruments have maturities of less than one year and are bought and sold in denominations of $100,000—but

---

* By 1986, money-market deposit accounts will have no legal minimum deposit requirement. However, banks will have the option to set minimum deposit requirements.

more often in $1-million units. So unless a saver or an investor is among the very wealthy or can afford to tie up large amounts of cash for a fixed time period, the best opportunity to get into the money market is to invest in a money-market fund. For a more detailed discussion on the above, *see* MONEY MARKET.

The Money-Market Fund. The money-market mutual fund (often just called "money-market fund") was created in 1972, but until 1974 few money-market mutual funds existed. Their origin is generally credited to the desire of smaller individuals and businesses to get into the money market. However, today, because of the range of benefits and uses offered by funds, even large banks, corporations, and other institutions are investing heavily for current income as well as using money-market mutual funds as a part of their cash-management programs.

A money-market fund is a MUTUAL FUND that operates on the principle of "pooling." A fund receives cash daily from many sources—both small and large investors. Each day this cash is pooled into one large sum and is used to purchase money-market instruments. Because these purchases are made each day throughout the year, and the purchases are of securities with various maturities and yields, *interest* is also earned each day. The interest, less expenses to pay for administering and managing the fund, is passed along to the investors.

Relative Safety. Many investors and savers ask: "How safe are money-market funds?" The answer is "Very safe," but, as with all investments, there is some risk, regardless of how small it may be. While investments in money-market funds are not insured by an agency of the federal government, they have an extraordinary record of safety.

By their very nature, money-market funds invest only in very short-term securities of the U.S. government, large corporate obligations, and certificates of deposit at major banks. It is a widely accepted principle that the shorter the maturity of an investment (the length of time a security is held for payment of face amount and/or any interest earned), the lower the investment risk. As of mid-1983, the average maturity of taxable money-market funds was about 37 days, but maturities ranged from as short as one day to as long as 82 days. The average maturity for a tax-free money-market fund was about 65 days.

Another feature ensuring the safety of money-market funds is the use of "approved investments" lists by portfolio managers. Money-fund managers analyze the relative financial strength of the issuers of money-market instruments and compile lists of corporations, financial institutions, and governments that meet their fund's standards. These lists are re-

viewed and updated on a regular basis, with deletions made anytime an issuer's creditworthiness is questioned.

In addition to the safety associated with very short maturities, money-market funds are regulated by the SECURITIES AND EXCHANGE COMMISSION (SEC), audits are performed at least annually by independent certified public accountants, and independent custodian banks hold the assets of the funds. Shareholder reports are issued periodically, making public the financial statements of the funds, and a prospectus containing complete and detailed information about each fund is updated annually and made available to shareholders. Thus, through a variety of "checks and balances," investors enjoy full disclosure of all material information relative to a fund.

Money-Market-Fund Yields. The yield of a money-market fund changes daily. It is not fixed or guaranteed for any period of time. The yield reflects current money-market rates earned by the underlying securities in the portfolio of the fund. The yield an investor receives is *net* of the expenses of the fund—that is, all the costs of operating the fund (management fees, administrative and possibly distribution costs) are subtracted from the *gross* yield each day to determine the *net* yield earned by the shareholders. For example, the average cost of operating a money-market fund in 1981 was 71/100 of 1%. Thus, if the gross yield of a fund was 12%, the net yield passed on to the shareholders would be 11.29% (12% less .71%).

Features. In addition to high yields and relative safety, money-market funds offer investors a variety of attractive features:

Daily income. Generally, dividends are calculated and credited to an account each day, and are paid to the shareholder in cash at the end of each month.

Liquidity. There is no minimum investment period and no early-withdrawal interest penalty. Generally, money-market-fund shareholders can withdraw money by mail, telephone, bank wire, or by writing themselves a check.

Automatic compounding. Rather than receive dividends in cash at the end of each month, investors have the option of having their dividend income automatically reinvested for them in additional fund shares. This allows shareholders to compound their income, thereby increasing the total return on their initial investment.

Stability of principal. Most money-market funds offer a constant share price (usually $1 or $10), so shareholders should not experience fluctuations in their principal value. This makes it easy for them to determine the value of their investment at any time.

Checkwriting. This service, offered by most funds (usually for free, but some funds require a minimum check of $250 or $500), can be used by shareholders to pay large bills or to replenish their regular checking accounts. Of particular importance to the shareholder is that his or her money continues to earn daily income until the check clears the fund's custodian bank.

No sales charges or redemption fees. Normally, the funds make no charge for buying or selling their shares. In 1983, funds generally were charging expenses of 0.7% a year—that is, about $7 for every $1,000 invested.

Low initial minimum investment. Generally, the minimum investment to open an account in a money-market fund ranges from $500 to $20,000, with most funds' minimums set between $1,000 and $3,000. Thus, almost anyone can open a money-market-fund account. It may be useful to note that most funds do not require shareholders to *maintain* the minimum investment as an average balance. However, most funds do have a limit as to how low a shareholder can take an account balance.

Convenience. In addition to the major services and features listed above, most funds try to make it convenient for their shareholders to conduct their business. (1) Most funds maintain a *toll-free telephone system* or allow a shareholder to *call collect.* This feature is especially helpful for shareholders who may need to contact a fund's customer-service department—to request current yield information, expedite redemptions, exchange shares, ask questions regarding their accounts, etc. (2) *Account statements* are sent to shareholders monthly (some funds send quarterly statements) and generally after every transaction (investment, redemption, or dividend payment). Thus shareholders are kept informed of the current status of their accounts. (3) *Automatic monthly investment plans* are available from most funds for savers who want to have a fixed dollar investment transferred from their regular bank checking accounts directly into their money-market-fund accounts. (4) *Systematic withdrawal plans,* whereby shareholders can instruct the fund to send a check (drawn on the account) to their home or office each month for any amount stated, are available from many funds. (5) *Shareholder reports* containing current financial data and portfolio listings are published and sent to shareholders at least twice annually. (6) *Customized services* are provided to many institutional investors—whether it is subaccounting, net transaction processing, or any other special need required by bank trust departments, investment advisers, trustees, and corporations.

Major Uses of Money-Market Funds. Generally, there is a place for a money-market-fund account in any individual's or organization's financial cash-management, savings, or investment program. Money-market funds can be used by all of the following:

Individuals

- As a place to accumulate cash for a major planned expenditure such as taxes, tuition, new home, new car, home improvement, vacation, etc.
- As a temporary place for depositing large cash inflows—proceeds from the sale of stock or real property, thrift-plan or retirement-plan payouts, an inheritance, a bonus, etc.
- As a place to keep investment capital working until a better opportunity arises.
- As an investment for funding an Individual Retirement Account (IRA), HR-10 Plan (Keogh), and/or a custodian account for dependents under the Uniform Gifts to Minors Act.

Investment Advisers, Accountants, and Attorneys

- As an income-earning alternative for conservative clients who wish to be "out of the market" during certain periods.
- As an account for the temporary deposit of dividends and coupon payments until cash accumulates toward a new investment.
- As a place to accumulate fee income until the cash is actually needed.

Businesses

- As a place to build cash reserves for regular periodic payouts such as payroll, taxes, lease payments, rent, etc., or for major capital expenditures.
- As a convenient place to keep cash for short periods, or until it is actually needed.
- As an account from which to draw current pension and profit-sharing payouts.
- As a part of the corporate employee thrift plan, payroll-deduction IRA, or 401(k) plan.
- As an alternative to a non-interest-bearing checking account.

Government Bodies and Agencies

- As a "cash account" for convenience in meeting short-term cash needs, or for emergencies.
- As a temporary holding place for large periodic inflows of tax revenues.
- As an alternative to a low or non-interest-bearing checking account.

Private Schools and Colleges

- As a convenient place to temporarily hold large, periodic inflows from tuition payments, gifts, etc.
- As a "cash account" to meet unexpected or emergency expenditures.

Churches, Clubs, Charitable Groups, Volunteer Organizations

- As an account for the temporary accumulation of contributions, gifts, proceeds from rummage sales, or cash raised from fund drives.
- As an alternative to a low- or non-interest-bearing checking account.
- As a place to build up cash for major, planned expenditures.

Selecting the Right Money-Market Fund. Selecting the right money-market fund today is not difficult, but does require some homework. First, an investor must select the "type" of fund. Within that type, the investor should evaluate and compare several funds on a few basic features.

For purposes of simplification, generally money-market funds can be categorized into three groups:

General-purpose money-market funds. These types of funds are available to any investor/saver—individuals and institutions. They can be obtained either from a broker or directly from the fund company. However, broker-affiliated funds may not offer all the service features of a "regular" fund and are generally suited for the more active investor. General-purpose funds invest primarily in nongovernment money-market securities (certificates of deposit, commercial paper, bankers' acceptances, etc.).

Governments-only money-market funds. These funds, too, are available to any investor and can be obtained either from a broker or directly from a fund company. They differ from general-purpose funds in that they restrict their investments to only U.S. government or federal-agency securities. They are perceived as less risky and their yields generally average ½% to 2% below those of the general-purpose funds.

Tax-free money-market funds. Again, these types of funds can be obtained directly from the fund company or through a broker. They invest, however, in only short-term tax-exempt municipal bonds. Consequently, their income is not subject to federal income taxes, but may be subject to some state and local taxes. Usually investors in higher tax brackets (above 35%) invest in such funds, since the tax-free nature of the dividends (which are substantially lower than taxable money funds) is most applicable to them.

In addition to the above basic categories, there are "institutional-only" funds and "special-purpose" funds. These funds are *not* open to all investors; they exist to meet the needs of institutional investors such as banks or brokerage firms or special-interest groups.

How to Compare Money-Market Funds. On the surface, all money-market funds within the basic categories (general-purpose, governments-only, and tax-

free) look alike. Therefore, investors usually compare one fund with another by simply checking the yield on each. This is a good beginning. If maximizing current income is an investor/saver's only objective, then higher yield would clearly be "better." But many investors are also interested in preservation of capital and liquidity as part of their investment objective. Consequently, it is necessary to get under the surface and check the factors that *influence* a fund's yield.

Quality of Securities. A money-market fund's yield can be increased simply by downgrading the overall quality of the instruments held in the portfolio. This practice involves the assumption of greater risk. For example, a number of government-only funds invest exclusively or primarily in U.S. Treasury and/or government-agency securities. Since there has never been a default on a U.S. Treasury or government-agency issue, these types of portfolios/funds are considered to offer the greatest amount of safety. Of course, the net yields of these funds generally range from ½% to 2% below those of general-purpose money funds.

Conversely, funds investing heavily in Eurodollar CD's (certificates of deposit issued abroad either by a branch of a U.S. bank or by a foreign bank) and/or Yankee CD's (certificates of deposit issued or payable in the United States by branches of major foreign banks) are generally viewed as less safe because they represent a form of "offshore" investing. However, these securities generally offer yields significantly higher than domestic CD's.

The quality of domestic certificates of deposit and bankers' acceptances is generally assessed by bank size and by evaluating several different financial measures. Generally, banks with assets of more than $2 billion are considered in the top tier of safety.

Many funds also invest in commercial paper, generally of the highest quality. Most commercial paper is rated according to the issuer's financial and competitive position. The ratings (highest to lowest) are as follows: P-1, P-2, P-3 for Moody's Investors Service; A-1, A-2, A-3 for Standard and Poor's; and F-1, F-2, F-3 for Fitch Investors Service.

Maturity and Timing. In general, "the shorter, the safer" is the rule of any fixed-income investment because "going long" (investing in a fund with a very long average maturity) in an effort to lock in higher money-market yields increases the risk of fluctuation in principal value of the underlying securities.

Most money-market funds maintain relatively short maturities (typically less than 50 days) and a stable net asset value (usually $1), in order to minimize any risk of fluctuation in principal.

Of equal importance, however, is the fund's "timing"—that is, structuring the maturities of the individual holdings in each portfolio so as to capture the highest yield for the longest time possible. This is where experienced professional money management plays a vital role. Most money-market funds employ full-time professionals who continually monitor changes in interest-rate levels in order to obtain the highest yield consistent with preservation of capital and liquidity.

Operating Costs. The first two factors—quality of the securities and the maturity and timing of the port-folio—affect a money-market fund's gross yield. The fund's operating costs, though, reduce the gross yield in order to arrive at the net yield an investor receives. The level of a fund's operating expenses is therefore an important factor in determining an investor's level of income; by minimizing operating expenses, the yield can be enhanced without increasing risk.

In 1981 the average money-market fund had an op-erating-expense ratio of 71/100 of 1%. Thus, as stated above, if the *gross* yield of all the securities in a port-folio of money-market securities was 12%, the net yield (earned by an investor) based on an expense ra-tio of .71% would be 11.29% (12% less .71%).

Investing in a Money-Market Fund. To invest in a money-market fund, an investor or saver must, of course, first get information about a fund, preferably more than one so that he can compare benefits and features. The information should include a prospec-tus. Although a prospective investor can find the pro-spectus challenging reading—primarily due to the document's length and detail—he should read careful-ly. In addition to a prospectus, most money-market-fund companies provide literature such as a brochure highlighting the principal features of their funds.

To get information about the more widely known money-market funds, an investor can simply buy a few daily editions of a current *Wall Street Journal,* the Sunday *New York Times,* and many other major con-sumer and business publications. There he will find advertisements for such funds as Vanguard Money Market Trust (Valley Forge, Pennsylvania), Dreyfus Liquid Assets (New York), Fidelity Daily Income Trust (Boston), and T. Rowe Price Reserve Fund, Inc. (Baltimore). He can also contact his broker.

More-complete listings can be obtained from sever-al publishers or associations. The No-Load Mutual Fund Association (Valley Forge, Pennsylvania 19481) provides an extensive listing of the majority of money-market funds as well as a directory of most no-load mutual-fund companies (funds that can be bought without paying a sales commission) at a cost of $1. Also, *Donohue's Money Fund Directory* (Box 540, Holliston, Massachusetts 01746) is available for $15.

It is relatively easy to open a money-market-fund account. You can do so in person (if you live near a money-market-fund company), or by mail or bank wire (money can be sent directly from your bank to most funds). Simply follow the instructions provided in the prospectus. For most funds, you will have to fill out an application. You should request *all* features/ services (such as checkwriting, telephone redemption, etc.) when initially opening the account, even if you have no immediate need for them. This will eliminate additional correspondence at some later date (because the fund company will require proof of identity and fund ownership) should you decide to use these ser-vices in the future.

In summary, money-market funds provide an op-portunity for both large and small investors to earn current money-market rates on their savings and/or investment dollars. However, not all money-market funds are alike. And while selecting the best money-market fund is not complicated, it does require basic knowledge about the money market and the variety of features offered by money-market funds. A saver or investor will need to do some homework to make an informed judgment as to which fund or funds are best suited to his financial objectives.

See also MUTUAL FUND.

Joseph F. Kissel

Money-Multiplier Municipal Trusts

The money-multiplier trust is a portfolio composed of tax-exempt current-coupon, discount, and zero-cou-pon bonds. The trust will have an average life of ap-proximately 30 years and will pay a rate of interest commensurate with the discount trust market plus approximately twice the principal invested if held to maturity. For example, an individual investing at a price of $760 per unit would receive interest income of approximately 11.00% current return annually plus $1,500 at maturity (approximately 30 years).

Moore & Schley Cameron & Company

Money Orders

Payment instruments commonly purchased for a fee. Anyone may purchase a personal money order from a bank, whether or not he or she has an account at the bank. The issuer of the order—not the seller—is re-sponsible for payment of a money order. The bank writes the amount of the order after payment and the purchaser fills in the name of the party to be paid and signs the order.

Phil Battey

Money Supply

The sum of all the funds that the public has immedi-ately available for spending in the domestic economy.

Monetary economists and the Federal Reserve use the money supply as a gauge for predicting and controlling the pace and direction of U.S. economic activity.

M-1 is the narrowest and most commonly used measure of money supply. It totaled $450 billion in mid-1982 and consists of the following:

1. Currency and coin outside the Treasury, Reserve banks, and commercial banks.

2. Demand deposits at all commercial banks except (a) those due to domestic banks, foreign commercial banks, and certain foreign official institutions, and (b) those due to the U.S. government. (In counting demand deposits at all commercial banks, the sum of all cash items in the process of collection [checks] and the sum of Federal Reserve float [credit that banks get for checks sent to Reserve banks for collection before collection is actually made] are subtracted from the total of demand deposits to avoid double counting and thus overstating the size of the money supply.)

3. NOW accounts at commercial banks and thrift institutions.

4. Credit-union share drafts.

5. Those savings deposits at commercial banks and thrift institutions that are subject to automatic transfers.

6. Demand deposits at mutual savings banks.

7. Traveler's checks.

M-2 is the broad measure of the money the public has immediately available for domestic spending. This measure, some $1,900 billion in mid-1982, consists of the following:

1. M-1.

2. Time deposits with minimum denominations of less than $100,000 and savings deposits at banks and thrift institutions.

3. Overnight "Eurodollar" deposits held by U.S. residents at Caribbean branches of U.S. banks.

4. Overnight "Repurchase Agreements" at commercial banks.

5. Money-market mutual-fund shares.

M-3 is a still broader measure of money supply, totaling $2,250 billion in mid-1982 and consisting of:

1. M-2.

2. Term repurchase agreements (those longer than overnight).

3. Time deposits with minimum denominations of $100,000.

L is a broad liquidity measure that consists of:

1. M-3.

2. Eurodollar holdings of U.S. residents not previously counted in the money-supply measures.

3. Bankers' acceptances.

4. Savings bonds.

5. Commercial paper.

6. Marketable liquid Treasury obligations.

This broadest of the money-supply measures totaled $2,650 billion in mid-1982.

About the Money Measures. All measures of the money supply share several definitional characteristics. Each successive (broader) measure of the money supply includes the measure that preceded it, and no measure counts moneys or near-moneys in the hands of banks or the government.

Banks hold money largely to meet Federal Reserve reserve requirements and/or for their own liquidity and business needs. The government manages the money it holds in a unique way, through a set of accounts at thousands of banks and thrift institutions into which all tax receipts and loan proceeds are deposited, called Treasury Tax and Loan accounts, and a set of accounts at the Federal Reserve banks from which all disbursements are made. To include moneys held by banks and the government in the "public" money-supply measures would distort the predictive link between money supply and commercial economic activity.

Checking accounts kept in the U.S. by foreign commercial banks and official institutions are also deleted from all money-supply measures, because these deposits are not generally maintained for use in domestic commercial transactions.

Money Supply and the Federal Reserve. In implementing monetary policy, the Federal Reserve sets a target for money-supply growth and then tries to influence bank lending and interest rates to achieve that target. The Federal Reserve's long-run objective is to provide the U.S. economy with a rate of money-supply growth consistent with its long-run production-growth needs and short-run business conditions. The Federal Reserve also uses money-supply growth rates as a measure of its own success or failure at achieving its operational objectives. A major problem for the Federal Reserve is that economists and statisticians do not know with certainty which measure of money supply is most accurate in predicting and controlling the course of the economy.

Coin, currency, and demand deposits represent America's functioning medium of exchange. However, consumer and business spending decisions are not based solely on the amounts of these three moneys being held. Most of the public's financial assets are not held in money form, but rather in scores of "near-moneys"—items that may be good stores of value and may even be good standards of value, but aren't generally accepted as money.

The public holds only a small fraction of its financial wealth in money form—only about $450 billion in 1982. Several trillion dollars are held in the form of such financial assets as government securities, life-insurance policies, pension funds, money-market funds, and various types of time and savings accounts in commercial banks and thrift institutions. The public held more than $1 trillion in time and savings deposits alone in the nation's banks and thrifts in 1982.

It has become increasingly apparent to monetary economists and to the Federal Reserve that consumers take at least some of these financial assets into consideration when facing major spending decisions. Consumers may look to their savings and time accounts to draw on "savings," or look to their credit cards as a source for borrowing funds, or convert a near-money asset into money to spend. What is not readily apparent, however, is just which financial assets are considered and which aren't.

Measuring Money Supply. The Federal Reserve's money-supply-measurement problem was complicated in the 1970s and 1980s by (1) banking innovations and changes in banking law that allowed banks and thrifts to offer new types of deposits that earn interest (and thus, as "time" deposits, would not be subject to instantaneous use), yet were checkable (subject to demand), and (2) rising deposit interest rates that induced consumers and business firms to transfer non-interest-earning demand-deposit money into interest-earning near-money. In 1980 Congress authorized all depositories across the nation to offer NOW accounts, automatic transfer service accounts, and for credit unions to offer share drafts, making the task of classifying "money" and "near-money" and measuring money supply all the more difficult.

In 1979 and 1981, the Federal Reserve redefined its measures of the money supply to accommodate these changes in banking and public practice. The new money-supply definitions, cited earlier, count similar deposits in the same measure whether they are liabilities of commercial banks or thrifts and include the near-moneys that were products of the financial-system innovations and regulatory changes of the 1970s and 1980s.

Interpreting the Measures. In the 1960s the growth of the narrow M-1 measure of the money supply seemed to offer better predictive results for the course of the U.S. economy than the broader money-supply measures. In the 1970s the M-2 measure came closer to the mark. By the mid-1970s, however, there were sharply divergent growth rates for the narrow M-1 measure and the broader M-2 money-supply measure—then defined as M-1 plus time deposits in commercial banks, except for large CD's. The M-1 money supply was growing slowly; the M-2 money supply quite rapidly.

The reason was that the public was reducing its checkbook balances, seeking to capitalize on the high interest rates offered by banks on time accounts and seeking to utilize the new interest-earning transaction accounts being offered by banks and thrifts. In transferring demand-deposit funds into NOW accounts, and in using such innovations as overdraft accounts, credit cards, and telephone transfers from savings to checking accounts to cover checks, the public effectively blunted the growth of the M-1 measure of money supply while increasing the M-2 measure.

No single measure of money supply can be adequately appraised without taking into account its interrelationship with the other measures. The rapid growth of money-market funds, the advent of nationwide NOW accounts in 1981, and the public's shift, in the early 1980s, from traditional savings-deposit and demand-deposit money into nontraditional near-moneys illustrate (1) the imprecision of the link between any one measure of the money supply and the future level of economic activity and (2) the difficulties monetary policymakers face in seeking to control money-supply growth in accordance with predetermined targets.

David H. Friedman

Moody's Investors Service, Inc.

Moody's Investors Service is regarded as a premier investment research and information service. Known in both the financial and business worlds for its bond ratings, Moody's is also one of the nation's largest publishers. In all, more than 15 million items of current financial and corporate data fill the more than 24,000 pages published by Moody's each year.

Among Moody's major services and publications are the following:

Moody's Manuals and News Reports. Seven individual manuals are published annually, and include a continuously updated series of news reports, published as often as twice weekly. This comprehensive library covers more than 20,000 U.S. and foreign corporations and over 14,000 municipal and government entities. The manuals and updated news reports together detail complete financial and operating data; company histories; comprehensive descriptions of products and services, plant locations, and properties; annual-report statistics, and officer listings. Widely used in the financial and commercial fields as a current source of corporate and government information, *Moody's Manuals* are published in these editions:

Bank and Finance covers over 10,000 organizations in the financial area, including national and state banks, insurance companies, mutual funds, real-estate trusts, finance companies, and other major financial institutions.

Industrial covers nearly 3,000 industrial companies listed on the New York, American, and regional exchanges.

OTC Industrial, a companion to the *Industrial Manual,* provides broad coverage of over 2,700 companies not listed on the exchanges.

Public Utility details every publicly held U.S. electric and gas utility, plus gas transmission, telephone and water companies, and many privately held utilities.

Transportation examines all travel and transportation-related entities, including airlines, railroads, auto/truck rental and leasing, oil pipelines, bridge and tunnel operators, bus and truck lines.

International details information on more than 3,000 major corporations and supranational firms in 95 countries on all continents.

Municipal & Government examines over 14,000 issuers of tax-free and taxable long-term debt, including nearly all taxing jurisdictions such as counties, cities, and the U.S. government. State agencies, foreign governments, and other municipal organizations are also covered, with data including Moody's bond ratings.

These seven *Moody's Manuals* form a complete library that meets virtually every corporate and individual need for up-to-date investment, business, and financial information.

Moody's Handbooks. Three soft-cover handbooks provide full-page reviews of the most widely traded exchange and OTC stocks, and also those companies with a record of outstanding dividend performance. The handbooks are as follows:

Handbook of Common Stocks, a quarterly, reviews 944 companies of high interest to both individual and institutional investors. One-page company reviews include a long-term stock-price chart and an analysis of both recent developments and prospects for long-term stock-price activity. A complete financial history and company description for 944 firms is supplemented with one-line tabular data on all NYSE companies not examined in detail.

Handbook of OTC Stocks, a reference guide, covers 550 over-the-counter securities that are actively traded, and also includes timely "new issues" of investor interest. Here, investors who are more speculative will find complete financial histories, stock-price charts, and an analysis of recent developments on well-known OTC-traded companies. Immediate access to new information and stock-price developments is provided through quarterly updating.

Handbook of Dividend Achievers contains full-page reviews of over 400 companies that have increased their dividend payout every year for the last ten years. More than 4,000 companies on all exchanges were researched in order to compile this data source for investors interested in reliable growth and income. Each of the 400 dividend achievers is analyzed in detail and ranked by growth rate, with complete business and financial histories, stock-price charts, and other background information provided.

Other Moody's Publications. *Commercial Paper Record* is a comprehensive reference tool covering over 1,000 issuers of commercial paper. Monthly issues provide concise write-ups of each company, including Moody's ratings and the latest information concerning the financial condition and operating trends of each firm. Detailed data include analytic opinions behind the ratings.

Bond Survey, published weekly, provides needed data and interesting commentary on both the economy and fixed-income markets. Other sections include comprehensive calendars of recent and pending corporate and municipal offers, Moody's commodity and scrap price indexes, Moody's yield averages, and commentary on the markets for various types of fixed-income securities. The *Bond Survey* is designed specifically to provide bond investors with a broad overview of the current marketplace.

Bond Record, known widely as the most authoritative source of current information for the bond investor, contains information on all currently outstanding corporate and municipal bonds, convertible bonds, preferred stocks, commercial paper, and international bonds. In all, more than 18,000 issues are analyzed as to interest rates, maturities, current prices, call prices, trading information, and the current Moody's rating. Published monthly, each issue is thoroughly updated in all categories of data.

Municipal Credit Report provides investors with insight as to why a municipal credit received its rating. The analysis, rating, opinion, and all financial factors of each municipality are clearly summarized for the investor.

Moody's Fixed Income Ratings rates a wide range of corporate and municipal bonds, preferred stock, and commercial paper. Since the early 1900s, Moody's has been one of the major RATING AGENCIES in the country.

The purpose of Moody's ratings is to provide investors with a system of grading the relative quality of investments. Grading of investment quality is indicated by a series of nine rating symbols. They range from *Aaa,* the highest, which is used to indicate least investment risk, to *C,* the lowest, which is used to denote greatest investment risk. In addition, each rating classification from *Aa* to *B* for corporate bonds may carry a numerical modifier. The modifier #1 indicates that the security ranks in the higher end of its rating category, #2 indicates a midrange ranking, and #3 indicates that the issue ranks in the lower end of its rating category. Finally, those municipal bonds in the *Aa* through *B* rating groups that are judged to possess the strongest investment characteristics will also carry a numerical modifier, #1.

Moody's debt ratings and their descriptions are as follows:

Aaa. Bonds rated *Aaa* are judged to be of the best quality. They carry the smallest degree of investment risk and are generally referred to as "gilt-edge." Interest payments are protected by a large or exceptionally stable margin, and principal is secure. While the various protective elements are likely to change, such changes as can be visualized are most unlikely to impair the fundamentally strong position of such issues.

Aa. Bonds rated *Aa* are judged to be of high quality by all standards. Together with the *Aaa* group, they comprise what are generally known as high-grade bonds. They are rated lower than the best bonds because margins of protection may not be as large as in *Aaa* securities, or fluctuation of protective elements may be of greater amplitude, or there may be other elements present that make the long-term risks appear somewhat larger than in *Aaa* securities.

A. Bonds rated *A* possess many favorable investment attributes and are to be considered upper-medium-grade obligations. Factors giving security to principal and interest are considered adequate, but elements may be present that suggest a susceptibility to impairment sometime in the future.

Baa. Bonds rated *Baa* are considered medium-grade obligations—i.e., they are neither highly protected nor poorly secured. Interest payments and principal security appear adequate for the present, but certain protective elements may be lacking or may be characteristically unreliable over any great length of time. Such bonds lack outstanding investment characteristics and in fact have speculative characteristics as well.

Ba. Bonds rated *Ba* are judged to have speculative elements; their future cannot be considered well assured. Interest and principal payments may be very moderately protected and thereby not well safeguarded during both good and bad times over the future. Uncertainty of position characterizes bonds in this class.

B. Bonds rated *B* generally lack characteristics of the desirable investment. Assurance of interest and principal payments or of maintenance of other terms of the contract over any long period of time may be small.

Caa. Bonds rated *Caa* are of poor standing. Such issues may be in default or there may be elements of danger with respect to principal or interest.

Ca. Bonds rated *Ca* are speculative to a high degree. Such issues are often in default or have other marked shortcomings.

C. Bonds rated *C* are the lowest class of bonds, and issues so rated can be regarded as having extremely poor prospects of ever attaining any real investment standing.

Sheila Lambert

Mortgage-Backed Bonds

See SECONDARY MORTGAGE MARKET.

Mortgage-Backed Securities

See GOVERNMENT NATIONAL MORTGAGE ASSOCIATION (GNMA).

Mortgage Banking

Mortgage banking is the origination, marketing, and servicing of long-term loans that are secured by real property. The property mortgaged can be land or structures, including but not limited to houses, office buildings, warehouses, stores, or apartments. This entry will focus on mortgages secured by one- to four-unit residential structures. A mortgage is a legal document that pledges real property as security for the payment of a debt. To gain a perspective of the current practices of mortgage banking, it is useful to understand the historical evolution of this industry over the past hundred years.

There are about 800 to 1,000 mortgage-banking companies operating in the United States today, including independent firms and subsidiaries of holding companies or other large corporations. Some mortgage bankers are small, local operations, but many are larger firms operating in markets all over the U.S. Some mortgage bankers deal only with residential loans, and a smaller number are devoted exclusively to the financing of income-producing property. Many mortgage bankers deal in both areas, and they also may be involved in related businesses, such as property management, real-estate brokerage, or land development.

History. The mortgage-banking function became necessary to real-estate financing after the mid-1800s. Prior to that time, land often was settled by homesteaders or passed down within a family, and land that was sold was often financed by the seller. Even as late as 1900, individuals rather than financial institutions were the primary source of funds for the purchase of real estate.

As early industrial America developed in the late

1800s, the major cities of the East, such as Philadelphia, Boston, and New York, became capital-surplus areas. The East generated capital through savings deposits by workers, profits of growing firms, and reserves accumulated by the life-insurance industry. In these bustling urban centers, the supply of loanable funds exceeded the loan demand, resulting in a local surplus. At the same time, the westward migration was creating a demand for credit outside these major cities to buy real estate, start businesses, and finance inventory. The supply of credit in the areas of westward migration was limited by the sparse population and absence of business savings. This relative shortage of credit outside the major cities created a need for financial intermediaries to bring surplus capital from the East to the developing areas. In the real-estate markets, mortgage bankers fulfilled this function.

The foundation of the mortgage banker's business was his knowledge of the local real-estate market and his long-term relationships with investors in the East. By knowing his local market, the mortgage banker could evaluate borrowers and property values to make prudent loans. While the loan remained in force, the mortgage banker would service the loan by collecting payments and periodically inspecting the collateral property to ensure that it was maintained to protect its value. If a borrower fell behind in payments, the mortgage banker would work out a refinancing plan or foreclose on the property if necessary. The mortgage banker's presence in and knowledge of the local market permitted him to represent the interests of the distant investor. The mortgage banker earned fees for making loans and for servicing them.

In order for the mortgage banker to make loans, it was necessary for him to have access to a source of funds. He accomplished this by maintaining a correspondent relationship with investors in the East. These investors—usually life-insurance companies or mutual savings banks—had surplus funds to invest, but did not have knowledge of the local market in the West. They relied on the knowledge and integrity of the mortgage banker to place their funds in secure investments, and to protect those investments through efficient servicing.

The investor would typically sell a commitment to the mortgage banker. The commitment was a contract to purchase mortgage loans from the mortgage banker during a specified period of time and subject to certain criteria, such as the interest rates on the loans, terms of the loans, credit rating of the borrower, size of the down payment, use and appraised value of the property, or any other condition important to the investor. Armed with the stipulations of the commitment, the mortgage banker would set out to make loans conforming to the investor's criteria, and would

deliver the loans against the commitment.

The investor and the mortgage banker typically enjoyed a long-term relationship, each gaining the respect and confidence of the other. Commitment controls often were verbal rather than written in the early days of mortgage banking. This arrangement benefited the investor, the mortgage banker, and the borrower. The investor could make plans to place his surplus funds, such as life-insurance premiums, in advance of their collection. The mortgage banker could process and close loan applications by lending from his own funds with the assurance that the loan would soon be sold and the funds replaced. The borrower, the mortgagee, could arrange a loan with known terms in a competitive market as much as several months in advance of the actual closing of the loan.

Mortgage banking typically was a highly leveraged business that operated on money borrowed from a local bank. The money borrowed from the bank, called a "warehouse line of credit," was used to make mortgage loans, and it was repaid as those loans were delivered to the investors for cash. The mortgage banker in effect recycled the money in his warehouse line of credit, earning a fee each time a loan was originated.

Because the mortgage banker continued to service the loans he originated for distant investors who had no servicing capability, he accumulated a servicing portfolio. He earned a fee from each loan serviced so long as it remained in force. While income from loan originations would fluctuate with the current demand for new loans, the servicing income would remain relatively steady. This relatively assured source of income helped the mortgage banker remain in business in bad economic times.

In these early days of mortgage lending, most real-estate-secured loans were secured by farm property rather than residential real estate. The typical loan was for three to five years, and a down payment of 40% to 50% usually was required. Payments were often for interest only and were payable semiannually or when the crops were harvested. It was not until after World War I that residential mortgage lending became widespread, although the short-term and high-down-payment features of mortgage loans remained common as late as the 1930s. Mortgage loans were not amortized over their term, so a large lump-sum payment was due at the end of the three- or five-year period.

Early in the 1920s, the economy grew rapidly, fueled by speculation in real estate that pushed up land values. The real-estate market began to falter by 1927, and after 1929 it suffered disastrous setbacks. In the early 1930s, the American banking system was in disarray and mortgage foreclosures became widespread. The distress in the real-estate market was due both to the high unemployment rate among mortgagees who could not make payments and to the shortage of deposits in the banking system that prevented many short-term mortgages from being rolled over, even though the mortgagees would have been able to make the payments. Many states established a foreclosure moratorium in 1930–33, and the breakdown of the banking system resulted in the closing of all banks for a time in 1933. This era marked a turning point for the real-estate finance markets as the government began to assume a new role of stabilizing the credit markets and guaranteeing the viability of depository institutions.

Perhaps one of the most important pieces of legislation to that end during this period was the National Housing Act of 1934, which created the FEDERAL HOUSING ADMINISTRATION (FHA). The FHA was created to help revive the devastated housing market by providing federally backed mortgage insurance, first for construction loans and then for long-term mortgage loans. By meeting certain credit-history and down-payment criteria established by the FHA, a borrower could obtain a 20-year, fully amortized mortgage loan. Not only was the loan attractive to home buyers due to its long term and fully amortized form, it also was attractive to lenders because of the federally backed mortgage insurance.

At the end of World War II, the combination of a flood of returning veterans and pent-up housing demand from the depression and war years unleashed a tremendous demand for housing. The federal government helped to facilitate this larger loan demand by incorporating in the Serviceman's Readjustment Act a provision that guaranteed a mortgage loan made to any qualified veteran, often with no down payment required. They were dubbed "VA loans." In addition, the Federal National Mortgage Association was established to purchase government-bonded mortgages, helping to establish the acceptance in the market of the long-term, low-down-payment, amortizing mortgage loan.

Both the FHA-insured and the VA-guaranteed loan programs instituted by the federal government produced a sense of security in the housing markets. They helped to create more-uniform mortgage instruments throughout the nation. These results were especially felt by the mortgage-banking community and contributed to the growing role of mortgage instruments throughout the nation. These results were especially felt by the mortgage-banking community and contributed to the growing role of mortgage banking in real-estate finance. Mortgage bankers sell the loans they make, and the government-insured and -guaranteed loans made their product more attractive to investors through standardization of documents, ap-

praisals, and terms, as well as the insurance feature.

The mortgage-banking environment continues to evolve. Today many mortgage-banking companies have become subsidiaries of large corporations, often bank holding companies. Although mortgage bankers continue to deal with their correspondent investors, they also sell many loans today in the secondary mortgage market in the form of pass-through securities. A pass-through security is a financial instrument backed by a pool of mortgages. The mortgage banker issuing the security pledges to "pass through" to the purchaser of the security the principal and interest payments due. The individual mortgages represent the collateral for the pass-through security, which may also be insured, and the real estate remains the collateral for the mortgages. This evolution of the market toward securitization has revolutionized the mortgage arena since the late 1960s, when fundamental market changes began to be felt.

Among the important changes that have influenced the mortgage market since 1960 were changes in the investment choices of life-insurance companies and the reduced growth of mortgage lending by depository institutions. Life-insurance companies in 1960 devoted 25% of their new investments to residential mortgages. That figure declined through the 1960s and 1970s as life-insurance investment managers sought higher returns in stocks, bonds, and commercial real estate. At the same time, the combination of generally rising market interest rates and restricted savings rates paid by depository institutions diverted part of the savings flow from such institutions to other financial intermediaries, such as the stock market and money-market mutual funds. As a result, banks and savings and loan associations made relatively fewer mortgage loans for their own portfolios, and life-insurance companies almost suspended residential lending by 1970. Savings and loan association market share of long-term residential mortgage loans originated fell from 51% in 1960 to 31% in 1982. Because of the securitization of the mortgage markets since the late 1960s, mortgage bankers and other issuers of mortgage-backed securities have been able to fill the void created by these fundamental institutional changes.

Government National Mortgage Association. Today's securitization of the mortgage markets began with the establishment, in its current form, of the GOVERNMENT NATIONAL MORTGAGE ASSOCIATION (GNMA) in 1968. This agency, "Ginnie Mae," is organized as a part of the U.S. Department of Housing and Urban Development. Its primary function is to guarantee residential mortgage pools, making them more attractive to investors because of the guarantee of timely payment of principal and interest. Lenders assemble pools of FHA-insured and VA-guaranteed mortgages and issue securities backed by these mortgage pools. The securities are then guaranteed by Ginnie Mae for a fee, and sold by the issuer into the market. Fees cover all costs and losses of the program and return a profit to the government. Sales of the securities replenish the funds of the lender for additional lending. This is a classic example of the mortgage-banking function.

Since 1968, more than $125 billion in Ginnie Mae mortgage-backed securities have been issued. The Ginnie Mae mortgage-backed security has provided a vehicle for lenders other than traditional mortgage bankers to engage in mortgage banking. In addition, Ginnie Mae's success has inspired the issuance of securities backed by conventional mortgages rather than FHA-insured or VA-guaranteed mortgages. Today, the huge volume of Ginnie Mae securities issued has created an active secondary market in these instruments. The conventional mortgage-backed-security market is not yet large enough to support an active secondary market.

Today, mortgage bankers make loans all over the country, but are concentrated mainly in the South and West, traditionally areas that are not strong sources of capital. Mortgage bankers originated $29.9 billion of long-term residential mortgage loans in 1982, 29% of the total market of all lenders. During 1982, mortgage companies originated 86% of all FHA-insured loans and 81% of VA-guaranteed mortgages. In the conventional loan area, mortgage bankers originated 16% of these loans, up from only 2% in 1970 and 7% in 1980. For the first time, mortgage bankers originated a larger volume in conventional mortgages than either FHA or VA loans. Clearly, mortgage bankers are an integral part of the mortgage industry in this country.

Mortgage-Banking Operations. A mortgage-banking firm has three major functions:
  1. Loan origination
  2. Loan marketing
  3. Loan servicing

Loan Origination. Loan origination is the process of bringing into being a loan secured by real property. Loan originators are the salespeople of mortgage banking, who often work on a commission basis. They deal with realtors to provide financing for the sale of existing homes, and they maintain close working relationships with builders or developers to finance new-home sales. Originators often arrange construction or land-development loans for builders, hoping also to provide the financing for the new homes to be built. There is some walk-in business, such as in the case of refinancing or second-mortgage lending. The originator strives to find lending situations that meet the requirements of commitments held by the mortgage-banking company from an investor.

Once the initial contact between a borrower and a mortgage company has been made, the mortgage banker accepts and processes the loan application. The applicant authorizes an investigation of his credit history and the mortgage banker arranges for an appraisal of the property involved. This phase of origination involves collecting all the information needed to evaluate the loan application so that an underwriting decision can be made. In the underwriting process, the mortgage company evaluates the credit risk of the loan and the value of the collateral property to determine if the mortgage will meet the investors' criteria for lending. The mortgage banker must be sure to comply with Truth in Lending regulations, the Equal Credit Opportunity Act, and other federal, state, and local laws.

When a loan has been deemed acceptable by the mortgage company and all the paper work is complete, the loan is ready to be closed. Closing is the legal procedure that establishes the mortgage and includes delivery of the deed, signing of notes, recording of the lien and other legal documents, and disbursement of funds to the appropriate parties. The mortgage banker earns fees for the work involved in loan origination.

Loan Marketing. Loan marketing is the purchase of commitments from an investor and the subsequent placement and sale of mortgages to the investor. Those investors might be life-insurance companies, pension funds, the Federal Home Loan Mortgage Corporation, the Federal National Mortgage Association, foreign investors, mutual savings banks, savings and loan institutions, commercial banks, state housing finance agencies, etc. The commitment for the delivery of loans can be either optional or mandatory.

Under the terms of a typical optional delivery commitment, the mortgage banker may choose to sell or not to sell mortgages to the investor, but the investor usually is obliged to purchase any qualified mortgages that are presented. This type of commitment is used by the mortgage banker to guarantee a market for loans that he may or may not actually originate.

A mandatory delivery commitment requires performance by both the mortgage banker and the investor. If the mortgage banker cannot originate sufficient loans to fill a mandatory commitment, he must purchase such loans in the market, and sell them at a loss if necessary, to fulfill his contract. Such a commitment assures the investor that he will in fact have a specified investment under specified terms within a certain period of time.

Loan Servicing. After the loan has been sold, the mortgage banker usually continues to service the loan for its term. Servicing involves collecting the monthly payment and forwarding it (less a servicing fee) to the investor, maintaining all records relating to the loan, forwarding taxes and insurance payments on the property, supplying the borrower with a periodically updated statement of the account, and making regular inspections of the property to verify that the collateral property is maintained. The mortgage banker monitors the payment record of the borrower and contacts any borrower who does not remain current. In cases where a borrower is temporarily unable to make payments, the mortgage banker works with him to refinance or otherwise correct the payment deficiency. When necessary, the mortgage banker takes legal action to foreclose on the property to protect the interest of the investor. In many cases the mortgage banker is required to remit principal and interest payments to the investor even when they are not received from the borrower. This arrangement encourages investors to lend against real-estate collateral, and it encourages the mortgage banker to carefully screen applications in the underwriting process to eliminate higher-risk borrowers.

The Secondary Mortgage Market. There are basically two different mortgage markets. The first, which we have been dealing with, is the primary market, where mortgages are originated. The other, the secondary market, is the market in which investors buy existing mortgages or securities backed by mortgages from an intermediary, such as a mortgage banker. By buying mortgages, investors replenish the funds loaned and thus make more funds available to the mortgage banker for additional mortgage lending. Because mortgage bankers have always marketed their mortgages, and because they have a high concentration of government-insured or -guaranteed loans, which are attractive to investors, they are a major force in the secondary mortgage market. In 1982, mortgage bankers sold about 30% of all loans sold in the secondary market.

The SECONDARY MORTGAGE MARKET is important for several reasons. First, if a primary mortgage lender is short of funds, it can sell mortgages it owns in the secondary market to create a new flow of funds to be used to make additional mortgage loans. Second, the secondary market provides an outlet for investors' capital by creating a secure liquid investment opportunity for them. Third, the secondary market provides a national mortgage market and thus allows for the efficient transfer of funds from capital-rich areas to capital-deficient areas.

The backbone of the organized secondary mortgage market consists of two organizations: the FEDERAL NATIONAL MORTGAGE ASSOCIATION (FNMA), known as "Fannie Mae," and the FEDERAL HOME LOAN MORTGAGE CORPORATION, known as "Freddie Mac."

Federal National Mortgage Association. The Federal National Mortgage Association began in 1938 as a part of the federal government's attempt to stabilize the housing market during the depression. In 1968 "Fannie Mae" became a private corporation owned by stockholders and traded on the New York Stock Exchange. Fannie Mae is the largest single owner of residential mortgage debt in the United States, with a portfolio that totaled $73 billion in early 1983.

Fannie Mae finances its purchases of mortgages by selling bonds in the private capital markets, and by selling conventional-mortgage-backed securities. With the money it raises in the financial markets, it buys and holds mortgages. Although Fannie Mae initially was permitted to purchase only FHA-insured and VA-guaranteed mortgages, since 1970 it has been allowed to purchase conventional mortgages. Fannie Mae is rapidly shifting its activities to the conventional mortgage market, as illustrated by a very active adjustable-rate mortgage-purchase program.

Federal Home Loan Mortgage Corporation. The Federal Home Loan Mortgage Corporation, known as "Freddie Mac," was established in 1970 as a part of the Federal Home Loan Bank Board. It originally was intended to provide a secondary mortgage market for members of the Federal Home Loan Bank Board System. Although Freddie Mac can purchase FHA-insured and VA-guaranteed mortgages, its primary function has been the purchase of conventional mortgages. Freddie Mac sells conventional-mortgage-backed securities, called "participation certificates" or PC's, that represent an undivided interest in a mortgage pool. There were about $50 billion worth of Freddie Mac PC's outstanding at the end of 1982, and they are sold to investors by Wall Street investment firms.

In addition to selling their PC's, Freddie Mac allows thrift institutions to swap their low-yielding mortgage loans for PC's that are more liquid and more marketable than the low-yielding loans. This program played an important role in helping thrift associations through the turbulent era of record high interest rates in 1980–82. Recently, Freddie Mac has expanded its program by eliminating the fee previously charged to lenders who were not members of its Federal Home Loan Bank System. This action is encouraging more mortgage bankers and other lenders to use Freddie Mac programs, which in turn is encouraging the growth and viability of the secondary mortgage market, especially in the conventional loan area.

Thomas R. Harter

Mortgage Insurance, Private

Private mortgage insurance is a relatively new entrant in the expanding world of housing finance. Yet, in just over two decades, the industry has grown so that the insurance in force on residential home loans at the end of 1982 was $125 billion.

Private mortgage insurance protects lending institutions (e.g., savings and loan associations, mortgage bankers, commercial banks, credit unions, and savings banks) from financial loss in the event of borrower default on a mortgage note. The insurance is purchased by the borrower and covers the high-risk portion of the mortgage. Private mortgage insurance provides an added layer of protection for the lender and assists many buyers in obtaining financing with as little as 5% or 10% down payment on the purchase of a home.

The foundation for the private mortgage-insurance industry was established through efforts made by the government in the early 1930s to improve the financing system for housing. The FEDERAL HOUSING ADMINISTRATION (FHA) was established to provide private lenders with an insurance against borrower default that would enable lenders to make loans with longer terms and higher ratios between the down payment and purchase price. Mortgage insurance helped stabilize and expand the mortgage market.

Progress in our housing finance system has always depended on support from private institutions. The housing policy of our government is based on the principle that private enterprise must be encouraged to play as large a role as it can in meeting total housing needs. This has become more important in recent years due to increasing costs of government assistance. Private companies have been able to take advantage of new opportunities to provide a private guaranty against borrower default. They have demonstrated their ability to deliver their product more efficiently to lenders, with a clear advantage to the homebuyer public.

The real key to success for the private insurance industry has been its financial solidity. Uncertainty as to whether our nation may endure another economic catastrophe that would seriously disrupt the housing finance system demands quality default protection from the private guaranty. State regulators, legislators, and other proponents of private mortgage insurance require mortgage-insurance companies (MIC's) to meet stringent capital and reserve minimums. MIC's are limited to a single line of insurance—namely, insuring amortized first liens on one- to four-family homes that do not exceed 95% of fair market value. MIC's are required to use their premiums conservatively, thus building a reserve base unique in the insurance industry. Today, private mortgage insurance provides a level of security for full lender and investor confidence.

The industry has grown from a single company with $250,000 in assets to 14 companies with combined assets in excess of $1.8 billion. The emergence and success of the private mortgage-insurance industry in taking over a major part of the government's role is a unique incident in the history of our nation's housing markets. This entry discusses the developing role of the private mortgage-insurance industry in today's modern housing finance system.

How the Industry Operates. The 14 private mortgage-insurance companies are actively engaged in insuring lenders against loss resulting from default on one- to four-family mortgages. All have met the qualifications of the FEDERAL NATIONAL MORTGAGE ASSOCIATION (FNMA) and the FEDERAL HOME LOAN MORTGAGE CORPORATION (FHLMC). These two government-sponsored secondary-market agencies purchase conventional loans in excess of 80% loan-to-value ratio (LTVR) on the strength of MIC insurance. FNMA and FHLMC require a qualified MIC to maintain a minimum policyholders' surplus of $5 million and limit outstanding insurance risk to 25 times its policyholders' surplus. The state regulators, along with FNMA and FHLMC, require that MIC's be monoline (offer one line with that corporation) and limit outstanding risk insurance on loans for real property other than the one- to four-family dwellings to 10% of the MIC's total outstanding risk. Thirteen MIC's are members of the Mortgage Insurance Companies of America (MICA).

The 13 MICA members conduct their insurance operations through more than 240 main and regional underwriting offices. Twenty-nine states are served by eight or more members, and no state is served by less than three.

Mortgage originators who seek the services of MIC's apply for master policies with one or more MIC. Insurance of a master policy is not perfunctory, since prudence, reinforced by requirements of FHLMC and FNMA, requires the MIC's evaluation of the lender's (1) net worth and quality of assets, (2) servicing ability, (3) methodology for handling delinquent loans, and (4) professional capability of appraisal and underwriting staffs. Moreover, once a master policy is issued, each application for insurance of a mortgage is subject to the MIC's underwriting procedures. Insurance commitments are issued generally within 24 hours of the MIC's receiving the following documents from the lender: application for insurance, credit report, appraisal, affidavit of purchase price, sales contract, and verification of income.

MIC's are chartered by the states and regulated by state insurance departments. State laws and regulations limit an MIC's exposure to not more than the top 25% of the mortgage. Most policies cover the top 20%, with 25% coverage generally limited to 95% LTVR mortgages. Actuarial experience supports the conclusion that 20% to 25% represents the risk portion of a low-down-payment mortgage and hence the valid insurable portion. The FHA 100% insurance has had an advantage in generating a viable secondary market; however, recent experience with increasing investor reception of conventional mortgage-backed securities indicates a continuing trend in the direction of private insurance.

The industry is highly competitive, and MIC's provide a variety of premium plans to their lender-customers. In all cases, initial-year premiums vary depending on the LTVR and whether coverage is 20% to 25%. For example, a premium could be 1% of the mortgage for the first year on a 95% loan with 25% coverage; 3/4 of 1% on a 90% loan with 25% coverage; or 1/2 of 1% on a 90% loan with 20% coverage. In most cases the premium for the second and subsequent years is lower—usually 1/4 of 1%. Single-premi-

Table 1
Typical Premium Schedule for Private Mortgage Insurers

COVERAGE	LOAN TO VALUE	ANNUAL PREMIUM PLAN	SINGLE PREMIUM PLAN						
			4 YEARS	5 YEARS	6 YEARS	7 YEARS	10 YEARS	12 YEARS	15 YEARS
25%	OVER 90-95%	1.00% [1]	1.40% [122]	1.50% [123]	1.75% [124]	2.00% [8]	2.375% [110]	2.45% [125]	2.50% [113]
	ALTERNATE OVER 90-95%	.50% each of 1st 3 years Renewal Rates thereafter [96]							
	OVER 85-90%	.65% [36]	1.00% [143]	1.25% [144]	1.50% [145]	1.60% [146]	2.00% [147]	2.35% [148]	2.375% [149]
	OVER 80-85%	.50% [38]	.95% [163]	1.20% [164]	1.30% [165]	1.40% [166]	1.70% [167]	2.00% [168]	2.15% [169]
	80% & UNDER	.35% [40]	.75% [182]	.90% [37]	1.00% [183]	1.10% [184]	1.45% [185]	1.80% [186]	2.10% [187]
22%	OVER 90-95%	.80% [27]	1.20% [126]	1.30% [121]	1.60% [127]	1.80% [116]	2.30% [128]	2.35% [129]	2.40% [200]
20%	OVER 90-95%	.75% [3]	1.15% [130]	1.25% [131]	1.50% [132]	1.75% [15]	2.20% [133]	2.25% [134]	2.30% [135]
	OVER 85-90%	.50% [4]	.80% [150]	1.10% [151]	1.375% [152]	1.40% [153]	1.80% [111]	1.90% [154]	2.25% [20]
	OVER 80-85%	.35% [41]	.75% [170]	1.00% [171]	1.15% [172]	1.20% [173]	1.50% [174]	1.80% [175]	2.00% [176]
	80% & UNDER	.25% [5]	.65% [188]	.70% [189]	.90% [190]	1.00% [22]	1.30% [118]	1.350% [191]	1.45% [192]
17%	OVER 85-90%	.40% [28]	.70% [120]	.80% [155]	.90% [156]	1.00% [117]	1.50% [112]	1.75% [114]	2.00% [201]
16%	OVER 90-95%	.625% [29]	1.10% [136]	1.20% [137]	1.40% [138]	1.60% [139]	2.10% [140]	2.15% [141]	2.20% [142]
12%	OVER 85-90%	.25% [30]	.60% [157]	.70% [158]	.80% [159]	.90% [160]	1.20% [161]	1.40% [162]	1.85% [202]
	OVER 80-85%	.175% [95]	.50% [119]	.60% [177]	.75% [178]	.80% [203]	1.00% [179]	1.375% [180]	1.75% [181]
	80% & UNDER	.15% [42]	.45% [193]	.50% [194]	.65% [195]	.70% [196]	.90% [197]	1.125% [198]	1.60% [199]

SPECIAL SINGLE PREMIUM PLANS
Insures to 75% of original value. Provides coverage until loan reaches 80%.

COVERAGE	LOAN TO VALUE	PREMIUM
25%	OVER 90-95%	2.50% [204]
22%	OVER 90-95%	2.40% [31]
20%	OVER 85-90%	1.85% [205]
17%	OVER 85-90%	1.75% [206]
12%	OVER 80-85%	.90% [207]

RENEWAL PREMIUM RATES

- Annual Renewal   .25% of current loan balance

  OR

- Level Annual Renewal — .24% of original loan balance for nine renewals, reduced to .125% beginning with the tenth renewal.

NOTE: 12% coverage (over 80-85%) annual renewal .175%, level annual renewal .165%.
12% coverage (80% and under) annual renewal .15%, level annual renewal .14%.

um plans are offered by most MIC's, and premiums for these vary from 1 1/2% for a five-year policy to 2 1/2% for 15 years with 20% coverage on an over-90% loan. Table 1 shows a typical rate structure for a private mortgage insurer.

The duration of mortgage insurance is determined by the lender, who at any time may opt not to renew the policy. However, the requirements of Fannie Mae and Freddie Mac and the private secondary markets dictate the continuation of insurance until the principal has been paid down to 80% of original appraisal value. The average term of an MIC policy is approximately eight years.

Claims Procedure. The essence of mortgage insurance is the protection of the lender against loss resulting from default of the borrower. MIC master policies require the lender to report delinquencies to the MIC and to institute foreclosure or other appropriate proceedings after continuing delinquencies. A lender must generally have evidence of salable title to the property at the time a claim is submitted. Upon receipt of a claim, the MIC will proceed according to one of the following options:

• Pay the entire claim to the lender and take title to the property.
• Pay 20% to 25% (depending on the policy) of the total claim.

The loss claim in most cases includes such lender costs as accumulated interest, real-estate taxes, fire- and hazard-insurance premiums, attorney's or trustee's fees, court costs, property-maintenance fees, and unpaid principal balance due on the mortgage.

Table 2 illustrates a claim settlement. The total claim in this example is $46,562. Under an MIC's first option, this amount would be paid to the insured

---

Table 2
Example of Claim Settlement

Principal balance due	$40,946
Accumulated interest (excludes penalty interest and late charges)	3,200
Subtotal	44,146
Attorney's fees (maximum 3% of subtotal)	1,324
Property taxes paid	584
Hazard-insurance premiums advanced	242
Preservation of property (includes such items as securing the property, winterizing, etc.)	160
Disbursement and foreclosure proceedings	386
Subtotal	$46,842
Less escrow balance and rent received	280
Total claims	$46,562

lender in return for salable title to the property. Under the second option, the lender would keep title to the property and receive a cash payment equal to that percentage of the total claim that is the percentage coverage originally selected in the lender policy. For example, if it were 25% coverage, the cash payment to the insured would be $11,640.50.

Solidity of the Industry. The question of soundness of the private mortgage insurance industry is subject to continuing evaluation by state insurance regulators as well as the government-sponsored secondary-market agencies. An investor in mortgages or mortgage securities must have no uncertainty as to the ability of the insurer to pay claims. Fannie Mae and Freddie Mac contracted in 1974 with Arthur D. Little, Inc., to conduct a study of the industry. The study concluded that the typical private mortgage-insurance company could survive economic conditions comparable to that of the early 1930s and still remain solvent.

The basis for MIC solidity is a contingency reserve required by state regulators, whereby half of each earned premium dollar goes into a reserve that is not available for loss payments for a ten-year period unless losses in a calendar year exceed 35% of the corresponding earned premiums and unless the insurance commissioner of the state where the MIC is domiciled concurs in the withdrawal. On December 31, 1982, the aggregate contingency reserves of MICA members was $1.052 billion.

In addition to the contingency reserve, MIC solidity is underlined by maintaining an "unearned premium reserve" and a "loss reserve." Premiums received for the term of a policy are placed in the unearned premium reserve. The method by which the premium is earned from this reserve is established by state law or regulation to match premium with losses and exposure. The loss reserve is established for losses or potential losses on a case-by-case basis as the company learns of defaults and foreclosures. It also includes a reserve for losses incurred but not reported. A key measure of financial strength is policyholder's reserves made up of uncommitted contingency reserves and policyholder surplus. This measure will determine the capacity of an MIC to write additional insurance. Most states have mortgage-guaranty insurance laws that prohibit exposure (risk) from exceeding 25 times total policyholder's revenues. Despite the growth rate, MIC's have stayed conservatively within this limit.

The capacity of the industry to write new insurance is based on policyholder reserves. The industry's capacity at the end of 1982 was in excess of $50 billion. FHA and VA new insurance written in 1982 totaled less than $20 billion. Thus, even without infusions of new capital, private insurers will for the foreseeable future be able to insure a greater portion of the loans that have relied upon the government insurance programs.

Market Served by MIC's. During 1982, 12 MIC's representing 99% of the market insured 313,000 home mortgages. The average insured mortgage was $57,225, and the average purchase price was $65,515. The average term was 28 years, and the average down payment 13%. Thirty-seven percent of the mortgages insured were 95% LTVR.

A sizable share of conventionally insured mortgages are for first-time and modest-income homebuyers, as illustrated by the fact that 30% of the mortgages insured by MIC's were below $40,000. Sixty-three percent of the mortgages were on existing homes, 37% on new; 73% on single-family detached units; and 18% on condominiums. MIC's serve this market without any caps restricting loan amounts, so conventionally insured loans are used by the entire spectrum of home buyers.

The mortgage insurance industry's customer base MIC's was made up in 1982 of the following lender types: 47% of the mortgages insured were originated by savings and loan associations, 37% by mortgage bankers, 10% by commercial banks, 3% by savings banks, and 3% by other lender types (e.g. insurance companies, brokers). By location, 29% of the homes were in urban areas (central cities within SMSA's); 65% within SMSA's but not in central cities; and 6% were rural or resort housing.

Future Challenges for the Mortgage-Insurance Industry. The major shift in importance from the primary to the secondary mortgage market occurring over the past several years provides the mortgage-insurance industry with its major challenges. Moving ahead aggressively, seeking new residential financing concepts that meet the needs of mortgage borrowers, loan originators, and institutional investors, MIC's face two major challenges: (1) encouraging pension-fund and other investment in conventional mortgages and mortgage-backed securities, and (2) prudently underwriting the risk in modern mortgage instruments that are workable for borrowers and lenders.

Mortgage insurance has been a major factor in bringing the necessary quality of investment security to high-ratio loans that are being packaged into mortgage-backed securities. The introduction some years back of mortgage-backed debt instruments heralded a substantial separation of the loan-origination function from the investment function, which should greatly enhance the marketability of loans. The GOVERN-MENT NATIONAL MORTGAGE ASSOCIATION (GNMA) program has had an important demonstration effect, which has paved the way for growth of the private pass-through market. GNMA's have become accepted as homogenous financial instruments, enhancing their marketability and attracting nontraditional investors such as pension funds and bank trust departments to participate in mortgage financing. Removing residual credit risk and guaranteeing the timely payment of principal and interest, whether or not there are underlying mortgage delinquencies, has helped make the securities fungible.

These and other GNMA packaging devices have been duplicated in large part by FNMA, FHLMC, and private security issuers. Conventional mortgages have affirmatively been shown to be able to gain access to the bond markets. The continued development of conventional mortgage-backed securities with the third-party guaranty of mortgage insurance will progress rapidly. The goal is to give mortgages the competitive edge they deserve in vying with other longer-term debt instruments.

MIC's are aggressively applying their expertise with that of the mortgage bankers and other progressive loan originators to provide the necessary investment security that will help create new funding opportunities. The creative ability to unearth new financial resources is essential if our nation is to adequately meet mortgage demands during this decade.

An important part of meeting these future demands will be finding new investors in conventional mortgage-backed securities. One potentially large source is the public and private pension funds. However, at this time, few pension investors have made serious commitments to mortgage-related instruments. This is not to say that pension funds are avoiding mortgages; there actually has been significant interest, especially in mortgage securities. But as a percentage of total pension assets, the volume of mortgages is small, especially in comparison to what one would expect based on the investment performance of mortgages.

There has been a great deal of political debate as to the question of using the capital potential of pension funds to make targeted investments. Directives for "socially useful investments" that involve nonfinancial purposes, however, raise legal, institutional, and practical constraints. Doing anything other than pursuing objectives that will maximize earnings with acceptable risk can financially hurt plan beneficiaries. It can also financially hurt plan sponsors, such as a local government that may have to make up for losses or poor earnings experience from social investments having lower returns or less safety.

Proponents of social investing in residential housing cite gains other than financial return, such as less unemployment or the economic multiplier from new construction. Although valid, these arguments need not be made. It is a myth that investing in housing somehow means lower performance. Investing in mortgages and mortgage-backed securities can bring direct financial rewards to pension portfolios.

Funds put aside for retirement by employees individually or through organized pension programs represent long-term asset formation, while mortgages obligating individuals to repay a debt represent the liquidation of long-term liabilities. These two flows of funds are similar. If the obligations of individual borrowers secured by their homes can be packaged in a process that (1) removes credit risk, (2) provides administrative simplicity, and (3) represents a market rate of interest, these securities could offer to individuals and beneficiaries of pension plans a superior investment opportunity. Social benefits and economic stimulus from the construction sector would accrue as extra dividends.

Pension-fund managers and sponsors need some basic education as to the substantial advances that have been and are being made due to new mortgage instruments and the secondary mortgage markets. In order to encourage their contribution to the flow of capital to housing, the instruments and institutions involved must be as efficient as possible. This implies a high degree of standardization, visibility, and accessibility nationwide. Because of these requisites, MIC's can fill a unique niche and help in the development of intermediary conduits to connect the home buyer with the capital markets. As an industry forced by competition to provide a valuable service at a reasonable price, MIC's help coordinate new alternatives and processes. Pension funds can invest to increase the housing stock and at the same time not sacrifice profitability. The challenge is to take the investment objectives defined by pension plans and find or develop mortgage investments that will accomplish these objectives.

Increased investment in conventional mortgage-backed securities will be affected by the type of mortgage backing the security. The various modern mortgage instruments being developed and introduced pose new challenges for the mortgage-insurance industry. Mortgage insurers are in the same position as borrowers—not knowing how the various instruments will affect the ability of the borrower to repay the loan as conditions change in the future. The shifting of the risk of volatile market interest rates from mortgage lenders to borrowers has meant a corresponding risk shift to the mortgage insurer. The new authority that has been granted to lenders for making adjustable rate-sensitive loans has been characterized as a "prudent man" lending rule. Lenders must dis-

close to borrowers how a new mortgage instrument will work, but a wide variety of instrument design features can be utilized, and the inherent uncertainty of their operation adds new levels of risks for all parties to the mortgage-financing process.

Mortgage insurers and borrowers should be especially cautious about some loans that carry design elements with special risks. Balloon loans, for example, have a condition calling for maturity sooner than if total amortization were to be permitted at the regular rate, and this condition creates the need for refinancing. If the lender does not guarantee, at the time the original loan is made, that a continued source of financing will be available, then the borrower faces not only interest-rate risk but default risk as well. Depending on circumstances, balloon loans could create severe hardships and greatly accelerate default.

Another example of a design element with serious risk features is found in loans where the initial monthly payment amount may not be sufficient to fully amortize the loan over the loan term. This is known as "negative amortization." Loans where borrowers are permitted to accrue the payment differential as interest due in addition to the principal balance of the loan may, again depending on circumstances, cause the borrower to become obligated for an amount in excess of the property value. If not properly understood and used appropriately, this design feature can generate unmanageable default risk.

This variety in modern instruments heightens the role of mortgage insurance. Insurance helps provide uniformity for loans, facilitating their pricing. When loans are viewed as more homogeneous, they can be more readily packaged and thus more marketable. Investors are able to look at their default and delinquency risks based on the insurance coverage rather than on uncertain projections as to how the various loan types will perform.

As the private mortgage-insurance industry meets the challenges of the future, the industry will be called on to take an active part in accessing and developing new sources of capital for the mortgage market. The role of mortgage insurers in housing finance is to guarantee against loss in the event of default and property foreclosure. This role will expand as a greater percentage of mortgages are sold as securities where the investor has a need to evaluate the quality of the underlying mortgages representing the pool collateral. Our housing markets must retain discipline as deregulation of the financial-services industry occurs. The regulatory requirements that must be met by mortgage insurers for capital as well as arm's-length underwriting practices are good examples of the type of discipline needed. Using the success of their current programs as a foundation, MIC's will continue their efforts to develop a mutually beneficial and supportive relationship among lenders, home buyers, investors, and the housing industry in general.

Steven P. Doehler

Mortgages

See HOME FINANCING, MORTGAGES.

Most Active Stocks

See COMMON STOCK.

Mother-Daughter Home

A single-family house that has been modified or designed to include a complete and separate living unit established for a family member or relative. Frequently, a separate entrance is provided for the unit.

Harley W. Snyder

Municipal and State Securities

Municipal securities are issued to obtain funds for the construction, repair, or improvement of *public* facilities, such as schools, streets, highways, bridges, and water and sewer works, or for any other accepted public purpose. The term *municipals* is used to broadly describe the bonds issued by states, territories, and possessions of the United States; by their political subdivisions (including cities, counties, school districts, and special districts for fire prevention, water, sewer, irrigation, and other purposes); or by a public agency or instrumentality, such as an authority or commission.

Types of Municipal Bonds. There are three basic types of municipal bonds. Each type, however, has a number of variations, and the features of more than one type are sometimes combined.

The General-Obligation Bond. This is secured by the pledge of the full faith, credit, and taxing power of the issuer. Sometimes the issuer's taxing power is limited by state law to a specified maximum tax rate, in which case the bond, while remaining a general obligation, is called a "limited-tax bond."

The Revenue Bond. This bond is payable from revenues derived from tolls, charges, or rents paid by the users of the facility constructed with the proceeds from the sale of the bonds.

The Special-Tax Bond. This bond is payable from the proceeds of a special tax, such as a gasoline tax. The special-tax bond becomes a general-obligation bond (thereby increasing its investment safety) when it is, in addition, secured by the full faith, credit, and taxing power of the issuer. A further variation of the special-tax bond is the *special-assessment bond,* which is payable only from assessments against those properties that benefit from the facility resulting from the sale of the bonds. These bonds, which may also become general obligations, are usually issued in connection with the construction of streets, sidewalks, and, less often, water and sewer works.

Investment Features of Municipal Bonds

Safety. Municipal bonds offer a high degree of safety concerning principal and interest payments. The comparative safety of municipal bonds as a group is evidenced by the volume of purchases of such bonds by commercial banks, trust companies, and insurance companies, which by law must be cautious in their investments. The safety of municipal bonds is often the key consideration in bringing the new investor into the securities market, because it minimizes the element of risk and affords a measure of stability in the investor's portfolio.

Flexibility. Municipal bonds offer a high degree of flexibility to the investor, with the opportunity to purchase various types of bonds with maturities ranging from 1 to 20 years or longer, and a wide choice of geographic locations, types of communities, and economic situations.

Marketability. There are two markets for municipal bonds: the new-issue market and the trading or secondary market. The distinction is simple. The new-issue market is the market that exists for bonds when they are inititally issued. The trading market in municipal bonds refers to the market in which older, seasoned issues are bought and sold before their maturity dates. The trading market in municipal bonds functions mainly through an over-the-counter system. This means that dealers throughout the country are in contact with one another via a nationwide wire network, thus assuring an active trading market.

Maturities. It is the generally accepted practice for municipalities to repay money borrowed for public improvements on the installment plan by issuing serial-maturity bonds. Some bonds come due each year until all have matured. For this reason the investor has a selection of maturities. From the standpoint of income, the greatest yield is customarily available in the longer maturities.

Forms of Payment. Municipal bonds are generally issued in $1,000 or $5,000 denominations. This is known as the bond's "face amount" or "par value" and is what the issuer promises to pay on the bond's maturity date. Municipal bonds are usually issued in the form of coupon bonds, which can be registered at the request of the buyer.

The *coupon bond* is also known as a "bearer bond" because it is presumed to be owned by the person possessing it. Usually every six months the bondholder clips a coupon attached to the bond and collects the interest due him from the issuer's paying agency or the bondholder's own bank. Transfer of ownership of this bond is effected simply by delivery.

The *registered bond* is actually registered in the owner's name, which appears on the bond and on the books of the issuer. Registered bonds offer greater protection to the owner than do coupon bonds in the event of theft, but coupon bonds are more easily marketable and provide better collateral. Interest on registered bonds is usually paid by check. Most bonds may be registered as to both principal and interest or to just principal.

Tax Exemption. The one element that most concerns individual investors is the exemption of municipal-bond income from taxation. Interest on municipal bonds is exempt from federal income taxes and generally from local and state taxes in the states where issued. Investors in these bonds may therefore receive returns that are often higher than after-tax returns on securities that provide far less safety. Individuals hold more than one-third of all municipal bonds outstanding.

Mechanics of Issuing Municipal Bonds. Many factors affect the marketing of municipal bonds: supply and demand; interest rates; and the quantity of competitive issues, such as corporate, federal, or other municipal issues. Because municipal-bond sales create inflexible obligations for long periods of time, it is clear that the utmost care must be exercised in the preparation and planning of an issue.

One of the first considerations is whether it is necessary to issue bonds at all or whether regular revenues will be sufficient to cover costs of the project involved. If it is decided that a bond issue is needed, the maturity schedule of the bond is established, with as short a maturity as feasible for the purpose of the issue. Then, prior to setting a marketing date, the responsible public officials must determine whether the sale will come at a favorable time. They determine this by discussion with experienced investment bankers and bank officials, and by reviewing the various financial journals that regularly report the news and trends in the bond market. Often, at unfavorable times, municipal bond issues have to be postponed.

Planning the Issue. The authority for the issuance of municipal bonds stems from the constitution or statutes of the state. In some instances the municipality may be required to submit a proposed bond issue to a vote by the electorate of the community. A majority is usually enough to approve the issue, but often a two-thirds vote is required.

Legal Opinions. After the Civil War, many cities and counties issued bonds to aid in the construction of railroads, believing that the railroad-building would greatly benefit the community. The results, however, were largely disappointing, with many bonds in default or repudiated. Bondholders brought bitterly contested suits in both state and federal courts to enforce the repayment of the bonds. However, because of irregularities in their issuance, some of these issues were held to be illegal.

Thereafter, investors demanded approving opinions of experienced attorneys in whom they had confidence before purchasing any more municipal bonds. As a result, bond houses began conditioning their bids for bonds upon approval as to their legality by their own counsel or a named attorney, who was generally referred to as a "municipal-bond attorney." Municipalities soon realized the advantages of employing such attorneys themselves to help in drafting legislation—including general law, special acts, charters, and charter amendments—so that the bonds issued would have a strong legal basis. In some states—notably Georgia, Florida, and Alabama—the bond attorney initiates court proceedings to have bond issues validated.

The bond attorney, prior to issuing an approving opinion, requires a complete transcript of all proceedings, affidavits of publication of notices, and many certificates as to the execution of the bonds and their delivery and payment.

The approving opinion covers the complete description of the bonds and states that in the opinion of the bond counsel the issue is exempt from federal income taxes under the then-existing law. If the bonds are general obligations, a statement is issued with reference to the taxing power on which the bonds are secured and any limitations on such powers. If the bonds are revenue bonds, statements are issued with reference to the particular revenues to be used in repaying the debt and to the document under which the bonds are authorized (trust agreement, ordinance, resolution).

It should be kept in mind that the revenues pledged to revenue-bond debt repayment constitute a trust fund maintained for the benefit of bondholders. The bond attorney therefore must protect the rights of the bondholders and at the same time protect the public body issuing the bonds.

Maturity Schedules. The majority of municipal bond issues are handled as a package, with different certificates bearing different interest rates and different maturities. The schedule of maturities is designed to retire the bond issue progressively, rather than keep all of the capital raised in the issue until the final maturity date. The maturity schedule is a balance of a number of factors. The bonds, according to legal requirements, should be retired within the useful life of the improvement to be financed by the bonds. If they are retired early, interest costs will be reduced accordingly. The total debt charge, which is the principal amount due at each maturity as well as interest to be paid at each maturity level, must reflect the issuer's ability to repay. In general, then, the maturity schedule for any new bond issue must be planned so that the maturity schedules for all outstanding debts of the issuer represent a reasonable, economical, and realistic plan for debt retirement.

Selling the Bonds

The Official Statement. Prior to selling a bond issue, the issuer furnishes comprehensive data about the community and its economic background and financial situation. The information is circulated to the financial press, thus providing the investment community with the facts pertaining to the issuer. In addition, most municipalities are required by law to publish paid notices concerning the sale. The Official Statement usually contains the issuer's financial statement, along with the "Notice of Sale," which gives complete information about the sale and sometimes about the general economic life of the community.

The Bond Sale. Bonds are generally sold at public sale by competitive bidding. However, from time to time, an issue will be negotiated. That is to say, where permitted by law, issuers negotiate directly with the underwriters for the sale of their bonds.

Most issues, however, are handled competitively. The various underwriters or underwriting groups may submit bids to the issuer in accordance with the "Official Notice of Sale." The winning bid is mainly determined by the lowest net interest cost to the issuer. The lower that cost, the more favorable the issue will be financially to the issuer. In some cases, however, such as in New York State school districts, the lowest coupon rate can be the determinant in computing lowest net interest costs. All bidders must adhere to the terms of the issuer's notice of sale, the Official Statement, or be disqualified. Once the sale is consummated, the issuer delivers the bonds to the winning underwriter as soon as possible, usually within 30 to 45 days.

The Bond Register. Prior to delivery of the bonds, the issuer will legally record the following information, which then constitutes the official bond register: the due dates and denominations of all bonds and coupons, and the interest due on each date to maturity. Interest is usually paid semiannually. The same information should be provided for payments of principal or payments into a sinking fund. The bond register provides a permanent record of all debt-service requirements, important for the preparation of budgets, reviewing of all outstanding debt obligations, and planning for future issues.

The Primary Market: Underwriting and Distributing. Underwriting may be described as the purchase of bonds from an issuer by an investment banker or group of investment bankers for resale to investors. An underwriter or underwriters may purchase an issue either through competitive bidding at public sale or by negotiation (*see* INVESTMENT BANKING). In most states, the law requires that issuers sell general-obligation bonds only by competitive bidding.

In bidding on an issue, the underwriters review the Official Statement to determine the procedure to follow in filing bids. If the size of the issue makes it unfeasible for one underwriter to handle it alone, he will form a syndicate with other underwriters to minimize the liability and risk placed on any one underwriter and to gain a wider distribution for the sale.

Syndicates, which are more generally known among underwriters as *accounts,* usually consist of the same underwriters who bid for a previous bond sale by the same issuer. If an issuer has no history of previous bond sales, the syndicate manager will form a new account to bid on the new issue on either a *divided account* or *undivided account* basis. The undivided account, also called the "eastern account," places liability for any unsold balances on all members in proportion to their participation. The divided account, also known as the "western account," limits members' liability to their share of the loan, regardless of the unsold balance.

In both forms of account, the syndicate profit is always based on the original participation. In some cases there is credit granted to oversellers in divided accounts, covered by an assessment against undersellers.

Accounts are generally set up to run for a period of 30 days, but on occasion may be extended to 60 days or even longer by majority agreement.

A day or two before the sale, it is necessary to decide preliminary prices at which the bonds will be offered to the public. If an underwriter is bidding alone, the municipal-bond traders in that firm will usually formulate the yield at which they think the bonds of each maturity can be sold. In a syndicate, each member establishes his own ideas as to the scale of offering prices. Then the account manager calls preliminary meetings of representatives from each of the syndicate members to discuss the final pricing. Based on the information gained at these meetings, the manager will, at a final meeting, suggest a bidding scale and profit margin. After all members agree on the prices, the dealer's "spread," or profit margin, is deducted, with the resulting price being the bid for the bonds.

Bidding Procedure. After the price has been set, a bid is formally submitted to the issuing body. On the day of the sale, the officials of this issuing body usually meet at a stipulated time to receive the bids, which may be presented in person or by mail. The winning bidder is determined by the lowest rate of interest with the highest premium bid by the lowest net interest cost offered to the issuer by the underwriter. The winning bidder, after accepting the bonds, reoffers them to investors at the scale of prices previously decided upon.

The Secondary Market: Traders and Brokers. Municipal bonds, like other securities, need a marketplace to accommodate purchasers of the original issues who wish to sell their holdings prior to the date of maturity. Therefore, the investment-banking industry provides facilities for investors to resell their bonds: the so-called secondary market.

There are actually two types of markets available for buying and selling outstanding bonds. The *auction market* functions for bonds listed on national exchanges. Here a broker competes with other brokers in open auction for the best possible execution of a transaction. However, relative to the total number of bond issues, there are few listed municipal bonds. Thus, the bulk of municipal-bond trading is handled in the *over-the-counter market.* Here an individual may act for his account or arrange for a recognized dealer to act for him to obtain the best bid for the securities.

The municipal-bond trader plays an important role in maintaining the secondary market for municipal bonds. He must have complete and accurate knowledge of the location of blocks of bonds, as well as up-to-the-minute information on bond prices, local credit, general market factors, and where to look for buyers of different maturities and different issues. Because of the specialized knowledge and skills needed in bond trading, a number of firms specialize in only the secondary bond market.

Municipal-bond trading shares with other securities a dependence on fast, modern means of communicating market information and of bringing buyer and seller together. Indeed, the two are closely allied. A network of private telephone and Teletype wires, supplemented by special-service telephone and Teletype lines, links bond dealers both for exchanging information on prices and for placing buy or sell orders. In addition, specialized publications, such as the *Blue List* and the *Bond Buyer,* act to keep buyers, sellers, underwriters, issuers, and dealers informed on the status of the secondary bond market.

Fundamentals of Analyzing Municipal Credit. The aim of credit analysis is the evaluation of the *ability* and *willingness* of the issuer to pay its debts. Through such analysis, it is possible to determine if there are significant weaknesses that may lead to trouble in the future. Furthermore, a standard as to the quality of an issue can be obtained for comparing one issue with another.

There are established guideposts for investors in municipal bonds. Quality ratings are published by independent authorities, such as MOODY'S INVESTORS SERVICE, INC., and STANDARD & POOR'S CORPORATION. These ratings broadly categorize nearly all municipal bonds by groupings, from those considered to be prime, with the least degree of risk, down to those considered to be of greatest risk, with speculative characteristics. These ratings are intended for use as guides to quality only, and they do not indicate market or price fluctuations. The ratings are the result of extensive analyses of the issuer's financial health, in terms of both ability and willingness to meet its debt obligations.

The ability of an issuer to pay its debts involves a study of both economic and financial statistics. Taken into consideration are geographic location, transportation facilities, population trends and characteristics, and other general civic information. When available, information on family income and education can prove of analytic value, as can individual wealth as measured by value of homeownership and per capita assessed valuation. Then there is the question of the character of the local economy. Is it industrial, residential, commercial, or agricultural? Or what sort of mix of these elements does it have? Is there sufficient diversification to afford economic stability? Are there stabilizing influences present, such as colleges, universities, and governmental establishments?

One important indicator of the strength of a bond issue is the financial condition of the issuer. What is the per capita debt as compared with that of other issuers of similar size? What is the relationship of debt to assessed valuation? What is the character of the debt? Are there tax limitations? Is state aid available?

In addition to all the factors that must be considered for evaluation of general-obligation bonds, special-purpose bonds require further information. For instance, a bond payable only from special assessments must be analyzed in view of the properties to be assessed and the relationship of the value of those properties to the assessments. Revenue bonds secured in varying degrees by income from the operation of facilities must be analyzed in terms of the facilities themselves, the rates to be charged, and the potential use of the facilities. The covenants covering these special bonds must be carefully examined.

As mentioned earlier, willingness to pay is a major consideration, but, obviously, willingness is more difficult to assess than ability. Some idea of willingness to pay can result from a study of the past record of debt payment, default, or delay in debt payment. Questions asked here include: What is the ability of the issuer to formulate realistic budgets and levy adequate taxes for current requirements? Is the governmental and political climate favorable?

The Mathematics of Municipal Bonds. Some investors are bothered quite a bit by the high-sounding math of yields, percentages, and so forth in bonds. They are impressed by their confirmations, which show the price carried out to many places. Many common-stock buyers found that the arithmetic involved there was quite simple. In fact, they even found that doing a price/earnings ratio was not difficult. If you mention bond math, however, they recoil in horror.

This reaction is unfounded because when you strip away all the fancy frills and the sophisticated calculators, it is just simple arithmetic. If you love gadgets, you can—if you haven't already done so—buy one of the new computers that are being used for everything including the grocery list. But pencil and paper and some of that old-time math are sufficient. Doodling with yields can be very stimulating.

The information below will explain whatever math you need for bonds. Of course, there is a lot more math in bonds than this—figuring out amortizations, for example—but what follows is all you will need.

1. Formulas for figuring out what the tax exemption means for you in your tax bracket.

2. How to figure interest.

3. How to figure yields—including current, to maturity, and discount yields.

The formula method for figuring tax equivalents came into use years ago when it was found that many people do not like to disclose their tax brackets. They were told to sit down with pencil and paper and taught how to use the formula, which works two ways: You can find the tax equivalent of either a tax-exempt bond or a taxable security. In either case the formula begins with ascertaining your tax bracket and then finding the differential:

$$
\begin{array}{r}
100\% \\
\text{Less:} \quad ?? \text{ (your tax bracket)} \\
\hline
?? \text{ (the differential)}
\end{array}
$$

Let's assume that you are in the 32% tax bracket. You have been offered a tax-exempt bond with an 8% yield. You want to know what the taxable equivalent is without looking at the chart, which you probably would not carry everywhere. The differential is 68%, and you divide this into the 8%:

$$
68 \overline{) 8.00 }^{11.76\%}
$$

Thus, you have found that the equivalent taxable yield is 11.76%.

Now suppose you were seeking to find what you must earn in a tax-exempt bond to equal an interest rate of 10.5% (taxable) being offered to you. Once again you use the differential, but this time you multiply as follows:

$$
\begin{array}{r}
10.50 \\
\times \quad .68 \\
\hline
7.14
\end{array}
$$

So you see that you require a 7.14% tax-exempt yield to equal the offering of the taxable security.

Knowing how to figure interest is a skill you can use in many endeavors, not only bonds. First of all, remember that tax-exempt bonds are figured on a 360-day year, while U.S. Treasury bonds and other transactions such as mortgages are figured on a 365-day basis. If you would like to check the interest on your confirmation, or if you would like to find out how much tax-exempt interest you made in a certain period, just follow this example. If you buy $5,000 of 7% bonds, you will earn $350 per year. The bonds are due January 1, 1975, and you are having them delivered to you on March 14. This means that you must pay two months and thirteen days' interest (you always figure up to the day before delivery). One day equals approximately $.9723. Multiply that by 73 days and your answer should be $70.98. You should be able to come within a penny or two of the figures on the confirmation. Actually, if you were to look at an interest table, you would find the official figure is $70.97. Close enough? Remember, the table was prepared with computers and the figures were carried out to many, many places.

There is another area where figuring yields can be very illuminating. Remember that the interest you earn and the discount or the premium you pay determine what yield you earn. All examples being used assume a $1,000 bond, even though most bonds are in denominations of $5,000.

One thing that confuses tax-exempt investors is that bond dealers do all their transactions either in dollars or in yield to maturity. As has been pointed out, most investors do not expect to be alive as long as some of their very long-term investments, which might mature as late as 2015. The yield most of them are interested in is the current return. You hardly ever see current return shown in an ad for bonds. However, many dealers show it in their offering sheets.

Current return has to do only with the interest that you earn. You need two factors. Let's say that you have purchased a 7% bond at 102. How do you determine the current return? It's simple. You divide the coupon by the amount paid, as follows:

$$
\begin{array}{r}
6.86\% \\
1020\,\overline{)7.000} \\
6\,120 \\
\hline
8800 \\
8160 \\
\hline
640 \\
612 \\
\end{array}
$$

Thus, 6.86% is what you are earning.

Since yield to maturity is the way bond dealers and banks express yields in ads, let's find out how this is arrived at. Let's assume that this is a bond with a 6.5% coupon due in ten years, and you purchased it at 105. What is the yield to maturity?

First you find the current return, which is:

$$
\begin{array}{r}
6.19\% \\
105\,\overline{)6.50} \\
6\,30 \\
\hline
200 \\
105 \\
\hline
950 \\
945 \\
\end{array}
$$

Then you divide that 5% premium you paid by ten years, and you find that this reduces your yield (5.0% ÷ 10 years) by .5% per year. Subtract this and you find:

$$
\begin{array}{r}
6.19\% \text{ (current yield)} \\
-\ .50\% \\
\hline
5.69\% \text{ (yield to maturity)} \\
\end{array}
$$

Now if the bond was a discount bond at 6.5% for 20 years and you purchased it for 90, you have two situations. You want to find the yield to maturity, but you also have to take into account that Uncle Sam demands a 25% capital-gains tax from you if you do hold those bonds for 20 years (which is possible). Again you find the current return:

$$
\begin{array}{r}
7.22\% \\
90\,\overline{)6.50} \\
6\,30 \\
\hline
200 \\
180 \\
\end{array}
$$

Taking the ten-point discount over the 20 years, you find that it is again worth .5% (10% ÷ 20 years), but this time, since it represents a discount, you add it to the current yield:

$$
\begin{array}{r}
7.22 \\
+\ .50 \\
\hline
7.72\% \\
\end{array}
$$

This is the yield to maturity, but this is not the yield you will earn, because you will have to pay that 25% capital-gains tax. After the capital-gains tax, all you will have gained from the 10% discount ($100) will be $75, or an effective discount of 7.5% instead of 10%.

Therefore the factor becomes .375 (7.5% ÷ 20) rather than .5, and this is the true yield to you:

$$
\begin{array}{r}
7.220 \\
+\ .375 \\
\hline
7.595\% \\
\end{array}
$$

Some of the above calculations may seem bothersome, but, in addition to being a good mental exercise, they give you a better look at bonds in the tax-exempt market. They also remove much of the mystery when you find out that these things can be figured out so easily and so quickly.

John M. Nash

Municipal-Bond Investments

See UNIT INVESTMENT TRUSTS.

Municipal Bonds

See MUNICIPAL AND STATE SECURITIES.

Mutual Fund

A mutual fund is a financial service organization that brings together investors with common financial goals and objectives. The operation of the fund is conceptually simple. The fund organization receives money from shareholders, and each day this cash is accumulated (pooled) together into one large sum. These dollars are then invested in stocks, bonds, money-market securities, and other types of investments according to the policies and objectives set forth in the fund's prospectus. The fund managers, whose job is to try to achieve the objectives laid out by the fund, attempt to make these individual investments grow through earnings such as interest, dividends, and/or capital gains.

The advantage of pooling money with thousands of other investors in a portfolio of securities is that it gives you a range of choice far wider than all but the wealthiest individuals would have. This might mean, for example, that together you can purchase an investment of such large size that it would be beyond your individual resources, and this in turn could mean a better return than you would otherwise have had.

Types of Mutual Funds. Mutual funds are also known as open-end investment companies. They continually offer for sale, or have outstanding, shares that are issued and redeemed by the fund at a price representing their underlying net asset value. Net asset value per share consists of the difference between the total market value of the fund's securities (common stocks, bonds, money-market instruments, etc.) and other assets less total liabilities, divided by the number of shares outstanding.

Closed-end investment companies have a *fixed* number of shares outstanding—that is, they do not normally redeem shares or issue new shares. The outstanding shares trade in the open market on a supply-and-demand basis at more or less than their underlying asset value.

This entry will discuss in detail only open-end funds.

Major Services and Features of Mutual Funds. Mutual funds offer a variety of services and fund features to meet the diverse needs of savers and investors.

Full-Time Professional Management. Mutual funds are managed by investment professionals. Managing security portfolios requires specialized skills, including the ability to gather and analyze information; the judgment to time critical buy and sell decisions without emotional ties; and the foresight to spot and react to trends in the marketplace. Results vary but the performance record of a fund manager is public and readily available for review by a prospective investor.

Diversification. It is a generally accepted investment principle that portfolio diversification reduces risk—and the increased risk to an individual of being undiversified does not justify the higher potential returns on his investment. Mutual funds invest in a large number of securities, thus reducing an investor's investment risk.

Exchange Privilege. Today most mutual-fund organizations offer a "family of funds" to meet current and future needs of investors. The exchange privilege enables shareholders in one fund to switch all or part of their investment to other funds in the same group with different investment objectives. The charge for this service is nominal, normally around $5 or $10 per exchange, whatever the size, and sometimes nothing at all. Also, most fund companies limit the number of exchanges into and out of a single account in a given year.

Liquidity. A mutual fund will redeem its shares at any time at the then-current share price. This provides investors with immediate access to cash as their personal needs demand or their investment objectives change.

Dividend/Capital-Gains Option. Investors in a mutual-fund company can either receive dividends and/or capital gains in cash or have them reinvested in additional fund shares. The reinvestment alternative allows investors to compound returns.

Automatic Investment and Withdrawal Plans. Many funds offer a service whereby additional shares can be automatically purchased each month according to a prearranged agreement involving the transfer of money directly from a regular bank checking account to the fund company. This service not only offers a measure of convenience but allows an investor to take advantage of "dollar-cost averaging." Dollar-cost averaging is a process whereby shareholders invest identical amounts of money at regular intervals; thus, they buy more shares when prices are low and fewer shares when prices are high. While there are no guarantees, this process tends to reduce the average cost of shares purchased.

Conversely, shareholders may arrange for a periodic transfer of cash—either from earnings or by liquidating principal—to their bank checking account. The amount withdrawn can be fixed or calculated as a predetermined number of shares. This feature is useful for those investors who require a steady monthly income from their investment, for example, many retired people.

Retirement Plans. HR-10 (Keogh) plans for self-employed individuals or partnerships and Individual Retirement Accounts (IRA's) for individuals with earned income are available from most mutual-fund organizations. You simply select the mutual fund(s) of your choice to be used in your retirement plan and fill out a Keogh and/or IRA application and beneficiary forms. Many fund companies also offer corporate payroll-deduction IRA's, 403(b)(7) plans for nonprofit organizations, and pension and profit-sharing plans as well. It is best to contact a fund organization and explore what retirement plans they offer to the public.

Shareholder Reports. At least twice annually, mutual funds publish financial data and portfolio listings for their shareholders. This information provides shareholders with detailed information on the performance of their investment.

Daily Price Listings. Most major daily newspapers provide current share-price listings of all mutual funds. This allows investors to track the value of their investments.

Wide Choice of Investments. Mutual funds reflect the variety of investments available. Their financial objective could be to produce the highest income for shareholders consistent with safety of principal; these are the money-market funds. At the other extreme, the objective could be to maximize capital appreciation; these funds might buy the shares of companies in high-technology industries, or the shores of small and emerging companies that they hope will have a considerable potential over the years, or companies where there have been changes of management and so only a relatively short track record. For these funds the risks are normally bigger than for those investing in long-established companies—but so are the possible rewards.

Between the extremes of these aggressive growth funds and money-market funds, there is every possible shade of investment objective. Some mutual funds will invest for capital growth but will only do so with blue-chip corporations; they are for people who want to share in the growth of the economy but want to limit their risks in doing so. Other mutual funds aim for a mixture of income and capital growth. Still others may choose to concentrate on particular industries where they have a special expertise, or on international corporations to take advantage of different conditions around the world. A fund may try to mirror the stock market as a whole by investing in the broadest possible range; or, on the other hand, it might deliberately seek to buy stocks that are currently unpopular in the expectation of getting a higher return when these stocks come back into favor. Some funds mix business with their own brand of social conscience and will not buy into, say, companies producing weapons or alcohol.

Other investors prefer not to put their money in common stocks at all. They may need income to meet current expenses, or they may be unwilling to take the risks inherent in investing in any common stock, or they just may feel that the way interest rates are moving will bring them not only income but the possibility of capital appreciation, too. For them, investing in a bond mutual fund is a natural choice; they get all the advantages of professional management and diversification in what can be a quite tricky market.

Here again there are plenty of differences. Some funds, for example, will deal only in top-rated bonds. Others buy lower-rated bonds because, although the issuers are not as highly thought of, they generally offer a higher rate of return. For some people the extra potential is worth the extra risk.

There is yet another major distinction within the bond funds. Those issued by local governments—which can be cities, states, or other public bodies—pay interest free of federal and, in some cases, state taxes. For those investors in high income brackets, a mutual fund that buys such bonds can be particularly attractive. Of course, returns on tax-free bonds are somewhat lower than corporate bonds precisely because they are free of tax, so investors should consider their own economic situations to determine if these funds make sense for their particular circumstances. These funds are not just an investment for the rich; inflation and higher money incomes have pushed millions of families into tax ranges that a few years ago they would not have expected to be in. Yet buying municipal bonds on your own is a complicated and possibly dangerous business. You need a lot of money and knowledge. Municipal-bond funds address both problems: The pool is big enough and its managers work full-time in this market.

Money-market funds are a different kind of investment again. Their aim is to provide the highest income they can by investing in securities whose prices scarcely vary over their lifetime. This stability is due partly to the stature of the issuer, but more particularly to the short-term nature of this type of money-market security. Typically, a money-market fund will invest in the paper of leading banks, blue-chip corporations, and the government—such as certificates of deposit, commercial paper, and Treasury bills. Minimizing even the remote risks of these securities, the typical money-market fund spreads its portfolio over a large number of them. On top of that, some funds buy only money-market securities of the federal government.

Money-market funds have the usual advantages over individual investing. For one thing, these securities are in such large sizes that usually only institutions can afford to buy them. But with a fund you can typically buy shares initially for $1,000, and in some cases with no minimum at all. The minimum for subsequent investments is frequently $100 or less. Second, the managers are buying and selling the securities all the time aiming for the best results. Third, you can cash in your shares at any time; you do not have to wait until the money-market securities you have bought mature.

Money-market funds have in fact proved to be the most popular new investment for the ordinary person in the whole post-World War II era. They have given literally millions of people market rates of return they could not have had otherwise, and millions of others have taken the first steps to investing through these funds. They have also revolutionized cash management for businesses of all kinds, which need no longer have cash lying idle; instead, the business can put money in and take it out to suit its day-to-day cash flow.

Mutual funds are sold in three different ways. First, from a stockbroker or financial planner. Many brokerage firms have their own mutual funds, but most will also deal with a range of funds that are managed independently. Second, a number of mutual funds have their own sales forces. To buy shares of these funds, you contact the fund or its local representative.

In both cases you will be charged a sales commission up to but not exceeding 8½% of your investment. What you are paying for here is the advice of the stockbroker or registered representative whose job is not only to buy shares in the fund for you but to guide you to the type of fund that is appropriate to your needs. Many sales representatives will want to build up a financial picture of you before they give you their recommendations.

Third, other funds sell directly to the public. You can buy their shares by replying to one of their advertisements or simply by contacting them directly. In this case you have to take the initiative, but there is no sales commission.

Both the number and types of mutual funds have grown enormously over the years as it has become apparent that the twin concepts of pooling money and managing it by professionals have almost infinite adaptability. In the early 1970s, 90% of the assets of the mutual-fund industry was in common-stock funds. This is now down to less than 25%. Yet these funds have not diminished in the meantime; it is simply that other types of funds, which did not even exist until recently, have come along to provide other sorts of objectives that present-day investors are looking for. Thus, the Investment Company Institute, the Washington, D.C.–based national association of mutual funds that compiles information of all kinds on mutual funds, had in 1983 some 900 members when only four years before it had around 500.

The great variety now available means that there are funds suited to almost every kind of economic condition. If interest rates are high, stable money-market funds are an obvious choice. When interest rates are coming down a bond fund can lock in current rates and produce capital appreciation. When interest rates are low and the stock market is rising, a common-stock fund (also known as "equity fund") can yield the best returns.

Similarly there are funds suited to all types of investors. Some investors, as a matter of personal preference or economic circumstances, want to run virtually no risk at all. For them, money-market funds have effected a true revolution. And for those who do not want to take even the remote risks of a run-of-the-mill money-market fund, those funds that invest only in U.S. government securities are an unparalleled opportunity. For those who are prepared to take more risks in order to try to build up a larger investment, long-term-bond funds and stock (equity) funds are appropriate. It is a good bet that whatever financial objective an investor has, there is now at least one mutual fund with that objective.

But, of course, economic conditions do not stay the same, and neither do people's investment outlooks. For this reason exchanges between funds have grown explosively over the last few years. This is particularly easy to do in a family of funds—mutual funds within the same management group. It gives unmatched flexibility, and investors are taking advantage of it in unprecedented numbers. In the mid-1970s, something like $1.5 billion was switched between funds in this

way in a year; by 1983 it was running at an annual rate of almost $40 billion.

Along with the growth in the number of funds has come an explosion in the number of people who invest in them. In mid-1983 there were more than 21 million shareholder accounts in mutual funds of all kinds. This was up from 11 million six years earlier.

Shareholders in mutual funds are of almost every type: all income groups, young and old, men and women, conservative and aggressive investors, large and small, people planning for their retirement through IRA's and Keogh plans, people laying aside money to pay the children's college costs, two-income families, and part-time workers.

One feature of a mutual fund that attracts all this variety is that, whatever type of shareholder you are, you get a share of the earnings exactly proportionate to your holdings. So the novice and the small investor get the same return on their money as the millionaire—an opportunity that is extremely rare in investing.

Millionaires in fact do invest in mutual funds. So, too, do pension funds, college endowments, banks of all sizes, companies varying from small partnerships to those in the Fortune 500. They do so because, for one reason or another, mutual funds give them results they find hard to get elsewhere. At the beginning of 1983, for example, institutions of various kinds had $114 billion invested in mutual funds. Since many of these institutions can afford the very best financial advisers of their own, their decision to go into a pool with thousands of others is regarded in the mutual-fund industry as a convincing tribute to its performance.

Clearly, expansion has to be grounded in results—that is to say, how mutual funds have performed over the years. That in turn depends on the type of fund. The most common of traditional mutual funds are those that invest in stocks. The Investment Company Institute has calculated how an investment of $10,000 in a representative sample of the most conservative of these funds, the growth-and-income funds, would have grown in the 25 years to the beginning of 1983. That period was chosen because it includes every type of economic condition except a great depression. It includes the good years and the bad years, the best- and worst-performing funds. It assumes all dividends and capital gains were reinvested by the shareholder, but is net of expenses, including the maximum sales charge. In that period $10,000 would have grown to $95,198. Clearly, it is a superior record. The average rate of return works out at around 9.4% annually, which was far ahead of the inflation rate during most of those years and indeed well ahead of most other investments available to the ordinary person.

As for money-market funds, high inflation in recent years has produced very high rates of return indeed. Again, the period chosen will affect the calculation—but over the five years to the beginning of 1983, these money-market funds averaged over 9% a year and in three of those years exceeded 12%.

Mutual funds give no guaranty about their rates of return. You can lose money in them. They are an investment. Still, their record is such that among financial observers there is scarcely any investment more highly rated for such a variety of needs.

Redemptions. Regardless of how you purchase shares in any type of mutual fund, you may redeem them in any amount, at any time, and, except in very rare cases, without any charge. You can redeem by mail always, and by telephone or wire often. In addition, shares in money-market funds (and some short-term municipal-bond funds) may also be redeemed by simply writing checks—actually drafts—for the amounts desired (in most cases minimum amounts are required). Specific redemption requirements for any fund appear in it prospectus.

Processing of a redemption begins the same day the request is received, so the amount of money you'll get is the amount your shares were worth at the close of that business day. Usually, a check is mailed within 24 hours, although a fund legally has up to seven days to complete your redemption.

See also MUTUAL FUND, HOW TO SELECT A.

Joseph F. Kissel and Reginald F. D. Green

Mutual Fund, How to Select a

Before investing in a MUTUAL FUND, you must first determine your objectives—aggressive growth, growth and income, preservation of capital, current income, liquidity, tax-sheltered income, etc., or some combination of these. Your objectives should reflect the purpose or use of the planned investment/savings program, your age, income, tax status, financial position, and your willingness to accept risk. Once these factors are identified, you are prepared to identify a fund or funds to meet your goals.

To get information on the mutual fund(s) that "match" your objectives, several sources are readily available. The local broker/dealer is one source. Checking with friends and associates will probably turn up the names of several area dealers.

The public library is a second source of information about mutual funds. Several publishers have produced listings, some with performance results, of mutual funds by objective categories. Two publications that regularly measure the performance of mutual funds are the *United Mutual Fund Selector* (Boston),

Wiesenberger Investment Companies Service (New York), and *Lipper Analytical Distributors, Inc.* (New York).

In addition, two trade associations offer directories of mutual funds. The No-Load Mutual Fund Association (Valley Forge, Pennsylvania 19481) provides an extensive listing of no-load mutual funds and money-market-fund companies at a cost of $1 for postage and handling. The Investment Company Institute (1775 K Street, N.W., Washington, D.C. 20006) will provide investors with free directory of its membership, consisting of 900 load and no-load mutual-fund companies, categorized by investment objective.

Once you have identified the various funds that appear to match your objectives, there are several steps to take before investing. First, you should read each fund's prospectus to determine if its investment objectives and policies are consistent with your own. Next, you should review the relative performance record of several funds for the past five, ten, and fifteen years versus the Standard & Poor's 500 stock index (a generally accepted measurement standard against which most equity/common-stock mutual funds' performance is compared) or the appropriate Salomon Brothers bond indexes (for comparisons of bonds and government-agency-security funds). If a fund has been operating for less than five years, you will simply have to make a judgment based on whatever performance record is available. At a minimum, a common-stock fund should outperform the S&P 500 (although this has not been easy in recent years) and a bond fund should at least equal its appropriate Salomon Brothers bond indexes. The next step is to compare one fund's performance against a similar fund's performance.

Comparing mutual funds on these major factors—investment policy, investment record, and performance against accepted industry indexes—is an excellent start in selecting the most suitable fund(s). However, it would be incomplete and unwise to stop there. These factors are best used to narrow the investor's fund choices down to a select few (three to five funds). A prudent investor will also thoroughly examine the following:

Comparative Risk. Risk is a crucial factor in deciding which of the many funds, all with the same investment objectives, is right for an investor. A fund that diversifies its holdings among many industries and companies is likely to have a less spectacular short-term record than one that concentrates on relatively few industries and companies. The diversified fund's longer-term record, though, can be far superior—particularly if the undiversified fund's management runs into a period of poor judgment. Portfolio makeup is vital to analyzing performance.

The Time Factor. The original idea of a mutual fund was to provide the means by which investors could acquire a diversified investment portfolio under constant professional management. A fund *can* produce large gains—or losses—over any short-term period, but it is not intended for short-term speculation; rather, it is designed to meet *long-term* investment objectives (except money-market funds).

Investment Strategy. "Timing" investments to catch highs or lows in the market is much less important than consistency in making investments. Since the fund's managers are investing to produce consistent results over the long term, the value of its holdings at any one point in time is less significant than a well-defined, time-proven investment strategy that is followed in good times and bad.

Management Structure. Management structure can vary from a one-person operation to a team operation. You should find out how the particular fund you are interested in is managed and make sure it is a system with which you are comfortable.

The Investment Record. On the face of it, it seems simple enough to say that Fund X has performed better than Fund Y, and that therefore one should buy Fund X. But, as any professional will testify, there is far more to an investment record than a simple comparison of percentage gains or losses.

When comparing investment performance, the investor should ask several questions, such as: For what periods are the investment records being compared? If it is a short-term period, what was the market environment? Was it a market dominated by speculative issues on the upside? If so, was Fund X, as compared to Y, in a position to take advantage of this environment?

In recent years, much has been made of the short-term investment record of a limited number of mutual funds. Again, the prospective investor must ask several questions: What actually produced the results? Was it the fact that the fund had a very small portfolio with a limited number of holdings, and a couple of these happened to be "star" performers? Or did the fund come on the scene just as a bull market was starting? Was it because the fund emphasized a given industry, which may soon cool off? Was the fund using borrowed capital? Did it invest in highly speculative and, to a great extent, unmarketable securities?

If the answer to any of these questions is yes, proceed with caution. You must avoid being deluded by short-term percentage gain figures. Ask, and get, clear, unqualified answers to such questions as are posed here. The central one is: What has been this fund's long-term record? The importance of this cannot be overemphasized, for an investor must know how the fund performs through bad markets and good ones. To the extent that it produces relatively favorable results through down markets as well as up, you can feel reasonably confident in management's ability. Figure on a ten-year record of performance as an appropriate yardstick for making comparisons.

Age. What about the "age" of the fund? The benefit of a long life is that the fund has had the obvious advantages of navigating through both up and down market cycles. Its management has become seasoned. A fund that has prospered only in up markets is unseasoned and you should investigate it carefully.

Makeup of the Portfolio. This point will give you vital clues to the operating philosophy of the fund's management as well as its investment goals. Among the factors you should analyze in this area are (1) whether the portfolio includes a great many or a limited number of holdings; (2) the fields in which this fund is investing; (3) the relative emphasis on investments in each field; (4) the size of the companies in which the fund invests; (5) the balance between seasoned companies and unseasoned ones; and (6) the holdings (or lack) of stocks, bonds, preferreds, and cash as a percentage of the portfolio.

Size of Fund. The size of a fund is *not* as important as many of the above factors, but can have an impact on whether, and how, investment objectives are achieved. A small fund may be less successful than a large fund in achieving the goal of income stability, for the larger fund can buy a more diversified portfolio and may be able to grow in a more orderly way than the smaller fund. On the other hand, a large fund is likely to be somewhat less successful in achieving the goal of big *capital gains,* for it cannot concentrate as a small fund can on a few small companies that have strong growth potential. In a small portfolio of around $10 million to $25 million, two or three hot stocks can do wonders for performance.

In summary, investing in a mutual fund is not complicated, but requires basic knowledge and some homework. By following the steps outlined above, you can make an informed decision about the open-end mutual fund or funds that best suit your investment objectives. If in doubt, you should contact an investment adviser, your accountant, or someone more knowledgable about your affairs.

Joseph F. Kissel

Mutual Savings Banks

See SAVINGS BANKS.

·N·

NASDAQ

See NATIONAL ASSOCIATION OF SECURITIES DEALERS AUTOMATED QUOTATIONS (NASDAQ).

National Association of Securities Dealers, Inc. (NASD)

The National Association of Securities Dealers, Inc., is the self-regulatory organization of the securities industry for the regulation of the over-the-counter securities market. The association was established under the authority granted by the 1938 Maloney Act amendments to the Securities Exchange Act of 1934, which allows voluntary associations of broker/dealers to regulate themselves under the oversight of the SE-CURITIES AND EXCHANGE COMMISSION (SEC).

Membership. Some 4,000 securities firms throughout the United States were members of the association in 1983, ranging from the nationally known giants to small and specialized local firms. Approximately 260,000 persons were registered with the NASD as registered representatives (or securities salesmen) and principals (or officers of firms).

Functions. The association has three broad functions:

- *Rule development.* It develops its own rules of fair practice, usually contingent on SEC approval, and it participates in the rulemaking of the SEC through comments and testimony regarding SEC rule proposals.
- *Regulation.* The association examines its members and enforces compliance with its own rules of fair practice and federal securities laws and regulations.
- *Services.* It provides services to the membership and to the over-the-counter market.

Organization. The NASD is controlled by its board of governors, two-thirds of whom are chosen from the securities industry and one-third of whom are selected from fields associated with the industry—insurance, mutual funds, accounting, law, and NASDAQ-quoted companies, among others.

Matters to come before the board are first studied by one or more of the many national standing and special committees appointed by the chairman of the board. The names of some of the committees reflect the scope of the association's interest and responsibility: Arbitration; Corporate Financing; Direct Participation (or tax-shelter) Programs; International; Investment Companies (or mutual funds); Municipal Securities; National Market System Design; Options, Qualifications; Real Estate; Trading; and Variable Contracts.

Beyond these national committees, the association has district committees in each of the 13 geographic districts into which the membership is divided for administrative purposes. The principal function of the district committees, which are elected by the members in the various districts, is to review the reports prepared by the NASD staff on the examinations of member firms. (Persons serving on the national and district committees also do so without compensation.)

The NASD's paid full-time professional staff consists of some 1,000 persons. Over 500 of these employees work on regulatory programs, principally in the district offices and at NASD headquarters in Washington, D.C.; approximately 220 are involved in the association's automated services to the NASDAQ market and the membership; and nearly 100 handle membership and registration administration.

The Rule-Development Function. Whenever the need for an addition or amendment to the NASD's rules of fair practice arises, the matter is referred to the appropriate standing committee. With staff assistance, the committee develops a proposed rule or rule change and submits it to the board of governors. If the board approves the proposal, it submits it to the NASD's membership for comment. After the comments have been taken into account, the proposal is presented to the membership for a vote. If the vote is favorable, the board then transmits the proposal to the SEC for its approval. When the NASD comments on a significant rule proposed by the SEC or another governmental body, the comment drafted by a committee is generally reviewed by the board of governors before it is officially transmitted.

The Regulatory Functions. The NASD fulfills its self-regulatory responsibilities by means of a nation-wide field-inspection program, carried out by the district offices, supported by the executive office in Washington, and reviewed by the district committees and the board of governors.

All NASD members are subject to examination by the association's district staff, which operates in a purely fact-finding capacity. The staff examination reports are reviewed by the appropriate district committees. In those instances in which a district committee finds an apparently serious violation of NASD or governmental rules, it will file a formal complaint against a firm and hold a hearing on the complaint. If the charge of a serious violation is sustained, the firm and the individuals involved in the violation will be penalized. In the gravest cases, a firm may be expelled from the NASD, an individual may be barred from association with any NASD member, and both may be fined. Disciplinary decisions by district committees are reviewed by the board of governors and are final only when the board has made its findings. NASD decisions may be appealed to the SEC, and the SEC decisions may be appealed to a U.S. Court of Appeals.

Other regulatory functions of the NASD include:

- development and administration of qualifications examinations for securities-industry professionals;
- review of public offerings of securities in which members participate to determine whether the terms and conditions of the offerings are reasonable; and
- review of advertising and sales literature published by NASD members for accuracy and fairness.

Service Functions. The principal service functions of the NASD are the ownership and operation of the NASDAQ System (*see* NATIONAL ASSOCIATION OF SECURITIES DEALERS AUTOMATED QUOTATIONS [NASDAQ]). This nationwide electronic service is largely responsible for the growth and efficiency of the NASDAQ market.

Another significant service, provided jointly by the North American Securities Administrators Association and the NASD, is the NASAA/NASD Central Registration Depository (CRD). This automated operation permits an individual to become licensed and/or registered with any of the participating states and/or exchanges and the NASD through the filing of a single form and the making of a single payment to the NASD. The CRD will eventually result in a substantial reduction in the amount of paper work caused by dual licensing and registration, to the benefit of the licensing authorities and the 260,000 securities professionals and their employers.

For the benefit of investors, the NASD operates a nationwide arbitration facility that is used by investors to resolve disputes with their broker/dealers and by broker/dealers to settle disagreements among themselves. The number of claims processed through the NASD's arbitration facility has increased significantly in recent years.

See also OVER-THE-COUNTER (OTC) MARKET.

Gordon S. Macklin

National Association of Securities Dealers Automated Quotations (NASDAQ)

A highly sophisticated, computerized communications system that stores and transmits up-to-the-second price quotations for approximately 4,000 domestic and foreign securities. In order to be quoted on NASDAQ, issuers of common and preferred stock, warrants, convertible debentures, and other financial securities must meet the financial requirements of this electronic system.

The electronic nationwide and international NASDAQ market is the prototype of the stock market of the future. It is also the most visible part of the vast U.S. OVER-THE-COUNTER (OTC) MARKET, whose combination of equity- and debt-securities trading makes it the biggest single financial market in the United States. This entry shall first cover the NASDAQ market and then deal with the other parts of the OTC market.

Growth of the NASDAQ Market. The NASDAQ market is the fastest-growing and the second-largest stock market in the United States. In late 1983, approximately 4,200 securities were traded in it—many more than on the New York Stock Exchange and the American Stock Exchange combined. The number of companies who list one or more issues on NASDAQ grew by nearly 50% from the end of 1977 to the end of 1983, from 2,456 companies to over 3,600. During the same period, the number of companies listing stocks on the NYSE was off slightly, from 1,575 to 1,537. The number of companies on the Amex fell by nearly 25%, from 1,098 in 1977 to 826 at the end of 1983.

The number of investors in NASDAQ and other OTC securities increased by almost 100% between 1975 and 1982, to 10 million, while investors in NYSE securities increased by only 45% and in Amex securities by 67%. In 1983, total share volume for NASDAQ securities was 75% of that of the NYSE and seven times that of the Amex.

Quality of NASDAQ Securities. Most significant for investors, the value of an average NASDAQ share, purchased at the end of 1974, was five times as much by late 1983. In the same time span, the Dow Jones industrial average only doubled.

Many large and nationally known companies have their stocks traded in the NASDAQ market: American Greetings Corporation, American International Group, Inc., Apple Computer, Coors (Adolph) Company, Intel Corporation, A. C. Nielsen Company, Nike, Inc., Pabst Brewing Company, Roadway Express, Inc., Tampax, Inc., and Tandem Computers, Inc., to name but a few. Also on NASDAQ are hundreds of banking, high technology, insurance, manufacturing, merchandising, oil, transportation, and utilities. A third category of NASDAQ companies consists of relatively new and small enterprises, some of which may turn out to be the growth stocks of the future. Finally, there are on NASDAQ some 250 foreign stocks and American Depository Receipts of Australian, British (Beecham), Canadian (Falconbridge), Dutch (Royal Dutch Petroleum), French (Perrier), German (Bayer), Israeli (Bank Leumi), Japanese (Toyota), South African (De Beers), South American (Telefonos de Mexico), and Swedish (Ericsson) enterprises.

Domestic NASDAQ companies, small and new or large and old, must generally conform to the same federal disclosure and reporting requirements that issuers of exchange-listed stocks do. To be included in the NASDAQ market, companies must have, at a minimum, $2 million in total assets, $1 million in capital and surplus, 300 public shareholders of record, and a public float (i.e., shares freely traded) of 100,000 shares. There are special requirements for foreign securities.

The 4,200 securities in the NASDAQ market in late 1983 were are of such quality that at least 600 of them could be listed on the NYSE if their issuers chose to list them, and approximately 1,600 NASDAQ securities could be listed on the Amex, whose criteria are less stringent than those of the NYSE.

Some years ago there was a fairly standard progression for a company and its stock: Start out in the OTC market, move to the Amex as the company grows, and list on the NYSE to show that it has arrived. Today, over 1,600 companies keep their stocks in the NASDAQ market instead of listing. They do so for three principal reasons:

- the competitive, multiple-market-maker system
- NASDAQ's state-of-the-art communications technology
- the NASDAQ National Market System

The Competitive, Multiple-Market-Maker System. The NASDAQ market is a dealer market, whereas the exchanges are auction markets. In an auction market, the buy and sell orders in a given security flow to a single specialist who "auctions" the orders off against each other. In return for his near-monopoly position, the specialist is subject to rules designed to keep the market in a stock orderly. In the NASDAQ dealer market, there are no single specialists. Instead, each NASDAQ security is traded by a number of competing dealers, known as "market-makers," who buy and sell the security they trade for their own inventories.

The average NASDAQ security has more than seven different dealers making a market in it. Some thinly traded securities have as few as two market-makers, which is the minimum required for initial listing on NASDAQ; at the other end of the spectrum, very active NASDAQ securities can have 20 to 30 market-makers, or more.

The competition between the market-makers, whose trading activities are closely monitored by the NASDAQ System and by NASD Market Surveillance professionals, keeps the markets for NASDAQ securities orderly. As the multiple market-makers compete for profitable order flow in a security, they express their differing judgments on the stock by the prices at which they are willing to buy and to sell it, and the quantities that they are willing to buy or sell at their quoted prices. This activity, combined with the activity of investors, determines the market price of a stock and the volume of trading in it.

Who the Market-Makers Are and Why. Well over 500 securities firms across the U.S. make markets in NASDAQ securities. They range in size from the nationally known giants, who each make markets in 500 to 1,000 stocks, to regional firms, making 50 to 200 markets, to local brokerage houses, making 1 to 10 markets in the stocks of local banks, manufacturing companies, merchandising enterprises, and utilities.

Large or small, securities firms make markets in NASDAQ securities for one or more of four reasons:

- *Wholesale interest.* A firm may seek profits from trading stocks with other broker/dealers.
- *Retail interest.* A firm must have good products (stocks) for its customers. Market-making is a way of acquiring at wholesale products to be sold at retail.
- *Research interest.* A firm's analysts may conclude that the stock of a NASDAQ company is a potentially rewarding investment. This could lead the firm to both make a market in the stock and recommend it to its customers.
- *Corporate finance interest.* When a firm has been an investment banker for a company, it generally considers it good business sense to be an effective market-maker in the company stock. This gives investors in the company an orderly market in which to sell and new investors one in which to buy. Also, a firm may make a strong market in a stock in the hope of attracting a company's investment-banking business.

Competing Market-Makers: Advantages for Issuers. Many issuers whose securities are eligible for exchange listing keep them in the NASDAQ market because they prefer the competitive, multiple-market-maker system to the specialist system. William G. McGowan, Chairman of MCI Communications Corporation, one of the most active NASDAQ securities, has said, "Why should we accept one [specialist] market-maker in our stock, when we can have 40? If your monopoly market-maker comes to work feeling bad, your stock will suffer, whereas if one of your (NASDAQ) market-makers feels bad, the others will make up for it."

In addition to the competition and diversity of the multiple-market system, NASDAQ issuers like three aspects of it: (1) the sponsorship that market-making firms provide to their stocks; (2) the retail sales efforts that market-making firms undertake on behalf of NASDAQ securities; and (3) the capital that firms commit to stocks in which they make markets.

The capital that market-makers commit to the maintenance of a security in their inventories provides support to the continuous and orderly marketability of the security. The combined capital that a number of market-makers in a NASDAQ security bring to its support is often greater than the capital that a single specialist on an exchange brings to the support of a listed security.

The market-makers' capital commitment is always helpful, but it is particularly important in maintaining stability in a security under adverse market conditions. For example, October 8–10, 1979, was a three-day period in which there occurred one of the most precipitous price drops recorded in recent years in the securities markets. During those three days, NASDAQ market-makers filled the void created by the absence of retail and institutional buyers. They committed estimated additional capital of over $100 million in acquiring for their own inventories more than 7.5 million shares of NASDAQ securities during the market decline. During this three-day market decline, investors benefited from the competitive market-maker system because it provided them with a number of places in which to sell their stocks even though other investors were not buying them.

Competing Market-Makers: Advantages for Investors. The competitive market-maker system allows their brokers to shop for the best price at which to buy or sell. When an investor is interested in buying, say, 100 shares of NASDAQ Company X, the broker can ascertain instantly, on his desktop terminal, what the lowest available selling price is among all the market-makers in the stock. If the customer then places his buy order, the trader in the securities firm locates on his NASDAQ terminal the market-maker who is quoting the lowest selling price and executes the customer's order with that market-maker. Thus, by means of the NASDAQ computer and the competitive market-maker system, the firm with the customer's order is able to get that customer the best price available at the time his order is placed.

NASDAQ Communications Technology. While the dealer or market-maker system has been around for a long time, it acquired its major advantages for issuers and investors and its ability to compete effectively with the specialist system of the exchanges only in the 1970s and early 1980s. The market-maker system was enabled to make this great forward leap through the communications technology introduced into it by the NASDAQ System, which was launched in 1971.

Before NASDAQ, price quotations from market-makers on over-the-counter stocks were hard to come by and often unreliable. Securities firms published or ascertained quotations in the so-called pink sheets, whose information was collected by messengers and distributed again by messenger and mail, often days out-of-date. For recent quotations, brokers had to reach market-makers by telephone or telegraph. Locating the best quotation among various market-makers was practical only for large orders. Under these circumstances, the market-maker system was not nearly as attractive to established or growing companies as it is today, and many of them listed their stocks on exchanges as they qualified for listing.

The NASDAQ System Today. In early 1971 the NASDAQ System was launched and electronically began the process of collecting and disseminating the quotations of market-makers on an up-to-the-second, nationwide and worldwide basis. The way NASDAQ works in the 1980s is this:

There are three giant central computers at the NASDAQ data center in Trumbull, Connecticut. The central computers are connected to some 2,000 NASDAQ terminals, located in the offices of market-makers, other broker/dealers, financial institutions, and regulatory organizations like the NASD, which owns and operates the NASDAQ System.

By means of their NASDAQ terminals, the more than 400 market-makers in the 4,200 NASDAQ securities enter price quotations at which they are ready to buy (bid) and sell (ask) into the NASDAQ computers. The computers store the information and make it available on demand to all subscribers of NASDAQ terminals. Thus, anyone with a NASDAQ terminal can see all the up-to-the-second quotes of all the market-makers on all the NASDAQ securities at any time.

The computers identify the best bids (the most a market-maker will pay) and asks (the least for which anyone will sell) for all the securities. This calculation not only is displayed on NASDAQ screens, along with the quotes of all the market-makers, but is also transmitted to market data vendor organizations. These organizations make the best bids and asks for NASDAQ securities available on 100,000 securities salesmen's desktop terminals in the U.S and the rest of the free world.

General market data is also provided by the NASDAQ computers to NASDAQ terminals and to desktop terminals through the vendors. This includes continuous display of the NASDAQ Composite Index and six subindexes (Banking, Industrial, Insurance, Other Finance, Transportation, and Utilities). At the end of the day, the computer collects and disseminates volume statistics on each NASDAQ security and the NASDAQ market as a whole, plus the advances and declines, most active stocks, etc.

Publication. The Associated Press and United Press International newswire services are also connected to the NASDAQ computer. They receive all the price and volume data in the computer, and then edit it in a variety of formats for transmission to their client newspapers. Some 100 leading papers receive and publish the NASDAQ National List of the 1,800 most prominent securities on NASDAQ; the *Wall Street Journal, Barron's* and the *New York Times* also publish all or part of an Additional List of 1,000 stocks; and dozens of newspapers carry abbreviated versions of the NASDAQ National List, or lists of stocks of particular regional interest. (In addition, hundreds of papers publish short lists of NASDAQ stocks of local interest.)

Market Surveillance. Besides collecting and disseminating data on NASDAQ securities for securities-industry professionals, investors, the press, and issuers, the NASDAQ computers are invaluable tools for policing the NASDAQ market, or market surveillance. For example, for each security on the NASDAQ System, the computers are programmed with a series of historical price parameters, which reflect the normal price range of the stock. The moment that any market-maker's quotation breaks one of those parameters on the high side or the low side, the computers alert the Market Surveillance Section at NASD headquarters in Washington, D.C., and print out the nature of the break. Market Surveillance professional analysts then go to work immediately to determine whether the parameter break was the result of legitimate market activity or whether it is suggestive of possible insider trading or stock manipulation or other violations of fair-practice rules that govern the securities industry.

To help the analysts, the NASDAQ computers also store second-by-second quotations data for each NASDAQ security. At the touch of a button, the analyst can review 60 days of activity in a security and reconstruct trading patterns as they occurred. Other Market Surveillance resources include overnight computer studies of NASDAQ activity, terminals that can retrieve 90 days' worth of news items on securities, and extensive files of reports from NASDAQ issuer companies.

In a given year, NASD Market Surveillance reviews over 5,000 on-line price-parameter breaks, conducts approximately 1,000 formal reviews of unusual price or volume activity, engages in upwards of 100 detailed investigations, and refers some 50 cases to the SEC or NASD district offices for further investigation and disciplinary action, where appropriate.

In the 1978–81 period, the SEC brought charges in 32 insider-trading cases of various kinds. Seven of the eight prosecutions involving insider trading in NASDAQ issues grew out of investigations initiated by NASD Market Surveillance and referred to the commission.

NASDAQ Technology, Issuers, and Investors. The development in NASDAQ communications technology have revolutionized the market for 4,000 securities, their issuers, and millions of investors. They have made the competitive market-maker system modern, efficient, and reliable. NASDAQ issuers have responded by keeping their securities on the NASDAQ market instead of listing them on the exchanges, and investors have responded by trading some 15 billion shares of NASDAQ securities in 1983, or over five times the volume five years earlier.

The NASDAQ National Market System. The third main reason why issuers keep their securities in the NASDAQ market, and why investors increasingly enter it, is the NASDAQ National Market System. The U.S. Congress, by the Securities Acts Amendments of 1975, mandated the creation of a national market system for stock trading and charged the Securities and Exchange Commission with overseeing its development by the securities industry. Among the objectives of a national market system, as envisaged by the Congress, was the combination of the best of the exchange markets and the best of the over-the-counter markets into one system. The SEC subsequently decreed that a number of NASDAQ securities should enter the National Market System, and become subject to real-time transaction reporting, as exchange-listed securities are.

Making certain NASDAQ securities subject to transaction reporting while being traded by competing multiple market-makers is a way of combining a popular feature of the exchange markets with the strength of the over-the-counter market. It is also a very acceptable idea to many NASDAQ issuers who welcome the increased information on their securities that transaction reporting provides (in addition to the continuing quotations information) and who also want to have their securities traded by multiple market-makers rather than by the single-specialist system.

Tier 1 NASDAQ/NMS Securities. The NASDAQ National Market System began experimentally in April 1982 with 48 of the most active NASDAQ securities, and with 13 more added by midsummer. The SEC's selection criteria for these so-called Tier 1 stocks included an average volume of 600,000 shares a month for six successive months and a bid price of at least $10.

The experiment was successful. The average number of market-makers per security actually increased. Investor interest in the Tier 1 securities continued high, and their total share volume over several months ran 80% of the volume of all 960 stocks on the Amex. For the month of July 1982, volume in these 48 Tier 1 stocks exceeded total Amex volume by more than 14%.

Tier 2. For the period beginning October 1, 1982, the SEC adopted less-stringent criteria for so-called Tier 2 NASDAQ/NMS securities, including 100,000 shares traded a month for six successive months and a bid price of over $5. In contrast to Tier 1 securities, which were mandated into NMS, Tier 2 designation is at the option of eligible issuers. A great many of the Tier 2 eligible issuers are applying for inclusion and their securities are being gradually phased into NMS. By the end of 1983, there were some 700 NASDAQ securities traded in NMS, and the aggregate share volume of these securities ran as high as 150% of the volume of all the securities on the Amex.

NASD Proposals for Tier 2. In addition, the NASD has proposed to the SEC a third set of criteria for the eligibility of NASDAQ securities for NMS. These criteria are comparable to those for listing on the American Stock Exchange. The NASD has pointed out that companies should be permitted to have the benefits of the dissemination of transaction information on their securities, which NMS designation provides, without having to list and give up the advantages of the competitive, multiple-market-maker system.

The SEC has supported the NASD-proposed criteria in principle, but has deferred action on the proposal until experience has been gained with NASDAQ/NMS under its own criteria. If the SEC rules favorably on the NASD proposal, another 1,000 NASDAQ securities will become eligible for NMS designation.

The Stock Market of the Future. The combination of electronically linked, competing market-makers with up-to-the-second transaction reporting—all without the use of the traditional exchange floor—puts NASDAQ on the leading edge of the securities industry. NASDAQ is the beginning of the stock market of the future, a highly visible and competitive market based on electronic links and executions rather than trading activity on an exchange floor. "The seemingly chaotic moving about and paper waving on stock exchange floors have become an exciting backdrop for stock market reports on nightly television news reports," Martin Baron wrote in the *Los Angeles Times,* "but some experts consider them anachronisms in the electronic age. The step taken by NASDAQ—the automated quotation network for over-the-counter stocks operated by the National Association of Securities Dealers—will provide investors in these securities more information than they ever had before. More important . . . it can be expected to furnish investors with better prices and faster trades."

See also NATIONAL ASSOCIATION OF SECURITIES DEALERS AUTOMATED QUOTATIONS (NASDAQ) INDEXES; STOCK EXCHANGES.

Gordon S. Macklin

National Association of Securities Dealers Automated Quotations (NASDAQ) Indexes

The NASDAQ Composite Index is a measure of all domestic common issues traded over the counter that

Table 1
NASDAQ Indexes

Index	Number of Securities	All-Time High	12/31/82	12/31/81	1982 % Change
Composite	2,961	240.70 (12/8/82)	232.41	195.84	+18.7
Industrial	2,254	283.03 (5/29/81)	273.58	229.29	+19.3
Bank	101	160.73 (11/12/82)	156.37	143.13	+9.3
Transportation	41	205.81 (11/5/82)	195.48	167.77	+16.5
Insurance	93	236.76 (12/6/82)	226.40	194.31	+16.5
Other finance	419	216.40 (12/8/82)	207.50	176.20	+17.8
Utility	53	316.17 (12/8/82)	286.23	181.67	+57.6

are included in the NASDAQ System, exclusive of those listed on an exchange and those with only one market-maker. It encompasses more securities than any other stock-market index or the Dow Jones averages.

Unlike the Dow Jones averages, in which each security has an equal effect on the average regardless of the number of shares outstanding, the NASDAQ Composite Index is weighted according to market value. The influence of each stock on the index is proportional to its price times the number of shares outstanding. The price is the best bid price at the time of computation of the index. The number of shares is adjusted immediately for stocks added to the NASDAQ system, for stocks removed from the system, and for changes in capitalization greater than 5% (annually for smaller changes).

The seven NASDAQ indexes were established at 100 on February 5, 1971, the Friday before the NASDAQ System became operational on Monday, February 8, 1971. Securities are grouped into the NASDAQ Index categories by using SEC classifications. At the end of 1982, the NASDAQ indexes stood as shown in Table 1.

Gordon S. Macklin

National Council of Savings Institutions

The council is the result of a consolidation of the National Association of Mutual Savings Banks and the National Savings and Loan League on November 1, 1983. Its initial membership consisted of some 600 savings banks and savings and loan associations located nationwide, with total assets of approximately $300 billion. The council sees its prime mission as representing the forward-looking, progressive savings institutions seeking to capitalize on the financial-services opportunities created by the GARN-ST GERMAIN DEPOSITORY INSTITUTIONS ACT OF 1982.

While federal legislation and regulation top the council's list of priorities, the organization also offers a full range of trade-association services to its members. Such programs are financed by fees paid by those institutions that choose to participate.

The council's publications are aimed at keeping its members up-to-date on emerging trends in areas of importance to progressive savings institutions. They include:

• *Bottomline*, a monthly magazine that reports on developments affecting the savings industry;
• *Washington Memo*, a weekly newsletter that gives an up-to-the-minute report on the legislative and regulatory scene;
• *Economic Update*, a monthly newsletter that inter-

prets economic and financial developments and provides a detailed report and analysis of savings-industry performance and trends; and
• *Special reports* that analyze regulations, legislation, tax matters, and accounting issues.

Many of these publications are also available to the general public.

The council also maintains a full schedule of meetings each year. These include:

• *The Annual Conference*, held in May each year at various locations across the country;
• *The Management Conference*, held alternately in New York and in other cities in December;
• *The Operations Conference/Exhibit*, held in late winter, with the location rotating between Boston, New York, and Washington, D.C.; and
• *The National Mortgage Conference*, held in September in Washington, D.C.

In addition, the council conducts a significant number of one- and two-day seminars on topics of current interest to savings-institutions executives, and 50 to 60 programs each year in the area of education and management development.

The National Council of Savings Institutions is headquartered in Washington, D.C.

Arthur M. Mikesell

National Credit Union Administration (NCUA)

The National Credit Union Administration is an independent financial regulatory agency of the federal government and is responsible for the chartering, supervising, examining, and insuring of all federal CREDIT UNIONS. Additionally, it insures the accounts of those state-chartered credit unions that choose this option or are required by state law to be federally insured.

At the beginning of 1983, there were 11,412 federally chartered credit unions and 5,139 federally insured state-chartered credit unions being served by the National Credit Union Administration. NCUA's central office is located in Washington, D.C., and it maintains six regional offices located in Boston; Washington, D.C.; Atlanta; Chicago; Austin; and San Francisco. Approximately 600 employees work for NCUA.

A credit union is a member-owned, nonprofit financial cooperative organized to promote thrift among its members and to make loans to its members from their accumulated savings. A credit union's members are associated by a common bond of occupation, association, or geography.

The credit-union movement in the United States traces its roots to cooperative credit societies founded in Germany in the mid-nineteenth century. Evolving out of a desire to combat usury and help the working class, these organizations spread to other countries of Europe and to North America.

The first credit union in the United States was established in 1908 in New Hampshire. In 1909, Massachusetts enacted the first "credit union act." Through the efforts of such people as the Boston department-store philanthropist Edward A. Filene, the movement quickly spread from New England to the rest of the country. Thirty-eight states and the District of Columbia had credit-union statutes on the books by 1934.

The Federal Credit Union Act was passed by the Congress and signed into law on June 26, 1934. The first federal credit union was chartered on October 1, 1934, by the Federal Credit Union Section, which was established in the Farm Credit Administration. This government agency was selected to administer the credit-union program after objections from the Treasury Department and the Federal Reserve to the Senate-passed version of the bill, which had provided that the authority should rest with the comptroller of the currency. Credit unions remained with the Farm Credit Administration until May 16, 1942, when the First War Powers Act of 1941 was used to transfer them to the Federal Deposit Insurance Corporation (FDIC). At this time there were approximately 4,100 federal credit unions with more than 1.3 million members.

For the next six years, credit unions were under the FDIC. In 1948 the FDIC, faced with the need to request appropriations for its credit-union responsibilities, decided against entering the appropriations process. As a result, on July 28, 1948, the Bureau of Federal Credit Unions (BFCU) was established and was transferred to the Federal Security Agency, the predecessor of the Department of Health, Education, and Welfare (HEW). At the end of 1948, there were 4,058 federal credit unions with 1.6 million members. By the end of 1952, federal credit unions numbered nearly 6,000 with 2.8 million members.

Reorganization Plan Number One of 1953 abolished the Federal Security Agency and created the Department of HEW. The BFCU became part of HEW and also became self-sufficient, operating from the fees of its member credit unions. During its 17-year stay in HEW, the number of federal credit unions jumped from 6,500 to approximately 12,700 and from 3.2 million members to 10.6 million members.

A bill to create an independent credit-union supervisory agency had first been introduced in November 1967 in the Ninetieth Congress by the chairman of the House Banking and Currency Committee, Wright Patman of Texas. Legislatively, no action was taken by the Ninetieth Congress on the measure, but federal credit unions and credit-union organizations were asked to submit recommendations and comments.

The CREDIT UNION NATIONAL ASSOCIATION, INC. (CUNA), the principal credit-union trade association, immediately took steps to publicize the measure to all federal credit unions. In 1968 CUNA adopted resolutions endorsing the concept of an independent federal credit-union regulator.

Chairman Patman and 23 other members of the House banking panel reintroduced the bill for the Ninety-first Congress in early 1969. It cleared both houses and was signed into law on March 10, 1970, thereby creating the National Credit Union Administration.

NCUA was established primarily to place the credit-union supervisory agency on a par with the federal agencies that supervise banks and savings and loan associations. The growth and maturity of credit unions was the major argument in support of the creation of a new, independent agency. Between 1950 and 1970, the number of federal credit unions grew from 4,984 to 12,977; assets rose from $405 million to nearly $9 billion; and members increased from 2 million to 12 million.

At first, NCUA was headed by a single administrator appointed by and serving at the pleasure of the president. A seven-member advisory board, consisting of "persons of tested credit union experience," was also appointed by the president. The administrator was enjoined to "seek the advice, counsel and guidance of the Board with respect to matters of policy. . . ."

In 1978 NCUA was restructured from a single-head agency to one governed by a three-person board. Board members, including the chairman, serve staggered six-year terms, are appointed by the president, and are confirmed by the Senate. No more than two board members may be from the same political party.

NCUA operates solely on funds received from credit unions in return for various services. It does not receive federal budget money. Essentially, the agency today is charged with the following responsibilities for federal credit unions: granting and revoking charters; prescribing regulations for federal credit-union operation; examining, liquidating, merging, or temporarily operating them (conservatorship); and establishing educational, experimental, and developmental programs. Additionally, the agency is called on frequently to testify before the Congress on credit-union matters, and it also administers the National Credit Union Share Insurance Fund and the Central Liquidity Facility.

The Share Insurance Program was created by Congress in 1970 as a reward to credit unions for their work in meeting the financial needs of millions of Americans. Presently, the fund insures credit-union member accounts up to $100,000. The program is mandatory for federal credit unions and open to voluntary participation by state credit unions. The fund operates entirely on premiums paid by the credit unions.

The NCUA Central Liquidity Facility was established in 1978 by Public Law 95-630. It functions as the central bank for the country's credit unions, providing funds to meet their liquidity needs when traditional sources of credit are not available. The CLF operates as a profit-making government corporation within the National Credit Union Administration. It is capitalized through stock purchases by its members.

NCUA's primary effort in recent years has been to reduce its involvement in the business decisions of credit unions. While stepping up examination of credit unions to ensure their safety and soundness, it has abolished or modified numerous rules and regulations that had governed the day-to-day operation of credit unions. Most notably, NCUA now allows federal credit unions to determine terms and conditions of all saving accounts, including dividend rates, maturities, penalties, and premiums.

Edgar F. Callahan

National Labor Relations Board (NLRB)

An independent federal agency created in 1935 to administer the National Labor Relations Act, the principal labor-relations law of the United States. The National Labor Relations Act defines and protects the rights of employees and employers, encourages collective bargaining, and seeks to reduce interruptions in commerce caused by labor disputes. The NLRB functions to prevent unfair labor practices by either employers or unions and conducts secret-ballot elections among employees to determine whether they wish to be represented by a union or not.

Harvey Rachlin

National Securities Clearing Corporation (NSCC)

See STOCK EXCHANGES.

Negotiable Order of Withdrawal (NOW) Account

Negotiable Order of Withdrawal accounts—or NOW accounts—allow a depositor to earn interest while at the same time issuing checks against the balance. In effect, a regular NOW account at a bank is a combination checking/savings account that yields 5¼%. Congress authorized depository institutions nationwide to offer NOW accounts in 1980, but institutions in the Northeast had been allowed to offer the account earlier.

See SUPER NEGOTIABLE ORDER OF WITHDRAWAL (NOW) ACCOUNT.

Phil Battey

Net, Net Profit, Net Loss, Net Worth

The "net" amount in a financial transaction is the amount remaining after all expenses and other necessary disbursements have been made. In the simplest example, an item that sells for $2, with the cost of manufacturing, transporting, storing, advertising, displaying, and selling, etc., accounting for $1, would give a net profit of $1. It is likely, however, that hidden costs and certainly taxes owed could reduce that amount even further, so that the $1 remaining might be called the "net receipts before taxes," and the real "net profit" would be a lower figure. Should there be a negative balance, or more money spent or disbursed than money taken in, the amount would be expressed as a "net loss."

When calculating one's net profit or net worth, which is one's total value (in cash, property, stocks, etc.) after deducting any outstanding expenses or amounts owed, it is important to present one's strongest position. The deductions, like depreciation on real estate, which are allowed on one's income-tax forms, are not always required to appear in a statement of one's net profits for a bank or creditor. An honest picture of one's worth, profits or losses, should reflect the real cash flow of a business or individual, though the IRS may allow or other contexts require certain extra deductions from the gross receipts.

For example, a person who owns rental property might gross (receive from all sources) $10,000 from the property. Maintenance, utilities, land taxes, insurance, and all other necessary expenses might account for $5,000 of that amount. When filing a tax return for rental income, however, the Internal Revenue Code allows one to deduct a reasonable percentage of the whole value of the property and certain renovations and contents of a building according to a schedule of depreciation. On one's income-tax form, the result of deducting depreciation might appear as an overall "accounting loss," as it is called.

While it is good for those who pay taxes to have accounting losses to balance against other income, it would blur the actual cash profile of a person applying for a loan to present an IRS form showing a net loss for tax purposes when in fact there was cash to draw from the property. One might do better to show the bank or creditor the "net profit" of $5,000 actual cash drawn from the property after expenses. The amount would reflect the cash flow from the property available toward repayment of a loan and in no way compromise the individual to the bank or IRS.

David B. Axelrod

Net Settlement

Settling payments among participants in CHECK CLEARING or similar arrangements by netting the claims presented by participants against one another and posting only the resulting credit or debit differences. In a net settlement, all accounting entries for the day's transactions net to zero among the group of participants (i.e., the debits offset the credits).

The twelve Federal Reserve banks provide net-settlement accounting services for participants in local check clearinghouses (*see* CLEARINGHOUSE) and regional county clearing arrangements, and provide a net settlement for clearing charge slips among participants in regional credit-card associations.

Because the Federal Reserve's credit and debit postings are considered final and irrevocable, private clearinghouses and similar clearing arrangements settle balances for participants on the books of the Reserve banks. In a Federal Reserve net-settlement arrangement, the participating financial institutions agree to have a third party designated as settlement agent (frequently one of the institutions themselves). Each day the settlement agent creates a listing of entries that will be posted to each participant's account at the Reserve bank and delivers the settlement sheet itself to the Reserve bank for posting, or transmits the settlement-sheet information to the Reserve bank electronically over the Fedwire.

Net settlement is considered by many economists and central bankers to be a governmental or central banking service that benefits the nation's banking system and the public as a whole by minimizing the number of payment transactions that must be made between banks to settle differences and by providing settlement in final and irrevocable funds. However, in the Depository Institutions Deregulation and Monetary Control Act of 1980, Congress designated Federal Reserve net-settlement service as one of eight banking services provided by Reserve banks that the Federal Reserve would be required to begin explicitly charging service users for. Net-settlement charges were first imposed in October 1981 and are assessed to settlement agents on a per-accounting-entry basis. Settle-

ment agents, in turn, usually prorate these charges to participating banks.

David H. Friedman

New York Cotton Exchange (NYCE)

A COMMODITY-FUTURES EXCHANGE on which cotton, frozen concentrated orange juice, and liquefied propane gas are traded.

History. The cotton industry, which suffered severely during the Civil War, began to revive by the late 1860s. Trading in cotton and in cotton futures was being conducted in brokers' offices, but by 1868 the flow of cotton bales through the Port of New York and the accumulation of supplies of cotton in the port's warehouses encouraged a group of New York brokers to organize a cotton exchange.

The first attempt by merchants and brokers to establish an exchange under the name of the New York Board of Cotton Brokers failed. A second attempt was successful, and the brokers signed an agreement on July 20, 1870, to support plans for the organization of a cotton exchange. A constitution and a set of bylaws were adopted at a meeting held on September 7, 1879, and the New York Cotton Exchange officially opened for business three days later. The first exchange occupied rented quarters at 142 Pearl Street, near Wall Street. Business prospered, and in 1872 the exchange moved to larger quarters in the building at the head of Hanover Square known as India House.

Cotton was initially traded in cents and fractions of a cent; but in response to competitiveness in the business, pricing was refined to hundredths of a cent in 1877. Trading volume continued to increase, and in 1885 the exchange was moved to a new building bounded by William, Beaver, and Pearl Streets. The exchange remained in this building until further growth made it necessary to enlarge facilities. Plans were disrupted by World War I and it was not until 1922 that the old building could be torn down and construction started on a new 23-story building on the same site. The new building was completed in 1923 to accommodate a membership that had expanded from 106 to 450 seats. In 1967 the exchange moved its premises once more, to 37 Wall Street.

Today the Cotton Exchange shares the trading floor of the Commodity Exchange Center with Commodity Exchange, Inc., the New York Mercantile Exchange, and the Coffee, Sugar and Cocoa Exchange in the World Trade Center. Each exchange has its own quadrant or floor area on the trading floor. The Cotton Exchange quadrant contains three trading rings, one each for cotton, frozen concentrated orange juice, and liquefied-propane-gas futures. The 25,000-square-foot trading floor serves more than 2,000 traders and support personnel who operate futures markets in over 20 different commodities. When the exchange first opened, seats could be purchased for $200 and annual dues were $25. In 1982, seats were valued at approximately $35,000.

The increased number of contracts traded resulted in the establishment of the certificate system in 1887. Previously, a cotton contract had to be delivered to the receiver, turned out of one warehouse, weighed, sampled, and carted by truck to another warehouse. Under the certificate system, the Classification Committee of the exchange issued a certificate detailing the grade of cotton bought or sold, the price, and the date of the transaction. The certificate could then be passed from person to person like a stock certificate. A clearinghouse was established in 1915 to safeguard the rights of market participants.

In the early 1930s, the exchange experienced its greatest ordeal when the impact of farm-support programs began to be felt. Farm-support programs decreased the role of the exchange by regulating the supply of cotton available and providing a price support. Later, the exchange's problems were further compounded by the activities of the Commodity Credit Corporation. By 1966–67 the total volume of trading in cotton-futures contracts was only 50,000 bales—less than one days' trading in normal times. By 1968, conditions in the cotton industry had worsened. Both domestic consumption and exports were at their lowest since 1957. Futures-trading volumes began to dry up as spot prices settled at government loan-support levels.

New legislation in the 1970s improved conditions, and trading volumes increased. The new law provided for the continuation of commodity programs on a scaled-down basis; limitations on the amount of money an individual producer could receive for participation in the program; land retirement and an increase in cotton acreage for the export market without the effects of price-support payments. Today, the exchange is once again suffering the effects of farm-support programs and the number of contracts traded has fallen to an average monthly level of 4,689 from an average monthly volume of 9,385 contracts traded in 1980.

A futures contract in frozen concentrated orange juice (FCOJ) was established by the Citrus Association of the New York Cotton Exchange in 1966 at the request of a group of Florida orange-juice processors. The group recognized that a futures contract would be beneficial to the growing manufacture and distribution of oranges and orange products. After 1967, the

first complete year of trading for the FCOJ contract, trading volume increased from 22, 860 contracts to a high of 387,182 contracts in 1981. Volume dropped sharply in 1982; for the period ending November 30, 1982, only 187,182 contracts had been traded.

In 1971 the New York Cotton Exchange further extended its activities to include a contract in liquefied-propane-gas futures, and Petroleum Associates was established. The LPG contract was revised in December 1981 and the unit of trading reduced from 100,000 gallons to 42,000 gallons.

Liquefied propane gas reemerged as an important fuel during the early 1970s when the energy shortage caused the industrialized nations to develop a mix of practical fuels to supply their future energy requirements. Today, propane ranks as one of America's four chief sources of energy, along with natural gas, oil, and coal. Almost 90% of America's propane is produced domestically—by natural gas, plants, and oil refineries. Propane's most common use is for both residential and commercial space heating. Propane has recently found a new market in dual fuel (gasoline and propane) or as straight propane for trucks and auto fleets in both Europe and the United States.

The Execution of a Futures Trade in Cotton, FCOJ, and LPG. The process of trading a futures contract in any of three commodities begins when a customer calls his broker, a FUTURES COMMISSION MERCHANT (FCM) and places an order to buy (or sell) a specific number of futures contracts. The futures commission merchant immediately transmits his customer's order to the floor of the Cotton Exchange, where a floor clerk or broker records the specific instructions on a trading slip, which is quickly passed to a trader standing at the ring. All orders received at the ring must be executed by "open outcry," which involves the continual voicing of offers to buy or sell. Traders also use hand signals to clarify communication with each other. Floor traders are required to record the details of each completed transaction on trading cards, which are time-stamped and become part of the exchange's daily record.

Once an order has been executed in the trading ring, the price is reported back to a floor clerk, who in turn reports back to the originating FCM. The FCM will often report the results of the transaction immediately to his customer by phone, followed by a written confirmation of the trade.

Throughout the trading day, exchange clerks stationed among the floor brokers use hand signals to transmit price changes to a recording clerk who is positioned in a rostrum overlooking the ring. A computer-terminal operator located within the propane-ring rostrum constantly sends updated trading information to the Commodities Exchange Center's central computer, which stores all data for subsequent retrieval from video display terminals located on the trading floor. Computer-activated wall boards, which surround the CEC trading floor, instantly display price changes in clear view of floor brokers and clerks. The CEC computer also feeds high-speed Teletype systems that deliver trading data to private price-quotations vendors and to national and international news media.

The amount of money needed to start trading commodity futures will vary with the type and quantity of contract to be purchased and the creditworthiness of the trader. On the New York Cotton Exchange, the minimum initial margin requirements are $1,000 for speculators and $500 for industry users for cotton futures and FCOJ. For liquefied propane gas, the margin requirements are $900 for speculators and $750 for industry users. Some brokerage firms will ask for a customer deposit of no more than $5,000, while others may request $30,000 or more to get started.

Structure. The Cotton Exchange is governed by a board of managers elected annually by the membership. The board is responsible for establishing and overseeing policy for the Cotton Exchange. In addition, it provides facilities for the Citrus Associates of the New York Cotton Exchange and the Petroleum Associates of the New York Cotton Exchange. Both the Citrus Associates and the Petroleum Associates are governed by boards of directors elected annually by the memberships. All these boards appoint separate committees to look after a wide range of matters, including business conduct, bylaws, physical deliveries, and finance.

The exchange itself is a not-for-profit organization. Income is generated by contract fees collected from member firms, and from interest on money invested.

All Cotton Exchange members and its 55 member firms must conform to the rules and regulations of both the exchange and the Commodity Futures Trading Commission (the federal regulatory agency for futures trading). The unique features of futures trading—ease of access to a centralized market; organized trading by public outcry; price discovery; and careful monitoring—assure a marketplace that is characterized by its fairness and efficiency.

The Clearing Corporation. All futures contracts are backed by a sophisticated clearing system that provides full performance guarantees to all market participants. The Commodity Clearing Corporation, Inc., is composed of exchange member firms who have agreed to honor the contract obligations of every individual clearing member.

At the end of each day, every executed trade must be recorded and matched within the Commodity Clearing Corporation. All data pertaining to a trade are recorded by both the buy and sell brokers' clerks on brokerage sheets. This information is fed into the Clearing Corporation's computer system. Once a trade is matched and reflected on the daily register, the Clearing Corporation guarantees its performance. Upon acceptance of the trade, the clearinghouse in effect becomes the seller to every buyer, and the buyer to every seller.

All clearinghouse members are required to deposit guaranty funds and fixed initial margins with the Clearing Corporation. At the close of each day's trading, a "settlement price" is established for each contract delivery month. Clearing members must replenish margins for each contract carried on their books where the settlement price has shown an adverse price movement.

Initial margin deposits, the guaranty funds, and the surplus reserves of the corporation are available against default by any clearing member. In addition, the members of the Commodity Clearing Corporation are jointly responsible in case of default. Because of these protective arrangements, New York Cotton Exchange futures-contract traders have never incurred a loss caused by the Clearing Corporation's failure to meet its financial obligations.

Memberships. There are 450 memberships on the exchange. Individual members, both trading and nontrading, are examined by the Membership Committee and approved by the board of managers. Trading members are allowed to trade in all three contracts on the exchange and are called "floor traders" or "brokers." A prospective trading member must show a liquid net worth of $100,000 before being considered for membership. A nontrading member of the exchange is usually an industry representative and must show a liquid net worth of $25,000. Members are also required to pay an initiation fee of $750 and annual membership dues of $250. At the end of 1982, memberships were quoted at $32,500 bid and $34,000 offered.

Trading Permits. Two-year trading permits are issued to nonmembers for trading liquefied-propane-gas futures. A prospective permit holder must show a liquid net worth of $50,000 and pay quarterly dues of $750.

Dana F. Ferrell

New York Federal Reserve Bank

The Federal Reserve Bank of New York is one of 12 regional Reserve banks that together with the board of governors in Washington, D.C., and Federal Open Market Committee, and the nation's depository institutions, comprise the Federal Reserve system, this nation's CENTRAL BANK. The New York Fed serves the Second Federal Reserve District, encompassing New York State, the 12 northern and central counties in New Jersey, and Fairfield County, Connecticut.

At the direction of the Federal Open Market Committee, the New York Fed conducts domestic open-market operations on behalf of the entire Federal Reserve system. The FOMC, composed of the seven board governors and five of the 12 Reserve Bank presidents, is the top monetary-policy-making unit of the system. Open-market operations—the buying and selling of U.S. government securities—are the means through which the system conducts monetary policy, by influencing the cost and availability of money and credit.

The president of the New York Fed is a permanent voting member of the FOMC and traditionally is selected its vice-chairman. The other 11 presidents serve one-year rotating terms. Thus, each year, four of the other presidents serve as voting members of the FOMC. However, the nonvoting presidents attend the meetings and participate in the discussions.

The first vice-president of the New York Fed traditionally is the only second-in-command who may substitute as a voting member of the committee in the absence of the Reserve Bank president. When other voting presidents are unable to attend an FOMC meeting, an alternate Reserve Bank president votes. FOMC meetings are held about eight times a year in Washington, D.C.

All foreign exchange trading for the Federal Reserve system is done at the New York Fed, which buys and sells foreign currencies in the New York exchange market at the direction of the FOMC. Similarly, the foreign desk operates in the exchange market for the U.S. Treasury.

The New York Fed also stores "official" gold owned by about 80 foreign nations, central banks, and international organizations. The vault, containing the largest known accumulation of gold in the world, rests on the bedrock of Manhattan, 80 feet below street level. It currently holds about $15 billion in gold bars, based on the official price of $42.22 per fine troy ounce. This represents about a quarter of the known gold reserves of the world.

Foreign official gold reserves have been held at the New York Fed since 1924 for numerous reasons, including the stability of the U.S. political system, the concentration of international trade and finance in New York City, and the convenience of centralizing gold holdings in a place where international payments can be made quickly. The New York Reserve Bank also holds more than $95 billion of marketable U.S. government securities in custody for foreign and international accounts. Through its domestic trading desk, the New York Fed, at the direction of the "official" customers, buys and sells U.S. securities on their behalf and provides them with a variety of investment and custodial services.

Though serving a geographically small area, the New York Fed is the largest Reserve bank in terms of assets and volume of activity. The New York Fed has a branch in Buffalo, New York, serving 14 western counties of the state. Additionally, there are five regional check-processing centers within the district— one at the Buffalo branch; one each in Utica, New York, and Cranford, New Jersey; and two in Jericho, Long Island.

Arthur Samansky

New York Federal Reserve Bank Services for Central Banks and International Institutions

The Federal Reserve Bank of New York provides a variety of banking services services for about 150 foreign central banks and for international official institutions such as the International Monetary Fund. As of January 1982, the New York Fed held for these accounts more than $100 billion in marketable and nonmarketable United States Treasury securities— primarily bills—and other dollar-denominated assets. It also held nearly 351 million fine troy ounces of gold, valued at $15 billion at the official price of $42.22 an ounce.

These assets are held at the New York Fed as a service to foreign official institutions. The New York Fed is the international arm of the U.S. central banking system. Administration of these official accounts, as well as other related services, is the responsibility of the bank's foreign-relations area, the only such unit in the Federal Reserve system. The open-market operations, government bond and safekeeping, and the foreign exchange areas of the New York Reserve Bank also have important roles in carrying out foreign account transactions.

The three areas also have other major responsibilities. The foreign exchange area conducts foreign exchange operations for the Federal Reserve system at the direction of the Federal Open Market committee. Similarly, it carries out exchange market operations for the U.S. Treasury. The government-bond area, like similar units at the other 11 Reserve banks, acts as fiscal agent for the U.S. government, and holds in safekeeping U.S. government, federal-agency, and other securities for district depository institutions. The open-market-operations area conducts domestic open-market operations for the system.

The most important services rendered on a day-to-day basis for official accounts are the receipt and payment of U.S. dollar funds and investment and custody transactions. Official institutions channel a significant portion of their U.S. dollar receipts and payments through their accounts at the New York Fed. Using special or standing instructions, the New York Fed carries out on its books transactions that official institutions may have with each other or with official U.S institutions.

In addition, the New York Fed acts as collection agent for items such as BANKERS' ACCEPTANCES submitted for collection and pays checks drawn by correspondents on their accounts. In 1981, overall payments and receipts exceeded $958 billion.

Funds are invested and custody services maintained under instructions received from correspondents. In 1981, the dollar volume of investment activity for correspondents exceeded $1.5 trillion.

Most investment activity for correspondents involves securities issued by the U.S. Treasury and federally sponsored agencies, and placements in the bank's repurchase-agreement pool. The New York Fed keeps correspondents current on financing operations of the U.S. Treasury and federally sponsored agencies and facilitates correspondent participation in such new offerings. The bank also acts as an intermediary between correspondents and the Treasury when it is mutually convenient that particularly large amounts of a correspondent's funds be placed directly in nonmarketable special treasury issues instead of being put into the secondary market.

Other related investment services include acting as custodial agent for U.S. government and agency securities and other instruments that official correspondents purchase through the New York Fed or through U.S. financial institutions.

In addition to these recurring operations, the New York Fed provides a number of other services in accordance with correspondent instructions. In its custodial capacity, the Reserve Bank transfers gold among accounts, arranges for export or local delivery of the metal, and clears gold through U.S. customs. Also, transfers related to International Monetary Fund gold auctions have been made by the New York Fed. The gold vault of the New York Fed holds a substantial amount of the foreign official gold reserves. The gold at the New York Fed belongs to about 80 correspondents.

The New York Fed also buys and sells foreign exchange for correspondents with corresponding debits and credits to their dollar balances.

Other services include providing a wide range of information requested by correspondents, making

available U.S. central bank personnel for technical assistance, and training foreign central-bank and related personnel.

Some New York Fed services are offered to correspondents without charge. However, the New York Fed attempts to recover its costs on investment and safekeeping transactions for correspondents through a small charge on repurchase-agreement transactions, suggested minimum uninvested working balances, and certain safekeeping charges. And although there isn't any charge for storing gold, there is a small charge for moving the metal.

Arthur Samansky

New York Futures Exchange (NYFE)

A COMMODITY-FUTURES EXCHANGE on which the New York Stock Exchange Composite Index futures contract and an option on this futures contract are traded.

The New York Futures Exchange was incorporated on April 5, 1979, as a wholly owned subsidiary of the New York Stock Exchange (NYSE). The NYFE trades futures contracts under the regulatory jurisdiction of the COMMODITY FUTURES TRADING COMMISSION (CFTC).

During August 1980, NYFE began trading futures contracts based on 90-day U.S. Treasury bills, 20-year U.S. Treasury bonds, and on five foreign currencies (the British pound, Canadian dollar, Japanese yen, West German mark, and Swiss franc). These futures contracts were traded on a floor at 30 Broad Street physically connected to the NYSE trading floor. Despite a successful beginning in Treasury bills and bonds, the NYFE products did not compete successfully with similar futures already trading in other markets. (The Chicago Mercantile Exchange previously traded futures contracts based on 90-day U.S. Treasury bills and the five foreign currencies, and the Chicago Board of Trade previously traded a somewhat similar contract based on 20-year U.S. Treasury bonds. All these contracts continue to be successful.) Consequently, the NYFE discontinued trading in these futures contracts.

During August 1981 the NYFE also listed a 90-day commercial bond certificate-of-deposit futures contract, but the Chicago Mercantile Exchange, which also listed a similar contract at approximately the same time, proved to be the dominant exchange in this market.

Recognizing that its greatest potential was in areas that capitalized on the synergism with its parent, the New York Stock Exchange, the NYFE submitted futures contracts to the CFTC in December 1981 based on the NYSE Composite Index, and the NYSE indus-

Table 1
NYSE Composite Index Futures and Options on Futures Trading on NYFE

Month	Average Daily Trading Volume (No. of Contracts)		Open Interest (End of Month)	
	Futures	Options on Futures	Futures	Options on Futures
May 1982	6,100	—	4,024	—
June 1982	6,756	—	4,384	—
July 1982	5,851	—	4,646	—
August 1982	7,568	—	4,690	—
September 1982	8,603	—	5,722	—
October 1982	10,877	—	5,459	—
November 1982	11,362	—	7,753	—
December 1982	11,069	—	5,273	—
January 1983	12,309	1,798*	6,841	1,478*
February 1983	13,783	1,445	10,781	5,338
March 1983	14,619	2,019	6,583	3,943
April 1983	13,518	1,197	9,120	7,512

* Based on two days of trading.

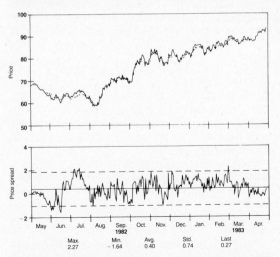

Max. Min. Avg. Std. Last
2.27 −1.64 0.40 0.74 0.27

Figure 1. NYFE nearby futures contract (solid line) versus NYSE composite index (dashed line).

trial, financial, utility, and transportation subindexes. The futures contract based on the NYSE Composite Index was approved by the CFTC and began trading on May 6, 1982. The NYSE Composite Index is a capitalization-weighted average of the prices of all common stocks listed on the New York Stock Exchange, approximately 1,500 stocks as of 1983.

With substantial support from the NYSE specialists and member firms, this futures contract enjoyed active retail and professional participation in trading from its beginning. This contract has become an inte-

gral part of the stock-market world and has established the NYFE as a viable and successful futures exchange. By March, the average daily volume reached nearly 15,000 contracts per day.

The NYSE Composite Index futures contract sometimes trades at a discount and sometimes at a premium to the actual Composite Index, as is depicted in Figure 1. The price spread of the futures minus the underlying index is referred to as the "basis," which provides profit potential for the successful arbitrager.

Subsequently, as part of the CFTC's commodity-options pilot program, the NYFE began trading an option on its NYSE Composite Index futures contract on January 28, 1983. The early trading activity of this option contract was substantial and has complemented the related futures contract.

Frank J. Jones and Karen M. Benedetti

New York Mercantile Exchange (NYMEX)

A COMMODITY-FUTURES EXCHANGE on which light "sweet" crude oil, New York Harbor No. 2 heating oil, New York Harbor regular leaded gasoline, platinum, palladium, and potatoes cash-settlement are traded.

History. The New York Mercantile Exchange, founded in 1872, has served the agricultural, industrial, marketing, and investment communities for well over a century by maintaining a market for commodity-futures trading. The exchange itself does not participate in trading; its function, like that of other futures exchanges and stock exchanges, is to oversee the trading and ensure that it is done in an open, fair, and orderly manner. To this end, the exchange provides the physical facilities, the trading rules, the mechanisms for their enforcement, and the necessary reporting and record-keeping systems.

Commodity-futures trading has experienced rapid growth over the past several years, and the NYMEX is no exception to the rule. Through the successful pioneering of energy futures, begun in 1978 when NYMEX introduced No.2 heating-oil futures, and the accelerated growth of the NYMEX precious-metals contracts, NYMEX has evolved into one of the largest established commodity-futures exchanges.

Membership. The exchange is a membership organization currently composed of more than 800 individual members. Some of the members are associated with brokerage houses; others represent businesses with interests in particular commodities; still other members are individuals trading on their own accounts.

There are well-qualified member firms who are granted clearing privileges. Clearing members are permitted to deal directly with the exchange in settling trades executed for their own accounts, and for the accounts of nonclearing members of NYMEX.

The exchange carefully regulates all members in terms of capital requirements, position limits, and several financial criteria to ensure the financial integrity of NYMEX.

Structure. The government of NYMEX and the control of its policies, property, and operations are vested in a board of governors. The members of the exchange elect these governors, including their chairman and vice-chairman, ensuring a fair representation of the various membership interests. The day-to-day activities of the exchange are administered by a highly qualified professional management team employed by the board of governors.

The president and his appointed staff have overall administrative responsibility, including responsibility for auditing the records of exchange members and member firms; responsibility for financial administration and for liaison between the exchange and its approved warehouses, depositories, and certifying agencies; the exchange's clearing and data-processing functions; research and information systems connected with exchange-traded commodities; investigation of the trading potential of various commodities; marketing of the existing contracts; and for general educational functions of the exchange. There are also NYMEX staff members responsible for the exchange's relationship with regulatory agencies, day-

to-day legal affairs, and the supervision of floor trading.

Additionally, there are several NYMEX member committees with staff liaison that deal with general administration policies, finances, business conduct, clearing activities, and the individual commodities.

Commodities Traded on NYMEX. The New York Mercantile Exchange offers unique trading opportunities to the industry hedger and the individual investor with its Energy Complex, Precious Metals Group, and the innovative "cash settlement" contract in potatoes.

The Energy Complex at NYMEX (which is often referred to by both press and traders as the "Energy Exchange") comprises a "paper refinery" of two major refined products—No.2 heating-oil futures and regular leaded gasoline futures—plus a major worldwide energy feedstock, light sweet crude oil.

Both the heating-oil and gasoline contracts are traded in 42,000-gallon contract units, quoted in dollars and cents per gallon, and specify New York Harbor delivery. The crude-oil contract is traded in thousand-barrel contract units, quoted in dollars and cents per barrel, and specifies Cushing, Oklahoma, delivery, as Cushing is the hub of domestic pipeline activity.

The NYMEX Energy Complex has for the first time made it possible for individual investors to have a say in the pricing of crude oil and petroleum products. These prices, which are reached by open outcry in the trading rings of the exchange, are a valuable source of price discovery and are internationally disseminated on a daily basis.

The precious metals traded at NYMEX are platinum and palladium. Both of these metals, best known for their myriad industrial applications, have experienced increased physical demand over the past few years as new uses are found for them on an almost daily basis.

Paralleling the increase in physical demand for platinum and palladium, futures trading in these metals on NYMEX has grown dramatically.

Platinum has a contract unit comprised of 50 troy ounces, sheet or bar, and is quoted in dollars and cents per troy ounce. Palladium has a contract unit comprised of 100 troy ounces and, like platinum, is quoted in dollars and cents per troy ounce.

The cash-settlement potatoes contract, introduced to trade on NYMEX in June of 1983, marks a major innovation in the traditional agricultural commodity-futures history in that no physical delivery of the underlying commodity is involved; rather, a cash-settlement mechanism is utilized.

The contract unit of the NYMEX cash-settlement

potatoes contract is 100,000 pounds and is quoted in dollars and cents per 50 pounds.

Where Trades Originate. Commodity-futures orders arrive in the trading rings of the New York Mercantile Exchange from all over the United States and from many parts of the globe. Clerks and brokers on the trading floor receive orders either directly from customers or indirectly via the nation's many brokerage firms that are exchange members. The leading brokerage houses, perhaps best known for trading in the stock markets, are very actively involved in commodity-futures trading.

Price inquiries and actual orders from exchange member firms come from their branch offices or their New York correspondents. A commodity specialist of the firm transmits them via private wire to the company's representative on the NYMEX trading floor. The requested information and reports of customers' purchases and sales are transmitted immediately from the floor to the New York order room of the member firm. Their order room then relays the information to its branch office, which in turn informs the customer. At each point in this circuit, the precise time of receipt is recorded. The entire process of a member firm receiving an order, executing it, and reporting the trade to its customers is frequently accomplished in less than a minute.

Trading in commodity futures offers solid risk management and investment opportunities. Trading in the unique configuration of contracts on the New York Mercantile Exchange offers opportunities rapidly being discovered by a realm of investors.

John Elting Treat

New York Stock Exchange (NYSE)

A major factor that accounts for the leading role played by the United States in world finance is the size and quality of its premier marketplace for securities—the New York Stock Exchange.

Founded in 1792, the exchange has for many years served more investors throughout the world and handled a greater money volume of stock purchases and sales than any other organized securities exchange. Recent dramatic upsurges of trading volume have given added emphasis to the NYSE's role of facilitating the transfer of ownership of shares in business enterprises.

The exchange's leadership in this aspect of finance rests on several unique attributes:

1. An overwhelming percentage of the nation's listed securities sales take place on the trading floor of the NYSE—about 85% in 1982.

2. Total value of securities traded on the NYSE dwarfs the size of other markets. In 1982, when exchange volume broke all previous records, 16.5 billion shares of stock worth $458 billion changed hands in the market at the corner of Broad and Wall Streets in New York.

3. Most of the leading corporations in the United States and some of the most prominent in other countries list their stock for trading on the NYSE.

4. The pool of capital available to professionals on the exchange trading floor is the largest of its kind in the world. It is not unusual for exchange professionals to assist in the transfer of as much as 1 million shares of stock in a single transaction.

5. Quality standards for the marketplace and for customer service are set by an extensive system of self-regulation that the members of the NYSE impose on themselves. It governs trading practices on the exchange floor and the way business is conducted in members' offices.

Function of the Exchange. The NYSE helps make the American private enterprise system work through its role in mobilizing capital this country needs for economic growth. Without a large, dependable, and liquid market for securities, it would be infinitely more difficult to raise the capital that helps provide new jobs and new industries.

The NYSE is a "secondary" market for securities, which means that its business is to trade shares *after* they have been purchased by the original investors. When stocks or bonds are offered for the first time to the investing public, the offering is made by investment bankers, who assume the risk of marketing a new issue of securities. This is the so-called primary market, where the new issues are purchased directly from the issuing company for resale to individual and institutional investors.

Without a strong secondary market, however, the primary market could not work. Buyers of securities must know that they can readily sell them, at a fair price, should the need arise. Thus, once the new securities are out in the hands of investors, they are traded on a secondary market, which may be one of the nation's stock exchanges or—in the case of newer, smaller companies—the over-the-counter market, which has no formal requirements for admitting stocks to trading. Most of the nation's large, widely owned companies rely on the New York Stock Exchange to provide the essential secondary market for their shares.

Auction Market. The exchange is an auction marketplace where prices reflect the basic laws of supply and demand. Through a member broker, an investor can sell any quantity of stock from a few shares to a million or more. The facilities are available at any hour of the business trading day to investors in any part of the free world.

The NYSE operates on the auction principle, but not the conventional kind of auction where there is just one seller offering goods to competing buyers. The exchange is a continuous two-way auction market, five days a week, six hours a day from 10:00 A.M. to 4:00 P.M. Bidders compete with each other to purchase the shares they want at the lowest possible price. Simultaneously, sellers compete with each other to get the highest possible price for the shares they are offering. All orders to buy or sell a given stock are taken or transmitted to an assigned location on the trading floor, the trading post for that stock. When the buyer bidding the highest price and the seller offering the lowest price agree on a figure acceptable to each, a transaction takes place.

In contrast, in the over-the-counter market, many issues of stock are handled only by dealers—if you want to buy, you must buy from a dealer; if you want to sell, you must sell to a dealer. On the New York Stock Exchange, most trades take place between brokers who represent public customers. The exchange itself neither buys nor sells stock. It is organized as a member-owned, not-for-profit corporation under the laws of New York State. A special category of members of the exchange, called "specialists" (see below), are authorized to act both as agents for public customers and also as dealers. Specialists have the responsibility to step into the market as buyers or sellers when there is a lack of public bids or offers for a stock at a given price range and point in time. Thus the specialist "backstops" the market by providing continuity so that (with occasional help from other floor professionals) there will *always* be a buyer available to take stock that is offered, and *always* a seller available to offer stock that is sought.

History. The exchange traces its origins to the late-eighteenth-century activities of New York merchants who gathered in lower Manhattan to trade securities. Their trading first involved U.S. bonds that had been issued to pay state debts assumed by the federal government in accordance with the new U.S. constitution. In 1792, under a buttonwood tree near the present site of the exchange, 24 of these merchant traders signed an agreement governing business principles and rates of commission. The so-called Buttonwood Agreement helped shape the early New York securities market.

Until 1817, trading continued informally in the street and nearby coffeehouses. In that year, the volume of sales was large enough to inspire organization of the "New York Stock & Exchange Board" with a written constitution. The quantity and variety of stocks steadily increased as the young nation grew: state-government bonds for construction of turnpikes, canals, and bridges; and stock sold by insurance companies and banks to raise capital for development.

The number of listed stocks grew from 30 in 1820 to more than 300 by the end of the Civil War, and membership expanded from 38 to 1,000 in 1869. The yearly volume of trading also grew dramatically in the great boom that followed the Union victory. During the war, the NYSE officially adopted its present name.

Until the early 1870s, the exchange used the "call market" system of trading. Under this system, brokers gathered two or three times a day in the trading room to hear an exchange official read off the list of stocks. As each security was called, brokers would cry out their bids or offers. Throughout the trading session, the brokers bid from assigned chairs, the origin of the "seats" that are now synonymous with membership.

Until the Civil War, the NYSE rented space in a succession of buildings in the financial district. In 1865 the NYSE moved to its present site on Broad Street. Its own elegant new building contained a trading room constructed like an amphitheater to accommodate the daily "call" sessions. In the immediate post–Civil War period, trading expanded enormously with the issuance of railroad stocks and other securities to finance the industrialization of the country. The large increase in the securities listed and in volume of trading made it impractical to continue with the call system, and in 1871 the present continuous auction method of trading was introduced, with business conducted on a large open trading floor.

In the new arrangement, stocks were assigned to permanent floor locations designated by a post with initials at the top (for example, U.P. for Union Pacific Railroad). Brokers circulated to trade while specialists stayed at a particular post to deal in specific stocks. Legend has it that the first specialist was a broker immobilized by a broken leg. Rather than walk about the trading floor, he offered to execute orders in Western Union stock left with him. His accidental occupation developed into one of the principal sinews of today's continuous auction market.

Introduction of the stock ticker in 1867 speeded the dissemination of accurate market information throughout the country and abroad.

By the turn of the century, the exchange needed a new building, which still houses the main trading floor and many staff offices. Opened in 1903, the elegant classical-revival-style building has a columned facade that has become a visual symbol of the stock exchange, instantly recognized from pictures and drawings around the world. In the exchange's central hall, new trading posts were installed with an interconnecting pneumatic tube system that also linked them to ticker-tape operators. An immense panel on one wall, with magnetically operated numbers that flapped incessantly, notified brokers by their badge numbers when a new order awaited them at their phone booths fringing the floor.

The extraordinary bull market of the 1920s impelled the exchange to expand its floor and modify its trading posts again, and during the ensuing years were constant changes to accommodate new business requirements.

The events of the 1929 stock-market crash and the Great Depression that followed led the exchange to reorganized its own governing structure, hire its first full-time paid president, and delegate to its staff more authority to oversee operations and enforce rules. In 1934 Congress passed the Securities and Exchange Act, and since then the exchange and other securities markets have operated under the aegis of the SECURITIES AND EXCHANGE COMMISSION (SEC). The SEC looks to the NYSE to oversee compliance by its members with the federal securities laws.

Exchange procedures were changed significantly again in the 1970s to deal with financial and operational problems that caused the failure of a number of brokerage firms, and to respond to important changes in securities laws enacted by Congress in 1975. During that period, the exchange's governing machinery was reorganized and self-regulation was made more comprehensive. Also in 1975 the practice of charging customers a minimum commission, which had prevailed since the exchange's beginnings in 1792, was abandoned. Commission rates are now negotiated between agent and customer.

Current Organization. Today, the exchange is governed by a 22-person board of directors elected by the members who own seats. Ten directors are chosen from the securities industry, ten from outside the industry. The chairman and president of the exchange, who serve as its chief executive and chief operating officers, are also board members. The exchange has about 1,750 employees, of whom about 600 work on the trading floor.

In 1980 the NEW YORK FUTURES EXCHANGE (NYFE) began operation as a wholly owned subsidiary to provide a marketplace for trading in financial futures. The principal products traded at NYFE are futures contracts on the New York Stock Exchange index, which measures the price movements of all listed securities, and subgroups. Recently, trading has been in-

augurated in options on the stock-index futures, offering still another way of participating in price changes in the stock market.

The late 1970s and early 1980s brought dramatic physical changes on the exchange's trading floor and in the worldwide network of equipment that is linked with the trading arenas. The exchange has fully embraced automation, as can clearly be seen from the exchange's public visitors' gallery, where one looks down not just on a sea of busy men and women in constant motion but also on a forest of highly sophisticated computer equipment.

Without computers, the exchange could not possibly handle its present volume, which has come close to 150 million shares on a single day and is anticipated to expand to 200, 250, and 300 million shares on peak days. Yet, as in years past, skilled professional people make the market work, assisted nowadays by modern electronic technology. Human judgment and willingness to risk capital in maintaining a market are still the key ingredients of the quality market at the NYSE.

Types of Brokers. Trading on the exchange is performed by approximately 1,500 brokers who are members of the exchange, assisted by their own clerical staffs and a staff of clerks, messengers, and technicians furnished by the exchange. The exchange's constitution fixes the number of equity members, who actually own a "seat," at 1,366. In addition, there are some members who pay an annual fee to rent a seat from another member, or to acquire the right on a year-to-year basis to personally transact business on the trading floor, or to have a direct electronic or wire connection from an office to the floor. A seat was priced recently at about $350,000, rental costs at around $55,000 to $60,000 a year, physical access $50,000, and electronic access $18,500 per annum.

Each broker on the trading floor has clearly defined functions and responsibilities defined in the constitution and rules of the exchange. A member may be a general partner or holder of voting stock in a brokerage concern, or an employee of a member organization. By virtue of his or her exchange membership, the firm is eligible to be designated as one of the more than 600 member organizations of the exchange. About two-thirds of the members of the exchange are associated with member organizations that do business with the public—so-called commission houses. This is the category of broker who usually executes orders on the floor from individual investors. Many firms transact sufficient business on the exchange trading floor to justify having several members.

The categories of membership are as follows:

Specialists. The responsibility of specialists, assigned by a special committee of the exchange board, is to maintain a fair and orderly market, insofar as reasonably practicable, in the stocks in which they are registered as specialists. In order to do this, the specialist is authorized to act in two capacities—both as broker and dealer.

As a broker, the specialist acts as agent for other brokers, who leave orders with him to buy or sell at a given price that is away from the currently quoted market. In that sense, today's specialist can clearly trace his professional ancestry to the nineteenth-century broker with the broken leg. For example, if you want to buy stock in XYZ Corporation now selling at $55 a share, and you want to pay only $52.50, your broker will leave the order with the specialist in XYZ. The specialist enters the order in his "order book" (now stored in a computer memory bank). When and if the price reaches $52.50, the specialist executes your order and notifies your broker. In return for this, the specialist receives part of the commission you pay to your broker.

As a dealer, the specialist is required by exchange rules, within reasonable limits, to improve the market in his assigned stocks whenever there is a temporary imbalance between supply and demand for those stocks. He does this by trading against the prevailing trend of the market—employing his own capital to buy for his own account when others are selling, and selling for his own account when others are buying. This explains why an investor, absent highly unusual circumstances, can *always* find a buyer or seller for his stock on the NYSE. In dealing for his own account, the specialist is also obliged by exchange rules to minimize price fluctuations from one trade to the next, to narrow the temporary spread between supply and demand, and to subordinate his personal interests in the market to the public's orders.

Floor Brokers. These members work for commission houses. They execute orders and represent the buying and selling interests of their customers and the member organizations with which they are associated.

Independent Brokers. Sometimes called "$2 brokers" (due to their fee per 100 shares years ago), they execute orders on their own behalf, or represent other member organizations.

Registered Competitive Market-Makers. Like specialists, they risk their own capital to provide additional depth and liquidity to the market, but they do not have a list of assigned stocks. Free to trade anywhere on the floor, they may be called upon by the exchange to assist a commission broker or a floor broker in executing a customer's order that might otherwise not be capable of execution.

Manual and Automated Trades. These skilled professionals now are backed up by an extensive array of computers and other electronic equipment that expedite transactions up to and away from the point of trade. Moreover, a growing percentage of smaller trades are now being automated.

Before automation, all trades were handled manually, and the larger trades still for the most part are handled this way. To illustrate: In a manual execution, an investor wanting to buy 100 shares of an oil stock (let's abbreviate it as OIL) gives his broker the purchase order. The order is sent by wire to the New York office of the brokerage firm (or its New York representative if it doesn't have its own office) and is relayed to a broker on the floor of the NYSE for execution. In the traditional method, the commission broker goes to the trading post where the stock is traded and asks the specialist, "How's OIL?" The specialist responds with a price quotation, which might be "A quarter and a half, two by four." This is oral shorthand for saying that the best price bid is 50¼ and best price offered is 50½ (dollars per share). In this quote the "50" was omitted because traders will be familiar with the main dollar amount, and more concerned with arriving at the best price expressed in eighths and quarters of a dollar (a pricing system that persists from the days of English shillings and pence). "Two by four" indicates the number of shares involved—200 shares are the number of shares an investor is willing to pay 50¼ for, and 400 the number of shares another investor is offering at 50½.

The difference between the bid and offer is called the "spread," and the number of shares is termed the "size." The broker who has been asked to buy 100 shares of OIL might then call out his bid, say at 50¼ for 100. Sellers in the crowd around the trading post, however, may not be willing to sell at that, and another broker may offer 100 shares at 50⅜.

If no commission broker makes an offer, the specialist customarily will step in and offer to sell 100 shares from his inventory, within the quoted price range. In this case, the buying broker will simply say "Take one hundred" at the compromise price.

The transaction is recorded by an exchange reporter, who makes a pencil mark on a card to indicate price and quantity of the stock sale, then drops the card into an electronic reader that instantly notes the information and translates it into signals. The signals go out over the exchange's worldwide ticker network and into countless computers that store and replay the information for brokers and investors everywhere.

The ticker now operates at a speed of 900 characters per minute—about as fast as the human eye can read. In busy markets, even this high speed lags behind the actual trading, but up-to-the-minute information is always available by means of electronic inquiry devices and by "flash prices" printed periodically on the stock ticker.

In addition to reporting prices on the New York Exchange, the ticker and electronic devices also carry price and volume information for transactions in exchange-listed stocks that take place in other market centers. The exchange feeds out data to its user network at a speed of 36,000 characters a minute.

The traditional face-to-face system of trading now is supplemented by a large array of automated systems. Among the most important:

DOT. An acronym for Designated Order Turnaround; it enables a member to transmit standard types of orders in virtually any listed stock directly from its office, through an electronic message switch, to the proper trading post on the exchange floor. The specialist receiving the order handles it, giving the DOT order the same status as other orders at this post, executing it as quickly as market interest and activity permit—and sends it back electronically to its originator. More than half the number of orders brought to the trading floor now are routed through DOT for execution. Currently DOT handles orders of up to 599 shares.

Odd Lot. A round lot, the normal trading unit on the exchange, is 100 shares or multiples of 100. Odd lots are for less than 100 shares (except for a few inactive stocks, where the round-lot unit is 10 shares). Odd lots are electronically priced at the trading post, at the price of the next round lot after receipt of the odd-lot order—plus or minus a fractional differential for handling the small order.

OARS (Opening Automated Report Service). Facilitates order handling at one of the busiest times of the trading day—before the opening of the market. OARS used the DOT system to enter smaller orders into the exchange's data bank and calculates any imbalance between orders to buy and sell, thus helping the specialist to determine the fair opening price for each of his assigned stocks. OARS considerably reduces the paper work involved in a market opening. The opening prices established with the aid of OARS are entered into the computer and all opening orders are automatically priced, with notice back to firms originating the orders.

Limit-Order System. A parallel automated pricing and execution system that is in late stages of planning to handle routine orders that carry a limit price. An example would be an order to buy 500 shares at 50¼ when the last price and current quote are still above that price. With LOS, the order would be stored in a computer and automatically executed when the desired price was reached—another step in drastically reducing paperwork and manual handling of routine transactions.

Certain other aspects of securities transactions benefit from user-owned automated facilities in which the exchange is a major participant and which developed out of services pioneered by the NYSE.

SIAC (Securities Industry Automation Corporation) is a large computer facility jointly owned by the New York and American Stock Exchanges. SIAC handles all the transaction data, operates the ticker and data-base networks, and supplies brokerages with the information they need for post-trade processing of transactions.

DTC (Depository Trust Company), originally founded by NYSE but now user-owned, is a central depository for actively traded securities. Ownership in an increasing number of transactions is changed by electronic bookkeeping entry at DTC, thus eliminating physical delivery of cash and securities. Large investing institutions are the primary users of DTC. Any individual who wants delivery of stock shares can still obtain them.

NSCC (National Securities Clearing Corporation) is an industry facility owned jointly by the NYSE, Amex, and National Association of Securities Dealers. It uses advanced automation to enable brokers, banks, and other financial institutions to automate the processing of securities transactions after the trade has taken place. NSCC compares and verifies trade information between brokers, automates clearance and settlement of transactions between clearinghouse members, and handles physical delivery and settlement of balances not eligible for processing in DTC or another central depository.

Intermarket Trading System. Other automated features of today's market stem from the work that has been done to establish a national market system that links together all national stock exchanges and the over-the-counter market in listed stocks. The NYSE, as the largest exchange, has played a leading role in carrying out the mandate of the U.S. Congress to assure investors an opportunity to get the best prices obtainable for listed securities wherever they may be available.

The Intermarket Trading System (ITS) is the mechanism for carrying this out. ITS is the key building block of the National Market System. In essence, it is an electronic communications network that effectively links trading on the New York, American, and regional stock exchanges. The system operates in conjunction with a composite quotation system that displays the bid and offered prices—as well as the number of shares sought and offered at those prices—from each of the participating market centers.

Through ITS, any NYSE member-firm customer is provided an opportunity to get the best price available at any particular moment within the total nationally linked trading network.

Maintaining Investor Confidence. The leadership of the New York Stock Exchange as a quality marketplace depends ultimately on its ability to retain the confidence of investors. The NYSE never loses sight of the fact that the public must continue to look to the exchange for high standards of excellence in three vital areas: the quality of the stocks traded in its market, the integrity of the trading process, and the integrity of the management of the network of its member firms. A major function of the exchange therefore is to maintain high standards for listing securities and for professional competence and performance that genuinely merit public confidence.

The Securities. Companies listed on the exchange must: give voting rights to all holders of common stock; make regular reports to stockholders on company operations; and make timely disclosure of corporate events likely to affect the value of their stock. The exchange monitors the accounting principles used in corporate reports, and also keeps a close eye on the manner in which corporations disclose significant events to investors. For example, it is common practice for the exchange to hold up trading in a stock pending important corporate news, such as a merger announcement, to give all investors time to evaluate the new development.

The exchange has stringent requirements for the quality of the companies its admits to trading. Normally, to qualify, a company should have earning power of over $2.5 million a year before taxes, a minimum of 1 million shares publicly held, with not less than 2,000 round-lot shareholders. The publicly held common shares should have a minimum aggregate value of $16 million, and all common stock must be voting shares. An analogous set of requirements applies to companies headquartered outside the United States.

The 5,200 stocks and bonds that are bought and sold on the NYSE are issued by more than 1,800 different enterprises, including most of the largest, best-known corporations in the United States. At the end of 1982, the exchange listed 39.5 billion shares of domestic and foreign stock with an aggregate market value of $1.3 trillion and, in its bond-trading room, listed the bonds of leading corporations and government entities having a par value of more than $680 billion. The list included 170 foreign securities, 47 of these being foreign stocks.

NYSE-listed corporations represent less than 1% of the nation's publicly owned companies, but together they provide jobs for about one-fifth of the U.S. labor force; produce practically all the domestically made cars and trucks, and more than 90% of U.S.-made copper, aluminum, and cement; and operate 97% of all telephones in service.

Market Surveillance. The exchange has developed a widely respected and emulated surveillance system for maintaining a vigilant watch on the way securities are traded on its marketplace.

The Division of Market Surveillance Services oversees the operation of the exchange marketplace, administering precisely detailed rules and regulations to ensure the maintenance of fair and orderly markets. Among many other functions, Market Surveillance conducts audits of specialists' records, which include analyses of sales and purchases for periods selected at random by the exchange staff. The staff checks these figures to determine the specialists' effectiveness in fulfilling their responsibilities. The exchange staff also administers questionnaires in which other trading-floor professionals regularly evaluate the quality of specialists' service and market-making performance. The staff also makes periodic detailed reviews of the performance of nonspecialist market professionals.

The market is continuously monitored by an on-line price-surveillance program called "Stock Watch." Using data from exchange computers that run the ticker tape, Stock Watch tracks every single trade reported on the ticker throughout each trading session. When the overall price movement of a stock exceeds predetermined guidelines, Stock Watch is alerted by a computer printout of the stock symbol and the price and time of the transaction in question; a trading floor official is also alerted to closely monitor the developing situation.

The surveillance section retrieves from the computer's memory bank and carefully examines the relevant chronological sequence of sales. Most frequently, an unusual price movement is readily explainable by a public announcement of changes in a company's sales, earnings or dividend pattern, introduction of a new product, or other entirely legitimate corporate development. Listed companies normally alert the exchange to such news, which, of course, provides a basis for evaluating the activity flagged by the computer. When no explanation of the unusual activity is readily available, exchange investigators conduct a more detailed inquiry. In the rare instances in which wrongdoing by any market participant may be discovered, the exchange initiates appropriate disciplinary action or, where the exchange lacks jurisdiction, requests the cooperation of the SEC.

Member-Firm Regulation. All member organizations of the New York Stock Exchange subscribe to a code of conduct set forth in the Constitution and Rules of the exchange, and also are required to adhere to federal and state securities laws. A public-opinion poll conducted a few years ago indicated that strict regulation of its firms is considered by the investing public to be one of the most important aspects of the NYSE.

Under exchange rules, all firms are subject to exchange inspection of their books and records at least once a year, and must have their books audited by an independent outside auditor also once a year. All firms that carry public accounts must file a monthly report on their finances and operations with the SEC. Firms that do not carry customer accounts file quarterly. The exchange's Division of Member Firm Regulatory Services analyzes these reports closely for signs of trouble and makes spot checks when market conditions require. The exchange also supervises sales practices, administers examinations to test professional qualifications of people in the securities business, and is responsible for registering member-firm personnel—in effect, a form of licensing.

The exchange's enforcement department follows up on complaints and other information on rules violations. Penalties can range from simple admonition to heavy fines and, in the gravest cases, expulsion from the securities business.

Much of the routine work of regulatory oversight now is automated, which enables exchange staff officials to keep up with the greatly increased volume and diversification of the securities business.

As the outgrowth of a program that started at the New York Stock Exchange, all broker/dealers must now belong to the Securities Investor Protection Corporation (SIPC), which insures customer accounts up to $500,000, including $100,000 in cash, in case of financial failure of a brokerage firm.

The Future. The exchange's latest estimate in mid-1981 indicated that some 32.3 million men, women, and children in the United States owned corporate stock and stock mutual funds. In addition, more than 133 million have an indirect stake in corporate equities through pension plans, insurance companies, and other institutions that invest money on their behalf. The ranks of shareowners are growing, and the exchange expects its volume of trading to reach new peaks in the years immediately ahead.

At the same time, the securities industry is rapidly developing an array of new financial services and products to serve the increasingly sophisticated financial requirements of individual and institutional investors.

To handle the much larger volume of business effi-

ciently, the exchange is introducing even more advanced automation systems. While preserving the vital element of human judgment at the point of trade, the exchange is rapidly automating all elements of the transaction chain that brings the order to the marketplace, and that handles necessary tasks after the trade, such as record-keeping, delivery, and settlement. The professionals who personally handle the flow of orders in the trading arena are also benefiting from very advanced automation systems. Many of the new technologies are already in use; others are in the development stage. Among the newest high-technology concepts now being worked on are a computer system that can be activated by human voice signals or by finger touch on a sensitive flat glass screen. Other projects involve small, hand-held terminals that can be used by the highly mobile people on the floor for such tasks as storing transaction information and transmitting it to the communications network.

One decision against change has been made: The NYSE has vowed, at least for the foreseeable future, to remain in its present premises at the corner of Broad and Wall Streets. Thus a strong link to the past will be preserved as the nation's largest stock exchange prepares for the future.

                                            John J. Phalen, Jr.

New York Stock Exchange Common-Stock Indexes

In 1966 the New York Stock Exchange began publishing stock-price indexes encompassing every common stock listed on the exchange. The development of the NYSE computer complex, recording and storing every transaction on the floor of the exchange, made possible for the first time the computation of price movements that would reflect not merely samples of the market but all issues listed.

The indexes consist of a Composite Index of all common stocks listed on the exchange and four subgroup indexes—Industrial, Transportation, Utility, and Finance.

The indexes are basically a measure of the changes in aggregate market value of NYSE common stocks, adjusted to eliminate the effects of capitalization changes, new listings, and delistings. The market value of each stock is obtained by multiplying its price per share by the number of shares listed. The aggregate market value, which is the sum of the individual market values, is then expressed as a relative of the base-period market value. The base value was purposely set at 50.00, because this figure was reasonably close to the actual average price of all common stocks on the base date of December 31, 1965.

The arithmetic procedure in calculating the index is

shown in the following simplified example: Current total market value, $770 billion, divided by adjusted base market value, $700 billion, multiplied by 50.00 equals the current index, 55.00.

Every measure of changes in stock prices—index or average—must frequently be adjusted to reflect only movements resulting from auction-market activity and eliminate the influence of corporate actions. Any change in the capitalization of an individual issue or of all issues in aggregate is dealt with in this index by making a proportionate change in the market value of the base figure.

For example, if 40 million shares are being added to the list for any company's stock and that company's stock closed at 50 on the night before listing, then the value of $2 billion would be related to the value of all common stocks on that night and the same proportion would be added to the base.

Assume the value of all common stocks on the night before listing to be $770 billion, and the base to be $700 billion. On the basis of the formula, this would give an index of $770 \div 700 \times 50$, or 55.00.

The added value of $2 billion related to $770 billion = 0.26%. Then 0.26% of 700, or 1.82 billion, is added to the base. The new calculation is $772 \div 701.82 \times 50$, giving an index of 55.00, the same as before.

Specifically, the procedures for adjustment are:

• Stock splits and stock dividends do not need adjustment in the base, since the aggregate market value is the same before and after the split or dividend.
• New listings and delistings require an increase or decrease in the base market value in direct proportion to the change in the aggregate market value of the list.
• Mergers between two listed companies resulting in no change in total value require no adjustment. When a listed company acquires an unlisted company, an adjustment is made for the additional value added.
• In rights offerings, an adjustment in the base is made to compensate for the value of the new shares being added to the current value of the issue.

The "Market." Also computed and published on the NYSE ticker tape is the change in the current average price of all common stocks. This is identified as the "Market," and stated in dollar and cents terms—e.g., up 16¢.

As the average price is affected by capitalization changes (stock dividends and splits), new listings, and suspensions, and as these occur almost daily, the current average price cannot be measured against any historical average price to indicate price change. It is measured against the preceding closing average price adjusted to compensate for any overnight changes in the list. To avoid confusion, the average price itself is not published.

The NYSE Composite Index has been computed on a daily-close basis from May 28, 1964. The discontinued index of the Securities and Exchange Commission was converted to the NYSE base on a weekly-close basis from January 7, 1939, to May 28, 1964. The component indexes have been calculated on a daily-close basis from December 31, 1965. Since July 14, 1966, the Composite has been computed every half-hour and the other indexes every hour. The Market change measure is calculated every half-hour.

The indexes are printed on the NYSE stock tickers and are available through commercial interrogation devices, on news tickers, in daily newspapers, and in financial and economic publications.

New York Stock Exchange

No-Fault Insurance

See AUTOMOBILE INSURANCE.

Note

An unconditional, written promise to pay a sum of money either on demand or at a definite time to a party specified in the document or to the bearer. It must be signed by the maker; therefore, the party signing the note assumes a legal obligation to pay according to the terms of the document. All bank loans are backed by notes.

Phil Battey

Nuclear Insurance

See INSURANCE.

Numismatics, Collection/Investment

Numismatics may be defined as the study, collection, or acquisition of coins, medals, paper money, and related items.

Collector/Investor Background. Coin collecting has been a popular hobby for centuries. In fact, the hobby has existed as long as there have been coins—dating back to the ancient Romans and Greeks. It has been a hobby with universal appeal, open and available to all people from kings to newspaper boys, with absolutely no barriers of discrimination. From rare, expensive four-dollar gold pieces to the most common of Lincoln pennies, there has always been an area in numismatics for every collector to invest his energies.

Numismatics as an investment field, however, is of recent origin, reaching a sophistication level relative to other, more traditional areas (i.e., stocks, bonds, real estate) only since the early 1970s. Interestingly, though, when old-time collectors are questioned about their numismatic "hobby" during the early years of the twentieth century, they invariably point out that they never bought a coin with any intention of parting with it at a future date *without making a profit.* And, in effect, this attitude represented the numismatic investment strategy adopted by most collectors in the mid-1930s. These numismatists really represented the embryonic stages of what has become an important and viable investment medium of the 1970s and 1980s.

Types of Coins. Though the word *numismatics* by definition includes not only regularly issued coins but also currency (paper money), medals, tokens, and other related items, it is the "standard" coins, both world and United States issues, that have been central to the numismatic investment environment of recent years. More specifically, United States coins, struck at U.S. government mints in Philadelphia, Denver, San Francisco, and other cities have been the key areas of modern-day collection/investment. There are more than 100 different U.S. coins (by denomination and design) that have been struck since the Philadelphia Mint first opened its doors for regular coinage production in 1793. These range in denomination from the half-cent through the twenty-dollar coin and were struck in various metals such as copper, bronze, nickel, silver, and gold. Coins that were issued in the past but are not currently coins of the realm include two-cent pieces, three-cent pieces, half-dimes, twenty-cent coins, and one-, two- and-one-half, three-, four-, and fifty-dollar gold pieces. Each specific denomination and series within each denomination has attracted its own collectors, investors, and researchers.

For convenience in categorization, the U.S. coin market is often broken down into these specific groups:

Type Coins. These are coins that display a major and specific variation of design within a given denomination. For example, a Buffalo nickel is a type coin within the five-cent denomination. It is, by design, different from the Liberty and Shield nickels that preceded it as well as the current Jefferson nickel design. A type coin is differentiated from the other coins in the series in that it is an example of one of the most common dates within the series. A 1937 Buffalo nickel, one of the most available and abundantly issued dates in this series, is regarded as a type coin. The 1931-S Buffalo nickel, because of its low mintage, is

considered a scarce date and hence does not qualify as a type coin. There are approximately 100 different U.S. type coins, ranging from the Liberty Cap half-cent of 1793 through trade silver dollars issued from 1873 through 1885.

Gold Coins. These are 90% pure gold coins struck at U.S. government mints for regular usage from 1795 through 1933 when the United States abandoned the gold standard. The basic designs are the Liberty Head type and the Indian type, but also include the beautiful Standing Liberty design created by sculptor Augustus St. Gaudens. Regularly issued denominations included the one-, two-and-one-half-, three-, five-, ten-, and twenty-dollar pieces. However, the excessively rare four-dollar and fifty-dollar gold pieces were also struck. When in 1934, it became illegal for U.S. citizens to own gold, most U.S. gold coins were called in and melted, the exceptions being those that found their way into collections or abroad, mostly in Europe.

Commemorative Coins. These are legal-tender U.S. coins struck in silver and gold that were specially issued to celebrate a specific person or event of significance in U.S. history. There were 142 different commemorative silver half-dollars issued; 1 silver quarter, 1 silver dollar, and 13 different gold commemorative coins.

Silver Dollars. Actually, these are really type coins; but because they have become so popular, not only in the United States but throughout the world, U.S. silver dollars, specifically the Liberty Head (Morgan) and Peace designs, occupy their own special category. Morgan dollars were issued from 1878 through 1921, and the Peace-dollar series saw issuance from 1921 to 1935. These two designs are probably the most popular and highly collected of all coins and are particularly attractive because of their large size, high silver content, availability, beauty, and affordability.

Colonial Coins. These are coins that were struck by the colonies prior to our country's independence, and by individual states through 1793. Many of the issues were struck on crude planchets and for the sole purpose of expediting commercial transactions in the New World. Most colonial coins were struck in copper, though a few of the rare ones were issued in silver.

Territorial Coins. Most of the coins in this category were gold coins struck by private mints in California and other western territories prior to these territories' becoming states. Most of these coins are very scarce and quite valuable and were struck during the 1850s, soon after the California gold rush. There were also territorial gold pieces struck in Georgia and North Carolina, also as a result of local gold discoveries in places far removed from the Philadelphia Mint.

Pattern Coins. These are fascinating trial pieces that were not meant for circulation but were examples of proposed designs for new regular issues. Most of these are very rare, as only a few pieces were submitted by mint engravers for official approval.

Proof Sets. These are government-issued, specially processed coins that were made with pristine mirror surfaces specifically for collectors. Included in this category are mint sets that have also been issued on an annual basis for direct sale to collectors.

Uncirculated Rolls. These are coins that have been bank-wrapped and purchased by investors and collectors prior to being dispersed for circulation. Depending on the denomination (50 pennies per roll, 40 nickels per roll, 20 half-dollars per roll, etc.), complete bank-wrapped rolls consist of anywhere from 20 to 50 pieces that are in mint condition, usually somewhat bag-marked.

Miscellaneous. Such items as Hard Times tokens, Civil War tokens, California fractional gold pieces, and error coins round out a miscellaneous yet important area of the coin market. These are specialized areas, but not without a strong following.

Collectibility, Investability: Which Are the Right Coins?

What is a rare coin? If only a dozen pieces of a specific coin were issued, and all are available, yet only ten people are actively interested in obtaining this issue, is this a rare coin? If a million pieces of another issue were originally struck and still are extant, yet 2 million people want to own this coin, can it be considered rare? In other words, must demand exceed availability in order for a coin to be considered rare? In determining a coin's value—which, in practicality, on today's market is equated with rarity—the answer to the above question is an emphatic *yes!* The three key factors in a coin's being considered a choice investment property are (1) demand, (2) rarity, and (3) condition.

Demand. For a specific coin or series to be considered investable, there must be an active marketplace of buyers and sellers. Collectors and investors must want this coin. A coin of tremendous popularity and widespread demand is the Morgan silver dollar. Even though this series is relatively plentiful, the demand factor has been so great for so many years that it has become the most transacted series on the numismatic market.

Rarity. The scarcity of a coin also plays a vital factor in its investability. If a specific issue is readily available in large quantities, it is considered common and thus has limited potential as an investment and limited desirability for the collector. Often a coin's rarity is directly related to its original mintage (population), though this can at times be misleading as some coins with large original mintages have not sur-

vived the battle of attrition and have become surprisingly rare. About 228,000 twenty-dollar gold pieces were struck at the Philadelphia Mint in 1920. Many are still around, and hence the 1984 catalog price in uncirculated condition is $750, which reflects its being a common date for this series. More than 550,000 pieces of the same denomination were struck the same year at the San Francisco Mint, but apparently very few escaped the melting pot, and perhaps only a dozen or so pieces survive. Its catalog price of $22,000 in uncirculated condition certainly attests to its true rarity!

Condition. This is the physical gradation or quality level of a coin and is a vital factor in determining both its rarity and its value. Coins may be graded on a numerical scale of from 1 to 70. Grades of 60 and above are considered to be in new or mint state (MS) condition, while coins lower than 60 are considered to be circulated, used, and, to a greater or lesser degree, in a worn state of preservation. MS70 is considered a perfect coin and, in the opinion of many numismatists, is a nonexistent Utopia. An MS60 coin will be uncirculated but will pick up the normal surface flaws—namely, bag and handling marks—from striking, packaging, and normal processing from point of issue at the mint through point of release at the bank. Choice and gem coins are those whose numerical grading would fall in the mid- to upper MS60s. An 1884 Morgan silver dollar struck at the San Francisco Mint in less than MS60 condition is considered a relatively common coin and is worth from $10 to $250, depending on the specific grade. However, an MS60 specimen of this issue is worth about $1,000, an MS63 about $3,000, and an MS65 $10,000 and up!

Of course there are other factors in determining a coin's attractiveness to the investor and collector, such as an esthetic and historical appeal, liquidity, and profit potential based on current value. But the overriding factors of demand, rarity, and condition are the vital ones studied by numismatists in decision-making and planning for the most suitable acquisitions.

Pros and Cons: The Advantages and Disadvantages of Rare-Coin Investments

Advantages

Fixed supply. Rare coins do not become more plentiful. Mint reports indicate the original population, and the supply becomes more limited through attrition as coins are locked into collections and investment portfolios, lost, or simply worn out in circulation.

Tangibility. Rare coins can be seen, held, taken possession of. They are visible hard assets, not certificates or pieces of paper that represent some type of equity.

Continually increasing demand. With new generations of collectors and investors, the demand for rare coins has increased in a gradual but constant manner over the last several decades.

Easy liquidation. Thousands of dealers, collectors, and investors comprise an active marketplace for the buying and selling of rare coins. Dozens of national auction houses sell coins on a regular basis. A relatively "new" field in spite of the recent boom (and the more recent decline), the numismatic investment field is still in its early stages. When there are trust funds, limited partnerships, and mutual funds of rare coins, and brokerage houses become more involved in rare coins, as they are just starting to now, the demand will dramatically increase as the supply factor decreases.

Continued increased promotion. In the past, rare-coin exposure was limited to technical trade journals. Now sophisticated marketing firms are reaching the average investor on a worldwide and nationwide basis, extolling the virtues of rare coins as an investment vehicle with a great track record and unusually good potential for continued long-term price appreciation. The *Wall Street Journal, Barron's,* and literally hundreds of investment newsletters have, via feature articles, introduced the public to the numismatic investment field.

Portability and safety. Rare coins are easily transported and stored in insured safe-deposit boxes or corporate vaults. The smallest safe-deposit box at a bank is big enough to hold $1 million in rare coins! And unlike gold bullion in the form of bars or coins, there is safety in the ownership and possession of numismatic material in regard to any form of government confiscation. During the 1934 U.S. gold recall, numismatic gold coins were given an exempt status and allowed to remain as collectibles.

Tax benefits. Profits made from the appreciation in value of rare coins are taxed at the preferred capital-gains rate and, under the IRS Like Property Ruling, profits taken from the sale of rare coins are tax-exempt if the proceeds are reinvested in other rare coins on an exchange basis.

Retirement-plan benefits. Until January 1, 1982, coins were an IRS-approved tax-deductible and tax-deferred investment for inclusion in a Keogh, IRA, or corporate pension plan. In this manner, a worthwhile numismatic investment/collection can be built over the long term and allowed to mature in value for the individual's retirement. (As of January 1, 1982, Section 314b of President Reagan's Economic Recovery Act withdrew the tax advantages the individual would receive from including rare coins in a Keogh or IRA account.)

Proven track record. Rare coins have increased in value consistently over the years, with just a few periods of price decline. During marked inflationary periods in our economy, rare coins have a solid record of not only outpacing the inflation rate but doing so dramatically, often appreciating at two to three times the annual rate of inflation. In 1981 the prestigious Wall Street Brokerage firm of Salomon Brothers concluded from their study that rare coins showed a 27.1% compounded rate of appreciation for the ten-year period beginning in 1971. And, of course, this figure includes the two depressed market cycles of 1975–76 and 1980–81.

Confidentiality. The rare-coin business has traditionally been well entrenched as a "cash" business and hence has always afforded the buyer and seller a status of utmost privacy and confidentiality.

Disadvantages

Risk. Although the chance of overall depreciation is minimal *over the long term,* it is possible, and there are a few coins that are worth less now than they were 20 years ago. Two examples are the 1950-D Jefferson nickel and the 1903-O Morgan silver dollar. These coins, considered twentieth-century scarcities in the early 1960s, were at one time worth $35 and $1,500 respectively (in uncirculated condition). Large hoards were subsequently discovered and the values drastically declined to the 1984 level of $12 and $300 per coin. However, this is certainly the exception; rare-coin prices are more apt to decrease as a result of profit-taking after a boom cycle than due to new discoveries of additional hoards.

Rare coins do not pay dividends and are not income-producing—they represent frozen assets whose benefits, however great they can be, cannot be realized (except on paper) until liquidation after being held for several years. The rare-coin investor thus has to be willing to tie up capital for long periods.

Rare coins do not stimulate industry or economic growth—although the money spent on a rare-coin portfolio represents an excellent hedge against inflation; and while it does *preserve* one's assets, an investment in rare coins is a personal investment and not one that stimulates industry and our country's economic growth.

Evaluation. Unlike the stock market, which pinpoints exact values on a daily basis, rare coins are not subject to exact values and are often quite difficult to appraise.

Numismatic "rip-offs." It is often difficult to implement a rare-coin investment program because the numismatic investment industry is plagued by an abundance of "rip-off" and unqualified dealers. This leads to the problem of getting fair value and accurate representation in rare-coin acquisitions.

Grading. This is not an exact science—a coin's value is based on its demand, rarity, and grade. The demand and rarity factors are relatively objective since information in these areas is available and well documented and understood. But the grade—the *physical condition*—of a coin is the most confusing and abused aspect of numismatics. It is the most difficult area of numismatics to learn; and to become competent in general grading, many years of experience are necessary.

How and why is grading considered a disadvantage of rare-coin investment? Simply stated, the higher the grading of the coin, the higher its value. And investment-grade coins (MS60 or better) are worth much more than the lesser-grade coins. If a dealer buys a coin as an MS63 and sells it as an MS65, this misrepresentation of grade, even by just two points, will often bring him several times what the coin is really worth. Though there has been tremendous enlightenment among investors and collectors during the last several years, there is still widespread abuse in grading practices among rare-coin firms and professional numismatists. It is generally agreed that the grading controversy looms as the single most negative factor in numismatics and the one with the largest impact on prospective investors and collectors.

How to Get Started. There is a saying in numismatics, "Buy the book before the coin," and this is basically good advice. Join the American Numismatic Association (ANA) by writing to its headquarters in Colorado Springs, Colorado. Membership includes free access to the ANA's library facilities as well as eligibility for technical seminars on such subjects as coin grading, coin photography, and counterfeit detection. You will also receive a monthly numismatic journal that is perhaps the finest in the business.

Two important books should be purchased. The first is *A Guidebook of United States Coins* by Robert S. Yeoman. This is the popular "Red Book," an annual that lists all U.S. coins, including values for different grades, specific grading qualifications for each series, and excellent historical information. The second important book to own is *ANA Grading Standards for United States Coins* (Whitman). It provides a detailed, coin-by-coin analysis of the grading standards for every series and grade level of regular-issue U.S. coinage.

Also, subscribe to (but do not initially buy from) *Coin World,* the most popular of the weekly numismatic newspapers. After reading through several issues of *The Numismatist* (the ANA's monthly journal), you will begin to become familiar with the names of many of the national dealers, firms, and auction houses. At this point you would be well advised to subscribe to auction catalogs from two or three of the larger national companies. Most of the auction catalogs are profusely illustrated, well researched and written, and offer a wide array of choice-quality rare coins. Continually adding auction catalogs to your numismatic library will keep you informed and up-to-date as to what is being sold and at what price levels.

There are also dozens of rare-coin advisory letters, but these are often misleading and confusing and are not suggested for the novice collector or investor. Many of the advisories tend to tout their own inventory or interests. When the above reading material has been acquired and studied and you are ready to initiate a rare-coin acquisition plan, you should also subscribe to the *Coin Dealer Newsletter,* a weekly and monthly summary of U.S. coin prices published in Hollywood, California. This "gray sheet" lists the dealer-to-dealer wholesale prices reflected by transactions that take place over a national Teletype circuit.

Selecting a source—a dealer who will represent you—may be the most difficult decision for the beginning collector and investor. No amount of advertising will carry as much weight in making an educated decision as will a strong reference from a personal friend or associate. Try to locate and meet a dealer who has been a nationally recognized professional numismatist for several years. Ideally, this will be an individual who is anxious to take full responsibility for the servicing of your rare-coin account. You will want a numismatist who will represent you in all aspects of your involvement—buying, selling, appraisals, exchanges, and, perhaps most important, the rendering of continued useful information. When you find the right numismatist, let him represent you in all transactions. If there are coins available from other sources or at auctions, get his advice and allow him to act on your behalf. In most cases he will be able to negotiate a better deal for you than you will for yourself in an attempt to avoid his commission.

Some Important Suggestions. Try to avoid relying on a relationship with a large national rare-coin firm. In most cases, though the principals are often very knowledgeable and competent, you will be dealing directly with a salesman who, by the nature of the position, tends to be both transitory and motivated more by his commission than by the desire to act in the very best interests of his customer.

Do not mail-bid at auction. Regardless of the reputation of the firm offering a mail-bid sale, it is important that you never bid on any coins that have not been personally examined by you or your representative. This relates to the problem of overgrading and the very real possibility of acquiring coins that are not accurately described and represented.

Buy the best-quality coins affordable. From an investment point of view, it is better to acquire a few investment-grade (generally MS60 or better) coins than a larger number of off-grade (less than MS60) specimens.

Go to public auctions and conventions. This will afford you an opportunity to get a firsthand look at what is selling, what isn't, who is buying, and at what price levels.

Concentrate on acquiring "blue-chip" coins. The standard, regular-issue coins are the ones that have traditionally been most in demand and are most easily liquidated. Try to obtain choice-quality-type coins, rare gold, silver dollars, commemoratives, etc., rather than overloading on the more esoteric areas of numismatics.

Review your collection each year. An annual evaluation will help you make sure that your acquisition strategy is consistent and that you are building on a nucleus of fine quality coins rather than accumulating a quantity of mediocre material.

Don't be tempted by "bargains." Bargain-hunting is probably the biggest trap for the beginning collector/investor. Be wary of *every* numismatic offering (in *Coin World,* journals, fixed price lists, and mail-order solicitations) that appears to be underpriced or available at less than the current market value. Under no circumstances should the beginner investor think that he can outwit a professional dealer. He cannot. When buying from a list in *Coin World* or other trade journals, remember that in most cases the coins offered have been around for a while, been picked over, and probably are the last choices of the educated buyer. The best coins often are not even included in advertisements but are immediately placed with a dealer's preferred customers.

Buy selectively. When buying coins, remember that the best coins are scarce and are not as subject to promotion and artificial manipulation and price run-ups as are the more common coins. Look for that rare individual piece or scarce high-condition coin rather than that always tempting "bargain" in a more common piece or bulk item (rolls, proof sets, etc.).

The Rare-Coin Market: A Review of the Last Decade and Prospects for the 1980s. The decade of the 1970s will always be remembered as the coming of age of the numismatic market. Hobbyists, part-time dealers, and little-known numismatists formed coin companies and numismatic investment firms that, by the end of the decade, became important forces in the new rare-coin investment industry. Rare coins appreciated in value at a far greater pace than the double-digit inflation rate of the times. Coins that were rare in the early 1970s and selling in the $1,000–$3,000 range became *very rare* by the end of the decade, when the unheard-of per-coin value of $100,000 was not only reached but far outdistanced by the sale of a Brasher doubloon at public auction in St. Louis in the summer of 1979 for an unthinkable $430,000!

But the boom period of the Seventies, with often staggering price increases, was not without its down cycle that sent prices plummeting during 1975–76. The rare-gold-coin market, which was relatively limited and was dominated by modest prices at the beginning of the decade, peaked with the fabulous Ullmer auction (Stacks, New York) in May 1974. For the two years after the Ullmer sale, rare-gold prices dropped off considerably, and analysts wondered whether the record prices achieved at that sale would ever be reached again. Meanwhile the type coin and nongold market continued to appreciate in value, but on a more modest level of about 20% per annum.

By 1979 a rampant inflation rate, the availability of millions of *new* investment dollars being channeled into the rare-coin field, and tens of thousands of new collectors and investors competing for a shrinking supply of rare coins caused the numismatic market to begin a growth period the likes of which had never been seen before! Practically across the board, choice-quality rare coins were virtually doubling in price overnight. The sale of famous collections at public auction created worldwide attention, and day-to-day trading was at a frenzied, chaotic level. By early 1980, hundreds of new dealers were frantically trying to acquire choice rare coins for tens of thousands of new investors and collectors.

The bubble burst midway through 1980, and prices dropped sharply and steadily over the next two years. By 1982, many rare coins, including some that approached the six-figure plateau, were worth as little as 10% of their 1980 peak. Still, from an overview, the bottom of the 1980–82 crash leveled off at a higher level than the peak of the 1974 boom cycle. Salomon Brothers reported that "the year 1982 notwithstanding, U.S. coins have proven most profitable for investors over the last decade, delivering annual profits of 22.5% second only to oil and leading 12 other tangible investment categories."

Unquestionably, the rare-coin market, like other investment alternatives, presents its share of risks. Still, the long-term performance has been outstanding and continues to show strong potential for the 1980s. There are, of course, many factors that created the significant numismatic crash of 1980–82: the decreased inflation rate brought about by the Reagan administration; continued very high interest rates; and, to a lesser degree, the effect of Section 314b of the 1981 Economic Recovery Act. All had negative effects on rare-coin valves. Still, the overriding factor may have been that prices increased too much and too quickly in a temporarily artificial market. The market readjustment was devastating but probably necessary and realistic.

By August of 1982, the bear market in numismatics had ended and the recovery period in rare-coin values had begun. The new optimism displayed by professional numismatists at the ANA convention in Boston proved to be well justified. A renewed concern with inflation and falling interest rates, and the general awareness that there were once again some excellent rare-coin values, were factors in the revitalization of the coin market. With many outstanding rare coins available at a small fraction of their 1980 peaks, and with the next bull market in rare coins promising to reach and exceed the previous price records, coin values firmed and began to steadily increase through 1983, indicating that the numismatic investment possibilities for the remainder of the 1980s appear to be bright.

Phil Kaufman

Nutrition Assistance for Puerto Rico

See SOCIAL WELFARE.

·O·

Office of Management and Budget

An agency of the Executive Office of the President whose purpose is to advise the U.S. president on government-wide budget and management policies. Its responsibilities include advising the president on fiscal and economic policies for the nation; preparing the budget and formulating the government's fiscal program; and evaluating the performance of federal programs.

Harvey Rachlin

Office of Personnel Management (OPM)

A federal agency that assists the U.S. president in carrying out his responsibilities for management of the federal work force. Activities of OPM include administering the retirement and insurance programs for federal employees and central examining and employment operations. OPM took over many of the responsibilities of the U.S. Civil Service Commission, which ceased to exist in December 1978.

Harvey Rachlin

Office of Revenue Sharing

See DEPARTMENT OF THE TREASURY.

Old-Age, Survivors, and Disability Insurance

See SOCIAL SECURITY.

Open Account

This is a traditional form of retail CREDIT in which payment for one or more purchases of goods and services is deferred for up to a month, with expectation by the creditor of receipt of payment in full for all charges on receipt of a periodic or monthly billing, usually without imposition of a finance charge. Such accounts may or may not have a credit ceiling for certain or all charge customers. It is primarily used for convenience in obtaining nondurable goods and services.

James A. Ambrose

Open-End Investment Company

See MUTUAL FUND.

Open-End Money-Market Fund

See MONEY-MARKET MUTUAL FUNDS.

Open-Market Operations, Techniques of

Federal Reserve System open-market strategy, since October 1979, has focused more intently on the supply of reserves to the banking community, and less on the cost of funds. Until the strategy was instituted, open-market operations in each statement week (Thursday through Wednesday) were aimed at maintaining a prescribed average rate for federal funds (*see* FEDERAL FUNDS, PURCHASE AND SALE OF). If monetary growth appeared different from that desired, the federal-funds rate objective was adjusted.

The Federal Open Market Committee, the top monetary-policy-making unit of the System, became dissatisfied with its performance in achieving its objectives through this approach. The new method is aimed at enabling the System to better control the growth of money and credit in the banking system and thus help slow inflation and promote desired economic growth.

The new supply-oriented approach tends to exert a greater degree of pressure, more quickly, on the banks and the money market when monetary growth extends desired paths. It also promotes a prompt relaxation of pressure when money growth falls short of the desired path. The procedure, however, doesn't guarantee an immediate return of money growth to desired levels. Money growth can still be too rapid, or too slow, for extended periods if demand for money is unexpectedly strong or weak.

In addition to, and in coordination with, open-market operations, the Federal Reserve will continue to adjust reserve requirements and the discount rate as well as its reserve paths.

In its new approach, the FOMC has sought to concentrate on controlling the supply of reserves through the government securities trading desk at the Federal Reserve Bank of New York. The New York Fed conducts open-market operations on behalf of the Federal Reserve, at the direction of the FOMC. Other things being equal, System purchases of securities add to reserves, while sales of securities absorb reserves. The FOMC establishes operating guides for the trading desk by choosing growth objectives for various measures of money, the funds available to the public for transaction purposes and liquid savings. The FOMC also sets a broad band within which the federal-funds rate is expected to move, such as 8–14%, which was selected by the FOMC at its August 1980 meeting.

The staff of the board of governors uses the monetary growth objectives as the basis for constructing growth paths for total and nonborrowed reserves that are consistent with desired money growth. Total reserves are assets depository institutions may count to meet central-bank reserve requirements. Most depository institutions must directly or indirectly maintain reserves with the central bank. Nonborrowed reserves represent total reserves less borrowings at the Federal Reserve DISCOUNT WINDOW. Initially, the staff decides how to divide the FOMC's two- or three-month growth objectives into monthly paths. The monthly pattern for money growth is then translated into nonseasonally adjusted weekly levels. Application of the appropriate required reserve ratios to the different categories of deposits results in an estimate of required reserves for the period between FOMC meetings, about once every four to six weeks. Addition of estimated excess reserves results in an estimate of total reserves for the period. Excess reserves is the difference between total reserves and required reserves. Deduction of the borrowing level indicated by the FOMC at its meeting produces the nonborrowed-reserve average the trading desk is expected to achieve.

Each week the trading desk has an objective for nonborrowed reserves. The reserve objectives for the intermeeting period are reviewed by senior FOMC and trading-desk staff, typically each Friday morning. The objectives may be revised to account for such factors as changes in the mix of currency and member and nonmember bank deposits in the money supply and other liabilities.

The path for nonborrowed reserves also may be revised to help speed the adjustment process if demand for total reserves is running well above or below the desired level. The nonborrowed path would be lowered if total reserves were running strong, and raised if total reserves were running weak.

Comparison of the projected demand for total reserves with the nonborrowed-reserve path for the interval indicates the amount of borrowing consistent with achieving the path. Borrowing in subsequent weeks needed to achieve the average is then deducted from the weekly estimates of the demand for total reserves to give the nonborrowed-reserves objective consistent with attaining the desired average for the interval.

Given the week's nonborrowed-reserve objective, along with an awareness of the excess and borrowed-reserve expectations, the trading desk devises an operating strategy. Each day, the desk receives projections of the supply of nonborrowed reserves for the statement week prepared by staff at the New York Fed and at the board of governors. The projected nonborrowed-reserve supply is compared with the objective to see whether reserves will need to be added or absorbed. Some factors, such as Federal Reserve FLOAT, are particularly hard to predict and often result in large projection errors.

Given this uncertainty about reserves, the trading desk also may draw information about actual reserve availability from the behavior of the market for reserves. For example, a sharp rise in the federal-funds rate may suggest reserves are in shorter supply than indicated in the projections; a sharp decline may suggest the reverse.

Pursuit of reserve objectives involves a daily judgment of when, and how much, to intervene with open-market operations to achieve the weekly reserve objective.

Arthur Samansky

Option Trading

Option trading is one of the oldest methods of investing, yet only became very popular in America with the organization of the listed option exchanges. In 1973 the Chicago Board Options Exchange introduced listed options; and since that time, options have been traded on the American, Philadelphia, Pacific, and other exchanges. The strength and flexibility of listed options lie in the fact that they have standardized expiration dates and striking prices. This standardization of contract terms allows options to be treated in a manner similar to stocks. Open trading and price reporting of option transactions show buyers and sellers where their investments stand at any given time. The liquidity of the market gives buyers and sellers a chance to close out or offset their original transactions.

Options can be used as a conservative investment vehicle or for speculations. Thus, as with any investment, a requisite for intelligent trading is a complete understanding of the risks involved. This entry does not deal with the tax considerations, margin requirements, and commission costs. Those factors should be considered *before* entering into an options contract.

Definition. There are basically two types of option contracts: puts and calls. Persons not familiar with option trading sometimes assume that a put and call are opposite sides of the same transaction. That is not true. Puts and calls have no relationship to each other. The call buyer buys the call from a call seller, and a put buyer buys from a put seller. A call option holder (or owner) has the right to *purchase* 100 shares of a specific stock at a predetermined price (striking price) up to the maturity date. A put option holder has the right to *sell* 100 shares of a specific stock at a predetermined price up to the maturity date.

The life of the option can be as long as nine months and expires quarterly in cycles beginning in January, February, or March. All options expire on the Saturday following the third Friday of the expiration month. Although each expiration cycle encompasses twelve months, only three of the four expiration months—i.e., nine of the twelve calendar months—are available at one given time. For example, in the second cycle, with option trading in February, May, and August, no November options would be available. Once the February option expires, the Option Clearing Corporation opens trading in November contracts. The OCC issues, guarantees, and provides the clearing facilities for option transactions.

Long and Short. Any position bought by an investor (i.e., any purchase of stocks, bonds, or options) is considered a "long" position. In dealing with stocks, bonds, and options, an investor can also sell something he doesn't own. Thus, it is possible to sell XYZ short (never owning the stock) at a given price, with the intention of buying it back sometime in the future at a low price. If that security should go up, the short seller would have to cover his short position at a higher price, thus sustaining a loss.

One cannot buy an option unless someone is selling it. That seller can either own the underlying stock (covered writing) or sell an option without ownership of the underlying stock (selling naked). Selling naked or uncovered calls is analogous to selling the stock short. It is done to benefit the investor from an expected decline in the price of the stock. Since securities have no maturity date, the only way to close out a short position is to buy back that security. Options have maturity dates and can be bought back at a profit or loss, or exercised upon maturity, or expire worthless.

Opening and Closing Transactions. Each time an option trader goes into a new position, whether long or short, it is called an "opening transaction." When that position is closed out, it is a "closing transaction."

The buyer and seller of options can close out their positions independently of each other. Options are not traded between individuals, but rather through a central clearing operation. This gives the option trader total flexibility—so that if Investor A sells a call to Investor B, he can close out his position by buying back the option from Investor C. This being the case, Investor A is totally out of the picture; in essence, Investor B now has a contract with Investor C.

Each option is either bought or sold against 100 shares of an underlying security. An ABC call option would give the owner the right to buy 100 shares of ABC common stock. The cost of buying the option is called the "premium" and should not be considered a down payment toward the purchase of the stock; it merely gives the holder of the option the *right* to buy the underlying stock. An ABC Apr 40 call is the right to purchase 100 shares of ABC at $40 up to the maturity date in April.

Strike Price. If the option is an ABC Oct 50 option, the contract thus reads that if the holder of the call exercises his option to buy, he will have to pay 50, and only 50, for the underlying stock. In the case of a put, the holder of the put would have the right to sell 100 shares for each put at a price of 50, remembering the original premium paid for those options was not a down payment toward the price of 50.

Premiums. The sum of money that the buyer of an option pays, and the seller of the option receives, is called the "premium." Therefore, if the premium is $3, the seller would receive $300 for each (100 shares) option written.

The cost of the option is determined by a number of factors that should be carefully considered—such as its intrinsic value, time, and volatility. The intrinsic value is the real value of the option in relation to the underlying security. Thus, an ABC Dec 40 call, with ABC common selling at 41, would have an intrinsic value of $100, because the holder could exercise his option to the stock at 40 ($4,000), and then sell at the current market price of 41 ($4,100). Once the stock goes below the strike price, the option has no intrinsic value and will sell at a price that reflects its time value and volatility.

Time Value. The time value can be related to the cost of the use of money in that the option buyer at the time he buys his option does not actually buy the security, and hence his cash outlay is relatively small. If he were to buy 100 shares of ABC common at 40, his cost would be $4,000. The cost of the use of money will vary, but assuming that it's 10% per annum, the mere cost of carrying that security for six months would be $200. Rather than buying the stock, he could buy a call for $300 and invest the balance of $3,700 in some income-producing vehicle, still retaining control over the 100 shares. Because time is money, the longer the life of the option, the costlier the premium is going to be. As time moves on, the time-cost factor loses its value, until maturity, when the time value disappears completely.

Volatility. The volatility of the underlying security is the third factor influencing the option premium. Obviously stocks that tend to be more volatile will command a greater premium. The option holder feels that he will get more movement from a volatile underlying security. Historically, growth stocks have been more volatile than, say, utilities, so that the premiums for options on underlying growth stocks selling at the same price as a more conservative investment will tend to be higher.

Options that sell strictly on their intrinsic (real) value are selling at "parity." This usually occurs when options are selling deep in the money or close to maturity.

Strategies. Buying options gives the investor a chance to have large capital gains with a relatively small investment, and limits the possible loss to the amount invested. Thus, an investor can control more shares for less money.

Buying Calls. If the investor feels that ABC common stock will go up, he can either purchase 100 shares at the market price of 40 or buy an option with a strike price of either 35, 40, or 45. If the option buyer, however, buys an ABC 40 call for $200 and ABC goes up to 50 a share, the option holder can either exercise his option and pay $4,000 for the stock or close out his option position for its intrinsic value, which would be $1,000. His profit, in this case, would be $800—$1,000, less the $200 original cost of the option—giving him a 400% gain, while the purchaser of the common stock would have had a 25% gain.

Assuming that ABC remained at 40, the option, at maturity, would have no value, thus incurring a loss ($200) to the holder. It is important to remember that the option buyer can never lose more than his investment. If ABC had gone down to $30 a share, he would still have lost only $200, while the stock purchaser would have had a paper loss of $1,000. Since stocks do not have a maturity date, the stock owner can elect to hold that security for as long as he wants. (Again, we are not considering dividends or commissions,

which would have an effect on the net returns of most transactions.)

In-the-Money Option. Most options are bought with the intention of reselling them before they mature rather than exercising them to purchase the underlying securities. Such investors anticipate that the increase in value of the underlying stock will more than offset the option's premium. We illustrated an ABC call at 40. This predetermined price—the strike price—is set by the exchange at $5 intervals. As the underlying security goes up or down, the exchange will institute new options, such as 35, 40, 45, etc.

The option buyer can choose the strike price he prefers, depending on how optimistic he is. With ABC common selling at 40, a call option with a strike price of 35 would have to sell for at least $5 (or $500 for 100 shares). This is called an "in-the-money option" because the exercise price is below the current market value. All things being equal, the total premium would reflect the fact that it has an immediate tangible value. With ample time remaining and the stock selling at 40, the ABC option at 35 would sell for around 6. This in-the-money option has an intrinsic value of 5, with the time factor and volatility factor being 1. Thus, the option price is 6. Like all investments, the option will either go up or down, or stay the same, depending on what the underlying security does.

Let's assume that ABC remains at 40. At maturity, the ABC call would have an intrinsic value of 5 ($500), the difference between its strike price of 35 and the market value of 40. In this case, he would have a loss of $100 ($500 value, less $600 option cost). If ABC went up to 45, he could sell his option for 10 or exercise the option at 40, thus having a net gain of $400 ($1,000 less his cost of $600). If ABC went below 35, there would be a loss of $600 because at that point the option would have no value.

Out-of-the-Money Option. With ABC selling at 40, the option buyer might decide to buy an ABC Apr 45 option for (½) $50 per 100 shares. Since the strike price is above the market price, this option is called "out of the money." ABC would have to go above 45 for the option to have a real intrinsic value. However, the option buyer could sell that option at any time prior to the maturity date. Let's assume that ABC went up from 40 to 44. It is quite possible that the 45 option would sell for 1. The holder could close out his position, realizing a 100% gain. Out-of-the-money options are bought by those people who are very optimistic, and they can thus control many more shares for less dollars.

Using the above illustration, the investor could buy six ABC calls at 45 for a total investment of $300 ($50

× 6). If ABC went up to 50 a share, the investor's profit would be $2,700 ($3,000 less the original $300 cost). Keep in mind, however, that ABC would have to have made a major move—from 40 to 50—to realize this profit.

Obviously, option buying is not for the conservative, long-term investor, because of the premium and maturity factors. Unless you have a well-thought-out plan and strong financial backing, option buying is not for you. Options, however, can be used to increase income and reduce risks.

Selling Options. Until now, we have discussed only the buying of options. But one cannot buy anything unless someone is willing to sell it. The individual who sells options is called the "writer." An option writer, or seller, can sell options on his existing portfolio. This is called "covered option writing." The typical writer is seeking two objectives: additional income from his portfolio, and some protection against the possible downside movement of the stock.

Let's take an example of an ABC Apr 40 call at 3. The investor buys 100 common at 40 and sells an option at 40 for $300. The $300 goes into his account immediately. Once again, the stock will either go up, go down, or stay the same. If ABC goes to 45 a share, the option writer can either buy back the option at any time or sit it out to maturity. If he elects to buy back the option, he will pay the current market price of that option. Assuming that ABC is now at 45 near or at maturity, he will pay $5—the intrinsic value of the option. He thus incurs a $2 loss ($5 less the $3 premium received at the opening transaction). By doing this, the owner of ABC absolves himself of all his obligations to sell his security at 40. His equity, however, is increased by $500, while his loss is only $200. If he decides to do nothing, he takes the chance that the buyer will exercise the option and that he will have to sell his stock for $4,000. In this case, it would really be as if he had sold the stock at 43, since he received the $300 premium.

If ABC remained at 40, he would still realize a profit of $300 (the original premium) and that option would mature worthless. The option seller's dream is to have little or no movement in the stock, because time is in his favor. As time moves on, if there is no change in the market, the option tends to lose value. If ABC stock should go down, the option seller will have no real risk until the stock drops below the premium received. In our illustration, ABC could go down to $37. Once the option expires, the owner of the security can either sell another option, hold, or sell the stock.

Frequently, people who own more than 100 shares will sell options on part of their holdings. Thus, if an investor who owns 1,000 shares of ABC common would like to increase his income, he could sell an option on only 500 shares. If ABC went much higher, his covered option would be exercised (thus selling 500 shares), and he would still hold 500 shares.

There are no set rules as to how often or on which proportion of a portfolio an investor should sell covered options. This depends on many factors, such as the investor's objectives, time, dividends, etc. If the investor feels confident about his portfolio, selling options makes sense because it reduces his cost and increases his income.

The drawback in selling options is the later regret, "I could have made more." The owner of ABC who sells an option at 40 is theoretically selling his stock at 43 or reducing his cost to 37. If ABC went up to 50, his strike price would, of course, not change. The option writer must condition himself to be satisfied with an above-normal return and not look for large capital gains. If he feels confident that ABC will have a moderate upside move, he could also elect to sell ABC 45 options. In this case, should ABC move higher, his obligation to deliver or sell would only begin at 45. By doing this, he would receive a smaller premium and have a larger capital gain.

Perhaps the most aggressive method of writing options, and one that carries the greatest amount of risk, is writing what are referred to as "naked," or uncovered, call options. This means selling the option without owning the underlying stock. Selling uncovered calls can be compared to selling stocks short, and can only benefit the investor in a declining market. Assuming the investor has no position in ABC, he could sell an ABC 40 call for $300. Should ABC go down or stay at 40, his profit would be the premium received. If he decides to buy back the call before expiration, he will, of course, subtract the repurchase cost from the original premium received.

The risk in this type of transaction is obvious. It is possible that ABC could have a fast upturn and the option writer would have an unlimited risk. At that point, assuming that ABC went to 60 a share, the naked-option writer could do one of two things: either buy back the option or buy an equivalent amount of shares. This would mean a loss of $2,000, less the $300 received. The investor should consider his possible exposure before entering into this type of contract.

Puts. Now that we understand the concept of calls, we will discuss the put option. Puts give the holder the right to sell the underlying security at a specified price up to a predetermined date. An IBM July 60 put gives the owner of the option the right to sell IBM up to the third Friday in July at $60 share. Once again, the option holder does not have to sell, but merely has the right or option to sell.

The put option can be very valuable if used correctly. It requires a positive temperament and some sophistication. Most investors do nothing to protect their portfolios, but just buy securities for possible appreciation. Over the years, many investors have become disenchanted with the market because they incurred losses without ever protecting their portfolio. In this respect, the put option can be very useful if considered as an insurance policy. Everyone buys insurance to protect his $10,000 automobile sitting in front of his home. Does it not make sense to protect oneself from possible market loss by buying insurance on one's portfolio, which might be worth many times the car?

Assume an investor owns 500 shares of IBM and 500 shares of ABC common, and is afraid that the market price of IBM might go down. He can choose to either liquidate his stock or buy a put option. By buying the put, he could lock in the value of his securities, so that if the market went down, he could sell his stock at the predetermined price of the put. Assuming the cost of buying the put on IBM was $300 while IBM was selling at 60, the stock could then go down to any level below 60 without his having any further loss. If IBM went down to 30 a share, the option holder could sell IBM at 60 by exercising his IBM 60 put. On the other hand, if IBM went up, he would still have all the advantage of that gain, less the $300 premium.

Put options can also be used by the investor who feels very optimistic about a particular security, yet wants to limit his exposure. Normally, he would buy only 100 shares at 60, thus investing $6,000. But because of special market conditions, he wants to take a much larger position with some limited risk. He might decide to buy 1,000 shares of IBM for $60,000, and also purchase ten put options for $3,000. He knows the limit of his risk. His total exposure would be $3,000 (the cost of the put); yet if IBM went up to 70, his profit would be $7,000.

An investor can also use put options to purchase securities below current market prices. If he wants to purchase 100 shares of General Motors below its market price of 40, he can sell a put option. The investor feels confident that General Motors is a good long-term investment. By selling a put on General Motors, he would receive a premium of $300. Assuming General Motors' stock went down to 35, the put holder would exercise his put, and our investor would have to buy the stock at 40; yet the total cost of General Motors would be only $3,700, because of the $300 received. By selling the put, he commits himself to the purchase of the underlying security. As the security goes lower and lower, he might continue to sell puts, thus reducing his costs in a declining market. The only "problem" in the above scenario would arise if General Motors immediately went up. In that case, he would receive the premium, but not buy the stock.

Straddles. Straddles consist of both a put option and a call option, with the same exercise price and the same expiration month. For example, a CBS Apr 65 put and a CBS Apr 65 call would be considered a straddle. Once an investor has mastered the skills of puts and calls, both buying and selling, he can widen his potential opportunities by use of the straddle. The advantage of writing a straddle versus writing only a call or put is that the straddle writer receives two premiums instead of one. If the straddle writer does not own the underlying security, he is a market straddle writer. He would be short one call and short one put. He may realize a profit even though one of the options is exercised.

Let's assume that in August CBS was selling at 65 and that the February 65 call was 6¾, while the February 65 put was 6. The option seller would receive both premiums. He is now in a position whereby he might have to sell 100 shares at 65 and also must be prepared to buy 100 shares at 65. As in all option strategies, the option seller does not have to own the underlying security, but must always be aware that he is liable to either buy or sell if the option is exercised. Remember that the option seller can close out his obligation by buying back any of his open positions. In our CBS illustration, the seller received a total of $1,275 from both options sold; thus, it would seem that the only way he would have any exposure would be if CBS went up more than 12¾ points or went down 12¾ points. The end result of writing a straddle is determined by the premium received less the movement of the underlying security, so that if CBS should go to 75, the naked call side of the straddle would result in a loss of $1,000, cutting his profit to $275. Theoretically speaking, it would seem that the straddle seller would have a gain if CBS stayed in a range of 53¼ to 77¾. Yet that might not be the case, as we will illustrate later.

The straddle writer should be aware that fluctuations in the price of the underlying security could result in both options being exercised. This does not mean that the total transaction would not be profitable. Assuming that CBS goes down to 60 and the put is exercised, the writer would now own 100 shares of CBS at 65. If subsequently CBS went to 80 and the call was exercised, the writer would then deliver the stock previously bought at 65 and still retain the $1,275 premium. If CBS went up to 75 and the call was exercised, he would then have to buy 100 shares at 75 or incur a $1,000 loss, because he would have to sell the stock at only 65. If CBS then went down to 60, he would be obligated to buy 100 shares (from the put buyer) at 65, thus incurring an additional $500 loss. In this scenario, the net loss would be $225 ($1,500 less $1,275 premium received).

Because of the limitless number of possibilities in option writing, it is impossible to predict the net profit or loss until all the options either expire or are bought or sold back. It thus appears that straddle writing is most profitable in a steady market.

Straddle selling can also be used in trying to achieve profits from securities held in a portfolio and to acquire the same or other securities at lower prices. Using our previous illustration, let's say the investor bought 100 shares of CBS at 65. He would like to sell his stock at around 75, yet would buy more if the price went down to 55. Selling straddles would be the perfect strategy. The writer received $1,275 premium, and since he owns the underlying security, he takes no risk on the upside, because he is now "short" a covered call. Should CBS fall sharply, he will be forced to buy additional stock at 65, but since he received a total premium of $1,275, the new stock would only cost him 52¼. If CBS went higher, he would sell (deliver) his original stock purchased at 65. This strategy is the most sophisticated and should be studied carefully.

Combinations. A combination is the same as a straddle, except that the put and call have different strike prices and/or different expiration dates.

A combination might consist of an NBC Apr 40 put and an NBC Apr 50 call. Just as in the case of a straddle, a combination may be written against a long stock position or can be sold naked.

The reason one would write a combination is that the stock would have to move in some direction before any of the options are in a range where they might be exercised. With NBC selling at 55, the investor would sell a combination of an NBC call at 50 and one NBC put at 40. NBC must move either five points up or five points down for the buyer of either side of the combination to have any intrinsic value in the option he bought, thus giving our combination seller more protection with less chance of being exercised. Since the writer's risk is reduced, his premium income is also reduced. As with all investments, the greater the risk, the greater the potential gain, and vice versa.

Ratio Writing. Ratio writing involves writing one covered call and one or more uncovered calls. This technique allows the option seller additional downside protection by receiving extra premiums. Assuming that TRW is selling at 60, the October 60 option would sell for around 3, while the October 65 call is around 1. The investor could buy one October 60 call and sell two October 65 calls for a net cost of $100. The investor has only a one-point risk should TRW go down, yet he would have a four-point gain if TRW went to 65. The long call would be worth $500, while the short calls would have no value at all. The investor's real exposure starts if the TRW stock should go above 70. Until 70, the risk is limited to the net cost of $100, because the call at 60 would be worth $1,000, while the short calls would each have a loss of $500, thus a $100 loss (the original cost differential of both options). Every point above 70 would be a point-for-point loss in the transaction.

It is important to do the mathematics when entering into a ratio-writing program. By treating the long position and the short position as separate entities, one can easily calculate the potential profit or loss. The ratio spread can also be one covered call and three naked calls, or any other ratio the investor desires. The greater the ratio on the naked side, the larger the income. However, there would be a greater risk should the stock go up.

There are various option spreads that can be used to reduce the degree of risk in a net long or net short position. The most common of all spreads is the vertical spread or price spread. In a vertical spread, the options that are bought and sold expire at the same time, but have different strike prices. The investor buys one XYZ call at 50 for $3 and sells one XYZ 55 for 1. This reduces the cost to $200 and limits his possible profit to $300. His maximum profit would be realized if XYZ sold at 55 at the time of expiration. His 50 call would be worth $500, while his short call would be worthless. After taking off his original cost of $200, he would be left with a $300 profit. Any move above that point would not create any additional profit, because the gain of the long call would be offset with the loss in the short call. The basic formula for profits in a vertical spread is the difference between the strike price and the net cost of the spread. The downside risk is limited to only the cost of the spread.

Conclusion. The examples of option transactions given here have deliberately been kept simple. There are many more-complex strategies that can be used. The strategies used should be based on the option buyer's or seller's portfolio and objectives. In calculating option strategies, it is important to treat each segment of the transaction separately. This will make it easier to determine potential profits and losses.

(A glossary of terms follows.)

Judah Munk

Glossary

assignment   The notice to the option writer that the option he has written has been exercised against him.

at-the-money   An option whose strike price is equal to the current market price of the underlying stock.

bear spread   An option strategy designed to allow an investor to participate, with limited risk and limited return, in a stock's decline.

bull spread   An option strategy designed to allow an investor to participate with limited risk and limited return, in a stock's advance.

buy back   See *closing purchase transaction.*

buyer   The holder of an option that, in the case of a call, gives the holder the right to buy stock and, in the case of a put, the right to sell stock, at a predetermined price for a predetermined period of time.

calendar spread   An option strategy that entails the purchase and sale of options on the same underlying stock, but with the option purchased having a longer amount of time to run than the option sold.

call   An option that gives its holder the right to buy, and its writer the obligation to sell, 100 shares of stock at a predetermined price for a predetermined period of time.

class   All options of the same type on the same underlying stock. For example, all calls on General Motors are the same class. All puts on IBM are another class.

closing purchase transaction   A transaction by which the writer of an option terminates his obligation to buy or sell stock.

closing sale transaction   A transaction in which the holder of an option terminates his right to buy or sell stocks.

combination   A put and a call on the same underlying stock having the same expiration date but different strike prices.

covered   A short option position that is hedged by a position in the underlying stock.

downside break-even   The price per share at which the option writer will not incur any loss in equity. This price is a direct function of the amount of premium received by the writer.

exercise   The process by which the holder of an option takes possession of the underlying stock, in the case of a call, or receives the proceeds of the sale of the stock, in the case of a put.

expiration cycle   The time frame in which listed options run. There are three expiration cycles: the months of January, April, July, October; February, May, August, November; and March, June, September, December.

expiration date   The last date on which the holder of an option can exercise his right to buy or sell stock. Similarly, the last day on which the writer of an option must fulfill his obligation to sell or buy stock.

expiration time   The time by which an option must be exercised before it expires. This time is 10:59 P.M. (Central Time) on the Saturday immediately following the third Friday of the expiration month.

intrinsic value   The amount by which the market price of a stock exceeds the strike price of the call. Similarly, the amount by which the market price of a stock is below the strike price of a put. Commonly referred to as the amount an option is "in the money."

leverage   The feature of options that provides limited risk but unlimited profit potential.

long   A term used to designate the position an option buyer has after he has purchased an option.

opening purchase transaction   A transaction in which the investor becomes the holder (buyer) of an option contract.

opening sale transaction   A transaction in which the investor becomes the seller (writer) of an option contract.

out-of-the-money   Describes a call option whose strike price is above the market price of the stock, or a put option whose strike price is below the market price of the stock.

parity   A condition that exists when the premium for an option consists strictly of intrinsic value. This usually occurs when the option is either deeply in the money or extremely close to expiration.

position limits   An exchange rule specifying that an individual or group of individuals acting in concert may not be long or short in excess of 2,000 contracts of the same class on the same side of the market.

premium   The amount of money a buyer pays, and a writer receives, for an option.

put   An option that gives its holder the right to sell, and its writer the obligation to buy, 100 shares of stock at a predetermined price for a predetermined period of time.

ratio call write   An option strategy that entails the sale of a number of calls in excess of the number of shares of stock held.

series   All options of the same class that have the same exercise price and expiration date.

short   A term used to designate the position the option writer has after he has written an option.

short sale   The sale of a security not in possession, in the hope of repurchasing it later at a lower price.

spread buying   The simultaneous purchase and sales of options on the same underlying stock but having different strike prices and/or expiration dates and resulting in a debit to the account.

spreads   The simultaneous purchase and sales of options on the same underlying stock but having different strike prices and/or expiration dates.

spread selling   The simultaneous purchase and sale of options on the same underlying stock but having different strike prices and/or expiration dates and resulting in a credit to the account.

straddle   A put and a call on the same stock having the same strike price and same expiration date.

strike price   The price at which the holder of an option has the right to purchase stock, in the case of a call, or sell stock, in the case of a put. Conversely, the price at which the writer of an option has the obligation to sell stock, in the case of a call, or purchase stock, in the case of a put.

time value   The amount by which the premium of an option exceeds its intrinsic or "in-the-money" value.

type   A term to designate whether an option is a put or a call.

uncovered   Describes a short option position that is not hedged by a position in the underlying stock.

upside break-even   The price per share at which the uncovered option writer will not incur any loss. This price is a direct function of the amount of premium received by the uncovered writer.

vertical spread   The simultaneous purchase and sale of options on the same underlying stock having different stikes prices but expiring in the same month.

writer   The seller or creator of an option contract.

Source: Judah Munk

Options on Futures

The advent of listed commodity options on October 1, 1982, has met with unprecedented acceptance. Individual investors who previously may have avoided commodities may now invest in commodity options and benefit from their leverage and volatility, with limited predetermined risk. Many institutional customers use commodity options to hedge their holdings and enhance their portfolios' yields.

Options on futures convey to the buyer, in the case of a call option, the right to take delivery of a futures contract at a specific price within a specified period of time. Put options convey to the buyer the right to assume a short position of a futures contract at a spe-

cific price within a specified period of time. Conversely, the seller of a call option has an obligation to assume a short futures position based on the call buyer's exercising his right, while the seller of a put option has an obligation to assume a long futures position based upon the put buyer's exercising his right.

The price at which this contract between buyer and seller is made is known as the "strike price" or "exercise price." The date at which the buyer's right and the seller's obligation terminate is known as the "expiration date." The specifications of the contract are prescribed by the specific exchange on which the contract is traded.

The variable that is not externally fixed is the price of the option, known as the "premium." Several factors affect the premium of an option.

The first is supply and demand. All things being equal, a strong demand for put or call options will cause an increase in their premiums. Conversely, a preponderance of supply will cause a decrease in premium levels for options. A strong bullish sentiment will cause an increase in call and a decrease in put premiums, while a strong bearish bias will cause an increase in put and a decrease in call premiums. It is critical to understand that insofar as call options convey the right to go long on a futures contract, they will be more attractive and therefore more expensive as premium levels rise in conjunction with an increase in futures prices. Of course, the opposite scenario would apply to put options.

The second factor is known as "intrinsic value"— that is, the amount by which the futures price is above the strike price in the case of a call, or below the strike price in the case of a put. Options will rarely, if ever, trade for less than their intrinsic value. The reason is that such circumstances would create arbitrage potential that the market would not tolerate. If it were possible to buy options at a discount to their intrinsic value, investors would do so, exercise the options, and sell the resulting futures positions for a profit in the open market.

The next factor is time value, or extrinsic premium. This represents an additional amount over and above the intrinsic value. For example, if the premium for a six-month 45 call option were three points and the futures price were $44\frac{1}{2}$, the option would have no intrinsic value and three points extrinsic value. If a six-month call with a strike price of 45 carried a four-and-one-half point premium and the futures price was $48\frac{1}{2}$, the option would have three and a half points of intrinsic value ($48\frac{1}{2}-45$) and one point of extrinsic value ($4\frac{1}{2}-3\frac{1}{2}$).

An option is a wasting asset. If it cannot be exercised or offset for a profit at expiration, it is worthless.

Table 1

Exchange	Contract	Date Trading Began
Chicago Board of Trade	Options on treasury bonds	10/1/82
Coffee, Sugar & Cocoa Exchange	Options on sugar futures	10/1/82
Commodity Exchange	Options on gold futures	10/4/82
New York Futures Exchange	Options on N.Y. composite index futures	1/28/83
Chicago Mercantile Exchange	Options on Standard & Poor's 500 index futures	1/28/83

Therefore, as expiration nears, the option's time value decreases. The erosion of the option's premium also accelerates significantly as expiration approaches. All other things being equal, the more time remaining until expiration, the higher the option premium. Also, the cost of being long an option from the ninth month to the eighth month before expiration is significantly less than the cost of being long from the third month until the second.

The final consideration affecting option premium is volatility. A high degree of price fluctuation in a given futures contract will result in the options commanding higher premiums. This is due to the fact that the greater the volatility, the greater the uncertainty as to whether the buyer will have a valuable right or the seller will have to make good on his obligation to deliver a futures position.

As of September 1983, options were traded on five different futures contracts (see Table 1).*

Options on futures are adaptive to the investment goals of both the speculator and the hedger. In the former case, the volatility in conjunction with limited risk allows speculation that is often much more attractive than other investments, such as specific commodities. The returns on capital are frequently appreciable given the small initial capital requirements.

The hedger has the opportunity through options on futures to protect himself from adverse price movements in the underlying portfolio.

There are a myriad of strategies available, including outright purchases and sales, vertical and horizontal spreads, and risk arbitrage through the use of long conversions and reverse conversions. A vertical or

---

* At this writing the CFTC is considering trading options or several other different types of contracts.

money spread employs two different strike prices on the same type of option within one expiration cycle to minimize risk. A horizontal or calendar spread uses options of the same type with common strike prices but with differing expirations to minimize risk. Long conversions involve a long future, short call, and long put to eliminate market risk and capture a specific credit at expiration. A reverse conversion uses a credit to accomplish the same goal as a long conversion, though each is a mirror image of the other—that is, the positioning of a reverse conversion is short future, long call, and short put.

Variations on these strategies foster innumerable trading opportunities for many different market participants, and it is this diversity that assures the continued growth and prosperity of options on futures.

Scott M. Krantz

Original Issue Discount (OID)

The original issue discount bond is a long-term bond issued with a lower coupon rate than other similarly rated long-term bonds issued at par. The tax-exempt capital appreciation realized at maturity compensates for the lower coupon rate. OID's are amortized yearly and when sold it is the accreted value, not the purchase price, that determines whether a loss or gain is realized. Example: An investor buys a 20-year new-issue OID at 80 and sells it five years later at 86; for tax purposes the seller of the bonds has approximately a one-point capital gain to report. On the other hand, if the same bond was sold at 84 five years after issue, the seller will have approximately a one-point capital loss to report. (In the secondary market, the purchase price will determine the tax consequences.) The OID is a good way to realize capital appreciation and still receive tax-free income.

Moore & Schley Cameron & Company

Overdraft Checking

An important checking-account variation that has become very popular is "overdraft checking." In effect, these plans allow a customer to write his or her personal loan without going into a bank. Under these plans, a bank will automatically make a loan to cover the difference when a person writes a check for more money than is in his or her account. Much of the time the credit is advanced in loans of either $50 or $100. Of course, there is always interest charged on the loan, and quite frequently there is also a service charge. The chief advantage of such plans is convenience.

Phil Battey

Overseas Private Investment Corporation (OPIC)

The developing nations are the world's fastest-growing markets and today they account for more than $90 billion in annual U.S. exports. Their potential is almost limitless—they contain more than two-thirds of the world's population and much of its natural wealth—but they lack the technical expertise needed to realize that potential.

The most effective vehicle for creating jobs, generating capital, and teaching new skills is foreign private investment, hence more Third World nations are seeking to attract investors from abroad. Since these markets offer such great opportunity for growth, it is clearly in the United States' interest, as well as the host country's, to accelerate the pace of private investment to sustain future growth.

The U.S. government has long recognized that private investment abroad is an effective tool for furthering host-country development and also for opening markets that will generate exports and create new U.S. jobs. In fact, it is estimated that for every $1 billion in exports, 40,000 jobs are created at home. Since U.S. overseas affiliates and subsidiaries account for some 40% of total U.S. exports, the role of private investment is obviously a critical one.

Recognizing that overseas investment entails unusual risks, Congress created the Overseas Private Investment Corporation in 1969 to consolidate and administer two major incentive programs designed to encourage U.S. investment in the developing nations.

First, OPIC offers political-risk insurance against three contingencies: inconvertibility of host-country currency; expropriation or nationalization; and war, revolution, insurrection, and certain types of civil strife. Policies are generally written for 20 years at a premium rate of $15 per $1,000 for all three coverages. Civil strife may be added to war coverage for an additional $1.50 per $1,000, but not taken out separately. Somewhat higher premiums may be charged for "large or sensitive projects."

Second, OPIC provides finance services in the form of direct loans of up to $4 million per project to small businesses, defined as companies with gross annual sales below the Fortune 1000 level; all-risk loan guaranties of up to $50 million to financial institutions providing funds for acceptable enterprises; and, as of 1983, partial funding of up to $100,000 for feasibility studies.

OPIC also offers a number of special programs to meet the specific needs of investors involved in contracting and exporting, energy exploration and development, and leasing arrangements. All OPIC contracts are backed by the full faith and credit of the United States of America.

Between the inception of the political-risk insurance program in 1948 and 1983, OPIC and its predecessor agencies had settled 147 insurance claims aggregating $399.7 million in cash payments and guaranties, and entered into an $8-million indemnity agreement in settlement of one other claim. OPIC is responsible for all but $3.8 million of the total.

OPIC operates on a self-sustaining basis and does not receive congressional appropriations. The president and executive vice-president of the corporation are nominated by the president of the United States and confirmed by the U.S. Senate. The 15-member board of directors includes seven members from the government agencies concerned with foreign economic policy and eight private-sector members nominated by the president and confirmed by the Senate. The government members include the Director of the International Development Cooperation Agency, chairman; the deputy U.S. trade representative, vice-chairman; the president of OPIC; the assistant secretaries of state, treasury, and commerce; and a representative of the U.S. Department of Labor.

The agency's programs are cleared for operation in more than 100 developing countries.

Craig A. Nalen

Over-the-Counter (OTC) Market

The over-the-counter market is by far the largest securities market in the United States, both in terms of the number of securities traded in it and in terms of the dollar volume of trading. Almost all trading in debt securities is done there—municipal, state, and U.S. government obligations, and corporate debt issues as well. It is also the market in which the stocks of most public corporations are bought and sold.

The equity securities traded in the OTC market include:

- all new issues of equity securities offered to the public for the first time
- the 4,200 securities quoted in late 1983 on the nationwide, electronic NATIONAL ASSOCIATION OF SECURITIES DEALERS AUTOMATED QUOTATIONS (NASDAQ) system, which comprise the most visible part of the vast OTC market
- some 20,000 common stocks of public corporations, less actively traded and not quoted on NASDAQ
- exchange-listed securities traded off the floors of the exchanges

Also traded in the OTC market are special categories of securities, which included:

- open-end investment company shares (mutual funds)
- variable contracts and certain other insurance-company products, which are legally classified as securities
- direct-participation programs, also known as tax-sheltered offerings

Technically, any securities transaction that does not take place on a stock exchange is effected in the OTC market. The market has no central physical site but consists of a nationwide network of competing dealers who "make markets" (i.e., maintain inventories) in the securities in which they elect to deal.

History. The term *over-the-counter* goes back to the middle of the nineteenth century. At that time, certain securities were traded at public auctions on the "stock exchange boards," as exchanges were then called. However, bonds issued by the federal government and many of the shares in the early corporations, banks, and insurance companies were generally distributed by merchant firms or banks. Investors would make their purchases and sales over the counters of these private institutions, which acted as dealers in the securities.

To this day, the methods of trading in the OTC and exchange markets are different. In the OTC market, the key figures are the dealers, who "make markets" by declaring their readiness to buy and sell certain securities. The dealers trade at their wholesale prices with other dealers; most of them also have retail departments, whose salesmen generate individual and institutional investor interest in the securities in which the firm makes a market.

By contrast, today's stock exchanges are essentially auction market. Orders from public investors for XYZ stock are transmitted to the floor of the exchange on which the stock is traded. On the floor, a "Specialist" in XYZ matches up the buy and sell orders he receives, to the extent that that is possible. If there is an imbalance between the orders, the specialist buys and sells for his own account to restore a balance.

The Advantages of the OTC Market. The OTC market and its trading methods have distinct advantages for many types of securities, and for their issuers and investors. Essentially, the OTC market is ideal for securities that do not have a continuing stream of public orders for them, since the dealers are prepared to hold such securities in their inventories to bridge the gaps in the order stream. For example, before any new issue of securities is offered, there is only a seller—the issuer—and there are no public buyers. The dealer, by

distributing the issue on behalf of the issuer, creates a trading market of buyers and sellers.

Issues of government and corporate debt tend to be very large, involving enormous amounts of money, and therefore are purchased primarily by financial institutions. A number of securities dealers have developed particular expertise in the placement of such big debt issues.

Less actively traded equity securities benefit from dealer sponsorship. Here, the function of the dealer is to present investment possibilities in these securities to investors who would otherwise not hear of them.

In addition, in the last decade the application of sophisticated automation and communications technology has made the OTC market the preferred market for many of the largest and most active issues of equity securities. Of the 4,200 securities quoted on the NASDAQ system in late 1983, 600 qualify for listing on the New York Stock Exchange and 1,600 for the American Stock Exchange. However, the issuers of these securities keep them on NASDAQ and in the OTC market because, instead of a single specialist on an exchange, they can have many competing firms acting as market-makers in their stock and sponsoring them with individual and institutional investors.

The Participants in the Market. More than 4,000 U.S. securities firms were active in the OTC market in 1983 and there were some 260,000 professionals registered to deal in OTC securities. The securities firms include the largest and best known: Merrill Lynch; Dean Witter Reynolds; E. F. Hutton; Paine Webber; Smith Barney; Prudential-Bache; Shearson/American Express; etc. All these firms have very large OTC departments, in addition to their other divisions. Also among the 4,000 OTC dealers are large and medium-size regional firms, local firms, "boutiques" specializing in certain types of securities, and firms with perhaps only a few employees.

Firms make markets in equity securities for three principal reasons, or a combination of them:

Research interest. A firm 's analysts may find that a security is attractive and has good prospects for price appreciation. This could make it profitable to accumulate the security, to create gains both for the firm and for its customers.

Retail interest. A firm must have good products—securities—for its salesmen to sell to its individual and institutional customers. Market-making is a way of acquiring at wholesale an inventory of products to be sold at retail.

Corporate financing interest. A firm may make a strong market in an equity security in the hope of attracting an issuer's investment-banking business. By the same token, a firm that has been the investment banker for a company generally considers it a professional obligation to be an effective market-maker in the company's stock. This gives investors in the company an orderly market in which to sell and new investors a market in which to buy.

Insurance companies play a large and growing part in the OTC market. About 100,000 of the 260,000 registered securities professionals in 1983 were insurance agents, who also sell variable annuities and other insurance-company products that are classified as securities. In recent years, insurance companies have made major acquisitions of securities firms, in the expectation of selling insurance to the customers of the securities firms, and vice versa.

Insurance companies and many other financial institutions—banks, money-market funds, mutual funds, pension funds, foundations, and endowments—are large investors in OTC debt and equity issues.

According to statistics compiled by the New York Stock Exchange, in late 1981 there were 10 million individual investors in NASDAQ and other OTC equity issues.

OTC Market Information. Investors may look to many sources for information on the OTC market. Current data on major issues of government and corporate bonds, on money-market funds and mutual funds, and on OTC equity securities can be found in leading national and regional newspapers and in financial periodicals. Background information on thousands of securities is provided by reference sources such as Standard & Poor's and Moody's, by any number of market letters, and by the research reports published by small, medium-size, and large securities firms. For the most active OTC equity issues, the nationwide NASDAQ system provides up-to-the-second quotations that securities salesmen can retrieve on their terminals.

Information on NASDAQ securities is also available in some 80 newspapers. The newspapers generally publish the previous day's closing best bid and asked quotations—i.e., the highest price that any dealer in a security will pay for it to another securities firm, and the lowest price at which any dealer will sell the security to another firm. However, for a growing segment of the NASDAQ market, the NASDAQ National Market System, the newspaper information is similar to that published for exchange-listed securities: Actual sale prices, not quotations, appear in the newspapers.

For the other 20,000 OTC securities, the National Quotation Bureau in New York provides two sources of information: a book called the *National Stock Summary,* which is periodically updated; and the daily "pink sheets," to which many securities firms subscribe. Both publications identify the dealers who are making markets in less-active OTC securities, and thus permit brokers and investors to find out their current prices.

Securities salesmen are, of course, key sources for many investors. The salesmen read and digest information on many securities and make it available to other customers, often with recommendations as to whether to buy, sell, or hold various securities.

OTC Trading. When an investor places an order to buy or sell an OTC security, his brokerage firm may handle the transaction as principal or as agent. If the firm is making a market in the OTC security, it may act as principal—i.e., it may sell the investor the security from its own inventory, or buy it from the investor for its inventory. In that case, the firm will usually deal with a retail customer at a price that will include a "markup" over its wholesale asked price, or a "markdown" from its wholesale bid price.

If the firm is not a market-maker in the OTC security, it will usually act as agent—i.e., it will buy the stock for the customer from a market-making firm, or sell it, on the customer's behalf, to a market-maker. In that case, the firm charges a commission for its work in affecting the transaction.

Whether it is acting as principal or agent, a brokerage firm has an obligation to buy or sell a customer's stock at the best price then available. The salesman dealing with the customer can ascertain the best wholesale bid or asked from the quotations terminal on his desk. If the customer is prepared to trade at that price, the salesman relays the order to the firm's trading room. There, a NASDAQ terminal displays the names of all the market-makers trading the stock, and the customer's order is negotiated with the market-maker displaying the best price.

Policing the OTC Market. The NATIONAL ASSOCIATION OF SECURITIES DEALERS, INC. (NASD) is the federally registered self-regulatory organization for the entire OTC market. Under the oversight of the SECURITIES AND EXCHANGE COMMISSION (SEC), the NASD conducts market surveillance of the trading of OTC securities, and it examines brokerage firms for their fairness in dealing with customers and for their compliance with federal securities laws and with the NASD's own rules of fair practice.

Gordon S. Macklin

·P·

Pacific Stock Exchange (PSE)

The Pacific Stock Exchange, like the New York Stock Exchange, is one of the nation's self-regulated securities centers. It is a public marketplace where corporate securities (stocks and bonds) and options may be purchased and sold.

The Pacific Stock Exchange is the largest securities exchange outside of New York City, based on the number of trades executed. Its guiding philosophy is to supply not only the best but the broadest scope of services to its members and member organizations. This includes providing a viable, competitive market in the 1,100 equity issues and 63 options stocks listed on the Pacific, as well as services in clearing and depository-related activities.

The Pacific plays no part in establishing the transaction price of any trade in which securities are bought and sold. Prices at which stocks are traded on the exchange reflect the basic law of supply and demand. A two-way auction market exists, where those seeking to buy compete with other sellers. The result is a constant adjustment of supply and demand for each stock and continual change in the price of the stock. When more people wish to buy than sell, prices rise. When more wish to sell than buy, prices fall.

The Pacific Stock Exchange is unique among U.S. securities markets, as it is the only exchange that trades equities on two floors, each located in a different city. Even though the floors are 400 miles apart—one in Los Angeles and the other in San Francisco—they work as one through a sophisticated telephone communications system. This unique wire system provides communication between the buyers and sellers on either trading floor within seconds. For example, a Los Angeles floor member need only pick up one of the six full-time voice-grade telephone lines that connect the two floors and announce the name of the security he wants to trade. His voice will be heard over speakers in San Francisco. All interested traders in San Francisco will pick up any of the many telephones on the floor and speak directly with the Los Angeles member to negotiate an execution.

The Pacific Stock Exchange's primary sources of income are the dues and associated fees assessed for facilities and services provided to members and listed corporations. Any profit realized by the exchange is reinvested in improved facilities and data-processing systems or retained for future investment.

Since its formation, the Pacific Stock Exchange has experienced rapid growth. This reflects the growth in California and the western region of the United States, which boasts the largest and fastest-growing population of shareholders nationwide. In 1957, in its first year of operation as a consolidated exchange, 35 million shares were traded on the exchange; 25 years later, in 1982, over 813 million shares were traded—representing a 23-fold increase in volume.

History. The roots of the Pacific Stock Exchange go back to the days of the Old West. Although the modern exchange was formed by the merger of the San Francisco Stock Exchange and the Los Angeles Stock Exchange in 1957, the marketplace has been shaped by attitudes that created the western expansion of the United States.

In San Francisco, the gold rush of the 1840s spawned legions of young mining companies. It was from this initial mining activity, and the subsequent boom in West Coast population, that the San Francisco Stock and Bond Exchange found its first business. Created September 18, 1882, the San Francisco Exchange traded the securities of these new silver- and gold-mining companies, and public utilities with names such as Omnibus Railroad and San Francisco Gas and Electric. Likewise, in 1899 the Los Angeles Oil Exchange was founded to handle the securities of companies that prospered from southern California's early oil explorations.

Initially, both of these exchanges operated essentially by appointment, meeting only several hours each day. The "call" system of trading was used by the original traders in each city, whereby the reader announced each issue for trading and the traders called out their offers to buy or sell stocks and found the appropriate buyer or seller for their trade to be executed. This system was eventually replaced by the specialist-post trading system, which is still in use today.

The exchanges operated separately (for most of their history known as the San Francisco Stock Exchange and the Los Angeles Stock Exchange) as the two principal securities markets in the West until January 1957, when they were combined to form the Pacific Coast Stock Exchange. The consolidated exchange created an active and broad marketplace providing many advantages for investors, corporations, member firms, and banks. In 1973 the exchange was incorporated and its name was changed to the Pacific Stock Exchange, Incorporated.

Beginning in 1961, a single governing board was established for the consolidated floors of the Pacific Coast Stock Exchange, and one president, Thomas Phelan, was elected. In 1964 the Pacific Clearing Corporation was established as a wholly owned subsidiary of the exchange to facilitate completion of trades and the paper work involved. Electromechanical trading boards were replaced on the Los Angeles floor in 1965, moving the Pacific into the fully automated electronic age of securities trading.

In April 1976 the Pacific Stock Exchange opened a listed options-trading facility adjacent to the San Francisco equities floor. Standardized options trading has generated both individual and institutional investor appeal and has furnished a valuable product for many member firms.

During this same period, the PSE endorsed and participated in the development of the National Market System through the creation of the Intermarket Trading System (ITS). ITS is the electronic linkage of the seven major national markets and the NASD. It was activated in 1978 and has proved its value to individual investors, corporations, and the securities community by allowing transactions to occur at the best price represented in any of the participating market centers. Participation in ITS is a key development in the Pacific's diversified trade operations. The Pacific in 1982 executed approximately 22% of all ITS trades and 20% of all ITS shares.

As the western financial community has expanded, so has the Pacific Stock Exchange. By continually introducing new concepts and more efficient and modern systems, the Pacific has served as a model exchange for the securities industry. Many PSE innovations have subsequently been adopted by the other national exchanges.

One of the first innovations in the securities industry was introduced in 1957, when the PSE expanded its trading hours beyond those of the New York markets. The PSE begins trading at 7:00 A.M. (Pacific Standard Time) in order to synchronize and coordinate with the New York and American Stock Exchanges' openings. When trading closes in the East, it is only 1:00 A.M. in California, and the PSE keeps trading another half-hour. Extended trading periods are particularly advantageous to western investors who frequently need the added margin of time to complete their transactions for the day. Also in 1957, the PSE began offering computerized broker services, competing interfloor specialists, and a composite tape linking market activity in Los Angeles and San Francisco—all firsts in the industry.

Many other innovations have set the Pacific and its subsidiaries apart as leaders in their fields. Among these are net-by-net clearing (eliminating the inefficient and time-consuming "delivery versus payment" system requiring direct matching and settlement on each transaction); clearing for over-the-counter securities; and clearing services for institutions.

But perhaps most significant, the Pacific Stock Exchange was the first to develop automated order processing. Introduced in 1969, the system initially executed odd-lot orders of up to 99 shares. In response to the changing needs of the brokerage community and the development of an integrated national market, the system was continually updated, improved, and expanded. In 1979 the Pacific introduced SCOREX, an acronym for the Securities Communication Order Routing and Execution system. SCOREX automatically executes market orders in dually traded issues up to 599 shares at the best available price nationwide within 30 seconds. With this capability, a firm can execute up to one-half of all orders written in dually traded stocks, thereby realizing substantial savings in execution costs.

The order process is fast, simple, and efficient. From any member-firm branch across the country, an order is entered by means of computer terminal or other input device. The order is routed to the firm's central switching computer, which is linked to the PSE's SCOREX computer system. It is then directed to the proper specialist, logged, executed, and compared. A report of the completed transaction is automatically sent back through this network. Reports of execution are also sent simultaneously to the specialist, the consolidated tape, and the Pacific Clearing Corporation for normal settlement. This entire process takes just a few short minutes for all agency market orders.

Membership. The Pacific Stock Exchange had as of September 1983, 500 memberships outstanding, representing over 300 member firms. PSE membership is not only national but international in scope. A number of member organizations are U.S. corporations that are wholly owned subsidiaries of banks or investment institutions in Japan, Canada, England, Germany, Switzerland, and the Netherlands.

Demand for memberships has steadily increased over the past several years. The price of a PSE membership reflects the current level of demand in the same way that the price of stock reflects the current demand for a particular issue.

Listings. There are two main types of stocks listed for trading on the Pacific Stock Exchange: those traded dually with either the American or the New York Stock Exchanges, and those traded exclusively on the Pacific. The PSE has dually listed most of the more active stocks (approximately 1,000) traded on the New York and American Exchanges. Exclusive issues number about 125.

Over the years, many smaller companies have first listed with the Pacific Stock Exchange before going on to become larger, well-known companies dually listed elsewhere. The Union Oil Company was one of the original PSE listings. In addition, other companies such as Standard Oil Company of California, FMC, Occidental Petroleum, AMFAC, and Southern California Edison Company listed solely and originally with the Pacific Stock Exchange. Although Big Board–listed companies still make up the bulk of the exchange's volume, the Pacific's exclusive issues such as OKC Limited Partnership, Mitral Medical International, and Commonwealth Oil Refining Company draws considerable national investor attention.

Any publicly held security that meets the Pacific Stock Exchange's listing standards is eligible for listing. An exclusive listing serves several purposes for the growing corporation. A corporation's stock receives national visibility by being quoted in major newspapers throughout the country. The company's stock becomes automatically marginable upon listing, allowing investors to purchase shares on credit. The trading in the issue is reviewed by the exchange's equity-surveillance department. Finally, federal regulations require the exchange specialist to maintain a fair, orderly, and competitive market in the stock. These benefits contribute to the successful growth of the corporation and its shareholder base, and help provide a regulated environment in which investors can trade.

Equity Trading. The equity-trading floors of the Pacific Stock Exchange are organized into two distinct components: booths and trading posts. Member booths serve as base offices for the members and their representatives who are responsible for the execution of customers' orders. These members are called "floor brokers." Each booth contains private wires and high-speed telecommunications printers through which the floor broker will receive orders to buy and sell stock for his firm's customers.

The trading posts are occupied by members designed as "specialists" and their assistants and clerks. There are a total of approximately 50 specialist posts on the two equity floors. Most of the Pacific's listed issues are assigned to a specialist, and it is only at the specialist's post that the stock may be traded. Each specialist is appointed by the exchange's board of governors, and the assignments of stock are made by a special exchange committee.

An exchange specialist performs two basic functions. His primary function is to maintain a fair and orderly market in the daily trading of assigned issues. This means committing his own capital when necessary to purchase stock from the public at a higher price than anyone else is willing to pay at that time, in order to minimize the volatility of the stock's price. In this way, there is always a bid and offer price for each stock. This provides price continuity and contributes to greater liquidity of the market. A specialist executing an order based on the current bid and offer price is executing a market order.

A specialist's second function is to act as a broker's broker on the floor. This means he will accept orders in stocks assigned to him from floor brokers. Floor brokers normally entrust orders to the specialist when the order to buy or sell is away from the current market price. This type of order is referred to as a "limit order."

On each trading floor, three electronic screens serve as the modern equivalent of the old ticker tape. One screen displays those trades done exclusively on the Pacific Stock Exchange. The other two screens show those trades done by all national exchanges in dually traded New York and American Stock Exchange issues.

Equity issues (common and preferred stock) and bonds are traded in basically the same manner. Suppose you decide to buy 100 shares of XYZ Corporation, last traded at $25 per share. You place an order with your account executive to buy at the market, which means to buy immediately at the lowest prevailing price. Your account executive will relay the order to the floor broker on the PSE equities-trading floor, who represents your brokerage firm. Upon receipt of that order, the floor broker will write up a buy-order ticket, time-stamp it, and proceed to the specialist post where XYZ is traded.

He calls out "XYZ" to announce his order. The specialist then announces his market in XYZ. Suppose the specialist's quote is 24⅝ bid, offered at 25. This means that at the moment the lowest price at which anyone is willing to sell XYZ is $25 per share, and the highest price at which anyone is willing to buy is 24⅝. The floor broker, acting in the best interest of his customer, will try to obtain a price that is lower than the available offer by bidding 24¾ per share. The specialist, who maintains an orderly market by allowing minimal variations between sales, might enter the market by offering XYZ for 24⅞ per share. The floor broker accepts this offer and a transaction is executed at 24⅞. Through the auction-market system, the floor broker has obtained a better execution.

Immediately upon the purchase, an exchange reporter is given a sell ticket by the seller. This ticket contains the elements of the trade: names of the firms representing the buyer and seller, name of the stock, number of shares, and price. The reporter time-stamps the ticket, and a Consolidated Tape System operator, located at various spots on the trading floor, puts this information into the exchange's computers, which are programmed to simultaneously report the trade to the Consolidated Tape Service and also generate a copy of the complete transaction blotter for both the buyer and seller to compare.

National Market System. In 1975, in an effort to begin creating a more unified system of stock trading, Congress and the Securities and Exchange Commission mandated the National Market System. In June 1978, motivated by the strong belief that this system is in the investing public's interest, the Pacific Stock Exchange began participating in the Intermarket Trading System (ITS).

The Intermarket Trading System is an electronic linkage of the Pacific Stock Exchange with the American, Boston, Cincinnati, Midwest, New York, and Philadelphia Stock Exchanges, as well as the NATIONAL ASSOCIATION OF SECURITIES DEALERS, INC. (NASD). It allows specialists or floor brokers on one exchange to execute against another market's bid or offer as shown through a composite computer quotation display. The success of the system in its first four years of operation clearly demonstrates the ability of regional stock exchanges to compete in dually traded securities, as over 50% of the volume passed through the system was attributed to markets outside of New York.

On the basis of total volume passed through ITS for execution, the PSE is second only to the New York Stock Exchange—accounting for 20–25% of share volume. However, the Pacific leads in the number of trades of New York–listed issues, with a total of more than 8%; and in 100-share trades, the Pacific does over 10% of the national total.

It is interesting to note the similarity of the ITS system to the existing linkage between the Pacific Stock Exchange's two equity-trading floors. In effect, the principle that united the Los Angeles and San Francisco markets in 1957 has been expanded, utilizing current technology to tie in all the nation's securities marketplaces. The concept of a specialist in each market center competing with specialists in other

market centers has also been carried over into the development of the national market system. Specialists of seven exchanges and the market-makers of the NASD now compete with each other, with the best bid or offer receiving the order.

PSE Options Trading. In April 1976 the Pacific Stock Exchange opened its options-trading facility. Options are used for a variety of investment objectives and have experienced rapid growth and increased investor interest over the past five years. The PSE began its options program with 10 underlying securities. As of September 1983, 63 options were traded on the PSE.

The Pacific Stock Exchange has combined several key features to offer the best execution in all 63 listed options. One of these features is a competing-market-maker system. Far different from the specialist system used on equity floors and certain other options exchanges, the Pacific provides several sources of capital rather than just one specialist's capital, thereby improving bids and offers while providing greater market depth. These market-makers compete among themselves while maintaining fair and orderly markets. Besides providing continuous markets for the public, this system improves liquidity and execution of orders handled by floor brokers representing member organizations.

Another Pacific innovation in options trading is the order-book official (OBO). All OBO's are employed by the exchange and are responsible for executing all limit orders for the public that are left with them by options members. This assures that all such public orders will be handled with the highest integrity.

In addition to the Pacific options facilities, three other exchanges trade call and put options. Unlike equities, where nearly all of the stocks listed on the Pacific are also listed on either the New York or American Stock Exchange, very few options are dually listed.

Pacific Clearing and Depository System. The Pacific Stock Exchange's Pacific Clearing and Depository System is the western link of a national clearance and settlement system. Electronic communication with the nation's major securities markets—New York, Philadelphia, and Chicago—makes it possible for trades to be executed on the exchange at the best possible prices the auction market can provide. Trades can be cleared and settled via the Pacific System regardless of the marketplace in which the trade is executed. This nationwide system is the result of a 1975 congressional mandate designed to minimize the extensive paper work involved in processing securities transactions and the physical handling of stock and bond certificates. Clearing a trade involves matching the accuracy of both the buy and the sell side of the trade. Settling involves completion of the paper work to transfer ownership of the stock.

A net-by-net clearance and settlement system is employed by Pacific Clearing and Depository, providing participants with a single net transaction per security. Pacific Clearing and Depository acts as a middleman, allowing participants to interact with one agency for the clearance and settlement of trades.

When trades are executed, the trade data is electronically recorded, producing a variety of reports that detail the transactions. The data on these reports are used to produce the "net sheet," which outlines settlement information for participants. The net sheet gives the participant a net position for each security bought or sold and a final money balance due to or from Pacific Clearing and Depository for all the transactions being settled that day. The participant simply uses the information on the net sheet to settle his position, thus settling a multitude of trades in a few simple steps. This process allows participants to settle trades rapidly and efficiently by eliminating the need for physical receipt, delivery, and transfer of certificates by mail services and costly armored couriers.

Pacific Clearing and Depository also provides participants with a centralized, highly secure storage facility for stock and bond certificates. This storage system, coupled with the Pacific's book-entry system, has markedly decreased paper work and reduced the possibility of loss and theft. The system has largely eliminated the need for participants to withdraw certificates. Participants can, however, physically deliver or receive certificates when desired.

The main facilities of Pacific Clearing Corporation and Pacific Securities Depository Trust Company are located in Los Angeles. Branch offices are maintained in Portland, Salt Lake City, Denver, and Seattle, with on-line terminals tying into the main facilities. Among other services the Pacific Clearing and Depository System offers its members are the following:

• The Securities Collection Division delivers physical securities and collects money for its customers throughout the United States and Canada, creating an efficient means for members to receive from or deliver to nonmembers.
• The Pacific Automated Communications System is designed to allow participants the use of participant terminals to check the status of their depository accounts and to make certain bookkeeping entries through on-line data processing.
• As a result of the handling and storage of certificates, Pacific Clearing and Depository processes cash and stock dividends and performs proxy and reorganization functions, including name changes, reverse splits, security redemptions, tender offers,

bankruptcy, corporate mergers, security conversions, corporate liquidations, and subscriptions.

James S. Gallagher

Participating Preferred Stock

See PREFERRED STOCK.

Partnerships

See BUSINESS ORGANIZATIONS, FORMS OF.

Par Value, Common Stock

See COMMON STOCK.

Par Value, Preferred Stock

See PREFERRED STOCK.

Passbook

A book kept by a depositor in which his or her deposits and withdrawals are entered by the bank. Also called a "bankbook."

Harvey Rachlin

Passbook Savings Accounts

Also called "regular savings accounts," these are accounts that (1) pay interest on funds deposited; (2) permit the addition or withdrawal of any amount at any time without penalty; and (3) require no minimum balance (although some financial institutions do impose a charge on accounts that fall below an established minimum). These accounts are called "passbook accounts" because transactions are commonly recorded in a PASSBOOK. Monthly or quarterly statements showing all transactions and current balance may be used in place of the traditional passbook. The maximum interest allowed on passbook accounts is established by law and is lower than the rate paid on longer-term certificate accounts. Until the 1960s, this was the only type of account offered by most savings and loan associations. With the increased competition for savers' dollars in the 1960s, new types of accounts paying higher interest rates were authorized. Until recently, most association savings were in regular savings accounts. Deregulation and the high interest rates of the early 1980s dramatically changed the types of savings accounts available, and most deposits at thrift institutions today are in accounts paying money-market rates.

Mary Ann Irvine

Pass-Through Securities

See SECONDARY MORTGAGE MARKET.

Payee

The person or entity to whom a check or note is made payable.

Harvey Rachlin

Penny Stock

See COMMON STOCK.

Pension Benefit Guaranty Corporation (PBGC)

The Pension Benefit Guaranty Corporation is a self-financing government corporation that insures the basic pension benefits of over 36 million workers and retirees in the U.S. PBGC was created by the EMPLOYEE RETIREMENT INCOME SECURITY ACT OF 1974 (ERISA).

PBGC is headed by a board of directors consisting of the secretaries of labor, the Treasury, and commerce. The secretary of labor is permanent chairman of the board. The PBGC's chief executive officer is its executive director, who is appointed by the board of directors. The corporation is aided in the development of its policies and programs by a presidentially appointed advisory committee, consisting of representatives of the public, labor, and management.

PBGC administers two pension-protection programs: a plan-termination insurance program for single-employer defined-benefit pension plans; and a plan-insolvency insurance program covering multiemployer defined-benefit pension plans. In each of these programs, PBGC's benefit guarantees are based on the pension plan's provisions. In addition, the PBGC guarantees are subject to limitations imposed by law. PBGC does not insure defined-contribution pension plans (such as money-purchase, thrift, stock-bonus, etc.).

The Single-Employer Program. Whenever a non-multiemployer plan insured by PBGC terminates, PBGC reviews the plan to ascertain whether it has sufficient assets to pay guaranteed benefits. If the plan's assets are sufficient, the plan administrator winds up the affairs of the plan and sees that participants receive their pensions. If plan assets are not sufficient to pay guaranteed benefits, PBGC assumes responsibility for the plan by becoming trustee, administering benefit payments and records, managing plan assets, and making up the financial insufficiency from corporate insurance funds. In all terminations,

assets of the terminated plan must be allocated as specified in ERISA. PBGC finances this program through insurance premiums that covered plans pay. In 1982, the premium for single-employer plans was $2.60 per person per year. In 1982, PBGC requested that Congress increase that premium to $6.00, because a deficit existed in the single-employer program.

The Multiemployer Program. PBGC's pension-protection program for multiemployer plans was revised by the Multiemployer Pension Plan Amendments Act of 1980. Multiemployer pension plans are maintained under collective bargaining agreements and provide benefits for the employees of two or more unrelated employers. Multiemployer plans that become insolvent may receive financial assistance from PBGC to enable them to pay guaranteed benefits to retirees. PBGC finances this program through premiums that the plans pay. In 1982, multiemployer plans payed $1.40 per person per year. That premium is scheduled to increase to $2.60 in future years. Increases beyond the $2.60 level will require approval by Congress.

Guarantees. Just as the FDIC limits the amounts it can insure in individual bank deposits, PBGC is limited in the amounts that it can guarantee to people whose pension plans terminate without sufficient assets or that experience financial difficulty. The law imposes maximum dollar amounts on monthly benefits and limits the extent to which recent benefit increases can be guaranteed. In 1983, for example, the maximum was $1,517.05 per month at age 65 in the form of a single-life annuity in PBGC's single-employer program. This maximum is adjusted each year. On average, PBGC's programs mean that workers and retirees receive about 85% of their vested pension benefits, where they might have received no pension or very little pension at all.

Edwin M. Jones

Pension Plans

There are many "tax shelters" in today's marketplace. However, all but one have some or all of the following disadvantages:

• lack of liquidity
• tax write-offs questionable
• high risk
• loss of control of money
• uncertainty as to when you may receive your money
• lack of economic realism

A pension plan has none of the above characteristics and is one of the best tax shelters available. The company is allowed a current deduction for its contributions to the plan; employees pay no tax on money contributed for their benefit until distribution is made; earnings from investments made with plan funds accumulate tax-free; and distributions from the plan may be afforded favorable income- and estate-tax treatment.

The following paragraphs give an overview of this complex area of the tax code.

ERISA. The EMPLOYEE RETIREMENT INCOME SECURITY ACT OF 1974 (ERISA) became law on September 2, 1974. ERISA completely overhauled the federal pension law after Congress found that (1) employees with long years of service were losing anticipated retirement benefits due to the lack of plan provisions relating to the vesting of benefits; (2) many plans lacked adequate funds to pay employees promised retirement benefits; and (3) plans were being terminated before enough funds had been accumulated to pay employees and their beneficiaries promised retirement benefits.

Accordingly, substantial changes were made in the employee-benefit structure by providing for minimum participation, vesting, and funding standards, in addition to providing other requirements, significantly with respect to fiduciary responsibility, the use of plan funds and other assets, and the imposition of penalties for deviating from the prescribed requirements.

TEFRA. On Thursday, August 19, 1982, Congress passed the TAX EQUITY AND FISCAL RESPONSIBILITY ACT (TEFRA) OF 1982, which contained perhaps the most extensive revisions of the pension-tax law since ERISA. Significant among the many changes was the addition of new Code 416, which set forth new qualifications for "top-heavy" plans. The requirements, which took effect beginning January 1, 1984, had an impact on all qualified plans.

Both defined-benefit and defined-contribution plans can be characterized as top-heavy. A defined-benefit plan is considered top-heavy for a given year if more than 60% of the current value of the aggregate accumulated benefit is given to key employees. A defined-contribution plan in which the account balances for key employees are more than 60% of the account balances of all the employees included in the plan is also considered top-heavy. A "key employee" is a plan participant who during the taxable year or any part of the past four years fell within one of the following categories of IRC 416(i): an officer; an employee owning one of the ten largest interests in the firm; an owner with more than a 5% interest in the

firm; or an owner with more than a 1% interest in the firm who earns at least $150,000 a year.

Once a determination has been made that a pension plan is top-heavy, certain requirements must be met to ensure that the plan remains qualified. These requirements will be explained in the appropriate sections below.

Eligibility Requirements. A plan must satisfy the minimum participation standards set out in the INTERNAL REVENUE CODE to qualify for favorable tax treatment. Generally speaking, a qualified plan that bases eligibility for participation on age and service may not deny or delay participation beyond the time the employee reaches age 25 and completes one year of service. If the plan provides for full and immediate vesting of benefits, however, participation may be denied until the employee reaches age 25 and completes three years of service.

A defined-contribution plan (a profit-sharing, stock-bonus, or money-purchase pension plan) may not impose a maximum age for participation. A defined-benefit plan or target-benefit plan may exclude an employee who starts to work for the company within five years of the plan's normal retirement age.

The employees of a controlled group of corporations [IRS Code 1563(a)] or of commonly controlled partnerships or proprietorships are to be looked upon as if they were employed by one employer. The intention is to make it impossible to avoid the coverage and antidiscrimination rules merely by operating a business through separate corporations rather than as a single entity.

In addition to meeting these age and service rules, a plan will qualify for favorable tax treatment if either (1) 70% or more of all employees participate in the plan, or (2) 70% or more of all employees are eligible to participate and at least 80% of the eligible employees actually participate. If the plan fails to meet either of these tests, it can still qualify if it covers a classification of employees that does not discriminate in favor of officers, stockholders, and highly paid employees (called the "prohibited group").

Types of Pension Plans. It is possible to classify all plans into two broad categories: defined-contribution plans and defined-benefits plans. Examinations of each follow.

A defined-contribution or individual-account plan (also called a "money-purchase plan") is one where the amounts of money contributed to the fund are fixed, but the actual money is contributed to each participant's separate account and invested. The amount received by the participant is determined by the amount of money in the account at retirement. Under the Internal Revenue Code and ERISA, a defined-contribution plan provides for an individual account for each participant and for benefits based solely on (1) the amount contributed to the participant's account and (2) any income, expenses, gains and losses, and forfeitures of accounts of other participants that may be allocated to the participant's account. The maximum allowable tax deduction for this type of plan is either 25% of compensation or $30,000 adjusted for cost of living (figures current as of 1983), whichever is less.

Two basic types of defined-contribution plans are the deferred profit-sharing plan and the target-benefit plan. A deferred profit-sharing plan is a program established and maintained by an employer to provide for the participation in his profits by his employees or their beneficiaries. The plan must have a definite, predetermined formula for allocating the contributions made to the plan among the participants and for distributing the fund accumulated under the plan after a fixed number of years, the attainment of a stated age, or upon the prior occurrence of some event such as layoff, illness, disability, retirement, death, or severance of employment. The contribution can be discretionary, per the employer. This flexibility is unavailable in other types of plans. For employer tax deductibility, the maximum limitation is 15% of compensation.

The target-benefit plan is a defined-contribution plan under which the amount of employer contributions allocated to each participant is determined by (1) a plan formula that does not allow employer discretion and (2) the amount necessary to provide a target benefit specified by the plan for each participant at normal retirement. This type of plan will make larger contributions for older employees but has all the other characteristics of a defined-contribution plan. The maximum allowable tax deduction for this plan is the same as for the defined-contribution plan.

A "defined-benefit plan" is one where the amount of pension benefits paid upon retirement is determined in advance but the amount of money paid into the fund varies through the years. Under a defined-benefit plan, there is a definite formula by which the employees' benefits will be measured. This formula may provide that benefits will be a particular percentage of the employee's average compensation over his entire service or over a particular number of years; it may provide for a flat monthly payment; or it may provide a definite amount for each year of service, expressed either as a percentage of his compensation for each year of service or as a flat dollar amount for each year of service. In plans of this type, the employer's contributions are determined actuarially.* The maximum allowable benefit is either 100% of compensation or $90,000 adjusted for cost of living, whichever is less. The maximum allowable tax-deductible contribution can be significantly higher than 25% of compensation as in a defined-contribution plan. It may run in excess of 100% of compensation (e.g., age 55, compensation $75,000, tax-deductible contribution $100,000).

Combining Dissimilar Plans. An employer may maintain both a defined-benefit plan (or plans) and a defined-contribution plan (or plans). A formula is applied each year to each employee to determine whether the limitations on contributions and benefits have been exceeded. The formula is the sum of a defined contributions fraction and a defined benefits fraction; the sum must not exceed 1.4. If 1.4 is exceeded, one or more of the plans maintained by the employer will be disqualified. A plan may contain a "fail-safe" provision that will freeze the annual additions or benefit accruals at a level that will prevent the limitations from being exceeded as to any employee. In a top-heavy plan, the aggregate limit for the combined plans is reduced to 1.0 (100%) from 1.4 (140%). Also, the defined-benefit plan and defined-contribution plan fractions used to compute the separate limits are revised.

Integration with Social Security. Although many retirement plans provide benefits that are entirely independent of Social Security, the Social Security–integrated plan has become very widely used among small and medium-size corporations. A private retirement plan superimposed on an employee's Social Security enables an employer to give higher-paid employees benefits proportionate to those received by lower-paid employees under the Social Security Act. Although such plans favor higher-paid employees, they are deemed nondiscriminatory if they combine with Social Security to form one comprehensive system of benefits that does not favor higher-paid executive personnel. The government has numerous requirements for establishing a nondiscriminatory Social Security–integrated plan.

An integrated plan enables an employer to take credit for contributions toward an employee's Social

---

*These calculations must be certified by an enrolled actuary as to their accuracy and reasonableness. The assumptions used by the actuary can be changed in order to accommodate the employer during difficult times (e.g., interest-rate changes, annuity-rate changes, etc.), provided they are reasonable, thereby allowing for lower contributions. This flexibility should be considered when one is choosing between a defined-contribution and a defined-benefit plan.

Security benefits. If the combined benefits of the private plan and Social Security do not discriminate in favor of the employer's higher-paid employees, the plan integrates properly.

A plan that provides an extension of Social Security benefits assumes that Social Security benefits credited to an employer's contributions are 37½% of the employees' compensation covered by Social Security. The employer may then install a private pension plan providing retirement benefits equal to 37½% of each employee's compensation in excess of Social Security–covered compensation. Thus, if an employee earns $20,000 a year and Social Security benefits are based on his first $10,000 of compensation, this employee would receive 37½% of salary in excess of $10,000 at retirement. Under this type of plan, only employees earning above the "covered compensation" level receive benefits from the plan.

A plan providing benefits equal to 10% of an employee's compensation covered by Social Security plus 47½% of excess compensation also would integrate properly since the combined benefits of Social Security and the private pension plan provide a proportionately equal benefit for all employees.

If a plan is top-heavy, there is a requirement that minimum benefits or minimum contributions be established in the plan, regardless of what the formula provides. In a defined-benefit plan, those who are not key employees must receive a minimum benefit that equals 2% of their compensation times the number of years of service (but an employee's minimum benefits needn't be more than 20% of his or her average compensation).

In a defined-contribution plan, the minimum contribution must be 3% of compensation unless the contribution for key employees is less than 3%. In those cases, the contribution for all employees can be lowered.

Vesting. An often neglected but very important element of plan design is that of vesting. Choices associated with vesting can have a significant impact on the ultimate cost of the plan. It is possible that two plans with identical benefit formulas and different vesting schedules will result in quite different costs to the employer.

Vesting is defined as the nonforfeitable interest of a participant in his account balance (under a defined-contribution plan) or in his accrued benefit (under a defined-benefit plan). When you become eligible to participate in your plan, you begin to earn or accumulate pension credits. Most plans provide that if you leave the employer that sponsors your plan before completing a specified number of years of service, you

will lose all or a part of the pension benefits you have earned. (For benefit-vesting purposes, a "year of service" means a 12-month period specified in the plan during which a participant completed at least 1,000 hours of service.) After a certain number of years of service, however, a percentage of your benefits becomes vested—that is, generally, you cannot lose these benefits, even if you leave your job. Some plans provide full and immediate vesting; in other words, your benefits become fully vested as you earn them.

Assume, for example, that a participant is 40% vested. In a profit-sharing or money-purchase plan, the participant's vested accrued benefit is equal to 40% of the balance in his account. In a defined-benefit plan, the participant has a nonforfeitable right to the portion of the normal retirement benefit that he has accrued—in this case 40% of his normal retirement benefit. If his normal retirement benefit is $150 per month, he has a nonforfeitable right to $60 per month.

Unlike the situation that prevailed under prior law, ERISA requires that employee's rights to accrued benefits derived from employer contributions must vest under one of three vesting schedules. His right to his normal retirement benefit must also be fully vested on attainment of normal retirement age. In addition, his rights to accrued benefits derived from his own contributions must be nonforfeitable at all times.

The three ERISA alternatives are deemed to be nondiscriminatory in form, but an employer must also show that the particular vesting schedule used is nondiscriminatory in operation. The three alternatives are:

1. *5–15-year vesting*—graduated vesting beginning with 25% after 5 years of service and increasing to 100% after 15 years of service.

2. *10-year vesting*—no vesting before 10 years of service but 100% thereafter (cliff vesting).

3. *Rule of 45*—graduated vesting beginning with 50% after 10 years of service or when the sum of participant's years of service and age equals 45, whichever comes earlier. Thereafter, the participant's vested interest increases 10% per year.

If the IRS determines that a plan's vesting schedule is or is likely to be discriminatory in operation, it may require more rapid vesting of benefits, but not more rapid than what is known as *4–40 vesting*. This vesting provision is based on total years of service with the employer, including years prior to the adoption of the plan. A 4–40 vesting schedule is shown in Table 1.

In practice, 4–40 vesting is the most commonly used schedule, primarily because it is considered beyond attack by the IRS. At each interval it provides more-liberal vesting than either the "5–15" or "Rule of 45" schedules. Only at the completion of ten years' service is "10-year cliff" vesting more liberal than the "4–40" schedule.

In a top-heavy plan, besides 100% immediate vesting, there are two alternative vesting rules. The plan must either vest in full after three years of service, or vest within six years on a graduated basis (20% vesting after two years and an additional 20% each following year, up to the sixth year).

Plan Terminations. The termination of a plan or the complete discontinuance of contributions to a profit-sharing plan can result in the retroactive disqualification of the plan, causing the disallowance of tax deductions for the company. This will depend on whether the plan was intended as a permanent program for the exclusive benefit of employees or as a temporary device to set aside funds for the benefit of officers, stockholders, or highly paid employees, or whether the plan was discriminatory in operation.

Generally, the IRS will not treat the termination as a device to benefit the "prohibited group" if the termination is caused by a change in circumstances that would make it financially impractical to continue the plan. Other valid reasons include a change in ownership by merger; the liquidation or dissolution of the company; a change in ownership by sale or transfer; the existence of adverse business conditions; or the adoption of a new, superseding plan.

According to ERISA, the practical effect of a plan termination is that each affected participant becomes 100% vested in his accrued benefit as of the date of the termination.

In the same way that there is no *legal* requirement to file a request for a "favorable determination" letter with the IRS with regard to a new or amended plan, neither is there a requirement regarding a plan's termination. However, a plan administrator must notify

the IRS on the annual report when a plan terminates by so signifying on the return for the year in which the plan terminates.

If the plan is covered by the insurance provisions of the PENSION BENEFIT GUARANTY CORPORATION (PBGC), the plan administrator must also notify the PBGC of the plan termination. The qualified plans that are exempt from PBGC coverage are the following: all defined-contribution plans (i.e., money-purchase, profit-sharing); defined-benefit plans established by professional service employers with no more than 25 active participants; and defined-benefit plans with only common-law employees (i.e., employees who are not owners of the business entity involved).

Pension Funds as Investments. The "prudent-man rule" requires a trustee or other plan fiduciary to act "with the care, skill, prudence, and diligence under the circumstances then prevailing that a prudent man acting in a like capacity and familiar with such matters would use in the conduct of an enterprise of a like character and with like aims." This rule governs the way in which plan assets may be invested.

There are no specific limits placed on the amount a pension plan can invest in any particular type of asset (other than employer securities or employer real property). Nor are there any limits on the types of investments that can be made. Investments in such tangible assets as real estate, gold, art, or diamonds are permitted, even though these investments might not generate current income for the plan and generally lack liquidity.

A trustee (or any other fiduciary responsible for investing plan assets) is required to discharge his duties by diversifying the investments of the plan so as to minimize the risk of large losses. The degree of risk that the trustee takes in making investments depends in part on the type of plan the employer maintains. In a defined-contribution plan, benefits received by a plan participant are based on the employer's contributions, increased or decreased by the return of plan investments. Thus it may be appropriate to consider some speculative investments in a defined-contribution plan.

In a defined-benefit plan, a rate of return on investments above that assumed by the actuary reduces required contributions, and a rate of return below the assumed rate increases required contributions. Thus investments will normally be of the type that will return at least as much as the actuary has assumed. It is likely, therefore, that speculative investments will have little appeal.

Another factor that may have an affect on the plan's particular investment philosophy is the size of

Table 1	
4–40 Vesting Schedule	
Total Years of Service with Employer	*% Vested*
0 to 4	0%
4	40%
5	45%
6	50%
7	60%
8	70%
9	80%
10	90%
11	100%

the plan. In a small plan, the objective often is to get the maximum tax deduction. A large return on investments will lower the cost. However, in a larger plan, costs become a factor. If you want to reduce costs in a defined-benefit plan, a more speculative investment might be in order.

Distribution of Benefits. At normal retirement age, the basic method of payment of retirement income will be a monthly benefit for life with a minimum of 120 monthly payments to the participant or his designated beneficiary. The actual amount of retirement income may be more or less than that stated above, depending on the option selected prior to the normal retirement date.

Following are examples of the income payable under different methods compared with the basic method:

1. *Life annuity.* Payments will be made to the participant for life; upon death, no further payments will be made to anyone.

2. *Joint and survivor option.* Payments will be made to the participant while both the participant and his beneficiary are living. On the death of either one, two-thirds of the amount of the monthly payments will be continued to the survivor as long as the survivor lives. No further payments will be made after the death of the survivor.

3. *Lump-sum option.* A cash payment equal to the present value of the normal-retirement basic option may be made with the consent of the Pension Committee.

For a disability retirement, a participant must be totally and permanently disabled in the opinion of a physician selected by the Pension Committee. The benefit would be the benefit earned to date, actuarially reduced to reflect the longer period of time over which payments are expected to be made.

A participant may, with the consent of the employer, remain employed beyond his normal retirement date. In such event, contributions on behalf of the participant shall cease as of his normal retirement date. On actual retirement, the participant will receive an actuarially increased benefit, payable in accordance with the option selected at least one day prior to the normal retirement date.

Taxation of Distributions. A lump-sum distribution to a terminated employee is taxed in the following way:

1. The ordinary income portion of the distribution (post-1973 plan participation) qualifies for special ten-year forward averaging; the rest of the distribution (pre-1974 plan participation) qualifies for favored tax treatment as a long-term capital gain.

2. The entire distribution may be reported as ordinary income subject to ten-year averaging.

3. The entire distribution may be reported as ordinary income without electing ten-year averaging.

4. All or part of the distribution may be rolled over to an IRA or to another qualified plan; no tax is paid on the amount rolled over, and the rest is taxed as ordinary income.

Note: Any part of the distribution not taxed under the ten-year averaging method may qualify for regular five-year averaging.

Louis A. Russo

Personal Financial Statement

A statement prepared from the financial records of an individual and listing that individual's assets, liabilities, net worth, and changes in net worth for a specific period of time.

Samuel C. Hoyt

Philadelphia Stock Exchange (PHLX)

The Philadelphia Stock Exchange, America's oldest, was founded in 1790. Initially, bank stocks and government bonds were traded on the Philadelphia Exchange. In 1792, the city served as headquarters for the only two nationally chartered banks—the Bank of North America and the United States Bank. This gave Philadelphia two advantages: one, as a financial center; and two, as a stimulant to trading in the two stocks on the Philadelphia Exchange. As a result, the PHLX was the nation's largest exchange for more than a quarter of a century.

The competition between the New York and Philadelphia Exchanges became more intense as our national economy grew and more securities became available for trading. With the opening of the Erie Canal in 1817, Philadelphia was eclipsed by New York as the nation's banking center and primary port. Fortunately, however, both exchanges prospered as the railroads grew and issued more and more securities.

Efficient communications were vital to the Philadelphia Exchange, even in the early 1800s. Boats from Europe reached New York before arriving in Philadelphia, and it was not unusual for New York traders with significant news from London or Paris to take a stagecoach and "make a killing" at the Philadelphia market.

In response to the problem, a private communications network was formed by a Philadelphia broker. The New York and Philadelphia Exchanges were linked by signal stations atop certain high points in New Jersey. New York Stock Exchange stock prices were flashed by mirrors during the day and by lights at night. The signals were watched by telescope, and information was relayed in as little as ten minutes. This system was supplanted in 1846 when the telegraph was introduced.

In 1870 the Philadelphia Exchange established the first clearing house system. And from the Civil War to the beginning of World War I, the Philadelphia Stock Exchange established itself as the second-largest organized exchange in the nation, after New York. Local and area railroads, coal, and insurance-company securities accounted for the bulk of the trading during this period.

A series of mergers and associate membership agreements, begun in 1949, transformed the Philadelphia Exchange from an organization with regional affiliations to one with nationwide participation. In 1949 the Philadelphia Stock Exchange merged with the Baltimore Stock Exchange. This was followed in 1953 by a merger with the Washington Stock Exchange. Associate membership agreements with the Pittsburgh exchange (1955), the Boston exchange (1957), and the Montreal exchange (1961) further expanded Philadelphia's trading base. A merger with Pittsburgh in 1969 gave Philadelphia the dual-trading-floor concept. This concept was expanded in 1974 with the establishment of the Southeastern Stock Exchange in Miami, Florida, a Philadelphia Stock Exchange trading division.

In 1968 the Philadelphia Stock Exchange began encouraging institutions to join the exchange. Competing specialist and third market-makers were brought to the Philadelphia Stock Exchange trading floor in 1971.

In 1975 the Philadelphia Stock Exchange operation was greatly expanded with the introduction of option trading. Since that time, the volume of options contracts traded on the Philadelphia Exchange has increased at a phenomenal rate. Additionally, those options traded on the Philadelphia Exchange are primary listings—that is, they are traded only on the Philadelphia Stock Exchange.

During 1982 the PHLX became the first exchange to trade options on foreign currencies. This new product, patterned after successfully traded options on common stocks, has been designed not as a substitute for forward and futures markets but as a new, additional, and versatile financial vehicle that can offer significant opportunities and advantages to those seeking either protection or investment profit from changes in exchange rates. Foreign-currency options provide a new useful service to multinational corporations, banks, investors, and virtually all companies engaged in international trade throughout the free world. At present, the Philadelphia Stock Exchange trades options on five foreign currencies: the British pound, the deutsche mark, the Japanese yen, the Swiss franc, and the Canadian dollar.

The Philadelphia Stock Exchange's central computer facility, called CENTRAMART, regulates the flow of incoming orders from across the nation. It is one of the most sophisticated trading support systems of any exchange. In 1977 CENTRAMART was expanded to include the Philadelphia Stock Exchange's Automated Communication and Execution System (PACE). PACE is an advanced order-processing system designed to speed equity orders and execution reports to and from the exchange floor. PACE accepts an order for a specific stock, scans information from the PHLX and NYSE stock quotes for the best price, then executes the order. Within 30 seconds after a market order is entered, it will automatically be executed, recorded on the consolidated tape, and reported back to its point of entry.

The Intermarket Trading System (ITS) was developed in 1977 by the American, Boston, New York, Pacific, and Philadelphia exchanges. ITS was formed in response to the congressionally mandated national market system. In 1978 the Philadelphia Stock Exchange joined with the New York Stock Exchange in implementing the first operational link for ITS.

The Philadelphia Stock Exchange has 505 members. In order to apply for membership, an individual must be affiliated with a partnership or corporation that is registered as a broker/dealer with the Securities and Exchange Commission (SEC). The prospective member must be at least 21 years of age and have knowledge of the exchange's financial rules and regulations. Additionally, he or she must have an understanding of securities accounting and reporting requirements. The applicant also must have had prior training or experience in the securities industry, or have been an apprentice on the exchange floor.

Candidates who meet all of the above requirements, and who have been approved by several committees at the exchange, can enter a bid to purchase a seat. A seat entitles the representative from the member organization to trade through the Philadelphia Stock Exchange or on the exchange floor.

Seats usually are sold on the open market; consequently, price depends on supply and demand. Two forms of membership are available. A regular membership gives the member access only to equity trading. An options membership offers both equity- and option-trading privileges.

One of the advantages of PHLX membership is that the investment in the membership and the cost of maintaining it through yearly dues are relatively low. A member organization also can earn money from its seat through a lease-type arrangement with another firm. The user must be a PHLX member, but does not have to pay the full price of a seat if this lease arrangement is utilized.

A Philadelphia Stock Exchange member has trading rights to over 1,200 securities, representing the most actively traded issues in American today.

The Philadelphia Stock Exchange has three subsidiaries: the Stock Clearing Corporation of Philadelphia (SCCP), the Philadelphia Depository Trust Company (PHILADEP), and the Financial Automation Corporation (FAC).

SCCP, formed in 1870, is the oldest established clearinghouse system in the United States. Basically, SCCP transports securities from seller to buyer and money from buyer to seller.

PHILADEP is a custodian for equity securities and corporate registered bonds. In conjunction with the Depository Trust Company of the New York Stock Exchange, PHILADEP established the first automated interface in the securities industry. By exchanging data between their computers, the two depositories are able to move stock positions between Philadelphia and New York on a same-day basis.

In 1980 FAC was formed to meet the growing demand for automation within the exchange. FAC has made substantial contributions to the exchange by upgrading CENTRAMART and PACE. As a result, those systems have handled peak volume days with relative ease.

See also STOCK EXCHANGES.

Nicholas A. Giordano

Point-of-Sale (POS) Systems

A means of using electronic fund transfers to pay for goods or services rather than paying with cash or check. Point-of-sale systems use terminals to electronically connect a merchant with a financial institution. By use of a plastic "debit card," a customer can transfer funds directly from his or her account to the merchant's account in payment for goods or services. These terminals also function as electronic cash registers that capture electronic data for the merchant's accounting, purchasing, and inventory-control needs. In addition to using the plastic card to make the transfer, the customer must normally also key in a secret personal identification number (or PIN) to authorize the transaction.

Such systems may link the merchant with either a single financial institution or several institutions through a shared system. In a single-institution system, both the customer and the merchant must have accounts at the same institution. In shared systems, several institutions are linked together through a computer switch, so that funds may be transferred electronically among institutions and the POS transfer

can be made even if the merchant and customer have accounts at different institutions.

Although once thought of as a means of rapidly moving to a "cashless society," POS systems have grown slowly, in part because the customer may be disinclined to use such systems since FLOAT is lost when funds are transferred immediately to the merchant. By contrast, payment by check gives the customer use of the funds until the check clears, and payment by credit card provides the customer with use of the funds until the credit-card bill must be paid.

Griffith L. Garwood

Portfolio Analysis (or "Modern Portfolio Theory")

A procedure for making investment decisions, based on the premise that diversification can reduce the risk of an investor's portfolio below the risk level of the individual securities comprising the portfolio.

For example, suppose that an investor is considering the purchase of two common stocks—an airline-company stock and an oil-company stock. The investor is not certain whether the price of fuel will increase substantially or remain relatively constant in the foreseeable future. He is confident that neither of the companies will experience operating losses, regardless of whether fuel prices increase. However, the airline company's profits will be substantial if fuel prices remain constant; there will be little or no profit if fuel prices rise. Conversely, the oil company's profits will have the opposite relation to fuel prices.

Given the fact that there is a significant probability for each company that profits will be close to zero, the investor might conclude that neither stock is attractive on its own merits. However, the portfolio-analysis procedure suggests that in such a situation the investor should consider investing in both securities, knowing that, regardless of whether fuel prices increase, one of the two companies will realize a substantial profit. Even though one company will not realize any profit, the average return on the two stocks might be acceptable. Furthermore, there is, in this example, very little risk for the portfolio of two stocks, while each security individually would leave the investor with a high degree of uncertainty regarding the future return on his investment.

Although the above example illustrates the premise of the portfolio approach, actual application of the procedure requires a relatively high degree of mathematical sophistication as well as extensive statistical calculations describing the relationships among securities. Such calculations cannot be efficiently performed without the aid of a computer, and therefore the individual investor will generally not be able to employ this technique directly in his investment decision-making. However, investors generally find the premise of diversification intuitively appealing and can apply the principle, if not the mathematical technique, to some of their investment decisions. Furthermore, since some investment advisers use the portfolio approach in formulating their recommendations, investors can employ the procedure indirectly by retaining the services of such an adviser.

R. Bruce Swensen

Portfolios

An investment portfolio can consist of common stocks, bonds, mutual funds, commodities, options, etc. Each portfolio should be custom-made to fit the needs of the individual investor; for example, a retired person's portfolio would generally be extremely conservative, while a younger person's portfolio would be much more aggressive.

A retired person who is looking for income and safety of principal should invest in BLUE CHIP-type securities that have a history of earnings and dividends. The bond portion of the portfolio should consist of high-quality bonds with various and continuing maturity dates, some maturing within six months, others maturing at a later date. The various maturity dates are beneficial because if interest rates fluctuate, the portfolio will have continuous money for reinvestment. If interest rates went down, the value of the long-term bonds would go up. Of course, if interest rates went up, the value of the portfolio would go down, but the investor would now have an opportunity to lock in those higher rates with the money coming due from the short-term bonds.

The investor looking for growth should divide his portfolio into long-term growth stocks and high-quality major-industry stocks. Each investor should decide what portion of his portfolio should be in stocks, in bonds, in commodities, etc. If he follows a strict investment philosophy rather than investing on impulse, the net result should be rewarding.

The investor should not invest all of his money at one particular time, but should hold a reserve so that if the securities of his choice should go down, he will have ample funds to dollar cost-average. Dollar cost-averaging is simply buying the same dollar value at lower prices, thus buying more shares at the lower rate.

Psychologically, it is difficult to buy when everyone is selling, but experience has shown that the investor who is not affected by short- and intermediate-term fluctuations usually will do much better than those who trade with the market trends. This requires discipline. The successful investor cannot follow crowds.

Each investor should split his portfolio into the investment vehicles that best suit him, then review his portfolio from time to time to make sure that his investment philosophy is consistent with his current or projected status. For illustrative purposes, let us assume that the investor, in splitting his portfolio, wants one-half of his money in growth stocks and one-half in bonds. (These proportions can change and/or can include other investment vehicles.) The portfolio should be reviewed every six months so that it maintains its equilibrium.

Maintaining the equilibrium (i.e., 50/50) is beneficial because it gives the investor the opportunity to sell stocks if they now represent more than 50% of the portfolio, and forces him to purchase more stocks if that portion then becomes less than 50%. The bond portion would be treated equally: If bonds represented more than 50% of the portfolio, that portion over 50% would be liquidated; and if bonds represented less than 50% of the total market value of the portfolio, more bonds would be bought. In view of the fact that bond prices go up when interest rates go down, and, conversely, bond prices go down when interest rates go up, the investor would force himself to sell at high prices because that portion of the portfolio would then represent more than its predetermined proportion. If bond values and security values both went in the same direction, the investor would take no action. As the investor's objectives changed, he might elect to change the proportions of his portfolio to suit his new circumstances.

Taxes should be a deciding factor in portfolio building. It is important to calculate to the bottom line and not invest on impulse. Many investors buy tax-free bonds just for the sake of not paying taxes, whereas they might be better off buying taxable bonds with high yields even though that income is taxable. To maximize income, money should be compounded at the highest rate possible, and this can be achieved by either reducing taxable income or deferring taxes through the use of tax-free bonds, deferred annuities, discount bonds, etc.

To summarize: In order to achieve success, investors should buy quality issues, get professional advice, and not look to maximize income by giving up quality. Don't be greedy and wait for the market to go up "higher." When securities are down, don't look for them to make bottoms. Average down and maintain a balanced portfolio.

Many investors keep large sums of money in savings accounts because they want maximum safety—that is to say, no risk. But if an investor leaves a large balance in a savings account at a rate of 5% to 6%, he is putting himself at risk. The risk is that he may lose purchasing power. With inflation running at a rate of around 10%, the investor should try to achieve at least a 10% return or sell; otherwise, inflation will eat up his capital. Why not buy Treasury bonds or other high-quality bonds yourself, rather than lending your money to a bank and having them buy the bonds for their own profit? Investigate before you invest. A little effort can be rewarding.

Judah Munk

Preexisting Condition

A health condition or problem that a person had prior to becoming insured for health coverage. An *exclusion* in connection with a preexisting condition means the policy will not pay benefits for illness arising from that condition. A *waiting period* means benefits will not be paid for a preexisting condition until after the policy has been in effect for a specified period of time.

See also HEALTH INSURANCE.

James L. Moorefield

Preferred Stock

Technically, preferred stock, like common stock, is a security that represents an ownership in a corporation. For most practical purposes, however, the rights of preferred stockholders are not the rights commonly associated with ownership. Common stockholders, as the owners of the corporation, have the right to vote in corporate elections and the right to share in corporate profits. Preferred stockholders usually do not have either of these rights and therefore should not be considered owners of the corporation. Under certain circumstances, preferred stockholders might have limited voting rights, but in general they do not participate in corporate decisions at all. Also, a preferred stockholder does not have a claim on a share of corporate profits; rather, he is usually entitled to a fixed annual dividend payment, which is specified by the issuing corporation before the stock is sold to the investor. For most preferred stockholders, this payment remains constant for an indefinite period.

Preferred stock is usually issued in denominations of $25, $50, or $100. This figure is referred to as the "par value" of the stock. The par value signifies the stockholder's claim on the assets of the firm in the event that the corporation is liquidated—that is, after all obligations to creditors have been met from the proceeds of the sale of the firm's assets, preferred stockholders have a claim on the remainder of the proceeds equal to the par value of a share. However, this claim is usually immaterial, because a firm that is liquidated does not usually have sufficient assets to satisfy all creditor's claims, much less those of preferred stockholders.

The dividend that a preferred stockholder receives is stated in one of two ways: either as a percent of par value or as a dollar amount per share. For example, a share of preferred stock with a $100 par value might have a dividend payment equal to 10% of par value. Or, the dividend might be stated as $10 per share. In either case, the stockholder receives $10 per year for each share that he owns.

Example: Jones and Smith invested a total of $1 million to form the Big Apple Corporation. As the holders of the firm's common stock, they are the owners of the corporation and therefore they vote in corporate elections and share the firm's profits.

Subsequent to the formation of the corporation, the owners decide to expand their business. The financing for this expansion will come in part from the sale of $500,000 of preferred stock. The shares of preferred stock will have a $100 par value and a dividend payment equal to 12% of par value, or $12 per year. If the Big Apple Corporation can sell this preferred stock for $100 per share, then 5,000 shares must be sold ($500,000 financing required/$100 per share). The firm's total dividend payment to preferred stockholders will be $60,000 per year ($12 dividends per share 5,000 shares).

Alternatively, if Big Apple sold shares with a $50 par value and a 12% dividend, 10,000 shares would be sold ($500,000 financing required/$50 per share). Each stockholder would receive a dividend payment of $6 (12% of $50 par value). Total dividends paid to preferred stockholders by the Big Apple Corporation would still be $60,000 per year ($6 dividends per share 10,000 shares).

Dividend Yield. The dividend yield for a share of preferred stock is calculated in the same manner as for common stock: dividends per share divided by price per share. While the significance of this figure is questionable when applied to common stock, the preferred-stock dividend yield provides a clearly useful basis for evaluation of the stock. This difference in interpretation stems from the difference in the nature of common-stock dividends and preferred-stock dividends. The common-stock dividend is usually a fraction of the firm's earnings per share and is therefore only a part of the shareholder's total claim on the firm's earnings. The remainder of the earnings is reinvested in the company on the stockholder's behalf. Furthermore, the common-stock dividend often fluctuates from one year to the next. Thus, a dividend-yield calculation based on the current level of dividends may have little or no relationship to the stockholder's anticipated yield.

In the case of preferred stock, the dividend payment is the investor's entire claim on the firm's profit, regardless of the size of that profit. This payment usually does not fluctuate from one year to the next; hence the dividend yield based on this constant dividend payment is the relevant anticipated yield for the preferred stockholder. He can use this dividend yield as a basis for comparison between one preferred stock and another, or between preferred stocks and other investments.

Example: The Big Apple Corporation intends to sell 5,000 shares of $100-par-value preferred stock with a 12% dividend. While the firm may desire to sell these shares to investors for $100, it may not be able to do so. It is not necessary that a share of preferred stock be sold at a price equal to its par value. If, for instance, investors are able to purchase comparable shares of preferred stock, issued by other corporations, which have a 15% dividend yield, there would be no reason to purchase the Big Apple shares for $100, with a 12% dividend yield ($12 dividends per share/$100 price per share). In fact, an investor would not be willing to pay more than $80 for a share of the Big Apple preferred stock; at a price of $80, the dividend yield would be 15% ($12 dividends per share/$80 price per share). Under these circumstances, the Big Apple shares would have a $100 par value with a dividend payment equal to 12% of par value, but the price of a share would be $80 and the dividend yield would equal 15%.

Cumulative Preferred Stock. A corporation is not legally obligated to pay a preferred-stock dividend in any given year; a dividend may be "passed" if, for instance, earnings are insufficient to meet the payment. This feature distinguishes preferred stock from a bond, because nonpayment of bond interest constitutes a default since it violates the contract with the bondholder.

The preferred stockholder does, nonetheless, have some protection against the possibility that dividends will be passed. First, common stockholders cannot receive any dividend payment unless preferred stockholders have received their dividend payment in full. Second, most preferred-stock issues specify that dividends are cumulative, which means that any dividend that is passed must be paid at a later date before common stockholders receive any dividends. Therefore, if a firm passes preferred-stock dividends of, say, $10 per share for two consecutive years, preferred stockholders must receive $30 in dividends the following year before common stockholders can receive any dividend payment. The $30 figure represents $20 of dividends in arrears plus the $10 current dividend.

See also CAPITAL STOCK; COMMON STOCK.

R. Bruce Swensen

Glossary

adjustable-rate preferred stock (or "variable-rate preferred stock" or "floating-rate preferred stock") A preferred stock issue whose dividend payment varies with changes in the level of interest rates in the economy. The dividend rate is based on the interest rate for various United States Treasury securities. For example, an adjustable-rate preferred stock issued by the Bank America Corporation in October 1982 specifies a dividend rate two percentage points lower than the highest rate paid on the following securities: three-month Treasury bills, ten-year Treasury notes, and twenty-year Treasury bonds.

call provision A provision of most preferred stock and corporate bond issues that gives the issuing corporation the right to retire the outstanding securities by purchasing them from investors at a specified price. The call price is specified when the security is issued and generally declines over time. It usually exceeds the par value or face value of the security; the difference between the call price and the face value is referred to as the "call premium." A call provision is usually exercised by a corporation for one of the following purposes: (1) to retire a security with a high yield in order to issue a new security with a lower yield; (2) to retire a security, without replacing it, in order to eliminate the obligation to pay dividends (in the case of preferred stock) or interest (in the case of a bond); (3) to force the holders of convertible preferred stocks or bonds to convert their securities to common stock.

convertible preferred stock A preferred stock issue which specifies that a share of preferred stock can be converted, at the stockholder's option, into a stated number of shares of the common stock of the same company. For example, if a preferred stock is convertible into five shares of common stock, the preferred stockholder can present a share of preferred stock to the issuing company and receive in return five shares of common stock. The "conversion value" of a share of preferred stock is defined as the total value of the common stock into which the preferred stock can be converted—that is, the conversion value equals the number of shares of common stock times the price per share of the common stock. When convertible preferred stock is issued, the conversion value is substantially below the price of the preferred stock. However, investors find the conversion feature attractive because they have the opportunity to receive a fixed preferred-stock dividend payment and also the potential to profit from increases in the value of the firm's common stock. This latter benefit will be realized if the price of the common stock rises to the point where the conversion value of a share of preferred stock exceeds its original purchase price.

guaranteed stock A stock issue (usually preferred stock) whose dividend payments have been guaranteed by a corporation other than the issuing corporation. Sometimes a corporation guarantees a preferred stock issue for a subsidiary. Also, railroad-company stock is sometimes guaranteed by another railroad company as part of a property-lease agreement between the two companies.

participating preferred stock   A preferred stock issue which specifies that preferred stockholders will receive dividends exceeding the stated dividend payment in the event that common-stock dividends exceed a specified limit. For example, a participating preferred stock might specify a dividend payment of $5 per share and also specify that if common-stock dividends exceed $5 per share, the preferred stockholder will receive the same dividend payment as the common stockholder. Most preferred stocks are nonparticipating, which means that the dividend payment cannot exceed the stated amount.

par value, preferred stock   A figure specified by the issuing firm which signifies the preferred stockholder's claim on the assets of the firm in the event that the corporation is liquidated. Also, preferred-stock dividends are often stated as a percent of par value; and when preferred stock is originally issued, it is usually sold at a price close to, or equal to, its par value.

rating, preferred stock   A rating, based on both quantitative and subjective factors, designed to indicate the likelihood that future dividends will be paid as scheduled on a particular preferred stock issue. A company whose earnings are expected to be substantially greater than its total preferred-stock dividends would have a very high rating, denoting a very high probability that preferred-stock dividends will be paid in the future. On the other hand, preferred stock issued by a company with low earnings relative to total preferred-stock dividends will have a low rating. Both Moody's Investors Service, Inc., and Standard & Poor's Corporation rate preferred stock issues.

sinking-fund provision   A provision of some preferred stock issues, as well as most corporate bond issues, requiring that the issuing corporation retire the outstanding securities by periodically purchasing a portion of the issue from investors. Usually the sinking-fund provision specifies that a certain percentage of the issue must be retired each year, either by purchasing the securities in the open market or by exercising a call provision.

Price/Earnings Ratio

The price/earnings ratio, or "p/e," of a stock is its market price divided by its per-share earnings. For example, take a company that earned $2 a share (net income less preferred dividend requirements, divided by the number of shares outstanding) for the most recent 12 months. If its stock is trading at $10 a share, the p/e multiple is 5. If the stock is at $20 a share, the multiple is 10. The p/e of a stock is often available in the market statistics sections of newspapers, along with its dividend yield and price information.

A high p/e indicates that investors are optimistic about a company's future in terms of its growth prospects, earnings, and dividends. A low p/e indicates less enthusiasm. However, there is no "right" or "best" p/e. Some industries traditionally command high ratios—the technology stocks, for example— while others are relatively low. The outlook for the stock market as a whole also affects individual price/earnings ratios.

Charles N. Stabler

Price Quotation

See COMMON STOCK.

Prime Rate

Banks began in the 1930s to publicize a base lending rate for their highest-quality, or prime, business customers. Rates on loans to borrowers of less than prime quality were scaled upward from the prime, making it the most important bank lending rate. The prime tended to be somewhat higher than most money-market interest rates, but during much of the post-depression era, money markets were far less significant sources of funds than the banks. Businesses were also willing to pay the higher bank rate because they received other financial services (checking accounts, for instance) in return, or because the effective cost of a loan could be altered by varying other lending terms (loan maturity or the size of non-interest-bearing deposits that the bank might require).

The prime rate became so important that many people, including politicians and public officials, latched on to it as representative of the whole spectrum of interest rates. Ironically, however, despite its great public notoriety, the prime rate has in recent years lost a good deal of its significance as the "price" of a bank loan. Bank lending practices in general have changed, largely because of the recurring bouts of tight money and high, volatile interest rates during the 1970s and early 1980s.

Early in the 1970s, discrimination (the loss of deposits because of ceilings on rates banks were allowed to pay) was severe. Due to the shortage of lendable funds, banks were forced to ration credit to even prime-quality customers, sending them scurrying to find other sources of short-term credit. They increased their borrowing from each other through the commercial-paper market, and they also began to obtain funds from foreign sources in the Eurodollar market. These practices stimulated the development of both of these financial markets. The high levels of interest rates also caused companies to try to find other ways to reduce their borrowing costs.

At the same time, the banks were facing different pressures. Regulatory changes permitted them to start paying market rates on growing portions of their deposits, lessening the disintermediation problem. But despite their then-higher cost of funds, they were restrained from raising the prime lending rate by the price-control program in effect in the early to mid-1970s. Negative interest-rate margins resulted on primed rate–based loans. When interest rates came down in 1975 and 1976, the banks were able to reestablish a positive spread between the prime and money-market rates, and they have since been hesitant to reduce that spread lest they have to face such negative spreads again.

Thus, prime customers, now with several alternative means of financing, began to demand cheaper pricing from banks at the same time that banks wanted to preserve their pricing margins. The result in many cases has been a new kind of loan pricing, with the lending rate on large loans set at a narrow spread over a money-market rate or a rate based on the bank's overall cost of funds. Some nonloan services formerly provided with a prime-based loan are now provided separately for a fee. The customer's borrowing cost is generally reduced, yet the bank obtains a profitable interest-rate spread and fee income.

This cost-of-funds loan pricing tends to be available only to large companies and for large loans. The banks continue to post a prime rate and to use it as a benchmark for pricing loans to small and medium-size companies and those companies and other customers in less stable financial condition. Administrative costs are higher and risks are generally greater in these lending situations, justifying the higher return now typical of loan rates set at a spread over the prime.

As a result of these market trends, the prime rate has been reduced from being a significant indicator of borrowing costs for top-quality bank customers to being just one of a number of formulas used to price loans to corporate and foreign borrowers.

Carol A. Stone

Probate

The procedure by which a document is proven to be the valid last will and testament of a deceased person (the "decedent") is known as "probate." *Probating of a will* is thus the legal term for the evidentiary process by which the appropriate court will determine whether or not all of the necessary statutory requirements were met when the will was made out.

If the will is admitted to probate—that is, approved by the court—legal title to all of the decedent's property will be transferred to the EXECUTOR named in the will. He or she will then be empowered to collect that property and settle the estate by paying the decedent's just debts and death taxes and distributing the balance to the beneficiaries named in, and in the proportions directed by, the will. The court will issue a document called a "Certificate of Letters Testamentary," which is proof that the will has been probated and that the person named in the Letters is the duly authorized executor.

On occasion there may be a probate contest—a proceeding in which one or more interested parties (usually family members who are required to be served with a court citation advising them of the impending probate proceeding) object to the alleged will. Their objections may be based on any one or more of the grounds specified in the state law, typically dealing with the mental capacity of the decedent when he signed the document in question or the manner in which it was executed (*see* WILL).

If the court is not satisfied that all legal requirements were met, the document will be denied probate, and the decedent will be adjudged to have died without a will—that is to say, "intestate." In this case, the distribution of the decedent's property will be in accordance with state law, and the court will appoint an administrator to perform the functions that would have been performed by the named executor had the will been admitted to probate.

A will can sometimes be admitted to probate without all of its provisions being given effect. If only certain provisions of the will have been challenged, the contestants and the person offering the will for probate may compromise by agreeing, with the court's approval, that the will should be probated but that the particular provisions in question shall be modified in a manner agreeable to all parties. If infants or persons not mentally competent are involved, the court will probably appoint a guardian (sometimes called a "guardian ad litem") to make sure that their interests are fairly represented. The guardian (who may also be appointed even in a noncontested probate, if persons under a legal disability are affected) usually will have to support the compromise (or the will itself, in a noncontested situation) or the court will not approve it.

Steven J. Wohl

Product-Liability Insurance

See INSURANCE.

Professional Corporation/Association

Conducting business under the form of a corporation is controlled basically by the statutes of each individual state. Often, states have prohibited certain "professionals"—such as doctors, lawyers, and architects—from operating through a corporate entity. The general theory has been that since corporations limit liability, and professionals should not have liability limited, they could not use a corporate form to conduct business.

Recently, many states have realized that this is inappropriate and have passed laws permitting professionals to practice their professions as corporate entities. However, these corporations have been specifically designated as professional corporations ("P.C.") or professional associations ("P.A."). Thus, a regular business corporation must be indicated by words such as *Corporation, Corp., Incorporated, Inc., Limited,* or *Ltd.;* and professional corporations must use the initials P.C. or P.A. to designate that they are professionals acting in a corporate entity. Other than those designations, and certain restrictions by the professional associations in the community, professional corporations and business corporations are basically treated the same.

Alan J. Pomerantz

Professional Liability Insurance

See INSURANCE.

Promissory Note

An unconditional written promise that the person signing the note, the "maker," will pay a certain sum on demand or at a specified time. The promissory note is frequently used in business transactions and is one of the essential documents in commercial banking, because every bank loan is supported by some form of note. The note thus provides legal evidence of debt.

Phil Battey

Property, Forms of Co-Ownership

There are two basic ways in which property can be owned outright by more than one person. These are by tenancy-in-common and by joint tenancy. These forms of ownership apply to all property, real and personal. A common example of personal property held in one of such tenancies is a bank account.

Under a *tenancy-in-common ownership,* each party, or tenant, owns a specific amount of the whole and can pass this property interest to a beneficiary of his choice through a bequest or devise in his will. He may also freely sell his interest during his life to a third party.

Under a *joint-tenancy ownership,* each joint tenant owns an equal share of the whole property. When one joint tenant dies, the surviving joint tenant (or tenants) automatically becomes the owner of the share of the deceased joint tenant. This property interest cannot be left to a beneficiary through a bequest or devise by will. Also, any transfer to a third party during life will retain the survivorship features of the original joint tenancy.

There is a special type of joint-tenancy ownership between spouses in New York, which is called a *tenancy by the entirety.* This ownership mode has the same survivorship features as the joint tenancy, except it cannot be unilaterally broken during life by either of the spouses. It can be severed only by agreement of the parties or by divorce. Upon divorce, the owners become tenants-in-common.

Paul Schimmel

Property-Casualty Insurance

One reason why Americans have the highest standard of living in the world may be that they are well protected against the financial disasters that otherwise could wipe out a family. Americans are better insured than people in any other nation. In 1980 total premiums were $189.8 billion, or 43.6% of the world total. Japan was second with 13.6%, West Germany third with 9.3%, Britain fourth with 7.1%, France fifth with 5.2%, and Canada sixth with 2.9%.

None other than Benjamin Franklin helped to get fire insurance off to its real start—in 1752—with the successful formation of the Philadelphia Contributionship for the Insurance of Houses from Loss by Fire (also known as the Hand in Hand). The company is still in existence.

When the automobile came along, insurance wasn't far behind. The first auto-insurance policy was issued before 1900.

Over the years, property-casualty insurers have expanded their horizons to cover almost all known perils, ranging from fires to hurricanes, tornadoes, and earthquakes . . . to the actions of criminals . . . to the consequences of one person's negligence resulting in harm to another. And repeatedly, insurers have found a way to deal with the highly specialized demands of advancing technology—the airplane, nuclear energy, offshore oil rigs, and spacecraft.

Competitive but Closely Regulated. Insurance is one of the nation's most competitive but closely regulated industries. There are more than 2,900 property-casualty companies, and no single company or group of companies with common ownership has more than 7.5% of the market. The ten largest companies combined can claim only a little more than one-third of the market.

Our society could hardly function without insurance. There would be so much uncertainty, so much exposure to sudden, unexpected, and possibly catastrophic loss, that it would be tough for anyone to plan with confidence for the future. It would also be difficult to obtain credit or financing since few lenders and investors would be willing to risk funds without a guarantee of safety for their investments.

The basic function of property-casualty insurance is the transfer of risk. Its aim is to reduce financial uncertainty and make accidental loss manageable. This is done by substituting payment of a known fee—an insurance premium—to a professional insurer for the insurer's assumption of the risk of a large loss, and a promise to pay in the event of such a loss.

The insurance product is a contract, known as a policy, which legally binds the seller (the insurer) and the buyer (the policyholder) to certain obligations. Insurers are obligated to pay for losses should a specific event covered by the policy occur. Policyholders pay a premium for the financial protection the policy provides.

Wide Range of Policies. Property-casualty insurance companies offer a wide range of policies covering the following:

- Losses of or damage to property from fire, windstorm, theft, vandalism, and other perils.
- The policyholder's legal liability to pay for injuries to other persons or damage to their property for which the policyholder is responsible.
- Costs arising from job-related illnesses and injuries.
- Protection for employers against losses caused by fraudulent or dishonest acts of employees (offered in the form of fidelity bonds).
- Failure of a contractor to perform specified acts within a stated period (suretyship).

In addition to regular liability coverage, insurers offer special policies known as "umbrella liability," which provide coverage ($1 million and more) over and above that provided in other policies. Many insurance policies contain a deductible—the amount the policyholder agrees to absorb before the insurance company takes over.

Auto Insurance. When you consider the tremendous toll in lives and property damage from auto accidents every year, it's little wonder that AUTOMOBILE INSURANCE is the largest single property-casualty coverage.

Of every $10 Americans spend for property-casualty coverages, $4 are for premiums for insuring motor vehicles and motor-vehicle liability.

Auto insurance has become an essential item in most family budgets. Many states require all registered car owners to carry insurance, and in every state there are laws under which a driver involved in an accident may lose the right to drive if he or she is unable to prove financial responsibility up to certain dollar amounts.

Home Insurance. Because a home is often the biggest single investment a family makes, most people purchase insurance as a safeguard against unforeseen financial losses resulting from damage to or destruction of property. Insurance coverages for the home and its contents and the homeowner's or tenant's liability to others usually are combined into a single package that is called HOMEOWNERS INSURANCE, although there are separate policies available for fire, theft, and other perils.

Major Role of Commercial Insurance. A huge chunk—nearly half—of all property-casualty insurance is commercial insurance—that is, insurance on businesses, organizations, institutions, and their properties. Coverages against a variety of perils are available for nearly all mobile and stationary business properties. Liability insurance also is available for a wide range of exposures, providing for the defense of lawsuits against the business, as well as payments for any claims, awards, or other settlements to workers or the public. Insurers also protect against losses due to interruption of business, employee dishonesty, failure in performance of another person or firm, and other risks.

The financial losses that a business or organization may be exposed to every day can originate from almost any aspect of the business. Along with safety and security, insurance can assure business owners that these losses will be minimized or made less debilitating than if the companies assumed the risks themselves.

There are many commercial multiple-line policies on the market, each with a common purpose—to cover the major property and liability exposures faced by a business. These policies are designed to meet virtually all insurance needs of typical businesses.

Agents and Brokers. The insurance buyer has a choice of agents or brokers, who often live or work nearby. It's the agent's job to advise the purchaser, to issue or arrange for issuance of the policy, and to provide follow-up service as needed.

The buyer may deal with any one of the following:

- An independent agent, who usually represents more than one company.
- An exclusive agent, who is an employee or a commissioned representative of a single company.
- A solicitor, an agency employee who may make sales and collect premiums, but whose authority stops short of issuing or countersigning policies.
- A broker who represents not the company but the customer. The broker deals with either agents or companies in arranging for the coverage required by the customer.

Although many people think of insurance as one giant industry, the two principal segments—life insurers and property-casualty insurers—market entirely different products. Often, however, the same agents or brokers handle both forms of insurance. Still other companies sell accident and health insurance exclusively, although many life insurers and property-casualty companies also compete in the accident and health market.

How Insurers Are Capitalized. In a business that is highly competitive, insurers are capitalized and operate in a variety of ways. As stated in the entry on INSURANCE, the principal categories of companies are capital stock companies and mutual companies. In addition, in the property-casualty insurance field, there are two other categories of companies: reciprocal exchanges and Lloyds associations.

Reciprocal exchanges are nonprofit organizations through which people pool their individual risks and share them proportionately. Each subscriber's premium is recorded in a separate account, from which the subscriber's share of each loss is paid. Unlike mutual companies, which are incorporated, reciprocal insurers are unincorporated organizations of "subscribers" who insure each other.

Lloyds associations are unincorporated organizations of individuals who accept a specific portion of liability under each policy issued. American Lloyds are named after but have no connection with Lloyd's of London, the world's largest firm of individual underwriters, and comprise only a minuscule part of the property-casualty insurance market in the United States. Each Lloyds association is administered by an attorney-in-fact, and much of the risk is reinsured by other insurance companies.

Rates Vary by States, Communities. For the major lines of property-casualty insurance, the rates vary from state to state and even from community to community, depending on the accident record of local motorists, the extent of fire protection available for property owners, the prevalence of crime, and other factors.

While many such factors are considered in rate-making, rates basically depend on two primary factors: the frequency of claims (which generally parallels the frequency of auto accidents, fires, and thefts), and the severity, as measured by the cost, of each claim (which in turn is affected by the costs of goods and services for which insurance pays). In their periodic review of rates, companies use this "loss experience," supplemented by factors reflecting economic trends, as a guide to the amount that will be required for future claims, to meet the costs of doing business (including taxes), and to realize a profit.

Why Underwriting Is Important. Underwriting is a cornerstone of the insurance process, but the term often is used to refer to the insurance business generally. Actually, an underwriter is an insurance-company employee who specializes in deciding whether to accept a risk, determining the conditions of accepting a risk, and reviewing the loss experience of an accepted risk to determine if it has been satisfactory.

Underwriting is a decision-making process. The underwriter must evaluate each application for coverage and decide whether to accept or reject it. A primary function of the underwriting department is to promote the company's growth by proper risk selection to achieve an acceptable balance of risks properly priced for each line of insurance.

Some risks that do not meet normal standards can be made acceptable by modifying the nature of the risk, and insurance companies frequently recommend such changes. Sometimes, for example, the installation of a sprinkler system in an old building will transform it from an unacceptable risk to an insurable property. (*See* UNDERWRITER, INSURANCE.)

The Claims Procedure. An insurance claim is filed when an individual or organization seeks to recover for a loss that may be covered under an insurance policy. Most property-insurance policies require notification in writing immediately or as soon as practicable after a loss has occurred. Liability policies require written notice as soon after an accident as is feasible, and require forwarding of all papers and documents pertaining to the accident as soon as they are received. Notification may be made to the insured's agent or broker or directly to the insurance company. The claimant may be required to produce accurate documentation of the loss, and estimates for replacement and repairs.

Once the insurer has determined that a policy is in effect and the loss is covered, an ADJUSTER is assigned to verify and determine the amount of loss. The adjuster may be an employee of the insurance company or an independent adjuster who handles losses for insurers. Some independent adjusters are highly trained specialists with wide experience in handling certain types of complicated losses.

Most insurance claims are adjusted promptly. However, some require prolonged investigation, often because the extent of loss or the cause of loss is unclear. Product-liability and professional malpractice claims are among the most difficult to adjust and the most likely to be decided before a judge and jury.

In startling contrast are settlements for claims from hurricanes and tornadoes. When these disasters strike, adjusters are on the scene within hours and often are able to issue partial payment checks within a day or two to policyholders whose homes have been damaged or destroyed. When a major disaster strikes, additional adjusters often are flown in from other areas of the country to expedite claims handling. Sometimes adjusters make advance payments on the spot to assist catastrophe victims.

Industry Regulation. Property and casualty insurance has long been subject to close regulation by authorities in every state, the District of Columbia, American Samoa, Guam, Puerto Rico, and the Virgin Islands. Because the industry has a high degree of competition, the safeguards embodied in the state regulatory system are recognized as being in the public interest.

The monitoring of insurance companies' financial conditions continues as a primary responsibility of regulators to assure that companies remain solvent and thus able to meet their policyholders' obligations. While their powers vary from state to state, regulators generally are charged with licensing and monitoring insurance companies, approving the form and conditions of policies, and reviewing rate changes to ascertain that customers are not overcharged or unfairly discriminated against and that rate levels are adequate to maintain a company's solvency.

The procedures for reviewing and putting into effect the rates on which policyholders' premiums are based are reflected in state rating laws, which provide varying degrees of flexibility. There are:

Prior-approval laws, under which companies must file statistically supported applications for rate changes, which then must be approved by the state regulator before they may be put into effect. Some of these laws have "deemer" provisions under which rates are deemed to have been approved if the regulator takes no action within a specified period.

Competitive-rating laws, which permit companies to make rate changes as needed, subject to competitive marketplace forces.

In turn, competitive-rating statutes take a number of forms:

Open-competition laws, under which companies are allowed to adjust rates without going through the formality of filing a notice with the regulatory agency.

However, in states with such laws, rates are subject to monitoring by the insurance regulator, who can take appropriate action if the rates are found to be excessive, inadequate, or discriminatory.

File-and-use laws, which require companies to file notice of rate changes but permit the use of the new rates upon filing until or unless the regulator subsequently disapproves them.

Use-and-file laws, a variation of file-and-use under which companies may put rate changes into effect and later submit an informational filing, which becomes subject to regulatory review.

Rate revisions may be filed either by individual companies or by rating organizations on behalf of groups of companies.

Consumers Raise Questions—and Get Answers. Invariably, consumers will have questions—where and how to shop for insurance; what kinds of protection are afforded by their policies; and what to do if they have an insurance-related problem.

The first step is to find the right agent, broker, or company representative, perhaps by consulting a friend or neighbor, or even the telephone book. Agents and brokers can answer questions about the insurance policies they sell and they serve as a liaison between the insurance company and the consumer. Many state insurance departments have personnel whose responsibilities include working directly with consumers who have complaints or differences of opinion with their insurers. The Insurance Information Institute has an active consumer-affairs program, including a national toll-free telephone hot line and free leaflets designed to provide answers to property-casualty insurance questions.

Mechlin D. Moore

Property Tax

A tax on real or personal property, assessed by state or local government. The right to tax real property in the United States rests primarily with the state. States in turn delegate taxing power to political and administrative subdivisions such as cities, counties, towns, villages, boroughs, and districts.

General real-estate taxes are levied for the support and operation of the government agency granted the power by the state to impose the taxes. These taxes are based only on the value of the real property; they are not related to the incomes or other assets of the property owners.

Most state laws exempt certain real estate from property taxation. Exemptions often include real estate owned by the government, religious institutions, hospitals, and educational institutions. Some state laws also sometimes allow special exemptions to decrease property taxes for homeowners, veterans, and senior citizens. Tax incentives such as special waivers or reductions are sometimes given by the state or municipality to attract new industries and business or to encourage the use of agricultural land.

Harley W. Snyder

Prospectus

See COMMON STOCK.

Proxy

See COMMON STOCK.

Public Employee Programs

These are programs of federal, state, and local governments that provide retirement, disability, and survivors' benefits for civilian employees. Other benefits may also be accorded by the jurisdiction, such as medical care, paid sick leave, and workmen's compensation in any case of injury, whether or not in connection with the job.

Harvey Rachlin

Public Liability Insurance

See INSURANCE.

"Put" Bonds

These are bonds issued with an optional feature entitling the holder to "put" the bonds back to the issuer at par on a set date, prior to maturity. The holder must notify the issuer in writing of the intention to "put" the bonds 60 days prior to the set date. The put date is usually ten years after the issue date, although more recently issued put bonds have an earlier date (three to five years). The put feature will vary form issue to issue in length of time before the put date. The put price is a factor. Whether the put is a one-time option, a yearly option, or a recurring option on any interest date are additional factors. This is an attractive vehicle with which to take advantage of longer-term rates with an "out" for the holder shorter-term. Put features add price support to the bond in the secondary market.

Moore & Schley Cameron & Company

Puts

See OPTION TRADING.

·R·

Railroad Social Insurance

Two federal laws provide social insurance protection nationally for employees of railroads, railroad associations, and railway labor organizations. Retirement annuities and survivor protection for aged or disabled railroad employees and their families are provided by the Railroad Retirement Act; unemployment and sickness benefits are covered by the Railroad Unemployment Insurance Act. Persons covered by this system receive hospital insurance and related medical-care insurance under the MEDICARE program. Until a railroad worker has ten years of creditable service as provided by the Railroad Retirement Act, the worker and his family are protected under the provisions of the Social Security Act.

Harvey Rachlin

Rating, Common Stock

See COMMON STOCK.

Rating, Preferred Stock

See PREFERRED STOCK.

Rating Agencies

The rating agencies are a vital link between the issuer of a fixed-income security and the investor. The definition of the role the rating agencies play is simple, but the implementation of that role is highly complex. Basically, a rating agency's responsibility is to determine the relative probability of an issuer paying the interest and principal on its debts at the time they are due. What makes the job complex is the wide range of variables that agency analysts must weigh in determining a rating for the long- or short-term issues of a corporation or a municipality.

One reason for the difficulty is the lack of precise criteria for determining a rating. There are no fixed mathematical formulas that automatically produce triple A or any other rating. Instead, a bond analyst must recognize and analyze the relationship between different financial ratios, and even that is only part of the rating process. Also to be considered are the nature of the industry in which a company operates; the position of that industry in relationship to the general economy; the position of a company within its industry; the company's market share; and the quality of the company's management.

There are two major agencies assigning ratings to fixed-income issues, and a number of smaller companies. Leaders in the field are STANDARD & POOR'S CORPORATION and MOODY'S INVESTORS SERVICE, INC. A third agency is Fitch Investors Service, which rates a small number of corporate issues compared to the majors, and is best known for its rating of banks. Comparatively new to the field is Duff & Phelps, which specializes in rating utilities.

The ratings assigned to issues by Standard & Poor's and Moody's are almost identical. For instance, S & P's designation for a top-quality bond is AAA, while Moody's will list it as Aaa. Both agencies consider any bond rated in the first four categories AAA/Aaa to BBB/Baa to be of investment grade, meaning that interest and principal are considered secure. But *secure* is a relative term, and bonds rated AAA are considered more secure than those rated BBB. A bond rated BBB is on the borderline between sound obligation and speculative, and ratings become more speculative and thus riskier as they descend from BB to CC. A rating of D indicates a bond in default.

For investors, a bond rating is a safety gauge; it is not a recommendation to purchase, sell, or hold a security. The rating evaluates the credit risk of the bond, but that should be only one element in the investor's overall buy-or-sell decision-making. Ratings do not concern themselves with such vital variables as market conditions or the suitability of the risk factor to a particular investor. The ratings are also not intended to measure potential investment returns. Whether a person gains or loses depends on the type of bond purchased and on whether the trend in interest rates is up or down. Whether a bond is rated AAA or A, the price of that bond will almost surely go down if interest rates go up.

A rating given to a fixed-income security is not a

permanent assignment. The rating agencies continually monitor the financial affairs of the companies and municipalities they rate; and if the agency sees a change in the issuer's ability to meet its interest and principal on time, the rating may be lowered—or, if there is an improvement in the issuer's financial condition, the rating could be raised.

Donald A. Moser

Real-Estate Agent

A real-estate agent is a person who is authorized to act on behalf of another person (called the "principal") in real-estate transactions and business. The agent is engaged by the principal (usually the property owner) to negotiate the sale, purchase, lease, or exchange of realty or to arrange financing for real estate, for a fee or commission. All real-estate agents must be licensed in the state where they work.

All agents come under the general law of agency, which concerns the legal rights, obligations, duties, and liabilities that are the result of business relationships between the agent, principal, and third party. An agent under the law enters into a fiduciary relationship (one of trust and confidence) with the principal and is obligated to perform faithful and honest service. Among the common law's principles is one that prohibits the agent from personally profiting from the position of agency other than through the agreed-upon fees or commissions. In addition, he or she cannot be a party to the transaction itself and must place the principal's interests above those of the persons dealing with the principal.

The commission is the compensation paid to a real-estate agent. (He or she usually does not get a salary.) The amount of commission is directly related to the amount of money involved in the real-estate transaction. Generally, a rate of commission is agreed upon between the principal and the agent. Every transaction is paid for separately and the financial success of a real-estate agent is dependent on his or her ability to bring about successful transactions.

To regulate the activities of real-estate agents, all states and the District of Columbia have licensing laws as well as real-estate commissions to administer those laws. Though the specifics of these regulations vary from state to state, all contain the same basic elements. The licensing statutes of many states are based on a model law recommended by the National Association of Realtors. Because many agents are becoming specialized in different areas—like appraisals, property management, and real-estate counseling—regulations have been broadened to include these specialties. All real-estate laws exist for the primary purpose of protecting the public. In addition, they protect honest and competent real-estate professionals from dishonest and illegal competition.

In order to obtain a real-estate license, an agent must pass a written examination that requires certain skills and knowledge developed through specific courses of instruction. Licensing courses are available to prepare a prospective licensee for the test. To keep the real-estate license, an agent must maintain certain standards of ethical conduct and in some cases participate in continuing education. The license must also be renewed at specified times.

A real-estate broker or agent who is also a member of the National Association of Realtors is called a "realtor." The term *realtor* is a registered service mark used to designate only those persons who belong to the National Association. All realtors must abide by the association's nationally recognized code of ethics. This code demands highly professional conduct and is enforced through professional-standards committees at local boards of realtors. The association strives to improve and enhance the professionalism of its members through continuing education as well. The National Association of Realtors, which recently celebrated its seventy-fifth anniversary, consists of local realtor boards and state associations that represent over 600,000 individual members nationally. A real-estate agent who is not a realtor is governed only by state licensing laws.

Advantages and Disadvantages of Working as a Real-Estate Agent. A career in real estate offers the following advantages:

Personal satisfaction and opportunity. A real-estate professional's services are needed in every community. Imagine the personal satisfaction an agent feels when he or she helps a young family purchase their first home.

Strong potential for above-average income. Considering the time involved, a real-estate agent has the potential for above-average earnings if he or she so desires.

Flexible hours. Working hours can often be adjusted to fit most individual situations.

Pleasant working conditions. Most real-estate offices have comfortable and well-located facilities.

Reasonable education requirements. A college degree is not needed to pursue a real-estate career. However, every real-estate agent must meet the educational requirements necessary to obtain his or her real-estate license. This can be accomplished by anyone who has the desire to put forth the necessary effort.

Minimum financial investment to get started. No large amounts of money are needed for education, equipment, or facilities. What *is* needed, however, is enough money for the cost of licensing, an automobile in good condition for showing property to prospects, and the ability to support oneself until commissions are earned.

Not desk- or office-bound. A real-estate agent meets a variety of people both in and out of the business office.

Equal opportunities for men and women of all ages. No heavy physical activity.

The disadvantages of pursuing a career in real estate include the following:

Irregularity of income. Most agents are paid by commission, and since real-estate sales can be seasonal or cyclical, irregularity of income is a real probability. The real-estate professional must be able to make psychological as well as financial adjustments for these slow periods.

Frustration associated with selling. Sometimes sales are lost for a variety of reasons. A person working in the real-estate business must accept this if he or she wants a successful career in the long run.

Working with a variety of personalities. Dealing with people can be very rewarding, but sometimes buyers, sellers, or even one's own associates can make the job a little harder by being uncooperative. If one can be patient and understanding, this problem can be handled with a minimum of difficulty.

Irregular working hours. While many people see this as an advantage, it can be a drawback in family situations. Many potential buyers will want to see property after they get off work or on the weekends, and contract negotiations usually take place at night when both husband and wife are present.

Forms, contracts, and financial detail work. These and other time-consuming tasks must be handled efficiently by the real-estate agent.

Lack of fringe benefits if one works independently.

Specialization. Many real-estate agents choose to specialize in a particular area of real estate. These specialties include:

Residential Brokerage (Sales). Agents sell single-family homes or vacant residential lots. Many real-estate agents begin in residential sales and then move on to other specialties. A professional organization of residential brokers is the residential division of the Realtors National Marketing Institute, an affiliate of the National Association of Realtors. The certified residential broker (CRB) is the professional designation awarded after five years' experience as a licensed broker or agent, and after the agent has completed the educational requirements.

Commercial-Investment Brokerage. These agents specialize in selling income-producing real estate like apartment buildings, office buildings, businesses, and warehouses. A professional organization for these agents is the commercial-investment division of the Realtors National Marketing Institute. The CCIM (certified commercial-investment member) is the professional designation awarded after stringent educational and practical requirements are met by members.

Appraisals. Many professional appraisers began as real-estate agents. A real-estate appraiser collects, studies, and interprets relevant facts and information in order to answer questions about the value, quality, and use of real property. The American Institute of Real Estate Appraisers (AIREA) is a focal organization for these real-estate specialists. All members hold either its MAI (member, Appraisal Institute) or RM (residential member) designation or are candidates for these designations.

Industrial Brokerage. Industrial brokers or agents specialize in the sale, development, and management of industrial properties. The Society of Industrial Realtors is an international organization serving these agents. The SIR (Society of Industrial Realtors) designation is awarded after the broker has successfully completed the educational and practical-experience requirements.

Securities and Syndication Brokerage. This type of brokerage has its origins in commercial and investment selling. Real-estate syndicators organize groups of investors for the purpose of investing in real-estate developments of various types. Syndicators can belong to the Real Estate Securities and Syndication Institute (RESSI), which sponsors the CRSS (certified real-estate securities sponsor) designation.

Farm and Land Brokerage. Farm and land brokers deal with the sale, lease, and management of farms and ranches and with the sale and development of raw land. The Farm and Land Institute serves as the trade organization for these agents.

Counselors. These real-estate agents become qualified to give competent and independent advice and guidance in real-estate matters. They work on a fee basis and will frequently function as a real-estate department within a corporation, municipality, or government agency. Each member of the American Society of Real Estate Counselors (ASREC), a professional organization for real-estate counselors, is authorized to use the professional designation CRE (counselors of real estate).

Property Management. The Institute of Real Estate Management (IREM) awards the CPM (certified property manager) designation to those members who have the required experience as property managers and have completed the specified course work.

(All of the above-mentioned real-estate organizations are affiliated with the National Association of

Realtors. To be a member of these organizations, the real-estate agent must belong to a local board of realtors.)

Harley W. Snyder

Real-Estate Investment Trust (REIT)

An investment in real estate has proven to be a consistently sound investment. Reasons for this include tax advantages (attributable to tax treatment of capital gains as well as depreciation and other deductions); appreciation of property value and rents; and the ability to leverage an investment (the use of borrowed funds to expand available capital with the expectation of earning income that exceeds borrowing cost).

One method of investing in real estate is through a real-estate investment trust or REIT (pronounced "reet"). A REIT is a business trust or corporation that operates by purchasing or financing primary real-estate projects, such as office buildings, shopping centers, hotels, apartment buildings, condominiums, industrial buildings, and warehouses. Investments have even included a steamboat, a racetrack, and a stadium. An investor participates by purchasing shares in a publicly owned REIT, often through the major exchanges. The REIT uses these funds plus borrowed funds to purchase or finance major real-estate projects.

A REIT is a unique business enterprise that combines the advantages of other investment vehicles while exhibiting some noteworthy distinctions. Like a corporation, a REIT offers centralized management, limited liability for its shareholders, and easy transferability of shares. Its shareholders have powers and duties similar to those of the shareholders of a corporation. But unlike a corporation, a REIT usually pays no federal taxes (and often no state taxes) on income or gains that are distributed to its shareholders. Like a real-estate partnership, a REIT thus offers its shareholders an investment whose income is taxed only at the investor level.

An investor in a REIT is also the beneficiary of other favorable tax treatment, including pass-through of capital gains, taxed only at the shareholder level at a lower rate than ordinary income; return of capital distributions (attributable to depreciation) that are taxed only when the shareholder sells his or her shares; and distributions that are not taxed (from the refinancing of mortgages or gains from the sale of property). This pass-through or conduit feature of the REIT differs from that of a partnership, however, in that a partner treats partnership losses and expenses as his own for tax purposes, while a REIT shareholder cannot.

The other important distinction between a REIT and a partnership is that an investor in a REIT is not compelled to expend a large amount of capital in order to participate, and may freely dispose of his or her shares. Usually bought and sold on major stock exchanges at per-share prices averaging $5 to $15, REIT shares are thus much more affordable and liquid than partnership interests. Low share prices are also attractive because the investor may spread risk by purchasing a portfolio of REIT shares.

Unlike many businesses that include an investment in real estate as one of many investment directions, a REIT participates in only one sector of the economy: real estate. Accordingly, it is managed by knowledgeable—and specialized—personnel. An investor with limited real-estate expertise often finds this element attractive.

A REIT is not restricted to investing or lending in one geographic area, as may be the case with a bank or savings and loan institution. A REIT is also able to offer a good variety of financing arrangements. Other features combining to make the REIT vehicle a unique one include the following:

- REIT investors (shareholders) are highly protected by rules and regulations imposed on REIT managers.
- REIT investments (properties and financing arrangements for the properties) are typically large and of high quality.
- REIT portfolios (types and places of investments) are often deliberately diversified to ensure the safety of invested funds.
- REIT current earnings (on investments), because they are untaxed and passed through directly to shareholders, are among the highest in all forms of investment.
- Appreciation in the value of REIT assets may be reflected in increasing REIT share prices.

Special Tax Status. The special tax-exempt status that distinguishes a REIT from other business trusts and corporations is a result of legislation passed by Congress in 1960. This legislation set aside previous rules for taxation of real-estate business trusts in order to afford the opportunity of real-estate investment to the general public and to direct more funds into the nation's real-estate market.

Provided a REIT complies with specific Internal Revenue Code requirements, it pays little or no federal taxes on its income or gains. To attain this exemption from taxation, the REIT must

- distribute at least 95% of net annual earnings to shareholders;
- hold at least 75% of its assets on real property,

shares in other REITS, cash, cash items, or government securities;

- derive at least 75% of its gross income from real estate (i.e., rents, mortgage interest, and gains from selling real estate);
- have 100 or more shareholders (more than half of outstanding shares cannot be owned by five or fewer individuals at any time during the last half of each taxable year);
- utilize independent real-estate professionals to perform specific management duties; and
- not engage in speculative, short-term holdings of real estate in order to sell for quick profits.

The Investor. REIT's provide an attractive investment choice for a varied clientele. In addition to appealing to investors of varying degrees of wealth and financial expertise and to those investors particularly interested in current income, REIT's have attracted the interest of the institutional investor (including certain profit-sharing plans, endowment funds, IRA and Keogh accounts, and charitable religious organizations) because of their specialized management and tax advantage (e.g., distributions received from leveraged portfolios are not subject to taxation as unrelated business income).

Foreign investors have exhibited recent interest in the REIT vehicle. Such investors value the long-term appreciation of REIT investments and the special tax advantages (in particular, nontaxable capital gains on sales of REIT shares).

REIT Structure. A REIT may be initially organized by groups with real-estate experience (mortgage banks, real-estate brokers, real-estate managers, etc.). Commercial banks and insurance companies have also sponsored REIT's.

Under present law, tax benefits are available to both REIT's that are organized as business trusts and those organized as corporations.

Legal existence is initially established and then guided by a "Declaration of trust" for a business trust and by articles of incorporation (or charter) for a corporation. The document sets forth the REIT's fundamental structure and operation. The declaration and articles also provide guidelines for the activities of REIT employees responsible for policies and daily management. Existence and organization are also controlled by statutes or common law, either in the state where the REIT's declaration or articles was initially filed or where the REIT's principal business office is located. Activities are additionally monitored by regulatory agencies, including the Securities and Exchange Commission (SEC) and the state securities administrators.

Regardless of the varying legal requirements, all REIT's share a similar internal structure. The trustees or directors of a REIT are its governing body. These individuals have overall management responsibility for the REIT, planning its investment objectives and overseeing its asset and liability management. In most states, the majority of a REIT's trustees must maintain no business or personal relationship with the trust, its affiliates, or its contractors. Most trustees are recruited from the real-estate, financial, business, professional, and academic communities.

The shareholders of a REIT own the trust and are endowed with voting privileges that are exercised to, among other things, approve trustees, endorse or reject proposed amendments to the declaration or articles (and their bylaws), and determine the fundamental business activity of the REIT. REIT shareholders are protected by disclosure rules and other antifraud and fiduciary-responsibility rules imposed on REIT management by the SEC and other regulatory agencies.

Because a REIT cannot manage its own properties directly, it employs management personnel to handle these functions. Trustees or directors may also recruit an outside organization to provide investment analysis, portfolio management, and other services on a contractual basis. This outside organization is called an "adviser."

REIT Types. Several types of REIT's have developed in response to investor interest and need. A REIT that specializes in the financing of real-estate projects is called a "mortgage REIT." Income for this type of REIT is derived from interest earned and discounts received.

Common financing arrangements in mortgage REIT's reflect their organizational flexibility and include short-term construction and development loans; first mortgages (long-term, secure, permanent), second mortgages, and other refinancings such as wraparound loans (REIT offers a second mortgage in an amount that includes the amount of the first mortgage, and assumes responsibility for payments to first lender); special short-term loans such as gap and bullet loans; and a variety of alternative financing arrangements that have developed during the recent period of high inflation.

A REIT that specializes in property ownership— either alone or jointly with other investors (joint venture)—is called an "equity REIT." Income for the equity REIT is derived from rent and in the form of capital gains on the sale of appreciated property.

An equity REIT acquires properties by purchase; by contracting for the construction of improvements on land (already owned by the REIT); by investing in a joint venture with a developer or other owners, entering into a tax-free exchange of property; by exchanging shares of stock for property; or by foreclosing on a mortgage. Payment for the properties may be financed by loans secured by short- or long-term mortgages. Financing the properties enables the REIT to preserve available cash and to leverage the investment for a greater return.

A REIT may also combine the advantages of both financing and owning to create a third type of REIT—a hybrid REIT.

Whether a REIT emphasizes equity and mortgages or operates as a hybrid, it may specialize further. For example, the REIT may invest in one kind of property (such as apartment complexes), one chief property (a stadium), one specific locale (the sun belt), one specific financing arrangement (first mortgages), or one specific type of ownership (land purchase/leasebacks).

Yet another variation is provided by a newcomer to the industry that is characterized by its intention to liquidate (dissolve and dispose of all assets at a specified time in the future, usually about ten years). The self-liquidating, "finite-life" REIT assures investors the opportunity to realize the fully appreciated value of the REIT's investments—at a specified date—and also maintains the safety, high return, and other advantages of REIT investment.

History and Future of REIT's. Professional management, portfolio quality, and national and local market conditions all have a great influence on investments in real estate, including real-estate investment trusts. Since 1960, when Congress enacted the special tax rules, REIT's have seen periods of prosperity and recession.

In the mid-1960s, the successful financing ventures of several mortgage REIT's attracted the interest of real-estate financiers, investment analysts, and brokers. Both the blessing from Wall Street and the rapid expansion of the construction market (and demand for financing) in the sixties and early seventies nurtured a boom in the REIT industry. Many new mortgage REIT's developed; many existing equity REIT's redirected their investment portfolios; and by 1973, 84% of REIT industry assets were concentrated in mortgages.

Considerable overbuilding ensued. Subsequently, the 1973 oil embargo and efforts by the federal government and the Federal Reserve Board to combat rising inflation (through tight monetary control) produced a nationwide recession in 1974. The entire real-estate industry, including REIT's, was seriously affected, with many companies cutting back operations or reorganizing.

Construction efforts were renewed in the late seventies and early eighties. Demands for financing simul-

taneously increased, if slowly, dampened by the effects of continuing high interest rates. REIT's began to place renewed emphasis on ownership rather than financing of properties.

The moderation of the early 1980s (in both construction and financing) has permitted the demand for commercial real-estate space to grow faster than supply, and occupancy rates for many income-producing properties have steadily increased. The growing shortage of space has increased rents and therefore produced higher asset valuations and better earnings for property-owning REIT's. Sixty percent of all REIT industry assets are now concentrated in property ownership.

In 1983 there were 118 REIT's in existence, with $7.5 billion of investments distributed across the United States, its territories, Canada, and Mexico. Most of these investments are located in the sun-belt states of California, Georgia, Florida, and Texas. Between 1979 and 1983 28 REITs had been formed.

Regular REIT dividend payouts totaled $274 million in 1982, representing a 13% increase over dividend payouts in 1977. The increase in dividends is due in large part to the renewal of older, cheaper leases, bringing increased rents and increased income. Many REIT's forecast continued increases in dividends, because increasingly sophisticated lending and leasing arrangements assure REIT's of variable or contingent interest or rental income that will keep pace with or exceed rates of inflation.

Real-estate investments—in particular, investments in real-estate investment trusts—have remained healthy and profitable, in spite of recent difficult market conditions. An investor in a REIT may be justifiably optimistic in looking forward to the benefits of current income, long-term appreciation (of the investment), and favorable tax treatment.

Thomas E. Robinson and Victoria J. Baker

Recording Fee

The service charge required when documents affecting the title to real property (deeds, mortgages, contracts for sale, liens, options, assignments, etc.) are placed on a public record, usually maintained by the county. The cost usually involves a basic fee for one or two pages and a lesser fee for each page thereafter. Each county office sets its own recording fees and procedures.

Harley W. Snyder

Refinancing

Refinancing means renegotiating the terms of a loan, frequently to reduce the amount of the installment payments and thus extend the length of the loan. Refinancing may also occur when a borrower has a "balloon" payment due, requiring a large lump-sum payment. Borrowers also sometimes refinance a loan in order to borrow more money. In addition, when interest rates decline, a borrower who had procured a mortgage at a higher interest rate may find it advantageous to renegotiate the loan at a lower rate.

Frances B. Smith

Regional Check-Processing Centers (RCPC's)

Regional check-processing centers are operated by Federal Reserve banks to expedite check collection. The centers clear checks and sort them according to the depository institution upon which the checks are drawn. This complements regional clearing arrangements established by depository institutions in the same locality to exchange checks and settle net balances.

In 1971 the Federal Reserve's board of governors recommended establishing RCPC's to help improve the nation's payments mechanism. The following year, the first center—the Baltimore-Washington RCPC of the Richmond Fed—became fully operational after a one-year pilot test.

RCPC's serve depository institutions within areas not necessarily confined to Federal Reserve district or state lines. Since the function of the centers is to accelerate nationwide check collection, RCPC boundaries are determined by check flows. For example, Fairfield County, Connecticut, is part of the New York Reserve district. However, many checks deposited in Fairfield County institutions are drawn on banks in the Boston Reserve district. Thus, Fairfield County is served by the Boston Fed's Southwestern New England RCPC in Windsor Locks, Connecticut.

RCPC's routinely receive checks drawn on participating institutions from four sources: other participating member banks; other RCPC's; Federal Reserve Banks and their branches; and "direct-sending" member banks. A direct-sending member bank is one authorized by its Reserve bank to send checks drawn on banks in other Reserve districts directly to the appropriate Reserve bank, branch, or RCPC. The direct-sending bank gets credit for those checks in its reserve account at its own Reserve bank.

As a result of the International Banking Act of 1978 and the Depository Institutions Deregulation and Monetary Control Act of 1980, all depository institutions in the U.S., except for certain agencies, have been granted limited deposit access to local facilities. Depository institutions include member and non-member commercial banks, savings banks, savings and loan associations, and credit unions.

Prior to the two acts, RCPC's also accepted checks deposited by local participating banks that weren't members of the Federal Reserve, providing the checks were drawn on other banks in the same RCPC area.

The primary objective of RCPC's is to collect checks overnight. To accomplish this RCPC's sort, clear, and deliver checks rapidly by eliminating various handling stages.

For example, a Newark corporation deposits a check drawn on a bank in Asbury Park, New Jersey, to its account at a Newark bank on a Wednesday. Because there is an RCPC serving the Asbury Park area, the Newark bank deposits the check at the RCPC Wednesday evening. The check is processed at the center on high-speed equipment during early morning and is presented for payment to the Asbury Park bank early Thursday. Payment is made by charging the Asbury Park bank's reserve account at the New York Fed. Simultaneously, the RCPC credits the account of the Newark bank. The Asbury Park bank charges the account of its customer—the check-writer—and the Newark bank credits the deposit to the account of the Newark corporation. Without the RCPC, the Newark corporation's check would have had to be processed at the New York Fed in Manhattan and at least one additional day would have been required.

Personal and corporate checks comprise the bulk of items deposited at RCPC's. These checks are generally delivered to the RCPC by private carriers hired by the participating banks. Other cash items deposited at RCPC's include checks drawn on the Treasury, postal money orders, and redeemed food coupons. These items are deposited by participating depository institutions. However, RCPC's don't handle cash or securities.

Finally, in addition to providing speedy clearance, the processing of checks at an RCPC results in quicker identification of fraudulent and other invalid items. Currently, the Federal Reserve system operates 46 RCPC's nationwide, of which 34 are located at a Reserve bank or branch. The other 12 are maintained off-premises.

In the Second Federal Reserve District (New York State, 12 northern counties in New Jersey, and Fairfield County, Connecticut) there are five RCPC's. One is the Western New York RCPC located at the Buffalo branch; another is the Northeastern New York RCPC at Utica; two are at Jericho, Long Island—the Long Island RCPC and the Downstate New York RCPC; the fifth is the North Jersey RCPC at Cranford.

As a result of the Monetary Control Act, Federal Reserve Banks were authorized to charge institutions, at explicit prices, for central bank services, including check-related operations.

Arthur Samansky

Regular-Way Delivery

See COMMON STOCK.

Regulation Q

See DEPOSITORY INSTITUTIONS DEREGULATION COMMITTEE (DIDC).

Rent Control

The concept of regulating rents has its roots in Europe and spread to the United States during World War I. The general population considered it only a wartime measure to shield the families of departed servicemen and industrial workers from the economic hardships of city life. Rent controls were reinstituted during World War II and supervised by the federal government. After the war, most measures were terminated. However, some states enacted their own rent-control enabling legislation. Until the early 1970s, the only state that had maintained rent control was New York. Today, some form of rent control is in effect in five states and the District of Columbia.

Rent-control programs are usually enacted by local jurisdictions to assist low-income households and the elderly in coping with shrinking real incomes. With inflation and other economic pressures, renters see rent control as one way to put a limit on their housing expenses. In theory, it is very beneficial.

However, research has shown that rent-controlling regulations can have long-term detrimental effects on a community and its residents. When rent-control programs have been initiated, communities generally have suffered from economic stagnation and declines in apartment and home development in the private sector. Because landlords are prevented from charging rents that reflect rising costs, tenants often suffer because many owners are forced to reduce expenditures for repairs and maintenance. Buildings may become run-down and decline in value, leading to neighborhood deterioration.

In addition, rent controls can create rental-housing shortages. Because of the increased risk, lenders are reluctant to loan money to build properties in areas where rent controls exist. Apartment-building investors may take their money elsewhere because they know rent control will not allow them to charge the rent they need to bring them a reasonable return on their investment. Often, new developers are discouraged from planning new apartment complexes for fear their newly constructed buildings will be included in rent-control legislation.

To add to the controversy surrounding rent control, it has been proved in a recent study that single-family-home owners can also feel the long-term effects of rent control in the form of higher property taxes. The study showed that apartment buildings deteriorate in areas where rent-controlling legislation exists, because landlords cannot raise rents to keep up with maintenance and repair costs. The buildings are then devalued by tax assessors, which creates a tax deficit in the community. The deficit must be made up through higher property taxes on single-family homes; otherwise the community has no choice but to cut municipal budgets for public services. The eventual effect is a gradual shift in the tax base to the single-family-home owner.

Harley W. Snyder

Reporting Dealers

In conducting open-market operations, the Federal Reserve Bank of New York buys and sells United States government and federal-agency securities through a number of securities dealers. Most of these dealers aren't associated with banks. These dealer firms are among those that voluntarily report their trading volume and portfolio positions to the Reserve bank's market-statistics area. They are designated by the Reserve bank as "reporting dealers."

Dealers, upon becoming significant market participants, may contact the New York Fed and begin reporting activity and positions informally. After evaluating these reports over a period to determine a dealer's capabilities and volume of business, the New York Fed's securities department may add the dealer to the reporting list. The manager of the System's open-market trading account makes the final decision.

A third criterion for establishing a trading relationship is that the dealer must be generally regarded as making sizable markets in government securities. The manager may then, or later, enter into a trading relationship if the dealer is adequately capitalized and achieves somewhat higher volume standards than those required for addition to the reporting list.

While all dealers trading with the Fed's desk for System open-market purposes are reporting dealers, not all reporting dealers necessarily trade with the Fed.

Reporting dealers are among those securities dealers called "primary dealers" by market participants. Primary dealers are institutions that buy new government securities directly from the Treasury and are ready to buy or sell outstanding U.S. government and agency securities. Securities dealers on the Federal Reserve's reporting list sometimes are referred to in the marketplace as "recognized dealers." This term isn't used by the Federal Reserve.

Open-market operations—the buying and selling of U.S. government securities to affect bank reserves—is the major tool used by the FEDERAL RESERVE SYSTEM to regulate the availability of money and credit. The New York Fed conducts open-market operations for the entire System at the direction of the Open Market Committee.

Arthur Samansky

Repurchase Agreements (RP's)

A significant financial development in recent years has been the rapid growth in repurchase agreements. RP's, or "repos," as they are frequently called, have existed for decades, but have grown substantially only in the late 1970s and early 1980s. Their importance now rivals that of other, better-known money-market instruments, such as commercial paper and negotiable certificates of deposit.

Description of the RP Market. A repurchase agreement, as the term is used in the financial markets, is an acquisition of funds through the sale of securities, with a simultaneous agreement by the seller to repurchase them at a later date. Basically, they are a secured means of borrowing and lending short-term funds. RP's are most frequently made for one business day (overnight), although longer maturities are not uncommon. A special type of RP is the continuing contract, which consists of a series of overnight loans that are automatically renewed each day unless terminated by either party to the transaction. The greatest share of all RP transactions consists of repurchase agreements involving U.S. government or federal-agency securities.

An illustration of a "typical" RP transaction is helpful in understanding this financial instrument. Suppose that the treasurer of a large corporation calculates his firm's cash position for the day and determines that the firm has funds that are not required immediately but will likely be needed to meet expected expenditures in a day or two. The treasurer, wishing to earn interest on these excess funds for a day, arranges to purchase a government security from a commercial bank with an accompanying agreement that the bank will repurchase the security on the following day. This type of transaction is illustrated in the accounting entries shown in Table 1.

At times the corporate treasurer may decide that excess funds will be available for a longer period. For example, if the corporation has just sold long-term bonds but will not make the capital expenditures for, say, 30 days, an RP can be arranged for this specific period. This would be beneficial because the transaction costs of a term RP contract are less than those for a series of daily contracts.

The advantages of RP transactions are numerous. Through the RP mechanism, corporations and other holders of large cash balances can earn a secured market rate of return on these balances until they actually are used for payments. At the same time, banks find RP's a useful source of short-term funds. Interest-rate ceilings do not apply to typical RP transactions. (Effective August 1, 1979, Regulation Q interest-rate ceilings were imposed on repurchase agreements of less than $100,000 with maturities of 90 days or more.) Moreover, there is no basic reserve requirement against funds obtained through RP's so long as the securities involved are obligations of the U.S. government or federal agencies. Effective in the reserve statement week beginning October 11, 1979, however, an 8% marginal reserve requirement was placed on

Table 1
Sample RP Transaction

	Bank	Corporate Customer
Before RP	$1 million deposit	$1 million deposit
Creation of RP	− $1 million deposit + $1 million RP borrowing	− $1 million deposit + $1 million collateralized loan (RP)
Completion of RP Agreement	+ $1 million deposit − $1 million RP borrowing	+ $1 million deposit − $1 million loan (RP)

managed liabilities of member banks, Edge corporations, and the U.S. branches and agencies of foreign banks. These liabilities include repurchase agreements against U.S. government and federal-agency securities as well as negotiable CD's with maturities of less than a year, Eurodollar borrowings, and federal-funds borrowings from nonmember institutions. The base for the marginal reserve requirement was initially set at $100 million or the average amount of managed liabilities held as of the two statement weeks ending September 26, 1979, whichever was larger. This amendment to Regulation D represented the adoption in modified form of a Federal Reserve proposal made in April 1979 to apply reserve requirements to RP liabilities. With the reserve statement week beginning April 3, 1980, Regulation D was again amended to raise the marginal reserve requirement to 10% and to lower the managed liabilities base. The marginal requirement was reduced to 5% in June 1980 and finally reduced to zero for the reserve week beginning July 24, 1980.

In an RP contract, the borrower pays interest at a rate negotiated with the lender. This interest rate is not determined by yields on or changing market prices of the government securities bought and sold. The role of government securities is only to provide collateral for the lender. The interest rate on RP's usually approximates the federal-funds rate, but frequently is slightly lower because RP's are collateralized borrowings whereas federal funds are not.

Most RP transactions are in amounts of $1 million or more, but a few are smaller than $100,000. Despite the large sums involved, there is little financial risk in RP transactions. This is because (1) securities issued or guaranteed by the federal government are used for collateral; (2) most transactions occur between institutions with high credit standings; and (3) repurchase is usually scheduled for only a short period after sale.

There is no central physical marketplace in which RP's are arranged. Transactions are negotiated by telephone, either directly between parties supplying and acquiring funds or through a small group of market specialists (U.S. government securities dealers). Most large banks and business firms employ traders who maintain telephone contact with potential suppliers (or borrowers) of funds, making offers to borrow (or lend) at specific interest rates.

RP transactions must be settled in immediately available funds such as deposits in Federal Reserve banks or collected liabilities of commercial banks that may be withdrawn in cash the same business day as the transaction occurs. A customer can make funds immediately available to a bank other than the bank where funds are deposited by having them transferred through the Federal Reserve wire transfer network. Securities that are purchased and sold under RP are transferred through the CPD (Commissioner of Public Debt) wire transfer system operated by the Federal Reserve.

The term *reverse repurchase agreement,* frequently used by participants in the RP market, signifies the same transaction viewed from the perspective of the lender. In an RP, the borrower sells a security in order to receive funds and repurchases it at maturity. In a reverse RP, the lender buys a security and resells it at maturity. Large commercial banks and government-securities dealers frequently arrange reverse RP's in order to obtain government securities with which to engage in an RP.

Participants in the RP Market. The major participants in RP market include commercial banks, government-securities dealers, nonbank financial institutions, business corporations, and state and local governments. In addition to its regulatory role, the Federal Reserve is also a direct participant in the RP market.

Large banks usually are borrowers of funds in the RP market. These institutions typically seek funds and have portfolios of government-issued and guaranteed securities with which to arrange RP's.

Government-securities dealers also are important participants in the RP market. They are generally net borrowers, using RP's to finance their sizable portfolios of government securities. Most dealer RP borrowing is very short-term—i.e., overnight or continuing contract. In addition to using RP's to finance their positions, dealers also act as financial intermediaries or brokers between demanders and suppliers of funds. The larger and better-known dealers are able to borrow in the repo market at more favorable rates than some smaller dealers and corporations. A profit can thus be made through arbitrage, by matching an RP transaction with a reverse RP transaction of equal maturity but higher rate. Also, dealers sometimes use reverse RP's to acquire securities in order to make a short sale; the net cost of obtaining the securities through reverse RP's is frequently less than the cost of borrowed securities.

Many types of investors supply immediately available funds in the RP market, including nonfinancial corporations and state and local governments. Business firms and municipalities with large cash balances are able to earn sizable returns on these funds by arranging RP's. Such a transaction converts the corporation's or municipality's demand-deposit balance into an interest-earning asset. Yet, since the funds are committed for only a brief period, they are still readily available for transaction purposes. For this reason, RP's are a more attractive investment than are newly issued negotiable CD's, which must have a minimum maturity of at least 14 days.

Another advantage of RP's to certain nonbank investors is the flexibility in recording these transactions on their books. Some investors choose to record the ownership of U.S. government securities rather than the ownership of RP's. This reporting feature is particularly appealing to those institutions, such as state and local governments, that are required by law to invest in Treasury securities.

Business firms and others hold cash primarily to bridge the periods when expenditures exceed receipts. Traditionally, most of these cash balances have been held in the form of demand deposits in commercial banks, and as a result have not earned explicit interest since 1933. This was not of great significance during the low-interest-rate periods prior to the 1960s. The higher interest rates in the Sixties and Seventies, however, created the incentive for businesses to develop better cash-management techniques just as banks were developing liability-management techniques. A variety of procedures were adopted to achieve a reduction in cash balances, including speeding up receipts, slowing down disbursements, and converting cash into interest-bearing liquid assets. RP's have become a particularly useful tool of cash management. They generate sizable income during periods of relatively high short-term interest rates. Moreover, they are relatively secure and liquid. In short, some corporations and municipalities treat RP's as income-earning demand deposits.

Federal Reserve system regulations play an important role in the RP market by limiting the types of transactions member banks may undertake. Federal Reserve actions may also influence federal-funds rates, which in turn dominate the interest rates available on RP's from day to day. The Fed is also a large direct participant in the RP market. Although the Federal Reserve supplies reserves to commercial banks primarily through outright purchases of government securities, it also uses RP's and reverse RP's to temporarily absorb or supply reserves.

Norman N. Bowsher

Repurchase and Matched Sale-Purchase Transactions

Among the tools used by the FEDERAL RESERVE SYSTEM to achieve its monetary objectives is the temporary purchase and sale of United States government securities, federal-agency obligations, and BANKER'S ACCEPTANCES in the open market.

In conducting these operations, the System uses REPURCHASE AGREEMENTS (RP's) and "matched sale-purchase" transactions, which have a short-term self-reversing effect on bank reserves. The trading desk of the System uses these techniques in open-market operations as a supplement to outright purchases or sales.

RP's and matched sale-purchase transactions are particularly useful in offsetting temporary swings in the level of bank reserves caused by such volatile factors as FLOAT, currency held by the public, and Treasury deposits at Federal Reserve banks.

In an RP agreement, the New York Reserve Bank, which conducts open-market operations for the System, buys a government security from a dealer who agrees to repurchase the obligation within a specified period up to 15 calendar days (usually 1 to 7 days). When repurchasing the obligation, the dealer pays the original price, plus an agreed-upon return to the Reserve bank.

The New York trading desk awards the agreements on a competitive basis. Under competitive bidding, each dealer is requested to present the rates the dealer is willing to pay for the agreements. The desk selects the best bids presented, ending when the total accepted is approximately equal to the volume of reserves to be added to the banking system. The bids submitted often reflect dealer transactions with their customers.

The New York Fed makes payment for the securities by directly crediting the reserve account of a member bank in which the dealer firm has its account. As a result, new bank reserves are created by the Federal Reserve.

When the transaction is reversed as agreed and the dealer repurchases the securities, funds are withdrawn from bank accounts to pay the Federal Reserve, thus reducing reserves in the banking system.

Repurchase agreements are made at the initiative of the trading desk. Under the usual type of arrangement, the dealer may prepay, thus completing the transactions prior to the original maturity; also, the contract permits the Fed to require early repayment, although this option has not been exercised in recent years. At times, the desk also arranges fixed-term or nonterminable RP's.

The proceeds of the RP are slightly less than the full value of the securities purchased. This difference in value is referred to as "margin" and serves as protection for the initial purchaser should securities prices decline.

In August 1982, as part of the effort to strengthen market practices, the desk announced it would take into account accrued coupon interest when valuing securities used in repurchase agreements, and urged other market participants to do the same. Under the new system, the New York Fed still pays a dealer slightly less than the market value of the security the dealer offers in a repurchase agreement, but adds whatever interest has accrued on the security to the proceeds it pays the dealer. If, for example, the New York Fed buys a $10,000 note that pays an annual interest rate of 9%—or $450 semiannually—the Reserve bank includes whatever portion of the $450 has accrued up to the Fed's transaction date with the dealer.

Matched sale-purchase transactions have the opposite effect on bank reserves: They withdraw reserves initially and later return them to the banking system. These transactions are sometimes referred to by market participants as "reverse repurchase agreements" or "reverse repos." In a matched transaction, the desk executes two transactions simultaneously, for different delivery dates. These contracts can't be terminated early.

When a matched sale-purchase transaction is executed, the trading desk sells Treasury bills from the System portfolio to dealers, simultaneously purchasing the same obligations for return within a short period—generally 1 to 7 days later. The desk also arranges the transactions competitively, starting with the best terms proposed.

In June 1982, as part of a general effort to strengthen practices in the government-securities market, the desk announced it was returning to a pricing method used from 1966—when matched sale-purchase agreements began—to 1975. Under the reinstituted method, the desk agrees to sell bills at a specified rate, which is the current market rate for the maturity. The dealer provides the rate at which the dealer will resell the securities to the Federal Reserve, which includes the dealer's profit.

The change in pricing occurred because dealers tended to set rates for the purchase at about their financing rate—the RP or federal-funds rate—leading to the central bank selling the bills at a rate higher than the market-bill rate.

Dealers purchase the obligations for cash on the day of the agreement, which immediately withdraws the reserves from the banking system. The Federal Reserve doesn't pay for its repurchase of the issue until the agreed-upon delivery date. When payment is made, reserves are returned to the banking system.

Arthur Samansky

Revenue Bond

See MUNICIPAL AND STATE SECURITIES.

Reverse-Annuity Mortgages (RAM's)

See HOME FINANCING, MORTGAGES.

Revolving Account

A hybrid form of open-end CREDIT that combines all of the advantages for consumers offered by both traditional 30-day, open accounts and traditional installment credit, but affords additional benefits for customers. Usually, an open-end line of credit is extended to consumers, which can be used optionally from time to time for purchases up to a customer's credit limit. Payment in full is allowed at any time for the outstanding balance or through fixed or fluctuating monthly repayment at or above the minimum monthly payment required by the creditor. Finance charges, when imposed by the creditor, are calculated by monthly rates. Finance charges not previously imposed at the time of billing can be avoided by payment in full of the outstanding balance within a time period in the billing cycle established by the creditor.

James A. Ambrose

Round Lot (Stocks)

See COMMON STOCK.

Rule of 78s

See INSTALLMENT LOAN, EARLY REPAYMENT OF AN.

·S·

Safe-Deposit Box

A container, usually metal, that a bank customer can rent to store valuables of all types. The safe-deposit box is in the bank's vault and generally has two keys, both necessary to open it. One key is held by the customer and the other by the bank.

Phil Battey

Sallie Mae

See STUDENT LOAN MARKETING ASSOCIATION.

Savings Accounts

See PASSBOOK SAVINGS ACCOUNTS.

Savings and Loan Associations

Savings and loan associations are specialized financial institutions that serve as a link between people who have funds to save or invest and those who want to borrow. Because of the business's well-known expertise, most savings and loan association customers borrow for real-estate purchases, most often single-family homes.

As of December 31, 1983, there were over 3,500 savings and loan associations in the United States. Some are called "homestead associations" (in Louisiana) or "cooperative banks" (in New England). They can be large institutions with assets of several billion dollars and many branches, or small associations with one office and assets of only a few million dollars. All have the same purpose: to promote thrift and home-ownership. To accomplish this, savings associations attract deposits from the public by offering a wide range of savings accounts and invest the bulk of these savings in mortgage loans, primarily residential mortgage loans.

History. Savings and loan associations were originally founded as "building societies" that pooled the savings of their members to provide them with funds to buy or build their own homes. These early associations were organized on a self-terminating basis, disbanding after all members had taken out and repaid home loans.

Banks during this time loaned funds mainly to commercial customers in business and industry and to well-to-do individuals; they had little interest in serving the needs of the small saver or in making small loans to individual tradespeople or skilled laborers.

To fill the need for a financial organization designed to make long-term mortgage loans at reasonable rates, the first savings and loan association, called the Oxford Provident Building Association, was founded in Philadelphia in 1831. Its 37 members pooled their savings to help one another acquire their own homes. Each member paid an initial fee and made a small deposit each month. When enough funds had been accumulated, an auction was held, with the loan going to the bidder willing to pay the highest premium for it. The borrower made small monthly interest payments in addition to his regular deposit. The association's operating costs were paid by the bid and the interest charge.

The first loan was awarded to Comley Rich, a lamplighter and comb maker who made the high bid of $10. His $375 loan was approved in May 1831.

Within 20 years, permanent associations were formed and borrowing was no longer restricted to a closed group of initial depositors. The associations operated independently, making new loans as funds became available. The incentive to save was no longer a loan for a home; it was the interest, the money paid to the saver for the use of his funds. In order to pay those dividends, associations began charging a competitive rate of interest on the loans they made.

The most spectacular growth in the savings and loan business came after World War II, coinciding with the greatest home-building and -buying demand in the nation's history. By 1982, savings and loan associations accounted for over 50% of all privately held mortgage debt.

In recent years, many savings associations have

broadened their operations by opening branch offices and by expanding their activity in the debit- and/or credit-card markets. In addition to providing extended hours and service locations, the increased use of plastic cards has added customer convenience and account accessibility—and has made possible the electronic transfer of funds.

Mergers. Although many new state and federal savings and loan charters are issued each year, the total number of savings associations has declined by about 20% over the past ten years. This trend toward consolidation has increased the size of merged associations and produced more economically efficient operating units—a necessity for savings institutions, which must compete in a newly deregulated environment in the 1980s.

Federal and State Laws and Regulations. Savings associations operate within a comprehensive framework of state and federal laws and regulations. These laws set general standards for the chartering of new associations and govern operating practices. They control the kinds of loans and other investments an association can make, and set broad parameters on the savings and investment services an institution can offer its depositors.

Both the federal government and state governments have supervisory agencies that establish detailed regulations governing operating procedures of savings and loan associations. These agencies require at least one annual report of financial conditions and provide examiners to verify compliance with the laws and regulations. States have specific savings association laws to govern state-chartered associations within the state, where supervision is vested in a board, a commission, or a designated state officer.

Federal Home Loan Bank System. Federal associations are governed by federal law and are chartered and supervised by the FEDERAL HOME LOAN BANK BOARD (FHLBB). The Federal Home Loan Bank system was established in 1932 by Congress to provide a central credit system for the nation's home-financing institutions. It is composed of three elements: the Federal Home Loan Bank Board (the governing agency), 12 regional Federal Home Loan banks, and member institutions.

All federally insured savings and loan associations are required by law to belong to the FHLB system. State-chartered savings associations, mutual savings banks, and life-insurance companies may become members if they qualify.

Insurance of Accounts. The Federal Home Loan Bank Board governs the FEDERAL SAVINGS AND LOAN INSURANCE CORPORATION (FSLIC), a government agency formed in 1934 to insure the safety of the funds of savers at savings and loan associations. The FSLIC assures that all members operate prudently and remain financially stable. All accounts in member associations are insured up to $100,000 by the FSLIC.

Federally chartered associations are required to have their accounts insured by the FSLIC, and state-chartered associations are allowed to become members if they qualify. Insurance of accounts is optional for many state-chartered institutions, although the vast majority of them are insured by the FSLIC.

There were 3,057 FSLIC-insured savings and loan associations as of November 1983. FSLIC members hold more than 98% of the total assets of the business.

Five states—Massachusetts, Ohio, Maryland, North Carolina, and Pennsylvania—have established insuring organizations by special statute. These state insuring agencies have duties and powers set forth by state law and answer to public officials and supervisory authorities. State-chartered institutions in those five states may choose to have deposits insured by the state agency rather than the FSLIC.

Framework, Structure, Annual Meeting. The most common type of ownership of savings and loan associations is the mutual association, where members—the savers and the borrowers—are the owners of the institution. They participate in the annual meeting where the directors are elected.

Publicly owned associations issue common stock, usually at the time of organization. Revisions of the regulations permitting conversions from mutual to stock associations in 1982 and 1983 gave greater flexibility and a source of new capital to converting institutions and resulted in a continuing trend toward stock ownership of savings institutions. At year-end 1982, 22% of all savings associated were stock owned.

Stock ownership is transferable, as in other publicly held companies. The stockholders are the owners of the association and elect the directors at the annual meeting. Although savers in a publicly held association have neither ownership nor voting rights, they do have a preferred position in case of liquidation.

Regardless of its form of ownership, each association is governed by a board of directors, typically made up of leading local business people and other citizens, who are elected at the annual meeting. Annual meetings are not usually widely attended and are commonly characterized by the use of proxy ballots. In addition to the election of directors, other business can also be addressed. The directors choose the association's officers and set broad policies for management. Monthly meetings of the board are usually held, with more-frequent meetings of board committees.

The chief executive officer, or managing officer, is appointed by the board of directors and is responsible for implementing the policies set by the board. Subordinate officers head other operating departments and report to the managing officer.

All associations, regardless of size, perform savings, lending, and accounting functions. Other departments generally include advertising, appraisal, branch operations, building management, collections, data processing, legal, marketing, and personnel.

As a corporation, an association must also have a secretary, who maintains the corporate records; and a treasurer, who maintains the financial records and receives and disburses money.

Savings and loan associations are fiduciary associations and have a legal responsibility to protect the deposits of their savers.

Assets and Taxation. Assets are the usual measure of the size of a savings institution and are comprised of what the savings and loan association owns, plus what is owed to it. As of December 31, 1983, the total assets of the savings and loan business were more than $760 billion.

Savings associations first became subject to federal corporate income tax in 1951 and are now among the most heavily taxed financial corporations in the United States. Provisions of the tax law are very complex, but, in general, savings associations are taxed like other corporations. The major difference is the provision that income which is added to reserves, up to specified limits, is tax-deductible. (Reserves provide financial institutions with an additional "cushion" to help absorb occasional operating losses.)

Savings Accounts. The major source of funds for loans at savings and loan associations are the savings deposits of individuals and families, which represent 80% of total liabilities for the savings and loan business as a whole. Money deposited in a regular or certificate account is a "loan" to the association. The saver becomes a creditor of the association; the institution is the debtor and owes the saver his or her money. Money can be withdrawn from the savings account in the manner provided for in the savings contract. Interest is the institution's cost of borrowing; it is paid to the saver for the use of his money.

Savings associations offer a wide variety of accounts that differ in the form of ownership, the maximum interest rate that may be paid, the term over which an account must be held, and the minimum balance required. Within the framework of regulations that govern basic categories and variations, each association can select the accounts and special features that best suit its situation.

Several types of ownership of a savings account are possible:

• An *individual savings account* is owned and controlled by one individual.
• A *joint-tenancy savings account* is owned by two or more persons who have equal rights to and control of the account with the right of survivorship. If one owner dies, the survivor(s) maintains all rights to the account.
• Funds deposited in a *trust account* are administered by a trustee and are deposited for the benefit of another person, the beneficiary.

Until passage of the Interest Rate Adjustment Act in 1966, the interest rate paid on savings accounts by associations had never been controlled by law or regulation. The 1966 legislation gave the Federal Home Loan Bank Board explicit powers to set the maximum rate that may be paid on different types of savings accounts.

Since banks then were able to offer a wider range of financial services, a rate differential was established. The differential was the additional interest amount that savings and loan associations could pay to help assure a steady supply of funds for home mortgage lending.

The Garn–St Germain Depository Institutions Act of 1982 mandated the elimination of all thrift institutions' savings rate differentials by January 1984. The Depository Institutions Deregulation and Monetary Control Act of 1980 called for the removal of all savings-rate ceilings by 1986. As a result of this legislation, interest rates on most savings accounts are deregulated.

Passbook Accounts. Passbook accounts were the major savings instrument issued by savings associations until the mid-1960s. They are losing popularity to higher-rate accounts and the major portion of the deposits of savings associations is now in market-sensitive accounts.

A regular *passbook account* is an "in-and-out" account that allows a saver to add to or withdraw from the account any amount at any time without a penalty. No minimum balance is required by regulation.

Statement accounts provide a periodic statement giving a concise picture of all account transactions during the period. It may include information on deposits, withdrawals, interest credits, beginning and ending balance, and preauthorized payments to the account and out of the account.

A *split-rate passbook* pays increasing rates of interest for increasing account balances.

A *club account* is a systematic savings plan characterized by small, fixed, weekly or biweekly deposits and a relatively short term. It is opened for a particu-

Table 1
Major Federal Laws Affecting the Savings and Loan Business

Date	Law	Key Provisions
1932	Federal Home Loan Bank Act	Established the Federal Home Loan Banks under the supervision of the Federal Home Loan Bank Board to provide a central credit facility for home financing institutions.
1933	Home Owners' Loan Act	Authorized the creation under the FHLBB of a system of federally chartered and supervised savings and loan associations.
1934	National Housing Act	Created the Federal Housing Administration to insure mortgage, and other loans made by private lenders; established the Federal Savings and Loan Insurance Corporation to insure savings accounts at member associations.
1944	Servicemen's Readjustment Act (The G.I. Bill of Rights)	Established a program of loan guarantees under Veterans Administration auspices to encourage private lending on generous terms to veterans of the armed forces.
1949	Housing Act	Established national housing goals of "a decent home and suitable living environment for every American family"; provided grants to municipalities for public housing and slum clearance; set up a program of financial assistance for rural areas under the Farmers Home Administration
1961	Housing Act	Authorized new programs for federal involvement in housing, including subsidized rental housing for low- and moderate-income families; expanded funding for FNMA special assistance functions.
1968	Housing and Urban Development Act	Gave federal associations the authority to invest in mobile home and home equipment loans; expanded their authority to issue a wide variety of savings plans, notes, bonds and debentures.
1970	Emergency Home Finance Act	Created the Federal Home Loan Mortgage Corporation, under the FHLBB, to provide a secondary market for conventional, FHA and VA mortgages; extended from 20 to 30 years the period allowed for associations to accumulate FSLIC-required reserves.
1974	Housing and Community Development Act	Liberalized the types and amounts of loans a federal association may make.
1974	Depository Institutions Amendments	Increased FSLIC insurance of association savings accounts to $40,000 for private funds, $100,000 for public funds.
1974	Equal Credit Opportunity Act	Prohibited discrimination in credit transactions on the basis of sex or marital status.
1974	Real Estate Settlement Procedures Act	Provided comprehensive guidelines for loan closing costs and settlement practices.
1975	Regulation Q and Home Mortgage Disclosure Act	Prohibited the elimination or reduction of the interest rate differential on existing types of savings accounts without prior congressional approval; required most financial institutions to disclose the number and dollar amount of mortgage loans made, by geographical area.
1976	Equal Credit Opportunity Act Amendments	Broadened the scope of ECOA to forbid discrimination in credit transactions on seven additional bases.
1976	Tax Reform Act	Reduced certain allowable federal income tax deductions for associations and increased the minimum tax rate; liberalized IRA and Keogh account provisions.
1977	Housing and Community Development Act	Raised ceiling on single-family loan amounts for association lending; liberalized the treatment of single-family and multifamily loans that exceed applicable ceilings; raised ceilings on conventional and FHA home improvement loans; required financial institution regulatory agencies to take into account an institution's record of serving the credit needs of its community when evaluating applications for new facilities, mergers and other matters.

Table 1   *(cont)*
Major Federal Laws Affecting the Savings and Loan Business

Date	Law	Key Provisions
1978	Revenue Act	Reduced certain corporate tax rates; permitted one-time exclusion of up to $100,000 capital gain on sale of home; liberalized IRA provisions.
1978	Financial Institutions Regulatory and Interest Rate Control Act	Increased FSLIC insurance limits for IRA and Keogh accounts from $40,000 to $100,000; amended Consumer Credit Protection Act establishing rights and responsibilities for electronic funds transfers.
1979	Housing and Community Development Act Amendments	Increased one-family home loan limits for federal associations; raised FHA loan limits and expanded the FHA GPM program; raised FNMA and FHLMC loan ceilings; exempted FHA loans from state usury ceilings.
1980	Depository Institutions Deregulation and Monetary Control Act	For all depository institutions, extended savings interest rate control and the thrift institution differential for six years; shifted rate-setting authority from individual agencies to a Deregulation Committee; increased FSLIC and FDIC insurance for individually owned savings accounts from $40,000 to $100,000; extended the federal override of state usury ceilings on certain mortgage and other loans; authorized nationwide NOW accounts effective at year-end 1980. For federal associations, authorized investment of up to 20% of assets in consumer loans, corporate debt securities and commercial paper; eased or removed lending restrictions; expanded authority to invest in service corporations; granted authority to invest in mutual funds, to issue credit cards and to engage in trust operations; granted authority to issue mutual capital certificates which can be counted toward federal insurance reserve requirements.
1980	Omnibus Reconciliation Act	Limited the issuance by states and municipalities of tax-exempt mortgage revenue bonds for housing purposes.
1981	Economic Recovery Tax Act	Created the All Savers certificate, a special tax-exempt savings account; substantially increased the annual contribution limits on IRAs, Keoghs and simplified employee pension plans; created a permanent income tax exclusion for interest income starting in 1985.
1982	Tax Equity and Fiscal Responsibility Act	Provided for 10% federal income tax withholding by payers of interest and dividends, beginning 7/1/83; reduced corporate pension plan contribution and benefit plan limits; scaled back certain corporate tax preference items, including certain additions to financial institution bad debt reserves.
1982	Garn-St Germain Depository Institutions Act	For all lenders, exempted insured or guaranteed loans from truth-in-lending requirements. For all depository institutions, authorized a new savings account directly competitive with money market funds; authorized public unit NOW accounts; preempted or severely limited state due-on-sale loan restrictions; granted broader powers to the federal deposit insurance corporations; mandated the phaseout of the savings interest rate differential by 1/1/84. For insured depository institutions with deficient net worth, provided for FSLIC and FDIC assistance to bring net worth to required levels, in the form of insurance corporation notes exchanged for net worth certificates issued by the institution. For federal thrifts, eased charter and conversion limits, prohibited one product or service from being tied to any requirement to buy or not buy another product or service from the institution, its subsidiaries or its competitors. For federal associations, created or expanded authority to invest in consumer, commercial and agricultural loans and other investments; authorized the acceptance of demand deposits from business and agricultural loan customers; removed mortgage loan-to-value ratio limits; permitted investment in tangible personal property for lease or sale up to 10% of assets.

Source: 1983 Savings and Loan *Sourcebook,* United States League of Savings Institutions.

lar purpose and has a definite goal for savings. Examples are Christmas Club, Hanukkah Club, and Vacation Club accounts.

A *notice account* is a passbook savings account on which the customer agrees to give specified notice before withdrawing funds. Funds earn at a rate higher than regular passbook accounts, but a penalty is incurred by early withdrawal.

A *bonus account* is a savings account that earns interest at a bonus rate if customers make regular deposits to the account or leave a specified amount on deposit for specified time.

A *NOW account* is a form of a savings account that allows checklike drafts, called "negotiable orders of withdrawal," to be drawn against the interest-bearing deposits and made payable to a third party. These accounts may be offered to individuals and to federal, state, and local governments.

A *super NOW account,* paying market interest rates on balances of $2,500 or more and offering unlimited checkwriting privileges, became effective in January 1983. This account is available to individuals and governmental units eligible for ordinary NOW accounts, but is not available to corporations.

Commercial Demand Accounts. Federal associations were authorized in 1982 to offer demand-deposit, or checking, accounts to persons or organizations that establish a business or commercial loan relationship with them. Such deposits cannot earn interest.

Utility companies and other business interests can open demand-deposit accounts to receive third-party payments from a federal association's nonbusiness customers.

Trust Accounts. IRA and Keogh plans were originally developed to provide retirement benefits to those individuals not covered under any existing plan.

An INDIVIDUAL RETIREMENT ACCOUNT (IRA) is a trust account that allows an individual to accumulate funds for retirement. Contributions to the account and interest earned are tax-deferred until withdrawn, typically when the saver has retired and is in a lower tax bracket. Beginning in 1982, IRA's were made available to every wage earner (and spouse), even those covered by an existing pension plan.

A Keogh account is a retirement account for self-employed persons and their employees. Contributions to a Keogh account and interest earned are also tax-deferred until withdrawn (*see* KEOGH PLANS).

Money-Market Deposit Accounts. A deposit account that requires a minimum initial deposit and pays a market rate of interest with no interest-rate ceiling; it allows immediate withdrawal privileges, either by check (draft), preauthorized transfer, or in person.

Certificate Accounts. Another major type of savings instrument issued by savings and loan associations is the certificate of deposit, or CD. Many variations of the certificate account are possible, featuring different combinations of term; minimum amounts of deposit; interest rates; and renewal provisions.

In certificate accounts, money is deposited with the association and earns interest over a fixed term at either a fixed or variable rate. Interest earned can be credited to the account, added to another account, or paid to the account holder by check. A penalty is charged for premature withdrawal, and the interest rate is higher than that on passbook accounts.

On October 1, 1983, all interest-rate ceilings and minimum-balance requirements were removed for new accounts with maturities greater than 31 days. At the same time, early-withdrawal penalties were changed and certain other savings-account regulations were phased out.

Additional Services. Savings associations offer a number of other services in addition to their savings programs. These services often include:

- A savings-account deposit plan that enables a customer to have checks—such as payroll checks, Social Security and other retirement checks, or stock dividends—sent directly to the savings association for deposit in his savings account or NOW checking plan.
- A payroll savings plan that authorizes an employer to deduct a specified amount from an employee's earnings each pay period to forward directly to the employee's savings association for deposit to his account.
- Safe-deposit boxes for safe storage of documents and valuables.
- Traveler's checks, which are signed by the purchaser at the time of purchase and again when cashed. They are used as a precaution against forgery and theft and if lost are replaced by the issuing company.
- Money orders, which are orders to pay a sum of money specified by the purchaser to a party named by the purchaser.
- An escrow account (also called a "reserve," "impoundment," or "trust" account), which is an account held by the savings association; the borrower makes a monthly payment to the account for a specific purpose, such as property taxes, insurance, or special assessments. The association (lender) disburses funds from the account as they become due.
- Life and mortgage life insurance.
- Stockbrokerage services.

Federal savings associations have consumer leasing powers and the authority to offer trust services. An association can act as a trustee, executor, administrator, or guardian for its trust customers.

Loans. This section discusses the various types of loans made by savings and loan associations.

Mortgage Loans. Home-purchase loans (mortgages) represent the major financing activity of savings and loan associations. They accounted for nearly 80% of the total assets of savings associations at year-end 1981. Associations held more than 53% of all mortgages on one- to four-family family homes and over 40% of all residential mortgages at the end of 1981.

A mortgage loan is a contract between a lender and a borrower in which the borrower gives the lender real estate as security in return for a loan for some of the purchase price of the property. The mortgagor is the borrower; the mortgagee, or lender, is the institution, group, or individual that lends the money.

Savings associations offer a broad range of mortgage options to help borrowers meet their home-financing needs. Until the late 1970s, the most common type of home loan was the standard, or conventional, loan, which has the interest rate set at the time the loan is made and has a fixed term, typically 25–30 years. Conventional loans are not insured or guaranteed by a government agency.

Savings and loan associations are now authorized to offer loans with adjustable rates, payments, and terms, and their popularity in the marketplace is increasing.

Effective in 1982, federal regulations condensed previous regulations for various types of alternative mortgage instruments to permit associations (including state associations where federal preemption is not specifically overridden by state law) to structure their mortgage loans to include any of the following: an adjustable interest rate; an adjustable payment; an adjustable term. Negative amortization, reverse annuity, and a balloon feature are other creative financing arrangements that can be offered.

A common feature of the adjustable mortgage loans (AML's) is the provision for periodic interest-rate adjustments. Many regulatory safeguards are provided to protect the borrower's interests.

Other mortgage plans, designed to accommodate borrowers in diverse circumstances, have varied features.

A *graduated-payment mortgage* permits mortgage payments to start at a low level and rise at a predetermined rate each year. This loan appeals to borrowers who expect their income to increase in the future.

A *reverse-annuity mortgage* can be structured in a variety of ways. Intended primarily for retired homeowners seeking to supplement their incomes, the reverse mortgage permits homeowners to borrow on the equity they have in their property and receive disbursements of the loan proceeds on a monthly basis.

A *growing-equity mortgage* (GEM), or early-ownership loan, features monthly payments that increase each year, with the additional funds going toward repayment of the principal.

Shared-equity or *shared-appreciation loans* permit a private investor to share part of the property's tax benefits and future appreciation in exchange for assistance in making the down payment and the monthly payments.

Savings associations also offer government-sponsored mortgages, including FEDERAL HOUSING ADMINISTRATION (FHA)–insured loans and VETERANS ADMINISTRATION (VA)–guaranteed loans. These loans are backed by government agencies and carry less risk for the lender. The FHA sets the limits on the principal, term and loan-to-value ratio, the interest rate, and other costs charged to borrowers.

Secondary Mortgage Market. Savings and loan associations are the largest buyers of loans in the secondary market and have recently been more active in originating mortgage loans for subsequent sale to investors such as pension funds and insurance companies. Savings associations participate in the SECONDARY MORTGAGE MARKET by buying, selling, and trading mortgages among originators and purchasers of whole loans and interest in blocks of loans. Secondary-mortgage-market activity accounts for 10–15% of total loan acquisitions by savings associations during a typical year.

Commercial Loans. Federal associations were authorized in 1982 to make secured or unsecured commercial, corporate, business, or agricultural loans.

A commercial, corporate, or business loan is any loan that is not a real-estate loan; not made to a person, family, or household; and not a participation in such loans. These can include inventory, floor-planning, and machinery loans.

Other Types of Loans. Besides mortgages, almost all associations make a variety of other loans. Construction loans are made to individuals or developers to finance the construction of homes, apartments, commercial buildings, or other improvements to real estate. A construction loan may include funds for land acquisition and terms for permanent long-term financing upon completion of the construction.

Consumer loans are loans typically not secured by a first mortgage on real estate and are made to an individual for nonbusiness (personal, family, or household) purposes.

Regulatory authority restricted these loan types to savings-account, student, mobile-home, and home-improvement loans for federally chartered associations; but because of financial reform legislation in the 1980s, federal associations are now allowed to finance a broad spectrum of common consumer needs, including vehicles, equipment and furniture, other tangible personal property, and credit-card purchases.

Other types of consumer loans include overdraft lines of credit loans on NOW accounts; marine, aircraft, and recreational-vehicle loans; and time-sharing loans.

A mobile-home loan has a term of up to 12-15 years, is made to finance the purchase of a new or used mobile home unit, and may include funds for associated costs such as transportation and setup. The loan generally is not considered a mortgage loan, because most state laws define a mobile home as personal property.

A home-equity loan is a junior (second) mortgage on the consumer's residence. The loan amount seldom exceeds the difference between 80% of the property value and the amount owed on the first mortgage.

Home-improvement loans are used to finance the repair, modernization, improvement, or equipping of residential real estate. These loans can be unsecured or secured by a junior mortgage on the property being improved.

Savings-account loans are loans secured by pledging the funds on deposit in a savings account or a savings certificate. Generally, these loans are for amounts up to 100% of the savings-account balance; the interest rate normally is approximately 2% higher than the account earns.

Education loans are loans made to students to finance tuition and other costs at a college, university, or trade or professional school. Most of these are made under one or more government student-loan-guarantee programs. Repayment normally does not begin until the student graduates from or drops out of school.

Service Corporations. A service corporation is a subsidiary corporation owned by one or more savings associations. It provides a broad range of services that savings associations are not permitted to offer; such services are closely related and incidental to the parent company's operations. Activities that service corporations can conduct include:

- originating, purchasing, holding, selling, and servicing mortgages
- appraisal, brokerage, clerical, escrow, research, and other services
- improved and unimproved real-estate acquisitions and sales
- developing, renovating, and holding real estate for investment purposes
- real-estate maintenance and management
- performance of insurance agent or brokerage services

- consumer loans, educational loans, and personal benefits programs

Because service corporations are subject to fewer regulations than savings and loan associations, they can be more flexible in the type and terms of the loans they make.

The Future. In the more than 150 years since their founding, savings and loan associations have grown to be a $700-billion business. Changes are taking place constantly as savings associations move from a regulated to a deregulated savings market. Modern technology will continue to affect operations at savings institutions, and expanded powers permitted by law and regulations will continue to change the nature of the savings business. The process of integrating the mortgage market more closely with the general capital markets will continue, as will the trend toward the homogenization of financial institutions.

New, broader lending powers and investment authorities granted to thrift institutions in 1982 will draw retail funds to broaden the business's financial underpinnings. Deregulation has changed the face of the financial-services business; and savings associations, equipped with new financial tools, are in the strongest position in many years to compete with other financial institutions as deregulation continues.

Mary Ann Irvine

Glossary

balloon mortgage A mortgage loan in which some principal and interest, or just interest, is paid periodically, but the major portion of the loan balance is paid in a lump sum at the end of the term.

fiduciary Any person or corporation with the responsibility of holding or controlling property for another.

negative amortization An arrangement in which interest due under a loan agreement is not paid, but rather added to the unpaid principal balance, all of which continues to earn interest until paid. Also known as "capitalization."

nonresidential property Commercial buildings, undeveloped land.

reserves The portion of earnings set aside to take care of any possible losses in the conduct of the association's business.

residential property One-to-four-family homes, multifamily 5+ units, cooperatives, and condominiums.

secondary mortgage market The aggregate buying,

selling, and trading of existing mortgage loans and mortgage-backed securities.

trust An arrangement in which an individual transfers legal title to property to another person, the trustee, who manages the property for the individual beneficiaries. It can be created by a will, agreement, declaration, or court order.

Source: Mary Ann Irvine

Savings and Loan Institutions

See SAVINGS AND LOAN ASSOCIATIONS; SAVINGS BANKS.

Savings Bank Life Insurance (SBLI)

Savings Bank Life Insurance is regular, legal reserve life insurance issued by mutual SAVINGS BANKS in Massachusetts, Connecticut, and New York State. The chief distinguishing feature is its method of distribution—through regular salaried savings-bank employees who have been trained in life-insurance matters. SBLI is traditionally low-cost and features liberal, early cash and loan values; annual dividends that begin with the first year as earned; and local personal service.

History. Savings bank life insurance had its beginnings in Massachusetts under the guidance of Louis D. Brandeis, who later became an associate justice of the United States Supreme Court. Mr. Brandeis's plan was an outgrowth of his investigation of life insurance and, at the same time, an investigation by a committee of the New York State legislature headed by Senator William W. Armstrong. The latter was the start of the famous Armstrong Investigation whose counsel was Charles Evans Hughes.

The investigation revealed that the cost of industrial insurance was far greater than the cost of ordinary insurance. In those days, industrial insurance was characterized by a very high lapse rate, expensive house-to-house collection, high selling cost, and considerable loss to policyholders when forfeiture occurred. The legislative committee sought to correct these abuses and set the pattern for other states.

Brandeis had long admired the theory and practice of mutual savings banks. They had a record of sound economic management, had proven their ability to invest funds safely, were directed by local trustees, and were held in high esteem by the community. With a slight enlargement of their powers, Brandeis felt that

mutual savings banks would be ideally suited to provide life insurance to thrifty buyers. Overhead expenses could be shared by the savings and life-insurance departments of the bank; earlier and larger cash and loan values would be possible; and because selling costs would be reduced, the working man could buy his life insurance at low cost.

With these ideas in mind, Brandeis developed a plan whereby life insurance could be issued at low cost to persons who would buy it at a savings bank on their own initiative.

In June 1907, in the state of Massachusetts, a savings-bank life insurance bill was passed into law, and the banks started selling life insurance in early 1909. The birth of SBLI was attended by conflict and controversy, fiercely opposed by the competing life-insurance industry. Yet the program endured. After operating for more than a quarter-century in Massachusetts, similar programs were started in New York and Connecticut.

In New York, insurance-industry opposition blocked attempts at SBLI legislation until 1938. That year, the plan erupted into the most controversial issue of the legislative session. When the struggle was finished, SBLI had been voted into existence. It had succeeded through the strong backing of Governor Herbert H. Lehman, support from both parties, plus prodding from an aroused public.

The first SBLI departments opened for business in January 1939. By the end of that month, an enthusiastic public had bought over $1 million in policies. Persuasive proof of the need for low-cost insurance was shown by the fact that many applicants owned no insurance at all. An entirely new group of people wanting insurance protection was now being reached.

How It Works. The system of savings bank life insurance is composed of savings banks that act as agency banks; savings banks that act as issuing banks; and a central office in each state to provide the technical expertise impractical for each bank on an individual basis.

Issuing banks are the backbone of the system. Each issuer is, in effect, a small life-insurance company within the structure of the savings bank. The bank's SBLI department performs most of the main functions of a life-insurance company. It takes applications, collects premiums, issues policies, invests funds, and pays claims. Assets of the department are required by law to be kept separate and distinct from those of the bank. Any earnings generated are distributed to policyholders after setting aside the necessary reserves, surplus, or contingency funds.

Agency banks are those that take applications and collect premiums. They do not, however, issue policies, invest funds, or pay death claims; those functions are handled by the issuing bank of their choice. Generally speaking, agency banks are those that do not normally generate enough SBLI business to support a life-insurance department of their own.

The central office in each state provides actuarial, underwriting, accounting, billing, legal, marketing, and advertising services for the banks. In Massachusetts those functions are provided by a division of the state insurance department and the Savings Bank Life Insurance Council. The Connecticut system is served by the Savings Bank Life Insurance Company, and New York has the Savings Banks Life Insurance Fund. In all three states, SBLI is surpervised by the State Banking and Insurance Department through regular audits of the banks' life-insurance departments.

The safety of the system in each state is provided by reinsurance agreements among the banks or through the central office. In that way, risks are shared so that no issuing bank would be affected by unusual lapses. In addition, each state has a central fund that acts as guarantor for the policies and contracts issued by the life-insurance departments of the banks.

SBLI Policies. Each state provides a variety of life-insurance policies, including whole-life; endowments; limited payment plan, such as 20-Pay Life; five-year renewable-term; decreasing-term policies; and, depending on the state, special nonsmoker plans, spouse riders, children's riders, group mortgage insurance, group creditor life insurance, and employer/employee groups.

Annual dividends are paid as earned on all individual SBLI policies beginning at the end of the first year, further reducing their low cost. Policyholders have five options as to dividends. They may either (1) Take them in cash, (2) used them to reduce premium payments, (3) used them to purchase more "paid-up" insurance (except on term policies), (4) leave them to accumulate at interest, or (5) use them to buy one-year term insurance (except on term policies).

Every effort is made to keep the purchase of SBLI attractively simple and convenient. Application forms are very brief. Medical exams are not required for certain ages and policy amounts. All plans, except term and certain children's policies at age 0, provide liberal cash and loan values at the end of the first year.

SBLI Investments. The ability of SBLI to offer low-cost life insurance stems in part from its investment operations. Over the years, SBLI's rate of return on investments has generally been higher than the average for the life-insurance industry as a whole.

The unique, decentralized organization of SBLI helps to account for this investment success. Reserves on policies, as well as most of the system's funds, are managed at the local level by each issuing bank. Each life-insurance department draws on the expertise of the professional investing staff of the savings bank. These investment staffs are experienced in managing the millions generated by the savings departments. The know-how is readily transferred to the similar money-management requirements for the bank's life-insurance operation.

SBLI's Growth. In its early days in all three states, SBLI struggled under some severe restrictions. Special legislation had to be obtained in each state to permit savings banks to sell life insurance. In that process, certain concessions had to be made pertaining to the amounts of insurance the banks would be allowed to sell.

For example, the initial limit in New York State in 1939 was $3,000 per life. Over the years, the limits have been raised in each state, but SBLI is still the only insurer with such state-imposed restrictions. In 1982 the limit per life for regular policies was $64,000 in Massachusetts, $75,000 in Connecticut, and $30,000 in New York.

In spite of these limits, each state has done well serving people who live or work in those states (another restriction). Total SBLI in force in each state reflects the size of the population or market in each state. In Massachusetts in 1982 it was over $3.7 billion; in Connecticut, just over $1.5 billion; and in New York, it $9.5 billion. For several years SBLI in New York has been among the top half-dozen insurers when measured by the number of policies sold. Similar sales success has been enjoyed in Massachusetts. The Connecticut system, with new limits, has begun to see rapid growth.

SBLI's Future Growth. The manner in which the life-insurance industry serves its public has changed considerably since SBLI started in Massachusetts over 70 years ago. The cost of selling and servicing industrial insurance has changed companies' attitudes toward further development of this kind of protection. The tendency of most companies is to sell larger policies to a more affluent segment of the market.

It would appear, then, that some other source will serve those people who formerly purchased moderate-size life-insurance policies. In the three SBLI states, the savings banks have been an answer for those people otherwise ignored by the life-insurance industry. It is reasonable to assume that similiar "retail" sources of life insurance will be developed in other states as people perceive their own needs for life insurance and look for convenient suppliers. With SBLI's firm foothold in three SBLI states, the large number of savings-banks offices in those states, and the public's continuing need for a convenient source of low-cost life insurance, the growth of SBLI is a strong possibility.

Ray E. Mauger, Jr.

Savings Banks

Savings bank is a generic term that historically has applied to a particular type of thrift institution belonging to an industry that is concentrated in the Northeast. Prior to the recent deregulation of the overall banking industry, savings banks differed from savings and loan associations in that they had much broader service and investment authority. However, they also differed from commercial banks in that they were not permitted to offer financial services to businesses and corporations. With deregulation, the distinctions among these different types of institutions have blurred considerably, but savings banks generally still have two important characteristics in common: (1) Most remain state-chartered, and (2) most are mutual in organizational form. (It should be noted, however, that many small commercial banks, particularly in the Midwest, have used the term *savings bank* in their names for many years, and that federal banking legislation enacted in 1982 authorizes any federally chartered savings and loan association to designate itself a "savings bank" if it so wishes.)

The $180 billion U.S. savings-bank industry consisted of about 400 institutions serving depositors with approximately 37 million accounts through more than 3,600 offices (figures current as of mid-1983). As of mid-1983, savings banks operated in 16 states (Alaska, Connecticut, Delaware, Indiana, Maine, Maryland, Massachusetts, New Hampshire, New Jersey, New York, Oregon, Pennsylvania, Rhode Island, Vermont, Washington, and Wisconsin), concentrated primarily in the Northeast.

The service and investment authority of savings banks may vary from one state to the next, because savings banks were limited to a system of state chartering until 1978. Legislation enacted by Congress in that year established an alternative system of federal chartering for existing savings banks, and several have since converted to a federal charter. However, the majority of savings banks still operate under state charters.

Federal legislation enacted in March 1980 granted federal savings banks significantly broader powers than those of state-chartered savings banks in many states, including the authority to make loans to and accept deposits from corporations and other businesses. Under parity legislation enacted at the state level, similar authority has since been extended to

savings banks in many states.

Since the late nineteenth century, savings banks have invested primarily in home mortgages. As of year-end 1982, savings banks had over $108 billion invested in mortgages and mortgage-type holdings, which represented more than 62% of the industry's total deposits. The majority of these loans were on single-family housing.

In addition to meeting consumers' savings and home-financing needs, savings banks also offer a broad range of other financial services. In various states, these include checking accounts, NOW accounts, credit cards, debit cards, telephone-bill payment, and other types of third-party payment services. Other savings-bank services include consumer installment loans, education loans, Individual Retirement Accounts (IRA's), Keogh plans, savings-bank life insurance (in Connecticut, New York, and Massachusetts), and trust services in several states. In recent years, savings banks have also been increasingly active in the commercial lending area under authority granted by either state or federal laws and regulations.

Early History. The concept of savings banking did not originate in the U.S., but was imported from Britain. The first savings bank was founded in 1810 by a thrift-conscious Scotch minister, the Reverend Henry Duncan, to serve his parishioners. The concept caught on quickly in the British Isles, and by 1817 some 200 savings banks were in operation there.

Meanwhile, word of this new idea spread to America, where it was received with enthusiasm by a number of civic-minded leaders in New York, Boston, and Philadelphia.

The founders of savings banks in this country were active in the reform programs of the time. They included the presidents of the American Bible Society, the American Lyceum, and the United States Temperance Union, together with the founders of the New York Free School Society, the American Anti-Slavery Society, and the American Unitarian Society. These reform-minded community leaders saw the concept of savings banks as a means of contributing to a better standard of living for the workingman and his family. However, they were also practical businessmen, and they clearly understood how a savings bank could benefit its community. At that time, the only banks in operation were commercial banks, whose prime function was to provide financial services to industry and commerce. In those days, commercial banks had little interest in "retail banking," since it necessarily involves the cumbersome and costly task of handling many very small sums of money.

In those early days of our country, however, there was also a pressing need for capital to finance the expansion and economic growth of a nation just entering the industrial age. The founders of the first savings banks in this country knew that new investment capital would become available by pooling the many small deposits of working people, which previously were simply withdrawn from circulation and hidden in cookie jars, mattresses, and the like. At the same time, they knew that the return on such investments would allow the payment of interest to these small depositors—a concept then regarded as a very innovative.

The first savings bank to "open for business" in the U.S. was the Philadelphia Savings Fund Society, now the largest institution in the savings-bank industry. PSFS accepted its first deposit on the morning of December 10, 1816. Only three days later, on December 13, the organizers of the Provident Institution for Savings in the Town of Boston received a charter to operate a savings bank from the Massachusetts legislature. Today, these two savings banks share the honor of being the industry's "founding" banks. Indeed, savings banks were the nation's first savings institutions.

Growth and Expansion. By the Civil War, there were nearly 300 savings banks operating in this country—primarily in the New England and Middle Atlantic states. In the period following that war, savings banking spread to the Midwest, and later to the Pacific Northwest.

From the Civil War on, however, the principal growth in terms of number of savings banks continued to be in the industrial Northeast. The reason for this geographic concentration was that the savings-bank concept was tailored to meet the special needs of a settled industrialized area, where the amounts that workers were able to save from their wages constituted a "capital surplus." The frontier states, on the other hand, were "capital-short" areas where money itself was in short supply and where there thus was little need for savings institutions.

Investment Patterns. While restricted in their investment latitude, the early savings banks made a vital contribution toward financing the country's growth through their purchases of municipal, state, and federal government bonds. They were also active in funding the construction of America's early transportation networks. In large part, it was savings-bank financing that helped make possible construction of the Erie Canal. Through their investment in railroad bonds, savings banks also helped finance the westward expansion of the nation's rail system.

Around the turn of the century, however, as savings banks responded to changing community needs, mortgage lending began to play an increasingly impor-

tant part in their investment activities. While savings banks' mortgage orientation was originally simply an investment decision, in later years it was increasingly a reflection of federal government housing policy, particularly in the post–World War II period.

In 1966, growing inflationary pressures and sharply rising interest rates produced heavy deposit outflows—"disintermediation"—from thrift institutions, effectively shutting off the flow of funds to housing. In that year Congress enacted legislation authorizing deposit-interest-rate ceilings in order to balance competition between commercial banks and thrift institutions, with the aim of increasing the availability of mortgage funds. Under that legislation, the federal regulatory agencies established a structure of deposit-interest-rate ceilings that authorized mortgage-oriented thrift institutions to pay a slightly higher rate on deposits than commercial banks were allowed to pay.

The Impact of Inflation on Mortgage Lenders. It soon became clear that the approach inherent in this new rate-ceiling structure failed to address an important underlying problem. While the rate differential did indeed improve the ability of thrift institutions to compete for savings with commercial banks, the ceiling structure as a whole afforded no protection against competition from the open market in high-interest-rate periods. As inflation accelerated in the 1970s, such periods became more and more frequent. And whenever federal anti-inflation monetary policies pushed open-market rates above deposit-interest-rate ceilings, more and more thrift-institution depositors withdrew their funds for investment in instruments not subject to rate ceilings, such as money-market mutual funds.

Adding to the problem was the fact that their federally mandated specialization in long-term mortgage finance made thrift institutions structurally incapable of competing for savings when interest rates rose sharply. Their portfolios were burdened with old mortgages made when rates were much lower. In many states, moreover, this burden was compounded by the long-term impact of unrealistic usury ceilings, which had prevented mortgage rates from keeping pace with other market rates. Given this handicap on portfolio earnings, savings banks were not in a position to bid for savings in a high-rate climate.

The Trend Toward Deregulation. The savings-bank industry had long been aware of the need to acquire the broader investment powers and increased operating flexibility necessary to compete in such an environment. Beginning in the early 1960s, savings banks began working toward these objectives, and made steady progress in acquiring broader consumer-service powers, primarily at the state level.

At the federal level, the savings-bank industry's major goal for almost 20 years was a federal charter alternative that would bring with it the progressive "checks and balances" benefits of a dual chartering system. This goal was finally achieved through federal legislation enacted in late 1978. Prior to that time, savings banks were alone among depository institutions in being limited to a system of state chartering. And this new federal charter option soon proved its value, for as the powers of federal savings banks were broadened by federal legislation, this encouraged the authorization of similar powers for savings banks operating under state charters.

Meanwhile, many banking developments in the 1970s were progressively weakening the deposit-interest-rate-ceiling structure. In 1973 the federal banking regulators attempted to stem the inflation-induced outflows from depository institutions by removing the ceilings on accounts of four-years-or-longer maturity. However, the result was a massive shift of funds from thrift institutions to commercial banks, whose portfolios of short-term business loans enabled them to pay much higher rates than mortgage-oriented thrift institutions could afford. The result was that the ceilings were hastily restored by congressional action.

In 1978 the regulatory agencies authorized all depository institutions to offer a six-month certificate of deposit with ceiling rates linked to the weekly auction discount rate on six-month Treasury bills. Instead of attracting substantial new deposits and stemming outflows, however, the primary consequence was a massive internal transfer of funds from lower-yielding accounts. This substantially increased thrift institutions' cost of funds, and contributed significantly to a sharp deterioration in their earnings.

Moreover, the introduction of market-linked rate ceilings intensified pressures to extend market rates of return to all savers on all types of accounts. This set the stage for a major change in the way rate ceilings were viewed by Congress. Instead of viewing rate ceilings as a beneficial tool for providing funds for mortgages, Congress increasingly began to see them as an obstacle preventing savers from receiving market rates of return.

The issue was initially addressed in the Depository Institutions Deregulation and Monetary Control Act of 1980, which was signed into law by President Carter on March 31 of that year. The most far-reaching banking legislation to be enacted since the 1930s, it provided for a six-year phase-out of deposit-interest-rate ceilings, together with broader powers for federal thrift institutions. However, it did not directly address the underlying problem posed by thrift institutions' portfolios of low-yielding mortgages and the resulting stubborn drain on earnings.

The Garn–St Germain Depository Institutions Act of 1982 took this process one step further. Signed into law by President Reagan on October 15, 1982, it provided for an even more significant expansion of thrift-institution powers and in effect virtually eliminated the distinction between savings banks and savings and loan associations at the federal level. However, it by no means completed the process of financial institutions' deregulation, and additional legislation is expected to be enacted that will have the effect of further blurring the distinctions among different types of institutions.

An Industry in Transition. Savings banks continue to face severe pressures on earnings as they move through the transitional period to a totally deregulated environment. Congress has increasingly recognized this problem, and has developed numerous legislative measures aimed not only at helping to smooth this transition but also at providing savings banks and other thrift institutions with a more realistic range of operating and investment authority.

At the same time, deregulation legislation is laying the foundation for a more competitive banking system, much more closely keyed to the rapidly changing needs of our nation's economy. Given that foundation, and once present difficulties are behind us, the long-term outlook for savings banks holds the promise of solid growth, dynamic development, and healthy diversification that responds to the changing needs of their customers and the communities they serve.

Arthur M. Mikesell

Savings Bonds

See UNITED STATES SAVINGS BONDS.

Seasonal Borrowing

The seasonal borrowing privilege is a credit arrangement available at Federal Reserve banks to assist smaller depository institutions in dealing with significant recurring variations in either loans or deposits each year. The privilege helps smaller institutions overcome strains placed on their limited resources by seasonal pressures so that legitimate credit needs in their communities can be accommodated. However, a seasonal line of credit is available from the Federal Reserve only if the borrower doesn't have access to another seasonal credit program.

The amount of credit available under the seasonal arrangement generally is limited to the amount by which the depository institution's seasonal needs exceed a certain percentage of its average total deposits in the previous calendar year. The percentage is established by the board of governors of the Federal Reserve system and is set to ensure that the institution makes an effort to help meet its seasonal needs from other sources and doesn't become totally dependent on the Federal Reserve for assistance. In addition, seasonal credit may be extended only if the Reserve bank is satisfied that the institution's needs for funds will persist for at least four weeks. If the need persists, advances under the program may be available for up to six months.

To obtain seasonal credit, an institution must negotiate a seasonal credit line with its Reserve bank, using information from recent years to demonstrate its need. Generally, seasonal credit isn't available to institutions with deposits in excess of $500 million, because of their access to the money markets. It also isn't available to institutions with access to other seasonal credit programs offered by other lenders, such as the Federal Home Loan Banks for member savings and loan associations and savings banks, and the National Credit Union Administration's Central Liquidity Facility for member credit unions.

Seasonal variations in the loans or deposits of an institution can result from a variety of factors, such as those related to crop cycles or the raising of livestock. College and resort communities also often have seasonal credit needs, as do other communities, because of seasonal variations in local tax collections and local credit needs. For example, farmers typically borrow from their local depository institutions to finance their operations until marketing their products. These financing needs are often greatest at the time when the institutions' deposit levels are low. As products are sold, the financing needs diminish, the loans get repaid, and excess funds are deposited into the institutions to be drawn upon to meet operating and other expenses.

Similarly, in areas largely dependent on resort business, depository institutions may experience seasonal fluctuations in deposits and loan demand. In these communities, as a summer vacation season or ski season approaches, local businesses, such as merchants acquiring inventories or hotel owners repairing and improving resort facilities, will normally increase their demands for credit from depository institutions. Once again, deposit levels are generally low at these times.

State and local governments, to cite another example, often borrow necessary operating funds from their local banks on a short-term basis in anticipation of tax receipts. As taxes are collected, these loans are repaid and excess funds are deposited. These deposits will then be drawn over several months as the municipalities meet their regular operating expenses, such as salary payments and suppliers' fees. Since some communities collect taxes only once or twice a year, seasonal variations in loans and deposits can, in these cases, last for several months.

Beyond helping smaller depository institutions to meet these typical seasonal needs, Federal Reserve credit also is available to those institutions to help satisfy unusual seasonal demands in a period of general liquidity strain. For example, during a period of monetary tightness, such credit might be used by a smaller institution to assist farmers, home builders, small businesses, and others.

The collateral requirements and, generally, the discount rate applicable to seasonal credit are the same as for regular credit obtained through the DISCOUNT WINDOW of Reserve Banks (*see also* DISCOUNT RATES).

Seasonal borrowing privileges were first granted to member banks in 1973, and the terms under which banks use these credit lines were liberalized in 1976. A principal feature of the liberalization was that member banks could borrow under the seasonal privilege while being net sellers of FEDERAL FUNDS.

In September 1980, Regulation A, which governs the extension of Federal Reserve credit, was amended to reflect changes brought about by the International Banking Act of 1978 and the Depository Institutions Deregulation and Monetary Control Act of 1980. Among other changes, those acts broadened eligibility for discount-window borrowing to all depository institutions, including U.S. branches and agencies of foreign banks, that have transaction accounts or nonpersonal time deposits. A "transaction account" is a deposit against which a depositor may make withdrawals by a transferable instrument to pay a third party. Among these accounts are checking accounts, negotiable order of withdrawal (NOW) accounts, savings deposits subject to automatic transfers, and credit-union share draft accounts. "Nonpersonal time deposits" are those of organizations, rather than persons.

Use of seasonal credit doesn't impair an institutions's ability to obtain additional temporary loans at the discount window to meet short-term adjustment credit needs.

Arthur Samansky

Secondary Distribution

See COMMON STOCK.

Secondary Market

See SECONDARY MORTGAGE MARKET.

Secondary Mortgage Market

The secondary mortgage market for home mortgages is a network of primary mortgage lenders who sell loans they have originated, and investors who buy loans or securities backed by groups of loans. Primary mortgage lenders make loans to property buyers and underwrite and service the loans, which can be held in lenders' own portfolios or sold to investors. Much of the money borrowed by home buyers comes from deposits of savers at savings and loan associations, mutual savings banks, and other thrift institutions. These funds, however, often are insufficient to meet demand of potential borrowers for new mortgage loans. Changes in demographics create demand that exceeds the amount of funds available. Also, in recent years high interest rates have caused savers, desiring higher-yielding investments, to take their deposits out of savings institutions.

Home buyers and mortgage lenders need a constant supply of mortgage money. A lender can raise money by selling to an investor loans already made. When a lending institution sells its loans, it has participated in a secondary market transaction and has recovered funds to reinvest in new mortgages. A variety of investors buy mortgage loans, attracted by the relatively high yields associated with mortgage investments.

Roles of the Secondary Market. The role of the secondary market in the past was primarily to redistribute the available mortgage money by transferring funds from capital-surplus to capital-deficit areas. The availability of mortgage money was heavily dependent on the deposit flows of thrift institutions, which traditionally have been the primary originators of conventional mortgages.

The secondary market accomplished this role through its purchases of mortgages in the newer, faster-growing regions of the country and sales of mortgages in the older, slower regions.

Today, the secondary mortgages market continues to redistribute funds, but also links the capital and mortgage markets more closely through its sales of mortgages in forms that attract investment from outside the traditional mortgage-investment community. The demand for mortgage credit nationwide has grown more rapidly than the deposit bases of traditional lending institutions and has increased the need for new sources of investment in residential mortgages.

Figures 1 and 2 (page 554) illustrate secondary-market activity in one-to-four family (nonfarm) and multifamily mortgage markets since 1970.

Participants in the Secondary Market. Three entities were created by Congress to serve the secondary mortgage market. They have become important elements in its development. They are the FEDERAL HOME LOAN MORTGAGE CORPORATION ("Freddie Mac"), the FEDERAL NATIONAL MORTGAGE ASSOCIATION ("Fannie Mae"), and the GOVERNMENT NATIONAL MORTGAGE ASSOCIATION ("Ginnie Mae").

Freddie Mac was created by Congress in 1970 under Title III of the Emergency Home Finance Act. Through secondary market operations, the corporation enhances the liquidity of mortgage investments and increases the availability of mortgage credit for conventional residential mortgage loans. It purchases conventional (without government insurance or guarantee) single-family (one to four units) fixed-rate and adjustable-rate loans, multifamily (more than four units) fixed-rate loans, and home-improvement loans. It buys these loans principally from savings and loan associations, as well as from mortgage bankers, commercial banks, and HUD-approved mortgagees. It finances most of its mortgage purchases through sales of conventional mortgage pass-through securities, called "Mortgage Participation Certificates." The corporation can also finance its operations by issuing short-term and long-term debt obligations and accessing lines of credit.

The corporation received initial capital of $100 million through the sale of nonvoting common stock to the FEDERAL HOME LOAN BANKS. Members of the FEDERAL HOME LOAN BANK BOARD (FHLBB), serving in a separate capacity, function as the corporation's board of directors. In 1982 Congress authorized Freddie Mac to issue preferred stock.

Fannie Mae was created by Congress in 1938 as a government corporation. In 1954 it became a mixed-ownership entity. Under 1968 legislation (Title III of the National Housing Act), it was partitioned into Ginnie Mae and Fannie Mae, with Fannie Mae owned by private shareholders. Initially, it provided a secondary market for FHA and VA mortgage loans only, but was authorized in 1970 to purchase conventional mortgage loans also. Fannie Mae purchases both single-family and multifamily FHA, VA, and conventional adjustable-rate, fixed-rate, and second mortgage loans. It has also provided secondary market support to federal housing-subsidy programs. It participates in construction and rehabilitation loans and makes direct loans to financial institutions. Fannie Mae finances its purchase activities primarily by the cash flow from its mortgage portfolio and high volume issuance of debentures and short-term discount notes. In 1981 the association began to sell conventional mortgage pass-through securities and it is increasingly relying on this form of financing. It also sells seasoned FHA and VA mortgage pass-through securities. A large and growing percentage of FNMA's earnings are generated from fees charged to lenders in

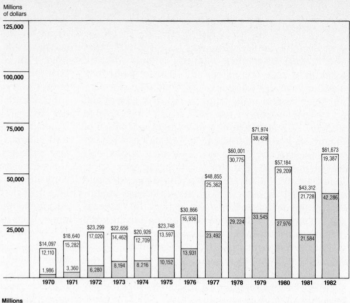

Figure 1. Secondary market activity in one-to-four family (nonfarm) and multifamily mortgage markets since 1970—lenders' sales. (Net of federal credit agencies and mortgage pools and of sales of seasoned mortgages made under swap programs.) Dark area = conventional; light area = FHA/VA. Note: columns may not sum to total due to rounding. (*Source:* HUD, "Survey of Mortgage Lending Activity." Reprinted with permission of the Federal Home Loan Mortgage Corporation.)

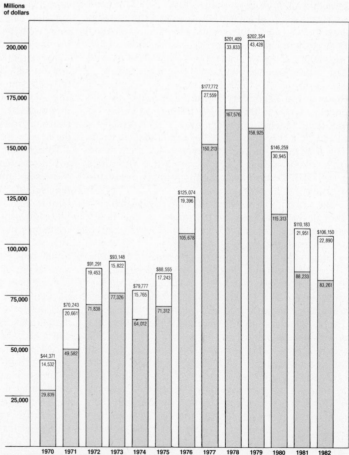

Figure 2. Secondary market activity in one-to-four family (nonfarm) and multifamily mortgage markets since 1970—organizations. (Includes commercial banks, mutual savings banks, savings and loan institutions, life insurance companies, private non-insured pension funds, mortgage companies, real estate, investment trusts, state and local retirement federal credit agencies, mortgage pools, and state and local credit agencies.) Dark area = conventional; light area = FHA/VA. Note: columns may not sum to total due to rounding. (*Source:* HUD, "Survey of Mortgage Lending Activity." Reprinted with permission of the Federal Home Loan Mortgage Corporation.)

its mortgage-purchase operations.

The organization is subject to regulatory authority of the secretary of the DEPARTMENT OF HOUSING AND URBAN DEVELOPMENT (HUD). It has a 15-member board of directors, 10 elected by shareholders and 5 appointed by the president of the United States.

Ginnie Mae was created by Congress in Title III of the National Housing Act of 1968. The agency supplies and stimulates, through secondary market mechanisms, mortgage credit that supports the government's housing objectives by assisting that segment of the housing market for which conventional financing is not readily available. GNMA guarantees passthrough mortgage securities representing interests in FHA, VA, and FmHA (Farmers Home Administration) mortgages. The securities are issued by lenders and guaranteed by GNMA. The agency is a governmental corporation within HUD. The president of GNMA, a presidential appointee, acts under general policy direction of the secretary of HUD.

Private mortgage-insurance companies (MIC's) are a major nongovernment participant in the secondary market. These companies insure conventional mortgage loans, thereby reducing the risk to the lender. They also arrange for and provide services in connection with the sale of conventional mortgage loans in the private secondary market. The companies finance their operations by premiums earned on individual mortgage-insurance policies, by premiums on pool insurance policies, by return on investments, and by stock or debt issues. MIC's are private corporations.

The Secondary Market Process. The secondary market for residential mortgages emerged over the decade of the 1970s and early 1980s as a multichanneled process. The number and types of both mortgage originators and investors have expanded as the secondary market has matured. Figure 3 shows the chain of finance from investor to home buyers. Terms used in Figure 3 are defined as follows:

Investors include thrift institutions, banks (for their own portfolios and for trust accounts), pension funds, life-insurance companies, and others.

Dealers are investment bankers.

Pass-through securities are mortgage-backed securities in which borrowers' monthly mortgage payments are passed by original lenders to a conduit such as Freddie Mac or Fannie Mae, which in turn passes the payments through to investors.

Participations are percentage interests (usually 50–95%) in pools of mortgages.

Mortgage-backed bonds are intermediate-term (five- to ten-year) bonds that pay interest semiannually and are collateralized by loans having an unpaid principal balance, evaluated at current market rates, in an amount of 150–200% of the indebtedness.

A *conduit* is an organization that buys mortgages and packages them to sell to other investors. In addition to the governmentally created institutions mentioned above, depository institutions and mortgage-insurance companies can function as conduits.

Lenders include savings and loan associations, commercial banks, mortgage companies, mutual sav-

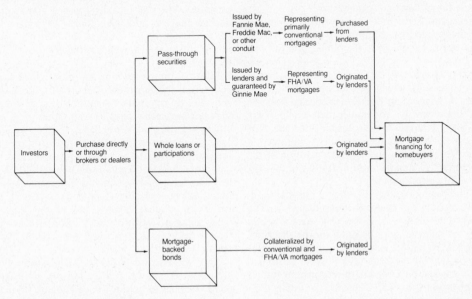

Figure 3. The secondary market process.

ings banks, credit unions, and others.

Federal Home Loan Mortgage Corporation

Second Mortgage

See HOME FINANCING, MORTGAGES.

Secretary of the Treasury

See DEPARTMENT OF THE TREASURY.

Secured Lending

See ASSET-BASED FINANCIAL SERVICES.

Securities, U.S. Government

See TREASURY SECURITIES.

Securities and Exchange Commission (SEC)

The United States Securities and Exchange Commission is an independent U.S. government agency that regulates the securities markets.

Historical Development. The decade leading up to the Great Wall Street Crash of 1929 was a period in which many fortunes were made and lost. The securities markets of the 1920s were characterized by hectic activity and an atmosphere of easy money. Often, the fortunes of a large number of investors were at the mercy of a handful of manipulators. There was much fraudulent activity and no regulation.

The Securities Act of 1933 was intended to remedy some of these abuses by requiring registration of securities that are to be offered to the public, and full disclosure of material corporate information. The following year, Congress passed the Securities Exchange Act (Exchange Act), which regulates the activities of securities exchanges and broker/dealers and requires periodic disclosure by companies that are publicly owned. The Exchange Act also established the SEC and gave the new agency responsibility for protection of investors, for the fair and orderly operation of the securities markets, and for administration of the corporate full-disclosure system.

From the beginning, the SEC drew to its staff a remarkably capable and energetic group of people. The staff worked diligently during the early years to set up the basis for the regulatory program for the securities industry, and to a great extent that program remains intact today. During the years 1935–40, four additional laws were enacted by Congress in response to studies and suggestions by the SEC. These are the Public Utility Holding Company Act of 1935; the Trust Inden-

ture Act of 1939; the Investment Company Act of 1940; and the Investment Advisers Act of 1940.

Organization. Directing the SEC are five commissioners appointed by the president and confirmed by the Senate, with one of the five designated as chairman. They set policy, direct the activities of the staff, and influence the course of securities legislation in Congress.

The SEC's staff numbers about 2,000 people who are located in the headquarters office in Washington, D.C., and in nine regional and six branch offices in various locations nationwide. Most staff members are divided among five major operating divisions, with the balance performing administrative, legal, planning, analytic, and other support functions.

Much of the commission's work involves developing and administering the rules that give form and substance to the broad provisions of the securities laws. This process is cooperative, incorporating the views of representatives of the securities industry, the corporate community, and investors through testimony before the commissioners and staff or the submission of written comments. Formal meetings of the commission at which proposed rules are discussed are generally open to observation by the public and press.

Functions

Enforcement. The Division of Enforcement is the law-enforcement arm of the SEC. Working out of Washington and the regional offices, the Enforcement Division responds to problems in all SEC regulatory programs. The staff includes lawyers, investigators, financial analysts, and accountants. They are responsible for detecting violations of the securities laws and taking whatever actions are necessary to prevent their recurrence.

Information concerning possible violations may come from the detection of unusual trends in market activities by the market-surveillance staff; from individual shareholders or others; and from press reports. Often, referrals are made from another government agency or from a self-regulatory organization that has jurisdiction over the activities of its members.

If a preliminary inquiry indicates that illegal activities may have taken place, the enforcement staff can utilize the commission's subpoena powers to compel people to produce records and to testify. Through painstaking investigative work, the staff establishes a record that substantiates violations of the securities laws.

The SEC is authorized to take several types of enforcement actions. It may bring a civil action in court, seeking to enjoin the defendants from further violative conduct. When appropriate, it may also ask the court to order "ancillary relief," such as disgorgement of ill-gotten gains. In cases involving securities-industry professionals or firms, the commission may order an administrative proceeding before one of its own administrative-law judges. This type of proceeding may result in a censure or in suspension or revocation of the defendant's registration to operate in the securities industry. Where there have been particularly flagrant violations, the SEC may recommend criminal prosecution by the Justice Department.

Full Disclosure. The Division of Corporation Finance is responsible for reviewing disclosure documents filed by corporations under the requirements of the Securities Act and the Exchange Act; for monitoring and evaluating the effectiveness of these disclosure requirements; and for providing interpretive and technical assistance to companies that are required to file.

Generally, companies must make disclosure to the SEC in three instances. The first is when securities are sold to the public. In that document, called the "prospectus," there is a variety of information about the business of the company, the use of the proceeds, and an analysis of the company's recent financial results.

The second type of disclosure is contained in periodic reporting documents. Companies of more than a certain size, with a substantial number of shareholders, are required to file certain reports with the commission on a regular basis. The annual report, on Form 10-K, is similar to the prospectus—it has detailed information with respect to business, property, and legal proceedings. The quarterly report, on Form 10-Q, is primarily composed of the financial results of the quarter and year to date.

The third type of disclosure is contained in proxy reporting documents. When a company solicits proxies (similar to absentee ballots) to elect directors or to conduct other major transactions, it must issue proxy statements to shareholders. These statements must also be filed in advance with the SEC.

Companies that file disclosure reports with the SEC are assigned, based on industry, to one of ten branches in the division. Not all reports are reviewed, but a significant percentage of them are. Once having reviewed the filing, the branch may call the company or send a letter giving its views as to the adequacy of the disclosure.

The objective of the full-disclosure program is to make available to investors and their advisers the background materials they need to make informed investment decisions. To assure that all corporate disclosures are accurate all the time is impossible. However, the securities laws do provide for fines or imprisonment for those making deliberately false or misleading statements in registration documents. In addition, an investor may be able to sue to recover losses in the purchase of a security if false or misleading statements were made in the prospectus.

Regulation of the Securities Markets. When an investor places a buy or sell order with a stockbroker, he sets in motion a complicated process through which millions of shares of stock change hands daily. The SEC's Division of Market Regulation has the responsibility for developing rules to protect the interests of all who participate in this process and assure that the markets operate in a fair and orderly manner.

Securities-industry regulation is a shared responsibility between the industry itself and the SEC. Membership organizations such as the New York Stock Exchange and the National Association of Securities Dealers (NASD) perform primary regulatory functions as well as conduct market activities. The SEC, in turn, closely oversees these regulatory efforts. This process of industry self-government under federal oversight is referred to as the securities industry's "self-regulatory system," and the private institutions involved are "self-regulatory organizations" (SRO's).

In general, individuals who buy and sell securities professionally must register with the appropriate SRO, must meet certain qualification requirements, and must comply with rules of conduct adopted by that SRO. The broker/dealer firms for which they work must register with the SEC and must comply with the SEC's rules relating to such matters as financial condition and sales practices. They must also comply with the rules of any exchange of which they are members and, usually, with the rules of the NASD.

In addition to overseeing the SRO's, the SEC has direct regulatory authority over broker/dealers in certain areas. The SEC can deny registration to securities firms and in some cases may impose sanctions against a firm or individual for violations of the federal securities laws, such as manipulation of the market price of a stock, misappropriation of customer funds or securities, or other abuse of customer trust. The SEC polices the securities industry through its own inspections and by working in conjunction with the SRO's and state securities commissioners.

Regulation of Investment Companies and Advisers. The Division of Investment Management is responsible for the administration of the federal securities laws insofar as they apply to regulation of and disclosure by investment companies and investment advisers.

Under the Investment Company Act of 1940, companies engaged primarily in the business of investing, reinvesting, and trading in securities are required to register with the SEC and are subject to certain statutory prohibitions and regulations designed to protect investors. The rules under the act cover such things as sales, management fees, composition of boards of directors, and capital structure. Also, various transactions of investment companies, including transactions with affiliated interests, are prohibited unless the SEC first determines that such transactions are fair. The securities of investment companies are also required to be registered under the Securities Act. Therefore, these companies must file the disclosure documents mentioned previously.

The Investment Advisers Act of 1940 establishes a pattern of regulation of investment advisers that is similar in many respects to Exchange Act provisions governing the conduct of broker/dealers. It requires, with certain exceptions, that persons or firms who engage, for compensation, in the business of advising others about their securities transactions shall register with the SEC and conform their activities to statutory standards designed to protect the interests of investors. The act prohibits certain types of fee arrangements; makes unlawful any practices of investment advisers that involve fraud or deceit; and requires, among other things, disclosure of any conflicting interests the advisers may have in transactions executed for clients.

Regulation of Public Utility Holding Companies. The Division of Corporate Regulation is responsible for the SEC's administration of the Public Utility Holding Company Act of 1935. The act provides for SEC regulation of the purchase and sale of securities and assets by companies in certain large electric and gas utility holding-company systems, and also for SEC regulation of their intrasystem transactions and service and management arrangements. It limits holding companies to a single coordinated utility system and requires simplification of complex corporate and capital structures and elimination of unfair distribution of voting power among holders of system securities.

(The SEC recommended to the ninety-seventh Congress the repeal of the Public Utility Holding Company Act, concluding that it had achieved its original purpose in that the industry had been geographically integrated and simplified. Furthermore, developments since 1935 in the form of new accounting standards, sophisticated financial analysis, increased disclosure requirements of other federal securities laws, and more effective regulation all ensure the soundness of the utility industry and the protection of utility consumers and investors.)

Corporate Reorganizations. Another responsibility of the Division of Corporate Regulation is the SEC's participation in corporate reorganizations. Reorganization proceedings in the U.S. District and Bankruptcy Courts are not initiated by the SEC but by a debtor

voluntarily, or by its creditors. Federal bankruptcy law allows a debtor in reorganization to continue to operate under the court's protection while it attempts to rehabilitate its business and work out a plan to pay its debts. Where a debtor corporation has outstanding publicly issued securities, the reorganization process raises many issues that materially affect the rights of its public investors. Therefore, the SEC may participate in corporate reorganization proceedings to protect the interests of public investors holding the debtor's securities and to provide independent, expert assistance to the courts and parties in a complex area of law and finance.

Andrew L. Rothman and Roxanne P. Fischetti

Securities Industry Automation Corporation (SIAC)

See STOCK EXCHANGES.

Securities Investor Protection Act of 1970 (SIPA)

A federal statute effective December 30, 1970, which created the SECURITIES INVESTOR PROTECTION CORPORATION (SIPC) and established procedures for liquidating financially troubled securities broker/dealers who are members of SIPC.

In passing SIPA, Congress's objective was to protect—up to certain defined limits—the customers of failed broker/dealers against loss of cash and securities. While protecting customers, SIPA's provisions for completion of open contractual commitments between broker/dealers limit the economic impact of failure on the brokerage community.

The Chandler Act (1938) was the first legislation recognizing the unique problems of a bankrupt broker/dealer's customers. An amendment to the Bankruptcy Act, that legislation addressed the priorities between a bankrupt broker/dealer's customers and other creditors.

In the late 1960s, existing customer protections proved inadequate and Congress passed SIPA. The legislation's general purposes were stated in the Senate report as follows:

... to protect individual investors from financial hardship; to insulate the economy from the disruption which can follow the failure of major financial institutions; and to achieve a general upgrading of financial responsibility requirements of brokers and dealers to eliminate, to the maximum extent possible, the risks which lead to customer loss.*

Jeffrey R. McCord

*S. Rep. 1218, 91st Cong., 2d sess. (1970), 4.

Securities Investor Protection Corporation (SIPC)

The United States Congress established the Securities Investor Protection Corporation in 1970 to provide customers of most registered securities broker/dealers with protection similar to that provided bank depositors by the Federal Deposit Insurance Corporation (FDIC). Unlike the FDIC, however, SIPC is neither a government agency nor a regulatory agency.

SIPC's creation followed a successful joint government and securities-industry legislative effort. Today, SIPC works closely with the securities industry's highly effective self-regulatory organizations, though it is subject to SECURITIES AND EXCHANGE COMMISSION (SEC) and congressional oversight.

SIPC's Origins. The operational and financial problems that securities brokers faced during the difficult years 1968 through 1970 posed a potential threat to the viability of U.S. securities markets. The "paperwork crunch," brought on by unexpectedly high trading volume followed by a sharp decline in stock prices, led hundreds of broker/dealers to either merge, seek to be acquired, or go out of business. Some were unable to meet their obligations to customers and went bankrupt.

The securities industry and Congress responded swiftly by designing a program to protect the funds and securities held for customers by broker/dealers. The SECURITIES INVESTOR PROTECTION ACT (SIPA) was signed into law in December 1970. SIPA created SIPC to afford certain protections against financial loss to customers of failed broker/dealers, and thereby promote investor confidence in the nation's securities markets. As of 1983 the limits of protection were $500,000 per securities customer, including up to $100,000 for cash claims.

SIPC is a nonprofit, membership corporation. Its members are, with some exceptions, all persons registered as brokers or dealers under Section 15(b) of the Securities Exchange Act of 1934 and all persons who are members of a national securities exchange.*

Today it is unlikely that many investors will need the protection afforded by SIPC. Since SIPC's creation in 1970, the corporation has initiated customer-protection proceedings for only 161—or about 1%—of the approximately 14,700 brokers who have been SIPC members. Nevertheless, all securities customers should know SIPC stands behind them.

SIPC maintains a customer-protection fund, underwritten by its member broker/dealers and which by law must aggregate at least $150 million in cash and U.S. government securities. Additionally, though never needed, the SEC has authority to lend SIPC up to $1 billion, drawn from the U.S. Treasury.

Customer Protection. SIPC goes into action the moment it learns from the SEC, NATIONAL ASSOCIATION OF SECURITIES DEALERS, INC. (NASD), or one of the STOCK EXCHANGES that a member broker/dealer is in or approaching financial difficulty. Before initiating a customer-protection proceeding—essentially, a liquidation—SIPC gathers and assesses financial data on the firm in question and determines whether or not the customers require protection.

If customers need protection, SIPC typically applies to a U.S. district court for the appointment of SIPC, or a person designated by SIPC, as trustee in a proceeding to liquidate the business of the failed member (hereafter referred to as the "debtor"). Promptly after appointment, trustees publish notice of a proceeding's commencement in one or more newspapers of general circulation. A copy is also mailed to all recorded customers of the debtor with open accounts within the preceding 12 months.

"Customer" Defined. SIPC's Section 16(2) defines *customers* as persons with claims on account of securities received, acquired, or held by the debtor in the ordinary course of its broker/dealer business from or for securities accounts of such persons (1) for safekeeping, (2) with a view to sale, (3) to cover consummated sales, (4) pursuant to purchases, (5) as collateral security, or (6) for purposes of effecting transfer.

The term *customer* also includes persons with claims against the debtor arising from sales or conversions of such securities, and persons who have deposited cash with the debtor for the purpose of purchasing securities. The term does not include, however, persons to the extent that they have claims for property that by contract, agreement, or understanding, or by operation of law, is a part of the capital of the debtor or is subordinated to the claims of the debtor's creditors. Nor does it include any person to the extent that that person's claim arises from transactions with a SIPC member's foreign subsidiary.

A customer must file a written statement of claim. A claim form accompanies each notice mailed to customers, and claims must be filed within six months after the publication of notice, with a few exceptions.

*Section 3(a)(2)(A) of SIPC excludes (1) persons whose principal business, in the determination of SIPC, taking into account business of affiliated entities, is conducted outside the United States and its territories and possessions; and (2) persons whose business as a broker or dealer consists exclusively of (*a*) the distribution of shares of registered open-end investment companies or unit investment trusts, (*b*) the sale of variable annuities, (*c*) the business of insurance, or (*d*) the business of rendering investment advisory services to one or more registered investment companies or insurance-company separate accounts.

Transfer of Customer Accounts. In certain cases, the trustee may transfer some or all customer accounts to another SIPC member if a transfer will facilitate prompt satisfaction of customer claims and liquidation of the debtor's business. A transfer's feasibility depends on several factors. These include the condition of the debtor's books and records, and the availability of an SIPC member interested in assuming the debtor's customer accounts, capable of handling the transfer, and effectively servicing the new accounts.

Account transfers minimize disruption of customers' access to their cash and securities. A customer whose account has been transferred may deal with the receiving firm or any transfer the account to another firm.

Satisfaction of Customer Claims. When a transfer is not feasible, customer claims are satisfied by the trustee in the following manner:

First, customers of a failed firm receive "customer name" securities registered in their names or in the process of being so registered, pursuant to instructions from the debtor. Not included are securities on hand registered in customer name and in negotiable form. Those securities are considered part of "customer property" (see below).* There is no limit on the value of such property returned.

Second, the customers receive all remaining customer-owned cash and securities held by the firm. There is no limit on the value of such "customer property" returned.† If there are insufficient securities to satisfy claims from "customer property," the trustee purchases the missing shares if a fair and orderly market exists. If that cannot be done, the trustee allocates the available securities pro rata and makes up the shortage by paying customers cash in lieu thereof. The amount paid is based on the value of the securities on the "filing date"—the day on which liquidation or bankruptcy proceedings commenced, or the date a receiver for the debtor was appointed.

Third, SIPC's funds are available to satisfy remaining claims of each customer up to a maximum of $500,000. There is a limitation on this maximum figure: On claims for cash (as distinct from claims for securities), not more than $100,000 may be paid from SIPC's funds. Cash protection is discussed in greater detail below.

Finally, any remaining assets after payment of liq-

uidation expenses may be available to satisfy any remaining portion of a customer's claims on a pro rata basis with other creditors.

Several Protected Accounts in "Separate" Capacities. Though this completes the discussion of SIPC's basic protection, substantial investors should know they may maintain more than one protected account with the same broker, providing each is held in a separate capacity. Consider a customer who deals with an SIPC member for himself and also maintains accounts as a trustee for another person. Under certain trust arrangements he would be deemed a different SIPC-protected customer in each capacity. A customer having several different accounts must be acting in a good-faith separate capacity with respect to each.

All such accounts, however, must meet the requirements of SIPC rules, identifying accounts of "separate" customers of SIPC members. The rules may be obtained by writing to SIPC and requesting the "Series 100 Rules."

A person who in a *single* capacity has several different accounts with the same firm—e.g., cash and margin—would be considered a single customer for purposes of applying the $500,000/$100,000 limits.

Cash Balances and Money Funds. Such broker/dealer products as money-market funds and various new cash-management services have become particularly popular with many individuals who have had little or no previous broker contact. Accustomed to FDIC protection of bank accounts and FSLIC savings insurance, such customers will be interested in the terms of SIPC protection of securities accounts, interest-bearing cash balances, and money funds.

Shares of money-market funds, although often thought of by investors as cash, are in fact securities when such funds are organized as mutual funds in which shares are issued and traded as securities. When held by a SIPC member in a customer's securities account, such funds are protected as any other covered security. It is important to remember, however, that SIPC protection does not cover decline in the value of securities.

Cash balances are protected under SIPA if the money was deposited or left in a securities account for the purpose of purchasing securities. This is true whether or not the broker pays interest on the cash balances. Of course, cash balances maintained solely for the purpose of earning interest are not protected.

SIPC presumes that cash balances are left in securities accounts for the purpose of purchasing securities. It would require substantial evidence to the contrary to overcome this presumption. Standing alone, the fact that a cash balance was earning interest and was

---

*SIPC protects most types of securities, such as notes, stocks, bonds, debentures and certificates of deposit. *No protection, however, is provided for unregistered investment contracts or for any interest in a commodity contract or commodity option.*

†*Customer property:* "Customer property" means cash and securities (except "customer name securities" delivered to the customer) at any time received, acquired, or held by or for the account of a debtor from or for the securities accounts of a customer. This includes the proceeds of any such property transferred by the debtor, including property unlawfully converted.

not used to purchase securities for a considerable period of time—say, four or five months—would not be sufficient to overcome the presumption.

SIPC Protection Exceeds $500,000/$100,000. As can be seen above, a securities customer's protection is greater than the dollar limits of SIPC advances alone suggest. SIPC's limits only come into play after customer property has been distributed. A customer with a remaining claim is a creditor of the general estate and may recover some or all of the balance owed him.

Higher limits and other protection improvements over the years have reduced the number of customers with claims over the SIPC limits of protection. Of 160,000 claims satisfied since SIPC's inception in 1970, only 260 were for property in excess of SIPC's limits.

In conclusion, investor protection has improved dramatically since 1970 as the self-regulatory apparatus has been refined, as member broker/dealer operations have been modernized, and as more stringent requirements for entry into the industry and higher minimum capital requirements have been instituted. The 1978 amendments to SIPA improved investor protection by providing more flexible and effective methods of conducting customer-protection proceedings, while increasing the amount SIPC could advance for each customer's claim. In 1980 the limits of SIPC advances were further increased to the current maximum of $500,000, with a limitation of $100,000 for claims for cash.

SIPA is a complex statute. Definitive answers to many questions concerning SIPA's application to various persons or situations will depend on future interpretations and administrative and court decisions.

Jeffrey R. McCord

Securities Markets and the Securities Industry

The basic job of the securities markets and the securities industry is to bring together the suppliers and users of long-term capital, matching their needs in the most efficient way possible.

An important part of the funds raised each year by U.S. business and state and local governments comes from the sale of securities. Typically, these funds are used to finance long-term projects and, in the case of corporations, to build a stronger base for generating profits. Capital raised through the securities markets can be especially important to smaller, emerging corporations, which frequently lack the internal resources to finance new facilities and products.

For investors, the securities markets serve the very important function of providing a mechanism through which securities can be bought and sold readily at fair prices. Through these markets, individuals and financial institutions can invest for current income and/or capital appreciation. Furthermore, investors can choose from an extremely broad array of instruments—from the most conservative investments to the most aggressive, depending on specific financial objectives.

How Capital Is Raised Through an Underwriting— The Primary Market. The essence of an underwriting is that a group of securities firms purchases securities directly from an issuer and assumes all risk of being able to resell them to investors. In this way, the underwriting group provides the issuer with a guaranteed amount of capital. In 1982, U.S. corporations raised $83.8 billion through the sale of stocks and bonds in the primary market.

Assume a corporation or government agency needs capital to construct a building, buy equipment, or finance practically any other major project. Though internal resources to cover the investment may be available, a decision might be made to raise part or all of the money externally. In considering this option, it is faced with a number of key questions:

- How much money does it want, and will it be able to raise the full amount?
- What is the relative feasibility of various external sources: public offerings of securities, private placements, commercial paper, bank loans?
- How much will the money being raised "cost"? What prospective rates of return will be needed to attract buyers?
- What is the best timing? Are market conditions most favorable for the offering now, or does it appear best to wait?

Typically, the securities firm that has been retained by the would-be raiser of capital will then seek out other securities firms to join in an underwriting syndicate. By joining together, syndicate members can combine their underwriting capital, spread the risks, and increase their distribution capability. This syndicate will be created expressly for the underwriting in question and will be disbanded when it is completed.

The underwriting syndicate is responsible for organizing the offering, negotiating the price and other terms with the issuer, putting up cash to buy the securities, marketing the securities, and absorbing any financial losses if the sale does not go as well as expected. For these services, the underwriters either charge the issuer a commission or purchase the securities from the issuer at a discount from the public offering price.

Unique Characteristics of the U.S. Securities Markets. The U.S. securities markets, generally regarded as the strongest in the world, are unique in three significant ways:

First, America has been described as the land of "people's capitalism" because of widespread public participation in the investment markets. In addition to the estimated 30 to 35 million Americans who own securities directly, approximately 130 million hold shares indirectly through pension funds and other institutions. The concept of people's capitalism has played a vital role in democratizing the nation's economic system, building individual wealth and converting huge amounts of individual savings to long-term capital for business and government.

Second, under the U.S. system, long-term capital is allocated to users through the diverse buy-and-sell decisions of investors. In most other nations, capital is allocated through a few giant financial institutions or through central planning and control. Major advantages of the U.S. free market approach include its ability to direct capital rapidly and efficiently to economic sectors with the brightest prospects.

Third, the American markets also are distinguished by their liquidity—that is, their ability to absorb large transactions with little or no distortion of securities prices. A high degree of liquidity means that investors can buy and sell securities—and corporations and government agencies can raise large amounts of long-term capital—rapidly and at fair prices.

The Role of the Securities Industry. Why should anybody be concerned about the viability of the securities industry, considering that its overall size—some 5,000 firms, more than 150,000 employees and annual revenues of $23 billion—is modest compared with any number of other primary U.S. industries?

One reason is that the securities industry stands at the middle of the critical relationship between suppliers and users of capital. If the industry fails to do its job well, there will be a variety of negative implications for the nation's economy—in terms of capital availability and, consequently, inflation, economic competitiveness, job creation, and other key economic concerns.

Broadly defined, the industry's responsibilities include:

- channeling funds to meet the long-term capital needs of business and governments
- raising short-term funds for the day-to-day operations of business and government through the marketing of commercial paper and various short-term government securities

- finding attractive opportunities for investors
- providing numerous services that, among other things, give the securities markets greater liquidity, enhance their valuation function, and help investors, corporations, and government bodies make intelligent financial choices

One of the industry's most important activities is the marketing of securities. Part of the industry's job is to create investment vehicles that will match the capital needs of corporations and government bodies to the available investment funds of individuals and institutions.

Money-market funds, bond funds, and mortgage pass-through securities are recent examples of innovative new vehicles that have attracted billions of dollars of capital. But even in the case of such long-standing vehicles as common stock and bonds, creativity and sensitivity to the interests of buyers are essential. In the "design" of new common-stock issues, for instance, securities firms advise clients on dividend rates, debt/equity ratios, and other elements relating to client needs and to the stock's attractiveness to prospective buyers. And in the case of bonds and other conventional debt instruments, yield, maturity, and call protection are among the many variables that investors consider before committing their funds.

The decision to save or invest is voluntary, which is why marketing is so important. People are free to allocate each dollar of disposable income in any way they see fit—toward a night on the town, for instance, or a new refrigerator, or "tangible" investments like gems and rare coins. To the extent that the securities industry is able to induce people to use some of their money to buy securities, it adds directly to the flow of funds available to business and government. The industry employs more than 60,000 salespeople, whose major function is to facilitate the process of investing and point out potentially rewarding opportunities to clients.

In addition, the industry is responsible for providing the liquidity that enables investors to resell—itself an important inducement for investing. Day in and day out, securities firms place billions of dollars of capital at risk in their market-making activities to help provide this liquidity. Unlike almost any other investment medium—real estate, art, antiques, coins, gems, etc.—securities can be resold rapidly and at an average commission of less than 2%.

Dozens of specific services are provided by the securities industry in fulfilling its basic functions:

- research services, economic forecasting, and advice on investment opportunities
- securities brokerage, or the execution of customer's

Table 1
Securities Products

Type of Security	Security of	Long- or Short-Term
Bankers' acceptances	Commercial banks	Short-term
Certificates of deposit	Commercial banks Savings banks Savings & loan associations Credit unions	Short-term
Commercial paper	Corporations	Short-term
Common stock	Corporations	Long- or short-term
Debt obligations (bonds)	Corporations Municipalities Government agencies	Long-term
Futures/options	Equity purchases in financial products or commodities of corporations or exchange indexes	Short-term
Mutual funds	Corporations U.S. government	Long-term
Puts/calls/warrants	Equity purchases of corporate preferred or common stocks/options to purchase additional shares	Short-term
Preferred stock	Corporations	Long- or short-term
Repos (repurchase of bonds)	U.S. government Municipalities	Short-term
Savings bonds	U.S. government	Long-term
Treasury bills	U.S. government	Short-term
Treasury bonds	U.S. government	Long-term
Treasury notes	U.S. government	Short-term

Source: Edward I. O'Brien.

buy and sell orders as agents on securities exchanges and in the over-the-counter markets
- market-making, in which a securities firm facilitates investor transactions by acting as buyer or selling securities out of inventory
- investor record-keeping and the "clearing" (processing) of transactions
- large "block" transactions, primarily for institutions
- safekeeping of customers' securities
- portfolio management
- financial-planning services

Edward I. O'Brien

Series EE Savings Bonds

See UNITED STATES SAVINGS BONDS.

Series HH Savings Bonds

See UNITED STATES SAVINGS BONDS.

Shared-Appreciation Mortgage (SAM)

See HOME FINANCING, MORTGAGES.

Shared-Equity Mortgage (SEM)

See HOME FINANCING, MORTGAGES.

Short Interest

See COMMON STOCK.

Short Sale

See COMMON STOCK.

Simple Interest

Interest computed and paid on the original principal only. It does not represent payment on the interest that has accumulated.

See also DAILY COMPOUNDING; INTEREST RATES, CALCULATION OF.

Harvey Rachlin

Sinking-Fund Provision

See PREFERRED STOCK.

Small Business Administration (SBA)

As one of the smallest federal agencies, the U.S. Small Business Administration is responsible for one of the largest, if not *the* largest, constituencies of the government. Created by Congress in 1953, SBA is an independent federal agency with a mandated responsibility to assist, counsel, and champion the more than 13 million small businesses in America.

The basic goal of SBA is to help people get into business and stay in business. In order to do this, the agency acts as an advocate on behalf of small businesses by supporting, encouraging, and marketing the cause of small business, explaining the roles of small businesses and the contributions they have made to our society and economy, and by advocating policies and programs that will benefit small businesses.

Historically, SBA's function has been to provide financial assistance to the prospective small-business owner and to both new and established small businesses. However, SBA has shifted that responsibility to the banking and finance community, through methods of preferred-lender status for banks and savings and loans, and by guaranteeing up to 90% of a loan made by a local bank to a small business. At the same time, SBA has concentrated on aiding small-business owners with management counseling and training, and with help obtaining direct government procurement contracts.

A targeted effort of the agency is assisting women, minorities, the handicapped, and veterans who desire to get into business; and once that is accomplished, SBA wants to assist them in every way possible to ensure they stay in business. In this regard, SBA works closely with lenders, other federal agencies, and state and local governments to encourage the assistance of small businesses throughout the country. SBA

also is responsible for loans to victims of natural disasters to help them repair or replace personal property, homes, and businesses that have been damaged or destroyed.

The agency has approximately 4,400 employees operating out of more than 100 offices nationwide. The location of the nearest SBA office can be found in the white pages of the telephone book under "U.S. Government."

James C. Sanders

Social Security

Social Security is the nation's basic method of providing a continuing income when family earnings are reduced or stopped because of retirement, disability, or death. It was enacted in 1935 during the Great Depression—a period that saw the nation's banking institutions collapse and the unemployment rolls swell from 1.5 million to 12 million people. In answer to those perilous times, President Roosevelt embarked upon the "New Deal," a proliferation of government programs designed to put America back to work and to provide income security for those most vulnerable in this society. Social Security was the cornerstone of that effort.

The original Social Security Act provided old-age retirement benefits, unemployment-insurance benefits, and cash assistance to needy aged and blind Americans. Today, Social Security generally refers to the old-age, survivors, and disability-insurance (OASDI) cash benefit programs and MEDICARE. So many changes occurred after 1935 that its operations now affect almost every man and woman in this country.

To illustrate, during 1983 about 116 million people worked in employment covered by the Social Security program. Workers paid into the system 6.70% of annual earnings up to $35,700. (Employers were taxed an equal amount.) On the outgo end of the scale, some 36 million people received Social Security benefits each month that year, the average monthly benefit amount totaling $411.

In contrast, during 1950—ten years after the program began paying benefits—48 million people worked in covered employment, paying Social Security taxes of 1.5% on annual earnings up to $3,000. Only 3.5 million people received Social Security benefits in December 1950; by December 1960, the fourth year that disability benefits were payable, the number of beneficiaries had increased fourfold to 14.8 million people. At the end of 1950, the average monthly benefit amount was $42.50.

To sum up this growth in yet another way, by 1983

an employee who had paid the maximum Social Security tax throughout his or her working lifetime would have contributed $19,328.39. In contrast, by 1950, no one could have paid more than $435 into the system. The maximum tax that year was $45. The average tax was only $38.

Who Is Covered. The original law covered virtually all workers in commerce and industry. Subsequently, coverage was extended to the vast majority of workers in the country. The 1950 act brought in agricultural and domestic workers, most self-employed workers, state and local government employees *not* covered by a retirement system (on an elective basis), and employees of nonprofit charitable, educational, and religious organizations. In 1954, coverage was extended to self-employed farmers and to employees of state and local governments covered by retirement systems (on an elective basis). Thus, in February 1983, of the approximately 13 million state and local government workers in the United States, some 9 million were covered by Social Security.

Extension of coverage to other small employment categories was accomplished in later years. Currently, the only major groups not covered are permanent federal civilian employees and those state and local government employees and nonprofit employees for whom coverage has not been elected. Railroad workers have a separate plan, which is closely coordinated with OASDI as to both benefit provisions and financing.

Age Requirements. The minimum retirement age for full benefits has always been 65. Early-retirement benefits at reduced rates became available at age 62 (with a 20% reduction) for women as a result of the 1956 act, and for men as a result of the 1961 act.

The minimum age for benefits for spouses of retired workers was initially 65. Reduced benefits are now available as early as 62.

Benefits for children of retired, disabled, or deceased workers are paid up to age 18 (19 if the child is in a secondary school), or longer if the child is disabled.

Benefits for aged surviving spouses were originally available only at age 65 and over. At present, however, widows and widowers can receive reduced benefits as early as age 60, or age 50 if they are disabled. Survivor children and their parents can receive benefits in the same manner as those of retirees.

Benefit Amounts. Benefits have always been related to average lifetime earnings, but they have been heavily weighted to provide *relatively* larger amounts to low-paid workers than to high-paid ones. The level of benefits has been changed frequently over the years so as to keep up to date, approximately, with changes in economic conditions. Until 1975 such changes were made in an ad hoc manner by legislation. However, beginning in 1975, benefits have been automatically adjusted each year to reflect increases in the consumer price index. Also, workers' earnings records are adjusted for years after 1950 up to the year of attaining age 60 (or at death or disability, if earlier) to reflect past changes in the general level of earnings.

How Earnings Affect Benefits. In general, benefits are not payable when beneficiaries have substantial employment. However, certain specified amounts of earnings are allowed, and any earnings over that amount result in a gradual reduction of benefits. The annual exempt amount in 1983 was $6,600 for persons age 65 or over and $4,920 for younger beneficiaries. These amounts will be automatically adjusted in the future in accordance with increases in average wages. (Any income from savings, investments, or insurance does not affect monthly checks.)

The earnings test applies to all types of beneficiaries. An exception to the earnings test applies to persons age 70 and over, for whom full benefits are payable regardless of the extent of employment.

Building Protection. The amounts of people's monthly Social Security checks are based on their earnings during their working lives. However, neither they nor their families can receive checks if a sufficient amount of credits have not been attained. The exact amount of work credit depends on one's age.

Social Security credit is measured in "quarters of coverage." In 1983, employees and self-employed people received one quarter of coverage for each $370 of covered annual earnings. No more than four quarters of coverage can be credited for a year. The amount of earnings needed to get a quarter of coverage will increase automatically every year to keep pace with average wages.

If individuals stop working under Social Security before they have earned enough credit, they cannot get benefits, but the credit they have already earned will remain on record and can be increased once they return to work covered under Social Security. Workers who reach age 62 in 1991 or later need 40 quarters of work in jobs covered by Social Security.

Work Credit for Disability. The work requirements are different for the disability-insurance program. Persons who become disabled before reaching age 24 will need credit for one and a half years of work in the three years preceding the disability. If they are between age 24 and 31, they must have credit for half the time between their twenty-first birthday and the time they become disabled. Those who become disabled at 31 or later generally need credit for at least five years of work out of the ten years ending when they become disabled. Workers disabled at age 42 or older, however, need more credit, depending on their age and when they become disabled, but never more than 40 quarters of work.

Those disabled by blindness do not have to meet the requirement of recent work, but they do need credit for one-fourth of a year for each year since 1950 (or the year they reached 21, if later), up to the year they become blind. A minimum of one and a half years of credit is needed.

Special Rules. Although almost all jobs in the United States are covered by Social Security, there are special rules that apply to some people. Individuals should check with a Social Security office about these special rules if they work in or about someone's home doing housecleaning, gardening, or baby-sitting; if they are students and also are employed by their school or college; if they own, operate, or work on a farm; if they are members of a religious order; if they have jobs that provide cash tips; or if they are employees of a state or local government or a nonprofit or international organization. Special rules also apply to people who work or are self-employed outside the United States. Leaving the United States for 30 days or more while getting checks may affect one's right to receive them.

Social Security Administration

Social Security Administration (SSA)

The Social Security Administration is a federal agency that is a division of the DEPARTMENT OF HEALTH AND HUMAN SERVICES. It is responsible for administering various social programs, including the Old-Age, Survivors, and Disability Insurance; SUPPLEMENTAL SECURITY INCOME (SSI); AID TO FAMILIES WITH DEPENDENT CHILDREN (AFDC); child-support enforcement; and refugee resettlement. Its headquarters are located in Baltimore, Maryland, but it has over 1,300 full-time offices located throughout the United States.

Social Security refers to the Old-Age, Survivors, and Disability Insurance (OASDI) program and was first established by the Social Security Act of 1935. Many changes have occurred in the program subsequent to 1935, so that it now affects almost every resident of the United States.

During 1982, about 116 million persons worked in employment covered by Social Security and about 36 million persons received cash benefits at a monthly rate of $13 billion. The total benefit payments under the Social Security program in 1982 amounted to about $156 billion.

Social Security is the nation's basic method of providing a continuing income when family earnings are reduced or stop because of retirement, disability, or death. In 1982, nine out of ten workers in the United States were earning protection under Social Security, and about one out of every six persons in the country received a monthly Social Security check.

Social Security Administration

Social Welfare

In the United States there are various federal, state, and local government programs whose purpose is to protect the public from the economic hazards of old age, disability, illness, unemployment, and death. These programs have evolved over a period of time as changing social and economic conditions warrant, and will presumably, continue to be modified, increased in scope, or diminished as future conditions dictate.

Early American history was characterized by pioneering individuals who battled a challenging physical world in carving out their economic niches. In the beginning the country's economy was primarily agricultural, and, perhaps in some measure because of the cooperative nature of such work and the need for people to stick together in the face of adverse conditions, family and community ties tended to be close. If economic disaster struck, financial assistance and other types of aid was readily obtainable from family and neighbors.

After the Civil War, however, industry grew rapidly, replacing agriculture as the predominant economic sector in the country. Hordes of people moved to the cities, where many individuals and families found themselves with less security against economic and personal misfortune. Poverty sprang up, and cities encountered such problems as slums and crime. Forms of relief were created to assist the needy and handicapped. In the early part of this century, public assistance and protection against economic insecurity were mostly limited to institutional arrangements for homeless children and for the disabled, the insane, and the needy aged. There were state workmen's compensation programs; old-age and mothers' pensions; retirement programs for certain government classes of work; veterans' benefits; and charity. The Social Security Act of 1935 established two national social-insurance programs (old-age and unemployment) and provided other forms of public relief. Through the years, legislation at all levels of government has generally expanded the scope and increased the benefits of existing programs as well as creating new ones intended to protect and aid citizens against any event or circumstance in which they cannot meet their economic needs.

The major Social Security, social-service, and public assistance programs, which have been classified here under the term *social welfare,* are summarized in Table 1 (pages 567–569).

Harvey Rachlin

Table 1
Social Welfare Programs

Program	Brief Description	Administered by	Where to Apply
Aid to Families with Dependent Children (AFDC)	A state-administered, federally regulated program of income support for families with dependent children. Its purpose is to protect dependent children in poor families that lack parental support and the resources to provide for them.	States; supervised by the Social Security Administration	Local public-assistance office
Child Nutrition Programs	The Child Nutrition Programs—the National School Lunch, School Breakfast, Summer Food Service, and Child Care Food programs—serve nutritious meals to children attending schools, child-care institutions, and summer recreational programs. Needy children can receive these meals free or at a reduced price. The Food and Nutrition Service works through state agencies, providing them with cash subsidies and commodities for use in preparing and serving meals.	States and Food and Nutrition Service (FNS) of the U.S. Department of Agriculture	Local public-assistance office
Child-Support Enforcement	A federal/state program to locate absent parents and help obtain support payments for their children.	Federal government and state child-support-enforcement agencies	Local welfare or social-service agency
Commodity Supplemental Food Program	USDA buys supplemental foods that state and local distributing agencies provide to low-income women, infants, and children free of charge. The Food and Nutrition Service also provides cash assistance to distributing agencies to help them offset their operating costs.	States and Food and Nutrition Service (FNS)	Local public-assistance office
Food Donations Program	The Food and Nutrition Service administers two food-distribution programs under the Food Donations Program: Commodities for Needy Families, and the Elderly Nutrition Program. Under the Needy Family program, FNS acquires and distributes agricultural commodities to needy persons on Indian reservations and in the Trust Territory of the Pacific. In the Elderly Nutrition Program, FNS provides cash and commodities to elderly feeding projects, which serve low-cost, nutritious meals to senior citizens.	States and Food and Nutrition Service (FNS)	Local public-assistance office
Food-Stamp Program	Food stamps are a form of currency issued to eligible low-income persons to help them buy a better diet. The Food and Nutrition Service administers the program in cooperation with state welfare agencies, and provides for the full cost of the food stamps themselves in addition to sharing all direct and indirect administrative costs incurred by the states on a 50-50 basis.	States and Food and Nutrition Service (FNS)	Local public-assistance office

(cont)

Table 1   *(cont)*
Social Welfare Programs

Program	Brief Description	Administered by	Where to Apply
General Assistance Programs	"General assistance" is the term most frequently applied to public financial assistance to those who cannot qualify under a federal/state assistance program. It is financed from state or local funds, or a combination of the two. It is also called "home relief," "outdoor relief," "direct relief," or "emergency relief."	States	Local public-assistance office
Low-Income Energy Assistance Program	A block grant to a state or tribe to help low-income individuals (households) meet *rising* costs of home energy. Each state devises its own plan for allocating benefits.	States and tribes on grants from the Department of Health and Human Services, Social Security Administration, Office of Family Assistance	Local public-assistance office
Lower-Income Rental Assistance	Aids lower-income families in obtaining decent, safe, and sanitary housing in private accommodations. HUD makes up the difference between what a lower-income household can afford and the fair market rent for an adequate housing unit. Lower-income families whose incomes do not exceed 50% of the median income for the area are eligible to occupy the assisted units. Project sponsors may be private owners, profit-motivated and nonprofit or cooperative organizations, public housing agencies, and state housing-finance agencies.	Department of Housing and Urban Development	Local housing authority
Medicaid	A federal/state assistance program for certain groups of needy, low-income people that helps pay their medical bills. Benefits vary somewhat by state.	States and Health Care Financing Administration of the U.S. Department of Health and Human Services	Local public-assistance office
Medicare	A federal health-insurance program that pays hospital and medical bills for most people age 65 and over, for certain disabled people under 65, and for patients with permanent kidney failure.	Health Care Financing Administration of the U.S. Department of Health and Human Services	Local Social Security office
Nutrition Assistance for Puerto Rico	The Food and Nutrition Service provides the Commonwealth of Puerto Rico with a Nutrition Assistance block grant to use in operating a food-assistance program for low-income people. This grant replaced the food-stamp program in Puerto Rico in July 1982.	Commonwealth of Puerto Rico on a grant from the Department of Agriculture	Local office of the Department of Social Services
Public Employee Programs	Federal, state, and local government programs that provide retirement, disability, and survivors' benefits for civilian employees.	Federal, state, and local governments	Personnel offices of federal, state, and local governments
Railroad Social Insurance	Comprehensive social-insurance protection for employees of railroads, railroad associations, and railway labor organizations.	Railroad Retirement Board	Local Railroad Retirement office

Table 1 *(cont)*
Social Welfare Programs

Program	Brief Description	Administered by	Where to Apply
Social Security	The nation's basic social-insurance program of providing a continuing income when family earnings are reduced or stop because of retirement, disability, or death.	Social Security Administration	Local Social Security office
Special Milk Program	The Special Milk Program helps schools, nonprofit child-care centers, and camps that have no federally assisted food programs serve milk to children at little or no cost. The Food and Nutrition Service provides cash subsidies to state-administered programs and directly administers the program in 19 states.	States and Food and Nutrition Service (FNS)	Local public-assistance office
Special Supplemental Food Program (WIC)	In the WIC Program, pregnant, postpartum, and breastfeeding women, and also infants and children up to 5 years of age who are found to be at "nutritional risk," receive free supplemental foods from their local health clinic. State departments of health receive cash grants from the Food and Nutrition Service for this activity.	States and Food and Nutrition Service (FNS)	Local public-assistance office
Supplemental Security Income (SSI)	A cash assistance program that provides a financial base for people 65 or over, or who are blind or disabled, and who have limited assets and income.	Social Security Administration	Local Social Security office
Temporary-Disability Insurance	Provides cash benefits to workers who lose wages due to temporary nonoccupational disability. Five states—California, Hawaii, New Jersey, New York, Rhode Island—and Puerto Rico have such a social insurance program.	State Workers' Compensation Board in New York; Department of Labor and Industrial Relations in Hawaii; and in California, New Jersey, Rhode Island, and Puerto Rico by the agency that administers unemployment insurance.	Appropriate state office
Unemployment Insurance	Cash benefits to regularly employed members of the labor force who become involuntarily unemployed and who are able and willing to accept suitable jobs.	U.S. Department of Labor	Local employment office
Vocational Rehabilitation Services	Provides grants to states for the development of comprehensive rehabilitation service programs specifically designed to reduce human dependency, increase self-reliance, and fully utilize the productive capacities of all handicapped persons.	States under grants from the Department of Education, Rehabilitation Services Administration	Local office of Vocational Rehabilitation
Workers' Compensation (Industrial Accident Insurance)	Cash benefits and medical care provided when a worker is injured in connection with his job, and monetary payments to his survivors if he is killed on the job.	Varies according to state; may be a state's labor department or an independent workers' compensation agency in the state.	Claims for compensation must be filed with the administering agency for due notice to the employer or insurer.

Sources: Virgil L. Conrad and Harvey Rachlin.

Sole Proprietorship

See BUSINESS ORGANIZATIONS, FORMS OF.

Specialist

See COMMON STOCK.

Special Milk Program

See SOCIAL WELFARE.

Special Supplemental Food Program

See SOCIAL WELFARE.

Special-Tax Bond

See MUNICIPAL AND STATE SECURITIES.

Speculation (Commodities)

See COMMODITY-FUTURES EXCHANGE.

Spokane Stock Exchange

It is 10:00 A.M. at the Spokane Stock exchange and the board marker begins calling such names as "Sunshine," "Hecla," "Callahan," and "Little Squaw Gold" and posting bids and offers for each as they are made from the floor by member mining brokers.

Thirty-eight registered stocks are called (as of September 1983), nearly all mining stocks, and most of the companies with properties in Idaho's famed Coeur d'Alene Mining District 80 miles east of Spokane. Speculators and investors view the daily auction from behind a railing in the public section of the exchange.

After the regular session ends at 11:30 A.M., the board quotations are printed on quotation sheets, as are interdealer quotations made earlier by exchange members on 105 unlisted over-the-counter mining stocks (as of September 1983). These issues are mostly of companies with mining properties in the Pacific Northwest, the majority in the Coeur d'Alene Mining District. They go by such interesting names as "Oom Paul," "Silver Surprize," "Amazon Dixie," and "Golden Chest."

The quotation sheets are distributed to clients of exchange members, to local newspapers, and to wire services, which provide the quotations to newspapers in other cities and to the electronic media. The *Spokane Daily Chronicle, Spokane Spokesman-Review, North Idaho Press,* and *Kellogg Evening News* are among the newspapers that carry the mining-stock quotations daily.

The Spokane Stock Exchange is the nation's leading registered stock exchange handling mining shares, and the only exchange, mining or otherwise, that allows open trading. It also is one of the oldest, having been in business 85 years. It was established on January 18, 1897, to meet a need for a central marketplace for buying and selling of shares of mining firms profiting from a number of rich copper and silver discoveries in southern British Columbia. The exchange started with 32 members and 37 listed mining stocks. It grew and flourished with new mining booms in the Republic gold camp northwest of Spokane, in Stevens County north Spokane, in the Coeur d'Alenes east of Spokane, and in the Metaline District northeast of Spokane.

Soon after the turn of the century, the fabulous Hercules mine at Burke, Idaho, and other Coeur d'Alene District properties began coming into production. Hercules dividends created half a dozen millionaires. The Coeur d'Alene District ore bodies proved to go deeper than those of the other mining districts and its mines have yielded more than $4,212,164,000 worth of silver, lead, zinc, gold, and copper (through 1982). It contains the largest underground silver mines in the United States. Silver production in 1982 was more than 13 million ounces. The district's mines have yielded more silver than any other district in the world—more than 964 million ounces from 1884 through 1982.

Volume of trading on the Spokane Stock Exchange has been up and down with the markets in precious and base metals. One of the exchange's best years was during the 1980 silver boom when 29 million shares, valued at $49.5 million, were traded.

See STOCK EXCHANGES.

Benjamin Harrison

Standard & Poor's Corporation

For more than 120 years, Standard & Poor's has been providing the public with investment guidance, and today S&P is considered a leading source of authoritative, objective financial information and analysis and bond ratings. S&P produces more than 50 publications and electronically disseminated services that are used by investors and businessmen around the world who need detailed information and statistics on the leading U.S. industries and corporations. Among S&P's major services are the following:

Corporation Records. A seven-volume, continuously updated library of detailed business and financial information covering the history, products, officers, debt and equity issues, and annual-report statistics of thousands of major corporations. One volume of the set is *Daily News,* which provides up-to-the-minute information five days a week on 10,000 publicly held corporations.

Stock Reports. This series of books provides the investor with analytic information on some 4,000 corporations. *Stock Reports* is divided into three sets of four volumes. The reports cover every company traded on the New York and American Stock Exchanges and some 2,000 companies sold over the counter. The two-page reports on each company are prepared by S&P's staff of stock and industry analysts and give the user ten years of company statistics; quarterly breakouts of sales; earnings and dividends; a summary of business operations; and forecasts of sales and earnings.

Industry Surveys. This two-volume, loose-leaf, continuously updated collection contains economic and investment reports on 65 of the country's leading industries, plus data on about 1,500 of their constituent companies. This material is published in a series of 32 surveys that graphically explore the environment in which the industries operate. For the investor or businessman, each survey is a primer on what has happened, what is happening, and what is likely to happen to the products, companies, and markets of each of the industries. The surveys cover all aspects of an industry, from the impact of tax and government policy to the labor situation.

Stock Guide. This is a pocket-size book that contains 44 columns of statistical and descriptive information on more than 5,000 common and preferred stocks. With the *Guide,* an investor gets current and historical stock data, plus indicators showing whether a stock's earnings—and the stock's S&P exclusive dividend and earnings ranking—are heading up or down.

The Outlook. This weekly advisory newsletter provides the investor with myriad current information, background, and forecasts for stocks, companies, and industries. Besides highlighting companies that are ripe for investment, *The Outlook* publishes a "master list of recommended issues." The list gives four distinct objective portfolios for investment guidance: Foundation Stocks for Longer-Term Gain; Stocks with Promising Growth Prospects; Cyclical/Speculative Stocks; and liberal Income with Inflation Protection. During the year, *The Outlook* comments on the investment merits of hundreds of stocks, and appraises its selections six months later.

Trendline publications. Three separate services publish marketing behavior charts on the most widely traded stocks on the New York, American, and OTC markets. These publications are the weekly *Daily Action Stock Charts,* with over 750 NYSE and American stock charts; the monthly *Current Market Perspective,* with 1,476 charts of the most widely traded listed stocks; and the *OTC Chart Manual,* a bimonthly compilation of 800 key OTC stocks. These publica-

tions not only give investors a graphic look at a stock's performance but also provide charts of highly significant indexes and indicators.

CreditWeek. This weekly publication comments on trends and outlook for fixed-income securities, and gives the investor in bonds a broad look at activity in this market. The publication also lists and explains all of the changes in credit ratings and new debt ratings S&P has made during the week. A section of the book vital to investors is "CreditWatch," which lists selected companies S&P is reviewing for rating changes, either upward or downward.

Bond Guide. A pocket-size book containing 41 columns of descriptive and statistical data gives the investor needed information on more than 5,000 corporate bonds. In addition, ratings are listed for nearly 10,000 municipal, general-obligation, and revenue bonds.

Commercial Paper Ratings Guide. This monthly service presents the vital data most critical for the informed selection of commercial paper of more than 1,000 issuers. Included is a rationale on the rating S&P analysts have given the paper.

CUSIP. These directories are the only available printed reference works of CUSIP Identification Numbers. The two hard-cover directories list over 1 million stocks, bonds, and warrants of 65,000 corporate and municipal issuers, domestic and foreign.

S&P handbooks. The company provides a series of handbooks that give immediate access to the facts and figures on stocks in a number of categories, including Growth, OTC, Oil & Gas, and High Yield. The handbooks contain concise two-page reports on the most widely traded stocks in these groupings.

Poor's Register of Corporations, Directors and Executives. A national directory of executive personnel listing over 400,000 company officials. In three volumes, the corporate volume provides executive rosters and business telephone numbers of 38,000 companies, plus principal product, number of employees, and names of primary bank and/or law firm. The directors and executives volume includes brief biographies of 70,000 officers and directors, with business and home addresses. The third volume lists companies in the register by SIC (industry) number and geographic location.

Security Dealers Directory. Issued twice a year, this volume lists more than 10,000 brokerage and investment-banking houses in the U.S. and Canada, along with their executive rosters.

Statistical Service. A comprehensive loose-leaf collection of the most important business, industry, and financial statistics, comprising over 1,000 statistical series, which are revised monthly. Among the series are long-term records of stock and bond prices, commodity prices, employment, foreign trade, product by industries, and many other government and industry figures.

Standard & Poor's also provides a number of electronically disseminated services. They include:

COMPMARK. Marketing and management information on 38,000 public and private companies, with listings, by function, of 405,000 executives.

COMPUSTAT. A data base of comparable financial statistics providing up to 20 years of annual income and balance-sheet, market, and supplemental statistics on nearly 6,000 companies, and up to 10 years of similar quarterly data on approximately 2,500 companies; available on magnetic tape or through time sharing.

Stock Guide Retrieval System. Provides ready or custom-made computer reports that are generated by screening the *Stock Guide* data base.

STOCKPAK. A system designed for use on a personal computer utilizing "diskettes" that provide access to 30 key financial statistics on 900 companies from the *Stock Guide.*

Fixed Income Management Systems. A computerized system that provides portfolio managers of fixed-income securities with analytic tools to better manage these portfolios, and also provides an accounting system that supplies amortization and accretion functions.

MarketScope. A real-time electronic information service that will provide registered representatives in brokerage houses with up-to-the-minute stock analyses, buy and sell recommendations, economic forecasts, and investment ideas.

Municipal Fund Pricing. Concerns itself with the evaluation of municipal bonds in unit trust funds. Currently, there is a par value of over $20 billion in these funds. There are approximately 25 active sponsors of these funds, which number 1,100.

Standard & Poor's Fixed Income Ratings. S&P is one of the major rating agencies in the country. It rates a wide variety of corporate and municipal bonds and commercial paper. There are now outstanding some 8,000 municipal ratings, 1,600 corporate ratings, and 950 commercial-paper ratings.

S&P rates bonds from AAA, the highest rating, to D, which is reserved for bonds in default. The company considers any rating from AAA to BBB to be of investment grade; those below BBB are listed as speculative. The S&P ratings and their descriptions are listed below.

AAA. Debt rated AAA has the highest rating assigned by Standard & Poor's. Capacity to pay interest and repay principal is extremely strong.

AA. Debt rated AA has a very strong capacity to pay interest and repay principal although it is somewhat more susceptible to the adverse effects of changes in

circumstances and economic conditions than debt in higher-rated categories.

BBB. Debt rated BBB is regarded as having an adequate capacity to pay interest and repay principal. Whereas it normally exhibits adequate protection parameters, adverse economic conditions or changing circumstances are more likely to lead to a weakened capacity to pay interest and repay principal for debt in this category than in higher-rated categories.

BB, B, CCC, CC. Debt rated BB, B, CCC, and CC is regarded, on balance, as predominantly speculative with respect to capacity to pay interest and repay principal in accordance with the terms of the obligation. BB indicates the lowest degree of speculation and CC the highest degree of speculation. While such debt will likely have some quality and protective characteristics, these are outweighed by large uncertainties or major risk exposures to adverse conditions.

C. The C rating is reserved for income bonds on which no interest is being paid.

D. Debt rated D is in default, and payment of interest and/or repayment of principal is in arrears.

Plus (+) or Minus (−). The ratings from AA to B may be modified by the addition of a plus or minus sign to show relative standing within the major rating categories.

The S&P 500 Stock Price Index. This measurement of stock performance has been used by professional and individual investors for more than 65 years. The index is one of the U.S. Commerce Department's 12 leading business indicators, and as such is an accepted barometer of economic conditions.

The S&P 500 comprises four major groups: 400 industrials, 40 public utilities, 20 transportation, and 40 financial. The majority of the stocks in these groups are traded on the New York Stock Exchange; but to give the index the broadest and strongest possible representation, some large banks, insurance companies, and corporations form the American Stock Exchange and over-the-counter market are included. Stocks making up the S&P 500 represent about 80% of the market value of the issues traded on the NYSE. Stocks that make up the index are divided among more than 90 industry subgroups that range alphabetically from Aerospace to Toys. These subgroups give investors a method of measuring industry performance.

The index is market-value-weighted rather than price-weighted. In the S&P Index, each stock is multiplied by the number of outstanding shares, thus each stock influences the index in proportion to its market importance.

The S&P Stock Price Index was introduced in 1917 as a weekly index, calculated on the basis of 200 common stocks divided into 26 subgroups. The S&P 500 was introduced 40 years later, in 1957. This index was supported by an expanded roster of 90 industry sub-indexes. Its base was set at 1941 − 1943 = 10, the same base used today.

Howard D. Hosbach

Statutory Disability Benefits Laws

Five states and Puerto Rico have statutory laws requiring the payment of weekly cash benefits to wage earners who are totally disabled as a result of *non-occupational* injury or sickness. This is entirely separate from and should not be confused with WORKERS' COMPENSATION insurance, which mandates benefits for *occupational* injury and illness. States with statutory-disability-benefits laws are California, Hawaii, New Jersey, New York, and Rhode Island. Employers can either purchase insurance through a private carrier or a state fund, or self-insure.

Sheila R. Wyse

Stepped Coupon Bond

This is a financing device that helps borrowers limit their costs while protecting investors against loss. Such bonds bear a rate of interest that is set prior to issuance and that increases or "steps up" from time to time during the life of the bond. The buyer of the bonds knows precisely what the rate is, and will be, on each maturity held. This feature helps distinguish these bonds from variable-rate issues, which peg coupon changes on a set formula geared to three-to-six-month Treasuries or the prevailing prime rate. The investor will know at the time of issuance what his coupon rate will be changed to at set dates for the life of the bond.

Moore & Schley Cameron & Company

Stock

See CAPITAL STOCK; COMMON STOCK; PREFERRED STOCK.

Stockbroker

A securities-firm executive whose function is to service clients seeking to buy and sell investment products. While the term *stockbroker,* in its narrowest sense, means one who acts as agent in putting together buyers and sellers of stocks, today such professionals, supported by the resources of sophisticated investment houses, are in a position to offer the public a much wider range of products, from annuities to zero-coupon bonds.

What role does the modern stockbroker play in dealing with his clients? That depends on how long

they've been investing—and their financial IQ. A very savvy customer may require merely the execution of a buy or sell order in the stock of a corporation traded on a major exchange, such as the New York or American Stock Exchange, and may not seek any counseling as to the wisdom of his investment decision. Even so, the skill of the broker and his firm is a vital ingredient in obtaining the best price for that client. Because he is called upon more and more to advise his accounts on how best to plan their lives financially, today's stockbroker usually refers to himself as an "account executive."

With the multitude of complex products and services available in the marketplace, how does he receive his training? The first step for the broker-to-be is applying to an investment firm to enter their training program. The large so-called wire houses, with coast-to-coast branch-office networks, provide extensive classroom work. Smaller firms offer a more personal program where one-on-one relationships with already successful account executives acting as mentors form the basis of an on-the-job training effort.

Regardless of the firm, each trainee, prior to being allowed to deal with clients, is required to pass the so-called Series 7 Examination as specified by the several regulatory bodies that govern the activities of the securities industry, including the New York Stock Exchange, American Stock Exchange, National Association of Securities Dealers, and Chicago Board Options Exchange. These groups, as well as the brokerage firms that comprise their memberships, come under the umbrella of the SECURITIES AND EXCHANGE COMMISSION (SEC), an agency of the federal government. Operating under the principle of self-regulation, the firms employing the account executives painstakingly ensure that clients are treated equitably and that only investments deemed suitable are recommended to them. After the trainee becomes "registered," he is permitted to solicit clients and to render investment advice. (Here the use of another term for stockbroker—*registered representative.*) Just as any professional's training never ceases—be he doctor, lawyer, etc.—so it is with the stockbroker. Via regular branch-office meetings, seminars run by firms or by the various securities exchanges, professional association activities, et al., the account executive's education is a continuing process. He now seeks to add the designation "Certified Financial Planner" to his business card. Being a C.F.P. signifies that the broker not only is well versed in the complexities of the investment products and services offered by his firm, but has also taken and passed a prescribed university course of study covering such subjects as personal budgeting, insurance, pension planning, estates, and taxation. This reflects the growing responsibility of the account executive of the future—namely, to become involved in an ongoing advisory relationship, *spanning virtually every phase of investing, as a means of executing a total financial plan for the client.*

In most cases, clients and their stockbrokers take a while to get to know one another before the total financial-planning concept comes into play. The relationship might begin with a recommendation from a friend who has benefited by the broker's advice. Sometimes an investor will respond to an advertisement or direct mail soliciation. In other instances, he'll seek out an account executive who specializes in a particular product.

How and where do you locate the right stockbroker? While there are nearly a thousand securities firms in the United States, not all of them deal with individual investors. Many service only banks, insurance companies, mutual funds, or other brokerages. These are known as "institutional" firms and their account executives don't service the public, otherwise known as the "retail" segment of the business.

One good source in the broker-selection process is the *Individual Investors Directory,* a booklet available from the New York Stock Exchange and containing a list of those member firms that serve the public. Determine which ones have conveniently located offices, pay them a visit, and discuss your investment objectives with the branch manager in charge. He'll assess your needs and recommend a suitable account executive on his staff.

The first several meetings will, of course, be exploratory; there's no obligation to disclose any financial information you don't care to, nor to purchase any security whatever. It's helpful, before discussing specific investments, to provide your stockbroker-to-be with some idea of the risks you can afford to take. This might include giving him or her some approximation of your overall net worth and how it's divided between securities, real estate, cash, and tangible assets.

The extent to which you have invested in the past will likely determine the posture your stockbroker will assume in initially laying out a strategy for the future. For example, if you already have a portfolio, your broker may suggest certain changes, depending on the goals you outline. Many clients use more than one broker, preferring to use different account executives for different types of investments, or preferring to mastermind their own financial plans with guidance from their accountants and attorneys. In such cases, that should be disclosed to the broker, who may wish to present specific products to both the client *and* his professional advisers.

Let's assume that you're a potential investor about to select a stockbroker. What kinds of investment possibilities is he or she likely to offer? Unless your net worth is so great that, even considering inflation,

you and your dependents can afford to live off the money provided by fixed-income securities such as bonds and preferred stock, you'll doubtless wish to discuss buying common stock in several diversified quality companies as an inflation hedge. Your investment goals may lie somewhere between maximizing capital appreciation and maximizing income. That will depend on the type of stocks you and your account executive ultimately select: basic industries versus high technology; large dividend-paying companies versus those that reinvest earnings; growth stocks versus cyclical ones. There are companies where earnings turnarounds are expected or where undervalued assets exist. The account executive may be aided in his selection process by the research staff of his firm. On the other hand, a number of excellent stockbrokers are also astute securities analysts in their own right and have the ability to identify companies whose securities are worth buying—or selling

Depending on your financial circumstances, your broker may suggest that you borrow money from his investment firm, at a predetermined interest rate, to buy securities. You'll have to put up a certain percentage of the purchase price, but the balance will be financed on "margin." Opening a margin account entails risk, which your stockbroker will explain.

After a long and successful relationship has developed, a customer may have sufficient confidence to give his broker discretion over the securities bought and sold for the account. Unless such permission is obtained in writing via a prescribed form, the client must give the broker verbal approval each time securities are bought or sold.

The account executive receives between 30% and 50% of the commission or markup paid by the client when a transaction takes place, depending on the firm's payout schedule and the annual production of the broker. Usually that constitutes his sole form of compensation; he receives no salary except in special cases. Successful account executives can earn in the mid–six-figure range.

But stocks and bonds aren't the only portfolio tools of the successful professional account executive. Here is a sampling of other major products that, depending on their clients' financial goals, may be suitable and accessible to the stockbroker:

Mutual finds—professionally managed securities portfolios that enable a client to diversify a small amount of capital into a wider variety of investments. There are mutual funds for just about every kind of security—bond funds, both corporate and municipal; common-stock funds, specific-industry funds, such as companies only in chemicals; option funds; and funds solely owning money-market instruments.

Securities whose underlying value is derived from that of other securities. These include preferred stock and bonds called "convertibles," which may be exchanged for common shares of the companies issuing them; options, warrants, and rights, which represent the right of their owner to buy or sell stocks, commodities, or certain indexes at specified prices prior to certain dates; futures, which are contracts for future delivery of a specific agricultural or industrial commodity (e.g., potatoes or silver), a stock index, such as that of the New York Stock Exchange, or on other debt instruments.

Insurance-company products—whole-life and term insurance as well as fixed and variable annuities. These are especially vital in comprehensive personal financial and estate planning.

Tax-sheltered investments, in which a percentage or multiple of the client's investment, usually as a limited partner, may be deductible for income-tax purposes. The most common ventures are oil and gas drilling or real-estate projects.

A stockbroker may have reason to suggest a number of different kinds of securities accounts other than the standard individual account. Joint accounts have special purposes, particularly in estate planning. A broker will probably also inquire as to whether the client has set up an INDIVIDUAL RETIREMENT ACCOUNT (IRA) and/or a KEOGH PLAN. If not, he or she can provide advice on taking advantage of these and other aspects of retirement planning.

Frequently, stockbrokers will want to know whether the individual client is also an officer of a corporation. If so, there are a number of important corporate services that the account executive, with the support of his firm, can render. One of these is raising needed capital from private sources or from the public via an underwriting. Another is seeking a merger or acquisition candidate. Of course, there are many others.

Whatever the particular assignment may dictate, the contemporary account executive, with his/her extensive array of financial wares, is a far cry from the "customer's man" of several decades ago.

The men and women choosing this exciting profession face several unusual challenges. The explosion of products brought about as competition intensifies among financial service industries calls for a high degree of expertise coupled with a comprehensive overview of swiftly changing economic conditions. Moreover, making intelligent investment decisions is sure to demand a level of computer literacy on the part of the stockbroker that is not required in other less information-intensive industries.

Steven A. Seiden

Stock Certificate

See COMMON STOCK.

Stock Exchanges

Organized marketplaces for securities where supply and demand are centralized and member brokers transact orders for individual and institutional investors and traders. Nearly 150 such marketplaces operate in countries all over the world.

In the United States, ten exchanges are registered with the SECURITIES AND EXCHANGE COMMISSION (SEC) as "national securities exchanges" under the terms of the Securities Exchange Act of 1934. No exchange operates under an exemption from registration. The registered exchanges and their locations are as follows: AMERICAN STOCK EXCHANGE (New York City), BOSTON STOCK EXCHANGE (Boston), CHICAGO BOARD OPTIONS EXCHANGE (Chicago), CINCINNATI STOCK EXCHANGE (Cincinnati), INTERMOUNTAIN STOCK EXCHANGE (Salt Lake City), MIDWEST STOCK EXCHANGE (Chicago), NEW YORK STOCK EXCHANGE (New York City), PACIFIC STOCK EXCHANGE (Los Angeles and San Francisco), PHILADELPHIA STOCK EXCHANGE (Philadelphia), and SPOKANE STOCK EXCHANGE (Spokane). Although it is registered to do so, the Chicago Board Options Exchange does not trade stocks or bonds; it is a marketplace for options to buy and sell securities.

The New York and American exchanges are the leading stock exchanges in this country. For the most part, they do not trade each other's securities. The Intermountain and Spokane exchanges deal primarily in the securities of low-priced speculative mining and extractive companies; they do not normally trade the securities listed on the various other exchanges. Stocks traded on the New York and American exchanges may also be traded on what are popularly known as the *regional exchanges*—Boston, Cincinnati, Midwest, Pacific, Philadelphia—either on a fully listed basis or on an unlisted basis. Stocks not traded on an exchange are traded in the OVER-THE-COUNTER (OTC) MARKET by dealers who are members of the NATIONAL ASSOCIATION OF SECURITIES DEALERS, INC. (NASD).

Economic Function. A stock exchange plays a vital role in a capitalistic economic system. It enables millions of people, directly or indirectly, to obtain a financial interest in the tools of production and distribution of goods and services through stock investment. As of the early 1980s, three out of four men, women, and children in the United States either owned shares of corporate stock or stock mutual funds directly in their own names or had an indirect stake through their pension funds, insurance policies, savings accounts, or other forms of institutional investment.

By providing a convenient mechanism for people

and institutions to put savings to work in business, a stock exchange makes possible additional economic growth, additional production, and additional jobs. By providing corporate businesses with a marketplace for their securities, an exchange makes it easier for companies to raise new money. Without such a marketplace, financing of industrial expansion would be sharply curtailed. At the same time, the ability of millions of individuals to plan for their own financial needs would be severely hampered.

In short, what the stock exchanges do is enable people to put their capital to work whenever they choose in a manner that gives them the opportunity to participate in the nation's economic growth. In a free economy, capital should be free to move from one enterprise to another. The stock exchanges provide the facilities for that freedom of movement. They give the saver a means by which he may convert his funds into securities that will benefit him through income, appreciation, or both—and, conversely, by which he may quickly convert those securities back into cash if his circumstances so require. Indeed, the key distinctions between U.S. and foreign stock exchanges are the high degree of liquidity and speed of transfer provided by a continuous auction-market system.

Listing Requirements. Each of the exchanges has listing requirements, which vary in degree of stringency. To be eligible for trading on a particular exchange, a corporation and its securities must meet certain standards. These standards deal with qualifications for initial listing and for continued listing thereafter. They typically cover such conditions as earnings, assets, market value, number of holders. In addition, the corporation must adhere to certain requirements for disclosure of information and protection of stockholder interests. To become listed, corporations submit their applications and pay the appropriate fees to the exchange on which they wish to list. They may list on more than one exchange.

In addition, the regional exchanges often apply to the SEC for the privilege of trading a particular company's stocks on an unlisted basis. In these cases, the company itself does not apply for the listing, nor does it pay listing fees. The SEC grants these requests readily. What sometimes happens, too, is that a company that originally may have had only local or regional interest remains listed on a regional exchange even after its growth and broader interest have enabled it to move to a listing on the New York or American Exchange.

In 1982, 85% of the dollar value of trading on exchanges in the United States took place on the New York Stock Exchange, about 3.5% on the American, and about 11.5% on all others combined. In terms of shares, the figures were 81%, 7%, and 12% respectively. The great bulk of the activity on the other exchanges is in issues listed on the NYSE.

Exchange Membership. Trading on an exchange takes place by or through members via oral agreements. Each of the exchanges has its own membership requirements that govern who may purchase a membership or "seat." The requirements deal with such matters as character, integrity, business experience, and financial capability.

A member may be a general partner or holder of voting stock in a member firm or member corporation. A brokerage firm doing business with the public—a so-called commission—may have more than one member, depending on the amount of its business and its consequent need for representation on the floor of the exchange. This type of member executes customers' buy and sell orders on the exchange, for which service their firms receive commissions.

Another group of members are called "specialists." They specialize in making and maintaining a fair and orderly market in one or more stocks. To narrow the price spread between public buy and sell orders and thus modify temporary imbalances in supply and demand for a particular stock, the specialist frequently risks his own capital, stepping in to buy at a higher price or sell at a lower price than the public may be willing to pay or accept at that moment. This arrangement makes for continuous markets with great liquidity.

Also important in the membership picture are the independent floor brokers, who assist the commission-house brokers in executing their public orders—for example, at times of unusually heavy activity. Other types of members perform more-limited functions, generally in trading for their own accounts. All member trading, however, is subject to careful surveillance by the exchanges and the SEC.

The cost of a stock-exchange membership fluctuates according to expectations for profitable use of the membership. In short, as in the stock market itself, the price depends on how much a prospective member is willing to pay and what the existing owner of a "seat" is willing to accept for relinquishing his membership. After acquiring the "seat," a member pays an initiation fee, annual dues, and various other fees for the use of the exchange's services and facilities.

The Trading Process. The first thing to remember in understanding the process of trading stocks on an exchange is that the stock exchange itself merely provides the marketplace; it neither buys nor sells, nor sets prices. The buyer purchases from another person or institutional investor; and likewise, the seller sells to another person or institutional investor. The individual investor's or trader's contact with the exchange is through a registered representative—sometimes known as an "account executive" or "customer's man."

Let's trace through a simple transaction to better understand the process. Assume, first of all, that Mrs. A. has decided to buy 100 shares of XYZ common stock. She calls her registered representative (RR) for the latest price of XYZ on the exchange where it is traded. An electronic interrogation device on his desk gives the RR instantaneous market information, including the fact that XYZ last traded at 52, or $52 per share, and that the current quotation is 52 to a half—i.e., $52 best bid to $52.50 best offer. Mrs. A. considers that a reasonable price for the stock and places a "market order"—an order to buy at the best price available to the RR firm's broker on the floor at the time the order reaches him. (Mrs. A. could have placed a "limit order," which would have specified the price she was willing to pay.)

As with each stock listed on the exchange, XYZ is assigned a specific location at a trading post on the exchange floor; all bids and offers in XYZ must take place at that location. Whether Mrs. A.'s order reaches the floor electronically or by telephone, it will be executed at that specific trading location. Meanwhile, Mr. B. has just placed a market order to sell 100 shares of XYZ, having been given the same information as to the current market situation. His order, too, is on its way to the exchange trading post.

At this point in our narrative, a slight digression may be enlightening. If XYZ were an over-the-counter stock—in other words, not traded on an exchange—the pricing of the transactions would probably have gone like this: Mrs. A. would have paid 52½ to the dealer making the market in XYZ, while Mr. B. would have received 52 for his shares. Both would probably have paid a commission, while the dealer profited from the half-point differential between what he bought and sold.

On the exchange, however, both brokers apply their experience, knowledge, and brokerage skill to try to obtain the best price for each customer. Assessing the current market in the "trading crowd" around the post where XYZ is traded (by open outcry in an auction procedure), the two brokers might very well have concluded a transaction between Mrs. A. and Mr. B. at 52¼. Completion of the trade would then be reported back to the brokerage office and the parties notified.

A relatively recent technological refinement that has been introduced into the process, as part of the development of a National Market System, is ITS—the Intermarket Trading System. ITS electronically links all the markets trading NYSE stocks, so that if a better price is available in a market other than the one to which the order was first routed, the order can benefit from that better price in another market. In the simple example of Mrs. A. and Mr. B., if the two orders had not arrived on the exchange floor to be executed against each other, the other side might have been found through bids and offers on one of the other markets linked into ITS.

Since 1975 the markets have also been linked via a Consolidated Tape, which reports transactions in NYSE- and ASE-listed stocks on all the markets in which they occur.

Related Organizations. The Securities Industry Automation Corporation (SIAC) provides certain communications, clearing, and data-processing operations and systems-development functions to both the New York and American Stock Exchanges and others. SIAC is two-thirds owned by the NYSE and one-third by the ASE. It charges the users of its services their respective shares of its costs.

The Depository Trust Company (DTC) is a central certificate depository that is organized as a trust company under various banking laws. Certificates are registered in the DTC nominee name—Cede & Co.—although beneficially owned by participants in the depository. The participant brokers or banks or other institutions instruct DTC to debit or credit buyer and seller accounts appropriately. Immobilizing securities in the vaults of DTC facilitates the transfer of enormous volumes of securities without necessitating physical delivery of the securities themselves. The transfers take place through computerized bookkeeping entries. Nevertheless, whenever requested, shares held on deposit can be transferred to the name of the customer.

National Securities Clearing Corporation (NSCC) operates clearing systems for its participants. Clearance of shares is a simple matching process for securities transactions, followed ultimately by delivery or receipt of net balances. Although the clearance operation is fairly complex, the end results are tremendous reductions in paper work and flows of certificates and money from one broker to another.

Regulation. The basic law governing the stock exchanges in this country is the Securities Exchange Act of 1934 and its amendments. The act operates on securities by requiring disclosure of information about a listed security and by requiring registration with the SEC of all securities listed on the national securities exchanges. The act operates on the exchanges primarily by banning various kinds of manipulative trading. In addition, the SEC has authority to require the exchanges to alter their regulations in the public interest.

The board of governors of the Federal Reserve system also affects the stock markets, by regulating the use of credit for the purchase and carrying of securities. These so-called margin requirements stem from the 1934 act. Another body with a regulatory interest in the stock market is the SECURITIES INVESTOR PROTECTION CORPORATION (SIPC). This nonprofit membership corporation, created by act of Congress, provides funds to protect customer cash and securities on deposit with a SIPC member brokerage firm in the event the firm fails and is liquidated.

Finally, the exchanges themselves exercise a stringent form of self-regulation. This regulation runs the gamut from qualifications for admission into the business, to financial responsibility in the form of capital requirements and auditing procedures, to the application of sophisticated computerized surveillance techniques that review stock trading as it takes place.

Stan West

Stock-Index Futures Contracts

Stock-index futures contracts began trading in 1982 in Kansas City, Kansas, far away from Wall Street, the stock-market capital of the world. These contracts represent a natural step in the evolution of futures markets and have, in their short history, become an integral part of the stock market.

A futures contract is an obligation to make or take delivery of a specified commodity at a price specified at the inception of the contract. FUTURES CONTRACTS are traded in the United States on organized commodity or futures exchanges under the regulatory jurisdiction of the COMMODITY FUTURES TRADING COMMISSION (CFTC).

Development. For many years, futures markets were based only on agricultural products. These markets were used by producers and purchasers of agricultural products to hedge the risk of future prices. Later, futures markets in precious metals, particularly gold and silver, were developed after the prices of these metals were allowed to float.

In 1972, after the breakdown of the Bretton Woods Agreement, the first financial futures began trading on foreign currency. Then, during 1975, after highly volatile interest-rate periods during the summers of 1973 and 1974, interest-rate futures were developed—first on GNMA's, and soon thereafter on U.S. Treasury bills and bonds. These financial-futures markets, in addition to being used by speculators who had never participated in the futures markets before, have been used extensively for hedging by professionals in the Treasury-security markets, particularly U.S. Treasury-security dealers. They have also been used to hedge underwritings and portfolio risk of not only Treasury securities but also corporate and municipal bonds. Interest-rate futures now represent an integral part of the U.S. Treasury-securities markets as well as the corporate and municipal bond markets.

These futures contracts have been used extensively for both speculation and hedging. Speculation is accepting a greater degree of risk in an investment in order to have the potential for greater profit. Hedging is a way of offsetting the risk in one position by assuming another, opposite position—that is, the loss on one position or transaction is offset by profits in the hedge, or vice versa.

After the development of futures markets in fixed-income securities, the development of futures markets in equity securities seemed a natural next step in the progression of the futures markets. Between February and May 1982, futures contracts began trading on three different stock-market averages—the Value Line Composite Index on the Kansas City Board of Trade; the S&P 500 Stock Index on the Index and Options Market of the Chicago Mercantile Exchange; and the NYFE Composite Index on the New York Futures Exchange. These three stock-index futures contracts are tied to broad-based stock-market averages or indexes, not on the prices of individual stocks. The specifications of these contracts are shown in Table 1.

These futures contracts have developed more quickly than any futures contracts previously introduced. They now frequently trade more in dollar value on a given day than the dollar value of stocks traded on the New York Stock Exchange, as illustrated in Table 2.

Futures-Contract Specifications. As we have said, these three futures contracts are all based not on the prices of individual stocks but on broad-based stock-market averages. A unique aspect of these contracts is that they are not settled by the delivery of stocks but by cash settlement.

Another important aspect of these futures contracts is their leverage. A fixed dollar deposit, called a "margin," equal to approximately 10% of the dollar value of the contract at the time it was listed for trading, is required to buy or sell a futures contract. The margins on the NYSE Composite Index, S&P 500, and Value Line futures contracts are $3,500, $6,000, and $6,500 respectively.

The examples in Table 3 show the daily profit and loss on the NYSE Composite Index futures contract and a cash settlement on the last day of trading.

Table 1
Stock-Index Futures Contract Specifications

Futures Exchange	Date Listed	Underlying Index	Type of Index	Level of Index*		Contract Multiplier		Dollar Value of Contract
New York Futures Exchange (NYFE)	May 6, 1982	New York Stock Exchange Composite Index	Capitalization-weighted All 1,500 stocks traded on NYSE	92.83	×	$500	=	$46,415
Chicago Mercantile Exchange (CME)	Apr. 21, 1982	Standard & Poor's 500 Index	Capitalization-weighted 500 stocks	161.80	×	$500	=	$80,900
Kansas City Board of Trade (KCBT)	Feb. 26, 1982	Value Line Composite Index	Geometric average Approximately 1,700 stocks	187.78	×	$500	=	$93,890

*Closing values on April 26, 1983.

Table 2
Dollar Value of Trading Comparison

Trade Date (1983)	CME Futures Volume × S & P Index Value Volume × Index × Cash Conv.	NYFE Futures Volume × NYSE Index Value Volume × Index × Cash Conv.	KC Futures Volume × Value Line Index Value Volume × Index × Cash Conv.	Total Futures Value	NYSE Volume × Estimated Aug. Share Price Volume × Aug. Price
3/28	23811*151.84*$500 = $1,807,731,100	12838*87.34*$500 = $560,635,460	2517*178.01*$500 = $224,025,590	$2,592,392,150	58,510,000*$35.00 = $2,047,850,000
3/29	23121*151.59*$500 = $1,752,456,200	14930*87.24*$500 = $651,246,600	3528*177.72*$500 = $313,498,080	$2,717,200,880	65,300,000*$35.00 = $2,285,500,000
3/30	28238*153.39*$500 = $2,165,713,400	14290*88.16*$500 = $629,903,200	3602*179.05*$500 = $322,469,050	$3,118,085,650	75,800,000*$35.00 = $2,653,000,000
3/31	31208*152.96*$500 = $2,386,787,800	17777*88.03*$500 = $782,454,660	4216*179.25*$500 = $377,859,000	$3,547,101,460	100,570,000*$35.00 = $3,519,950,000
4/4	26542*153.01*$500 = $2,030,595,700	13876*88.06*$500 = $610,960,280	2548*178.75*$500 = $227,727,500	$2,869,283,480	66,010,000*$35.00 = $2,310,350,000
4/5	29115*151.90*$500 = $2,211,284,300	15282*87.47*$500 = $668,358,270	3250*178.46*$500 = $289,997,500	$3,169,640,070	76,810,000*$35.00 = $2,688,350,000
4/6	36591*151.05*$500 = $2,763,535,300	18805*86.97*$500 = $817,735,430	3504*177.04*$500 = $310,174,080	$3,891,444,810	77,140,000*$35.00 = $2,699,900,000
4/7	30372*151.77*$500 = $2,304,779,200	16291*87.32*$500 = $711,265,060	2524*177.23*$500 = $223,664,260	$3,239,708,520	69,480,000*$35.00 = $2,431,800,000
4/8	27727*152.85*$500 = $2,119,036,000	11237*87.87*$500 = $493,697,600	2750*178.03*$500 = $244,791,250	$2,857,524,850	67,710,000*$35.00 = $2,369,850,000
4/11	29018*155.14*$500 = $2,250,926,300	12912*89.07*$500 = $575,035,920	2100*179.80*$500 = $188,790,000	$3,014,752,220	81,440,000*$35.00 = $2,850,400,000

Table 3
Daily Adjustment (Except Last Day of Trading)

Accounts maintaining long (futures buyer) or short (futures seller) positions are adjusted (marked to the market) to reflect the futures-contract settlement price of that day.

	Futures Price	Value of Contract
Previous day's settlement contract value	90.00 × $500	$45,000
Today's settlement contract value	92.00 × $500	$46,000
Difference	2.00 × $500	$ 1,000
Long position credited		$ 1,000
Short position charged		$ 1,000

Cash Settlement
(Adjustment on Last Day of Trading)

Positions held through the close of trading on the last day of trading are adjusted to reflect the closing value of the NYSE Composite Index on that day. Actual transfer of funds is made on the following day (Settlement Day).*

	Futures Price	Value of Contract
Settlement contract value of day prior to last day of trading	85.80 × $500	$42,900
Final value of NYSE Composite Index on last day of trading	85.22 × $500	$42,610
Difference	.58 × $500	$ 290
Long position charged		$ 290
Short position credited		$ 290

*Cash settlement for contracts purchased or sold on the last day of trading and held to the close of business on that day is based on the difference between the price of such purchase or sale and the closing value of the NYSE Composite Index on that day, to the nearest .01.

Thus, on a $3,500 margin, a $1,000 profit is made due to a two-point move in the NYSE Composite Index.

Uses. As indicated above, these futures contracts have grown quickly and have become an integral part of the stock-market world. Their growth has been due principally to three features. The first is leverage. Due to margins that, while large relative to other futures contracts, are small relative to the stock market, many investors have used stock-index futures contracts to supplement their stock-market strategies. The margin requirements for the NYSE stock-index futures contracts are substantially smaller than the 50% margin required for stock positions and the 30% required for stock-options positions.

The second feature is liquidity. Stock-index futures contracts have become very liquid. As indicated above, they frequently trade more in dollar value than is traded on the entire New York Stock Exchange, and thus are significantly more liquid than the market for individual stocks.

The third aspect is commissions. The commissions on stock-index futures contracts are significantly less per dollar value than those on stocks.

Due to leverage, liquidity, and commission, stock-index futures contracts have been extensively used by participants in the stock and stock-options markets to enhance their stock-market strategies.

Another important advantage of these contracts relates to stock-market risk. There are two types of risk in the stock market: stock-specific risk—the risk that the price of a specific stock will outperform or underperform the overall market; and market risk—the risk of the overall market increasing or decreasing. When an investor buys a particular stock, he buys a "bundle" of both stock-specific and market risk. Stock-index futures contracts, however, represent only market risk, since they are based on broad stock-market averages. Thus, stock-index futures contracts permit stock-market participants to "unbundle" market risk from stock-specific risk.

For example, if an investor is bullish or bearish on the market, but does not have a view on an individual stock, he can buy or sell, respectively, stock-index futures to implement these views. Or if he is bullish on an individual stock relative to the overall market, but does not have a view on the market, he can buy the stock and sell the futures contract (to hedge the market risk in the stock), thereby bearing only stockspecific risk. The fact that stock-market participants can unbundle stock-specific risk and market risk has been an important advantage of stock-index futures.

Stock-index futures contracts have been extensively used for speculation and for hedging. Many stock- and stock-options-market investors who had never participated in the futures market in the past have become active speculators in the stock-index futures markets. Stock-market professionals have used stock-index futures to hedge risk arbitrage transactions, stock underwriting, and block positioning. In addition, pension funds and other institutions have used stock-index futures to hedge their portfolios.

Frank J. Jones and Karen M. Benedetti

Stock-Index Options Contracts

Options on individual stocks began trading on April 26, 1973. Originally, only call options were traded. (Stock-options calls are the right, but not the obligation, to *buy* a stock at a specified price, the strike price of the option, within a specified time period.) A limited number of puts on individual stocks were introduced in June 1977. (Puts are the right, but not the obligation, to *sell* a stock at the strike price, within a specified time period.) Today, calls and puts are traded on the Chicago Board Options Exchange (CBOE), the American Stock Exchange (Amex), the Philadelphia Stock Exchange (PHLX), and the Pacific Stock Exchange (PSE). All these exchanges are regulated by the Securities and Exchange Commision (SEC) and all trade stocks, except the CBOE.

Development of Stock-Index Options. The development of options on indexes did not directly follow options on individual stocks. Instead, these options first began trading as derivatives of futures contracts a few months after the futures contracts on indexes were widely accepted by the investment community (*see* STOCK-INDEX FUTURES CONTRACTS).

Under the Commodity Futures Trading Commission's pilot program on commodity options, the New York Futures Exchange (NYFE) and the Chicago Mercantile Exchange (CME) began trading options on their underlying stock-index futures contracts on January 28, 1983. Somewhat later, on March 11, 1983, the Chicago Board Options Exchange, under the regulation of the Securities and Exchange Commission (SEC), began trading an option on an index of its own construction, the CBOE-100. On April 29, 1983, the American Stock Exchange began trading an option on the Major Market Index (MMI), also an index of its own construction. The New York Stock Exchange (NYSE) began trading an option on its Composite Index on September 23, 1983. As of January 1984, the NYSE was awaiting approval on 14 industry-index options. Upon approval, it will join the Amex, CBOE, PHLX, and PSE in trading such options.

Nature of Contracts. The New York Futures Exchange (NYFE) option on the NYSE Composite Index futures contract and the Chicago Mercantile Exchange (CME) option on the S&P 500 futures contract are very similar in composition. Both options are based on capitalization-weighted indexes on which futures are traded.

The SEC-regulated stock options on broad indexes were traded, as of January 1984, on three exchanges: the Chicago Board Options Exchange, the American Stock Exchange, and the New York Stock Exchange.

The first such index was the CBOE-100 trading on the CBOE, a market-value-weighted index of 100 stocks on which CBOE trades options. Shortly following was the Amex Major Market Index, a simple average index of 20 stocks, 15 of which are included in the Dow Jones industrial average.

The NYSE Composite Index option is based on the NYSE Composite Index, which has been calculated since 1965. The index is capitalization-weighted and includes all 1,500-plus common stocks traded on the NYSE.

The levels of all three indexes would be multiplied by $100 to convert to the actual dollar value. While futures contracts are received on the CFTC-regulated options, the SEC-regulated options are settled in cash. Options on the futures contracts and options on indexes and stocks have some important technical differences that are not discussed here. The specifications of the options contracts on the commodity and securities exchanges are summarized in Table 1.

Uses of Options on Stock Indexes. Options provide similar opportunities to profit from, and obtain protection against, increases or decreases in futures contracts on stock indexes, but with a known and limited risk. Whereas participants in the futures market must possess substantial financial and psychological tolerance for risk, the buyer of an option knows in advance that the most he can lose is the cost of the option.

The buyer of a call option of the types mentioned above obtains the right—but not the obligation—to purchase a futures contract on an index or directly purchase the value of a portfolio of stocks convertible to cash, at a specified price at any time during the life of the option. That is, he obtains the right to acquire a "long" position in the futures or stock portfolio. For example, a "NYFE June 88 call" is an option to purchase an NYSE Stock Index futures contract at a price of $88 at any time before the option expires in June.

In contrast to a call option, which gives the option buyer the right to buy a stock-index futures contract or stock-index convertible to cash, the buyer of a put option obtains the right to sell a futures contract or the value of a stock portfolio at any time during the life of the contract. That is, he obtains the right to acquire a "short" position in the futures or stock portfolio. For example, a "NYFE June 88 put" is an option to sell a NYSE Stock Index futures contract at a price of $88 at any time before the option expires in June.

Options on futures and stock indexes can be used in creative strategies with futures contracts to hedge against stock-market risk. Stock portfolios can also be hedged with options alone. By hedging, an investor offsets, wholly or in part, the effects of future price

Table 1
Stock-Index Options Contract Specifications

(a) *Options on Futures*

Exchange	Date Listed	Underlying
NYFE	January 28, 1983	1 NYSE Composite Index futures contract
CME	January 28, 1983	1 S&P 500 Index futures contract
KCBT	March 1, 1983	1 Value Line composite index futures contract

(b) *Stock and Stock-Options Exchanges (SEC)*

Exchange	Date Listed	Underlying Index	Type of Index	Level of Index*	Contract Multiplier	Dollar Value of Contract
Chicago Mercantile Exchange (CME)	March 11, 1983	S&P 100	Capitalization-weighted 100 stocks	166.38 ×	$100 =	$16,638
Chicago Mercantile Exchange (CME)	July 1, 1983	S&P 500	Capitalization-weighted 500 stocks	165 ×	$100 =	$16,500
American Stock Exchange (Amex)	April 29, 1983	Major Market Index	Simple average of stock prices 20 stocks (15 in DJIA)	118.61 ×	$100 =	$11,861
American Stock Exchange (Amex)	July 8, 1983	Market Value Index	Capitalization-weighted 839 stocks	232.47 ×	$100 =	$23,247
New York Stock Exchange (NYSE)	September 23, 1983	NYSE Composite Index	Capitalization-weighted 1,500 stocks listed on NYSE	92.83 ×	$100 =	$ 9,283

*Closing values on September 2, 1983.

changes in a diversified portfolio of stocks. The investor's aim is to offset the loss on the stock portfolio by the profit on his option position. The premium paid for an option is the cost of insurance against adverse changes in the price of the underlying group of stocks.

Assume an investor holds a diversified stock portfolio currently at a level of 90, as measured by a broad-based index. He will *buy* a put option at a premium of 5, for example, to hedge his position. If the market goes to 80, he will lose $10 on his portfolio. However, he will profit on his put, thereby limiting part of the loss on his portfolio. If the market increased, the investor would gain money on the stock portfolio and lose money on the option. For example, a rise in the market to 100 would result in a $10 stock profit. However, the $5 he paid for the option would be lost. Therefore, the net profit would be $5. The investor can never lose more than the $5 option premium, but can gain any appreciation, less the pre-mium paid for the put. Figure 1 graphically depicts the profits and losses associated with buyers of put options.

Another way to hedge a portfolio is to *sell* a call option. By selling a call, the investor receives a fixed premium, in this case 5, but is liable to deliver the underlying stock at 90 if the price increases above this value. If the market declines, there will be a loss in the portfolio. However, the call will not be exercised by the buyer. The investor who sold the call gets to keep the $5. Figure 2 graphically depicts the profits and losses associated with selling a call option.

Despite the newness of these contracts, stock-market professionals have used the stock-index futures and options markets to hedge their securities positions and transactions to a significant extent. A rapid rise in participation in these markets by both individuals and institutions is expected over the next few years, as more choices of instruments are avail-

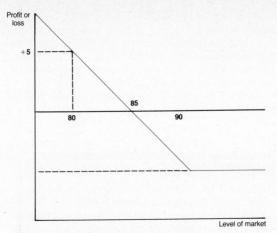

Figure 1. Profit/loss graph of long put option.

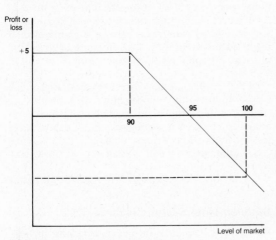

Figure 2. Profit/loss graph of short call option.

able, knowledge is increased, and investor confidence grows.

Frank J. Jones and Karen M. Benedetti

Stock-Market Indicator

See COMMON STOCK.

Stop Order

See COMMON STOCK.

Student Loan Marketing Association

The Student Loan Marketing Association ("Sallie Mae") is a federally chartered, stockholder-owned corporation that is the major intermediary to the education credit market. Created by the 1972 amendments to the Higher Education Act of 1965, the corporation provides a national secondary market (that is, a market in which previously issued loans or securities are traded) for insured student loans made by financial and educational institutions, state agencies, and other organizations under the federally sponsored Guaranteed Student Loan Program (GSLP) and Health Education Assistance Loan Program (HEAL), and other financial services to assist the credit needs of students generally. Since beginning operations in 1973, Sallie Mae had, as of the beginning of 1984, provided more than $11 billion in liquidity to more than 1,800 GSLP lenders and direct or indirect financial assistance to over five million students. Headquartered in Washington, D.C., Sallie Mae is owned by its stockholders. Holders of voting common stock consist of approximately 1,000 financial and educational institutions eligible to participate in the GSLP and HEAL programs; holders of nonvoting common stock consist of about 1,500 institutional and individual investors.

Under the GSLP, which is the nation's largest single source of student credit for postsecondary educational financing, undergraduate students can borrow up to a maximum of $2,500 a year and graduate students can borrow up to a maximum of $5,000 a year. These loans are insured by state agencies and reinsured by the federal government or are directly insured by the federal government in the event of death, disability, default, or bankruptcy. The HEAL Program provides insured loans to help meet the financing needs of students attending a variety of graduate programs in the health professions, including medical, osteopathic, and dental students.

Sallie Mae offers GSLP and HEAL lenders a number of products and services in order to enhance the availability of financing for postsecondary education throughout the nation. These products and services include purchases of GSL and HEAL loans from lenders; "warehousing advances," or loans to an institution for the purpose of making insured student loans; and commitments to purchase student loans or to extend credit to an institution for making additional student loans in the future. The corporation also provides commitment and letter-of-credit services as well as loans to state student-loan agencies.

Under Sallie Mae's Loan Purchase Program, an institution can sell GSLP and HEAL loans from its portfolio to Sallie Mae. The funds obtained from the sale can then be used to fund additional student loans or for any other purpose. This allows lenders to continue originating student loans without increasing the funds invested in the program. In most instances, Sallie Mae assumes the responsibility for servicing and collecting the loans, thus relieving the seller of the expense and difficulty of loan servicing.

Under Sallie Mae's Warehousing Advance Program, an institution can borrow funds from Sallie Mae using its guaranteed-student-loan portfolio or U.S. Treasury or agency securities as collateral. Funds are usually borrowed at rates that, like the total return on student loans, are indexed to the 91-day U.S. Treasury bill rates, so that an institution can be assured of the positive "spread" between the return on its student loans and the interest it pays on the funds used to support those student loans.

Sallie Mae also offers purchase commitments, which enable an institution to sell up to a specified amount of student loans to Sallie Mae within a certain period. Purchase commitments are particularly useful for state agencies that finance their student lending activities with bond issues, since the commitments assure the agencies of a market for their student loans when the bonds mature. A newer letter-of-credit service enables bond issuers to obtain the highest investment quality ratings on their issues. In addition, Sallie Mae offers commitments to lend funds, or lines of credit. Particularly during periods when the money market is tight and the availability of funds is uncertain, a line of credit offers a student-loan originator the assurance that it will be able to obtain funds to support its lending activities.

Sallie Mae also works closely with other organizations to develop programs for providing student loans to groups of students with limited access to traditional sources of student credit.

Sallie Mae receives no state or federal appropriations and pays federal income taxes at the full corporate rate. Beginning in 1974, the corporation met its funding needs through borrowings from the Federal Financing Bank (FFB), an arm of the U.S. Treasury. However, in 1981 Sallie Mae agreed to discontinue borrowing from the FFB and now meets its funding needs in the capital markets. The corporation utilizes a variety of financial instruments, including adjustable-rate preferred stock, discount notes, floating-rate notes, and fixed-rate securities. The corporation pioneered the use of two particular financing techniques: the sale of floating-rate notes with a weekly interest-rate adjustment; and the use of interest-rate swaps, whereby the payment streams on its fixed-rate securities are swapped for the payment streams on floating-rate securities issued by another corporation. These funding techniques are designed to strengthen Sallie Mae's balance sheet by closely matching the interest-rate sensitivity of the corporation's floating-rate assets and liabilities, both of which are indexed to the 91-day U.S. Treasury bill.

Since beginning operations, Sallie Mae has maintained a record of strong earnings and asset growth. For the year ended December 31, 1983, Sallie Mae recorded net income of $66.6 million, up 76.4% from the previous year; and on a per-common-share basis, net income was $1.37, a 27.1% increase over the previous year. At year-end 1983, the corporation's total assets were $9.1 billion.

Edward A. Fox

Super Negotiable Order of Withdrawal (NOW) Account

Authorized by the federal government on January 5, 1983, Super Negotiable Order of Withdrawal (NOW) accounts allow banks and other depository institutions to meet competition from money-market mutual funds by offering a market-rate, federally insured transaction account to customers. There are no government-set interest-rate ceilings on such accounts as long as a $2,500 minimum balance is maintained. If the balance falls below $2,500, an interest-rate ceiling of 5¼% will apply on the balance until it returns to $2,500.

Unlike MONEY-MARKET DEPOSIT ACCOUNTS, there are no limits on the number of transfers on this account. An important point to remember about both accounts, however, is that banks will probably charge fees for transactions written to them.

See also NEGOTIABLE ORDER OF WITHDRAWAL (NOW) ACCOUNT.

Phil Battey

Supplemental Security Income (SSI)

Supplemental Security Income is a federal income-maintenance program for the aged, blind, and disabled in the 50 states, the District of Columbia, and the northern Mariana Islands. The program provides monthly payments to aged, blind, and disabled people who have little or no income and resources.

The federal government administers the SSI program through the SOCIAL SECURITY ADMINISTRATION (SSA). It makes the basic payments to recipients, determines eligibility of claimants, and maintains a master record of recipients. States have the option of supplementing the federal payments to other recipients. The states also provide MEDICAID, FOOD STAMPS, and various social and rehabilitation services.

Even though the Social Security Administration runs the federal program, SSI is not the same as Social Security. It is financed from general funds of the U.S. Treasury—personal income taxes, corporation taxes, and other taxes—whereas Social Security is funded through the Social Security taxes paid by workers, employers, and self-employed people. The two programs also differ in other areas, such as the conditions of eligibility and the method of figuring payments.

To be eligible for SSI, an individual may have resources (assets) of up to $1,500, and a couple may have resources of up to $2,250. However, not all resources are counted in determining the amount of a claimant's resources for SSI purposes. A home (and adjacent land) that is the claimant's principal place of residence is not counted, regardless of its value. Personal effects or household goods with a total equity value of $2,000 or less are not counted. If the total equity value exceeds $2,000, the excess counts. The equity value is what an item can be sold for, less the amount of any legal debt against it. There are also other exclusions, such as an automobile and a life-insurance policy.

An individual is eligible for Federal SSI if he or she has income of less than $284.30 a month; a couple is eligible with income of less than $426.40 a month. If only one member of a couple qualifies for SSI, part of the ineligible member's income is considered to be the eligible spouse's. If an unmarried child living at home is under 18, some of the parent's income is considered to be the child's. However, there are certain exclusions from income.

Social Security Administration

Suretyship

See INSURANCE.

Surplus and Excess Line Insurance

See INSURANCE.

Swap Network

The swap network is a series of short-term, reciprocal credit lines. It enables the Federal Reserve to exchange (swap) dollars for the currencies of 14 foreign nations through their central banks up to previously agreed amounts. The BANK FOR INTERNATIONAL SETTLEMENTS (BIS) is also part of the swap network for specified currencies it holds.

Any participant can initiate swap drawing. Transactions are conducted through the Federal Reserve Bank of New York, which acts for the FEDERAL RESERVE SYSTEM and the United States Treasury in foreign currency operations. As in domestic money-market operations, the New York Fed acts under authorization and a directive from the Federal Open Market Committee (FOMC). It also consults closely with the U.S. Treasury on all operations. Credit lines

between the Federal Reserve and foreign participants have totaled $30.1 billion since late May 1981.

The first swap line of $50 million was established with the Bank of France in March 1962. Similar agreements with other central banks followed in 1962 and 1963. The last lines were established in 1967. However, most credit lines have been increased since then.

The agreements establishing swap lines are limited to one year, but can be renewed annually, by mutual consent, for additional one-year periods.

Funds drawn under swap agreements are created by central banks. The Federal Reserve, for example, creates dollars through authority granted by Congress. Of course, any undesired bank-reserve creation can be offset by domestic open-market operations. Other foreign central banks have similar power to create national currency. The BIS, however, acquires its swap funds either through borrowings from participants or through exchange-market operations.

Use of the swap facilities was heavy through the early 1970s, as foreign central banks often drew on the lines to obtain dollars needed to finance exchange-market intervention. The Federal Reserve obtained foreign currencies either for exchange-market intervention or to purchase dollars that central banks would otherwise have converted into gold or other U.S. reserve assets. Throughout periods of heavy borrowing, swap drawings reduced the need for central banks to rely on gold and other reserve assets to settle their accounts.

Federal Reserve use of the swap network was suspended temporarily on August 15, 1971, when the U.S ended dollar-gold convertibility. The Federal Reserve resumed swap drawings for market-intervention purposes in August 1972. With the move to floating exchange rates by the major countries in 1973, the Federal Reserve and other central banks have subsequently made use of swap lines on numerous occasions to finance exchange-market intervention. The objective of these interventions has been to counter disorderly trading conditions. In keeping abreast of market developments, the New York Fed maintains close communications with other central banks in the network, on a daily basis in many instances.

A drawing will usually be initiated by telephone, followed by an exchange of cables specifying terms and conditions. A swap is in the form of a foreign-exchange contract—the sale of dollars by the Federal Reserve for the currency of the foreign central banks, with the simultaneous agreement to reverse the transaction three months later. The appropriate bookkeeping entries are made by the New York Fed and the foreign central bank involved.

Arthur Samansky

Swap Network and Bank Reserves

A swap drawing by the Federal Reserve to finance sales of foreign currencies in countering disorderly exchange-market conditions for the dollar doesn't have any net influence on reserves of depository institutions in the United States or on the nation's money supply. In essence, the drawing leads to two opposite and offsetting effects on bank reserves, given the current operating procedures of the Federal Reserve.

First, the sale of a foreign currency for dollars in the exchange market causes an initial reduction in bank reserves. Second, a swap drawing to finance the foreign-currency sale starts a process that leads to an offsetting increase in bank reserves. The mechanism by which the reserves are replenished will vary, depending on the course of action chosen by the securities trading desk at the Federal Reserve Bank of New York. The New York Fed conducts day-to-day domestic market operations for the Reserve system at the direction of the Federal Open Market Committee. It similarly acts for the U.S. central banking system and the U.S. Treasury in foreign-exchange operations.

A swap drawing generally begins with a telephone call from an officer on the foreign-exchange trading desk of the New York Fed to an exchange officer at the foreign central bank participating in the swap network to discuss the Federal Reserve's planned intervention. The call is placed at the direction of the manager of the System's open-market account for foreign operations, who also is a senior officer of the New York Fed.

For example, a swap might be arranged if the Federal Reserve plans to intervene in the U.S. exchange market by selling West German marks. Officials at the New York Fed would call officials of the West German central bank (Bundesbank) and arrange to draw marks on the swap line, if marks are needed to finance the operation.

Once arrangements are completed, the New York Fed begins intervening in the New York foreign-exchange market, making contracts to sell marks for dollars.

After all the contracts are arranged, Reserve Bank officials telex Bundesbank officials, formally requesting to draw on the swap line for the exact amount of marks needed for delivery. The agreements between the Federal Reserve and the foreign central bank usually call for the foreign currency to be delivered two business days later and for the Fed to repay the foreign currency at the same exchange rate three months later.

On the second business day, the Bundesbank credits a Federal Reserve account at the German central bank with the agreed-upon marks. In making the bookkeeping credit entry, the Bundesbank creates the marks.

Central banks influence the availability of the money as part of their responsibility to regulate the cost and availability of credit within their respective nation. Immediately, the Bundesbank, following payment instructions of the Federal Reserve, puts the newly created marks into the commercial bank accounts in Germany of the purchasers of marks from the Federal Reserve. All credit entries are in a bookkeeping form; mark bank notes aren't physically delivered. In the process, West German commercial bank reserves increase.

While the marks are moving through the Bundesbank, a series of entries are made on the books of the New York Fed.

On the same day, the Federal Reserve removes dollars from the appropriate bank's reserves at the New York Fed in payment for the marks. The commercial bank, in turn, debits its customer's account. Also, the New York Fed credits the Bundesbank's account at the Reserve with an amount of dollars equivalent to the marks created in the Bundesbank and simultaneously debits the account, investing the Bundesbank's dollars in a special interest-bearing nonmarketable U.S. Treasury certificate of indebtedness. As a result, Treasury cash balances at the Reserve Bank increase and the Treasury issues a bookkeeping IOU to the Bundesbank.

In crediting dollars to the Bundesbank, the Federal Reserve has created dollars, which are then debited and paid to the U.S. Treasury. Generally, the Treasury uses the funds either by spending the money or by transferring the funds to its commercial bank accounts. Thus, the dollars move into the banking system and bank reserves increase, offsetting the previous drain in reserves brought about by the sale by the Federal Reserve of marks for dollars.

In a few cases, the Treasury doesn't immediately disburse the funds. Thus, its cash balances at the New York Fed will be temporarily high. That increase is essentially the same amount as the drain on bank reserves from the System's exchange intervention.

An increase in the Treasury's balance is one of many factors the domestic trading desk takes into consideration in determining day-to-day open-market operations. Other things equal, the domestic desk will react to an increase in the Treasury's balance as a signal to provide reserves to the banking system to achieve its objectives. However, System swap operations represent only one of many factors that lead to fluctuations in the Treasury's account; in turn, changes in the Treasury's account are but one of many factors affecting bank reserves. The effect of even large swap drawings is normally overshadowed by other sources of variation in bank reserves. In practice, there isn't any effect on bank reserves, and the nation's money supply doesn't change as a result of System intervention in the exchange markets financed by a swap drawing.

When the swap is repaid, the Federal Reserve may create dollars and buy marks in the marketplace, thus increasing bank reserves. The marks are repaid to the Bundesbank, and the Reserve system's debt in marks is reduced. Simultaneously, the Bundesbank repays the Federal Reserve by redeeming the certificate of indebtedness.

The Bundesbank is paid from the Treasury's account at the New York Fed. If the Treasury's account is replenished, through borrowing in the market or receipts from other sources, bank reserves decline. That directly offsets the expansionary effect on reserves of the System's mark purchases.

If the Treasury's account isn't replenished, the decline in its balance will be considered by the domestic trading desk as a factor increasing bank reserves. The desk typically will respond to appreciable declines in the Treasury's balance, or to other factors leading to increased reserve supplies, by absorbing bank reserves. That response neutralizes the expansionary effect of the System's purchases of marks to repay swap commitments to the Bundesbank.

Arthur Samansky

System Open-Market Account

The Federal Reserve system open-market account is composed of the central banking system's portfolio of United States Treasury and federal-agency securities, and BANKERS' ACCEPTANCES acquired in conducting open-market operations.

Open-market operations involve buying and selling securities in the marketplace. The open-market operation is one of three basic tools the central bank uses to conduct monetary policy—which influences the cost and availability of money and credit. Other things remaining equal, a purchase of government securities in the market by the Federal Reserve adds reserves to the commercial banking system, enabling banks to expand their lending and investment activities. A sale of securities by the Federal Reserve withdraws reserves from the banking system, limiting the ability of banks to make loans and investments.

The other major tools of monetary policy are the discount rate and reserve requirements. The discount rate is the interest charge depository institutions must pay when they borrow from the Federal Reserve (*see* DISCOUNT WINDOW; SEASONAL BORROWING). Reserve requirements are the reserves various depository in-

stitutions must keep in their vaults or on deposit in their accounts at the Federal Reserve, based on a percentage of customers' demand, time, and savings deposits.

A specified portion of the System's outright holdings in the portfolio is allocated to each of the 12 Reserve banks, but is held by the New York Fed. The securities trading desk at the New York Fed is the control center of the System's market activities, which are directed by the FEDERAL OPEN MARKET COMMITTEE (FOMC), the top monetary-policy-making unit of the System. The percentage allotments of the portfolio are adjusted annually to reflect movements of deposits among Reserve banks.

The power to buy and sell government securities was granted to each Reserve bank by the Federal Reserve Act. However, not until the 1920s was the monetary-policy impact of changes in the portfolio generally understood. The structure of the FOMC itself wasn't established in its present form until passage of the Banking Act of 1935.

Following the first full year of open-market purchases in 1916, two years after the Federal Reserve began operations, the portfolio amounted to $184 million at face value. The System's holdings of government bonds and acceptances remained below $500 million until the early 1920s. In 1930 the System's holdings of government securities and acceptances reached $1 billion. By 1942 the portfolio was valued at more than $5 billion, and it increased to $20 billion in 1945. The portfolio reached $50 billion in April 1968 and $100 billion in June 1976. In May 1980 the face value of the portfolio reached a record $134 billion.

The composition and value of the portfolio fluctuates daily in response to the central bank's market operations. However, the FOMC usually limits the change between meetings to $3 billion. The meetings take place about ten times a year.

The FOMC is composed of the seven members of the board of governors and five Reserve bank officials, usually presidents. The chairman of the Federal Reserve Board of Governors also serves as FOMC chairman. Because of the New York Fed's special role in managing the account, that bank's representative is a permanent voting member of the FOMC and, by tradition, the committee's vice-chairman. The other Reserve bank presidents serve on a one-year rotating basis beginning March 1.

Each year, one president or first vice-president is eligible to be elected to the committee by one of the boards of directors of one of the Reserve banks in each of four groups of Reserve banks. Group one consists of Boston, Philadelphia, and Richmond; group two—Cleveland and Chicago; group three—Atlanta,

St. Louis, and Dallas; and group four—Minneapolis, Kansas City, and San Francisco. Customarily, only presidents have been elected to the FOMC.

The Reserve bank presidents who aren't voting members of the committee also attend the meetings to offer their views on economic conditions and policy approaches. Should one of the voting presidents be unable to attend a meeting, an alternate president, designated each March from the remaining seven, may cast a vote in the place of the absent president. If the New York president is absent, the first vice-president of the New York Fed attends the meeting and votes. Traditionally, the New York Fed first vice-president is the only such officer designated as an alternate. Voting alternates must be from the same group as the presidents they replace.

On a daily basis, the securities portfolio is directed by the manager of the System open-market account for domestic operations. The manager is appointed by the FOMC and customarily is a senior officer of the New York Fed. The account manager attends the FOMC meetings to report on domestic operations, as well as to be fully informed of the discussions leading to adoption of the committee's directive to him. In addition, the manager participates daily in a telephone conference call with a designated Reserve bank president and the senior staff of the board of governors. The account manager proposes a plan for the day and receives comment from the president on the call. Each day the board staff sends a telegram to the voting and nonvoting members of the FOMC covering the discussion of the call.

The interest received by the Federal Reserve on its portfolio holdings constitutes virtually all of System earnings. However, unlike individuals or private institutions, the central bank acquires or sells securities purely to implement monetary policy and not in pursuit of profit. The interest earned on those holdings is apportioned to the individual Federal Reserve banks according to the percentage of the portfolio each owns.

A portion of the earnings is used for the salaries and other operating expenses of the banks, with a small amount set aside in a surplus account. In recent years these expenses have amounted to about 8.4% of the annual earnings on the portfolio of the Federal Reserve banks. After additions to surplus and dividends on Federal Reserve Bank stock, the remaining earnings are paid to the U.S. Treasury on a weekly basis as interest payments on Federal Reserve notes at a rate established by the board of governors.

Arthur Samansky

·T·

Take-Back

See HOME FINANCING, MORTGAGES.

Tax

A tax is a compulsory contribution exacted by a government for public purposes. It is an involuntary or forced levy on persons or property, transferring wealth from private persons or organizations to meet the needs of government.

By virtue of their sovereign status, all U.S. state governments have the inherent power of taxation. Local governments, as creatures of the states, have only those taxing powers delegated to them by the states. Since the federal government has no "inherent" powers of sovereignty giving it the power to tax, it was necessary to provide such powers in the U.S. Constitution. Article 1, Section 8, gives Congress the power to impose taxes, with four limitations: (1) Any tax must be used "to pay the debts and provide for the common defense and general welfare of the United States"; (2) a tax may not be imposed on articles exported from any state; (3) direct taxes (generally those on income and wealth) must be apportioned among the states according to numbers of people; and (4) all indirect taxes must be uniform. In addition, some taxes may be authorized or prohibited elsewhere in the Constitution, as for example under the Fifth Amendment provision that no person shall be "deprived of life, liberty, or property without due process of law." The income tax, based on taxable income, was not feasible under the original Constitution since it would have had to be apportioned according to population. The Sixteenth Amendment, approved in 1913, gave Congress the power to levy the income tax.

The major purpose—and some observers contend the only proper role—of taxation is to raise money to support government. There are no rules of thumb or guidelines as to the amounts governments "need" to spend for public purposes and thus to the amounts required in taxes; such decisions are left for legislative

bodies, who presumably represent the collective wishes of their constituencies.

In the United States, about four-fifths of all government revenue comes from taxes. Although the provision of public funds is the major purpose of taxes, they are often viewed as means for achieving various social or economic objectives that promote the general welfare. For example, the tax system may be seen as a way of facilitating economic stabilization and growth; redistributing income to aid the poor; maintaining price stability; and encouraging such goals as capital formation, homeownership, individual savings, research and development, and many others.

Taxes may also be imposed as a regulatory device, as for example to discourage consumption of harmful commodities. So-called sin taxes are justified in part by the fact that the items or activities on which they are levied—such as cigarettes, gambling, and alcoholic beverages—may be harmful. To the extent that regulatory taxes are successful in accomplishing their aim, they will provide little revenue.

Classifications of Taxes. One of the oldest bases for classifying taxes distinguishes *direct* and *indirect* levies. Generally, direct taxes are those levied on individual income and wealth, the tax burden of which cannot be shifted to anyone else. Indirect taxes are exemplified by those on commodity transactions or sales. Federal excise taxes on cigarettes are paid to the government by manufacturers in the tobacco-producing states; but the tax on cigarettes and tobacco products is passed on to the ultimate consumers of those products in all states. Attempts to determine who actually bears the final burden of a tax involves the study of tax incidence, which is defined as the ultimate resting place of a tax upon one who cannot shift it further.

Taxes levied on business are considered indirect levies, since business as such has no taxpaying capacity in and of itself. Studies attempting to ascertain the incidence of business taxes—such as those on corporate income and business property or the employer's share of Social Security taxes—have not yielded definitive answers. Generally, it is reasonable to assume that some portion of indirect business taxes is shifted forward to consumers in the form of higher sales prices; that some of the burden falls on the owners of the business; and that other portions are shifted backward to employees in the form of lower wages, or to suppliers and creditors.

Based on their incidence, taxes may be *progressive, regressive,* or *proportional.* A progressive levy commands a higher share of the income of well-to-do individuals than of those less well off. The principal source of progressivity in the U.S. tax system is the individual income tax, with graduated rates that rise as incomes increase.

Regressive taxes follow the reverse pattern, taking a larger share of income from lower-income persons than from those in higher income brackets. Sales taxes are viewed as regressive: Those with lower incomes spend larger portions of their income for items subject to consumption taxes than do higher-income individuals. Even though a tax is inherently regressive, adjustments can be made so as to temper its incidence. To this end, many states exempt food and medicine from the general sales tax so as to alleviate its burden on poor families. Similarly, property taxes on owner-occupied homes are believed to be regressive, and thus are often lowered for the elderly and/or poor by special relief provisions.

Proportional taxes are neither progressive nor regressive; they claim the same percentage of income from families at all levels. A flat-rate income tax, without allowance for personal exemptions (which inject an element of progressivity into the tax), is an example of a proportional tax. Sales taxes, with exemptions for necessities, may also be structured as proportional levies.

Another classification involves the breadth of the tax base. *Broadly based* taxes—such as comprehensive individual income taxes and general sales taxes covering most consumer purchases—clearly produce more revenue than those levied on comparatively narrow bases, such as the excises on specific commodities. In some states, even personal income taxes are quite *narrowly based,* touching only income from investments or capital gains. Similarly, general sales taxes can become so riddled with exemptions that they apply to limited portions of consumer purchases and thus have a narrow base.

Taxes may be classified as *general* or *earmarked,* depending on the use to which they are put by the government authority. General taxes go into a jurisdiction's general or overall budget, which supports all functions of government. Earmarked taxes are dedicated by law or constitution to specific purposes, often those linking benefits to the item taxed, and are set aside in separate funds. Included in earmarked taxes are social-insurance levies, notably Social Security and unemployment-compensation taxes that are supported by taxes on employment, with benefits reserved for former workers. Taxes on motor fuels and other highway-related items, often regarded as "user taxes," are set aside in the highway trust fund at the federal level and often go into funds dedicated to highway purposes in the states. Particularly at the state and local levels, the practice of earmarking to maintain many separate funds, each for different uses, has been subject to criticism because of its adverse effect on the overall budget process.

Taxes may be levied on an *ad valorem* or *specific* basis. Ad valorem taxes are imposed according to the value of the taxed item. General sales taxes at 5% of the selling price and property taxes at $1.40 per $100 of assessed valuation are examples of ad valorem taxes. Specific taxes apply at a given amount per unit of volume: gasoline at 14 cents a gallon, cigarettes at 20 cents a pack, and so on. In a period of rising prices or real values, ad valorem taxes will rise more rapidly than the specific taxes, and are thus more desirable when a growing source of income is needed.

Types of Taxes. The terms applied to individual taxes generally indicate the economic base on which they are levied—either income, commodity transactions, or wealth. Some levies touch upon more than one base.

Individual and corporate income taxes, measured by net income, are imposed by the federal government, by most states, and by some local units. Income taxes provide almost 50% of all tax revenues. Definitions of what income is subject to tax vary according to the laws of different jurisdictions, as do allowances for personal exemptions, deductions, exclusions, and the rates and brackets for tax computation. The income-tax laws of most states conform to a considerable degree with provisions of the federal INTERNAL REVENUE CODE. State and local income taxes may be included in itemized deductions in computing federal tax liability. A few states allow deductibility of federal income taxes in determining the amount of tax due to the state.

Taxes on payrolls are the second-largest category of U.S. taxes, with yields exceeding 20% of all tax collections. The largest block of these taxes falls under the federal Old-Age, Survivors, and Disability Insurance Program and may be designated as FICA taxes (for Federal Insurance Contributions Act, under authority of which the taxes are imposed). Currently the taxes are imposed on all wages up to $35,700. Employers and employees each pay 6.7% of taxable earnings; the maximum combined employer and employee tax is $4,784. The self-employed are assigned a different rate. Another sizable lump of payroll taxes is levied under the Federal Unemployment Tax Act (FUTA), under which employers pay federal and state taxes on a specified maximum amount of earnings for each employee, at rates jointly determined by federal and state laws.

General sales taxes, used in the United States exclusively by state and local governments, apply on all retail transactions of goods and services except those specifically exempted. In practice, the tax falls largely on consumption goods; most services (housing, professional, financial, etc.) are free from tax. General sales taxes are looked upon with favor because they can provide large and stable revenues that will grow as the economy expands. For states alone, sales taxes constitute about one-third of the tax revenues.

Selective sales or excise taxes are imposed only on transactions of specific items. In the states, separate levies apply to items such as motor fuels, alcoholic beverages, cigarettes and other tobacco products, and public utilities, which altogether furnish almost 20% of state tax revenues. A 1964 law eliminated or reduced many federal excise taxes, but dozens of others remain, including those on gasoline, cigarettes, alcohol, certain sporting goods, air transportation, telephone service, and still others, including the lucrative "windfall profits" tax on oil that was imposed in 1980. Such taxes constitute about 6% of all federal revenues.

The property tax, used mainly by local governments, has been referred to as a "family of taxes" because of its broad range. The levies include general property taxes relating to property as a whole, realty and personalty, tangible and intangible, including property owned by businesses as well as individuals. All property may be taxed at the same rate per dollar of assessed value, or a graded or classified system may be used, under which certain types of property—farms, owner-occupied homes, etc.—receive preferential treatment. At the turn of the century, the property tax was virtually the sole support of state and local governments; and as recently as 1940, it provided more than half of state and locally raised taxes. Although reliance on the tax has declined sharply (to less than one-third of state/local taxes), it is still by far the largest source of state/local tax revenues. For all local governments combined, the property tax provides two-thirds of tax receipts; state governments do not use the property taxes to a significant extent.

License taxes are levied (either for revenue-raising or for regulation) as a condition to the exercise of a privilege. They may be imposed at a flat rate or measured by such bases as capital stock. A great variety of these levies are imposed, chiefly by the states. They include license taxes on motor vehicles (for the right to use public highways), motor-vehicle operators (for the privilege of driving motor vehicles), public utilities, alcoholic-beverage dealers, various occupations and businesses, hunting and fishing, and extend to animal licenses and marriage licenses. License taxes on business, such as those imposed on corporations for the right to do business in a jurisdiction, may also be referred to as "franchise taxes."

Death taxes are imposed by the federal government and most states. They include estate taxes, levied at graduated rates on a decedent's estate before it is divided among heirs, and inheritance taxes imposed on the value of the inheritance. Closely related are gift taxes, levied on the transfer of property as a gift in contemplation of death.

Severance taxes, which assumed special importance among energy-rich states in the 1970s and early 1980s, are imposed on the removal of natural products—e.g., oil, gas, minerals, timber, etc.—from land or water, and measured by the value or quantity of products removed and sold.

(See Table 1, pages 593–594.)

Principles of Taxation. The criteria used today in evaluating taxes rest heavily on rules enunciated more than two centuries ago by the noted philosopher Adam Smith. In his 1776 book, *An Inquiry into the Nature and Causes of the Wealth of Nations,* Smith set forth four "canons" of taxation that, he wrote, "have recommended themselves to all nations." He summarized these maxims as equality, certainty, convenience of payment, and economy of collection. While there remains broad agreement that taxes should meet these criteria, the terms have lent themselves to a considerable degree of subjective interpretation.

Smith's first principle—equality—is considered interchangeable with such terms as *equity, fairness,* and *ability to pay.* All of these are hard to define in practical ways. Economists recognize two separate types of equity—horizontal and vertical. Horizontal equity requires that "equals shall be treated equally." Those with the same income and otherwise in similar or equal circumstances should pay the same tax. If incomes are equal but taxpayer circumstances differ in ways relevant to the costs of government, the rule implies that tax burdens be modified. Such adjustments constitute a large part of tax laws. Income taxes, for example, make allowances for family size (through personal exemptions) and for unusual claims on family incomes (such as heavy medical expenses).

Vertical equity would require that a tax be "fair" to those with different amounts of income, and relate in some way to ability to pay. Some economists view equity as synonymous with the notion of progressivity. This has been the guiding principle behind graduated-rate income taxes imposed by the federal government and most states. While it is relatively easy to structure a tax so that it becomes progressive, there is little agreement on just how much difference in tax should be imposed for a given difference in income.

Smith's second canon of taxation—certainty—raises fewer questions of interpretation. The taxpayer should know when the tax payment is due, the manner in which it is to be paid, and the amount that is due.

Many modern taxes are levied so as to fulfill the principle of the taxpayer's convenience, Smith's third principle. Sales and excise taxes are paid little by little, as purchases are made, so that payment is relatively convenient. Pay-as-you-go or withholding is almost universal under modern income taxes. Somewhat in opposition to the convenience notion is another view held by some economists—that taxes should be imposed in such a way that taxpayers will be fully conscious of the taxes they pay. Payment of annual property taxes in a lump sum, for example, provides considerable taxpayer awareness of the tax burden and the costs of government.

Finally, Adam Smith's fourth rule of taxation—economy of collection—held that "every tax ought to be so contrived as both to take out and keep out of the pockets of the people as little as possible over and above what it brings into the public treasury of the state." Implicit in this principle are several rules widely used in evaluating taxes. Administration of the tax by government should be efficient and relatively inexpensive as compared to the amount collected. Many economists believe that taxes should be neutral in their effects on resource allocation and should have as little adverse effect as possible on the operation of free markets. Taxes alone should not encourage the use of one resource over another, should not penalize one industry, one occupation, one form of business organization, or one region in comparison with others. Where there are good reasons for interference with the market economy in the public interest, tax adjustments to alter resource allocation may be considered desirable. This departure from the neutrality criterion is evidenced in many incentive devices built into the tax system that are aimed at encouraging various social and economic goals.

Overall Tax Considerations. Revenue needs for a jurisdiction usually require the imposition of a variety of taxes, none of which conforms fully to the requisites of an ideal tax. Moreover, taxpayers are at once subject to levies of national and subnational jurisdictions. Flaws in one tax may be offset by superior aspects of other taxes. The mix of taxes thus becomes important in judging the equity of the system. Income taxes at progressive rates, for example, may counterbalance the effect of sales taxes that tend to be regressive. By and large, the combination of progressive, proportional, and regressive levies imposed in the United States leads to a system of taxation that is proportional throughout the range that includes the large majority of families.

In judging the fairness of a tax system, it also seems appropriate to examine the way in which government benefits are distributed. Studies of tax incidence show that low-income families typically have high tax burdens relative to their incomes, because all or nearly all of their purchases are for taxed consumption items. On the other hand, the benefits they receive from government spending far outweigh their taxes. A Tax Foundation study, based on the 1972–73 Bureau of Labor Statistics Consumer Expenditure Survey, found that families in the lowest income bracket received government benefits equal to more than three times their tax bills, while those in the highest income group paid taxes equal to almost twice the amount of government benefits allocable to them.

Tax-writing groups in Congress, state legislatures, and city councils devote considerable attention to ways of improving individual taxes and the overall tax system. Their overriding concern, however, continues to be that of raising adequate revenues to meet the rising costs of government.

Elsie M. Watters

Taxable Income

The federal government, for tax purposes, defines *gross income* as all income from whatever source, except for those items specifically excluded. The INTERNAL REVENUE CODE lists the most common types of gross income as follows:

1. Compensation for services including fees and commissions
2. Gross income from business
3. Gains from dealings in property
4. Interest
5. Rents
6. Royalties
7. Dividends
8. Alimony and separate maintenance payments
9. Annuities
10. Income from life insurance and endowment contracts
11. Pensions
12. Income from discharge of debt
13. Partners' share of partnership income
14. Income "in respect of a decedent"
15. Income from an interest in an estate or trust

Table 1
Types of Taxes (Summary)

Consumption tax	A general term describing taxes on commodities and/or services sold for direct consumption, usually paid at the time of purchase. Includes general sales and excise taxes. May also refer to a consumption or expenditure tax that is similar to an income tax except that savings are excluded from taxation.
Corporate income tax	Imposed by the federal government and 45 states on net income of corporations, usually at progressive rates that rise as income increases. Paid monthly or quarterly. Corporate income is subject to "double taxation" since it is taxed both at the corporate level and again to the recipient of corporate dividends.
Customs duties	Imposed by the federal government on imported goods, usually as a percentage of value. Paid by the importer but added to the selling price paid by the consumer. Also known as "tariffs."
Estate tax	Levied at progressive rates on the value of the entire estate of a deceased person before it is divided among the heirs. Imposed by the federal government and most states; payment is due within a legally specified period after the estate is settled. Also known as a "death tax."
Excise tax	Levied on specific goods such as cigarettes, gasoline, and alcohol and based on a percentage of value or a stated amount per unit; may be levied on producers or distributors but is generally shifted to consumers.
FICA tax	Imposed as a specified percentage of wages and salaries up to a certain amount. Paid equally by employers and employees. Better known as "Social Security tax." Employers withhold employee share of tax and submit periodic payments to the federal government. Authorized under the Federal Insurance Contributions Act to finance the Old-Age, Survivors, Disability, and Health Insurance Program (formerly by the Social Security Act of 1935).
FUTA tax	A joint levy imposed by federal and state governments at a specified percentage of wages up to a legal base; paid by employers. Rates and taxable base above the federal amount vary among states and employers. Proceeds of the tax pay benefits to qualifying unemployed persons. Authorized by the Federal Unemployment Tax Act (formerly by the Social Security Act of 1935).
Gift tax	A federal or state tax imposed on transfers of property by gift, paid by the donor. Now combined with the inheritance tax.
Individual income tax	Levied by the federal government, 43 states, and some localities on net income as defined by law. Rates are generally progressive. Tax returns are due annually, but earnings are subject to current withholding by the employer. Quarterly payments are made to the government on nonwage income.
Inheritance tax	Levied by the federal government and most states on the value of property received by the heir to a decedent's estate, as a percentage of value. Also known as a "death tax."
Luxury tax	A sales tax generally at high rates on nonessential consumption items such as furs, jewelry, cosmetics, and leather goods. Formerly levied by the federal government as a means of wartime finance.
Payroll tax	Applies mainly to taxes levied on employers and/or employees under the Social Security and unemployment-insurance programs. See FICA and FUTA.
Property tax	A levy conditioned by the ownership of real and personal property and based on its value. May be imposed at the same rate for all properties or at different rates where property is classified for tax purposes. Used primarily by local governments, some 67,000 of which have the power to levy property taxes.
Real-estate tax	The part of the property tax that falls on land, buildings, and permanent fixtures.

(cont)

Table 1 *(cont)* **Types of Taxes (Summary)**	
Sales tax	A levy on purchases or sales of goods and services at the manufacturer, wholesaler, or retailer level, but usually shifted to the final consumer. May be levied as a percentage of selling price or at a flat rate per unit. Includes general sales and excise taxes.
Social Security tax	See FICA.
Unemployment tax	See FUTA.

Source: Elsie M. Watters.

Judicial decisions have developed a concept of "income" that is quite different from what might ordinarily be expected. The courts have defined *income* as the gain derived from capital, from labor, or from both combined, provided it be understood to include profit gained through a sale or conversion of capital assets.

The Internal Revenue Code sets forth certain "exclusions" from gross income, which will not be taxed. Certain types of expenses and costs—such as medical expenses, personal exemptions, charitable gifts, and the payment of income to another—are generally deductions against one's own income.

After computing the amount of gross income and deducting the exclusions from income, what is left is the "net" income or "taxable" income upon which each taxpayer is required to pay taxes.

Alan J. Pomerantz

Tax-Anticipated Notes

The Constitution of the United States, as amended, and the constitutions of various states and localities permit the governments to tax their citizens for the purpose of conducting government business. Certain taxes, like sales taxes, are collected periodically throughout the year; others, like income tax, are due and payable only in the year after they are earned. To finance their business, governments often borrow money from people and promise to repay the loans (sometimes without interest) directly from the anticipated taxes to be collected. For example, in January the government may borrow from the public the money that it anticipates receiving the following year from income taxes. The government evidences this borrowing by issuing a note or IOU. The note may bear interest depending on the market rate. When the government collects the taxes, it uses the proceeds of the taxes to repay the loan plus any interest that may be due.

Alan J. Pomerantz

Tax Court

Governments in the United States are the only entities empowered to raise taxes. This right was given to them by the Constitution of the United States and the various constitutions of the states. In addition, governments are the only entities permitted to create courts. Because of this unique combination, governments have the power to designate in which courts certain matters will be heard. To hear certain matters involving taxes, the federal system has established a "tax court." Thus, for certain types of hearings, such as challenges to assessments of taxes to individuals and companies, proceedings may be brought against the government only in a tax court.

Alan J. Pomerantz

Tax-Deferred

This term describes income that will be taxed at a future time.

As a general rule, if a taxpayer earns money, the tax is due the year after he earns it. However, under certain circumstances the payment of these taxes can be put off (deferred) to a later year. This is economically advantageous because it permits a taxpayer to have the use of his money for a longer period of time.

Examples include Series HH United States Savings Bonds, deferred annuities, and retirement plans such as Individual Retirement Accounts and Keogh plans. The aforementioned produce a certain return, but tax on the income is put off until some future date when the participant redeems the bonds or decides to receive distributions from the plan.

Alan J. Pomerantz

Tax-Deferred Annuities (TDA's)

These *qualified* retirement plans, available to employees of certain organizations, are also called "tax-sheltered annuities" (TSA's), which is somewhat misleading since tax will have to be paid later (deferred) rather than being partly or completely avoided (sheltered). Nevertheless, the two names for this plan are interchangeable in practice.

Organizations that are exempt from business income tax to begin with lack the tax incentive of deductibility of employer contributions to a pension plan. Thus, until 1942, retirement arrangements for these tax-exempt, "nonprofit" organizations were, at worst, nonexistent and, at best, haphazard and variable. In that year, the Internal Revenue Service established this retirement plan (amended a number of times since), which is at least tax-favorable to employees and consistent for all these organizations as defined in Section 501(c)(3) of the INTERNAL REVENUE CODE. The most common examples are charities, private universities and colleges, private schools and school systems, private hospitals and medical facilities, churches and religious affiliates, research setups, and organizations devoted to the protection of children or animals. Generally, state or local public institutions are not eligible. A major exception is public school systems. Some public hospitals can also qualify, if independent. Your employer knows if your organization qualifies.

One of the reasons TDA's are included in this reference book is that 501(c)(3) organizations often offer "employment" opportunities to professionals and specialists *in addition to* their primary source of income. In this case, another pension plan may also become available to them.

The major advantage of a TDA is that the contribution by the employer or employee is excludable from taxable income in the year made. In addition, as in all qualified plans, the interest earned in the plan is not taxable until received, at which time any contributions withdrawn are also taxable. Money can be withdrawn from a TDA without penalty at any time prior to or at retirement (but is then taxable income); and if the funding vehicle permits loans, they are now treated as nontaxable distributions (at that time) up to the normal, pension-loan limits permitted by the Tax Equity and Fiscal Responsibility Act (TEFRA).

Although some other funding instruments have been added to the permitted list over the years, most TDA plans are funded by annuities. Virtually any annuity can be used (*see* ANNUITY). Although the contribution must actually be made by the employer, the money can come from the employer, the employee, or both. You should put this in writing with the employer, and a new agreement can be made each year (which gives TDA's considerable flexibility). The employer is not obliged to have a formal plan, and in fact often doesn't because the regulations do not require any coverage or inclusion of participants. Thus, the employer can be selective. A "salary reduction" agreement is very common (a portion of your salary goes to the annuity) and the employer can give raises to or make employment arrangements with whomever desired. Only the net income after TDA reduction is taxable income. Both part-time and full-time employees are eligible. The maximum permitted contribution is determined by several formulas, which are too complicated for discussion here. The choice among them, however, can affect the future as well as the present. You should seek counsel from your financial adviser or the insurance company on this as well as the current tax status of TDA's.

A warning is in order. Due to the nature of many 501(c)(3) organizations, they often make varied arrangements with the people with whom they affiliate. Only *employees* can qualify for TDA's. Thus, for example, a salaried staff doctor in a hospital, who has FICA and income taxes withheld, does qualify; while an "affiliated" doctor, who bills his patients himself, does not. There is a gray area in between, and if you fall into it, you should seek expert advice and perhaps change your working arrangement if you want a TDA.

Some people who might be eligible for a TDA may also qualify for other tax-favored plans (e.g., doctors and dentists). If the TDA is not the best alternative, it at least deserves serious consideration. For clerical and administrative employees of eligible organizations, a TDA may be the only qualified plan available (other than IRA's, which everyone can have). Investigate!

Harold C. Luckstone, Jr.

Tax Equity and Fiscal Responsibility Act of 1982 (TEFRA)

If the ECONOMIC RECOVERY TAX ACT OF 1981 (ERTA) was the largest tax reduction ever enacted in this country, TEFRA was the largest tax increase. Thus, Congress gave with one hand in 1981 and took back with the other only one year later. This should surely make clear why you should always check out current taxation.

Much of TEFRA deals with qualified PENSION PLANS. Tax benefits in *corporate* plans were generally reduced, while plans for the *self-employed* (KEOGH PLANS) were improved (basically making them equal to corporate plans). Church pension plans were also improved. There are many other pension changes in TEFRA that won't be discussed here since most of us can do little about our pension plans. However, your financial planner can advise you, if necessary.

Of greater concern to the average person's pocketbook are stiffer "minimum tax" rules; 10% withholding tax on interest and dividends; withholding tax on pension income; a penalty tax on certain withdrawals from deferred annuities before income starts; tax on part of loans made from deferred annuities; taxation of some unemployment benefits; and, for those who itemize deductions on their income-tax returns, the near elimination of casualty and theft losses (unless very large) and further limitations on medical expenses. In addition, cigarette excise taxes have been doubled through 1985; telephone excise taxes have been tripled; the tax on air tickets has been increased and an additional $3 imposed on international flights; and penalties for taxpayers who abuse or avoid tax laws have been increased (be careful of shady "tax shelters"), with criminal fines for the promoters of these schemes now going as high as $500,000.

Harold C. Luckstone, Jr.

Taxes, History of U.S.

Taxes have been with the world almost as long as there has been organized society. Well before Caesar demanded that people render unto him all that he declared was his, the Egyptians, among other ancient people, were paying tribute, tariffs, and various excises to their pharaoh. We use the verb *tax* to mean placing a burden or a strain on a person. In the monetary sense, "to tax" is to assess a person's income or to apportion a part of it to another, usually the prevailing government or ruler. A "tax," then, is a demand made on a person, and the more one is pressed to pay—the more that is demanded—the more one is likely to cry out against taxes.

It was to assert some equity in taxes that the British drafted the Magna Carta in 1215; and again in Britain, a Bill of Rights was adopted in 1689 to help assure some sense of fairness and consent among the taxed. Adam Smith (1723–90), in his book *The Wealth of Nations,* reduced the argument over taxes to its essence. He stated simply that those imposing a tax must be careful that the tax is equitable, certain, and economical to collect. If a tax applies equally to all, is not imposed arbitrarily, and is sufficiently convenient to collect, it has a chance of succeeding. Others have tried to define *taxes* as an assessment on the whole public for its general betterment. To be equitable, by that definition, the assessments would have to be applied equally to all citizens, as would the benefits.

In the United States, a tax on direct income was not approved until 1913, when the Sixteenth Amendment to the Constitution was ratified (*see* INCOME TAX, HISTORY OF U.S.). Land taxes, estate or death taxes, and other selective assessments, coupled with the wealth of newly discovered or developed territories, seemed to serve well enough to fill the coffers of kings in other countries and pay the bills of our own new nation.

There were vague attempts in England and in the American colonies to impose a direct tax on income, but they failed. The U.S., in its fourscore years, received the vast proportion of its federal income from customs duties, excises, and other indirect (not direct income) taxes. Indeed, all but .5% of the U.S. government's income until 1812 came from tariffs and excise taxes.

George Washington, presiding over his new citizenry, was immediately faced with a growing insurrection against the excise tax levied on whiskey. Tax collectors were lucky to get away with their lives and some tar and feathers. By 1794, President Washington was forced to call out the militia, under the old warhorse with the memorable name Lighthorse Harry Lee, who managed to end the Whiskey Rebellion with at least a minimum of bloodshed.

Article 1 of the Constitution had empowered Congress to levy and collect taxes, duties, and excises; and soon after, in 1791, that power was given over directly to the first secretary of the Treasury, Alexander Hamilton. The number of regional collectors quickly proliferated, functioning under a newly established Office of the Commissioner of Revenues.

In 1798 a tax was passed on slaves, houses, and land. That tax was much like the colonial "faculty tax," which required that each colonist pay a tax based on his "estate or faculties" (slaves, machinery, etc.). Even that tax turned out to be too much like a direct income tax, and by 1801 Thomas Jefferson and his Democrats abolished it, together with the Office of the Commissioner of Revenues. Except for a few aberrations of the War of 1812, anything approaching an income tax, and its consequent extension of federal power, was resisted in the United States until the Civil War, when an income tax was passed that lasted until 1872. At that time, and subsequently, when the courts declared an attempt to revive the income tax unconstitutional, an income tax was the least popular form of taxation in this country.

Of our own tax philosophers, Edwin R. A. Seligman stands out for his *Essays in Taxation,* first published in 1895. His book was precipitated by an ongoing debate in this country over the efficacy and justness of an income tax. In his first pages on the development of taxation, he notes that voluntary payments, or donations, to the group or the social community were probably the earliest approximation of taxation. "But," says Seligman, "with the weakness of human nature, in the face of a diversity of interests, even the feeling of duty fails to produce adequate revenue. The moral obligation soon becomes a legal obligation."

If people would no longer give out of a sense of duty, a more formal "duty" was required, and leaders usually showed little restraint in imposing a variety of duties and indirect taxes on their subjects. The "indirect" or hidden tax was, of course, more easily imposed in proportion to how well it was disguised. A direct tax on income was viewed as a tyranny. Even a direct tax on personal property was a difficult step for a ruler to take.

In his overview of taxation, Seligman offers the following rationale for a direct tax on income:

Just as a man's ability to support himself or his family is seen in his income or revenue, so in the same way, it is recognized that the test of a man's ability to support the state is to be found in this same income or revenue. From the modern point of view, it is the duty of the citizen to support the government according to his capacity to support himself.

One may note an echo of Marx's "from each according to his ability, to each according to his need" in this rationale, and indeed arguments for a direct income tax in the United States stirred controversy over the communistic and socialistic direction of such a tax.

David B. Axelrod

Tax Haven

From the earliest days of taxation, people have been devising schemes to avoid paying money to taxing authorities. In addition, as a result of political upheavals, there was a need to move currency to havens that promised financial and political stability. In order to attract these currencies, it was often necessary for the localities to create laws and regulations that would not tax capital placed in these political entities, nor income generated "offshore" or from local sources.

There are four basic categories of tax havens:

1. Political entities that have virtually no taxes at all.

2. Countries and political entities that impose taxes at a relatively low rate.

3. Countries that tax income from domestic sources, but exempt all income from foreign sources.

4. Countries that allow certain privileges and do not tax certain types of transactions, but generally tax other transactions.

Currently, tax havens fill two basic needs. First, they provide a place to secrete capital where it can be securely held and put to income-producing use without its owner's home country being aware of its existence or use. Second, tax havens provide the ability to earn income that, as a result of the tax laws or certain tax treaties, is not taxable by the country in which it is earned and not taxable by the country of residence of the income earner, even if they are aware of it.

An example of the first situation is a country such as Switzerland, which has very strict secrecy laws. By use of numbered bank accounts and strictly enforced criminal statutes imposing secrecy on banking transactions, Switzerland has traditionally attracted capital from people outside the country who wish to have their financial transactions kept wholly private.

An example of the second situation is a country that creates exemptions from tax for certain activities. If properly structured, business transactions can occur openly and not be taxed. Hong Kong, for example, generally does not tax activities of Hong Kong corporations that occur outside of Hong Kong. The United States generally does not tax foreign (non-U.S.) corporations that do not do business in the United States or generate general income from the United States, even if such corporations are owned by United States citizens. Thus, if a United States citizen owns a Hong Kong corporation that buys merchandise manufactured in Japan and sells the merchandise in France, there will be no income tax on the transaction anyplace.

Alan J. Pomerantz

Tax Reform

Just as sure as we are of death and taxes, we may also be sure of constant proposals for tax reform. Plans to alter the means by which a government collects its revenues have taken many and varied forms, but more recently, in the United States, tax reform has been linked with a few major proposals. Some favor revising the tax code to do away with provisions that benefit special-interest groups. Others have been enthralled with the idea of a direct, fixed percentage (1%, for example) of income tax payable by every income earner, thus eliminating complex systems for deductions and any arguments over our present system of graduated income taxes. Yet another category of tax reform would mandate that a government (local, state, federal) spend no more than it takes in—an absolute prohibition against budget deficits.

Perhaps the most popular notion of tax reform to come out of the Seventies was the movement begun in California in 1978 with the passage of Proposition 13—also known as the Jarvis-Gann proposal, after the two private citizens who placed the proposal on the ballot. The bill limited the amount of real-estate (property) tax to 1% of the property's value, and further specified that the government would need the approval of two-thirds of all registered voters to levy any new or "special" taxes.

While the immediate effect was to cut California's real-estate-tax income from approximately $12 billion to $5 billion, many of the catastrophic layoffs and cutbacks within the government were avoided with an infusion of state surplus funds into local governments. Subsequently, however, Californians have experienced noticeable cutbacks in government services, with a concurrent saving of perhaps $300 for the average homeowner in the state.

Though it can be argued that Proposition 13 provided only very modest tax relief compared to the whole burden of local, state, and federal taxes, the seeds of that reform spread quickly to other states, so that dozens more states within just a few years had passed similar laws limiting taxes.

The main complaints of the tax reformers are, of course, the increasingly high amounts of taxes, per capita, that we pay. This argument is followed closely by complaints about the increasing costs of providing government services, pointing to what seems to be growing inefficiency of the government. It is still accurate to say that, with all the real-estate and other budget and tax reforms proposed since 1978, the northeastern states, together with California and Alaska, still take the biggest per capita tax bite at the state and local level. A Commerce Clearing House, Inc., chart indicates that states like New York and Massachusetts still assess state and local taxes well over $1,000 per capita, compared to the lowest tax areas in the South, where rates are half that or less.

David B. Axelrod

Tax Shelters

A tax shelter is an investment that allows the investor to realize significant tax benefits in terms of reducing or deferring taxable income. The purpose of a tax shelter is to accelerate any tax benefits into the present and defer the burden of tax repayment as long as possible. The effect of this tax savings is to lessen the actual out-of-pocket cost of the investment and thus improve its return potential. By converting dollars that would otherwise be taxed into assets that could have real economic potential, the investor has in effect let the federal government pay for part, if not all, of the investment. This is the appeal of tax shelters—using pretax dollars to reduce the taxpayer's current tax bill and at the same time provide ownership in a meaningful asset.

Tax shelters, as a class of investment, provide necessary capital to certain sectors of the economy in exchange for government-sanctioned tax benefits. Legitimate tax shelters are not loopholes in the tax law; they are genuine incentives created by Congress to encourage private capital funding for industries vital to this country's growth and independence, such as real estate, energy, transportation, agriculture, and research and development. Of course, tax shelters have been formed around just about all types of business, from baseball teams to Bibles. If there is economic justification for the investment, it's possible to create a tax shelter around it.

Most tax shelters work on a common premise. Generally, a new business venture will initially produce tax deductions and operating losses in excess of the income derived from it. A general partner, or operator of the venture, by structuring the business in such a way that the investors contributing the capital are allocated substantially all of the tax benefits, is able to meet all, or a great part, of the financing needs of the venture without having to use capital from within the company or from outside sources, such as a bank.

Also, for accounting purposes, there is usually a benefit to the company for not having to carry the depreciation or other tax losses on the balance sheet, since on paper they lower corporate profits. This is important for a public company concerned with "dressing up" its earnings. That is why this type of financing is often referred to as "off–balance sheet." It is an excellent means of attracting interest-free capital to fund the venture, yet allows the operator to maintain a proprietary interest in the operation.

To the investors, the up-front tax benefits help to reduce the dollars of risk exposure one would otherwise have in the program. Less dollars at risk means a greater opportunity for profit. As an example, if an individual were to invest $10,000 in a real-estate limited partnership that provided a 50% write-off in the first year—that is, a $5,000 deduction—this tax deduction could be used to offset other income the investor might have. And if this individual were in the 50% tax bracket, that $5,000 deduction would help to reduce his out-of-pocket cost in the program to only $7,500 ($10,000 minus the 50% tax savings on $5,000, or $2,500 = $7,500) Therefore, any return received would be enhanced because of this lower actual amount of capital at risk.

As Table 1 illustrates, a $1,000 return on a $10,000 bond yields a 10% return. The same $1,000 return on a $10,000 tax shelter, where the investor has only $7,500 of after-tax risk capital invested, yields a

Table 1 Yield Comparison Chart	
Bond Investment	*Tax Shelter*
$10,000 bond	$10,000 shelter −2,500 tax savings 7,500 net Investment
1,000 return	1,000 return
10% yield ($1,000 divided by $10,000)	13.33% yield ($1,000 divided by $7,500)

13.33% return. So the operator benefits from the tax shelter, and the investor benefits from the tax shelter; both accomplish their objectives without either suffering severe economic trade-offs.

There are three components that make up the basis of any tax-shelter investment: (1) tax savings, (2) economic return, and (3) risk/return ratio. *Tax savings* are the benefits gained by the realization of tax deferrals, tax deductions, and tax credits, all of which help to offset the inherent risks of investing. The *economic return* is represented by material gains arising from either the profitable operation of the venture or appreciated value of the assets employed in the business, or both. The *risk* and *return* characteristics of the investment are important because, owing to the varied nature of each particular venture, every investment must be judged on the level of risk an individual finds acceptable, proportionate to its potential return. The higher the risk, the higher should be the anticipated return. Ultimately, the decision as to whether a venture is an acceptable tax-shelter investment becomes a subjective one, based on the level of risk one is willing to assume commensurate with the tax motives and economic expectations.

Most tax shelters are set up as limited partnerships (*see* BUSINESS ORGANIZATIONS, FORMS OF). A limited partnership has the principal advantage of allowing for the direct "pass-through" of cash flow and tax benefits to the investors. Because a limited partnership itself is not a tax entity, the tax obligation instead rests with the individuals who own interests in the partnership. Limited partnerships thus avoid the double taxation of corporations.

In a limited partnership, there are two classes of partners—the general partner and the limited partners. The general partner is the one responsible for managing the day-to-day operation of the venture. It is his experience and ability that will guide the course of the investment. The general partner also assumes an unlimited financial liability for partnership obligations. The limited partners are the investors. It is their pooled resources that supply the necessary capital for the venture. In turn, the limited partners are granted limited liability, limited to their capital contributions.

As previously stated, in the initial years of most tax-shelter operations, the amount of tax deductions and other tax benefits from the new venture will normally be in excess of any income that it produces. This results in a tax loss. It is this tax loss that creates the "shelter" effect as investors apply their share of the losses against other income. The net result is an offsetting of a tax liability on income that would otherwise be taxed. If the venture becomes profitable, investors are normally entitled to a share of the cash flow. Usually, because of the nature of most tax-shelter businesses, these distributions of cash are to some degree sheltered from tax. In the case of real estate and equipment leasing, where the investor owns real property, the depreciation of the asset produces deductions that can be used to offset a portion of this income. Oil and gas income can be partially sheltered because of the depletion allowance.

Various tax incentives play a role in most tax shelters. Obviously, the business activities of tax shelters are varied, but most center around the ownership of property—real property like buildings, or investment property like cattle or movies. Certain common tax incentives apply to most of these types of property. The three that are the source of most benefits are *depreciation,* the *investment tax credit*, and the *depletion allowance.*

Because of the tax codes, certain business costs cannot be fully deducted in the year in which they are incurred; they must be recovered over a period of years through depreciation. The theory is that business assets become obsolete or eventually wear out through use and must be replaced. The depreciation deduction enables a business to write off the cost of these investments over some predetermined period of time. Depreciation applies to a broad range of property, buildings (but not land—land doesn't wear out), machinery and equipment, farm animals, transportation vehicles, even baseball players' contracts. The 1981 Tax Act greatly simplified the determination of just how many years over which one must spread the depreciation deductions. Under the ACRS—Accelerated Cost Recovery System—assets now fall into one of four classes: 3-year property, such as cars and light trucks; 5-year property, like most machinery and equipment; 10-year property—for example, public-utility property; and 15-year property, which applies to most real estate. Table 2 shows the schedule of depreciation allowance for each class of investment.

In addition to the schedules for the "straight-line" method of depreciation shown in Table 2, ACRS permits the use of "accelerated" depreciation methods, which can speed up the write-offs in the first few years. For instance, for all property other than low-income housing, you can use the 175% declining-balance depreciation method. This means you can deduct 175% of each remaining year's depreciation, thus speeding up the write-offs. Table 3 compares the effects of accelerated versus straight-line depreciation on a 15-year real-estate property.

The investment tax credit (ITC) is not actually a deduction; it is a credit. There is a big distinction. A deduction permits one to offset a corresponding amount of income against the deduction in order to reduce one's taxable income base. A credit, on the other hand, applies directly against one's tax obligation, reducing dollar-for-dollar the actual tax owed. For example, if a taxpayer had taxable income of $85,000 and received a tax *deduction* of $10,000, that

---

Table 2
ACRS Schedule of Depreciation*

Ownership (year)	Class of Investment			
	3-year	5-year	10-year	15-year
	%	%	%	%
1	25	15	8	6.66
2	38	22	14	6.66
3	37	21	12	6.66
4		21	12	6.66
5		21	10	6.66
6			10	6.66
7			9	6.66
8			9	6.66
9			9	6.66
10			9	6.66
11				6.66
12				6.66
13				6.66
14				6.66
15				6.66
	100	100	100	100

*Schedule applicable through 1984.

Table 3
Accelerated versus Straight-Line Depreciation

Year	Accelerated*	Straight-Line
1983†	$11,667	$6,667
1984	10,306	6,667
1985	9,103	6,667
1986	8,041	6,667
1987	7,103	6,667
1988	6,274	6,667
1989	5,542	6,667
1990	5,245	6,667
1991	5,245	6,667
1992	5,245	6,667
1993	5,245	6,667
1994	5,246	6,667
1995	5,246	6,667
1996	5,246	6,667
1997	5,246	6,667
Total	$100,000	$100,000

*Using 175% declining-balance method in '83 with optimal change to straight-line in 1990 (you are permitted to change over from accelerated to straight-line, but once done, you can't switch back).

†Calculations assume building was placed in service on January 1.

---

amount could be used to offset an equal portion of the person's taxable income, and thereby reduce this person's taxable income to $75,000. However, a tax *credit* of $10,000 can be applied directly against any tax owed on the $85,000 of taxable income, consequently making a credit worth about twice as much as a deduction. The ITC was designed to foster new capital investment in equipment and certain forms of property. An investment tax credit is generally allowed for qualified investment property in the first year the taxpayer places the property in service. Property in the 3-year ACRS class has a 6% investment credit; property in the 5-, 10-, and 15-year classes is eligible for the full 10% investment credit. There are also special tax credits for energy investments and historic structures.

The 1982 Tax Act requires that taxpayers who choose to take the investment tax credit reduce the depreciation basis of the property by 50% of the amount of the credit. The depreciation basis of an investment is that amount used for accounting purposes to determine the extent of depreciation deductions that can be applied against a property. However, a taxpayer may elect not to have the basis reduced as described above, and instead take a reduced ITC (rather than using the 10% credit, one can use 8%, 4% in the case of 3-year property).

The depletion allowance is similar to depreciation in that both are means of amortizing a wasting asset. In the case of depreciation, that asset is usually a building or piece of equipment. With depletion, the asset takes the form of a natural resource like oil and gas. Again, much like depreciation, the government has established specific rules on depletion. There are two methods of computing the depletion allowance—*percentage depletion* and *cost depletion*. With newly discovered reserves, you can choose either method. With "transferred" properties—wells already discovered—the government allows cost depletion only.

Under the percentage-depletion method, 15% of gross revenues produced from a property may be excluded from tax. This allowance is permitted over the life of the property. Under cost depletion, that portion of the reserves that are drawn out of a property in a particular year, as they relate to the total amount of reserves, becomes the proportionate share of the cost one can use to offset income. For instance, if 20% of the reserves are drawn in a given year, the investor would be entitled to a depletion allowance equal to 20% of the cost of acquiring those reserves.

A few other tax considerations affect tax shelters. The first is the "at risk" rule. This tax law prohibits individuals from deducting tax losses from an investment in excess of the amount of actual dollars the investor has risked. The genesis of the law came from "nonrecourse" borrowing. A number of years ago, shelters were organized wherein the majority of the capital supposedly required for the investment was "lent" to the investor in the form of a "nonrecourse" note, or a loan. The investor had no legal obligation to repay it—it was simply a means of increasing, on paper, the investor's capital contribution to the venture, and thus increasing the deductions available. Today, with the exception of real estate, an investor must be fully "recourse-liable" on an investment to receive deductions up to that amount.

Another tax rule to consider is "recapture." If you sell an asset on which you have previously taken deductions for such things as depreciation, your tax position on the sale proceeds may be altered.

Normally, when you sell an asset that has been held for over one year, the profit on it is subject to a favorable long-term-capital-gains tax, in which 60% of the gain is excluded from taxation. If, however, that property is sold and a portion of the gain is subject to recapture, the recapture portion is treated as ordinary income taxable at ordinary tax rates. Recapture rules are complicated and vary according to the type of property. Generally, though, they come into play when an asset is sold prior to the end of its depreciable life. In the case of real estate, recapture is based on the type of property. For residential buildings, recapture applies only to that portion of the depreciation taken in excess of the straight-line method. With nonresidential property, if an accelerated depreciation schedule was used, all depreciation taken must be recaptured upon sale. For this reason, most investors prefer to use the straight-line method of depreciation for nonresidential real estate.

"Investment interest" is another potential tax problem. Investment interest is money borrowed to acquire investment property such as stocks, bonds, or tax shelters. There are limitations on the amount of investment interest one can claim in a tax year. The limit is $10,000, to the extent it exceeds investment income.

One tax provision that effects many tax-shelter investments is "Tax-preference items," which are subject to a "special alternative minimum tax." Tax preference was created as a means of assuring that everyone paid some tax. Many wealthy individuals used to claim tremendous deductions in an effort to reduce their tax liability to zero. Congress determined that everyone should pay something into the federal tax system, so it enacted laws that hold certain deductions to be items of preference, subject to this alternative minimum tax. Examples of preference items are the accelerated portion of depreciation on real property, the untaxed portion of capital gains, and that portion of intangible drilling cost deductions taken in excess of ten-year straight-line depreciation. This special tax is computed on "alternative minimum tax-

able income" at a rate of 20% on amounts exceeding $30,000 for individuals and $40,000 for married people filing jointly.

Tax shelters can be divided into four main groups: (1) real estate, (2) oil and gas, (3) equipment leasing, and (4) venture capital (a catchall for everything else).

Real-estate tax shelters can be anything from mobile homes to 100-story office complexes. Real-estate deals have been organized on hotels, motels, factories, apartments, shopping centers, public housing projects, fast-food restaurants, historical structures—you name it (if it doesn't move, someone has probably done a real-estate tax shelter on it already).

The types of real estate most often used for tax shelters, though, center on (1) commercial properties, (2) conventionally financed projects, and (3) government-assisted housing. These properties can be new or existing. Generally, new construction is considered to have a higher risk/reward profile, since there are more potential problems associated with it, such as cost overruns and an inability to rent out the property. Existing properties are thought to be safer, but provide less upside potential. The first rule of real estate, though, is that there are no rules. Each property is unique. Different location, different tenants, different building, different management—what may apply to one building may not work with another. The key to real-estate tax shelters is location and management—these two variables will have the greatest effect on the outcome.

Commercial properties encompass shopping centers, office buildings, and industrial properties, all of which are normally leased to corporate tenants. The attraction of this type of real estate is the relatively long-term leases associated with commercial occupancy. Unlike apartments, which commonly lease year-to-year, commercial leases typically run 3 to 15 years and even longer (most have escalation clauses that allow for rent increases with inflation.) Because many of these buildings are "leveraged"—meaning that a part of the overall cost of the property was financed with borrowed funds, such as mortgage—most if not all of the cash flow should be sheltered from taxes by depreciation and interest expense.

Table 4 illustrates the investment in a medical building. It was purchased for $75,000, of which $45,000 was borrowed on a 12%, 30-year mortgage. The building is fully rented for $9,000 per year. This is a perfect example of how a property can have positive cash flow and yet show a tax loss. It should be emphasized that this model exaggerates the point of tax deductions and cash flow because (1) no allowance has been made for a "reserve fund" to take care of any contingencies, such as repairs to the building; (2) no management fees, insurance costs, general expenses, etc., are assumed; and (3) we used the first

---

Table 4
Commercial Property Model, 1st Year Projection

Cost of building	$75,000
Cash invested	30,000
Mortgage	45,000
Rent	9,000*
Mortgage interest payment	−5,400
Mortgage principal payment	−1,500†
Cash flow	2,100
1st year straight-line depreciation	4,500‡
Tax deductions (interest and depreciation)	9,900

* This example assumes the tenant has a "net" lease, which requires the lessee to pay all property taxes, maintenance, and utilities.

† For purposes of this example, 1/30 of principal is paid down yearly.

‡ Assumes $7,500 of the $75,000 purchase price is attributable to land costs.

---

year's depreciation, which is the greatest, since subsequent years will be calculated on a continually smaller depreciable base. Of course, it should also be pointed out that rents can be expected to increase over time, and hopefully faster than expenses.

Somewhere down the road, you will probably want to sell your property, either because a substantial portion of the tax benefits have been used up or because a sale would realize a profit. Most commercial buildings are valued on a multiple of cash flow. Increase the rents, and you increase the value of the property. Property held over one year is subject to favorable long-term capital-gains treatment. It should be remembered that, as with most tax-sheltered investments, liquidity and the timing of the disposition of partnership assets rest with the general partner. Tax shelters should not be considered short-term investments; they are generally illiquid long-term propositions.

A form of commercial real-estate shelter popular with wealthy individuals is the "net lease" arrangement. Under the terms of a net lease, the tenant will pay, in addition to the rent, the property taxes, maintenance, and utilities. Many major corporations use this as a means of financing their buildings. When a corporation builds and owns its own building, they (1) tie up capital and (2) can deduct mortgage costs and depreciation on the building only, not the land. If they have a group of investors erect or purchase the building and lease it back to them, the company can deduct the full cost of the lease payments. The advantage to the investors is that they have a long-term tenant and a locked-in rate of return, having negotiated a spread of profit between their costs and the lease payments. Because this type of investment creates a substantial

amount of "investment interest," net-lease deals are recommended only for investors with high amounts of unearned income that can be used to offset the investment interest.

A conventionally financed property is usually an apartment building or a complex of buildings. Unlike commercial leases, apartment leases are generally for one year or less. The increased frequency of tenant turnover affords the owner an opportunity to increase rents, assuming the supply of apartments in that area will competitively allow it.

Most conventionally financed properties have as their objectives a combination of cash flow, tax benefits, and capital appreciation. The tax benefits of apartments are quite favorable. For all real estate other than low-income housing, you can use the 175% declining-balance depreciation method (accelerated depreciation).

The amount of cash flow a property generates is to a great extent a function of the leverage (borrowing) applied to the purchase. A low level of leverage usually produces a higher level of cash flow since there is little or no debt to service. The trade-off is that you buy less property. Highly leveraged deals are more tax-oriented—they offer more deductions from interest expense and depreciation—but they usually produce little cash, because of the need to pay off borrowings.

Capital appreciation is a result of two things: the increased value of the property and the amount of leverage. Balancing the leverage factor is a matter of investment temperament. Leveraged properties have more upside, but they generally react more poorly in a weak economic environment. Nonleveraged deals are safer because they are unencumbered by mortgages, but appreciation potential is less. Every investor has to fit his investment to his own acceptable level of risk and reward.

Government-assisted housing has always been an attractive tax shelter because it can apply a tremendous amount of leverage and permits 200% declining-balance depreciation methods (government-assisted property held over 100 months is not subject to recapture upon sale). Many government housing programs will have arranged guaranteed mortgages substantially below market interest rates, for up to 90% of the cost of the project, with the investors supplying only 10% of the capital. The government does this to encourage developers to construct lower-cost housing for low- to moderate-income families as well as the elderly and the handicapped. Besides attractive rates, these government-assisted mortgages are usually spread out 40 years in length. On the negative side, because of the attractive financing available, the government requires the project developers to maintain low rents, and therefore most government housing programs have little or no distributable cash. The government compensates for this by supplying generous tax benefits, which for the high-taxed individual can be just as beneficial.

Recent laws have been enacted to encourage another type of real-estate development, the rehabilitation of older buildings and historically designated structures. Incentives are provided in the form of special tax credits of up to 25% depending on the age of the building. Certain guidelines must be followed in the restoration process, but the tax credits can supply substantial economic justification for complying.

Another big area for tax shelters is oil and gas. The energy industry's constant need for capital has compelled Congress to maintain certain tax benefits for individuals and companies engaged in the discovery and production of these vital resources. Although this area should rightly be called "natural resources" because tax shelters are formed on all natural energy sources, including timber and coal, the majority of activity centers on the discovery of oil and natural gas, both found in prolific quantities in the United States. Drilling programs are the biggest part of this business. "Exploratory" drilling involves the greatest risk, and of course the greatest reward. Exploratory wells are drilled in areas where no known quantities of hydrocarbons (oil and gas) exist. "Development" wells are wells drilled near existing producers. Usually they are drilled around the site of a successful exploratory well, in an effect to expand the field's draining capacity. These wells usually involve a lower degree of risk, but the rewards are usually less, too. Many drilling programs have a balanced approach, spending some of the money to drill a few exploratory prospects, and the remainder for development work. Obviously, the idea behind this is to balance the risks inherent in drilling. Diversification by participating in a number of wells is also a means of balancing risk: The more wells you participate in, the greater your chances of achieving an acceptable return.

The attractions of a drilling program, from the tax standpoint, are the "intangible drilling cost" deductions (IDC's) and the depletion allowance. Certain costs incurred in the drilling and developing of oil and gas properties are immediately deductible. "Intangible costs" for items that in and of themselves have no salvage value—such as labor, fuel, and drilling-rig rental—can be expensed in the year they are incurred. Tangible or capital items—such as pipe and wellhead equipment—must be capitalized and depreciated. Most drilling partnerships are set up with an allocation of costs that allows the investor to pay for all the intangibles and the operator to pay for the tangible items. In this way, a substantial portion of the capital

contributed by the investors can be deducted during the first couple of years, while the initial drilling takes place. For someone in a 50% tax bracket, able to write off 100% of the investment in IDC deductions, it means that "Uncle Sam" is really paying for half the investment. And should oil or natural gas be discovered, a portion of the revenues will be untaxed, thanks to the depletion deduction. As Table 5 illustrates, even though the depletion allowance is 15%, because it is based on gross revenues from the wellhead, and investors receive net revenues after expenses, the amount of sheltered cash flow will actually be above 15%.

One other form of oil and gas investment that has popular appeal is the "income fund." Unlike drilling programs that look for new reserves of oil or gas, income funds purchase interests in producing wells— wells that have already been discovered and are producing or capable of producing. Sometimes these income funds finance a small amount of development drilling or enhancement work on the producing properties, but most of the money is spent to buy reserves. Consequently, little or no intangible drilling-cost deductions are gained, and most of the investment must be acquired with after-tax dollars. The production of the reserves does offer depletion allowances, which help shelter a portion of the income stream. Income funds are more conservative than drilling programs in their tax-shelter ability and their upside potential; but for someone interested in tax-sheltered income with little or no drilling risk, income funds provide a means of playing the energy game.

Equipment leasing makes up the third big segment of the tax-shelter industry. Equipment leasing is a popular way for industry to acquire expensive capital assets necessary for doing business—everything from computers, to airplanes, to buses, to machinery, to windmills. In short, if it can be leased for business

---

Table 5
Benefit of Intangible Drilling Costs on a $10,000 Investment in a Drilling Shelter

Capital investment		$10,000
IDC deductions	10,000	
Tax Savings @ 50% bracket		−5,000
After-tax cost of investment		$ 5,000
Depletion-Allowance Model		
Oil or gas gross revenues		$100
Expenses		20
Net revenue		80
15% depletion (15% of $100)		15
Depletion as a percentage of net revenue		19%

purposes, it can probably be used in a tax shelter.

The principal benefit to the investor is the availability of depreciation deductions and the investment tax credit, as well as the cash flow from the rental. For the lessee (the person or company it is leased to), the advantage is they need not tie up vital capital that can be used for other things, and since the lease payments are fully deductible, it creates a favorable situation much the same as a net lease—namely, it's more attractive for accounting reasons and it has its economic rationale, too.

Equipment-leasing deals can be made for a single piece of equipment or for several pieces, under a "pooled" arrangement. In the latter case, a number of investors pool their money to purchase a number of pieces of equipment—say, 20 long-haul buses—rather than just one. This is a form of diversification. If one bus breaks down or goes off lease (the lease expires and is not renewed), it is not as great a hardship as if the investor had an interest in just a single bus.

Because the tax law requires that the length of a lease be half the useful life of the equipment in order to claim the investment tax credit (corporate investors are not subject to this requirement), investors must seriously consider whether the equipment will be leasable when the lease term expires. Obsolescence and new technology are prime considerations in equipment leasing.

Equipment leases are on either an "operating" basis or "net lease" basis. Under a net-lease arrangement, the equipment is leased to a lessee who pays the rent, the maintenance, and any other costs related to that equipment. In an operating lease, the operator or sponsor of the program will use the equipment himself or will lease it out on a short-term basis for whatever market conditions will allow. Operating leases carry a higher amount of risk, but since they are not tied into a fixed-rate contract, in an inflationary economy, assuming supply stays in line with demand, higher usage rates are possible.

Equipment leasing is really a means of tax deferral—the postponement of tax liability until sometime in the future. In a typical leasing deal, the accelerated amount of depreciation deductions come in the early years, tapering off drastically in later years. Because interest payments will normally continue beyond this period there may actually be a point where, although the lease is generating taxable income, the investor is seeing no cash flow since it is going to service debt. And with the tax deductions pretty much exhausted, it creates a situation known as "phantom income." This is sometimes also referred to as the "crossover point," and is the most serious drawback of equipment leasing. One other tax consequence common to equipment leasing is depreciation recapture. Upon the sale of the equipment, a substantial portion of the proceeds are taxed as ordinary income, even though the asset has been held over one year. The amount of depreciation recapture will be equal to the amount of depreciation already taken and any gain realized on the sale.

On the positive side, equipment leasing, if properly structured, can be an excellent way to derive significant early tax benefits while at the same time providing the potential for high annual returns should the equipment show good utilization and residual resale value.

As an example, let's say you were to acquire a computer for $30,000, paying $7,500 in cash and borrowing the rest from a bank on a seven-year loan at 12% (interest-only payments of $300 per month for three years, at which time amortization will begin). We will also assume that, simultaneous with the purchase, the computer is leased for two years at an annual rate of $4,800. Table 6 shows what the first two years of ownership might look like.

Assuming the equipment is re-leased with good utilization, hopefully at an increased rate, and that somewhere in the future the equipment is disposed of at a reasonable price, equipment leasing can be very advantageous for both individuals and corporations seeking the benefits of a leveraged investment.

In addition to real estate, oil and gas, and equipment leasing, there are many other types of tax-shelter investments, most of them involving "venture capital." Venture capital is money invested in fast-growing young companies. This country was built on the willingness of investors to back the dreams and promises of a growing nation. Today, venture capital still survives and thrives—but, much of the investment

Table 6 **Equipment-Leasing Example, First Two Years Projection**		
	Year 1	*Year 2*
Cost of computer $30,000		
Cash invested 7,500		
Bank loan 22,500		
Computer lease income	$ 4,800	$4,800
Investment tax credit (ITC)	(3,000)	
Depreciation (5-year ACRS)	(4,275)*	(6,270)
Interest payment on loan	(3,600)	(3,600)
Tax deductions in excess of income	$ 9,075†	$5,070

*Assumes full year depreciation on depreciable base of $28,500.

†This amount reflects treatment of a tax "credit" of $3,000 as the same as $6,000 in deductions.

motive has to do with the tax benefits available.

Research-and-development (R&D) shelters are popular because the costs of developing new products and processes can be written off immediately. If the project is successful, investors usually receive their share of profits in the form of royalties. Royalties generally are taxed as long-term capital gains.

Many ventures are really variations of real-estate or equipment leasing. Cable TV is a good example. A growing industry, cable TV could be called "electronic real estate," since the majority of tax benefits come from depreciation and ITC on the cable and equipment. And like real estate, when a cable-TV system is sold, its sale price is usually based on a multiple of cash flow, much like the pricing of conventional properties.

It's very likely the sports team in your town is a tax shelter. Whether it's baseball, hockey, football, or basketball, they are all assets. The players' contracts are assets which are depreciable, as is their equipment. Other common shelters are timber, cattle, mining, fruit groves, horse breeding, movies, books, records, and artwork. All have tax incentives to encourage investment—all have a profit motive.

In the end, deciding which tax shelter to invest in should be largely a matter of economic consideration. The tax benefits are there to mitigate the inherent risks. After a few years, most shelters exhaust the tax incentives, and the investor is left with only the underlying investment. Tax motives aside, a tax shelter is like any financial product—it must be a sound business investment. Failure as a business will ultimately mean failure as a tax shelter.

David M. Geliebter

Technical Analysis

A procedure for evaluating common-stock investments, based on the premise that future price changes can be predicted by analyzing historical information from the stock market itself. This information includes, for example, patterns in price changes and data on trading volume and short sales. Technical analysts (also referred to as "technicians" or "chartists") evaluate information for the stock market as a whole, as well as for individual securities, in order to forecast both the overall trend of stock prices and the price behavior of an individual security.

Technicians, unlike fundamental analysts, believe that information regarding a firm's anticipated earnings or the relationship between general economic conditions and a firm's profitability is not useful to the individual making investment decisions. While fundamental analysts believe that the desirability of a particular stock depends on the prospects for the firm, which are affected by general economic conditions, technical analysts contend that all such fundamental data have been evaluated by market participants in determining the current price of a stock; therefore, since the current market price reflects all currently available fundamental data, this information cannot be used to predict future price changes. On the other hand, technicians believe that prices follow predictable trends and patterns; hence, an investor who studies historical patterns and market information can forecast future price change with reasonable accuracy.

While technical analysts employ a wide variety of techniques and data, a few specific examples can convey the general nature of the technician's methods. The most widely known approach to technical analysis is the Dow theory, originally proposed by Charles Dow, the founder of the *Wall Street Journal.* According to the theory, a major trend in the stock market, lasting as long as several years, can be discerned by observing the behavior of a market average over a period of time. (It was in connection with this theory that Dow developed the Dow Jones industrial average in 1896.) Intermediate trends move in a direction opposite to the major trend, and the investor can determine whether a major trend will continue by comparing successive intermediate trends. Proponents of the Dow theory believe, for example, that a major trend upward will continue if successive intermediate trends downward start and end at price levels higher than the previous intermediate trend.

Technical analysts use charts and graphs (hence the name "chartists") to study trends and patterns such as those suggested by Dow. These charts display the movements of market averages and indexes, as well as the prices of specific securities, and volume data both for the market as a whole and for individual securities. The charts are analyzed to identify patterns that, according to the chartists, repeat themselves in a reasonably predictable manner. Hence, chartists observe phenomena such as resistance levels (price levels at which the analyst expects that prices will usually decline), support levels (where he expects prices to rise), and various formations with descriptive titles including "head and shoulders," "double tops," "flags," and "channels." These, and many other formations, are significant to the chartist because he expects that historical patterns will be repeated.

Volume data is also essential to the technician's evaluation. For example, a declining price accompanied by light trading volume is not as significant an indicator of future price declines as is a declining price and heavy volume. Therefore, technicians are interested in data on the total volume of stock-market transactions and the trading activity of specific stocks in a particular time period.

Many technical analysts also believe that the size of the short interest outstanding can be a useful indicator of future price changes because it represents a source of demand for stock purchases by short sellers, who must eventually cover their short sale. Therefore, a large short interest indicates a potential for price increases.

Numerous other aspects of stock-market trading—including odd-lot transactions or the number of securities increasing and decreasing in price on a given day—are also used by technical analysts as indicators of future price changes.

R. Bruce Swensen

Temporary Disability Insurance

Temporary disability insurance, also referred to as "cash sickness insurance," provides cash benefits to workers who lose wages due to a temporary nonoccupational disability. Five states, Puerto Rico, and the railroad industry have such social-insurance programs.

The worker must be disabled as defined by law to qualify for benefits. There are also certain requirements regarding past earnings or employment. If certain other types of income are received during the disability period, the claimant may be disqualified.

Benefits are paid weekly, usually replacing at least half of the weekly wage loss for a limited time, with minimum and maximum amounts. The temporary-disability-insurance programs cover most of the commercial and industrial workers in private industry, although certain classes of workers are excluded, such as the self-employed, domestic servants, government employees, and members of the employer's family.

The five states with temporary-disability-insurance laws are California, Hawaii, New Jersey, New York, and Rhode Island. In New York the program is administered by the state Workers' Compensation Board; in Hawaii by the Department of Labor and Industrial Relations; and in the remainder of the states and Puerto Rico, by the same agency that administers unemployment insurance.

Harvey Rachlin

Tenancy by the Entirety

See PROPERTY, FORMS OF CO-OWNERSHIP.

Tenancy-in-Common Ownership

See PROPERTY, FORMS OF CO-OWNERSHIP.

Thrift Institutions

Thrift institutions are depository financial intermediaries organized to encourage thrift, particularly among small savers, by offering savings-deposit facilities to consumers. They channel the flow of money between savers and borrowers and offer liquidity, convenience, interest income, and safety of principal. The institution invests funds in its own name and is responsible for its investment management.

The operation and practices of all thrift institutions are similar, the greatest differences being the types of assets held and the kinds of loans and investments made.

Savings and Loan Associations

Description. SAVINGS AND LOAN ASSOCIATIONS are also called "homestead associations" (in Louisiana), "cooperative banks" (in New England), and some have recently converted to savings banks. They were originally founded in 1831 as building societies that pooled the savings of members in order to provide the members with funds to buy or build their own homes. That early thrift and homeownership orientation continues, and today they provide the major source of residential credit in the United States by accepting savings deposits from the public and investing those savings primarily in residential mortgage loans.

Chartering and Supervision. Savings and loan associations operate under a dual system of chartering: Federally chartered associations are chartered and supervised by the FEDERAL HOME LOAN BANK BOARD (FHLBB); state-chartered associations are chartered under state statutes and supervised by an agency of the state.

Insurance of Accounts. Federal associations and state-chartered associations who are members of the Federal Home Loan Bank system are required by law to have their accounts insured by the FEDERAL SAVINGS AND LOAN INSURANCE CORPORATION (FSLIC). Insurance of accounts is optional for many state-chartered institutions, although the vast majority of them are insured by the FSLIC. Five states—Massachusetts, Ohio, Maryland, North Carolina, and Pennsylvania—have established insuring organizations by special statute.

Services Provided. Savings and loan associations provide a broad range of financial services to both savers and borrowers. Services may include passbook and statement savings accounts; money-market deposit accounts; certificates of deposit, including market-rate CD's; IRA & Keogh retirement-plan accounts; NOW and Super NOW checking accounts; commercial demand accounts; Eurodollar certificates; home mortgage loans; commercial, corporate, business, or agricultural loans; consumer loans; overdraft loans; home-improvement loans; mobile-home loans; education loans; commercial mortgage loans; credit and debit cards; stockbrokerage services; life insurance; pay-by-phone and other bill-payment services;

financial counseling; traveler's checks; money orders; and direct deposit of paychecks, Social Security checks, and the like.

Location. Savings and loan associations are located in every state of the union, the District of Columbia, Puerto Rico, the Virgin Islands, and Guam—and in virtually every community.

Ownership. Most savings and loan associations were traditionally mutually owned by their members. Changes of regulations in 1982 and 1983 controlling conversions of mutual to stock association has increased the number of associations with some type of stock ownership.

Savings Banks

Description. SAVINGS BANKS are financial institutions originally founded to encourage thrift among working people with modest incomes by providing a safe place for individuals to save. Like savings associations, savings banks today serve a broad segment of the public in the states where they operate. Today, savings-bank depositors' funds are invested in mortgage loans, stocks, bonds, and other securities.

Chartering and Supervision. Prior to 1979, all savings banks were state-chartered corporations. Since 1979, savings banks have been allowed to apply for federal charters, although most are still state-chartered. State-chartered savings banks are subject to state laws and regulations and state regulatory authorities; federally chartered banks are supervised by the Federal Home Loan Bank Board. Mutual savings banks are the only intermediaries cross-regulated by federal authorities serving commercial banks and savings associations.

Insurance of Accounts. Most state-chartered banks are insured by the FEDERAL DEPOSIT INSURANCE CORPORATION (FDIC). Most Massachusetts mutual savings banks are insured by the Massachusetts state deposit insurance program. Savings banks that belong to the Federal Home Loan Bank system are insured by the Federal Savings and Loan Insurance Corporation (FSLIC) or the Federal Deposit Insurance Corporation.

Services Provided. Savings banks provide thrift services for savers and offer loans to borrowers. Services may include savings accounts; checking accounts; NOW and Super NOW accounts; commercial demand accounts; money-market deposit accounts; IRA and Keogh accounts; real-estate loans; commercial, corporate, business, or agricultural loans; overdraft loans; consumer loans; student loans; home-improvement loans; passbook loans; pay-by-phone bill payments; credit cards; financial counseling; and a wide variety of family-money-management services. They are authorized to sell individual and group life insurance in some states.

Location. Traditional savings banks were mainly located in the middle Atlantic states and New England. Because of federal legislation permitting the conversion of savings and loan associations to federal savings banks, savings banks are now be found across the United States.

Ownership. Except for a small number of stock associations, most savings banks are mutually owned corporations.

Credit Unions

Description. CREDIT UNIONS are financial cooperatives whose members share a common bond. They operate by collecting the savings of their members and making these funds available to the members for loans, generally at interest rates lower than market rates. A saver must usually pay a small membership fee and purchase a single share to join. Credit-union earnings are exempt from federal income taxes but may be subject to some state taxes.

Chartering and Supervision. A credit union can have either a federal or a state charter. Federal credit unions are supervised by the National Credit Union Administration; state-chartered credit unions are supervised by their respective state superintendent of banks.

Insurance of Accounts. Federally chartered credit unions are insured by the NATIONAL CREDIT UNION ADMINISTRATION (NCUA); state-chartered credit unions are insured by NCUA or state insurance programs.

Services Provided. Services that may be provided by credit unions include savings accounts, consumer and personal loans, home mortgage loans, life and automobile insurance, traveler's checks, money orders, direct deposit of paychecks, financial counseling, and credit cards.

Location. Credit unions operate in all 50 states and the District of Columbia.

Ownership. A credit union is mutually owned by its members.

Mary Ann Irvine

Time Accounts

Time accounts are, in general, accounts in which the depositor agrees to limitations on withdrawals in exchange for payment of interest.

There are many types of time accounts—including certificates of deposit, time savings accounts, and Christmas or Hanukkah clubs.

In recent years the line between demand accounts and time accounts has become blurred with the creation of the NEGOTIABLE ORDER OF WITHDRAWAL (NOW) ACCOUNT, the SUPER NEGOTIABLE ORDER OF WITHDRAWAL (NOW) ACCOUNT, and MONEY-MARKET

DEPOSIT ACCOUNTS—hybrids of demand and interest-bearing accounts. The important thing to remember about the time account, however, is that its terms call for either a specific maturity or notice of withdrawal.

Phil Battey

Timesharing

A form of ownership or a license to use that involves two or more purchasers of different time intervals, with each purchaser paying for only the time interval in which he or she will use a unit (for example, a two-week period). It is ideally suited for a vacation residence or setting, such as a recreational condominium development or a hotel.

There are many advantages to timesharing. The management firm that sells or licenses the time shares is responsible for upkeep and maintenance—mowing the lawn, repairing broken windows, fixing a leaky faucet, etc. In addition, the right to use recreational facilities like swimming pools and tennis courts is often included in the same way common areas are handled in a condominium. Purchasing a timesharing unit with a built-in kitchen saves the expense and bother of eating out.

Basically, there are two types of timesharing arrangements available. One is the "interval ownership" contract. Under this agreement, the buyer actually owns the unit. Ownership may be indefinite (fee simple) or for a specific number of years (leasehold estate). In either case, occupancy privileges each year are limited to a specific time period—e.g., two weeks. In the leasehold-estate type, at the end of the specified number of years, all owners of the time periods in a particular unit automatically become "tenants-in-common." They can then enter into a new interval agreement, sublet the property, or sell it.

The second type of ownership is the "right-to-use" contract. In this arrangement, participating families are allowed occupancy rights for a specified number of years but do not have any ownership interests or equity. When the contract term expires, the occupancy rights revert to the owning entity unless the contract is renewed. For example, in a hotel, you would buy the right to use a particular room or suite of rooms for a designated time interval each year—e.g. the first two weeks of September.

Harley W. Snyder

Title Insurance

An insurance contract indemnifying an owner or mortgagee of real property against loss resulting from specified matters related to the title of the property.

What Is Title? In any real-estate investment—whether it is the purchase of a home, the lending of money on the security of real estate, or the buying of shares in a corporation or partnership that owns a shopping center or office building—it is impossible to avoid three important questions:

1. Who "owns" the property?
2. What is the exact quality of that ownership?
3. Have all of the technical steps been taken to transfer to the investor the exact interest for which the investor has bargained?

The answers to these questions can be determined in a number of ways, but the questions themselves must be understood in order to adequately appraise the value of the investment and the risks involved.

Title and Ownership. Unlike the ownership of an automobile, which in most states is conclusively determined by a certificate of title issued by the state, there is no single piece of paper or document that conclusively demonstrates who owns a piece of real estate. A DEED is a legal document by which ownership rights in land are transferred from one person to another, but the possession of one such piece of paper does not, of itself, determine or prove who the owner may be. There may be dozens of such deeds in the history of a piece of land. In determining the ownership of that land, it is necessary to make an analysis of all the transactions that have affected the property.

The term *title* is applied not to a document but to the conclusion reached by this analysis. When real-estate people say that "title is vested in John Jones" or "John Jones has title," this is a shorthand way of saying that a careful legal analysis of the transactions affecting the property has led to the conclusion that all of the rights of ownership are held by that person. It is also possible, however, that John Jones holds title "subject to" rights held by other people.

The Quality of Ownership. The ownership of real estate is sometimes referred to as a "bundle of rights." When one "owns" real estate, one has the legal right to occupy or use the property, to dispose of the property through a voluntary transfer, to use the property as security for a debt, or to dispose of the property at death through a WILL (or, if the owner dies without a will, through application of the laws of succession).

One or more of these rights can be separated from the others so that many people can have interests in the same piece of real property simultaneously. Real estate can be divided *physically,* with one person owning the east half of the tract and another owning the west half, or with one person owning the surface of the land and someone else owning the air rights above it or the mineral rights below it. While buildings are normally part of the real estate, the ownership of the buildings and improvements can be separated from the ownership of the land.

The property can be divided *quantitatively,* with one person owning an undivided one-half interest in the property (or one-third or one-hundredth) and one or more other people owning the balance. Or it can be divided *on the basis of time,* with one person owning the property as long as that person lives (a "life estate") and someone else owning it thereafter.

Individual ownership rights can be separated as in a lease, in which the right of possession is given to the tenant for a specified period of time, all of the other rights of ownership remaining in the landlord. Or the owner of a piece of property can give someone else an "easement"—a right to use the property for a particular purpose (such as the granting of a private road or the granting of the right to maintain part of a building or improvement on the property).

Property can be granted with restrictions on the type of use to which the property can be put, or on the locations or types of buildings that will be permitted, and the party imposing these restrictions can retain the right to take back the property in the event of a violation of the restrictions.

The land may be used as security for a loan by granting to the lender a mortgage, trust deed, or similar claim against the property. In addition, the statutes of the various states create liens or claims against real estate to secure money that is due. An example of this is a mechanic's lien, which gives a person providing labor or materials for the construction of an improvement on land a claim against the land in the event the bill is not paid. The lien can be enforced by a judicial sale of the real estate in order to pay the debt.

Each of the kinds of interests just described constitutes a share in the "ownership" of the property. This flexibility contributes to making real property such a useful medium for investment, but it also makes real-estate transactions more complicated than the purchase of an automobile. It is imperative that anyone investing in real estate be sure that all of the ownership rights are accounted for.

The Transfer of Real-Property Rights. If one is buying a piece of land, acquiring a mortgage on the land, or acquiring some other interest in the land, the proper, formal procedures must be followed in order to accomplish this in a legally recognized way. The forms of deeds, mortgages, and other documents differ from one state to another, so it is important to get competent advice as to the legal requirements. In addition, it is essential to verify the identity of the parties signing a deed or mortgage and, if they are acting on behalf of a corporation or other artificial entity, to determine their authority to do so.

How does one determine the answers to these three questions? In each case, it is necessary to analyze all the prior transactions affecting the property. This is facilitated by the recording laws of the various states. Unlike the system that exists in most European countries, under the American legal system it is possible for the owner of land to transfer an interest in the land without having the transaction approved by a government agency. The transaction is completed as soon as the owner fills out a deed or mortgage form, signs it, and delivers it to the purchaser or lender. An additional step is required, however, to make sure that the rest of the public knows that the transaction has taken place. Each state has set up a system of public offices in which these documents can be filed for public reference. In most instances the offices are maintained on a county level and are operated by a county recorder or county clerk or by some court official. The act of recording a document consists simply of delivering it to the appropriate office and having it numbered and indexed. Once this is accomplished, the document is usually returned to the party who delivered it. Possession of the document is not critical, however, since a copy is maintained by the public office, and additional certified copies can always be obtained.

Other matters affecting the land (such as claims of the government for unpaid taxes) and matters affecting the power of the owner to deal with the property (such as bankruptcy or mental-illness proceedings) frequently appear in different public records.

Evidence of Title. In dealing with land, everyone is legally responsible for knowing whatever would be disclosed by the public records. Therefore, in preparing to buy real property or to make an investment secured by a mortgage on real property, it is necessary to have a search made of the public records and a legal analysis of all of the matters disclosed by that search. The result of the search and analysis is referred to as "evidence of title," and there are three basic forms in use:

Abstract and Opinion. In many parts of the country, the process of searching the records is carried out by a professional searcher called an "abstracter." The abstracter looks through the appropriate records and briefly summarizes each document or entry relating to the ownership of the land in question. These summaries, or abstracts, are bound into a book called *Abstract of Title.* The abstracter carefully certifies exactly which records have been searched and the date to which the search extends. The *Abstract of Title* is then delivered to an attorney acceptable to the buyer so that the transactions can be subjected to a legal analysis. On completing this examination, the attorney writes his "opinion of title," frequently in the form of a letter, stating his conclusion as to who owns the property, what outstanding claims there may be against the property (such as liens, easements, use restrictions, etc.), and any defects he observes in the recorded evidence of the ownership. The *Abstract of Title* obtained by the purchaser in one transaction can be expanded at a later date when the property is sold again. For this reason, an *Abstract of Title* may consist of numerous pieces prepared by one or more abstracters over intervals of many years.

Attorney's Certificate. In some parts of the country, both the searching of the records and the analysis of the items found are done by attorneys without the use of an abstracter. In such a situation, the attorney does not prepare an entire *Abstract of Title* but instead prepares notes for his own use and delivers to the purchaser only the attorney's certification that a search has been done and the attorney's conclusions as to the ownership and condition of title.

Title Insurance. In both of the preceding approaches, the abstracter and the attorney have a duty to apply the highest standards of their profession in doing their work. They are legally liable to the purchaser for any loss or damage that results from negligence in the making of the search or examination. It is possible, however, that loss can occur without such liability. For example, no matter how careful the abstracter and how diligent the attorney, it is not possible to know from the public records whether deeds or other documents related to the ownership of the property bear forged signatures. Such a document would be totally worthless to transfer an interest in real property, and the true owner could continue to assert rights in the property. Other "hidden risks" of this kind include problems related to undisclosed or missing heirs, deeds by minors or persons of unsound mind, deeds by persons supposedly single but actually married, confusion of names in documents related to the title, etc. One source lists over 50 such risks.

In addition, even where a loss does result from negligence on the part of the abstracter or attorney, in order to recover the damages suffered, the purchaser of the property would have to assert a claim or even file a lawsuit against the abstracter or attorney. At the time of such a claim, the abstracter or attorney may no longer be alive or they may not have the financial ability to pay the claim.

The existance of "hidden risks" such as those mentioned and the question of financial responsibility led to the development of title insurance. The title-insurance policy is a contract between an insurance company and a named insured under which the insurer indemnifies the insured against loss or damage resulting from defects in the title. Unlike a claim against an abstracter or attorney, it would not be necessary for the injured party to prove whose fault caused the loss, but only to show that the ownership of the property is different from that described in the title-insurance policy. Since the title-insurance company is regulated by the appropriate state authorities and is required to maintain insurance reserves, the insured party has the security of knowing that the insurer will be financially able to meet any claims payable under the policy.

There are many title-insurance companies operating in the United States, but over the years a great degree of standardization has taken place in the terms of basic title-insurance policies. In New York and Texas, the policy forms are standardized by the state insurance commissioners. In California the customary forms are those developed by the California Land Title Association. In most parts of the country, however, the basic title-insurance forms available from most companies are those developed by the American Land Title Association.

Regardless of the state, there are two basic types of policies: One is designed for property owners; the other for mortgage lenders. The typical owner's policy insures against loss or damage to the named insured as a result of (1) title being vested other than as designated in the policy, (2) the presence of defects, liens, or encumbrances not otherwise known to the insured or excepted from the coverage of the policy, and (3) the absence of a legal right of access to the property. Many forms also insure that the title is a "marketable title." This last phrase assures the owner that the examination of title by a subsequent purchaser or lender will show that the records are sufficiently clear that the purchaser or lender cannot legally refuse to accept the title on that ground. The policy issued to a mortgage lender insures virtually the same points and also assures the lender that the mortgage documents are sufficient to create a valid and enforceable lien that is superior to any other lien not specified in the policy.

There are three ways in which title insurance is distinctly different from other forms of insurance.

First, title insurance focuses primarily on *eliminating* risk related to a *particular piece* of property rather than calculating *average* losses for a certain *class* of property. The title search and examination may disclose certain defects or restrictions on the ownership, and these must be either excluded from the coverage of the policy or dealt with in some way. Much of the work of title-insurance companies consists of working with the parties and their representatives to devise ways to eliminate these problems or substantially reduce their effect.

The second difference is that, in contrast to life insurance and fire insurance, which insures against loss resulting from a future occurrence, title insurance protects against loss relating only to the status of the title on the date of the policy. That is, it guarantees the legal effect of all of the preceding transactions affecting the ownership of the property, but it does not insure against loss resulting from matters that occur *after* the date of the policy.

The third difference is that, rather than paying an annual premium for the insurance coverage, one pays for title insurance with a single premium at the time the policy is issued. The policy continues in effect for as long as the insured or the heirs or devisees of the insured continue to own the property. Many policies continue to protect the named insured even if the insured has transferred the ownership by means of a warranty deed. The policy issued to a mortgage lender continues in effect while the mortgage continues to be unpaid, or, if the loan goes into default and the lender acquires ownership of the property through a foreclosure or the taking of a deed in lieu of foreclosure, for the time that the lender continues to have a legal interest in the property.

An additional benefit of title insurance is that the insurer not only pays for loss resulting from the described title defects but also pays the cost of defending the title against such claims (even where the claims are ultimately found to be groundless).

In preparing title-insurance policies, the insurer may rely on the work done by outside abstracters and attorneys or may utilize its own staff of trained employees for the searching and evaluation of the title. Some title insurers or their agents have extensive "title plants" in which copies of many of the public records are kept and indexed for rapid access.

Who pays for the title insurance depends on local practice and the terms of the contract between the buyer and seller. In some places the cost is paid by the buyer; in some places by the seller; and in some places it is divided. The costs of various policies differ from one part of the country to another, depending on the extent to which each state regulates minimum or maximum charges and whether the charge includes the cost of the title search and examination in addition to the insurance premium.

Title Registration Systems. In a few parts of the country (Massachusetts; Hawaii; the Minneapolis area; and parts of Cook County, Illinois, for example), the state has established one or another form of title registration system. These systems are alternatives to the recording system previously described. The principal distinction between a title registration system and a recording system is that while the recording sys-

tem creates merely a depository for documents related to the ownership of land, the title registration system designates or creates a public authority that is required to pass on the validity of each transaction affecting the land. The records kept under title registration systems ordinarily include a book or compilation of certificates showing the name of the current owner and all liens, claims, and encumbrances that have been registered against the property. Such a book or certificate is an additional form of evidence of title, and the accuracy of this material is the responsibility of the state authority.

In many jurisdictions, title insurance is also used in connection with the purchase and mortgage of property that has been subjected to the title registration system. In some areas this is done because the particular registration system does not cover as many outstanding risks as can be covered by title insurance, and because the protection given by the state authorities does not include a duty to defend the owner or lender against adverse claims (as required by the standard title-insurance policy). In addition, lenders often insist upon title insurance because the title registration system does not specifically insure the validity and enforceability of the lien of the mortgage.

Additional Aspects of Title Insurance. One of the special benefits of title insurance is that it can be used to facilitate a transaction by helping to protect one or another of the parties on points of special concern. For example, an attorney may recognize that the interpretation or effect of a particular old document is open to question, and that this potential defect in the title leaves an element of risk to the attorney's client. Depending on surrounding facts, the title insurer may be willing to give special coverage to the client, protecting against some or all of the loss that might result from that risk. As financing and investment arrangements become more complicated, title insurers are frequently asked to consult with the attorneys for the parties in order to find a legal structure that the company will insure as creating valid and enforceable interests in the land, thus carrying out the objective of the parties.

The availability of title insurance has also helped mortgage lenders to sell their mortgages to the institutional investors who constitute the SECONDARY MORTGAGE MARKET. This has the effect of developing new funds for new investments.

Title-insurance companies also frequently provide escrow and closing services that assist the parties in the mechanics of actually completing the transaction with speed and safety.

By providing a variety of insurance products and

services, title-insurance companies are able to remove or minimize many of the legal risks and practical problems inherent in real-estate investments.

See also HOME, PURCHASING A.

Hugh A. Brodkey

Trade and Professional Associations

There may be exceptions, but every field of interest in this country seems to be organized for united action (Table 1). According to Gale's *Encyclopedia of Associations,* there are 16,519 national associations in America. When you add regional, state, and local associations, the number jumps to about 40,000.

An association is a not-for-profit organization of firms or individuals who have joined together voluntarily to exchange ideas, to share information, to protect their mutual interests, and in general to strengthen the economy and contribute to the good of society.

There are two kinds of associations: trade associations and professional societies.

What Is a Trade Association? A trade association concentrates on providing services of practical value to its members. For example:

- It keeps its members informed about trends and developments affecting their businesses, their profits, and their future.
- It conducts research programs designed to improve products and services, to reduce waste, to encourage recycling, to conserve energy, to build greater public goodwill—and to increase sales.
- A trade association provides special services such as insurance programs at a lower cost to members.
- It makes the views of its members known to Congress, government agencies, and state legislatures.

What Is a Professional Society? A professional society is an organization made up of individuals who are recognized as professionals in a particular field such as medicine, law, accountancy, and so on. Such a society concentrates on helping the individual member grow, develop, and advance in his profession. Typical services include:

- Programs of continuing professional education
- Accreditation
- Government relations
- Public relations
- Research
- Help and counseling in publishing and communications

The Role of Associations in the Economy. According to research conducted for the American Society of Association Executives, Washington, D.C., for its *1980 Association Operating Ratio Report,* 45% of all U.S. associations are national or international in scope, with 44% falling into the state or regional category and the remaining 11% being local organizations.

The same ASAE study found that almost 900 associations have an annual budget of $1.2 million or more, with most of those being national or international associations. The study analyzed the average budgets of all associations in 1980 and projected that total expenses for associations represented by ASAE was $7 billion.

The American Society of Association Executives—an association of associations—estimates that national associations employ 495,570 people for an aggregate payroll of more than $9.8 billion. In Washington, D.C., where the largest number of associations are based, the association business constitutes the city's largest employer after the federal government and tourism. The 3,100 national trade associations and professional groups in the Washington area account for upwards of 80,000 employees.

After Washington, D.C., the two cities where most associations are headquartered are New York and Chicago with some 2,600 and 900 respectively.

The impact of associations on the national economy is reflected in what they spend yearly on products and services. Based on a 1977 market study conducted for ASAE, associations are a major market for the insurance industry, audiovisual and office equipment suppliers, the printing industry, computer services, and allied industries. Using the 1977 ASAE study as a barometer, the following was spent by associations in one year:

- Insurance premiums—$3.9 billion
- Office equipment—$49.9 million
- Hotel accommodations—$126.5 million
- Air transportation—$52.8 million
- Printing—$185.4 million
- Typesetting—$44.7 million
- Artwork/graphics—$28.1 million
- Computer services—$73 million

The most visible influence that the association industry has on the economy is in the area of meetings and conventions. Here, associations spend more than $16 billion a year and account for more than two-thirds of the total convention market. Each convention generates substantial income for the city where it is held. For example, when ASAE held its 1982 convention in Chicago, the event netted about $3 million in revenues for the city. Convention attendees spent about $1.25 million on housing, food, miscellaneous items, and transportation. The exhibitors and ASAE spent an additional $1,750,000 on food, labor, exhibit service contractor fees, and other services. The total dollars in revenue for any convention city reflect the combined money spent by the association, the exhibitors, and the convention delegates.

The scope of today's associations goes far beyond the billions of dollars they contribute to the U.S. economy. Recent research by ASAE shows that the average national trade association represents 765 company members, and that the average national professional and individual membership society represents 24,507 individuals. Extending these figures to national groups only (because the same company or person may belong to the same organization at the national, state, and local level simultaneously), ASAE projects that more than 55 million individuals and firms hold association memberships.

Associations Today. Associations today are an increasingly important part of the private sector. They represent a diverse and powerful constituency of America's business executives and professionals. Working together, associations are seeking—successfully—to solve social and economic problems that plague not only their members but society as a whole.

R. William Taylor

Table 1
Major U.S. Trade and Professional Associations in Finance, Real Estate, Insurance, and Related Areas

Finance

American Bankers Association	Commercial banks
Investment Company Institute	Mutual funds
Securities Industry Association	Investment bankers, securities underwriters
Association of Investment Brokers	Securities representatives
U.S. League of Savings Institutions	Savings and loan associations and savings banks
National Council of Savings Institutions	Savings banks and savings and loan associations
Independent Bankers Association of America	Independent banks
Mortgage Bankers Association of America	Mortgage bankers
No-Load Mutual Funds Association	No-load mutual funds
American Institute of Certified Public Accountants	Accountants
Society of Actuaries	Individual-probability mathematicians

Table 1 *(cont)*
Major U.S. Trade and Professional Associations in Finance, Real Estate, Insurance, and Related Areas

Finance

American Academy of Actuaries	Individual-probability mathematicians
American Collectors Association	Collection agencies
National Commercial Finance Conference	Commercial planners
Investment Council Association of America	Investment-counseling firms
Public Securities Association	Securities dealers
International Consumer Credit Association	Consumer-credit executives
National Association of Credit Management	Credit and financial executives
National Consumer Credit & Finance Association	Companies involved in direct credit lending
Associated Credit Bureaus	Credit bureaus
American Financial Services Association	Financial services companies
International Consumer Credit Association	Consumer-credit executives

Real Estate

American Institute of Real Estate Appraisers	Real-estate appraisers
American Society of Appraisers	Personal-property appraisers
American Society of Home Inspectors	Home inspectors, architects
National Association of Realtors	Real-estate agents
Institute of Real Estate Management	Property managers
National Association of Real Estate Brokers	Real-estate representatives
National Association of Home Builders	Single multifamily commercial builders

Insurance

Health Insurance Association of America	Health insurers
American Council of Life Insurance	Legal reserve life insurers
Insurance Information Institute	Property-casualty insurers
American Institute of Property & Liability Underwriters	Insurance personnel, educational standards
Casualty Actuarial Society	Insurance actuaries

(cont)

Table 1 *(cont)*
Major U.S. Trade and Professional Associations in Finance, Real Estate, Insurance, and Related Areas

Insurance

American Institute of Marine Underwriters	Marine-insurance representatives
National Association of Life Underwriters	Life-insurance representatives

Related

Futures Industry Association	Futures commission merchants
American Institute of Architects	Architects
Financial Management Association	Academic and corporate individuals interested in financial management
International Association of Financial Planners	Individual financial planners
National Association of Estate Planning Councils	Life underwriters, trust officers, attorneys, CPA's

Source: R. William Taylor

Transaction Account

A deposit account from which the holder can withdraw money to make a payment or a transfer to another party through such means as a check, draft, payment order of withdrawal, or telephone transfer. Examples of transaction accounts are demand deposits; NEGOTIABLE ORDER OF WITHDRAWAL (NOW) ACCOUNTS; savings deposits subject to automatic transfer; share draft accounts; deposits that can be accessed through AUTOMATED TELLER MACHINES (ATM's), and deposits from which payments can be made with a DEBIT CARD.

The term *transaction account* was created by Congress in the Depository Institutions Deregulation and Monetary Control Act of 1980 to describe all deposits against which depository institutions would have to maintain reserves. The inclusion of interest-earning checking account–type deposits in the definition represented a significant change in the government's regulation of those deposits. Prior to the 1980 law, such accounts were treated as "savings deposits," which carried lower reserve requirements than demand-deposit accounts. The Monetary Control Act exempted personal time and savings deposits from reserve requirements. Congress excluded from the definition of *transaction account* those deposits from which account holders make three or less preauthorized transfers per month and those accounts that banks establish for depositors from which funds can be withdrawn to repay a loan at the same bank.

David H. Friedman

Traveler's Checks

A convenience item sold by many banks. Issued by well-known banks and other institutions, traveler's checks enable people to carry money without risk of loss. The issuer guarantees payment of these checks, and the purchaser pays a fee for the convenience. At the time of purchase, the buyer signs each one. When he cashes a check, he signs his name again in the presence of the casher. Traveler's checks are generally about the size of a common, personal check and are issued in many denominations.

Phil Battey

Treasury Bills

See TREASURY SECURITIES.

Treasury Bonds

See TREASURY SECURITIES.

Treasury Issues, How to Compute Returns on

The "yield" on a security represents the return, or income, the owner receives. There are a variety of measures used to specify yields for U.S. government securities bought at auction at Reserve banks. Among the methods of computing the return are the bank-discount basis and the bond-equivalent basis.

Since Treasury bills are sold at auction at a discount price—i.e., at less than face value—and redeemed at maturity at face value, the return equals the difference between the purchase price and the face value. This return is termed the "discount" or "bank discount."

Because the "discount" method is based on the return as a percentage of the face value of the bill, rather than the purchase price, it understates the actual return. Thus, an alternative measure, called the "bond equivalent yield," is often used. That measure uses the purchase price as the amount invested rather than the face amount of the bill. The bond equivalent yield also is called the "investment yield," the "interest yield," or the "coupon equivalent yield."

The exact formulas used by the Treasury are long and complicated. The results are precise to several decimal places. In addition, the formulas vary, depending on the maturity of the security.

Generally, for bills with maturities of three months or six months, the bond-equivalent-yield formula can be simplified as follows: Yield equals $10,000 (face value of the bill) minus the purchase price, divided by the purchase price, times the quotient of the number of days in the year following the issue date, divided by the number of days to maturity.

For example, assume a six-month bill (182 days) was auctioned at an average price of $9,521.90 per $10,000 face value. The high, low, and average prices are announced by the U.S. Treasury after the auction.

In this example, if the formula is taken in sections: 10,000 minus 9,21.90 = 478.10; 478.10 divided by 9,521.90 = .0502105.

Next: 366 (number of days based on 1980 being a leap year) divided by 182 days = 2.0109.

Then: .0502105 times 2.0109 = .100968. To change the number into a percent, the decimal is moved two places to the right (i.e., multiply the result by 100), resulting in 10.0968%. The number may be rounded to a bond equivalent yield of 10.10%. In that auction, the bank discount rate was 9.457%. Both yields are specified in the Treasury announcement following auctions. The bond equivalent is shown as the "investment rate."

The formula for the discount basis is considerably different because it relies on the face value of the bill.

To determine the rate on a three- or six-month bill on a discount basis, the formula is: rate equals the face value minus the purchase price times 360 days (the numerator), divided by the face value times the number of days to maturity (the denominator.)

For a three-month (or 13-week) bill, the days to maturity generally are 91, while for six-month (or 26-week) bills, days to maturity usually are 182.

In the example, a 182-day Treasury bill was auctioned at an average price of $9,521.90 per $10,000 face value. Thus, the numerator is $10,000 minus $9,521.90 times 360, or 172,116. The result is divided by the denominator: 10,000 times 182 = 1,820,000. The result is .0945692. The decimal is moved two places to the right, resulting in a 9.45692% bank discount rate. The rate may be rounded to 9.457. Note that the bond equivalent yield was 10.10%.

For the three-month bill, the same formula is used, but rather than multiplying $10,000 by 182 days, the face amount is multiplied by 91 days.

The formula to determine the approximate yields for coupon-bearing bonds and notes also can be simplified as follows: Yield equals the annual interest coupon, plus or minus the Treasury-announced discount or premium, divided by the number of years to maturity. The result is divided by the average investment.

The average investment reflects the additional return from buying the security at a discount, or the reduced return from buying the security at a premium.

The average investment equals the par (face) value at maturity, plus or minus the cost of the security (depending on whether the security is purchased at a premium or discount), divided in half.

For example, a 9⅝% two-year note auctioned at an average price of $99.955 per $100 had an average yield of 9.65%. This information is announced by the Treasury after the auction.

To compute the yield in this example, the coupon interest rate (9⅝%) is converted to a decimal, 9.625. The purchase price (99.955) is subtracted from 100 and divided by the maturity of the security (2 years). The result in this example is .0225.

The equation used is:

$$\text{Yield} = \frac{9.625 + .0225}{\frac{100 + 99.955}{2}}$$

The numerator is 9.6475. The denominator is the purchase price per $100 (99.955) plus 100 (face-value proxy), divided in half. The result is 99.9775.

The numerator (9.6475) is divided by the denominator (99.9775), and equals .0964967. The result is multiplied by 100 to convert it to a percent, 9.64967. Rounded, the average yield equals 9.65%.

Arthur Samansky

Treasury Notes

See TREASURY SECURITIES.

Treasury Securities

One of the primary responsibilities of the United States Treasury Department is to provide for the financial needs of the federal government. This responsibility includes the function of *debt management,* which involves raising funds to cover the difference between revenues and outlays and providing for the refunding or repaying of maturing debt. The Treasury raises much of its funds by selling marketable securities to the general public. These securities may be purchased, *without service charge,* from any of the 12 Federal Reserve banks (or branches of these banks) or the U.S. Treasury Department Bureau of Public Debt. These banks and the Treasury receive applications from the public for the purchase of securities, allot the securities among bidders, deliver the securities, collect payment from the buyers, redeem the securities later when they mature, and pay interest coupons. Federal Reserve Bank personnel can answer questions on the purchase, exchange, or redemption of Treasury securities, but they are not permitted to offer investment advice.

New Treasury securities may be purchased also through commercial banks and other financial institutions. These institutions, however, usually charge a fee based on each transaction. Previously issued Treasury securities may be purchased privately or in the securities market through a dealer.

Among the attractive features of Treasury securities are their safety and salability. Treasury securities are backed by the full taxing power of the federal government, thus the interest payments and the return of principal are fully guaranteed. Also, there is always an active secondary market for Treasury securities, which renders them salable at all times. The seller of such securities earns interest up to the day the securities are sold.

Interest earned from Treasury securities is exempt from state and local income taxes. Such interest, however, is subject to the federal income tax. For specific federal-income-tax liability, you should consult the INTERNAL REVENUE CODE.

Individuals seeking to buy Treasury securities may submit either a competitive or a noncompetitive bid. Those electing to submit a *competitive bid* must specify not only the amount of the securities that they want to purchase but also the price or yield that they are willing to pay. In a price auction (such as Treasury bills), the price must be expressed on the basis of 100, with not more than three decimals—e.g., 99.925.* Because Treasury bills are purchased at a discount and paid off at par, the lower the price, the higher the yield to the buyer or holder.

Competitive bidders should be quite skilled in the buying of securities or should have professional advice on how to make a proper bid. Many competitive bidders are money-market banks, dealers, and other institutional investors who buy large quantities of Treasury securities. The prices that these bidders submit for securities depend both on the rates yielded by outstanding money-market instruments and on what (if any) movement they think is occurring in short-term or long-term rates.

Small bidders or inexperienced investors may be better off submitting a *noncompetitive bid.* With the noncompetitive bid, prospective purchasers are not

required to state a price or yield; instead, they simply indicate the amount of securities they wish to purchase and agree to accept the average price or yield established in the auction. Thus noncompetitive bidders are protected against the risk of paying a price that is higher than the going market price. Yet they are also assured that their bids will be accepted within certain limitations if below specified dollar amounts. For Treasury bills, noncompetitive tenders in any one name are limited to $500,000 for each new offering. For Treasury notes and bonds, the limitation is $1,000,000.

After the auction closes (or the deadline for submitting tenders has passed), the bids are forwarded to the Treasury Department in Washington and are tabulated for each issue. The Treasury satisfies all *noncompetitive* bids first. The remainder of the offering is allocated among the competitive bidders, beginning with those that bid the highest prices and ranging down in price until the total amount is issued. The lowest accepted price is called the "stop-out" price. *Noncompetitive* bids are awarded at the *average price* of accepted competitive bids.

Treasury Bills. Treasury bills are short-term securities issued with maturities of 13 weeks, 26 weeks, and 52 weeks respectively. They are sold in minimum amounts of $10,000 and in multiples of $5,000 above the minimum. Treasury bills are issued only in book-entry form. In effect, this means that purchasers will receive a receipt rather than an engraved certificate as evidence of their purchase. Ownership will be recorded in a book-entry account established for purchasers at the Treasury. Book-entry securities protect the purchaser against loss, theft, and counterfeiting. Moreover, book-entry securities are advantageous to the Treasury because they substantially reduce the processing costs of managing the public debt.

Subsequent to their original issue, Treasury bills may be purchased or sold at prevailing market prices through financial institutions, brokers, and dealers in investment securities. Except for issues that carry a special tax-anticipation privilege, Treasury bills are not redeemable before maturity.

Offering Schedule. Three series of Treasury bills are offered on a regular basis. Two series of bills, one having a 13-week and the other a 26-week maturity period, are offered each week. Except when holidays or special situations occur, the pattern for weekly issues is as follows:

1. The offering is announced on Tuesday.

2. The bills are auctioned the following Monday.

3. The bills are issued on the Thursday after the auction.

Treasury bills with a 52-week maturity period are

---

* The prices of Treasury securities are quoted on a 100-face-value basis even though the actual face value is some multiple of 100. For example, a $1,000-face-value bond with a quoted price of 99.925 would sell for $999.25; a $10,000-face-value security would sell for $9,992.50.

also offered on a regular basis every four weeks as follows:

1. The offering is announced every fourth Friday (for exact date, contact your local Federal Reserve Bank).
2. The bills are auctioned the following Thursday.
3. The bills are issued on the following Thursday.

When a normal auction date falls on a holiday, the auction is generally held on the preceding business day.

Purchase Procedures. To purchase Treasury bills, a prospective purchaser must first submit a *tender,* which is nothing more than a special form to be completed for submitting a bid. A copy of a tender for 26-week bills, along with instructions, is shown in Figure 1 (pages 618–620). The tender is in quadruplicate, with one copy to be retained by the purchaser. Located on the tender is a place for purchasers to indicate whether they are submitting a competitive or noncompetitive bid. For a *competitive bid,* purchasers must specify the price they are willing to pay. In the case of a *noncompetitive bid,* purchasers do not have to specify a price; instead, they agree to pay the average price of the competitive tenders accepted by the Treasury. By submitting a noncompetitive bid, a purchaser is assured of receiving the amount of bills requested up to a maximum of $500,000.

A bid must be submitted in advance of the auction. Prospective purchasers will not know the results of the auction—and consequently the return on their investment—until an announcement is made by the Treasury, usually the day after the auction. This announcement frequently appears in the local newspaper. If a particular local newspaper does not carry such announcements, individuals may find the results in the *Wall Street Journal* or one of the other prominent newspapers.

A purchaser may submit a tender directly to one of the Federal Reserve banks, or to one of its branches. The tender may be submitted in person (between 9:00 A.M. and 2:00 P.M.) or by mail. A tender may be submitted on the auction date, but it must reach the Federal Reserve Bank (or its branch) by 1:30 P.M., Eastern time, to be eligible, or, in the case of direct submission by mail to the Treasury, it must be postmarked no later than midnight the prior day and received no later than the date of issue. (Normally, this requires mailing during the week before the auction.) Any tender received after the deadline is automatically held for the next auction unless the purchaser specifically requests that it be returned. Purchasers who submit a letter rather than a tender form should be sure to type or print it carefully and should include the following information:

1. The face amount of bills requested

2. The maturity desired (3, 6, or 12 months)
3. Whether they are submitting a noncompetitive or competitive bid, and if competitive, the price
4. Whether they want to reinvest the funds at maturity
5. The account identification, which includes the purchaser's name and mailing address
6. The Social Security number of the purchaser (two Social Security numbers are required for co-ownership)
7. The purchaser's telephone number during business hours
8. The purchaser's signature

The tender and payment should be mailed to: Fiscal Agency Department, the name and address of the Federal Reserve Bank in the area. The purchaser should print or type the words *Tender for Treasury Bills* at the bottom of the envelope.

Payment. Payment for the full face value of the Treasury bills must accompany the tender. The payment can be made in one of the following forms:

1. In U.S. currency
2. By certified personal check
3. By check issued by a commercial bank, savings and loan association, savings bank, or credit union (provided such checks are drawn to the order of a specified Federal Reserve bank or the U.S. Treasury)
4. With redemption checks issued by the Bureau of Public Debt in payment of matured Treasury bills, provided the tender is submitted in the name(s) of the payee(s)
5. In matured U.S. Treasury securities (notes or bonds)

The difference between the payment for the face value of the bills and the issue price as determined by the auction will be refunded to the purchaser shortly thereafter. For example, the purchaser would receive a check for $150 if the issue or purchase price of the bill turns out to be $9,850 for a $10,000 bill. This check for $150 is in fact *a refund* and *not prepaid interest.*

Book-Entry. When Treasury bills are issued in book-entry form, the Treasury Department will establish an account for the purchase within 10 to 60 days after the issue date and will mail the purchase Form PD 4949, a "statement of account" (Figure 2, page 621). This statement will include relevant information about the purchaser's transaction, such as the account number, amount of securities, interest earnings, date of issue, and date of maturity. The first copy of the statement, marked "duplicate," is intended for use in corresponding with the Bureau of Public Debt, U.S. Treasury Department. The second copy is the statement that purchasers should retain for their own records. This copy does not have a carbon back and

"26-WEEK BILLS"

FORM PD 4632-2
Dept. of the Treasury
Bur. of the Public Debt
(Rev. Jan. 1980)

INSTRUCTIONS FOR COMPLETING FORM PD 4632-2
"TENDER FOR TREASURY BILLS IN BOOK-ENTRY FORM
AT THE DEPARTMENT OF THE TREASURY
26-WEEK BILLS ONLY"

USE OF TENDER FORM
This form should be used only to submit a bid for the purchase of 26-week Treasury bills in book-entry form if the Department of the Treasury is to establish and maintain the book-entry account for the securities. If bills are to be held in book-entry form by a financial institution or a dealer in securities, the institution or dealer will supply the form to be used.

TENDERS MUST BE SUBMITTED IN ACCORDANCE WITH THE INSTRUCTIONS IN THE CURRENT PUBLIC ANNOUNCE-MENT. REGULATIONS GOVERNING BOOK-ENTRY TREASURY BILLS ARE CONTAINED IN DEPARTMENT CIRCULAR, PUBLIC DEBT SERIES NO. 26-76.

The following instructions are keyed to the headings on the form:

FOR OFFICIAL USE ONLY
Do not write in these spaces.

MAIL TO
This tender may be submitted either to the Bureau of the Public Debt, Securities Transactions Branch, Room 2134, Main Treasury, Washington, D C 20226, or to the Federal Reserve Bank of your district. If the latter, indicate the name of the Bank or Branch. Tenders must be timely submitted, as provided under "Type of Bid".

TYPE OF BID
NONCOMPETITIVE
Check this block if the tender is being submitted on a noncompetitive basis. To be considered timely, a noncompetitive bid must be received by the Treasury or a Federal Reserve Bank or Branch no later than 1:30 p.m., Eastern time, on the auction date, or, in the case of direct submission by mail to the Treasury, postmarked no later than midnight the prior day. Do not enter a price.

COMPETITIVE
Check this block if the tender is being submitted on a competitive basis. If this block is checked, enter the price offered, which must be expressed on the basis of 100, with three decimals, e.g., 99.920. Fractions may not be used. To be considered timely, a competitive bid must be received by the Bureau of the Public Debt or a Federal Reserve Bank or Branch no later than 1:30 p.m., Eastern time, on the auction date.

IF NEITHER BLOCK IS CHECKED OR IF NO PRICE IS ENTERED THE TENDER WILL BE CONSIDERED NONCOMPETITIVE.

AMOUNT OF TENDER
Enter the total par amount of bills being requested. Amount must be a minimum of $10,000 or a multiple of $5,000 over the minimum amount.

ACCOUNT IDENTIFICATION
a.   Print the name or title of the Depositor for whom the account is to be maintained on the books of the Bureau of the Public Debt. Accounts will be established in the name or names of individuals, executors, trustees, partners, officers of corporations or unincorporated associations, natural or voluntary guardians, etc. Accounts for individuals must be shown in one of two forms: (i) single name, or (ii) two names joined by the connective "or". No other form of recordation in the names of individuals is permitted. Accounts for corporations, associations, fiduciaries, partnerships, etc., must show the name of the entity. In order to facilitate transactions which may be necessary prior to maturity, the name of a corporation or association should be followed by the name of one individual authorized to request transactions. By identifying an authorized individual as part of the recordation, the Treasury Department will recognize the request by that individual to dispose of the account without requiring any other supporting evidence such as resolutions, powers of attorney, etc. Paragraphs 2.a. and b. on the back of this instruction sheet provide examples of the forms in which accounts will be maintained.

b.   Enter the Depositor's home address or the address to which the Bureau of the Public Debt is to mail notices and payments.

c.   Enter the Depositor's taxpayer identifying number. If recordation in the names of two individuals is requested, enter the appropriate number for each Depositor. Treasury bills will not be recorded on the books of the Bureau of the Public Debt unless the appropriate number(s) is furnished. Paragraph 2.c. on the back of this instruction sheet provides information regarding the number to be used.

DISPOSITION OF PROCEEDS
Reinvestment (roll-over) may be authorized by checking this block. After issue, reinvestment may be cancelled by completing Form PD 4633 "Request for Transactions in Book-Entry Treasury Bills Maintained by the Bureau of the Public Debt." Reinvestment may also be authorized after issue by completing Form PD 4633-1 which is mailed with the statement of account.

METHOD OF PAYMENT
PAYMENT IN FULL MUST ACCOMPANY ANY TENDER SUBMITTED DIRECTLY TO THE BUREAU OF THE PUBLIC DEBT OR A FEDERAL RESERVE BANK OR BRANCH. The amount of the payment should be shown on the form. If payment is made by check, the check must be issued by a commercial bank, savings or thrift institution, savings and loan association, or credit union; or the check must be certified. Checks must be drawn to the order of (a) the Bureau of the Public Debt if this tender is submitted to the Bureau of the Public Debt, or (b) a Federal Reserve Bank or Branch if the tender is submitted to one of them. If matured or maturing Treasury securities are submitted for redemption and the proceeds are to be applied to the purchase price of Treasury bills, enter the par amount of securities presented. Describe the securities by title in the space above the words "Maturing Treasury Securities", e.g., Treasury Bills Due 6-2-77.

DEPOSITOR'S AUTHORIZATION
Sign and date the tender. A telephone number, including area code, is requested so that you may be contacted in the event questions arise concerning the account.

Figure 1.

GENERAL INFORMATION REGARDING
TREASURY BILL BOOK-ENTRY ACCOUNTS
MAINTAINED AT TREASURY

1. SCOPE OF TREASURY BOOK-ENTRY SYSTEM — The book-entry system maintained by the Bureau of the Public Debt, Department of the Treasury, is designed to serve those who invest in Treasury bills with the intention of holding them to maturity. The Treasury WILL NOT:

   a. Arrange for, conduct or handle cash transfers incident to transactions after original issue;

   b. Recognize the pledge of book-entry Treasury bills deposited with it; or

   c. Transfer bills between accounts it maintains, except in the case of lawful succession.

2. RECORDATION — The Bureau of the Public Debt will maintain book-entry accounts in the forms prescribed in Sections 350.7 and 350.14 of Department Circular, Public Debt Series No. 26-76.

   a. Individuals. Accounts for book-entry Treasury bills may be held in the names of individuals in either of two forms: single name, i.e., "John A. Doe (123-45-6789)"; or two names, i.e., "John A. Doe (123-45-6789) or Mary B. Doe (987-65-4321)".

   b. Others. Accounts for book-entry Treasury bills may be held in the names of fiduciaries and other entities in the forms indicated by the following examples:

   John Smith and First National Bank, ex uw of James Smith (456-78-9123)

   John Smith, Tr u/a Sara E. Coe dtd 5-27-76 (12-3456789)

   Smith Manufacturing Co., Inc., James Brown, Treas (98-7654321)

   Grey and White (21-3456789), John Grey, Gen Partner

   John Doe, Secy-Treas of Local 100, Brothd of Locomotive Engineers, uninc assn (89-1234567)

   John R. Greene, as natural gdn of Maxine Greene (321-45-6789)

   John A. Jones, as voluntary gdn of Henry M. Jones (789-12-3456)

   c. Taxpayer Identifying Numbers. The appropriate taxpayer identifying number (the number required on tax returns and other documents submitted to the Internal Revenue Service) must be furnished for each account established at the Bureau of the Public Debt. In the case of an individual, it is the social security number of the Depositor, i.e., "123-45-6789". In the case of a partnership, company, organization, or trust, it is the employer identification number, i.e., "12-3456789". In the case of a guardian, it is the social security number of the beneficial depositor, i.e., "987-65-4321". In the case of a deceased person, it is the social security number of the decedent, i.e., "231-45-6789", or the employer identification number of the estate, i.e., "89-1234567".

3. TRANSFERS FROM THE BUREAU OF THE PUBLIC DEBT — The Bureau of the Public Debt will transfer book-entry securities under the following conditions:

   a. A book-entry account will be transferred through the Federal Reserve Bank communications system to a book-entry account established and maintained by (i) a member bank of the Federal Reserve System, or (ii) an entity providing securities safe-keeping services for customers (e.g., a nonmember bank, thrift institution, securities dealer, etc.) which has a related book-entry account at a member bank. The transfer will be made only in the name or names of the Depositor(s) as recorded on the books of the Bureau of the Public Debt.

   b. To obtain a transfer, a request certified by an officer authorized generally to certify assignments of registered Treasury securities under Department Circular No. 300, current revision, must be submitted by or on behalf of the Depositor. (Form PD 4633 should be used for this purpose.) CERTIFICATIONS BY NOTARIES PUBLIC ARE NOT ACCEPTABLE FOR TRANSFERS. Each request must (i) identify the account by name(s), address and taxpayer identifying number(s); (ii) specify the amount, maturity date and CUSIP number of the bills to be transferred; and (iii) specify the name of the member bank to or through which the transfer is to be made, the type of account at the member bank, the name of the commercial bank's branch, to whose attention the transfer should be sent and, when appropriate, the entity which is to maintain the book-entry account.

   c. Transfers of bills from accounts maintained by the Bureau will not be made earlier than twenty (20) business days after the issue date or the date the bills were transferred to the Bureau, nor later than twenty (20) business days before maturity.

   d. All transfers must be in the minimum amount of $10,000 or a multiple of $5,000 above that amount. Withdrawals may be made in whole or in part, provided that partial withdrawals do not reduce the balance in the account below $10,000.

4. OTHER TRANSACTIONS — To insure the proper delivery of checks, all requests for change of address, change of name, recognition of fiduciaries or persons entitled, etc., must be received no later than twenty (20) business days before maturity. (Form PD 4633 should be used to provide such notices.) The signature to such requests must be certified by an authorized certifying officer. A notary public is considered an authorized certifying officer in these cases.

5. CONFIRMATION OF TRANSACTION — The Bureau of the Public Debt will issue to each Depositor a statement of account confirming the establishment of a book-entry account or any transaction or change affecting such an account.

6. CORRESPONDENCE — All inquiries regarding book-entry accounts or requests for transactions after original issue should be addressed to Bureau of the Public Debt, Book Entry, Washington, D.C. 20226.

Figure 1.

FORM PD 4632-2
Dept. of the Treasury
Bur. of the Public Debt

**TENDER FOR TREASURY BILLS
IN BOOK-ENTRY FORM AT THE
DEPARTMENT OF THE TREASURY
26-WEEK BILLS ONLY**

FOR OFFICIAL USE ONLY

FRB Request No. _____

Issue Date _____

Due Date _____

Cusip No. 912793

MAIL TO:

☐ Bureau of the Public Debt, Securities Transactions Branch
Room 2134, Main Treasury, Washington, D. C. 20226
☐ Federal Reserve Bank or Branch
of your District at: _____

**BEFORE COMPLETING THIS FORM READ THE
ACCOMPANYING INSTRUCTIONS CAREFULLY**

Pursuant to the provisions of Department of the Treasury Circular, Public Debt Series No. 27-76, the public announcement issued by the Department of the Treasury, and the regulations set forth in Department Circular, Public Debt Series No. 26-76, I hereby submit this tender, in accordance with the terms as marked, for currently offered U.S. Treasury bills for my account. (Competitive tenders must be expressed on the basis of 100, with three decimals. Fractions may not be used.) I understand that noncompetitive tenders will be accepted in full at the average price of accepted competitive bids and that a noncompetitive tender by any one bidder may not exceed $500,000.

TYPE OF BID

NONCOMPETITIVE ☐   or   COMPETITIVE ☐   at: Price _____

AMOUNT OF TENDER $ _____
(Minimum of $10,000. Over $10,000 must be in multiples of $5,000.)

ACCOUNT IDENTIFICATION: (Please type or print clearly using a <u>ball-point pen</u> because this information will be used as a mailing label.)

Depositor(s) _____

_____

_____

Address _____

_____

_____

PRIVACY ACT NOTICE
The individually identifiable information required on this form is necessary to permit the tender to be processed and the bills to be issued, in accordance with the general regulations governing United States book-entry Treasury bills (Department Circular PD Series No. 26-76). The transaction will not be completed unless all required data is furnished.

DEPOSITOR(S) IDENTIFICATION NUMBER

FIRST NAMED   SOCIAL SECURITY NUMBER   ☐☐☐ - ☐☐ - ☐☐☐☐   OR   EMPLOYER IDENTIFICATION NO.   ☐☐ - ☐☐☐☐☐☐☐

SECOND NAMED   SOCIAL SECURITY NUMBER   ☐☐☐ - ☐☐ - ☐☐☐☐

DISPOSITION OF PROCEEDS

The par amount of the account will be paid at maturity unless you elect to have Treasury reinvest (roll-over) the proceeds of the maturing bills. (See below)

☐ I hereby request noncompetitive reinvestment of the proceeds in book-entry Treasury bills.

METHOD OF PAYMENT

TOTAL SUBMITTED $ _____   Cash $ _____   Check $ _____   Maturing Treasury Securities $ _____

DEPOSITOR'S AUTHORIZATION

Signature _____   Date _____   Telephone Number During Business Hours (_____) _____   Area Code

FOR OFFICIAL USE ONLY

Received by _____   Date _____

STATEMENT OF ACCOUNT		Issue Discount Price $		Amount of Discount $	
Date	Transaction	Par Amount Transacted		Account Balance	Authority Reference	Validation
		Decrease	Increase			
		$	$	$		

A: Department of the Treasury Copy

Figure 1.

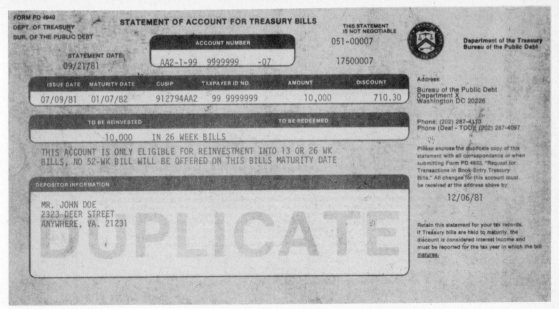

Figure 2.

has relevant information printed on the reverse side. The duplicate copy should be included with all correspondence and transaction requests affecting the account except Forms PD 4633-2 (computer reinvestment cards).

To request a change in the account, such as change in address or cancellation of a previous request for reinvestment, the purchaser should request Form PD 4633 (Figure 3, pages 622–624) from a Federal Reserve bank. The completed form should be mailed to the Bureau of Public Debt, U.S. Treasury Department, along with the *duplicate copy of Form PD 4949.* The Treasury Department will not make an account change unless the change can be effected 20 business days prior to maturity.

For individuals, accounts for book-entry Treasury bills may be held in their names in one or two forms as follows:

One name	John A. Doe (123-45-6789) (Address)
Two names	John A. Doe (123-45-6789) (Address) or (Mrs.) Mary C. Doe (987-65-4321).

No other forms of recordation in *two names,* whether individuals or others, will be permitted, except in the case of cofiduciaries.

Accounts for book-entry Treasury bills may be held in the names of fiduciaries and other entities in the forms indicated by the examples shown in Subpart C, *Federal Register* Volume 41, Number 235—Monday, December 6, 1976.* Several key regulations governing book-entry Treasury bills are in this volume of the *Federal Register.*

Transfer or Sale of Treasury Bills. While the Treasury bills are held in a Treasury account, any owner of such bills who wishes to sell them must have the bills transferred through the Federal Reserve communications system to an account maintained by or through a Federal Reserve member bank. A request for withdrawal must be made sufficiently in advance of the maturity date of the bill to permit its timely transfer. The Treasury *will not* (1) arrange for conduct of or handle cash transfers involved in transactions after original issue; (2) recognize a pledge of book-entry securities for collateral; (3) transfer securities among book-entry accounts it maintains, except in case of legal succession.

To effect changes other than ownership transfers, the purchaser's signature must be certified by a notary public. To transfer ownership through a private financial institution, the purchaser's signature must be certified by an officer or employee of a bank or trust company, a federal savings and loan association, or

*Also listed as Department of the Treasury, *Department Circular, Public Debt Series No. 26—76.*

INSTRUCTIONS FOR COMPLETING FORM PD 4633,
"REQUEST FOR TRANSACTIONS IN BOOK-ENTRY TREASURY BILLS
MAINTAINED BY THE BUREAU OF THE PUBLIC DEBT"

The following instructions are keyed to the numbered items on Form PD 4633.

1.   Enter the requested information as shown on the Statement of Account. Please submit a separate form for each Treasury bill account.

2.a.   Check this block and complete this item if the Bureau of the Public Debt is being requested to wire transfer all or any part of the account to a commercial institution. A wire transfer must be in a minimum amount of $10,000 or a multiple of $5,000 above that amount. A withdrawal may be made in whole or in part, provided that a partial withdrawal does not reduce the balance in the account below $10,000. The account will be transferred in the same form in which it is maintained by the Bureau of the Public Debt. The commercial institution to which the account is to be transferred must agree in advance to accept the transfer and should provide the remainder of the information necessary to complete this item, including the wire routing number of the member bank to which the wire is to be addressed. Special routing instructions to the Federal Reserve Bank and member bank should be shown, where appropriate. A wire transfer will not be made before twenty (20) business days after the issue date or after twenty (20) business days before the maturity date. (Due allowance should be made for the time needed to transmit this form to the Bureau.)

2.b.   Check this block to authorize the noncompetitive reinvestment of the bills, rather than their cash redemption, at maturity. This action will constitute the submission of a noncompetitive tender for the issue of new bills of the term indicated which are offered concurrently with the maturity of the outstanding bills. A request for continuous reinvestment will not be accepted.

2.c.   Check this block to cancel a previous reinvestment authorization and to request that the proceeds of the Treasury bill be paid to the depositor(s) at maturity.

2.d.   Check this block if the address on the account is to be changed. Also complete item 3.b. Indicate "SAME" in 3.a. and 3.c. if there is no other change in the account designation. An address for a check mailed to financial institutions should include the name of the office when appropriate, and the account number.

2.e.   Check this block if the status of the depositor(s) has changed due to death, incompetency, etc. In the event of death of one of two named depositors, a certified copy of a death certificate is necessary to obtain recognition of the survivor as sole depositor. If there is no surviving depositor, and an executor or administrator has been appointed, submit a copy of letters of appointment, certified under seal as of a recent date. If the decedent's estate will not be administered, a completed Form PD 4634 must be submitted. If a guardian or other fiduciary has been appointed for the depositor, a copy of the appointment, certified under seal as of a recent date, must be submitted.

2.f.   Check this block if the depositor's name has been changed. If the name was changed other than by marriage, attach a certified copy of the court order. If the name was changed by marriage, no evidence is required, but the signature to the request should show both names, e.g., "Shirley J. Smith, changed by marriage from Shirley S. Jones". Also complete item 3.a. Indicate "SAME" in 3.b. and 3.c. if there is no change in either address or taxpayer identifying number.

2.g.   Check this block to request any other change or correction in the account, such as a misspelled name, erroneous taxpayer identifying number, etc. Complete item 3. as appropriate. If necessary, identify changes on a separate sheet and attach it to the form.

3.   Complete applicable portions if item 2.d., 2.e. or 2.f. is checked. "SAME" can be used in a., b. or c., if there is no change.

4.   Sign the form and, if acting in a fiduciary capacity, enter the appropriate title. A telephone number including area code, is requested so the submitter can be contacted promptly in the event questions arise concerning the request.

5.   If item 2.a. is checked, the signature to this request must be certified by an officer or employee of a bank or trust company chartered by or incorporated under the laws of the United States, or a Federal savings and loan association, or other organization which is a member of the Federal Home Loan Bank System, who has been authorized to (i) generally bind their respective institutions by their acts, (ii) unqualifiedly guarantee signatures to assignments of securities, or (iii) expressly certify assignments of securities (See Subpart F of Department of the Treasury Circular No. 300, current revision.) A complete list of classes of authorized officers may be obtained from any Federal Reserve Bank or the Bureau of the Public Debt. If transfer is not requested, and item 2.a. is not checked, the signature may be certified by either a notary public or one of the officers or employees described above.

NOTE:

A single Form 4633 may be used to request a change of name, address, or status of the depositor(s), as well as the wire transfer, reinvestment or revocation of a previous reinvestment request.

Figure 3.

FORM PD. 4633
Dept. of the Treasury
Bur. of the Public Debt
(Rev. Mar. 1980)

(For Official Use Only)

REQUEST FOR TRANSACTIONS IN
BOOK-ENTRY TREASURY BILLS MAINTAINED
BY THE BUREAU OF THE PUBLIC DEBT

REQUESTS FOR TRANSACTIONS CONCERNING TREASURY BILLS ISSUED PRIOR TO JANUARY 15, 1980 MUST BE RE-
CEIVED BY THE BUREAU OF THE PUBLIC DEBT NOT LATER THAN TEN (10) BUSINESS DAYS PRIOR TO MATURITY. RE-
QUESTS FOR BILLS ISSUED AFTER JANUARY 15, 1980, MUST BE RECEIVED NOT LATER THAN TWENTY (20) BUSINESS
DAYS PRIOR TO MATURITY' (NOTE: DO NOT COUNT SATURDAYS, SUNDAYS OR FEDERAL HOLIDAYS.)

BUREAU OF THE PUBLIC DEBT
DEPT. X   TELEPHONE: (202) 287-4113
WASHINGTON, D. C. 20226   (TTY) TELEPHONE FOR THE DEAF: (202) 287-4097

The undersigned hereby requests that the action indicated below be taken on the following described book-entry Treasury bills maintained at the Bureau of the Public Debt:

1.   **CURRENT ACCOUNT IDENTIFICATION (as shown on Statement of Account):**   Amount _____

   a.   Description of bills:
         Account No.   Issue Date _____

   _____   Due Date _____

   b.   Depositor(s) _____

   _____

   c.   Address _____

   _____

   d.   Depositor's Taxpayer Identifying Number

   SOCIAL SECURITY NUMBER   EMPLOYER IDENTIFICATION NUMBER
   FIRST   [ ][ ][ ] – [ ][ ] – [ ][ ][ ][ ]   OR   [ ][ ] – [ ][ ][ ][ ][ ][ ][ ]
   NAMED

2.   **ACTION REQUESTED [Check appropriate block(s)]** :

   a. ☐ Wire Transfer (see footnote 1) $ _____ of the above described bills through the

      Federal Reserve Bank or Branch at _____

      to [ ][ ][ ][ ][ ][ ][ ][ ][ ]
          (Wire Routing No.)   (Member bank name and address, including branch or office)

      If account is not to be maintained at member bank shown above, furnish name and address of financial institution or se-
      curities dealer which will act as custodian. Please include branch or office and to whose attention the transfer should be
      directed.

      _____

      _____

      _____

   b. ☐ Reinvestment of the redemption proceeds at maturity into bills then being issued for the term checked; this request will consti-
      tute a noncompetitive tender for such new bills which are offered concurrently. Only one type of bill may be selected when
      requesting reinvestment. Please note that 26 week and 13 week bills are interchangeable. Fifty-two week bills maturing on or
      before October 14, 1980 may be reinvested in 52 week bills only. Fifty-two week bills maturing on or after November 6, 1980
      may be reinvested in 52 week, 26 week or 13 week bills.

      Check one type only: (2) ☐ 52 week bill   (6) ☐ 26 week bill   (3) ☐ 13 week bill

   c. ☐ Payment of the redemption proceeds at maturity instead of reinvestment as previously requested. (See footnote 2)

   d. ☐ Change of address. (See footnote 2 and complete item 3.b. on reverse)

   e. ☐ Recognition of fiduciary or other change in status of the Depositor(s) (evidence required). (See footnote 2 and complete
      item 3. on reverse)

   f. ☐ Change of name (evidence may be required): (See footnote 2 and complete item 3.a. on reverse)

   g. ☐ Other (See footnote 2 and complete item 3. as appropriate)_____
                                                                        (specify)

   1/   Signature must be certified. Certification by a notary public WILL NOT be accepted. See instruction 5.
   2/   Signature must be certified. Certification by a notary public will be accepted.

Figure 3.

3. **REVISED ACCOUNT IDENTIFICATION** [Complete applicable portion(s) if item
    2.d., 2.e., or 2.f. is checked]

    a. Depositor(s) _____
        _____
        _____

    b. Address for mailing Statement of Account   Address for mailing checks (If different
                                                      from address for mailing Statement of Account)

        _____   _____
        _____   _____
        _____   _____
        _____   _____

                                            (Please include account number if this is a
                                            financial institution)

    c. Depositor's Taxpayer Identifying Number

    FIRST   SOCIAL SECURITY NUMBER   EMPLOYER IDENTIFICATION NUMBER
    NAMED   [ ][ ][ ] — [ ][ ] — [ ][ ][ ][ ]   OR   [ ][ ] — [ ][ ][ ][ ][ ][ ][ ]

    PRIVACY ACT NOTICE

    The individually identifiable information re-
    quired on this form is necessary to permit the
    request to be processed in accordance with
    the general regulations governing United
    States book-entry Treasury bills (Department
    Circular PD Series No. 26-76, as amended).
    The transaction will not be completed unless
    all required data is furnished.

4. _____   Telephone Number and Area Code
          (signature)   during the hours of 8:30 am and 5:00 pm
                                              Eastern time.
    _____
       (fiduciary capacity, if any)

5. I CERTIFY that the above-named person as described, whose identity is well known or proved to me, personally appeared before
    me this_____ day of_____ at _____
    and signed this request.   (month and year)   (city and state)

                                            _____
                                            (signature and title of certifying officer)

    (OFFICIAL SEAL
    OR STAMP)
                                            _____
                                                       (address)

    FOR NOTARY USE ONLY
    My Commission Expires _____

Figure 3.

other organization belonging to the Federal Home Loan Bank System.

Interest or Rate of Return. Treasury bills do not bear a stated interest rate. The purchaser's earnings are calculated by taking the difference between the price paid for the bills and the amount the purchaser receives for them, which is either (1) the face value of the bills if they are held until maturity; or (2) the market value of the bills if they are sold before maturity.

The difference between what is actually paid for the bills and the face value of the bills—assuming the bills are held until maturity—is called the "discount." For example, the purchaser's earnings or the discount on the 26-week bills determined from the auction held on September 15, 1980, as shown in Figure 4, would be $549.73 because the purchase price is $9,450.27 and the face value of the bill is $10,000.*

The results of the auction of Treasury bills are usually reported in the daily newspaper on Tuesday, the day after the auction. Although all newspapers do not report as much detail on the auction as the *Wall Street Journal,* most of them report the yield on both an investment-yield basis and a bank-discount basis (see Figure 4). With the rate given on a bank discount basis, purchasers can compute their actual earnings by using the following formula:

$$\text{Discount rate} \times \text{face value of the bill}$$

$$\times \; \frac{\text{no. of days of maturity}}{360} = \text{earnings}$$

Using the information in Figure 4, the earnings would be computed as follows:

$$10.875\% \times 10,000$$

$$\times \; \frac{182 \text{ days}}{360} = \text{earnings}$$

$$1,087.50 \times .5055 = 549.73$$
(or approximately $550)†

If purchasers desire to compare their earnings or rate of return from Treasury bills with the earnings or rate of return from other investments, they need to convert the discount rate to an *investment yield* or *coupon-equivalent rate,* which can be directly compared with the stated annual rate of interest on investments that are not quoted on a discount basis. In contrast to the discount rate, the coupon-equivalent rate is based on the actual purchase price of the bills, and thus reflects the actual yield on the purchaser's investment. From the information in Figure 4, for example, a good estimate of the investment rate or coupon-

*The bids are submitted on the basis of price per 100, with not more than three decimals. In this auction, the purchase price was set at the average price of 94.503.
†For 13-week bills, use 91 days.

Rates Increase On Treasury Bills

Richmond Times Dispatch, 9-16-80

WASHINGTON (AP) — Interest rates on short-term Treasury securities climbed to their highest levels in nearly five months in yesterday's auction.

The discount rate on 13-week Treasury bills averaged 10.628 percent, the highest since 10.788 percent on April 28. The rate was up from 10.06 percent last week.

Rates on 26-week bills averaged 10.875 percent, the highest since 11.892 percent recorded on April 21. The rate a week ago was 10.234 percent.

The interest financial institutions may pay on 26-week money-market certificates is tied by law to the discount rate on 26-week Treasury bills.

As a result of yesterday's auction, commercial banks and thrift institutions may pay as high as 11.125 percent on those certificates starting Thursday.

The discount rate on Treasury bills represents an investor's return based on the face value of the securities.

At yesterday's auction, the investment rate was 11.08 percent on the 13-week bills and 11.67 percent on the 26-week bills. The investment rate is based on the investor's cash outlay for the securities, which is less than their face value.

The department also announced that the average yield of its 30-month securities over the past five days was 11.3 percent. The figure is the basis for calculating the interest rates financial institutions may pay on 30-month "small-saver" certificates of under $100,000.

As a result of yesterday's announcement, thrift institutions may pay as high as 11.3 percent interest on 30-month certificates sold during a two-week period beginning Thursday. Commercial banks may pay as high as 11.05 percent.

Figure 4.

equivalent rate can be computed as follows:

$$\frac{550}{9450} \times \frac{365}{182} =$$

$$.0582 \times 2.0055 = .11672$$
(or 11.7%)‡

The reader will notice that in this example the coupon-equivalent yield exceeds the rate on a discount basis. This is always the case because the coupon-equivalent yield is computed on the basis of the initial purchase price of the Treasury bill, whereas the discount rate is based on the face value of the bill. Because the purchase price of a Treasury bill is always slower than the face value, it follows that the coupon-equivalent yield will always exceed the yield on a discount basis.

‡Note the use of the 365-day year instead of a 360-day year.

Payment at Maturity or Reinvestment (Roll-Over). The face amount of Treasury bills held in a book-entry account will be paid at maturity by Treasury check unless the purchaser has indicated on the tender form that he or she wishes to reinvest the funds (roll-over) automatically at maturity. No statement is mailed to the purchaser when an account is closed. When the account matures, the purchaser will receive either a redemption check or a discount check and a Statement of Account for the issue into which the maturing account was reinvested. *Discount checks are mailed separately from the statements on reinvested accounts.*

There are a number of ways in which purchasers can request a roll-over. With the initial or original purchase of Treasury bills, the purchaser can request a single roll-over on the tender form (Form PD 4632-2). If the request for a roll-over is not indicated on the tender form, the purchaser can request a roll-over by completing Form PD 4633-2, "Request for Reinvestment of Book-Entry Treasury Bills." This form is actually a preprinted, prepunched card that will be sent after a new account is established. The front and back of this card are shown as Figure 5. The card will be mailed to purchasers separately, rather than with the Statement of Account. *No card will be mailed to depositors when the account is already scheduled for reinvestment.*

If purchasers do not receive the special card (Form PD 4633-2) within a reasonable period of time after the account is established, or if they receive the card and subsequently misplace it, they should submit a request for a roll-over on Form PD 4633-1 (Figure 6). This form, as well as Form PD 4633, which must be used to request cancellation of a previous request for a roll-over and other changes to an account, can be

---

This is NOT a check

REQUEST FOR REINVESTMENT OF BOOK ENTRY TREASURY BILLS

This is NOT a check

This card should be used in lieu of a Form 4633-1 to request the reinvestment of a book-entry bill account maintained by the Treasury. If you desire reinvestment, check the appropriate block, sign the card and return it to: BUREAU OF THE PUBLIC DEBT, DEPT. X, WASHINGTON, D.C. 20226. Requests for reinvestment must be received on or before the cut-off date indicated below. A request for continuous reinvestment will not be accepted. Please note the additional instructions on the reverse side of the card.

CUT-OFF DATE:
AMOUNT:
TITLE OF SECURITIES:

TREASURY ACCOUNT NO:

I hereby request that the proceeds of the above Treasury bill be reinvested at maturity on a noncompetitive basis for the number of weeks indicated.

_____
Signature and Date

NECS/HP-30415

CHECK
ONE BOX ONLY:
☐ 52 week bill
☐ 26 week bill
☐ 13 week bill

PLEASE DO NOT FOLD, STAPLE OR MUTILATE

FORM PD 4633-2 - Dept. of Treas.- Bur. Public Debt

BUREAU OF THE PUBLIC DEBT
DEPT. X
WASHINGTON, D.C. 20226

TELEPHONE: (202) 287-4113
TELEPHONE FOR THE DEAF: (202) 287-4097

IMPORTANT

This form **cannot** be used to:
(a) Change an address.
(b) Add or delete a second named depositor.
(c) Cancel a previous request for reinvestment.
(d) Submit any other request other than to reinvest an account currently scheduled for redemption. (Use Form PD 4633 to request such changes.)

Before you check which type of bill you want issued at reinvestment, please note that
(a) <u>Only</u> one type of bill may be selected when requesting reinvestment.
(b) 26 week and 13 week bills are interchangeable.
(c) 52 week bills maturing on or before October 14, 1980 may be reinvested in 52 week bills only.
(d) 52 week bills maturing on or after November 6, 1980 may be reinvested in 52 week, 26 week or 13 week bills.

If you do not desire reinvestment or your account is already scheduled for reinvestment, please dispose of this card.

PLEASE DO NOT FOLD, STAPLE OR MUTILATE

NECS/HP-304158

Figure 5.

FORM PD 4633-1
Dept. of the Treasury
Bur. of the Public Debt
(Rev. Jan. 1980)

BPD NO._____
(FOR OFFICIAL USE ONLY)

REQUEST FOR REINVESTMENT OF
BOOK ENTRY TREASURY BILLS

SEND TO: BUREAU OF THE PUBLIC DEBT
DEPT. X
WASHINGTON, D.C. 20226

TELEPHONE: (202) 287-4113
TELEPHONE FOR THE DEAF: (202) 287-4097

This form can only be used to request the reinvestment of a book-entry bill account maintained by the Treasury. A reinvestment represents an investment of the proceeds of a maturing security into a newly issued security. This form must be submitted each time you wish to reinvest your account. A request for continuous reinvestment will not be accepted.

This form **cannot** be used to:
(a) Change an address.
(b) Add or delete a second named depositor.
(c) Cancel a previous request for reinvestment.
(d) Submit any other request other than to reinvest an account currently scheduled for redemption. (Use Form PD 4633 to request such changes.)

This form **must be received** by this office not later than:
(a) Ten (10) **business** days before maturity for bills issued prior to January 15, 1980.
(b) Twenty (20) **business** days before maturity for bills issued after January 15, 1980.
(**NOTE:** Do not count Saturdays, Sundays or Federal holidays.)

Before you check which type of bill you want issued at reinvestment, please note that
(a) **Only** one type of bill may be selected when requesting reinvestment.
(b) 26 week and 13 week bills are interchangeable.
(c) 52 week bills maturing on or before October 14, 1980 may be reinvested in 52 week bills **only**.
(d) 52 week bills maturing on or after November 6, 1980 may be reinvested in 52 week, 26 week or 13 week bills.
(e) Your account number must be shown.

I hereby request that the proceeds of maturing Treasury bills as identified by the following account number be reinvested at maturity on a noncompetitive basis for Treasury bills then being offered for the number of weeks indicated.

☐☐☐ - ☐ - ☐☐   ☐☐☐   ☐☐☐ - ☐☐
(Account No. as shown on Statement of Account)

CHECK ONE BOX ONLY:
(2) ☐ 52 week bill
(6) ☐ 26 week bill
(3) ☐ 13 week bill

Print name and mailing address below:

_____

_____

_____

_____

_____

Social Security Number or
Employer Identification Number

Telephone no. and area code during the hours of 8:30 a.m. to 5:00 p.m. Eastern Time

Signature and Date
(This form does not require certification)

Figure 6.

obtained from the nearest Federal Reserve bank or branch or by writing to the Bureau of Public Debt, Dept. F, Washington, D.C. 20226.* Individual requests from purchasers for Form PD 4633-2, "Request for Reinvestment of Book-Entry Treasury Bills," will not be accepted. Also, requests for duplicate forms will not be processed.

Although the Treasury will accommodate a purchaser's request to reinvest the funds (roll-over) automatically at maturity, the Treasury will not accept requests from purchasers who want to increase their accounts at maturity. Purchasers who wish to increase their investment in Treasury bills by $10,000 or more may do so by submitting a tender to a Federal Reserve bank (or branch) or to the Bureau of Public Debt for a new purchase.

The Treasury will process a request to decrease an account at maturity in a multiple of $5,000, as long as the minimum amount in the account remains at $10,000. Also, the Treasury will process a request to wire-transfer all or any part of the account to a commercial institution. A wire transfer must be in a minimum amount of $10,000 or a multiple of $5,000 above that amount. A withdrawal may be made in whole or in part provided that a partial withdrawal does not reduce the balance in the account below $10,000.

Treasury Notes and Bonds. Treasury notes and bonds have longer maturities than Treasury bills. Notes have a fixed maturity of not less than one year and not more than ten years from date of issue. Bonds normally have a fixed maturity of more than ten years. Most Treasury notes and bonds are not redeemable prior to maturity. Periodically, however, bonds are issued with a *call provision* as a part of the agreement with the purchaser. This provision permits the Treasury to redeem the bond prior to maturity. A bond with a call provision carries a *call date* in addition to a maturity date, such as in the following example: August 15, 1944—August 15, 2002.

Although August 15, 2002, is the maturity date for the issue in the foregoing example, the Treasury reserves the right to redeem the bonds at face value plus accrued interest anytime between the two dates.

$1,000 and $5,000 Denominations. Periodically, Treasury notes and bonds are issued in minimum denominations of $1,000 and $5,000 (see Figure 7). Notes maturing in four years or longer, and all bonds, are usually available in a minimum denomination of $1,000. Notes maturing in less than four years are usually offered in a minimum denomination of $5,000, and purchases may be made in any higher multiples of $5,000.

Treasury Note Auction Planned

The Washington Post, 3-15-80.

The Treasury will raise $733 million in new cash through sales of $3.5 billion in two-year notes and $2.5 billion in four-year notes in separate auctions to redeem more than $5.2 billion of maturing notes.

The two-year notes will be sold next Thursday and the four-year notes on March 25. Tenders for the two-year notes, in minimum denominations of $5,000, and the four-year notes, in minimum amounts of $1,000, must be received by 1:30 p.m. EST on the day of each auction at the Treasury or Federal Reserve banks or branches.

Figure 7.

A Treasury note or bond may be registered in any of the following forms:

ONE NAME	John A. Doe (123-45-6789)
TWO NAMES	John A. Doe (123-45-6789) and/or (Mrs.) Mary C. Doe (987-65-4321)
JOINT TENANCY	John A. Doe or Mary C. Doe (either party's social security number is acceptable)
MINORS.....................	John R. Jones as natural guardian for Henry B. Jones, a minor (789-12-3456) William C. Smith, a custodian for John A. Smith, a minor (456-78-9123) minor's number under the Virginia Uniform Gifts to Minors Act

Note: Treasury securities may not be registered solely in the name of a minor. A custodian must be named.

Figure 8.

Forms of Issuance. Treasury notes and bonds are currently issued in registered, coupon, and book-entry forms. In the registered and coupon forms, these securities are issued as *engraved certificates.* The ownership of registered notes and bonds appears on the engraved certificate (see Figure 8). This ownership is also recorded on the records of the Department of the Treasury, providing a measure of protection to the owner if the note or bond should be lost, stolen, or destroyed. Registered notes and bonds may be transferred by assignment executed by the owner or the owner's authorized representative.

The ownership of coupon notes and bonds is *not recorded* on the books of the Department of the Treasury, and they and their interest coupons are payable to *bearer.* Title to coupon notes and bonds passes by delivery without endorsement and without notice. Because coupon securities are by their very nature negotiable, it is extremely important that they be kept in a

* Please note that requests to cancel a previous request for reinvestment or a roll-over must be submitted over the certified signature of the purchaser (or depositor).

safe-deposit box or otherwise protected.

Notice of Offering. A forthcoming sale of Treasury notes and bonds is announced publicly in the daily newspapers (Figure 7) and in a communication entitled *Highlights of Treasury Offering* sent by Federal Reserve banks to individuals and financial institutions. To receive a newsletter, a prospective buyer must first request a Name and Address Card from a Federal Reserve bank (see Figure 9). Among other information, the two-page newsletter lists the following:

1. Amount of securities offered
2. Description of the securities
3. The terms of sale
4. The key dates (see Figure 10, page 630)

Occasionally the Treasury announces an *exchange offering* in which notes and bonds may be issued in exchange for other outstanding Treasury notes or bonds. Only those issues specifically mentioned in the announcement by the Treasury will be eligible for the exchange. Subscriptions from persons not owning those issues cannot be accepted. An additional payment may be required from or a refund may be due the purchaser, depending on the terms of the offering.

Purchase Procedures. When the sale of Treasury notes or bonds is publicly announced, a prospective purchaser may subscribe (apply) in person at a Federal Reserve bank (or branch); the Bureau of Public Debt, Treasury Department; or by mail, according to the time limits set by the Treasury for that particular offering. Competitive tenders must be received by the deadline established in the announcement offering the securities to the public, usually 1:30 P.M., Eastern time. Noncompetitive tenders will be considered timely, even if received after the deadline, provided they are postmarked no later than the day prior to the auction. The form used for subscribing to the issue of

PLACE
STAMP
HERE

FEDERAL RESERVE BANK OF RICHMOND
FISCAL AGENCY DEPARTMENT
P. O. BOX 27622
RICHMOND, VA.   23261

*FA 1054 (Orig. 7-79)

NAME AND ADDRESS CARD

Please forward information concerning the next offering
of Treasury Notes and/or Bonds.

PLEASE INSERT NAME AND ADDRESS

Figure 9.

FEDERAL RESERVE BANK OF RICHMOND
FISCAL AGENT OF THE UNITED STATES
RICHMOND, VIRGINIA 23261

May 14, 1981

TO ALL BANKING INSTITUTIONS AND OTHERS CONCERNED
IN THE FIFTH FEDERAL RESERVE DISTRICT:

There is printed below for your information, a press statement issued by the Treasury Department on May 13:

TREASURY TO AUCTION $4,250 MILLION OF 2-YEAR NOTES

The Department of the Treasury will auction $4,250 million of 2-year notes to refund $2,131 million of notes maturing May 31, 1981, and to raise $2,119 million new cash. The $2,131 million of maturing notes are those held by the public, including $627 million currently held by Federal Reserve Banks as agents for foreign and international monetary authorities.

In addition to the public holdings, Government accounts and Federal Reserve Banks, for their own accounts, hold $411 million of the maturing securities that may be refunded by issuing additional amounts of the new notes at the average price of accepted competitive tenders. Additional amounts of the new security may also be issued at the average price to Federal Reserve Banks, as agents for foreign and international monetary authorities, to the extent that the aggregate amount of tenders for such accounts exceeds the aggregate amount of maturing securities held by them.

Details about the new security are given in the highlights of the offering printed on the reverse side of this announcement and in the official offering circular which is available upon request.

FEDERAL RESERVE BANK OF RICHMOND
Fiscal Agent of the United States

HIGHLIGHTS OF TREASURY OFFERING
TO THE PUBLIC OF 2-YEAR NOTES
TO BE ISSUED JUNE 1, 1981

May 13, 1981

Amount Offered:	
To the public	$4,250 million
Description of Security:	
Term and type of security	2-year notes
Series and CUSIP designation	Series R-1983 (CUSIP No. 912827 LX 8)
Maturity date	May 31, 1983
Call date	No provision
Interest coupon rate	To be determined based on the average of accepted bids
Investment yield	To be determined at auction
Premium or discount	To be determined after auction
Interest payment dates	November 30 and May 31
Minimum denomination available	$5,000
Terms of Sale:	
Method of sale	Yield auction
Accrued interest payable by investor	None
Preferred allotment	Noncompetitive bid for $1,000,000 or less
Payment by non-institutional investors	Full payment to be submitted with tender
Deposit guarantee by designated institutions	Acceptable
Key Dates:	
Deadline for receipt of tenders	Wednesday, May 20, 1981, by 1:30 p.m., EDST
Settlement date (final payment due from institutions)	
a) cash or Federal funds	Monday, June 1, 1981
b) readily collectible check	Thursday, May 28, 1981
Delivery date for coupon securities	Tuesday, June 9, 1981

Figure 10.

securities is called a "tender" and is shown in Figure 11 (pages 632–633). If a prospective purchaser does not have a tender and decides to submit a subscription letter, it should contain the following information:

1. Home address and zip code
2. Telephone number
3. Amount of securities desired
4. Whether bid is noncompetitive or competitive
5. Preference for form in which securities are to be issued (if preference is registered form, name(s) for registration and the social security number(s) must be furnished)
6. Whether the purchaser plans to take delivery of the securities in person or have them mailed
7. Address(es) for delivery of the securities and interest checks
8. Purchaser's signature

In addition to supplying the above information, the purchaser should: (1) enclose the proper payment; (2) indicate on the outside of the envelope the following legend, "Tender for Treasury Notes (Bonds)"; and (3) mail the letter to a Federal Reserve bank (or branch), or to the Bureau of Public Debt, Treasury Department.

Treasury notes and bonds are usually sold at auction. Competitive and noncompetitive bids are accepted by the Federal Reserve Bank according to the terms announced by the Treasury. Prospective purchasers who submit competitive bids must specify the price they are willing to pay, expressed on the basis of 100 to two decimal places (e.g., 99.01, 100, etc.). Those who decide to submit noncompetitive bids are not required to indicate a specific price. Again, as in the case of Treasury-bill auctions, all noncompetitive bidders for notes and bonds agree to pay an undetermined price set by the competitive bidders according to the specific terms of the offering. This price may be above or below par. *Above par,* for example, would mean that the price of a $1,000 face-value note is set at an amount more than $1,000, and that the purchaser must send additional funds if the initial payment covered only the face value of the note. *Below par* would mean that the price of a $1,000-face-value note is set at an amount less than $1,000, and that the purchaser will receive a check for the difference if he or she has made an initial payment covering the face value of the note.

Payment and Delivery. Purchasers of Treasury

notes and bonds are required to make full (face value) payment when submitting a tender or a letter of subscription for these securities. Payment may be made in cash; by personal check; by check issued by a commercial bank (savings bank, savings and loan association, or credit union), provided such checks are drawn to the order of a specific Federal Reserve bank or the U.S. Treasury; or with redemption checks issued by the Bureau of Public Debt in payment of matured Treasury securities, provided the tender is submitted in the name(s) of the payee(s); or with matured U.S. Treasury securities (notes and bonds); or with checks or drafts drawn on money-market or mutual-fund accounts.

After payment has been made, a purchaser may arrange to receive the note or bond certificates in person at the Federal Reserve Bank (bearer form only) or have the certificates sent to the home or office by registered mail at the expense of the Treasury Department. Registered securities are inscribed by the Treasury Department at the time the issue records are established. Therefore, depending on the size of the issue, the delivery of registered securities could take at least three weeks or even several months.

Earnings or Rate of Return. Treasury notes and bonds carry a fixed-interest coupon rate. This enables purchasers to determine their coupon interest rate quickly by applying this rate to the *face* value of the note or bond.

Depending on the actual price of the note or bond set by the Treasury after all bids are considered, the purchaser's annual interest earnings may amount to an investment yield that is greater or less than the coupon interest rate. If the actual price is set below par, the securities are sold at a *discount* and thus the investment yield will be greater than the coupon rate. On the other hand, if the price is set above par, the securities are sold at a *premium,* and thus the investment rate will be less than the coupon rate. Usually when the Treasury announces the results of an auc-

tion on notes or bonds, the announcement emphasizes the investment yield. The interest coupon rate, however, is also mentioned (see Figure 12, page 634).

Payment of Interest (to Owners of Registered Securities). The interest earnings on Treasury notes and bonds are payable twice a year, or every six months, either by a check from the Treasury or, in the case of a bearer instrument, by the cashing of a coupon. The coupons may be cashed through any commercial bank or through a Federal Reserve bank.

There are occasions when the payment for notes or bonds must include the principal amount of the securities and the accrued interest on the securities from the date of the last scheduled interest payment to the effective date of purchase of the securities. Notice of this additional part of the payment usually appears on the front page of the tender in fairly bold type (see Figure 13, page 635). The amount of this additional payment is always expressed as the amount per $1,000 of the securities purchased, along with the precise period of time for which the interest has accrued. The amount of this accrued interest will be included in the next scheduled interest payment.

Occasionally, under the terms of the official offering circular, the period from the date of issue to the first interest-payment date may be more or less than six months. When this occurs, the first interest-payment check will be an amount larger or smaller than the remaining payments. All subsequent interest-payment checks will be computed on a six-month period and will be one-half of the dollar amount to be paid annually under the terms of the offering.

Redemption at Maturity. Treasury notes and bonds may be redeemed at maturity for face value at any Federal Reserve bank (or branch), or at the Bureau of Public Debt. These securities do not earn interest after their maturity dates. If the securities are to be mailed, registered mail should be used. The securities should be accompanied by a letter indicating that payment is requested, showing the address to which the

---

Can Treasury Bills Be Pledged as Collateral?

The Treasury will not recognize a pledge of book-entry securities for collateral, nor will the agency transfer securities among book-entry accounts that it maintains.

If John Doe owns a $10,000 Treasury bill on book-entry account and wishes to pledge this bill as collateral for a loan from his commercial bank, one of the procedures that he might use to achieve his objective would begin with the processing of Form PD 4633, shown as Figure 3. In the section marked "Action Requested," John Doe would request the transfer of his Treasury bill from the book-entry account at the Treasury to the account of a commercial bank (member bank) held at a regional Federal Reserve bank. It should be noted that when this transfer is made, the Treasury bill *is no longer held in the name of John Doe.* Rather, it becomes part of the Treasury bills held in the name of the commercial bank at the Federal Reserve Bank.

After the transfer is complete, the commercial bank will usually maintain internal records showing that $10,000 of the Treasury bills held in its account at the Federal Reserve Bank constitute collateral for a loan made to John Doe. If and when the loan is paid, the bank will credit John Doe's checking account for $10,000 after the bill matures.

Tender for Treasury Notes of Series R-1983

Dated and bearing interest from June 1, 1981

TO ....
(Insert—Head Office, Baltimore Branch or Charlotte Branch)

Federal Reserve Bank of Richmond,
Fiscal Agent of the United States :

Due May 31, 1983

Date ....

Pursuant to the provisions of the Treasury Department Offering Circular the undersigned offers to purchase the Treasury Notes as indicated below and on the reverse.

NONCOMPETITIVE TENDER* $............................ .... $............................

FOR USE OF FEDERAL RESERVE BANK
$............

*Tenders for $1,000,000 or less without stated yield from any one bidder may be accepted in full at the average price of accepted competitive bids. This price will be at or more or less than 100.000.

COMPETITIVE TENDERS {
.... @ .... % $............................
.... @ .... %
.... @ .... %
.... @ .... %
}

$............

Payment for notes allotted hereunder to financial institutions must be made or completed on or before Monday, June 1, 1981 in cash or other funds immediately available by that date as indicated below. **Payment in full must accompany tenders from individuals and non-financial institutions.**

METHOD OF PAYMENT
(Payment cannot be made by credit to Treasury Tax and Loan Account)

☐ Charge our reserve account $............

☐ Draft or check on ....
(A. B. A. Number)

☐ Payment to be made by............
(Name of Bank)

☐ Maturing securities $............

Held by ....

DELIVERY INSTRUCTIONS

☐ Hold in safekeeping for our account $............
(member banks only)

☐ Hold in our General Account $............
(member banks only)

☐ Hold in our Trust Account $............
(member banks only)

☐ Hold in our Dealer Account $............
(member banks only)

☐ Hold as collateral for Treasury Tax $............
and Loan Account

☐ Deliver to ....

COUPON SECURITIES TO BE ISSUED

Serial Numbers	No. Pieces	Denom.	Amount
		$ 5,000	$
		10,000	
		100,000	
		1,000,000	

Total coupon securities . . . . $............

Total registered securities . . . . . . $............
(listed on reverse)

Total coupon and registered securities . . . $............

THIS TENDER MUST BE MANUALLY SIGNED BY SUBSCRIBER

TO BE COMPLETED BY INDIVIDUALS AND OTHERS
Certification

WE HEREBY CERTIFY that we have not made and will not make any agreements for the sale or purchase of any securities of this issue prior to one-thirty p.m., Eastern Daylight Saving time, Wednesday, May 20, 1981.

(Name of Individual or Other Subscriber)

(Street and Number)

(City or Town)   (State)   (Zip Code)

SIGN HERE ....
(Signature)

If you wish your name removed from our mailing list for Treasury Bonds or Notes, please check the block, sign the form and return it in the enclosed envelope.   ☐

☐ **This is an original tender**

☐ **This is a confirmation**

TO BE COMPLETED BY COMMERCIAL BANKS ONLY
Certifications

WE HEREBY CERTIFY that we have not made and will not make any agreements for the sale or purchase of any securities of this issue prior to one-thirty p.m., Eastern Daylight Saving time, Wednesday, May 20, 1981.

WE FURTHER CERTIFY that we have received tenders from customers in the amounts set opposite their names on the reverse which is made a part of this tender, and that we have received and are holding for the Treasury, or that we guarantee payment to the Treasury, of the deposits stipulated in the official offering circular.

WE FURTHER CERTIFY that tenders received by us, if any, from other commercial banks or primary dealers for their own account, and for the account of their customers, have been entered with us under the same conditions, agreements, and certifications set forth in this form.

(Name of Bank)

(City or Town)   (State)   (Zip Code)

BY ....
(Official Signature)   (Title)

IMPORTANT: In order that tenders may be received promptly they should be sent under separate cover and not included with other mail to the Federal Reserve Bank. Tenders may be addressed to the Head Office or nearest Branch of this Bank, and the envelope should be marked "Tender for Treasury Notes".

PRIVACY ACT STATEMENT—The individually identifiable information required on this form is necessary to permit the tender to be processed and the securities to be issued. If registered securities are requested, the regulations governing United States securities (Department Circular No. 300) and the offering circular require submission of social security numbers; the numbers and other information are used in inscribing the securities and establishing and servicing the ownership and interest records. The transaction will not be completed unless all required data is furnished.

IMPORTANT— Tenders are invited and will be received up to one-thirty p.m., Eastern Daylight Saving time, Wednesday, May 20, 1981. Noncompetitive tenders mailed will be considered timely if they are postmarked no later than Tuesday, May 19.

Figure 11.

IMPORTANT — List name and address of each subscriber indicating by number, in the first column the class of investor, in accordance with the schedule below as required by Treasury Department regulations:

INVESTOR CLASSES AND NUMBERS

01 Individuals.
11 Personal trusts, estates, and partnerships.
21 Non-profit and tax-exempt organizations, foundations, and endowment funds. (Do not include pension and retirement funds.)
02 Mutual savings banks.
13 Life insurance companies.
23 Casualty and liability insurance companies.
33 Other insurance companies.
14 Primary dealers (excluding commercial bank primary dealers) in U. S. Government securities as currently designated by the FRB of New York.
24 Other nonbank dealers and brokers.

18 Commercial bank primary dealers in U. S. Government securities as currently designated by the FRB of New York.
28 Other commercial bank dealer departments.
38 Commercial bank investment accounts (including investment accounts of dealer banks).
05 Pension and retirement funds of State and local governments.
06 Private pension and retirement funds.
07 State and local government funds other than pension and retirement funds.
09 Non-financial corporations.
19 Mutual funds (including money market funds).

29 Financial corporations other than insurance companies, banks, savings and loans, and mutual funds (includes finance companies, REITs, and other financial corporations).
10 Savings and loan and building and loan associations.
20 Credit unions.
91 U. S. Government accounts and Federal Reserve Banks.
92 Government deposit accounts not included in the unified budget of the U. S. and government-sponsored agencies.
93 Official foreign and international accounts.
94 Other foreign and international accounts.

SCHEDULE FOR ISSUE OF COUPON SECURITIES

Investor Class No.	Name and address of subscriber	Amount	NUMBER OF PIECES				
			Yield	5,000	10,000	100,000	1,000,000
		$					
	Should additional space be needed use a separate sheet and attach. TOTAL	$					

SCHEDULE FOR ISSUE OF REGISTERED SECURITIES

Investor Class No.	NAME IN WHICH SECURITIES SHALL BE REGISTERED AND ADDRESS FOR INTEREST CHECKS, INCLUDING ZIP CODE (Taxpayer's identifying number must be shown opposite name to which it applies)	Amount	NUMBER OF PIECES				
			Yield	5,000	10,000	100,000	1,000,000
		$					
	Should additional space be needed use a separate sheet and attach. TOTAL	$					

SCHEDULE FOR ISSUE OF BOOK-ENTRY SECURITIES

Investor Class No.	Name and address of subscriber	Amount
		$
	Should additional space be needed use a separate sheet and attach. TOTAL AMOUNT	$

Figure 11.

4-Year Notes Average 10.52%

The Washington Post, 12-21-79.

The Treasury paid an average yield of 10.52 percent yesterday on the $2.5 billion of 4-year notes it sold to the public. The notes will carry a coupon paying 10.5 percent on the face value. To reach a yield of 10.52 percent, the notes were sold at a slight discount from their face value. The average investor would pay $999.36 for a note with a face value of $1,000.

Figure 12. © 1979 The *Washington Post.* All Rights Reserved.

check is to be sent. A telephone number at which the submitter can be reached during business hours should be provided. To ensure timely payment, the securities should be sent in no later than two to three weeks before the maturity date.

The assignment form on the back of each registered security may be left blank if the redemption check is to be issued in the same name(s) as the registration. If the check is to be issued in another name, assign the securities to "Secretary of the Treasury for redemption for account of (name[s] and address[es] of payee[s]). The signature to the assignment should be certified by an authorized certifying officer.

See UNITED STATES GOVERNMENT SECURITIES QUOTES, HOW TO READ.

James F. Tucker

Treasury Tax and Loan Program

Treasury tax and loan (TT&L) accounts are maintained for the United States Treasury Department at more than 14,000 depository institutions throughout the nation. Generally, the balances in these TT&L accounts consist of federal tax payments by business firms and, for note-option depositories, the proceeds from the sale of U.S. savings bonds. Under the TT&L investment program, which was initiated on Noverber 2, 1978, certain depositories holding these funds began paying interest on these balances to the Treasury. Similarly, the Treasury began paying fees to those depositories for specific services performed on

behalf of the Treasury. Previously, depositories had interest-free use of funds in TT&L accounts for several days as a form of compensation for services provided to the Treasury.

The Treasury maintains accounts at each of the 12 Federal Reserve banks and writes checks against these balances to pay federal government expenses. As money is needed by the Treasury to pay for goods and services, TT&L depositories are notified through the Reserve banks to transfer funds to the Treasury's accounts at the Reserve banks. These notifications are known as "calls." When a "call" is made on a depository, the transfer is made through the depository's direct account at its local Federal Reserve bank, or through the account of a correspondent.

The system of TT&L accounts and the manner in which the Treasury "calls" (or reduces) its balances in these TT&L accounts moderate the flow of Treasury funds (tax receipts) from the public to the Treasury. If all funds were deposited directly and continuously into the Treasury's Reserve Bank accounts, there would be abrupt changes in bank reserves. This would lead to large swings in credit availability and volatility in the money and securities markets. The use of TT&L accounts prevents an immediate loss in reserves in the banking system, since the funds remain in banks, although they change from private to government ownership.

To qualify as a depository, an institution must file an application with its local Federal Reserve bank. This application, when approved, constitutes a formal agreement under which the depository agrees to conform to all pertinent Treasury rules and regulations concerning TT&L accounts. When the depository begins to receive tax deposits, it must pledge collateral, as specified in the Treasury's rules and regulations, to secure these deposits.

Under the 1978 TT&L investment program, depositories may participate as either a remittance-option or note-option depository. Remittance-option depositories credit all tax deposits to their TT&L accounts, which are demand-deposit accounts, on the day of receipt and forward advices of credit to their local Federal Reserve bank. When the advices are received by the local Federal Reserve bank, the funds are immediately credited to the Treasury's account maintained at that Reserve bank.

Remittance-option depositories with total tax deposits in excess of $4 million for the prior year (designated remittance-option class 1 depositories) are assessed a charge equal to the interest rate paid on note-option balances for each day an advice of credit isn't received timely. All depositories are paid a 50-cent fee for all federal tax deposits fully processed by the Internal Revenue Service. In the case of remit-

Tender for 13⅞% Treasury Bonds of 2006-2011

ADDITIONAL ISSUE

Dated May 15, 1981 with interest from August 17, 1981   Due May 15, 2011

TO ....
(Insert—Head Office, Baltimore Branch or Charlotte Branch)

Federal Reserve Bank of Richmond,   Date ....
Fiscal Agent of the United States:

Pursuant to the provisions of the Treasury Department Offering Circular the undersigned offers to purchase the Treasury Bonds as indicated below and on the reverse.

	FOR USE OF FEDERAL RESERVE BANK

NONCOMPETITIVE TENDER* $ _____ $ _____ $ _____

*Tenders for $1,000,000 or less without stated yield from any one bidder may be accepted in full at the average price of accepted competitive bids. This price will be at or more or less than 100.000.

COMPETITIVE TENDERS
$ .... @ .... $ .... $ ....
.... @ ....
.... @ ....
.... @ ....

Payment for bonds allotted hereunder to financial institutions must be made or completed on or before **Monday, August 17, 1981** in cash or other funds immediately available by that date as indicated below. Payment in full must accompany tenders from individuals and non-financial institutions. Payment from all classes of investors must include the principal amount and accrued interest of **$35.44158 per $1,000** from **May 15, 1981 to August 17, 1981.**

METHOD OF PAYMENT
(Payment cannot be made by credit to Treasury Tax and Loan Account)

☐ Charge our reserve account $ _____

☐ Draft or check on _____ $ _____
(A. B. A. Number)

☐ Payment to be made by _____
(Name of Bank)

☐ Maturing securities $ _____

Held by _____

DELIVERY INSTRUCTIONS

☐ Hold in safekeeping for our account $ _____
(member banks only)

☐ Hold in our General Account $ _____
(member banks only)

☐ Hold in our Trust Account $ _____
(member banks only)

☐ Hold in our Dealer Account $ _____
(member banks only)

☐ Hold as collateral for Treasury Tax and Loan Account $ _____

☐ Deliver to _____

COUPON SECURITIES TO BE ISSUED

Serial Numbers	No. Pieces	Denom.	Amount
		$ 1,000	$
		5,000	
		10,000	
		100,000	
		1,000,000	

Total coupon securities . . . . . . $ _____

Total registered securities . . . . . $ _____
(listed on reverse)

Total coupon and registered securities . . $ _____

THIS TENDER MUST BE MANUALLY SIGNED BY SUBSCRIBER

TO BE COMPLETED BY INDIVIDUALS AND OTHERS
Certification

WE HEREBY CERTIFY that we have not made and will not make any agreements for the sale or purchase of any securities of this issue prior to one-thirty p.m., Eastern Daylight Saving time. Thursday, August 6, 1981.

_____
(Name of Individual or Other Subscriber)

_____
(Street and Number)

_____
(City or Town)   (State)   (Zip Code)

SIGN HERE _____
(Signature)

If you wish your name **removed** from our mailing list for Treasury Bonds or Notes, please check the block, sign the form and return it in the enclosed envelope.   ☐

☐ **This is an original tender**

☐ **This is a confirmation**

TO BE COMPLETED BY COMMERCIAL BANKS ONLY
Certifications

WE HEREBY CERTIFY that we have not made and will not make any agreements for the sale or purchase of any securities of this issue prior to one-thirty p.m., Eastern Daylight Saving time, Thursday, August 6, 1981.

WE FURTHER CERTIFY that we have received tenders from customers in the amounts set opposite their names on the reverse which is made a part of this tender, and that we have received and are holding for the Treasury, or that we guarantee payment to the Treasury, of the deposits stipulated in the official offering circular.

WE FURTHER CERTIFY that tenders received by us, if any, from other commercial banks or primary dealers for their own account, and for the account of their customers, have been entered with us under the same conditions, agreements, and certifications set forth in this form.

_____
(Name of Bank)

_____
(City or Town)   (State)   (Zip Code)

BY _____
(Official Signature)   (Title)

IMPORTANT: In order that tenders may be received promptly they should be sent under separate cover and not included with other mail to the Federal Reserve Bank. **Tenders may be addressed to the Head Office or nearest Branch of this Bank, and the envelope should be marked "Tender for Treasury Bonds".**

PRIVACY ACT STATEMENT—The individually identifiable information required on this form is necessary to permit the tender to be processed and the securities to be issued. If registered securities are requested, the regulations governing United States securities (Department Circular No. 300) and the offering circular require submission of social security numbers; the numbers and other information are used in inscribing the securities and establishing and servicing the ownership and interest records. The transaction will not be completed unless all required data is furnished.

(left margin, rotated) IMPORTANT—Tenders are invited and will be received up to one-thirty p.m., Eastern Daylight Saving time, Thursday, August 6, 1981. Noncompetitive tenders mailed will be considered timely if they are postmarked no later than Wednesday, August 5.

Figure 13.

tance-option depositories with deposits of less than $4 million (class 2), any similar charges (analysis credits) associated with the late receipt of advices of credit are netted against the fee payments. If the amount is negative, no fees are paid and no charges are assessed.

Note-option depositories also credit all tax receipts to their TT&L accounts on the day of receipt and forward advices of credit to their local Federal Reserve bank. On the following business day, these funds are transferred into open-ended note accounts, representing funds acquired from the Treasury. In effect, these depositories are borrowing funds from the Treasury under an open-ended note. The interest rate payable to the Treasury under this arrangement is determined by subtracting 25 basis points from the average weekly federal funds rate for the period during which the balances were held.

Note-option depositories may establish a maximum balance for their TT&L accounts based on their anticipated flow of tax deposits and their ability to maintain adequate collateral to secure a given level of deposits. All tax deposits received in excess of the maximum balance are automatically transferred to the Treasury.

"Calls" (withdrawals of funds from note-option depositories) are initiated by the Treasury for all or a portion of the note-account balances. The Treasury classified the note depositories into the following three categories:

- Class "C" note-option depositories are those that had $70 million or more in federal tax deposits credited to their TT&L accounts during the previous calendar year and whose total time and demand deposits exceeded $60 million on September 30, 1980.
- Class "B" depositories are those that had federal tax deposits credited to their TT&L accounts totaling $7.5 million to $70 million; or those that had $70 million or more of federal tax deposits, but whose total time and demand deposits were $60 million or less on September 30, 1980.
- Class "A" depositories are those that had federal tax deposits credited to their TT&L accounts totaling less than $7.5 million.

"Calls" (withdrawals) of Treasury funds can be based on book balance, previous uncalled balance, or deposit balance (also known as "accelerated calls").

Under a book-balance or previous-uncalled-balance withdrawal, a future payment date is specified by the Treasury on the date the call is announced, the call date. On the payment date, the portion of the TT&L account balances previously specified on the call date is paid to the Treasury.

Under a withdrawal based on a deposit-balance call, all or part of a given day's TT&L account balances are paid to the Treasury on the call date.

Finally, a direct investment procedure exists whereby excess Treasury funds may be returned to the note-option depositories that have previously agreed to participate in direct investments. Direct investments are made on both a one-day and a same-day basis.

Arthur Samansky

Trust Account

An account administered by a trustee, in which funds are deposited for the benefit of another person, the beneficiary.

Mary Ann Irvine

Trusts

A trust is a form of property ownership involving two different types of ownership rights with respect to the property that is subject to the trust. The person (or institution, if a bank is involved) who holds legal title to the trust property is the *trustee.* The trustee is the owner of the stocks, bonds, cash, real estate, or other properties that form the principal (sometimes called the "corpus" or "res") of the trust. It is the trustee who can legally sell, borrow against, exchange, invest, reinvest, or otherwise deal with the principal, just as an individual deals with his own property.

However, there is one critical difference between how a trustee manages property and how an individual deals with his property. Whereas the individual is free to invest or otherwise dispose of his assets as he likes, without regard to safety, speculativeness, or the interests of anyone else, a trustee must act prudently and in the best interests of the *beneficiaries*—those persons for whose benefit the trust was established.

In this sense, the beneficiaries are also owners of the trust property; they have what is called the "beneficial ownership," since they have a right to challenge the propriety of what the trustee has done. If the trustee has acted improvidently or in a self-interested fashion, the court having jurisdiction over the trust has the power to "surcharge" (or fine) the trustee, deny him his compensation (ordinarily fixed by statute or by common law) for acting as trustee or even order his removal from office, especially if the beneficiary has suffered pecuniary loss as a result of the trustee's negligence.

In sum, there are three essential requirements for every trust: There must be at least one trustee; one or more beneficiaries; and property that forms the trust corpus.

Sometimes—even frequently—one or more of the beneficiaries is or are also the trustee(s). For instance, a husband may set up a trust under his WILL for the benefit of his wife, and name his wife and his eldest daughter as the trustees to manage the trust for the wife's benefit. In this illustration, the wife and daughter will jointly have the legal right to deal with the trust property. Some states will require them to act unanimously; others will permit either to act separately and to bind the cotrustee.

If there are more than two trustees, many state statutes specify that majority action will control. However, if there is only one trustee, who happens also to be the sole beneficiary, a valid trust will not have been created. Instead, the law will find either that the trustee/beneficiary owns, outright, all of the "trust" property, or that he has a legal "life estate" in that property—that is, the right to use it or the income it produces for his lifetime.

Just as every trust involves two forms of ownership of property (legal and equitable), most trusts also create two different types or classes of beneficiaries. First, there is the *income* beneficiary—the person who receives, or is eligible to receive, the interest, dividends, rents, or other money produced by the trust property. There may be more than one income beneficiary, and their income interests can extend either for a period of years, or for a period ended by the occurrence of a particular event (e.g., marriage), or for the respective lifetimes of the beneficiaries involved.

Moreover, the right to income can be mandatory (that is, under the terms of the trust, the income *must* be paid to the beneficiary); or it can be discretionary, if the person who established the trust (called the "settlor," "grantor," or "trustor") conferred a flexible power upon the trustee to decide if, to what extent, and when a single named beneficiary should receive income, or, if there is more than one income beneficiary, who among a group of potential beneficiaries should receive income, in what amounts, and at what times. Such a trust, in which the trustee has the right to allocate income among a group of beneficiaries, is frequently referred to as a "sprinkle" or "spray" trust. (Sometimes, in a sprinkle trust, the trustee also has the right to make discretionary distributions of the trust principal to the persons who are income beneficiaries.) A major advantage of a sprinkle trust is that income may be spread among a number of beneficiaries, thus reducing the income taxes payable by the group as a whole.

The second type of beneficiary designated in a trust is called the "remainder beneficiary," or "remainderman." It is the remainderman who ultimately will receive legal title to the trust principal, upon termination of the trust in accordance with its terms and distribution of the corpus to him or her.

Sometimes the income beneficiary and remainderman are the same person (or same group of persons).

One typical example is a trust for a minor child established by will (called a "testamentary trust" to differentiate it from a trust set up during one's lifetime, which is known as an "inter vivos" or "living" trust). A testamentary trust for the testator's child frequently will provide that the trustee, at his discretion, may pay the trust's income to the child, or apply it directly for the child's benefit, until the child reaches age 18 or 21; or, alternatively, that the trustee can accumulate any income not currently paid or applied until the child reaches either of those ages; then the accumulated income will typically be paid out to the child.

However, the trust itself may not end at age 18 or 21; instead, it may continue on until the child reaches a subsequent age—e.g., 35—at which the testator feels the beneficiary will be able to deal more competently with the responsibility of owning and managing a larger fund. Along the way, the testator may specify that the beneficiary shall be paid current income, on a mandatory basis, together with interim distributions of principal at stated ages—for instance, one-third at age 25, one-third at age 30, and the balance at age 35.

A further proviso of the trust—the "default provision"—ordinarily will specify to whom the trust principal will be paid should the child die before attaining the final principal-payout age. Alternatively, the default provision, instead of naming particular persons who will receive the trust principal upon the beneficiary's early death, may instead give the beneficiary the right to name substitute beneficiaries by his own will, or by an acknowledged document signed by him during his lifetime. This right to designate who shall receive property at a future date is called a "power of appointment," and many trusts include such a power (rather than specifying particular "default" beneficiaries) because the power of appointment lends added flexibility to the trust, permitting as it does an alteration in the disposition of the trust property long after the death of the person who established the trust. On the other hand, it is often argued that the naming of specific "default" beneficiaries is preferable to the granting of a power of appointment, in that the former mechanism lends certainty and finality to the scheme of disposition decided upon by the grantor (or testator) originally.

In any event, in the example given above, it can be seen that the income beneficiary—the testator's child—is also, to a large extent, the remainderman of the trust; the child has both an interest in income and, if he or she reaches age 25, an interest in one-third of the principal. If he or she lives to age 35, the interest in the principal extends to the entire trust, since he or she stands to receive all of the fund.

This analysis as to who is the income beneficiary and who the remainderman is significant in virtually every trust, since the trustee's balancing of the interests of these two types of beneficiaries is perhaps his most difficult and perilous task, and the one that may most often catch him in the cross fire of litigation between persons having equal but vastly different rights and interests in the trust and in the way it is invested and managed.

The income beneficiary almost always desires that the trustee invest the trust assets in a way that produces maximum income. He or she is little concerned with, for example, "growth" stocks, and would instead prefer to see the principal devoted entirely to a secure investment with good income, such as Treasury bills or high-rated corporate bonds. The remainderman, on the other hand, ordinarily will opt for investments that are somewhat more on the speculative side, or that at least hold out the likelihood or possibility of growth of principal.

It is the trustee's task to make this delicate investment decision; to balance the beneficiaries' conflicting desires; and to deal as impartially and fairly as possible between them. Thus, if and to the extent that the income beneficiary and the remainderman is or are the person(s), as described in the example given above, the trustee's job is made that much easier, since presumably the potential conflict between the beneficiaries will be reduced or eliminated.

Kinds of Trusts. Trusts can be broadly divided into two groups: those primarily established for property-management purposes; and those motivated by a desire to minimize one or another of the income, gift, or estate taxes. Of course, there is usually some overlapping of objectives, particularly where a tax-oriented trust is involved, since it would hardly benefit the grantor or his family to create a trust that saves money from a tax viewpoint but loses it all back through poor management.

The trust most often associated with the property-management concept is the *revocable inter vivos trust,* which the grantor establishes either for his own personal benefit (sometimes called a "housekeeping trust") or for the benefit of family members or friends. This type of trust may be amended or revoked by the grantor at will; as a result, it has no tax advantages (or disadvantages) whatsoever. It does not exempt the property in the trust from estate or inheritance taxes, nor does it achieve economies in family income taxation. What it does do, however, is allow a grantor who is perhaps too busy, old, or ill to properly manage his finances to create a vehicle by which others of his selection may do so for his or his family's benefit.

In addition, a grantor establishing and funding a revocable trust while he is alive has an opportunity to see how the trust (and its trustees) function during his lifetime. If there are things he doesn't like, his power to revoke or amend permits him to make the necessary corrections. Then, in his will, he may simply direct that the balance of his property be paid to the previously established trust. (A will of this type is sometimes called a "pour-over" will.) The grantor of the revocable trust thus will frequently use the trust as a substitute for a probate estate by combining it with a pour-over will. An additional advantage of this plan is that probate administration expenses may be reduced, since attorneys' fees and fiduciary commissions sometimes (although not always) are reduced when assets pass at death to a revocable trust, rather than through the probate estate.

The types of trusts created for tax-minimization purposes are many, and include sprinkle trusts (discussed above), Clifford trusts (also called "short-term" or "ten-year" trusts), minors' trusts, marital-deduction trusts, insurance trusts, charitable remainder trusts, and charitable lead (or "front-end") trusts, to name some of the more prominent ones. A common element in all of these tax-oriented trusts is that each is and must be irrevocable, meaning that the grantor may not retain, in the trust document, the right either to revoke or to amend the trust he has created. (Curiously, despite the requirement that the trust contain language as to its irrevocability, some states have laws that nevertheless permit revocation if all of the parties having a financial interest in the trust are adults and agree to a revocation.)

A *Clifford trust* is an income-tax-savings device established by a high-bracket grantor ordinarily for the benefit of a lower-bracket family member. The duration of the trust must be at least ten years, at the end of which time the principal reverts to the grantor. (For this reason, the value of the reversion is an asset includable in the grantor's estate for federal estate-tax purposes.) The law also permits the trust to end if the income beneficiary dies, or if the grantor dies, as long as he had an actuarial life expectancy of at least ten years when he created the trust.

During the period of the trust, the income must either be paid to the income beneficiary or be accumulated for later distribution to him or her. The typical beneficiary is a minor child or an elderly parent living on a fixed income or in need of additional income to cover medical expenses.

An example will demonstrate the substantial savings that can be achieved through use of a Clifford trust. Suppose a taxpayer in the 50% bracket desires to build a college fund for his daughter, age 8, but does not wish to make a permanent gift to her, because he does not know how well she will be able to handle property as a young adult, age 18. The taxpayer (who is married in this example) transfers property worth $45,000 to a ten-year Clifford trust he has created, giving the trustees the right either to pay out the income to his daughter or to accumulate it.

Various gift-tax laws will shield the taxpayer from having to pay any federal gift taxes on his transfer to the trust. Suppose the fund is invested in a Treasury bill paying 10%. Had the grantor retained the bill, he would have earned $4,500 per year; after 50% taxes, however, he would have been left with only $2,250, or $22,500 after the ten-year period. In a properly drafted Clifford trust, however, the income taxes are paid either by the beneficiary (if income is distributed) or by the trust (if accumulated). Assuming the daughter (or the trust) has no other income, her (or its) bracket will be about 16%. Thus, after tax, the $4,500 will be reduced only to $3,780, or $37,800 for the ten-year period—an increase in "family dollars" of $15,300 over the $22,500 that would have been available had the taxpayer not created the trust.

It should be carefully noted, however, that in order for the Clifford trust to be effective for tax purposes, complicated and precise tax rules must be followed to the letter. Among other things, none of the income from the trust may be used to satisfy the taxpayer's own legal obligations—e.g., his obligation to support his daughter by paying her food, shelter, and clothing.

A *minor's trust* (technically referred to as a "2503(c) trust") is similar in some ways to many Clifford trusts: It is frequently set up to provide for a child's health or medical needs or to establish a college fund; it is irrevocable; it can permit current income distribution or accumulation; and often it can be planned and drafted to escape gift taxation. It differs from the Clifford trust, however, in that the principal does not return to the grantor at the end of the trust period. (For this reason, the minor's trust is not included in the grantor's estate for estate-tax purposes.) Instead, the trust principal must be paid to the child, to his or her estate, or to those whom the child designates by a power of appointment, should the child die before receiving the principal.

Marital-deduction trusts are used in ESTATE PLANNING, in order to minimize gift and estate taxes, in situations where one wishes to utilize (in whole or in part) the marital deduction available for transfers to one's spouse, but where, for whatever reason, an outright gift or bequest is not desired. Thus, instead of giving property to the husband or wife, or leaving it directly by will, a trust may be created under which the spouse is the sole income beneficiary, and the principal either passes to the spouse's estate upon his or her later death, or is distributed as the spouse directs by exercise of a power of appointment. With one exception, no other person may be interested in the

trust, or the marital deduction will be forfeited.

The exception referred to is the so-called QTIP marital-deduction trust, which was created by a revision of the tax laws in 1981. The QTIP trust permits a tax election to be made that will qualify the trust for the marital deduction for estate- and gift-tax purposes, even though, for the first time, the principal (remainder) of the trust is designated for persons other than the spouse or the spouse's estate. The advantage is that one can use this type of trust to make tax-free lifetime or death-time transfers for the benefit of a spouse, yet still control who ultimately obtains the property, thus preventing second spouses and children of later marriages from acquiring one's property after the transfer to one's spouse.

Insurance trusts are designed to exclude the proceeds of life insurance from estate and inheritance taxes, not only when the insured person dies but also upon the subsequent death of the insured's spouse. It is a common misconception that life insurance is not subject to death taxes. In fact, the opposite is true, unless the insured person both gives up all ownership rights over the policy (e.g., the right to change the beneficiary) *and* makes certain that the beneficiary of the insurance is not the insured's estate.

One way to achieve this result is for the insured to transfer ("assign") his policy to his wife, naming her as the beneficiary. Since both of the above tests for excludability will be met, the insurance is not subject to death taxes when the insured dies—provided he has lived at least three years after having made the transfer. However, since the spouse has received the insurance proceeds, they will ultimately be subjected to estate taxes upon her death, unless she has consumed them.

The insurance trust avoids the later tax on the wife's death. Instead of assigning his policy to his spouse, the insured creates an insurance trust and names (typically) his spouse and an independent third-party trustee as owners and beneficiaries of the policy. Again, assuming the passage of three years before death, no estate taxes are incurred when the insured dies. Moreover, no taxes are payable when the surviving spouse dies, because she is only the income beneficiary (and, perhaps, the beneficiary of discretionary principal) of the insurance trust, and not the owner of the policy proceeds. While the insurance trust sometimes will provide that the children (or other beneficiaries) will benefit only after the surviving spouse's death, more frequently it will be drawn to function as a sprinkle trust (with wife *and* children as "permissible beneficiaries") while the surviving spouse is still living, thus providing the usual income-tax advantages of a sprinkle trust discussed previously.

Charitable lead and *charitable remainder trusts* are usually created by will and are designed to secure deductions from the estate tax (although such trusts may also be created during one's lifetime to obtain gift- or income-tax advantages). A charitable lead trust is one in which a named charity or charities (or one or more charities designated by the trustees) receives a set percentage or dollar-amount payout from the trust for a determinate number of years. Upon the termination of the trust, the principal reverts to the deceased's family or other beneficiaries. If properly drafted, 100% of the value of the trust can be exempted from estate tax, even though the family ultimately regains title to the property in the trust. Huge tax benefits are possible, since not only the estate taxes saved but also capital gains and accumulated income in excess of the amount required to be paid to charity will be transferable to the beneficiaries at the end of the trust period. The drawback is that a lead trust is practicable only where the family can afford to do without the trust property or its income for a lengthy period of time (such trusts usually are devoted to charities for about the first 20 years).

The charitable remainder trust is exactly the opposite of the lead trust. Here, family members or other individuals receive the required payment for the specified period; *then* the principal is paid, upon termination, to a named or trustee-designated charity or charities. Again, as with the lead trust, a sizable estate- or gift-tax charitable deduction may be obtained, although, unlike the lead trust, the deduction can never equal 100%.

The advantage of the charitable remainder trust is that the deduction is obtained immediately upon the making of the gift (or upon death, in the case of an estate), even though the charity may not receive the property for years. The disadvantage is that the trust property ultimately passes out of the family. Thus, this trust frequently is suitable only in a situation where the grantor has no immediate family other than a spouse (who receives the payout prior to the ultimate distribution to charity), or where, if there is family, they are provided for from other sources.

In both types of charitable trusts—lead and remainder—careful planning and drafting by an estate-planning attorney is absolutely essential. The regulations, rulings, and cases governing the use of these trusts are among the most sophisticated and complex in the entire field of tax law. As with all of the other trusts discussed above, use of these trusts should be completely integrated with the individual's overall estate plan.

Steven J. Wohl

Truth in Lending Act

See CONSUMER-CREDIT REGULATION

·U·

Underwriter, Insurance

In the early days of international commerce, men of means used some of their funds to insure the safe arrival of ocean shipments. Each man who accepted a share of the risk of a given voyage would note on the policy the amount he assumed. By *writing* his name *under* the amount, he would become an *underwriter.* During the late seventeenth century, underwriters tended to gather in places like Edward Lloyd's coffeehouse in London, a custom that gradually expanded into the insurance operation well known today as Lloyd's of London.

Today, underwriters perform a vital function in the insurance industry. The profits or losses of any insurance company depend largely on the abilities of its underwriters, who determine what risks to accept and under what terms and conditions coverage will be offered. Sound judgment is essential. If an underwriter is too strict, the insurance company will pass up too much business; if he or she is too liberal, insurance claims will exceed premium and investment revenues.

Underwriting is much more than risk selection. Launie, Lee, and Baglini, in the book *Principles of Property and Liability Underwriting,* define *underwriting* as "the process of hazard recognition and evaluation, risk selection, pricing, and determination of policy terms and conditions." Some underwriters, referred to as "line" underwriters, pass judgment on individual applications for insurance. Higher-level underwriters, sometimes referred to as "staff" underwriters, develop the guidelines that help line underwriters recognize and evaluate hazards. Staff underwriting guidelines may also set limits on the prices, terms, and conditions the line underwriters may offer. Of course, insurance underwriters must also operate in compliance with a variety of state laws.

As an example of underwriting, suppose Elliott applies for a fire-insurance policy on his restaurant. A line underwriter will review his application in order to recognize and evaluate any unacceptable hazards connected with Elliott's restaurant. It may be necessary to obtain additional information to complete this evaluation. If Elliott's requested coverage is found acceptable in view of the guidelines provided by staff underwriters, the line underwriter will agree to provide the insurance. The underwriter may have made a good decision, yet there may be a claim to pay. This could happen if all hazards in Elliott's restaurant are well controlled but the restaurant nevertheless has a fire, resulting in a covered claim that will be paid. On the other hand, a restaurant loaded with hazards may be fortunate and have no fires—and thus an underwriter who overlooked serious hazards and agreed to provide insurance coverage made a bad decision that, only through luck, resulted in no claims to pay.

The above example involves property insurance. Underwriters also review life- and health-insurance applications, evaluating such factors as the health and age of the prospective insured. But this is not the only way the term *underwriter* is used in the insurance business. Especially in life and health insurance, the term is often applied to sales personnel. Many life-insurance sales personnel have earned the professional designation "chartered life underwriter" (CLU) by completing a challenging five-year educational program and meeting other requirements. Not all CLU's are sales personnel, however.

The property-liability insurance industry's professional designation, "chartered property-casualty underwriter" (CPCU), is not limited to sales personnel or to people in underwriting occupations. A chartered property-casualty underwriter is an insurance professional with any insurance-related occupation who has successfully completed a five-year series of challenging courses and has met certain experience and ethics requirements.

Sometimes the term *underwriter* is also used to denote the person in an insurance agency or brokerage firm who contacts insurance-company line underwriters to "place" applications received from the agent's or broker's customers.

Underwriters perform a similar evaluation, selection, and pricing function in connection with fidelity and surety bonds, which are insurance-like products.

However, underwriters involved with the issuance of corporate or municipal bonds serve an entirely different function from that of insurance underwriters.

Eric A. Weining

Underwriter, Securities

See INVESTMENT BANKING.

Unemployment Insurance

There are unemployment-insurance programs in each of the 50 states, the District of Columbia, and Puerto Rico.* Federal-state in character, their objective is to provide partial replacement of wages during the involuntary unemployment of persons who were regularly employed members of the labor force.

State unemployment programs must meet certain requirements as set forth by federal law if employers are to be able to credit the state tax against the federal levy (industrial and commercial employers who meet certain standards pay a national tax) and if the state is to receive federal grants for administration. However, each state is responsible for the content and development of its own law. Each state individually decides what the amount and duration of the weekly benefits shall be and, with minor limitations, what the eligibility requirements, disqualification provisions, and contribution rates shall be. Administration of the laws—including collecting contributions, taking claims, and paying cash benefits—is handled directly by the states.

Eligibility. Although unemployment laws vary from one state to another, generally speaking there are certain conditions an unemployed worker must meet to be eligible for benefits. The person must be registered for work at a public employment office and be ready, willing, and able to work. The unemployed worker must also have had a certain amount of recent work and/or earnings in employment covered by the state law.

An unemployed wage earner may be disqualified from benefits for various reasons, including discharge from previous employment due to misconduct; voluntary termination without good cause; refusal to apply for or accept employment without good cause; and unemployment due to a labor dispute.

The occupational groups covered by state law are generally limited to those covered by the Federal Unemployment Tax Act (FUTA), which primarily relates to industrial and commercial workers in private industry. The act excludes certain categories of workers, such as the self-employed, agricultural workers, domestic help, and members of the employer's family. However, some states have special provisions that cover some of these excluded classes. Special federal legislation has brought federal civilian employees and ex-servicemen under the unemployment-insurance system, and a separate insurance law enacted by Congress covers railroad workers.

Benefits. All the states pay benefits on a weekly basis; the amount varies with the worker's past wages, with minimum and maximum limits. The states have formulas for determining the amount of benefits, which in most cases results in weekly benefits equal to half of the person's usual weekly wage, up to a specified dollar maximum. Most states have a waiting period of one week after filing a claim before the benefits can begin. Some states will pay benefits for this period if the unemployment continues for a certain amount of time or if the person returns to the labor force within a specified period.

Harvey Rachlin

United States Bullion Depository

See FORT KNOX.

United States Customs Service

See DEPARTMENT OF THE TREASURY.

United States Government Securities, Special

The United States Treasury occasionally issues special, nonmarketable government securities to foreign governments. Generally, they are issued as the dollar counterpart of a swap drawing by which the U.S. acquires foreign exchange for use in intervention operations (*see* SWAP NETWORK, FINANCIAL INSTITUTION REGULATORS, BANK FOR INTERNATIONAL SETTLEMENTS). The special securities also may be issued to aid a foreign monetary authority's investment of dollars purchased in its exchange market. The securities usually are issued by the Treasury through the Federal Reserve Bank of New York.

The funds acquired through the swap network in return for a certificate of indebtedness are reflected on the Consolidated Statement of Condition of all Federal Reserve banks under "liabilities," as a deposit in the U.S. Treasury general account, or in deposits-other, which includes the special checking account of

---

* Puerto Rico's unemployment insurance program was incorporated into the federal-state system in 1961.

the EXCHANGE STABILIZATION FUND (ESF). The "certificate" itself is reflected in the Treasury's Monthly Statement of the Public Debt of the United States, under nonmarketable securities.

Since October 1961, when these securities were initiated, four types of nonmarketable debt instruments have been used: bills, with maturities of one to nine months; certificates of indebtedness, with maturities of three to six months; notes, with maturities up to seven years; and bonds, with maturities exceeding seven years. The type of debt instrument issued is determined by the nature of the transaction and mutual agreement between the U.S. Treasury and foreign government acquiring the security.

The nonmarketable securities have been issued in two forms. Those denominated in dollars, officially are called "foreign series" securities. Those denominated in a foreign currency, with interest and principal payable in the foreign currency, are called "foreign currency series" securities, or "Roosa bonds." They are named after Robert V. Roosa, who, as undersecretary of the Treasury for monetary affairs, was primarily responsible for their initiation. Both series are governed by special rules: They can't be sold to other governments or traded in the open market, and they can be purchased from and redeemed by only the U.S. Treasury through the Federal Reserve. However, if notice is given to the Treasury, they can be redeemed before they mature.

The issuance of nonmarketable securities may avoid substantial movements of funds into and out of the government securities market that could result in sharp changes in interest rates. Such large swings could have a deleterious effect on U.S. financial markets. The primary means by which the Fed carries out its monetary policy is through the buying and selling of marketable Treasury securities in the open market. Wide swings in interest rates would complicate this operation. By agreement with foreign governments, the special securities can't be exchanged for marketable U.S. government securities.

In addition to earning interest for the holder, the foreign-currency series securities insure the owner against the risk that the dollar might decline in relation to the foreign currency involved, since the foreign government will receive a specified amount of foreign currency at redemption. However, if the dollar rises, the foreign nation loses the benefit of that appreciation.

"Roosa" securities in the "fixed-exchange-rate" system were originally sold with the agreement that if the currency of the buyer were to be revalued against the dollar before the security matured, the Treasury's redemption price would be based on the value of the foreign currency at the time the security was purchased. Securities issued currently don't include the agreement.

The price paid by the foreign government for the nonmarketable security varies according to the type of security issued. Bills are sold at less than the face (par) value, as are certificates of indebtedness. This means they are sold at a discount. If the foreign government holds the security to maturity, the face value is paid. If the security isn't held until maturity, the foreign government is paid a market rate based on the time the security was held.

The purchase price of the notes and bonds is based on the price of an outstanding marketable Treasury issue of the same type and maturity on the day that the nonmarketable security is issued. The foreign government may therefore pay less than the face value or more than the face value. The foreign government will be paid the face value at the maturity date or the market value at any time prior to maturity. The interest on bonds and notes is payable semiannually.

On November 1, 1978, as part of the U.S. government's announcement of its intention to acquire foreign currencies to support intervention by the U.S. in foreign exchange markets, the Treasury said it would introduce an additional type of special security, denominated in foreign currency, which would be sold only to private foreign residents. These bonds have been called "Carter" bonds, after President Carter.

The first of these new securities, Treasury notes denominated in West German marks, were sold to private West German residents in December 1978. A total of 3,039 million marks, equivalent to $1,595 million, were sold in two issues. The three-year bonds totaled 1,774 million marks, equivalent to $931 million, and carried an interest rate of 5.95%. A four-year issue totaled 1,265 million marks, equivalent to $664 million, paying 6.20% interest. Interest is paid annually.

The notes in denominations of 500,000 marks equal to $262,000 at the exchange rate on the day the securities were paid for, were offered through the German Federal Bank (Bundesbank) as agent and registered with that central bank. The owners of the notes are allowed to transfer them to other West German private residents. However, only four such transfers can be made following the initial purchase. The transfer is made at a negotiated price. The Bundesbank must be notified each time a transfer is made.

In January 1979 the Treasury sold to private Swiss residents two issues of notes denominated in Swiss francs totaling 2,015 million Swiss francs, equivalent to $1,203 million. These notes, in 500,000 Swiss franc denominations equivalent to $299,000 at the exchange rate on the day the notes were paid for, were offered through the Swiss National Bank as agent. The two-and-one-half-year issue totaling 1,247 million Swiss francs, equivalent to $744 million, carried an interest rate of 2.35%. The four-year notes totaled 768 million Swiss francs, equivalent to $459 million, and pay 2.65% interest. Interest is paid annually. Unlike the mark notes, the Swiss-franc notes aren't transferable.

A second mark-denominated issue was sold in February. The special "Carter" bonds carried the interest rates prevailing at the offering date in the two countries where they were sold, rather than the rates prevailing in the U.S. for outstanding issues of Treasury securities—the policy for "Roosa" bonds. Two additional mark-denominated issues were sold through mid-1980.

Arthur Samansky

United States Government Securities Quotes, How to Read

Approximately $10 billion of U.S. government securities (see TREASURY SECURITIES) are traded every business day. The bulk of these secondary market transactions in treasury bills, notes, and bonds is among banks, dealers, and brokers that buy and sell securities after original issuance for their accounts or for customers. A list of prices of marketable issues is made available each afternoon by the Federal Reserve Bank of New York in the "Composite Closing Quotations for U.S. Government Securities" report.

The prices listed for the bills, bonds, and notes are obtained from five securities dealers. From time to time, one or more of these dealers are changed. The New York Fed determines the listed price from the range of quotations received. Actual purchases or sales may have taken place at higher or lower prices.

There are six groups of numbers under five headings for each note or bond. For example:

Issue	Bid	Asked	Change	Yield
7⅜ 5/15/81-N	104.8	16	+6	6.20

Numbers under the first heading identify the issue by interest rate (7⅜%) and maturity date (May 15, 1981). The "N" means the security is a note. In the market, this note is referred to as "7⅜s of May 1981." "Bid" is the price a buyer is willing to pay for the issue, and "asked" is the price a seller is willing to accept. Both numbers are abbreviations.

Note and bond issues are usually quoted in 32nds of a point, and bid of 104.8 is 104 8/32 of a point. For

each $1,000 of face value, a full point equals $10 and a 32nd equals 31.25 cents. Thus, a quote of 104.8 means a dollar price on a $1,000 security of $1,042.50, or: (104 × $10) + (8 × $0.3125) = $1,042.50. Denominations other than $1,000 are quoted in multiples of this price.

The number 16 that appears under "asked" is an abbreviation for the price asked, which is 104.16. Asked prices are also expressed in 32nds of a point. Thus, 16 means 16/32 of a point, or $5.00 on $1,000 of face value. The full dollar price on a $1,000-face-value security with an asked of 104.16 thus is $1,045 or: (104 × $10) + (16 × $0.3125) = $1,045.00. Asked prices are always higher than bid prices. If the asked-price digits after the decimal are lower than those for the bid, the whole number must be moved to the next-highest whole number. For example:

Issue	Bid	Asked
7⅜ 5/15/81-N	104.27	3

The 3 is lower than the 27, indicating the asked price is 105.3 or $1,050.93, not 3/32 more than 104.

Following the asked price is the change in the current day's bid price from the closing bid price of the preceding business day. It, too, is a shorthand reference to the number after the decimal. In the example, it denotes an increase of 6/32 or about $1.88. Often, the change is the same for bid and asked prices. A plus sign (+) may appear to the right of the price or its change. It means dealers are also quoting an issue in 64ths. A quote of 104.8+ means 104 8/32 plus 1/64— or 104 17/64.

The yield, 6.20 in the example, is the annualized percentage return an investor receives if the note is purchased on the day of the quotation at the asked price and held until maturity. However, when a security is callable before maturity and quoted above par, the call date, rather than maturity, is used to calculate the yield.

Bills are quoted differently from notes and bonds since they don't pay a stated rate of interest. An investor's return on a bill is the difference between the purchase and subsequent sale price or, when held to maturity, the face value paid by the Treasury. Consequently, bills are quoted at a discount from face value, with the discount expressed as an annual rate based on 360 days. Quotations are thereby comparable regardless of maturity of a specific issue.

As with notes and bonds, numbers on the report are abbreviated. But Treasury-bill numbers have different meanings from those for notes and bonds. For example:

Issue	Bid	Asked	Change	Yield
2/24/77	4.63	4.59	−1	4.69

The first numbers refer to the bill's maturity date, February 24, 1977. Assume that date is 55 days from the delivery date. The bid, 4.63, is the annualized percentage return the buyer is seeking. In the example, to get a 4.63% annual return, the buyer would pay $9,929.27 for a 55-day $10,000 Treasury bill. When held to maturity, the holder would receive $10,000, which is $70.73 more than paid. That $70.73 represents a 4.63% annualized return on $10,000.

The asked quotation is the annualized percentage return the seller would like the buyer to accept. In the example, the seller would receive $9,929.87 for the $10,000 Treasury bill if the buyer was willing to accept a return of 4.59%. The return offered by a seller would give a seller 60 cents more than what a buyer is bidding, the difference between $9,929.87 and $9,929.27.

To determine bid and asked dollar prices for each $10,000 of face value, multiply the bid or asked return (excluding decimals) by the number of days to maturity and divide by 360 days. Subtract the result from the $10,000 face value. In the example, the bid dollar price per $10,000 face value would be:

$$\$10,000 - (463 \times 55)/360 = \$9,929.27$$

The asked dollar price would be:

$$\$10,000 - (459 \times 55)/360 = \$9,929.87$$

The change of minus 1 in the quotation is the change in the closing bid from the preceding day's bid in 1/100 of a percentage point. Thus, the change in this example means the previous day's bid was 4.64. One-hundredth of a percentage point is also described as a "basis point."

The yield is based on the asked rate and is the annualized rate of return if held to maturity. The yield is calculated on a coupon equivalent (the amount invested, not the face amount of the bill). In the example, the investor, receiving $70.13 more at maturity than the price he paid, obtains a 4.69% annualized rate of return on the $9,292.87 he paid.

Arthur Samansky

United States League of Savings Institutions

The United States League of Savings Institutions is the largest trade association serving the nationwide thrift business. Its primary function is to further the concepts of thrift and homeownership.

Organized in 1892, the U.S. League has nearly 3,500 member institutions, representing approximately 98% of the more than $900 billion in assets in savings institutions in the United States. Members are located in all 50 states, the District of Columbia, Puerto Rico, the Virgin Islands, and Guam, and represent approximately 99% of total savings and loan assets.

The U.S. League was born during a two-day organizational meeting in Chicago on April 14–15, 1892. Most savings associations of that time were completely local in character, but a few hundred "national" building and loan associations were formed using the savings and loan name. These speculative operations threatened to endanger public confidence in savings institutions. To combat this threat, various statewide building and loan leagues banded together to form a new trade organization—the U.S. League of Local Building and Loan Associations. The group's first annual convention was held in June 1893 in Chicago and a motto for the new organization was chosen: "The American Home, The Safeguard of American Liberties."

The newly formed organization was successful in obtaining the passage of savings and loan "codes" in various states and eliminating the threat posed by the "nationals."

The objectives of the U.S. League are to encourage savings and private homeownership; to assist in the development of safe, efficient operating methods for member institutions; and to work for the improvement of statutes and regulations affecting the savings and loan business and the public interest.

The U.S. League has maintained a full-time operation at its headquarters in Chicago since 1929. A second office in Washington, D.C., has been in operation since 1950. The U.S. League has a staff of 237—202 staff members in the Chicago office and 35 in the Washington office.

The U.S. League's policymaking structure consists of the board of directors, the Executive Committee, the officers, and such standing and special committees as the board or the Executive Committee may designate. A chairman and vice-chairman are elected each year by the membership. The president, appointed by the Executive Committee, is the league's chief executive officer.

Publications of the U.S. League include *Savings Institutions,* a monthly magazine for savings association and savings bank management; *Directors Digest,* a bimonthly publication providing specific information for savings and loan association directors; *Savings and Loan Sourcebook,* a yearly comprehensive data reference book for the savings and loan business including history and trends; *Washington Notes,* a weekly report covering the latest legislative and regulatory activity of interest to savings and loan associations; and the *Capital Guide,* an extensive reference source on Congress, the executive department, and independent and regulatory agencies, updated yearly. *Construction: Principles, Materials & Methods,* a comprehensive reference for the home-building industry, has developed into a text used in many colleagues and universities. Also published by the U.S. League are the *Federal Guide,* a four-volume loose-leaf publication, updated monthly, containing all federal laws and regulations affecting savings associations; and the *Legal Bulletin,* a bimonthly publication that provides information on savings and loan law and reviews of current court decisions and state legislation.

The league holds an annual convention in November; an annual legislative conference in Washington, D.C.; a secondary-mortgage-marketing conference in January; a series of management conferences in the spring; and dozens of specialized seminars, clinics, regional meetings and workshops, and legal clinics.

U.S. League Affiliated Organizations. Closely affiliated with the U.S. League are several organizations that provide specialized services to their members and member institutions and the entire savings and loan business.

The Institute of Financial Education has been the educational affiliate of the league since 1919. The institute provides multilevel professional education and training programs for savings association personnel through 260 chapters and study clubs and through home study courses. The institute has a total membership of 60,000 savings association employees and conducts resident schools and workshops at major universities.

The International Division of the institute offers consulting services in housing, residential finance, and institutional development to financial institutions and housing agencies in Latin America, Africa, the Far East, and the Middle East.

SAF Systems and Forms, a wholly owned subsidiary of the Institute of Financial Education, is the specialized source of internal operations information, forms, franchise funds transfer systems, and other services designed exclusively for savings and loan associations and cooperative banks.

The Advertising Division, Inc., develops advertising and promotional materials for use by member institutions. Its wholly owned subsidiary, Advertising Southeast, Inc., provides full advertising-agency service.

The Financial Managers Society is a professional organization whose membership is made up of 4,500 financial officers, controllers, treasurers, internal auditors, and electronic-data-processing managers. It sponsors local chapters throughout the United States

for the advancement of accounting and auditing techniques.

The Financial Institutions Marketing Association is a professional society for marketing executives in the thrift business. Its basic purpose is the advancement of thrift marketing practices and principles. FIMA sponsors educational programs and conferences and publishes a range of periodicals and special marketing reports for its 1,700 members.

Three new affiliate groups were organized by the U.S. League in 1982.

U.S. League Services, Inc., offers several insurance programs to participating associations.

U.S. League Financial Services, Inc., offers noninsurance income-producing services to participating associations including a traveler's-check program in cooperation with Thomas Cook.

U.S. League Investment Services, Inc., sponsors an institutional money-market fund for thrift institutions, called Liquidity Fund for Thrifts, Inc.

Mary Ann Irvine

United States Savings Bonds

History. The U.S. savings bonds program is but one of several ways the Treasury Department meets its need to borrow. It has its roots in the securities issued to the public in small denominations during the Civil War and Spanish-American War. Its immediate predecessor, the "Liberty Bonds" of World War I, set the stage for today's savings bonds by showing the Treasury how small-denomination bonds could be sold in large quantities, and showing that small savers and unsophisticated investors need nonmarketable securities to avoid losses.

During the 1930s, as borrowing needs increased for programs to combat the effects of the Great Depression, the Treasury drew on its past experience to create a new form of security—the savings bond. This security, unlike the "Liberty Bond," would be nonmarketable, and thus safe against market fluctuations such as those that led to losses for many bond buyers during World War I. The bonds would be small enough to be purchased by any potential saver, they would draw interest on a fixed schedule of payments, and they would be redeemable at any time after a short holding period.

The resulting "baby bonds" were issued between 1935 and 1941, with denominations set at between $25 and $1,000. They were sold by post offices and by the United States treasurer. Promotion was through direct mail and magazine ads. During the six years they were offered, about $4 billion worth of "baby bonds" were sold.

World War II Growth. The approach of World War II brought a need for even greater government spending and borrowing. Encouraged by the evident success of "baby bonds," the Treasury expanded that effort and created the modern bond program. Its aims were several: (1) to raise money for the government primarily from small savers; (2) to encourage personal saving in general; (3) to take surplus money out of the spending stream and store it for future needs, thereby helping to reduce inflationary pressures; (4) to educate people about government securities; and (5) to unify the country by providing a concrete way for each citizen to help with the common defense effort.

On May 1, 1941, three new series of savings bonds were issued, the most important of which was the Series E. The E bond—which was to last until 1980, when it was replaced by the EE—had a ten-year maturity and drew interest on a rising scale that averaged 2.9% if held the full ten years.

E bonds were registered securities and could be replaced in the event of loss. They were exempt from state and local income taxes. Most important, they were sold by thousands of financial institutions, as well as post offices and the Treasury. Soon, employers began offering their employees the opportunity to buy bonds in small installments taken automatically from their pay. This payroll savings plan made it easy for all workers to save, even if they didn't have the $18.75 needed to purchase a $25 bond, the smallest denomination. Payroll savings quickly formed the core of bond sales, and remains so today.

Payroll savings complemented the Treasury's savings-stamp program, begun in 1942, which allowed schoolchildren and others to buy bonds in installments as small as 10 cents. (The sale of savings stamps was discontinued on June 30, 1970.)

Postwar Changes. The end of the war let loose the long-deferred spending desires of the American people, and, thanks in part to savings bonds, there was a lot of money to spend. But the bond program did not end with the war. Millions of Americans continued the thrift habit they had developed, and continued to buy bonds. The Treasury also found that savings bonds had become an important part of debt-management efforts, and so continued to promote their sale and retention.

To keep bonds attractive to the public, and to reduce the erosion in sales that reached a low of $3.2 billion in 1951, a series of interest-rate increases began in 1952. Most rate changes reduced the length of time a bond had to be held to maturity and, beginning in 1959, higher rates were applied to all outstanding bonds. Also during the 1950s, interest extensions were granted to older bonds and tax deferral on the bonds' interest was extended to the time a bond was cashed or reached final maturity. As a result, many people held on to their older bonds, while sales held steady in the $4- to $5-billion range throughout the 1950s and early 1960s.

In 1952 a current-income bond, the Series H, was introduced. This bond, along with the Series E, remained on sale through the end of 1979. The H bond paid interest by check every six months. In 1960 it became possible to exchange Series E bonds for H bonds with a tax deferral on the E bond's interest income. This made H bonds an integral part of retirement planning for many E-bond buyers.

The late 1960s brought a new security into the savings-bond family. The U.S. savings note, or "Freedom Share," was sold in denominations of $25 to $100 along with E bonds of the same or larger denomination. Savings notes yielded slightly higher interest, had a shorter maturity period, and had a very tight limitation on the amount that could be purchased in any one year. In the three years they were sold, 30.8 million notes were issued.

Meeting Market Changes. Between 1968 and 1973, as inflation drove interest rates offered by banks and saving and loans upward, the Treasury moved to keep bond interest rates competitive. A series of increases brought rates from 4.15% on bonds held seven years to 6% when held five years. The increases had their intended effect—sales soared from $4.5 billion in 1970 to a peak of $8 billion in 1978.

The late 1970s brought two developments that had a profound effect on the future of the bond program: double-digit inflation and the onset of bank deregulation. Inflation made the interest rate on bonds, long under a congressionally imposed ceiling, too low to be very attractive. Financial institutions, on the other hand, were given freer rein to offer higher-interest options than they had previously, and most quickly responded to market pressures to offer certificates of deposit that were at or near market rates.

Changing Series. The approach of the 1980s also brought the approach of the end of the third interest-extension period for E bonds issued during the 1940s, and the end of the second extension for early H bonds. The Treasury, buffeted by ever-increasing record-keeping costs, decided not to further extend the early E and H bonds and to issue new series to replace them—the Series EE and HH.

The two new series, first issued on January 2, 1980, were similar to the ones they replaced. The major differences were a longer initial holding period and longer maturity (with 7% interest) for EE bonds, and a flat interest-payment schedule with penalty for early redemption for Series HH.

During 1980 the combination of high inflation, high interest rates, confusion over which E and H bonds would stop earning interest and when, and the introduction of the two new series sent bond sales into a tailspin and redemptions rocketing upward. With nearly $80 billion worth of bonds outstanding, playing a significant role in debt management, the Treasury recognized the need to improve the bond product. Millions of individuals still bought bonds through payroll savings plans, and nearly a third of all American families owned bonds. The Treasury felt that it had to give these people a better deal.

In late 1980, legislation was enacted enabling the Treasury to respond more quickly with rate increases as necessary. Briefly, the legislation removed the rate ceiling fixed by statute and now authorizes the secretary of the Treasury, with the president's approval, to increase the yield on savings bonds by up to 1% during any six-month period. The full authority (1%) was exercised in November 1980, raising the yield to maturity to 8% for new issues of Series EE bonds and 7.5% for issues of Series HH bonds, and again, in May 1981, raising the rates to 9% and 8.5% respectively. Outstanding savings bonds and savings notes also received two 1% increases in yield for the remaining period to their next maturity.

This rate system also proved unsatisfactory in the highly volatile market situation of 1981 and 1982. To remedy the problem once and for all, the Treasury proposed that Congress remove the interest ceiling for savings bonds entirely to make way for a market-based system. Following enactment of the enabling legislation, this system was implemented effective November 1, 1982.

Under the market-based system, savings bonds held five years or longer receive 85% of the so-called five-year Treasury (marketable) rate. The market-based rate is compiled from the daily five-year Treasury rate, averaged semiannually, and implemented for the subsequent six-month period. At the end of five years (or longer), the average of all semiannual rates to date are averaged to figure the overall yield and current redemption value of the bond.

As an added protection for savers, a minimum guaranteed rate of 7.5% was set for bonds held at least five years. Bonds held less than five years continue to receive interest on a fixed, graduated scale.

The market-based rate is effective for all new issues of Series EE bonds. In addition, it is effective for Series E and EE bonds purchased before November 1, 1982, and held at least five years after that date. Bonds redeemed or reaching final maturity before being held the required period receive a fixed interest yield.

Series EE and HH Bonds. Series EE bonds are accrual-type securities sold at one-half their face amount. Denominations range from $50 to $10,000, and there is an annual purchase limitation of $30,000 (face amount). Series EE bonds may be purchased over the counter or through the "Bond-a-Month" plan at financial institutions and the payroll savings plans offered by employers. Most banks and other financial institutions are qualified to issue and redeem Series EE bonds.

Interest accrues at a graduated rate through scheduled increases in redemption value. For example, Series EE bonds yield 5.49% if redeemed after one year and 7.5% if redeemed after five years, and the market-based rate or the minimum guaranteed rate (7.5%) if held longer. Series EE bonds issued on or after November 1, 1982, have a term to original maturity of ten years; EE bonds issued prior to that date have original terms of eight, nine, or eleven years, depending on issue date. Series EE bonds may be redeemed, at purchase price plus accrued interest, at any time after six months from issue date.

Series HH bonds are current-income bonds available only in exchange for Series E and EE bonds and savings notes with a total current redemption value of at least $500. HH bond denominations range from $500 to $10,000. The bonds are issued and redeemed at par only by Federal Reserve banks and branches and the Bureau of the Public Debt (Treasury). Interest is paid semiannually by Treasury check, currently at the rate of 7.5% per annum. The term to original maturity is ten years. Series HH bonds are eligible for redemption six months after issue.

Series HH bonds issued on exchange are not subject to an annual purchase limitation or to any interest adjustment for early redemption. Any combination of eligible Series E and EE bonds and savings notes may be presented for exchange, provided they have a total current redemption value of at least $500. Series E bonds are eligible for exchange until one year after final maturity; Series EE bonds are eligible six months after issue. Owners making such an exchange may continue to defer federal-income-tax reporting of accrued E/EE/savings-note interest until the HH bonds reach final maturity, are redeemed, or are disposed of otherwise, whichever comes first.

Series EE and HH bonds are nontransferable securities that may be registered in single-ownership, co-ownership, or beneficiary form. They may not be pledged as collateral. The bonds may be issued under conditions specified in the governing regulations.

The interest on all savings bonds is subject to federal income tax but is exempt from state and local income taxes. For federal-income-tax purposes, interest on Series EE bonds may be reported each year as it accrues or reporting may be deferred until the bonds are cashed, reach final maturity, or are disposed of otherwise, whichever occurs first. Interest on Series HH bonds must be reported annually for the year in which it is paid. Series EE and HH bonds are subject to estate, inheritance, and gift taxes, both federal and state.

For further information, the following circulars may be requested from the Bureau of the Public Debt or from Federal Reserve banks: Department of the Treasury Circular, Public Debt Series No. 1-80 (Series EE offering), No. 2-80 (Series HH and exchange offering), and No. 3-80 (governing regulations).

Series E and H Savings Bonds and Savings Notes. Series E bonds were offered for sale from May 1941 through June 1980; Series H bonds, from June 1952 through December 1979; and U.S. savings notes

("Freedom Shares"), from May 1967 through October 1970. All of these securities have received a number of ten-year extensions beyond their original maturity dates. Outstanding bonds and notes will continue to earn interest until they reach final extended maturity dates.

As shown in Tables 1, 2, and 3, Series E bonds issued between May 1941 and April 1952 are the first bonds to reach final maturity, exactly 40 years after issue. For example, a May 1941 bond matured and ceased to earn interest as of May 1981; an April 1952 E bond reaches final maturity as of April 1992. Series H bonds issued between June 1952 and January 1957 are the first H bonds to reach final maturity, exactly 29 years and 8 months after issue. For example, the

---

Table 1
Series E Extended Maturities (First Day of Month Shown)

Date of Issue	Date of Maturity	Term of Bond
May 1941–April. 1952	May 1981–Apr. 1992	40 yrs.*
May 1952–Jan. 1957	Jan. 1992–Sept. 1996	39 yrs., 8 mos.
Feb. 1957–May 1959	Jan. 1996–Apr. 1998	38 yrs., 11 mos.
June 1959–Nov. 1965	Mar. 1997–Aug. 2003	37 yrs., 9 mos.
Dec. 1965–May 1969	Dec. 1992–May 1966	27 yrs.
June 1969–Nov. 1973	Apr. 1995–Sept. 1999	25 yrs., 10 mos.
Dec. 1973–June 1980	Dec. 1998–June 2005	25 yrs.

Source: U.S. Savings Bond Division, Department of the Treasury.
*The Department of the Treasury has announced that no further extensions will be given to these bonds.

Table 2
Series H Extended Maturities (First Day of Month Shown)

Date of Issue	Date of Maturity	Term of Bond
June 1952–Jan. 1957	Feb. 1982–Sept. 1986	29 yrs., 8 mos.*
Feb. 1957–May 1959	Feb. 1987–May 1989	30 yrs.*
June 1959–Dec. 1979	June 1989–Dec. 2009	30 yrs.

Source: U.S. Savings Bond Division, Department of the Treasury.
*The Department of the Treasury has announced that no further extensions will be given to these bonds.

Table 3
Savings Notes Extended Maturities (First Day of Month Shown)

Date of Issue	Date of Maturity	Term of Note
May 1967–Oct. 1970	Nov. 1991–Apr. 1995	24 yrs., 6 mos.

Source: U.S. Savings Bond Division, Department of the Treasury.

final interest payment on a June 1952 H bond was made on February 1, 1982.

All Series E bonds held at least five years after November 1, 1982, and still earning interest, receive the market-based rate or previously guaranteed yields, whichever is more. Series H bonds, not eligible for the market-based rate, earn either 8.5% per annum or 7.5% per annum, depending on date of purchase. Series E bonds less than five years old and Series H bonds less than ten years old are still in their original maturity period, during which time yields are graduated. Series E bonds and savings notes issued after December 1950 will also receive a .5% bonus if held until their first interest-accrual date in 1991.

Series E bonds and savings notes may be exchanged for Series HH bonds with continued tax deferral of the accrued interest, as noted in the description of Series HH bonds above.

The interest on Series E and H bonds and savings notes is subject to federal income tax but is exempt from state and local income taxes. For federal-income-tax purposes, interest on Series E bonds and savings notes may be reported each year as it accrues, or reporting may be deferred until the securities are cashed, reach final maturity, or are disposed of otherwise, whichever occurs first. Interest on Series H bonds must be reported annually for the year in which it is paid. Series H bonds issued on exchange may include tax-deferred E bond/savings-note interest, which must also be reported when the H bond is cashed or reaches final maturity. In such cases, the amount of deferred interest is printed on the face of the H bond. Series E and H bonds and savings notes are subject to estate, inheritance, and gift taxes, both federal and state.

Most banks and other financial institutions are qualified to redeem Series E bonds and savings notes. Series H bonds may be redeemed only by Federal Reserve banks and branches and the Bureau of the Public Debt.

For further information, the following circulars may be requested from the Bureau of the Public Debt or from Federal Reserve banks: Department of the Treasury, Circular No. 653 (Series E offering), No. 905 (Series H offering), No. 3-67 (savings-note offering), No. 530 (governing regulations), and No. 2-80 (Series HH exchange offering).

Other Series of Savings Bonds. Over the years, other series of savings bonds have been offered for sale by the Treasury—namely, Series A, B, C, D, F, G, J, and K. All of these earlier series have matured and no longer earn interest.

Any bonds of Series A–D still outstanding may be presented for redemption, at face value, to an author-ized paying agent for savings bonds. Series F, G, J, and K bonds still outstanding are redeemable only by a Federal Reserve bank or branch or the Bureau of the Public Debt. Series F and J bonds will be paid at face value; Series G and K bonds will be paid at face value plus the final semiannual interest payment.

Stephen Meyerhardt

United States Secret Service

See DEPARTMENT OF THE TREASURY.

Unit Investment Trusts

Introduction and History. A "unit investment trust," as defined in the Investment Company Act of 1940, is a type of investment company that (1) "is organized under a trust indenture," (2) "does not have a board of directors," and (3) "issues only redeemable securities, each of which represents an undivided interest in a unit of specified securities." This type of investment company is usually formed by professional depositors or sponsors, who assemble a fixed portfolio of securities, deposit them with a trustee for units, and then offer the units to investors. Each unit represents a fractional undivided interest in the specified securities deposited. After the initial securities are deposited, except in limited circumstances, the trust sponsors are prohibited from making further purchases or trading the securities in the portfolio.

Over the past 20 years, the largest number of these unit investment trusts have been composed of fixed portfolios of tax-exempt state and municipal securities. The first municipal bond trust—Municipal Investment Trust Fund, Series A—was introduced in 1961 by Ira Haupt & Company. This firm, starting in 1955, had submitted several ruling requests to the Internal Revenue Service for a determination that interest income from municipal bonds held by such a trust would continue to be tax-exempt when received by unit holders. A favorable ruling was finally received in 1961. During the early 1960s, the concept of these unit investment trusts developed slowly as many brokers and potential investors did not fully understand the concept or the benefits of the trust.* In fact, a prominent Wall Street municipal-bond underwriter predicted that the concept would go the way of the dinosaur. The total annual volume of municipal investment trusts, however, began to soar in the mid-1970s as investors became familiar with the special investment characteristics of these trusts. Annual sales of units expanded to over $2 billion in the mid-

---

* Another type of unit investment trust, periodic payment plans, involves the sale of mutual funds with a front-end load. Sales of this type of unit trust have fallen off sharply following 1970 Investment Company Act amendments. This entry discusses only the fixed portfolio type of unit trust.

1970s and in 1982 exceeded $14 billion in municipal trusts and $8.8 billion in corporate trusts. The total face amount of municipal trusts issued through July 29, 1983, was $50.5 billion.* Unit trusts issued with other types of securities totaled $43.4 billion as of the same date.† See Table 1 for a list of sponsors of municipal tax-exempt unit investment trusts and the total face amount issued through July 29, 1983, and Table 2 for sponsors of corporate taxable unit investment trusts and the total face amount issued as of the same date.

Creation of Unit Investment Trusts. A unit investment trust is formed when a sponsor or group of sponsors who are broker/dealers registered under the Securities Exchange Act of 1934 decide to create a trust.

The sponsor will first select the type of securities to be acquired and establish investment criteria for the trust. Research bond analysts will then carefully evaluate the creditworthiness of all the securities contemplated for purchase in the trust. Once securities are selected, professional traders will go into the open market to purchase them, taking advantage of any institutional-size discount offered. After all of the securities have been purchased for the size trust desired, the sponsor will deposit the securities with a bank trustee. In exchange, the trustee will then deliver to the sponsor units of fractional undivided interest (units) representing the entire ownership of the trust. The units are then offered to investors at the public offering price, which is equal to the aggregate offering-side evaluation of the underlying securities (usually determined by an independent evaluator), divided by the number of the units in the trust, plus a sales charge. A proportionate share of the accrued and undistributed interest on the underlying securities up to the settlement date for units is added to the public offering price paid by the investor.

Administration of the Trusts. The sponsors and the trustee are responsible for the administration of the trusts. The trustee maintains records of transactions of the trusts, names and addresses and holdings of all purchasers, and a list of the securities held. In addition, the trustee is responsible for the collection of the interest or dividends and any cash receipts as a result of redemptions, maturity, or sales of securities in the trust. Scheduled periodic (i.e., monthly, quarterly, or semiannual) cash distributions of all the income after expenses are then made to each holder of units as of each record date in proportion to each holder's invest-

* *Source:* Standard & Poor's Corporation.
† *Source:* Merrill Lynch, Pierce Fenner & Smith and Interactive Data Services, Inc., a subsidiary of Chase Manhattan Bank.

ment. Cash distributions of any capital received are generally made at the same time. Instead of the cash distribution, the unit holder may elect to have distributions reinvested either in a separate mutual fund holding similar securities or in later series of his unit investment trust, whichever is offered by the sponsors. The trustee is also required to furnish each unit holder a statement with each distribution, showing the amount of interest or dividends and any other receipts that are being distributed. In addition, to each investor who at any time during the calendar year was a unit holder of record, the trustee is required to furnish an annual statement, including a statement of condition—a statement of all income and disbursements and any changes in the trust's securities.

Portfolio Supervision. A unit investment trust does not have a board of directors and is not managed. The sponsor, however, is normally authorized to direct the disposition of securities upon default in payment of principal or interest or in the event of certain other adverse market conditions. Sponsors often maintain research departments to evaluate the creditworthiness of issuers for initial purchase and also to maintain a continuing surveillance of all securities in the trusts in order to anticipate possible defaults and take appropriate actions in the interest of the unit holders.

Types of Unit Investment Trusts. Unit investment trusts were at first utilized to sell interests in fixed portfolios of tax-exempt municipal securities. The concept was later expanded to sell interests in fixed portfolios of taxable corporate securities, and today the concept is used to offer interests in portfolios of almost every type of security. The following summarizes the investment characteristics of many of the types of unit investment trusts.

Municipal Fixed-Income and Adjustable-Rate Unit Trusts

Municipal Bond Fixed-Rate Unit Trusts. Trusts formed for the purpose of providing federal-tax-exempt income through investment in a portfolio consisting of fixed-rate state, municipal, and public-authority debt obligations. This type of trust may be long-term (over 15 years), intermediate-term (5–15 years), or short-term (less than 5 years). Certain trusts are formed for the purpose of providing income that is also exempt from state and certain other taxes for residents of a specific state. For example, an investment in a trust consisting of bonds issued by the state of New York, its political subdivisions and municipalities, and certain U.S. territories and possessions would be exempt from federal, New York State, and New York City income taxes to an investor who is a resident of New York City.

Municipal Bond Floating-Rate Unit Trusts. Trusts formed for the purpose of providing federal-tax-exempt income through investment in a fixed portfolio consisting of floating-rate debt obligations issued by states, municipalities, and public authorities. The floating-rate nature of the underlying bonds in the trust will decrease changes in the value of the underlying securities and lessen the risk of capital depreciation as well as the potential for capital appreciation in comparison to fixed-rate trusts. The floating rates are usually set as a fixed percentage of the prime rates of various banks and will change up or down as those prime rates change. Many securities in floating-rate trusts also have minimum rates, for example 7%, below which the interest rates will not fall, regardless of how low the prime might fall; and maximum rates, for example 25%, above which the interest rates will not rise, regardless of how high the prime might rise. Payment of principal and interest on the bonds in most floating-rate trusts is also guaranteed by or backed by letters of credit from major banks.

Market Discount Bond Trusts. Trusts formed for the purpose of providing federal-tax-exempt coupon income and taxable capital gains from market discounts through investment in a fixed portfolio of state, municipal, and public-authority debt obligations.

Insured Municipal Trusts. Trusts formed for the purpose of providing federal-tax-exempt income through investment in a fixed portfolio of state, municipal, and public-authority debt obligations that are insured as to payment of principal and interest when due. The market value of such debt obligations and units of the trust, however, is not insured. Some trusts contain bonds on which the insurance is prepaid and remains in effect until the bonds mature. Other trusts pay annual insurance premiums on their underlying bonds that are not otherwise insured. Such insurance is effective only while the bonds are held by the trust. If there is a default, the bonds may not be sold without losing their insured value.

Corporate Fixed-Income and Adjustable-Rate Unit Trusts

Bonds and Preferred-Stock Trusts. Trusts formed for the purpose of providing a high level of income through investment in a portfolio of long-term, fixed-rate corporate debt obligations or preferred stock. This type of trust is usually long-term (more than 15 years) or intermediate-term (5–15 years).

Original-Issue Discount-Bond Trusts. Trusts formed to provide a high yield to maturity on an investment in a fixed portfolio consisting primarily of debt obligations of corporations originally issued at a substantial discount from face value and bearing a zero coupon. The zero-coupon bonds pay no current income and are purchased at deep discounts. Since the issuer of the bond is required to pay the full face amount at maturity, the principal is in effect compounded at a stated rate of interest over the life of the bond. However, as the accrual of the discount is currently taxable, these trusts are best suited for tax-deferred retirement plans, such as an Individual Retirement Account (IRA).

Adjustable-Rate Preferred-Stock Trusts. Trusts formed for the purpose of providing current income constituting dividends for federal income-tax purposes, such dividends being eligible for the $100 dividends-received exclusion for individuals and the 85% dividends-received deduction for eligible corporations. This type of trust is invested in a fixed portfolio consisting primarily of preferred stocks that adjust their dividend rates quarterly based on specified relationships to certain indexes of U.S. Treasury securities. The adjustable- or floating-rate nature of the underlying securities will decrease changes in the value of the underlying securities and lessen the risk of capital depreciation as well as the potential for capital appreciation in comparison to fixed-rate trusts.

Short-Term Unit Trusts. Trusts formed for the purpose of providing current income through investment in a fixed portfolio of domestic and/or foreign bank certificates of deposit maturing in three or six months.

GNMA Unit Trusts. Trusts formed for the purpose of obtaining safety of capital and current monthly distributions of interest and principal through investment in a fixed portfolio consisting primarily of mortgage-backed modified pass-through certificates fully guaranteed as to principal and interest by the GOVERNMENT NATIONAL MORTGAGE ASSOCIATION (GNMA). All of these securities are backed by pools of long-term mortgages on one-to-four-family dwellings. Since principal is paid on an amortized basis and the underlying mortgages are subject to prepayment at any time at par (face value), the investor in this type of trust does not have the call protection or the cash-flow predictability that is present in most other trusts. He must recognize that GNMA's are amortizing securities paying both interest and principal every month. The monthly principal distributions he receives will therefore fluctuate, depending on mortgage prepayments, and his dollar amount of monthly income will decline to reflect the reduced principal outstanding after each monthly payment.

GNMA-Collateralized Bond Unit Trusts. Trusts formed for the purpose of obtaining safety of capitol and current monthly interest income through investment in a portfolio of corporate bonds collateralized by mortgage-backed certificates, whose principal and interest are fully guaranteed by GNMA. These trusts generally provide some call protection.

Equity Income Unit Trusts

Utility Common-Stock Trusts. Trusts formed for the purpose of providing current income constituting dividends for federal income-tax purposes, such dividends being eligible for the $100 dividends-received exclusion for individuals and the 85% dividends-received deduction for eligible corporations, through investments in a fixed portfolio consisting of common stocks issued by domestic public utility companies. Income from such trusts even when reinvested will not qualify for the $750 tax exclusion available to individuals participating in qualified public utility dividend reinvestment plans. The value of the trust will fluctuate with the value of the underlying utility stocks, and income of the trust will tend to increase as dividends increase. Based on the past history of public utility dividends, this type of trust offers potential income growth.

S&P 500 Index Trusts. Trusts formed to give investors the opportunity to purchase units representing proportionate interests in a portfolio that consists of substantially all of the common stocks comprising the Standard & Poor's 500 stock-price index. Such trusts are designed to produce investment results that generally correspond to the price and yield performance of the common stocks listed in the Standard & Poor's index.

New Directions Trusts. Trusts with a portfolio of common stocks believed by the sponsor to be undervalued; such a trust terminates at a specified time within two years.

Variations of some of the above types of trusts have also been issued by various sponsors. One such variation is a municipal-bond trust, in which bonds are backed by letters of credit or guaranties issued by major banks as additional security. Other types are likely to be issued in the future as other types of investment securities are introduced to the market.

Investment Advantages of Unit Investment Trusts

Professional Selection and Diversification. A trust's portfolio is composed of many different securities of the same type to provide investors with a professionally selected, diversified group of bonds or other types of securities, from different issuers and with different maturities and yields. Investing in a broadly diversified trust does not eliminate the risk of an investment, but does reduce it substantially. Sponsors typically reduce the risk further by selecting only those securities rated "BBB" (or "Baa") or "A" or better by one of the nation's major rating agencies. the lower

"BBB" rating implies a somewhat greater risk for a slightly higher interest rate. In addition, by buying institutional-size quantities, the sponsors can purchase securities for the trust at volume discount prices, the savings from which are then passed along to the unit purchaser in the form of a lower price and therefore a higher return on the units.

Convenient Low Unit Price. Bonds and other fixed-income securities have generally been considered investments for the wealthy individual or for institutional investors. The minimum round-lot investment (on which a better price can be obtained) is generally $25,000. (For certain types of securities, such as certain Treasuries or Ginnie Maes, the minimum round lot is $100,000.) Even though many bonds are issued in minimum denominations of $5,000 each, the individual investor often finds himself at a disadvantage when buying or selling an odd lot, and those investors who wish to invest less than $5,000 may be precluded from buying any bonds. A unit trust, however, allows the small investor to purchase a fixed-income diversified investment for as little as $1,000, although some sponsors offer units for a minimum initial purchase of $5,000 and in incremental amounts of $100 above $5,000. A purchaser of trust units, therefore, can obtain both a diversified portfolio and perhaps a favorable market rate through the savings the trust may be able to realize by making large, institutional-size purchases.

Convenient Periodic Income Payments. Although most bonds pay interest semiannually or annually, payment dates on unit trusts vary. Some unit trusts are available with monthly, quarterly, or semiannual distributions, while others offer any one of these three different options. Trusts making payments less frequently offer slightly higher returns because of compounding.

Portfolio Supervision. The sponsors for the trust provide for the overall supervision of the trust and its portfolio of securities. A trust is usually designed to be liquidated as the securities in the portfolio mature or are redeemed by their issuers. When a liquidation occurs, the trustee will distribute to each unit holder his proportionate share of the proceeds. In limited circumstances, the sponsors may direct the trustee to sell a security before its maturity in the event of default or if, in the opinion of the sponsor, there are certain other adverse credit developments. Some trusts may use the proceeds to acquire other securities meeting criteria similar to those for securities originally acquired. The money distributed from a sale, redemption, or maturity of a security will represent a return of principal and could result in some gain or loss for tax purposes. Regular periodic interest payments will, of course, change as securities mature, are redeemed, or are sold, or as the expenses of the trust change.

Reinvestment Option. Distributions of interest, principal, and premiums, if any, are usually paid by the trustee to the unit holder in cash. However, holders of most trusts may elect to have such distributions reinvested. Some sponsors offer a separate investment-accumulation program, usually an open-ended management investment company, sold without sales charge, whose primary objective is to obtain current income through investment in a fixed portfolio consisting primarily of securities with investment characteristics comparable to those in the trust from which the income was earned. Other sponsors allow reinvestments in small units of subsequent series of the trust, charging either a transaction fee or a reduced sales charge.

Ease of Redemption and Sale of Units. The sponsors of unit investment trusts not only offer unit holders liquidity without a fee at then prevailing market values, but can also offer a way to avoid the "odd-lot" price differential on transactions in small quantities of bonds.

Unit holders are normally offered two distinct ways to cash in their units. Many sponsors of unit trusts, although not legally obligated to do so, maintain secondary markets in the trusts they sponsor. Most of the sponsors offer to pay prices for the units based on the "bid-side" evaluations of the underlying securities (in contrast to the higher "offer-side" evaluations at which units are initially sold). Some sponsors offer to pay the "offer-side" evaluations. What this means is that a unit holder can normally sell some or all of his units to the sponsors at any time on a regular five-business-day settlement basis. Because many trusts provide that portfolio securities will be sold in institutional quantities to meet redemptions, unit values would be based on higher prices usually obtainable on those larger institutional-size lots. There is no charge or interest penalty when units are sold. A holder would receive accrued interest up to, but not including, the settlement date of the sale. The price a holder receives, however, may be more or less than originally paid, since it is determined by the current market value of the securities in the portfolio at the time of sale or redemption.

The second way to cash in units is to tender them to the trustee for redemption at prices based on the "bid-side" evaluations of the underlying securities.

Exchange Option. Certain sponsors offer unit holders an option to exchange units for those of another trust offered by the same sponsor, at a reduced sales charge and subject to certain conditions. Such an exchange of units will normally constitute a "taxable event" for federal income-tax purposes unless the characteristics of the two trusts are substantially similar or the exchange has no significant purpose or utility apart from the anticipated tax consequences. The investor should consult his own tax adviser. Any gain or loss from an exchange of units will be of capital or ordinary income nature, depending on the length of time he has held his units and on other factors.

The Secondary Market for Unit Trusts. Sponsors maintaining the secondary markets described above for repurchase of previously issued units attempt to resell units purchased at the current repurchase price plus the applicable sales charge. These resales require delivery of prospectuses with financial information no older than 16 months before the date of sale. An investor can often find attractive offerings of older unit trusts in the secondary market: For example, units of trusts issued in the early 1970s at 6% to 7% may be available in the secondary market when rates are higher (perhaps 10% to 12%) at substantial discounts from face value, with a potential for capital gains. The secondary market offers the investor not only the many different types of trusts that have been issued to date, but also a wide variety of maturities, prices, and yields.

Charles J. Terrana

Table 1
Sponsors of Municipal Tax-Exempt Unit Investment Trusts Issued Through July 29, 1983

Sponsor	Number of Trusts	Total Face Amount (Millions)
Bear Stearns & Company New York, N.Y.	60	$ 758,500
Clayton Brown & Associates, Inc. Chicago, Ill.	117	2,288,255
Craigie, Inc. Richmond, Va.	3	16,500
Dain Bosworth, Inc. Minneapolis, Minn.	12	38,280
Dean Witter Reynolds, Inc. New York, N.Y.	48	575,620
Donaldson Lufkin & Jenrette Securities Corporation New York, N.Y.	1	9,750

Table 1 *(cont)*
**Sponsors of Municipal Tax-Exempt Unit
Investment Trusts Issued Through July 29, 1983**

Sponsor	Number of Trusts	Total Face Amount (Millions)
Fidelity Distributors Corporation Boston, Mass.	1	7,700
First of Albany Corporation Albany, N.Y.	1	6,000
First of Boston Corporation New York, N.Y.	1	25,000
First of Charlotte Corporation Charlotte, N.C.	5	5,000
First of Michigan Corporation New York, N.Y.	13	47,000
Foster & Marshall, Inc. Seattle, Wash.	3	10,176
Glickenhaus & Company New York, N.Y.	84	738,986
E. F. Hutton & Company New York, N.Y.	129	1,854,681
Kemper Financial Services, Inc. Chicago, Ill.	56	987,810
Legg, Mason, Wood, Walker, Inc. Baltimore, Md.	4	16,600
Manley, Bennett & McDonald, Inc. Detroit, Mich.	2	13,500
Merrill Lynch, Pierce, Fenner & Smith, Inc. Dean Witter Reynolds, Inc. Prudential-Bache Securities, Inc. Shearson/American Express, Inc. New York, N.Y. As cosponsors	607	19,576,649
Moore, Leonard & Lynch, Inc. Pittsburgh, Pa.	1	3,000
Moseley, Hallgarten, Estabrook & Weeden, Inc. New York, N.Y.	106	1,236,800
John Nuveen & Company Chicago, Ill.	360	10,041,750
Ohio Company Columbus, Ohio	32	157,600

Table 1 *(cont)*
**Sponsors of Municipal Tax-Exempt Unit
Investment Trusts Issued Through July 29, 1983**

Sponsor	Number of Trusts	Total Face Amount (Millions)
Paine Webber, Jackson & Curtis, Inc. New York, N.Y.	218	3,354,289
Prescott, Ball & Turben Cleveland, Ohio	26	144,300
Rauscher Pierce Securities, Inc. New York, N.Y.	1	5,000
Robinson Humphrey/American Express, Inc. Atlanta, Ga.	8	37,000
Rotan Mosle, Inc. Houston, Tex.	12	75,000
John L. Ryan & Company West Orange, N.J.	1	5,000
Shearson/American Express, Inc. New York, N.Y.	36	440,750
Smith Barney, Harris Upham & Company New York, N.Y.	141	2,928,270
Stephens, Inc. Little Rock, Ark.	1	2,300
Tax-Exempt Bond Trust, Inc. Los Angeles, Calif.	1	10,000
Thompson McKinnon Securities, Inc. New York, N.Y.	113	1,809,181
Tucker Anthony & R. L. Day, Inc. New York, N.Y.	9	24,700
Van Kampen Merritt, Inc. Naperville, Ill.	143	3,211,884
B. C. Ziegler & Company West Bend, Wis.	75	75,000
Total	2,431	$50,537,831

Note: The preceding information was obtained from Standard & Poor's Corporation and other sources that we believe to be reliable, but it may not be entirely complete, nor is any of the information guaranteed.

Table 2
Sponsors of Corporate Taxable Unit Investment Trusts Issued Through July 29, 1983

Sponsor	Number of Trusts	Total Face Amount (Millions)
Bear Stearns & Company New York, N.Y.	1	$ 6,000
Drexel, Burnham, Lambert, Inc. New York, N.Y.	1	20,755
The Dreyfus Service Corporation New York, N.Y.	16	1,410,000
E. F. Hutton & Company New York, N.Y.	44	824,104
Merrill Lynch, Pierce, Fenner & Smith, Inc. Dean Witter Reynolds, Inc. Prudential-Bache Securities, Inc. Shearson/American Express, Inc. New York, N.Y. As cosponsors	516	39,788,577
Moseley, Hallgarten, Estabrook & Weeden, Inc. New York, N.Y.	7	93,000
John Nuveen & Company Chicago, Ill.	8	87,000
Ohio Company Columbus, Ohio	1	5,000
Paine Webber, Jackson & Curtis, Inc. New York, N.Y.	14	179,600
Prescott, Ball & Turben Cleveland, Ohio	2	28,000
Prudential-Bache Securities New York, N.Y.	15	152,500
Shearson/American Express, Inc. New York, N.Y.	3	42,000
Smith Barney, Harris Upham & Co. New York, N.Y.	33	501,500
Thompson McKinnon Securities, Inc. New York, N.Y.	5	82,000
Van Kampen Merritt, Inc. Naperville, Ill.	18	197,551
B. C. Ziegler & Company West Bend, Wis.	9	27,000
Total	693	$43,444,587

Note: The preceeding information was obtained from Interactive Data Services, Inc., a subsidiary of Chase Manhattan Bank, and other sources that we believe to be reliable, but it may not be entirely complete, nor is any of the information guaranteed.

Universal Life Insurance

See LIFE INSURANCE.

Usury

In its modern meaning, usury is the receiving and taking of excessive and illegal interest for credit or the forbearance of a debt at a rate or in an amount above the limit specified in and authorized by the laws of each state. Interest, which is a charge for the rent of money, has been regulated since ancient times by either civil or religious laws. In the United States, interest has been regulated since the earliest colonial days. Consequently, these earliest usury statutes were probably the first price-control laws in the U.S.

Each of the states has a law called the "general usury statute" that sets a maximum interest charge for credit contracts and agreements that are unwritten or are written but otherwise unregulated. These laws are enforced only through civil suits brought by debtors and specify forfeiture of interest and sometimes also the principal as penalties for violation. In most states, commercial credit is exempt; in the others, it is regulated. Agricultural credit is unregulated, but not exempt. All forms of consumer credit are regulated either by a series of laws that set a maximum authorized rate of interest, finance charge, or time-price differential for each class of consumer credit, or by a uniform consumer-credit code, a single, comprehensive law that regulates all forms and nearly all aspects of consumer credit.

Until modern times when the concepts of capitalism were adopted, interest as the cost of pure rental of money was regarded as usurious because money in and of itself is not productive. Even until rather recent years, a myth persisted that interest in excess of 6% was usurious, even though the general usury statutes of all the states even then permitted maximum rates ranging from 8% to 10% per year. Since the early 1980s, recognition has begun to grow that interest rates should be set by competition in the marketplace, rather than specified by laws.

Today, all forms of credit are beginning to be recognized as a valuable service in which the interest or the rental of money is but a part of the cost of providing financing to consumers. It is also being recognized that ceilings on the cost of credit tend to result in legal evasion of such ceilings. And if the ceiling rates are too low, they become the "going" rates and credit availability is cut off except to the most profitable and least-risky credit users.

At the beginning of the 1980s, concepts of usury began to break down more rapidly. Financial markets in the U.S. became volatile as the Federal Reserve

Board tightened the money supply to restrain inflation. This led to pressure on interest rates for commercial, agricultural, and home-mortgage credit. To restore equilibrium to a faltering national economy, Congress passed laws preempting state laws that set interest ceilings for those forms of credit, so that rates would be set by competition and the demand for credit. As the availability of consumer credit began to be cut off, the states either authorized so-called market rates or raised their rate ceilings for consumer credit. Both the federal laws preempting state interest ceilings and the revised state statutes have provisions requiring legislative review, so that, in the future, interest rates for various forms of credit, including consumer credit, can be expected to rise and fall, with revisions in ceilings lagging behind changing economic conditions and public concepts of usury.

Even in colonial days, it was recognized that the use of credit may or may not be discretionary, depending on whether or not credit use is optional for the debtor.

As a result, it was felt that the public need not be protected from excessive charges for the use of credit if informed, rational, and discretionary choices could be made. This led to the concept of the time-price differential, under which retail credit purchases were regarded by the courts, even the U.S. Supreme Court, as exempt from general usury statutes. But that concept has broken down with the realization that time-price differentials (charging of a higher price for future payment in full for a credit sale than for immediate payment for a cash sale) fail to protect the nondiscretionary use of sales credit by the poor, so now time-price differentials are regulated by ceilings much like interest.

Concepts of usury have been changing more rapidly in modern times, but they have been evolving since ancient times. The semantics of this term are still in a state of flux and can be expected to continue to change as public attitudes are modified.

James A. Ambrose

·V·

Value Line, Inc.

Value Line, Inc., an independent investment adviser registered as such under the Investment Advisers Act of 1940, publishes one of the nation's major investment advisory services, *The Value Line Investment Survey,* as well as three other investment advisory publications: *The Value Line OTC Special Situations Service, Value Line Options,* and *Value Line Convertibles.* The company also provides financial information via computer tape and computer time-sharing services. Value Line manages six open-end mutual funds, all of which bear the Value Line name and have varied investment objectives, and provides investment counseling and asset-management services to private and institutional clients. Value Line and its parent, Arnold Bernhard & Company, Inc., have been in the investment advisory business since 1931.

Publications. *The Value Line Investment Survey,* published since 1935, is a weekly investment advisory service that rates common stocks for future relative performance based primarily on computer-generated financial statistics and stock-market performance. *The Value Line Investment Survey* is published in a two-volume set of binders, divided into three sections.

The first section, *Ratings and Reports,* contains full-page reports on each of 1,700 common stocks, classified into 92 industry groups. Each report contains extensive statistical data, statistical analyses, estimates of future performance, and a textual discussion. Each week approximately 130 stocks are reviewed on a preset sequential schedule. All 1,700 stocks are reviewed in a 13-week period, after which the cycle begins again. The 1,700 stocks under regular review account for most of the trading volume on all stock exchanges in the United States.

The second section, *Summary & Index,* is a weekly alphabetical catalog of all 1,700 stocks at their most recent prices, with their current rankings for "timeliness" and "safety" (as described below). The *Summary & Index* also contains lists of stocks that meet a variety of specialized investment criteria. Used in conjunction with the full-page analyses in *Ratings and Reports,* these lists are organized according to such factors as timeliness, stocks trading at discounts from book value, and stocks that have the highest earned return on net worth, to help subscribers tailor portfolios to meet their personal investment goals.

The third section, *Selection & Opinion,* provides Value Line's assessment of business prospects, the stock-market outlook, and advisable investment strategy. Each week's *Selection & Opinion* features detailed analyses of one or more stocks that are believed to be especially suitable for year-ahead relative performance ("Performance Stock Highlights") or income ("Income Stock Highlights"). It also features articles and computer screens on investment ideas that the company believes merit special attention, and articles on other matters of public interest.

The key evaluations for each stock covered by the Survey are timeliness and safety. "Timeliness" relates to the probable relative price performance of a stock over the next 12 months, as compared to the rest of the 1,700 covered stocks. Rankings are updated each week, and range from Rank 1 for the expected best-performing stocks to Rank 5 for the expected poorest performers. "Safety" rankings are a measure of risk avoidance and are based primarily on the issuer's relative financial strength and the stock's price stability. "Safety" ranges from Rank 1 for the most stable stocks to Rank 5 for the riskiest.

Established in 1951, *The Value Line OTC Special Situations Service* concentrates on fast-growing, smaller companies whose stocks are perceived as having exceptional appreciation potential. Typically, these stocks involve a high degree of risk.

The *OTC Service* is published 24 times per year. Each issue includes a report recommending a new "Special Situation," follow-up "supervisory reviews" of previously recommended special situations, and a summary-index containing the past performance record of all open recommendations (and Value Line's current advice on each).

Value Line Options evaluates and ranks almost all

options listed on United States exchanges (currently more than 9,000) while *Value Line Convertibles* evaluates and ranks for future market performance approximately 580 convertible securities (bonds and preferred stocks) and approximately 75 warrants. *Value Line Options,* begun in 1975, and *Value Line Convertibles,* begun in 1971, utilize the ranking of underlying stocks as they appear in the *Value Line Investment Survey.* They then attempt to search out underpriced and overpriced convertibles and options on those stocks.

Value Line intends to make the data bases of both the VL options and the VL convertibles available via computer timesharing in the future.

The Value Line Data Base II contains historic annual and quarterly financial records for over 1,600 industrial, transportation, utility, real-estate, banking, insurance, and finance companies, savings and loan associations, and securities brokers. *Data Base II* contains annual and quarterly data beginning with 1969 and is available via computer tape and computer timesharing.

Other Businesses. The company publishes the *Value Line Index,* a daily index of the stock-market performance of the 1,700 common stocks contained in *The Value Line Investment Survey.* The calculation of the index is done by a firm unaffiliated with the company. Futures contracts based on fluctuations in the Value Line Index are traded on the Kansas City Board of Trade. Options on Value Line Index futures are traded on the Chicago Board of Trade. The company receives fees in connection with this activity. The company also provides independent appraisal to determine the value of closely held companies and restricted or not otherwise marketable securities of publicly held corporations.

Value Line, Inc.

Variable Life Insurance

See LIFE INSURANCE.

Variable-Rate Preferred Stock

See PREFERRED STOCK.

Velocity

Money in very liquid form that is immediately available for spending—cash and checking accounts—totaled about $500 billion in the spring of 1983. But spending (defined as the GROSS NATIONAL PRODUCT [GNP]) is running at a rate of over $3 trillion. The operation of the financial and monetary system makes it possible for each dollar in the money supply to be spent over and over; this turnover of the money supply is called "velocity." A simple equation illustrates this relation of money and GNP:

$$V = \frac{PY}{M}$$

PY, or prices times real income, is the same as gross national product, so velocity is just GNP divided by the money supply.

Velocity is determined by factors affecting the operation of the financial system; for instance, the advent of home banking through computer terminals will speed the processing of transactions, increasing velocity. Velocity also shifts with forces that affect the public's demand to hold money balances. In 1982, for example, great uncertainty followed several major bankruptcies and a surge in unemployment, causing people to want to keep more liquid assets rather than longer-term securities. As a result, money-supply measures grew very rapidly and velocity fell.

Over the long run, swings in velocity tend to average out. Indeed, the monetarist economists' conclusion that, over time, money-supply growth will equal inflation (the rate of price change) is based on the assumption of steady growth in velocity. A steady velocity trend, or at least stable, predictable velocity is also assumed by the Federal Reserve Board and other countries' central banks, which try to stabilize business cycles and reduce inflation by targeting the money supply. They believe that if they achieve a certain growth rate of the money supply, a stable velocity trend will translate that money-supply growth into desired amounts of real economic growth and inflation. Thus, the Federal Reserve was confounded in 1982 by the unexpected drop in velocity and the strong growth of the money supply. It then reduced its reliance on monetary targeting until velocity returns to its normal trend.

Carol A. Stone

Vesting

See PENSION PLANS.

Veterans Administration (VA)

A federal agency that administers a system of benefits and services for veterans of the U.S. armed forces and their dependents or beneficiaries. A great variety of benefits and services are available for persons who served during wartime, and a limited number for those who served in the military forces during peacetime. These benefits include compensation for disabilities or death related to military service; pensions based on financial need for disability or death not related to military service; a comprehensive medical system, including the hospitalization, nursing-home care, domiciliary and restorative care, and prosthetic devices; burial expenses, including cemetaries, markers, and flags; vocational rehabilitation services; educational assistance; loans for the purchase of homes, farms, and businesses; grants for specially adapted homes and cars; and low-cost government life insurance.

History. The Veterans Administration was established as an independent agency under the president by Executive Order 5398 of July 21, 1930, in accordance with the act of July 3, 1930 (46 Stat. 1016). This act authorized the president to consolidate and coordinate the U.S. Veterans Bureau, The Bureau of Pensions, and the National Home for Volunteer Soldiers, thus bringing together under a single agency responsibility for the various veterans' programs passed by Congress over the years.

GI Loans for Homes, Condominiums, and Mobile Homes. For eligible veterans who are buying a home, condominium, or mobile home, the VA guarantees loans made by private lenders that help the veteran obtain a purchase featuring (1) an interest rate usually lower than current market mortgage rates; (2) no or very low down payment; (3) a long amortization or repayment period. The purpose of these GI loans is to enable eligible veterans to purchase a home; buy a residential unit in certain new or proposed, existing or converted condominium projects; build a home; repair, alter, or improve a home; refinance an existing home loan; and buy a mobile home with or without a lot.

Harvey Rachlin

Vocational Rehabilitation Services

See SOCIAL WELFARE.

·W·

Warrant

An option to purchase, at a specified price, a specified number of shares of a corporation's common stock. Warrants are often issued by a corporation to its creditors as an additional incentive, or "sweetener," to encourage a creditor to provide financing to the corporation. A creditor who is otherwise unwilling to extend credit, due to a significant risk of default on the part of the borrower, might be willing to take such a risk if he receives warrants for the corporation's common stock. The exercise price of a warrant is the price per share at which the warrant holder can purchase common stock from the issuing corporation. When the warrants are issued, the exercise price is significantly below the market price of the firm's stock. However, if the market price of the stock rises above the exercise price of the warrant, the warrant holder can realize a profit by exercising his option to purchase stock at the exercise price and then selling the stock at the higher market price. It is this potential profit that sometimes makes warrants attractive to creditors. The expiration date of a warrant is the last date on which the warrant can be exercised. Usually, the expiration date is several years after the warrant is originally issued, although some warrants do not have an expiration date and are therefore perpetual.

R. Bruce Swensen

Will

Sometimes more formally referred to as a "last will and testament," a will is the legal document by which a person (called a "testator") disposes of all property he owns or in which he has an interest in his own name at the time of his death. It is important to emphasize that the will distributes only property that is neither governed by some other legal document nor owned by another person jointly with the testator. For instance, insurance proceeds, pension benefits, trust bank accounts, and jointly owned real estate all typically pass "outside of the will"—that is, as dictated by the insurance policy, pension beneficiary designation, bankbook, or deed, respectively—rather than under any provision of the will.

With respect to the property in the testator's own name, however, it is the will that determines not only who will inherit that property and in what proportions but also whether the inheritance is to take the form of a trust (see TRUSTS) or is to be distributed outright to the beneficiary.

The will also designates who is to serve in one or more of several fiduciary capacities usually required to be filled for the orderly administration of the testator's estate, or for the welfare of his family. Thus, the will nominates an EXECUTOR, whose job it is to offer the will to the appropriate surrogate's court for PROBATE and, upon admission of the will to probate, to collect the decedent's assets; pay his debts, funeral expenses, and the expenses of administering the estate (including any death taxes); and distribute the remaining balance to those entitled to the property under the will. Trustees may also have to be appointed if the will establishes one or more trust funds; and if minor children are involved, the will should provide for guardians "of the person" of the minors (i.e., those responsible for the children's upbringing) and for guardians of the minors' property (similar to trustees). In all cases, a thorough will should designate substitute or "successor" fiduciaries in case those originally named fail or refuse to accept their appointments, or die afterward.

A comprehensive will typically also contains clauses designed (1) to minimize death taxes (see ESTATE PLANNING) and to specify which beneficiaries are to bear the burden of such taxes as may be payable; (2) to relieve the named fiduciaries of the necessity of filing a surety bond; (3) to specify the manner in which the estate will be distributed in the case of "simultaneous death" of two spouses; (4) to effect the disposition of specific items of property of sentimental or special economic significance to the testator (so-called specific bequests); (5) to select the law of a state other than that of the testator's domicile to govern the administration of his estate, if such selection is desirable; and (6) to deal with particular problems inherent in the individual testator's family or financial situation—e.g., a trust for a retarded child, tax-qualified charitable dispositions, or provisions dealing with the postmortem management of the testator's "closely held" family business.

A will is said to be "ambulatory"—that is, it may be revoked or amended (an amendment to a will is called a "codicil") at any time prior to the testator's death, in order to reflect significant changes in his family situation (e.g., marriage, divorce, childbirth) or in the composition or valuation of his assets. However, there are two exceptions to the principle that a will is always ambulatory. First, if the testator becomes incompetent, his will cannot be altered unless and until he regains his "testamentary capacity." Second, if the testator has made a "joint will" with his or her spouse (or with any other person)—that is, a single document that both have signed, with the understanding that neither will revoke without the other's consent—the will generally cannot be revoked or amended without that consent; and this is especially true once the other person has died. It can readily be seen that the inherent lack of flexibility in a joint will suggests that only rarely (if ever) is it a good idea, and that each person should have his or her own will.

In order to make a valid will, rigid statutory requirements must be scrupulously observed (see below, "How to Make a Valid Will"). In addition, the will must be the free and voluntary act of the testator. If he is deceived by another person into making either the will itself or specific provisions thereof, the document as a whole may be denied probate, or the specific offending provisions may be invalidated on the grounds of fraud or of "undue influence." Likewise, if force or "duress" (mental *or* physical) has been used, the same consequences may result.

Of course, as noted above, a person must also be mentally competent to make a will—that is, he or she must be an adult under the laws of the state of his or her domicile and, in addition, must possess what is called "testamentary capacity." This means that the testator must have knowledge of the approximate value and nature of his estate; must know who are the "natural objects of his bounty" (that is, the identities of those family members to whom a person ordinarily would be expected to leave his or her property); and must understand the actual dispositions of property he or she has made in the alleged will.

Once a valid will has been signed, it may be revoked either by a subsequent will or by the testator (or another person, upon his instructions) destroying or mutilating the old will. It should be noted that in most states, the subsequent revocation of the latest will does not automatically "reactivate" any prior will that had itself previously been revoked by the will

that is now being revoked. For this reason, and others as well, it is usually preferable to revoke a will not by destruction but rather by execution of a new will. In this way, it can be assured that the testator always has a valid will in effect.

As to amendments, or codicils, to wills, these must always be executed with the same degree of formality (see below) as the will itself; changes informally written into an existing will (called "interlineations") will ordinarily be denied effect by the probate court, and may even result in the invalidation of the entire will itself.

How to Make a Valid Will. Although the laws of each state vary somewhat, there are certain common principles that ordinarily apply regardless of the domicile of the testator. Needless to say, a will should be drawn only by a competent attorney who is familiar both with the laws of the particular state involved and, at least to a moderate degree, with applicable federal and state estate-tax laws (*see* ESTATE PLANNING). Although in limited circumstances (usually, where one is in the military service) an individual may make an oral, or "noncupative," will, or may write out his or her own unwitnessed will by hand (called a "holographic will"), as often as not such wills lead to a contested probate or, at best, to a valid but ambiguous document requiring court interpretation (called a "will construction" proceeding).

The written document prepared by the attorney must be signed by the testator in the presence of at least two and sometimes three "attesting witnesses." (Alternatively, many states permit the testator to "acknowledge," or state verbally, to the witnesses that he or she has previously signed the will.) The witnesses themselves (who preferably should not be persons who are beneficiaries under the will) must each sign, as witnesses, in the presence of the testator (although most states do not require that each witness sign in the other witnesses' presence). All signatures should be physically placed at the end of the will, since many states will give no effect to provisions added after the signatures.

Two of the most important requirements for the valid execution of a will are that the will be "published," and that each witness sign the will at the specific request of the testator. The latter criterion will usually be satisfied if the testator's attorney, in the presence of the testator, asks the witnesses to affix their signatures in that capacity.

As to the former condition, a will is said to be "published" when the testator declares to the witnesses, either directly or in response to his attorney's question, that the document he and they are signing is in fact his will. Although the witnesses need not read or have any knowledge whatsoever of the contents of the will, they *must* be told by the testator, directly or in response to the attorney's question, that it is his will. The failure to observe this requirement—as, for example, by a person taking a will to two friends, neighbors, or business associates and merely asking them to sign this "legal document"— has perhaps led to more invalidations of proposed wills than any other failure. In passing, it may be remarked that few, if any, states require that the signatures to a will be notarized.

Only one original will should be signed by an individual (although photocopies can of course be made). This is because many states will presume a testator has revoked all of his wills if he or she executed duplicate originals and only one can be located at the time of death. The original will should be kept in a safe place (perhaps in the lawyer's vault), but *not* in a safe-deposit box of the testator, since state laws frequently require the "sealing" of these boxes upon the bank's receipt of notice of death.

Steven J. Wohl

Workers' Compensation

Workers' compensation, also referred to as "industrial accident insurance," provides cash benefits and medical care to a wage earner who is injured in connection with his job, or financial payments to his survivors if he is killed. There are workers' compensation programs in each of the 50 states and Puerto Rico and these operate independent of any federal law. There are also three federal programs covering federal government employees, private employees in the District of Columbia, and longshoremen in the United States.

Workers' compensation laws vary widely from state to state. Some states exempt certain classes of workers or limit coverage to workers in certain specified, hazardous occupations. A number of states also exclude from coverage employers who do not have a specified minimum number of employees.

The cash benefits paid for injury or death of a worker are usually a percentage of weekly earnings at the time of accident or death. Most often this is 60%, 65%, or 66⅔%, but in some states the percentage varies with marital status and number of dependent children, particularly in the case of death. Most state laws permit lump-sum settlements.

Administration of workers' compensation laws is performed in 26 states by an independent workers' compensation agency, in 19 states and Puerto Rico by the state's labor department, and in 5 states by court administration. Federal provisions are all administered by the U.S. Department of Labor's Office of Workers' Compensation Programs. It is with these agencies that a claim for compensation is filed, for

due notice to the employer or insurer. Such a claim must usually be filed within a year of the injury, onset of disability, or of death; and under certain conditions, particularly with regard to occupational diseases, there are specified time limits.

Harvey Rachlin

World Bank

This term is commonly used to refer to the International Bank for Reconstruction and Development (IBRD) and one of its affiliates, the International Development Association (IDA). The IBRD has a second affiliate, the International Finance Corporation (IFC). The common objective of these institutions is to help raise living standards in developing countries by channeling financial resources from developed countries to the developing world. In addition, they play an important nonfinancial role through the analytic work and policy advice they provide to their member countries.

IBRD. The IBRD, founded in 1945, is owned by the governments of 144 countries. Like private companies, it has shareholders—member governments, whose shareholdings are related to the economic weight of each country. All powers in the Bank are vested in a board of governors, which consists of one governor appointed by each member country. Typically, a governor is his country's finance minister or CENTRAL BANK governor. This board has delegated current operations to a board of executive directors. The president of the Bank is selected by the board of executive directors and serves as chairman of the board. The headquarters of the World Bank and the IFC are located in Washington, D.C.

The IBRD finances its lending operations primarily with funds it borrows in the international capital markets. Paid-in capital from its members, its retained earnings, and loan repayments also add to its resources. IBRD loans generally have a grace period of five years and are repayable over 15–20 years. The interest rate is calculated against the cost of the Bank's own borrowings. A "front-end fee" is also applied to IBRD loans.

The World Bank finances high-priority projects in developing countries. Projects are designed in close collaboration with national governments, often in cooperation with other multilateral assistance agencies. The Bank makes loans only to the extent that borrowers are creditworthy, assisting only those projects that promise reasonable rates of economic return to the borrowing country. It does not finance military expenditures, nor exports of any particular country. The World Bank (including IDA) has suffered no losses on its loans. As of June 30, 1982, the IBRD had made loans totaling over $78 billion.

World Bank projects are in a wide variety of sectors, such as agriculture and rural development, energy (these sectors account for roughly 50% of total lending), education, industry, population, transportation, health, and nutrition. The Bank's work is performed principally by country specialists and a "projects staff," among whom are a substantial number of economists, financial analysts, and engineers, as well as agronomists, educators, sociologists, architects, demographers, and urban planners.

The World Bank begins its operational cycle with a study of the economy of the borrowing country and the needs of the sectors in which lending is contemplated. These analyses provide the basis for long-term development strategies that will lead to the formulation of individual projects. The life cycle of a project usually consists of six stages: identification, preparation, appraisal, negotiation and approval, implementation and supervision, and ex post evaluation. The cycle typically takes 11 years.

The World Bank is an important source of technical assistance. The demand for such assistance—especially to strengthen, rather than merely augment, a developing country's capabilities—has grown in recent years. This is a result of the expansion and diversification of lending activities, the intensification of institution-building efforts, and the increasing complexity of the development tasks in which the Bank has become involved as the emphasis of its work shifted from traditional infrastructure to poverty-oriented projects.

The Bank also plays the role of a catalyst by attracting cofinancing of its projects from other lenders. In the fiscal year ending June 30, 1982, cofinancing of World Bank projects totaled $7.4 billion, nearly double the fiscal year 1981 figure of $4.1 billion. Sources of cofinancing include commercial banks, government agencies and multilateral insitutions, and export credit agencies. Commercial banks have become the largest source of cofinancing; in fiscal year 1982, it amounted to $3.3 billion.

In 1980 the World Bank inaugurated a new type of loan, for structural adjustment, that supports programs of policy changes and institutional reforms designed to achieve more efficient use of resources. In February 1983 the Bank launched a special action program that aims to further expand structural-adjustment lending, increase the World Bank's share of projects costs, enhance policy dialogue with member countries, and intensify coordination with other lending institutions. Its purpose is to help developing countries maintain the momentum of their investment programs during a period of financial constraints.

IDA. IDA was established in 1960, primarily to transfer funds to the poorer developing countries on terms that would bear less heavily on their balance of payments than IBRD loans. IDA's assistance is concentrated on countries with per capita GNP of less than $795 (in 1981 dollars). More than 50 countries are eligible under this criterion. Membership in IDA is open to all members of the IBRD, and 131 of them have joined to date. Although legally and financial distinct from the IBRD, IDA is administered by the same staff. The same rigorous standards in IBRD project work are applied to IDA operations.

IDA funds come essentially from general replenishments provided by the more developed member nations, and transfers from the net earnings of the IBRD. IDA credits (so-called to distinguish them from IBRD loans) are made to governments only, with 10-year grace periods, 50-year maturities, and no interest. There is a small annual service fee on both the disbursed and undisbursed portions of each credit. Cummulative IDA lending amounted to $26.7 billion at the end of June 1982.

IFC. IFC was established in 1956, specifically to help promote and assist productive private enterprises in the developing countries. With its special role of helping to mobilize resources, on commercial terms, for business ventures and financial institutions where a market-oriented approach is not only applicable but economically preferable, IFC is indispensable to the World Bank's development strategy. Membership in the IBRD is a prerequisite for membership in IFC, which totals 122 countries. Legally and financially, IFC and IBRD are separate entities. IFC has its own operating and legal staff but draws upon the IBRD for administrative and other services.

A. W. (Tom) Clausen

Wraparound (Wrap)

See HOME FINANCING, MORTGAGES.

·Y·

Yield

Refers to either the profit (or return) derived from investment or the return received by daily compounding when the original principal and earned interest are left to accumulate for a year (yield percentages are stated in annual terms).

Certificates of deposits are often advertised as having a particular annual interest rate (e.g., 12.300%) and a higher effective annual yield (e.g., 13.279%). The stated annual interest rate is the percentage of interest the certificate pays. The effective annual yield is the amount of interest earned if the principal and interest remain on deposit for the full term of the certificate. This rate is earned for the entire period of the certificate, unlike money-market funds, whose rates fluctuate daily.

Harvey Rachlin

·Z·

Zero-Coupon Bonds

These are debt instruments sold at significant discounts from their face values with no annual payout. No interest is paid for the life of the bond, but a significant capital appreciation is realized at maturity. Example: A 30-year zero-coupon bond issued at 4 ($40 per bond) will return 100 ($1,000 per bond) at maturity. Existing IRS rulings state that the capital appreciation on Municipal Bonds originally issued at a discount is tax exempt. These instruments provide a better vehicle for goal-oriented investors to reach their objectives than traditional tax-free, fixed-income investments. They can be used as a supplement to IRA's or as a planning vehicle for a child's education, etc.

See also BONDS: COUPON STRIPPING.

Moore & Schley Cameron & Company

Appendix

Acronyms and Abbreviations

AAA	American Arbitration Association
ABA	American Bankers Association
ACH	Automated clearinghouse
ADR	American Depository Receipt
AFDC	Aid to Families with Dependent Children
AFDC-UP	Aid to Families with Dependent Children-Unemployed Parents
Amex	American Stock Exchange
AML	Adjustable mortgage loan
AMVI	Amex Market Value Index
APR	Annual percentage rate
ARM	Adjustable-rate mortgage
ATM's	Automated teller machines
ATS	Automated transfer service
BBB	Better Business Bureau
Big Board	New York Stock Exchange
BIS	Bank for International Settlements
BLM	Bureau of Land Management
BLS	Bureau of Labor Statistics
BSE	Boston Stock Exchange
CAB	Civil Aeronautics Board
CBOE	Chicago Board Options Exchange
CBOT	Chicago Board of Trade
CD	Certificate of deposit
CEA	Council of Economic Advisers
CFA	Chartered financial analyst
CFTC	Commodity Futures Trading Commission
CHIPS	Clearing House Interbank Payments System
CLU	Chartered life underwriter
CME	Chicago Mercantile Exchange
COMEX	Commodity Exchange, Inc.
CONDO	Condominium
Co-op	Cooperative housing
CPA	Certified public accountant
CPCU	Chartered Property-Casualty Underwriter
CPD	Commissioner of the Public Debt

CPI	Consumer price index
CPSC	Consumer Product Safety Commission
CSCE	Coffee, Sugar and Cocoa Exchange
CUNA	Credit Union National Association
DBA	Doing business as
DBL	Disability Benefits Law
DIDC	Deposit Institutions Deregulation Committee
DJIA	Dow Jones industrial average
DTC	Depository Trust Company
EEOC	Equal Employment Opportunity Commission
EFTS	Electronic fund-transfer system
EMCF	European Monetary Cooperation Fund
EPA	Environmental Protection Agency
ERISA	Employee Retirement Income Security Act of 1974
ERTA	Economic Recovery Tax Act
ESF	Exchange Stabilization Fund
ESOT	Employee Stock Ownership Trust
EXIMBANK	Export-Import Bank of the United States
Fannie Mae	Federal National Mortgage Association
FAS	Freight alongside
FCA	Farm Credit Administration
FCC	Federal Communications Commission
FCIA	Foreign Credit Insurance Association
FCM	Futures commission merchant
FDIC	Federal Deposit Insurance Corporation
FHA	Federal Housing Administration
FHLBB	Federal Home Loan Bank Board

FHLMC	Federal Home Loan Mortgage Corporation	LGIP	Local government investment pool
FICB's	Federal intermediate credit banks	LIBOR	London interbank offer rate
FLB	Federal Land Bank		
FLRA	Federal Labor Relations Authority	MACE	MidAmerica Commodity Exchange
FmHA	Farmers Home Administration	MCA	Monetary Control Act of 1980
FOB	Free on board	MGE	Minneapolis Grain Exchange
FOMC	Federal Open Market Committee	MIC	Mortgage-insurance company
FRB	Federal Reserve Board	MMC	Money-market certificate
FRCD	Floating-rate certificate of deposit	MMDA	Money-market deposit account
Freddie Mac	Federal Home Loan Mortgage Corporation	MMF	Money-market fund
		MSB	Mutual savings bank
FRN	Floating-rate note	MSE	Midwest Stock Exchange
FRS	Federal Reserve System		
FSLIC	Federal Savings & Loan Insurance Corporation	NACHA	National Automated Clearing House Association
FTC	Federal Trade Commission	NAHB	National Association of Home Builders
GA	General assistance	NAR	National Association of Realtors
GEM	Growing-equity mortgage	NASD	National Association of Securities Dealers, Inc.
Ginnie Mae	Government National Mortgage Association	NASDAQ	National Association of Securities Dealers Automated Quotations
GMC	Guaranteed mortgage certificate		
GNP	Gross national product	NCRB	National Labor Relations Board
GPARM	Graduated-payment adjustable-rate mortgage	NCUA	National Credit Union Administration
GPM	Graduated-payment mortgage	NLRB	National Labor Relations Board
GSCA	Government securities clearing arrangement	NOW Account	Negotiable Order of Withdrawal account
		NSCC	National Securities Clearing Corporation
HHS	Department of Health and Human Services	NYCE	New York Cotton Exchange
HUD	Department of Housing and Urban Development	NYFE	New York Futures Exchange
		NYMEX	New York Mercantile Exchange
		NYSE	New York Stock Exchange
IBA	International Banking Act		
IBF's	International banking facilities	OASDI	Old-Age, Survivors, and Disability Insurance
IBRD	International Bank for Reconstruction and Development	OCC	Office of the comptroller of the currency
ICC	Interstate Commerce Commission	OECD	Organization for Economic Cooperation & Development
IDA	International Development Association	OID	Original issue discount
IFC	International Finance Corporation	OPEC	Organization of Petroleum Exporting Countries
IMF	International Monetary Fund	OPIC	Overseas Private Investment Corporation
IMM	International monetary market		
IRA	Individual retirement account	OPM	Office of Personnel Management
IRS	Internal Revenue Service	OSHA	Occupational Safety & Health Administration
ISE	Intermountain Stock Exchange		
ITS	Intermarket Trading System	OTC	Over-the-counter
KCBT	Kansas City Board of Trade	PA	Professional association

PAC	Participation certificate	SEP	Simplified employee pension plan
PBGC	Pension Benefit Guaranty Corporation	SIA	Securities Industrial Association
		SIAC	Securities Industry Automation Corporation
PC	Professional corporation		
PCA	Production credit association	SIPA	Securities Investor Protection Act of 1970
P/E	Price/earnings ratio		
PHLX	Philadelphia Stock Exchange	SIPC	Securities Investor Protection Corporation
POS	Point of sale		
PSE	Pacific Stock Exchange	SPDA	Single-premium deferred annuity
		SSI	Supplemental security income
RAM	Reverse annuity mortgage	STIP	Short-term investment pool
RCPC	Regional check-processing center	STIT	Short-term investment trust
REIT	Real-estate investment trust		
ROG	Receipt of goods	TDA	Tax-deferred annuity
ROI	Return on investment	TDA	Time-deposit account
RP	Repurchase agreement	TEFRA	Tax Equity and Fiscal Responsibility Act
S&L	Savings and loan association	TSA	Tax-sheltered annuity
S&P Index	Standard & Poor's stock-price index	TT&L	Treasury tax and loan
Sallie Mae	Student Loan Marketing Association	USITC	United States International Trade Commission
SAM	Shared appreciation mortgage	USLSI	United States League of Savings Institutions
SBA	Small Business Administration		
SBIC	Small business investment company	VA	Veterans Administration
SBLI	Savings bank life insurance		
SDR's	Special drawing rights	WATS	Wide area telecommunications service
SEC	Securities & Exchange Commission	Wrap	Wraparound mortgage
SEM	Shared-equity mortgage		